The Selected Papers of
Elizabeth Cady Stanton and Susan B. Anthony

The Selected Papers of Elizabeth Cady Stanton and Susan B. Anthony

VOLUME V

Their Place Inside the Body-Politic
1887 to 1895

Ann D. Gordon, EDITOR

Lesley L. Doig, EDITORIAL ASSISTANT
Patricia L. Hampson, EDITORIAL ASSISTANT
Kathleen Manning, EDITORIAL ASSISTANT
Shannen Dee Williams, EDITORIAL ASSISTANT

RUTGERS UNIVERSITY PRESS
NEW BRUNSWICK, NEW JERSEY

LIBRARY OF CONGRESS CATALOGING-IN-PUBLICATION DATA

Stanton, Elizabeth Cady, 1815–1902.
    [Selections. 1997]
    The selected papers of Elizabeth Cady Stanton and Susan B. Anthony / Ann D. Gordon, editor.
    p.   cm.
    Includes bibliographical references and index.
    Contents: v. 5. Their place inside the body-politic, 1887 to 1895
    ISBN 978-0-8135-2321-7 (alk. paper)
    1. Feminists—United States—Archives.   2. Suffragists—United States—Archives.   3. Stanton, Elizabeth Cady, 1815–1902—Archives.   4. Anthony, Susan B. (Susan Brownell), 1820–1906—Archives.   5. Feminism—United States—History—19th century—Sources.   6. Women—Suffrage—United States—History—19th century—Sources.   I. Anthony, Susan B. (Susan Brownell), 1820–1906.   II. Gordon, Ann D. (Ann Dexter)   III. Miller, Tamara Gaskell.   IV. Title.
HQ1410.A25   1997
016.30542—dc21   97-5666
                                                                                                                     CIP

BRITISH CATALOGING-IN-PUBLICATION information is available from the British Library.

Copyright © 2009 by Rutgers, the State University of New Jersey
All rights reserved

No part of this book may be reproduced or utilized in any form by any means, electronic or mechanical, or by any information storage and retrieval system, without written permission from the publisher. Please contact Rutgers University Press, 100 Joyce Kilmer Avenue, Piscataway, New Jersey 08854. The only exception to this prohibition is "fair use" as defined by U.S. copyright law.

TEXT DESIGN: Judith Martin Waterman of Martin-Waterman Associates, Ltd.
Manufactured in the United States of America

Publication of this volume was assisted by a grant from the National Historical Publications and Records Commission.

∞ This paper meets the requirements of ANSI/NISO Z39.48-1992 (R2002) Permanence of Paper.

Frontispiece photograph of Elizabeth Cady Stanton and Susan B. Anthony, probably 1891. Taken by John H. Kent, Rochester, New York. Library of Congress, Prints and Photographs Division, LC-USZ62-37938.

*To the memory
of
Constance Knowles Eberhardt Cook
1919–2009*

*Attorney
Educator
Assemblywoman
Co-author of New York State's abortion rights law*

Contents

Illustrations XVI
Preface XVII
Acknowledgments XVIII
Introduction XX
Editorial Practice XXVIII
Abbreviations XXXIV

1. 9 February 1887 — Franklin G. Adams to SBA *1*
2. 18 February 1887 — SBA to Rachel G. Foster *2*
3. 28 February 1887 — ECS to Clara Bewick Colby *7*
4. 10 March 1887 — ECS to SBA *9*
5. 18 March 1887 — Oliver Johnson to SBA *14*
6. 23 March 1887 — SBA to Rachel G. Foster *15*
7. 25 March 1887 — SBA to Rachel G. Foster *17*
8. LATE March? 1887 — SBA to Rachel G. Foster *18*
9. 5 April 1887 — ECS to Benjamin F. and Sara Francis Underwood *20*
10. c. 13 April 1887 — ECS to Sara Francis Underwood *22*
11. 16? April 1887 — ECS to Nora S. Blatch *23*
12. 19? April? 1887 — Draft call to International Council of Women *24*
13. 25 April 1887 — SBA to Rachel G. Foster *26*
14. 1 June 1887 — Call to International Council of Women *27*
15. 6 June 1887 — SBA to Frances E. Willard *29*
16. 15 June 1887 — ECS to Flora McMartin Wright *31*
17. 17 August 1887 — SBA to Elizabeth Smith Miller *36*
18. 28 August 1887 — SBA to Lillie Devereux Blake *37*
19. 6 September 1887 — SBA to Harriet Taylor Upton *39*
20. 25 October 1887 — SBA to Anna H. Shaw *41*
21. 26 October 1887 — Speech by SBA in Leavenworth, Kansas *42*

22.	7 November 1887	Lucy Stone to SBA, with enclosure *52*
		Editorial note *54*
23.	13 December 1887	SBA to Lucy Stone *57*
24.	15 December 1887	SBA to Thomas B. Reed *58*
25.	21 December 1887	Minutes of informal conference between Lucy Stone and SBA *59*
26.	23 December 1887	Lucy Stone to SBA *68*
27.	24 December 1887	SBA to Rachel G. Foster *69*
28.	25 December 1887	ECS to Clara Bewick Colby *70*
29.	26 December 1887	SBA to Lillie Devereux Blake *74*
30.	7 January 1888	SBA to Henry W. Blair *75*
31.	12 January 1888	ECS to Rachel G. Foster *77*
32.	20 January 1888	SBA to Caroline Healey Dall *78*
33.	24 January 1888	SBA to Caroline Healey Dall *80*
34.	1–4 February 1888	Diary of SBA *82*
35.	6 February 1888	SBA to Frederick Douglass *83*
36.	12–14 February 1888	Diary of SBA *85*
37.	27 February 1888	SBA to Lillie Devereux Blake *86*
38.	6 March 1888	ECS to Helen Taylor *90*
39.	7 March 1888	Helen Taylor to SBA *91*
40.	26 March 1888	Address by ECS to International Council of Women *93*
41.	27 March 1888	International Council of Women, Temperance Session *107*
42.	3 April 1888	Executive Sessions of National Woman Suffrage Association *109*
43.	8 May 1888	SBA to Francis J. Garrison *122*
44.	30 May 1888	Remarks by SBA to New England Woman Suffrage Festival *123*
45.	13 July 1888	Matilda Joslyn Gage to ECS *126*
46.	BEFORE 14 July 1888	SBA to Unknown *131*
47.	7–11 August 1888	Diary of SBA *132*
48.	13 August 1888	Article by ECS: Parties or Platforms *135*
49.	15 August 1888	Frances E. Willard to SBA *139*
50.	2 November 1888	ECS to Clara Bewick Colby *140*
51.	5? November 1888	ECS to Clara Bewick Colby *141*

52.	10 November 1888	ECS to Elizabeth Smith Miller *142*
53.	3 December 1888	Speech by ECS: Woman's Duty to Vote *143*
54.	BEFORE 15 December 1888	ECS to Clara Bewick Colby *159*
55.	22 December 1888	Call to Washington convention *160*
56.	31 December 1888	SBA to Frances E. Willard *163*
57.	6 January 1889	SBA to Olivia Bigelow Hall *164*
58.	21–24 January 1889	Executive Sessions and Executive Committee of National Woman Suffrage Association *166*
59.	1 February 1889	ECS to Hartford Equal Rights Club *175*
60.	11 March 1889	SBA to Olympia Brown *177*
61.	13 March 1889	Speech by SBA in Leavenworth, Kansas *181*
62.	14 March 1889	Speech by SBA in Leavenworth, Kansas *189*
63.	17 March 1889	Article by ECS: Let the Blue Laws Rest *191*
64.	30 March 1889	Remarks by SBA in Leavenworth, Kansas *194*
65.	March 1889	ECS to Sara Francis Underwood *196*
66.	14 April 1889	Article by ECS: The Great Trial *198*
67.	8 May 1889	ECS to Olympia Brown *200*
68.	4 June 1889	Matilda Joslyn Gage to ECS *201*
69.	7 July 1889	SBA to Laura Carter Holloway *204*
70.	12 July 1889	Speech by ECS to Seidl Society *205*
71.	BEFORE 10 August 1889	ECS to Clara Bewick Colby *208*
72.	30 August 1889	Speech by SBA to Seidl Society *209*
73.	AFTER 30 August 1889	ECS to Clara Bewick Colby *210*
74.	12 October 1889	ECS to Olympia Brown *211*
75.	19 October 1889	ECS to Matilda Joslyn Gage *214*
76.	1 November 1889	SBA to Lillie Devereux Blake *215*
77.	23 November 1889	Call to Washington convention *217*
78.	25 November 1889	SBA to Rachel Foster Avery *220*
79.	November 1889	ECS to Clara Bewick Colby *223*
80.	21 December 1889	SBA to Rachel Foster Avery *225*

81.	23 December 1889	SBA to Editor, *Woman's Tribune* 226
82.	6 January 1890	Gideon J. Tucker to SBA 228
83.	7 January 1890	ECS to Elizabeth Smith Miller 230
84.	17 January 1890	SBA to May Wright Sewall 231
85.	31 January 1890	SBA to Isabella Beecher Hooker 234
86.	5 February 1890	SBA to Eliza Wright Osborne 236
87.	13–14 February 1890	Diary of SBA 237
88.	15 February 1890	Birthday celebration for SBA 240
89.	15–16 February 1890	Diary of SBA 245
90.	17 February 1890	Remarks by SBA to National Woman Suffrage Association 246
91.	17 February 1890	Diary of SBA 248
92.	18 February 1890	Speech by ECS to National-American Woman Suffrage Association 249
93.	18–21 February 1890	Diary of SBA 268
94.	11 March 1890	SBA to Sarah Burger Stearns 269
95.	21 March 1890	SBA to Frances E. Willard 274
96.	21 March 1890	ECS to Clara Bewick Colby 278
97.	27 March 1890	Diary of SBA 280
98.	29 March 1890	SBA to Samuel A. Ramsey 281
99.	30 March 1890	SBA to Henry L. Dawes 283
100.	19 April 1890	Article by ECS: What Should Be Our Attitude towards Political Parties 285
101.	1 May 1890	ECS to Hannah Whitall Smith 293
102.	AFTER 30 May 1890	SBA to Alice Alt Pickler? 294
103.	4 June 1890	Emilie Ashurst Venturi to ECS 295
104.	6 June 1890	ECS to SBA and Clara Bewick Colby 297
105.	10 June 1890	SBA to Harriet Taylor Upton 300
106.	12 June 1890	Priscilla Bright McLaren to ECS 302
107.	14 June 1890	SBA to Alice Alt Pickler 304
108.	BEFORE 2 July 1890	SBA to Alice Alt Pickler 306
109.	7 August 1890	ECS to SBA 308
110.	15 August 1890	ECS to Clara Bewick Colby 311
111.	September 1890	Article by ECS: Wyoming Admitted as a State 312
112.	1 September 1890	SBA to Harriet Taylor Upton 319

113.	3 September 1890	SBA to Olympia Brown *321*
114.	5 September 1890	SBA to Harriet Taylor Upton *324*
115.	9 October 1890	Speech by ECS to Bristol Women's Liberal Association *327*
116.	27 October 1890	ECS to Margaret Stanton Lawrence *328*
117.	9 November 1890	Inscription by SBA *332*
118.	1 December 1890	ECS to Margaret Stanton Lawrence *333*
119.	BEFORE 13 December 1890	SBA to Clara Bewick Colby *334*
120.	21 December 1890	ECS to Clara Bewick Colby *334*
121.	January 1891	Article by ECS: Patriotism and Chastity *336*
122.	12 January 1891	ECS to Clara Bewick Colby *343*
123.	12? January 1891	ECS to Margaret Stanton Lawrence *345*
124.	15 January 1891	ECS to Lucy Stone *346*
125.	18 January 1891	ECS to William T. Stead *355*
126.	21 January 1891	William T. Stead to ECS *356*
127.	30 January 1891	Lucy Stone to SBA *356*
128.	11 February 1891	Isabella Beecher Hooker to SBA *357*
129.	BEFORE 21 February 1891	ECS to Clara Bewick Colby and SBA *358*
130.	26 February 1891	Speech by ECS: Degradation of Disfranchisement *360*
131.	28 February 1891	ECS to Clara Bewick Colby *369*
132.	6 March 1891	ECS to Clara Bewick Colby *370*
133.	11 March 1891	SBA to Lucretia Longshore Blankenburg *373*
134.	28 March 1891	Article by ECS: Lord Chancellor *374*
135.	7 May 1891	SBA to Olivia Bigelow Hall *376*
136.	21 May 1891	SBA to Mary Post Hallowell and Sarah Kirby Willis *378*
137.	24 May 1891	Lady Rosalind Carlisle to ECS *379*
138.	27 May 1891	Speech by SBA to New England Woman Suffrage Festival *380*
139.	June? 1891	ECS to SBA *385*
140.	8 July 1891	SBA to J. Merritt Anthony *386*

141.	8 September 1891	Harriette Robinson Shattuck to SBA *389*
142.	14 September 1891	ECS to Harriot Stanton Blatch *390*
143.	22 September 1891	SBA to Lillie Devereux Blake *392*
144.	22 September 1891	SBA to Salome Merritt *394*
145.	BEFORE 1 October 1891	ECS to Editor, *Voice* *396*
146.	15 October 1891	Reception for ECS in Rochester, New York *398*
147.	22 October 1891	SBA to Harriet Taylor Upton *403*
148.	6 November 1891	ECS to Eliza Wright Osborne *404*
149.	10 December 1891	SBA to George F. Hoar *406*
150.	10 December 1891	SBA to Harriet Taylor Upton *407*
151.	11 December 1891	Thomas B. Reed to SBA *409*
152.	1 January 1892	SBA to Harriet Taylor Upton *410*
153.	15 January 1892	Eliza Wright Osborne to ECS, with enclosure *412*
154.	16 January 1892	Executive Committee of National-American Woman Suffrage Association *414*
155.	18 January 1892	Speech by ECS: Solitude of Self *423*
156.	21 January 1892	Business Meeting of National-American Woman Suffrage Association *436*
157.	February 1892	Article by ECS: Sunday at the World's Fair *439*
158.	13 February 1892	SBA to Lillie Devereux Blake *442*
159.	15 February 1892	SBA to Elizabeth Smith Miller *446*
160.	29 February 1892	Diary of SBA *448*
161.	30 March 1892	SBA to Elizabeth Smith Miller *450*
162.	10 April 1892	SBA to William Sulzer *452*
163.	10 April 1892	Henry B. Blackwell to SBA *454*
164.	16 April 1892	SBA to Harriet Taylor Upton *460*
165.	26 April 1892	Isabella Beecher Hooker to ECS *463*
166.	AFTER 26 April 1892	ECS to Olympia Brown *465*
167.	7 May 1892	Speech by ECS to New York City Woman Suffrage League *465*
168.	10 May 1892	Statement by SBA *471*
169.	C. 17 May 1892	ECS to SBA *473*

170.	26 May 1892	Remarks by SBA to Ohio Woman Suffrage Association *473*
171.	8 June 1892	Remarks by SBA at meeting during Republican National Convention *475*
172.	8, 21 June 1892	Diary of SBA *477*
173.	22 June 1892	ECS to Ellen D. Eaton *479*
174.	22 June 1892	Diary of SBA *480*
175.	30 June 1892	Remarks by SBA to Kansas Republican Convention *480*
176.	30 June 1892	Diary of SBA *482*
177.	2 July 1892	Remarks by SBA at meeting during People's Party National Convention *483*
178.	2–4 July 1892	Diary of SBA *485*
179.	28 July 1892	SBA to Thomas B. Reed *486*
180.	7–9 August 1892	Diary of SBA *487*
181.	20 September 1892	Remarks by SBA to Mississippi Valley Conference *490*
182.	15 October 1892	ECS to Olympia Brown *493*
183.	21 October 1892	SBA to Harriet Taylor Upton *494*
184.	25 October 1892	ECS to Clara Bewick Colby *495*
185.	25–27 October 1892	Diary of SBA *496*
186.	27 November 1892	SBA to ECS *499*
187.	24 December 1892	ECS to SBA *502*
188.	16 January 1893	Remarks by SBA to National-American Woman Suffrage Association *503*
189.	30 January 1893	SBA to Laura Clay *505*
190.	1 February 1893	ECS to Alice S. Blackwell *507*
191.	20 May 1893	Speech by SBA: Organization among Women *509*
192.	23 May 1893	Remarks by SBA to Public Press Congress *513*
193.	27 May 1893	Speech by SBA: Moral Leadership of the Religious Press *516*
194.	14 June 1893	Ellis Meredith to SBA *521*
195.	22 June 1893	SBA to Lydia Avery Coonley *529*
196.	22 June 1893	SBA to Albion W. Tourgée *532*
197.	25 June 1893	SBA to Frederick Douglass *534*

198.	16 July 1893	SBA to Ellis Meredith *535*
199.	11 August 1893	SBA to Ellis Meredith *538*
200.	12 August 1893	Speech by ECS: Suffrage a Natural Right *539*
201.	5 October 1893	SBA to Harriet Taylor Upton *546*
202.	23 November 1893	SBA to Ellis Meredith *548*
203.	25 November 1893	Plan of work for New York *551*
204.	11 December 1893	SBA to Lillie Devereux Blake *553*
205.	29 December 1893	SBA to Lillie Devereux Blake *556*
206.	December 1893	Appeal by ECS to women of New York *559*
207.	1–7 January 1894	Diary of SBA *563*
208.	8 January 1894	Speech by SBA at rally in Rochester *566*
209.	8–26 January 1894	Diary of SBA *569*
210.	15 February 1894	Remarks by SBA to National-American Woman Suffrage Association *580*
211.	28 February 1894	ECS to Clara Bewick Colby *582*
212.	23? March 1894	SBA to Clara Bewick Colby *583*
213.	1 April 1894	SBA to Franklin G. Adams, with enclosure *586*
214.	22 April 1894	SBA to Lillie Devereux Blake *593*
215.	24 April 1894	Remarks by ECS at parlor meeting in New York City *595*
216.	26 April 1894	ECS to Editor, New York *World* *596*
217.	4 May 1894	Speech by SBA at rally in Kansas City, Kansas *598*
218.	4–5 May 1894	Diary of SBA *616*
219.	7 May 1894	ECS to Mary Rice Livermore *618*
220.	7 May 1894	Remarks by ECS at mass meeting in New York City *619*
221.	24 May 1894	Remarks by SBA to committee on suffrage *621*
222.	5–11 June 1894	Diary of SBA *625*
223.	12 June 1894	Remarks by SBA to Kansas People's Party Convention *629*
224.	12–13 June 1894	Diary of SBA *631*
225.	22 & 23 June 1894	Interviews with SBA *632*

226.	26 June 1894	ECS to Lillie Devereux Blake *635*
227.	9 July 1894	ECS to Anna H. Shaw *637*
228.	19 July 1894	SBA to ECS *638*
229.	20 July 1894	ECS to John Bigelow *639*
230.	25 July 1894	SBA to Elizabeth Smith Miller *640*
231.	19 August 1894	SBA to ECS *641*
232.	21 August 1894	ECS to Editor, New York *Sun* *643*
233.	22 August 1894	Speech by SBA at Cassadaga Lake Free Association *645*
234.	BEFORE 1 September 1894	ECS to Editors, *Woman's Journal* *647*
235.	7 September 1894	SBA to Thomas E. Bowman *650*
236.	3 November 1894	Article by ECS: Educated Suffrage JustiWed *655*
237.	18 November 1894	Remarks by SBA to gospel suffrage meeting *658*
238.	18–23 November 1894	Diary of SBA *660*
239.	24 November 1894	Frances E. Willard to SBA *662*
240.	BEFORE 22 December 1894	ECS to Editors, *Woman's Journal* *664*
241.	2 January 1895	Article by ECS: Educated Suffrage Again *665*
242.	13 January 1895	SBA to Mary S. Anthony *669*
243.	19 January–11 February 1895	Diary of SBA *671*
244.	16 February 1895	ECS to Clara Bewick Colby *677*
245.	25 February 1895	Funeral of Frederick Douglass *679*
246.	4 March 1895	ECS to Clara Bewick Colby *681*
247.	29 March 1895	Lillie Devereux Blake to SBA, with reply *683*
248.	2 April 1895	SBA to Eliza Gray Whiting *685*
249.	4 April 1895	Meeting of Political Equality Club of Rochester *687*
250.	4–9 April 1895	Diary of SBA *689*
251.	26 April 1895	ECS to Clara Bewick Colby *692*
252.	AFTER 26 April 1895	ECS to Clara Bewick Colby *693*
253.	5 June 1895	Lady Isabella Somerset to ECS *694*
254.	6 June 1895	ECS to Augusta J. Chapin *695*
255.	C. 22 July 1895	SBA to Nannie Wright Lyon *698*

256. ⇝ 24 July 1895   SBA to ECS   *699*
257. ⇝ 29 July 1895   ECS to Clara Bewick Colby   *701*
258. ⇝ 1 August 1895   Frances E. Willard to ECS   *703*
259. ⇝ 10 August 1895   ECS to Robert L. Stanton   *704*
260. ⇝ 26 August 1895   SBA to Clara Bewick Colby   *706*
261. ⇝ 21 September 1895   Parker Pillsbury to SBA   *707*
262. ⇝ 30 September 1895   SBA to ECS   *709*
263. ⇝ 1 November 1895   SBA to Ascha Harter Reynolds   *711*
264. ⇝ 5 November 1895   SBA to Anna E. Dickinson   *713*
265. ⇝ 6–9 November 1895   Diary of SBA   *715*
266. ⇝ 10 November 1895   Statements by SBA and ECS: If Women Came to Congress   *717*
267. ⇝ 10–11 November 1895 Diary of SBA   *718*
268. ⇝ 12 November 1895   Speech by ECS to Reunion of Pioneers and Friends of Woman's Progress   *719*
269. ⇝ 12–13 November 1895 Diary of SBA   *730*

  Appendix A   *733*
  Appendix B   *735*
  Index   *747*

Illustrations

Laura M. Johns, Anna Howard Shaw, Rachel G. Foster, and Susan B. Anthony in Kansas

Family and friends on the porch at 17 Madison Street, Rochester, New York

Emma Smith DeVoe

Alice Alt Pickler

Alonzo A. Wardall

Carrie Chapman Catt

Laura Clay

Harriet Taylor Upton

"Elizabeth C., Susan B. and the Rochester U."

"Stay Out! Come In."

Mary Seymour Howell

Jean Brooks Greenleaf

Harriet M. Mills

Metropolitan Opera House, 12 November 1895

Ida B. Wells

Funeral of Frederick Douglass, Rochester, New York

~ Preface

THIS IS THE FIFTH IN A SERIES of volumes publishing selected papers of Elizabeth Cady Stanton (1815–1902) and Susan B. Anthony (1820–1906). Like the earlier volumes, this one builds upon the work of Patricia G. Holland, Ann D. Gordon, Gail Malmgreen, and Kathleen McDonough in preparing the microfilm edition, *Papers of Elizabeth Cady Stanton and Susan B. Anthony* (1991). The underlying search for the papers of Stanton and Anthony is described in detail in the *The Papers of Elizabeth Cady Stanton and Susan B. Anthony: Guide and Index to the Microfilm Edition* (1992).

This series brings the most important documents of that comprehensive collection to print. The *Selected Papers* focuses on the public careers of two co-workers in the cause of woman suffrage, beginning with the start of their activism in the 1840s and pursuing the story of their ideas, tactics, reputations, and impact until the end of their lives in the twentieth century. Volume five draws on the papers dating from 1887 to 1895; it documents the collaboration of two aging friends; the union of their suffrage association with that of their rivals; the challenges of a reform movement made more complicated by size, ambition, and a changing political landscape; and pervasive tension over the impact of religion on women's lives.

Acknowledgments

It is a pleasure to acknowledge and thank the people who made this volume possible. The title page credits the people whose work is most evident in the pages of this volume. Many more people contributed their time and talents to the completion of specific tasks. Kate Sell worked several months as a researcher. Michael David Cohen, a postdoctoral fellow in historical editing, joined the staff in time to help complete this book. Graduate students at Rutgers who helped at different times are Vanessa Holden, Rebecca Tuuri, Damian Miller, and Laurie Marhoefer. Two terrific undergraduate interns contributed to the work; Lindsey Wilson of Rutgers worked with us for a semester; Tamar Weinstock of Cornell worked with us for a summer.

We acknowledge in the notes the archivists, librarians, and local historians across the country who answered our queries about people, places, and sources. In addition, we want to thank Virgil Dean, Kansas State Historical Society; John P. Joergensen, Library of the Rutgers Law School–Camden; Janice E. Ruth, Library of Congress; and Amy Zimmer, Colorado State Library. At the University of Washington, Jessica Lee, read the Wardall diaries for us; in the city of Rochester, Christine L. Ridarsky read newspapers, searched probate records, and chased down illustrations; at Smith College, Corey F. Borenstein read the *Queen Isabella Journal*; at the New York State Library, Ann E. Pfau read newspapers; and to take advantage of the resources of the Kansas State Historical Society, we employed Dale Nimz and Abby Pierron. Scholars who offered special assistance are Nancy Sinkoff of Rutgers University and Jill E. Martin, Quinnipiac University.

We extend our gratitude to the owners of manuscripts who allowed us to publish items from their collections: Stephen H. Hart Library, Colorado Historical Society; The Huntington Library; Connecticut State Library; Harriet Beecher Stowe Center; Frances E. Willard Historical Library and Archives; Indiana State Library; Library and

Archives Division, Kansas State Historical Society; University of Kentucky Library; Schlesinger Library, Radcliffe Institute for Advanced Study, Harvard University; George J. Mitchell Department of Special Collections and Archives, Bowdoin College Library; Massachusetts Historical Society; Sophia Smith Collection, Smith College; Missouri Historical Society; Brooklyn Collection, Brooklyn Public Library; Division of Rare and Manuscript Collections, Cornell University Library; Special Collections and University Archives, Rutgers University Libraries; Manuscripts and Archives Division, New York Public Library, Astor, Lenox and Tilden Foundations; Archives and Special Collections, Vassar College Libraries; Local History and Genealogy Division, Rochester Public Library; Department of Rare Books and Special Collections, University of Rochester Library; Special Collections, Schafer Library, Union College; Special Collection Research Center, Syracuse University Library; Chautauqua County Historical Society; Bryn Mawr College Special Collections; State Archives, South Dakota State Historical Society; Archives and Rare Book Library, London School of Economics and Poltical Science; Special Collections Division, University of Washington Libraries; Wisconsin Historical Society; The Gilder Lehrman Collection; the Jenkins family; Stephen I. Rudin; and Sy Sussman.

This volume was produced with major financial support from Rutgers, the State University of New Jersey; the National Historical Publications and Records Commission; the Blanche and Irving Laurie Foundation; and Patricia G. Holland. We have also received generous gifts from the following: Kathleen Alaimo, American Lives Film Project, Jean H. Baker, Richard A. Baker, Paul E. Barnes, Elizabeth R. Bodine, Carolyn Blatch Boulter, Irene Bowers, Philander C. Chase, Margaret Davidson, Carol DeBoer-Langworthy, Helen R. Deese, Ellen C. DuBois, Faye E. Dudden, Carol Faulkner, Lawton W. Fitt and James I. McLaren Foundation, Liz and Ken Fones-Wolf, Ann Forfreedom, Tammy Gaskell, Carolyn DeSwarte Gifford, Vivan Gornick, Nancy and Jesse Green, the late William L. Holland, Mary M. Huth, Coline Jenkins, the late Rhoda Barney Jenkins, Kathi Kern, Martha J. King, Edward T. Kole, Gary Kornblith, Susan G. Lane, Carol Lasser, Maurice DuPont Lee, Jr., J. Perry Leavell, John E. Little, Barbara Craford Manning, Gail Malmgreen, Maeva Marcus, Barbara Marhoefer, Carol Nadell, Jill Norgren, Mary Beth Norton, Barbara Oberg, Ann E. Pfau, Sherrill

Redmon, Leslie S. Rowland, Nancy A. Sahli, Shelah Kane Scott, Stacy Kinlock Sewell, Fredrick E. Sherman, Sarah L. O. Smith, Allison Sneider, Claire M. Stern, Lisa M. Tetrault, Judith Martin Waterman, Judith Wellman, and Jean Fagan Yellin.

Many people in the list of donors stepped in at a moment of crisis, when a major funder withdrew support for the project. At the same time, a team of people at Rutgers University made it possible for the work to continue. For that support, we owe an especial thanks to Paul G. E. Clemens, Ann V. Fabian, Philip Furmanski, Ziva Galili, Ruth B. Mandel, Barry V. Qualls, and Harvey Waterman.

A. D. G.

INTRODUCTION

Their Place inside the Body-Politic, 1887 to 1895, like earlier volumes in this series, documents the lives and work of Elizabeth Cady Stanton (1815-1902) and Susan B. Anthony (1820-1906). Imbedded in the design of this edition is an assertion or hypothesis that the *Selected Papers* of these great reformers belong together. It might be said that, as a private matter, their friendship warrants an intermingling of the historical record, and that, as a public matter, the interconnectedness of their work is best told in a single narrative. But during the years treated in this volume, the accuracy of those claims was the subject of speculation and experiments by contemporaries of Stanton and Anthony. Furthermore, modern biographers and historians of the two women have read changes in their daily lives in this period as evidence of sharp disagreements and divergent interests between them. To a significant degree, this volume of the *Papers* interrogates its own design.

At the banquet marking Susan B. Anthony's seventieth birthday in 1890, Elizabeth Cady Stanton and the guest of honor testified to their enduring friendship. Before an audience of family members, co-workers, senators, and congressmen, they each described how the other had acted as a catalyst in the discovery of her own better nature. Each of them also traced their political work back to that intimate connection. Speaking first, Stanton proclaimed,

> If there is one part of my life that gives me more intense satisfaction than another, it is my friendship of forty years' standing with Susan B. Anthony. . . . I do believe that I have developed into much more of a woman under Susan's jurisdiction, fed on statute laws and constitutional amendments, than if left to myself reading novels in an easy-chair, lost in sweet reveries of the golden age to come, without any effort of my own.

Anthony reciprocated. "If I have ever had any inspiration she has given it to me," she confessed. "I want you to understand that I never could have done the work I have if I had not had this woman at my right hand." Behind the scenes, private festivities continued into the wee hours, as Stanton and her daughters shared champagne with Anthony and her brother.[1]

By 1890, the four-decade friendship of Stanton and Anthony was no private matter. So long as they appeared to be teamed in the same harness, it was simplest to treat them as Theodore Tilton did in 1871. "It has been sometimes suspected," he wrote, "that Mrs. Stanton and Miss Anthony are two distinct persons, united by a cartilege like the Siamese twins, but in the absence of any medical or other scientific proof of this hypothesis, I remain of the opinion that, like Liberty and Union, they are 'one and inseparable.'"[2] Two decades later, their teamwork was less obvious to some of their collaborators and less benign to others. As Matilda Joslyn Gage complained after failing to set them against each other in 1891, "It has always been the policy of Susan & Stanton to play into each other's hands and to hold each other up at the expense of all other workers."[3]

Elizabeth Cady Stanton (ECS) and Susan B. Anthony (SBA) spent very little time together between 1887 and 1895; they embarked on no large collaborations comparable to the books they produced in the previous decade, and they often disagreed. Age treated SBA more kindly. Sixty-six, to ECS's seventy-one, when this volume opens in 1887, she persisted as a vagabond, loosely based at her sister's house in Rochester, New York, but willing and able to stay on the road for months at a time. SBA's pace sometimes appalled the immobile ECS; while SBA whirled through the Midwest attending state suffrage conventions in 1889, ECS reported, "I tried to pursuade her not to go as she needs rest more than excitement, but in vain, although I assured her that the earth would turn on its axis after she & I ascended to Abraham's bosom."[4]

[1] See documents number 88 and 109 within.
[2] *Golden Age*, 1 July 1871.
[3] Matilda J. Gage to Lillie D. Blake, 14 March 1891, Lillie D. Blake Papers, Missouri Historical Society.
[4] ECS to Clara Bewick Colby, 29 September 1889, in Patricia G. Holland and Ann D. Gordon, eds., *Papers of Elizabeth Cady Stanton and Susan B. Anthony* (Wilmington, Del., 1991, microfilm), reel 27, frames 444–47. Cited hereafter as *Film*.

ECS had given up her own home and her independence. Family members opened their houses to her, her rare trips required escorts, and on a stage, she lacked the strength to stand through her own lecture. Unable to make the trip to Washington after 1892, she lost influence with younger generations of activists. By 1894, if stairs stood between her and a meeting, she stayed home.

Of course the activities of their daily lives diverged. Immobility recreated the circumstances of ECS's early collaboration with SBA. In the 1850s, when children and housework tied her down, ECS relied on SBA to be her legs and voice. But late in life, SBA had her own projects, ideas, and schedule; she was not so easily recruited to serve ECS's needs. ECS's frustration can be heard in rude remarks about SBA that were often as much about SBA's autonomy as they were about substantive differences between old friends.[5]

These aging leaders of women navigated a complicated political situation. The rejection of a constitutional amendment for woman suffrage by the United States Senate on 25 January 1887 shook up the suffrage movement and forced its transformation.[6] At first the event seemed almost routine. Insults voiced by senators during debate were familiar ones. The solid opposition of Democrats was predictable. SBA found comfort in the fact that the Senate, after nearly twenty years dawdling and dodging the amendment, brought it to a vote. Honored were the stalwart supporters who voted aye. But in the ranks of organized womanhood, the senators' vote ruptured a complex coalition built by the National Woman Suffrage Association over the course of its ten-year campaign to bring the federal amendment to a vote.

In the three years after the amendment's defeat in the Senate, the political forms of suffrage activism changed. As if released by the failure to win senators' support, the suffrage movement revealed its complexity and presented competing claims for the attention and loyalty of women who wanted to vote. Nothing was brand new. State suffrage associations grew in size and produced accomplished and

---

[5] See, for example, document number 257 within, where ECS undercuts SBA with the remark, "Susan has one idea & she has no patience with any one who has two."

[6] *Congressional Record*, 49th Cong., 2d sess., 25 January 1887, pp. 978–1003; Ann D. Gordon, ed., *When Clowns Make Laws for Queens, 1880 to 1887*, vol. 4 of *The Selected Papers of Elizabeth Cady Stanton and Susan B. Anthony* (New Brunswick, N.J., 2006), 545–48. Cited hereafter as *Papers*.

ambitious leaders over many years. Frances Willard had cultivated an alliance between the temperance union and the Prohibition party since the early 1880s. The Farmers' Alliance recognized its women before it joined talks on forming the People's party. The Republican party employed women in national campaigns before its leaders granted official status to the new Woman's Republican Association. And the American Woman Suffrage Association declined for a decade before its leaders asked to merge with the National association late in 1887. But each of these political projects reached a critical point between 1887 and 1890.[7]

SBA first used the phrase "their place inside the body-politic" in a letter to Senator Henry L. Dawes in 1890 to describe an unrealized goal; that sometime in the future, voting rights would allow women to cross over into the "body-politic." The Fifty-first Congress had just convened in Washington, and she hoped Dawes would resume work for the constitutional amendment. His effort, she promised, would cause women to flock back to the Republican party from the Prohibitionists. Without any indication that she detected dissonance between her distant vision of women entering politics and the carrot she held out for Dawes of women's political realignment, SBA aptly described a suffrage movement increasingly shaped by women's partisan commitments and political behavior.[8]

In the competitive circles of the woman suffrage movement, the idea that these old friends might at last be "two distinct persons" encouraged critics and opponents to hope that one of them could be enticed to act against the other. Back at the birthday party on 15 February 1890, their reaffirmation of friendship had clear political purposes. A difficult two-year negotiation about incorporating Lucy Stone's American Woman Suffrage Association into their National Woman Suffrage Association was drawing to a close that week. Opponents of union

---

[7] The transformation of women's political behavior in this period is suggested in Jack S. Blocker, Jr., *Retreat from Reform: The Prohibition Movement in the United States, 1890–1913* (Westport, Conn., 1976); Rebecca Edwards, *Angels in the Machinery: Gender in American Party Politics from the Civil War to the Progressive Era* (New York, 1997); Michael Lewis Goldberg, *An Army of Women: Gender and Politics in Gilded Age Kansas* (Baltimore, Md., 1997); and Melanie Susan Gustafson, *Women and the Republican Party, 1854–1924* (Urbana, Ill., 2001).

[8] Document number 99 within.

among members of the National had worked for several months to cast the change as antithetical to ECS's values and an act of blind ambition on SBA's part. Matilda Joslyn Gage went so far as to call for a rival organization and claim ECS endorsed it. Lucy Stone expressed her reluctance to merge the historic rivals into a new National-American association by pitting SBA against ECS in the upcoming vote for the new society's president. While SBA pressed the National's members to support ECS, Stone and her husband urged members of the American to defeat ECS by casting their votes for SBA. The performance of ECS and SBA at the birthday party signaled that they would not be set against each other. A few days later, the two societies joined, and ECS became president of the new National-American. The friends had demonstrated that they were still a formidable force.

Though they took distinct roads during the years from 1887 to 1895, one can hear ECS and SBA calling out to each other time and again, acknowledging each other's work and protecting each other as best they could. Responding to ECS's request in 1895 that she give her name to the *Woman's Bible* committee, SBA refused: "You fight that battle— and leave me to fight the secular—the political fellows," she wrote. She worried about the Bible project spilling over into the political project, but she nevertheless encouraged her friend. "I know your doing good because you are making Rome Howl— So go ahead."[9] For her part, ECS was attuned to the political project even while complaining about SBA's fixation with suffrage. When, for example, SBA's agreement to campaign for the Kansas People's party in 1894, in recognition of the party's endorsement of woman suffrage, caused the Republican press and Henry Blackwell to turn against her, ECS defended her decision. Rejecting customary partisanship for disenfranchised people, she asked, "What is silver coinage, tariff, or income tax to us compared with our inalienable rights to life liberty & happiness?"[10]

The Stanton children, customarily identified in each volume's introduction, enter this volume as caretakers of their aging mother. In the winter of 1887, ECS lived in England with Harriot Stanton Blatch

---

[9] Document number 256 within.
[10] Documents number 226 and 227 within.

(1856–1940), Harry Blatch, and their daughter Nora. For several months in 1887, ECS relocated to Paris and the house of Theodore Weld Stanton (1851–1925), a writer. Back in the United States in 1888, she settled for nearly a year in Omaha, Nebraska, with Margaret Stanton Lawrence (1852–1930) and Frank Lawrence. That visit was cut short when Frank became gravely ill and needed Maggie's full attention. In his only appearance in his mother's papers for this period, Daniel Cady Stanton (1842–1891) escorted ECS to the East Coast. Neil, as ECS addressed him, was probably living in Iowa at the time. While in the Midwest, ECS made a final visit to the Iowa ranch of Gerrit Smith Stanton (1845–1927) and Augusta Hazleton Stanton. Gat, as he was known in the family, had decided to return east and live on Long Island. There he welcomed his mother in the summer of 1889. Hattie arrived that fall with plans to fetch ECS back to England. After Frank Lawrence's death in 1890, Maggie moved to the New York City house of her aunt Tryphena Bayard. In the city she lived near two brothers. Henry Brewster Stanton, Jr., (1844–1903) and Robert Livingston Stanton (1859–1920), known as Kit and Bob, lived together until 1891 and practiced law together until 1893. When ECS returned to New York in 1891, she set up housekeeping with Maggie and Bob in an apartment. The threesome lived together until ECS's death in 1902. Kit Stanton surprised everyone by marrying at age forty-six into a prominent Catholic family.

Editorial Practice

Principles of selection

This volume selects less than ten percent of the documents available for the period of time from February 1887 to November 1895. Documents are printed in their entirety with two exceptions: entries from diaries are selected from the larger document; ECS's and SBA's contributions to meetings are occasionally excerpted from the fullest coverage available.

The high cost of producing and publishing historical editions creates an editorial imperative to bulldoze most of the trees while leaving an attractive and useful forest in place. The selection of documents to include in each volume often boils down to arbitrary choices between equally valuable items. There are, however, guidelines. Selection is governed first by the mission to document the careers of the two coworkers. Drawn from the papers of two people, the selections must next represent differences in the documentation of each one. Although writings by ECS and SBA have priority, incoming mail is included if it documents the other voice in longstanding friendships with ECS or SBA or supplies unusual evidence about their lives. The dominant stories evident in the documents of any year or era are also retained. The inclusion of discussions in which people other than ECS and SBA participate reflects the editors' conviction that in the battle of ideas waged by these women, exchanges with opponents and allies give critical evidence about political style, intellectual influences, and differences of opinion that the principals might otherwise have failed to mention.

A considerable "selection" of documents for the years of this volume occurred long before the editors began their work. For example, SBA's diaries for the years 1887, 1889, and 1891 disappeared. Letters written by ECS are in very short supply. More than in previous volumes of this series, ECS here speaks primarily in her public voice as a writer and lecturer.

Arrangement

Documents are presented in chronological order according to the date of authorship, oral delivery, or publication of the original text. Documents dated only by month appear at the start of the month unless the context in surrounding documents dictates later placement. Documents that cover a period of time, such as diaries, are placed at the date of the earliest entry, and the longer text is interrupted for the placement of other documents that fall within the same period of time.

If a diary entry appears on the same date as another document, it is assumed that the entry was written at day's end. When two or more documents possess the same date, ECS and SBA authorship takes precedence over incoming mail, and SBA's papers appear before those of ECS unless the context dictates otherwise.

Selection of Text

Most documents in this edition survive in a single version. When choices were required, original manuscripts took precedence over later copies, and the recipient's copy of correspondence was used. A speech reported by a stenographer, however, took precedence over the manuscript. The newspaper to which SBA or ECS submitted a text took precedence over newspapers that reprinted it.

When letters survive only in transcripts made by editors and biographers, the earliest transcript was used as the source text. Typescripts by Harriot Stanton Blatch and Theodore Stanton took precedence over their published texts; considerable rewriting occurred between the two.

For the text of meetings and other oral events, the official report, or in its absence, the most comprehensive coverage, is the primary source text. If reports differ widely, composite reports were created. Additions to or substitutions from a second source are set off by angle brackets. The sources are separated by a semicolon in the endnote.

The goal with speeches is to publish a text as close as possible to the version delivered at a particular date, but how to achieve that varies in nearly every case, depending on what has survived. A stenographic report of a speech is usually regarded as the most authoritative text. Stenographers reported several speeches and discussions in this volume; the evidence is clear for documents at 26 and 27 March 1888, 3 and 4 April 1888, and 27 May 1893. The majority of the speeches are based on a local reporter's own notes. Manuscripts for three of ECS's speeches—at 26 March 1888, 18 February 1890, and 26 February 1891—survive; their differences from other sources were recorded in notes.

Format

Some features of the documents have been standardized when set into print. The indentation of existing paragraphs was consistently set. The dateline of each letter appears as the first line of text, flush to the right margin, regardless of its placement in the original. The salutation of letters was printed on one line, flush left. Extra space in the dateline or salutation indicates the author's line break. The complimentary close of letters was run into the text itself, regardless of how the author laid it out, and signatures were placed at the right margin beneath the text. The dash is uniformly rendered even though the lengths vary in the originals.

Each document is introduced by an editorial heading or title that connects the document to ECS or SBA, except in cases of meetings at which both women participated and texts to which they both contributed.

Following the text, an unnumbered endnote describes the physical character of the document and the source or owner of the original. The endnote also explicates unusual physical properties of the document and explains the uses made of square brackets in the transcription. In the case of diary entries, this note appears at the end of the series. Numbered notes follow the endnote, except that numbered notes for diary entries follow each entry.

Transcription

The editors strive to prepare for print the most accurate transcription that reproduces the format of the original as nearly as possible. However, the greater the remove from the author, the less literal is the representation.

LETTERS AND DIARIES. The editors retained the author's punctuation, including the absence of customary symbols; emphasis by underlining, although not occasional use of double or triple underlines; spelling and capitalization; mistakes; abbreviations; superscripts; and paragraphing, or its absence. The author's form of dating was retained. Opening or closing quotation marks have been supplied in square brackets when the author neglected to enter them.

Emendations in the original text are marked by symbols to show cancelled text, interlineations, and other corrections and additions. A minimum number of exceptions were allowed when the interlineation obviously resulted from slip of the pen or thought, as when an infinitive was clearly intended but the "to" was added above the line. Strike outs and other erasures are indicated with a line through the text. Interlineations, above or below the line, are framed in up and down arrows. Text from the margin is moved into place with an editorial notation about the original location.

SBA's dashes can usually be distinguished as pauses or full stops, and the distinction is represented by spacing. The em-dash is flush to the words on either side in a pause; extra space is added after the dash at a full stop. SBA made no visible distinction when capitalizing letters "a," "m," and "w," and in haste, often lost the distinction for other letters. When her customary practice could not be found, the editors resorted to standard usage. Haste also affected SBA's ending syllables. Her rendition of "evening" became "evenng" and then something resembling "even^g." A similar evolution occurred with the "ly" ending. These compressions and contractions were ignored and the invisible letters supplied. Readers may notice that the numbers of mistakes in SBA's letters rose in this period; she often left out words, syllables, and letters.

When SBA kept her diary in commercial appointment books, the printed date is set in capitals and small capitals to distinguish it from her entry.

ECS's letters contain a form of implied punctuation; if a comma or period were required and she had reached the right margin of her paper, she omitted the punctuation. Rather than supplying what she left out, extra space was introduced into the text, larger for a full stop.

THE TYPEWRITER. With money from the National-American, SBA hired secretarial help off and on after 1890 and dictated some letters to be typed. She did not easily cede control of her correspondence, and most of her typed letters show her intervention with a pen, as she checked the typist's punctuation, revised her own sentences, and scribbled postscripts. To preserve this collaboration between SBA and her clerks, new procedures were required. For typewritten incoming letters, such as those from Franklin Adams and Frances Willard, handwritten corrections are silently incorporated into the typed text. SBA's typed letters are published as emended texts, without indication of the collaboration between author and typist. Substantial additions she made, usually positioned like postscripts, are marked as in her hand. Her revisions are reserved for textual notes: alterations are listed by paragraph and line numbers, referenced to paragraph numbers printed beside the text. The textual notes detail significant changes in wording that SBA made, either to improve a phrase or to alter meaning; the notes do not indicate every comma or underline that she added.

PRINTED TEXTS. In printed texts, obvious typographical errors have been silently corrected. When new words were substituted, the original wording was recorded in a numbered note. The original titles of articles and appeals were retained as part of the text. The practice of typesetters to use small capitals for emphasis and for highlighting the names of speakers has been ignored. To preserve the emphasis, italics have been substituted.

ANNOTATION

In numbered notes, the editors provide the information they think necessary for readers to understand the document. Editorial notes placed either beneath a document's heading or interjected in the transcription provide context for texts excerpted from reports of a meeting.

To incomplete place and datelines, the editors have added, in italic type within square brackets, the best information available to complete the line. The basis for supplying a date is explained in a note.

The numbered notes principally identify references in the text, explain textual complexities, and summarize documents omitted from the edition. People are identified at the first occurrence of their names in the documents. The editors have tried to identify every person and reference, but they have not added notes simply to say "unidentified" or "not located." Biographical notes about people identified in previous volumes of this series do not recapitulate earlier information; if previous volumes contain useful references to the individual, readers are directed to them.

Research on the Internet has become an important part of the editors' work on annotation, especially for constructing biographies. Rather than citing sources by the Uniform Resource Locator (URL) or address in annotation, the editors recorded the name of the database and the host institution. Addresses changed too often. More ephemeral information with no institutional connection was described and copied for retention in the project's files.

Unless otherwise indicated, documents published in this volume may be found at their date in the microfilm edition of the *Papers of Stanton and Anthony*. A citation to the film (as *Film*, reel number:frame numbers) appears in the endnote only if the document is filmed at a different date. *Film* citations are included for documents mentioned within the numbered notes. An indication that a text is "not in *Film*" signifies that it has been acquired since publication of the microfilm edition.

Textual Devices

[roman text]	Text within square brackets in roman type is identified in the unnumbered endnote.
[roman text?]	The question mark indicates that the editors are uncertain about the text within the square brackets.
[roman date]	Date when a speech was delivered or an article published.
[*italic text*]	Editorial insertion or addition.
[*italic date*]	Date supplied by editors. In most cases, the basis is explained in a numbered note.
↑text↓	Authorial interlineation or substitution.
~~text~~	Text cancelled by the author.
~~*illegible*~~	Text cancelled by author that cannot be recovered.
<roman>	Addition to the source text from a second source.

≈ Abbreviations

Throughout the volume Elizabeth Cady Stanton is referred to as ECS and Susan B. Anthony as SBA.

In notes only the National Woman Suffrage Association is abbreviated as NWSA and the National-American Woman Suffrage Association as NAWSA.

Abbreviations Used to Describe Documents

ALS ❦ Autograph Letter Signed

AMs ❦ Autograph Manuscript

ANS ❦ Autograph Note Signed

TL ❦ Typed Letter

TCL ❦ Typed Copy of Letter

TLS ❦ Typed Letter Signed

TMs ❦ Typed Manuscript

Standard References, Newspapers, and Journals

ACAB ❦ James Grant Wilson and John Fiske, eds., *Appletons' Cyclopaedia of American Biography*, 6 vols. (New York, 1888–1889)

ACAB Supplement ❦ James Grant Wilson, ed., *Appletons' Cyclopaedia of American Biography*, (1901; reprint, Detroit, Mich., 1968)

Allibone Supplement ❦ John Foster Kirk, *A Supplement to Allibone's Critical Dictionary of English Literature and British and American Authors*, 2 vols. (Philadelphia, 1891)

American Women ❦ Frances E. Willard, *American Women: Fifteen Hundred Biographies with over 1,400 Portraits*, 2 vols. (New York, 1897)

American Women: Standard Biographical Dictionary ↢ Durward Howes, ed., *American Women: The Standard Biographical Dictionary of Notable Women, 1939–40* (1939; reprint, Teaneck, N.J., 1974)

ANB ↢ John A. Garraty and Mark C. Carnes, eds., *American National Biography*, 24 vols. (New York, 1999)

Anthony ↢ Ida Husted Harper, *Life and Work of Susan B. Anthony*, 3 vols. (1898–1908; reprint, New York, 1969)

Appleton's Annual Cyclopaedia ↢ *The American Annual Cyclopaedia and Register of Important Events of the Year 1871, 1882, 1899* (New York, 1872-1900)

Banks, *Biographical Dictionary of British Feminists, 1800–1930* ↢ Olive Banks, *The Biographical Dictionary of British Feminists*, vol. 1, *1800–1930* (Brighton, England, 1985)

BDAC ↢ *Biographical Dictionary of the American Congress, 1774–1971* (Washington, D.C., 1971)

BDAmerEd ↢ John F. Ohles, ed., *Biographical Dictionary of American Educators*, 3 vols. (Westport, Conn., 1978)

BDGov ↢ Robert Sobel and John Raimo, eds., *Biographical Dictionary of the Governors of the United States, 1789–1978*, 4 vols. (Westport, Conn., 1978)

BDTerrGov ↢ Thomas A. McMullin and David Walker, *Biographical Directory of American Territorial Governors* (Westport, Conn., 1984)

Connecticut Reports ↢ *Connecticut Reports. Cases Argued and Determined in the Supreme Court of Errors of the State of Connecticut*, 150 vols. (Hartford, Conn., 1817–1966)

DAB ↢ Allen Johnson and Dumas Malone, eds., *Dictionary of American Biography*, 20 vols. (New York, 1928–1936)

DAB, Supplement 1 ↢ Harris E. Starr, ed., *Dictionary of American Biography, Supplement One, To 1935* (New York, 1944)

DAB, Supplement 3 ↢ Edward T. James, ed., *Dictionary of American Biography, Supplement Three, 1941–1945* (New York, 1973)

DANB ↢ Rayford W. Logan and Michael R. Winston, eds., *Dictionary of American Negro Biography* (New York, 1982)

DBF ❧ J. Balteau et al., eds., *Dictionnaire de biographie française* (Paris, 1939–)

Dictionary of Canadian Biography ❧ *Dictionary of Canadian Biography*, 14 vols. (Toronto, Canada, 1966–)

DNB ❧ Leslie Stephen and Sidney Lee, eds., *The Dictionary of National Biography*, 22 vols. (1885–1901; reprint, London, 1973)

Douglass, *Papers* ❧ Frederick Douglass, *The Frederick Douglass Papers. Series One: Speeches, Debates, and Interviews*, ed. John W. Blassingame et al., 5 vols. (New Haven, 1979–1992)

1894. Constitutional-Amendment Campaign Year ❧ New York State Woman Suffrage Association, *1894. Constitutional-Amendment Campaign Year. Report of the New York State Woman Suffrage Association* (Rochester, N.Y., 1895)

Eighty Years ❧ Elizabeth Cady Stanton, *Eighty Years and More: Reminiscences, 1815–1897* (1898; reprint, Boston, 1993)

Encyclopedia of Mormonism ❧ Daniel H. Ludlow, ed., *Encyclopedia of Mormonism*, 5 vols. (New York, 1992)

Federal Reporter ❧ *The Federal Reporter. Cases Argued and Determined in the Circuit Court of Appeals and Circuit and District Courts of the United States*, 141 vols. (St. Paul, Minn., 1892–1911)

Film ❧ Patricia G. Holland and Ann D. Gordon, eds., *Papers of Elizabeth Cady Stanton and Susan B. Anthony* (Wilmington, Del., 1991, microfilm)

Garrison, *Letters* ❧ William Lloyd Garrison, *The Letters of William Lloyd Garrison*, ed. Walter M. Merrill and Louis Ruchames, 6 vols. (Cambridge, Mass., 1971–1981)

History ❧ Elizabeth Cady Stanton, Susan B. Anthony, Matilda Joslyn Gage et al., *History of Woman Suffrage*, 6 vols. (vols. 1–2, New York, 1881, 1882; vols. 3–4, Rochester, 1886, 1902; vols. 5–6, New York, 1922)

McPherson, *Hand-Book of Politics* ❧ Edward McPherson, *A Hand-Book of Politics for 1888, 1890, 1892, 1894* (Washington, D.C., 1888–1894)

Michigan Reports ❧ *Michigan Reports. Cases Decided in the Supreme Court of Michigan*, 446 vols. (Chicago, 1878–)

Mill, *Collected Works* ⚐ John Stuart Mill, *Collected Works of John Stuart Mill*, ed. J. M. Robson, 33 vols. (Toronto, Canada, 1963–1991)

"Minutes of the Twentieth Annual Convention, 1888" ⚐ "The Twentieth Annual Convention of the National Woman Suffrage Association: Minutes of the Meetings of the Executive Committee and Executive Services [sic], April 3 and April 4, 1888," typescript, National American Woman Suffrage Association Papers, DLC

Mt. Hope and Riverside Cemetery Interment Records ⚐ on-line images, Mt. Hope and Riverside Cemetery Interment Records, Department of Rare Books, Special Collections, and Preservation, NRU

National Party Platforms ⚐ Kirk H. Porter and Donald Bruce Johnson, eds., *National Party Platforms, 1840–1968* (Urbana, Ill., 1970)

NAW ⚐ Edward T. James, Janet Wilson James, and Paul S. Boyer, eds., *Notable American Women, 1607–1950: A Biographical Dictionary*, 3 vols. (Cambridge, Mass., 1971)

NAW Modern Period ⚐ Barbara Sicherman and Carol Hurd Green, eds., *Notable American Women, The Modern Period: A Biographical Dictionary* (Cambridge, Mass., 1980)

NCAB ⚐ *National Cyclopaedia of American Biography*, 63 vols. (New York, 1891–1984)

New York Reports ⚐ *Reports of Cases Decided in the Court of Appeals of the State of New York*, 264 vols. (Albany, 1872–1956)

Oxford DNB ⚐ H. C. G. Matthew and Brian Harrison, eds., *Oxford Dictionary of National Biography*, on-line edition (Oxford, England, 2004)

Papers ⚐ Ann D. Gordon, ed., *Selected Papers of Elizabeth Cady Stanton and Susan B. Anthony*, vol. 1, *In the School of Anti-Slavery, 1840 to 1866* (New Brunswick, N.J., 1997); vol. 2, *Against an Aristocracy of Sex, 1866 to 1873* (New Brunswick, N.J., 2000); vol. 3, *National Protection for National Citizens, 1873 to 1880* (New Brunswick, N.J., 2003); vol. 4, *When Clowns Make Laws for Queens, 1880 to 1887* (New Brunswick, N.J., 2006)

Quaker Genealogy ⚐ William Wade Hinshaw, *Encyclopedia of American Quaker Genealogy*, 3 vols. (Ann Arbor, Mich., 1936–1940)

Queen's Bench ↭ *The Law Reports of the Incorporated Council of Law Reporting. Queen's Bench Division and on Appeal therefrom in the Court of Appeal, Decisions on Crown Cases Reserved and Decisions of the Railway and Canal Commission*, 20 vols. (London, 1891–1900)

Register of Federal Officers ↭ *Register of Officers and Agents, Civil, Military, and Naval, in the Service of the United States . . .* (Washington, D.C., 1865–1892)

Report of the International Council of Women, 1888 ↭ *Report of the International Council of Women, Assembled by the National Woman Suffrage Association, Washington, D.C., U.S. of America, March 25 to April 1, 1888* (Washington, D.C., 1888)

Report of the Twenty-fifth Annual Convention, 1893 ↭ *Proceedings of the Twenty-Fifth Annual Convention of the National American Woman Suffrage Association, Held in Washington, D.C., January 16, 17, 18, 19, 1893*, ed. Harriet Taylor Upton (Washington, D.C., 1893)

Report of the Twenty-sixth Annual Convention, 1894 ↭ *Proceedings of the Twenty-Sixth Annual Convention of the National-American Woman Suffrage Association, Held in Washington, D.C., February 15, 16, 17, 18, 19 and 20, 1894*, ed. Harriet Taylor Upton (Warren, Ohio, n.d.)

Report of the Twenty-seventh Annual Convention, 1895 ↭ *Proceedings of the Twenty-Seventh Annual Convention of the National-American Woman Suffrage Association, Held in Atlanta, Ga., January 31st to February 5th, 1895*, ed. Harriet Taylor Upton (Warren, Ohio, n.d.)

Rev. ↭ *Revolution* (New York)

SEAP ↭ Ernest H. Cherrington, ed., *Standard Encyclopedia of the Alcohol Problem*, 6 vols. (Westerville, Ohio, 1925–1930)

Stanton ↭ Theodore Stanton and Harriot Stanton Blatch, eds., *Elizabeth Cady Stanton, as Revealed in Her Letters, Diary and Reminiscences*, 2 vols. (1922; reprint, New York, 1969)

Sumner, *Works* ↭ Charles Sumner, *The Works of Charles Sumner*, 15 vols. (Boston, 1870–1883)

Temperance and Prohibition Papers ↭ *The Temperance and Prohibition Papers, Microfilm Edition*, eds. Randall C. Jimerson and Francis X. Blouin (Ann Arbor, Mich., 1977)

TroyFS ⇐ Mrs. A. W. Fairbanks, ed., *Emma Willard and Her Pupils, or Fifty Years of Troy Female Seminary, 1822–1872* (New York, 1898)

TwCBDNA ⇐ Rossiter Johnson, ed., *The Twentieth Century Biographical Dictionary of Notable Americans*, 10 vols. (Boston, 1904)

United States Reports ⇐ *United States Reports: Cases Adjudged in the Supreme Court*, 438 vols. (New York, 1884–)

Wallace ⇐ John William Wallace, *Cases Argued and Adjudged in the Supreme Court of the United States*, 23 vols. (Washington, D.C., 1866–1876)

Washington Territory Reports ⇐ *Reports of Cases Determined in the Supreme Court of the Territory of Washington, 1854–1888*, 3 vols. (1879; reprint, Seattle, Wash., 1906)

WhNAA ⇐ *Who Was Who among North American Authors, 1921–1939*, 2 vols. (Detroit, Mich., 1976)

Who's Who of British Members of Parliament ⇐ Michael Stenton and Stephen Lees, eds., *Who's Who of British Members of Parliament: A Biographical Dictionary of the House of Commons*, 4 vols. (Atlantic Highlands, N.J., 1976–1981)

Wisconsin Reports ⇐ *Reports of Cases Argued and Determined in the Supreme Court of the State of Wisconsin*, 1st ser., 275 vols. (Chicago, 1853–1957)

Woman's Who's Who 1914 ⇐ John William Leonard, ed., *Woman's Who's Who of America, 1914–1915* (1914; reprint, Detroit, Mich., 1976)

Women Building Chicago ⇐ Rima Lunin Schultz and Adele Hast, eds., *Women Building Chicago, 1790–1990: A Biographical Dictionary* (Bloomington, Ind., 2001)

WWW1 ⇐ *Who Was Who in America*, vol. 1, *1897–1942* (Chicago, 1942)

WWW2 ⇐ *Who Was Who in America*, vol. 2, *1943–1950* (Chicago, 1950)

WWW3 ⇐ *Who Was Who in America*, vol. 3, *1951–1960* (Chicago, 1966)

WWW4 ⇐ *Who Was Who in America*, vol. 4, *1961–1968* (Chicago, 1968)

Archives and Repositories

CSmH ⇐ The Huntington Library, San Marino, Calif.

CoHi ⇐ Colorado Historical Society, Denver

ABBREVIATIONS

Ct ❧ Connecticut State Library, Hartford

CtHSD ❧ Harriet Beecher Stowe Center, Hartford, Conn.

CtY ❧ Yale University Libraries, New Haven, Conn.

DLC ❧ Library of Congress, Manuscript Division (unless otherwise noted), Washington, D.C.

DNA ❧ National Archives and Records Service, Washington, D.C.

ICIU ❧ University of Illinois at Chicago, Special Collections

IEWT ❧ Frances Willard Historical Association, Evanston, Ill.

In ❧ Indiana State Library, Indianapolis

Ia-HA ❧ State Historical Society of Iowa, Des Moines

KHi ❧ Kansas State Historical Society, Topeka

KyU ❧ University of Kentucky Library, Lexington

MeB ❧ Bowdoin College Library, Brunswick, Maine

MCR-S ❧ Schlesinger Library, Radcliffe Institute, Harvard University, Cambridge, Mass.

MHi ❧ Massachusetts Historical Society, Boston

MNS-S ❧ Sophia Smith Collection, Smith College, Northampton, Mass.

MnHi ❧ Minnesota Historical Society, St. Paul

MoSHi ❧ Missouri Historical Society, St. Louis

MtHi ❧ Montana Historical Society, Helena

NjR ❧ Rutgers University Libraries, New Brunswick, N.J.

NB ❧ Brooklyn Collection, Brooklyn Public Library, N.Y.

NIC ❧ Cornell University Library, Ithaca, N.Y.

NJost ❧ Johnstown Public Library, Johnstown, N.Y.

NN ❧ New York Public Library

NPV ❧ Vassar College Library, Poughkeepsie, N.Y.

NR ❧ Rochester Public Library, Rochester, N.Y.

NRU ❧ University of Rochester Library, Rochester, N.Y.

NSchU ⇝ Union College Library, Schenectady, N.Y.

NSyU ⇝ Syracuse University Libraries, Syracuse, N.Y.

NWefHi ⇝ Chautauqua County Historical Society, Westfield, N.Y.

PBm ⇝ Bryn Mawr College Library, Bryn Mawr, Pa.

PSC-Hi ⇝ Friends Historical Library of Swarthmore College, Swarthmore, Pa.

SdHi ⇝ South Dakota State Historical Society, Pierre

UkL ⇝ London, England

WaU ⇝ University of Washington Libraries, Seattle

WHi ⇝ Wisconsin Historical Society, Madison

Manuscript Collections

Blackwell Papers, DLC ⇝ Blackwell Family Papers

ECS Papers, DLC ⇝ Elizabeth Cady Stanton Papers

ECS Papers, NjR ⇝ E. C. Stanton Papers, T. Stanton Collection, Special Collections and University Archives

Gage Collection, MCR-S ⇝ Matilda Joslyn Gage Collection

Garrison Papers, MNS-S ⇝ Garrison Family Papers

NAWSA Papers, DLC ⇝ National American Woman Suffrage Association Papers

Rare Books, DLC ⇝ Rare Books Division

Papers of ECS, NPV ⇝ Papers of Elizabeth Cady Stanton

SBA Collection, NR ⇝ Susan B. Anthony Collection

SBA Papers, DLC ⇝ Susan B. Anthony Papers

SBA Papers, MCR-S ⇝ Susan Brownell Anthony Papers

SBA Papers, NRU ⇝ Susan B. Anthony Papers

The Selected Papers of Elizabeth Cady Stanton and Susan B. Anthony

1 ❦ FRANKLIN G. ADAMS[1] TO SBA

[*Topeka, Kan.*] Feb. 9, 1887.

My Dear Miss Anthony,

I am very tardy in making the acknowledgment inclosed.[2] The work of the State Historical Society has been very great this winter and other matters have hindered me.

I rejoice with you at the prospects of municipal suffrage in Kansas resulting from your good work and that of those associated with you.[3] Mrs. Johns[4] especially has been exceedingly attentive and faithful, and her work has been done in such a discreet manner that it seems as if every act has counted.

It was a matter of extreme regret on the part of every body that illness prevented you from reaching Topeka,[5] but all seem to have redoubled their efforts so as to in some measure compensate for the loss of your help.

I say all this simply from outside glances, for I have done nothing myself—have only been a distant observer, but having a heart-felt interest I could not but help see something of the work. Yours sincerely,

❦ *F. G. Adams.*

❦ TLS letterpress copy, Records of the Kansas State Historical Society, Letterpress Books, Department of Archives, KHi.

1. Franklin George Adams (1824–1899) was a founder of the Kansas State Historical Society and its secretary from 1876 until his death. He corresponded regularly with SBA about state history and woman's rights. He became the authority on women's use of the municipal franchise with his book, *Woman Suffrage in Kansas. An Account of the Municipal Elections in Kansas in 1887, As Told by the Newspapers of the State. With a Brief Account of the Suffrage Movement in the State, and Statistical Tables of the Women's Votes in 1887–88* (1888). (Alfred Theodore Andreas, *History of the State of Kansas, Containing a Full Account of Its Growth* [Chicago, 1883], 283–85, 554; *NCAB*, 6:498; *Topeka Daily Capital*, 3 December 1899, SBA scrapbook 31, Rare Books, DLC. See also *Papers* 4.)

2. Enclosure omitted. Adams sent a receipt for SBA's latest donation to the

historical society of books, pamphlets, and newspapers produced by the woman's rights and woman suffrage movements.

3. A bill granting municipal suffrage to women in Kansas awaited the governor's signature. Passed with strong majorities, overwhelmingly Republican, in both houses of the legislature, the bill was a triumph for the two-year campaign conducted jointly by the Kansas Equal Suffrage Association and the state's Woman's Christian Temperance Union, with the aid occasionally of SBA. (*History*, 4:638-40; Michael Lewis Goldberg, *An Army of Women: Gender and Politics in Gilded Age Kansas* [Baltimore, Md., 1997], 86-96; Carolyn De Swarte Gifford and June O. Underwood, "Intertwined Ribbons: The Equal Suffrage Association and the Woman's Christian Temperance Union, Kansas, 1886-1896," unpublished paper in editor's possession. See also *Papers* 4.)

4. Laura Lucretia Mitchell Johns (1849-1935) was recruited into the Kansas Equal Suffrage Association in 1884, not long after her move from Illinois to Salina, Kansas. Her lobbying for municipal suffrage began the next year, and she won election as president of the association in January 1887. Johns retained that position until 1895. In the meantime, her loyalties and duties grew more complex: she simultaneously served for several years as superintendent of the franchise for the Kansas Woman's Christian Temperance Union and organized the Kansas Woman's Republican Association. Johns and her husband left Kansas for California in 1911. (*American Women*; *Woman's Who's Who 1914*; Amy A. Mitchell, "Reminiscences of Laura Lucretia Johns," typescript, Alma Lutz Collection, NPV; "Laura M. Johns," *Chronicle Monthly Magazine* 2 [September 1894]: 3-5; Goldberg, *Army of Women*, 72-74, 88.)

5. SBA was scheduled to attend the annual meeting of the equal suffrage association in Topeka on 11 January 1887, but she telegraphed from her brother's house in Leavenworth to say she was ill. (*Woman's Tribune*, February 1887.)

2 ⇝ SBA TO RACHEL G. FOSTER[1]

The Riggs House   Washington D.C. Feb. 18/87—[2]

Darling Niece Rachel

Yours from 748—is here—came last evening— Glad to think of you at home—again!!

1st—about Kennett Square Society— It was in connection with my advice to keep State Societies <u>independent</u> ↑that I said what I did to Mary Grew!—↓ but—<u>no matter</u> for that—the <u>now</u> is the question[3]   As Mrs Pennock[4] states the matter—<u>she</u> will have to advise auxilliaryship

to the Penn. society of Phila—though it really is not a state society—
Still it has always assumed to be— As I understood you—most of the
young members—feel kindly to the National—and are likely—ere long—
to be ready to vote the Penn society—independent—if so—then making
the Chester County society Auxilliary to the Penn—will bring to it
added power to make itself independent!! It seems to me, therefore,
that to "lie low"—that is organize all the new societies auxilliary to the
Penn—and when you get enough representation↑ve↓ societies thus
allied to it—↑and you↓ move for independence—you will have a strong
alliance to help the Penn. out of its narrow position!!

I see the advantages of the other course—that is—of insisting on
↑the↓ independence of each new society—but fear that there is not
intelligence enough as to the two societies to prevent its making ↑a↓
division— You see—you couldn't carry the Ameses'[5] now—for either
indepence or auxiliaryship to the National—now—but by working
right along without raising the question you may, by & by, be able to
do so!— Still the Americans are bringing their annual meeting to Phila.
next October!!—[6] So—as you see & say—it is a very delicate & difficult
thing to decide— If Mrs Pennock hadn't had the money voted specially
to form a branch society to the Penn—but then—can it not be a branch
society—without being formally ↑made an↓ auxilliary?— So you see I
leave you to act as seemeth best when you are with the Kennett people—
I cannot decide for you at this ↑distance.↓

2^d—as to my speaking at Parkersburg, Westchester &c. &c.—[7] I
cannot possibly give a day to that work— I must close up here at Wash.
as quickly as possible—and then talk up work with you & get home at
earliest day—to set about getting out 2^d edition of Vol. I. History—[8]

3^d I sent you, last night—specimens of envelopes—that we have
here—square ones—and the larger letter sheets—plenty of both are
here—while there are but two or three sheets of the square envelope
paper—and not a single envelope for the large letter sheets— No—I am
wrong—while there are none here—there are plenty of them at Rochester—& I write Mr Charles Mann[9]—8 Elm st—Rochester—N.Y—to
send you a 1000 of them—at once— I had entirely forgotten that he
printed a lot while I was out West—

3^d↑4th↓—Yes—you may call your self—"manager"

4↑5th↓—It rains to-day—still—I will try & go to see the Opera Houses
& their renters—[10]

5↑6↓th—Yes—<u>You may</u> have some <u>Penn. manager's</u> paper printed—

7th There is <u>no money</u> in the treasury to pay for printing the promised pamphlet report!!—[11] It ought to be done!! But whence will come the cash? For 1885 & 1886—I have Ellen Burrs[12] stenographic report—and for this year's—we should have to depend upon Mrs Colby's!![13]

6↑8↓th—About Blairs[14] speeches—75 cts a ~~1.00~~ ↑hundred↓ will do—the actual cost to us is 50 cts— The entire report of the speeches discussion & vote—pamphlets actual cost is 7 cts apiece—[15] So we will sell them at 10 cts single copy—& $1. for 12 copies— How is that?

7↑9↓th—I have talked over the envelope heading[16]—& thought & thought it over—and as you say—40th anniversary cannot be added to it without lumbering it— So let it go— Only the envelope—if it doesn't have all the P.O. addresses of the Committee—<u>must have</u> at least <u>one address</u> to whom, in case of miscarriage of any kind—the Post Masters could return the letters ~~to~~ You see <u>that</u> is an absolute necessity—

8↑10↓th—When I come we will call on Mary Grew together—

11th—As Lucy E.[17] wrote you last night—I take it for granted she answered all your questions to her— Now—Lucy E. comes—and says she wrote you she would go up to Phila. Saturday— Niece Maude[18] expects to leave Sunday or Monday—and shall go northward as soon after as may be!!

Haven't I hit every point this time?—

Love to dear Niece Julia—[19] What a delightful thing it is for her to be mother as well as sister to you—and make that lovely home— She seemed so <u>like</u> "<u>Mama</u>" as she sat there that morning with her work in hand— Lovingly yours

> *Susan B. Anthony*

> ALS, on NWSA letterhead, Anthony-Avery Papers, NRU.

1. Rachel G. Foster (1858–1919), later Avery, a wealthy single woman living at 748 North Nineteenth Street in Philadelphia, became corresponding secretary of the National association in 1881 and continued in that post. Her responsibilities grew rapidly as she took over many chores once performed by SBA. SBA's use of "niece" for Rachel and her sister Julia reciprocated their decision, as much younger friends, to call her "Aunt Susan." (*NAW* and *ANB*, s.v. "Avery, Rachel G. Foster"; *Film*, 25:219–20.)

2. After the close of the National Woman Suffrage Association's convention and a subsequent state and national meeting in Philadelphia, SBA returned to Washington and the Riggs House, a hotel owned and managed by her close friends Caleb and Jane Spofford.

3. Foster led a new Woman's Suffrage Committee for Organizing Pennsylvania, created by the National Woman Suffrage Association but intended to bridge the historic divide between its loyalists and the Pennsylvania Woman Suffrage Association, an affiliate of the rival American Woman Suffrage Association headed since 1869 by Mary Grew (1813-1896). The state society had no presence outside Philadelphia; suffragists in western Pennsylvania had worked separately for more than a decade; and the National's affiliate in Philadelphia, the Citizens' Suffrage Association, to which Rachel Foster belonged, showed no sign of life. Its founder, Edward M. Davis, died later in 1887. (*NAW*; Ira V. Brown, *Mary Grew: Abolitionist and Feminist, 1813-1896* [Selinsgrove, Pa., 1991]; *History*, 3:457-68; *Film*, 25:219-20; *Papers*, 4:358-59, 383-84, 544-45. See also *Papers* 2 & 3.)

4. Deborah Ann Yerkes Pennock (1831-1912), the wife of Samuel Pennock, a manufacturer, lived in Kennett Square, Chester County, west of Philadelphia. She and her husband were active in the Underground Railroad and the Progressive Friends of Pennsylvania, or Longwood Meeting. In 1886, she served on the National association's executive committee for Pennsylvania, but in 1884, she also served as an officer of the American-affiliated, state suffrage association. SBA always advised local and state societies to vote themselves independent of the national societies in cases where a vote on affiliation might cause a division. (Winfield Scott Garner, ed., *Biographical and Portrait Cyclopedia of Chester County, Pennsylvania, Comprising a Historical Sketch of the County, by Samuel T. Wiley* [Philadelphia, 1893], 665-67.)

5. Charles Gordon Ames (1828-1912) was pastor of Philadelphia's Spring Garden Unitarian Society. His wife, Fanny Baker Ames (1840-1931), was a founder and the president of the city's New Century Club. Although staunch loyalists of Lucy Stone since 1869, since their move to Philadelphia in 1880, Charles and Fanny Ames had cooperated with Rachel Foster on more than one suffrage meeting, including most recently the one called by the National association on 31 January 1887. (*ANB* and *NAW*, s.v "Ames, Fanny Baker"; *NCAB*, 23:317; *History*, 2:758-60, 765, 3:753-55; *Papers*, 2:294, 295n, 399, 400n; *Film*, 22:304-15, 25:219-20.)

6. The American Woman Suffrage Association met in Philadelphia from 31 October to 2 November 1887.

7. Probably events to further Deborah Pennock's organizing in Chester County, these were in the village of Parkesburg (not Parkersburg) and the borough of West Chester.

8. The first edition of volumes one and two of the *History of Woman Suffrage* were published by Fowler & Wells in New York City. After SBA published volume three, working with the printer Charles Mann in Rochester, she planned to reissue the earlier volumes in the same way.

9. Charles Mann (c. 1861-1899), a son of Rochester's Unitarian minister, Newton Mann, headed the Charles Mann Printing Company. Besides odd

printing jobs for the National association, his firm published the third volume of the *History of Woman Suffrage*. He, and sometimes his father, read the manuscript very closely and proposed changes. SBA conceded that he "often very much improves even Mrs Stanton's best sentences." (Federal Census, 1880; Rochester *Post Express*, 21 November 1899, SBA scrapbook 31, Rare Books, DLC; SBA to Elizabeth B. Harbert, 26 October 1885, *Film*, 24:585-94.)

10. SBA changes the subject here to her search for an appropriate hall for an international meeting in Washington in 1888 to mark the fortieth anniversary of the Seneca Falls woman's rights convention. At its recent convention, the National association agreed to call the meeting and placed SBA at the head of its committee of arrangements.

11. In 1884, ECS and SBA published *National Woman Suffrage Association. Report of the Sixteenth Annual Washington Convention, March 4th, 5th, 6th and 7th 1884, With Reports of the Forty-Eighth Congress*, and announced a plan to prepare annual reports thereafter to supplement the record in the *History of Woman Suffrage*. Although the National issued no more reports, the National-American Woman Suffrage Association resumed the practice in 1892. See *Papers*, 4:333-34.

12. Frances Ellen Burr (1831-1923), Connecticut's senior advocate of woman suffrage and founder of the Hartford Equal Rights Club, was the sister of the publisher of the *Hartford Times*, the state's leading Democratic paper. She often used her stenographic skills to prepare reports of the National association's meetings. (Charles Burr Todd, *A General History of the Burr Family*, 4th ed. [New York, 1902], 305; *New York Times*, 10 February 1923; *History*, 2:538-43. See also *Papers* 2-4.)

13. Clara Dorothy Bewick Colby (1846-1916), of Beatrice, Nebraska, edited the *Woman's Tribune*, which, though not an official organ of the National association, covered the work of its members and affiliates. SBA did not think her reports of meetings were very good. (*NAW*; *ANB*.)

14. Henry William Blair (1834-1920), Republican from New Hampshire, served in the Senate from 1879 to 1891. Named to the new Select Committee on Woman Suffrage in 1882 in the Forty-seventh Congress and reappointed in the Forty-eighth and Forty-ninth Congresses, he wrote its report in favor of the suffrage amendment in 1886 and brought the amendment to a vote in January 1887. The National association purchased and distributed copies of *Woman Suffrage. Speech of Hon. Henry W. Blair, of New Hampshire, in the Senate of the United States, December 8, 1886* (1886), delivered when he asked the Senate to take up the amendment. (*BDAC*. See also *Papers* 4.)

15. *Debate on Woman Suffrage in the Senate of the United States, 2d Session, 49th Congress, December 8, 1886, and January 25, 1887, by Senators H. W. Blair, J. E. Brown, J. N. Dolph, G. G. Vest, and Geo. F. Hoar* (1887).

16. The topic is envelopes for the international meeting's committee of arrangements.

17. A real niece, Lucy Elmina Anthony (1860-1944) was the daughter of SBA's brother Jacob Merritt Anthony of Fort Scott, Kansas. After graduation from the Rochester Free Academy in 1883, she found a variety of roles in the suffrage movement—at this time, as assistant to the committee organizing the international meeting. (Charles L. Anthony, comp., *Genealogy of the Anthony Family from 1495-1904* [Sterling, Ill., 1904], 189; *New York Times*, 6 July 1944.)

18. Another real niece, Maude Anthony (1865-1950), later Koehler, was the eldest child of SBA's brother Daniel Read Anthony of Leavenworth, Kansas. Maude studied at the Gannett Institute in Boston, but opted not to fulfill SBA's hopes that she would continue her education at the University of Kansas. (Anthony, *Anthony Genealogy*, 185, 187; *Los Angeles Times*, 24 January 1950; SBA to Lucy E. Anthony, 27 August 1883, and SBA to Kate Stephens, 8 June 1884, *Film*, 23:276-88, 784-88.)

19. Julia T. Foster (c. 1849?-1890), Rachel's older sister, took an interest in the woman suffrage movement and helped out with the work of the National association. Their mother, Julia Manual Foster (c. 1830-1885), died while traveling with her daughters in Europe. (Federal Census, Pittsburgh, 1870, and Philadelphia, 1880; Samuel W. Durant, *History of Allegheny Co., Pennsylvania* [Philadelphia, 1876], 127, 128, 138; Adelaide Mellier Nevin, *The Social Mirror; A Character Sketch of the Women of Pittsburg and Vicinity* [Pittsburg, Pa., 1888], 30; *Anthony*, 2:701; SBA to R. G. F. Avery, 18 November 1890, *Film*, 28:737-41. See also *Papers* 4.)

3 ~ ECS TO CLARA BEWICK COLBY

Basingstoke Hants, England, Feb. 28th [1887].[1]

Dear Mrs. Colby: I send you by to-day's mail a copy of the London *Daily News* containing the report of a meeting to organize a Woman's Liberal Federation.[2] The Ladies' Primrose League was so successful in helping the Tories to carry the last election, that the Liberals decided to avail themselves of this reserved force to help boost themselves again into power. So they called a meeting of Liberal men and women and in secret session of delegates alone from local societies formed for this purpose they decided on a central organization, their principles of action, and plan of campaign. The great work was to be for the success of the Liberal party and all such "pet crotchets" as woman suffrage were to be held in abeyance. This produced a division in starting. Some of the women, and one member of parliament, Mr. Walter McLaren, a nephew of John Bright[3] scorned the idea of women working for a party that ignored their rights, and in a Liberal Federation that would not inscribe woman suffrage on its banner. The delegates had a hot discussion over the matter in the morning, but the public meeting in the afternoon was seemingly harmonious, aside from Mr. McLaren's protest. All the speakers you will see by the report, from Mrs. Gladstone[4] who presided, to the gentlemen who closed the meeting, all deplored the questionable measures of the Primrose League and claimed that the Liberal Federation should be carried on, by honest, straight-forward merits only, by direct open measures. Now there is only one way to exert direct influence in politics and that is through and by the ballot. Who can for a moment suppose that this Liberal Federation of women all over the kingdom will be one whit more scrupulous than the Primrose League, with men controlling both organizations, and to make the plan for carrying a close and heated election. If these women had votes they might feel some responsibility for their action. But when the whole movement is based on indirect influence, no one can be made accountable. Thus you see the women of England are to be placed in battle array, organized catspaws in the hands of either party.

And yet the men and women who spoke at this last meeting enlarged on this Liberal Federation as such a great school for women to study practical politics. You will see by the speech of the distinguished Professor Stuart[5] that he takes a financial view of this new power, he congratulated the Liberal party that the women would be so *useful* because they would give their *services for nothing*. They could hold meetings and distribute tracts in all the obscure localities and do faithful service, asking no reward!! I cannot tell you my indignation in reading their speeches, and my daughter who sat through the whole farce said she blushed for her sex, that women could be so dead to all self respect as to complacently listen to such insults, and worse still, echo them in their own speeches. I leave further comments for your brilliant pen. Pray give your readers a few extracts. Cordially yours,

~ *Elizabeth Cady Stanton.*

~ *Woman's Tribune*, April 1887.

1. ECS wrote from the home of her daughter Harriot Stanton Blatch, known as Hattie. Basingstoke lies in Hampshire County, abbreviated as Hants.

2. Clara Colby published ECS's letter without reprinting the article in the *Daily News*. On 25 February 1887, after nearly a year of planning, forty local

Women's Liberal Associations came together in London to inaugurate the Women's Liberal Federation. Having lost its parliamentary majority in 1886, the Liberal party thought it wise to engage women in electoral politics and looked to the Conservative party's Primrose League as a model. Founded in 1883 to build a popular base of support and provide volunteers during elections, the league admitted women a year later and created the Ladies Grand Council of the Primrose League in 1885, in time to help the party win control of the government in 1886. (London *Daily News*, 26 February 1887; Linda Walker, "Party Political Women: A Comparative Study of Liberal Women and the Primrose League, 1890-1914," in *Equal or Different: Women's Politics, 1800-1914*, ed. Jane Rendall [Oxford, England, 1987], 165-91.)

3. John Bright (1811-1889) was the leading Radical in Parliament for three decades and the senior member of a large, extended political family. Walter Stowe Bright McLaren (1853-1912), who entered Parliament in 1886, was a son of Bright's sister Priscilla Bright McLaren and, unlike his uncle John, a strong supporter of woman suffrage. The press was excluded from the morning meeting to which ECS refers, but in the afternoon, Walter McLaren reiterated his point, that a "desire to get just legislation for all" was commendable, but "it would have been better if they had confined their efforts to the obtaining of just legislation for themselves." (*Oxford DNB*, s.v. "Bright, John"; *Who's Who of British Members of Parliament*, vol. 2, s.v. "McLaren, Walter Stowe Bright"; Bertha Mason, *Walter S. B. McLaren: An Appreciation* [London, n.d.], Women's Library, London; London *Daily News*, 26 February 1887.)

4. Catherine Glynne Gladstone (1812-1900), wife of the Liberal party's leader, William E. Gladstone, presided over not only the inaugural meeting but also, for many years, the Women's Liberal Federation itself. (Joyce Marlow, *Mr and Mrs Gladstone: An Intimate Biography* [London, 1977], 251-52, 268.)

5. James Stuart (1843-1913), professor at Cambridge University, was a Liberal member of Parliament and advocate of woman suffrage. (*Who's Who of British Members of Parliament*, vol. 3; London *Daily News*, 26 February 1887.)

4 ~> ECS TO SBA

[*Basingstoke, England*] March 10th [*1887*]

Dear Susan,

Reading your last epistle over again this morning & seeing the difficulty about large buildings why not have the two small ones you speak of The Foundry & the Universalist church.[1] Then two meetings can be going on at the same time. We shall want two days for suff. the temperance people will want the same. You & I can speak at both if we see fit. If the Boston people[2] would unite with all their associations we could keep two meetings going easily. It would be like the old anniversary weeks in New York.[3] Thus our foreign friends would have the opportunity of seeing our women in the different reforms, & we could have a grand social gathering at the close. Let every President preside & manage her own association   Perhaps we could induce the Woman's Congress[4] to hold their meetings there at the same time   How would "International Federation" do for a name   The English women are just forming a "Liberal Federation" If you think Congress too hackneyed what think you of <u>Federation</u>   "International Federation" sounds well. If we could get all associations of women to meet in Washington at that time representing suffrage, temperance, education, industries, science, art, social purity   religion, it would be a grand idea. Hattie & I have talked together over the speech question again & feel that your plan would indeed be herculean & wholly impracticable. Ask for their subjects & limit them to twenty minutes or half an hour & that is I think all you can do[5]

Now as to circular letter, do not I pray you let one go out until you & Mr Mann put every sentence through your metaphysical, rehetorical & common sense tweezers. Our women are in general too verbose they leave nothing to be understood. The call for the Wash con. was ridiculous.[6] Do not let a circular letter of that style go out. I wish you could have seen the call Mrs Gage[7] sent me. Woman about fifty times. It makes me nervous to think of a circular letter. If you will write me <u>all</u> you want said   Hattie & I will put it in shape, or at least let me see it before it is published. Our young women will not take the trouble you & I do with sentences. You must not trust them. A letter to circulate in Europe as well as America should be put in the best English of which we are capable   As to Mrs Gage's documents I need say nothing, long experience has shown us that she will not ponder sentences. I think the 10th of April is as late as we should hold the International Federation. But few women know how to make a synopsis of their speeches, & the papers will make their own synopsis anyway. Don't get up more machinery than you can manage. You err on the side of details, & I on the opposite extreme   let us try & strike the happy medium & leave something to peoples common sense, though Train[8] says they have none. I shall be home in June Hattie will come over one month before the Congress whenever that may be. We shall want one or two of the <u>last days</u> for the religious phase of our movement[9] we will take the last so that all those who are not interested in that phase of the question can leave when their work is done. I shall manage this meeting, my speakers as it looks to me now will be Adler,[10] Conway,[11] Newton[12] Ingersoll,[13] Mrs Gage, Helen Gardener[14] Clara Neyman[15] & myself, Hattie & Miss Müller[16] & Gerald Massey[17] if he will go over. But whether to have men or not I am not quite clear. I half incline to shut them out entirely as they have had their say if we do I shall ask Olympia,[18] Florence Kollock,[19] & others in their stead. Hattie will prepare herself on both the religious & political phase of the movement. Lady Haberton[20] will want one day for the dress question. Are you fully decided all things considered that Washington is better than New York? I like it better, because there are fewer cranks in Wash. Well I think I have said my say if I think of anything else will write

~ E. C. S.

[*Written on the envelope*] Would it not be well to discuss the Irish question one session & invite Miss Tod[21] Mrs Parnell[22] Mrs Sullivan[23] & Helen Taylor[24] to take part   These are simply suggestions! As soon as you decide on the time make sure of Francis Williard[25] & Hannah Whitehall Smith[26]

~ ALS, Anthony-Avery Papers, NRU. Envelope addressed to Rochester, New York.

1. SBA's missing letter solicited ideas for the international meeting in 1888. ECS suggests locating the events at two of Washington's churches, the Methodist Episcopal Foundry, at G and Fourteenth streets, Northwest, and the Universalist Church of Our Father, at Thirteenth and L streets, Northwest.

2. A reference to the American Woman Suffrage Association, based in Boston.

3. During anniversary weeks, usually scheduled in May, religious and reform societies convened in the same city to allow their leaders and members to hear a variety of speakers.

4. The Woman's Congress was convened annually by the Association for the Advancement of Women to discuss topics of intellectual and social concern.

5. ECS elsewhere described SBA's idea that speeches for the international meeting be "sent to a committee for inspection" in advance. "Who," ECS asked, "would be on a committee to look over fifty manuscripts?" (ECS to Clara B. Colby, 9 March 1887, *Film*, 25:279-86.)

6. See *Film*, 25:125.

7. Matilda Joslyn Gage (1826–1898) of Fayetteville, New York, had worked with ECS and SBA since the 1850s, and most recently she joined them as an editor of the *History of Woman Suffrage*. She held office in the National association as a vice president. (*NAW*; *ANB*.)

8. George Francis Train (1829–1904), a successful financier, railroad promoter, and advocate of Irish nationalism, founded the *Revolution* in 1868 for ECS to edit and SBA to publish. (*DAB*.)

9. For earlier discussion of this plan to call a meeting on women and religion in conjunction with the fortieth anniversary meeting, see ECS to Harriet H. Robinson, 30 September 1886, *Papers*, 4:519–20.

10. Felix Adler (1851–1933), lecturer and social reformer, founded the New York Society for Ethical Culture in 1876. (*ANB*.)

11. Moncure Daniel Conway (1832–1907), a Unitarian minister and writer, who lived in England from 1863 to 1885, became a friend of ECS in London in 1883. (*ANB*. See also *Papers* 4.)

12. Richard Heber Newton (1840–1914), an Episcopal clergyman, was rector of All Souls' Church in New York City and a defender of critical studies of the Bible. (*ANB*.)

13. Robert Green Ingersoll (1833–1899) was an agnostic, whose lectures against the Bible and fundamentalism were enormously popular. (*ANB*.)

14. Helen Hamilton Gardener (1853–1925), a disciple of Ingersoll, published *Men, Women and Gods, and Other Lectures* in 1885. To freethought, she brought a sharp critique of religion's role in degrading women. (*NAW*; *ANB*.)

15. Clara Low Neymann (c. 1840–1931), whose name often appeared as Clara B. Neymann, was a widow, German-American freethinker, and noted lecturer, active in the New York city and state suffrage societies. Neymann later served on the Woman's Bible Revising Committee. (Federal Census, 1880; city directories, 1880 to 1891; *Woman's Who's Who 1914*, s.v. "Glucksmann, Olga Neyman"; *Woman's Journal*, 23 February 1884; *New York Times*, 28 May 1931.)

16. Frances Henrietta Müller (1846?–1906) was born in Valparaiso, Chile, the daughter of a German-born businessman who became a British subject. Henrietta, as she was known, stood for election to the London School Board in 1879 and served on the board until 1885. Using the nom de plume Helena B. Temple, she edited the *Women's Penny Paper* from 1888 to 1890, renamed it the *Woman's Herald*, and continued publishing until 1892. (*Oxford DNB*. See also *Papers* 4.)

17. Gerald Massey (1828–1907) was a poet and writer with a strong interest in Christian socialism, spiritualism, and mysticism. (*Oxford DNB*.)

18. Olympia Brown (1835–1926), an ordained Universalist minister, was pastor of the church in Racine, Wisconsin. She served as a vice president of the National association. (*NAW*; *ANB*. See also *Papers* 2–4.)

19. Florence Ellen Kollock (1848–1925), later Crooker, was a Universalist minister, trained at St. Lawrence University. She established the churches in

Pasadena, California, while on a visit in 1885, and Englewood, Illinois, where she preached at this time. In 1884, she spoke at the National association's Washington convention and at a hearing before the House Judiciary Committee. (St. Lawrence University, *General Catalogue of the Officers, Graduates, and Non-Graduates, 1856-1925* [Canton, N.Y., 1926], 121; *American Women*, s.v. "Kollock, Florence E."; *WWW1*, s.v. "Crooker, Florence Kollock"; *Film*, 23:685-88.)

20. Florence Wallace Legge Pomeroy, viscountess Harberton (1843?-1911), founded the Rational Dress Society in 1881 to promote dress reform and her own reform costumes. She also participated in the National Society for Women's Suffrage. (*Oxford DNB*. See also *Papers* 4.)

21. The Irish Question at this date was concerned principally with Home Rule. In 1886, Liberal Prime Minister William Gladstone proposed a parliament for Ireland. The idea divided his own party, leading Gladstone's government to resign in July 1886. Isabella Maria Susan Tod (1836-1896) of Belfast was a Protestant Unionist, who devoted the last decade of her life to advocating Ireland's union with Britain. In earlier days, she helped to found the Belfast Women's Temperance Association, formed the Northern Ireland Society for Women's Suffrage, and was prominent in the National Society for Women's Suffrage. (Maria Luddy, "Isabella M S Tod (1836-1896)," in *Women, Power and Consciousness in 19th-Century Ireland*, eds. Mary Cullen and Maria Luddy [Dublin, 1995], 197-230. See also *Papers* 4.)

22. Delia Tudor Stewart Parnell (?-1898) was the American mother of the Irish leader and member of Parliament Charles Stewart Parnell. With her daughters, she founded the Irish Ladies' Land League in the United States, and she made occasional appearances at suffrage meetings. In 1886, the National association named her honorary vice president for New Jersey. (Federal Census, Burlington County, New Jersey, 1880; *New York Times*, 27, 28 March, 2 April 1898; *History*, 3:956, 4:840.)

23. Margaret Frances Buchanan Sullivan (1847-1903) was an Irish-born journalist from Chicago, who wrote *Ireland of To-day; the Causes and Aims of Irish Agitation* (1881). (*WWW1*; D. J. O'Donoghue, *The Poets of Ireland: A Biographical and Bibliographical Dictionary of Irish Writers of English Verse* [1912; reprint, Detroit, Mich., 1968].)

24. Helen Taylor (1831-1907), the stepdaughter of John Stuart Mill and an early advocate of woman suffrage, supported Home Rule and the nationalization of land. (*Oxford DNB*. See also *Papers* 4.)

25. Frances Elizabeth Caroline Willard (1839-1898) was president of the Woman's Christian Temperance Union and the most influential woman among American Evangelicals. (*NAW*; *ANB*. See also *Papers* 3 & 4.)

26. Hannah Whitall Smith (1832-1911) was an evangelist, temperance advocate, and suffragist, based in Philadelphia but often in London, where she and ECS rekindled their acquaintance. (*NAW*; *ANB*. See also *Papers* 4.)

5 ⇝ OLIVER JOHNSON[1] TO SBA

209 W. 45th St.,   New York, March 18, 1887.

My Dear Susan,

I feel somehow as if I did not half deserve to be remembered so kindly by you. I have been severely critical of some things in your career, not in public so much as in private. But you are a generous, great-hearted woman, in spite of every ~~ful~~ fault, as I always knew you were, and so you overlook all my rough edges and take me for what is best in myself. I do greatly admire your life-long devotion to the cause of woman, and your bravery as well. There is no discount here.

Yes, thank you, I have your first two volumes in red cloth on my shelves, and would be most glad of the third to keep them company; but in truth I don't deserve the gift at your hands. My pecuniary assets are, however, so small as to forbid me the luxury of buying ~~my~~ books in my old age.

You ask after my wife. I am glad to say she is in usual health, in spite of long and wearisome watching over me. I have been very ill more than once in the last two years, and should not now be alive on the earth but for her angelic devotion. Ah, what do we men <u>not</u> owe to women! As for the little girl, I wish she might know ↑you↓ as one of her father's oldest friends. She is a bright, happy, loving girl of almost 13 years, and she makes us <u>very</u> happy. Yours admiringly,

⇝ *Oliver Johnson.*

⇝ ALS, HM 10604, Ida Harper Collection, CSmH. Noted on sheet that *History* was sent to Johnson 21 March 1887.

1. Oliver Johnson (1809–1889), abolitionist, early supporter of woman's rights, and editor of the *National Anti-Slavery Standard* during the Civil War, worked for various newspapers in the New York area in the postwar decades. Although claimed as their own by the American Woman Suffrage Association, Johnson spared neither suffrage association when he disapproved of tactics or advice. After the death of his first wife, Mary Ann White Johnson, in 1872, Johnson married Jane Maria Abbott (1833–1900) in 1873. Their daughter Helen Hunt Johnson, later Daly, was born in 1874. (*ANB*; Steven M. Raffo, *A*

Biography of Oliver Johnson, Abolitionist and Reformer, 1809–1889 [Lewiston, N.Y., 2002], 317, 330; *Woman's Journal*, 29 December 1900. See also *Papers* 1 & 2.)

6 ❧ SBA TO RACHEL G. FOSTER

Rochester March 23/87

Dear Niece Rachel

I send you this from Mrs Stanton¹—and I want you not to condemn until you get to the end—because you will see that after suggesting— <u>she</u> <u>sees</u>—it wont do—herself— But I think you had better not send it to May²—because she may take her <u>sentence</u> <u>making</u> criticism as personal!! I want <u>you</u> to study & become a <u>non</u>-<u>repetitious</u> writer— Mrs Stanton <u>may</u> go to the extreme ↑one way↓—but it sure most of go to the other— And I want Lucy³ to see Mrs Stanton's letter—for I do want her to study good sentence making— I would like to have a whole year of practice with Mrs Stanton as teacher— You see I want <u>all</u> of <u>my</u> <u>nieces</u> to excel where their aunt makes a lamentable failure—

Why do you not send me Mrs Sewall's draft of letter of invitation— she writes she sent it to you long ago—thinking I was there!!

I tell you, this cold, snowy, blowy weather—so late in March—as 23—makes me feel shivery about the days we have upon for our 40th anniversary—March 25 to April 1— But still I suppose it is not this disagreeable in Washington now— I doubt if we change our week— even if we thought it best to—

Let Lucy return Mrs Stanton's— Did I send you hers about sister Mary⁴ <u>& I</u> <u>sharing</u> <u>the</u> the expenses of her <u>Tenafly</u> house & home?— which I most respectfuly declined!!—

Do send me a specimen of your column— I am sorry to have you give your time & strength to that—when Mrs Colby—with very little additional expense could do it for you—& all of the Nationals!

Mrs Harbert⁵—to day—tells me of her plan to get out her "<u>New</u> <u>Era</u>[">]—as a <u>Quarterly</u>!! and asks my opinion—and I have "<u>sat</u> <u>down</u>["]⁶ on the propal <u>heavy</u>—telling her if any of us had money or brains to invest in ↑the↓ newspaper line—we ought to concentrate both upon the one paper now in existence— It does seem a craze to start papers— Mrs Blake[7] writes as if she expected me personally to set about working for The Question— Well, "every pig will burn its nose in the hot swill"

I hope all the scientists will concentrate their metaphysical powers upon our Committees secretary[8]—clerk—so as to put a stop to such excesses as to time and quantity both—else our Committee wont have a very strong & lasting helper in that little personage! I think she ought to lie on her back for a time, at least, until the new remedial agency can get the ascendency ove the evil thought that possesses the trouble!

And I hope she is telling you when she is not feeling equal to work— For crime as it is to be ailing—the first failure necessitates the next step—and I do hope that my niece Rachel wont outrage even the science—by overdoing— Because the fires of the Richmond Hotel[9] no more surely took the life—than too great violation of material law will produce it throug over-work or over carelessness— So don't be reckless nor prodigal of your strength my dear— Lovingly yours

~ *Susan B. Anthony*

[*written on envelope*] N.B. Do send to Mrs Colby every item of your Penn. work—so she can have Penn. news in her paper every time

~ ALS, on NWSA letterhead, Anthony-Avery Papers, NRU. Envelope addressed "748—North 19th street Philadelphia."

1. Above at 10 March 1887.
2. May Eliza Wright Thompson Sewall (1844–1920) was principal of the Girls' Classical School in Indianapolis. A cofounder of the Indianapolis Equal Suffrage Society in 1878, and active in the National association since 1880, she chaired the National's executive committee. (*NAW*; *ANB*; Ray E. Boomhower, *"But I Do Clamor": May Wright Sewall, A Life, 1844–1920* [Zionsville, Ind., 2001].)
3. That is, her niece Lucy E. Anthony.
4. Mary Stafford Anthony (1827–1907), the youngest of the Anthony sisters, retired from the Rochester public schools in 1883. She lived in the house on Madison Street which had belonged to her mother. ECS decided to sell rather than return to her house in Tenafly, New Jersey. (Anthony, *Anthony Genealogy*, 173; *Anthony*, 1489; Rochester *Post Express*, 6 February 1907; Warranty deed, 26 May 1887, *Film*, 25:482–84.)
5. Elizabeth Morrison Boynton Harbert (1843–1925), a journalist, presided over the Illinois Equal Suffrage Association until 1884 and frequently served on the National's executive committee. When her monthly *New Era* ceased publication in December 1885, she told readers the paper would be back. (*American Women*; *NCAB*, 18:232; *Women Building Chicago*.)

6. This placement of SBA's missing close to her quotation marks may not encompass all of the words she deemed slang.

7. Lillie Devereux Blake (1833–1913), a writer and president of both the New York State Woman Suffrage Association and the New York City Woman Suffrage League, had recently taken on the job of associate editor of *The Question*, a small New York paper committed to suffrage and better conditions for working women. Blake retired from the state presidency in 1890, after eleven years in office, but she presided over the city league until 1897. (*NAW*; *ANB*; *Woman's Journal*, 12 February 1887. See also *Papers* 2–4.)

8. Lucy Anthony suffered some form of menstrual pain that incapitated her for at least a week every month. SBA had recently sent money for Lucy to continue unspecified experimental treatments, and in this warning about exhaustion, she explores the concepts and language of Mind Cure. (SBA to R. G. Foster, 19 March 1887, *Film*, 25:311–17.) Although Christian Science and Mind Cure had attracted adherents for more than a decade, they were surging in popularity and organization during 1887, both in New England and the Midwest. For their growth in the late 1880s, see Beryl Satter, *Each Mind a Kingdom: American Women, Sexual Purity, and the New Thought Movement, 1875–1920* (Berkeley, Calif., 1999), 79–110.

9. Buffalo's new Richmond Hotel burned on 18 March 1887, killing twelve guests and injuring many more. (*New York Times*, 19, 20, 21, 22, 23, 24 March 1887.)

7 ❧ SBA TO RACHEL G. FOSTER

Rochester March 25—P.M. 1887—

Dear Rachel—

Your note with package of May's first draft is here—[1] I do not ↑know↓ but such a recapitulation is needed—but my first impression is that it is too much an enlargement on the Call—less strongly put—while there is nothing of what I most wanted to see—that is the subjects to be discussed— The delegate, not only to tell what her society had done in its specific line—but also what it had done to draw its members to the ballot— Well it is here & I will study it—but surely this letter should be <u>instructions</u> as ↑to↓ the meeting & not a report of womans progress in 40 years—

❧ S. B. A.

[*on face of postcard*] April—17— my sister just finds this card in the bottom of one of her boxes!!— And now—I am still amazed at the results of this long delay—

↘ ANS on postal card, Anthony-Avery Papers, NRU.

1. This was a draft of the invitation addressed to national and international organizations to send a delegate to the international meeting in 1888. The call and an appeal for funds were mailed out in June. The invitations were sent out in July and August. (*Report of International Council, 1888*, pp. 447, 454n, *Film*, 26:154ff.)

8 ↘ SBA TO RACHEL G. FOSTER

[*Rochester, late March? 1887*]¹

Dear Rachel—

If you take Mrs Stanton's <u>thinking</u> <u>aloud</u> to S. B. A.—so seriously I shant send on any more of them— I just laughed at her suggestions— for they were only her <u>first</u> thoughts—and before she got to the end of one she evidently saw its impracticability— Her last note <u>implored</u> me to come strait over & go to Paris to a great women's meeting with her— & then come home with her in June!! Nothing will settle our plan & program—like giving <u>them</u> to people <u>on paper</u>—

So I trust our "<u>May</u>" will soon send us her first mappings out— I hope my throwing her first <u>ten</u> pages overboard—didn't hurt her feelings—but I was so set back—that of the whole 12 pages—there wasn't the first glimmering of the plan of procedure—as to the calling, organizing or conducting of the Council— The Rhetoric & reason for the gathering are in the call already—and the letter wants only <u>clear</u> statements of—of whom the Con. is to to be composed &c— I begged her to make a program of subjects & societies for each day of the eight— <u>without</u> names of speakers—so that we could get some notion of her thought of the way things should be—and I understood her to say she had the whole thing thought out!!

If we don't get things into shape before—I think you had better go to Indianapolis—too—then three of us can be together for a few days— May hasn't written a word since I told her I had repented me—and <u>would</u> go to her May 3 & 4 meeting—but I suppose she still wants me—

or she would let me know—[2] I have to day settled upon May 10th to lecture at Evansville[3]—and Dr Mary F. Thomas[4] wants me at Richmond—but if you go to Ind. I shall want all of the first 10 days at 343 with the trio of the Com—[5]

But never you fear about the <u>helm</u> of our good craft being surrendered to any one outside of <u>our own</u> National officers—and as Mrs Stanton will not be <u>bored</u> to preside the whole eight days—& S. B. A. stands next in order—R. G. F. M. W. S. et all <u>can manage no. 2</u>—there wont be any foundering of the ship— But I do not want to say to Mrs Stanton, any more than to May, Rachel or Spofford[6]—that she <u>shan't</u> have things so & so!!— <u>Time</u> good work & <u>very</u> <u>little</u> talk—as to what shall & what shant be—will make all the machinery & their owners run like clock-work— Mrs Stanton is always <u>very</u> <u>pliable</u> unless sets up <u>shan't</u> be or do!! She is very human—that is— So I await May's idea as to how & of whom the council shall be made up—and what subjects shall be assigned to each day—morning & evening—&c—&c— I must admit that I have not yet been able to get a clear plan into my head yet— So I wait for her—or you—or any one who can—to present it to me— I sent all I had of Mrs Gage's as well as of Mrs Stanton's—

Yes I fully agree that if Mrs Stanton shall present her that to the Church & Priests is due all of woman's degradation—then Miss Williard & the Church women [should?] be permitted to put in their claim that to the Church is due the credit for all that woman is & is to be!!— I <u>have</u> written Mrs Stanton on all the absurdities of her suggestions— [*in margin of first page*] Lovingly yours

S. B. A—

ALS, on NWSA letterhead, Anthony-Avery Papers, NRU. Square brackets surround word guessed by editors.

1. The date is speculative. Rachel Foster had responded to SBA's letter of March 23, and SBA had already edited May Sewall's draft of the invitation that she received on March 25.

2. For the second annual convention of the National Woman Suffrage Association of Indiana. May Sewall chaired the executive committee. See *Film*, 25:432-35.

3. See *Film*, 25:438-39.

4. Mary Frame Myers Thomas (1816–1888), a physician in Richmond, Indiana, rose to prominence in the local woman's rights movement in the 1850s and remained active in the state suffrage association and the state

temperance union's franchise department. She served as president of the American Woman Suffrage Association in 1880. (*NAW*.)

5. SBA refers to Sewall's house at 343 North Pennsylvania Street, Indianapolis, where she spent at least two weeks during May 1887.

6. Jane H. Snow Spofford (1828–1905) was the National association's treasurer and an active member of suffrage societies in the District of Columbia. She and her husband ran the Riggs House. (Jeremiah Spofford, *A Genealogical Record, Including Two Generations in Female Lines of Families Spelling the Name Spofford, Spafford, Spafard, and Spaford* [Boston, 1888], 247; research by Katherine W. Trickey, Bangor, Me.; *Woman's Journal*, 6 January 1906. See also *Papers* 3 & 4.)

9   ECS TO BENJAMIN F. UNDERWOOD AND SARA FRANCIS UNDERWOOD[1]

Basingstoke Hants [*England*]   April 5th [*1887*]

Dear Friends

I am very glad to get a line direct from you, to know that you have a local habitation & a name in the Great West, & that you are fairly started in a new venture. Success to you. I am quite tempest tossed just now, not having decided whether to return to America this spring, or to go to Paris for the summer, or to stay where I am, but whatever I do I will write as you propose for The Open Court.

You ask about Miss Lord.[2] She is also editing a paper in Chicago & has gone over hook & line into mind cure. In her present mental bewilderment I do not think it worth while for Mrs Underwood to expend any force on her as she would no doubt prove very unsatisfactory, unless perchance she too is suffering with the same epidemic, which is certainly very contagious & spreading in many latitudes. I have been concentrating my attention on Biblical commentaries this winter & have just read the Bishop of Lincoln's (Mr Wordsworths) notes on the Pentetuch.[3] Though written from an orthodox standpoint, he views the whole thing as figurative & allegorical, even the march of the children of Israel through the wilderness, is but the wanderings of the human soul. But the one point in which ecclesiastics make no change or progress, is in the status of woman. All The critics leave us in hopeless degradation, one point at least in which all religions & sects agree, under all circumstances woman is the scape goat for the sins of the people. With kind regards & best wishes for your success Sincerely yours

~ *Elizabeth Cady Stanton*

~ ALS, Papers of ECS, NPV. Year 1884 added in error to date.

1. Benjamin Franklin Underwood (1839–1914), a prominent freethinker, lecturer, and author, and his wife, Sara A. Francis Underwood (1838–1911), a writer and woman suffragist, left Boston for Chicago in 1886, when the Free Religious Association's decision to terminate the Boston *Index* cost them their jobs. In Chicago, they were hired to edit the *Open Court*, a new biweekly journal "devoted to establishing ethics and religion on a scientific basis." They moved into a house at 3024 Lake Park Avenue. (*DAB* and Gordon Stein, ed., *The Encyclopedia of Unbelief* [Buffalo, N.Y., 1985], s.v. "Underwood, Benjamin Franklin"; *WWW1*, s.v. "Underwood, Sara A. Francis"; Sara A. Francis Underwood, "Memories of Elizabeth Cady Stanton," *Free Thought Magazine* 21 [January 1903]: 20–22; city directory, 1887; *Papers*, 2:200–201, 4:passim.

2. Henrietta Frances Lord (c. 1848–?), best known as the English translator of Hendrik Ibsen's plays *The Doll's House* and *Ghosts*, was ECS's earliest collaborator on the *Woman's Bible*, when she came to the United States from England in 1886, but her passion for the project was short-lived. She moved to Chicago to study Christian Science, or Mind Cure, with Emma Curtis Hopkins, and stayed to edit a Christian Science journal for women. After Lord's return to England later in 1887, she published *Christian Science Healing: Its Principles and Practice*. (Cambridge University, Girton College, *Girton College Register, 1869–1946* [Cambridge, England, 1948], 8; Census of Britain, 1881; Allibone Supplement; Kathi Kern, *Mrs. Stanton's Bible* [Ithaca, N.Y., 2001], passim; *Eighty Years*, 374, 377, 390–92. See also *Papers* 4.)

3. In his six-volume commentary on the Old Testament, *The Holy Bible, in the Authorized Version, with Notes and Introductions*, published first in the 1860s, Chrisopher Wordsworth (1807–1885), bishop of Lincoln, devoted the first volume to the five books of Moses, or the Pentateuch.

10 ❧ ECS TO SARA FRANCIS UNDERWOOD

[*Basingstoke?, England, c. 13 April 1887*][1]

Dear Mrs Underwood,

Yours & Mr Underwoods letters both received I was very glad to hear from you. Why dont you send me some numbers of "The Open Court" that I may see what you are thinking & saying. I send you an article on the exciting topics here at this hour.[2] Be sure & read the proof carefully as my words are some times obscure. I am so disgusted with the extremes of wealth & poverty, & this hateful distinction of classes, that I cannot write of anything in this old world with patience. The utter contempt of labor, & the laborer is truly pitiful. Do not overtax yourself to do anything in haste on the Bible   There is no hurry. It will be a longer job than I supposed.[3] As to Miss Helen Gardner I supposed Mrs Gage was to fill that office, as she had requested to be made chairman of that committee, but she got some crotchet in her head & would not act & I not being on the spot was obliged to leave matters to take care of themselves. Women are still so undeveloped that it is very difficult to work with any half dozen together. But until we can make men & women to order, we must make the most of them as they are. I am very glad that you are so well started in Chicago. It is a good central point. I think you will find a large circle of progressive women there. Francis Lord is a very cultivated woman she is absorbed just now in mind cure   still you might enjoy her acquaintance. She spent six weeks with me just before I left America & I enjoyed her society very much. I am going to Paris to morrow[4] so write me & send some copies of "The Open Court" to my sons Theodore's care of 9 rue de Bassano, Paris, France. With best regards for Mr Underwood & yourself sincerely ever

~ *Elizabeth Cady Stanton*

~ ALS, Anonymous Private Collection. Not in *Film*.

1. In *Eighty Years*, ECS recorded that she went to Paris on 14 April 1887, "my daughter escorting me to Dover, and my son meeting me at Calais." (*Eighty Years*, 399.)

2. "Jails and Jubilees," *Open Court* 1 (12 May 1887): 175-77, *Film*, 25:447-48. ECS objected strongly to the Conservative government's disregard for the civil liberties of Irish protesters and their sympathizers as expressed in the Coercion Act under consideration in Parliament. She also criticized taking pennies from an impoverished people to build monuments to mark Queen Victoria's Jubilee.

3. ECS had assembled a revising committee, including Sara Underwood, to write commentaries on biblical passages about women for what she called the "Woman's Bible." In December 1886, Matilda Gage told her son that she chaired "the Historical committee" for the project. Perhaps Helen Gardener assumed that job. (M. J. Gage to Thomas Clarkson Gage, 2 December 1886, Gage Collection, MCR-S; *Papers*, 4:510-11, 528-29; Kern, *Mrs. Stanton's Bible*.)

4. To visit the family of her son Theodore Stanton.

11 ⇾ ECS to Nora S. Blatch[1]

[*Paris*] Saturday afternoon [*16? April 1887*]

Dear Nora,

Well here I am in Paris. I came into this great walled city last night just as the clock struck eight. Lizette[2] would sit up to see me. After I was seated at the head of four flights, she ran down to meet me. She is a beautiful little girl, with dark curling hair & beautiful large dark eyes, rosy cheeks pretty nose & mouth. She is only one inch taller than you are $39\frac{3}{4}$ we have not had her weighed yet, but intend to take her to be weighed on Monday   The boy, little Bob[3] is very pretty too, he looks like his father, & is about the size of Jackanapes. Well my precious babe, I find myself often thinking of you, & all you said & did, you hold a large place in my heart. Now I suppose you would like to know how large my heart is, that you may be able to appreciate your possessions. Well viewing it physicologically, (say Physicologically) it comprizes the globe, my motto being, "the world is my country & all mankind my countrywomen"[4]   So you may imagine a fraction of my heart to be the size of Basingstoke & that you own all you can see from the chimney top on The Mount bounded by the <u>horizon</u>. What is the horizon. What is the zinith? This dog at the head of the sheet is to remind you of our big white dogs in the sleigh ride. I told Jocko & Minnette & the sleigh of the sleigh ride to Lizette this morning. She looked at me steadily, but never said a word, but when I had finished she said tell me again   [*in margin of first page*] She takes everything quietly. I should like to see you together. lovingly

~ Queen Mother

~ ALS, in the collection of Coline Jenkins, Greenwich, Conn.

1. Nora Stanton Blatch (1883-1971) was ECS's granddaughter, the child of Harriot and William Blatch, with whom ECS had lived at The Mount in Basingstoke for the previous six months. ECS's stationery bore a portrait of an attentive dog. (*NAW Modern Period* and *ANB*, s.v. "Barney, Nora Stanton Blatch.")

2. Elizabeth Cady Stanton, Jr., (1882-1909), the daughter of Theodore and Marguerite Stanton, known into adulthood as Lizette or Lisette, was a few months older than Nora Blatch. (Genealogical notes of Robert and Francis Stanton, Mazamet, France; *Woman's Journal*, 29 February 1910.)

3. Robert, or Robert Livingston, Stanton (1885-1974) was born in Paris on 2 August 1885 to Theodore and Marguerite Stanton. (Genealogical notes of Robert and Francis Stanton, Mazamet, France.)

4. Adapted from William Lloyd Garrison's motto for the *Liberator*.

12 ~ EARLY TEXT OF THE CALL TO THE INTERNATIONAL COUNCIL OF WOMEN

EDITORIAL NOTE: SBA asked Charles Mann to print this proofsheet of a call to the international meeting of 1888 when she thought members of the planning committee had at last agreed on a text based on ECS's second draft. By March 19, ECS's draft had been sent to May Sewall, who returned it to SBA with significant changes. Some of those changes were reversed by SBA before she gave the manuscript to Mann. She acted on her conviction that because an international council did not yet exist, it could not convene an event. She also deleted something that Sewall added. An undated and edited entry from her (lost) diary for 1887 indicates that SBA "struck out the paragraph saying, 'no one would be committed to suffrage who should attend,'" adding, "I can't allow any such apologetic invitation as that!" (ECS to Clara B. Colby, 9 March 1887; SBA to Rachel G. Foster, 19 March, 26 March, 18 April 1887; all in *Film*, 25:279-86, 311-17, 356-63, 400-406; *Anthony*, 2:634.)

[*19? April? 1887*]

The Fortieth Anniversary
OF
The First Woman Suffrage Convention.

In commemoration of the first public demand for the political rights of women, made at Seneca Falls, N.Y., in 1848, an International Council of Women, under the auspices of the National Woman Suffrage Association, will be held in Albaugh's Opera House, Washington, D.C., opening Sunday, March 25, and closing Sunday, April 1, 1888.

The far-reaching influence of such a convention cannot be estimated. It will arouse the women of all civilized lands to perceive what power there is in association; it will intensify their love of liberty by interchange of sentiment and opinions on the great questions of human rights now agitating the world; it will help to further that application of the principles of common justice for which women have been so long and earnestly contending.

However the governments and religions, customs and habits, of nations may differ, they are alike agreed on one point, namely: Man's sovereignty everywhere, as head of the State, the Church, and the Home.

It is to challenge this tyranny of sex on which society is built, that delegates from all associations of women are invited to meet in solemn council, and send forth their declaration of rights, demanding justice, liberty and equality in every department of life for her who as mother of the race is unquestionably a coequal factor in civilization.

In considering the disparity of their achievements as compared with their labors, most women will no doubt agree that they have been trammeled in their efforts by political subordination. Those active in great philanthropic enterprises, sooner or later, realize that so long as women are not acknowledged the political equals of men, their judgment on public questions carries but little weight.

Women of the Old World and the New, recognizing the fact that their interests are the same, should in the spirit of universal sisterhood unite in harmonious effort to destroy this worst form of aristocracy— caste in sex.

The sixteen sessions will afford ample opportunity for discussion of the various phases of women's work and progress in all parts of the world during the past forty years. Not only will Suffrage Organizations be represented in the Council, but also Scientific and Literary Clubs, Art Unions, Temperance Unions, Missionary, Peace and Moral Purity Societies, Charitable, Professional, Educational, Industrial and other Associations of Women.

Formal invitations will be issued to all representative organizations, and it is hoped that all friends of woman's advancement will lend the support of their presence. On behalf of the National Woman Suffrage Association,

> ≈ *Elizabeth Cady Stanton,*
> *President.*
> ≈ *Rachel G. Foster,*
> *Corresponding Secretary.*

≈ Proof sheet, SBA scrapbook 13, Rare Books, DLC.

13 ≈ SBA TO RACHEL G. FOSTER

Rochester N.Y. April 25, 1887

Dear Rachel

Here is May's "<u>soliloquy</u>" on the Call & all—[1] She is right—perhaps as to putting the call on Commercial note sized paper—and it easy enough to have it run over to meet that demand— But surely she cannot mean or if she does—she must be wrong—that ↑it is↓ the <u>International</u> Council that extends the Invitation— It is surely the <u>National W.S.A.</u> that extends invitation to all the different organizations to send ↑their↓ delegates to Washington to form the <u>proposed</u> International— I still think to say

The <u>International Council of Women to the</u>—National Woman's Christian Temp. Union—

You are invited &c

would be absurd—

But I am utterly <u>non-plussed</u> and all at sea—so that I feel discouraged—<u>no</u> two of our Com. are where they can consult—and no two agree on any one point by writing—so it looks utter hopeless getting settled upon anything!! May thinks ↑she had↓ everything all right—when she sent to you—but none of the rest of us think with her—

↩ S. B. A

↩ ALS, on 40th anniversary letterhead, Anthony-Avery Papers, NRU.

1. Enclosure omitted. It was May Sewall to SBA, 21 April 1887, *Film*, 25:411–24. Impatient with SBA's changes to the call's heading, Sewall explained that the call summoned people to an international council and that point should be evident in the heading; moreover, she insisted, "this point was formally settled by the Com. at its regular meeting in Phil." Sewall went on to dispute SBA's characterization of her words about welcoming non-suffragists as "an apology or in the nature of one." It was "a simple statement of fact—for this is not an International Council of <u>Suffragists</u> . . . this is a much <u>broader</u> and <u>noble</u> thing than a Council of Suffragists only, and by conceiving and planning such a Council has the N.W.S.A demonstrated its breadth." For Sewall's later narrative of this dispute, see "Minutes of Twentieth Annual Convention, 1888," pp. 8–10, *Film*, 26:638ff.

14 ↬ CALL TO THE INTERNATIONAL COUNCIL OF WOMEN

June 1, 1887.[1]

INTERNATIONAL COUNCIL OF WOMEN.

The first public demand for equal educational, industrial, professional and political rights for women was made in a convention held at Seneca Falls, New York, (U.S.A.), in the year 1848.

To celebrate the Fortieth Anniversary of this event, an International Council of Women will be convened under the auspices of the National Woman Suffrage Association, in Albaugh's Opera House, Washington, D.C., on March 25, 1888.

It is impossible to over-estimate the far-reaching influence of such a Council. An interchange of opinions on the great questions now agitating the world will rouse women to new thought, will intensify their love of liberty, and will give them a realizing sense of the power of combination.

However the governments, religions, laws and customs, of nations may differ, all are agreed on one point, namely: man's sovereignty in the State, in the Church and in the Home. In an International Council women may hope to devise new and more effective methods for securing in these three institutions the equality and justice which they have so long and so earnestly sought. Such a Council will impress the important lesson that the position of women anywhere affects their position everywhere. Much is said of universal brotherhood, but, for weal or for woe, more subtle and more binding, is universal sisterhood.

Women, recognizing the disparity between their achievements and their labors, will no doubt agree that they have been trammeled by their political subordination. Those active in great philanthropic enterprises sooner or later realize that, so long as women are not acknowledged to be the political equals of men, their judgment on public questions will have but little weight. It is, however, neither intended nor desired that discussions in the International Council shall be limited to questions touching the political rights of women. Formal invitations requesting the appointment of delegates will be issued to representative organizations in every department of woman's work. Literary Clubs, Art Unions, Temperance Unions, Labor Leagues, Missionary, Peace and Moral Purity Societies, Charitable, Professional, Educational and Industrial Associations will thus be offered equal opportunity with Suffrage Societies to be represented in what should be the ablest and most imposing body of women ever assembled.

The Council will continue eight days and its sixteen public sessions will afford ample opportunity for reporting the various phases of woman's work and progress in all parts of the world, during the past forty years. It is hoped that all friends of the advancement of women will lend their support to this undertaking. On behalf of the National Woman Suffrage Association,

Elizabeth Cady Stanton, President, 8 W. 40th St., New York.

Susan B. Anthony, First Vice President, Rochester, N.Y.

Matilda Joslyn Gage, Second Vice President, Fayetteville, N.Y.

May Wright Sewall, Chairman Ex-Committee, 343 N. Penn. St., Indianapolis, Ind.

Ellen H. Sheldon,[2] Recording Secretary, 811 Ninth St., N.W. Washington, D.C.

Jane H. Spofford, Treasurer, Riggs House, Washington, D.C.

Rachel G. Foster, Corresponding Secretary, 748 N. Nineteenth Street, Philadelphia, Pa.

↩ *Woman's Tribune*, July 1887.

1. Together in Indianapolis in May 1887, SBA and May Sewall revised the call and sent it to Rachel Foster for typesetting. (SBA to R. G. Foster, 5, 12 May 1887, *Film*, 25:436-37, 442-46.)

2. Ellen Harriet Sheldon (1841-1890), formerly a clerk in the War Department, studied medicine at Howard University from 1879 to 1884 and practiced in Washington. She had been active in suffrage societies since at least 1874, and the National association first elected her recording secretary in 1878. (Gloria Moldow, *Women Doctors in Gilded-Age Washington: Race, Gender, and Professionalization* [Urbana, Ill., 1987], 19, 24, 139; *Register of Federal Officers, 1873, 1876, 1878*; Daniel Smith Lamb, comp., *Howard University Medical Department, Washington, D.C.: A Historical, Biographical, and Statistical Souvenir* [Washington, D.C., 1900], with assistance of Clifford L. Muse, Jr., Howard University; city directories, 1876 to 1890. See also *Papers* 3 & 4.)

15 ↭ SBA TO FRANCES E. WILLARD

Rochester N.Y. June 6/87

My Dear Miss Willard

Among my huge piles of papers—I find a roll of <u>Washington Territory</u> Papers & clippings—with request that they be forwarded to Miss Willard[1]

I wonder if you have had the full summary of all these made into a <u>leaflet</u>?! If you have not—and do not wish to use them—will you please forward the whole of them to Mrs Clara Bewick Colby—Beatrice—Neb— <u>She</u>—<u>surely</u> ought to make a full & clear resume of the case in her paper— It is clearly a put up job of the <u>Whiskey</u> <u>Powers</u>— Dont you think so!!

Do you note our plan of <u>enrollment</u>[2] of <u>all</u> <u>friends</u> of <u>woman's enfranchisement</u>—in <u>each</u> <u>state</u>—not to a petition—specially—to make a <u>count</u>—and then to have all copied into a book—or two books—one to be kept at the State Capital—and another to be kept at Washington—so that when Legislator or Congressman says—<u>none</u> of the women of ↑among↓ my Constituents want to vote—we can <u>turn</u> to his state—& to his Congressional <u>District</u>—& show him the <u>long</u> <u>lines</u> of his own constituents who do want to vote

Wont your women's unions help roll up these names—& send to our <u>National</u> <u>State</u> <u>Vice</u>-<u>Pres</u>— I enclose a list of them—[3] I believe we can get a good list of names—this way—<u>and</u> <u>keep</u> <u>them</u>— instead of having them buried in the vaults of State & National Capitol buildings—

I am very sorry the Wisconsin Women are carrying their <u>School</u> <u>Law</u> into the courts—for in all probability it will result in an <u>adverse</u> <u>decision</u>—that will shut <u>every</u> <u>ballot</u> <u>box</u>—even those that there were open at this spring's elections![4] What they should do—it seems to me—is to let their vote on "<u>School Matters</u>"—rest—and just push forward & get a Municipal suffrage from their next Legislature!!—

<u>Suppose</u> <u>they</u> get a favorable decision—it is only to vote on "<u>School</u> <u>Matters</u>"—and what the women most long for—is to vote on <u>Whiskey</u>, <u>gambling</u> &˙<u>prostitution</u> <u>matters</u>!!— Lovingly yours

                              Susan B. Anthony

N.B—Since scribbling the within—I came across the National W.C.T.U's 13th annual report—1886—and a stupendous work it tells of—[5] I shall read it thoroughly— Your thorough organization is my pride—it is the result of <u>one</u> <u>head</u> working to one end during the <u>thirteen</u> <u>years</u>— What a revolution has come to the <u>church women</u> in those years—as to <u>speaking in public</u>—how the <u>old</u> <u>style</u> <u>St</u> <u>Paul</u> must weep over his sisters in the Church of St Frances!!

ALS, on NWSA letterhead, IEWT, from *Temperance and Prohibition Papers*.

1. On 3 February 1887, the Supreme Court of the Territory of Washington declared the law of 1883 enfranchising women to be unconstitutional, basing the decision on a technical standard about how laws should be titled. The case was brought by a convicted gambler who had been indicted by a grand jury that included women, and SBA was not alone in suspecting that he received encouragement from liquor interests. Women had voted in the election for the incoming legislature, and their representatives drafted a new statute, properly titled, that was signed into law in January 1888. The supreme court struck down the new law in August 1888, in time to prevent women from participating in Washington's final steps toward statehood. (Clippings, SBA scrapbook 12, Rare Books, DLC; Harland v. Territory of Washington 3 Wash. Terr. 131 [1887]; Bloomer v. Todd 3 Wash. Terr. 599 [1888]; Nelson A. Ault, "The Earnest Ladies: The Walla Walla Woman's Club and the Equal Suffrage League of 1886-1889," *Pacific Northwest Quarterly* 42 [April 1951]: 123-37; Alan Hynding, *The Public Life of Eugene Semple: Promoter and Politician of the Pacific Northwest* [Seattle, Wash., 1973], 79-82; John Fahey, "The Nevada Bloomer Case," *Columbia* 2 [Summer 1988]: 42-45.)

2. The National's executive committee decided in January 1887 to ask the association's vice presidents "to secure an enrollment for their states, of names of persons who desired woman suffrage." As May Sewall wrote in a circular sent to the vice presidents after the meeting, "the work of securing signatures to petitions is, to a great extent, wasted labor, and [the officers] have decided to make the enrollment now determined upon a matter of permanent and available record." (*Woman's Tribune*, April 1887, *Film*, 25:198-202; M. W. Sewall to Vice Presidents, n.d., SBA scrapbook 12, Rare Books, DLC.)

3. Enclosure missing.

4. Olympia Brown was deciding whether to sue the inspectors of election in Racine, Wisconsin, after they refused her ballot in municipal elections in April 1887. A new state law, approved by the voters in November 1886, granted women the right to vote "in any election pertaining to school matters." Woman suffragists, including some legislators and lawyers, thought the indefinite language opened the door to municipal and some statewide suffrage, and Brown's attempt to vote in a city where municipal officers managed the schools tested that interpretation. SBA urged officers of the state suffrage association not to sue "unless you *know* you will get the broadest decision upon it." Brown won her case in circuit court in November 1887, but the inspectors appealed the decision to the state supreme court. There she lost; in an opinion issued in January 1888, the court's majority ruled that the law could not be put into effect until the legislature provided for ways to separate the votes of women from those of men. (SBA to O. Brown and Almeda B. Gray, June? 1887, *Film*, 25:579; *Woman's Journal*, 23, 30 April, 2 July, 19 November 1887; Brown v. Phillips 71 Wisconsin Reports 239 [1888]; *Wisconsin Citizen*, Supplement, April 1889; *Papers*, 4:526-28.)

5. *Minutes of the National Woman's Christian Temperance Union, at the Thirteenth Annual Meeting in Minneapolis, Minn., October 22 to 27, 1886, With Addresses, Reports and Constitutions* (Chicago, 1886).

16 ~> ECS TO FLORA MCMARTIN WRIGHT[1]

Paris June 15th [*1887*]

Dear Flora,

I was delighted to get a line from you once more, & especially an epistle of such humor   I could just see Aunty Had[2] with her facial muscles all set to grief rushing round to funerals & being chief mourner in the procession. Well funerals have always been the great feature in the life of our native town. But why did you not go too is the question?

As to weather we have had the same here, cold & rainy all through May. I have not put on summer clothing yet. Theodore says they never have such hot weather here as in America, so I trust it will remain cool all summer. I had a long letter from Nettie Smith & her husband[3] a few days since. They had just been hulling strawberries for tea. A sweet calm scene in their domestic life! I suppose they ate them afterwards a far more pleasant occupation   Nettie has done well. Mr Grover was a lawyer in Chicago I used to see every winter in my western travels. He is well off, good looking, an intelligent, well educated man. His children are all grown except one boy 13, the only one at home. I recommended her to him & he went straight for her. He visited me last summer at Tenafly to consult me about a wife. I do hope & pray she will prove a good one. You might say to the inquiring friends, that you hear she has done well. They will think you hear from the west & not from Paris. Cady has gone to Germany.[4] I saw him the day before he started, he was well & in good spirits, & was living like a nabob at the Maurice Hotel.[5] Mr Bigelow[6] & his daughters are near us, we have exchanged calls several times. The Madame remains in London until after the Jubilee. I am having a delightful time here alone with Theodore. Our cook is a treasure she manages everything. She keeps accounts counts the cloths that go to the laundry, & does all there is to be done in the home. She brings us chocolate & bread & butter at half past eight. I am generally bathed & half dressed by that time   at nine o'clock I pose for the painter[7] one morning, the sculptor[8] the next until 12 o'clock when we breakfast. After that I take a nap, then read, write, walk on the balcony take an occasional stitch. At half past six we dine & then drive for an hour   then sit or walk on the balcony, read or write letters. Sometimes we go out, sometimes receive visitors. Theodore persists in pulling me [round?] as if I were forty. Last week we were out to two breakfasts one dinner, one reception & one evening party where we stayed until one o'clock. The next day I felt like a squeezed sponge. I met Mrs Wilbour[9] at one breakfast. She had just returned from Egypt. They spent the winter on a boat sailing up & down the Nile   Mrs Bullard & Mr Tilton[10] called yesterday. She is on her way to Switzerland. Marguerite[11] & the children are enjoying themselves in their southern home. Hattie has been trying a kindergarten teacher who has a little boy just Nora's age, but the experiment is a failure Nora does not like either mother nor boy. Harry[12] hates them Hattie only tolerates them. The three months is up the middle of July. I told Hattie it would not do when she begun it, but it all looked rose colored to her for <u>two weeks</u>. Now we are in pursuit of a German governess Lizette talks French German & English. She used to look so astonished when I asked her to tell [Lucie?] & Jean[13] what I wanted. Why grandmother can't you talk? Not French ɳor German, then she would laugh, & say why Robbie can, & see how little he is. She could not understand how it was that I could be so large & could not talk as well as she could. She is a beautiful child. Madame de Barrau[14] is very attentive we exchange visits & drive out together frequently. All the new streets here are beautiful wide with half a dozen rows of trees either side grass & seats fountains & flowers, what a charming city this is. Imagine seats all round the streets in Johnstown, the church yards with the trees, grass close cut, & seats where people could sit on Sunday & in the evening, & all over the cemetery, then one could walk & rest with comfort. With love [*in margin*] good night

↭ *Aunty Lee*

↭ ALS, Scrapbook 2, Papers of ECS, NPV. Square brackets surround uncertain readings.

1. Flora McMartin Wright (1843–1898) was a niece of ECS who married William Pelham Wright, the son of Martha Coffin Wright. Usually resident in Florida, Flora visited her Cady relatives in Johnstown, New York, in the summer. ECS signed this letter with the nickname Lee, used only within her family. (Wright genealogy, Garrison Papers, MNS-S; Orrin Peer Allen, *Descendants of Nicholas Cady of Watertown, Mass., 1645–1910* [Palmer, Mass., 1910], 174.)

2. Harriet Eliza Cady Eaton (1810–1894) was an older sister of ECS who married their cousin Daniel Cady Eaton. A widow since 1855, she often spent summers in Johnstown. (Allen, *Descendants of Nicholas Cady*, 174–75; Gravestones, Johnstown, N.Y.; genealogical files, notes from Presbyterian Church Records, NJost.)

3. Nettie Corrine Smith had recently married Alonzo Jackson Grover (1829–1891), formerly of Earlville, Illinois, and now of Atchison County, Kansas. He was a good friend of both SBA and ECS, who had written for the *Revolution*, hosted SBA, lined up ECS to be a contributing editor to his *Earlville Transcript* in the 1870s, and published several pamphlets on woman suffrage. According to family members, he and Octavia Elmira Norton Grover (1839–1904) divorced about 1885, after thirty years of marriage. The youngest of their four living children was Alonzo Jackson Grover, Jr. (1873–1938). If, as ECS implied, Nettie Grover came from Johnstown, she was probably a

member of the Cady family. The Nettie C. Smith in Johnstown in 1880 was an eleven-year-old residing with her widowed mother, Lucy B. Cady Smith; an aunt, Grace E. Cady; and a younger sister. (Alfred Theodore Andreas, *History of Chicago, from the Earliest Period to the Present Time* [Chicago, 1884], 3:693; *Rev.*, 3 December 1868, 18 February 1869, *Film*, 1:380, 467-68; *Atchison Daily Champion*, 13 February 1891, in SBA scrapbook 17, Rare Books, DLC; Federal Census, 1880; with the assistance of the Earlville Public Library; Betty J. Mortland, East Lansing, Michigan; and Delbert Grover, St. Ann, Missouri.)

4. This Daniel Cady Eaton (1837-1912), one of several in the family, was Flora's cousin and ECS's nephew, the son of Harriet Cady Eaton. He was an art historian who taught at Yale from 1869 to 1876 and again after 1902. (Allen, *Descendants of Nicholas Cady*, 175; *WWW1*; D. Cady Eaton Papers, CtY.)

5. Hôtel Meurice on Rue de Rivoli was counted among hotels of the highest class in Paris.

6. John Bigelow (1817-1911), an author and lawyer in New York, was former ambassador to France. His wife, Jane Tunis Poultney Bigelow (1829-1889), stayed in London for celebrations on 20 and 21 June 1887 marking the fiftieth year of Queen Victoria's reign. ECS did see her in Paris at another time on this trip. Which of their four daughters accompanied the Bigelows is not known. (*ANB*; *New York Times*, 9 February 1889, 20 December 1911; *Eighty Years*, 401.)

7. Anna Elizabeth Klumpke (1856-1942), an American painter living in Paris, stayed with Theodore Stanton's family in southern France in the summer of 1886, where she completed a portrait of Lisette and made sketches for "Catinou Knitting," the painting she submitted to the Salon in 1887. Her portrait of ECS, completed in 1889, is now at the National Portrait Gallery in Washington. (Anna Elizabeth Klumpke, *Memoirs of an Artist*, ed. Lillian Whiting [Boston, 1940], 25; Britta C. Dwyer, *Anna Klumpke: A Turn-of-the-Century Painter and Her World* [Boston, 1999], 47-48.)

8. Paul Wayland Bartlett (1865-1925), born in Connecticut, studied sculpture at the École des Beaux Arts in Paris and showed his first major work, "Bear Tamer," at the Salon in 1887. Though he completed many commissions in the United States, Paris remained his principal home until 1908. His bronze medallion of ECS was pictured in *New England Magazine* in 1905 and displayed in an exhibit of Barlett's work at the American Academy of Arts and Letters in 1931, but its current location is unknown. (*ANB*; *New England Magazine* 33 [December 1905]: 374; *Catalogue of Memorial Exhibition of the Works of Paul Wayland Bartlett, at the American Academy of Arts and Letters* [New York, 1931].)

9. Charlotte Beebe Wilbour (1833-1914) and Charles Edwin Wilbour (1833-1896) moved to Paris from New York City in 1874, when Charles, a lawyer, came under scrutiny for his associations with the Tweed Ring. There he pursued his interest in Egyptology, amassing a great collection of books and

artifacts, while living part of each year with his wife and children aboard a boat on the Nile. Charlotte Wilbour had been a leading organizer of women in New York before their move: she was secretary of the Women's Loyal National League, an officer in the New York and National suffrage associations, a founder of the woman's club Sorosis, and planner of the first Woman's Congress in 1873. (*NCAB*, 13:370; *ACAB*, s.v. "Wilbour, Charles Edwin"; *New York Times*, 26 December 1914; file on C. B. Wilbour, Sorosis Collection, MNS-S. See also *Papers* 1–4.)

10. Laura J. Curtis Bullard (c. 1834–1912) and Theodore Tilton (1835–1907) were both Americans living abroad. Bullard was an ally of ECS and SBA in the American Equal Rights Association and at the Woman's Bureau, before she succeeded ECS as editor of the *Revolution* in 1870. (Federal Census, 1870, 1880; *New York Times*, 20 January 1912. See also *Papers* 2–4.) Tilton was a respected editor, lecturer, and reformer and a close friend of ECS and SBA during and after the Civil War. His success came to a dramatic end when Henry Ward Beecher prevailed in the hearings and trials that investigated charges of Beecher's affair with Tilton's wife. He moved to Europe in 1883 and stayed until his death. (*ANB*. See also *Papers* 1–4.)

11. Marguerite Marie Berry Stanton (1857–1951) of Paris married Theodore Stanton in 1881. Her family owned an estate in the south of France, where ECS had stayed on her previous trip. (Genealogical notes of Robert and Francis Stanton, Mazamet, France; Harriot Stanton Blatch and Alma Lutz, *Challenging Years: The Memoirs of Harriot Stanton Blatch* [New York, 1940], 55–58. See also *Papers* 4.)

12. William Henry Blatch, Jr., (1851–1915), known as Harry, married Harriot Stanton in 1882. He was employed in his family's breweries in Basingstoke, England. (*New York Times*, 3 August 1915.)

13. Presumably these are servants in the Stantons' house.

14. Caroline Françoise Coulomb de Barrau de Muratel (1828–1888), active in the education of girls, the protection of young women seeking work in Paris, the improvement of women's prisons, and the reform of prostitutes, shared a house in Paris with the Berry family, Theodore Stanton's in-laws. As SBA noted with gratitude when Caroline de Barrau escorted her around Paris in 1883, she spoke English. (*DBF*. See also *Papers* 4.)

17   SBA to Elizabeth Smith Miller[1]

Rochester N.Y. Aug. 17, 1887

My Dear Mrs Miller

    Your note from Saratoga is just here—also—one from Miss Müller of London— I shall be delighted to meet Miss M. at your delightful home on that lovely lake—or—if she should come through to Rochester—to go there with her— She does not give me any address sufficiently definite for me to hope to consult with her farther—nothing save the Adirondacks—& Boston—both rather vauge—but you doubtless know how to reach her—it will make no difference to me—as I am now to be at home until the middle of September—and will hold myself in readiness to receive Miss Müller here at my home or to meet her at yours—as she shall decide—

    I do not know what to say of the Mental Science[2]—only that the prefix of <u>Christian</u> to it—repels every sense of me!! makes it seem like a <u>catch</u>-<u>trap</u> for the unwary & unthinking—of the old creeds!! Still I cannot discredit the most wonderful works reported of its advocates—it stands with me about as Spiritualism always has—I like its <u>theology</u>—its theories—but cannot accept their logical conclusions in practical matters. There must be a great deal of truth mixed up with it—but I doubt if they—its leaders—are not claiming far too much for it—when they insist that <u>broken bones</u> and other <u>organic</u> difficulties are mended by <u>thought alone</u>—but I <u>can</u> believe in its efficacy in all functionary disturbances—but we'll talk it over when we meet—

    It is very pleasant that Mrs Stanton can enjoy her Theodore, <u>alone</u>, this summer—but I miss her very much—in the work needing to be done for the International— Sincerely yours

                                Susan B. Anthony

I reached home yesterday—after a six weeks with my friend Miss M. A. Thomson[3] of Phila.—at Cape May ↑N.J.↓, South Adams, Mass—my birth place—Magnolia, Mass—and Newport R.I.—

    ALS, on 40th anniversary letterhead, Smith Family Papers, Manuscript Division, NN.

1. Elizabeth Smith Miller (1822–1911) invited SBA to her lakeside house in Geneva, New York, at the time of a visit from Henrietta Müller. Miller, the daughter of ECS's cousins Gerrit and Ann Smith and one of ECS's best friends since childhood, was a reformer and philanthropist who sometimes held office in state and national suffrage associations. (E. S. Miller to SBA, 15 August 1887, *Film*, 25:606-9; *NAW*; *ANB*. See also *Papers* 1–4.)

2. Miller asked the question about Mind Cure and continued, "It seems to have a strong element of truth, but there must be a limit to ignoring evil—it is hard to believe in setting a broken leg by ignoring it. But these are marvellous days."

3. Mary Adeline Thomson (1812?–1895) of Philadelphia, known as Adeline, was a close friend of SBA since their meeting at a woman's rights convention in 1854. She represented Pennsylvania at the founding of the National association in 1869 and served on the executive committee in the 1870s. With her late sister Anna, she often hosted ECS and SBA, and since Anna's death, she occasionally traveled with SBA. (*Friends' Intelligencer* 52 [1895]: 109; *Woman's Journal*, 9 March 1895; *Anthony*, 1:122, 327n, 2:264, 814; *History*, 3:468n; with assistance of the Estate of J. Edgar Thomson, Philadelphia.)

18 ~ SBA TO LILLIE DEVEREUX BLAKE

Rochester N.Y. Aug 28/87

My Dear Mrs Blake

Your two last notes must now be answered— So all you say of the Phila. Convention to celebrate our 100 years of Constitutional life—is very true— We—the National W.S.A. should have planned for a "big" <u>appeal & protest there</u>—but at this late day—with the time less than a month ahead—and our women all <u>engaged</u> so as to make it impossible to do a <u>big</u> <u>thing</u>—it strikes me we may as well say & do nothing—[1] If I—or any one <u>could</u> write an "<u>able</u> & eloquent" statement of the nation's failure—with a powerful demand for recognition now—we could sign it—& send it into the meeting of the Governors of the States—that is <u>we</u>—the officers of the National who are on this side— We couldn't get it over to Mrs Stanton & back—nor would she be likely to put <u>her</u> <u>name</u> to any document any of us could write—even if there were time to get it to her— So—if <u>you</u> <u>will</u> <u>write</u> the paper as best you can & send it to me—I will sign it—send it to Mrs Gage—Mrs Sewall, Mrs Colby &c—it ought to have the signatures of all the <u>State</u> <u>Vice</u>

Presidents of the National—to make it at all proper & imposing— Dont you think so?— Even to do this will require that some of the most remote <u>ones</u> should send their <u>signatures</u> to be pasted upon it—taking it for granted—the paper was right— <u>You</u>—are the only one who <u>can write it</u>—because you are the only one who has seemed to feel it a thing to be done—hence—without delay—if it is to be done—put your best thoughts into your tersest sentences—& have two or three <u>type writer copies</u>—made of it—despatch a copy to Mrs Gage—& to me—instanter—& let us see—if we can put our names to it— I wish you could do it with Mrs Gage—

We surely cannot go to Phila. to join in the procession—or make any <u>personal</u> <u>show</u> <u>there</u>— I shall be in the West then—[2] Mrs Sewall will be just entering upon a new school year— Miss Foster will be in Phila. then—and if you could go on—she & you and what others you could muster could go before some committee—& <u>see</u> that the paper was duly presented to the meeting—there will undoubtedly be some man present—who is friendly—& who would help get the paper presented— So—the whole burden of getting the proper document—& the presentation of it—must rest with you & Miss Foster—[3] Sincerely yours

⚜ *Susan B. Anthony*

⚜ ALS, on NWSA letterhead, Lillie D. Blake Papers, MoSHi.

1. On the events in Philadelphia marking the centennial of the United States Constitution, see Gary B. Nash, *First City: Philadelphia and the Forging of Historical Memory* (Philadelphia, 2002), 303-13. Blake presented her protest on behalf of the National Woman Suffrage Association to President Grover Cleveland at a reception in City Hall on 17 September 1887. (SBA to L. D. Blake, 7, 11, 29 September 1887; L. D. Blake to SBA, 6 September 1887; SBA to Rachel G. Foster, 28 August, 5, 7 September 1887; and "Protest against the Unjust Interpretation of the Constitution," 17 September 1887; all in *Film*, 25:640-45, 671-73, 678-92, 706-7, 715-19, 743-45; *Woman's Journal*, 24 September 1887.)

2. After meetings and lectures in Wisconsin in the final weeks of September, SBA moved on to a series of congressional district meetings across Kansas through all of October, followed by congressional district meetings across Indiana through November and the first week of December.

3. Omitted here is SBA's enclosure, a letter from M. R. Leverson to Ellen H. Sheldon, 21 April 1887, with advice about pressing labor parties to include woman suffrage in their platforms. In a separate note on the enclosure, SBA asked Blake to follow up.

19   SBA to Harriet Taylor Upton[1]

Rochester N.Y. Sept. 6th 1887

My Dear Mrs Upton

Yours of August 29th came duly, and sent me forthwith down-town for the Forum—[2] I had seen the speech of Senator Ingalls, made at Abeline, before a large and intelligent audience—which gave him no cheers of approval—and which called down upon his devoted head the entire press of Kansas—with only two or three exceptions— ~~"Minors~~ "Women children & other <u>dependent</u> classes"!!—enrages me mo[re] than anything in his articl[e—] Who makes the wife, the daugh[ter] dependent? Man's laws—bu[t] I never write— I wish you would send an article to t[he] Forum—in reply— All I c[an] do is to work & talk— an[d] I shall do some of both not [only?] in Kansas—but in <u>Atchiso[n]</u> the home of the Senator—↑where↓ we [are?] to hold a three days Convention—[3] [I?] devote the lovely month of October to that lovely state—and now t[hat?] its women have the Municipal vo[te] I hope they'll soon get the full ballot— And when they do posses[s it?] I trust there'll be an end to the promotion of men to highest offices who denounce women as inferior and rank them with children & imbecile men!!

But even Ingalls will have a sudden conversion to equality of the sexes—when he needs the votes of women to carry him to the place he seeks—

I am very thankfu[l] that you called my attention to the Forum articles— Miss Mulock[4] vies with the Senator in her depreciation of women— What sort of stuff can the woman be made [of?]

I shall hope to meet you in Washington next w[inter] and also that your fat[her] and other M.C's who believ[e] in woman's enfranchisement— will [work?] to bring our question to a direct v[ote] during the 50th Congress—

Please give my best regards to your father & believ[e me?] Sincerely yours

           Susan B. Anthony

⇜ ALS, on 40th anniversary letterhead, SBA Papers, NRU. Letters in square brackets obscured by mounting of letter.

1. Harriet Taylor Upton (1853-1945) was the daughter of Congressman Ezra Booth Taylor (1823-1912), Republican of Ohio, who served in the House of Representatives from 1880 to 1893. He, a member of the House Judiciary Committee, was a key supporter of the federal suffrage amendment. In 1886, he prompted SBA to correspond with his daughter, in an apparent attempt to convert Harriet Upton to the suffrage cause. Her conversion came quickly; she organized suffrage events in Ohio in 1888 and provided informal help to the National association in Washington in 1889. In 1891, when Ohio sent her to the National-American meeting as a delegate, she was named to the association's new congressional committee. (*NAW*; *ANB*; *BDAC*; *Papers*, 4:505-6.)

2. To read John James Ingalls, "The Sixteenth Amendment," *Forum* 4 (September 1887): 1-13. Ingalls (1826-1905), the Republican senator from Kansas from 1873 to 1891 and president of the Senate, with a long record of opposition to woman suffrage, voted against the amendment in January 1887. His article in the *Forum* expanded a speech he delivered in Abilene, Kansas, on 20 May 1887, to explain his vote against the amendment. For SBA's full reply to Ingalls, see below at 26 October 1887. (*BDAC*; *Abilene Gazette*, 26 May 1887, SBA scrapbook 12, Rare Books, DLC; *Woman's Journal*, 25 June 1887. See also *Papers* 4.)

3. A three-day congressional district meeting in Atchison opened on October 20, and despite SBA's speech against his views, Senator Ingalls and his wife hosted a reception for her during the event. Although congressional district meetings, managed jointly by the National and state associations, occurred in Kansas and Wisconsin in 1886, the idea entered the National association's plan of work in 1887. May Sewall instructed state vice presidents that to realize its goal of national legislation, the association needed to work with national legislators. Vice presidents should, she continued, "hold a convention in each of the Congressional Districts in her state, during the coming year, and through such conventions to influence voters to send men to Congress who entertain just opinions upon this question." (M. W. Sewall to Vice Presidents, n.d., SBA scrapbook 12, Rare Books, DLC; *Woman's Tribune*, October, November 1887; *Papers*, 4:521-24, 524-25, 526-28, 533, 535.)

4. Dinah Maria Mulock Craik (1826-1887), the English writer, signed her essay "Concerning Men," *Forum* 4 (September 1887): 38-48, simply as the author of *John Halifax, Gentleman*, a successful novel she published as Miss Mulock in 1856. Her essay emphasized essential differences between men and women and warned, "The instant they begin to fight about their separate rights they are almost sure to forget their mutual duties, which are much more important to the conservation of society." (*Oxford DNB*.)

20   SBA TO ANNA H. SHAW[1]

Hiawatha Kan.[2] Oct. 25/87

Dear Rev. Anna

I shall arrive at Leavenworth Wednesday P.M. 7. Oclock—to serve up Ingalls—at the Baptist Church[3]—that evening—and I left word with Mr & Mrs Fred. Willard[4]—that I wanted you to speak the first <u>half hour</u>—sure—say answer the Mass. women <u>not</u> voting[5]—& every voting class making itself felt—or such say two points as you prefer—

My brother Col. D. R. Anthony[6]—is to introduce me— And I have written him that if the train <u>should</u> be late—he must go ahead at 8 P.M. and introduce you—& you will talk till I come—but I do hope the train will arrive on time—so I can hear you & get inspiration to start me off right— But I want you to open the meeting whether I am on time—or a little late—any way— Sincerely yours

                        Susan B. Anthony

ALS, SBA Papers, NRU.

1. Anna Howard Shaw (1847–1919) had just begun her career in the suffrage movement, after completing advanced training in medicine and divinity. Rather than practicing either profession, she used her oratorical talent as the basis of a career. At this time, she was a national lecturer for the American Woman Suffrage Association, brought to Kansas as a guest of the Kansas Equal Suffrage Association. Henry Blackwell, who had also traveled to Kansas, wrote home that Shaw cut "a bigger figure out here than SBA herself. She is greatly admired & could have entirely spiked Susan's guns if she had chosen." (*NAW*; *ANB*; H. B. Blackwell to L. Stone and A. S. Blackwell, 16 October 1887, in Leslie Wheeler, ed., *Loving Warriors: Selected Letters of Lucy Stone and Henry B. Blackwell, 1853 to 1893* [New York, 1981], 309-10.)

2. The seventh of SBA's congressional district meetings in Kansas took place in Hiawatha, in the northeast corner of Kansas, 24 to 25 October 1887. With a break before her next meeting in Garnett on October 27, she accepted an invitation to lecture in Leavenworth. Rather than join SBA, Shaw lectured at the same time at the African Methodist Episcopal Church. (*Leavenworth Times*, 26 October 1887.)

3. SBA was scheduled to speak in the First Baptist Church on Sixth Street.

4. Frederick W. Willard (1857–1917), a printer employed in the newspaper

trade and a Republican activist, was married to Julia H. Dustin Willard. In 1889, he was appointed sheriff of Leavenworth County, and in 1891, he won election to the state legislature. (Federal Census, 1880; Frank W. Blackmar, ed., *Kansas: A Cyclopedia of State History, Embracing Events, Institutions, Industries, Counties, Cities, Towns, Prominent Persons, Etc.* [Chicago, 1912], 3:1218-19; Debra Graden, comp., *Leavenworth County, Kansas Death List, 1870-1920 and 1923-1930* [Leavenworth, Kan., 1997], 52.)

5. In his article "The Sixteenth Amendment," John J. Ingalls made use of disputed statistics about how many women in Massachusetts voted in school elections. By their low turnout, he argued, the women "have betrayed an insensibility and indifference to their enfranchisement which is shocking to the philanthropist and discouraging to the patriot." In the *Woman's Journal*, Henry Blackwell retorted that women lacked real school suffrage, having only the right to vote for school committees, and they faced onerous requirements for poll taxes and annual registration. Local issues also caused the turnout of women to vary considerably from year to year. (John James Ingalls, "The Sixteenth Amendment," *Forum* 4 [September 1887]: 11-12; *Woman's Journal*, 10 September, 8 October 1887; Lois Bannister Merk, "Boston's Historic Public School Crisis," *New England Quarterly* 31 [June 1958]: 172-99.)

6. Daniel Read Anthony (1824-1904), one of two younger brothers of SBA in Kansas, lived in Leavenworth, where he published the *Leavenworth Times*. (Anthony, *Anthony Genealogy*, 185-91; *United States Biographical Dictionary: Kansas Volume* [Chicago, 1879], 56-63.)

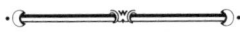

21 ❧ Speech by SBA in Leavenworth, Kansas

EDITORIAL NOTE: Between four and five hundred people heard SBA speak in Leavenworth's First Baptist Church in the evening of 26 October. Paraphrasing D. R. Anthony's introduction of his sister, the press reported him presenting "one who inherited from her ancestors a love of the principles of humanity, justice and equality and who had passed her life in advocating the rights first of the bondman and then of women." The newspaper described this text of SBA's speech as "the substance of her lecture."

[26 October 1887]

Thirty years ago an able and brilliant lawyer of New England, in order to deny to the negro freedom and equality of rights, called the Declaration of Independence a "string of glittering generalities."[1] That brilliant lawyer was Rufus Choate, seeking to overthrow the arguments of the abolitionists. But in spite of his pronunciamento against it the world has continued to put into practical application the doctrines of this same declaration.

And now to-day we have another brilliant lawyer, *not* of Boston but of Kansas. The state which fought the border warfare in order to make itself the home of freedom—from that state comes this said lawyer, who, in order to hinder the application of these great principles of justice and equality to the other half of this people, the women—has valiantly denied the principles themselves.

In his Forum article[2] Senator Ingalls says: "The dogma that suffrage is a natural right has no support, either in reason or experience." In another place he says: "The *dogmatism* which asserts that suffrage is a natural right and that government rests upon consent has naturally led to a vigorous demand for the enfranchisement of women." Think of a Representative of Kansas asserting that the doctrine of the consent of the governed has no support, either in reason or experience? Still farther on, not satisfied with throwing overboard the Declaration of Independence, he says: "Thomas Jefferson,[3] the father of modern Democracy, borrowed his ideas of the social contract from Rousseau[4] and the French philosophers." Who ever heard Thomas Jefferson charged with plagiarism before? (Laughter.)

But that is not enough, and the senator continues: "His dreamy imagination," (Thomas Jefferson, he means), "his *dreamy* imagination was captivated by their vague phrases and imperfect generalization." Then further on he says: "He"—still referring to Thomas Jefferson—"He had no conception of the moral forces which give a nation strength, duration and grandeur."

We've waited 111 years since the Declaration of Independence was issued; we have gathered every Fourth of July and have heard our statesmen and states*women* make speeches based on this Declaration of Independence as expressive of a grand and glorious truth, and *now* we have found a Kansas senator who announces to us that Jefferson borrowed his ideas from others, and was only a dreamer! And further along he says, "The proclamation of emancipation disposed of the fallacious rhetoric of the composer of the Declaration of Independence."

The Declaration of Independence knocked in the head!!

And now, having thrown Jefferson overboard as a mere dreamer, he goes back and says: "If the premises are granted, the argument is conclusive. If voting is a natural right, then everybody has the same right to vote that he has to exist and the disfranchisement of women, minors, aliens, paupers and polygamists is indefensible tyranny."

If government rests upon consent, *then* to disfranchise women is indefensible tyranny. So, lest our argument should be based on this, he says further on, "The South, in 1861, endeavored to act upon the theory that government rests upon consent." Who ever heard *such* a statement with regard to the rebellion?

He says of the Southerners: "Dissatisfied with the lawful expression of the will of the majority at the polls, they refused to consent to the administration of the government by the Republican party under the presidency of Lincoln."[5] What *does* the consent of the governed mean? Does Senator Ingalls mean that to act in accordance with the doctrine of the consent of the governed each man is to knock down any other man who doesn't agree with him? Does he mean to say the logical result of the doctrine of the consent of the governed would be for the men who belonged to the party in the minority in this city to refuse to abide by the laws or live under the officers made and elected by the party in the majority and to strive by physical force to overthrow the city government?

For that is precisely what the South tried to do. When unable to carry its opinion to victory at the polls, the South *refused* to abide by the decision of the majority and appealed to arms. Yet even Senator Ingalls would hardly say that the *real* meaning of the doctrine of consent was to struggle against the rule of the majority. I was taught at school that the doctrine of consent meant that those of us who found ourselves in the minority on any question should abide by the decision of the majority, meanwhile working with might and main to bring others to our way of thinking until we in our turn became the majority, and it seems to me, that to say that the South in 1861, in trying to carry its opinion by force of arms and precipitating the whole country into a bitter, bloody war, was acting upon the theory that government rests upon consent is the most *absurd statement that mortal man* has ever made. (Applause.)

Then he says: "Had this government rested upon the consent of the governed, slavery would not have been abolished nor would the eleven seceded states have returned to the Union."

Who *are* the governed in this country? Who were the governed in the eleven seceded states? He must know that if the negroes could have been counted *they* would have voted themselves into freedom. When he says, "Had this government rested upon the consent of the governed slavery would not have been abolished," does he include in the governed the four million slaves, or does he mean only the masters of these slaves? So the senator there either doesn't speak plainly what he means, or else he doesn't know what he really does mean.

Then he goes back after denying that suffrage is a right, and says: "But if suffrage is a privilege conferred from considerations of expediency and *if* government rests primarily and ultimately upon force, *then* there is a rational and satisfactory explanation of the universal exclusion by all nations of *women*, children and other dependent classes from participation in legislation and politics." Now then, again, isn't it the highest respect when he classes women with "children and other dependent classes," you'd think *any* man would be willing to name his wife in some other connection than with children and "other dependent classes." And what wonderful audacity a man must possess to call women a dependent class when he knows they have performed their full quota in creating the wealth of the world, and that men have usurped the power and legislated into their own possession the result of the labor of woman's hands and brain. I think I felt the insult in that sentence more than any other in the entire article.

* * *

But now, the senator, after saying suffrage is a privilege, goes on to state authoritatively that "Suffrage *is* a privilege, conditioned upon age, sex, birth, property or intelligence, conferred by the state upon such citizens as are considered most likely to aid in the accomplishment of the fundamental objects for which government is established."

Now what *is* the state?

The state was at first composed only of white, male citizens worth a certain amount of property, all others were excluded from voting. It was a white male aristocracy of wealth. The state finally went forward and opened its doors to take in poor white men and then we had a white male aristocracy. Then the state went forward again [*and*] took in all black men, so that to-day we have an aristocracy based not upon wealth or color, but upon sex. So the state is a moveable feast and the question now is whether it shall open its doors again and take in the women.

* * *

Then the senator says *further*: "The most passionate pleader for female suffrage (I hate that phrase, *Female* suffrage) has never affirmed that women would make valuable judges, public[6] executioners, guards, jailors, policemen, militia or regular soldiers." How he's mistaken (laughter). Jailors, that's what we've been pleading for, we want good women in some capacity to follow unfortunate women into every place where misery or crime can take them.

In Rochester we are pleading to have women police matrons appointed. They have them already in Boston, Chicago and Philadelphia. Common decency requires that women serve in this capacity. Valuable judges, yes we *do* believe in them and Mrs. Esther Morris[7] who was appointed justice of the peace in Wyoming, which is the same as judge here, during the entire three years of her term, never had a single one of her decisions reversed by the higher court. We don't ask for women to shrink any responsibility of citizenship.

Mr. Justice Miller[8] has just appointed as United States marshall, that brilliant orator Miss Phoebe W. Couzins,[9] of St. Louis. This is something we never thought of asking but then the senator goes on to tell us how men and women differ intellectually saying "between the mental faculties and activities of the sexes there is a great gulf fixed, bridged only by the sentiments, the emotions and the passions."

Doesn't it throw a wonderful disrespect for the proprieties of sex on the part of Justice Miller? (Laughter.) *Jurors, yes I want* women as jurors, and if you had women as your jurors here in Kansas, you would have no difficulty in carrying out your prohibition laws, in finding juries who would bring a verdict of guilty for offense against such laws.[10]

In illustration of this I want to tell you an anecdote.[11] In 1871 I went by invitation of a Lecture Bureau to speak at Sioux City Iowa on my usual theme. On my arrival there in the morning I noticed a good deal of a stir and excitement and asked what it was about. I was told that the decent women of the town had during the night set fire to a house in which their husbands and brothers had domiciled a half dozen demimondes whom they had brought up from St. Louis. In my lecture that evening I made a point of this incident and described the terrible position of the wives who were forced by the laws and by consideration for their children to live with men whom they knew were faithless to their marriage vows, and spoke of this as a condition in which no self-respecting woman could live. The next morning's papers said that Miss Anthony had insulted the respectable women of Sioux City and that if she ever came there again she would be treated to a coat of tar and feathers. In 1877 I went there again to speak. I picked up one of the local papers and there I saw the report of a recent trial. A woman was accused of keeping a house of ill fame and numerous complaints entered against her. The jury were thirteen hours and finally returned with the verdict "No cause for indictment." When there was not a man on that jury who did not know that the accused was not only guilty of all which was charged against her but that never a young man came into that city who was not approached and tempted in some way through her servants, that she was a pitfall to their own sons. Think you if there had been half a dozen women, nay *one* woman on that jury, such a verdict could have been rendered, or that the local wives of that city would have been left to defend their homes as they had done at the time of my other visit, for the accused was a Madame Shaw, the very woman whose house they had burned over the very heads of its inmates six years before. Yes, we do want women on juries and good women must not shrink from such responsibilities.

Now, *don't* you think there *might* be an intellectual plane on which even Senator Ingalls might meet such a woman as George Eliot?[12] Don't you think such a woman might be able to comprehend and appreciate even a masculine intellect?

The senator says "It is impossible to conceive of a female Blackstone, Webster, Napoleon, Shakespeare, Gladstone or Bacon."[13]

Well as to Napoleon, there's been only one among men. Then about Shakespeare, you don't know as you have had *even* one among the men! (Laughter.) As for Webster, whom you feel was a king among legal minds, I would pit my friend, Elizabeth Cady Stanton, as his peer any time. But, strangely enough, after telling us of this great gulf fixed between the intellectual possibilities of men and women, he goes on to say that women could have been Shakespeares and Gladstones, etc., if they'd only wanted to. He says "Opportunity and capacity have not been wanting, but inclination and disposition have been absent."

Then in the very next line he says "It cannot be claimed that the faculties of woman are under duress for the tendency from subordination to equality has been irresistible, and her emancipation has long been complete." In one breath he says women might have been great in various lines, that only inclination was lacking, and in the next he says they have been emancipated—emancipated from what? If women always were freely welcomed to equal opportunity with man, how can they have been emancipated? Only six years since the high school of Boston, the city of culture, was opened to girls,[14] and girls were admitted to the public schools in the first place to enable the districts to draw more money, as the public moneys were distributed per capita, so as to get public money they let the girls into the school during the summer, while the boys were in the hay fields.

Only in 1836 did Oberlin open its doors to negroes and white girls—negroes have always been a little ahead of women.[15] Now would you think the senator had ever read histories.

First he says there's been nothing in our way and then he says *it's just been abolished!* (Laughter.)

But now let me come to the Sixteenth amendment argument. Mr. Ingalls says: "In considering the wisdom or expediency of enlarging the voting classes in this country by compelling all the males peremptorily to confer suffrage upon all women under penalty of forfeiting representation in congress and the electoral college as is proposed by the champions of the Sixteenth amendment to the constitution, it is not necessary to affirm nor to imply that woman is incompetent or disqualified for the ballot by reason of moral or intellectual infirmity."

Now I have the honor to be one of these "champions of the Sixteenth amendment." I circulated the first petition that was ever presented to congress for such an amendment and this is the first time in all the history of the movement that I've been told that those who are working for a Sixteenth amendment expect to force it upon reluctant states under any such penalty as is here mentioned.

Now either the senator is himself befogged or he means to befog other people.

The second section of the Fourteenth amendment says: "If any state shall disfranchise any of its male citizens all of that class shall be counted out of the basis of representation."

Under the old regime of slavery the negroes were not fully counted in the basis of representation—there was only a three-fifths count. The enfranchisement of the negro in its first section, was accompanied by this second section, this threat that the South should lose some of its representatives in congress by its refusal to allow the negro to vote.

Now, perhaps, Senator Ingalls is thinking of the Fourteenth amendment and has forgotten that women are now fully counted in the basis of representation. He seems to have forgotten that the proposed Sixteenth amendment contains no such clause—yet he repeats in another paragraph: "No amendment to the constitution is necessary nor could it have any other effect except to force the enfranchisement of women upon reluctant states that are not prepared for it and do not wish for it, under the penalty of a *reduction* of representation in Congress and the Electoral College."

Now if anyone can tell me what the Senator means by repeating thus *three* times that we suffragists propose to reduce the representation in Congress of those states which refuse to accept the situation, you can tell me more than I can now understand. After admitting to the ballot box every possible class of men, educated and uneducated, black and white, drunk and sober, native and foreign, Senator Ingalls turns to intelligent, American women, asking for the ballot and says to them: "We have reached the danger line." You have taken in the negro, the foreigner, ignorant of our institutions; you admit to the ballot box every possible man, except criminals, not pardoned, lunatics and the arch traitors of America—and then you turn to wives, mothers and sisters and say, "We have reached the danger line!"

* * *

Farther on the Senator says: "The opponents of the measure have [*been*] held up to scorn and derision, as cowards who were afraid to allow women to vote. Those who have ventured upon the right of private judgment have been denounced as intellectual felons, punishable by outlawry." Now doesn't this sound like "squealing" coming from the man who has exhausted his store of uncomplimentary names upon us as suffragists?

Why, just remember his Topeka speech in 1882, when he paid his compliments to us after this fashion: "That obscene dogma, whose advocates are long-haired men and short-haired women, the unsexed of both sexes, human" but [*I*] could not quote to any audience his terms of nature's monstrosities, and now the senator objects because we have tired of this treatment at his hands, and have replied to his attacks.[16]

* * *

Says the senator "social and political institutions are a growth and development to meet the requirements of some antecedent and pre-existing aspirations of the human soul."

Now here he grants the whole question. Social and political institutions *are* a growth—and there is a *pre-existent* and *antecedent* aspiration on the part of women to have these political institutions so enlarged as to include them; so we may believe that our cause will win, "whenever woman wants the ballot and society needs her enfranchisement, then the Sixteenth amendment will be adopted." You see how completely he yields. He grants all we demand.

Now this is beautiful. Just listen to this wisdom we have at the end. "There is no legislation that can annul the ordinances of nature,—(how profound) or abrogate the statutes of the Almighty," that is just what *he* has been trying all this time to do. One of the statutes of the Almighty is *justice*, and that God created man and woman equal, "male and female created he them and gave to *them* dominion."[17]

The senator has been trying to reverse the wheels of progress and with his little mop and broom a la dame Partington,[18] to sweep back this mighty tide of public sentiment for the full recognition of equality of rights for woman—but you see even *he* has given up his attempt to abrogate the statutes of the Almighty, and annul the ordinances of nature.

↦ *Leavenworth Times*, 27 October 1887, SBA scrapbook 12, Rare Books, DLC. In *Film*, in error, at 4 October 1886. Ellipses in original. Words in square brackets supplied by editors.

1. Calling on the Whigs of Maine to oppose the new Republican party in 1856, lest its triumph drive the South out of the union, Rufus Choate (1799-1859), former Massachusetts congressman and senator, characterized Republican ideals as "the glittering and sounding generalities of natural right which make up the Declaration of Independence." (*The Old-Line Whigs for Buchanan! Letters of Rufus Choate and George T. Curtis, of Massachusetts* [Boston, 1856], 4.)

2. John James Ingalls, "The Sixteenth Amendment," *Forum* 4 (September 1887): 1–13. SBA quotes liberally and accurately from his text in what follows.

3. Thomas Jefferson (1743–1826) authored the Declaration of Independence in 1776 and later became the third president of the United States.

4. Jean-Jacques Rousseau (1712–1778), French philosopher, upheld the idea that political authority owed its legitimacy to the general will rather than divine right.

5. Abraham Lincoln (1809–1865) was sworn in as sixteenth president of the United States in 1861.

6. The *Leavenworth Times* reads "police executioners"; with "public executioners," the text matches what Ingalls wrote.

7. Esther Hobart McQuigg Slack Morris (1814–1902) lived in South Pass City, Wyoming, when the territory enfranchised women, and in February 1870, she became the first American woman to hold judicial office, when county officials appointed her justice of the peace. SBA is correct about Morris's exemplary record in office, but Morris held the post for less than a year. (*NAW*; *ANB*.)

8. Samuel Freeman Miller (1816–1890) served as an associate justice of the Supreme Court of the United States from 1862 until his death. (*ANB*.)

9. Phoebe Wilson Couzins (1839?–1913), the first woman to enter the law school of Washington University in St. Louis, was named United States Marshal of the Eastern District of Missouri in September 1887 to succeed her father at the time of his death. The appointment lasted only until November 1887. A founder of the National Woman Suffrage Association in 1869 and occasionally one of its officers, Couzins was an accomplished lecturer who was plagued by ill health. (*NAW*; *ANB*. See also *Papers* 3 & 4.)

10. Kansans amended the state constitution in 1880 to prohibit the manufacture and sale of liquor. Enforcement of the provision was uneven and in dispute in state and local elections.

11. On this oft-told tale about Sioux City, Iowa, see SBA diary, 14 June 1871, 8 November 1877, *Film*, 15:91ff, 19:12ff; *Papers*, 3:167, 174n, 301; and *Papers*, 4:185.

12. George Eliot was the penname of the English novelist Mary Ann Evans (1819–1880).

13. For his eclectic list of intellectual giants Ingalls selected the English jurist William Blackstone (1723–1780); American lawyer and politician Daniel Webster (1782–1852); Napoléon I, emperor of France (1769–1821); English playwright William Shakespeare (1564–1616); leader of Britain's Liberal party William Ewart Gladstone (1809–1898); and English philosopher Francis Bacon (1561–1626). Francis Bacon was suggested as a likely author of the plays of William Shakespeare.

14. Possibly a reference to the Girls' Latin School for college preparation, that opened in 1878 and graduated its first class in 1880. A practical high school education intended primarily for teachers had been available to Boston's girls for many decades.

15. Oberlin College admitted white girls at its start in 1833 and enrolled African-American boys in 1835 and girls a few years later.

16. Despite SBA's precision, it is not clear when and where Ingalls spoke these words, though his love of invective and hostility to woman suffragists are not in doubt. His biographer quotes similar language from an undated manuscript in his papers. In a letter of 10 April 1886, SBA implied that he had recently used this language in a speech that echoed one he delivered two years earlier. The *New York Times*, 14 September 1884, quoted the words while reporting on a disagreement in Kansas about whether Ingalls thus described prohibitionists or woman suffragists. (Burton J. Williams, *Senator John James Ingalls: Kansas' Iridescent Republican* [Lawrence, Kan., 1972], 155; SBA to Hartford Equal Rights Club, 10 April 1886, *Film*, 24:985–90.)

17. Gen. 1:27–28.

18. The image of Dame Partington stemming floodwaters with her mop symbolized the futility of resisting political progress, after Sydney Smith used the image to taunt the House of Lords about their rejection of the Reform Bill in 1831.

22 ❧ LUCY STONE[1] TO SBA, WITH ENCLOSURE

> Office of American Woman Suffrage Association,
> 3 Park Street, Boston, November 7, 1887.

Dear Miss Anthony: I inclose to you the certified vote of the American Woman Suffrage Association, at its late meeting in Philadelphia, in regard to a union of the National and American Associations. I shall be glad to have this accomplished.

Will you let me know your movements and when you can most conveniently meet with me to consider the matter?[2] Yours sincerely,

❧ Lucy Stone.

ENCLOSURE

> Office of American Woman Suffrage Association,
> 3 Park Street, Boston, November 7, 1887.

At the nineteenth annual meeting of the American Woman Suffrage Association, held in Philadelphia, October 31, November 1 and 2, 1887, the following resolution, recommended and reported by the Business Committee, was unanimously adopted:

Whereas the woman suffragists of the United States were all united until 1868 in the American Equal Rights Association; and whereas the causes of the subsequent separation into the National and American Woman Suffrage Societies have since been largely removed by the adoption of common principles and methods; therefore

Resolved, That Mrs. Lucy Stone be appointed a committee of one from the American Woman Suffrage Association to confer with Miss Susan B. Anthony, of the National Woman Suffrage Association, and, if on conference it seems desirable, that she be authorized and empowered to appoint a committee of this association to meet a similar committee appointed by the National Woman Suffrage Association, to consider a satisfactory basis of union, and refer it back to the Executive Committees of both associations for final action.

I hereby certify to the accuracy of the above as printed.

~ Henry B. Blackwell,
Corresponding Secretary American Woman Suffrage Association.

~ *Negotiations between the American and National Woman Suffrage Associations in Regard to Union*, ed. Rachel G. Foster (N.p., 1888), 2. In *Film* at 20 April 1888.

1. Lucy Stone (1818–1893) and her husband, Henry Browne Blackwell (1825–1909), known as Harry, shared editorial duties at the Boston *Woman's Journal* and controlled the powerful executive committee of the American Woman Suffrage Association. (*NAW*, s.v. "Stone, Lucy"; *ANB*, s.v. "Blackwell, Henry Browne" and "Stone, Lucy." See also *Papers* 1–4.) The text of this communique was published in April 1888 by the National association and May 1888 by the American association, as each society offered the public its own version of events. For the American's history, see *Woman's Journal*, 5 May 1888.

2. SBA was still in the Midwest. On November 11, although she had not yet received this letter, she knew that Lucy Stone had authority to pursue union, and in that, SBA detected a trap for herself. "[I]f she makes the overture—& nothing comes of it—the failure, as niece Lucy E. sees will be thrown upon Susan B. A—!!" (SBA to Rachel G. Foster, 11 November 1887, *Film*, 25:787–91.)

EDITORIAL NOTE: There is a great deal not known about how and why the American Woman Suffrage Association reached the decision to propose union with its rival. Reporters at the annual meeting described the vote as a routine matter that won the delegates' approval without debate. After the vote was taken, the association's president, William D. Foulke, "congratulated the association on this harmonizing step and predicted rich results from the union of the two bodies," according to the Philadelphia *Evening Bulletin*. The *Woman's Journal* offered its readers no explanation.

If a plan for union circulated among state presidents and delegates in advance of the annual meeting, then it is likely that someone alerted SBA. The historic division of suffragists was still solid among leaders but highly permeable in the states, and few activists would have felt obliged to keep a secret. However, there is nothing in the record to confirm that SBA knew what was afoot. The public call to the American's meeting gave no hint about the decision to be made.

Just two weeks before the event in Philadelphia, at a meeting of the Kansas Equal Suffrage Association, Henry Blackwell busied himself with a plot to perpetuate division. The Kansas society's constitution declared its affiliation with the National association, yet friends of Blackwell and Lucy Stone encouraged them to believe that the loyalty could be switched. Despite Blackwell's efforts at the meeting in Newton, the Kansas society not only rejected affiliation with the American association, but also recommended that the American unite with the National and voted to send a delegation to the American's annual meeting. As Blackwell reported to Stone, the Kansans kept that vote for union off the record and out of its minutes. Two years later, Laura Johns, president of the Kansas association, recalled it with pride. We "take unto ourselves much credit for our part in bringing about this happy denouement" of union, she told her members. We were, "I think, the first to decide upon the union of the parent societies as a most desirable way out of the difficulties that beset our association as the child of two mothers."

SBA also attended the meeting in Kansas in October 1887, saw Blackwell at his divisive work, and no doubt helped her allies defeat the scheme to change the society's affiliation. That Kansans would recommend union need not have surprised her: by this date, union was the hope and aim of many suffragists.

Frances Casement of Ohio had taken the idea to a meeting of the American association in 1884. William Lloyd Garrison, Jr., of Boston had pressed Lucy Stone to reconcile with SBA. Matilda Hindman of Pittsburgh offered cooperative projects to competing societies in Pennsylvania. Rhode Island's society repeatedly scheduled national leaders from both societies to speak together at its annual meetings. No doubt there were more activities underway. SBA had cooperated with these efforts to build fragile bridges between the rivals.

That Lucy Stone had union or cooperation on her mind in 1887 is indisputable. Ill health led her to leave Boston for the South that winter; a final, written good-by to her husband before she left suggests she thought her end was near. In letters home to her daughter, Stone toyed with the idea of greater cooperation between the suffrage associations but not at the expense of cultivating her dislike for her rivals. Alice Blackwell later took most of the credit for overcoming her parents' resistance to union, but Stone's letters belie that role in the early stages. The mother tried to teach her daughter how to rise above personal dislike for the competition and serve the cause.

Little had changed in Stone's view of the National's leaders. There "does seem to be something not quite honest, frank, and straight in the whole of them," she wrote Alice on 12 April 1887 from Georgia. "It really is the dividing characteristic between the two societies." Nonetheless, in the same letter she spelled out the kind of cooperation she could abide. Neither association would give up its identity or leaders; "each [would] be responsible for the management of its work, but all *meeting* upon occasion." By such a loose affiliation, she wrote, the Americans could escape "for the most part, any indiscretions which the National Branch might run into." Stone's idea had not shifted much by July 1887: the National and American would become "branch societies" of an umbrella organization, she wrote a friend; an annual meeting would "tak[e] away the feeling that there is opposition between suffragists."

When the American association's executive committee met in Philadelphia three months later, they agreed on a plan for union that far exceeded Lucy Stone's earlier ideas about arms-length cooperation. Whose proposal was it that Stone sent to SBA? Did executive committee members debate and craft its objectives and details? Who prepared delegates to accept the recommendation? At this point, the answers to those questions are unknown. The historian who studied most closely the suffrage associations founded by Lucy Stone concluded that the American association was sputtering to its end and had little choice but to unite with its larger and more popular rival. If she is correct, Henry Blackwell's adventure in Kansas might have sounded the alarm that the American association could not be revived by recruiting dissidents to realign the state affiliates.

The plan put forward by the American association's executive committee conceded nothing to weakness or inevitability, however. Presumptuous in its detail, the resolution directed not only Lucy Stone but also the entire National Woman Suffrage Association about how to proceed. It stipulated that SBA was the person to whom Stone should talk, instructed the National to form a committee, prescribed that two ad hoc committees define a basis for union, and instructed that neither conference committee consult its executive committee until after that basis was drawn. Those details proved useful to Lucy Stone and Henry Blackwell over the next year as grounds for protesting actions taken by the National association during negotiations. Equally problematic for SBA and the National association was the sudden reversal of roles between the two associations. The American association had rejected union for two decades. As soon as its leaders reversed themselves and made an offer, they put SBA and the National association in a difficult and unfamiliar position. If the National proceeded to reject the offer, the blame for division would be transferred from Lucy Stone and Henry Blackwell to SBA and ECS, while the call from suffragists for unity would still be unanswered. (L. Stone to A. S. Blackwell, 12 April 1887, and H. B. Blackwell to L. Stone and A. S. Blackwell, 16 October 1887, in Wheeler, *Loving Warriors*, 303-5, 309-10; L. Stone to Antoinette B. Blackwell, 23 July 1887, in Carol Lasser and Marlene Deahl Merrill, eds., *Friends and Sisters: Letters between Lucy Stone and Antoinette Brown Blackwell, 1846-93* [Urbana, Ill., 1987], 253-54; *Woman's Journal*, 24 September, 5, 12 November 1887; Philadelphia *Press*, 31 October, 1, 2, 3 November 1887; *Public Ledger*, 1, 2, 3 November 1887; *Philadelphia Record*, 1, 2, 3 November 1887; *Evening Bulletin*, 1, 2, 3 November 1887; *Wichita Eagle*, 2 October 1889, *Film*, 27:450-55; Alice Stone Blackwell, *Lucy Stone, Pioneer of Woman's Rights* [Boston, 1930], 229; Lois Bannister Merk, "Massachusetts and the Woman-Suffrage Movement," [Ph.D. diss., Radcliffe College, 1956], 238-40; Samuel J. Tamburro, "Frances Jennings Casement and the Equal Rights Association of Painesville, Ohio: The Fight for Women's Suffrage, 1883-1889," *Ohio History* 108 [Summer-Autumn 1999]: 173; *Papers*, 4:156-60, 181-83, 333-35, 376-78, 383-84.)

23   SBA to Lucy Stone

Philadelphia Pa.[1] Dec. 13th 1887

Dear Lucy Stone

Since no letter is here—if agreable—I will go to you on Tuesday night's New England train—Dec. 20th—reaching Boston Wednesday A.M.—[2] Miss Rachel Foster will accompany me—and we shall be the guests of Mrs H. S. Purinton—88 West Newton Street[3]

I should like to have Alice[4] present at the interview—that each of us may have a <u>suffrage</u> <u>daughter</u> to help bring about the desired end

I should like our talk to be Wednesday afternoon or evening—and just where it will best suit you.

I think it desirable to have a Stenographer present—that each of us may have an exact report.[5] If you agree with me—please engage the best one you can and I will pay half the expense— Yours Hopefully

                         ❧   *Susan B. Anthony*

❧ ALS, on 40th anniversary letterhead, Blackwell Papers, DLC. Marked by Stone "Rec'd Dec. 14, 1887—Philadelphia."

    1. At the home of Adeline Thomson.

    2. Stone had earlier announced that she was too ill to travel to Philadelphia to meet SBA. (*Negotiations between the American and National*, p. 2, *Film*, 26:746–51.)

    3. Harriett S. Furguson Purinton (1824–?) hosted SBA during her summer vacation with Adeline Thomson earlier in 1887. She was the wife of James Purinton, Jr., a retired manufacturer of shoes in Lynn, Massachusetts. (*Vital Records of Lynn, Massachusetts, to the End of the Year 1849* [Salem, Mass., 1906], 2:312; Federal Census, Lynn, 1880; *Anthony*, 2:624.)

    4. Alice Stone Blackwell (1857–1950) was the daughter of Lucy Stone and Henry Blackwell, and since her graduation from Boston University in 1881, she had assumed more and more responsibility for editing the *Woman's Journal*. (*NAW*; *ANB*.)

    5. Stone did not accept this suggestion. Notes taken by Alice Blackwell and Rachel Foster at the meeting on December 21 formed the basis for later negotiations.

24 ~ SBA to Thomas B. Reed[1]

Philadelphia Pa. Dec. 15, 1887

Hon. T. B. Reed   My Dear Sir

May I not depend on you to present the resolution for the 16th amendment—at an early day—and have it duly placed with the Judiciary Committee—

If the Republican Party deems woman's good wishes & work for its success in 1888—it would be well for that <u>party</u> to make some sign of good will toward her—after this fashion—

1st—Bring the 16th am't Bill to a discussion & vote—in <u>Both Houses</u> <s>of Congress</s>, during this first session of the 50th Congress—with as nearly a <u>party vote</u> for it as possible—and

2^d—Have a Municipal Suffrage ↑bill↓ presented in every State Legislature in session—<u>this</u> <u>winter</u>—and brought to a vote—and <u>carried</u>—wherever the party is strong enough!!—and

3^d—Have a fairly good promise in the National party platform at Chicago next June!!

With three party line demonstrations of this sort—I feel that even the ↑majority of the↓ Miss Willard Temperance women would be drawn ↑back↓ toward <u>praying</u> & <u>working</u> for the success of the Grand Old Party,[2] and of all the rest of us—I am sure it would ↑cause us to work for it!!↓

I believe the <u>enthusiasm</u> of the <u>grand army</u> of <u>women</u> who <u>want</u> to <u>vote</u> for one reason or another—and for principle's sake—on the side of the Republican party & its nominees—would be a source of strength to it in the coming campaign—and I <u>know</u> it will not be given to them—unless the party makes some decided sign of determination in the direction of their complete enfranchisement.

I talked this over with Representative Morrill[3] of Kansas—when at his home in Hiawatha last October—and I do hope you will talk over the matter with the leaders of the party— We have a hundred women and more—<u>good</u> <u>campaign</u> <u>speakers</u>—who would gladly work for the Republican Party—but with no <u>promise even</u>—how can they be expected to rally around it—

Hoping to be able to "shout" for the Republican Party—as well as for its best members—Very sincerely yours

~ *Susan B. Anthony*

~ ALS, on 40th anniversary letterhead, Thomas Brackett Reed Papers, Special Collections, MeB.

1. Thomas Brackett Reed (1839-1902), Republican of Maine, who served in the House of Representatives from 1877 to 1899, provided leadership for woman suffragists in Congress. The first session of the Fiftieth Congress, under Democratic control, began 5 December 1887, and the constitutional amendment for woman suffrage needed to be introduced anew. Reed took care of that on 4 January 1888, when he proposed House Resolution No. 16. Following its usual practice, the House referred the resolution to the Judiciary Committee, but Reed no longer served on that committee. (*BDAC*; *Congressional Record*, 50th Cong., 1st sess., 218; *Papers*, 4:155, 318-19, 426-27, 467, 490-91.)

2. Frances Willard had worked since 1881 to lead the Woman's Christian Temperance Union into an alliance with the Prohibition party, on whose executive committee she held a seat from 1882 to 1891. By this date, the national union and most of the state unions had endorsed the party, and in the next year's presidential campaign, Willard and union members worked hard for the party's candidate. Willard's designs were quite different from SBA's: she expected to lure woman suffragists into the Prohibition party. (Ruth Bordin, *Woman and Temperance: The Quest for Power and Liberty, 1873-1900* [Philadelphia, 1981], 123-31; Ruth Bordin, *Frances Willard, A Biography* [Chapel Hill, N.C., 1986], 134-37; F. E. Willard to SBA, 11 May 1887, and SBA to Willard, after 11 May 1887, *Film*, 25:440-41.)

3. Edmund Needham Morrill (1834-1909), long active in Kansas politics, served as a Republican in Congress from 1883 to 1891. SBA stayed with him in Hiawatha, Kansas, on October 24 and 25, during the congressional district meeting. (*BDAC*.)

25 ~ MINUTES OF INFORMAL CONFERENCE BETWEEN LUCY STONE AND SBA

EDITORIAL NOTE: Alice Blackwell prepared these minutes after the meeting of herself, Rachel Foster, SBA, and Lucy Stone in Boston on 21 December 1887, but the people who negotiated union may not have seen them. Rather than send the minutes to the National association, Blackwell sent her mother's list of conditions for union, drawn up after the meeting (Appendix A in this volume), and Rachel

Foster distributed that list to the National's conference committee. Foster received the minutes late in January after making a special request to see them, and she wrote Blackwell, "As I found your report correspond with my own memory of the occasion, with the exception of several points which I should wish to make fuller, my report will be practically yours, slightly enlarged upon." Foster included neither her own minutes (if she ever wrote them) nor Blackwell's in the history of negotiations she wrote in April 1888. Henry Blackwell included them in his version of the history of negotiations, published in May 1888. By that time the negotiations had, from his perspective, broken down. To place the onus of failure on the National association, he inserted commentary into the minutes, which here appears in notes to the text. (*Woman's Journal*, 5 May 1888, *Film*, 26:756-61.)

[21 December 1887]

After the preliminary civilities, Mrs. Stone invited Miss Anthony to make suggestions. Miss Anthony said she should prefer not to make any at that time, but to hear what Mrs. Stone had to suggest. Mrs. Stone said that the first point would be the question of a name for the united society.

Miss Anthony said she should object to the adoption of any name that would destroy the historical continuity of her society in the announcement of annual meetings as 19th, 20th, etc.

Mrs. Stone said that as the united society would be neither the National nor the American, but a new body, a combination of the two, it would necessarily have a new name. She had thought of three names, any one of which might do, viz: The United Woman Suffrage Societies, the National American (or American National) Woman Suffrage Association, or the American Equal Suffrage Association.

Miss Anthony and Mrs. Stone agreed that they both liked "Woman Suffrage" much better than "Equal Suffrage."

Mrs. Stone liked "The United Woman Suffrage Societies" best.

Miss Anthony expressed a preference for "The National American Woman Suffrage Association." She asked Miss Blackwell what she thought about it. Miss Blackwell said she liked the name "National American Woman Suffrage Association" best.

Mrs. Stone said, "Then let it be 'The National American.'"

Miss Anthony said: "How would it be written? National-American with a hyphen? Very well."

Mrs. Stone suggested that in the united society there should be no distinction of sex in membership or eligibility to office.

Miss Anthony said that that was now the case in the National Association.

Mrs. Stone said that she had been under a contrary impression. Miss Blackwell said she had always heard that a by-law or other provision was adopted at the first meeting of the National Association, excluding men from holding office.

Miss Anthony said she would not say that there never had been such a regulation, but it certainly had not been in existence for the last fifteen years. She said: "We have not elected any men to office simply because no men have offered us much help. We have treated them as they treat us."[1]

Mrs. Stone suggested that the united society should have a delegate basis; that duly accredited State delegates should be alone entitled to vote at business meetings;[2] that the presidents of State societies should be ex-officio vice-presidents of the general society, and the chairmen of executive committees of State societies be ex-officio members of the general executive committee.

Miss Anthony said that Mrs. Shattuck[3] had been engaged for a year or two in working up a plan for a delegate basis for the National Woman Suffrage Association, and had now got it into a shape where she (Miss Anthony) thought it was perhaps as good a one as could be devised. The Woman Suffrage Association really ought to be organized thoroughly, like the W.C.T.U.; every local society paying a portion of its annual fee to the State Association, and the State a part to the National Association. As for the presidents of State societies, a good many of them had been made vice-presidents of the National.

Miss Anthony took up the list of National officers and went over them, naming the National vice-presidents who were State presidents, and where this was not the case, assigning reasons.[4]

Mrs. Stone called attention to the fact that the sole object of the National Society, as now defined by its constitution, was to obtain a sixteenth amendment. She thought that the scope should be so far widened as to include all kinds of suffrage work.[5]

Miss Blackwell said she thought, in case the union were accomplished, there should be an understanding that Miss Anthony would help to push the movement for municipal and presidential suffrage,[6] which had always been our specialty, and that we should do all we could, on the other hand, to aid the effort for a Sixteenth Amendment.

Miss Anthony said she approved of the effort to get municipal suffrage; she did not take much stock in presidential suffrage, but, if any State wanted to try for it, she had no objection.

Mrs. Stone suggested that the object of the united association should be defined to be "to secure suffrage to the women of the United States."

Miss Anthony thought there would be no objection to that.

Miss Foster suggested that the general officers and chairman of the executive committee of the united association for the first year be elected by the individual members of the two associations on joint ballot—the vote to be taken by mail. She said that in important matters of this kind, the individual members were apt to feel better satisfied if they had all been consulted, and that the National Executive Committee had not been elected with a view to their acting on this particular matter, as it had not been known at the last National Annual Meeting that the American W.S.A. would make an overture for union.

This idea impressed Miss Blackwell favorably at first. After a little reflection, however, she saw and pointed out to Miss Foster that to decide anything by joint ballot would not ensure a result mutually satisfactory to both associations, but only a result satisfactory to the association which cast the most votes. To secure a mutually satisfactory result, every matter of importance connected with the union must be accepted by each association separately. This was what was contemplated by the vote of the American Association at Philadelphia. Miss Blackwell added that under the newly adopted regulation of the National Association by which all the individual members of some of its auxiliary State societies were reckoned as *ipso facto* members of the National W.S.A., the American would be placed at an undue disadvantage on such a ballot. The individual members of those State societies would all be entitled to vote on the question, while the individual members of the American auxiliary State societies would not.[7] Miss Blackwell added that the American Executive Committee had been authorized by the society to take final action on the question of union on such a basis as should have been previously agreed upon by the Conference Committees. As the National Executive Committee had not been so authorized, if they thought fit to refer the report of the Conference Committees back to their individual members for ratification, there could be no objection to their doing so.

The question of States where there were two State societies was discussed.[8] Mrs. Stone thought that, in such cases, the original State society should be the one recognized by the united association.

Miss Anthony thought that the State societies should be left to settle their own quarrels.

Miss Foster said that the formation of a second State society where one already existed was generally due more to local causes than to any special sympathy either with the National or the American. If the two general societies united, the pretext for keeping up two State societies would be removed, and she thought that they (the State societies) would undoubtedly unite also.

Mrs. Stone said that since many persons in the National Association regarded her as responsible for the original division, and since many persons in the American Association regarded Mrs. Stanton and Miss Anthony as responsible for it, and more or less feeling still existed in regard to the matter, she thought it would help to promote the union if they were all three to enter into a mutual agreement in advance that they would none of them accept the presidency of the united society.

Miss Anthony expressed strong repugnance to this proposal, and so did Miss Foster.

Miss Foster said that she herself would like to see Miss Anthony president, but rather than not have that office filled by some one of the three ladies named, she should prefer a triple presidency composed of all of them.

Miss Anthony said she was not willing to retire from the work as long as she could be of any use in it.

Mrs. Stone said she had had no idea either of proposing that Mrs. Stanton and Miss Anthony should retire from the work, or of retiring from it herself. She said: "We could all be together on the executive committee."[9]

Miss Anthony said that in sending out notices and public documents, it was important that the women whose names were signed as officers should be persons of national reputation.

Mrs. Stone said that Mrs. Julia Ward Howe[10] and Mrs. Mary A. Livermore[11] were both of them women of national reputation.

Miss Foster said that that was true, but their reputation was not solely as suffragists. She added that there were many women in the National Association who would not be willing to work under the presidency of Mrs. Livermore, or of any other person whom they regarded as just about on a level with themselves, but who were willing to work under Miss Anthony on the ground of her priority in service.

Miss Blackwell suggested that the constitution of the united society should contain a proviso like that of the National Woman's Christian Temperance Union by which no department of work recommended by the general association should be binding on State associations or individuals; also that if the associations united upon a constitution satisfactory to both, that constitution should not be changed afterwards without full notice given a good while in advance to all the members of the exact change proposed.[12]

Miss Anthony said that another question which would come up would be that of the papers. She said: "Mrs. Colby has struggled on with her paper for four years, and we cannot ask her to give it up," or words to that effect.

Miss Blackwell said: "We had not thought of asking her to give it up. She could not be expected to do so. Neither could we be expected to give up our paper, which has been going on for nearly twenty years, and has always kept out of debt. What I should propose, would be that the *Woman's Journal* and the *Woman's Tribune* should be dealt with on an equal footing, without discrimination for or against either, and left to make their way on their merits, as lower price, or superior interest, or other similar considerations may determine. They could both be offered at the national meetings, and the lower price of the *Woman's Tribune* would always give it a considerable advantage."

Miss Anthony said that she thought if the papers were both offered, the result would be that subscriptions would not be got for either.

Miss Anthony said that if she appointed a committee, it would consist of Mrs. May Wright Sewall, Mrs. Laura M. Johns, Mrs. H. R. Shattuck, Mrs. Clara B. Colby, Miss Rachel Foster, Rev. Olympia Brown, Mrs. Helen M. Gougar.[13]

As we all rose to go, Mrs. Stone recurred to her suggestion about the presidency, and said she wished it could be favorably considered, as she was sure it would greatly promote harmony. If Miss Anthony's objections to it were insuperable, she (Mrs. Stone) thought it would be necessary for her to consult again with her auxiliaries.

Mrs. Stone wishes me to add that she is perfectly willing to leave the whole question of officers, etc., to be agreed upon by the respective conference committees and ratified by the associations.[14]

↝ *Woman's Journal*, 5 May 1888. In *Film* at 5 May 1888.

1. This presumed difference between the two associations figured prominently in the propaganda of Lucy Stone and Henry Blackwell for two decades. "It was proposed to confine membership to <u>Women</u>," Blackwell wrote of the National's founding meeting in 1869 from which he was absent; "Mr & Mrs Stanton & others advocated this. It was voted down— But a bye-law was then, or subsequently, adopted <u>excluding</u> men <u>from</u> holding office—<u>all</u> the officers were made <u>women</u>." He offered this description as a reason for Isabella Hooker to affiliate with the American association. At their meeting in May 1869, the National's delegates did reject Henry Stanton's suggestion of excluding men. Evidence that they then or later excluded men from leadership is lacking. In 1882, the National took the step of urging men to join the association in order to increase their numbers. (H. B. Blackwell to I. B. Hooker, 6 December 1869, Isabella Hooker Collection, CtHS-D; *Papers*, 2:242–43, 4:143, 144–45n.)

2. Stone here took aim at a major difference between the two associations. The American adopted a federal system, based on state suffrage societies, represented by delegates to the association's annual meetings. In this fashion, it intended, as stated in the call to its founding convention, to "embody the deliberate action of the State organizations." However, rather than allotting delegates by the size of membership in state societies, the American set the number of delegates to match each state's congressional delegation, whether or not a state society existed and regardless of its size. The National association was made up principally of individual members, but as SBA replied to Stone, changes were underway. Since 1882, members had tried various forms of representation through delegates. At an executive session in 1886, Harriette Shattuck's plan to limit the voting rights of individual members won unanimous approval. Each state and territory would be entitled to one delegate for every twenty-five resident members of the association. In addition, state suffrage societies would be permitted two delegates. When fifty individual members who lacked status as delegates protested at the Washington convention of 1887, they were granted the privilege of voting at that meeting. The 1888 convention was also to consist of delegates, but individual members could be allowed to vote at the meeting by a unanimous vote of the executive committee. (*Constitution of the American Woman Suffrage Association and the History of Its Formation* [Boston, 1881], NAWSA Papers, DLC; *Papers*, 4:143, 476–77, 487n; *Woman's Tribune*, April 1887 and 21 April 1888, and *Washington Critic*, 26 January 1887, and Rachel G. Foster to Olympia Brown, 6 January 1888, and "Minutes of the Twentieth Annual Convention, 1888," pp. 2–7 and unnumbered pages following p. 88, all in *Film*, 25:198–202, 211–12, 1027–32, 26:633–36, 638ff; and May W. Sewall to Vice Presidents, undated circular from spring 1887, SBA scrapbook 12, Rare Books, DLC.)

3. Harriette Lucy Robinson Shattuck (1850–1937) of Massachusetts collaborated with her mother, Harriet Robinson, in challenging the American

association's dominance in New England. They arranged for the National to hold its annual meeting in Boston in 1881 and a year later, they founded the National Woman Suffrage Association of Massachusetts. (*WWW4*; *New York Times*, 23 March 1937; Claudia L. Bushman, *"A Good Poor Man's Wife": Being a Chronicle of Harriet Hanson Robinson and Her Family in Nineteenth-Century New England* [Hanover, N.H., 1981], passim. See also *Papers* 4.)

4. SBA's discussion was beside the point: the National customarily selected state presidents to be vice presidents, but a state president, elected locally, was not ex officio an officer of the National. Moreover, a state or territory could have a vice president in the National when no state or territorial suffrage society existed, as was the case, for example, with Marietta Bones, vice president for Dakota Territory. Members of the National's executive committee were separately selected.

5. The National association's statement of purpose evolved. In 1869, its object, stated in article two of its constitution, was "to secure the Ballot to the women of the nation on equal terms with men." By 1872, article two promised "to secure State and National protection for women citizens in the exercise of their right to vote." In 1876 at the start of the sixteenth amendment campaign, the reference to state protection was dropped, leaving the clear purpose "to secure National protection," and that language remained until 1890. Article two of the American association's constitution began with the general object of "concentrat[ing] the efforts of all the advocates of Woman Suffrage in the United States" and proceeded into details about forming auxiliary societies, holding meetings, publishing tracts, and circulating petitions. Blackwell's examples did not come from constitutional language but from plans of work. (*Film*, 13:748–50, 16:313–14, 18:790–91, 22:165; *Constitution of the American Woman Suffrage Association and the History of Its Formation*.)

6. By presidential suffrage, its advocates meant the right to vote for members of the Electoral College in each state. Because the Constitution of the United States directed state legislatures to determine the manner of their selection, it was asserted that the enfranchisement of women for this purpose required changing only a state's election laws rather than its constitution. Henry Blackwell was its most conspicuous advocate.

7. Rachel Foster explained this exchange in her letter to the National's committee on union. "Miss Blackwell objected that as they do not recognize members of their auxiliaries as members of the American W.S.A. (as the National does) this would place them at a disadvantage." The American's consideration of union and election of officers would be the business of its executive committee. The National's provision for treating members of auxiliaries as members of the parent organization was included in the basis of representation in effect for the convention of 1888. When the practice began is not known. (R. G. Foster to Olympia Brown, 6 January 1888. See also Appendix B.)

8. Rival suffrage societies in some states, such as Missouri and California,

were short-lived, but in Indiana and Massachusetts, rival societies with strong identities were thriving.

9. An additional paragraph at this point in the text was probably inserted by Henry Blackwell when he placed the minutes in his history of negotiations for union. It read: "From this remark, which was several times repeated in the course of the conversation, Miss Foster got the idea (which she expressed to Miss Blackwell on the following Friday) that Mrs. Stone proposed that they should none of them hold office except on the executive committee, or even be chairman of that. Miss Blackwell understood Mrs. Stone to be referring to the presidency only, and it is so set down in her notes. Mrs. Stone, being asked, says that her suggestion referred solely to the presidency."

10. Julia Ward Howe (1819–1910), author most famously of the "Battle Hymn of the Republic," was the first president of the New England Woman Suffrage Association and a staunch ally of Lucy Stone for two decades. (*NAW*; *ANB*.)

11. Mary Ashton Rice Livermore (1820–1905) was a very popular lecturer and former editor of the *Woman's Journal*. Like Julia Howe, she became an advocate of woman suffrage only after the Civil War. (*NAW*; *ANB*.)

12. Article five of the American's constitution permitted amendments "at any annual meeting by a vote of three-fifths of the delegates present," without prior notification. Alice Blackwell's far stricter proposal for a united society would forestall immediate changes to the new constitution by majority vote. (*Constitution of the American Woman Suffrage Association and the History of Its Formation*.)

13. This list matched the appointments SBA made in early January. May Sewall chaired the committee, and Rachel Foster served as its secretary. Helen Mar Jackson Gougar (1843–1907) of Indiana was a prohibitionist who joined the suffrage movement in 1880. She was a very effective lecturer, and in her home state and Kansas, she showed talent as an organizer. (*NAW*; *ANB*. See also *Papers* 4.)

14. Again it is probable that Henry Blackwell authored this paragraph, which appears without typographical distinction as the next one in his history of negotiations: "Mrs. Stone thought the arrangement suggested in regard to the presidency very desirable, as she had reason to believe that there were persons in both associations who would not be willing to join the union society if anyone whom they regarded as responsible for the original division were placed at the head of it. But of course such an agreement could only be made by mutual consent; and as Miss Anthony decidedly preferred not to enter into it, that ended the matter."

26   Lucy Stone to SBA

Boston, December 23, 1887.[1]

Dear Miss Anthony: In thinking over the points raised at our informal conference, it seems to me that the substantial outcome is this: The committees appointed by us respectively, if we conclude to appoint them, must each agree upon a common name, a common constitution, and a common list of officers for the first year. A subsequent acceptance of these by each association will thereafter constitute the two societies one society.

If you think that there is a fair probability of coming to an agreement I will proceed to appoint my committee; but the selection will be a matter requiring care and thought, and I must take a week or two about it.[2]

As the formal overtures for union have come from the American Woman Suffrage Association, it will be appropriate that our committee should draw up the plan for union which appears to them the most feasible, and forward it to Miss Foster, to be submitted to your committee. The chief points will probably be those we spoke of on Wednesday, of which Alice will write out a statement for Miss Foster, so that your committee may be thinking them over in advance.[3] Then your committee will suggest such modifications as they may think needful; and, if a mutually satisfactory result can be reached, the name, constitution, and list of officers will go to the Executive Committee of each association for the final action. Yours truly,

                                 Lucy Stone.

Negotiations between the American and National Woman Suffrage Associations in Regard to Union, ed. Rachel G. Foster (N.p., 1888), 2–3. In *Film* at 20 April 1888.

1. When SBA called at the offices of the *Woman's Journal* on this date, Alice Blackwell handed her this letter, and Henry Blackwell engaged her in further conversation about terms of union. Alice Blackwell later admitted, "as Miss Anthony made no objection, I supposed she assented." (A. S. Blackwell to Rachel G. Foster, 27 December 1887, in *Woman's Journal*, 5 May 1888, *Film*, 26:756–61.)

2. Members of the American association's conference committee were Julia Howe (chairman), William Foulke, Hannah Cutler, Margaret Campbell, Mary Thomas, Anna Shaw, and Henry Blackwell (secretary).

3. Rather than send her minutes of the meeting (above at December 21), Alice Blackwell extracted from her notes a list of conditions for union, added points discussed between SBA and her father, and mailed it to Rachel Foster on December 25, who in turn forwarded it to SBA (see Appendix A in this volume). Foster, not regarding the list as a proper report of the meeting, asked on December 27 for the minutes. She still had only the list of conditions on 6 January 1888, when she sent material to members of the National's committee on union. During the National's discussions of union, members referred to the memorandum, not the minutes. The earliest extant copy of Blackwell's minutes is that published in the *Woman's Journal* in May. (*Negotiations between the American and National*, p. 3, *Film*, 26:746–51, and *Woman's Journal*, 5 May 1888.)

27 ~ SBA TO RACHEL G. FOSTER

[*Rochester, 24 December 1887*]¹

I cannot think of any stipulation that I wish to make the basis of union of all suffrage friends—save that we unite and after that discuss all measures, ways and means, officers and newspapers, and cheerfully accept and abide by the rule of the majority. I do not wish to exact any <u>pledges</u> from Lucy Stone and her adherents—nor can I give any for Mrs Stanton and her followers. When united we must trust to the good sense of each and all of us—just as each has trusted during the existence of the division. As Greely said about resuming specie payments, "The way to unite is to unite" and trust the consequences.²

~ Extract in hand of Lucy E. Anthony, Olympia Brown Papers, MCR-S. In *Film* at 6 January 1888.

1. The date of this letter is that assigned on the copy published in April in *Negotiations between the American and National*. The copy here was included in materials sent on 6 January 1888 to members of the committee named by SBA to discuss the American association's proposition for union. On December 27, Rachel Foster also sent it to Alice Blackwell to indicate that SBA had no stipulations to add to Stone's list. Blackwell, however, read it as a rejection of her mother's conditions. "The vote of our society," she replied, "authorized my mother to appoint a committee to agree with a similar committee

from the other side on a basis of union; but did not authorize either her or the committee to form a union unless a satisfactory basis could be agreed upon beforehand; and she is limited to that." (*Woman's Journal*, 5 May 1888, *Film*, 26:756–61.)

2. Although credit for this sentence about resumption of the gold standard in currency is often given to Horace Greeley (1811–1872), longtime editor of the *New York Tribune*, it originated in a letter to Greeley by former Treasury Secretary Salmon P. Chase dated 17 May 1866. (Jacob William Schuckers, *The Life and Public Services of Salmon Portland Chase* [New York, 1874], 410.)

28 ECS TO CLARA BEWICK COLBY

Basingstoke Hants   England Dec 25th [*1887*]

Dear Mrs Colby,

A Merry Christmas & Happy New Year to you, & the readers of The Tribune.

The best wishes of the season, for the success of the Journal, in its new satin dress, good clear type, & its promise of weekly ministrations.[1]

I have just read it through, every word from beginning to end, & thoroughly enjoyed its courageous tone, its radical thought & its evident determination to go to the root of the evils that block woman's path to freedom.

I was specially pleased with the articles by Mrs Chandler,[2] May Rogers[3] & "The plan of work for suffrage clubs"[4] all showing that women having proved their right to vote, at least to their own satisfaction, are now beginning to think in what manner that right shall be exercised

Some knowledge of the principles of political ↑economy↓ of the American system of Jurisprudence, & of the secular nature of our government are surely important subjects, on which women should inform themselves.

The brave heroes of our revolution, seeing the evils in the old world from a union of church & state, laid the foundations of our Republic so securely against all ecclesiastical power as to show us, that they understood the work they had in hand.

Such fear had they of priestcraft & religious fanaticism in politics that at first the clergy were not allowed to vote or express any opinions on politics in their pulpits.

But at length, having no established church with its emoluments & places of honor in government, it was deemed safe, for them to have some opinions & to express them at the polls as other men did, with no added ↑power↓ or authority because of their profession

Since then as citizens, they now have their legitimate influence in the state, surely there ↑is no↓ reason why as members of the various sects, their theological dogmas should be recognized in our ~~laws &~~ ↑national↓ constitutions.

As all shades of religious opinions are represented in the American people, Jews & Gentiles, Roman Catholics & Protestants Deists, Theists & Athesists, our first duty is to see that each & all stand equal before the law: their rights of conscience & individual judgement fully protected.

Those who asks for religious tests, in our rulers & party platforms would desire to frame such tests to suit their convictions, & thus the dogmas of a fraction of the people would disqualify the rest, ~~of~~ ↑for↓ equal rights in the state, & equal joys in Heaven.

If the ignorance superstition & fanaticism of women are to be used by crafty priests, either Protestant or Roman Catholic to this end, their enfranchisement will prove no blessing to themselves nor the nation.

The movement on the part of prohibitionists to introduce the name of God into our political platforms, our state & national constitutions, shows at least a very narrow idea of the essential elements of the central person in the Trinity. To the cultivated mind the Godhead embodies the cardinal virtues: justice mercy goodness & truth & it would be no special honor to the Supreme Being, to have his name in our party platforms as constituted at present, nor in our national constitution a document ~~even~~ to human eyes ↑still↓ so imperfect, even after fifteen amendments as to ~~still~~ need further improvements

When some form of government is evolved, approximating more nearly to the divine ideal ↑than any we have yet seen↓, it will be time enough to stamp its Magna ~~Carta~~ ↑Charta↓ with the seal of Jehovah.

Our imperative duty at this hour, is to see that all the citizens of this republic stand equal before the law & thus truly honor their Maker. "If ye love not man whom you have seen how can you love God whom you have not seen"[5]

The Bible in our public schools, rigid Sunday laws and the ↑non-↓taxation of church property, religious tests in politics, are all questions to be settled ~~by~~ perchance by the votes of women, & it is of vital consequence to know what their action will be.

One of the arguments the conservative party in England is now using for woman suffrage, is that women would favor the established church, the coercion of Ireland, ~~the~~ ↑a↓ royal family, a landed aristocracy & the Tory police in general [*added in margin*] It is said the Primrose Dames carried the last election

We who understand the dangers threatened in the prohibition movement, as shown by Mrs Chandler in The Tribune of December 10th, "the rock ahead for woman suffrage," must not be dazzled by the promise of a sudden acquisition of numbers to our platform, with the wide spread influence of the church behind them, if with all this is coming a religious proscription, that will undermine the secular nature of our government.

One of our best speakers in a recent suffrage convention was quite severely criticised, by a member of the christian temperance union, because in quoting the opinions of some great men, favorable to woman suffrage, she made no mention of Jesus.[6] Why should she have done so, since he never expressed any opinion on the question, as Republics did not exist in his day.

It would be quite as sensible to complain that Tyndall, & Huxley & Spencer[7] make no reference in their lectures to Jesus ~~who never expressed~~ seeing that he never expressed his views on the natural sciences.

The mission of the great Nazarine was not to build up governments, nor collect statistics in material phenomen~~on~~↑a↓, but to give the world a spiritual gospel, & illustrate the purest moral principles in his life as well as teachings. ~~Sincerely yours Elizabeth Cady Stanton.~~ I do not agree with some of May Rogers propositions, but of her next time, when her paper is fully published, but I am glad that women are considering the labor question anyway   Sincerely yours

❧ *Elizabeth Cady Stanton*

❧ ALS, Clara B. Colby Papers, Archives Division, WHi. Marked for typesetter, "Letter from Mrs. Stanton, President of the National Woman Suffrage Association." Also published in *Woman's Tribune*, 21 January 1888.

1. With its issue dated 10 December 1887, the start of its fifth volume, the *Woman's Tribune* debuted as a weekly rather than monthly paper. Aiming for "general circulation," as Colby explained, the issue was printed with a larger typeface and wider columns.

2. Lucinda Banister Chandler (1828–1911), an active member of the National association since 1872, was a reformer chiefly known for her ideas about enlightened motherhood and a uniform sexual standard for men and women. Beginning in 1880, when she was a voting delegate to the Greenback-Labor party's national convention, Chandler turned her attention to economic reforms. In "Liberty; and The Ballot for Woman," she warned against new attempts to "revolutionize our institutions and forms of government in the name of religion." In particular, she condemned resolutions by state branches of the Woman's Christian Temperance Union promising to favor political parties that recognized in their platforms Christ's headship of government. It began, she wrote, as an effort of the National Reform Association to press the Prohibition party for such a plank. To Chandler the dangers were twofold: women undermined their hopes for enfranchisement by acting in ways that threatened freedom of conscience, and Protestant women paved the way for Roman Catholicism to "achieve its supreme ambition to obtain temporal dominion." (*ANB*. See also *Papers* 3 & 4.)

3. May Rogers (1852–?) was a writer, lecturer, and club woman from Dubuque, Iowa, best known for *The Waverly Dictionary* (1879), a guide to the characters in Walter Scott's novels. In this issue, the *Tribune* published the first of five parts of her lengthy "Woman in Relation to Labor Reform," a call "for conservative and patriotic women to condemn any coalition between woman suffrage and the conspiracy to coerce our free nation into State socialism." (*WWW4*; *Woman's Tribune*, 17 and 24 December 1887, 7 and 14 January 1888.)

4. The "Plan of Work for Suffrage Clubs" was Colby's own proposal that suffrage societies form study clubs. For clubs that adopted the study of either law or the science of government, the *Tribune* provided questions suggested by editorials in each issue.

5. 1 John 4:20.

6. ECS earlier identified this woman as Clara Neymann, who spoke on "Sceptics and Scepticism" at the National association's convention in January 1887. Whether the attack on her omission occurred at the meeting or later is not evident. (*Woman's Tribune*, March 1887, and ECS to Sara F. Underwood, 10 September 1887, *Film*, 25:192–97, 697–705.)

7. These English writers, who used the natural sciences to explain social as well as natural phenomena, were John Tyndall (1820–1893), physicist; Thomas Henry Huxley (1825–1895), biologist; and Herbert Spencer (1820–1903), philosopher.

29   SBA to Lillie Devereux Blake

Rochester N.Y. Dec. 26, 1887

My Dear Mrs Blake

Your letter of the [*blank*] met me in Phila. a week ago— As well might the poor old hen pledge that her Ducklings <u>wouldn't go into the water</u>—as S. B. A. that the speakers & members of the National W.S.A. will or will not—shout for the Republican Party if it shows its hand direct in Congress for 16th amt—& in State Legislatures for Municipal Suffrage—but I surely should hope to be able to influence some of them to stand by & hope & pray & talk for the success of the party that <u>by its works</u> promises most for woman!!

I am awfully sorry—we missed putting our appeal into the Council of Republican Clubs in New York a two weeks—or ten days ago—[1] But I came east so rusty & ragged that I was not presentable either in Washington among the members—or in New York among the Clubs— So the opportunity was & is lost— I do not believe—However—that there is yet any general feeling among the leaders of the Repub. party of the need of <u>our help</u> to <u>save them</u>—and until that time comes—they wont speak or act <u>officially</u> for us—though many of them <u>as individuals</u> will ~~do so~~ be & are on our side—

Miss Foster & I went on to Boston to see when & how the "pipe of peace" could be smoked—and Mrs Stones conditions are soon to be sent us as written out by her daughter Alice—[2] while my proposal was & is like that of Horace Greeley—~~If you~~ "The way to resume is to resume"— So I said—"The way to unite is to unite"—and trust to the <u>majority vote</u> of the <u>members</u>—who are actually <u>paid members</u>—of the two societies at the time of the union—to decide upon every question— name—Constitution—basis of representation—officers—plans of work &c. &c.—yes and Newspaper Organ also— Neither Stone, Stanton & Anthony—nor any Committee appointed by them—nor yet the Executive Committees <u>can</u> settle the terms of the union—they can only formulate them—& submit them to the vote of the rank & file of the members—that is if the job is done Democratic fashion!! With a Happy New years I am as ever sincerely

~ *Susan B. Anthony*

[*sideways in margin of first page*] I shall be at home till new years

~ ALS, on NWSA letterhead, Lillie Devereux Blake Papers, MoSHi.

1. The National Convention of Republican Clubs met in New York City, 15 to 17 December 1887. (*New York Times*, 13, 16-19 1887.)
2. Still without any report from Boston on December 28, SBA wrote to Rachel Foster: "The more I think of the scene at No 3 Park st—a week ago this very hour—the more cheeky it looks to me!— But let us patiently wait the full developement— What we saw & heard is but the corn in the blade!— What it will be ↑in↓ the full ear—who can tell?" On the next day, upon receiving Alice Blackwell's statement of her mother's terms for union, SBA wrote, "It really is of no sort of use to go farther—except to allow each one of the Committee and after them—each friend ↑of↓ our cause—↑to↓ see for themselves—just what the plan of union is with the so called American—Boston—wing! . . . not one of our women could or would believe such modest demands could be made." (SBA to R. G. Foster, 28, 29 December 1887, *Film*, 25:851-60.)

30 ~ SBA TO HENRY W. BLAIR

Phila. Pa. Jan. 7, 1888

Dear Senator Blair

I see you presented our Bill the first thing—[1] Now who will prepare the report—if not yourself? I have not written senator Chase or Bowen[2]— about the matter—because I didn't think it would look a bit pretty—for me to interfere with what is really our honored Chairman's business[3] Hence—if you feel that you cannot prepare it—or that you want one of the others to take turn-about—you will ↑yourself↓ propose it to the one you choose—but really—I do not think ↑for↓ Senator Bowen to do it— will add weight to the testimony—this is sub rosa of course—but if Senator Chase would do it—his name would be a different one from yours or Palmers[4]—and really would not at ↑least↓ lessen the weight of the reports already given

But of course I leave the matter, wholly, with you— I would say—

however—<u>confidentially</u> that I do not believe any one of the Com. can do any better—than your own self— the only need of thought of getting either Mr Chase or Mr Palmer—~~wa~~ is that <u>you</u> may be relieved from the <u>drudgery</u> of doing it— So don't think that my suggestion of any other member's making the report, than yourself—is because I think any one else can make a better one—or his name give more weight to it—for it is from no such cause that I have thus suggested!! You believe me—dont you?—

But my main point in writing you—is to urge that you present the report at an early day—and then ask or give notice that you'll call it up for discussion & vote—at the earliest reasonable day— What <u>I want</u> to <u>make</u> <u>sure</u> of <u>this</u> <u>session</u> of <u>this</u> <u>Congress</u>—is that <u>both Houses</u> bring our 16th am't bill to a discussion & vote—without fail—so as to give the women of the Country—not only <u>Woman</u> <u>Suffrage</u> women—but the Prohibition <u>Party</u> <u>women</u>—is to give the Republicans a chance to show <u>their hand</u> on the Woman Suffrage <u>question</u>—as a party— I know nothing will do so much to ensure their, the womens, <u>prayers & tears</u> on the Republican side—as such showing—

I see—too—that Mr Reed has presented our bill—[5] It isnt worth while for us to have a <u>hearing</u> before the Committees— Do you think it is?

Wont you send me a Congressional Directory—or Record—with the <u>House</u> Committees—to 114—North 11th street—Phila— I shall have to stop here a few days before going to Washington—unless you see & say I ought to be there sooner— But the main thing now is to get the Com's of both Houses to report at once—

I wish I could make the Repub's in Congress & State Legislatures see & believe how much good would come to their <u>party</u>—by speaking & acting as I have indicated to several of them— Sincerely yours

                 Susan B. Anthony

ALS, on NWSA letterhead, GLC 3300, Gilder Lehrman Collection, Gilder Lehrman Institute of American History. Envelope addressed "H. W. Blair—U.S.S. Washington D.C." Not in *Film*.

1. Blair introduced Senate Resolution No. 11, extending the right of suffrage to women, on 12 December 1887. It was referred to the Committee on Woman Suffrage. (*Congressional Record*, 50th Cong., 1st sess., 34.)

2. Thomas Mead Bowen and Jonathan Chace were Republican members of the Committee on Woman Suffrage and co-signatories with Blair of the committee's report recommending the suffrage amendment in 1886. Bowen

(1835–1906) of Colorado served in the Senate for one term beginning in 1883. Chace (1829–1917) of Rhode Island entered the Senate in 1885 to fill the seat of Henry Anthony and served until 1889. (*BDAC*; Senate, Committee on Woman Suffrage, *Report to Accompany S.R. 5*, 2 February 1886, 49th Cong., 1st sess., S. Rept. 70, Serial 2355. See also *Papers* 4.)

3. Francis Marion Cockrell (1834–1915), Democrat from Missouri and former Confederate army officer, served in the Senate from 1875 until 1905. He continued to chair the Committee on Woman Suffrage, despite his intense opposition to the federal amendment. He coauthored the reports against suffrage in 1884 and 1886. (*BDAC*. See also *Papers* 4.)

4. Thomas Witherell Palmer (1830–1913), Republican of Michigan and a supporter of woman suffrage, also sat on the Senate committee and signed the report of 1886. He served in the Senate from 1883 to 1889. (*BDAC*.)

5. On 4 January 1888. See note above at 15 December 1887.

31 ~ ECS TO RACHEL G. FOSTER

Basingstoke Hants [*England*]   Jan 12th [*1888*]

Dear Rachel,

I have only one suggestion to make on the programme you sent me, & that is that Miss Helen Gardner should be invited to speak at the coming con. She wrote some admirable articles in the Science Monthly on the size of woma[n's] brain in answer to Dr Hammond.[1] She is logical & at the same time amusing. I think one speech on our heads, as to their size & contents would be interesting   I have written her & directed to the Office of The Freethinker[2] Clinton Place N.Y. as I have lost her address. Unless you know [it] you can do the sam[e] as her books are published there. She is a very pleasing little woman. Helen Gardner is her nom de plume, but her real name is Mrs Alice Chenworth Smart[3]   As her nom de plume is well known, & her real one to but few you better address her & announce he[r] as Helen Gardner   Hattie & I have been attending a course of lectures on "Mind Cure" & are deeply interested in its basic principles. We are not fanatical on the question but searchers after truth. I hope to sail for my native land early in March. I shall be very happy to see all your earnest young faces once more. With much love for Julia [& y]ourself sincerely ever

~ *Elizabeth Cady Stanton*

↛ ALS, Anthony-Avery Papers, NRU. Letters in square brackets torn away. In *Film*, in error, at 12 January 1887.

1. William Alexander Hammond (1828–1900), formerly surgeon general during the Civil War, was a neurologist with a penchant for applying his medical theories to social phenomena. (*ANB*.) Writing in *Popular Science Monthly*, he asserted, without irony, that civilization brought with it a greater differentiation of the sizes, and consequently the power, of the brains of men and women because in civilized nations "the differentiation between the sexes is far more distinctly marked than it is with nations low in the scale of progress." Helen Gardener challenged his sources as well as his reasoning, wondering why he overlooked "the fact that [women] have never been allowed the very training and opportunities which he claims produced the desired change in the males of their race." In an emotional riposte, Hammond repeatedly mocked Gardener's pretension to understand the scientific literature on which she relied to challenge him. (William A. Hammond, "Brain-Forcing in Childhood," *Popular Science Monthly* 30 [April 1887]: 721–32; Helen H. Gardener, "Sex and Brain-weight," ibid. 31 [June 1887]: 266–68; Hammond, "Men's and Women's Brains," ibid. 31 [August 1887]: 554–58; Gardener, "More about Men's and Women's Brains," ibid. 31 [September 1887]: 698–700; Hammond, "An Explanation," ibid. 31 [October 1887]: 846.)

2. ECS gives the address of the *Truth Seeker*, a journal of free thought since 1873, not that of the *Freethinker*. The Truth Seeker Company, at 33 Clinton Place in New York City, published Gardener's book, *Men, Women and Gods*.

3. Gardener grew up as Alice Chenoweth and added Smart to her name at the time of her first marriage, but her penname became her name.

32 ↬ SBA to Caroline Healey Dall[1]

The Riggs—Washington D.C. Jan, 20, 1888[2]

My Dear Mrs Dall

Enclosed is the Call for the celebration of the 40 years of womas crying in the wilderness of disfranchisement—[3]

Our plan is to have about two papers of 25 or 30 minutes each—at each session—and following these a discussion of 10 minute speeches by as many as will fill the time—

I do not venture to <u>ask you</u> to take part with us—but do want you to know—or rather to ↑be↓ re-assure↑d↓ ~~you~~—that the National's platform is—as always from the beginning—broad enough to welcome all who earnestly seek woman's enfranchisement—hence that you will be now as ever most welcome—if the spirit shall move you— The Saturday A.M. session[4] will be called—a Conference of the Pioneers—and you surely began your good work early enough to entitle you to ↑belong to↓ that class— Mrs Stanton will open the session—& Lucy Stone follow her—after them then will be 10— minutes—or less speeches I hope from 10 or 20 of the valiant old Soldiers of the Cross!! Will you be one of the number—whose names shall be announced?

I go all around this way—because you have so many times told me you did not wish to be identified with us—and all I want to do—is to tell you the door is open—

My day this winter will be Wednesday—so I may hope for a call from you may I not?—[5] I never go out for calls except Mrs Spofford escorts me—and you can see that ↑it↓ is very embarrassing for me to ask her to take me to call on any one who does not recognize her—by calling on her— So if I have seemed not to pay my respects to you as you feel due from me—you can see one reason—why it is not easy to take you in our course as we make calls— I think you are the only one of my friends who never recognizes my best friend—helper & co-worker—the woman—but for whose love & generous hospitality to both the cause & me—I could not have lived in Washington the last ten years to ↑do↓ what I could for woman's enfranchisement— I not complain—nor criticise—but simply explain— So I am very sincerely yours

~ *Susan B. Anthony*

[*sideways at bottom of page*] N.B.—I would not have you mention what I have said to my dear hostess for anything!!

~ ALS, on 40th anniversary letterhead, C. H. Dall Collection, MHi. Inscribed in Dall's hand "Jan 23/88."

1. Caroline Wells Healey Dall (1822–1912), writer, reformer, and woman's rights activist, moved from Boston to Washington, D.C., to live with her son, a scientist at the Smithsonian Institution. (*NAW*; *ANB*. See also *Papers* 1–3.)

2. Although SBA's number looks like "20," she mentioned this invitation to Caroline Dall in her diary on January 23. Dall endorsed the letter as received on January 23 and apparently replied that same day. (SBA diary, 1888, *Film*, 25:869ff.)

3. Enclosure missing. SBA quotes Deut. 8:2.

4. On Saturday, March 31.

5. At the Riggs House, under Jane Spofford's tutelage, SBA tried to follow

the intricate etiquette of making social calls and setting her own day to receive visitors, though here and in the letters that follow, the rules conflict with her own social instinct.

33   SBA TO CAROLINE HEALEY DALL

Riggs House, Washington, D.C., Jan. 24 1888

My Dear Mrs Dall

Yours of yesterday is before me—[1] I surely must have told you—in reply to your letter—two years ↑ago↓—asking me why Mrs Spofford did not invite you to her receptions given in honor of Mrs Stanton—the same reason!![2] I cannot imagine what other one I could have given you—& I well remember your writing to know what you <u>could</u> <u>do</u>—or <u>not</u> do—to secure the invitation! & at my special request you were invited—

I cannot—<u>shall not</u>—show your letter to Mrs Spofford—as I told you I wrote without her knowledge and I shall feel that you betray me—if you should tell her—or speak to her on the subject— When you went into ↑her↓ room—that you tell of—& didn't speak to her!!—but a truce to the whole ↑of↓ it—only I want to say for <u>her</u>—that <u>I</u> as good as <u>know</u>—your informant as to her declaring she would not call on you &c was mistaken— at least <u>I</u> have never heard ↑her↓ say anything of that sort—and it doesn't sound a bit like her— There is but this—to leave behind—& untalked—the past—and go ahead in the present & future on the basis of good will— I <u>know</u> it is the true way— So I beg of you do not when you make your call refer to the past— She did invite you two years ago—& you came—last winter she neither made calls or received—save informally— So let the dead past bury the dead—and you just make it pleasant to me, to yourself & all—

After receiving tomorrow P.M. and a tea at the Hamilton[3]—of Mrs Snowden and Mrs Russell[4]—I take the 10 Oclock train to go to Milton Pen. to lecture[5]—& shall not be at home until Sunday— I tell you this—because I hope you'll steal away—or bring your visitors to call tomorrow— Oh yes—we expect a call from the 6— young women at the National Deaf-Mute college between 2 & 3—[6] I ask all my <u>special</u>

friends to come before 3 so we can chat at our leisure— Very sincerely yours—

~ *Susan B. Anthony*

[*sideways on first page*] Please give me the exact title for your 10 minutes speech at the Pioneer session— Of course if you should fail to fill the program—we shall have to explain you absence— I wouldn't under circumstance put a thing in the notice or program about any woman's liability not to be able &c—⁷ Let men talk about poor health but let us not do it!! so we will run the risk of your being able to make the speech!! S. B. A

~ ALS, on 40th anniversary letterhead, C. H. Dall Collection, MHi. Inscribed in Dall's hand, "Jan 25/88. an absurd letter from beginning to end."

1. In her diary, SBA described this missing letter as "a tart reply." (SBA diary, 24 January 1888, *Film*, 25:869ff.)

2. SBA apparently refers to Jane Spofford's reception on 16 February 1886, when three hundred political and social notables called at the Riggs House to meet delegates to the National's Washington convention.

3. The Hamilton House was a hotel located at the corner of Fourteenth and K streets, Northwest.

4. This was probably Elizabeth B. Russell, who became matron at the District of Columbia jail in 1884, when the position was created in response to a campaign by local activists. Mrs. Snowden is unidentified. (*Report of the Sixteenth Annual Washington Convention, 1884*, p. 13, *Film*, 23:573ff; *History*, 4:571; *Washington Post*, 22 December 1883, 21 February, 16 March 1884; city directories, 1888, 1889; *Papers*, 4:317.)

5. SBA earned fifty dollars for a lecture to a small audience in Milton, Pennsylvania, on 26 January 1888. (SBA diary, 1888, *Film*, 25:869ff.)

6. In the fall of 1887, the National College for the Deaf, now Gallaudet University, admitted six female students on an experimental basis, four of whom paid a call on SBA at the Riggs House during her visiting hours on October 25. (SBA diary, 1888; Edward Miner Gallaudet, *History of the College for the Deaf, 1857-1907*, eds. Lance J. Fischer and David L. DeLorenzo [Washington, D.C., 1983], 166-67.)

7. Dall's name stood in the program for the session of pioneers through many editions circulated into March. It was removed in the final edition.

34 ~ FROM THE DIARY OF SBA

[*1–4 February 1888*]

WEDNESDAY, FEBRUARY 1, 1888. Received Postal from Mrs Stanton saying it was doubtful if she came to Council— Was too incensed to write—so waited—

THURSDAY, FEBRUARY 2, 1888. Received Mrs Stanton's letter to Rachel bidding her to get <u>Susan</u> ready to make the opening speech & get along without her— I was more on fire than ever—

FRIDAY, FEBRUARY 3, 1888. At Riggs— At 9.30—this eve—mailed most terific letter to Mrs Stanton—in response to her Postal to me & letter to Rachel Foster—say she might <u>not</u> come to Council—

SATURDAY, FEBRUARY 4, 1888. Francis Miller Esq.—burried this A.M. his wife—Caroline Hallowell Miller always an invalid—he a st[rong?] man![1]

~~At 9.30 P.M. mailed most terrific letter~~ [*No entries for 5–11 February.*]

1. Francis Miller (1829–1888) died on February 2 at his home in Sandy Spring, Maryland. With Caroline Hallowell Miller (1831–1905), his wife, he taught school until 1867, when he began the study of law with Albert G. Riddle in Washington, and Caroline Miller took charge of their school. Francis Miller and Riddle, who represented the plaintiffs in the District of Columbia voting rights cases in 1871, later worked together in the office of the attorney for the District of Columbia from 1877 to 1885. Under Caroline Miller's care, the school at Sandy Spring became a school for girls. An active member of the National association in the 1880s, she gained a reputation as an excellent speaker. Through local, state, and national suffrage societies, she pursued suffrage until the end of her life. (*Yale Obituary Record 1888*, from Archives, CtY; *Woman's Journal*, 16 September 1905; *Friends' Intelligencer* 62 [1905]: 575; *History*, 3:254–55, 956; 4:20, 72, 114, 147, 263, 267, 296, 695, 697, 1100; *Papers*, 2:526n, 604–5, 607–8, 3:45–46, 286.)

~ Excelsior Diary 1888, n.p., SBA Papers, DLC. Square brackets surround uncertain reading.

35   SBA TO FREDERICK DOUGLASS[1]

Riggs House, Washington, D.C., Feb. 6, 1888

My Dear Friend

The only session in which these "<u>horrid women</u>" propose to give the "<u>poor men</u>" a chance to speak in the Council—is to be on Saturday morning ↑March 31st↓—when there is to be a "Conference of the Pioneers"—[2] Of all the men who signed that famous Declaration of 1848— I think <u>you</u> are the <u>only one</u> left <u>this</u> <u>side</u> the big river— Hence—we want you to make a 20 minutes address—on that morning— Mrs Stanton will preside & make the <u>first</u> talk of course—and I want ↑you↓— as her stay & support in the 48 Con. to be the same on this occasion of its 40th Anniversary— Your wife can't claim to be a <u>pioneer</u>—any more than can the wife of Robert Purvis[3]—but since husband & wife are one—and now-a-days that one is getting to be <u>the wife</u>—Mrs Douglass will of course accept this as an invitation to ↑be one↓ of us at the Council—

If it were in the possibilities—I should go over the river to you[4] but my time is so crowded—& I shan't get a half of the old & new friends written telling them I hope they'll be at the Council— Mr & Mrs Sam'l Sewall[5] of Boston intend to come—& I hope our dear Amy Post[6] of Rochester— Parker Pillsbury's wife[7] is very ill again—so I fear he wont be able to come—

Now—my dear old friend—& <u>earliest</u> <u>stand-by</u> of Mrs Stanton's—I want you to make <u>the</u> <u>speech</u> that Saturday A.M. that shall kindle the fires of freedom & equality afresh in all hearts—<u>young</u> as well—& <u>more</u>—than the old ones!!

Let me see you—or hear from you at least— My day to be <u>certainly in</u>—is Wednesday—and I shall be very grateful to you & Mrs D. if you will count me <u>socially</u> as <u>already</u> ↑possessing↓ a Congressman's claim— that of being first called upon—[8] Sincerely yours

                                  Susan B. Anthony

P.S. Lucy Stone—is to speak Pioneer's day—her title is to be—"The advance of the last fifty years"—just why she puts it 50—instead of 40—

I do not know— All of the "seceders" are coming now upon the invitation of the Old National W.S.A.!!!

[*in margin of first page*] Robert Purvis will speak a few words if he is able to get here—also Antoinette Brown[9]—Mrs Gage—there are very few of us left— May I put your name in program to speak March 31st—
S. B. A.

~ ALS, on 40th anniversary letterhead, Frederick Douglass Papers, DLC.

1. Frederick Douglass (1818–1895), former slave, abolitionist, and early supporter of woman's rights, moved from Rochester, New York, to Washington in 1872. ECS credited him with gaining acceptance at the Seneca Falls convention for the controversial demand for woman suffrage. In 1884, after the death of his first wife, Douglass married Helen Pitts (1838–1903), a graduate of Mount Holyoke College, former teacher of freedmen in the South, and member of suffrage societies and the Moral Education Society in Washington. (*DANB*; *ANB*; Mount Holyoke College, *One Hundred Year Biographical Directory of Mount Holyoke College, 1837–1937* [South Hadley, Mass., 1937], 95. See also *Papers* 1–4.)

2. Filed with this letter are a call to the International Council of Women and a printed flyer, undated, listing some of the speakers.

3. Robert Purvis (1810–1898) of Philadelphia, a prominent African-American abolitionist and one of the few who argued that the rights of his daughters were as important as those of his sons, was a member of the Citizens' Suffrage Association of Philadelphia and active in the National association. After the death of his first wife in 1875, Purvis married Tacy Townsend (c. 1827–1900), a Philadelphia Quaker and author of children's books. (*DANB*; *ANB*; *Friends' Intelligencer* 57 [1900]: 759. See also *Papers* 1–4.)

4. Douglass's house, Cedar Hill, is in southeast Washington, across the Anacostia River from Capital Hill.

5. Samuel Edmund Sewall (1799–1888), lawyer, and Harriet Winslow List Sewall (1819–1889), poet, were early abolitionists and supporters of woman's rights. When ECS lived in Boston in the 1840s, she counted Harriet Winslow among her friends. The Sewalls, who married in 1856, were founding members of the New England Woman Suffrage Association and stockholders in the *Woman's Journal*. (*NCAB*, 10:347, 466–67; *Papers*, 1:40–43, 2:452–53, 536.)

6. Amy Kirby Post (1802–1889), early abolitionist and signer of the Declaration of Sentiments at Seneca Falls in 1848, was at the center of reform in Rochester before and after the war. (*NAW*; *ANB*. See also *Papers* 1–4.)

7. Parker Pillsbury (1809–1898), another early abolitionist who had retired to New Hampshire, edited the *National Anti-Slavery Standard* before joining ECS as coeditor of the *Revolution* in 1868. In 1840, he married Sarah H. Sargent (1818–1898). (Stacey M. Robertson, *Parker Pillsbury: Radical Aboli-*

tionist, Male Feminist [Ithaca, N.Y., 2000]; *Woman's Journal*, 23 April 1898. See also *Papers* 1 & 2.)

8. Compounding the difficulties of etiquette in Washington were rules of social precedence adjusted to a hierarchy of government officials. SBA's quip alludes to the custom that congressmen and their wives did not initiate the exchange of social calls; to receive them, SBA would have to call on each one first.

9. Antoinette Louisa Brown Blackwell (1825–1921) was the first American woman to be ordained a minister. While living in Henrietta, New York, before her marriage, she worked closely with ECS and SBA in the movement for woman's rights. (*NAW*; *ANB*. See also *Papers* 1–4.)

36 ~ FROM THE DIARY OF SBA

[*12–14 February 1888*]

SUNDAY, FEBRUARY 12, 1888. Heard Prof. Peabod[1] of Harvard College— Met Senators Hoar[2] & Palmer at Church [*No entry for 13 February.*]

1. Andrew Preston Peabody (1811–1893), a Unitarian minister, retired in 1881 from his post as professor of Christian morals at Harvard and spent his time as a lecturer and writer. (*ANB*.)

2. George Frisbie Hoar (1826–1904), Republican of Massachusetts, served in the Senate from 1877 until his death. A supporter of suffrage for women, he was chiefly responsible for the creation of the Senate's Select Committee on Woman Suffrage, and he voted in favor of the suffrage amendment in 1887. (*BDAC*. See also *Papers* 3 & 4.)

TUESDAY, FEBRUARY 14, 1888. Riggs House Wash. D.C. Got Cablegram from Mrs Stanton this P.M. saying simply—"Coming"—↑showing that she had received mine of the 3^d—↓ so my heart is relieved— sent word immediately to Miss Foster—Mrs Sewall—& ran down stairs to tell news to Mrs Spofford

~ Excelsior Diary 1888, n.p., SBA Papers, DLC.

37 ✎ SBA TO LILLIE DEVEREUX BLAKE

Riggs House, Washington, D.C. Feb. 27, 1888.

Dear L. D. B.

I sent you the name of Mrs L. Ormiston Chant[1]—of London—who is the delegate of the Scotch W.S. Societies—and who writes she is coming— Miss Caroline A. Biggs[2] writes that ↑she knows of↓ "several of our ablest speakers ↑who↓ are going"—but doesn't name one— I think those English women surpass all I ever tried to do any sort of business with in their <u>lack</u> of business management—

Baroness Gripenberg[3] and Miss Alli Trygg[4]—are ~~coming~~ ↑to sail↓ from England—(they represent Finland)—on March 8th—so they will be at your reception if you can intercept them—[5] I should think Miss Taylor & Mrs Scatcherd[6] would notify me—if they were <u>not</u> coming— ↑both accepted invitation without an if!↓ I have again written them—begging each to <u>Cable</u> me at once on receipt of my letter—and I have asked that each one shall <u>Cable</u> ↑<u>name</u> of↓ ship & <u>date</u> of sailing—but with my experience with them thus far—I don't feel sure of their doing it!![7]

About <u>Woodhull & Claflin</u>—[8] If <u>our</u> <u>own</u> <u>National</u> <u>officers</u> & <u>members</u> will but possess their souls in <u>quiet</u>—they'll not trouble ↑us↓— while any manifestation of <u>fear</u> of them—judging from their old habits—would be sure to bring them out in the papers with some disagreeable things!!— We of the National—have carried our good ship through a good many <u>tidal</u>-<u>waves</u>—and thus far kept her abreast the sea—and we shall now—↑do so↓ with worse <u>threatenings</u>—even—than the Woodhulls!!— But what I <u>most</u> <u>beseechingly</u> <u>beg</u> <u>of</u> <u>you</u>—<u>is</u> <u>not</u> <u>to</u> <u>talk</u> <u>with</u> <u>the</u> <u>reporters</u> ↑or anybody else↓ about them & their scandals—or about any other parties whose names may be rushed into print— I tell you <u>now</u>—as I did with their shadow—[<u>La Fever?</u>][9]—in 1874—don't talk—don't seem to see or hear or know—of them—<u>absolute</u> <u>silence</u>—& seeming <u>indifference</u> are the <u>only</u> <u>weapons</u> with which to meet them—& put them to flight!!— <u>You</u> <u>needn't</u> <u>to</u> <u>fear</u> <u>me</u>—<u>my</u> <u>fear</u> <u>is</u> <u>of</u> <u>you</u> <u>and</u> <u>the</u> <u>other</u> <u>scared</u> <u>women</u>!— If you'll all keep still—& leave me to see & say & act—with regard to them—& others that may be brought down upon us—I'll promise you—we shall neither run into Carybdis or Scylla!!¹⁰

Just go ahead & hold your meetings ↑there↓—as we will here—& nobody from outside ↑will or↓ can harm us— The National is the strong—the popular association—and every one sees it is to be made more so—& of course envious ones will try to bring us down!!

You remember once, before the House Com., how aghast every woman was at the sight of Dr Mary Walker¹¹—& how I went round & said to each—"be still—and I'll manage it!!"—and so one can—but all ↑trying to↓ are sure to defeat the very end they seek— So all I can say is—"be still"—I have heard all—& have my eyes open!!—

~ S. B. A

~ ALS, on 40th anniversary letterhead, Lillie Devereux Blake Papers, MoSHi. Square brackets surround uncertain reading.

1. Laura Ormiston Dibbin Chant (1848–1923), a nurse, author, and activist, came to the International Council with other credentials too from the Edinburgh and British Women's Temperance Associations, National Vigilance Association, Women's Peace and International Arbitration Society, Edinburgh Purity and Vigilance Association, and the Edinburgh Branch of the Federation for Repeal of State Regulation of Vice. She spent many months in the United States after the council lecturing on social purity. (*SEAP*; *Oxford DNB*.)

2. Caroline Ashurst Biggs (1840–1889) was a member of the Central Committee of the National Society for Women's Suffrage; editor, from 1870 until her death, of the *Englishwoman's Review*; onetime foreign corresponding secretary of the National Woman Suffrage Association; and author of the chapter on Great Britain for the *History of Woman Suffrage*. SBA spent time with her in London in 1883. (*Oxford DNB*; *Women's Suffrage Journal* 20 [1 October 1889]: 125; Mill, *Collected Works*, 17:1698, 1823–24, 1825, 1836, 1842–43, 1849, 1851, 1860; *History*, 3:833–94. See also *Papers* 4.)

3. Alexandra Gripenberg (1857–1913), a Finnish writer, attended the International Council as a delegate of the Finnish Women's Union. Although she attended some sessions and took part in the Committee on Organization, she was too ill to deliver her speech on woman's work in Finland. Nonetheless it was included in the council's final report. Gripenberg stayed in the United States for six months, and her account of that visit was published in Helsinki the next year (and translated into English in 1954). A proponent of making the council a permanent body, she later served as treasurer of the council from 1893 to 1899 and organized the National Council of Finnish Women in 1911. (*Report of the International Council of Women, 1888*, pp. 44, 49, 388–92, *Film*, 26:154ff; Alexandra Gripenberg, *A Half Year in the New World:*

Miscellaneous Sketches of Travel in the United States, trans. Ernest J. Moyne [Newark, Del., 1954]; Margaret H. McFadden, *Golden Cables of Sympathy: The Transatlantic Sources of Nineteenth-Century Feminism* [Lexington, Ky., 1999], 171-80; *Kuka Kukin Oli. Who Was Who in Finland: Henkilötietoja 1900—Luvulla Kuolleista Julkisuuden Suomalaisista* [Helsinki, 1961].)

4. Maria Alexandra Trygg (1852-1926), known as Alli, was studying social work in London at the time she traveled to the council, not as a delegate of any society but as an interested observer. She credited her encounters with Frances Willard at the council meetings with her conversion to temperance, and she went on to become a leading temperance advocate in Finland. After her marriage in 1897 to another temperance activist, she was known as Alli Trygg-Helenius. (*SEAP*, s.v. "Helenius-Seppälä, Maria Alexandra Trygg"; McFadden, *Golden Cables of Sympathy*, 177; *Kuka Kukin Oli. Who Was Who in Finland*.)

5. Because the international delegates would land in New York, Blake assumed the role of first hostess for their American visit. The New York City Woman Suffrage League held a reception for them at the Park Avenue Hotel on 21 March 1888; they were honored guests at the annual meeting of the New York State Woman Suffrage Association on 22 March; and, according to Blake's daughter, they were also guests at Blake's house on 23 March. (*Woman's Journal*, 10 March 1888; *New York Times*, 22 and 23 March 1888; Katherine Devereux Blake and Margaret Louise Wallace, *Champion of Women: The Life of Lillie Devereux Blake* [New York, 1943], 168-69.)

6. Alice Cliff Scatcherd (1842-1906) of Leeds, an effective speaker and organizer, made particular contributions to the British movement by her attention over many decades to working women. When SBA met her in 1883, she remarked in her diary how much she liked Scatcherd, adding, she "is less bound by old customs than any woman I have met here." (Sandra Stanley Holton, *Suffrage Days: Stories from the Women's Suffrage Movement* [London, 1996], passim; E. Sylvia Pankhurst, *The Suffragette Movement: An Intimate Account of Persons and Ideals* [1931; reprint, London, 1977], 118; Patricia Hollis, *Ladies Elect: Women in English Local Government, 1865-1914* [Oxford, England, 1987], 35-36, 155; *History*, 3:866n, 868n, 875, 923, 929, 941; SBA diary, 18-19 October 1883, *Film*, 22:814ff.)

7. Slowly SBA learned about the storm over delegates to the International Council from the United Kingdom. On January 11, she heard that the Central Committee of the National Society for Women's Suffrage had rescinded its appointment of three delegates—"a most extraordinary action!!" On January 20, she wrote twenty letters to Englishwomen "begging each to come to Council." And on January 24, she learned from Alice Blackwell that Helen Taylor "wouldn't speak at Council—if Mrs Ashton-Dilke was allowed!!"

That Alice Blackwell delivered messages to SBA from Helen Taylor pointed to another thread of the story: by her own account, Taylor introduced the Central Committee's final resolution to rescind the appointment of delegates, and although she did not tell SBA her plans until March, in January she opened communication with Lucy Stone through the extended Blackwell family, seeking advice about how to respond to SBA's invitation. She wanted in particular to learn if the American and National associations were cooperating on the council and if the council might be the work of American advocates of "sexual license."

The council idea exacerbated differences over politics and personalities throughout the British movement. The society in Edinburgh, lead by close friends of ECS and SBA, ignored the vote in London and sent delegates, as did several local branches of the Women's Liberal Association. (SBA diary, 11, 20, 24 January 1888, and A. S. Blackwell to SBA, 31 January and 27 February 1888, *Film*, 25:869ff, 25:1095–97, 26:72; Helen Taylor to Mrs. Blackwell, 7 January 1888, and Elizabeth Blackwell to Helen Taylor, 4 February 1888, Mill-Taylor Papers, British Library of Political and Economic Science, UkL; Holton, *Suffrage Days*, 64–65, 73–74; Holton, "'To Educate Women into Rebellion': Elizabeth Cady Stanton and the Creation of a Transatlantic Network of Radical Suffragists," *American Historical Review* 99 [October 1994]: 1125; *Papers*, 4:299–300, 349–50.)

8. Parentheses open at the start of this paragraph and close at its end. They appear to be a later addition in another hand. Victoria Claflin Woodhull (1838–1927) and Tennessee Celeste Claflin (1845–1923) were allies of ECS and SBA in the early 1870s, but public reaction to their advocacy of free love and personal experience with their misuse of information to threaten critics made the sisters more liability than asset. Both had moved to England and married wealthy gentlemen by this date. Blake and SBA seem to react to rumors of a visit to the United States, perhaps to the International Council. Evidence suggests that the sisters stayed abroad in 1888. (*NAW*; *ANB*; with the assistance of Randy L. Bixby, Special Collections Research Center, Southern Illinois University. See also *Papers* 2 & 3.)

9. This person is unidentified.

10. Rocks in the water between Sicily and Italy, Charybdis and Scylla posed equal danger to the sailor who avoided one of them, only to collide with the other.

11. Mary Edwards Walker (1832–1919), a physician and dress reformer, had often attended Washington suffrage conventions, interrupting the proceedings and in the opinion of ECS and SBA, distracting the press from the political purposes of the events. (*NAW*. See also *Papers* 2–4.)

38 ~ ECS TO HELEN TAYLOR

Basingstoke Hants [*England*]   March 6th [*1888*]

My dear Miss Taylor

The enclosed letter from Miss Anthony to my daughter speaks for itself.[1]

I can only add that it is a grave mistake if you do not go. Do you realize what it is to have the House of Representatives granted to you & me, the first women who have been so honored.[2] Do not I of beg you let the gossip about any other delegate prevent you from going. Do you think the sainted John Stuart Mill[3] if pledged to go to a great International Congress would have declined at the last minute because Sir Charles Dilke[4] was to be there? On the contrary would he not have felt it more imperative to do his best to see that England was grandly represented. Would he not have felt greater instead of less individual responsibility? It is in this light I [regard?] you. Mrs Dilke[5] is not a speaker equal to such an occasion. It is as if you & I were invited to address the House of Commons, & two young untrained speakers were sent to fill our places   No one in either country would make you responsible for the character of other delegates, nor that of their ancestors. The only persons responsible for Mrs Dilke are the members of the society in New Castle who sent her.

I do hope you will see your duty clearly in this matter & redeem your pledge to Miss Anthony. Do get ready & sail with me from Southhampton on the 8th. The special train for the steamer leaves London at 12 o'clock. The London Office is 32 Cockspur street of the German Lloyd steamers is 32 Cockspur street. From the letter I received ↑from you two weeks ago I thought you were going.↓ If you cannot get ready so soon another steamer of the same Line leaves on Sunday the 11th Mrs Scatchard & Mrs Chant go from Liverpool in a few days. Our friends in America have made herculean efforts to make the occasion a grand one, & we depend on you to help make it a success. It is not Miss Anthony's fault, that fitting delegates were not early chosen by English societies, & the blunders this side should not be visited on her. You pledged yourself to go, you are extensively advertized & you cannot in honor now decline. Hoping to meet you soon in the New Republic Sincerely yours

~ *Elizabeth Cady Stanton*

~ ALS, Mill-Taylor Papers, British Library of Political and Economic Science, UkL. Square brackets indicate uncertain reading.

1. Enclosure missing.

2. ECS implies that she and Helen Taylor were expected to address the House of Representatives. Possibly someone made an attempt to secure such an invitation; it had been tried in previous years. Foreign delegates to the council did address the Senate Select Committee on Woman Suffrage. (*Papers*, 4:466; *Film*, 26:577–631.)

3. John Stuart Mill (1806–1873), Helen Taylor's stepfather, was a philosopher, champion of woman suffrage, and member of Parliament from 1865 to 1868.

4. Charles Wentworth Dilke (1843–1911) lay at the root of Helen Taylor's protest. A rising leader in the Liberal party and a strong supporter of woman suffrage in Parliament, he was named corespondent in a divorce case in 1885, and though the case against him was dismissed early in 1886, the divorce in question was granted nonetheless. The ambiguity of this result opened the way for a scurrilous campaign against Dilke's morals and political future that dragged on for years. (*Oxford DNB*; David Nicholls, *The Lost Prime Minister: A Life of Charles Dilke* [London, 1995]; Walker, "Party Political Women," 176-77.)

5. Margaret Maye Smith Dilke (1857–1903), a London suffragist inextricably linked to the Dilke scandal, bore the brunt of Helen Taylor's hostility. She was the widow of Ashton Wentworth Dilke (1850–1883), the younger brother of Charles, and a sister of Virginia Crawford, the woman who named Charles Dilke as her lover. When the Central Committee rescinded Dilke's appointment to the council, she became the delegate of the Newcastle Women's Liberal Association. (*Oxford DNB*; Nicholls, *Lost Prime Minister*, 189-90.)

39 ~ HELEN TAYLOR TO SBA

13 Harrington Road South Kensington   London 7 March 1888

Dear Miss Anthony

It grieves me to be compelled to disappoint you by withdrawing my acceptance of the invitation to the Washington Conference. Owing to my time having been fully occupied this winter by meetings and Lectures on the Land question¹ and to my consequent long absences from home, your last letter and the one preceding it only reached me together, or I should have telegraphed to you sooner.

It has been a matter of unbounded surprise to me to hear that Mrs Ashton Dilke is going to Washington with Mrs Stanton. Had I been assured of this I should have at once written to you to cancel my acceptance of Miss Foster's official invitation; and therefore I consider that the responsibility of my absence from the Washington Convention rests upon Mrs Stanton rather than upon myself.

It should ill express the reverence I feel for my beloved mother² and my step-father were I to allow myself to appear associated with a lady who having publickly declared her beleif in the guilt of Sir Charles Dilke, appears to condone it, and who, bearing the name of his brother, keeps alive the disgraceful scandal by seeking occasions of publicity when the natural instinct of a refined woman would be to studiously avoid them. Her appearance at the Washington Convention must necessarily excite the amused attention of the enemies of women's suffrage, and I had hoped that Mrs Stanton would have seen the unwisdom of it. As however Mrs Stanton seems not to see the unsuitability of being publickly associated with Mrs Ashton Dilke, and is taking her out under the auspices of the President of the Convention, it would be wrong of me to appear to sympathize with such a proceeding when I strongly condemn it.

However much I may regret to come ↑to this decision↓ I regret still more that the action Mrs Stanton is taking in this matter may cause the Convention to do as much harm as good to the cause of women's Suffrage as well as to that of Moral progress (the root of all progress) and I feel compelled to withdraw my acceptance of the invitation which I accepted under totally different circumstances to those now existing.

If the loss of my name has only half the importance your letter attributes to it, the obligation upon me to withdraw it is only the more imperative now that the circumstances under which I gave it are altered. Believe me, dear Miss Anthony, to remain, Yrs sincerely

Helen Taylor

ALS, HM 10610, Ida Harper Collection, CSmH.

1. From supporting the Irish Ladies' Land League, Taylor moved on to advocacy of nationalizing land and taxing its value in England.

2. Harriet Hardy Taylor Mill (1807–1858), mother of Helen Taylor, married John Stuart Mill as her second husband. Interest in newspaper reports of the First National Woman's Rights Convention, in Massachusetts in 1850, led her to write "The Enfranchisement of Women," *Westminster Review* 55 (July 1851): 149–61, widely reprinted in the United States.

40   Address of Welcome by ECS to the International Council of Women

EDITORIAL NOTE: Delegates to the International Council of Women met for business at the Riggs House on Saturday, March 24 and for pleasure at a reception for hundreds of guests that evening. They represented fifty-two associations ranging across a wide spectrum of women's activism, including the American Red Cross, Universal Peace Union, Woman's National Indian Association, Woman's Relief Corps, and Christian Women's Board of Missions. Sunday was given over to religious services led by ministers in attendance. The formal opening at Albaugh's Opera House took place Monday morning, and, according to the *Washington Post*, "As the ladies did not have to wait for their husbands they arrived promptly." It is difficult to discover precisely what ECS said to welcome the crowd. Stenographers were present at this as at every session of the weeklong meeting, and the *Woman's Tribune* claimed to publish what the stenographers supplied. When the official report of the council appeared several months later, ECS's speech was described as condensed from the stenographer's report. Yet the "condensed" report restored several paragraphs missing from the *Tribune* and repositioned a key point. Despite the stenographers, neither the *Tribune* nor the report included ECS's ad-lib remarks. Meanwhile the *Woman's Journal* published a longer version of the speech that matches what survives of ECS's manuscript and includes twelve paragraphs missing from the *Tribune*. Though it is possible that ECS omitted those paragraphs at the podium, the reporter for the *Washington Post* heard them. The *Journal* remarked that ECS, "at several points in her address, drifted away from her manuscript and sailed out into the realm of spontaneous oratory. At such times she always got applause." Its report paraphrased some of those flights but omitted one that stirred controversy for several days. The *Washington Post* noted a warning ECS delivered: "'If the wrongs of our sex are not righted,' said Mrs. Stanton, speaking extemporaneously for a moment, 'women will join hands with laboring men, with Socialists, and with Anarchists and the scenes of the French Revolution will be repeated within this fair land of ours.' This remark was received with perfect silence, although nearly every previous sentence had been punctuated with applause." In reports filed after ECS repeated this prophecy to the Senate Committee on Woman Suffrage on April 2, it was said that she conjured up the French Commune, not the French Revolution. The *Woman's Journal*'s text provides the basis of what is published here, though ECS's paragraph breaks are restored from the manuscript, and any misreadings of her handwriting are corrected. (*Woman's Tribune*, 27 March, 5 April, 5 May 1888; *Woman's Journal*, 31 March 1888; *Report of the International Council, 1888*, pp. 31-39; *Washington Post*, 27 March 1888; ECS, "Address of Welcome," AMs; all in *Film*, 26:154ff, 390-92, 403-75, 589-94, 632.)

[26 March 1888]

We are assembled here to-day to celebrate the fortieth anniversary of the first organized demand ever made by women for the right of suffrage. The initiative steps were taken in my native State. In 1848 two conventions were held in Central New York, and the same year the married woman's property bill passed the legislature.[1] Other conventions were soon called in Ohio, Indiana, Massachusetts, Pennsylvania,[2] and the other States, one after another, adopted New York's advance legislation.[3] Thus started the greatest movement for human liberty recorded on the page of history; a demand for freedom to one-half the entire race, and the keynote struck in this country in '48 has been echoed round the world. And to-day, to celebrate our fortieth anniversary, we have representatives in person or by letter from nearly every State in the Union, from Great Britain, France, Finland, Italy, Sweden, India, Denmark and Norway.

It has been our custom to mark the passing years by holding meetings of the members of the suffrage societies on each decade,[4] but for this we decided a broader recognition of all the reform associations that have been the natural outgrowth of the suffrage agitation in the old world as well as the new.[5]

Four years ago, at a reception in Liverpool, given to Miss Anthony and myself, the question of an international convention was discussed, and so favorably received, that committees of correspondence were appointed to ascertain what the general feeling might be.[6]

While the response from the different countries was encouraging, the general feeling seemed to point to America as the country to make the first experiment. Accordingly the National Suffrage Association assumed the responsibility of calling this International Council.

Those only who have been behind the scenes can estimate the herculean undertaking which the correspondence has involved. Though we cannot all share in the honor of the toil that has made this grand gathering possible, we can share in the joy of welcoming to our shores the noble women of foreign lands. We can benefit, too, in the broader interests and more liberal opinions that association with the people of other countries must necessarily bring to us.[7]

"The world is my country and all mankind my countrymen," is a motto[8] that cannot be echoed and re-echoed round the globe too often, to keep our sympathies alive to the weal and the woe of the human race. In welcoming representatives from other lands here to-day, we do not feel that you are strangers and foreigners, for the women of all nationalities, in the artificial distinctions of sex, have a universal sense of injustice, that forms a common bond of union between them.

Whether our feet are compressed in iron shoes, our faces hidden with veils and masks, whether yoked with cows to draw the plow through its furrows, or classed with idiots, lunatics, and criminals in the laws and constitutions of the State, the principle is the same, for the humiliations of spirit are as real as the visible badges of servitude. A difference in government, religion, laws and social customs makes but little change in the relative status of woman to the self-constituted governing classes, so long as subordination in all nations is the rule of her being. Through suffering we have learned the open sesame to the hearts of each other. There is a language of universal significance, more subtle than that used in the busy marts of trade, that should be called the mother-tongue, by which, with a sigh or a tear, a gesture, a glance of the eye, we know the experiences of each other in the varied forms of slavery. With the spirit forever in bondage, it is the same whether housed in golden cages, with every want supplied, or wandering in the dreary deserts of life, friendless and forsaken. Now that our globe is girdled with railroads, steamships and electric wires, every pulsation of your hearts is known to us. Long ago we heard the deep yearnings of your souls for freedom responsive to our own. Mary Wollstonecraft, Mesdames de Staël and Roland, George Sand, Frederica Bremer, Elizabeth Barrett Browning[9] and George Eliot have pictured alike the wrongs of woman in poetry and prose.

Though divided by vast mountain ranges, boundless oceans and plains, yet the psalms of our lives have been in the same strain, too long, alas! in the minor key; for hope deferred has made the bravest hearts sometimes despairing. But the same great oversoul has been our hope and inspiration. The steps of progress already achieved in many countries should encourage us to tune our harps anew to songs of victory. It is with great satisfaction we also welcome here to-day representatives of our own countrywomen, from thirty different associations of moral and philanthropic reforms.[10]

Although all these are the natural outgrowths of the demands made, and the basic principles laid down by those who first claimed equal, civil and political rights for women, yet this is the first time we have met on the same platform to advocate the same measures in carrying on the varied reforms in which we are mutually interested. I think that most of us have come to feel that a voice in the laws is indispensable to achieve success; that these great moral struggles for higher education, temperance, peace, the rights of labor, religious freedom, international arbitration, are all questions to be finally adjusted by the action of government, and that without a direct voice in legislation, woman's influence will be essentially lost.[11]

Experience has fully proved that sympathy as a civil agent is vague and powerless until caught and chained in logical propositions and coined into law. When every prayer and tear represents a ballot, the mothers of the race will no longer weep in vain over the miseries of their children.

The active interest women are taking in all the great questions of the day is in strong contrast with the apathy and indifference in which we found them half a century ago, and the contrast in their condition between now and then is equally marked.

Those who inaugurated the movement for woman's enfranchisement, who for long years endured the merciless storm of ridicule and persecution, mourned over by friends, ostracized in social life, scandalized by enemies, denounced by the pulpit, scarified and caricatured by the press, may well congratulate themselves on the marked change in public sentiment, that this magnificent gathering of educated women from both hemispheres so triumphantly illustrates.

In the great national and State conventions for education, temperance and religion, even thirty years ago, woman's voice was never heard.[12] The battles fought by the pioneers in the suffrage movement to secure a foothold for woman on those platforms have been eloquently described many times by Susan B. Anthony, Lucy Stone and Antoinette Brown, and I hope during this council they will be rehearsed once more for the benefit[13] of those who, while holding the vantage-ground they secured, are afraid of the principles by which it was gained. The protracted struggle through which we have passed, and our labors not yet crowned with victory,[14] seems to me in review like a painful dream, in which one strives to run and yet stands still, incapable alike of escaping or meeting the impending danger. The civil and political position of woman, when I first understood its real significance, was enough to destroy all faith in the vitality of republican principles. Half a century ago the women of America were bond-slaves, under the old common law of England. Their rights of person and property were under the absolute control of fathers and husbands. They were shut out of the schools and colleges, the trades and professions, and all offices under government; paid the most meagre wages in the ordinary industries of life, and denied everywhere the necessary opportunities for their best development. Worse still, women had no proper appreciation of themselves as factors in civilization. Believing self-denial a higher virtue than self-development, they ignorantly made ladders of themselves by which fathers, husbands, brothers and sons reached their highest ambitions, creating an impassable gulf between them and those they loved, that no magnetic chords of affection or gratitude could span.

Nothing more common forty years ago, than to see the sons of a family educated, while the daughters remained in ignorance; husbands at ease in the higher circles, in which their wives were unprepared to move. Like the foolish virgins in the parable: Women everywhere in serving others, forgot to keep their own lamps trimmed and burning, and when the great feasts of life were spread, to them the doors were shut.[15]

Even married women enjoy, in a measure, their rights of person and property.[16] They can make contracts, sue and be sued, testify in courts of justice, and with honor dissolve the marriage relation when it becomes intolerable. Now most of the colleges are open to girls, and they are rapidly taking their places in all the profitable industries and in many of the offices under government. They are in the professions, too, as lawyers, doctors, editors, professors in colleges, and ministers in the pulpits.

Their political status is so far advanced that they enjoy all the rights of citizens in two Territories, municipal suffrage in one State and school suffrage in half the States of the Union.[17] Here is a good record of the work achieved in the past half century,[18] but we do not intend to rest our case until all our rights are secured. And noting the steps of progress in other countries, on which their various representatives are here to report, we behold with satisfaction everywhere a general uprising of women, demanding higher education and an equal place in the industries of the world.

Our gathering here to-day is highly significant, in its promises of future combined action. When, in the history of the world, was there ever before such an assemblage of able, educated women, celebrated in so many varied walks of life, and feeling their right and ability to discuss the vital questions of social life, religion and government?

When we think of the vantage-ground woman holds to-day, in spite of all the artificial obstacles she has surmounted, we are filled with wonder as to what the future mother of the race will be when free to seek her complete development. Thus far women have been the mere echoes of men. Our laws and constitutions, our creeds and codes, and the customs of social life are all of masculine origin. The true woman is as yet a dream of the future: a just government, a humane religion, a pure social life, await her coming. Then, and not till then, will the golden age of peace and prosperity be ours.

This gathering is significant, too, in being held in the greatest republic on which the sun ever shone, a nation superior to every other on the globe, in all that goes to make up a free and mighty people: boundless territory, magnificent scenery, mighty forests, lakes and rivers, and inexhaustible wealth in agriculture, manufactures and mines, a country where the children of the masses in our public schools have all the appliances of a complete education, books, charts, maps, every advantage, not only in the rudimental, but in many of the higher branches, alike free at their disposal. In the Old World the palace on the hill is the home of nobility; here it is the public school or university for the people, where the rich and poor, side by side, take the prizes for good manners and scholarship. Thus the value of real character above all artificial distinctions, the great lesson of democracy, is early learned by our children. The number and circulation of our daily papers and magazines is fabulous, and so cheap as to be available for the laboring classes. There is no excuse for ignorance here.

This is the country, too, where every man has a right to self-government, to exercise his individual conscience and judgment on all matters of public interest. Here we have no entangling alliances in church and State, no tithes to be paid, no livings to be sold, no bartering for places by dignitaries among those who officiate at the altar, no religious tests for those elected to take part in government. Here under the very shadow of the Capitol of this great nation, whose dome is crowned with the Goddess of Liberty, the women from many lands have assembled at last, to claim their rightful place as equal factors in the great movements of the nineteenth century. So we bid our distinguished guests welcome, thrice welcome to our triumphant democracy. I hope they will be able to stay long enough to take a bird's-eye view of our vast possessions, to see what can be done in a moral, as well as material point of view, in a government of the people. In the Old World they have governments and people; here we have a government of the people, by the people, for the people; that is, we soon shall have when that important half called women are enfranchised, and the laboring masses know how to use the power they possess. You will see here for the first time in the history of nations a church without a pope, a State without a king, and a family without a divinely ordained head, for our laws are rapidly making fathers and mothers equal in the marriage relation.[19] We call your attention, dear friends, to these patent facts, not in a spirit of boasting, but that you may look critically into the working of our republican institutions; that when you return to the Old World you may help your fathers to solve many of the tangled problems to which as yet they have found no answer. You can tell the Czar of Russia and the Tories of England that self-government and "Home Rule" are safe and possible, proved so by a nation of upward of 60,000,000 of people.

Since the inauguration of our movement most of our noble coadjutors, men and women, have passed to the unknown land: Garrison, Phillips, Channing, Rogers, Burleigh, Edward M. Davis,[20] Lucretia Mott, Josephine Griffing, Clarina Nichols, Frances Gage, Paulina Davis, Abby Foster, Lydia Maria Child,[21] and many others, together far outnumbering those who still remain to watch and wait. The vacant places on every side warn us in the sunset of life that we, too, are passing away, and that younger hands must soon take up our work. To achieve equality for woman in every position in life and fit her to maintain that position with wisdom and dignity, is a work worthy to unite all our energies and attune our hearts in harmony.

Those who, like the children of Israel, have been wandering in the wilderness of prejudice and ridicule for forty years,[22] must feel a peculiar tenderness for the young women, on whose shoulders we are about to leave our burdens. Although we have opened a pathway to the promised land, and cleared up much of the underbrush of false sentiment, logic and rhetoric, intertwisted and intertwined with law and custom, blocking all avenues in starting, yet there are still many obstacles to be encountered before the rough journey is ended. I think, however, you will find in the bound volumes of "The Revolution" and the "Woman's Journal,"[23] and the three huge volumes of the "History of Woman Suffrage,"[24] all the necessary arguments to silence any reasonable opponent. If these fail, we shall hope much from the youngest born of all our papers, the "Woman's Tribune." If it finds that arguments fail, with the daring of youth it may use some more powerful ammunition to drive all opposing forces from the field of battle, and overthrow forever an aristocracy based on sex. The younger women are starting with great advantages over us. They have the results of our experience; they have had superior opportunities for education, and will have a more enlightened public sentiment for discussion, and more courage to take the rights that belong to them; hence we may look to them for speedy conquests.

In calling this Council we anticipated many desirable results. Aside from the pleasure of mutual acquaintance in meeting face to face so many of our own country-women, as well as those from foreign lands, we hoped to secure thorough national and international organizations in all those reforms in which we are mutually interested. To come together for a week, and part with the same fragmentary societies and clubs, would be the defeat of one-half the purpose of our gathering.

Above all things that women need to-day in their reform work is thorough organization, and to this end we must cultivate some *esprit de corps* of sex, a generous trust in each other. A difference of opinion on one question must not prevent us from working unitedly in those on which we agree. Above all things, let us hold our theological speculations of a future life in abeyance to the practical work of the present existence, recognizing all sects alike, and all religions—Jew and Gentile, Catholic and Protestant—to be held equally sacred in their honest opinions.

We sincerely hope that the proceedings of this Council, as a whole, will be as successful and satisfactory as our conventions in Washington invariably have been, and that marked courtesy in public and private will be generously extended to all our guests. We trust this interchange of sentiments and opinions may be a fresh inspiration to us all in our future work, and that this convocation may be long remembered as among the most pleasant and profitable days of our lives. As the character of this convention must depend, in a large measure, on what those who called it may do and say, it would be well for us to keep in mind the responsibility that rests on each and all. If it be true that we can judge of the civilization of a nation by the status of its women, we may do much during this convention to elevate our institutions in the estimation of the world.

Our form of government is being studied by leading statesmen in the old world, as never before, alike in the chamber of deputies and the house of commons; the powers of our executive, legislative and judicial departments have been freely discussed and recommended as worthy of adoption.[25]

Mr. Gladstone says: "The American constitution is, as far as I can see, the most wonderful work ever struck off by the brain and purpose of man."[26]

Lord Salisbury says: "The Americans have a senate. I wish we could institute it here. Marvellous in its strength and efficiency. . . . Their Supreme Court gives a stability to their institutions, which, under the vague and mysterious promises here, we look for in vain."[27] Such writers and historians as Sir Henry Maine, Mackenzie, Froude and Matthew Arnold[28] have all commented on our democratic institutions in the most complimentary terms. Indeed, the whole tone of English writers and travellers has entirely changed since they amused the world with ridicule of our people fifty years ago. It is the dignity of the republic, as viewed to-day, we are here to represent. Closer bonds of friendship between the women of different nations may help to strengthen the idea of international arbitration in the settlement of all differences;

that thus the whole military system, now draining the very life-blood and wealth of the people in the old world, may be completely overturned, and war, with its crimes and miseries, ended forever.

The question is continually asked, if women had the right of suffrage, how would they vote on national questions? I think I might venture to say that the women on this platform would all be opposed to war. As to the much-vexed question of the fisheries we would say, in view of our vast Atlantic and Pacific coast, thousands of miles in extent, do let Canada have three miles of the ocean if she needs it.[29] If the cod is the bone of contention, as it is the poorest of all fish, let the Canadians eat in peace[30] so long as we have oysters, shad, bass, and the delicate salmon from our Western lakes and California. Among other questions now up for consideration we should probably be of one mind. As to a treaty with Russia, to send back her political prisoners to be tortured in her prisons and the mines of Siberia, our verdict would be no, no; America must ever be the great university, in which the lovers of freedom may safely graduate with the highest honors, and under our flag find peace and protection.[31] The able statement by Stepniak, a Russian nihilist,[32] laid before our Senate, should be carefully read by all of us, that our influence may be used intelligently against all treaties, compromising, as they would, the honor of a nation upholding the right of free speech and free press in the criticism of their rulers by the people. As to international copyright, we should, no doubt, say, let us have a law to that effect, by all means, because it is fair and honest.[33] Moreover, since we now have our own historians, philosophers, scientists, poets and novelists, and England steals as much from us as we do from her, it is evident that sound policy and common honesty lie in the same direction. As to the overflowing treasury that troubles the conscience of our good President,[34] our wisest women would undoubtedly say, pay the national debt and lighten the taxes on the shoulders of the laboring masses. As to amendments of the Constitution now asked for by a body of the clergy and some reformers,[35] to recognize the Christian theology in the Constitution and introduce religious tests into political parties and platforms, in direct violation of Article 6, Clause 3, of the National Constitution,[36] I think the majority in our woman suffrage associations would be opposed to all such amendments, as they would destroy the secular nature of our government, so carefully guarded by our fathers in laying the foundation of the republic. This freedom from all ecclesiastical entanglements is one of the chief glories of our government, and one of the chief elements of its success. We cannot too carefully guard against all attempts at a retrogressive policy in this direction. If there is one lesson more plainly written than another on the institutions of the old world it is the danger of a union of church and state; of civil and canon law; of theological speculations in the practical affairs of government. If the majority of women on the suffrage platform would vote thus wisely on five questions, they may show equal wisdom on others that may come up for future legislation.

On questions of land, labor, prohibition and protection, there would, no doubt, amongst us be many differences of opinion. But I think we should all agree that that system of political economy that secures the greatest blessings to the greatest number must be the true one, and those laws which guard most sacredly the interests of the many rather than the few, we should vote for. When woman's voice is heard in government our laws will be touched with some emotion, our legislation become more humane, and judgments in our courts tempered with mercy. Surely the mothers who rocked the cradle of this republic may be safely trusted to sustain their sires and sons in all their best efforts to establish in the new world a government in which the sound principles of our Constitution and Declaration of Independence may be fully realized, in which there shall be no privileged classes, but equal rights for all.

Under a government and religion recognizing in rational beings the rights of conscience and judgment in matters pertaining to their own interests, above all authority of church and State, it needs no argument to prove the sacredness of individual rights, the dignity of individual responsibilities. The solitude of every human soul, alike in our moments of exaltation and humiliation, in our highest joys and deepest sorrows, into which no other one can ever fully enter, proves our birthright to supreme self-sovereignty. As in all the great emergencies of life we must stand alone, and for final judgment rely upon ourselves, we cannot over-estimate the necessity for that liberty by which we attain our highest development and that knowledge that fits us for self-reliance and self-protection.

↞ *Woman's Journal*, 31 March 1888, corrected with AMs, ECS Papers, DLC.

1. For the woman's rights conventions at Seneca Falls and Rochester, New York, in July and August 1848, see *Film*, 6:702-40, 742-57; and *Papers*, 1:75-

88. On 7 April 1848, New York's governor signed into law the Married Women's Property Act, granting women separate contol of the real and personal property they brought into marriage. On the property act, see Norma Basch, *In the Eyes of the Law: Women, Marriage, and Property in Nineteenth-Century New York* (Ithaca, N.Y., 1982), 113-61, and Peggy Rabkin, *Fathers to Daughters: The Legal Foundations of Female Emancipation* (Westport, Conn., 1980), 85-99. On the laws of married women's property in other states, see Elizabeth Bowles Warbasse, *The Changing Legal Rights of Married Women, 1800-1861* (New York, 1987).

2. The earliest conventions in these states were: Salem, Ohio, April 1850; Akron, Ohio, May 1851; Dublin, Indiana, October 1851; Worcester, Massachusetts, October 1850 and October 1851, the First and Second National Woman's Rights Conventions; and West Chester, Pennsylvania, June 1852. (*History*, 1:103-15, 220-42, 306-7, 350-67.)

3. ECS had revised this sentence, and the manuscript does not match the *Journal*'s rendition: "Other conventions were soon called in Ohio, Indiana & Massachusetts ↑Pennsylvania↓ & the↑se↓ younger ↑with other↓ states, one after another, as they came into the union, adopted New York's advance legislation."

4. The *Journal* reads "meetings of the suffrage societies".

5. The manuscript shows a change of mind; it reads "outgrowth of the antislavery & suffrage agitations in the old". The next twelve paragaphs were omitted in the *Tribune*.

6. *Papers*, 4:299-300.

7. At some point ECS envisioned the next paragraph as the opening one of her address, with the heading "Address of Welcome."

8. See note at 16 April 1887 above.

9. This list of intellectuals who established the modern, international language for discussing women's rights includes, in addition to George Eliot, Mary Wollstonecraft (1759-1797), author of *A Vindication of the Rights of Women*, published in London in 1792; three influential Frenchwomen, writer Germaine de Staël (1766-1817), revolutionary Jeanne-Marie Philipon Roland (1754-1793), and novelist George Sand (1804-1876); the Swedish novelist Fredrika Bremer (1801-1865); and the English poet Elizabeth Barrett Browning (1806-1861).

10. Fifty-two associations were represented in the Council, according to the *Report of the International Council of Women, 1888*, pp. 8, 49-50, *Film*, 26:154ff. From outside the United States, twenty-one associations were represented.

11. The *Journal* reads "woman's influence will be eventually lost."

12. In the *Report of the International Council of Women, 1888*, this and the next paragraph were moved into a new position as the second paragraph of ECS's address.

13. The *Journal* reads "will be rehearsed for the benefit".

14. The *Journal* reads "through which we have passed, with our labors not yet crowned".

15. Matt. 25:1-13.

16. The *Woman's Tribune*, having omitted twelve paragraphs from ECS's manuscript, picked up here, making this the second paragraph of ECS's address.

17. School suffrage gave women the opportunity to vote on issues regarding public education, though states differed in listing which issues those were. Some form of school suffrage existed in Arizona Territory, Colorado, Dakota Territory, Kansas, Kentucky, Massachusetts, Michigan, Minnesota, Montana Territory, Nebraska, New Hampshire, New Jersey, New York, Oregon, Vermont, and Wisconsin. Wyoming and Washington were the two territories with full political rights for women. Washington women lost their rights in August 1888; see note above at 6 June 1887.

18. The *Journal* and the *Tribune* read "Here is a great record of the work".

19. ECS here struck out a paragraph welcoming leaders of the American Woman Suffrage Association. In her manuscript, it ends mid-sentence. "We would also extend the right hand of fellowship to some of our coadjutors who are with us for the first time in many years. Our estrangement has been a matter of deep regret to many who have harmonized with those on either side. The individual idiosyncracies, misunderstandings, & inconsequential differences that separated us years ago, time has still further minimized & changed. Speaking for myself I would say if word or act of mine, has helped to widen the chasm between us, I would gladly atone for the past, by doing all in my power, for that reconciliation, which the best friends of our".

20. Leading opponents of slavery too, these allies in the cause of woman's rights were William Lloyd Garrison (1805-1879), editor of the *Liberator*; Wendell Phillips (1811-1884), lawyer and orator; William Henry Channing (1810-1884), Unitarian minister; Nathaniel Peabody Rogers (1794-1846), editor; Charles Calistus Burleigh (1810-1878), editor and lecturer; and Edward Morris Davis (1811-1887), founder of the Citizens' Suffrage Association. For Garrison, Phillips, Channing, and Davis, see also *Papers* 1-4.

21. Like the men named by ECS, these women were outstanding abolitionists as well as leaders of the antebellum and postwar agitation for woman's rights. They were Lucretia Coffin Mott (1793-1880), Josephine Sophia White Griffing (1814-1872), Clarina Irene Howard Nichols (1810-1885), Frances Dana Barker Gage (1808-1884), Paulina Kellogg Wright Davis (1813-1876), Abigail Kelley Foster (1811-1887), and Lydia Maria Francis Child (1802-1880). See also *Papers* 1-4.

22. Deut. 8:2.

23. The *Revolution*, a weekly paper based in New York City, was published from 8 January 1868 through 17 February 1872. From its start until late May 1870, SBA was its proprietor and ECS one of its editors. The *Woman's Journal*, a weekly based in Boston and controlled by the New England Woman

Suffrage Association, Lucy Stone, and Henry Blackwell, appeared first on 8 January 1870. It survived beyond passage of the Nineteenth Amendment in 1920.

24. Elizabeth Cady Stanton, Susan B. Anthony, and Matilda Joslyn Gage, eds., *History of Woman Suffrage*, three volumes published in 1881, 1882, and 1886.

25. Two pages of ECS's manuscript are missing (pages forty-four and forty-five), beginning with "Mr. Gladstone" and ending in the next paragraph with "we are here to represent."

26. William E. Gladstone, "Kin beyond Sea," *North American Review* 264 (September–October 1878): 185.

27. Robert Arthur Talbot Gascoyne-Cecil, marquess of Salisbury (1830–1903), was Britain's prime minister from 1886 to 1892. ECS probably found this quotation in Andrew Carnegie, *Triumphant Democracy, or Fifty Years' March of the Republic* (1886), where it appears on pages 369 and 377. Lord Salisbury, then leader of the Conservative opposition to William Gladstone, was speaking to the Scottish Conservative Club in Edinburgh on 23 November 1882. (*Oxford DNB*; *New York Times*, 24 November 1882.)

28. These Englishmen were Henry James Sumner Maine (1822–1888), jurist and student of comparative law; Robert Mackenzie (1823–1881), journalist and author of books on the United States; James Anthony Froude (1818–1894), historian; and Matthew Arnold (1822–1888), poet and critic.

29. On 20 February 1888, President Cleveland submitted to the Senate a treaty on American fishing rights in British North American waters, negotiated by Thomas F. Bayard, the American Secretary of State, and Joseph Chamberlain, a member of Parliament. In May the Senate Committee on Foreign Relations reported against ratification. (McPherson, *Hand-Book of Politics for 1888*, 114–22.)

30. The *Journal* and the *Tribune* read "let the Canadians eat it in peace".

31. In March 1887, the United States and Russia signed a treaty on the extradition of criminals that would, if ratified, include in the list of extraditable crimes attempts on the life of the czar and his family. Such attempts were defined as non-political crimes, comparable to any charge of murder. As a tool to help the czar capture and punish revolutionaries in his own country, the treaty was very unpopular in the United States, where perpetrators of political crimes received protection. Not until 1893 did the Senate ratify the treaty. (McPherson, *Hand-Book of Politics for 1894*, 83–85; *New York Times*, 27 March, 3, 14 April, 20 May 1887.)

32. Sergej Mikhajlovich Stepniak-Kravchinskij, or Sergei Stepniak (1852–1895) was a Russian writer and revolutionary, living in exile in London. His letter to the House and Senate committees on foreign affairs, sent through Senator Joseph Hawley, made a passionate argument against an extradition treaty between Russia and the United States, appealing to the country's own

revolutionary tradition and justifying acts of violence as necessary when seeking the end of absolute power. (*Washington Post*, 30 January 1888.)

33. The Senate Committee on Patents reported an international copyright bill on 19 March 1888. See *Report*, 50th Cong., 1st sess., S. Rept. 622, Serial 2520.

34. Grover Cleveland (1837–1908), the twenty-second president of the United States, held office from 1885 to 1889. He opened his third annual message to Congress in December 1887 with a call for lower taxation because federal revenues exceeded "the sum necessary to meet the expenses of the Government." (Fred L. Israel, ed., *The State of the Union Messages of the Presidents, 1790–1966* [New York, 1967], 2:1587–88.)

35. The *Tribune* dropped "and some reformers". ECS struck out an earlier version that read "by a body of the clergy & some temperance organizations".

36. Section three of article six concludes, "no religious Test shall ever be required as a Qualification to any Office or public Trust under the United States." On repeated efforts to introduce Christianity into the Constitution, see Gaines M. Foster, *Moral Reconstruction: Christian Lobbyists and the Federal Legislation of Morality, 1865–1920* [Chapel Hill, N.C., 2002].

41   International Council of Women, Temperance Session

EDITORIAL NOTE: Frances Willard chose some of her most accomplished leaders to speak at this evening session on the many-sided work of the Woman's Christian Temperance Union. At the conclusion of a report on the union's effort to place matrons in urban police stations, Anna Shaw rose to introduce a resolution saying the International Council rejoiced in the union's work. While the audience demonstrated its approval, Willard cautioned that the demonstration was simply an expression of personal opinion and not "politics." Before permitting a rising vote, SBA reminded Willard that only delegates could vote on official actions of the International Council. A short time later, the evening's final speaker, Mary H. Hunt, introduced another resolution at the conclusion of her speech about which states required temperance education in their schools. Hers praised the Blair Education Bill, a measure for federal aid to common schools recently passed in the Senate. Laws about temperance education were not much use, she pointed out, without schools. ECS took the floor to begin this discussion, omitted from the official report of the meeting. (McPherson, *Hand-Book of Politics for 1888*, 122–25; Foster, *Moral Reconstruction*, 42–43.)

[27 March 1888]

Mrs. Elizabeth Cady Stanton. Ladies and Gentlemen: Although I am thoroughly in favor both of education and temperance, yet, as this is an International Council, where many subjects are being considered, I do not think it fair to have any resolutions passed unless all those who are represented here are in favor of them. I see no particular objection, of course, to these resolutions, only I do not wish the International Council pledged to any particular thing. We all are here on equal grounds to talk in favor of all these subjects. I know [*I*] have many opinions that I should be unwilling to insist upon the women here pledging themselves to believe in; and I do not wish to be pledged to any of the things which I have not considered beforehand, and the resolutions which have not passed under the eye of a committee. I hope you understand me. I have no particular objection to the resolution presented by Miss Willard as far as I understood it, nor to this resolution; only it is not the fair thing to do.

Miss Anthony. I think I fully explained it before, that any resolution that should be presented by the leaders of any particular session is simply the embodiment of their thought; that any such resolution ratified by this audience does not in any way commit the International Council. The Council is composed of delegates, what we term the Council, who are officially appointed by the great national organizations from the different nationalities that are represented here, and I think there is no misunderstanding on that matter; I am going to ask— I have been thinking of it all the way through—thinking that it would be a most magnificent thing for the delegates to prepare resolutions which should be the epitome the best thought on each one of these great branches that shall be discussed, that might be adopted by the delegates in committee meeting assembled to go out to the world as the best thought. Of course there has been no intention to commit anybody to anything here tonight.

Mrs. Mary B. Clay. I would like to suggest that these resolutions being brought up as they are, while we understand them, I don't think the country at large would understand them, and therefore I would rather not have the resolution passed.

On motion of Mrs. Blake, of New York, it was voted that the resolution together with others that have been presented, or any that may be presented by any of the speakers during this Council, be referred to a committee, and by them referred to the delegates for careful consideration.

Miss Frances E. Willard. I know that Mrs. Stanton does not believe that there was the slightest intention to take advantage of anybody. The Woman's Christian Temperance Union is a great, free-hearted organization, and in the resolution to secure the thought of the people present in a general way, there was no thought of taking any advantage. But I believe Mrs. Stanton has meant the utmost justice, and that the serious consideration of the delegates would give added weight to the opinion that might go forth. I say this in explanation with the same kindly feeling that Mrs. Stanton expressed in what she said.

The motion of Mrs. Blake was seconded and carried unanimously.

~ *Woman's Tribune*, 29 March 1888. Word in square brackets supplied by editors.

42 ~ EXECUTIVE SESSIONS OF THE NATIONAL WOMAN SUFFRAGE ASSOCIATION

EDITORIAL NOTE: Henry Blackwell waited in Washington on March 27 for the opportunity to meet the National association's conference committee in session for the first time that day. Five days earlier, he had mailed to each member a constitution with thirteen articles, a list of nineteen bylaws, and a slate of thirty-three officers, comprising the proposal of the American's conference committee for union.

Discussion by the National's committee did not go as he imagined. May Sewall later described how the members quickly abandoned Blackwell's proposal and agreed "that if we determined to unite, what we had to do was to unite and then convene the executive officers of both associations" to take the next steps. After the committee debated the desirability of union, Blackwell was informed by a note on March 28 that, because its decision "was such as must be first referred to the executive committee," they had "nothing to offer for your consideration."

On April 3, the National association's executive committee convened to hear Sewall's report on the work of her committee since the fall of 1887 and its recommendation "that no attempt at a union be made." Union made sense, Sewall told the group, if the standard was likeness of political principles; neither society any longer limited itself to working for state or federal legislation. In that regard the National and American associations had grown alike. But the American proposal exposed tension, suspicion, and jealousy that undercut the offer to unite and could cripple future work. Sewall pointed to the American association's insistence that all critical decisions be made in advance of the new society's birth, to Lucy Stone's plea that experienced leaders be barred from office, and to a constitutional provision that segregated different facets of suffrage work into different cities—congressional work in Washington, a lecture bureau in Chicago, and oversight of suffrage literature in Boston.

At the conclusion of Sewall's report, Lillie Blake moved that the discussion of union be continued in the larger forum of a business meeting, or what the National association called an executive session. ("Minutes of the Twentieth Annual Convention, 1888," pp. 13-23; and H. B. Blackwell, "The Negotiation for Union," *Woman's Journal*, 5 May 1888, *Film*, 26:638ff, 756-61.)

[3 April 1888]

EXECUTIVE SESSION.

Mrs Elizabeth Cady Stanton presiding:

On motion of Mrs Blake, of New York, the reading of the Minutes was dispensed with.

A motion was then made that Mrs Sewall be requested to present the Report of the Conference Committee on the plan of the union of the National Woman Suffrage Association with the American Woman Suffrage Association. After having repeated the statement which appears in the report of the meeting of the Executive Committee, Mrs Sewall said in addition to this: "It was stipulated and desired that the letter which the Chairman of the Committee of Conference was requested to prepare to be sent to the American Association, after having been submitted to the Executive Board of the National Association, should bear the signature of all the members of the Committee."

After stating the original points of difference between the two Societies, one working for amendments to the State Constitution and the other for an amendment of the United States Constitution, she said: "Originally we made that difference. As each Society has seen the success of the other, both organizations have come to labor in both directions. It was through the effectual labors of the officers of the National Association that municipal suffrage was pushed in Kansas. On the other hand the American Association in the amendment of the

U.S. Constitution has seen perhaps a shorter road for securing political rights to the women of the United States, and has lent its emphatic aid in securing that amendment. Yet in these two societies, although working for the same object, the methods and views of things are after all different. It was the conclusion of your Committee, considering how well managed both of these organizations now are, the ability they have to carry on the work and also the fact that they can, as we have shown in our International Council, work in harmony when brought together in large meetings for some great object, that it was better to preserve this harmony and friendliness between two distinct organizations, than to run the risk of crippling both by bringing about a formal union, when there is sufficient difference in ideas and conditions to indicate that there would not be the mutual confidence that ought to exist among the leaders of a great organization. The permanent National Council is the form in which the National and the American Associations will, if they desire, have a place. The plan of this union is open under this statement for discussion."

Mrs Blake: In view of the great importance of union between these two societies, in view of the fact that the deliberations of this Committee are evidently not complete and not formulated in such shape as we would wish to present them to the general public; in view of the courtesy due to a society working for the same object as our own, I move that the time of this Committee be extended so that it may, within the coming year, make a report on this question, commensurate with the dignity of this Convention. I move that the time of this Committee be further extended with power.[1]

The Motion of Mrs Shattuck for the amendment that the time of the Committee be extended until the afternoon session of April 4th, was accepted by Mrs Blake.

A suggestion was made by Mrs Isabella B. Hooker[2] that another Committee be appointed to confer with the Committee which had just reported.

Mrs Blake: My idea in making the motion was that we want some discretion and courtesy exercised towards the other Society. We do not wish to dismiss the proposition too hastily.

Mrs Sewall: The members of this Executive Session have a very erroneous idea if they think anything has been done with haste. This Committee has worked since last October in this matter. What we report today is the result of deliberations with leading officers of both Associations. It is the result of a dozen close conferences with the President of the American Association[3] by the Chairman of the Committee, and an extensive correspondence which has covered the time since October. We have had all the time we want except time to finish the report in proper shape. I think if this Committee should meet for years its report would remain what it is today. I wish to ask, as Chairman of that Committee, that we may be permitted to have until the last Executive Session to submit the letter which we have decided to read. We have no objections to having the Committee enlarged, indeed we would be glad to have it enlarged. We have the views of the absent members of our Committee which are as clear as the views of those present. I wish you to know as far as the Committee is concerned, whatever you think of the result, the work was done with great care and deliberation and with every opportunity to draw upon the opinions of the officers of our own and of the American organization.

Mrs Blake: I did not mean hasty, I meant incomplete.

Mrs Sewall: It is only incomplete in its verbal form; the spirit we abide by.

Mrs. Clay[4] moves that the meeting be adjourned until the next morning, and the whole time then devoted to the discussion of this subject.

Mrs. Perkins:[5] I think this subject has been carefully considered. We ought to act upon it. It seems to me any sensible woman could decide it in her own mind in ten minutes. It is not best to unite unless we can work in harmony. It appears best that each Society should work in its own way. I am not in favor of unity. Our Pioneers have done too much for the cause ever to be set aside until we permit them. Do not waste all day tomorrow on this subject.

Mrs Clay: Haste sometimes makes waste. I propose we dismiss this Committee and hear the voice of the people and appoint a Committee to confer with the American and decide this matter.

(*Name Unknown*) It strikes me that prolonging the time would not hurt anybody. As the lady says "Everything cometh to him who waiteth." Perhaps some political emergency may arise, some measure in which we shall want union very badly.

Miss Shaw:[6] Mrs. Perkins said in her remarks, "The pioneers have done too much to be set aside." As a member of the American Association Committee, I have never heard a proposition of that kind—a demand of that kind. I have heard a suggestion, not a proposition as having been submitted to the Committee of the National from the American Society.

Mrs Sewall: In the original proposition sent out by Mrs. Lucy Stone Blackwell on the first conference between Miss Anthony and Mrs. Stone, that was one of the first propositions made in writing.[7] It was sent in writing to every member of the National Committee. The proposition was not at all intended in the spirit of setting anybody aside. I shouldn't have framed my statement in that way. It was this: That Mrs. Stanton, Miss Anthony and Mrs. Stone should agree not to permit their names to be brought forward for the Presidency of the Association, should a new Association be formed. I was at that time anxious for union, thinking we might work better as one than as two organizations, but I was not willing to have any stipulations made about officers until we were united, and certainly not a stipulation that seemed to discredit any of these three women who have done most to carry on the suffrage work.

Miss Shaw: This was a suggestion and not a proposition. The propositions do not include this. As a member of that Committee I would not have permitted it. There were thirteen propositions sent to me. They were numbered in that way, from one to thirteen.

Mrs. Minor:[8] I endorse the remarks of the lady from Ohio, Mrs. Perkins.

Mrs. Shattuck: There were submitted to the members of the National Conference Committee 13 propositions. I do not know what was submitted to the American Committee—13 propositions in writing upon which we acted in Committee and in our correspondence. The 13th proposition is in substance as follows "As many members of the American Society regard Mrs. Stone as the cause of division, and as many members of the National Society regard Miss Anthony and Mrs. Stanton as the cause of division, it is therefore proposed that these three should agree in advance that none of them will take the presidency of the united association."[9] It has been stated that there was a fairness about this proposition, because they proposed to remove Mrs. Stone. Neither Mrs. Stone nor Miss Anthony is at present the President of either of these Associations. With the exception of one year Mrs. Stone has never been President of the American.[10] Mrs. Stanton is

President of the National Association. They propose that we shall agree to remove our President while they remove an inferior officer. I cannot see any fairness in that. In regard to this question it is a philosophical and broad one. The whole trouble with the proposition as read to you is that there is no element of progress in it at all. If we accepted any such proposition as that we should be bound, and have to consider ourselves in a vise where we couldn't act at all. The National Association standing on a broad platform must so stand as long as we stand by it. We could not live under any such proposition. Then with regard to their proposition as to the list of officers before any Union has been effected. I feel, as a member of the Committee feeling much stronger than any of them on the question of union at first, that the methods of the American Association from beginning to end are such that we as a National organization cannot positively endorse.

Mrs Clara Neymann, of New York: I think it is a perfect impossibility to form a union between these two societies. I feel very kindly towards the American, although I am a member of the National; but I think both societies are doing such splendid work in different ways and with different methods, it would cripple the work of both to unite them. As long as we have these faithful workers who have pioneered the movement and to whom the younger members owe so much, let each Association continue to do its own work in its own way.

Mrs. Johns (of Kansas): I would like to say, as a member of the National Committee, that I object to the use of the words "proposition" or "stipulation" as applied to these articles of agreement. I think they are intended only for suggestions. It puts the matter too strongly. It is not quite fair to call them by any possible name but suggestions. The only stipulation is that there should be a common board of officers, a common constitution and a common name.

Mrs. Isabella Beecher Hooker: I understand that "suggestion" is the proper word to use; but, friends, those of us who have been working in the National organization for twenty years at any rate, the meetings for conference to try to prevent a split in our ranks occurred in my house. I invited the leaders of both sides to come together, and I begged those who thought of leaving the National not to organize,—not to make another organization, because I had that feeling in favor of unity. I fairly implored them, with tears, at my own breakfast table, where they were gathered at the time of that convention which I had called at

Hartford; but, as the old Abolitionists split and became Garrisonians and Americans and were benefited by it, it has turned out to honor of the whole cause; a greater amount of work has been accomplished than could have been otherwise done. I was terribly against it. How hard I worked! It is no discourtesy for one who has watched the signs of the times to say women are human as well as men. People work for party harder than for principle. These two organizations are like parties. You have got attached to them. You work harder than you would if you were one party. You have a greater scope for individual expression. In performing this national work under our leader, Mrs. Stanton, if before we shall have a plan of union we are going to cut her head off, it strikes me there is something in the suggestion—I call it a mere suggestion—it seems to me we can work better alone. I have never said a word against anybody founding this new organization. I have never said a word against the work of the American; but now, for them to come with a suggestion—I don't care from whom—that, in order to form a new organization, we shall drop, not only our name, but our President, who has borne the burdens of our cause for forty years, it fills me with disgust. I mean the mere suggestion. You may count me now and forever against union with anybody or in any work as a National Society. We are friendly, I do not mean to say otherwise. This is only the expression of my present feeling.

Mr. [blank] Wilcox:[11] It strikes me, ladies, there are two considerations which ought to be taken into account; neither of which, as far as I have heard, has been touched upon this afternoon. This is the presidential year. Several parties have adopted women suffrage planks, as they call them. It certainly seems to me that far the wiser course would be to postpone action until the developments of this year are known to us. In the state of New York there is a condition of things somewhat peculiar. There is no law there which forbids women to vote. Some have voted during the past year. We have a suit now pending to defend one of them, as a test case, against any infliction of punishment for thus voting. We have the opinion of some forty or fifty eminent lawyers that our ground is true. The case has been tried in one of the courts and has been appealed to another. The judgment has not yet been rendered, but will probably be rendered this week. We intend if the decision is adverse, to carry it to the highest court of the state.

There are several states, New Jersey, for instance, in a similar condition. In none of them can it be said that women violate any law by voting. If we can act more wisely in six months hence than we can now, let us take advantage of that delay. There will certainly [*be*] no injury to the result if we act with deliberation.

Mrs. Clay: My proposition was that we should take time to discuss this matter.

Mrs Swain:[12] It seems to me both organizations are necessary for the success of the cause.

Mrs. Chambers:[13] As a member of the National Organization, Mrs. President, I think that I express the sentiments of the majority of this association by endorsing every word that Mrs. Hooker has said. We have in Mrs. Stanton a lady, an honorable gentlewoman, who has carried our banner for forty years, and I shall endorse nothing that will put her name from still leading in that office. We want just such a leader as Mrs. Stanton is. She is without spot, without blemish, without prejudice and without selfishness, spending her time and her money without reward except the love of the National, which will never forget her. We endorse no platform that suggests such a thing as putting her name aside from still being the head of this organization.

Mrs. Clay: I don't see any use of discussing this matter as if we were putting Mrs. Stanton on the market. We are not working for individuals; we are working for all. We should deliberate on this matter. It is a question of great importance. If it is necessary, we ought to devote the whole time to this business. My motion was that this house should adjourn until to-morrow morning for the purpose of discussing this matter, and elect a committee to confer with the American Association, who shall present a plan of work for us to approve in a year from now. I don't think it ought to be decided now. In the Northern States you don't feel the need of this union as we do in the South and West, where we simply do individual work. We have nobody to appeal to, to work with us, unless we have a national organization and work in that way together and can be identified in our work. I think we ought to have this matter discussed; simply appoint a committee to decide this question with the American, and have our endorsement next year. That, I think, is Miss Anthony's opinion.

The Chairman: Miss Anthony said, in a hasty way, that she had appointed this Committee of Seven just as the American had appointed their Committee of Seven, and, if we decline this overture, it will all come back on her. That is her hasty view of it. She wants the responsibility of replying to this overture to be shouldered by this whole Society, and not have it depend on this Committee of Seven appointed by her. There should be a separate committee to meet with this committee, to have a chairman, and see on the whole what is best that they should recommend.

Mrs. Sewall: As Chairman of the Committee appointed by Miss Anthony it will be gratifying to have this meeting appoint another committee to confer with us. Before a small committee it would be much more possible for the Committee of Seven to give all the information in our hands, and explain all the manifold and complicated changes of circumstances which have led to our conclusion.

Mrs. Blake: I move that we proceed to appoint a Committee of Seven to confer with this other committee and report at the morning session, if possible.

Mrs. Gage moves, as an amendment, that the committee be eight instead of seven in number.

The amendment being accepted, the motion was seconded and carried.

The following persons were appointed to form said committee: Mrs. Isabella Beecher Hooker, Mrs. Matilda Joslyn Gage, Mrs. Lillie Devereux Blake, Mrs. Perkins, Mrs. Clara Neymann, Mrs. Clay, Miss Mary Eastman,[14] and Mrs. Harbert.

On motion, the meeting was adjourned to April 4th, at 10 A.M.

> EDITORIAL NOTE: In the morning of April 4, the executive session reviewed credentials and began the election of new officers. With ECS presiding, the election continued into the afternoon session. Then the conference committee and its advisors returned with a report.

[4 April 1888]

Mrs Isabella Beecher Hooker, Chairman of the Committee on Union, reported as follows: "The Committee on the proposed union between the American Society and the National Society have written this letter to Henry B. Blackwell in response to the overtures of the American Society."

April 4, 1888.

Mr. Henry B. Blackwell, Sec'y of the Conference Committee of the American Woman Suffrage Association.

Dear Sir:

The Committee of Conference on the part of the National Woman Suffrage Ass'n, appointed to consider overtures from the American W.S.A. toward the union of both Societies in suffrage work, having made a statement of their views to the Executive Committee of the N.W.S.A. asked advice before making a formal reply to the communications received from the A.W.S.A. The Executive Committee immediately appointed a Committee of eight to meet the Conference Committee for consultation and this Joint Committee, after due deliberation do now report:

That since the Conference Committee on the part of the Nat'l W.S. Ass'n found it impossible to consider the Constitution, by-laws and list of officers presented by the Conference Committee of the American W.S.A., inasmuch as Constitutions, By-laws and lists of officers for an organization that does not exist are beyond the powers of a Committee from an existing organization, and this action of the Conference Committee being approved by the Joint Committee, this Committee do now further report:

That they rejoice in the desire for union now manifested by the American W.S.A. and wish cordially to unite with them in measures which shall bring the constituency of both parties into fraternal relations and harmonious plans of work. To this end they propose that the officers of both Societies shall unite in calling a joint Convention to consider the terms of union, which Convention shall be empowered, after due deliberation, to proceed to the formation of a new Constitution and the election of officers for the first year.

This Convention to be composed of the officers of both Societies and of regularly accredited delegates from the membership of both, based on the bona fide, paid up membership of each Association for the current year—one vote to be allowed for every twenty-five members as they appear on the Treasurer's books of each Society at this date, April 4, 1888, these books to be submitted to the officers who unite in calling the Convention. The action of this Convention shall be final, both Societies agreeing to abide by its decision and make its proceedings their own.

MAY WRIGHT SEWALL,
CH. OF CONFERENCE COMMITTEE.

RACHEL G. FOSTER, HARRIETTE R. SHATTUCK,
LAURA M. JOHNS, HELEN M. GOUGAR,
OLYMPIA BROWN, CLARA B. COLBY.

ISABELLA BEECHER HOOKER,
CH. OF THE ADVISORY COMMITTEE.

MATILDA JOSLYN GAGE, MARY B. CLAY,
SARAH M. PERKINS, LILLIE DEVEREUX BLAKE,
MARY F. EASTMAN, CLARA NEYMANN,
ELIZABETH BOYNTON HARBERT.

A Motion to accept the report of the above Committee was seconded and carried unanimously.

~ TMs, prepared by Mary F. Seymour, Stenographer, "The Twentieth Annual Convention of the National Woman Suffrage Association. Minutes of the Meetings of the Executive Committee and Executive Services [sic], April 3 and April 4, 1888," pp. 24-38, 79-82, NAWSA Papers, DLC.

1. On Blake's views of union, see Blake and Wallace, *Champion of Women*, 169-70; and Grace Farrell, *Lillie Devereux Blake: Retracing a Life Erased* (Amherst, Mass., 2002), 161-64.

2. Isabella Beecher Hooker (1822-1907) of Hartford, Connecticut, tried to reconcile the divided suffrage movement in 1869, when Lucy Stone and Henry Blackwell were recruiting her to help found their American Woman Suffrage Association. Loyal to ECS, SBA, and the National through all the years of division, she was most active on the national scene in the 1870s and always a mainstay of the movement in Connecticut. (*NAW*; *ANB*; Jeanne Boydston, Mary Kelley, and Anne Margolis, *The Limits of Sisterhood: The Beecher Sisters on Women's Rights and Woman's Sphere* [Chapel Hill, N.C., 1988], passim. See also *Papers* 2-4.)

3. William Dudley Foulke (1848-1935), a Republican lawyer from Richmond, Indiana, became president of the American Woman Suffrage Association in 1885 and held the position until 1890. Foulke gave up the practice of law in 1889 or 1890 to devote his time to reform, principally to civil service reform. (*DAB, Supplement 1*; *NCAB*, 26:429-30.)

4. Mary Barr Clay (1839-1924), who divided her time between Ann Arbor, Michigan, and Lexington, Kentucky, joined the National association in 1879 and was chosen president of the American association in 1884. A leader in state associations in both Kentucky and Michigan, she contributed the report on Kentucky to the *History of Woman Suffrage*. Clay's marriage to John Frank Herrick ended in divorce in 1872, and she resumed use of her maiden name. (*American Women*; *History*, 3:818-22; H. Edward Richardson, *Cassius Marcellus Clay: Firebrand of Freedom* [Lexington, Ky., 1976], 31n, with assistance of the Filson Club, Lexington, Ky.; *Papers*, 3:477-80, 4:157, 312-14.)

5. Sarah Maria Clinton Perkins (1824-1905), an ordained minister in the Universalist church and an experienced lecturer on woman suffrage and temperance, moved to Cleveland in 1880 after the death of her husband. She held positions of leadership in Ohio's suffrage association, and at this meeting of the National association, she served on the committee on resolutions. (*SEAP*; *American Women*; *Woman's Journal*, 16 December 1905; *Papers*, 3:100-102.)

6. Anna Shaw served on the American association's conference committee, but she may also have been a member of the National association.

7. See Appendix A in this volume for this message from Alice Blackwell to Rachel Foster.

8. Virginia Louisa Minor Minor (1824-1894) presided over the Woman Suffrage Association of Missouri, the first such society in the country, at its founding in 1867. Driven out by a nasty fight to affiliate the group with the American association in 1871, she collaborated with her husband on a test case of women's right to vote under the federal Constitution. In *Minor v. Happersett* (1875), the Supreme Court of the United States affirmed the right of states to bar citizens from voting. As president of the new National Woman Suffrage Association of Missouri in 1879, Minor regained a position of leadership. (*NAW*; *ANB*. See also *Papers* 2-4.)

9. Shattuck or the stenographer reversed the elements in this proposition; the passage she quoted reads that members of the *National* regarded Stone as the cause and those of the *American* regarded ECS and SBA as the cause.

10. Lucy Stone presided over the American Woman Suffrage Association only in 1872.

11. John Keappock Hamilton Willcox (1842-1898), known as Hamilton, whose activism dated back to the Universal Franchise Association in postwar Washington and continued when he returned to his native New York City to practice law, led New York's Woman Suffrage party. The state suffrage association collaborated with him earlier in the 1880s in an attempt to gain legisla-

tive recognition of women's existing, common law right to vote. Inspired by the joint effort, Lucy Sweet Barber of Alfred, New York, voted in a federal election in the fall of 1886 and was arrested by federal marshals in January 1887. The fact that in the end neither federal nor county authorities pressed charges against her encouraged Willcox to believe that his ideas were gaining support. (Columbia University, *Alumni Register, 1754–1931* [New York, 1932]; *Woman's Journal*, 4 December 1898; *History*, 3:959–61, 4:856; *Papers*, 2:140n, 3:399n, 4:208–9n, 465–66, 551n; Hamilton Willcox, "Political Status of Woman in New York and at Common Law," *Chicago Law Times* 1 [October 1887]: 341–61.)

12. Adeline Morrison Swain (1820–1899) lived in Illinois, where she moved sometime after the death of her husband in 1877, but her work for woman suffrage dated back to her early days in Fort Dodge, Iowa, where she settled in 1858. There she hosted SBA on 23 April 1872, and the two met again on 17 March 1878, when SBA lectured in the town. Swain was the Greenback party's candidate for Iowa superintendent of public instruction in 1881 and a delegate-at-large to the party's national convention in 1884. (*American Women*; *History*, 3:144n, 617, 623, 4:1102; SBA diary, 1872 and 1878, *Film*, 15:888ff, 19:791ff; biographical files courtesy of the Iowa Women's Hall of Fame, Iowa Commission on the Status of Women.)

13. Eliza Anne Chambers (c. 1844–?), from the District of Columbia, graduated from the Howard University Law School in 1886, gained admission to the bar in 1887, and began a practice in Washington. Boone Chambers, her husband, was chief clerk in the auditor's office of the department of the post office. (Federal Census, 1880; *Report of the Sixteenth Annual Washington Convention, 1884*, pp. 11–13, *Film*, 23:573ff; city directories, 1886 to 1891; Virginia G. Drachman, *Women Lawyers and the Origins of Professional Identity in America: The Letters of the Equity Club, 1887 to 1890* [Ann Arbor, Mich., 1993], 48, 216–17; *Washington Post*, 28 April 1897.)

14. Mary F. Eastman (c. 1834–1908) of Massachusetts was a teacher before discovering her talent as a lecturer. Though identified with the American Woman Suffrage Association for many years, she made her first appearance at meetings of the National association in 1886. (Federal Census, 1880; Julia Ward Howe, ed., *Sketches of Representative Women of New England* [Boston, 1904], 484–89; *Woman's Journal*, 21 November 1908; *Woman's Tribune*, March 1886, *Film*, 24:900–908.)

43 ❧ SBA TO FRANCIS J. GARRISON[1]

Riggs House, Washington, D.C., May 8, 1888.

My Dear Frank Garrison

Your lovely note arrived last evening—and made me feel dreadfully ashamed I had never answered your first— But alas it has been impossible for me to do anything save the imperative—ever since the Council was over— Mrs Stanton Miss Foster & myself have remained here at the Riggs—by the invitation of its Hostess—Mrs Spofford—to get out the pamphlet report of the Council— And such a time—with the most imperfect reports of the Daily Tribune!! Well—we have simply agonized over the whole thing—I have—because we had to supply so much out of our true inwardness—[2]

Of all of the first letter—we will talk when we meet—

Mrs Stanton now promises to go on to Boston with me—and I so write Lucy Stone—[3] The "<u>book</u>" is now half done, only, and Mrs Stanton feels that she must return to New York—so she leaves Miss Foster & me to-day— I have promised to be in Chicago June 9th—so you see I am not likely to die of "<u>rust</u>" just yet—[4]

So—I will write Mrs Purinton—shall I—that I should like to be sheltered during that week under her most hospitable roof— Dear Ella's[5] house is always so crowded—that—though I long to be with her & William—I feel I should accept Mrs Purinton's invitation—as she has no family but herself, husband & one son—[6] Lovingly your friend

❧ *Susan B. Anthony*

❧ ALS, on 40th anniversary letterhead, Miscellaneous Bound, MHi.

1. Francis Jackson Garrison (1848–1916), the youngest son of the abolitionist William Lloyd Garrison and chairman of the executive committee of the New England Woman Suffrage Association, invited SBA to attend the group's twentieth anniversary meeting and popular Suffrage Festival at the end of May. Noting the appointment in her diary, SBA wrote, "invited by Lucy Stone." (Garrison, *Letters*, 6:18; SBA diary, 30 May 1888, *Film*, 25:869ff.)

2. This was the *Report of the International Council of Women, Assembled by the National Woman Suffrage Association, Washington, D.C., March 25 to April 1, 1888*, a "pamphlet" of four hundred and seventy-one pages, including

its index, printed by Rufus H. Darby in Washington in 1888. See *Film*, 26:154ff.

3. ECS changed her plans, leaving Boston suffragists without one of their advertised speakers.

4. She had agreed to preside at the farewell meeting in Chicago's Farwell Hall for Laura Ormiston Chant. See *Film*, 26:801-6.

5. Ellen Wright Garrison (1840-1931), William Lloyd Garrison, Jr., (1838-1909), and their five children often hosted SBA at their home near Boston. Growing up in Auburn, New York, the daughter of Martha Coffin Wright, Ellen Garrison had adored SBA, and she remained a friend for life. In recent years, William Garrison, a businessman and reformer, had taken the lead in trying to reconcile SBA and Lucy Stone as a prelude to reuniting the suffrage movement. (Wright genealogical files, Garrison Papers, MNS-S; *New York Times*, 13 September 1909. See also *Papers* 1-4.)

6. James Purinton, Jr., (1821-1891), retired shoe manufacturer, and Charles S. Purinton (1848-?), a stock broker in Boston, boarding with his parents. (*Vital Records of Lynn, Massachusetts*, 1:334, 2:312; Boston city directory, 1890.)

44 ~ SPEECH BY SBA TO THE NEW ENGLAND WOMAN SUFFRAGE FESTIVAL

EDITORIAL NOTE: The New England Woman Suffrage Festival offered at a price a social hour with prominent reformers, an elegant banquet, and a short program of speeches. A tradition during Boston's Anniversary Week, the festival raised money for the *Woman's Journal* and other projects of the New England Woman Suffrage Association. Mary Livermore presided; speakers would be limited to ten minutes, she told the crowd, except in two instances. "We will hear all Clara Barton has to say, if we 'don't go home till morning, till daylight doth appear'; and we won't attempt to muzzle Susan B. Anthony, though she were to talk by the hour." (*Boston Daily Globe*, 31 May 1888, *Film*, 26:795.)

[30 May 1888]

I have made every possible inquiry this evening if there was not some way in which to ventilate Music Hall,[1] and I was answered, "No; you have all the air you can get." Now, my good men and brethren, when we women get to be architects, if we cannot devise some plan by which a little fresh air can be introduced into an audience chamber of any sort, whether it is the House of Representatives at Washington or Music Hall in Boston, I shall then certainly be compelled to give up that women are no smarter then men. (Laughter.) But you must first give us a chance. Miss Anthony related something of her early experience in the suffrage movement, stating the reasons which first led her to become an advocate of the cause. She referred to the time when, in a meeting of school teachers in the State of New York, she, as one of the teachers, had risen to address the meeting. She said, "Mr. President," and the chairman came to the front of the platform and leaning forward inquired in a solicitous voice, "What will the lady have?"[2] When it was found that she desired to address the meeting a storm arose which lasted for half an hour, during which time she remained standing, and at the close of which she was, by a small majority, given permission to speak. She told how, little by little, advances had been made, until women were freely allowed to speak in such a meeting, were put upon its committees, and made its officers. And now we have come to another demand. Instead of demanding simply the right to speak, simply the right to express an opinion, we are demanding the right to have our opinions counted at the ballot-box. (Applause.) And there will be no rest, there will be no cessation of this magnificent warfare, of this grandest battle that was ever fought since the sun began to shine, until our demand is granted. (Applause.) Men of Massachusetts, if you want to get rid of us, if you don't want us to be forever scolding you, you must take down the bars, take down all the barriers, and give to women perfect freedom to have their opinions counted equally with men's opinions. What is this little thing that we are asking for? It seems so little; it is yet everything. I remember when your silver-tongued orator said, "To talk of freedom to the negro without the ballot is mockery."[3] Never was truer utterance made; and I have said from that day to this, and all women of this movement say to-day, that to talk of freedom to women without the ballot is mockery, precisely as it is mockery, and always has been considered mockery, to talk to men of freedom without the ballot. What is this ballot? What does your right to vote in this country, men and brethren, say to you? What does that right say to every possible man, native and foreign, black and white, rich and poor, educated and ignorant, drunk and sober, to every possible man outside the State prison, the idiot and the lunatic asylums? What does it everywhere under the shadow of the American flag say to every man? It says, "Your judgment is sound, your opinion is worthy to be counted." That is it. And now, on the other hand, what does it say to every possible woman, native and foreign, black and white, rich and poor, educated and ignorant, virtuous and vicious, to every possible woman under the shadow of our flag? It says, "Your judgment is not sound, your opinion is not worthy to be counted." Do you not see how this fact that every possible man's opinion the moment he arrives at the age of twenty-one is thus respected, and thus counted, educates all men into the knowledge that they possess the political authority of every other man? The poorest ditch-digger's opinion counts for just as much as does the opinion of the proudest millionaire. It is a good thing; I believe in it. I would not take from the most ignorant man under the shadow of the flag the right to vote, but I do want to make you understand the difference in our position. I want to say to you what all of you know, that if there was still left under the shadow of the flag any class of men who are still disfranchised, that class would rise in rebellion against the government before it would submit to the outrage. We women cannot rise in open rebellion. Men are our fathers and brothers and husbands and sons. But we shall stand and plead and demand the right to be heard, and not only to be heard but to have our votes counted and coined into law, until the very crack of doom, if need be. (Applause.)

⇜ *Woman's Journal*, 9 June 1888.

1. The Boston Music Hall, built in 1852, was home to the Boston Symphony Orchestra. It survives as the Orpheum Theater. Dreadful ventilation was one factor in the decision to build Symphony Hall. (Richard Poate Stebbins, *The Making of Symphony Hall, Boston: A History with Documents* [Boston, 2000], 14.)

2. SBA had quickly seen the power of retelling this story about the New York State Teachers' Association meeting of 1853 in Rochester. She recounted it in one of her earliest speeches, at the New York Woman's Rights Convention in September 1853, and continued to tell it for decades. Charles Davies (1798–1876), a college professor of mathematics who received his education at the United States Military Academy, had presided at the meeting of school teachers. (*BDAmerEd*; *New York Teacher* 1 [September 1853]: 367–68, *Film*, 7:792ff; *Papers*, 1:226–29, 2:326, 3:300.)

3. Although SBA had attributed the quotation to Wendell Phillips for many years, and although possibly Phillips did incorporate the words into a speech, Frederick Douglass was the author. At the Massachusetts Anti-Slavery Society

meeting in January 1865, when Phillips insisted that the society's mission was not yet done, he described the need to guarantee the freedmen's citizenship. Douglass rose to second and expand the idea, and said, during the course of his speech, "I am for the 'immediate, unconditional and universal' enfranchisement of the black man, in every State of the Union. Without this, his liberty is a mockery; without this, you might as well almost retain the old name of slavery for his condition." (*Papers*, 2:574; Douglass, *Papers*, 4:62.)

45 ~ MATILDA JOSLYN GAGE TO ECS

Fayetteville, N.Y., July 13, 1888.

Dear Mrs Stanton:—Your two letters are received. I do not at all favor the Prohibition party—was about to write you.¹ Mrs. Wallace² writes me: "It has now passed into history that we were treated by all parties in their platforms with silent contempt, the Labor parties and Prohibition party alone paying us any attention." She thinks all self-respecting and conscientious woman suffragists should seek to destroy those parties which have ignored our claims, and intends herself to work henceforward for the success of the Prohibition party.

I am more in line with the Labor people, who are struggling for their own rights, but deem it worse than folly to offer and offer ourselves to any party.

Miss Anthony says: "If you and the leading women had been at Chicago with headquarters at the Grand Pacific Hotel, we could have gotten the words 'male or female' in the Republican ballot plank, and that not until we go to their conventions in force can we expect anything."³

Susan is wild on the subject of Republicans—always was.⁴ I was very sorry to see your and her pronunciamento in '84, when we had nothing from them.⁵ It places our association in a false light. The Democrats were as politic as the Republicans this year, and much more so in '80 when we did have headquarters at one of the first hotels—the Palmer House—with seventy-six delegates who received no consideration, not even as far as the *reception* of our address.⁶ The Democrats gave seats among their own delegates to sixteen of ours, placed a committee room in the Opera House at our disposal, and Susan, with our address in her hand, was escorted by Carter Harrison[7] to the platform, where it was read aloud to the convention by a secretary. Numerous other courtesies were accorded us. Even the Greenbackers treated us with more respect than the Republicans; listening to our address to them in open convention.[8]

I can never work with the Prohibitionists. Their preamble says: "The Prohibition party in National convention assembled, acknowledging *Almighty God as the source of all power in government*, does hereby declare, etc."[9]

The first five planks solely concern the liquor traffic; the sixth is on civil service reform; the ninth prohibits combinations of capital; the eleventh is on arbitration; the twelfth, monopoly of land and equal wages for equal work to both sexes; tenth, immigration and citizenship; eighth, for the abolition of polygamy and the establishment of uniform laws governing marriage and divorce; tenth, for the preservation and defense of *the Sabbath* as a civil institution without oppressing any who *religiously observe the same or any other day in the week*; the ninth (and suffrage plank) reads: "That the right of suffrage rests on no mere circumstance of race, color, sex or nationality, and that where, from any cause, it has been withheld from citizens who are of suitable age and mentally and morally qualified for the exercise of an intelligent ballot, it should be restored by the people through the legislatures of the several states on such educational basis as they may deem wise."

Here, you see, is no specific mention of women—as was noted by a Methodist elder in writing upon it. All suffrage is relegated to the States, with moral and educational qualifications,—the "moral" evidently to be twisted church-wise.

Suffrage, like revolutions, never moves backward. The earlier states had church, educational and other restrictions. The tendency now is to perfect freedom. With great inconsistency, while placing suffrage with the states, the Prohibitionists wish "the Sabbath," "polygamy," "marriage and divorce" to come under national law, thus turning the body politic feet uppermost.

The "United Labor Party"—the Henry George party—has no suffrage plank, such being opposed by their "prominent men."[10] This party, which is the latest labor development in a political line, has split since its nominations, Henry George favoring the democrats on the ground that free trade is the first step towards free lands. There is besides the

Union Labor party and the Socialist Labor party, neither of whose platforms have I seen, though I have heard that the first has a woman suffrage plank.[11]

Belva's party[12]—whatever it is—put Alfred Love[13] in nomination for Vice-President, but he declined the honor. As I recall its platform, even that is *not out and out* woman suffrage. Yes, I think it quite ridiculous that Belva should have kept up that presidential idea another year. In '84 it was really educational, and she actually received the electoral vote in Indiana, but that bee in her bonnet must be insane now.

This seems an hour when we must labor and wait. To be sure we have "waited" forever and a day. I should like to knock together the Republican and Democratic parties and sink them both forever. I am of your opinion, and Mrs. Wallace, that it is a derogation of dignity to appeal more or again to Republicans, and so felt over Susan's Chicago pronunciamentos.

I neglected to say that several of the state prohibition conventions refused to put in a suffrage plank at all. The New York convention was held in Syracuse not long since and a battle occurred over woman—who was defeated. You should have seen some of the delegates—Methodist brethren, too holy to exist.[14] Another thing which makes this party one of *extreme danger* is the W.C.T.U., upon which the Prohibition party depends for success. Mrs. Chandler,[15] in an open letter to Miss Willard, shows that the W.C.T.U., at the Vermont convention, declared its belief in Christ as "the author and head of government," who should be recognized in all political platforms. Six or more state conventions have since endorsed this resolution, while the National Reform Association,[16] through its secretary, distinctly states that the party that acknowledges the authority of God in civil government pledges itself "to choose for office only such as fear God."

This looks like a return to the middle ages and proscription for religious opinions, and is the *great danger of the hour*. The Catholics are full of it, the Episcopalians alongside of them, the Presbyterians not far off, the Methodists falling into line.

The great dangerous organization of the movement is the W.C.T.U.; and Frances Willard, with her magnetic force, her power of leadership, her desire to introduce religious tests into the government, is the most dangerous person upon the American continent to-day. The Council opened my eyes as never before. I am glad, oh, so glad, that Susan does not favor the Prohibition party. I have some hope for her yet, although she does not see the *real* danger.[17]

You and I must stand firm; we have a great tide to stem, a great battle yet before us. We must have no religious test for anything. Get ready for a strong fight, Sincerely yours,

~ Matilda Joslyn Gage.

~ *Woman's Tribune*, 18 August 1888. In *Film* at 20 July 1888.

1. ECS sent this letter, along with a cover note, to Clara Colby, who published them both in the *Woman's Tribune*. ECS's note said that Gage's letter "expresses fully my own ideas."

2. Zerelda Gray Sanders Wallace (1817–1901), a leader of the Indiana Woman's Christian Temperance Union and a cofounder of the Indianapolis Equal Suffrage Society, was an early promoter of woman suffrage within the Woman's Christian Temperance Union. Wallace's letter to Gage as well as one from SBA to Gage were said by ECS to be enclosed in the mailing to Colby, but Colby did not receive them. (*NAW*. See also *Papers* 3.)

3. SBA wrote to Gage after discovering that she, in her capacity as chair of the executive committee, had called off the National association's plans to petition the Republican National Convention. No doubt the rest of her letter was less temperate. In deciding to make Gage's letter public, ECS knew what Gage had done and also that Gage blamed ECS for making her decision necessary. At the National's Washington convention, Gage was put in charge of three committees whose members were to arrange hearings and present a memorial for woman suffrage at the Democratic, Republican, and Prohibition presidential conventions. Gage was certain that ECS was simultaneously directed to write the memorial, but the written record was contradictory: the minutes said nothing about ECS's assignment, while the report in the *Woman's Tribune* supported Gage's recollection. When Gage learned in May that ECS had no intention of writing a memorial, she refused—"for my own self-respect"—to write one herself, and she instructed the committee in Chicago that without a memorial from ECS, they lacked the authority to go before the convention. Chicago committee member Caroline Huling repeated the essentials of Gage's private letter in her newspaper, that ECS was instructed to write the memorial, that "Mrs. Stanton declined to prepare the memorial, and the committees were not authorized to take other action." (*Woman's Tribune*, 21 April 1888; "Minutes of the Twentieth Annual Convention, 1888," unnumbered pages after 88; *Justitia*, 1–15 July 1888; all in *Film*, 26:633–36, 638ff, 809; and M. J. Gage to Caroline A. Huling, 9 June 1888, Caroline A. Huling Papers, IUCi.)

4. When Isabella Hooker and SBA, in Chicago on other business in the week before the Republican convention, learned what had happened, they took matters into their own hands. They arranged for parlors in which to meet

with delegates; Hooker spoke to the Republican National Committee; they obtained the Cook County suffrage association's endorsement of a resolution; Hooker, Caroline Huling, and SBA all testified to the resolutions committee; and Hooker and SBA wrote a memorial to the delegates that they signed as individuals. One reason for SBA's belief, in the passage Gage quoted, that suffragists had lost a good chance, was a rumor that the vote on woman suffrage in the resolutions committee resulted in a tie, broken by the chairman. After the convention, SBA called on Benjamin Harrison, the presidential candidate, with one final appeal for his support. (*Chicago Daily Tribune*, 20 June 1888; Chicago *Inter-Ocean*, 20 & 22 June 1888; and *Justitia*, 1–15 July 1888; all in *Film*, 26:807–14.)

5. *Papers*, 4:361–64.

6. On events at the Republican National Convention in 1880, see *Papers*, 3:539–40. Potter Palmer provided parlors at the Palmer House where members of the National association met with delegates.

7. On the Democratic National Convention in 1880, see *Papers*, 3:545–49 and *Film*, 21:306–10. Carter Henry Harrison (1825–1893) represented Illinois in the House of Representatives from 1875 to 1879 and served as mayor of Chicago from 1879 to 1887 and again in 1893 until his assassination. (*BDAC*; Melvin G. Holli and Peter d'A. Jones, eds. *Biographical Dictionary of American Mayors, 1820–1980: Big City Mayors* [Westport, Conn., 1981], 151.)

8. Gage and SBA were two of the suffragists invited to speak at the Greenback-Labor party convention in 1880. See *Film*, 21:285–93, and *Papers*, 3:346–49.

9. Gage quotes the opening sentence of the Prohibition party's platform. In what follows, she correctly lists, and often quotes, the planks of the platform, but she invented her own numbering of them. The suffrage plank, quoted in full, was number six. (*National Party Platforms*, 78–79.)

10. For the United Labor party's platform, see *National Party Platforms*, 84–85. Henry George (1839–1897), reformer and advocate of a single tax imposed on land, ran for mayor of New York City in 1886 and secretary of state of New York in 1887. He supported Grover Cleveland in the election of 1888. (*ANB*.)

11. The Union Labor party was made up of farmers and labor radicals, many of them former Greenback party members. Its platform proclaimed, "The right to vote is inherent in citizenship irrespective of sex, and is properly within the province of state legislation." (*National Party Platforms*, 84.)

12. Belva Ann Bennett McNall Lockwood (1830–1917), a Washington lawyer and at one time a key member of the National Woman Suffrage Association, was running for president on the Equal Rights party ticket, repeating her effort of 1884 but with fewer supporters. Gage had supported her earlier candidacy. (*NAW*; *ANB*; Jill Norgren, *Belva Lockwood: The Woman Who Would Be President* [New York, 2007], 162–68. See also *Papers* 2–4.) Gage's misstatement of the Equal Rights party's platform was corrected by an indignant party member from Iowa who sent the text for publication in the *Woman's Tribune*, 27 October 1888. It promised that "if our party and candidates come into power, equal rights shall be meted out to all citizens without regard to sex

or color," and asked Congress "to pass an enabling act giving women the right to vote in all elective precincts of the United States."

13. Alfred Henry Love (1830–1913), president of the Universal Peace Union, received the Equal Rights party's nomination for vice president on the Lockwood ticket, but he firmly declined the offer. (*ANB*; Norgren, *Belva Lockwood*, 164–65.)

14. The New York Prohibition party convention not only omitted a plank for woman suffrage from its platform, but delegates also objected to seating the women elected by the New York Woman's Christian Temperance Union as delegates. (*New York Times*, 27, 28 June 1888.)

15. Lucinda B. Chandler said substantially this in her article in the *Woman's Tribune*, 10 December 1887, described above at 25 December 1887. That article did not take the form of an open letter to Frances Willard.

16. The National Reform Association's objectives were to make government Christian and legislate personal morality, and a proposal to amend the Constitution to acknowledge the divine origins of government was one of its projects. On its collaboration with the Woman's Christian Temperance Union during the election campaign of 1888, see note above at 25 December 1887. (Foster, *Moral Reconstruction*, 81–84, 88–89.)

17. In a letter to Frances Willard, SBA reacted to the publication of Gage's attack. "I am more vexed than I can tell you—that Mrs Stanton should send that wretched scribble... to the Woman's Tribune—and I am chagrinned that Mrs Colby should publish it—even if Mrs S. did send it to her— It is too idiotic for anything—it is complimentary to you—in comparison to its fling at 'Susan'—the vulgar way in which it calls me 'Susan' and pities my lack of sight & insight!! Well you & I can stand it!— But the National W.S.A. platform is not agnostic any more than it is Roman Catholic or Methodistic—women of all beliefs have perfectly equal rights upon it—and it is on this point that both Mrs G. & Mrs S. are at fault—it seems to me— They, to my face—charge me with having become weak & truckling ↑not only↓ to the Church Women—but also to society women!—they say I am eaten up with desire to make our movement popular &c" (SBA to F. E. Willard, 23 August 1888, *Film*, 26:859–74.)

46 ❧ SBA TO UNKNOWN

[*Rochester, before 14 July 1888*]¹

I hope, if you have occasion to allude to my political position, you will save me from any report of having gone over to the Third Party Prohibitionists, who have made the most fatal of concessions in submitting the right of citizens to vote to the will of the majority of the States. Look at their suffrage plank, which, after declaring that the right of suffrage inheres in citizenship, coolly says it is the duty of the

States to restore it. Isn't that a sop to the ex-rebels? Isn't that surrendering the vital principle on which the war was fought, and which we have been wont to say we gained by the sword, and secured by the fourteenth and fifteenth amendments?—that it is the right and the duty of the national government to protect the right of the citizens of the United States to vote in every State of the Union? No, I shall not shout for a party that remands my inherent rights.

~ *Woman's Journal*, 14 July 1888.

1. Henry Blackwell, who incorporated this undated extract in a lengthy editorial about the presidential campaign, described it as "a private letter quoted by the [Boston] *Traveller*." SBA's rejection of the Prohibition party's plank on woman suffrage provided Blackwell with an occasion to reiterate his faith that the "U.S. Constitution leaves the regulation of suffrage wholly to the States." (*Woman's Journal*, 14 July 1888.)

47 ~ FROM THE DIARY OF SBA

[*7–11 August 1888*]

TUESDAY, AUGUST 7, 1888. Mrs Stanton & self took 4.30 train for Byron Center—took tea at Mr J. Peckams—spooke in Presbyterian Church to good audience[1]—& rode two miles to Mrs Newton Greens—[2] very warm day—

1. En route to Nebraska with her daughter Margaret Lawrence, ECS spent several days visiting SBA in Rochester. Before leaving the state, she spoke in two western New York counties with SBA in tow. In Genesee County, where they accepted an invitation from the Byron Woman Suffrage Association, ECS talked for forty minutes on the need for woman suffrage, and SBA took questions from the audience. J. Peckam is unidentified. (*Batavia Daily News*, 8 August 1888, SBA to Frances E. Willard, 12 August 1888, *Film*, 26:843–47.)

2. Sylvina M. Dewey Newton (1832–1911), founder and president of the Byron association, was the wife of Newton H. Green, a former state legislator who farmed and grew fruit on four hundred acres. He was known for extensive research and experimentation in his agricultural practices. Sylvina Newton presided over the local suffrage society into the twentieth century. (Federal Census, 1880; Safford E. North, ed., *Our County and Its People; A Descriptive and Biographical Record of Genesee County, New York* [Boston, 1899], pt. 3, p. 66; Batavia *Daily News*, 17 April 1899, 24 October 1911.)

WEDNESDAY, AUGUST 8, 1888. Spent the day at Mrs Green's lovely farm home— some 60 or 70 women & one man called in P.M. they came from LeRoy & Batavia—[1]

1. Genesee County towns to the south of Byron.

THURSDAY, AUGUST 9, 1888. Left Mrs Greens at 8.30—reached Buffalo 11.45— lunched with Julia England Johnson[1]—Maggie Stanton there— at 2 went on to Jamestown—arrived 6.30—& were met by Mrs Henderson[2] & escorted to the palatial home of Mrs Reuben E. Fenton—[3] she has two splendid daughters, Mrs Gilbert & Mrs Gifford

1. From Byron to Jamestown in Chautauqua County, they continued west by rail to Buffalo and changed lines. Julia England (c. 1856–?), a daughter of the late Isaac W. England of the New York *Sun*, grew up with the Stanton children in Tenafly, New Jersey. The given name of her husband Mr. Johnson is not known. (Federal Census, 1880; *Eighty Years*, 322–23; *Papers*, 3:256, 259.)

2. Martha Y. Tiffany Henderson (1839–1903) belonged to the Jamestown Political Equality Club, one of the most active local societies in the state, and she became the president of the Chautauqua County Political Equality Club at its founding later in 1888. Her husband was a pharmacist and local historian, who held several federal appointments in the county. (Federal Census, 1880; William Richard Cutter, ed., *Genealogical and Family History of Western New York* [New York, 1912], 1:434–35; John P. Downs, ed., *History of Chautauqua County, New York, and Its People* [Boston, 1921], 1:351–52, 354; *Jamestown Evening Journal*, 24 February 1903.)

3. Elizabeth Scudder Fenton (1824–1901), widow of New York governor and senator Reuben Eaton Fenton (1819–1885), lived in an elegant mansion known as Walnut Grove. As a member of the Political Equality Club, she signed the call in October for a mass meeting of citizens "favorable to 'Impartial Suffrage.'" The Fentons' daughters also lived in Jamestown. Josephine Fenton Gifford (1845–1928) married Frank Edward Gifford, a banker and manufacturer of furniture who went into business with her brother. Jeannette Fenton Hegeman Gilbert (c. 1848–?) returned to her parents' house from New York City before 1880 with two young children from her marriage to Johnston Niven Hegeman and later married Albert Gilbert, Jr., who also worked in a Fenton-family business. (Downs, *History of Chautauqua County, N.Y.*, 1:106, 2:4, 6; "To the Citizens of Western New York," 13 October 1888, unidentified and undated clipping, SBA scrapbook 13, Rare Books, DLC; Federal Census, 1880; Jamestown *Post-Journal*, 9 July 1976, on-line at site of Prendergast Library, Jamestown, N.Y.; *New York Times*, 4 October 1875, 30 July, 13 November 1895.)

FRIDAY, AUGUST 10, 1888. Mrs Fenton & 8 or 10 others dined with us at Mrs C. W. Schofield's—at the Sherman House[1]—& at 2.30 we had meeting in Opera House of a 100 hundred women—& at 8 the house was packed—[2] [*added later above date*] Little Annette died this P.M.[3]

 1. Anna Bishop Scofield (c. 1835–?), treasurer of the Jamestown Political Equality Club, sometimes hosted its meetings in her "parlors" at the Sherman House, the city's hotel. Carl Wylie Scofield, her husband, described as an "oil producer," was active in the oil fields of McKean County, Pennsylvania. (Federal Census, 1880; New York State Census, 1892; M. A. Leeson, *History of the Counties of McKean, Elk, Cameron and Potter, Pennsylvania* [1890; reprint, Bowie, Md., 1994], 93–94; Downs, *History of Chautauqua County, N.Y.*, 1:351; Daughters of the American Revolution, *Lineage Book* [Washington, D.C., 1915], 40:91–92.)
 2. Allen's Opera House was located at East Second and Pine streets.
 3. SBA tipped into her diary a notice in the *Leavenworth Times*, 11 August 1888, that her niece Annette Anthony (1883–1888) died this day at Mackinaw, Michigan, while on vacation with her mother. SBA described this child, many years younger than her siblings, as "a perfect pet of the household." SBA did not receive the *Times* until August 14, and it was August 16 before she received word of the death directly from D. R. Anthony. (SBA diary, 15 December 1883, 12, 14, 16, 22 August 1888, *Film*, 22:814ff, 25:869ff.)

SATURDAY, AUGUST 11, 1888. I took 8.50 train for Salamanca[1] & thence to Rochester arriving at 2 P.M.—to find all—Miss Thomson,[2] Lucy & Louise[3] & Sister Mary gone to the Lake— the weather is lovely—& the trip has been lovely—

 1. East of Jamestown in Cattaraugus County, Salamanca was a railroad junction where SBA could board a northbound train for Rochester.
 2. That is, Adeline Thomson.
 3. Helen Louise Mosher (1862–?), known as Louise, was the daughter of the late Hannah Lapham Anthony Mosher. SBA and Mary Anthony provided her a home after the death of her mother in 1877. When she completed high school in Rochester in 1883, she moved to Philadelphia, and by 1888, she had opened a private kindergarten. Her address in the city was that of Edith C. James, a widowed sister-in-law of the man Louise married in 1889. (Anthony, *Anthony Genealogy*, 185; Mildred Mosher Chamberlain and Laura McGaffey Clarenbach, comps., *Descendants of Hugh Mosher and Rebecca Maxon through Seven Generations* [Warwick, R.I., 1980], 312, 550; city directory, 1889; SBA to Sarah I. Cooper, 10 September 1888, *Film*, 26:891–94; *Friends' Intelligencer* 46 [June 1889]: 408. See also *Papers* 3 & 4.)

 ⚘ Excelsior Diary 1888, n.p., SBA Papers, DLC.

48 ARTICLE BY ECS

[13 August 1888]

PARTIES OR PLATFORMS.

There seems to be a broad difference of political opinion among thoughtful women, as to which party they should give the influence they possess. The key to the solution of this question is the comparative moral importance of the platforms they represent. To those who see the need of an entire social and industrial re-organization of society, on the basis of co-operation, all specific reforms, though tending in the right direction, seem fragmentary and unsatisfactory. But as humanity moves forward by these slow and solitary steps of progress, each earnest thinker must give her energies to the one she deems most important. In a critical review of the different party platforms, I find more promise of social re-organization in the Prohibition platform than in either of the others.[1] As tariff, or free-trade, is the chief vital issue of the two great parties in this campaign,[2] and as they are equally divided on them, some Republicans for free-trade, and some Democrats for high tariff, and as the arguments and statistics are so contradictory on either side as to puzzle the most clear-sighted, it is with a feeling of relief that the ordinary woman turns with hope to a party that proposes to attack the two colossal crimes of the centuries: the wrongs of woman and the vice of intemperance.

While there is no reference to woman, directly or indirectly, in the Republican or Democratic platforms, we have honorable mention three times of what most deeply concerns our interests, in that of the Prohibition party. In the sixth, eighth and eleventh planks, it demands suffrage for women, equal wages with men in the world of work, and uniform laws of marriage and divorce. Those who have had any experience in life's struggles, understand the bearings of these three questions on woman's freedom and happiness. She has felt the injustice of having no voice in the government, the hardship of unequal wages for equal work, and the slavery of the present laws on marriage and divorce. Marriage, instead of being an equal compact, is still made a condition of subjection for the wife, in a greater or less degree, in the different states of the Union. Homogeneous and equal laws for this important social institution are at the basis of all public morality. On these grave questions of individual happiness, the Prohibition party now proposes to give woman a voice. It recognizes our fundamental right to legislate on all questions in which our interests are involved.

Some say beware of the temperance hosts; they propose to put God in the Constitution; to make religious tests for nominees to office; to pass rigid Sunday laws, and completely overturn the secular nature of our Government. The Prohibition platform foreshadows none of these dangers. According to the sixth plank of their platform, the next person they propose to put into the Constitution is woman. When justice, liberty, and equality are secured to all the human family, then, and not till then, will the essential elements of the God-head be found in the Constitution. "If you love not [woman] whom you have seen, how can you love God whom you have not seen." I. John 4:20.

I notice that all the platforms alike, even the liquor dealers, declare their intentions of guarding the morality of the people. If these promises are fulfilled by all parties, the people will have reason to look for a speedy millennium.

Some object to the sixth plank because it leaves the question of suffrage to be settled by the state. They say to demand national protection for the liquor traffic, and leave the inalienable rights of half the people to the states, is an undue estimate of their comparative importance. Nevertheless the shortest way to secure suffrage may be by state action, through an enabling act by the legislature. It has been conceded by learned judges and publicists that the state legislature has the power both to limit and extend the suffrage. There are many instances on record in the history of the older states, in which they have exercised this power.

As the action of the Republican party has been retrogressive on this point in its judicial decisions, and the speeches of its leaders, it is fair to say they have individually and collectively abandoned the ground they took during the war, "That suffrage is a national question, to be protected by the General Government." Hence the Prohibition party occupies as high ground in the abstract as any other, and higher in the concrete, as it has taken some action on the question.

Women have had equal honor with men in their presidential nominating conventions. They were accorded seats as delegates, and as members of the resolution committee. They are welcomed everywhere, North and South, as speakers by that party, and considered important factors in the present canvass.

We have nothing to hope of the old parties, now rent with factions, in a struggle simply to save their lives. They are alike in the process of disintegration; as the Republican party rose from the ashes of the Whigs and Barnburners, as the radical branch of the Democratic party was then called, combining the best elements of both, so the party of the future, ready for other onward steps in civilization, is now in the process of formation.[3]

Just as the third party in 1848, bent on the abolition of slavery, held the balance of power, and roused the indignation of the people against that system, so the Prohibition party with its vital issues of equal suffrage, equal wages, temperance, arbitration for all national differences, and land for those who cultivate it, will hold the balance of power in the coming Presidential campaign, and in combination with other reform parties now looming on the political horizon will organize the new Liberty Party for the next generation.

No woman with a proper self-respect can longer kneel at the feet of the Republican party. We have patiently watched and waited for national action at their hands for twenty years, and as yet they have granted us nothing. They have simply played with our petitions and arguments as a cat does with a mouse, giving us neither "liberty nor death."

In the face of the fourteenth and fifteenth amendments, in every test case in the Supreme Court, we have been remanded to the state by Republican judges. Susan B. Anthony was arrested by Republican officials, imprisoned by a fiction of the law, tried by Republican judges, and was condemned and fined for voting a clean Republican ticket, under the provisions of the fourteenth amendment.[4] She has attended with other of her coadjutors, two of their Presidential conventions and asked in vain for seats in their conventions and a plank in their platforms,[5] and yet she preserves a childlike faith in the final justice of that party towards woman. She still points with triumph to the fact that we have twenty Republican votes in the United States Senate.[6] But what does that avail so long as in their conventions, state and national, they ignore the whole question and never suggest any measures for an enfranchisement. Like the old family clock in the corner they tick gently in their accustomed places, and strike once a year when shaken up with our annual Washington convention. On the temperance question the old parties propose no measure of relief. While liquor dealers are undermining the stability of both the home and the state, in their defiance of law and social order, politicians propose to license the evil and get the highest possible revenue out of the traffic.

In the dwellings of the poor, bloated monsters make the lives of helpless women and children a hopeless struggle with ignorance, poverty, and vice, while our palace homes are but so many stately mausoleums of human hopes; idiots, lunatics, the blind, the deaf, the dumb, shadowing every hearthstone.

While mothers give the hey-day of their lives to bring up sons for the state, surely fathers should make it their duty to see that our towns and cities are safe for them to live in, guarded by wise laws from the present dangers and temptations. If they have not the power to do this, then place the ballot in the hands of women, the reserve force in society, ever ready to unite with good men to enforce law and order.

~ *Union Signal*, 13 August 1888. Square brackets in original.

1. *National Party Platforms*, 78–79.
2. Tariffs versus free trade became defining issues of the presidential campaign of 1888 when President Cleveland devoted his entire annual message in December 1887 to the need to lower tariffs and thus put an end to government protection of wealth and capital. The Democratic platform endorsed Cleveland's view, while the Republican platform supported protection for American manufacturers against European competitors.
3. Barnburners, the antislavery wing of New York's Democratic party, helped form the Free Soil party in 1848, absorbing the earlier Liberty party, mentioned by ECS below.
4. See *Papers* 2 & 3.
5. ECS did not include 1888 in her count. For SBA's attendance at the Republican convention of 1872, see *Papers*, 2:499–502, 507-11; and of 1880, see *Papers*, 3:539–40.
6. A reference to the Senate vote on the sixteenth, woman suffrage amend-

ment on 25 January 1887. Sixteen Republicans voted aye, but, as Henry Blair reported to SBA, seven additional votes were paired and not counted. See *Papers*, 4:545-48.

49 ❧ FRANCES E. WILLARD TO SBA

Evanston, Ill., August 15, 1888.

Miss Susan B. Anthony, Rochester, New York.
My Dear Susan:—

I have heard from all except May Wright Sewell.[1] Not hearing from her for weeks, I can but think she has gone off somewhere for a vacation, and fear the address will be indefinitely delayed. You and Sister Thomas[2] and Sister Eastman[3] have dealt with me in great mercy.[4] I rather suspect that May will make hash of my manuscript.

I am sorry that there is one subject on which we do not at all agree, because on every other we seem to be almost of one mind and spirit; but I am confident some day we shall be in unity on this subject also. The only draw-back now is, that you have so plainly shown your preference for the Republican party, whereas if you had simply not come out for any, no one could have complained. It hurts us with the Prohibition party for you and Lucy Stone to take the attitude you have done;[5] and I only fear they may throw us off, for the conservatives among them are very fond of saying, "You see how little backing-up we get from the old liners," and it seems as if we are wounded in the hearts of our friends, which is the most trying of all experiences. If I say a word in public on this subject I know you will not take it as personal, but simply as the expression of my great regret that you feel it incumbent openly to stand with the Republicans. No matter how we may differ, we are always, I am sure, sincerely attached friends. Believe me, Ever yours most affectionately,

❧ *Frances E. Willard.*

❧ TLS, on Woman's National Christian Temperance Union letterhead, HM 10612, Ida Harper Collection, CSmH. Endorsed by SBA "August/88 about criticism of Call—"

1. Willard had circulated among officers of the new National Council of

Women of the United States a draft of the circular *An Address to the Organizations of Women in the United States*. At the council's founding in March, she was elected president, SBA vice president at large, and May Sewall corresponding secretary. For the address as published in November 1888, see *Film*, 26:965-66.

2. Maria Louise Palmer Thomas (1822-1907) was the widow of Abel C. Thomas, a prominent Universalist minister, and a woman whose wide interests included entomology, soil science, animal husbandry, criminal justice, and women's clubs. She was at this time president of Sorosis in New York City and treasurer of the National Council of Women. (*NCAB*, 13:602; E. R. Hanson, *Our Woman Workers: Biographical Sketches of Women Eminent in the Universalist Church for Literary, Philanthropic and Christian Work*, 2d ed. [Chicago, 1882], 301-10; *Business Woman's Journal* 3 [February 1891]: 48-49; *New York Times*, 16 February 1907.)

3. That is, Mary F. Eastman, recording secretary of the National Council.

4. See SBA to F. E. Willard, 12 August 1888, *Film*, 26:844-47.

5. Neither Lucy Stone nor Henry Blackwell urged readers of the *Woman's Journal* to support the Prohibition party. Blackwell saw no prospects for woman suffrage in the campaigns of 1888: "Woman suffrage, we are sorry to say," he wrote for the issue of July 14, "has not been made a direct issue by any party in the present presidential campaign. It ought to be made the main question, and all others should be secondary. But the fact is otherwise." In her most recent signed editorial on August 11, Stone detected disdain for woman suffrage in the Democratic and Republican parties, but saw no promise in the Prohibition party, which "cannot hope to elect their candidates." Suffragists "are still to toil on, trying to create the public sentiment which will compel the admission of their claim to equal rights." (*Woman's Journal*, 16, 23, 30 June, 14 July, 11 August 1888.)

50 ❧ ECS TO CLARA BEWICK COLBY

706 North 19th street N.Y.¹   Nov 2nd [1888]

My dear Mrs Colby,

Do not have a convention here until we have time to get up a good one.

I am told that the last one left so bad an impression with all Phoebe Couzins threats about her big father & brother, that it will take time to efface the memory.² We ought to have time to get good speakers & advertise &c

Then too people will be so tired out with political excitement that they will not care to hear us. As to Miss Anthony & myself we are "lagging superfluous on the stage"³ the times demand more finished speakers. I am tired of conventions & suffrage per see. I am more interested in other phases of the question, & desire to read & think on other subjects. The chief block in our way, those on our platform are not ready to attack. I feel more deeply than any other the religious bondage of woman, & would fain strike my blows at that   I am not in voice for speaking & find it hard to stand. All I ask now is what the poor devils in the scripture asked let me alone.⁴ I feel that I have a right now to sit in my easy chair & read & write. Don't have a convention here until I get some hold socially on the people With love yours

~ E. C. S.

~ ALS, on NWSA letterhead, Clara B. Colby Papers, Archives Division, WHi.

1. The address of Frank and Margaret Stanton Lawrence in Omaha, Nebraska, not New York. ECS arrived there at the end of September. Clara Colby hoped to take advantage of her presence in the state to invigorate the Nebraska suffrage association.

2. On this very public incident of ill temper at the conclusion of the Nebraska amendment campaign in 1882, see *Film*, 22:715–16, and *Papers*, 4:207n.

3. A common adaptation of a line from Samuel Johnson, *The Vanity of Human Wishes. The Tenth Satire of Juvenal, Imitated* (1749): "Superfluous lags the Vet'ran on the Stage."

4. Luke 4:33–34.

51 ~ ECS TO CLARA BEWICK COLBY

[*Omaha, Neb.*] Monday morning [5? *November 1888*]

Dear Mrs Colby,

If you are resolved on a convention, I urge you to invite some one on whom you can definitely depend. Do write Helen M. Gougar   I dare say she would come & pay her own expenses, & she is the most effective speaker we have. Would not Mr Poppleton¹ or Senator Manderson² speak in the evening at the Opera House.³ I feel that Miss Anthony is very uncertain & I know my capacity to speak is doubtful. I cannot stand to speak over five minutes & my voice is very husky. It has always been a pitiful sight to me when old people lag superfluous on the stage[4] to parade their infirmities & I do not feel like being dragooned into doing it myself. You need not be surprized if I leave town to escape the mortification   I know I cannot do myself nor the cause justice. Is it too late to postpone or throw up the sponge altogether? At all events have Mrs Gougar here, she would be some inspiration to me. Yours sincerely

~ *Elizabeth Cady Stanton*

P.S. Next to myself of all things I dislike to hear my beloved Susan

~ ALS, on NWSA letterhead, Clara B. Colby Papers, Archives Division, WHi.

1. Andrew Jackson Poppleton (1830–1896) of Omaha, who was known for his oratorical skill, had recently retired from the Union Pacific Railroad after two decades as its general attorney. A lawyer of national reputation, who argued numerous cases before the Supreme Court of the United States, Poppleton was also tied closely to Nebraska's history, beginning with his service in the territorial legislature in the 1850s. (*ACAB Supplement*; James W. Savage and John T. Bell, *History of the City of Omaha, Nebraska* [New York and Chicago, 1894], 570–72.)

2. Charles Frederick Manderson (1837–1911) of Omaha served in the United States Senate from 1883 to 1895. He voted in support of the sixteenth, woman suffrage amendment in January 1887. (*BDAC*.)

3. Boyd's Opera House, at the corner of Fifteenth and Farnam streets, opened in 1881 with a seating capacity of seventeen hundred.

4. See note above at 2 November 1888.

52 ~ ECS TO ELIZABETH SMITH MILLER

Portsmouth, Iowa, November 10, 18[88].[1]

[D]ear Julius:[2]

I have enjoyed Omaha very much thus far. Everybody has called on me, [i]nvited me to dinners, drives, receptions, theatres, concerts, etc., etc. [Th]ere are many charming people in this western world. Susan spent a day [w]ith us enroute for Kansas and will stop again on her return.[3] I have read ["R]obert Elsmere" and enjoy it very much. It is rather singular that an [A]merican and English woman should have written on the same theme at the [sa]me time. Did you read "John Ward, Preacher"?[4] It is strange that people [ca?]n feel so intensely on matters so speculative as any system of religion [ne]cessarily is. I was out of all patience with that silly Catherine. I [w]as glad the American author made the man orthodox and the woman liberal. [I]t is a great step towards woman's freedom when she gets rid of her [su]perstitions. Lovingly,

~ *Johnson.*

~ Typed transcript, ECS Papers, NjR. Letters within square brackets obscured by binding.

 1. ECS celebrated her birthday with her son Gerrit Smith Stanton, known as Gat, on his ranch near Portsmouth, Iowa. (*Eighty Years*, 416.)
 2. Since 1851, ECS and Elizabeth Smith Miller had called each other Johnson and Julius after characters in a show by the Christy Minstrels. Julius was the wit, while Mr. or Missur Johnson played the philosopher.
 3. SBA visited ECS in Omaha October 20 to 22 on her way to the annual meeting of the Kansas Equal Suffrage Association in Emporia and returned to Omaha to attend the Nebraska meeting on December 3 and 4. (SBA diary, *Film*, 25:869ff.)
 4. ECS contrasts *Robert Elsmere* by Mrs. Humphry Ward and *John Ward, Preacher* by Margaret Deland, both published in 1888 and both explorations of how incompatible religious beliefs affected a marriage. In Ward's novel, the evangelical Catherine marries a skeptical preacher. Deland's agnostic heroine marries a strict Calvinist. Mary Augusta Arnold Ward (1851–1920) was an English writer and antisuffragist, always known by her husband's name. Margaret Wade Campbell Deland (1857–1945) was a prolific writer in Boston. (*Oxford DNB*; *Woman's Who's Who 1914*; *New York Times*, 14 January 1945; "Theology in Fiction," *Atlantic Monthly* 62 [November 1888]: 699–706.)

53 ~ "WOMAN'S DUTY TO VOTE": SPEECH BY ECS TO THE NEBRASKA WOMAN SUFFRAGE ASSOCIATION

EDITORIAL NOTE: The annual meeting of the Nebraska Woman Suffrage Association opened in the evening of 3 December 1888 at Boyd's Opera House in Omaha. At seven o'clock, Amelia Bloomer and a committee of local women hosted a reception to introduce ECS, SBA, and Clara Colby. By eight o'clock, five hundred people had gathered in the auditorium to hear short speeches by Colby and SBA and, as the main attraction, a lecture by ECS. She spoke while sitting next to a speaker's table. (*Film*, 26:967-75)

[3 December 1888]

The exercise of the right of suffrage by woman is not a new idea in the history of nations. Women have voted and held office in times past in many countries as they are doing to-day.

Judge Charles B. Waite, of Chicago, has just issued a pamphlet,[1] showing the position of the original thirteen colonies, according to the language of their constitutions, on this question.

As the suffrage in these constitutions was not restricted to "male citizens," women possessed the right, and exercised it on various occasions in the different colonies. In New Jersey the women voted as late as 1807, when they were deprived of the right by an arbitrary act of the Legislature, without going through the form of a constitutional amendment.[2]

This idea of woman's political equality we inherited from the mother country, with her literature, her system of jurisprudence, and her principles of constitutional liberty. Women of wealth and nobility have voted and held important offices in England from time immemorial. This ancient right which had fallen into disuse was reaffirmed and reestablished, by the Gladstone government, by two acts, one securing municipal suffrage to women on a property qualification, and the other by the married woman's property bill, giving all wives the absolute right and control of their own inheritance.[3]

During the prolonged discussion of the last half century in this country some of our most able lawyers, judges, senators, legislators, and editors have declared that the broad principles of republican government must logically apply to women as well as men. And we are yet to see the first logical argument by the opposition. That women have the right to vote is unquestioned by all intelligent people who are governed by reason rather than prejudice, and this right is so far recognized by the present generation, that school suffrage is secured to women in twelve states of the union, municipal suffrage in one state, and full suffrage in two territories, though the constitutionality of the measure is questioned in one territory.[4] But the right is so far conceded that the debate on that point may be regarded as closed.

Hence, I propose to talk this evening to women *on their duty to vote*; to take an active part in government; to cultivate the virtue of patriotism, and thus stimulate their fathers, husbands, brothers, and sons to a conscientious discharge of their public duties.

The majority of men are so absorbed in the daily struggle for wealth that the most important interests of the masses are left to the management of a small minority of politicians. We need every influence we can summon to-day to rouse men to their duty. If women would use as much persuasion to get men to the polls and primary meetings, as they do to get them to the church, the opera, or evening parties, we should have better government. But women use no influence in this direction because they have no appreciation of the importance of suffrage for themselves. Many men never go to the polls, many more never attend a primary meeting, and many, right or wrong, simply vote with their parties, quite regardless of platforms or candidates. The consequence is corruption and imbecility in every department of government.

Our journals, like faithful watchmen on the towers, are continually warning the people of the danger of this apathy and indifference of good men to their public duties, but few heed the warning.

An editorial in *The Bee* of November 27, urging good men to attend the primary meetings and reconstruct your city council, shows the pressing need of rousing men to their public duties.[5]

"It is the duty of every citizen, whether he be republican or democrat, to attend his respective primary. He should see to it that only reputable and trustworthy men receive the nomination of his ward. This ought to be no idle appeal. The welfare, the prosperity, the future greatness of Omaha hang in the balance. Nine honest councilmen can infuse vigor and honesty in the city government. But nine boodlers can sink the city into corruption and hurry it into bankruptcy. It remains in the taxpayers' hands which of the two he will take. The exertions of a few hours at the primaries and the polls on the part of our citizens for the selection of men of character to the council will be worth more to the city of Omaha than all the endeavors made by our business men to attract capital and immigration."

This appeal from one who understands the situation is an admission of the fact that those who constitute the governing power of this city are not faithful to their trusts.

Now one reason of this is the ignorance of women in regard to questions of government and their indifference to all interests outside the home. There has been so much said and written on the sphere of woman, that she is as much afraid of getting outside the prescribed circle, as an Andersonville prisoner was of crossing the dead line.[6] To my mind the sphere of man and woman is the same, only with different duties in that sphere. Their life work is side by side. Men should take more interest in their homes and women more in the state. John Stuart Mill says, wherever the strongest interests of women are centered, there men will be attracted also.[7] If woman's desires and ambitions are limited to personal adornment and family aggrandizement, we need not look for much public spirit or lofty patriotism in the men of their families. If we would cultivate a higher political virtue in the men of this nation, women must be made to feel their responsibility in the success of the grand experiment of republican government. Woman has the same interest in good government that man has, and suffers equally from its mismanagement and corruption.

What should we think of a woman, who having inherited a splendid estate should through the inefficiency of a husband, allow everything to run to waste and ruin, house dilapidated, leaks in the roof, water in the cellar, lawn and garden overgrown with weeds, grapery and conservatory dismantled, fences down, orchards and woodland plundered, children playing in the streets and highways in rags, ignorance and vice. What should we think of a woman if under such circumstances, she imagined the sum of her duties consisted in being well dressed, always greeting her husband and friends with smiles on the threshold, and with occasional fasting and prayer cultivating a pious resignation to her misfortunes.

Sensible people would consider her as great a failure as the man by her side, and far more guilty, if possessed of ordinary common sense and executive ability. It would clearly be her duty to supplement if possible her husband's incapacity with her superior ability; to take the helm of domestic government, to repair the buildings, plant the garden, cut the lawn, protect the orchards, feed and clothe the children and transplant them from the highways to the schools, and when her rights were vindicated, her duties all fulfilled, it would be time enough to smile complacently and pray.

The religion of women is too often a sickly sentimentality, born of apathy and superstition, leading them to accept with patience their present condition, rather than meet the necessary friction in getting out of the old grooves of thought and action to conscientiously assume the new duties, that in this transition period, woman is called on to discharge.

The family is but the nation in miniature, and the duty of the wise wife and mother in the supposed case, is the duty of the wise women of this republic in the present hour. There is a large department of legislation that belongs specifically to women. Questions of education and religion, the sanitary conditions of our homes, school houses, jails and prisons, temperance, charities, the treatment of criminals, marriage, divorce, prostitution, the rights of children, and the protection of our domestic animals that cannot protect themselves. Our daily papers are filled with crimes of every variety and degree, that thousands of women weep and pray over in their homes, without a thought that they are in a measure responsible for their existence.

The question is often asked why it is that the moral and spiritual progress of the race does not keep pace with its intellectual and material achievements. I would answer, the moral and spiritual world belongs specifically to woman, and she is not yet awake to her duty in this realm of thought and action. The world of trade and commerce, of material wealth, exploration, discovery, invention, belongs specifically to man, and we can look with pride and thankfulness on the wonders he has achieved in the last half century. He has ploughed up our vast prairies, bridged our chasms, and with his railroads linked the Atlantic and Pacific, the Rocky and Allegheny mountains together. With his iron steamers and ocean cable he has anchored continents side by side, and melted the nations of the earth in one.

With his inventions and discoveries, the fable of Atlas and Hercules is more than realized,[8] the burdens of labor heavy on human shoulders for centuries, are now shifted on muscles of iron, and tireless machinery throws off the work of the world. The sun, moon and stars, the winds and the waves, that mysterious, erratic force in nature called electricity, are now all bridled and harnessed to do man's bidding. Like an eagle in his eyrie the clerk of the weather sits in the clouds, to warn us when the storms, the cold and hot waves are coming; when it is safe to visit our neighbors, and when for the laundress to hang out our clothes. The wildest dreams of fancy are now fully realized, the elfs, the gnomes and the fairies no longer waste their lives dancing by moonlight, but are active in the service of man. With an electric spark they illuminate our houses and streets, and carry our messages of business and pleasure hither and thither to the ends of the earth.

While the sun now in the blue-curtained attic of the photographer takes all the family pictures, and the telephone orders our dinners to be cooked by an unseen agent in the bowels of the earth, electricity adjusts the switches on all our great railroads and with steam we circumnavigate the globe. In fact man has accomplished all he ever proposed, with two exceptions. He has failed to find out the nature of woman, and the latitude of the north pole. Now I do not think I could throw any new light as to the voyage of the north pole, but I could help him in his researches as to the idiosyncracies of Eve's daughters. The key to the whole situation is found in the golden rule.[9] If man will simply accord woman precisely what he would desire for himself under similar circumstances, he will understand her nature as well as his own. Had woman fulfilled her duties in the world of morals as well as man has in the material realm, we should now welcome as marvellous changes in social ethics, in the progress of the race toward a true manhood and womanhood, in that inner life seen by the eye of Omnipotence alone.

Professor Fiske,[10] in his Destiny of Man, says: "We have almost reached the ultimatum of physical discovery; henceforth our work will be more and more the varied application of known laws. And now comes the period for psychical discoveries, in which woman will take an active part." Dr. James C. Jackson[11] says:

> Make woman intelligent and free as man claims the right to be, and is constantly striving to be, and you create and bring into existence for human good, a new and hitherto unknown potential element to be used in the management of human affairs. This new agent is spirituality. It answers in the world of mind to electricity in the world of matter. Like the latter, it is as yet chiefly known by its effects. From these it is inferable that as human beings are at present developed, other things being equal, its highest expression is through woman. Its manifestation is seldom seen in any considerable measure in men at large. Here and there among multitudes of men are to be seen individuals who possess it. Such men are remarkable. Their influence on

other men is indescribable. They are the men who remove mountains, and in the sphere of thought and sensibility build mighty fabrics that never decay. Emancipate woman, give her the freedom of her person and the ownership of herself, bid her take her proper place by the side of man as his helpmeet in the world's work, limit the use of her powers only by her extent of possession of them, and you make her the incarnation of this divine potency which is destined in due to time to change the face of the world.

When woman awakes to beauty of science, philosophy and government, then will the first note of harmony be touched, then the great organ of humanity be played on every key, with every stop rightly adjusted, and with louder, loftier strains, the march of civilization will be immeasurably quickened.

As citizens of this great republic we have an inheritance, unsurpassed in the history of nations, boundless acres, majestic forests, lakes and rivers, inexhaustible mines of wealth and the institutions of a continent, to make and mould to our will. In our Federal constitution, Declaration of Independence and republican theory of government, we have a magna charta of rights, such as the daughters of Kings and Emperors were never pledged. Andrew Carnegie,[12] in his Triumphant Democracy, has painted in glowing colors the grandeur of our present outlook as a nation, and the infinite possibilities of our future. Russia and America are the only nations still in the act of growth. The rest have reached the zenith of their power, and are looking toward the setting sun.

We are the only nation that has proclaimed the true idea of government. In the old world they have governments and people; here we have in theory at least a government of the people, by the people, for the people, to be fully realized as soon as women, one-half the people, are enfranchised, and the laboring masses know how to use the power they possess. In the old world, the palace on the hill is the home of nobility, here it is the public school or university where the children of rich and poor side by side contend for prizes for scholarship. Thus the value of character above all artificial distinctions, the great lesson of democracy, is early learned by our children. There is no excuse for ignorance here; the circulation of our journals and magazines is fabulous and so cheap as to be available to all. The Czar of Russia and the tories of England might learn from our experience that self-government and "Home Rule" are safe and possible, proved so by a nation of 65,000,000 of people.

Our institutions are being studied by leading statesmen in the old world as never before. Alike in the Chamber of Deputies and the House of Commons, the powers of our Executive, Legislative and Judicial departments have been discussed and recommended as worthy of adoption. Mr. Gladstone says: "The American Constitution is, as far as I can see, the most wonderful work every struck off by the brain and purpose of man."[13]

Lord Salisbury says: "The Americans have a Senate, I wish we could institute it here, marvellous in its strength and efficiency.... Their Supreme Court gives a stability to their institutions, which, under the vague and mysterious promises here, we look for in vain." Such writers and historians as Sir Henry Maine, Froude and Matthew Arnold, have all commented on our Democratic institutions, in most complimentary terms. Indeed the whole tone of English writers and travellers, has entirely changed, since they amused the world with the ridicule of our people fifty years ago. It is the dignity of the republic as viewed from this standpoint, that I urge the women of this nation to defend and maintain. You have an equal share to this rich inheritance and it is your duty to vindicate your rights. Would that I could awake in the minds of my countrywomen the dignity of this demand for the right of suffrage: what it is to be queens in their own right: intrusted with the power of self-government, possessed of all the privileges and immunities of American citizens. The ballot is the crown of honor and the scepter of power in a republic; by it our social, religious and political relations are all regulated. Are not the educated women of America as capable of wielding this power as Victoria of England,[14] and is not individual sovereignty in a republic as exalted as in a monarchy? What American woman would scorn the position of Britain's Queen? And yet the position of an American citizen is prouder far, if the duties of self-government are fully discharged. Whoever heard of an heir apparent to a throne in the old world abdicating his rights because some conservative politician or austere bishop doubted woman's capacity to govern. History affords no such example. Those who have had a right to a throne have invariably taken possession of it, and against intriguing cardinals, ambitious nobles and jealous kinsmen fought to the death even to maintain the royal prerogatives that by inheritance were theirs. When I hear American women, descendants of Jefferson, Hancock and Adams,[15] say they do not want to vote, I feel that the blood of the revolutionary heroes must have long since ceased to flow in their veins. When I heard that a body of Massachusetts women had actually been before their Legislature to beg that the women of the state might not be enfranchised, I blushed for my sex.

Suppose, when the day dawned for Victoria to be crowned queen of England, she had gone before the House of Commons and begged that such terrible responsibilities might not be laid on her, declaring that she had not the moral stamina nor intellectual ability for the position; that her natural delicacy and refinement shrunk from the encounter; that she was looking forward to the all-absorbing duties of domestic life, to a husband, children, home, to her influence in the social circle where the Christian graces are best employed. Suppose with a tremulous voice and a few stray tears in her blue eyes, her head drooping on one side, she had said she knew nothing of the science of government; that a crown did not befit a woman's brow; that she had not the physical strength to even move her nation's flag, and much less to hold the sceptre of power over so vast an empire; that in case of war she could not fight, and hence she could not reign, as there must be force behind the throne, and the force must be centered in the hand that governed. What would her Parliament have thought? What would other nations have thought? All alike would be astounded and said: "The girl is demented; the blood in the House of Hanover has run out." Instead, however, of making such a pitiful spectacle of herself, she prepared herself by study and reflection for the exalted position she was to occupy, and when the hour for her coronation arrived, though only seventeen years of age, she walked down the spacious aisles of Westminster Abbey, surrounded by the dignitaries of church and state, lords and ladies, and foreign diplomats, with a grace and dignity becoming the grandeur of the occasion. And there at the altar she took the oath "to support the civil laws, customs, and statutes, the laws of God, the Protestant reformed religion, the church of England, and promised security for the church of Scotland," the Archbishop of

Canterbury administering the oath, and placing the crown worn by a long a line of kings upon her brow. Thus she accepted her high honors with dignity, and the nation rang with plaudits for their youthful queen.

Neither did the burdens of government destroy her domestic tastes and affections. She no doubt enjoyed the attentions of Prince Albert as a lover, was as loyal to him as a husband, and as devoted to her children, and as happy in the round of her social duties as any unknown beauty in the most remote corner of the British Isles.

In the year of 1776, when our fathers sent forth their Declaration of Rights, booming at the mouth of the cannon, it was heard round the world, electrifying the lovers of liberty everywhere and making every crowned head tremble on his throne. And when later they issued our national constitution reasserting the broad principles of justice, liberty and equality, it was the coronation day of our virgin republic. Then government and religion clasped hands. Luther's[16] inspiring motto in the Reformation, individual rights, individual conscience and judgment, was reasserted, and has been echoed and re-echoed through the last two centuries.

Thus was humanity dignified, all caste and class, all bills of attainder, all royal prerogatives abolished, and the oath administered in old Independence Hall pledged the right of self-government to every man and woman under our flag. The time has fully come when the principles of our government must be vindicated. The moral necessities of the hour demand the direct influence of the educated women of this nation in government. The recent presidential canvass shows that men are quite ready to avail themselves of woman's help in emergencies, and she is equally ready to give it. There were women speaking on different platforms for different parties throughout the campaign. Women marching in the processions, too, carrying flags and banners, some adding enthusiasm to public meetings by playing on musical instruments and singing quartettes. Their pens have been busy, too, discussing the merits of different parties and questions under consideration. There has never been a time in the history of our nation when women manifested so much interest in an election. If all this interest could have been represented in votes the Republicans and Prohibitionists would have had larger majorities, and a far greater number of women would have been aroused to their duties as citizens.

I do not say that the possession of the ballot will revolutionize the nation and transfigure womanhood *instanter*, but it is the first step in that direction; it is the outpost to the temple of learning and power. To abolish all invidious distinctions of sex, will inspire woman with greater self-respect, and give her opinions new weight in public affairs.

To dignify woman, is to give our sons new lessons of reverence for the mothers of the race, for those who have gone to the very gates of death, to give them life and immortality.

The recent tragedy in our midst has its lessons of warning and wisdom.[17] As this case is but one among many thousands occurring in all civilized countries its special merits and demerits concern us but little. It is but the wreck of one man and one woman, but the causes that lead to such results are what we are bound to consider. The question for us to decide is whether the present status of woman in our social life is a true one, if according to Divine and human law there must of necessity be two codes of morals, one for man and another for woman.

Thus far we have had a distinctively masculine civilization based on the idea that society is constructed for the best interests of man alone. As he has been the dominant power thus far during the reign of physical force he has naturally in all his arrangements consulted his own tastes and inclinations. Our best legal authorities from Blackstone down to Kent and Story,[18] all take the ground that man and woman are not to be judged by the same moral code. This idea runs through all our laws and judicial decisions in all cases in which man and woman as plaintiff and defendent appear in our courts, and the popular sentiment in social life reflect these decisions.

Many jurists, says Kent, Vol. 2, page 88,[19] are of opinion that infidelity of the husband ought not to be noticed or made subject to the same animadversions as that of the wife, because it is not evidence of such entire depravity, nor equally injurious in its effect upon the morals, good order and happiness of domestic life. Montesquieu, Pothier and Dr. Taylor[20] all insist that the cases of husband and wife ought to be distinguished, and that the violation of the marriage law on the part of the wife, is the most mischievous, and the prosecution ought to be confined to the offense on her part. (Elements of Civil Law, page 254). Lecky, in his History of European Morals, says, Vol. II, page 283:[21]

> There has risen in society a figure which is certainly the
> most mournful, and in some respects most awful upon

which the eye of the moralist can dwell. That unhappy being who is scorned and insulted as the vilest of her sex, and doomed to disgrace, wretchedness and an early death, appears in every age as the perpetual symbol of the degradation and sinfulness of man. Herself the supreme type of vice, she is ultimately the most efficient guardian of virtue. But for her, the unchallenged purity of countless happy homes would be polluted, and not a few, who in the pride of their untempted chastity, think of her with an indignant shudder, would have known the agony of remorse and despair. On that one degraded and ignoble form, are concentrated the passions that might have filled the world with shame. She remains, while creeds and civilizations rise and fall, the eternal priestess of humanity, blasted for the sins of the people.

Such are the sentiments and opinions of men who are quoted as authority on this question, and yet these "high priestesses of humanity," while their profession is considered a necessity, have no protection in church or state, under the Canon or Civil law. Though the victims of men, they are hounded like wild beasts by men from one shelter to another, dragged into the courts, taxed by the state, robbed of their property, shunned by society at large, and left to perish on the highway.

While the women of wealth and position who shed tears over George Eliot's portrayal of such wrongs in "Adam Bede,"[22] and in Hawthorne's "Scarlet Letter,"[23] shun the hapless victims of our social system, they welcome the destroyer to their domestic altars.

Alas! the cheapest article of commerce to-day is womanhood. A vast organized company circumnavigating the globe has a profitable business buying and selling young girls in every market of the world, and like cattle the prices rise and fall according to the demand, now east, now west, now north, now south, according as the tide of emigration tends, or as new sources of wealth are discovered; they form a recognized fraction of the army and navy, alike in peace and war. When the terrible revelations were made in London three years ago, the world was startled with the iniquities in high places.[24] That was but a rift in the dark clouds that surround all womanhood, giving casual observers but a hasty glance into the world of misery and crime. Speaking from woman's standpoint of this dark problem, one remedy I see is the thorough education of our daughters for self support and financial independence.

Open to them all the higher advantages and opportunities of life; free access to the universities of learning, the trades and professions, the positions of profit, honor and distinction. Let us reverence the woman who honestly earns her own bread, rather than her who lives in luxurious ease on the toils of another. Virtue and independence go hand and hand. Alexander Hamilton[25] said long ago, "Give a man a right over my subsistence and he has a right over my whole moral being."

And while planting woman's feet on the divine heights of purity and peace, we must sedulously educate our sons into higher sentiments of chivalry and reverence for the whole sex. It is the duty of every man to treat all women as he would wish his own mother, wife, sister, or daughter treated. Surely if honor is demanded anywhere it is in the relations of men and women. If a gentleman in a game of billiards finds his friend cheating, he lays down his cue, and plays with him no more. If in business he finds him guilty of questionable honesty, he avoids all relations thereafter, but if a man enters home after home and despoils the daughters of the people, it does not close the doors of good society to him, nor lessen his chance of holding the highest position under government.

Ah! my friends so long as this is our moral code, we shall have the social chaos we now suffer, yea worse still, for in woman's transition from slavery to freedom, she will more surely year by year avenge her own wrongs, feeling that she has no protection elsewhere. The antagonism between the sexes is daily increasing and will until justice, liberty and equality are vouchsafed to woman.

And yet in natural conditions they are bound to each other by every law of attraction. It is this fine, almost invisible, cobweb of faith that men and women have in each other that binds society together. A faith though often disappointed and betrayed, that makes for the few a love and friendship that may endure through time and eternity. Whether for weal or for woe, woman must be an equal factor in civilization, hence she has a right to a voice in the laws that affect her welfare. From our standpoint we say, one code of morals for man and woman; and nature, by the terrible penalties she has inflicted on the race, for the violation of this law, has set the seal of her condemnation on the present system, and verified the warning given amid the thunders of Sinai: "the sins of the fathers shall be visited upon the children to the third and fourth generations."[26] This whole social problem is too vast for man to adjust alone; the interests of both parties most be equally regarded in any valid contract and surely in the one on which rests our whole social fabric.

Galton[27] says, the brain of man is already overweighted with the requirements of this intense civilization, and to meet the still more complicated problems awaiting his solution, the race must by some means be lifted up a few degrees higher.

Where can we look for this new force, but in the education, elevation, and enfranchisement of woman.

~ *Woman's Tribune*, 15 December 1888.

1. Charles B. Waite, "Who Were Voters in the Early History of This Country?" *Chicago Law Times* 2 (October 1888): 397–412, was reprinted as a pamphlet of the same title. Charles Burlingame Waite (1824–1909) was a Chicago attorney and writer who had served as a justice of the supreme court of Utah Territory during the Civil War and federal district attorney of Idaho Territory after the war. At the time of his move to Chicago in the late 1860s, Waite became convinced by the argument of Francis Minor of St. Louis that women were already voters, and he oversaw a test case originating in his wife's attempt to vote in local elections in 1871. In the article to which ECS refers, Waite reviewed the common law and statutory rights of women to vote in the original thirteen colonies and some states. "Next to negro slavery," he wrote, "the denying to the women of their right to the elective franchise which they had in England by the common law, has been the great political crime of the age." (*ACAB*; *United States Biographical Dictionary: Illinois Volume* [Chicago, 1876], 298–99; *Chicago Legal News*, 25 November 1871, 13 January 1872.)

2. On women's voting rights in New Jersey, see *History*, 1:447–51; and Judith Apter Klinghoffer and Lois Elkis, "'The Petticoat Electors': Women's Suffrage in New Jersey, 1776–1807," *Journal of the Early Republic* 12 (Summer 1992): 159–93.

3. By the Municipal Franchise Act of 1869, women who met the residency and rate-paying qualifications for men could vote in England's municipal elections. The act was widely described as "restoring" rights removed by a nineteenth-century addition of sex to franchise qualifications. Courts later limited the right to unmarried women. Women in Scotland gained municipal suffrage by separate and later acts of Parliament. By the Married Women's

Property Act of 1882, English wives gained new control over and protection of their separate property, but Parliament rejected language that would grant them the legal standing of single women. (Helen Blackburn, *Women's Suffrage: A Record of the Women's Suffrage Movement in the British Isles, with Biographical Sketches of Miss Becker* [1902; reprint, New York, 1970], 12–13, 91–95; Hollis, *Ladies Elect*, 1–10; Lee Holcombe, *Wives and Property: Reform of the Married Women's Property Law in Nineteenth-Century England* [Toronto, 1983], 195–205, 247–52; Mary Lyndon Shanley, *Feminism, Marriage and the Law in Victorian England, 1850–1895* [Princeton, N.J., 1989], 102–30.)

4. On states and territories with school suffrage, see note above at 26 March 1888.

5. ECS incorporated the editorial in its entirety from the *Omaha Bee*, 27 November 1888.

6. Union Army soldiers held by the Confederacy at Andersonville Prison were shot if they crossed the dead line, past which they came too near the prison walls.

7. ECS restates a key point in John Stuart Mill's "Subjection of Women," that the uneducated wife causes deterioration of her husband's mental activity. "He ceases to care for what she does not care for; he no longer desires, and ends by disliking and shunning, society congenial to his former aspirations, and which would now shame his falling-off from them; his higher faculties both of mind and heart cease to be called into activity. . . . [A]fter a few years he differs in no material respect from those who have never had wishes for anything but the common vanities and the common pecuniary objects." (Mill, *Collected Works*, 21:335–36.)

8. Ideals of human strength, Atlas supported the world on his shoulders, and Hercules completed the twelve tests of his strength that guaranteed him immortality.

9. Matt. 7:12.

10. John Fiske (1842–1901) was an American historian who used evolutionary theory to sustain a view of inevitable historical progress. ECS refers to *The Destiny of Man Viewed in the Light of His Origin* (1884), though she quotes from a different and unidentified source.

11. James Caleb Jackson (1811–1895) was the founding physician of the water-cure in Dansville, New York, and an old friend of ECS and SBA. ECS quotes from *The Outlook for Women, A Sermon* (Dansville, N.Y., 1888), 11–12. (*ANB*. See also *Papers* 2–4.)

12. Andrew Carnegie (1835–1919) owned the Homestead Steel Works that he later consolidated into the Carnegie Steel Company. He published *Triumphant Democracy, Or Fifty Years' March of the Republic* in 1886. This early edition paid little attention to Russia's rate of growth, but in a revised edition in 1893, Carnegie described Russia as the country's only economic competitor.

13. For the source of quotations from Gladstone and Lord Salisbury, see above at 26 March 1888.

14. Victoria, queen of the United Kingdom of Great Britain and Ireland and Empress of India (1819–1901), came to the throne in 1837. In 1840, she married Albert of Saxe-Coburg-Gotha (1819–1861), known as Prince Albert. ECS first wrote this fantasy about Victoria refusing the crown in an attack on the Massachusetts Remonstrants, women who petitioned against granting their right to vote, in 1885. Much of that article, "Republican Queens Abdicate Their Thrones," *Boston Index*, 2 April 1885, *Film*, 24:223–24, is incorporated into this speech from this point forward.

15. In a reference to leaders of the American Revolution, Thomas Jefferson is joined by John Hancock (1737–1793) and John Adams (1735–1826), members of the Continental Congress from Massachusetts. Adams was later second president of the United States.

16. Martin Luther (1483–1546), German reformer and founder of Protestantism.

17. On 17 November 1888, Elizabeth Biechler King stepped off the train from Chicago, checked into the Paxton Hotel in Omaha, located her husband's room, and shot him dead. She had learned from newspapers that Henry W. King, Jr., had taken another wife. The sensational case, that would not come to trial until spring, captivated newspapermen as a tale of conflicting moral standards. From Chicago, Harry King's wealthy parents defended their profligate son's reputation by instructing the press that the murderess was a known prostitute with no legal claim to the status of wife. In Omaha, that narrative found limited support. Citizens divided into two camps, described by a local minister as defenders of marriage who sympathized with the wronged wife, on the one side, and men of Harry King's type who wanted to see the criminal hung, on the other side. (*Omaha Bee*, 18, 19, 20 November 1888, 8 April 1889.)

18. Along with the *Commentaries* of William Blackstone, American lawyers relied on works by two American jurists, James Kent (1763–1847) and Joseph Story (1779–1845). Kent published *Commentaries on American Law* (1826–1830). Story wrote many books, including *Commentaries on the Constitution of the United States* (1833).

19. ECS quotes, with very minor changes, from James Kent, *Commentaries on American Law*, lecture 27, "Of the Law Concerning Divorce." In the fourth edition of 1840, the passage appears at 2:105–6. The parenthetical citation at the end of her quotation is within Kent's text.

20. Kent referred to Charles-Louis de Secondat, Baron de La Brède et de Montesquieu (1689–1755), citing his *Défense de l'Esprit des lois* (1755); Robert-Joseph Pothier (1699–1772), citing his *Traité du Contrat de Mariage* (1768); and John Taylor (c. 1704–1766), citing his *Elements of the Civil Law* (1755).

21. William Edward Hartpole Lecky (1838–1903), British historian, published his two-volume *History of European Morals from Augustus to Charlemagne* in 1869. ECS omits a few phrases from his paragraph.

22. *Adam Bede* (1859), George Eliot's first novel, is a story of frustrated love, illicit sex, pregnancy, and shame. Sentenced to death for leaving her child to die, Hetty Sorel is rescued by the child's father who has the sentence changed to transportation out of the country.

23. Nathaniel Hawthorne (1804-1864), American author, published *The Scarlet Letter* in 1850. Set in Puritan New England, adultery results in social isolation and eternal damnation, though Hester Prynne manages to raise her child and eventually move her beyond the reach of local condemnation.

24. In the summer of 1885, William T. Stead published a series of articles about the "Maiden Tribute of the Modern Babylon," the results of his investigations of the forced prostitution of large numbers of girls in London. (*Pall Mall Gazette*, 4-10 July 1885; Ray Strachey, *The Cause: A Short History of the Women's Movement in Great Britain* [1928; reprint, London 1978], 218-21.)

25. Alexander Hamilton (1755-1804) wrote in *The Federalist Papers*, no. 79, that "a power over a man's subsistence amounts to a power over his will."

26. Exod. 19:16, 20:5, 34:7.

27. Francis Galton (1822-1911), a cousin of Charles Darwin and a scientist in his own right, founded the science of heredity. ECS paraphrases his *Hereditary Genius: An Inquiry into Its Laws and Consequences* (London, 1869), 345. See also *Papers*, 4:174, 259.

54 ❧ ECS TO CLARA BEWICK COLBY

[Omaha, Neb., before 15 December 1888]

Dear Mrs Colby,

Be sure & get the sentence on the Connecticut & New York Legislatures right.[1] I copied it in the margin so that you cannot mistake. "<u>Party</u>" occurs so often substitute "<u>association</u>" I have linked some sentences that can go together. When printed on a sheet of paper such short sentences would look badly. Mr Lawrence[2] started for California this morning   Maggie & I are busy picking up the odds & ends after his sickness. Poor Maggie is completely tired out with all her care & nursing. When people violate law & break down their health, others beside themselves must pay the penalty. Thus the innocent suffer for the sins of the guilty, & the guilty think the innocent cannot do & suffer too much for them. Hence invalids are always exacting. In haste

❧   E. C. S.

❧ ALS, Clara B. Colby Papers, Archives Division, WHi.

1. With this letter, ECS returned a proofsheet of the call to the Washington convention on which her sentences about votes in the Connecticut and New York legislatures had been misunderstood. (See 22 December 1888 below.) Colby failed to make the correction, and the text in the *Woman's Tribune*, 15

December 1888, reproduced the error. In a subsequent letter, ECS instructed Colby to correct and reissue the call; "The point you lose entirely is that Democrats in Connecticut voted for woman suffrage & republicans against." (Call, 15 December 1888, and ECS to C. D. B. Colby, after 15 December 1888, *Film*, 26:979–81.)

2. Frank Eugene Lawrence (1848–1890) married Margaret Stanton in 1878. Raised in Council Bluffs, Iowa, he met Margaret at the home of Amelia and Dexter Bloomer. The couple started married life in Red Oak, Iowa; lived for a time in Council Bluffs; and were at this time settled across the river in Omaha, where Frank worked for the Nebraska Grain Dealers Association. Despite her stay at his house in October, SBA first learned of Frank Lawrence's illness when she had lunch with Margaret and ECS in Omaha on December 4: "Mr Lawrence ill—& going to California with his father & mother." He was suffering from Bright's disease. (Marriage return, New Jersey State Department of Health; Chicago *Inter-Ocean*, 22 June 1878, and SBA diary, 1888, *Film*, 20:295, 25:869ff; Federal Census, Iowa, 1870; *History of Pottawattamie County, Iowa* [Chicago, 1883], pt. 2, p. 37; Council Bluffs *Daily Nonpareil*, 19, 25 April 1890, with assistance of the Pottawattamie County Genealogical Society. See also *Papers* 3 & 4.)

55 ~ CALL TO THE NATIONAL WOMAN SUFFRAGE ASSOCIATION'S TWENTY-FIRST WASHINGTON CONVENTION

[22 December 1888]

The National Woman Suffrage Association will meet in Washington, D.C., January 28th, 29th, and 30th, 1889, at the Congregational church, corner of G. and 10th streets.[1]

Delegates from all the states are invited to be present. The question of uniting the two societies will be again under consideration, as the resolutions passed at the recent annual meeting of the American society, held at Cincinnati, demand some action on the part of the National Association. For this and other reasons a large gathering of the friends of this movement is desirable.[2]

For twenty years in succession these conventions have been held at the national capital, with hearings before committees of the Senate and House Judiciary, and able minority reports thereon, which have been extensively circulated throughout the nation and thus a great educational work has been accomplished. We see the effect in the gradual extension of the suffrage to woman, and a growing interest on her part in public affairs.

In the presidential canvass just ended, women have taken a more active part than ever before, and shown that they are by no means a unit on political questions. For the first time large delegations of women have marched with banners, in various processions, and spoken on the platforms of different political parties.

Neither among politicians, nor women themselves, is this in any sense a party movement. While the prohibition party incorporated woman suffrage in its platform, the Republicans of Kansas made it a fact by extending municipal suffrage to the women of that state. The Democrats of Connecticut on several occasions voted for woman suffrage while Republicans voted against it. In the New York Legislature, Republicans and Democrats have alike advocated and voted for the measure. In Congress the last vote in the House was eighty Republicans for woman suffrage, and four Democrats against it, and not a single Democrat voted in favor of it on the floor of the Senate. Both the Labor and Greenback parties have uniformly recognized woman suffrage in their platforms.

There are movements now in the political horizon pointing to the formation of a national party in the near future, combining the interests of labor, woman, temperance and other reforms. Our strength for future action lies in the fact that woman suffrage has some advocates in all parties, and that we, as a party, are pledged to none.

The denial of the ballot to woman is the great political crime of the century, before which tariff, finance, land monopoly, temperance, labor, and all economic questions sink into insignificance, for the right of suffrage involves all questions of personal and property rights.

While each party in power has refused to enfranchise woman, being sceptical as to her moral influence in government; yet with strange inconsistency they alike seek the aid of her voice and pen in all important political struggles, as shown in the late presidential campaign. While not morally bound to obey the laws made without her consent, yet we find woman the most law-abiding class of citizens in the community. While not recognized as a component part of the government, she is most active in all great movements for education, religion, philanthropy and reform.

The magnificent convocation of women from the world over, held at Washington last March, a council more important than any since the Diet of Worms,[3] was proof of woman's marvelous power of organization, and her clear comprehension of the underlying principles of all questions of government. With such evidence of her keen insight and executive ability, we invite all interested in good government to give us the inspiration of their presence in the coming convention.

      ❧   *Elizabeth Cady Stanton, Pres.*
      ❧   *Susan B. Anthony, Vice-Pres.*
  ❧   *Matilda Joslyn Gage, Ch. Ex. Com.*
    ❧   *Rachel Foster Avery, Cor. Sec.*[4]

❧ *Woman's Tribune*, 22 December 1888.

1. Though she managed to fix ECS's sentence about votes in the Connecticut legislature in this version of the call, Colby incorrectly changed the dates of the convention scheduled to begin on 21 January 1889.

2. At its annual meeting in November, the American association took up the terms of union proposed by the National association in the letter addressed to Henry Blackwell on 4 April 1888 (in minutes above at 3 April 1888). The delegates at the American's meeting renewed their commitment to "union, on equitable terms," but rejected the National's terms. "It was pointed out," Alice Blackwell reported, "that the National W.S.A. at its last annual meeting had elected about two hundred officers, more than double the number of the officers of the American W.S.A.; that the time set for counting up the respective membership of the two associations was fixed at a date when the National was swelled much beyond its usual numbers by the International Council, while the American had only its average membership; and finally, that the way in which the membership of the two associations was counted (the American voting strictly as a delegate body) was so different as to make any sort of joint ballot impracticable as long as they retained their separate constitutions." In a counter offer, the delegates acceded to the election of officers by a united society, rather than in advance of union, if a new constitution and bylaws were drawn up in advance and approved by each society independently. To this end, delegates authorized the president to appoint a new committee on union and agreed that a vote on a new constitution could be conducted by mail. They also removed Lucy Stone and Henry Blackwell from the negotiations. (*Woman's Journal*, 1 December 1888.)

3. In 1521, Martin Luther was summoned to this assembly of the estates of the Holy Roman Empire to defend his teachings. After hearing his defense, the diet declared Luther an outlaw and banned his writings from the empire.

4. On 8 November 1888, Rachel Foster married Cyrus Miller Avery.

56 ❦ SBA TO FRANCES E. WILLARD

Rochester—N.Y.   Dec. 31, 1888—

My Precious St Frances

Your lovely Sisterly greetings Card is just her—how nice of you to do so pretty a thing—poor <u>Quaker</u> <u>Susan</u> never dreamed of such doings to her dear friends!! But she loves them all the same, though!

Well—I did want to see you so much that week I was a prisoner in Chicago—but I could neither go to you nor invite you to come to me—for <u>my</u> doctor—the splendid Julia Holmes Smith[1] commanded be to keep still—<u>tongue</u> & all—and it was a real hardship

My cold is now lifting & loosening— So Richard will be ~~him~~↑her↓self[2] & ready to go to Phila. to see darlings Rachel & niece Lucy E. and thence to Washing—early next week—

Our Con. is to be Jan. 21, 22, 23, <u>for sure</u>—and in spite of Mrs Colby's unaccountable "<u>correction</u>"! of the dates— How I would love to announce you as one of our <u>star</u> speakers—but I know—so long as you lead your Church woman host—it would not be the wise thing for you to do!—but when you get ready to stand <u>for</u> <u>Suffrage</u> <u>pure</u> & <u>simple</u>—<u>apart</u> <u>from</u> <u>all</u> <u>other</u> <u>questions</u>—come <u>few</u> or come <u>many</u> of the white ribbon army—<u>then</u>, no one will rejoice—no one will hug you closer than this very "<u>Aunt</u> Susan"! But till then—she will rejoice with you in every step you in accordance with <u>your own</u> convictions of head & head—whether in accordance with hers—or not— She'll believe in St Frances—and wish her ever & ever so many new years for the best & truest work she is capable of doing—

With Love to your precious mother[3]—& darling Anna Gordon[4]—and the whole circle in ~~the~~ Rest Cottage—and ever & ever so many bushels of it to your own dear self   I am trustfully & gratefully

❦ *Susan B. Anthony*

❦ ALS, on NWSA letterhead, IEWT, from *Temperance and Prohibition Papers.*

1. While SBA lectured in Illinois, a bad cold progressed into a terrible cough, and when she reached Chicago on December 15, Julia Holmes Smith

ordered her to cancel future lectures and remain quiet at the home of her cousin Melissa Dickinson. Released on December 20 to take the overnight train back to Rochester, SBA continued a slow recovery to year's end. Julia Holmes Abbot Smith (1838–1930) completed her medical training at the Chicago Homeopathic College in 1877. She was a director of the Illinois Training School for Nurses, former president of the Chicago Women's Club, and woman suffragist, who would soon help organize the Queen Isabella Association. (SBA diary, 13–25 December 1888, *Film*, 25:869ff; *Women Building Chicago*.)

2. Adapted from Colley Cibber, *Richard III*, act 5, sc. 3. Richard revives "in arms, and eager for the fray."

3. Mary Thompson Hill Willard (1805–1892), a widow, lived with her daughter Frances at Rest Cottage, their home in Evanston, Illinois. (*American Women*.)

4. Anna Adams Gordon (1853–1931) was Frances Willard's personal secretary and companion. (*Women Building Chicago*.)

57 ❧ SBA TO OLIVIA BIGELOW HALL[1]

Rochester N.Y. Jan. 6/89

My Dear Mrs Hall

I have carried your good letter of Oct. 15/88—in my port-folio—ever since it overtook me in my wandering through four western states last Autumn—Kansas—Nebraska Illinois & Iowa— Because you said—"Please accept this <u>little</u> gift" ($100!) "for your own personal use"—my niece[2] and sister tucked the draft into my personal bank here— But I have made it a point—all my life—to pass all such contributions over to the treasury of the Society whose work I was & am trying to farther— I do this—because if ↑I↓ had ever accepted a tithe of the sums thus sent—lots of dear good friends would have been robbed of the <u>public acknowledgement</u> of their generous help to our cause— I know you say this—as do all others—because ↑of↓ your faith in me—that I'll use every dollar ↑to↓ help along the cause—and so I have & always shall—but there is no way I can use it better than through the <u>National</u> W.S.A. Treasury—except it might be—to have a fund upon which I might draw—to get out a 2^d Edition of the History of Woman Suffrage—that I may have a 1,000 or more sets to place in the leading public Libraries of the nation— The financial power to do that thing—before my 3 score & 10—& more or less—years are done—is one of my ambitions— But—alas—I shall go hence—when I go—no matter whether later or sooner—with mountains of ambitions to do the impossible, no doubt!! So unless—you send me your annual contribution to the National treasury—and command me to let the magnificent $100. you so kindly sent last October—remain ~~to~~ ↑in↓ my personal account for my History dream—I shall put it into the Treasury of the National—where I feel it belongs—unless you <u>positively</u> command otherwise—

How I wish I could see ↑you↓ once ~~once~~ more to chat over—the <u>Saints</u> of our W.S. movement— I go to Washington this week— Why can you not drop down upon us Jan. 21, 22, 23—and give us your wise counsel in the <u>conference</u> <u>about</u> <u>Union</u>—with Lucy Stone & Co— I told her—if <u>I</u> or <u>the National</u>—had ever <u>refused</u> to cooperate with her—or any one—I should feel that it would be <u>for</u> <u>me</u> to <u>make</u> <u>overtures</u>—but since it was <u>she</u> who had shaken the dust of us of the <u>National</u> from her feet—& gone off & formed a new society—the <u>move</u> to <u>join</u>—must come from her & hers—and so it does—but ↑it comes↓ asking us of the National—to surrender ↑our↓ name—and Mrs Stanton as our President—and make the <u>Woman's</u> <u>Journal</u>—that has for the whole score of years—either ignored us & our work altogether—or reported so meagerly & crookedly as to give its readers no just idea of ↑us or↓ our work—equally the organ of the Union—<u>with the Woman's Tribune</u>—that takes special pride & pains to do us full justice— The demands are indeed the <u>essence</u> of <u>modest</u> self-appreciation—

But I would so love to have ↑you↓ there with us to see & hear the overtures of the American Committee—and help—us to say & do wisely—We <u>never</u> <u>made</u> the <u>separation</u>—never felt there was any just cause for it—and now we must not <u>prevent</u> their uniting with us whom they ostracised—twenty years ago!! That is the way I feel—and yet—I am disposed to stand for justice to Stanton & Co. & the National—<u>now</u>—With love to Mr Hall & all the family Sincerely & gratefully yours

∾ *Susan B. Anthony*

∾ ALS, Olivia Bigelow Hall Papers, DLC.

1. Olivia Bigelow Hall (1822–1908) lived in Ann Arbor, Michigan, where she was active in local and statewide suffrage associations and frequently hosted ECS and SBA. She and her husband, Israel Hall (c. 1813–1889), were

founding members of the Toledo Woman Suffrage Association in 1869. Israel Hall ran a large nursery business and developed commercial property, which he continued to manage from Ann Arbor after their move around 1871. (Clark Waggoner, ed., *History of the City of Toledo and Lucas County, Ohio* [New York, 1888], 712; Samuel W. Beakes, *Past and Present of Washtenaw County, Michigan, Together with Biographical Sketches* [Chicago, 1906], 458; obituaries, SBA scrapbook 14, Rare Books, DLC; Patricia Bigelow, *The Bigelow Family Genealogy*, vol. 2, *Seventh and Eighth Generations of John Biglo (1617-1703) of Watertown, Massachusetts* [Flint, Mich., 1993], 77; *History*, 2:377, 4:219, 758; *Papers*, 2:419-22.)

2. It is not evident which niece was resident at Madison Street in the fall of 1888. Most likely, Lucy E. Anthony was visiting.

58 ❧ EXECUTIVE SESSIONS AND EXECUTIVE COMMITTEE OF THE NATIONAL WOMAN SUFFRAGE ASSOCIATION

[21-24 January 1889]

FIRST SESSION.

The usual order of things was reversed and the executive session held in the afternoon of each day, in the parlors of the Riggs House. In the absence of Mrs. Gage, chairman of the executive committee, Miss Anthony presided.[1]

Committees were announced as follows: *Nominations*, Miss Anthony, Mesdames Shattuck, Johns, Brown and H. C. Miller;[2] *Resolutions*, Mesdames Duniway, Hooker, Minor;[3] *Amendment to Constitution*, chairman, Mrs. Sewall.

After a discussion in which Mrs. Gougar claimed that the old committee on union held over with power to act, it was ruled that it did not,[4] and the following conference committee of thirteen was selected: Miss Anthony and Mesdames Hooker,[5] Minor, Duniway, Johns, Sewall, Perkins, Colby, Spofford, Brown, Blake, Gougar and Avery.[6] Mrs. Clay[7] asking that Mrs. Caroline Hallowell Miller be appointed to give the South better representation, Mrs. Colby resigned in her favor.

Mrs. Sewall moved a resolution "that in case an honorable union can be effected upon such conditions as will be accepted by the committee of conference and afterwards by a two-thirds vote of the executive session, union is desirable." Mrs. Hooker and others spoke against the resolution and it was not carried.

[22 January 1889]

Second Session.

The price at which the report of convention could be obtained was stated, and Miss Anthony urged the Saturday sale of the *Tribune*.

On motion of Mrs. Blake the time of speakers was limited to five minutes. The Basis of Representation was reported by Mrs. Shattuck, chairman of committee, discussed and adopted. The main difference between this and as it was afterwards embodied in the *new* constitution is that the Representation committee had carefully guarded the right of members to vote.[8]

Mrs. Blake moved a resolution relating to union, which was tabled by a vote of 32 to 16. The tenor of the discussion was that the executive session should not express an opinion on the subject of union of the two societies until it had listened to a report of the conference committee. Mrs. Duniway reported for the resolution committee.[9]

Mrs. Colby reported the work of the National Enrollment. Some names had been sent from each of the thirty-four states and territories. 65,212 names are in the hands of the superintendent, including the 13,600 brought from Ohio by Miss Sara Winthrop Smith.[10] Several vice-presidents present reported additional names, and it is thought the total number will not fall short of 100,000. The value of the enrollment being questioned, it was warmly endorsed after Miss Smith presented the beautiful enrollment prepared under the direction of Mrs. Southworth,[11] national vice-president for Ohio, and showed its advantages in state legislative work. It was decided to prosecute the work another year, making each vice-president responsible for the preparation of the enrollment of her own state. Enrollment headings and directions to be obtained from the office of the superintendent, Clara B. Colby, Beatrice, Nebraska, who will also take charge of names from states where there is no active vice-president.

[23 January 1889]

Third Session—Thursday Afternoon.

The report of the nominating committee was first in order. Mrs. Shattuck moved that we vote by ballot upon the principal officers. Carried.

Mrs. Elizabeth Cady Stanton was re-elected president, Susan B. Anthony, vice president; Hannah B. Sperry[12] and Sara Winthrop Smith, secretaries; Rachel Foster Avery, corresponding secretary; Jane H. Spofford, treasurer. May Wright Sewall was elected chairman of the executive committee, by a vote of 44 to 16. The minority vote was cast for Rev. Olympia Brown. The other officers were elected *viva voce*. As each state was called, members present from the state were asked to make nominations. The full official list will be published later. The committee on resolutions completed its report. Resolutions were under discussion at each session, and some of them were the topics of lively debate. They will be published in full in the next issue of the *Tribune*.[13] Mrs. Sewall then reported for the committee on Constitution and By-Laws.[14]

THURSDAY EVENING.

The first business was the hearing of the report of the conference committee which was in substance as follows:

Alice Blackwell and Rev. Annie Shaw had been present on behalf of the American Association, and had accepted the deviations made from the proposition as presented by the American, and felt reasonably certain that their Association would endorse their action.[15]

Name, etc.—The Association is to be called the National American Woman Suffrage Association. The annual convention to be held at Washington.

Chronology.—The next annual meeting of the joint society to be—as it would be for the National—the twenty-second annual Washington convention.

Work.—To be for National and State legislation protecting women in the exercise of their right to vote.

Representation.—As provided in the new National constitution.

Where two Associations exist in one State and will not unite, both are to be accepted as auxiliary societies.

An earnest debate followed. Miss Anthony threw her influence strongly in favor of union, which carried many with her, even some who openly expressed themselves that their judgment would be to continue the two societies.

Mrs. Colby moved that after the points had been considered, if the propositions were accepted by the executive session, the vote on the question of union should be taken of the entire membership in writing. Mrs. Colby maintained that the important questions involved in union should not be settled by the vote of the small number present for an Association of two thousand members. The motion was lost by a vote of 9 to 27.[16]

The vote was then taken on union, thirty voting for, eleven against. Mrs. Colby explained her vote against, by stating that she thought: *1st*, the Associations on account of difference of methods would do better work separately; *2d*, that absent members had a right to be heard upon this important question. Miss Hindman[17] said she voted "no" because she could not approve the constitution.[18]

After the vote was announced, there was some discussion as to its present effect. It was stated that if the union was completed by the American Association accepting the action of the committee, the National would carry on its work in its individual capacity until the joint convention. Mrs. Johns said she supposed this was the betrothal of the Associations and the wedding might be expected to take place at the next convention.

A letter from Mrs. Gage was read and referred to the executive committee.[19]

On motion, all unfinished business was referred to the executive committee and the convention adjourned.

[24 January 1889]

Executive Committee.

A meeting of the committee was held Friday afternoon, May Wright Sewall in the chair.

A letter was read from Mrs. Gage, giving the suggestions for work which had been furnished by members of the executive committee in response to communications.

It was voted to employ three women to act as national organizers. Names were placed in nomination and balloted upon. Those receiving the election were Elizabeth Lyle Saxon,[20] Abigail Scott Duniway, and Mary Seymour Howell.[21]

Committees were appointed as follows:
Credentials; Shattuck, Howell, Harper.[22]
Congressional; Anthony, Brown and Sewall.

Work of Organizers; Anthony, Spofford, Brown, Hindman and Avery. *Program;* Avery, Blake, Shaw.

It was voted to appropriate $500 for clerk of corresponding secretary. Roberts' Rules of Order were adopted for the Association.[23]

Mrs. Colby gave notice that at the next annual meeting of the Association she would present an amendment to the Article in the Constitution relating to the manner of electing vice-presidents for the National Association.[24]

All unfinished business was referred to the general officers.

↭ *Woman's Tribune,* 16 February 1889.

1. Matilda Gage offered different explanations for her decision to stay in South Dakota on a visit to her children rather than chair the National's executive committee meeting. In advance, she said she would be there "had I the money to go & come with," implying that the association should pay her way. After the fact, she explained "that at time of the Wash. Con. I was confined to a wrapper, from a Carbuncle on my back, which was obliged to be dressed five or six times [a day?]." (M. J. Gage to Harriet H. Robinson, 26 December 1888, 23 March 1889, Robinson-Shattuck Papers, MCR-S.)

2. That is, Harriette Shattuck, Laura Johns, Olympia Brown, and what is probably a typographical error for Caroline Hallowell Miller.

3. On this committee, Isabella Hooker and Virginia Minor were joined by Abigail Jane Scott Duniway (1834–1915) of Portland, Oregon, the preeminent advocate of woman suffrage in the Pacific Northwest from 1871 until her death. (*NAW; ANB.*)

4. Some details and emotions of the discussion about union that are lacking in Clara Colby's report for the *Woman's Tribune* can be supplied from a manuscript by Harriette Shattuck that served chiefly to document her efforts to derail plans for union. The few pages written in the form of minutes open with a record of discussion at this point in the meeting. "The proposition of the 'American' for Union was brought forward by Mrs. Blake (L D)   S. B. A. ↑who presided at all the meetings↓ said she would proceed to appoint a committee, as she supposed no one would question (her right) that was understood.

"H R S. asked who authorized her to appoint the committee. She understood that to be the proposition of the American and that they certainly would not instruct the National or its officers

"Johns of Kansas made the motion to appoint the committee as proposed.

"H R S of Mass. raised the question whether this Committee was to consider proposition of union & report, or whether it was to form a union and report. Discussed." (Shattuck notes on Union, *Film,* 27:24–59.)

5. A week earlier, Isabella Hooker wrote that she had lost interest in union because she saw no advantage to working with Henry Blackwell. In an editorial in *Woman's Journal*, 22 December 1888, he sneered at the idea dearest to Hooker, that Congress had authority enough to grant woman suffrage. (I. B. Hooker to William Lloyd Garrison, Jr., 14 January 1889, Garrison Papers, MNS-S.)

6. In addition to members named above, the committee included Sarah Perkins, Clara Colby, Jane Spofford, Lillie Blake, and Rachel Avery.

7. That is, Mary Barr Clay.

8. Colby's elliptical sentence about members' voting rights is all that survives of the report from the committee on a basis of representation. Despite Harriette Shattuck's years of service at the head of that committee, she omitted the discussion from her minutes. For the plan in effect at this meeting in 1889, see Appendix B in this volume. The decision about whether to allow an individual member to vote at the annual meeting now rested with her state delegation rather than with the executive committee.

9. Shattuck's notes on this second session begin: "Blake of N.Y. offered a resolution I that we unite, II that we instruct ↑the↓ committee to report a form of union. Nothing said of equitable terms.

"Blake was informed that her resolution↑s↓ must be submitted to Com. on Resolutions   She then changed it into 'a motion, in the form of a resolution,' and objection being made to second clause withdrew that, a large majority voted the motion down/ including most of the Committee (Sewall absent)."

Shattuck then recorded a vote of six yeas to thirty-one nays on her own motion to table something not specified in her notes.

10. Sara Wisner Winthrop Smith (1851–1902) lived in Ohio at this date, though her name is associated also with Seymour, Connecticut, where she lived in 1892, and Nantucket, Massachusetts, where she moved after the death of her father in 1894. In Seymour, she founded the Woman's Club, and in Nantucket, she founded the Goldenrod Club for girls, the Boys' Industrial Club, and a chapter of the Daughters of the American Revolution. She was an illustrator whose work appeared in many magazines and several books. Within the National association she was described "as a woman of rare executive ability," and rumors circulated that she might soon chair the executive committee. (Thomas Bellows Peck, *The Bellows Genealogy; or, John Bellows, the Boy Emigrant of 1635 and His Descendants* [Keene, N.H., 1898], 361; Jane C. Croly, *The History of the Woman's Club Movement in America* [New York, 1898], 309; Matilda J. Gage to Harriet H. Robinson, 26 December 1888, Robinson-Shattuck Papers, MCR-S; Nantucket *Inquirer and Mirror*, 4 January 1902, and *Woman's Journal*, 11 January 1902; with research assistance from Suzanne Gardner, Nantucket Historical Association Research Library.)

11. Louisa Stark Southworth (1831–1905), known in Cleveland for her philanthropic and woman's rights work, became active in the National Woman

Suffrage Association in 1885 and later also served as Ohio superintendent of the franchise for the Woman's Christian Temperance Union. Both ECS and SBA were her guests on many occasions. (Mrs. W. A. Ingham, *Women of Cleveland and Their Work: Philanthropic, Educational, Literary, Medical, and Artistic* [Cleveland, Ohio, 1893], 338–42; Cleveland Necrology File, Cleveland Public Library. See also *Papers* 4.)

12. Hannah Bassett Sperry (1841–1923), a journalist and typographer, moved to Washington early in the 1880s from Ashtabula, Ohio, with her husband and their two sons. Andrew F. Sperry, who published *History of the 33d Iowa Infantry Volunteer Regiment, 1863–6* in 1865 and edited newspapers in Iowa and Ohio, began work at the capital as managing editor of the *Washington World and Citizen Soldier* and later secured a job in the post office. In their new home, Hannah Sperry wrote Washington news for newspapers in several states, but she also became a reliable leader in numerous women's organizations. In addition to offices in the National association, she held the posts of treasurer and president at different times in the District of Columbia suffrage association, the District's Federation of Women's Clubs, and the Woman's National Press Association. (Pension File of Andrew F. Sperry, Military Service Branch, Record Group 94, Records of the Adjutant General's Office, 1780–1917, DNA; "Editor's Introduction," in A. F. Sperry, *History of the 33d Iowa Infantry Volunteer Regiment, 1863–6*, eds. Gregory J. W. Urwin and Cathy Kunzinger Urwin [Fayetteville, Ark., 1999], xvii–xxx; *Washington Post*, 14 August 1890, 12 January, 22 October, 9 December 1895, 14 January, 31 October 1896, 6 May 1923.)

13. See *Film*, 26:1076, for text of resolutions; no newspaper reported discussion of them. Notable are ones about common law voting rights, federal suffrage, and partisan politics. Before reiterating support for a sixteenth amendment in the fifth resolution, the delegates pointed to other avenues of relief, beginning with echoes of the views of Hamilton Willcox and Charles Waite about voting rights: "*Whereas*, Women possessed and exercised the right of suffrage in the inauguration of this government; and *Whereas*, They were deprived of this right by the arbitrary acts of successive state legislatures in violation of the original compact as seen in the early constitutions; therefore *Resolved*, That it is the duty of the several states to make prompt restitution of these ancient rights." In the next, delegates instructed Congress on its duty "to pass a declaratory act, compelling the several states to establish a 'republican form of government' within their borders by securing to women their right to vote." In the wake of several arguments during the convention about partisanship, the final resolution reasserted the association's position of nonpartisanship.

14. Omitted here is the text of the National association's new constitution and bylaws. See Appendix B in this volume.

15. Reference to the American's proposition seems to point back to the constitution sent by Henry Blackwell in 1888. See Appendix B.

16. After noting the committee's report, Shattuck recounted this discussion: "<u>Blake</u> of N.Y. moved that we 'unite under the name of the Nat. Am. W.S.A.[']

"Colby of Neb. moved that the vote on Union be submitted by a circular letter to every National member and answers received by a certain date determine the vote of the N.W.S.A.

"Blake withdrew her res. for Colby

"Long discussion, in which it was <u>shown</u> <u>that</u> <u>the</u> <u>advocates</u> <u>for</u> <u>Union</u> <u>had</u> <u>combined</u> <u>together</u> <u>and</u> <u>agreed</u> <u>to</u> <u>support</u> <u>each</u> <u>other;</u> <u>also</u> <u>that</u> <u>they</u> <u>were</u> <u>afraid</u> <u>to</u> <u>submit</u> <u>the</u> <u>question</u> <u>to</u> <u>the</u> <u>vote</u> <u>of all</u>. This <u>last</u> <u>statement</u> was made by H.R.S

"Colby's motion was lost by yeas 9, nays 27."

A motion to put the question to a vote of the National's members was unprecedented, however wise it might have been as policy. The association had always conducted business and elections by a vote of members present or represented at its annual meeting. Evidence about polling in the American association is confusing: at each step of negotiations, its leaders restated the fact that there were no voting members of that association. At the annual meeting in October 1888, delegates agreed to a future mail ballot on a new constitution, but they did not amend their existing constitution to enfranchise any individual members. When Henry Blackwell announced on 2 March 1889 that the new constitution "is now submitted to a vote of the members of the Association," he did not explain who were these so-called "members." It is possible that he chose his words to taunt discontented members of the National association. In a rare reference to a sort of polling that did occur, Charles and Catherine Waite were said to have received a copy of the new constitution from Alice Blackwell and asked what they thought of it. (*Woman's Journal*, 1 December 1888, 23 March 1889; Merk, "Massachusetts and the Woman-Suffrage Movement," 242–43; Matilda J. Gage to Harriet H. Robinson and Harriette R. Shattuck, 9 February 1889, Robinson-Shattuck Papers, MCR-S.)

17. Matilda Hindman (?–1905) of western Pennsylvania had worked as a lecturer and organizer for woman suffrage since 1872, sometimes in the employ of the New England Woman Suffrage Association and other times paid by state associations. By 1884, she was collaborating with ECS, SBA, and the National association. She was an early proponent of union between the rival suffrage societies and used her column in the *Pittsburgh Commercial Gazette* to publish writers from each group. (*Woman's Journal*, 26 August 1876, 6 December 1879, 1 April 1905; *History*, 2:819, 832, 849, 857, 3:241, 458–59, 461, 469, 522, 615, 622, 624–25, 719, 4:24, 61–62, 628, 970; Henry B. Blackwell to Lucy Stone, 26 August 1890, in Wheeler, *Loving Warriors*, 355; *Papers*, 4:383–84, 388–89.)

18. Shattuck's record of discussion leading up to the vote reads: "<u>Blake</u> then moved that we 'unite under the name of the N.A.W.S.A.[']

"Miss Anthony stated the motion, 'that we unite on equitable terms.'

"There was ~~some~~ confusion for some could vote for one and not the other.

"Anthony's motion taken with one dissenting (Miss Ward) H. R. S. and others refusing to vote on such a motion 'on the terms laid before us.'

"Then <u>Blakes</u> motion was put, by consent, in place of former motion, and a rising vote shewed Yeas 30, Nays 11."

19. In a letter read to the public session on Wednesday morning, Gage urged individuals to continue petitioning Congress for removal of their political disabilities, a tactic that she believed "compel[ed] thought upon the just principles of government" and showed fruit. (*Woman's Tribune*, 16 February 1889, *Film*, 26:1063-75.)

20. Elizabeth Lyle Saxon (1832-1915), a southern writer who helped to launch the woman's rights movement in Louisiana after the war, moved north late in 1879, and worked as an organizer for the Woman's Christian Temperance Union and a lecturer on woman suffrage. A frequent presence at meetings of the National association, she joined campaigns in Nebraska and Kansas in the 1880s. By then she lived in Tennessee and was named that state's vice president by both the National and the American associations. (*NCAB*, 16:207; *American Women*; Carmen Lindig, *The Path from the Parlor: Louisiana Women, 1879-1920* [Lafayette, La., 1986], 43-44; Marsha Wedell, *Elite Women and the Reform Impulse in Memphis, 1875-1915* [Knoxville, Tenn., 1991], 60-65; *History*, 3:956, 4:409. See also *Papers 3 & 4*.)

21. Mary Catherine Seymour Howell (1844?-1913) of Albany, New York, was both an effective lobbyist and strong lecturer whose abilities were put to use by state and national suffrage associations as well as the Woman's Christian Temperance Union. In New York, where her husband's job as state librarian enlarged her political connections, she was a well-known figure to legislators who consulted her about bills affecting women. As a national lecturer, she joined the campaign in South Dakota in 1890, delivering forty-five lectures in twenty-five counties, and she assisted the Kansas Equal Suffrage Association in its canvasses leading up to the amendment campaign of 1894. Three different birthdates for Howell circulated in her lifetime (1844, 1848, and 1850), and none appears on her gravestone. An obituary described her as born "sixty odd years ago." (*American Women*; *WWW1*; "Mary Seymour Howell," Rochester Regional Library Council website, *Western New York Suffragists: Winning the Vote*; *History*, 4:839-73; Elizabeth Murray Wardall, "Woman Suffrage in South Dakota," p. 9, *Film*, 28:871ff; with assistance of Terry Mistretta, Mount Morris, N.Y.)

22. Ida A. Husted Harper (1851-1931), a journalist from Indiana, became secretary of the National Woman Suffrage Association of Indiana at the time of its organization in 1887 and was making her first appearance at a meeting of the National association. She later became famous as SBA's biographer. (*NAW*; *ANB*; *History*, 4:615.)

23. Henry M. Robert, *Pocket Manual of Rules of Order for Deliberative*

Assemblies, was first published in 1876 and gained wide popularity in the final decades of the nineteenth century as a national standard for the conduct of meetings. On its impact, see Don H. Doyle, "Rules of Order: Henry Martyn Robert and the Popularization of American Parliamentary Law," *American Quarterly* 32 (Spring 1980): 3-18.

24. The National's new constitution designated the president of any state auxiliary society to be a vice president of the National. The National's president retained the power to name a vice president for a state without an auxiliary. To critics of the constitution, the advent of ex officio vice presidents, elected at the state rather than national level, weakened the National association.

59 ECS TO THE HARTFORD EQUAL RIGHTS CLUB

Omaha, Neb., February 1, 1889.

The discussion in your club as to the duties of mothers to themselves and children is timely and interesting.[1] Every brave, well organized woman with an ordinary sense of justice and love of liberty must utterly repudiate the teaching of the Rev. Knox Little[2] on marriage, and that of the moralist in the "Christian Union"[3] as to the rights of fathers. (Knox Little says no woman should ever oppose her husband under *any* circumstances.) The idea that a wife under no circumstances should seek a divorce, nor defend her children against the cruelty of a father, is out of harmony with all the lessons of human rights taught by the fundamental principles of republican government. America has illustrated the possibility of a state without a king, a church without a Pope, a currency without a gold basis, and a family without a divinely ordained head. Individual rights, individual conscience, judgment, are the soul and center of our government and religion. The family unit with man's headship, received its death-blow when the women of this republic repudiated the old common law of England and demanded in the several States their personal and property rights.

The status of a woman is no longer that of a slave, but an equal. Self-development for her is a higher duty than self-sacrifice in this age of individual responsibility. To live with a man who treats his wife with cruelty and contempt, and for whom she can have neither love nor respect, is to degrade the institution of marriage, to destroy her self-respect, and to reproduce in the children the hatred for the father she herself feels.

If all men had "the three necessary elements of sovereignty" as defined by Blackstone,—"wisdom, goodness and power,"—they might be trusted with absolute government in the family.[4] But inasmuch as they have not, being ignorant of human nature, selfish, unreasonable and passionate, it is not safe to back their superior brute force with the authority of law and gospel.

I think the natural impulse of every true mother is to defend her children against harm at all hazards. What a picture to behold—a mother calmly seated with folded hands while a trembling little child is being kicked and cuffed by a brutal man; the child so frightened and confused that it cannot understand the point of resistance or obedience! This conception may please the artist of the "Christian Union," but I should turn from it in disgust. It does not lessen the shock to a compassionate heart to know the man is the child's father, but intensifies four fold our surprise and condemnation that he who should be a shield and protection against all danger and oppression to those under his care, should be such an arrant traitor to his trust, and become the one enemy to be feared above all others in the family. No! no! this cannot be morality in our civilization. Parents have tried to whip the cardinal virtues into their children long enough; now let us try moral suasion and good example. Yours ever,

~ *Elizabeth Cady Stanton.*

~ *Hartford Times*, 18 February 1889, in Hartford Equal Rights Club Records, 1885-1919, Minute Book 1; Archives, History and Genealogy Unit; Ct.

1. Since its founding in 1885, the Hartford Equal Rights Club occasionally asked ECS to provide a letter that would be the basis for discussion. Though the minutes of the biweekly meeting on 16 February 1889 indicate that F. Ellen Burr read the letter, no discussion of it is recorded. Burr, the club's corresponding secretary, published the letter in her report of the meeting for the *Hartford Times*. The club was Connecticut's principal society for discussions and education about women's rights. (*History*, 3:338; *Papers*, 4:411-15, 496-98, and *Film*, 24:226-28, 969-71.)

2. William John Knox-Little (1839-1918), a popular Anglican preacher and High Churchman who frequently riled some American women with his pronouncements on their duties, spent several weeks of December 1888 preach-

ing in New York City. According to a clipping reproduced in the *History of Woman Suffrage*, he preached during his trip in 1880 that wives owed "the duty of unqualified obedience" to their husbands. "It is her duty to subject herself to him always, and no crime that he can commit can justify her lack of obedience." (*DNB*; *New York Times*, 3, 9 December 1888, 6 January 1889; *History*, 1:782, 3:471-72; *Papers*, 4:252, 397.)

3. The *Christian Union*, once the paper of Henry Ward Beecher, was a journal of opinion with wide circulation, edited by Lyman Abbott, a firm believer in the duty of wives to mold their lives to their husbands'.

4. William Blackstone, *Commentaries on the Laws of England in Four Books* (New York, 1841), 1:33.

60 ~ SBA TO OLYMPIA BROWN

Leavenworth, Kansas,[1] March 11, 1889

My Dear Olympia

Your several letters relative to the <u>unsigned</u> check found me in my wanderings a three weeks since—and your Postal Card is also received—saying the two $25. Drafts were duly received— So far—so good—

Then—also—I have before me your good word of sympathy & hope of the future—on the reading of the sad & fatal accident to my darling niece Susie B. ↑which occurred↓ just four weeks ago this very afternoon[2]—and last night—I slept alone—in the very bed—in ↑which↓ <u>she slept with Aunt Susan</u>—the last night I was here last Autumn—the 16th of October November—it was—and on the morning that I left at 8 Oclock, she drove me to the R.R. Station— She had a gentle horse & ↑nice↓ buggy—and drove alone—or with a school-mate—or Mama or sister—every day after school—and she was so bright that morning—& so proud showing off her skill in driving—but alas that fatal ice pond— & the <u>last</u> <u>skate</u> on it—[3] She is no more here— She looked at rest— when we last saw the blanched-cold face—it was & is too cruel—but it is ↑one↓ of the inevitable things that must be submitted to— She was 16 years & five months old—and five feet six inches tall— She didn't <u>walk</u>—she <u>skipped</u> & <u>danced</u>— My hopes were set on her making a splendid womanly woman of great independence & power— But they are dashed to the earth— No my dear—I know of no change in my ideas of the present or future life— Instinctively—I feel that the <u>vital</u> <u>thing</u>— <u>the breath</u>—<u>the spirit</u>—the <u>something</u> that <u>thinks</u> & <u>feels</u>—<u>enjoys</u> & <u>suffers</u>—<u>must</u> <u>survive</u> the <u>part</u> <u>that</u> <u>decays</u>—before our eyes but how or where it exists—I know not—and none of the various theories have ever made feel that I <u>knew</u>!! So I have always been—& still am—content to trust—as my dear & noble & good father[4] said on his dying bed—that "the same power that orders all things well for the children of this life— will do the same for them in the next"— Whatever is the next—will be right—will be the inevitable—be it what & how it may— But I cannot like our dear Isabella—see & know—as it were face to face—the <u>spirits</u> of my departed loved ones—[5] I shall have to wait <u>certain</u> <u>knowledge</u> until I go hence—as I fear all others will have to— No! no! my dear Olympia—I have not changed my views—and I do not know as I should be any the happier & better if I had or could change them— I am content to do all I can to make the conditions of this life better for the next generation to live in—assured that right living here is not only the best thing for me & the world here—but the best possible fitting for whatever is to come in the hereafter— I suppose your feeling of my change—is the same as that of Mrs Gage & Mrs Stanton—that is because I am not as <u>in</u>tolerant of the ↑so called↓ <u>Christian</u> <u>women</u>—as are they—that therefore I have gone—or am about to go over ↑to↓ the the popular church— I do not approve of their system of fighting ↑the↓ religious dogmas of the people I am trying to convert to my doctrine of equal rights to women— But if they can afford to distrust my religious integrity—I can afford to let them— But what matters it—our puny notions of things—dont—can't make or change one fact of the universe— I believe—<u>absolutely</u> in <u>law</u>— and that there is no mortal of us that can escape the penalty of any violation of law!!

 As to the Proposal for Union—I do not pretend to fathom the motive of the Stone-Blackwell firm in allowing it to be made—but I do now know—as I have felt from the beginning that it would be <u>suicide</u> to us of the National to <u>flatly</u> <u>reject</u> <u>the</u> <u>proposal</u>—because to do so—would place the National & its leaders in precisely the same position that the American & Stone-Blackwell have held for their 20 years & more—and which has proved so disastrous to them that they are bound to get out of it— They have always been on the <u>defensive</u>—compelled forever to show cause why they didn't & nobody else should—stand on our

National platform & work side by side with those women—Stanton & Co— they haven't gotten ahead with the people just because of their refusal to cooperate with us— While we, ↑were↓ all all the time— declaring ourselves perfectly willing to work with them—inviting them from year to year through all of their naughtiness—have gone on from triumph to triumph—until they see & feel & want to share our glory & power— Of course, what they expected—perchance hoped—was that we in our pride of success would refuse to unite with them—or to permit them to come under the aegis of our National—but I saw from the first—that our true position was that of cheerful welcome to the proposal—and I still believe it to be the right attitude— But I do want all of our women—especially you—& Mrs Hooker—& all of the women ↑who↓ know of the true inwardness of the Stone Blackwell twain—to be on hand ↑at↓ our next annual Wash. Con. to stand firm as a rock for perfect freedom in the Union & for Mrs Stanton as President of it.

If the Nationals should fail to be fully represented at our 22^d Wash. Con. or being there—should vote for any other woman for President than Mrs Stanton—I shall feel sadly—not because of the Union—but because of our own womens lack of loyalty to the one woman living who started—or called the 1st Con. and who has made it possible through all these years of struggle for me to be & ↑to↓ do the little I have been able to— I hear that even Lucy Stone has brought herself down to being willing—or at least not to rebel—if Miss Anthony should be elected Pres—but that she & others will never submit to be over ↑under↓ Mrs Stanton as President— And because of this very fact—I want the test made at the very first moment of the attempted Union!— Then if any wont stand it—let them secede again—then will come the odium to them that wont work with the majority—that is all will be as ↑there will be↓ nothing but reproach for those who ↑shall↓ go on the "rule or ruin" principle—

Now—my dear I do ↑not↓ want you to tell ↑any one of↓ all these thoughts of mine—but I feel sure—there will come a revolt—if Mrs Stanton shall be elected—and hence—I want them to have a second chance to show themselves to be the ones who wont submit to the wish & will of the Majority— I want them caught in their ↑own↓ trap— that is—

And yet—you know—there is a possibility that the "Leopard has changed his spots"⁶—and that they have resolved to <u>abide by majority-rule</u>— I hope they are changed— But the best evidence they can give us—will be submission to the overwhelming election of Mrs Stanton!!

Now—keep this to yourself—& plan to be on hand with a strong vote behind you— I havent heard a lisp from Alice since she left Washington—but we shall see what we shall see— All I want is for us to do the <u>fair thing</u> & that openly— Lovingly yours—

~ *Susan B. Anthony*

~ ALS, on stationery imprinted with address, Olympia Brown Papers, MCR-S.

1. SBA arrived in Leavenworth on this date after lecturing in Arkansas and Missouri.

2. Susie B. Anthony (1872-1889) and a high school classmate, Edwin Pierce, drowned when the ice gave way on a pond where they were skating with friends after school on February 11. SBA learned of the accident while on the train from Cincinnati to St. Louis and proceeded to Leavenworth. Although little evidence survives of SBA's connection to her namesake, in his funeral sermon on February 14, the family's minister chose to speak directly to SBA's loss. "As a mother's hopes and ambitions and expectations are bound up in a child of especial promise, so Miss Anthony was waiting for her heart longing to be realized in Susie. Away from each other much of the time, yet ever remembered and in constant communication. A mutual bond, a mutual taste, a mutual sympathy held them as one in loving bands. But Susie is gone; yet in her busy life the aunt shall ever feel the old heart throb, the tender affection; for to her shall the Master say in words of exquisite blessing, 'Not dead; not dead; only sleeping.'" (Clippings, SBA scrapbook 14, Rare Books, DLC; SBA diary, 1 December 1890, and 11-15 February 1892, *Film*, 27:679ff, 29:655ff.)

3. On these events, some of them noted after the fact, see SBA diary, 23-26 October, 12, 15, 18 November 1888, *Film*, 25:869ff. Susie was the daughter of Anna E. Osborne Anthony (1845-1930), who married Daniel Read Anthony in 1864. (Anthony, *Anthony Genealogy*, 185; *U.S. Biographical Dictionary: Kansas Volume*, 56-63; biographical files, KHi. See also *Papers* 1-4.)

4. Daniel Anthony (1794-1862).

5. On Isabella Hooker's spiritualism, see Barbara A. White, *The Beecher Sisters* (New Haven, Conn., 2003).

6. Adapted from Jer. 13:23.

61 ❧ Speech by SBA to Women's Meeting in Leavenworth, Kansas

EDITORIAL NOTE: While SBA returned to lecturing after her niece's funeral, women in Leavenworth prepared for the municipal election on April 2. Because state law required that voters register each year, a campaign to get eligible voters registered before the March 22 deadline was the first step. On 7 March 1889, at a meeting open to all interested women, the work of canvassing the city's six wards to register voters was assigned to ward committees, and coordination of effort with African-American women was assigned to a special committee. Finally, the group agreed that an address "to the ladies of Leavenworth" by SBA should launch their registration drive, and they asked the chairwoman of the First Ward Committee to extend the invitation. For the event in the afternoon of March 13, women and a few men filled Chickering Hall. The *Leavenworth Times* described its report of SBA's speech as a synopsis. (*Leavenworth Times*, 8 March 1889.)

[13 March 1889]

Mrs. President[1] and Ladies: This is the first time I have been called upon to address an audience of women who are in possession of the right of suffrage and to speak to them upon their duties in the exercise of that right. For over forty years I have been addressing men and women pleading for this boon—this inestimable boon for women. For forty years the women have been pressing, urging and demanding a practical application of the principles of our government to the condition of women.

I am at a loss how to begin or what I shall say to the women who possess a right of which I am deprived, living as I do in the state of New York. Once and twice you have exercised this right in municipal elections. For the third time you are called upon to exercise this right, this inalienable right, this political privilege (whatever you may call it), this sign and token of citizenship in this American republic and under this American flag.

No one not possessed of this right of suffrage is considered a citizen with an equal share in all privileges of citizenship. No man is denied this right, by which all other rights are protected, without reason. He must be either an idiot or a criminal. One-half of our people, without being either idiots or criminals, have been denied this right.

The legislature of Kansas has removed this bar, and given the women of your state a right to vote in municipal elections. The Republican party, by a strict party vote, extended this right to you. The Democratic party has supported neither the prohibitory nor the suffrage law. But when any class is in possession of this right, every party will make haste to put itself in line with that class.

I remember when the law was passed, that judges and men in influential positions took pains to ascertain what laws the women would like to have enacted and to what laws they were opposed. It is not until women have the right to make and unmake laws that they are of any political significance.

You can all vote. You all believe you ought to vote. Since in your city I have seen a good many things in which you are or ought to be vitally concerned. There is nothing in the details of municipal government, the streets, schools, laws, etc., which any woman cannot help to change. If she does not, she is to blame for mismanagement. The right of suffrage is a wonderful power.

Why do you have in Kansas 283 chartered cities, while in New York we have but 23? I want to give you a little history on this point. In 1867 the Kansas legislature passed a law allowing women to sign, or withhold signature to, saloon licenses.[2] A license could not be issued without the consent of half the women of any locality. Mrs. Stanton and myself passed through your state that year (1867). As we traveled every man we met said this law was utterly prohibitory in its effect. The women would not sign.

While this was true in rural districts, in the cities the law was a dead letter, because the officers being elected by men, ignored the law requiring the consent of the women. But it did not stop here. The obnoxious provision was an annoyance to the liquor men, who went to the legislature and secured the passage of an act exempting cities of the first and second classes from this requirement. They capped the climax by afterwards getting an act creating every city of 250 inhabitants a city of the third class and exempting such cities also.[3]

The liquor traffic to save its life from the touch of woman's hand disfranchised her. So that the control of affairs relapsed to the man.

Then came the prohibitory law, successful in rural districts but a dead letter in cities. The men elected to office were not anxious to have the law enforced. But we are witnessing an application of the old saying, "He who seeks to save his life shall lose it." The women of today have actually the power to dispose of this question.

When you had no rights, no power to say yea or nay, you had no duty, no responsibility. But from that hour when the legislature conferred upon you rights and power to say yea or nay, your duty and your responsibility began. If there is a city or settlement in the state where the law is not enforced, it is the fault of the women as much as of the men. New rights bring new duties.[4]

Not only have you power over the liquor traffic but there are other sinks of iniquity in this city, as there are in every city in the nation and in the world. There are brothels and gambling houses. You have plenty of law but not enough exercise of it. You have the power to shut up every brothel and gambling hall as well as every grogshop. You cannot say it is the duty of the men alone. The women in Kansas must exercise their rights and not wait for the men.

I know how hard it will be. It will be a hundred years before the women are educated to a full feeling of the responsibility resting upon them. Having the right to vote, you have the responsibility thrown upon you first, to exercise that right and set a good example.

I have told you how adroitly the liquor interest got rid of women and how now the women have the power of which they were once deprived. I wonder how many here today have registered and [are] ready to vote for the best party and the best men and women. I shall not ask you to stand up for I have heard how many registered and not many here would stand up, but all who have registered are here without doubt.

I would like to have some woman here who is indifferent on this question to tell me what she thinks is her duty as a citizen of Leavenworth.

I remember being at the seashore two years ago and meeting a Leavenworth lady. I told her I supposed she had voted. She replied that until too late she had not thought it of any importance to register, but that she deeply regretted not having done so, as the tide was turned by a very narrow margin. You do not know but that your vote may turn the tide.

The world doesn't care whether the men vote or not. They have the right and nothing can deprive them of it. But it does care whether you vote.

I remember after the election of last September in this state, in which 28,000 ladies had voted, our senior senator said in a great speech at Abilene that he did not know of any respectable body of women who had voted at all or who would vote, if able, for president. We have lots of such men.[5]

The women of the east are looking to the women of Kansas. Much rests upon you and I appeal to you to vote whether you want to vote or not. Vote because it is your right as a citizen. Did you ever think what it is to vote? The law which gave you that right said to each of you that your judgment was sound and your opinion worthy to be counted.

I live where disfranchisement is my portion, where the law says to me, "your judgment is not sound and your opinion is not worthy to be counted." I wish every woman could feel the crown of glory which is upon you by virtue of possessing this right.

I don't care who is mayor or councilmen.[6] It matters little whether you can vote for president. Home matters are of the greatest importance. I would rather have a voice in the affairs of my native city than be able to vote for president. But you don't have this choice, you cannot vote for president. The law says to every man, native or foreign, high or low, educated or ignorant, drunk or sober, rich or poor, that his judgement is sound and his opinion worthy to be counted. It is not possible for woman to be respected by the lower classes of men so long as she is denied the right of suffrage. Every boy feels that he is superior to his mother and sisters, and boasts that when he is 21 he will make their laws for them. No boy in Kansas can look his mother or sister in the face and feel in that manner. It is an object lesson.

We must go further. Women must not only vote, but must sit on juries. The law will never be enforced vigorously as long as men alone are on the juries. In 1871, I was speaking one night in Sioux City, Iowa. The women of that city burned down a house of ill fame that very night, whose inmates had been brought from St. Louis by the men of the town. I made some comments in my speech upon the affair, expressing my wonder that women would live with their husbands, knowing them to be guilty of such acts as these. The papers said I had traduced everybody in town, and said if I came back I would be summarily dealt with. I did go back in '77. The first thing I heard was that the grand jury was investigating charges against Madam Short, the keeper of the very house burned six years before. It took the jury thirteen and one-half hours to decide that there was no cause for complaint, when every man on the jury knew Madame Short to be guilty.[7]

Would this have occurred if women had been on the jury? It is impossible for any class to get justice until it is represented at the ballot box and in the jury box.

In Wyoming and Washington territories women have been enfranchised for twenty years. Judge Howe,[8] chief justice, said that no verdict had ever been given contrary to the evidence, and that women discharged their duties with equal intelligence with the men. Every testimony was to good effects. With the experience we have had it seems to me that every one must believe that the suppression of vice demands the presence of women in the jury box.

When women in every state are working with might and main, willing to make any sacrifice, to secure this right, to establish this fundamental principle; when the legislature has granted half what has been asked for, do you not think it would be a gracious act for you to go solidly to the ballot box? Can you not encourage us who live where there is less hope than here and hold up our hands and help us to refute the argument used against us that women will not vote when they have the right?

But the objection has been made that women will vote as their husbands vote. If the men believed this, would not every man be a ranting woman suffragist? (Applause.) Neither of the two great parties believes it can control the woman vote. It is because they know woman has a will of her own that they will not champion her cause. If the Democratic party had believed that it could have controlled the woman vote and used it to offset the negro vote when the negro was enfranchised, it would have taken up our cause years ago. And so with the Republican party.

I am anxious that you exercise this right of yours well. No woman should vote contrarily to her own convictions. In my state every farmer expects to get $5 for his vote. I hope no woman would sell her vote. But if she did, would it argue more against her than it does when a man sells his vote?

If there is a woman here who thinks she need not register, I wish she would let me know. (A gentleman in the audience called out that his wife thought he could attend to that for her.) "Oh! You represent her, do you?" asked Miss Anthony.

"Yes."

"Well, then, while you are representing her, who represents you?" (Laughter and applause.)

"We think that the head can attend to the affairs of the branches. Husband and wife are one."

Miss Anthony continued:

It is always husband and wife one—and that one the husband. No man can represent his wife; if he does, he does not represent himself. That idea was exploded when the property law of 1846 was passed, and when that law made husband and wife two in law, two in land and two in brains.[9]

Woman is only of any significance when she has a ballot in her hands. In 1876 a petition signed by 7,000 women of Illinois was laid on the table by the legislature, and one of the members made a motion that the sergeant at arms clear the hall of the mob, as he characterized the committee of ladies who brought the petition.[10] Every year before and since the liquor men of Illinois have gone down to that same legislature. They have never been called mobs. Their petitions have never been laid on the table. They could vote.

In California in 1861 a petition from negroes was ordered thrown out of the window by a member of the legislature. In 1871 a petition from the same race was most respectfully received and granted, and the chairman bringing it invited to address the legislature. They could vote in 1871.[11]

In your own city two years ago I was glad that not only colored men but colored women helped to elect a council of good men.[12] I cannot talk to you about the candidates this time because they are not named. I see the Democrats in the Second ward have nominated a woman for the school board.[13] The Republicans ought not to nominate anybody against her. They ought to nominate a lady for the school board. Somebody has said no woman would run on a city ticket. I am ashamed for the Leavenworth women if there are not twenty who would run.

At the close of the address a vote of thanks was extended to Miss Anthony. Upon motion of Mrs. Slosson,[14] Mrs. Cushing announced that Miss Anthony would speak this evening at the colored Methodist church on South Fifth avenue.

It was Miss Anthony's intention to have offered a resolution requesting the ministers of the city to preach a sermon on the necessity of the women registering and voting, but she forgot it. The suggestion is an excellent one and the various clergymen of the city are requested to act upon it.

☞ *Leavenworth Times*, 14 March 1889. Word in square brackets supplied by editors.

1. Harriet Smith Cushing (1826–1897) was the leading organizer of women in Leavenworth, where she settled in 1865. Building on her experience in Chicago before and during the war, she founded a Home of the Friendless in 1868, acquired a state charter, and gained state and city appropriations to support its work. In the 1890s, the home expanded to include a training school for nurses and a hospital. After establishing the city's Saturday Club, Cushing convened women from other parts of the state to found the Social Science Club of Kansas and Western Missouri, an umbrella group for women's clubs. She also presided over the short-lived Kansas Council of Women, formed by the state's equal suffrage association and temperance union in 1888. (J. H. Johnston, *They Came This Way* [Leavenworth, Kan., 1988], 73–81; unidentified clipping, November 1888, SBA scrapbook 13, Rare Books, DLC.)

2. *Laws of the State of Kansas, 1867*, chap. 56. The law applied to licenses issued in townships and chartered cities. A majority of residents, male and female, were needed to approve the license.

3. SBA describes how laws to incorporate ever smaller cities eroded the license law of 1867. In 1868, legislation about the incorporation of cities both of the first class (more than fifteen thousand inhabitants) and the second class (fifteen hundred to two thousand inhabitants) empowered the city councils to license liquor sellers, without any reference to the law of 1867. A year later, cities of the third class (as small as eight hundred inhabitants) were created and given the same authority. After adoption of statewide prohibition in 1880, the laws about incorporation were amended to remove councils' authority to license liquor sales. (*Laws of the State of Kansas, 1868*, chap. 18, 19; *1869*, chap. 26; *1881*, chap. 37, 40.)

4. Leavenworth was notorious for its defiance of prohibition. Since the granting of municipal suffrage to women, the city's Republican minority focused on prohibition in the hope that women would give its candidates a majority.

5. SBA describes the spring, municipal elections of 1887 but confuses the publication of John Ingalls' article in September of that year with his speech at Abilene on May 20. The closest Ingalls came in that speech to uttering the words SBA attributes to him falls near the end: "I hope the women of Kansas, when this subject is confided to them, will say not only that they do not require the sixteenth amendment to the constitution of the United States, but are unwilling to participate in any other degree than that in which they now mingle in the affairs of the state by accepting the ballot, no matter with what

majority it may be tendered to them." (*Abilene Gazette*, 26 May 1887, SBA scrapbook 12, Rare Books, DLC.)

6. This disinterested stance became more difficult for SBA's audiences to believe once her brother won the Republican nomination for mayor on March 18.

7. On this oft-told tale, see *Papers*, 3:167, 174n, 301, 4:185. In earlier renditions, the name appears as Madame Shaw, not Short.

8. John Homer Howe (1822–1873), the chief justice of Wyoming Territory's supreme court from 1869 until the fall of 1871, favored woman suffrage and insisted that women were also entitled to serve as jurors. Myra Bradwell's *Chicago Legal News* paid close attention to the experiment and published Howe's account of its effects. SBA's refers to twenty years of voting in Wyoming, not Washington. (*ANB*; *Chicago Legal News*, 12 March, 9 April 1870, 11 March 1871.)

9. SBA here switched her attention away from Kansas to New York and its Married Women's Property Act of 1848, on which see note above at 25 March 1888.

10. On this early episode in Frances Willard's career in 1879, not 1876, see her account in Frances E. Willard, *Woman and Temperance, or the Work and Workers of the Woman's Christian Temperance Union*, 5th ed. (Chicago, 1886), 362–65.

11. Events in Kansas usually provided SBA's model of the change wrought by voting rights for black men. Her dates only approximate the political history of California's African Americans, who petitioned in the 1850s and 1860s for access to public schools, the right to offer testimony in court, and the right to vote. As late as 1865, the Democratic-controlled legislature rejected petitions for suffrage from the state's Convention of Colored Citizens. After California rejected the Fifteenth Amendment in 1870, a number of cities followed the attorney general's directive to turn away black would-be voters from the polls in local elections. Black men voted in their first state elections in 1871. (Larry George Murphy, "Equality before the Law: The Struggle of Nineteenth-Century Black Californians for Social and Political Justice," [Ph.D. diss., Graduate Theological Union, 1973], 106–64.)

12. In 1887, the Democratic, anti-prohibition candidate won the election for mayor by less than two dozen votes, but a tough campaign to register women as a voting bloc for enforcement of prohibition resulted in Republicans taking every seat on the city council. Women made up thirty-eight percent of the electorate in the municipal election that year. On that campaign, spearheaded by Helen Gougar's organizing among the city's women, see Goldberg, *Army of Women*, 104–11, and SBA scrapbook 12, Rare Books, DLC.

13. Democrats had just nominated Elizabeth Geyer (c. 1847–?), a single woman and the daughter of German immigrants, who lived in the Second Ward. At their nominating convention on March 18, the Republicans did indeed second her nomination, and with the dual endorsement, Geyer won a seat on the school board. (Leavenworth city directories, 1890 to 1893; Federal Census, 1900; *Leavenworth Times*, 14 March 1889.)

14. Achsah Louise Lilly Slosson (1836–1906) was a relative newcomer to Leavenworth, having arrived in 1882 after two decades at Sabetha, Kansas. She and William B. Slosson grew up in Broome County, New York. William moved to Kansas in 1857 and returned to New York to be married in 1860. Achsah Slosson presided over the temperance union in Sabetha, organized Sunday schools, served on the state women's board of Congregational church missions, and, once she moved to Leavenworth, joined the board of Harriet Cushing's Home of the Friendless. She was also active in the Social Science Club of Kansas and Western Missouri. (Andreas, *History of Kansas*, 955; *Sabetha Herald*, 18 October 1906; William B. Slosson, "A Letter to Friends of My Wife," 10 August 1907, KHi.)

62 ~ Speech by SBA at the Colored Methodist Church, Leavenworth, Kansas

EDITORIAL NOTE: SBA spoke next in the evening of March 14, probably in the Methodist Episcopal Church (Colored) on Fifth Street. Church names were inconsistently rendered. All campaign events in Leavenworth were not segregated, and social practice was not the only reason to convene African-American women separately. Local black leaders protected their political base and, in this campaign, objected to a cross-racial alliance of women as divisive. "Colored voters" were called together on 11 March 1889 for, among other things, planning how to achieve full registration of women, and black women continued to hold separate meetings right up to election day. (*Leavenworth Times*, 9 March 1889; Goldberg, *Army of Women*, 113–14; with the assistance of the Leavenworth Public Library.)

[14 March 1889]

Mrs. Keyes[1] presided over the meeting and introduced Miss Anthony who delivered one of her characteristic speeches, bristling with argument and powerful in persuasion.

The address was along the line discussed by Miss Anthony Wednesday afternoon, and was an earnest, powerful appeal to the colored women to exercise the rights which the legislature had bestowed upon them. The necessity for registering and voting was forcibly urged. Miss Anthony carried her audience with her, convincing them how vitally essential it was to their every interest to assert and exercise every right in their possession.

At the conclusion of the lecture proper, which was listened to with the most rapt attention, Miss Anthony called for questions regarding the duty of the women or any other phase of the question not clearly understood by the colored people. One colored woman said that after the last election, when a Republican council was elected, a large amount of work requiring laborers was done in the city. The contractors went outside the city and imported laborers from abroad, while Leavenworth laborers stood by idle. What good had come from their voting?[2]

Miss Anthony answered the question by saying that if they were cheated once, that was all the more reason they should not be discouraged, but try again. Weed out the bad; the good will get in by and by. No man should be voted for for councilman or mayor who was not pledged to be loyal to the laboring interests of the city, and who would not bind himself to use his influence to secure employment for Leavenworth labor. When work was to be done in Leavenworth, Leavenworth labor ought not to be idle while imported labor took the bread from its mouth.

Miss Anthony told the women that even after they had the right to vote eternal vigilance was the price of justice. Before they had the right they had not the ghost of a show. The fact that immediate betterment of their condition did not spring from the first exercise of suffrage was no argument against such exercise.

Miss Anthony said she expected to speak in every ward in the city. She wanted the colored people to bring all questions they did not understand, all faults they found with the way they were treated by their white brethren to her. She was the friend of the colored race. She advised the women not to work for and support an idle, lazy husband, who smokes up, drinks up, or chews up enough in one year to support his family. She closed her remarks by urging every man and woman present to go to the clerk's office at once, register, and on election day vote, each man and woman, his or her honest conviction.

A vote of thanks was extended to those who had given the use of the church for the meeting and to Miss Anthony for her address.

Leavenworth Times, 15 March 1889.

    1. Mrs. Keyes is unidentified.

    2. During the campaign of 1887, Republicans addressed this recurring complaint in Leavenworth about city officials importing white workers to

avoid hiring resident African Americans. Addressing "our colored friends" at a campaign rally in 1887, one party activist "guarantee[d] that the laboring men of our city will not have to go idle while outside men can come and do our work and take our money with them." (Unidentified clipping, 1 April 1887, SBA scrapbook 12, Rare Books, DLC.)

63   Article by ECS

[17 March 1889]

Let the Blue Laws Rest.

The existence of a national reform party in this country, proposing a union of church and state, has been well styled "A conspiracy against the republic."[1] The members of this party say they do not propose a union of church and state, but when they ask to have the christian religion taught in the schools, its God recognized in the United States constitution, more restrictive legislation for the observance of the Sabbath, suppressing Sunday papers, the mails, freight trains, street cars, and all innocent amusements, it looks very much as if we were going back to the old Puritan blue laws of Connecticut, when, it is said, a man could not kiss his wife nor a hen lay an egg on Sunday.[2]

With the experience of the union of church and state in the old world before their eyes, the fathers of this republic laid the foundation of our government carefully, as they thought, on a secular basis, free from all ecclesiastical entanglements. They were so afraid of the influence of the clergy, that at one time they were not allowed to vote or discuss political questions. When during the early temperance, anti-slavery movements they began to express their opinions on public affairs in their pulpits, many churches were sundered in twain. Now they not only preach on all that concerns the daily life of the people but they propose to dominate the state in the most arbitrary and unreasonable manner.

A few years ago a gentleman of wealth in Pittsburg offered to give $20,000 to build a conservatory in the park, with the proviso that it should be opened freely to the public on Sunday.[3] Several clergymen called on the common council and urged them not to accept the gift on that basis, as it would be a desecration of the Sabbath. Fortunately the common council could not see the sin in the laboring masses walking in the park and looking at rare plants and flowers on Sunday, so they turned a deaf ear to the clerical advisers and accepted the gift.

That this reform party can accomplish all it proposes at a time when liberal ideas are so rapidly spreading, is doubtful. Nevertheless it is wise to resist the first encroachments on the liberties of the people as there is no tyranny so insidious as that in the name of religion. When bills to enforce Sunday rest, and to have the christian religion taught in our schools, are introduced into the United States senate, it is time to rouse popular thought on these questions.

Inasmuch as we have in our schools the children of Catholics, and innumerable sects of protestants, Jews, Gentiles, infidels, agnostics, the safe ground is to teach no theological speculations. The moment we begin to teach religious dogmas we introduce endless discussion and dissension among the parents. Protestants would ignore the pope, Universalists the inferno, Jews and Seventh Day Baptists the christian Sunday, and agnostics all the creeds and ordinances as of no significance whatever.

Lessons in the exact sciences and moral duties to themselves, their fellow beings, and their country, would be of more practical value to the children in our public schools than speculations as to the unknown and the eternal future.

As to the constitution, as long as that document is based on the principles of justice, liberty and equality, we have the essential elements of our highest ideal of a Supreme Being, already recognized in that Magna Charta of human liberties.

We must beware of giving the pulpit too much authority over the press or our institutions of learning. Its power has always been aggressive and proscriptive.

No end of sermons have been preached and essays written against the Sunday newspapers, one of the greatest blessings to our people, especially in the large cities.[4] The audiences of country clergymen average about 400, while our newspapers speak to thousands.

The American Sunday newspapers, with their able editorials on the questions of the hour, and letters from the old world, are marvels of literary ability, and extensive news, from every quarter of the globe. There is not to be found in London, Paris or Berlin a Sunday paper that can compare with those published in the chief cities of the United States.

The objections the national reform party makes to the Sunday paper have no special force nor merit.

First, they say it depletes the churches. This is the real ground of hostility also against opening the libraries, picture galleries, concert halls, and all places of amusement—a tacit admission that the church cannot stand competition with any other form of instruction or entertainment. It is true that the multitudes who never go to church read the Sunday papers in hotels, saloons, on the cars, in the open air on the only day they have leisure to read. What would take the place of the paper for all these for whom there is no room nor attraction in the churches.

Second, they say the labor involved in printing and distributing the papers compels a large force to desecrate the Sabbath. The labor on the Sunday papers is done on Saturday. It is the Monday issue, if any, that should be tabooed on that ground. As to the boys who distribute the papers, it takes no more time nor strength for their duties than for those who ring the bells for all the churches. These reformers wish to suppress the omnibuses, street cars and bands of music on account of the noise, so distasteful to those who enjoy the holy stillness of the Sabbath day. All these together cannot possibly be so great a nuisance in any community, especially to invalids or those who live near churches, as the doleful ringing and tolling of those bells all day. I once lived on a corner within one block of five different churches, and with the meetings, funerals and Lenten seasons, all punctuated and emphasized with those bells, I was nearly distracted.

I cannot see that setting type in order to provide some intellectual pabulum for a community is more a desecration of the Sabbath, than setting tables and cooking food for the family. To be consistent, those who insist on Sunday being a day of rest, should make it a season of fasting and self-denial for themselves and of freedom for their wives and servants from all manual labor. The dinner should be cooked on Saturday and served cold on Sunday with primitive simplicity. But the clergy as a class (to say nothing of most of the sons of Adam), are proverbial for their love of good eating, hence we hear very little from the pulpit as to the sin of good dinners on the "Lord's day."

According to what system of morals is it more sinful for Patrick to set type and read his paper, than for Bridget to cook a turkey and plum pudding and read nothing on Sunday?

~ *Elizabeth Cady Stanton.*

~ *Omaha Bee*, 17 March 1889.

1. That is, the National Reform Association.
2. The Blue Laws of Connecticut set the standard for absurdity in the enforcement of sabbath observance, though historians doubted that the extreme examples cited by ECS were ever enacted.
3. Henry Phipps, Jr., (1839-1930), a partner of Andrew Carnegie in the steel firm of Carnegie, Phipps & Company, made the offer. His conservatory opened in Allegheny City's West Park in 1887. (*DAB*; *Memoirs of Allegheny County Pennsylvania: Personal and Genealogical, with Portraits* [Madison, Wis., 1904], 1:18; *Papers*, 4:499–501.)
4. The Sunday newspaper grew in popularity after the Civil War, especially when publishers realized that it sold more copies than any other issue of the week. But this new direction in business and leisure collided with new evangelical pressure for stricter observance of their sectarian Sabbath. ("Boston Monday Lectureship: Mr. Cook's One Hundred and Eighty-first Lecture," *Independent* 38 [25 February 1886]: 5–8; Michael Schudson, *Discovering the News: A Social History of American Newspapers* [New York, 1978], 99–100; Foster, *Moral Reconstruction*, 94–95.)

64 ~ Speech by SBA at Republican Rally in Leavenworth, Kansas

EDITORIAL NOTE: SBA had spoken nearly every day during the campaign, including Sundays when ministers offered her their pulpits. Although her request to speak at a Democratic Ladies' Meeting was refused, she had invitations to speak at Republican rallies; a meeting of the Ladies' Law and Order League, a Republican front; and a Gospel Temperance Meeting, called by the Woman's Christian Temperance Union. As election day neared, the pace quickened: she addressed a mass meeting of women on March 29, this Republican gathering on March 30, and a final rally on the night of April 1. In those final days, the campaign also took a nasty turn. As happened in 1887, Democrats deployed sexual and racial politics, accusing Daniel Anthony of slandering the reputations of Democratic women and SBA of arousing among African Americans "a passion which will soon be unable to be restrained." At the start of this rally on March 30, William D. Matthews, describing himself "as the representative of the negro race in this city," paid tribute to SBA, a friend of his since 1865; "the result of her teachings," he said, "was not anarchy and lawlessness but an elevation of negro citizenship." SBA took the stage late in the evening, after her brother addressed the crowd. (*Leavenworth Post*, quoted in *Leavenworth Times*, 29 March 1889.)

[30 March 1889]

Miss Susan B. Anthony was received with applause. At a meeting in this city it was said that Colonel Anthony has brought his sister here to take a part in the municipal election. I have talked in favor of the enforcement of the temperance laws in this hall and the churches. In all these speeches I have not spoken my brother's name as a candidate for mayor. What a compliment the Democratic party pays to woman suffrage, when it expresses fear that a woman will turn the election.

The speaker next proceeded to assert that no mother could be in favor of the grogshop. The Republicans gave Kansas the prohibitory law and the Democratic party opposed it. Do you believe that these Democrats will better enforce the temperance laws than the Republicans? The Democratic party repealed the ordinance enforcing the liquor law—can their repentance be trusted so soon after it has been declared?

Miss Anthony proceeded to say that the ballot in the hands of the women was the only power that can put the grogshop and the brothel under a ban, because women are instinctively against these evils. The speaker proceeded to make an argument for woman suffrage, warning women that it behooves them to use well the right of suffrage, lest it be taken from them by the power that gave it. It is a good omen for the future that we meet and discuss principles. Let us stick to principles. She urged the women to vote early—to give their husbands the best early breakfast of the year, and then go to the polls to vote in your turn because some may fail to get the chance when there are 1,200 or 1,500 voters in a ward.

Miss Anthony continued to urge voters to do their duty and to be on their guard and to do their duty.[1]

❧ *Leavenworth Times*, 31 March 1889.

1. When the votes were counted, the success of mobilizing women was evident: women cast more than forty percent of the ballots, and in some wards, they came close to fifty percent. However, in all but two wards a

majority of women voted for Daniel Anthony's opponent, one factor in his loss of the election. (*Leavenworth Times*, 4, 6 April 1889.)

65 ✎ ECS to Sara Francis Underwood

706 North 19th Omaha [*Neb. March 1889*]¹

Dear Mrs Underwood,

You must not judge my pleasure in hearing from you, by the length of time your letter has laid unanswered   I have been busy criticising sermons on Divorce & Sunday amusements²   I send you a paper containing my last effort. I get the papers you send & am much obliged. I have been urged by several friends to write "reminiscences" so I am reviewing my childhood³   youth &c &c to give you young fry something to laugh at when I am the other side talking with Ruth & Naomi, Deborah & Huldah &c &c.⁴ What shall we say to Paul when walking some day arm in arm on the banks of the Jordan we meet him face to face? Of course we will show our sense of superiority by speaking to him <u>first</u>, in a condescending manner. We will wear no masks, veils, nor bonnets   no emblems of subjection whatever, we will each have a Greek testament in hand, discussing perchance his gross ideas on marriage. I might introduce you as from Chicago the state where liberal divorce laws prevail,⁵ & ask him his views on that question. Then if ↑he↓ airs any of those narrow theories he promulgated in Joppa, Epesus & Demascus,⁶ we will have a discussion. Perhaps just then Mr Underwood & the Rev Patton⁷ will come along on one side Solomon David Moses & Aaron⁸ on the other, & then what a convocation we shall have   But with all the clubs you have on hand you have no time to speculate about the next sphere of action, & I know I better keep my mind on the affairs of this planet yet for a season. I have started a woman's department [*in margins of second sheet*] in a paper here, in the most liberal paper, no doubt like the scriptural grain of mustard seed it will be [*in margin of first sheet*] productive like yours in the Religio Philosopico of great results in time.⁹ With kind regards for Mr Underwood & yourself sincerely ever

✎ *Elizabeth Cady Stanton.*

↝ ALS, Papers of ECS, NPV.

1. Can be dated late March or early April by references to ECS's own writing.

2. ECS's weekly articles in the *Omaha Republican* began in February 1889 with discussions of divorce that lasted into late March and ended with the article below at 14 April 1889. During the same months she wrote at least two articles for the *Omaha Bee*, including "Let the Blue Laws Rest," above at 17 March 1889. See *Film*, 27:103, 114, 116, 120, 137-38, 142, 151-52, 161, 166.

3. The first chapter of ECS's "Reminiscences," subtitled "Childhood," was published in the *Woman's Tribune*, 6 April 1889, *Film*, 27:159-60.

4. Frequently cited by ECS as biblical examples of women's possibilities, Naomi's loyalty to Ruth is recounted in the Book of Ruth, Deborah's courage in Judges 4, and Huldah's learning in Second Kings. ECS proceeds to imagine conversation with the apostle Paul, on whose views about silence in the churches and subordination to husbands rested much of modern Christian teaching and practice.

5. Illinois led the states in the number of divorces granted from 1867 to 1886, according to the new report by the federal Bureau of Labor Statistics. Newspapers began to comment on the data as soon as the report was transmitted to Congress on 20 February 1889. (Carroll D. Wright, *A Report on Marriage and Divorce in the United States, 1867 to 1886*, rev. ed. [Washington, D.C., 1891], 442-43.)

6. Joppa, Ephesus, and Damascus are critical sites in the early history of Christianity, though not all of them are associated with the apostle Paul.

7. If ECS refers to William Weston Patton (1821-1889), a Congregational minister and president of Howard University from 1877 until his death, her fantasy seems asymmetrical. Patton was a notorious critic of woman suffragists, who thought their greater freedom led to religious skepticism and immorality. (*NCAB*, 10:165; *Papers*, 4:402-3.)

8. Major figures in the Old Testament, David and his son Solomon were kings of Israel, and Moses and his brother Aaron were religious leaders.

9. According to the *Omaha Republican*, 31 March 1889, Sara Underwood had taken charge of the woman's department in the *Religio-Philosophical Journal*. Later, Benjamin Underwood became the journal's editor.

66   Article by ECS

[14 April 1889]

The Great Trial.

The great trial that has just closed in this city will in future legal reports furnish many remarkable precedents for reference and action. One of the most important principles enunciated which I do not remember ever to have heard stated before in a court of justice, is woman's right to a trial by a jury of her peers. In his address to the jury Judge Baldwin said:[1] What are we doing here to-day? There is under trial for the highest crime known to law—a woman. She, nor one of her sex, has aught to do with the administration of the law; not one of her sex sit in the jury box to try her; not one of them has anything to do with it, but she, by the powers vested in the opposite sex, sits there to be tried by those who know nothing of a woman's love. Still we would do violence to our feelings if we did not here and now congratulate that unfortunate woman that the prosecution has been conducted in a most honorable way, and that this court is presided over by a gentleman who is so well known for his endeavors to do what is right not only by her, but by the community as well. Gentlemen, never did you occupy the position you do to-day. You sit in a holy place. You sit in the temple of justice, where no woman's voice is heard, and yet topmost on the pinnacle of the temple is the form of justice—a woman's form.

It is a serious consideration that in the whole history of the past, except in the little territory of Wyoming, no woman has ever as yet been tried by a jury of her peers. And yet this right has been held so sacred far back in English history that it is difficult to trace its origin. The commons always demanded a jury of their own class, the nobles of theirs, and royalty protested against the injustice and presumption of a trial by either church or state, unless royal blood flowed in the veins of their jurors. Let those who say the acquittal in the King case was a "sentimental verdict" remember the helpless condition of woman before the law. Our civil and criminal codes are all made by man: expounded by man, administered by man, placing woman in the courts wholly at the mercy of man, where the judges, the jurors, the advocates are all men. Surely there is room for sentiment when the fundamental principles of justice are denied all womankind. The eloquent defense of Judge Baldwin and Mr. Cowin,[2] the chastened tone of the judge's charge;[3] the summing up of the prosecution, the haste with which the twelve jurors brought in the verdict of acquittal and the intense enthusiasm of the audience, all herald the dawn of a new day for woman when the same moral code shall apply to both sexes. The sermon of the Rev. J. E. Ensign,[4] preached during the trial is worthy of note as reflecting the public sentiment of the community. When the bar and the pulpit unite in demanding of young men more truth and honor in their relations with women, the fires of love will burn with a clearer, purer flame on every domestic altar. It is this fine cobweb of faith, that men and women have in each other, that holds society together.

I hope the time is not far distant when Shakspeare's beautiful dream of Portia at the bar will be fully realized, and we shall have judges, jurors and advocates of our own sex,[5] not that we could do better than men have done, on this trial, but simply as a matter of justice.

A frail woman being tried before a court composed of men does not make a pleasing picture on canvas.

The gentle, loving Jesus before Pilate and his stern coadjutors is not more touching than those of Jean d'Arc, Charlotte Corday, and Mary, Queen of Scots[6] before their bearded accusers. In gazing at these pictures in the galleries of the old world how many times I have wondered if the monstrous injustice of the scene ever entered into the minds of the artists, or the multitudes who through long years have beheld them.

Judge Baldwin has at last voiced a thought—under circumstances to make a deep impression—that has long agitated the minds of many earnest women.

~ *Elizabeth Cady Stanton.*

~ *Omaha Republican*, 14 April 1889.

1. The jury rendered a verdict of not guilty in the murder trial of Elizabeth King on 10 April 1889. Charles A. Baldwin (1825-?), a former judge, a specialist in criminal defense, and one of King's two defense attorneys, spoke these words as he opened his summation for the jury on 6 April. (*Omaha Bee*, 7 April 1889; Savage and Bell, *History of the City of Omaha*, 238-39.)

2. John Clay Cowin (1846-1918), a prominent lawyer in Omaha who served

as the city's district attorney from 1868 to 1872, was King's defense attorney from the time of her arrest in November 1888. He addressed the jury on April 8 and 9. (*WWW1*; *Omaha Bee*, 20 November 1888, 9, 10 April 1889.)

3. Lewis A. Groff (1841–1928), justice of the state's third district court since 1887, heard the criminal case. He charged the jury on April 10. Later in 1889, Groff was named Commissioner of the General Land Office in President Harrison's administration. By 1900 he had moved to California, where he served as postmaster of Los Angeles in 1900, and later worked as dean and professor at the College of Law, University of Southern California. (Savage and Bell, *History of the City of Omaha*, 241–42; *Omaha Bee*, 11 April 1889; *New York Times*, 17 September 1889, 27 January 1928; with assistance of Claude B. Zachary, University of Southern California)

4. James Edwin Ensign (1851–1929) moved to Omaha from New York State to become secretary of the Young Men's Christian Association and stayed for several years to serve as a pastor. Preaching at the Methodist Episcopal Church on 7 April 1889, Ensign expressed sympathy for King and ventured the opinion that "a jury of women would acquit her and not leave their seats, and I believe the men will." The sin in Omaha, he continued, "is the unfaithfulness of men to the most sacred vows they have ever made, and that to their wives." (*Omaha Bee*, 8 April 1889; Hiram G. Burley, "James E. Ensign," *Official Minutes, Sixty-Third Session, Central New York Annual Conference, Methodist Episcopal Church, 1930*, 555–56, with the assistance of Jocelyne Rubinetti, United Methodist Archives Center, Drew University.)

5. In William Shakespeare's *Merchant of Venice*, Portia disguises herself as a lawyer to defend a friend against Shylock. Her name became synonymous with female attorneys.

6. These victims of execution were deemed political martyrs: Joan of Arc (1412?–1431), national heroine of France; Charlotte Corday (1768–1793), French revolutionary; and Mary, Queen of Scots (1542–1587), the Catholic queen executed by Elizabeth I.

67 ❧ ECS TO OLYMPIA BROWN

Hempstead Long Island N.Y.[1]   May 8th [*1889*]

Dear Olympia,

I am always sorry to say nay to anything my friends urge, but really I could not promise to take so long a journey, except for some imperative ↑necessity↓[2]   When you are 73 years old, you will appreciate my reluctance to leave your own bed   rocking chair, & writing desk. The word "go" has lost all charm for me. I think my future work must be done with the pen   Our cause has become too popular, our numbers too large for me as a leader. I am a leader of thought rather than numbers. The National association has been growing politic & conservative for sometime. Lucy & Susan alike see suffrage only   They do not see woman's religious & social bondage, neither do the young women in either association, hence they may as well combine for they have one mind & one purpose. I would rather be a free lance outside, to say my say as opportunity offers as an individual, than to speak as the President of an association. When the Union is consummated one of original conditions was that I should retire, which I am quite willing & happy to do. You shall have my best wishes for the success of your convention. I will write a letter on whatever point you desire. With kind regards for Mr Willis[3] & yourself sincerely ever

                                  Elizabeth Cady Stanton

ALS, Olympia Brown Papers, MCR-S.

    1. By the time Margaret Lawrence decided in April to join her ailing husband in California rather than care for her mother, her brother Gerrit had abandoned ranching in Iowa and moved to the East Coast, starting out in Hempstead. Gat, as he was known, resumed the practice of law in New York City. Daniel Stanton was commissioned to escort his mother from Nebraska to Long Island, where she spent the summer. (*Eighty Years*, 417-18.)

    2. Apparently Olympia Brown had acted early to invite ECS to the Wisconsin Woman Suffrage Association's annual meeting in Milwaukee in October. For more on this invitation, see below at 12 October 1889.

    3. John Henry Willis (1825-1893) married Olympia Brown in 1873. When the family moved to Wisconsin in 1878, he reestablished himself in business, eventually to become a partner in a publishing company. (*Portrait and Biographical Album of Racine and Kenosha Counties, Wisconsin* [Chicago, 1892], 702-3; Charlotte Coté, *Olympia Brown: The Battle for Equality* [Racine, Wis., 1988], 135.)

68   Matilda Joslyn Gage to ECS

                                  Fayetteville N.Y. June 4 1889

Dear Mrs Stanton

    I am alone in my house sitting by a grate fire, while the rain drops plaintively on the tin roof of the Bay window.[1]

So you have really bought up, like, a newly married person, & gone to house-keeping again. Alas! where are the fine mugs, the coffee urn, the finger glasses of yore?

Elias and Carrie have given up their home,[2] on which was a big mortgage,—have sold horses, carriages sleighs—dismissed the coachman and cook and are living in a Troy Hotel—The Phoenix.

To the consternation, dismay and regret of Mrs R. Elias suddenly sold out the rest of his Laundry to the cheating partner, who had already secured the advantage of one-half; and that haven of rest sociality and welcome is no more. What should I say? <u>Sic</u> <u>transit</u> ↑<u>gloria</u>↓ <u>mundi</u> or something to that effect.

The one great social disadvantage of growing old, is that we are compelled to witness so many changes on the part of our friends. I do not think Elias will recover

Yes, I enjoy your <u>Reminiscences</u> but you should copy-right them.[3] I think, <u>without doubt</u>, they will have a nice sale in book form. At present they are at the mercy of any pirate. Have Mrs Colby print you two copies of the title, with your name, and do you send them to the Librarian of Congress, Mr Spofford,[4] accompanied by one dollar and you will get your copy-right. Then have Mrs Colby put "Librarian of Congress," on her subscription list for <u>two</u> copies, of her paper; also placing the words "copyrighted" below the title of <u>each</u> article, and you will be all right. I think there is <u>money</u> in them.

What do you think of Bellamy's <u>Looking</u> <u>Backward</u>?[5] I feel imprisoned upon reading it. While it has some good thoughts, its ultimate is radically wrong. It strikes me that all spontaneity—all individuality would be lost under such a system. And where could a government be found or created in 113 years, so perfect as to be best trusted with the people' industrial arrangements. The book is creating some stir, and people seem to find in it the solution of all evils. I hope to be enjoying <u>Devachan</u> ere that time.[6]

Who is with you? Are you on the sound? Tell me all about yourself. I am alone & expect to be. There seems no likelihood of a visit from either one of my children.[7]

It is nearly half past eight, the rain drips more and more rapidly, and I came home to-day to find that the floods had undermined the wall in front of my barn,—the platform succumbed to the water, and a moderate line of destruction with a dozen—more or less—men at work upon repairs.

Have you seen Judge Waite on Springer,[8] uniform marriage & divorce amendment? I tell you few people realize the growing danger to individual freedom. Afft.

~ *M. J. Gage*

~ ALS, on 40th anniversary letterhead, Clara B. Colby Papers, Archives Division, WHi.

1. Since the death of her husband in 1884 and the emigration of her children to Dakota Territory, Gage occupied her house in Fayetteville only a part of each year, otherwise staying in rooms in Syracuse and passing the winter with her children.

2. By this account, Caroline Gilkey Rogers (c. 1837-1899), known to friends as Carrie, gave up her comfortable house in Lansingburgh, New York, when her husband, Elias F. Rogers, sold out his share of the custom laundry that he ran for many years with Thomas P. Dowling in Troy. Caroline Rogers, a portrait painter, was active in the New York State Woman Suffrage Association through the 1880s and 1890s, noted especially for her skills as a speaker. ECS was but one of many suffragists entertained by Rogers at the mortgaged house. (*Woman's Journal*, 25 November 1899; *Albany Argus*, 12 March 1884, in SBA scrapbook 10, Rare Books, DLC; Arthur James Weise, *Troy's One Hundred Years, 1789-1889* [Troy, N.Y., 1891], 424.)

3. By this date, ECS had published seven installments of her "Reminiscences." See *Film*, 27: 159-60, 162-65, 168-70, 181-84, 190-93, 202-4, 227-29.

4. Ainsworth Rand Spofford (1825-1908) was named sixth librarian of Congress by President Abraham Lincoln in 1864. (*ANB*.)

5. Edward Bellamy (1850-1898) published his utopian novel *Looking Backward* in 1888, and it quickly became a bestseller and the inspiration for a Nationalist movement. Its vision of a cooperative commonwealth in which women enjoyed economic and political equality as well as freedom from domestic toil appealed especially to a female audience. By the summer of 1889 women, including local suffrage leaders in many states, were conspicuous members and leaders of Nationalist clubs. (Mari Jo Buhle, *Women and American Socialism, 1870-1920* [Urbana, Ill., 1981], 75-82.)

6. Evidence of Gage's ongoing study of Theosophy, Devachan is the term for the state of consciousness into which the ego goes after the body dies.

7. At this date all four of the Gage children lived in Dakota Territory: Helen Leslie Gage Gage (1845-1933), Thomas Clarkson Gage (1848-1938), Julia Louise Gage Carpenter (1851-1931), and Maud Gage Baum (1861-1953).

8. Charles B. Waite, "Springer Amendment to the Federal Constitution," *Chicago Law Times* 3 (July 1889): 237-52. William McKendree Springer (1836-1903), a Democrat from Illinois, served in the House of Representatives from 1875 to 1895. On 5 January 1889 he introduced his own sixteenth amendment to the Constitution that would give Congress "power to make a

uniform law of marriage and divorce." Waite thought this an odd act for a Democrat, as it would force states to cede authority over laws of marriage to the federal government. His own research into state laws on the causes of divorce, he wrote, demonstrated that less diversity existed than Springer thought. (*BDAC*; McPherson, *Hand-Book of Politics for 1890*, 25.)

69   SBA to Laura Carter Holloway[1]

Rochester N.Y. July 7, 1889

My Dear Friend

Your two telegrams are before me—and much as I would love to say "yes" and be with you next Friday the 12th inst—I have to deny myself the pleasure—

1st Because I am but just settled into being lazy at home—and

2d Because that very day I am expecting the arrival of my brother D. R's only surviving daughter[2]—and

3d Because my purse groans with emptiness from too many such acceptances already!!

I didn't answer by <u>wire</u>—yesterday—because the operators of neither office would send it without some more definite address than Brooklyn—N.Y—though my niece assured them over & over you were sufficiently known—

Our Grand Commander in Chief—Elizabeth Cady Stanton is at Hempstead—Long Island— Why do you not levy upon her—she is so very near to you—and always can say just the beautiful word in the most beautiful way—

I saw you were to have <u>Anna Dickinson</u>[3]—do tell me how she is—and whether you feel that she will return to her pre-eminently proper sphere—the platform!! We have no young woman that at all matches her powers of oratory— I do hope she is well now—and full of new hope & life to resume her old sphere of usefulness— I would love to see her & hear her—as of yore!

Regretting I cannot comply with your most flattering invitation—I am very sincerely yours

  Susan B. Anthony

↩ ALS, on NWSA letterhead, Laura C. Holloway Collection, NB.

1. Laura Carter Holloway (1848?-1930), later Langford, was a lecturer, author, and journalist, and an editor for many years at the *Brooklyn Daily Eagle*. At SBA's invitation, she spoke at the International Council of Women in the session on professions. She now wanted SBA to speak to the Seidl Society at Brighton Beach in Brooklyn. The society's chief purpose was to offer orchestral music, under the baton of Anton Seidl, to a largely female audience at low prices. But Holloway, its founder and president, also organized events with well-known lecturers and added a philanthropic project of taking city children and working girls on holidays to the beach. (Lucian Lamar Knight, comp., *Biographical Dictionary of Southern Authors* [1929; reprint, Detroit, Mich., 1978]; Oscar Fay Adams, *A Dictionary of American Authors* [Boston, 1897]; Tennessee Historical Society, *The Tennessee Encyclopedia of History and Culture*, on-line edition [Knoxville, Tenn., 2002]; *History*, 1:49; *Brooklyn Daily Eagle*, 26 July 1902, 11 July 1930; research by staff of Brooklyn Public Library; *Papers*, 4:120-21; *New York Times*, 7 September 1889; Joseph Horowitz, "Laura Langford and the Seidl Society: Wagner Comes to Brooklyn," in *Cultivating Music in America: Women Patrons and Activists since 1860*, eds. Ralph P. Locke and Cyrilla Barr [Berkeley, Calif., 1997], 164-83.)

2. That is, Maud Anthony.

3. Anna Elizabeth Dickinson (1842-1932) was in her youth one of the most successful lecturers in the country on political and cultural subjects. During and after the Civil War, the Republican party employed her to campaign for their candidates. (*NAW*; *ANB*.)

70 ↪ SPEECH BY ECS TO THE SEIDL SOCIETY

EDITORIAL NOTE: Two hundred women of the Seidl Society gathered for lunch and a speech by ECS at the Brighton Beach Hotel on 12 July 1889. In this report on the occasion by the noted stenographer and editor Mary F. Seymour, ECS's gift for extemporaneous speaking won high praise: "while she speaks extemporaneously with perfect ease and fluency," Seymour wrote, "her language has the vigor and finished style of a written address." After Laura Holloway's introduction, ECS "was greeted with enthusiastic applause." Many years later, in a letter to Harriot Blatch, Laura Holloway Langford recalled, "There were women at Brighton at the time your mother was there, who knew nothing of womens suffrage, and to these Mrs Stanton was an education. She did us all good." (L. C. H. Langford to H. S. Blatch, 14 June 1911, ECS Papers, DLC.)

[12 July 1889]

She opened her address by saying that she was glad to know that the Seidl Society was the first club ever organized on a basis of complete equality, and that it especially honored women who were capable of self-support. Said she, "When Lord Coleridge[1] visited this country, the one thing that filled him with the most astonishment was the intelligence of our women in regard to the great questions of government." She advised her hearers to consider carefully and discuss frequently all the great problems of the day, among others, the labor question, the opening of art galleries on Sunday, as to whether religion should be taught in our public schools, etc. Said she, "Morality is one thing and religion is another. We can always give lessons in morals without interference. On questions of morals all religions agree, but in the great dogmas and doctrines there is the greatest difference. Let us use our influence to promote the teaching of exact sciences in our schools and leave the speculations of religion to be settled in our homes and the various churches to which we belong. This is the only way we can preserve our schools and make the whole community harmonize in their [appetites?]."

Alluding to the bad condition of the streets of New York she said: "Men have given up and admit they find it impossible to keep them clean. I think if you would make Mrs. Holloway Commissioner of Streets in New York they would not be dirty long. She could clean out New York City in less than three months. Now, if you had the right to vote you could make her Commissioner of Streets."

She described in a very amusing way a discussion which she had with Bishop Coxe,[2] who said that he never expected women would be able to take an equal share in the government on account of their disabilities. Being requested to state what the leading disabilities were, he asked: "Isn't maternity a disability?" Said she: "Maternity a disability! Don't you chant the Magnificat daily in every cathedral in the land, glorifying motherhood? Maternity a disability!" "Well," said he, "you must admit that petticoats are a disability." "But," said Mrs. Stanton, "my good Bishop, you are aware that we were not born with petticoats, and can wear them or not at our pleasure. You acknowledge the flowing robe to be the robe of dignity. When you go into the pulpit to preach you put on long flowing robes, the judges on the bench of the United States Supreme Court all appear in flowing robes. When you want to be specially dignified you adopt our costume. You don't find it a disability in the pulpit or on the Bench. Our women who ride on the bicycle have thrown the petticoat aside and appear in tights."[3] Then the Bishop didn't know what to say. "I want every woman to deny that she is a bundle of disabilities or she will become so in reality after awhile. I believe that men and women are created equally and so intended to be. God said: 'Let us make man in our own image, male and female, and give them dominion over every creature on the earth.'[4] Nothing was said about giving man dominion over women. That was an interpolation of men afterward. It is as necessary that the influence of both men and women should be felt in the government and in all the affairs of life as that we should have both the centrifugal and centripetal forces in nature to preserve us from chaos. I do not mean that men and women are just alike, the fact that they are not alike makes it all the more important that each should be represented."

The speaker advised American girls to protest against the custom of wearing decollete dresses when presented at the English court. She said the Chinese and Japanese are allowed to wear their national costume and suggested that American girls should adopt as their national costume a modest dress. She said that this custom of displaying bare arms and necks originated at the time when women were bought and sold at auction and when men purchased them for wives as they would a horse or an ox. Said she, "Shall we make our drawing rooms auction blocks for our daughters?"

At the close of the address she said she was ready to answer any questions which the ladies wished to present to her, and some of the ladies availed themselves of this opportunity. In reply to a question as to the status of women in the Bible, she said: "When Josiah was king some wise men wished to know the interpretation of a certain part of the 'Book of the Law' and he sent them to Hulda. They found her in a college where her duty was to expound the great principles of statesmanship and jurisprudence. Her husband was keeper of the roads."[5]

⇜ Unidentified clipping, 13 July 1889, SBA scrapbook 14, Rare Books, DLC. Square brackets surround uncertain reading.

1. John Duke Coleridge, Baron Coleridge (1820–1894), England's Lord Chief Justice from 1880 to 1894, toured the United States for several months in 1883. By the time he reached Washington in October, his praise for American women was legendary and "imperilled the lord chief justice's chances of

ever again finding favor in the eyes of English beauty," according to the *Washington Post*. "Wherever he went the American lady was the same charming personage and the American girl the same self-possessed bundle of independent anomalies." (21 October 1883.)

2. Arthur Cleveland Coxe (1818–1896), bishop of the Episcopal diocese of western New York, was a leader of the Anglo-Catholic movement that sought to restore Catholic practice in the Episcopal church. The Magnificat, also known as the Song of Mary, forms a part of both Catholic and Episcopal services. (*ANB*.)

3. This recognition of women's growing interest in the new safety bicycle was timely. American production of the safety began late in 1887; the first women's bicycle club in the United States started in Washington in 1888; and by the spring of 1889, clubs were found in many other cities. (David V. Herlihy, *Bicycle: The History* [New Haven, Conn., 2004], 235–45.)

4. Gen. 1:27–28.

5. 2 Kings 22:13–20. Huldah's husband was keeper of the *robes*, not the roads.

71 ECS TO CLARA BEWICK COLBY

[Hempstead, N.Y.?, before 10 August 1889][1]

Have you read "Looking Backward"? If not, do so at once. Bellamy's beautiful ideal of the future is to me full of hope and inspiration. I fully believe the time is near when all God's children will be educated, fed, clothed, and sheltered. When the good things of life will be equally distributed among the whole human family. When poverty, ignorance and vice will be known no more. If all this is not to be realized, to what purpose has the race endured its fierce struggle for the centuries.

Read the book. It is the new gospel of equality which we must carry to the nations of the earth.

Woman's Tribune, 10 August 1889.

1. Dated with reference only to the issue of the *Woman's Tribune* in which it was published.

72   Speech by SBA to the Seidl Society

EDITORIAL NOTE: The Seidl Society welcomed SBA at its luncheon for about two hundred and fifty women in the Brighton Beach Hotel on 30 August 1889. Laura Holloway introduced her, and according to the *New York Times*, SBA's "voice was clear and pleasant, and could be heard throughout the large dining room, though she spoke in low tones." Mary Seymour's report of this speech for the *Business Woman's Journal* alluded to the portion printed by the *Times* but focused on an opening that repeated well-known anecdotes SBA used on many occasions to distinguish charitable actions for women from reforms to empower women by giving them "an equal chance with every man to earn money." (*Film*, 27:417–18.)

[30 August 1889]

Men have always been more democratic than women because for every man there is one day on which all men are equal—election day. This fact that each man's opinion is equal to every other man's opinion makes all equal. I am glad to see it, because I like to feel that the opinion of every man on all subjects can have effect at least once a year. The converse is true of women. Women are aristocratic because there is never a day on which the opinion of each one has the same value as that of others. We have been divided into classes with different ideas, and now we are being educated into the knowledge of the fact that we must have organization for fellowship. The Woman's Convention at Washington last year[1] educated us to believe that our special and particular hobbies might not be more important than other hobbies. Miss Willard, for example, learned that temperance or prohibition was only one spoke in the wheel of woman's progress. We Woman Suffragists also lost some of our hobbies there by finding that other women were equally interested in other questions, and were doing famous work for the world. We women have been taught that the object of a woman's life is to help a man. No one seems to have suspected that any man was ever born for any purpose except his own happiness and self-development. Now, after forty years of agitation, the idea is beginning to prevail that women were created for themselves, for their own happiness, and for the welfare of the world. Therefore it is not their work to repair the damages made by men in the homes.

My mission is to prove that it is not women's duty to repair damages. I would work a revolution for this effect. The reason why women are doomed to subordination and financial dependency is that they are disfranchised. Give them the power to hold wealth and all the objections to a woman's proposing marriage to a man will disappear, for then, if the husband becomes a sot, she can turn him out of her house instead of his turning her out.

~ *New York Times*, 31 August 1889.

1. That is, the founding meeting of the International Council of Women.

73 ~ ECS TO CLARA BEWICK COLBY

[*Hempstead, N.Y., after 30 August 1889*][1]

Dear Mrs Colby,

I send you a scrap just found that if I remember ↑I↓ intended to improve a certain point in the way I put it in this.[2] Perhaps you can polish it up. It is a little more artistic to say Mrs Garrison was performing the last act in the opera of "Lullabye" than putting her children to bed

Susan has just spent two days with me. We talked over the coming Washington Convention & prepared the call[3]   She starts for the west in about two weeks to attend all the state conventions.[4] She had just returned from Brighton Beach were she had a grand ovation. Though the "Napoleon" of our movement will be seventy next February, she skips round as lightly as a girl of sixteen, while I roll about like a Dutch Brig. Oh that this too solid flesh would melt,[5] but it will not, like poor Jane in "Patience."

> "I fear there still will be
> In twenty years too much of me"[6]

~ AL incomplete, Clara B. Colby Papers, Archives Division, WHi. Marked for typesetter at "Though the 'Napoleon'" and published in part in *Woman's Tribune*, 5 October 1889.

1. Dated by reference to SBA's Seidl Society lecture.
2. Enclosure missing. ECS revised a sentence in "Reminiscences: Boston,"

Woman's Tribune, 21 September 1889, *Film*, 27:436-41, about a visit to Helen Eliza Benson Garrison (1811-1876), the wife of William Lloyd Garrison.

3. See below at 23 November 1889.

4. In October, SBA attended, and ECS wrote letters to, the annual meetings of state societies in Kansas, Indiana, Wisconsin, and Minnesota. At each one, members voted on whether to become auxiliary to the new National-American association. On the meetings, see *Film*, 27:450-66, 479-92, 505-6. Of the same visit ECS later wrote, "Susan spent a day with me on her way west to attend all the state conventions   I tried to pursuade her not to go as she needs rest more than excitement, but in vain, although I assured her that the earth would turn on its axis after she & I ascended to Abraham's bosom." (ECS to C. B. Colby, 29 September 1889, *Film*, 27:444-47.)

5. Shakespeare, *Hamlet*, act 1, sc. 2, line 285.

6. *Patience, or Bunthorne's Bride*, a comic opera by Arthur Sullivan and W. S. Gilbert, was first performed in 1881. In the lament "Sad Is That Woman's Lot," Lady Jane details how "her beauties disappear," ending with "Stouter than I used to be, / Still more corpulent grow I— / There will be too much of me / In the coming by and bye!"

74 ❧ ECS TO OLYMPIA BROWN

Hempstead, L.I., [*N.Y.*] Oct. 12th, 1889.

Rev. Olympia Brown, Dear Friend:—As I am unable to attend your state convention,[1] I would press on your consideration just two points:

First—The necessity of the union of our National Associations and thorough organization of our forces from Maine to California. If our suffrage movement were as well organized as the Woman's Temperance Association, we should have ten fold the power we have to-day.[2]

But as the first step toward organization is union, it is of vital consequence that all our coadjutors should see the wisdom of united action. Two associations advocating precisely the same measures yet seemingly in antagonism have been distracting forces in our cause for the last twenty years. Hence, when the proposition from the party that seceded came for "union," I readily assented, because in union I saw added strength as well as an immense saving of money and force.[3]

As many who took part in the division have passed to another sphere of action, and the work is gradually slipping from the hands of those who remain, it is a pity to hand down a heritage of discord to the brave young women on whose shoulders the future labors are to rest. The many apprehensions I hear expressed of the crippling effect of the proposed union seem to my mind wholly groundless, inasmuch as all measures will be settled by the vote of the majority. (The new organization can make and amend its constitution as it sees fit, choose its officers, and decide its plans of action all by the vote of the majority.) There is no room for clap-trap and political manoeuvering, and I do not see in any of the steps thus far taken the least disposition in that direction. Hence I heartily advocate union, and a thorough organization in all the states, and that each and all state societies become auxiliary to the National American Association, to hold its first union convention in Washington the coming winter.

Second—The next point to which I would call your attention is the present status of woman in the church. Such writers as Sir Henry Maine[4] clearly show that wherever the canon law has touched the civil law for woman it has degraded her, and that the church is the most powerful influence to-day in perpetuating the bondage of woman. Those who advocate both temperance and woman suffrage should be consistent and carry their principles just as fully into the religious sects as they do into the political parties. It is not consistent for such advocates of both measures as Frances Willard and Helen M. Gougar to make the fierce war on the political parties they do for their inaction on the temperance question, when their total neglect of the greater question, the fundamental rights of half the people, is still more glaring. If political parties are to be reined up for such violations of principle, how much more the churches of different sects for their pronounced hostility to the equal rights of women.

I cannot see the consistency of denouncing political parties that make no claim to superior virtue for certain violations of principle, while urging silence in regard to the action of church organizations, their priests and bishops claiming to be the great leaders of morals in every community. Whatever the church impresses upon the people as their religious duty from generation to generation, that will they obey. No law so powerful as religious superstition. See how long it has taken England to get rid of "the deceased wife's sister bill," and she is still struggling with it.[5] A few bishops in the House of Lords hold the common sense of the nation at bay because it has been taught a deadly sin by the tenets of the church, for a man to marry his wife's sister.

It is clear to my mind that the hostility of the church is our greatest barrier to the recognition of woman as an equal factor in civilization.

When in the great convocations for the different sects, woman's claims to recognition as an equal are ridiculed and denied, the lesson of contempt for her is taught in every department of the world's work. Seeing the devotion and enthusiasm of woman are the chief support of the churches in every community, a proper self-respect on the part of women should move them to make the same demands of the church now that we have made of the state in the last half century:—justice; liberty; equality. Yours sincerely,

~ *Elizabeth Cady Stanton.*

~ *Woman's Tribune*, 2 November 1889.

1. The Wisconsin association's annual meeting opened in Milwaukee on October 15. It was well known that the association would decide whether to affiliate with the new National-American, and ECS wrote to that point. Neither minutes of the meeting nor reports in newspapers mentioned this letter; whether it arrived too late or it did not suit Olympia Brown's purposes is not known. By the time Clara Colby published the letter in the *Woman's Tribune*, the association had made a decision. According to the minutes, a motion to affiliate was amended to refer the matter to local societies in the state. The *Milwaukee Sentinel*'s reporter detected "considerable sentiment expressed in favor of" becoming auxiliary. (*Film*, 27:484-91.)

2. ECS means the Woman's Christian Temperance Union.

3. This sentence brought Henry Blackwell to a boil, and he wrote "A Correction," in the *Woman's Journal*, 25 November 1889. Since the organizers of the American association had never belonged to the National, they could not secede from it, he pointed out. Offering his usual historical narrative, he constructed a detailed account of the National association's founding in 1869 at a meeting he did not attend, explained the reasons why self-respecting people could not join its founders, and reviewed the generous terms on which the American association began. While announcing his own self-restraint near the end of his lengthy article, he made the unusual statement that bitterness between the two associations came *after* both were founded: "Into the causes of disagreement which arose afterward, and greatly embittered the division, it is not necessary to enter."

4. Henry Sumner Maine, *Ancient Law, Its Connection with the Early History of Society and Its Relation to Modern Ideas* (1861). Maine wrote that common law borrowed most of its principles about marriage from the canon law (pages 158-59 in edition of 1863).

5. Until 1907 British law forbade the marriage of a widower and his wife's sister, but Parliament repeatedly debated Marriage with a Deceased Wife's

Sister bills. One such bill passed in the House of Commons only to fail in the House of Lords while ECS was in England in 1883. (Margaret Morganroth Gullette, "The Puzzling Case of the Deceased Wife's Sister: Nineteenth-Century England Deals with a Second-Chance Plot," *Representations* 31 [Summer 1990]: 142–66; *Papers*, 4:250, 260, 263–64n.)

75   ECS TO MATILDA JOSLYN GAGE

Hempstead, L.I., [*N.Y.*] October, 19, 1889.

Dear Mrs. Gage:

Helen Gardener has just spent a day with me and we talked the matter over, pros and cons, and came to the conclusion that there was more to be said in favor than against.[1] How might it be to fight the battle *within* the suffrage lines, claiming that we have the same right to vote in the church as in the State.

Claim one session for this branch, thus avail ourselves of suffrage audiences and finances. I do not know that this is feasible, but the thought suggests itself. We might call it "The Liberal Suffrage League," that will be free to discuss religious and social questions. The suffrage movement languishes to-day because the new-comers and many of the old ones are afraid to take an advance step. We are just in the position of the churches, dead. You cannot arouse enthusiasm any longer on the old lines, hence they are revising their Bibles, Prayer Books, catechism, creeds and discipline, and we must consider some onward steps.

Now this is your inspiration, your work. I am sick of all organizations and will not pledge myself to do one thing, except to join and speak when you say I must. How to get the needed dollars, how to get a mouthpiece in some paper, all this you must plan and manage. I will speak and give the highest truth I see on all religious and social questions, but I will not take any office in any organization. Once out of my present post in the suffrage movement I am a free lance to do and say what I choose and shock people as much as I please. With love,

  E. C. S.

Liberal Thinker, January 1890.

1. When Matilda Gage published this letter in January 1890, she said ECS wrote it "in reply to a letter asking her opinion in regard to forming a new liberal-thought organization." This organization was one of two challenges to the union of suffrage societies that Gage mounted in the fall of 1889. After she wrote to ECS, Gage found money to call a convention in Washington in February 1890 to establish the Women's National Liberal Union. By year's end, she defined its purposes as direct opposition to existing suffrage societies, all of which "cater to their worst enemy, the Church," and resistance to the "encroachment of 'The Church Party in Politics,' composed of both Catholics and Protestants." While she gathered support for her new society, Gage also circulated a protest against union, charging that the decisions made at the meeting she skipped in January 1889 were improper and in violation of the National's constitution. She circulated the *Liberal Thinker* and the protests against union together to members of the National association in a last minute effort to stop the merger. (*Liberal Thinker*, January 1890; M. J. Gage to Thomas Clarkson Gage, 6 November 1889, Gage Collection, MCR-S; M. J. Gage to Harriet H. Robinson, 17 December 1889, and M. J. Gage to H. H. Robinson and Harriette R. Shattuck, 18 January 1890, Robinson-Shattuck Collection, MCR-S; Olympia Brown, Charlotte F. Daley, Marietta M. Bones, and Matilda Joslyn Gage, *A Statement of Facts. Private* [N.p., 1890], *Film*, 27:661-68.)

76 ~> SBA TO LILLIE DEVEREUX BLAKE

Minneapolis Minn.¹ Nov. 1, 1889

Dear Mrs Blake

Your letter & list of local societies &c were forwarded me by my sister Mary— I meant to have written you long ago—but this flying about from point to point is not conducive to business matters—

Mrs Sewall thinks the new Constitution is so very specific—in saying "an added delegate for every 25 members above the first 50"—that only actual $1. or ↑50 ct—↓ state members—will be counted as the basis of representation—² I wrote Alice Stone Blackwell for her opinion—some time since—and hope soon to get an answer— But it is the one safe thing for the local societies to vote themselves auxilliary to the state society ↑& pay their dues to it—↓ and then—if the majority decide the basis shall be on the membership of the auxilliaries—as well as the direct members of the state societies—all will be ready—for that—or for the direct state membership basis— It ought to be decided—at once—but as I am bound up here in the Northwest—going South Dakota from Nov 12 to 22³—& thence work eastward—I cannot call a meeting officers—or write each & get the majority opinion—but if we are to ~~coul~~ reckon only upon the <u>actual members</u> of the state societies—who have paid the 50 cts—or $1. fee into the state treasury direct—each state ought—at once—to know this & thus have a chance & time to get all the <u>local</u> <u>society</u> members—to join the state direct—

I wish you—& the others who have an abiding place would settle this question—it won't make much difference in the results—only all the states must reckon from same basis—either of local members—or only from state members—

I go to Duluth the 4th & can hear from you to care of Mrs Sarah B. Stearns⁴ Duluth—Minn—until the 10th inst— The first rough draft for ↑call for↓ Wash. Con.—made by Mrs Stanton—was sent to Mr Blackwell two months ago—to add to—take from & make over to his mind—& return to Mrs Stanton for final rounding out & issuance—and as yet—I hear not a lisp from him—other than that the paper was received—This puts back the call hopelessly—& a letter should go out with it definitely stating basis &c   Sincerely yours

❧ Susan B. Anthony

[<i>sideways on first page</i>] Write Rochester Club what you think is the <u>basis</u> on which to reckon number of delegates—before Nov 8th when they hold their next meeting!

❧ ALS, Lillie D. Blake Papers, MoSHi.

1. SBA spent more than two weeks in Minneapolis and Duluth, visiting, lecturing, and attending the annual meeting of the Minnesota Woman Suffrage Association. See <i>Film</i>, 27:505-6, 519, 528.

2. May Sewall and SBA quote from the National association's second bylaw on basis of representation as adopted in Janunary 1889. See Appendix B in this volume. Sewall read it as assigning delegates to state auxiliaries of the National on the basis of individual memberships in a state society. Blake and SBA raised the question, might state societies also count the individual members of their local auxiliaries in establishing a basis for delegates to the National?

3. South Dakota became a state on 2 November 1889. While in Minneapolis, SBA was invited by leaders of the Dakota Farmers' Alliance, its president Henry Loucks and vice-president Alonzo Wardall, to help prepare for a referendum on woman suffrage. Wardall was also an officer of the new South

Dakota Equal Suffrage Association. The new constitution, like that of Colorado in 1876, directed the legislature at its first session to submit to the voters the question, "Shall the word 'male' be stricken from the article of the constitution relating to elections and the right of suffrage." On this preliminary visit, the suffrage association arranged SBA's schedule of lectures, and the Farmers' Alliance welcomed her to its convention. (South Dakota Const. of 1889, Art. 7, sec. 2; C. H. Ellis, *History of Faulk County, South Dakota, Together with Biographical Sketches of Pioneers and Prominent Citizens* [Faulkton, S.D., 1909], 239-40; Dorinda Riessen Reed, *The Woman Suffrage Movement in South Dakota* [Vermillion, S.D., 1958], 20; Wardall, "Woman Suffrage in South Dakota," p. 3, *Film*, 28:871ff; Howard Roberts Lamar, *Dakota Territory, 1861-1889: A Study of Frontier Politics* [New Haven, Conn., 1956], 244-84; Herbert S. Schell, *History of South Dakota* [Lincoln, Neb., 1968], 219-27.)

4. Sarah Burger Stearns (1836-1904) of Duluth was president of the Minnesota Woman Suffrage Association. As a young woman, she led a challenge to the University of Michigan's exclusion of women, after educating herself to exceed the entrance requirements. Later, she earned her degree at the Michigan Normal School. During the war, before and after her marriage in 1863 to a soldier and Michigan graduate, she earned notice for her service to soldiers' aid and sanitary work. In 1866, she and her husband moved to Rochester, Minnesota, and in 1872, relocated to Duluth. A leader in winning school suffrage for women in the state, Sarah Stearns served three years on the Duluth School Board. She was active in both the Woman's Christian Temperance Union and the National association. (*American Women*; *NCAB*, 5:656, 10:230; L. P. Brockett and Mary C. Vaughan, *Woman's Work in the Civil War: A Record of Heroism, Patriotism and Patience* [Philadelphia, 1867], 760; Barbara Stuhler, *Gentle Warriors: Clara Ueland and the Minnesota Struggle for Woman Suffrage* [St. Paul, Minn., 1995], 20-30; *Woman's Journal*, 21 May 1904.)

77 ~ CALL TO THE WASHINGTON CONVENTION OF THE NATIONAL-AMERICAN WOMAN SUFFRAGE ASSOCIATION

[23 November 1889]

The Twenty-Second Annual Convention will be held at Washington, D.C., in the Church of Our Father, corner of 11th and L Streets, Feb. 18, 19, 20, and 21, 1890.[1]

This Convention should be one of the deepest interest to all American women, coming as it does in the midst of so many historic events which mark the life of this nation. We have just celebrated in 1889 one hundred years of constitutional government; the coming Congress opens the second century of our national life; and in 1892 we round out 400 years since Columbus discovered America.[2] The memories of the great events of the past should inspire women with increased love of country, and arouse them to a sense of their duty in helping to maintain our free institutions.

While four great States just admitted into the Union have freely discussed women's right of suffrage in their conventions, they have all failed to incorporate it into their constitutions.[3] Nevertheless, the steps of progress already achieved should encourage the timid, and stimulate the brave to renewed efforts. The concessions made in the world of work, the trades and professions; in the department of education, opening colleges and universities; in the civil status of woman, securing to wives their rights of property, and many other individual responsibilities denied under the old common law; school suffrage in sixteen States,[4] municipal suffrage in Kansas, and, best of all, full suffrage in Wyoming Territory, where, after twenty years' experience, equal franchise has just been submitted to the people, both men and women, and has been incorporated in the new constitution by a vote of eight to one,[5]—all these steps of progress herald a new day for woman. But let us remember that these are so many privileges which those who gave may take away, unless women have some representatives in the councils of the nation. We are not secure until we have the ballot in our own hands,—that pivotal right of citizenship by which we can protect what we already possess or may attain.

This is pre-eminently a time when woman's co-operation is needed in the great work of government. Statesmen are mourning over the corruption in politics, in the legislative, executive, and even judicial departments; prophets are warning us of coming dangers; philosophers tell us that the problems of civilization are too complicated for man to solve them unaided, that his brain is already overweighted, and that some new force must be summoned. Where shall we look for this moral power that will bring order out of chaos, harmony out of discord, peace out of war, but in the education and elevation of women?

Hence we urge the friends of woman suffrage everywhere to renewed earnestness in their demands, and to a more thorough organization of State and local societies than we have ever had before. Each

State Woman Suffrage Association should seek to increase its membership, in order to prepare for the most efficient work possible. We also urge every State society, whether it has hitherto been auxiliary to the National or to the American Woman Suffrage Association, or to neither, to become auxiliary now to the united society, elect its representative on the National-American Executive Board, and send delegates to the annual meeting at Washington to plan for organized and united work.

NATIONAL.
- Elizabeth Cady Stanton, President.
- May Wright Sewall, Chairman Ex. Com.
- Hannah B. Sperry,
- Sara Winthrop Smith, Rec. Secretaries.
- Rachel Foster Avery, Cor. Secretary.
- Jane H. Spofford, Treasurer.

AMERICAN.
- William Dudley Foulke, President.
- Lucy Stone, Chairman Ex. Com.
- Henry B. Blackwell, Cor. Secretary.
- Martha C. Callanan,[6] Rec. Secretary.
- Julia Ward Howe, Foreign Cor. Secretary.
- Margaret W. Campbell,[7] Treasurer.

Woman's Journal, 23 November 1889.

1. It is not known whether Henry Blackwell ever returned the call to ECS before publishing it on 23 November 1889. Not until December 7 did the *Woman's Tribune* publish it. Differences in the later text are small ones and include locating the Universalist Church of Our Father at the correct corner, L and Thirteenth, Northwest. But the *Tribune*'s publication omitted officers of the American association entirely, concluded with the statement "On behalf of the National Woman Suffrage Association," and named only ECS, May Sewall, Jane Spofford, and Rachel Avery as signatories.

2. Christopher Columbus (1451–1506), the explorer of the New World.

3. South Dakota, North Dakota, Montana, and Washington.

4. See note at 26 March 1888 above. The higher number in 1889 was reached by the admission of Montana and the Dakotas to statehood.

5. Anticipating statehood in the near future, voters in Wyoming approved a new constitution on 5 November 1889 that guaranteed woman suffrage.

6. Martha Coonley Callanan (1826–1901), the wife of one of the richest men in Des Moines, Iowa, held sway in the state's suffrage and temperance movements for twenty-five years. Her opposition to the National association and more personally to friends of ECS or SBA, informed her local leadership.

(Benjamin F. Gue, *History of Iowa, from the Earliest Times to the Beginning of the Twentieth Century* [New York, 1903], 4:38-39; Louise R. Noun, *Strong-Minded Women: The Emergence of the Woman-Suffrage Movement in Iowa* [Ames, Iowa, 1969], 265-67; *Woman's Journal*, 24 August 1901.)

7. Margaret West Campbell (1827-1908) was a confidante of Lucy Stone, who became a lecturing agent for the Massachusetts Woman Suffrage Association and an organizer for the American association in the 1870s. After years of moving around, she settled in Iowa and helped to bring the state's independent suffrage association into affiliation with the American. (L. Stone to M. W. Campbell, 30 March 1874, 17 March 1888, in Wheeler, *Loving Warriors*, 249, 313; *Woman's Journal*, 28 February, 4 April 1874, 13 March, 26 June 1875, 28 July 1894, 12 December 1908; *History*, 2:766, 3:269, 622.)

78 ~ SBA TO RACHEL FOSTER AVERY

Pierre—South Dakota¹   Nov 25/89

My Dear Rachel

Mrs Spofford sends me the enclosed—² I have written Mr Mallon³—asking him to write to you—giving him your address—what will be his terms—and what are the forms necessary for the society—to make its claim good &c— I made it very <u>non</u>-committal—because you told me you had the matter in advisement— If you have not engaged a Lawyer to push our claim—I should think well of entrusting it with Judge Mallon— But surely we should not lose it by default of proper legal counsel!—

That $600. would give us a mighty lift in this Dakota work the coming year— It looks here as if ~~it~~ ↑we↓ might possibly carry the vote in South Dakota next November—if we begin our work early & in earnest & can keep out & ↑in the↓ <u>background</u> the 3ᵈ Party-Prohibition fanatics who want to vote as they pray—& everytime vote to bring into power the Whiskey party!!⁴— The Republicans are solid here—made Prohib. am't a plank in platform—and if we can hold our lecturers' heads level—will do the same for woman suffrage am't—& if they do it—the question will be carried—but it will take wise work—& no mistakes—⁵

It does seem so queer that when the Temp. people get their laws from the Repub's they turn round & try to kill the goose that laid the golden egg— The Repub. Prohib. Com. here—didn't allow 3^d Partyism to be advocated in their campaign—every lecturer—man & woman— was instructed <u>not</u> to obtrude it upon their audiences—& not one of them Mary Lathrap[6] or Col. Baine[7] said "<u>Vote as you pray</u>["] <u>non-sense</u>!! St John[8] came & made <u>one</u> <u>speech</u>—and though he did <u>say</u> 3^d Party—his very name & presence carried it—brought it into the meeting—and the Com. asked him not to speak again—& all say if the 3^d party people hadn't been kept <u>silent</u>—the Prohib. am't would have been lost

And now all agree that the success of the W.S. am't will depend upon whether the state suffrage Com. can be equally successful in keeping all 3^d Partism out of the state— Why Helen Gougar's last winter's Washington speech would tear things to fritters here—[9]

But I long to get to you— I think of my darling & rejoice with you every single night as I lay my head on my pillow & take a review of all I love & hope for[10]—& among them none has a dearer place than has the <u>first</u> adopted niece of your devoted Aunt

≫ *Susan B. Anthony*

My stops now are—[11]
    Nov. 25—St Lawrence, S.D.
      "   26—Aberdeen   "
          29—Detroit—Mrs Jenkins[12]
          30—Ann Arbor—Mrs Israel Hall
    Dec. 1—   "   "
      "   5—Rochester—Lecture—
         6—Geneva—N.Y. to see Mrs Stanton & Hattie
        & then to Phila—& Washington

≫ ALS, SBA Papers, DLC.

  1. SBA spoke in Pierre on November 23 and 24. (*Film*, 27:547-48, 552.)
  2. Enclosure missing.
  3. Patrick Mallon (1823-1896), an attorney in Cincinnati and an old acquaintance of Henry Blackwell, was handling the estate of Elizabeth Amanda McConnell (c. 1815-1889), a member of the National Woman Suffrage Association. McConnell bequeathed six hundred dollars to the *Woman's Journal* and another six hundred to the National association. (The *Woman's Journal* erred in announcing it shared honors with the temperance union.) The Butler County Probate Court accepted a redirection of the National's gift to the National-American, but the money was not paid until 15 December 1890. In

1880, McConnell, a widow who boarded with relatives in Oxford, Ohio, had answered the National's call for postcards of support directed to the Republican National Convention; other evidence of her commitment has not been found. (*History of Cincinnati and Hamilton County, Ohio; Their Past and Present* [Cincinnati, 1894], 552-53; *Cincinnati Commercial Tribune*, 9 December 1896; Records, Spring Grove Cemetery, Cincinnati; research assistance from the History and Genealogy Department, Public Library of Cincinnati and Hamilton County; Federal Census, 1880; E. A. McConnell to ECS, 31 May 1880, *Film*, 5:188; *Woman's Journal*, 23 March 1889; Will and Estate File of Elizabeth A. McConnell, Will Record 5 NEW, pp. 356-58, and Estate File No. 1852, Butler County Records Center and Archives, Hamilton, Ohio, with special thanks to Robert L. McMaken.)

4. In a separate ballot at the election on their state constitution in 1889, South Dakota's voters approved the prohibition of the manufacture and sale of liquor. SBA draws an analogy between the prohibitionists' campaign and the campaign she thinks necessary to carry woman suffrage. Republicans, under pressure from the Farmers' Alliance, endorsed prohibition in the earlier election, but, she learned, they would have bolted if the measure became identified with the Prohibition party. National lecturers from the Prohibition party and Woman's Christian Temperance Union campaigned for the measure along nonpartisan lines. Prohibition remained critical to state politics, with standards of enforcement still to be written and opponents talking about repeal. (South Dakota Const. of 1889, Art. 24; George W. Kingsbury, *History of Dakota Territory*. With *South Dakota, Its History and Its People*, ed. George Martin Smith [Chicago, 1915], 3:735-37.)

5. In a letter of November 17, SBA qualified her confidence: "The Republican party here stood for prohibition, and if it will stand for woman suffrage we can carry it, and not otherwise." (*Film*, 27:543.)

6. Mary Torrans Lathrap (1838-1895) was a licensed preacher in the Methodist Episcopal church and president of the Michigan Woman's Christian Temperance Union. She was also one of the founders of the state's suffrage association in 1870 and a worker in the amendment campaign of 1874. (*American Women*; *SEAP*; *The Poems and Written Address of Mary T. Lathrap, with a Short Sketch of Her Life*, Julia R. Parish, comp. [N.p., 1895]. See also *Papers* 3.)

7. George Washington Bain (1840-1927), a Prohibition party activist and temperance lecturer from Kentucky, campaigned in South Dakota for the prohibitory amendment. (*SEAP*; *WWW1*.)

8. John Pierce St. John (1833-1916), former governor of Kansas and a popular speaker, was the Prohibition party's presidential candidate in 1884. SBA meant to say "though he did *not* say 3^d party". (*ANB*.)

9. SBA refers to Helen Gougar's pitch for the Prohibition party at the National association's convention, "Partisan and Patriot." Gougar arraigned the major parties for their lockstep hostility to the Prohibition party and their tendency to act only in partisan opposition to each other. According to the

Washington Post, 24 January 1889, she "attacked every phase of politics under the sun save woman's suffrage" for at least ten minutes past her time limit, and SBA called her to order. An unidentified clipping, possibly from the Chicago *Lever*, a Prohibition party paper for which Gougar was associate editor, characterized SBA's action as "a clear case of Republican gag law for fear of the truth being told, which would not redound to the glory of Republican methods." (*Film*, 26:1081–82; unidentified and undated clipping, SBA scrapbook 14, Rare Books, DLC; Robert C. Kriebel, *Where the Saints Have Trod: The Life of Helen Gougar* [West Lafayette, Ind., 1985], 119.)

10. Presumably SBA rejoices in Rachel Avery's pregnancy. Rose Miller Avery was born 31 May 1890.

11. For coverage of Aberdeen, Detroit, and Rochester, see *Film*, 27:556–57, 569–70.

12. Helen Mar Philleo Jenkins (1833–1913) had known SBA since they collaborated to reform the New York State Teachers Association in the 1850s, when she taught school in Utica. After her marriage in 1862, she moved to Buffalo, Pittsburgh, and Detroit, making a name for herself in each city as a suffragist and local organizer. An occasional writer for the *Revolution* in 1868 and 1869, she served on the advisory committee of the National Woman Suffrage Association in the early 1870s. She hosted SBA on this visit to lecture in Detroit. (D. H. Van Hoosear, comp., *The Fillow, Philo and Philleo Genealogy. A Record of the Descendants of John Fillow, a Huguenot Refugee from France* [Albany, N.Y., 1888], 116; Nevin, *Social Mirror*, 32; *History*, 3:396, 4:298, 331, 756, 5:31n; *Film*, 1:444, 492, 2:18, 312, 9:35–43, 356–66, 766–77.)

79 ⇒ ECS TO CLARA BEWICK COLBY

Geneva New York [*November 1889*]¹

Dear Mrs Colby,

I should have written you ere this on the point on which you asked my opinion but I have been quite ill for a month, in bed much of the time, but am now better. I have about made up my mind to go to the Dansville Sanitorium & be rejuvenated.² In regard to Mrs Gages movement:—it seems to me that just as we have accepted the offer of union of the two national associations, it would not be honorable for me as President of one to take part in immediately organizing another without even making the experiment for one year to see how we can work together. Mrs Gage's idea is to combine those who are religiously free in a Liberal League   I see many difficulties in such an organization

1st There is but a small number at best & many of those would not be willing to be known as representatives of a new religion

2nd To accomplish anything we must have money   women are paupers.

It is a great struggle for the men to maintain a League. Ingersoll told me that all the expense of conventions & papers fell on a few rich men & that it was very difficult to get them to act against their worldly interests. These difficulties are doubled in the case of women.[3] Hence I suggest that we labor within our suffrage lines, to gradually liberalize our coadjutors without any separate action, bringing them on step by step. They would move the faster if they do not know just where they are going. I feel as strongly as Mrs Gage does that religious superstitions more than all other influences put together cripple & enslave woman, but so long as women themselves do not see it & hug their chains, we have a great educational work to do for them before they can see the chains that bind them & be willing to throw them aside. I would fain do all I can to make the Union of our forces a success. It seems desirable to me from every standpoint. It is time enough a year hence to organize a Liberal League if the experiment of Union fails   With kind regards yours ever

Elizabeth Cady Stanton

ALS, Clara B. Colby Papers, Archives Division, WHi.

1. Written late in November 1889. At the end of October, ECS was reported to be ill in Buffalo. From there she traveled to Geneva for a month-long stay with her cousin Elizabeth Miller. Still plagued by a severe cold, she went to Dansville about December 1, where SBA visited her on December 7. (Interview, *Buffalo Express*, 3 November 1889, *Film*, 27:510; *Eighty Years*, 418–20.)

2. The Sanatorium at Dansville, New York, once known as Our Home on the Hillside, was thought to be the premier water-cure of the time. Founded by James Caleb Jackson, abolitionist, lecturer, physician, and old friend of ECS and SBA, the facility was by 1889 in the charge of his son and daughter-in-law. After her visit to Dansville, SBA described ECS's purpose as "trying to get some of her adipose washed out." (William D. Conklin, comp., *The Jackson Health Resort: Pioneer in Its Field* [Dansville, N.Y., 1971]; SBA to Olivia B. Hall, 12 December 1889, *Film*, 27:588–93.)

3. Gage had just secured her scheme's immediate financial future by accepting gifts from the wealthy and eccentric pair William Farrington Aldrich, developer of mining and manufacturing in Alabama and later a congressman,

and his wife, Josephine W. Cables Aldrich, spiritualist, Theosophist, and former editor of *The Occult World*. Neither of them, Gage remarked, had ever "been in suffrage or liberal work of this character." Josephine Aldrich became the publisher of Gage's *Liberal Thinker*, and the couple's pet reforms dominated the meeting of the Women's National Liberal Union. (M. J. Gage to Thomas Clarkson Gage, 6 November 1889, Gage Collection, MCR-S; M. J. Gage to H. H. Robinson, 17 December 1889, Robinson-Shattuck Collection, MCR-S.)

80 ❧ SBA to Rachel Foster Avery

Washington D.C.—Dec. 21st 1889

My Dear Rachel

A letter from Mrs Stanton this A.M. says Harriot has decided to remain until after the Convention—¹ So no one need calculate on filling Mrs Stanton's place—<u>this time</u>—not even S. B. A. who— report says— is <u>very anxious</u> to supersede her old friend E. C. S.!!—² she says she cannot be in Phila Jan. 2^d—that they will stay at Dansville two or three weeks longer—and then visit Hempstead & New York—& bring round here by the <u>last</u> of January—but I want her here to go before the Congressional Committees before that date—if I secure Hearings!!

The appeals for money from South Dakota are very strong—and I feel like sending them my last dollar—but even that wouldn't be a drop in the bucket to what must go there— Lovingly yours

❧ *Susan B. Anthony*

❧ ALS, on NWSA letterhead, SBA Papers, DLC.

1. Harriot Blatch arrived in the United States in September 1889, and spent much of the next few months with her ailing mother. Having determined that she should take ECS to England to live, Blatch resisted SBA's pleas that their departure be delayed until after the Washington convention. (*Eighty Years*, 418–20; Ellen Carol DuBois, *Harriot Stanton Blatch and the Winning of Woman Suffrage* [New Haven, Conn., 1997], 70.)

2. Matilda Gage was one conduit for this rumor. Passing it along to Harriot Robinson, with the claim she had it straight from ECS, she wrote: "she— Susan—was as I had always supposed—to be the President. I think that was planned last winter—and I am at liberty to think so without injustice to Susan, who publicly proclaimed from our platform in 88 that she 'believed in rings.'"

But with gossip piling up in the same letter, Gage backed away: "Then again some members of the N.W.S.A bro't such pressure to bear ↑on Susan↓ in regard to Mrs Stanton that it has now been arranged between them that she [ECS] is to stand. The whole thing is a dirty muddle." (M. J. Gage to H. H. Robinson, 17 December 1889, Robinson-Shattuck Collection, MCR-S.)

81 ❧ SBA TO THE EDITOR, *WOMAN'S TRIBUNE*

Riggs House, Washington, D.C., December 23, 1889.

Dear *Woman's Tribune*:

Allow me to add to what I said in your last,[1] that my fourteen days in South Dakota were well filled: November 12th at Redfield; 13th, Huron; 14th, Mitchell; 15th, Yankton; 16th and 17th, Sioux Falls; 18th, Madison; 19th, Brookings; 20th, De Smet; 21st, Watertown; 22d, Parker; 23d and 24th, Pierre, the present capital of the State; 25th, St. Lawrence;[2] 26th, Aberdeen, where I was the guest of Mr. Thomas Clarkson Gage, the only son of Mrs. Matilda Joslyn Gage, and where I spoke before 475 delegates of the Farmers Alliance, with an immense assemblage of people who were not delegates, in their largest public hall.[3] I never saw an audience so alive to every point of my argument, responding with the heartiest "Yes" or "No" to my every appeal for justice to the women of that young State. At the close of my lecture I attended a meeting of their Equal Suffrage Executive Committee, where I reported my splendid meetings throughout the State and my most sanguine hope, nay, expectation, that a good majority of the men of South Dakota will, at the election of 1890, vote for the enfranchisement of the women of the State.[4]

On the morning of the 27th I left South Dakota for lectures in Detroit and Ann Arbor, Mich.; Toronto, Canada; and Rochester, N.Y., in all of which places I was greeted by fine audiences.[5]

I was most happy to assure our Canadian friends that, however it might be as to the union of our Governments, the National American Suffrage Association of the United States would most gladly welcome the Equal Enfranchisement Association of Canada into our union. And their President, Dr. Emily H. Stowe,[6] will be present at our twenty-second Washington convention in February, 1890.

On December 9th I arrived in Washington, where I shall remain to do all in my power to secure a discussion and vote on the floor of both Houses of Congress, as well as to make our coming convention overtop all of its predecessors, splendid as they have been for the past score or more of years. And may I not appeal to every friend of our good cause to send on to me not only their good words but their good dollars also, and thereby help along not only the convention, but aid also in carrying forward the great work that lies before us the coming year; that of helping the friends in South Dakota to educate every elector in that State into an understanding of the right and need of the enfranchisement of the women of their own households.

~ *Susan B. Anthony*

~ *Woman's Tribune*, 28 December 1889.

1. *Film*, 27:529.
2. For reports on Huron, Sioux Falls, Madison, and Pierre, see *Film*, 27:534, 538, 544, 547–48, 552. See also Mary Kay Jennings, "Lake County Woman Suffrage Campaign in 1890," *South Dakota History* 5 [Winter 1975]: 390–409.
3. At what the press called "a monster meeting" in Aberdeen's opera house on 26 November 1889; see *Film*, 27:556. Members of the equal suffrage association, including Elizabath Wardall and Marietta Bones, also appealed to the meeting. On the day after SBA addressed the meeting, the alliance adopted a resolution in support of woman suffrage and selected representatives to propose the same plank to a regional convention in the next month. When the alliance's vice president Alonzo Wardall went to Washington as a delegate to the National-American Woman Suffrage Association meeting in February 1890, he reported unanimous support in the state alliance, a resounding vote for suffrage in the ten-state Northwestern Farmers' Alliance, and a combined effort by the alliance and the Knights of Labor "to put into the field fifteen organizers, and their first qualification for the work must be that they were in favor of the ballot for women." (Lamar, *Dakota Territory*, 274–82; Schell, *History of South Dakota*, 225–26; Larry Remele, "'God Helps Those Who Help Themselves': The Farmers Alliance and Dakota Statehood," *Montana: The Magazine of Western History* 37 [Autumn 1987]: 22–33; *Aberdeen Daily News*, 1 December 1889; Wardall, "Woman Suffrage in South Dakota," p. 4, and *Woman's Tribune*, 1 March 1890, both in *Film*, 28:63–77, 871ff.)
4. Members of the executive committee of the South Dakota Equal Suffrage Association were Samuel Ramsey, Alonzo Wardall, Moses Barker, Sarah Richards, William Fielder, and Emma DeVoe. As state organizer, Helen Barker was no doubt included in the discussion. To document the plan made at this meeting, historians rely on a single source—SBA's recapitulation in a

letter to Samuel Ramsey, below at 29 March 1890. By that account, the committee agreed to visit every election district in the state by 1 May 1890. Emma DeVoe, assistant state organizer, went to work on the plan immediately. (Wardall, "Woman Suffrage in South Dakota," p. 4; *Woman's Journal*, 18 January 1890; Jennifer Ross-Nazzal, "Emma Smith DeVoe and the South Dakota Suffrage Campaigns," *South Dakota History* 33, no. 3 [2003]: 241-42.)

5. On her engagements in the United States, see notes above at 25 November 1889. In a last minute addition to her schedule, SBA accepted an invitation to address the Dominion Women's Enfranchisement Association in Toronto, Ontario, on 2 December 1889. See *Film*, 27:565-67 for coverage of her speech, 27:568 for an interview, and Catherine L. Cleverdon, *The Woman Suffrage Movement in Canada*, 2d ed. (Toronto, 1974), 25.

6. Emily Howard Jennings Stowe (1831-1903) studied at Clemence Lozier's New York Medical College for Women and was the first Canadian woman to practice medicine. After founding the Dominion Women's Enfranchisement Association early in 1889, she served as its president until her death. (*Dictionary of Canadian Biography*, 13:506-10.)

82 ❧ GIDEON J. TUCKER[1] TO SBA

New York, 6 Jan. 90

Miss Susan B. Anthony Respected Madam,

I have not the honor of your personal acquaintance although I am a convert of yours on the ↑question of↓ Woman Suffrage. I heard your address to the New York Legislature in 1866,[2] and I voted for Woman Suffrage in the Constitutional Convention of 1867.

I say this that I may prove my favorable prejudice in favor of justice to your sex, and because I want to express my surprise and disappointment at the language attributed to you in respect to ↑so unworthy a member of your sex as↓ Queen Isabella of Castile, in this day's ↑(N.Y.)↓ Morning World.[3] You will find you are wrong in saying that Isabelle sold her jewels to assist Columbus,—as much wrong as Mr. Purcell,[4] Editor of The Rochester Union, was, the other day, when he said she pawned her jewels for that purpose. She did neither: she borrowed church moneys to fit out Columbus, on the credit of her kingdom, Castile, and used no personal credit, no pawn, and no sale of any of her individual property. I have shown this fact in publications in this State, the fame whereof has probably not reached you, and I call your attention to facts of history which lie as open to you as to myself, that this sentimental story may be dismissed from your mind.⁵

Isabella was a selfish, cruel, faithless and bloody tyrant: she has no claim to honor at the hands of American free women of the Nineteenth Century. She persecuted the Jews, Mahomedan Moors, & West Indian natives. She founded the Inquisition, and established negro slavery in America. We have now not a statue of a king or queen, I think, on this continent, and hers should be the last that ever should be erected here. I am, madam, with high respect, Yours,

 Gideon J. Tucker.

 ALS, AF 69, Anthony Family Collection, CSmH.

1. Gideon John Tucker (1826–1899) was a Democratic lawyer and journalist who had served as secretary of state, surrogate judge, member of assembly, and delegate to the constitutional convention of 1867. (*Appleton's Annual Cyclopaedia, 1899*, 643.)

2. Tucker was mistaken in thinking SBA addressed the New York legislature in 1866. At the constitutional convention of 1867, he was, however, one of nineteen delegates to vote in favor of removing the word "male" from the state constitution. (*History*, 2:304n.)

3. As fast as a commemoration of the "discovery" of America by Christopher Columbus caught the public imagination and stirred politicians, women talked about his sponsor, Isabella (1451–1504), queen of Castile and Léon, and weighed how she might be incorporated into the national celebration. Tucker saw one of two statements attributed to SBA on the subject. From Washington, where she organized a petition to Congress on the subject of women's participation in the national celebration, she was reported to say, "People seem to forget that to a woman was due the discovery of America, for it was Isabella of Spain whose assistance enabled Columbus to pursue his journey, and who sold her jewels to secure him the necessary funds. So after Columbus, it is Isabel whom we should honor." A week later, similar remarks appeared in the *Washington Post*. (*New York World*, 6 January 1890, not in *Film*; *Washington Post*, 12 January 1890, *Film*, 27:1044.)

4. William Purcell (1830–1905) edited the Democratic *Rochester Union and Advertiser*. His statement about Queen Isabella pawning her jewels led Tucker to write on the subject, in articles and letters reprinted across the country. (*New York Times*, 28 December 1905.)

5. The introduction of Queen Isabella triggered a popular debate about her suitability as an icon for nineteenth-century Americans. William H. Prescott, *History of the Reign of Ferdinand and Isabella, the Catholic* (1837) informed the dominant, romantic view, while Eliza Ann Starr, *Isabella of Castile, 1492–1892* (1889), published for the Queen Isabella Association, reinforced the romance. Many contrarians relied on Alex C. Ewald, *Stories from the State*

Papers (1882), that exposed horrors of Isabella's reign. Popular journals carried articles on the subject, and debates about Isabella raged for weeks in the *Woman's Journal*, after the editors praised the Queen Isabella Association and its plans for a statue. Tucker's lessons for SBA in this letter cover most points of contention. (*Woman's Journal*, 12 October, 16, 30 November, 28 December 1889, 11 January, 8, 15 February, 26 April 1890; *Woman's Tribune*, 25 January 1890; *Albany Weekly Times*, 2 January 1890; *Syracuse Sunday Herald*, 26 January 1890; *Dallas Morning News*, 26 January 1890; *Kansas City Star*, 22 February 1890; with assistance from Ann E. Pfau.)

83 ❧ ECS TO ELIZABETH SMITH MILLER

Hempstead, Long Island, [*N.Y.*,] January 7, 18[90].

[D]ear Julius:

At last Hattie and I have reached Hempstead. We shall stay here until [w]e leave for England, unless we go to Washington and postpone England until March. Susan is pulling for Washington, Hattie for England, and like [M]icawber I am hoping something will turn up.[1] At our last evening at the [S]anatorium we had a great performance in the chapel, which holds about four [h]undred people.[2] We had music, recitations, charcoal sketches, etc., etc. [H]attie and Maggie both recited and I gave my medley, getting up some amusing [s]tories, which brought down the house every time.

My children here[3] have just commenced experimenting with the incubator [a]nd they have already hatched 150 chicks. What a wonderful invention it is. [I] should not be surprised if in the near future Eve's curse were removed forever! Lovingly,

❧ *Johnson*.

❧ Typed transcript, ECS Papers, NjR. Letters in square brackets obscured by binding.

1. In Charles Dickens, *David Copperfield*, Micawber's failures are not cause for despair but occasions for renewing his faith that something will turn up.
2. For undated reports of her speech at the sanatorium, see *Film*, 27:655-57.
3. Along with her son Gat, she refers to his wife, Augusta E. Hazleton Stanton (1850-?). (William A. Stanton, *A Record, Genealogical, Biographical, Statistical of Thomas Stanton, of Connecticut, and His Descendants, 1635-1891* [Albany, N.Y., 1891], 463; *Papers*, 3:306-7.)

84 ⇒ SBA TO MAY WRIGHT SEWALL

Washington D.C. Riggs House—Jan. 17, 1890

My Dearest May

Mrs Seward[1] of Bloomington has written me of Helen's[2] refusal to attend an Ex. Com. meeting called by her &c— I trust she cannot entirely block Indiana's wheels!!— All it needs is for the Treasurer to make out an accurate list of the members who have paid their dues this—or last year—& send the money on here— Mrs Gougar has no more power—by right of her office—than has Mrs Seward by right of hers, to forbid—or command the treasurer— But whatever Mrs Gougar does or doesn't do—Mrs Sewall is the Indiana member of National-A. Ex. Com.—hence you can speak & vote for Indiana— And then, too, as the Chair, Ex. Com. of Old National—you will have a vote in the election of the officers— You see the new Con. really disfranchises all of the old officers of both societies—and leaves only the State Presidents, members of Ex. Com. and delegates—with the right to vote & decide matters until after or before the election of officers—

I wrote ↑asked↓ Alice Blackwell—how she interpreted the matter—& she thought—by common consent—the general officers of both the National & American societies would be accorded the right to vote, until the new officers were elected— Now—I have that much—and do not propose to ask any farther questions—but when we get here together—I shall move—or get some delegate to do so—that all of the official boards of both old societies, shall be ex-officio delegates—with equal ↑the↓ right to vote on all questions until after the election of officers for the ensuing year—which according to the Constitution cannot be until!— I thought the Constitution specified the time for the election of officers—but I can't find a word of it—[3]

Now for the National— We surely should hold an Executive session—some-time—to receive the Treasurer's report—and wind up our business—as becometh a body who has made a will of itself to somebody else than itself—and it should be the Chair. Ex. Com. who should call this meeting—should it not? And should it be Monday A.M. 10

Oclock—the 17th of February?— I think so! But if you prefer—it might be on Saturday the 22^d—after we shall have seen the Union fairly inaugurated!— If it shouldn't <u>unite</u>—we might like to have our old ship standing at the dock ready for us to jump aboard again!

Alice writes me there is no requirement that the <u>state treasurers</u> should send the N.A. treasurer the names & P.O. addresses of their members—but I say there is—for the Con. says "a list—of the members of said organization["]—surely a list of names without the P.O. address would be of little avail!! So I have written every President to require her treasurer to write both names & Post Office addresses— That is the only way to <u>fore-arm</u> against all cheating!! I learned in Minnesota that there is very much of the W.C.T.U. membership after this fashion—a woman in a town gets some one to give her $10— and she sends it on to the National W.C.T.U and that $10. counts for 100 members of a local union—and gives the state <u>one</u> vote— I am told that a great many of dear Frances' quarter of a <u>million</u> <u>dear</u> W.C.U's are of that mythical class—and we want our 25 cts to come to us on ↑nothing but↓ bona-fide—human beings—who are actual members of a state society & its auxiliaries— Do you see—therefore—that we must insist on the names & P.O. addresses of all who are reckoned in the basis of representation

I have secured the $^1/_3$ R.R. fare on the Trunk Line & Southern Association Roads—which include all the middle & southern states—Buffalo—Pittsburg & Ohio—and am expecting the Central—which covers all east of Chicago & St Louis—and the Western—all west of those cities—& the New England—but they are awfully slow in getting ready to answer—[4]

And for Board rates—$2.50—at the Riggs—which is no more than the fith rate Hotels usually charge— Mr Spofford[5] is not willing I should <u>announce</u> that low write— So you can tell all—<u>free homes</u> will be found for a few—but the D.C. women all live in the smallest quarters—

I now have to say to you that it looks as if my hopes of Mr Stanton's being here were <u>false</u>— Hattie writes me she has never consented to stop until after the Con—and feels that she cannot stay away from her husband & child any longer—[6] If <u>you</u> will promise to Mrs Stanton across with you next summer—I think she would stay—but she is feeling far from well—& no one here can give her so good a home as can Hattie—so I cannot scold—nor importune her ↑not↓ to go—because I cannot offer her what she must have a home— If it wasn't for the South

Dakota work—I would say to her—go with me to Rochester & we'll live [*sideways on first page*] there together to the end— Lovingly yours

↝ S. B. A

↝ ALS, Grace Julian Clarke Papers, Indiana Division, In.

1. Elizabeth Irene Helton Seward (1837-1915) chaired the executive committee of the new Indiana Woman Suffrage Association, formed in October 1889. A resident of Bloomington, she was married to Williamson Brewster Seward of the Seward Foundry and was the mother of nine children. Seward and Helen Gougar had belonged to the National association's affiliate. When Indiana's rival societies met to merge in 1889, they were both candidates for president. The official report of that meeting did not hide Gougar's maneuvers with respect to how the election of officers would proceed, but it quoted nothing she said to indicate her motives. After electing Gougar, the association voted to affiliate with the National-American and chose May Sewall its delegate to the Washington convention. The difficulties described in this letter signaled Gougar's future course. Her name stood as the National-American's vice president for Indiana in 1890 and several years later, but the state society moved, in step with her, closer to the cause of prohibition; Seward was replaced as chair of the executive committee in 1890 by Mary Haggart, president of the state temperance union, and in 1891, Gougar pushed to disband the state society and concentrate the work in the temperance union's franchise department. For the next decade, Indiana delegates to the National-American more often represented city suffrage clubs than the state society. By 1897, the association was no longer an auxiliary of the National-American, and in 1899, national leaders stepped in to reorganize the state. (Federal Census, 1880; United States, Work Projects Administration, Indiana, *Index to Death Records, Monroe County, Indiana, 1882-1920, Inclusive* [Bloomington, Ind., 1940]; on-line family records, copy in editor's files; *Woman's Journal*, 8 June, 2 November 1889, 27 December 1890, 15 July 1893; unidentified clipping, c. November 1891, SBA scrapbook 17, Rare Books, DLC; *History*, 4:615-16; SBA to M. W. T. Sewall, 20 December 1897, *Film*, 37:502-6.)

2. That is, Helen Gougar.

3. When Ella Marble and Anna Shaw of the National association took this question to the final executive session of the American association, Alice Blackwell reluctantly agreed to allow old officers of both societies to vote for officers of the National-American. (*Woman's Journal*, 1 March 1890, *Film*, 28:78-82.)

4. Railroads granted price breaks for the purpose of travel to specific meetings. SBA describes negotiations with trunk line associations, groups of railroads that shared territory and limited their competition by agreements on rates charged for freight and passengers. The Trunk Line Passenger Committee

covered eastern railroads; SBA also refers to committees for the Southern Passenger, Central Traffic, and Western States Passenger associations.

5. Caleb Wheeler Spofford (1823–1901), husband of Jane Snow Spofford, became a proprietor of the Riggs House about 1877 and the sole owner a year later. He left the hotel and the business by 1892. (Spofford, *Genealogical Record of Spofford Families*, 247; city directories, 1877 to 1892; SBA diary, 11 February 1901, *Film*, 41:649ff.)

6. SBA received a telegram from ECS on 21 January 1890 saying she would come to Washington later that week and a letter on January 25 saying that she was delayed until January 27. (SBA diary, 1890, *Film*, 27:679ff.)

85   SBA to Isabella Beecher Hooker

The Riggs House   Washington D.C. Jan 31/90

My Dear Mrs Hooker

Of course I want you at the whole weeks doings—& wish Mr Hooker[1] could be here, too, on the 15th— And I want you at the Riggs too—and ↑as↓ close to Mrs Stanton & me as I can get you—for your head is so level on all pertaining to the work of cooperation— Mr Spofford puts his price down to $2.50 a day—& no one can get a fifth rate hotel for less ~~than that~~—

I note what you say about the C't state society not being auxilliary— Are you sure that all the local clubs of a state can each become auxilliary— while the state society does not— Ok—yes—I have read the Con. over—[2] I never did see such a bundle of a muddle as it is— I hope you will so manage as to secure the largest possible vote for Connecticut— I do want the old Nationals to try & stand solid—but Mrs Gage is doing her level best to defeat a real solid Union— Mrs Stanton the ↑first of↓ December—flatly refused to go into any secession movement with Mrs Gage—and then to humiliate her ↑& punish her↓ for such refusal Mrs Gage gets out her leaflet & publishes that October letter of Mrs Stanton— written half ironically—& fully at random—never dreaming that Mrs Gage could or would make a public [word?]![3] Mrs Gage is a most malicious person—always means to ↑have↓ revenge ↑upon↓ those who thwart her—and this is her way of paying off Mrs Stanton for standing by the Union— Of course none but those of ↑us↓ who know Mrs

Stantons suave way of evading a collision—can understand her writing such a reckless harum-scarum letter!!

Yes—I have received your two Centennial letters—but the ↑women in↓ Official circles were pushing the women on the Board of Managers—so that I felt it wisest for us suffrage women to leave all to them— But of all this when you come[4]   Mrs Stanton just come in—and says I shall be rejoiced to see Isabella once more—

My Dear do put down every point for resolutions—and do let us have one—stating the purpose—the breadth—the freedom of our platform— Now is the time to have a fixed & solemn declaration—that shall make all women—who are really for woman's political emancipation stand shoulder to shoulder in this one N. A. associati[on]— I want it to show the twenty years ago seceders that we are ↑fully↓ as broad & free as then—and the Gage seceders that our platform is as free now & then & therefore is broad enough for all who work for the ballot pure & simple— If a lot of women want to halt by the way to knock something ↑else↓ down—befor[e] they get freedom—let them go— Lovingly yours
≈ Susan B. Anthony

[*in margin of enclosure*] The reduction will do you no good—except you purchase your ticket in New York—but you will want to come before the 12th & stay longer than the 24th—hence wont care for any of this—[5]

≈ ALS, 920 An87, Archives, History and Genealogy Unit, Ct. Square brackets surround one uncertain reading and letters missing at margin. Envelope addressed to Hartford, Conn.

1. John Hooker (1816–1901), husband of Isabella Hooker, was a lawyer and useful ally of Connecticut's suffragists. Alongside his wife, he drafted women's rights legislation and lobbied for its passage. (Obituary Sketch of John Hooker, 73 Connecticut Reports 745. See also *Papers* 2 & 3.)

2. This discussion about the Connecticut Woman Suffrage Association's inaction on becoming an auxiliary of the National-American contradicts a list of auxiliaries published in the *Woman's Tribune*, 11 January 1890, that included Connecticut. SBA notes that local clubs could affiliate with the National-American when the state society did not, according to section one of the second bylaw, on the basis of representation. See the constitution of 1889, appendix A, in this volume.

3. See above at 19 October 1889. Gage also announced on the front page of the *Liberal Thinker*, January 1890, that ECS would be among the speakers at the meeting.

4. Neither a location nor a governing structure for the Columbian celebration had yet been settled by Congress, but a large lobby was at work in Washington to ensure that whatever the plan, women were included. SBA joined the work in December 1889, and much of her time in Washington in January 1890 was given over to social calls on the wives of officeholders. On January 13, Senator Orville Platt presented a petition signed by female relatives of justices of the Supreme Court, cabinet officers, and senators and members of Congress, as well as by a few women prominent in their own right, all seeking the appointment of women to the exposition's board of managers. SBA's calls on the wives continued after January 13, suggesting that pressure on politicians continued at home. Hooker later became involved in the exposition, both as one of Connecticut's members on the Board of Lady Managers and as a member of the unofficial Queen Isabella Association. (Jeanne Madeline Weimann, *The Fair Women* [Chicago, 1981], 21–33; *Report of the Twenty-sixth Washington Convention, 1894*, pp. 131-37, and SBA diary fragment, December 1889, and SBA diary, entries for January 1890, all in *Film*, 26:1001, 27:679ff, 32:326ff; *Congressional Record*, 51st Cong., 1st sess., 499.)

5. Omitted here is the enclosure, a printed flyer detailing how to obtain the special rates for travel to the Washington convention.

86 ～ SBA TO ELIZA WRIGHT OSBORNE[1]

Washington D.C. Feb. 5, 1890

My Dear Friend

I am delighted that you & Ellen[2] will both be here—& dear Wm Garrison too—it is almost too good to believe!— Mr Spofford will give you a single room opening from theirs—a double one—he has put his price down to $3. & $2.50—a day— I want you three to have real nice rooms—& have so told Mr S.—and dear Mrs Lord[3]—too—how glad I shall be to see you all— Maria Davis & Anna Hallowell[4] decline to come— I am very sorry—but am very very glad you all will come— You will doubtless see Mrs M. J. Gage's movement to make a secession—but never mind— Come & stand by <u>Susan once</u> more—just as your precious mother always did— Mrs Stanton has been here a week & is delighted that you are all coming— I do not believe any considerable number will follow Mrs Gage—to form a <u>Liberal religious Woman Suffrage Association</u>!! You ↑see↓ that would be just as ridiculous a <u>Christian W.S.A.</u>— It cannot be that our women can be cajoled or deceived into such a foolish step— But we shall see— I tell them I have ↑worked↓ 40 years to make the W.S. platform broad enough for Atheists & Agnostics to stand upon—& now if need be I will fight the next 40—to keep it Catholic enough to permit the verriest ↑Orthodox↓ religionist to speak or pray & count her beads upon— I shall hope Mr Spofford can give you rooms near to Mrs S. & me— Lovingly & rejoicingly

↝ *Susan B. Anthony*

[*in margin of first page*] Do come to visit before the 15th do!!

↝ ALS, on NWSA letterhead, year corrected, Garrison Papers, MNS-S.

1. Eliza Wright Osborne (1830–1911) lived in Auburn, New York, where she grew up, a daughter of Martha Coffin Pelham Wright (1806–1875). Wright served as the National association's president at the time of her death. Osborne was active in the New York State Woman Suffrage Association, following in the footsteps of her mother who was its first president. (*NAW* and *ANB*, s.v. "Wright, Martha Coffin"; Wright genealogical files, Garrison Papers, MNS-S; Garrison, *Letters*, 6:214n; *Woman's Journal*, 12 August 1911. See also *Papers* 1–3.)

2. That is, Eliza Osborne's sister, Ellen Wright Garrison.

3. Martha Mott Lord (1828–1916) was the youngest child of Lucretia and James Mott and first cousin of Eliza Osborne and Ellen Garrison. (*Selected Letters of Lucretia Coffin Mott*, ed. Beverly Wilson Palmer [Urbana, Ill., 2002], xlviii; *Papers*, 2:606.)

4. Maria Mott Davis (1818–1897), another of Lucretia Mott's daughters, was the widow of Edward M. Davis, a longtime ally of ECS and SBA. (*Selected Letters of Mott*, xlvi.) Her daughter Anna Coffin Davis Hallowell (1838–1913) of Boston edited *James and Lucretia Mott: Life and Letters* (Boston, 1884). (*WWW4*; Garrison, *Letters*, 5:418n; *Selected Letters of Mott*, xlvii.)

87 ↝ FROM THE DIARY OF SBA

[*13–14 February 1890*]

THURSDAY, FEBRUARY 13, 1890. In Washington   Brother D. R. Sister Annie O. & Mary S. and Niece Maude arrived at 4 P.M—

Mary Hallowell & Sarah Willis[1]—& Lucy Boardman Smith[2] Mrs L. C. Smith[3]—Jenny Marsh Parker all of my own city—[4]

Surely my own family—my own city & my own Suffrage friends do me more honor than I can deserve—

1. Guests arrived to attend SBA's birthday celebration, organized by May Sewall and Rachel Avery. Mary H. Post Hallowell (1823-1913) was one of SBA's closest friends and an activist for woman's rights since the convention at Seneca Falls in 1848. Sarah L. Kirby Hallowell Willis (1818-1914) was a member of the same extended family of reformers in Rochester and also attended the convention at Seneca Falls. (*Quaker Genealogy*, 3:434, 483, 489, 507; William F. Peck, *History of Rochester and Monroe County, New York, from the Earliest Times to the Beginning of 1907* [New York, 1908], 2:1242-44; Nancy A. Hewitt, *Women's Activism and Social Change: Rochester, New York, 1822-1872* [Ithaca, N.Y., 1984], passim; Hewitt, "Amy Kirby Post," *University of Rochester Library Bulletin* 37 [1984]: 4-21. See also *Papers* 1-4.)

2. Lucy Boardman Smith (1820-1901) and her husband, a retired lawyer and former assemblyman from Livingston County, moved to Rochester in the 1870s, probably about the time their son entered the University of Rochester. SBA knew them as members of the Unitarian Church, and although documents of their friendship are scarce, there are hints: SBA sat with Lucy Smith on the night before her death; the *New York Times* made their friendship the centerpiece of Smith's obituary; and a few years later, Smith's son was a pallbearer at SBA's funeral. (Federal Census, 1880; *New York Times*, 5 December 1901; SBA diary, 5, 6 December 1901, *Film*, 41:649ff; on-line transcription of Grove Cemetery Records, Ulysses, N.Y., in editor's files.)

3. Lewia C. Hannibal Smith (1811-1909), better known as Mrs. L. C. Smith, moved to Rochester as a widow in the 1850s and became a local activist. At her ninety-fourth birthday party, SBA called her "the champion worker in the way of begging money in this city." (Federal Census, 1880; *History*, 3:413; Hewitt, *Women's Activism and Social Change*, 208, 210-11, 214; Rochester *Democrat and Chronicle*, 14 June 1905, *Film*, 44:561; Garland Cemetery, Clarkson, N.Y., tombstone transcription.)

4. Jane Marsh Parker (1836-1913) of Rochester was a prolific writer under the name Jenny Marsh Parker, who helped establish SBA's role in Rochester's history. She emerged in the next few years as a strong opponent of woman suffrage. (*ANB*; *Papers*, 4:350-52.)

FRIDAY, FEBRUARY 14, 1890. In Washington   Cousins Hannah Boyles, Melissa Dickinson   Dr. Fannie & Charles all came from Chicago[1] and Cousin Lucien & Ellen Hoxie Squier from Brooklyn[2]—& on Saturday Nephew Arthur Mosher—& Niece Louise & husband & Mrs James[3]— Miss Thomson[4]—Eliza Wright Osborn & Ellen Wright Garrison— So [many?] many of my friends

1. The Dickinsons were children of SBA's aunt Ann Eliza Anthony Dickinson, her father's youngest sister. Hannah Dickinson Boyles (1838–1920), the eldest, was married to a Chicago merchant. (Anthony, *Anthony Genealogy*, 216–17; Frederick A. Virkus, ed., *The Compendium of American Genealogy* [1930; reprint, Baltimore, 1968], 4:67, s.v. "Boyles, Katherine.") Melissa Dickinson (1839–1910) joined her brothers in the family business, the Albert Dickinson Seed Company. By the 1890s, she was spending each winter in Florida, where she acquired considerable property. (Anthony, *Anthony Genealogy*, 218; Will of Melissa Dickinson, signed October 1906, NAWSA Papers, DLC.) Frances Dickinson (1856–1945), known as Fannie, and Charles Dickinson (1858–1935) were the youngest and had traveled abroad together in 1883 and 1884, encountering SBA along the way. Frances graduated from the Woman's Medical College in Chicago, studied opthamalogy abroad, and launched a distinguished medical career. Her Chicago office also provided headquarters for the Queen Isabella Association. Charles worked in the family seed business. (F. M. Sperry, comp., *A Group of Distinguished Physicians and Surgeons of Chicago: A Collection of Biographical Sketches of Many of the Eminent Representatives, Past and Present, of the Medical Profession* [Chicago, 1904], 150–53, and obituary in unidentified paper, 24 May 1945, both courtesy of the Chicago Historical Society; *The Book of Chicagoans: A Biographical Dictionary of Leading Living Men and Women of the City of Chicago, 1917* [Chicago, 1917]; *Who's Who in Chicago* [Chicago, 1926]; *Chicago Daily Tribune*, 3 September 1935. See also *Papers* 4.)

2. Ellen Hoxie Squier (1833–1904), another first cousin, was a daughter of Hannah Anthony Hoxie. She and her husband, Lucien Bertrand Squier (1829–1904), lived in Brooklyn, New York. (*Friends' Intelligencer* 61 [16 January 1904]: 40, [3 December 1904]: 779; Anthony, *Anthony Genealogy*, 191, 197; *Quaker Genealogy*, 3:173.)

3. SBA groups together the family of her late sister Hannah Mosher. Louise Mosher married Alvan T. James (c. 1852–1924) on 20 June 1889, by Quaker ceremony at the home of Edith C. James, where Louise had been living. The couple stayed on at that address for several more years. Although SBA's biographer described James as "a prominent business man" of Philadelphia, salesman was the occupation given in city directories. (*Friends' Intelligencer* 46 [1889]: 408, and 81 [1924]: 198; *Anthony*, 2:652; Federal Census, 1880, 1910; city directories, 1888 to 1893.) Elizabeth Knight James (1813–1890) of Byberry Township, Philadelphia, was Louise Mosher's mother-in-law who died only a month after this event. (*Friends' Intelligencer* 47 [1890]: 201.) Arthur Anthony Mosher (1851–1932) was one of Louise's older brothers. After learning the insurance business with D. R. Anthony in Leavenworth, he was sent to St. Louis by the Travelers Insurance Company and headed the firm's southwest regional business. In 1891, he became vice president of the Missouri, Kansas, and Texas Trust Company in Kansas City, Missouri. (Anthony,

Anthony Genealogy, 183; *Insurance Times*, February 1891, SBA scrapbook 17, Rare Books, DLC; *New York Times*, 20 May 1932.)

4. That is, M. Adeline Thomson.

❧ Excelsior Diary 1890, n.p., SBA Papers, DLC.

88 ❧ Birthday Celebration for SBA

EDITORIAL NOTE: For the birthday party on 15 February 1890, guests gathered at nine o'clock in the evening at the Riggs House, where May Sewall and ECS received them. After an hour of conversation, SBA, on the arm of Senator Henry Blair, led the way into the dining room, with ECS on the arm of Robert Purvis close behind. Then nearly two hundred guests, each of whom paid four dollars to attend, found their seats at small tables in the room. After the meal, rhymes were read, and toasts and responses were given. Someone with a sense of humor assigned the toast "Miss Anthony as Fellow-Worker" to Matilda Gage. ECS responded to the toast "The Friendships of Women."

[15 February 1890]

Mrs. Stanton then responded to "The Friendships of Women." "Friendship, like the Immortality of the Soul, is too good to be believed. Therefore the cynic world has denied it in women." Mrs. Stanton's address is given in full.

It has been said "that women are incapable of lasting friendship."

This is one of those oft-repeated masculine slanders, that has passed into a proverb. But the innumerable instances of tender friendships between women, lasting through life, contradict the time-worn assertion.

It may be true of the fashionable, frivolous classes, as a rivalry of wealth, position, and charms, with their jealousies and envies, would necessarily soon produce most strained relations. In friendship as well as in love, we must first have units, complete men and women, before we can have enduring friendship.[1]

An old Latin motto says: "The good only are capable of lasting friendship." Earnest women, engaged in serious pursuits, to whom life is not a tournament, but as Mazzini says, "a march and a battle," must have warm friendships;[2] indeed, to such they are imperatively necessary. How many such instances history might have given, we know from what we see in our own day. But as men in the past were the only writers of history, they have simply recorded their own deeds of heroism; not thinking it worth while to record anything concerning women, except their evil deeds. The Scriptures give a few glimpses of possible friendships between Ruth and Naomi, Mary and Elizabeth, Phoebe and Priscilla, and Tryphena and Tryphosa,[3] but the general silence in secular history shows that it is written on Caesar's idea, that "the highest praise for a woman is that her name be never mentioned."[4] Fortunately, the time has come for women to write history themselves, and thus we are able to refer to many friendships, especially among single women, in whose homes one finds the most perfect harmony and freedom. George Eliot,[5] Frances Power Cobbe,[6] Charlotte Bronte,[7] Harriet Martineau,[8] all had their intimate, steadfast friends.

Our sainted Lucretia Mott had a group of young disciples, whose love and friendship knew no shadow of turning during her long life. Our own Sallie Holley and Caroline Putnam,[9] who have spent twenty years together in teaching the freedmen, are as true to their work and each other as on the first day they clasped hands and dedicated themselves to their mission.

If there is one part of my life that gives me more intense satisfaction than another, it is my friendship of forty years' standing with Susan B. Anthony. Her heroism, faithfulness and conscientious devotion to what she thinks her duty has been a constant stimulus to me to thought and action. Ours has been indeed a friendship of hard work and self-denial. I always know when Susan appears on my threshold that we are to gird our armor on and attack some stronghold of the enemy.

Emerson says, "it is better to be a thorn in the side of your friend than his echo."[10] If this adds weight and stability to friendship, then ours will endure forever, for we have indeed been thorns in the side of each other. I helped to convert my dear friend to the suffrage gospel, little dreaming what an expansive, explosive element I had uncorked on this Republic, in creating that power, so long sought for by philosophers, "perpetual motion," for Susan is always at her post, never caught napping.

Sub rosa, dear friends, I have had no peace for forty years, since the day we started together on the suffrage expedition, in search of woman's place in the National Constitution. Alas! we have had no greater success than the heroes who have been searching for the North Pole, and never found it.

She has kept me on the war-path, at the point of the bayonet, so long that I have often wished my untiring coadjutor might, like Elijah, be translated, a few years before I was summoned,[11] that I might spend the sunset of my life in some quiet chimney-corner, and lag superfluous on the stage no longer.[12] But after giving up all hope of her sweet repose in Abraham's bosom, I sailed some years ago for Europe. With an ocean between us I said, now I shall enjoy a course of light reading, I shall visit all the wonders of the Old World, and write no more calls, resolutions, or speeches for conventions, when, lo! one day I met Susan face to face in the streets of London, with a new light in her eyes, and broader plans for execution. Lo! there were new worlds to conquer. She had decided on an international council in Washington, so I returned with her to the scenes of our conflict.

Now I am about to make another experiment, and I do hope you will keep our Napoleon busy in the Dakotahs and Washington, long enough for me to take breath, and visit my children and grandchildren on the other side. But alas! there is little hope, for Susan told me in confidence that she should use her influence to have the next International Council in London. I trust the young disciples will put down their official foot and insist on having it under the dome of our own Capitol. I am constantly told that I am completely under Susan's thumb. Well, as all women are supposed to be under the thumb of some man, I prefer a tyrant of my own sex, so I shall not deny the patent fact of my subjection, for I do believe that I have developed into much more of a woman under Susan's jurisdiction, fed on statute laws and Constitutional amendments, than if left to myself reading novels in an easy-chair, lost in sweet reveries of the golden age to come, without any effort of my own.

At the close of Mrs. Stanton's remarks "the Guest of the Evening" was announced, and Miss Anthony arose amid a tumult of applause, clapping of hands, and waving of handkerchiefs. It took some time to restore quiet. When this was done, Miss Anthony said:

I have been half inclined, while listening here to-night, to believe that I had passed on to the beyond. But I don't mean to go there yet.

Then I thought that, perhaps, the next time we meet together you may all denounce me, for it is so easy, just by one little slip of the tongue, to be misunderstood. To-night you sing my praises, but how easy it is for the world to turn around and say the other thing! I think if there is one thing I would like more than another, it is, if I should stay on this planet thirty years longer, that I may be worthy of the wonderful respect you have manifested for me here to-night. But I am going to try to behave as well as I can. The one thought I wish to express is how little my friend and I could accomplish alone. What she has said is true; I have been a thorn in her side, and in that of her family, too, I fear. Mr. Stanton[13] was never jealous of any one but Susan, and I think my going to that home many times robbed the children of their rights. But I used to take their little wagon and draw them round the garden while Mrs. Stanton wrote speeches, resolutions, petitions, etc., and I never expect to know any joy in this world equal to that of going up and down, getting good editorials written, engaging halls, and advertising Mrs. Stanton's speeches. After that is through with, I don't expect any more joy. If I have ever had any inspiration she has given it to me. I want you to understand that I never could have done the work I have if I had not had that woman at my right hand. If I had had a husband and children I never could have done it. And if I had had opposition in my own home I never could have done it. My father and mother,[14] my brothers and sisters, those who have gone and those who are here to-night, have been a help to me! In all my forty years of labor I have had the sympathy and help of my family. I never could have done my work if I had had to go home to a disagreeing family on this question. How much depends on the sympathy and co-operation of our friends and those about us! I see John Hutchinson[15] here. What would he have done without it? Every woman presiding over her table in the homes where I have been has helped to sustain me. It isn't necessary for all to make sacrifices and go to the front. I want them to realize how they have supported and helped me in their own homes. It is my hope that we are to do a grander work than ever before—a work in which the women from over the water shall join hands with us.

~ *Woman's Tribune*, 22 February 1890.

1. With the word "unit," ECS revives a term of Ralph Waldo Emerson about the solitary individual, complete in his character, and able "to yield that

peculiar fruit which each man was created to bear." To Emerson, true unions, whether civic or romantic, required prior attainment of this state of self-reliance and fulfillment. See especially his essays "The American Scholar" and "Love."

2. Guiseppe Mazzini (1805-1872) was the champion of the unification of Italy under a republican government. In the form "a battle and a march," this description of life was more closely associated in the nineteenth century with the English historian Thomas Carlyle, though its use was widespread.

3. Accounts of these biblical pairs are found, for Ruth and Naomi, in the Book of Ruth; Mary and Elizabeth, in Luke 1:5-90; Phoebe and Priscilla, in Romans 16:1-4; and Tryphena and Tryphosa, in Romans 16:12.

4. ECS alludes to a story about Julius Caesar (100-44 B.C.), who decided to divorce his wife over suspicions about her adultery even though he believed her to be innocent, giving rise to the phrase, Caesar's wife must be above suspicion.

5. Probably a reference to Sara Sophia Hennell (1812-1899), a close friend of George Eliot. (*George Eliot Letters*, ed. by Gordon S. Haight [New Haven, Conn., 1954], 1:lv-lix.)

6. Frances Power Cobbe (1822-1904) was an English writer, reformer, and leading figure in the antivivisection movement with whom ECS visited in England. Mary Charlotte Lloyd (1819-1896), a sculptor and friend of Harriet Hosmer, was Cobbe's companion. (Sally Mitchell, *Frances Power Cobbe: Victorian Feminist, Journalist, Reformer* [Charlottesville, Va., 2004]. See also *Papers* 4.)

7. Charlotte Brontë (1816-1855), the English author of *Jane Eyre*, among other novels, was close friends for twenty-four years with her schoolmate Ellen Nussey (1817-1897). (*The Letters of Charlotte Brontë, with a Selection of Letters by Family and Friends*, ed. by Margaret Smith [Oxford, 1995], 1:93-95.)

8. Harriet Martineau (1802-1876), an English writer and abolitionist, enjoyed a close friendship with Elizabeth Jesser Reid (1789-1866), a widow and pioneer in women's education. (R. K. Webb, *Harriet Martineau, a Radical Victorian* [London, 1960], 17; Garrison, *Letters*, 2:663n.)

9. Sallie Holley (1818-1893) and Caroline F. Putnam (1826-1917) were companions from their days at Oberlin College until Holley's death. They worked together at the Holley School in Lottsburg, Virginia, funded by Emily Howland for the education of African Americans. (*NAW* and *ANB*, s.v. "Holley, Sallie"; Patricia Harland Gaffney, *The Emily Howland Papers at Cornell University: A Guide to the Microfilm Publication* [Ithaca, N.Y., 1975], 14-15; New York *Evening Post*, 27 January 1917.)

10. In his essay "Friendship," Ralph Waldo Emerson (1803-1882) advised it was better to be a nettle than a thorn.

11. In 2 Kings 2:8, when his life comes to an end the prophet Elijah is swept

to heaven in a tornado. In Luke 16:22-25, to rest on the bosom of Abraham while awaiting judgement was the highest honor.

12. For the source of this phrase, see note above at 2 November 1888. The *Tribune* printed "lay superfluous," prompting ECS's fierce retort at 21 March 1890, below.

13. Henry Brewster Stanton (1805-1887).

14. Lucy Read Anthony (1793-1880). Two of SBA's sisters died young: the oldest, Guelma Penn Anthony McLean (1818-1873), and the one born next after SBA, Hannah Lapham Anthony Mosher (1821-1877).

15. John Wallace Hutchinson (1821-1908) was the last surviving member of the original Hutchinson Family Singers, who first performed at gatherings of reformers in 1843. (Family tree, in Dale Cockrell, ed., *Excelsior: Journals of the Hutchinson Family Singers, 1842-1846* [Stuyvesant, N.Y., 1989].)

89 ~ FROM THE DIARY OF SBA

[*15-16 February 1890*]

SATURDAY, FEBRUARY 15, 1890. At the Riggs—Washington—D.C— This closes my allotted <u>three</u> <u>score</u> & <u>ten</u> <u>years</u>—and starts me on the last decade of my fourth score— Many friends come in time for the Banquet gotten up by Mrs May Wright Sewall & dear Rachel Foster Avery—the one sorrow was that the latter couldn't be here—[1]

1. Rachel Avery was detained in Philadelphia to care for her older sister, Julia Foster, who apparently suffered a nervous breakdown. SBA rushed to Philadelphia on February 23 to help Rachel move Julia to a new medical facility. Julia died before the end of the year. (SBA diary, 23-25 February, 4 March 1890, *Film*, 27:679ff.)

SUNDAY, FEBRUARY 16, 1890. In Washington   The Boston Party arrived this A.M—and all day the delegates & friends kept arriving—

Sunday evening our National's held a meeting to talk up who should be President—neither Mrs Stanton nor Miss Anthony were allowed in—

~ Excelsior Diary 1890, n.p., SBA Papers, DLC.

90 ❧ REMARKS BY SBA TO THE FINAL EXECUTIVE SESSION OF THE NATIONAL WOMAN SUFFRAGE ASSOCIATION

EDITORIAL NOTE: At the Riggs House, delegates from the American and National associations filed into separate rooms for their final executive sessions. To the American delegates Henry Blackwell explained the day's significance: "that upon all the points of difference in methods" between the two associations, "the National had now accepted the position originally occupied by the American. . . . Above all, it had expressly determined to take for its watchword woman suffrage pure and simple, and to exclude side issues." The delegates then voted that in a presidential contest between ECS and SBA, "the American delegates be recommended to cast their votes for Miss Anthony." Back in the National's meeting, delegates heard reports from committees, discussed the disposition of the treasurer's papers, and heard SBA make an impassioned plea to elect ECS and sustain the National's long history of tolerance. (*Woman's Journal*, 1 March 1890, *Film*, 28:78-82.)

[17 February 1890]

Mrs. Chairman,[1] officers and members of the National Association. There was a meeting last evening of the Nationals in the private dining room, and a long discussion as to whom the Nationals preferred for President of the National American. I will say to every woman who is a National, and who has any love for the old association, or for Susan B. Anthony, that I hope you will not vote for her for President. I stand in a delicate position. I have letters which accuse me of having favored the union solely from personal and selfish considerations. I have letters accusing me of trying to put Mrs. Stanton out. Now what I want to say is, don't you vote for any human being but Mrs. Stanton. There are other reasons why I want her elected, but I have these personal ones. When the division was made 22 years ago, it was because our platform was too broad, because Mrs. Stanton was too radical. A more conservative association was wanted. And now if we divide and Mrs. Stanton shall be deposed from the presidency you virtually degrade her. If you have any regard for the National from the beginning, that has stood like a rock without regard to creed or politics, without regard to any possible consideration, that every woman should be allowed to come on our platform to plead for her freedom; if you have any regard for that grand old principle, vote for Mrs. Stanton.

When Mrs. Stanton went to Europe before, she went as the representative of a quarrel. Now we want to send her as the representative of union and harmony. Our association has always allowed the utmost freedom to vote against everything that would block our way, no matter whether it was the church, or what it was. Anything and everything that stood in the way of progress was always likely to get its head knocked off on the platform of the National Woman Suffrage Association. I want every one who claims to be a National to stand for this broad principle. I want our platform to be kept broad enough for the infidel, the atheist, the Mohammedan, or the Christian. I remember thirty years ago George William Curtis[2] said to me: "If you want your platform to succeed you must not allow Mrs. Ernestine L. Rose[3] to stand upon it, she's a pronounced atheist." I said: "We shall never turn her out." Now we have come to another phase of the fight, and if it is necessary, I will fight another forty years to make it broad enough for the Christian to stand upon, whether she be a Catholic, and counts her beads, or a Protestant of the straightest orthodox creed. I shall fight for the rights of the Christians to-day, as for the rights of the infidels forty years ago. We have also delegates from Utah on our platform. Let not the Nationals go back on their record. Every woman, whether she be Mormon or Gentile, has the right to vote. It was a dastardly act of Congress in disfranchising the women of Utah. They are here to-day with a magnificent delegation.[4]

These are the broad principles I want you to stand upon, that our platform may be kept as broad as the universe, that upon it may stand the representatives of all creeds and no creeds—Pagan, Jew, Gentile or Christian, Protestant or Catholic. (Applause.)

Woman's Tribune, 22 February 1890.

1. May Sewall chaired the meeting.
2. George William Curtis (1824–1892), a prominent essayist, provided suffragists with a powerful voice at New York's constitutional convention of 1867 to which he was elected a delegate-at-large. His convention speech for equal rights remained in circulation as a pamphlet. (*ANB*. See also *Papers* 2.)
3. Ernestine Louise Siismondi Potowski Rose (1810–1892), one of the first

women to petition for reform in the laws regarding married women's property, was a powerful speaker on the antebellum woman's rights platform. Born in Poland and married in England, Rose arrived in New York in the 1830s. After the Civil War, she and her husband settled in England. (*NAW*; *ANB*. See also *Papers* 1-4.)

4. The National association, often in collaboration with Mormon women, had long defended the voting rights of women in Utah Territory against congressional plans to disenfranchise them. In a sweeping renunciation of woman suffrage, the Edmunds-Tucker Act of 1887 disenfranchised polygamous males in the territory and all women, whether or not polygamous. SBA chose this example of tolerance with good reason: Lucy Stone regarded the National's cooperation with Mormon women as reprehensible. In her lists of inappropriate activity by ECS and SBA, Stone by 1882 included welcoming Mormon women to the suffrage platform. As recently as 1888, she refused to join the National Council of Women because polygamous Mormon women were involved. (Sarah Barringer Gordon, *The Mormon Question: Polygamy and Constitutional Conflict in Nineteenth Century America* [Chapel Hill, N.C., 2002], 147-81; Lucy Stone, statement about divisions, 4 February 1882, NAWSA Papers, DLC; L. Stone to Frances E. Willard, 23 August 1888, in Wheeler, *Loving Warriors*, 314-15.)

91 ~ FROM THE DIARY OF SBA

[*17 February 1890*]

MONDAY, FEBRUARY 17, 1890. In Washington— When 10 Oclock came the Nationals packed the Private Dining room to suffocation—& the Americans looked lost in the great parlor—so I proposed to the A's to exchange with the N's—which they did very cheerfully— Mrs Gage was present—& I made her understand—in my speech on Mrs Stanton for Pres—that all of <u>her</u> <u>mean</u> <u>efforts</u> to persuade our members that I favored Union—from ambition to supersede Mrs Stanton—were fully known to me—& I appealed to all—as they would do me personal honor to vote solid for Mrs Stanton—at the National American union meeting in the afternoon— I was filled with most Rigteous indignation at her—

~ Excelsior Diary 1890, n.p., SBA Papers, DLC.

92   Address by ECS to the National-American Woman Suffrage Association

EDITORIAL NOTE: From the stage in the new Lincoln Music Hall, ECS called to order the first meeting of the National-American Woman Suffrage Association at eleven o'clock in the morning of 18 February 1890. After thanking delegates for electing her their president, she explained that she had written resolutions for the convention to consider; "The reason I do this," the *Evening Star* reported her saying, "is that this is the only session I will be here, and I will be unable to be present in the committee of resolutions and discuss them there." She then asked Clara Colby to come forward to read them. At that moment, John W. Hutchinson caught SBA's attention with a request that he start the meeting with a song. When he finished, Colby read the resolutions, but another interruption delayed ECS's address: men arrived to decorate the stage with a large shield with the seal of Wyoming and a circle of flags. When she began her address, ECS sat down to speak, holding her manuscript under a table lamp. She had organized her speech as an argument for her resolutions. At its conclusion, she had crossed swords with a significant number of the delegates in her audience. (Washington *Evening Star*, 18 February 1890, and *Washington Post*, 19 February 1890, *Film*, 28:50-51, 83.)

[18 February 1890]

As I sail for Europe tomorrow morning, and may not have the honor of standing on this platform again for some time, and in view of my age perhaps never, yet I shall hope to see again all these familiar faces, so dear to me through many years of mutual struggle.

But in saying farewell for the present I ask the privilege of expressing my opinion on a few practical questions that I would like to bring before our Union Association for consideration.

As in the nature of things our work must soon pass into the hands of a younger generation, it would not be amiss before parting to give them the keys to our archives, explain to them our genealogical tree, that they may know something of their ancestors, and tell them of our experiences in the past and our hopes in the future. We might point out to them the defects in the old house, and its management, and wherein it needs repairing, if our suffrage children had not already so clearly pointed them out themselves.

But I trust that while they try to cover all minor defects with paper and paint, they will use brick and mortar and enduring cedar plank, for all the dangerous places that I shall make known to them.

Though this movement was inaugurated by some of the most cultured men and women of the nation, and carried on with rare ability and heroism, yet the great truths proclaimed have been received with profound indifference by the vast majority.

Though such men as Emerson, Theodore Parker, Channing, Alcott, Garrison, Phillips and Gerrit Smith[1] have all with matchless eloquence graced our platform, yet they seemingly failed to rouse any enthusiasm in our behalf. Caroline M. Severance,[2] Ernestine Rose, Paulina Wright Davis, Isabella Beecher Hooker, Elizabeth Oakes Smith,[3] Abby Kelley, all as beautiful women in form and feature as one ever sees in a fashionable drawing room, brought to our platform their wit, their logic, their rare executive ability and their inspiring prophecies of speedy victory, but their words fell on those who had ears but heard not, eyes too had they but saw not,[4] and seemingly they too did not create a ripple on the surface. Then came a simple, childlike looking girl from a remote town in the old Bay State, with a plump form, a rosy face, and a voice sweet as any nightingale, fresh from the inspiration of college life, armed and equipped with pathos, wit and argument so earnest and persuasive and yet at times so vehement, that it seemed as if she must move the hearts of the people. They listened, cried and laughed over the experiences in woman's life held up before them and remembered Lucy Stone but not the lessons she taught them. They went home to their usual occupations and seemingly no lasting impression was made. The sainted Lucretia Mott with her gentle manners and persuasive speech and her noble sister Martha Wright were pillars of strength to our movement all through the darkest days of the early struggle.

There too were Frances D. Gage, a brilliant speaker and writer of prose and verse, Clarina Howard Nichols, who was considered the best Whig editor in Vermont for many years, Caroline H. Dall, who has published several interesting works that give her as a writer and thinker a worthy place in our literature. Oberlin college gave us Antoinette Brown, Antioch gave us Olympia Brown, the first women regularly ordained ministers in the nation.

Matilda Joslyn Gage speaks for herself in the History of Woman Suffrage. We must not forget our devoted friends Samuel J. May,[5] Samuel E. Sewall, Frederick Douglass, Robert Purvis, Thomas Wentworth Higginson[6] and George William Curtis, who with pen and tongue gave the weight of their literary position at an early day to the cause of woman, and continue to do so at this hour.

Many other noble men and women, time fails me to mention, joined us in what we may call the sub-soiling, under-draining, deep-ploughing period, when ridicule and persecution frightened cowards to silence and places of safety. I must not forget to mention her whom William Henry Channing styled the Napoleon of our movement. Yes, friends, "Susan and I" came also, and tormented the Legislature of New York for twenty years, until a member proposed, one day on the floor of the Senate when they heard we were coming to hold a protracted meeting in Albany, that the military be ordered out, whether to protect us or the Legislature did not clearly appear in the record. In due time we handed the State over to Mrs. Devereux Blake, and our legislators have had no more peace under her dynasty than ours. And yet with such an array of gifted men and women it seemed for a long time as if no one heeded the new gospel of woman's equality; with waiting ears we heard only the echo of our own voices, though thousands were all along pondering in their hearts all that had been said on our platform. After a few years we began to see some signs here and there that labor had not been wholly lost, a stray blade of grass or flower marked the path our friends had trodden.

The chief barriers in the way to a more pronounced success in our movement have been:

1st. The apathy and indifference of society to all reforms.

2nd. Our lack of thorough and widespread organization.[7] Lecky has well said the success of a movement, "depends much less upon the force of its arguments, or upon the ability of its advocates, than on the predisposition of society to receive it."[8] Conservatives are made up largely of those who are afraid of everything new, and of those who are too lazy to entertain a new line of thought and action. They take it for granted, that our earthly arrangements are permanently established for all time. Though they see the marked changes made, from the remote past to their day, yet they can not believe that as marked changes will be made in the future.

The apathy of society is a large factor in every step of progress. Each reform demands an entire change in popular thought and a new line of action. This, to that large class who accept things as they find them, who believe implicitly in the traditions of their fathers, and never do any thinking, is troublesome and heretical.

From want of use the muscles of their minds are flabby, they can not entertain a new idea. You might as well ask those who are not trained gymnasts, to stand on their heads, as this class, to gird up their minds to thinking. To their vision the principles of government, religion and social life all run in parallel lines together. Now a proposition to change one of these lines, they readily see puts it out of joint with the remainder, but they do not understand, that change in all directions is the law of progress, and that in due time, with a new current of thought, on many other vital questions, all the lines will be changed, until parallel once more, when woman's political equality will be in harmony with the changes in all other directions.

3rd. As to organization, for many years we had no forces to organize. Each individual was a free lance to say or do whatsoever she listed. The few states that took any action whatsoever, did so independently of the rest. Though the methods and specific demands were the same, they were so, not from any concert of action but from the same injustice suffered. Until the war, a National Committee that rarely met was the only bond of union. When the slaves of the South were emancipated, and their political status was the same as ours, we urged the abolitionists to unite with us in an Equal Rights Association. But they, believing that the Freedman stood a better chance for enfranchisement than the woman, refused the proposed affiliation. However our Equal Rights Association was formed, but owing to divisions on the anti-slavery question and the pending 14th amendment and some personal differences, it lived but a brief period, and from its ashes sprang the National and American organizations.

And now, after twenty years of grand work on different lines, we have come to the conclusion that in union there is strength, and added power in thorough organization. In uniting all our forces to-day under one banner, with the hearty co-operation of every friend of the movement victory might soon be ours.

The Union may be a difficult and delicate relation in starting, but if we can hold all personal differences in abeyance for a few years, I think we shall have no farther need of any organization. For if the great western states now coming into the Union shall, in harmony with the spirit and letter of the National constitution, recognize women as citizens of the United States, and hence legal voters for all United States officials, and as citizens of their respective states also, with the right to vote for all state officials, our work will soon be accomplished. And these rights are clearly guaranteed by the 14th and 15th amendments. But to this end we must have thorough organization. Isolated effort is of little value in carrying any great measure. For evil purposes, as well as good, there must be combination. The Molly McGuires in Pennsylvania held all law at defiance, and terrorized that State for years.[9] Labor with its strikes has compelled proud monopolies to grant fairer terms, and organized capital holds the nation in the hollow of its hand to-day.

A small minority of Irishmen under the lead of Parnell[10] in the House of Commons has kept the question of Home Rule before Parliament for years, upset Ministries, and compelled even the Tory party to talk of doing justice to Ireland. When the anti-slavery sentiment was at last organized in a political association it overturned old parties, precipitated the war and set the slaves free. These examples show us our primal duty at this hour. With all our forces welded together and concentrated on one point, our influence on the near future will, I know, prove irresistible. And never did we need united, determined action more than at this time when, by the admission of so many western states in which the question of woman suffrage is pending, our future labors must be indefinitely multiplied. Fortunately the press of national and state work comes at different seasons. From June to November, we can work with reference to state elections; and from December to May, with Congress, conventions in Washington and hearings before committees, with Majority and Minority Reports franked by the thousands and scattered through the states, again to influence the fall elections. With the state societies planning their own campaigns, and the National Association the movements in Washington, there need be no conflict in action.

In view of the many vital questions now up for consideration in which women are especially interested, it seems to me that the time has come for more aggressive measures, more self assertion on our part than was ever manifested before. Those of us who feel it most keenly have never been able to portray the monstrous crime of woman's disfranchisement, nor the grievous humiliation we feel, in view of our degraded position as native born American citizens under a foreign yoke, increasing in weight with every ship-load landing on our shores, until it is indeed grievous to be borne.

It is an arrogant assumption of power, by those administering the government to hold us another day in such bondage.[11] Our title to a voice in this government is as clear as that of the man by our side. We were accounted as "people" and "voters" in the constitutions of thirteen original colonies. We find no mention of a privileged class of "white male citizens," in those early documents, we hear only of "people" "persons" "inhabitants" and "tax-payers." Accordingly women voted in some of the colonies until as states their constitutions were so framed as to limit the suffrage with qualifications of property, education, color and sex in violation of every principle in our government. It is a patent and oft repeated fact that

> in the State of New Jersey women voted at all elections from 1776 to 1807 upon terms of equality with men. They helped to elect the delegates from that State to the constitutional convention. They voted to ratify the instrument when submitted. They voted at the first five presidential elections—twice for Washington,[12] twice for Jefferson and once for John Adams. Their descendants are only claiming the exercise of a right as old as the constitution itself.
>
> The contest in the year 1800 was bitter beyond all precedent, and we are told that all the women of the State who were entitled to vote did so.[13] One of these voters, the late Mrs. Cumback, mother of the Hon. Wm. E. Cumback of Indiana, died only a few years ago.[14]

This right in the colonies was but following the precedent established far back in English history, showing that women voted and held office throughout that Kingdom at an early day. It is clear then that women have been cruelly robbed of rights they once possessed and exercised.

For fifty years we have been plaintiffs at the bar of justice, and three generations of statesmen, judges and reformers, have exhausted their able arguments and eloquent appeals in the courts and before the people. But as the Bench, the Bar and the Jury are all men, we are nonsuited every time.

Some men tell us we must be patient and persuasive; that we must be womanly. My friends, what is man's idea of womanly? It is to have a manner that pleases him, quiet, deferential, submissive, that approaches him as a subject does a master. He wants no self-assertion on our part, no defiance, no vehement arraigning of him as a robber and a criminal. While the grand motto "Resistance to tyrants is obedience to God,"[15] has echoed and re-echoed round the globe electrifying the lovers of liberty in every latitude, and making crowned heads tremble on their thrones; while every right achieved by the oppressed has been wrung from tyrants by force; while the darkest page on human history, is the outrages on women, shall men tell us to-day to be patient, persuasive, womanly? What do we know as yet of what is womanly? The women we have seen thus far have been, with rare exceptions, the mere echoes of men. Man has spoken in the state, the church, and the home, and made the creeds and codes and customs that govern every relation in life, and we have simply echoed all his thoughts and walked in the paths he prescribed, and that they call womanly. When Joan d'Arc led the French army to victory I dare say the carpet knights of England thought her unwomanly. When Florence Nightingale,[16] in search of blankets for the soldiers in the Crimean War, cut her way through all orders and red tape, commanded with vehemence and determination those who guarded the supplies to "unlock the doors" and not talk to her of the proper authorities when brave men were shivering in their beds, the nobles of Russia would no doubt have called her unwomanly, but doors opened! the blankets were forthcoming! and the men in their tents slept warmer that night than if she had waited with patience and persuasive eloquence to convince the authorities that the thermometer was 20 degrees below zero, and that British soldiers unused to the cold climate of Russia might be a little chilly in their tents.

To me "unlock the doors" sounds better than any words of circumlocution, however sweet and persuasive, and I consider that the womanly way of accomplishing her object.

Now this is the metaphorical force and dynamite that I am ever and anon recommending to my co-adjutors in securing the right of 20,000,000 of women on this green earth.

Patience and persuasiveness are beautiful virtues in dealing with children and the feeble-minded adults, but with those who have the gift of reason, and understand the principles of justice, it is our duty to compel them to act up to the highest light that is in them, and as promptly as possible.

We have rehearsed the great principles of our government on the popular platform, until the leading journals are wont to say that the same old arguments have been made to do duty once more, and the literati ask us if like Poe's Raven we intend to sit and sing suffrage on every door-post forevermore.[17]

One thing is sure, our arguments have not done their whole duty until the nation is converted to freedom, and crowns 20,000,000 women with their rights of self-sovereignty. When that is done we shall come down from our perches and sing suffrage no more. Then will a new song be put in our mouths, for our year of jubilee will indeed have come.

We might get some agitation by trying a new field for our labors, demanding equality for woman in the church.[18] As women are the chief supporters of the church, get up all the fairs, donation parties, do all the begging to build churches, support missionaries and theological seminaries, many of them making large bequests to these various institutions, one would think the time had fully come for women to demand of the church the same equal recognition she demands of the state. She should assume her right and duty to take part in the revision of Bibles, Prayer Books, and Creeds; to vote on all questions of business and to fill the offices of deacon, elder, Sunday School Superintendent, Pastor and Bishop, and have the right to sit and vote as delegates in all ecclesiastical conventions, synods, and assemblies, that thus our religion may no longer reflect only the masculine element in humanity, and that woman,—the mother of the race,—may be honored as she must be before we can have a happy home, a rational religion, and an enduring government.

If educated women had exerted any enlightened influence on the religious thought of the world, leading men in the 19th century would not stand debating the damnation of infants at this hour, harrowing up the souls of pale mothers, sorrowing over the loss of their first born. Men not endowed with the paternal instinct may pass unscathed through the ordeal of such a discussion, but alas! for the young mothers all over this land, who read these atrocious sentiments in cold type, as they decorate with flowers the little graves of their loved ones.

Our insane asylums are full of susceptible, imaginative young women, whose reason has been dethroned by these religious superstitions.

Surely the yearning mother-love once set free from old creeds and dogmas, must bring to humanity new light and hope, both for this world and the one to come.

As women are taking an active part in pressing on the consideration of Congress many narrow sectarian measures, such as more rigid Sunday laws, to stop travel and the distribution of mail on that day; and to introduce the name of God into the constitution; as this action on the part of some women is used as an argument for the disfranchisement of all, I hope this convention will declare that the Woman Suffrage Association is opposed to all Union of church and State and pledges itself as far as possible to maintain the secular nature of our government. As Sunday is the only day the laboring man can escape from the cities, to stop the street cars, omnibuses and railroads would indeed be a lamentable exercise of arbitrary authority. No, no, the duty of the state is to protect those who do the work of the world in the largest liberty, and instead of shutting them up in their gloomy tenement houses on Sunday, we should open wide the parks, horticultural gardens, the museums, the libraries, the galleries of art and the music halls where they can listen to the divine melodies of the great masters. All these are questions of legislation, and what influence women will exert as voters is already being canvassed; hence the importance of this association expressing its opinions on all questions in which woman's social, civil, religious, and political rights are involved.

Consider the thousands of women with babies in their arms year after year, who have no change to the dull routine of their lives, except on Sunday when their husbands can go with them on some little excursion by land or sea, suddenly compelled to stay at home by the passage of a rigid Sunday law, secured by the votes of those who can drive about at pleasure in their own carriages, and go wherever they may desire.

It is puerile to say, "no matter how we use the ballot, the right is ours," but if the presumption that we will use it wisely, enters into the chance of our obtaining it, it is desirable for the public to know our opinions on practical questions, of morals and politics.

We must demand a voice too in another field of labor, thus far bounded, fenced and tilled by man alone; where according to his own statistics one may now gather more thorns and thistles than fruits and flowers, and this is in the home.[19] Many propositions are now floating about as to the laws regulating our family relations. We have had several symposiums in popular reviews by leading minds both in England and America from the pens of men and women, from Mr. Gladstone,[20] England's greatest statesman down to our own Helen Gardener.[21]

The message I should like to have go out from this convention is, that there should be no farther legislation on the questions of Marriage and Divorce until woman has a voice in the state and national governments. Surely here is a relation in which above all others there should be equality; a relation in which woman really has a deeper interest than man, and if the laws favor either party it should be the wife and mother. Marriage is a mere incident in a man's life. He has business interests and ambitions in other directions, but as a general thing it is all of life to woman where all her interests and ambitions centre. And if the conditions of her surroundings there are discordant and degrading, she is indeed most unfortunate, and needs the protection of the law to set her free rather than to hold her in bondage.

And yet it is proposed to have a national law restricting the right of divorce to a narrower basis. I doubt whether the states would concede this power over private contracts between their citizens, to Federal authority; though Congress has already made an appropriation for a report on the question, which shows that there are 10,000 divorces annually in the United States and other statisticians say the majority, asked for by women.[22] If liberal divorce laws for wives are what Canada was for the slaves, a door of escape from bondage, we had better consult the women before we close the avenues to freedom. Where discontent is rocked in every cradle and complaints to heaven go up with every prayer, talk not of the sacredness of such relations, nor of the best interests of society requiring their permanent establishment. The best interests of society and the individual always lie in the same direction, hence the state as well as the family is interested in building the home on solid foundations.

Some may say that none of these questions legitimately belong on this platform, but as they always have been discussed on the woman's rights platform from the beginning they probably always will be. Wherever and whatever any class of women suffer whether in the home, the church, the courts, in the world of work, or on the statute books, a voice in their behalf should be heard in our conventions. We must manifest a broad catholic spirit for all shades of opinion, in which we may differ and recognize equal rights of all parties, sects and races, tribes and colors. Colored women, Indian women, Mormon women, Christians and Infidels and women from every quarter of the globe have been heard in these Washington conventions and I trust they always will be.[23]

The enfranchisement of woman is not a question to be carried by political clap-trap, by stratagem or art, but by the slow process of education, by constant agitation and in new directions attacking in turn every stronghold of the enemy.

The Paris milliners and dress-makers show their knowledge of human nature by getting up new fashions for every season. Let us imitate them and stir up a whole group of new victims from time to time, by turning our guns on new strongholds. Agitation is the advance guard of education. When any principle or question is up for discussion, let us seize on it and show its connection, whether nearly or remotely, with woman's disfranchisement. There is such a thing as being too anxious lest some one "hurt the cause" by what he or she may say or do; and perhaps the very thing you fear is exactly what should be done. It is impossible for any one to tell what people are ready to hear. Let me give you an example to show how little we can judge of what it is at all times best to say and do. When I was last in England a daughter of the great statesman, the Hon. John Bright,[24] invited me to her house to spend a few days as she proposed to have a parlor meeting and wished me to tell her friends the status of our cause in America.[25]

"But," said she, "I want you to be very careful as to what you say. You must remember we have municipal suffrage for widows and spinsters, but not for married women, so say nothing about them. Don't say anything about marriage or divorce, nor about the church, nor the Bible, for our people are not prepared for any radical ideas." I was so afraid that I might get outside the narrow limits that I said, "The best thing is for you and your friends to ask questions, and thus keep me on the line you desire." That was agreed on, and after I had talked about fifteen minutes on the condition of women in America, one of the Reverend Gentlemen present asked if the sphere we proposed for woman was in harmony with the teachings of the Bible. I said our Bible like our constitutions and statute books, was susceptible of various interpretations, but its general principles of justice, liberty, and equality, illustrated in the characters of such grand women as Huldah, Deborah, Vashti, and Esther,[26] fully warranted women in assuming all honorable positions in the college, the state, or at the head of the army. As they listened, apparently with interest, to my commentaries, I gave them the most favorable view for our movement that can be drawn from the scriptures. I made no reference to Paul's epistles nor the contemptuous disposition of everything of the feminine species in the Pentateuch.

When the audience dispersed my hostess said: "I am afraid you shocked these christian people, they never heard such latitudinarian ideas before."

"Well," said I, "perhaps it is time they did hear them, for my part I like to rouse people to some new thought even if at first it does shock them." As Mrs. Margaret Lucas,[27] a sister of John Bright who has just passed away, was of our party, we talked by the fireside late that night as to the wisdom of uttering the highest truth we saw as opportunity offered. The next morning to my surprise the Methodist minister called to invite me to occupy his pulpit in the afternoon and give exactly what I said the previous evening. I accepted the invitation.

When Mrs. Clark and Mrs. Lucas returned from church I told them of my afternoon engagement. "Why," they exclaimed, "that will never do, the minister will lose his place; the General Conference would reprimand him severely for allowing so heretical a teacher to preach in his pulpit." "Well," said I, "go and tell him what you think, I will not be offended if he reconsiders the invitation." She returned saying he was quite determined. So I gave my Bible argument and the congregation received it with enthusiasm. The women were particularly pleased to hear that they were not an afterthought in the creation; that they were not the authors of sin, from the beginning in collusion with the devil; that maternity was not intended as a curse, nor marriage necessarily a condition of slavery. The minister wrote me a letter afterwards telling me how much pleased his people were with all I had said. Here is an evidence of how little we can judge of what the people are ready to hear, and of the wisdom of uttering at all times the highest truth we see.

In this way we make of ourselves mediums through which the great souls of the past may speak again. The moment we begin to fear the opinions of others and hesitate to tell the truth that is in us and from motives of policy are silent when we should speak, the divine floods of light and life flow no longer into our souls. Every truth we see is ours to give the world, not to keep for ourselves alone, for in so doing we cheat humanity out of their rights and check our own development.

Another question demanding consideration on our platform, is the race problem that was supposed to be settled a quarter of a century ago by the proclamation of emancipation, as Wendell Phillips said when Abraham Lincoln went up to heaven with four million chains in his hands.[28] Then, statesmen said emancipation is a mockery without the ballot, and enfranchised the Freedman, and secured all his civil and political rights by a civil rights bill and the XIV. and XV. amendments to the National Constitution. He was declared to be a citizen of the United States, with the right to vote in every state in the Union.

How comes it then with all these safe guards thrown about him, that the race problem is again up for discussion in Congress and the civil rights bill in our hotels?[29]

Because every fundamental principle by which he was emancipated and enfranchised was immediately denied in its application to woman.

Able statesmen and lawyers at once said on the passage of the XIV. amendment, that woman as well as the freedman was made by it a United States citizen possessed of the right to vote. We begged abolitionists and the friends of woman suffrage to press this new demand. But those most deeply interested in the Freedman's fate, with bated breath begged us not to press our claims, lest in making other complications, we should endanger his chances. Republicans, Abolitionists and even those in the woman suffrage ranks, begged us to discontinue our conventions for a season and give all our thoughts and energies to get the Freedman into the political kingdom. Accordingly, we did so, and for one year devoted ourselves wholly to his service sending the largest petition, in his behalf, ever presented in Congress.[30] But as the XIV. amendment was a national topic of conversation in the Halls of Legislation and at every fireside, we saw the wisdom of putting in woman's claims under it and extorting from the framers the full significance of its spirit and letter. Those were the darkest days that the few of us who stood by this principle experienced in the whole course of our movement. Colored men reproached us for being false to them; Abolitionists for being false to them; and Republicans for having gone over to the democracy, in the supreme moment of the nation's need; in pressing the claims of woman, which had no political significance whatever, during the war, nor the period of reconstruction.

But in the full belief that we had the right to vote under the XIV. amendment a few of us obstinately persisted in the discussion. In many places, too, women voted, and in many more their ballots were refused. Then some women were sued for voting, and others sued the inspectors for denying their right and refusing to receive their ballots.

Test cases were carried to the supreme courts of the states, and the United States, and all the decisions rendered were in flat contradiction of the principles laid down in the amendments, as well as the spirit and letter of the whole constitution. While the United States had just made 2,000,000 Freedmen voters, and forbade any state to deny or abridge the right of any citizen on account of color, in the case of women they said the United States had no voters, and that the status of woman was settled by the state.[31] We said then that the Republican party in thus stultifying its own principles was confusing the moral sense of the nation, and showing southern politicians that the XIV. amendment was merely a piece of political clap-trap, meaning one thing for the North and another for the South. And we predicted that the time would come when these Supreme Court decisions would react against the Freedmen themselves.

And our prophecies have been fulfilled. The South has kept a watchful eye on these decisions. In a recent trial in Georgia the case of Virginia L. Minor was referred to, to show that the Freedmen were not United States citizens and had no right to vote for United States officers.[32] All over the South to-day they are driving the Freedmen from the polls and denying United States authority for him exactly as the North has done in the case of women.

Thus the results of the war have been all frittered away by political manoeuvering, and we shall have the battle of State rights and Federal power to fight over again.

Now suppose in '68 the Republicans had been true to their principles and enfranchised women also; what an educational work would have been going on all over the nation, for the past quarter of a century with our feet firmly based on principle. As they considered woman a dangerous element they might have limited our numbers and commenced the experiment with qualifications of property, education, or on the English ground excluding married women and according the right only to widows and spinsters.

They might have done that with some show of principle, as suffrage was granted to men at first on educational and property qualifications. But as it is now the denial of principle in the case of women at the North has reacted in the denial of the same principle in the case of the Freedmen of the South. And now our statesmen are at their wits end to know what to do with the Freedman, and are actually proposing to colonize him.

If the Russian system is to be adopted and all discontented citizens are to be sent to some Siberia, our turn will come next. Hence we should make a stand on the Freedman and demand justice for him as well as ourselves. It is justice, and that alone that can end the irrepressible conflict between freedom and slavery, going on in every nation on the globe. That is all the nihilists, the socialists, the communists ask; that is all Ireland asks, and the Freedmen, and the women of this Republic ask no more.

~ *Woman's Tribune*, 22 February 1890, with minor corrections based on AMs, ECS Papers, DLC.

1. Not previously identified are Theodore Parker (1810–1860), Transcendentalist clergyman and author; Amos Bronson Alcott (1799–1888), educator and utopian; and Gerrit Smith (1797–1874), philanthropist, abolitionist, and radical reformer.

2. Caroline Maria Seymour Severance (1820–1914), active in the early woman's rights movement in Ohio and Boston, founder of the New England Woman's Club, and an organizer of the American Woman Suffrage Association, had lived in Los Angeles since 1875. (*NAW*; *ANB*. See also *Papers* 1 & 2.)

3. Elizabeth Oakes Prince Smith (1806–1893), a writer and one of the first American women to earn a living as a lecturer, was active in the woman's rights movement in the early 1850s. (*NAW*; *ANB*. See also *Papers* 1 & 2.)

4. Adaptation of Isa. 42:20.

5. Samuel Joseph May (1797–1871), an early abolitionist and the Unitarian minister at Syracuse, New York, was a key ally in the state's movements for woman's rights and equal rights. (*ANB*. See also *Papers* 1 & 2.)

6. Thomas Wentworth Higginson (1823–1911), a former minister who was active in the antebellum woman's rights movement, became an editor of the *Woman's Journal* after the war. (*ANB*. See also *Papers* 1, 3 & 4.)

7. The first of her resolutions read: "*Whereas*, Our labors with Congress and State Legislatures should henceforward be carried on with renewed

determination, zeal and consecration; therefore, *Resolved*, That a thorough and widespread organization of our forces must be secured, that by concentrated action we may make our united powers irresistible at any given time and place."

8. From a sentence in the first paragraph of the introduction to William E. H. Lecky, *History of the Rise and Influence of the Spirit of Rationalism in Europe*, revised edition, 1879. The *Tribune* mistakenly read the closing words as "of society to secure it."

9. Molly Maguires was the name given to Irish perpetrators of violence in the anthracite coal region of Pennsylvania during and after the Civil War. ECS's use of their history is unusually benign; the prevailing narrative of the nineteenth century described them as a vast, dangerous conspiracy, not workers seeking to right wrongs. See Kevin Kenny, *Making Sense of the Molly Maguires* (New York, 1998).

10. Charles Stewart Parnell (1846–1891), Irish nationalist leader and member of Parliament, switched his own and his followers' allegiances from the Liberal to the Conservative party and back again in the mid-1880s, in the quest for Home Rule. He was credited with placing the Irish question at the center of British politics. In February 1890, Parnell seemed to be vindicated of charges of adultery that came to light when William O'Shea named Parnell as co-respondent in a filing for divorce. Early in the month Parnell won an action for libel against the *Times* of London for publishing his name in connection with the divorce. (Robert Kee, *The Laurel and the Ivy: The Story of Charles Stewart Parnell and Irish Nationalism* [London, 1993], 533–40.)

11. Her second resolution read: "*Whereas*, The constitutions of the original thirteen colonies made no distinctions of sex, and women in the early days exercised the right of suffrage; and *Whereas*, By the principles laid down in the Declaration of Independence, and by the letter and spirit of the National constitution women are citizens and voters; therefore *Resolved*, That the disfranchisement of one-half the people of the nation is, and always has been, an arrogant assumption of power, by those administering the government."

12. George Washington (1732–1799), first president of the United States.

13. The election of 1800 was a tight contest between Thomas Jefferson and John Adams.

14. Only in ECS's manuscript is it possible to tell that this passage is a quotation; she clipped and pasted into her manuscript the final paragraph of Francis Minor, "Woman's Legal Right to the Ballot," *Forum* (December 1886): 351–60. William Cumback (1829–1905), Republican of Indiana, served in the House of Representatives from 1855 to 1857. This story about his mother is just barely possible: from the 1850 federal census for Indiana, it is evident that she lived in New Jersey when at least two of her sons were born, about 1811 and 1813, and that she was born about 1786 and thus reached voting age just before women were disenfranchised. (*BDAC*.)

15. An epigram attributed to Thomas Jefferson.

16. Florence Nightingale (1820–1910), English pioneer in nursing.

17. ECS adapts the popular poem "The Raven" by Edgar Allan Poe (1809–1849), in which the bird repeatedly says "Nevermore."

18. The second part of her fourth resolution read: "*Resolved*, That the time has come for woman to demand of the church, the same equal recognition she demands of the state: to assume her right and duty to take part in the revision of Bibles, prayer-books and creeds; to vote on all questions of business, to fill the offices of elder, deacon, Sunday-School superintendent, pastor and bishop, and have the right to sit in ecclesiastical synods, assemblies and conventions as delegates, that thus our religion may no longer reflect only the masculine element of humanity, and that woman, the mother of the race, be honored as she must be before we can have a happy home, a rational religion and an enduring government."

19. Her fourth resolution began: "*Whereas*, It is proposed to have a national law, restricting the right of divorce to a narrower basis, and *Whereas*, Congress has already made an appropriation for a Report on the Question, which shows that there are 10,000 divorces annually in the United States and the majority demanded by women; and *Whereas*, Liberal divorce laws for wives are what Canada was for the slaves—a door of escape from bondage; therefore *Resolved*, That there be no farther legislation on this question until woman has a voice in the state and national government."

20. William E. Gladstone, "The Question of Divorce," *North American Review* 149 (December 1889): 641–44.

21. Perhaps ECS had early access to Helen H. Gardener, "Divorce and the Proposed National Law," *Arena* 1 (March 1890): 413–22.

22. On 3 March 1887, Congress directed the Bureau of Labor Statistics to report "the statistics of and relating to marriage and divorce," and after Carroll Wright completed the report in February 1889, Congress appropriated funds for the Government Printing Office to publish twenty thousand copies. Wright's report was intended to be an alternative to federal legislation or a federal amendment, though it did not stop the most ardent opponents of divorce from introducing new measures. ("Introduction," Wright, *Report on Marriage and Divorce*, 9–22; *Congressional Record*, 50th Cong., 2d sess., 27 February, 1 March 1889, pp. 2373, 2543; Foster, *Moral Reconstruction*, 69–70.)

23. Her final resolution read: "*Whereas*, The greatest question before the American people to-day is the enfranchisement of woman, involving as it does the civil and political rights of one-half the people; and *Whereas*, The sole object of the National-American Association is to accomplish this purpose; therefore *Resolved*, That our platform in the future as in the past must recognize the equal rights of all parties, sects and races, manifest a broad, catholic spirit, for all shades of opinion in which we may differ, and ever hold our personal differences subordinate to the greater good that can be accomplished by harmonious and concentrated action."

24. Helen Priestman Bright Clark (1840–1927), John Bright's daughter by

his first wife, married William Stephens Clark in 1866 and settled with him at Street, where he ran the C. & J. Clark Company. She followed her Bright and Priestman aunts in supporting woman suffrage. (J. Travis Mills, *John Bright and the Quakers* [London, 1935], 1:474-78, 2:60-63; Percy Lovell, *Quaker Inheritance, 1871-1961: A Portrait of Roger Clark of Street, Based on His Own Writings and Correspondence* [London, 1970], 1-5, 260-61; Sandra Stanley Holton, "From Anti-Slavery to Suffrage Militancy: The Bright Circle, Elizabeth Cady Stanton and the British Women's Movement," in *Suffrage and Beyond: International Feminist Perspectives*, eds. Caroline Daley and Melanie Nolan [New York, 1994]; *Times* [London], 17 January 1927. See also *Papers* 4.)

25. For other accounts of these events in mid-May 1883, see *Eighty Years*, 372, and ECS diary, 21 May 1883, *Stanton*, 2:206-7. The visit began with ECS participating in a meeting of the Bristol Women's Liberal Association on May 17, in *Film*, 23:156.

26. Vashti's disobedience of her husband's command is in the Book of Esther. Esther herself was said to have saved the Jews by revealing to her husband a plot to kill them.

27. Margaret Bright Lucas (1818-1890) was a younger sister of John Bright and Priscilla McLaren. Active in reforms since childhood, Lucas supported woman suffrage, worked to repeal the Contagious Diseases Acts, and presided over the British Women's Temperance Association. She died on February 4. (*DNB*; *SEAP*; *Women's Suffrage Journal* 21 [1 March 1890]: 33; Holton, "From Anti-Slavery to Suffrage Militancy: The Bright Circle." See also *Papers* 4.)

28. Her third resolution read: "*Whereas*, The principles declared by the 14th amendment, making the southern slaves citizens and voters, were all reversed for women, by the decisions in the test cases carried to the supreme court; therefore *Resolved*, That the persecutions of the Freedmen to-day are due to the narrow policy of their defenders, a quarter of a century ago, making justice one thing for the black man, and another for woman, thus confusing the moral sense of the nation, and by denying the application of a principle to one class, jeopardizing the rights of all. *Resolved*, That as the fathers violated the principles of justice; in consenting to a three-fifths representation, recognizing slavery in the constitution, and thereby made a civil war inevitable; so our statesmen and supreme court judges, by their misrepresentations of the 14th amendment, declaring that the United States has no voters, and that citizenship does not carry with it the right of suffrage; have not only prolonged woman's disfranchisement but undermined the status of the Freedman, and opened the way for another war of races."

29. In his first annual message in December 1889, President Harrison pointed out that "where the colored population is large the people of that race are by various devices deprived of any effective exercise of their political rights and of many of their civil rights." He went on to ask Congress to consider "such measures within its well-defined constitutional powers as will secure to all our people a free exercise of the right of suffrage and every other civil right under

the Constitution and laws of the United States. . . . The power to take the whole direction and control of the election of members of the House of Representatives is clearly given to the General Government." Three senators introduced bills to reform federal election laws at the start of the Fifty-first Congress, while in the House, steps were taken to form a select committee to consider additional bills. Just days before ECS spoke, Henry Cabot Lodge, chairman of the select committee, used the occasion of Abraham Lincoln's birthday to affirm a citizen's right to vote and promise an end to fraudulent elections. In March 1890, Lodge introduced the bill that came to be known as the Force Bill. (Israel, *State of the Union Messages*, 2:1651-52; Stanley P. Hirshon, *Farewell to the Bloody Shirt: Northern Republicans and the Southern Negro, 1877-1893* [Chicago, 1968], 202-5; *Newark Daily Advertiser*, 13 February 1890.)

30. On this work through the Women's Loyal National League, see *Papers* 1.

31. ECS paraphrases the decision of the United States Supreme Court in *Minor v. Happersett* 21 Wallace 162 (1875).

32. *Ex parte Yarbrough* 110 U.S. 651 (1884). White Georgians who had attacked a black voter cited the Supreme Court's decision in *Minor v. Happersett* that "the Constitution of the United States does not confer the right of suffrage upon any one," to argue that they committed no federal crime because only state law governed the right to vote for members of Congress. ECS omits the court's interpretation in *Yarbrough* of what was intended in *Minor*: in that earlier opinion, the court meant that "the right is not definitely conferred on any person or class of persons by the Constitution alone, because you have to look to the law of the State for the description of the class. But the court did not intend to say that when the class or the person is thus ascertained, his right to vote for a member of Congress was not fundamentally based upon the Constitution, which created the office of members of Congress, and declared it should be elective, and pointed to the means of ascertaining who should be electors." Setting up an argument useful for women to pursue federal suffrage, the court declared that the states, "in prescribing the qualifications for the most numerous branch of their own legislatures, do not do this with reference to the election of members of Congress," and that the right to vote for members of Congress "is guaranteed by the Constitution, and should be kept free and pure by congressional enactments whenever that is necessary." Francis and Virginia Minor brought the opinion to the attention of woman suffragists. Francis Minor's article, "The Right of Women to Vote at Congressional Elections" appeared in the *Woman's Tribune* in 1888; he published the pamphlet *The Law of Federal Suffrage; An Argument in Support of* in June 1889; Virginia Minor reviewed the court's opinion at a hearing about legislation to allow women to vote for members of Congress in February 1890; and Francis Minor returned to the subject in an article published in December 1891. (*Woman's Tribune*, 28 January 1888; *St. Louis Spectator*, n.d., SBA scrapbook 15, Rare Books, DLC; Francis Minor, "Citizenship and Suffrage; the Yarbrough Decision," *Arena* 5 [December 1891]: 68-75.)

93   From the Diary of SBA

[*18–21 February 1890*]

TUESDAY, FEBRUARY 18, 1890. The National-American Assn met publicly for the first time—in the 22^d annual Washington Woman Suffrage Convention this A.M—and Mrs Stanton as <u>its</u> President made the opening speech— her daughter Harriot came to the stage & said a few words—in look & manner she showed herself worthy her mother & her mothers life long friend & co-worker— It was a proud moment for me—& for all of us of the old National—and ought to be to all who truly love the cause fully— Wm Dudley Foulke followed with a very fine address—[1] at 4 P.M. Mrs Spofford & self saw Mrs Stanton & daughters Maggie & Hattie off for New York—& we though sad at the parting were full of joy that Mrs S. went crowned [*along margin*] with the Presidency of the whole suffrage society[2]

  1. For William Foulke's address, see *Woman's Tribune*, 22 February 1890, *Film*, 28:55–62.
  2. Harriot Blatch's concession to the schedule of the suffrage association extended only to the opening day of the National-American's meeting; ECS and Harriot sailed from New York the next day.

WEDNESDAY, FEBRUARY 19, 1890. 22^d Annual—Wash. Con. Lincoln Music Hall— Though fine looking is surely sadly wanting in good acoustic properties—[1]

I presided at the A.M. Public Session—and at the 3 P.M. Executive Session—and again at the evening Public Session—

  1. Old Lincoln Hall, at Ninth and D streets, Northwest, burned down in 1888, and Lincoln Music Hall was constructed on the same site. After the opening night concert on 20 December 1889, a reviewer expressed similar criticism of the hall's accoustics. (*Washington Post*, 21 December 1889.)

THURSDAY, FEBRUARY 20, 1890. <u>Third</u> day of the 22^d Wash. Con— Everything seems moving smoothly—though no doubt there is at heart some chagrin that Mrs Stanton is the chosen Standard bearer—& that by a vote of 131 to 90— I sprang to make it a unanimous vote—but was too late—so the first informal vote—was made the formal one 131 to 90—[1]

Mrs Julia Ward Howe seemed to me to speak better than ever before[2]—as did H. B. B[lackwell]

All called on Mrs Harrison[3] at 4 P.M to day—

1. The election took place on February 17. Ninety votes were cast for SBA.
2. For Julia Howe's address, see *Woman's Tribune*, 1 March 1890, *Film*, 28:63-77.
3. Caroline Lavinia Scott Harrison (1832-1892), the First Lady, invited the executive committee to call on her at the White House. (*NAW*; Washington *Critic*, 20 February 1890.)

FRIDAY, FEBRUARY 21, 1890. 4th Day of the 22d Con We rounded out with Mrs Wallace—Olympia Brown & Rev Annie Shaw this last evening—& closed with seeming good feeling all round— Mrs Howe made most lovely word to me—

~ Excelsior Diary 1890, n.p., SBA Papers, DLC. Letters in square brackets expand initials.

94 ~ SBA TO SARAH BURGER STEARNS

March 11th—Wash. D.C. 1890

Dear Mrs Stearns

Yours of Feb 19th is now before me—

If your Minnesota W.S.A. Cannot raise the money necessary for Mrs Nelson[1] to work in South Dakota—The N.A. S.D. Com. must lend a hand[2]—for I think Mrs Nelson a very important person— Now—On what terms will she go into the localities of the foreign born people— It is among such that she seemed to feel she could go to good advantage— The foregin men will be hard to convert—but it is best to do all in our power to win them over—[3] How soon will Mrs Nelson go into the state— I think she should be taken care of by the Farmers Alliance men—or the Republican Committee—in the Foreign Districts— She shouldn't go under the wing of Prohibitionists or W.C.T.U. folk— since she mustn't carry but just the one question to them—that is

Equality of political rights for woman—but dear Mrs Nelson has the sconce & tact I am sure to see & to do the wise thing—[4]

Mrs Grubb[5] is Sup't of <u>Foreign</u> affairs of the National W.C.T.U.— I do not know whether she lectures— If she does—she ought to help in S.D.— She wishes me to send her $80. to pay for tracts she has had printed to send to S.D.— I write her I first want to know what the matter is &c— When I reached the end of your letter I find Mrs Nelson's & her terms— I will accept them—for the N.A. South Dakota Committee—that is $50— a month & her travelling & Hotel expenses— she counting her Collections & contributions to make up as much of her expenses as possible—they will probably pay all & more too Now if she can commence work the first of April—I shall be very glad— I will correspond with the S.D. State Ex. Com—and decide <u>where</u> she had better begin— My plan is—for her first to go into each of the <u>voting precincts</u> of each County—& hold meetings & organize local societies— and then—after she has compased the several precincts of the county— and at each meeting had ↑two↓ delegates appointed to go up to the County Seat City—to organize a County Convention & association— Just the way that Mrs De Voe[6] has been doing in Hyd, Hand & Beadle counties & is now doing in Spink county—

So my dear—Please tell Mrs Nelson—the ↑S.D.↓ State & National Com's—accept her terms—& hope she will begin work at her earliest safe moment—

So far as I can learn—no canvassing has been done during the winter months in the State—save that done by Mrs De Voe!! And I cannot understand ~~why~~—if she could go ahead & canvass a county in each month—& round it out with a County Convention—why other women in other counties could not have done the same— So much valuable time has been lost—by the other counties—that I now feel anxious to see women at work in every county—as soon as possible—

Well—the Union is in working trim—and if only H. B. B's tongue & pen could be kept from harping upon the <u>causes</u> of <u>their</u> old secession—all would go ~~as~~ ↑mery↓ as May— But I suppose he'll have to keep both wagging—spitting back to & about every one who says a word he doesn't like— Well let him—his daughter Alice does her level best to keep him still—he behaved—on the whole—very well—when here at the Con—and Alice & Mrs Howe were beautiful in all their ways—

Well—how is Wendell[7]—has he thrown Aunt Susan overboard absolutely—

How I should have loved to see him & his beloved Caroline at the family table on Sunday night the 16th— When we had a long table spread for it—there were first—Susan—Mary & Daniel R. of the original six children—then there were D R's wife Annie & daughter Maude—Sister Hannah's son Arthur & wife Mattie[8]—daughter H. Louise & husband Alvin James, Cousin Ellen Hoxie & her husband Lucien Squier, and Cousins Hannah Boyles, Melissa, Frances, & Charles Dickinson—and Mrs James—made 16—at our table— It is many years since we have so many of us been together—and it was a very great pleasure

Then so many of my dearest & oldest friends came—Mrs Hallowell & Mrs Willis of Rochester—also Mrs L. C. Smith & 8 or 10 others of my own city—Martha C. Wright's daughters—Mrs Osborn & Mrs Garrison—Richard Motts daughter—Annie C. Mott[9]—of Toledo Ohio—all nieces of the Sainted Lucretia Mott—then dear Adeline Thomson of Phila—& dear Mrs Bartol—[10] It was a proud day for Aunt Susan—tell Wendell— With love to the Judge & Susan B. & the University twain[11]—& to Wendell & Caroline   Lovingly yours

~ *Susan B. Anthony*

[*in margin of first page*] Did I ever tell you that I put a V. of yours to S. B. A. birth-day pile &—a V. to South Dakota—many thanks for both

~ ALS, on NWSA letterhead, year corrected, in the collection of Sy Sussman, Las Vegas, Nev.

1. Julia Bullard Nelson (1842-1914), a widow from Red Wing, Minnesota, a longtime teacher of African-American students in the South, and a member of the National association, moved back to Minnesota in 1888 and turned to organizing and lecturing for temperance and suffrage. She was at this date vice president of the Minnesota Woman's Christian Temperance Union. The Minnesota Woman Suffrage Association pledged four hundred dollars to send her into South Dakota, where she delivered one hundred and fifty lectures during the campaign, a record topped only by Emma DeVoe. From 1890 to 1896, Nelson presided over the Minnesota suffrage association. (Julia Wiech Lief, "A Woman of Purpose: Julia B. Nelson," *Minnesota History* 47 [Winter 1981]: 303-14; *Woman's Journal*, 1 March 1890, and Wardall, "Woman Suffrage in South Dakota," p. 8, *Film*, 28:88, 871ff.)

2. At the urging of Alonzo Wardall, Alice Pickler, and John Pickler, all of

whom attended the National-American meeting in February 1890, the association agreed to focus its resources during the year on an amendment campaign in South Dakota. The executive committee then crafted a plan for raising and spending money to that end: SBA would chair a new South Dakota Campaign Committee, and all funds raised by and for that committee would remain in the National-American's control. This decision to control the money rather than pass it along to the state association was deliberate; just before voting on that question, the committee discussed a public letter by Helen Gougar alleging that leaders of both the American and National associations had misused funds and insisting that control of all campaign funds be given to local officers in South Dakota. The executive committee ignored her advice. (*Woman's Journal*, 1 March 1890; *Woman's Tribune*, 1 March 1890; and *Washington Post*, 21 February 1890; all in *Film*, 28:53, 63–82.)

3. Twenty-eight percent of South Dakota's population was foreign born in 1890, and percentages in many counties ran much higher. In Campbell and McPherson counties, foreign-born settlers were the majority, and in sixteen additional counties, their strength exceeded the state average. The largest groups were, in descending order, Norwegians, Germans, and Russians. South Dakota's constitution allowed non-citizen, adult males to vote, provided they had sworn their intention to become citizens. Nelson's aptness for assignment to foreign-born voters probably derived from her experience as an organizer among Minnesota's immigrants; possibly she spoke Norwegian, the language of her husband's family. (U.S. Census Office, *Report on the Population of the United States at the Eleventh Census: 1890* [Washington, D.C., 1895], 1:427–28, 655–56; South Dakota Const. of 1889, art. VII, sec. 1.)

4. Most woman suffragists in Dakota Territory had pursued their goal as members of the Woman's Christian Temperance Union. When the territorial union met in September 1889 for the last time, officers reported three hundred and nine local unions and just over three thousand members. At that meeting, members renewed their support for woman suffrage. Only in October 1889 did the first statewide suffrage association organize, and its relationship to the temperance union would be a persistent problem during the amendment campaign. (Kingsbury, *History of Dakota Territory*, 3:764–65.)

5. Sophronia Farrington Naylor Grubb (1834–?) became national superintendent of the Woman's Christian Temperance Union's work among foreigners in 1883 and oversaw an immense publishing program in seventeen languages. She left St. Louis for Kansas in 1887, settling first at Chanute and moving to Lawrence in 1893. In the latter year, she became president of the Kansas temperance union. In both South Dakota and Kansas, suffragists did not always welcome Grubb's generous offers of tracts because each one displayed the temperance union's name on its cover, advertising a connection between prohibition and woman suffrage. (*American Women*; Mary Simmerson Cunningham Logan, *The Part Taken by Women in American History* [Wilmington, Del., 1912], 677–78.)

6. Emma Smith DeVoe (1848-1927) of Huron was the most effective organizer in the South Dakota campaign. She moved from Illinois into the territory in 1880, after her marriage to John Henry DeVoe, and joined both the territorial temperance union and the Women's Relief Corps. In October 1889, she and John signed the call for an equal suffrage association, and she went to work immediately, forming local suffrage clubs in the three counties SBA names. After a change in the association's leadership in July 1890, she was named state lecturer. The DeVoes also provided music for the campaign as composers and performers; Emma, a singer, led the music department at Eureka College in Illinois before her marriage. The DeVoes left South Dakota after the campaign, settling in Illinois and Washington State. For many years, the National-American association relied on Emma DeVoe to campaign wherever lectures and organizing were needed. (*American Women*; Ross-Nazzal, "Emma Smith DeVoe and the South Dakota Suffrage Campaigns," 235-62; E. S. DeVoe to SBA, before 11 January 1890, *Film*, 27:1027.)

7. Wendell Phillips Mosher (1858-1946), the third son of SBA's late sister Hannah Mosher, was soon to marry Carolyn Louise Mixer (1861?-1933) of Cleveland, Ohio. After working with his older brother Arthur in the insurance business in St. Louis, Wendell became an agent in Philadelphia and settled in Duluth as district agent of the Missouri, Kansas, and Texas Trust Company, the Employers' Liability Company, and Travelers Life and Accident Insurance Company. (Bertha Bortle Beal Aldridge, *Laphams in America* [Victor, N.Y., 1932-52], 156, 223; St. Louis city directories, 1879, 1880; Duluth city directories, 1890, 1891; *Papers*, 4:286-88; SBA diary, 17 April 1890, *Film*, 27:679ff. See also *Papers 3*.)

8. Martha Beatrice Brown Mosher (1857-1926) was the wife of Arthur A. Mosher and mother of their three sons. In 1898, she published a well-regarded book, *Child Culture in the Home, A Book for Mothers*. (Anthony, *Anthony Genealogy*, 183; *WhNAA*; *New York Times*, 11 July 1926.)

9. Richard Mott (1804-1888), brother-in-law of Lucretia Mott, a mayor of Toledo, Ohio, and one-term congressman helped organize the Toledo Woman Suffrage Association in 1869. His daughter, Anna Caroline Mott (1835-1902), known as Cannie, was active in local, state, and national suffrage societies. She often hosted SBA in her Toledo home. (*BDAC*; Thomas Clapp Cornell, *Adam and Anne Mott: Their Ancestors and Descendants* [Poughkeepsie, N.Y., 1890], 386-87.)

10. Emma Jemima Welchman Bartol (1821-1908) was a charter member of Philadelphia's New Century Club, founded in 1876; a donor to many of the city's charities; and a world traveler who published books about her trips. Her husband, Barnabas Henry Bartol, an engineer who died in 1888, took over the Southwark Foundry in Philadelphia in the 1850s and extended his business into Cuban sugar refineries, for which the foundry made equipment. Bartol probably came to know SBA and ECS through her friendship with Rachel Foster Avery's mother, and on the eve of SBA's departure for Europe in 1883,

she hosted a grand dinner in SBA's honor. She was also a patron of the International Council of Women in 1888. (Emma J. Bartol, *Recollections of a Traveller* [Philadelphia, 1906]; *Anthony*, 2:548; records of West Laurel Hill Cemetery, Bala Cynwyd, Pa.)

11. Ozora Pierson Stearns (1831–1896), who served in the United States Senate for about five weeks in 1871, trained in law at the University of Michigan and served from 1874 to 1895 as a judge of the eleventh judicial district of Minnesota. In 1890, he became a regent of the University of Minnesota. He and Sarah Stearns had three children. Susan M. (1867–1953) married John Beckett Esden before 1904, lived many years in Chicago, and spent her last years in Berkeley, California. Victor Alonzo (1870–1942) graduated from the University of Minnesota in 1891 and Harvard Law School in 1894, and returned to Duluth to practice law. Stella Burger (1872–1948) graduated from the University of Minnesota in 1892, enrolled as a graduate student at Bryn Mawr College the next year, and became a high school teacher of English and Latin, working in Minnesota, Maryland, Idaho, and California. (*BDAC*; *NCAB*, 5:656, 10:230; clippings files, Duluth Public Library, with thanks to Linda Rau, Reference Division; Charles Warren, *History of the Harvard Law School and of Early Legal Conditions in America* [1908; reprint, Union, N.J., 1999], 3:218; *Program, Bryn Mawr College, Academic Year 1900-01* [Philadelphia, 1900], 60; on-line index to California Death Records; and with assistance of Lorett Treese, Bryn Mawr College Archives.)

95 ~ SBA TO FRANCES E. WILLARD

Riggs House, Washington, D.C., March 21st 1890

My Dear Miss Willard

About South Dakota—and what the National W.C.T.U will do—and what the National American W.S.A. will do to help carry suffrage there next November—

When I closed my "sweep ↑swing↓ round the circle"¹ at the annual meeting of the Farmers Alliance, at Aberdeen—the 27th of last November—I was present at their E.S.A. Executive meeting—at which I presented a plan for winter work by the Home people—that is—that Mrs Barker² as W.C.T.U. President—should cause her District V̶i̶c̶e̶ Presidents to cause each of her County Presidents to call local W.C.T.U meetings in her respective county—and there urge that the franchise spoke in their wheel should be worked as the main one—and that those locals should appoint delegates to go up to an ↑Equal Suffrage↓ Convention at the county seat—& there organize a <u>county</u> association for the suffrage campaign—and that from that point on—all should pull together as a suffrage band to the end of the campaign— They of the state were to do this school-District-organizing work—by the friends driving out when the weather was suitable—from the county towns—

And, meanwhile, <u>I</u> was to go east & do all in my power to raise money—before ~~the~~ ↑our↓ annual Washington Convention—Print Senator Palme's admirable speech[3]—& send it broadcast over South Dakota under the <u>frank</u> of a S.D. M.C.—and also to buy as many papers of Mrs Colby as I could get the money for—& have her mail copies to everybody—

These two things I did—1st had 50,000— copies of Senator Palmers speech <u>printed</u>—had <u>volunteer</u> <u>women</u> for <u>the</u> <u>love</u> of <u>the</u> <u>cause</u>—come to my <u>hotel</u> <u>parlor</u>—two & three at a time—working for whole weeks—franking & addressing very nearly ↑fully↓ 40,000 of them—& when you remember that one pair of hands can address only about 5 or 6 hundred a day—you can see it has been a big job— Then I have purchased & had mailed by Mrs Colby 45,000 copies of the Woman's Tribune—so that there can be scarcely a household in all South Dakota that hasn't received these two documents— Letters come to Major Pickler[4] to Mrs Colby daily telling how much good these papers are doing—

Well—to make a long story short—only <u>one</u> district W.C.T.U. President has called ↑her↓ local W C.T.U's together—and organized County suffrage societies—& she has accomplished the work in only 4 out of her 10 counties—

And now comes to me the word that the reason the local organizing has not been done is that the women who should do it <u>must</u> <u>be</u> <u>paid</u> <u>therefor</u>— And I am asked to send money to the <u>District W.C.T.U.</u> <u>Presidents</u> ↑Treasures↓—to enable them to go to work—which—you can see our <u>suffrage</u> <u>association</u> <u>cannot</u> <u>do</u>—since the only hope of carrying the election lies in keeping <u>our</u> suffrage canvass entirely apart from the W.C.T.U. and Enforcement League societies—[5] And this is important—because while those two societies can & must, if it is done at all—convert the <u>Prohibition</u> <u>foreign</u> born men—to vote for woman suffrage—they can but repel the <u>Anti</u> <u>prohibition</u> ↑men↓ from the question— And ↑too↓ since, with their <u>best</u> persuasion—they'll fail to convince many of the prohibition foreigners—who gave that measure its six thousand majority last year—we <u>must</u> convert at least <u>6 or 8 thousand men</u> out of those who voted against Prohibition!! We must get enough out of ~~that~~ the Anti Prohibs—to balance those of the ↑foreign↓ Prohibs. who will stick to their anti woman suffrage—

Therefore you will see—while the W.C.T.Us must work with might & main with all of the Prohibition men—native & foreign—Our Suffrage association in its Canvass must know no democrat no republican—no prohibitionist no License man—high or low— We must know nothing but <u>woman</u> suffrage—else we might as well never spend a dollar in South Dakota

Now—my dear—What I want of you as Pres. of the National W.C.T.U. is—to rouse the members of your national—of ↑all↓ your State and local Unions—so that they will at once send <u>speakers</u> & <u>money</u> to S.D.—to help <u>that</u> <u>state</u> W.C.T.U. to work ~~in~~ ↑the↓ <u>franchise spoke</u> ↑in its wheel↓—or ↑its↓ franchise department—for all it is worth from top to bottom—

The people are <u>so poor</u>—<u>that they can't move</u>— I am told every W.C.T.U. is in debt & can't move— So if they work to help carry the election <u>your</u> <u>National</u> <u>must</u> <u>help</u> them <u>financially</u>— Now—Can you—will you—send them money—not <u>you</u> <u>personally</u>—but the <u>Unions generally</u>—

I have offered to pay ↑local↓ organizers the very least they can go for—but they must work ↑go↓ in the name of and for the suffrage society— You see the point— We of the suffrage Campaign—must be able to say—& say <u>truly</u>—that our association is not a <u>part</u> & <u>parcel</u> of the <u>Prohibition Law</u> & <u>its enforcement</u>— We shall say that whether the majority of the women of S.D. shall vote for or against Prohibition—we want them to have the right to vote all the same—

Now—my dear—don't repeat a single word of this to Mrs Barker—or to any one—as coming from me— But draw your own conclusions—and say to her & all the W.C.T.U's your <u>own</u> say—not quoting me— If Mrs Barker is going to run her district & county W.C.T.U. conventions—she should <u>not</u> run the suffrage campaign that is sure—& she & all ought to see that for her to attempt to run both—will be disastrous—
Yours Lovingly

Susan B. Anthony

↝ ALS, on NAWSA letterhead, IEWT, from *Temperance and Prohibition Papers*.

1. SBA added the word "sweep" above the word "swing" without indicating a final decision. In the fifth paragraph, she did the same thing, writing "Treasures" above the word "Presidents."

2. Helen Morton Barker (1834–1910) was president of the South Dakota Woman's Christian Temperance Union and state organizer and lecturer of the South Dakota Equal Suffrage Association. She joined the temperance union in its early days in western New York and presided over the Alleghany County union until she and her husband moved west. She led the territorial union until it divided into state unions in 1889, and the success of prohibition in the state redounded to her credit. She did not, however, shine as an organizer of the suffrage association. As early as 6 March 1890, SBA observed, after writing to Barker about the plan of campaign, "she doesn't seem to me to grasp situation!!" In the fall of 1890, Barker hinted that she was, at some point, offered a salary to concentrate on the suffrage campaign but refused to abandon her temperance work. Barker later served on the Board of Lady Managers for the Columbian Exposition and became national treasurer of the temperance union. (*SEAP*; Federal Census, Alleghany County, N.Y., 1880; H. M. Barker to Editor, *White Ribbon Journal*, SBA scrapbook 16, Rare Books, DLC; SBA diary, *Film*, 27:679ff.)

3. *Universal Suffrage. Speech of Hon. Thomas W. Palmer, of Michigan, in the Senate of the United States, Friday, February 6, 1885* (Washington, D.C., 1885).

4. John Alfred Pickler (1844–1910), as a member of the territorial legislature, managed the woman suffrage bill that both houses adopted in 1885 but the governor vetoed. A Republican, he entered the House of Representatives on 2 December 1889 as one of South Dakota's two members and served until 1897. During the National-American's Washington convention in February 1890, he made a few appearances and spoke briefly to thank the association for its support of the South Dakota campaign. (*BDAC*; *Washington Post*, 21 February 1890, *Film*, 28:53.)

5. Once voters approved the constitutional article for prohibition, the South Dakota Enforcement League led the movement for its enforcement, drafting and lobbying for legislation, bringing suits against dealers, and occasionally taking direct action against the trade. (Kingsbury, *History of Dakota Territory*, 3:737–41.)

96 ECS TO CLARA BEWICK COLBY

Basingstoke Hants [*England*]   March 21st [*1890*]

Dear Clara,

I have just sent a package off to you criticising that discussion on parties & our attitude towards them.[1] I am so sorry I was not there to maintain the dignity of our platform. I never did hear such twaddle where were you & Susan that you did not interject a little common sense into that one sided discussion   May Wright Sewall was simply ridiculous in her position, & fulsome on Folke   Who did compose the committee on resolutions? They read as if they had been thrown together on the way to the hall.[2] That twaddle about Christ sounds like that rattled brained Mrs Bennett.[3] I should think you & Susan would feel ashamed of the Resolutions, & that discussion. I am I assure you. Fortunately but few people will read either resolutions or discussion   Be sure & publish my errata "lag superfluous on the stage" instead of lay   I am not a hen hence never lay.[4] I should object even to lie as my proportions could not be gracefully bestowed, before a crowded house. Your "devils" will be the death of me. I wonder if you have received all the packages I have sent. Three ↑Rems↓ & shall send another to morrow[5]   What ails Susan? I have not had one line from her yet. Can you send me a complete sett of my Rems I want to paste them in a book. I would like my two speeches just made in Washington. Well Matilda's convention seemed to go off all right & no one was hurt.[6] How groundless all these fears are about "hurting the cause." How we exaggerate the influence of trifles. When will you go west? Let me know that I may send my fulminations to the right center. Hattie & I are well. She made a speech last night at a meeting of laboring men & received much applause. Kind regards to Miss Smith,[7] if she can find time I wish she would give me her impression of the convention yours as ever

E. C. S.

ALS, Clara B. Colby Papers, Archives Division, WHi

1. Below at 19 April 1890.

2. For the resolutions adopted by the meeting, see *Woman's Journal*, 1 March 1890, *Film*, 28:78-82. They incorporated most of the topics and many phrases found in ECS's own resolutions, but delegates rejected her claim that women voted in the thirteen colonies and "are citizens and voters"; dropped her reference to narrow interpretations of the Fourteenth Amendment as the cause of "the persecutions of the Freedmen to-day"; and modified her statement about divorce while retaining her insistence that "there should be no further legislation on this subject until woman has a voice in the National Government." Delegates not only omitted her familiar call for women to insist on equal rights within churches, they also inserted the remarkable passage ECS mentions: "That we rejoice in the growing recognition among Christians that the teachings of Christ inculcate the equality of the rights of women and men, and that every righteous liberty is to be enjoyed by women as well as men; and since freedom is one of the most inspiring promises of Christ to his disciples, we urge upon women who call Christ Lord, to consider how greatly it is their duty to labor earnestly to attain this high gift, and not to be deterred by ignoble indifference to it or by cowardly conformity to the world."

3. Sarah Lewis Clay Bennett (1841-1935), known as Sallie, was the second of the daughters of Cassius M. Clay. From her home in Richmond, Kentucky, she joined her older sister Mary in state and national suffrage work before 1880. Bennett was an early proponent of federal legislation to permit women to vote for congressmen, a right she believed the Constitution guaranteed without need for amendment. (Richardson, *Cassius Marcellus Clay*, 31n, with assistance of the Filson Club, Lexington, Ky.; *History*, 3:176, 180, 957, 4:6, 234, 665. See also *Papers* 3 & 4.)

4. Above at 18 February 1890.

5. Due to Colby's need to make room in her paper for coverage of the Washington convention, no chapters of ECS's reminiscences were published between 18 January 1890, when the section entitled "A General Commotion" concluded, and 29 March 1890, when "Marriage and Divorce" began.

6. No doubt ECS received letters now lost about the meeting that formed the Woman's National Liberal Union. By this date, she would have also seen the *Woman's Tribune*, 8 March 1890, but probably not the more detailed report in the *Tribune*, 15 March 1890. From the resolutions published at the earlier date, she would have learned that efforts to found an alternative suffrage society had failed: suffrage did not appear in the group's name, and suffrage was not mentioned in the resolutions. Only Olympia Brown made a speech about woman suffrage. If ECS read the *Truth Seeker* while she was in England, she would have seen Richard B. Westbrook's sarcastic commentary on the meeting's failure, also published on 8 March 1890. Westbrook, president of the American Secular Union, longtime acquaintance of Gage, and husband of a former officer in the National Woman Suffrage Association, found Gage's autocratic management of the meeting intolerable. He did offer an explanation for it: Gage "had been repressed and suppressed by Susan B. Anthony and her

compeers so often through a large number of years that she was determined to hav everything her own way for once." (The *Truth Seeker*'s modest spelling reform insisted on the spelling "hav".) Many freethinkers disagreed with Westbrook's assessment, but free thought journals waited until April to publish more favorable reports. The *Woman's Tribune* of 15 March shifted ground: Colby had to defend her decision to publish the anti-Christian resolutions against sharp criticism from some of her readers, and she made space for Clara Foltz's attack at Gage's meeting on woman suffragists, including her opinion that "the women who have been the leaders of the woman suffrage question have led to its defeat. . . . Mrs. Gage has shown that she appreciates the situation. The others, I am told, (those on the National American platform) offer all sorts of opposition to this convention. They know they have made a most ridiculous failure. . . . After all sorts of argument and clap-trap for fourteen years, their attempts to obtain the suffrage have at last fallen flat." (*Truth Seeker* 17 [8 March 1890]: 148.)

7. Sara Winthrop Smith had joined the *Tribune*'s staff, identified on the masthead as assistant.

97 ~ From the Diary of SBA

[*27 March 1890*]

THURSDAY, MARCH 27, 1890. In Washington The Bill for the Admission of <u>Wyoming</u> into the Union was passed to-day at 4.30 P.M—by a vote of 139 to 127 after the voting down one after another three amendments proposed by Springer of Ill. each aiming at the disfranchisement of the women—before allowing it to come into the Union—[1]

1. SBA used her diary sparingly while in Washington in the winter of 1890. The pages are blank for 27 January through 12 February, 9 through 26 March, and 28 March through 16 April. The newspapers noted her presence on this day at the Capitol. William Springer's amendments embodied the "Views of the Minority" in the Committee on the Territories. The first one would undo the steps toward statehood and cause a new election for delegates to a new constitutional convention in which only male inhabitants would vote. It was defeated by a vote of 131 to 138. The second one would accept the proposed constitution but limit voting in November 1890 to males and put to them a referendum on woman suffrage. In another defeat, the vote was 133 to 139. His third proposal would amend the proposed constitution to add the word 'male' through all descriptions of voters. The House defeated this amendment 132 to 138. (*Congressional Record*, 51st Cong., 1st sess., 2707–12; House, Committee

on the Territories, *Admission of Wyoming into the Union, Views of the Minority*, 21 March 1890, 51st Cong., 1st sess., H. Rept. 39, Pt. 2, Serial 2897.)

↬ Excelsior Diary 1890, n.p., SBA Papers, DLC.

98 ↬ SBA TO SAMUEL A. RAMSEY[1]

[*Washington, D.C., 29 March 1890*]

Immediately on the receipt of your answer to my first letter to your executive committee, instead of sending you a personal reply I wrote again to the entire committee, answering the various points presented by you, Mr. and Mrs. Barker[2] and others. This I did to save writing the same thing to half a dozen different people, as well as to make sure that I should get your official action upon what seemed to me most important matters; but to this date I have received not only no official answer, but no information which shows my letter to have been acted upon. Nor have I heard from any member of the committee that you have mapped out any plan of campaign, or have accepted and proposed to work on the one which I outlined last November at the Aberdeen meeting,[3] and twice over have stated in my letters.

You, personally, say to me that you must have the national funds put into your treasury before you can plan work. Now, my dear sir, as a business man you never would give your money to any person or committee until they had presented to you a plan for using it which met your approval. Then I have had no indication of any intention on the part of your executive committee or State organizer to hold any series of suffrage meetings or conventions. The only ones written of are W.C.T.U. county and district conventions. California's suffrage lecturer, I am informed, is to be introduced to the State at the First District W.C.T.U. Convention.[4]

Now, I want to say to you individually, and to the executive committee generally, that the National-American South Dakota committee will pay the money entrusted to them only to *suffrage* lecturers and *suffrage* conventions. We shall not pay it to any individual or association for any other purpose, or in any other name, than suffrage for women, pure and simple. We talked this over fully in your executive committee meeting at Aberdeen last fall, and all agreed that, while the temperance societies worked for suffrage in their way, the suffrage campaign should be carried forward on the basis of the one principle. Our national money will not go to aid Prohibition leagues, Grand Army encampments, Woman's Relief Corps, W.C.T.U. societies or any others, though all, we hope, will declare and work for the suffrage amendment. We can not ally ourselves with the Prohibition or Anti-Prohibition party—the Democrats or the Republicans. Each may do splendid work for suffrage within its own organization, and we shall rejoice in all that do so; but the South Dakota and the National-American Associations must stand on their own ground.

Co-operation is what our committee desire, and we stand ready to aid in holding three series of county conventions with three sets of speakers, at least one of each set a national speaker, beginning on May 1 and continuing until the school election, June 24. I am feeling sadly disappointed that every voting precinct of every county has not been visited, and will not have been by the 1st of May, as was agreed upon at Aberdeen. Still, I want to begin now and henceforth push the work; but the entire fund would not pay every single man and woman in the State who helps, hence every one who can must work without cost either to the State or national committee.

~ *Anthony*, 2:681–82.

1. Samuel Albert Ramsey (1856–1924), a law graduate of the University of Michigan, settled in Woonsocket, South Dakota, in 1883 and practiced there until his death. Both a Democrat and a prohibitionist, Ramsey served in the constitutional convention in 1889 and was named president of the South Dakota Equal Suffrage Association later that year. During the amendment campaign, he was somewhat distracted by his appointment to and meetings of the Board of Managers of the Columbian Exposition. (University of Michigan, *Catalogue of Graduates, Non-Graduates, Officers, and Members of the Faculties, 1837–1921* [Ann Arbor, Mich., 1923]; *NCAB*, 3:351; Sarah A. Richards to Alice A. Pickler, 23 June 1890, Major John A. Pickler Family Papers, 1865–1976, SdHi; with assistance from the Bentley Historical Library, University of Michigan.)

2. Moses Barker (1829–1911), the husband of Helen Barker, was a Baptist minister who resigned his pastorate to become general secretary of the equal suffrage association at a salary of one hundred dollars per month. His salary might have escaped scrutiny if he had performed well in the job; late in June 1890, Helen Gougar described him as "grossly negligent in his duties," which

included scheduling speakers and dispatching their mail and campaign literature. By 10 June 1890, Samuel Ramsey had secured Barker's resignation and awaited the executive committee's decision about further payments to him. (Federal Census, Alleghany County, N.Y., 1880, and Evanston, Ill., 1900; *SEAP*, s.v. "Barker, Helen Morton"; on-line Illinois Statewide Death Index; SBA diary, 10, 20 June 1890, and Wardall, "Woman Suffrage in South Dakota," p. 5, *Film*, 27:679ff, 28:871ff; H. J. Gougar to Alice A. Pickler, 23 June 1890, Major John A. Pickler Family Papers, 1865-1976, SdHi; *Union Signal*, 19 June 1890.)

3. A reference to the meeting SBA described above at 21 March 1890.

4. This was Matilda Hindman, who spoke about equal suffrage to a district temperance meeting at Parker, South Dakota, on 4 April 1890. Though she was not, as a reporter described her, "of California," Californians contributed the money that paid her for work in South Dakota beginning on March 25. The record is confused as to whether that money came from temperance unions or suffrage associations. While in the state, Hindman held one hundred and fifty meetings in thirty-five counties. (Helen M. Barker to Editor, *White Ribbon Journal*, December 1890, and *Sioux Falls Press*, n.d., in SBA scrapbook 16, Rare Books, DLC; Wardall, "Woman Suffrage in South Dakota," p. 9, *Film*, 28:871ff.)

99   SBA TO HENRY L. DAWES[1]

The Riggs House   Washington D.C. March 30/90

My Dear Friend   Senator Dawes

Yours of yesterday was a delightful message to me—because my friends who invited the guests to my Banquet assured me they had invited you—and that you had not deigned to even send regrets—and your good words are all that mortal could desire—   Still I shall always regret that the invitation was thus waylaid—and thereby your & Mrs & Miss Dawes presence lost—at that memorable gathering—that marked my arrival at the three score & ten limit of mortal man—

Please say to ↑your↓ wife & daughter—the above—

And now <u>Wyoming</u>—with <u>full</u> <u>woman</u> <u>suffrage</u> guaranteed—is half into the Union—and all say the senate will complete her entrance—the moment the bill reaches that body!!

Well—I rejoice that at last the Republican Party has drawn its line outside of Woman Suffrage—and so in a measure committed itself to the principle of the right of women to their place inside the bodypolitic— It was a proud day to me—as I listened to the ↑manly↓ speeches on the Republican side—& watched the <u>vote</u>, <u>over</u> & <u>over</u>, on the several Democratic amendments to cheat us of woman's enfranchisement—and saw every Republic↑an↓ member but one—Dunnell[2] of Minnesota—shout nos on every call—and at last—on the final vote—in good clear tones shout "aye"—

I wonder if you have thought of the wonderful sign of the times—<u>this strict party</u> ↑vote↓ <u>is</u> to our army that has been marching up & down—over & across the wilderness of disfranchisement lo! these forty years?— Well—may I not entreat you to ↑do↓ all in your power to make the Senate vote just as pronounced—as is that of the House— Again thanking you I am very sincerely & gratefully

~ *Susan B. Anthony*

~ ALS, Henry Laurens Dawes Papers, DLC.

1. Henry Laurens Dawes (1816-1903), Republican of Massachusetts, served in the House of Representatives from 1857 to 1875 and in the Senate from 1875 to 1893. In the House, he had assisted in attempts to legislate woman suffrage in the District of Columbia, and in the Senate, he was respectful of suffragists' petitions. In 1844, he married Electa Allen Sanderson (1822-1901). (*BDAC*; *Papers*, 3:38, 282.) SBA also mentions their daughter, Anna Laurens Dawes (1851-1938), a journalist and social reformer who served in the leadership of the antisuffragists in Massachusetts. (*WWW1*.)

2. Mark Hill Dunnell (1823-1904), Republican of Minnesota, served in the House of Representatives from 1871 to 1883 and again from 1889 to 1891. He joined the Democrats in voting against the admission of Wyoming, the only Republican to do so. (*BDAC*; *Congressional Record*, 51st Cong., 1st sess., 27 March 1890, p. 2712.)

100   Article by ECS

[19 April 1890]

WHAT SHOULD BE OUR ATTITUDE TOWARDS POLITICAL PARTIES.

I regretted very much that I could not have been present during the discussion on the attitude the Woman Suffrage Association should maintain towards political parties, especially, as none of the speakers represented the side of the question I should have taken. It seems marvellous to me that not one word was said in the opposition, unless the presence of three gentlemen, all on one side, awed those ladies who might have differed to silence.[1]

The discussion, if discussion it might be called by courtesy, with all on one side, reminded me of the preface of an old book on etiquette I once owned which said, "never discuss politics, religion, or social problems in the presence of ladies, for men seldom appear like gentlemen in controversy."

As the platform of the suffrage association is one for the discussion of the broadest political questions, namely: the civil, political, religious, social, educational, and industrial rights of one-half the people, it is folly to say that we will have nothing to do with political parties, that our safety is to hold ourselves free from all "entangling alliances."[2]

Nothing easier to do, as all the parties in turn have clearly shown that they desire no "entangling alliances" with us, and that is our misfortune. Our association is like a helpless little craft at sea, tossed about for forty years, in a vain search for the beautiful Atlantis.

Though the poor little craft has been long buffeted by the winds and the waves, riddled by the shafts of the curious to find out whether it was a vessel or a whale, though it owns no coaling station, no flag, no country, yet the passengers will not consent to any nautical affiliations, even to send up signals of distress, lest through "entangling alliances" with some of the great lines of steamers it should be swallowed up.

A rope from a great vessel in the hour of danger, a calculation by their chart and compass for latitude and longitude, some knowledge of the path across the ocean might all be reassuring and suggestive, did not the fear of some "entangling alliance" drive the little craft into a dreary isolation to encounter fogs, cyclones, and icebergs, unaided and alone.

Now friends, what are we as an association after? a flag, a country, a political party, education in the science of government, to be recognized citizens in a republic.

Does any sane person suppose we can conquer all this by sweet words and a non-partisan position, by standing aloof from all parties and sects? No, no, our demands are to be made and carried like all other political questions, by the aid of and affiliations with parties. Where is the truth on any given point is a greater question than the route we take in quest of it. If "our platform," as one gentleman tells us, "is to be strictly educational" must we not discuss all the vital issues of the hour?[3] The day is not distant when we are to vote on all questions up for consideration, and now is the time for preparation.

Mr. Hinckley warns us against narrow methods and prohibition.[4] Mr. Foulke, against expressing any opinion on marriage and divorce, or taking part in any ordinary political discussions.[5] And Mr. Blackwell warns us against the deceitfulness of political parties and platforms and the danger of an "entangling alliance" with prohibition.[6] There really is more danger if we obey these gentlemen implicitly that we shall be too exclusive for any earthly affiliation whatsoever.

Mr. Foulke says he should regret to see the suffrage association taking a position advocating any kind of divorce. As the question is up for consideration both in England and America, and as all the laws and customs of society make marriage a most unequal contract between man and woman, it seems to me, that this is preeminently the association, above all others, that should take the lead, and point the way to a true relation.

Where is there a body of men as well educated in the rights of women as those women who have stood forty years on this platform, that we should trust them to take the initiative in the discussion of this question?

We have had man's idea both in his canon and civil laws. We have had his example experimenting in every form of social relation, and now shall men tell us that on the only political platform where woman has a right to express her opinion, that it does not behoove us at this time and place, to send forth the true clarion note on any question concerning the civil, political, and social rights of women? Are we to stand humble petitioners forty years longer with bated breath to hear what man may say on any given question before an opinion from woman's own standpoint is opportune on her own platform? Man has expressed his opinion fully and freely on the question of divorce, from Milton down to Gladstone,[7] and a respectful silence best becomes him now until woman is free to give an intelligent opinion. But Mr. Foulke further says that if the question were submitted to the suffrages of women the laws would be tightened rather than relaxed. What data has Mr. Foulke on which to form such an opinion?[8] And suppose his assumptions were true? If wives generally feel that they need added guarantees for the faithfulness of husbands, why should they not have them? But statistics show that the majority of divorces are asked for by women. When M. Naquet's bill[9] passed the Chamber of Deputies in 1882, 3000 divorces were asked for the first year, and the majority by women. I do not think I could agree with Mrs. Sewall in accepting Mr. Foulke as my representative.[10] In fact I have never yet seen or heard the man that I thought understood "the woman question" in all its bearings unless I should make an exception in favor of William Lloyd Garrison, who was the clearest sighted reformer this or any other country ever produced.

The woman question precipitated into the anti-slavery conflict was the severest strain the anti-slavery movement ever had. Yet Mr. Garrison stood by the principle of human rights in the conventions both in New York and London.[11] Not even for the sake of the cause so near his heart would he purchase peace for his association at the expense of woman. No warning words through all that bitter controversy on the woman question ever escaped his lips as to that "entangling alliance" injuring the anti-slavery cause. As to the divorce question, which I introduced into one of our early conventions, he was equally clear and liberal, even in opposition to Mr. Phillips.[12]

Mr. Garrison said he fully concurred in opinion with his friend, Mr. Phillips, that they had not come together to settle definitely the question of marriage, as such, on that platform; still, he should be sorry to have the motion adopted, as against the resolutions of Mrs. Stanton, because they were a part of her speech, and her speech was an elucidation of her resolutions, which were offered on her own responsibility, not on behalf of the Business committee, and which did not, therefore, make the convention responsible for them. It seemed to him that, in the liberty usually taken on that platform, both by way of argument and illustration, to show the various methods by which woman was unjustly, yet legally, subjected to the absolute control of man, she ought to be permitted to present her own sentiments. It was not the specific object of an Anti-Slavery Convention—for example—to discuss the conduct of Rev. Nehemiah Adams,[13] or the position of Stephen A. Douglas, or the course of *The New York Herald*; yet they did, incidentally, discuss all these, and many other matters closely related to the great struggle for the freedom of the slave. So the question of marriage came in as at least incidental to the main question of the equal rights of woman.

Mr. Hinckley lays down a broad platform when he says "Equality of rights in all respects for men and women." Very good! This allows the discussion of all laws and customs where there is the least disparity between men and women. This is the most extreme radical position I have ever advocated.

But on the heel of this he warns us against prohibition. When Frances Willard marshalls an army a hundred thousand strong on our platform I think we gain in the affiliation more than we lose. Liquor dealers are not so blind to their interests as not to have seen the ultimate effect of woman suffrage on the temperance movement long before the Rhode Island election. Conservatives always see more clearly than radicals themselves where their principles ultimately lead. They told us in the beginning that the woman's rights movement meant a complete revolution in the state, the church, and the home; and those who have the least prescience now see that it does, although we denied the impeachment when starting. We cannot carry woman suffrage by clap-trap, by pretending that we have no strong proclivities on any other question. The woman-suffrage gospel is not like blown glass, so frail that we must guard it carefully and continually lest it be shattered; nor is our platform made of such elastic timber that it cannot bear the weight of the whole mountain of sorrows that oppresses the souls of women.

My idea of political parties is to affiliate in some way with them whenever and wherever we have opportunity, if any feel inclined to affiliate with us. If I lived in Kansas I should use my voice and pen to help the Republican party, above all others, simply because it has taken one step in the right direction on woman suffrage. I should not care whether it was for or against land monopoly, free trade, paper money, or prohibition, because I consider woman suffrage, involving as it does the fundamental rights of one half the people, a larger question than any one of these, or all put together.

If the Prohibition party in some other State put a well-seasoned plank in its platform for woman suffrage, I would help that party all I could in that State. If the Labor party in another declared itself unmistakably for woman suffrage I would go for that party in that State. If the Democratic party in New York would declare itself for woman suffrage I would use all my influence to help that party carry the State election. If at a Presidential election all the parties should adopt an equally strong plank for woman suffrage, I would go for the party most likely to succeed in carrying woman suffrage.

I think it is wise to try them, each and all, every Presidential campaign, and see what recognition we can get out of them, and it is good policy too to hold one of our National conventions right under their eyes every time. Even if they do behave as badly as Mr. Blackwell represents, we get some agitation out of it, and agitation is primary school in political education. When we get the suffrage it will be through some political party, so we may as well begin to study the nature and assailable points of such organizations, first as last, and the more entangling the alliance the better, so that they cannot sever it. Justin McCarthy[14] in a recent speech on the woman-suffrage platform said: "Women will never get the suffrage until, like the Irish party, they aim at the point of seating and unseating ministries."

Look at all the rebuffs the Irish members have had in the House of Commons and how slowly step by step they have climbed into power.

When we can seat and unseat Congressmen by affiliating with some party and thus making our influence seen and felt, all parties will stand ready to do us honor. Woman suffrage will be our test of political friendship, and we shall express our opinion freely on all parties and politicians and the vital questions of the hour. But where can we do this if not on our own platform?

It is very well for the three gentlemen who led in the discussion, who are members of the ruling class, who have their political platform outside the suffrage association, for the expression of their opinions on general topics, to set limits to our freedom, to tell us what does and does not legitimately belong to our platform, it is very well for those women who have implicit confidence in man's judgment, who feel that men can and do represent them, to accept their advice, but I, for one, should accept the advice of members of the masculine aristocracy with great reservation on all questions regarding women. We must remember that men came into our association with the ordinary feelings of men, as to their own superiority, and our natural position of subjection; as to their strength, and our weakness; their wisdom, our folly; their gift of reason, and our blind instinct.

They cannot throw off nor disguise the education of centuries, and women naturally accord to them whatever position they take.[15]

I should be very sorry to see all discussion of the liquor traffic forbidden on our platform. Woman has rights and duties in this reform that cannot be trusted to any body of men to accomplish. Thus far man has had all legislation on the question in his own hands. He has tried high license, local option, and prohibition, wherever and whenever he has seen fit. He makes liquor as a beverage in all possible varieties, and sells it under all sorts of attractive names, and sets his nets for the unwary in every street and highway in the land. His victims shadow every fireside, fill our jails and prisons, and cause death and destruction on every side. If they fear woman suffrage as the avenging angel to end all this, I trust the fear may soon be a fact, and that to woman suffrage may be the glory of abolishing the most terrible evil that has ever cursed mankind. If an "entangling alliance" with prohibition should delay woman's enfranchisement; for a final victory over such an enemy to all her most sacred relations, as mother, daughter, sister, wife, to the peace, permanency, and prosperity of the home; we can afford to wait.

Woman needs the discussion of this question on our platform, fully and freely, before she can decide whether the best mode of attack lies through high license, local option, or prohibition, and may the Spirit of all Good anoint our eyes to see what is right on every question.[16]

~ *Elizabeth Cady Stanton.*

~ *Woman's Tribune,* 19 April 1890.

1. On the morning after ECS's departure from Washington, the National-American's convention debated "the Attitude of This Association Toward

Political Parties." The discussion was reported at length in the *Woman's Tribune*, 1 March 1890, *Film*, 28:63-77. By invitation, Alice Pickler and Frederic Hinckley opened the session with their answers to the question, and at the request of the audience, SBA asked William Foulke to speak before she invited delegates to join in. Henry Blackwell chimed in during the discussion.

2. The term was Frederic Hinckley's: the association's "attitude should be one of righteous demand upon all and entangling alliances with none." Frederic Allen Hinckley (1845-1917), a Unitarian minister, left the American association in 1880 to join the National. While he lived in Providence, he held office in the Rhode Island state association, collaborating with loyal adherents of the American association and setting an example of the unity that he favored at the national level. He moved to Northampton, Massachusetts, in 1888. (*WWW1*. See also *Papers* 3 & 4.)

3. William Foulke recommended that for the present time the association "be strictly educational." By way of example, referring back to ECS's address of the previous day, he said he would "regret to see this Association take a position advocating any kind of divorce."

4. Still smarting from the defeat of woman suffrage by Rhode Island's voters in 1887, Hinckley ascribed it to the perception of woman suffrage as a tool in the hands of prohibitionists. He also warned against the "narrow, and small, and degrading" habit of reformers to see their cause as "the great panacea."

5. Foulke also wanted to steer away from "any ordinary political discussions of the day" that "would only distract our councils."

6. Blackwell railed against political parties: a plank endorsing woman suffrage in a party's platform had no effect on how the party's politicians behaved, and it was "nonsense" to talk about supporting parties that supported their cause. He also seconded Hinckley's remarks about the damaging connection between prohibition and woman suffrage; it has "cost us the entire Northwest," he concluded.

7. John Milton (1608-1674), the English poet, wrote several essays in support of divorce. On earlier occasions, ECS cited specifically *The Doctrine and Discipline of Divorce* (1643). She also refers to William E. Gladstone, "The Question of Divorce," *North American Review* 149 (December 1889): 641-44.

8. Rather than offering data to support his position, Foulke posited that "a consciousness of the sacredness of" marriage was "more deeply implanted in the minds of women than in the minds of men."

9. Alfred-Joseph Naquet (1834-1916), a strong advocate of secular republicanism, wrote the law of 1884 that reestablished divorce in France. In an interview in Paris with James Gordon Bennett for the *Chicago Tribune*, 14 October 1888, Naquet provided this number of three thousand divorces annually since the bill's passage. ECS's source on women's role in initiating those divorces is unknown, but her information is consistent with data from France during an earlier era of legal divorce, when overwhelmingly women were the petitioners for divorce. (David S. Bell, Douglas Johnson, and Peter

Morris, eds., *Biographical Dictionary of French Political Leaders Since 1870* [New York, 1990]; Wesley D. Camp, *Marriage and the Family in France Since the Revolution: An Essay in the History of Population* [New York, 1961]; Patricia Mainardi, *Husbands, Wives, and Lovers: Marriage and Its Discontents in Nineteenth-Century France* [New Haven, Conn., 2003], 11–12.)

10. May Sewall praised Foulke as a man who "never speaks without really representing women. He does thoroughly understand both the woman's and the man's side of this great question."

11. Note from the source: "See History of Woman Suffrage, Vol. I., p. 61."

12. Here ECS pasted onto her manuscript the text of the following paragraph, clipped from *History*, 1:733. The *Woman's Tribune*'s typesetters made no distinction between the handwritten and printed text. The topic arose at the Tenth National Woman's Rights Convention in May 1860, on which see *Papers*, 1:418–31, 438–39, and *Film*, 9:612–75.

13. Nehemiah Adams (1806–1878), Congregational clergyman, was an apologist for slavery and the chief author of the "Pastoral Letter" in 1837, attacking the public appearances of Sarah and Angelina Grimké. Stephen Arnold Douglas (1813–1861), Northern Democrat, thought settlers should decide whether new territories would be slave or free. The *New York Herald* was a proslavery paper.

14. Justin McCarthy (1830–1912) was an Irish writer and Liberal member of Parliament for both Londonderry City and Longford. The source of this quotation has not been found. (*Oxford DNB*; *Who's Who of British Members of Parliament*, vol. 2.)

15. This paragraph continues in ECS's manuscript: "Hence I do not agree with Mr Foulke when he says 'it would be a source of weakness, for the suffrage association to be composed entirely of women.' I think we need no better proof of it, than this discussion, in which the women who did speak simply echoed what the men said beside paying ↑one of↓ them the most fulsome compliments." (*Film*, 28:282–97.)

16. Clara Colby chose this point to conclude ECS's article and so marked the manuscript. ECS went on to say: "Mrs Sewall says 'We have no right, even impliedly, to say, because a political party will pledge itself to put into our hands the ballot, that therefore we shall deposit that ballot for the advancement of that political party and for the retaining of that political party in power. I think that we should always place ourselves so squarely there could be no danger of misunderstanding our position.' I think under such circumstances, we should show very little political knowledge, if we did not sustain such a party, with all the influence we could muster. It would be very difficult to understand common sense women taking such a position.

"A party of saints & angels would not stand by us in the face of such ingratitude. I must say I was grieved & disappointed with the discussion on this point."

101   ECS to Hannah Whitall Smith

Basingstoke Hants [*England*]   May 1st [*1890*]

Dear Mrs Smith,

You will no doubt be surprized to know that I am again in England. This makes five times that I have crossed in seven years.[1]

My daughter & I are going up to London for a week to visit several friends & attend some meetings   I write particularly to say that if you are to be at home any time from the 8th to the 16th we will spend one night with you, if you are not otherwise engaged   I want to talk with you, both about our movements in America, & England. You have no doubt heard the great news about Wyoming   That is a great triumph, a true republic at last, where women too are full fledged citizens. I had the pleasure of meeting your daughter[2] when I was last in England & hope to meet her again   Mrs Blatch joins me in kind regards. Yours Sincerely

Elizabeth Cady Stanton.

ALS, Letters and Documents Collection, PBm.

    1. The conjecture that this letter was addressed to Hannah W. Smith is based on a reading of this and two related letters from the same season and same collection at Bryn Mawr College. The strongest clue is ECS's invitation on 5 June 1890 to visit and bring "Mrs. Costelloe," another reference to Smith's daughter. Smith also fits the profile of interests and activism that ECS assumed in her correspondent: a transatlantic engagement with woman's rights, interest in details of the suffrage movement in the United States, and involvement with the Women's Liberal Federation in London. See *Film*, 28:366–69, 393–95.

    2. Mary Smith Costelloe (1864–1945), later Berenson, the oldest of Hannah Smith's surviving children, had lived in London since her marriage to Frank Costelloe in 1885. (Barbara Strachey, *Remarkable Relations: The Story of the Pearsall Smith Family* [London, 1981], 76–99.)

102 ❧ SBA TO ALICE ALT PICKLER?[1]

[*after 30 May 1890*]

Passed May 30, 1890

Resolved: That to promote harmony and facilitate ↑the↓ prompt and thorough organization of the suffrage work in the state, Miss Anthony be requested to take charge of the appointments of the speakers under the control of the National of the National association, and the state executive Committee to attend to the appointments of speakers under their control—full lists of appointments be made in duplicate and furnished to each other—and perfect cooperation maintained—[2]

This is the resolution passed at the last Ex. Com. meeting to cut off S. B. A. & I scolded all hands roundly therefor—& they promised to re-consider & repeal!!—

❧ AL, on verso of printed schedule of SBA and Mary Howell for May and June, Major John A. Pickler Family Papers, 1865–1976, SdHi.

1. Found in the papers of Alice Mary Alt Pickler of Faulkton, South Dakota, what was once an enclosure now has no obvious cover letter. Pickler (1848–1932) met her husband John while they attended the Iowa State University. After the couple married in 1870, she accompanied him to Ann Arbor, where he studied law at the University of Michigan, and moved with him around the Midwest several times before joining him in Dakota Territory in 1883. An early member of the Woman's Christian Temperance Union, she worked through the territorial union to achieve woman suffrage in advance of statehood. At the National-American's convention in January, she tempered Alonzo Wardall's enthusiasm, warning the delegates not to think from his remarks "that they expected plain sailing for the amendment. It was to be submitted at a general election with all the political and personal interests." On April 29, Alice Pickler and SBA began filling engagements made for Anna Shaw who left the state earlier than planned. (Doane Robinson, *History of South Dakota, Together with Personal Mention of Citizens of South Dakota* [Logansport, Ind., 1904], 2:1618–19; Linda M. Sommer, "Dakota Resources:

The Pickler Family Papers and the Humphrey Family Papers at the South Dakota State Historical Society," *South Dakota History* 24 [Summer 1994]: 115-34; *Woman's Tribune*, 1 March 1890, *Film*, 28:63-77.)

2. SBA was not present at the meeting of the equal suffrage association's executive committee on 30 May 1890; she returned to Huron on June 2. The resolution adopted in her absence differed in tone and procedures from the one adopted when she arrived in the state in late April, reported by Moses Barker on 1 May 1890: "*Resolved*, That the committee cordially welcome Miss Susan B. Anthony, as a representative of the National American Woman Suffrage Association, to the work in South Dakota, and that she be given a voice and a vote at our executive meetings." Between the time of her arrival in South Dakota on April 23 and the end of May, SBA had attended at least twenty meetings in as many towns stretching from the state's northern to its southern border in the eastern half of the state, crossing paths with Mary Howell, who followed a similar schedule. Both of them were denied use of halls they were announced to speak in, and at Yankton, SBA griped to her diary she "was advertised for 10 A.M. & 2 & 8 P.M.—this on Saturday & in a county where 9 out of 10 women do their own work." Responding on June 3 to Julia Nelson's frustration with poor planning and insufficient assistance from headquarters, SBA asked "Is it not a little queer that the State Ex. Com. here doesn't feel the need of inviting you or Miss [*illegible*] & me or Mrs Howell in to their Councils?" But until they found "a good planning brain devoted to this Campaign," she urged Nelson to find her own way of working and "feel your way along." (*Woman's Journal*, 10 May 1890; SBA to J. B. Nelson, 3 June 1890, *Film*, 28:385-89.)

103 ❧ EMILIE ASHURST VENTURI[1] TO ECS

Carlyle Cottage King's road, Chelsea S.W. June 4/90

Dear M[rs] Stanton

I hope you have not quite forgotten me as I want to add my word of earnest longing to hear you once again, to the official letter which has been sent to me to forward to you.

Pray let me say how great an honour I should consider it for our Association for you to speak from our platform and, especially, on the subject of our "<u>over</u> government" as you only can do.[2] The desire of every individual democrat to become an autocrat and to turn the power which partial freedom has given him to the oppress[io]n and coercion of those who differ with him, is to me the saddest sight of our day. That slaves made the cruelest slave-drivers I had learned when a young girl from W. L. Garrison's lips; but that the sons of ↑working↓ men who won their own freedom for themselves, should strive to enslave others—now about temperance, now about what <u>they</u> call purity, and now about religion, is indeed disheartening. Crimes committed in the name of God are far more terrible and far-reaching in their consequences, than crimes committed in the name of the devil. Hoping that I may once again hear you sound your silver trumpet for liberty, <u>quand même</u>,—and with best remembrances to Mrs Blatch I am, dear Mrs Stanton most sincerely and respectfully yours

~ *Emilie A Venturi*

It may interest you to know that I am devoting my ↑remnant of↓ time to the copying & preparing for the press of Mazzini's letters to our family; in which labour of love I have much help and sympathy from Frank Garrison.[3]

~ ALS, ECS Papers, DLC. Letters in square brackets faded from original.

1. Emilie Ashurst Hawkes Venturi (1819?–1893), an English activist with many interests, invited ECS to address the Personal Rights Association, a group that opposed overuse of state power to enforce morality. Raised in an antislavery household, Venturi also committed herself to the Italian republican movement, becoming a secretary, translator, and biographer of Giuseppe Mazzini. She was a member of the Married Women's Property Committee from 1876 until it won its objective in 1882, and for many years she edited the journal of the Ladies' National Association for Repeal of the Contagious Diseases Acts. ECS probably met her through the new Women's Franchise League. (*Oxford DNB*; Joseph O. Baylen and Norbert J. Gossman, eds. *Biographical Dictionary of Modern British Radicals*, vol. 2, *1830–1870* [Sussex, U.K., 1984]; E. A. Venturi to ECS, 23 June 1890, *Film*, 28:437-38.)

2. See *Film*, 28:440, for a bit of ECS's speech on June 25.

3. A preview of this project appeared in the American *Century Illustrated Magazine* 43 (November 1891): 67–76. Although Venturi did not live to complete it, three volumes were later finished by Elinor F. Richards and published as *Mazzini's Letters to an English Family* (1920–1922).

104 ~ ECS to SBA and Clara Bewick Colby

Basingstoke Hants [*England*]   June 6th [*1890*]

Dear Susan,

The Woman's Journal has another two column article of falsehoods on Train in Kansas, contradicting all my statements.[1] He is bound to pitch into me. He does not mention you because it is his policy now to play you off against me.[2] Just what I told you they would do, if I was made President. Now the question is if <u>I</u> am to keep silent & let Blackwell go on with his lies & insults giving as he says the facts of history!! I answered his editorial on our movement in which Mrs Hooker saw three lies.[3] I saw five, but Mrs Spofford & Mrs Colby thought best not to publish it & I assented. now I think it was a mistake to let him off, for here he comes again reasserting his falsehoods. I think it is unwise to let him go on & say what he chooses hypocritically saying that "he is sorry to refer to the past, but ↑the↓ truth of history makes it necessary."[4] Now I know as much about the history of the division & the struggle in Kansas as he does. You say Alice asked you to prevent me if possible writing anything that would rouse antagonism. ~~What~~ ↑Why↓ not ask her to prevent her father doing & saying anything to rouse antagonism especially not to falsify the facts of history. He made a direct & rude attack on me in Washington, then he went home & penned that insulting editorial. Then he pitches into my Reminiscences. Can Alice in justice ask silence on our side while The Woman's Journal allows these attacks in its columns. Blackwell is determined if possible to kill me, & you all say sit still & let him do his worst. So long as I am the target no matter. I have just read the Kansas chapter with all Harry & Lucy's letters showing how utterly we were deserted by all the eastern philanthropists & editors on whom we relied, Greeley, Tilton, Higginson, Phillips, Frothingham, & how unreliable the Kansas Republicans were.[5] Gerrit Smith Garrison Douglass all watched Kansas with bated breath lest our movement should defeat the negro. Train thrashed them one & all & so do Lucy & Harry in their letters. That was the chief thing they all felt in our affiliation with

Train, that he held up the mirror before their faces in which they could see themselves. Blackwell tells a different story in his letters about Kansas politicians, from what he tells to day.

You & I had nothing to do with Train's coming into the state.[6] I always understood that he was urged to do so by some St Louis ladies who went with him in that railroad excursion where the golden spike was driven half way across the continent   I never heard anyone say that he came under the auspices of the "the Equal Rights association." The first I heard of his coming was in a conversation between Gov Robinson[7] & Mr Blackwell who seemed much pleased with the prospect of his advent

The fact is we were so utterly deserted by eastern friends & so, doubtful of the action of Kansas politicians, that we were all glad of help from any quarter

<u>Read</u> & <u>send</u> <u>to Susan</u>. I enclose references in Vol II to Harry & Lucy's letters.[8] When negro suffrage was defeated [*sideways in margins*] the Blackwells joined with rest in blaming Susan & me, for its failure. Yours ever

~ E. C. S.

Dear Mrs Colby,

As you do not wish <u>me</u> to notice Blackwell you better correct his misstatements in as mild a way as you choose yourself. The History & what I have written here & in that long article will give you the true facts in the case. What he says is false altogether. Yours E. C. S.

~ ALS, Clara B. Colby Papers, Archives Division, WHi.

1. *Woman's Journal*, 24 May 1890. Blackwell reacted to chapters of ECS's reminiscences about the Kansas amendment campaign of 1867, the most contentious topic in suffrage history. Although he appropriated the title of the chapter published on 3 May 1890, "Kansas, Train, The Revolution," Blackwell focused on the earlier one, "My First Experience of Pioneer Life," published on April 26. There ECS stayed close to the theme of her title, describing land, modes of transportation, and people she met in her three-month tour of Kansas. She referred readers to her chapter in the *History of Woman Suffrage* for background on the campaign, but she included a few sentences from that source to set the scene of her personal experience. Chief among Blackwell's objections were sentences praising the assistance provided by George Francis Train; he had, she wrote, gained Democratic votes for a campaign abandoned by most Republicans. ECS stood nearly alone, Blackwell replied, in thinking

Train useful; Train "was regarded by most people simply as a lunatic"; and as a Democrat, he was "the last person who could be expected to do good" in Republican Kansas. (*Film*, 28:318–19, 352–53; *History*, 2:229–50. See also *Papers* 2.)

2. ECS speaks literally: while attacking SBA in an editorial on 8 March 1890, Blackwell referred to her simply as "a speaker"; in the May 24 editorial about ECS's history, he mentioned "the two ladies who now stand alone (so far as we know) in defending the alliance with Mr. Train," but never uttered SBA's name.

3. *Woman's Journal*, 8 March 1890. ECS's unpublished reply has not been found. Blackwell's editorial, occasioned by the publication of SBA's remarks at the National's final executive meeting, above at 17 February 1890, pronounced "her account of the division . . . not in harmony with the facts." The American association practiced only one form of exclusion, he wrote: "persons of conspicuous absurdity or notorious immorality ought not to be invited to speak from suffrage platforms." He named George Train and Victoria Woodhull as prime examples.

4. ECS paraphrases elaborate apologies in both the objectionable editorials.

5. *History*, 2:229–68; letters from Lucy Stone and Henry Blackwell, written before ECS and SBA reached Kansas in 1867, are on pages 232–39. Blackwell assured ECS on 10 and 21 April 1867 that though Republicans would not endorse the amendment, "the Democrats all over the State are preparing to take us up." Stone announced to ECS on April 20, "I have been for the last time on my knees to Phillips and Higginson," and she complained repeatedly about eastern reformers and Republicans who would not use their influence in support of the amendment, naming most of the men in ECS's list. Not previously identified is Octavius Brooks Frothingham (1822–1895), clergyman and author. (*ANB*; *Papers*, 2:57–58.)

6. Blackwell's editorial attack on ECS continued with charges that the American Equal Rights Association was sullied by an invitation to George Train, issued in its name, without consent of its executive committee, "and altogether against their judgment." In this he was mistaken; he described an uproar that came after the Kansas campaign, when ECS and SBA traveled and lectured with Train as they headed back to the East Coast, and Blackwell and Stone mobilized a faction in the executive committee to denounce them. The association's name did appear on publicity at that time. No one from the equal rights association invited Train to Kansas; as ECS recalls, a group in St. Louis extended the first invitation, and invitations from men in the Kansas Impartial Suffrage Association followed. As a railroad man, Train was influential in St. Louis and parts of Kansas after years of promoting the transcontinental connection. His invitations coincided with a wide push to muster Democratic support for the amendment. When Blackwell returned to Kansas in October, he boasted of his own negotiations with Democrats and voiced no objections

to working in the state alongside Train. (*Woman's Journal*, 24 May 1890; H. B. Blackwell to L. Stone, 29 October 1867, Blackwell Papers, DLC; *Papers*, 2:92–121.)

7. Charles Robinson (1818–1894) was the first governor of Kansas and one of the few Republicans who worked for impartial suffrage in the Kansas campaign. He served on the executive committee of the Impartial Suffrage Association and toured with ECS to win support from voters for black and woman suffrage. (*BDGov*; Don W. Wilson, *Governor Charles Robinson of Kansas* [Lawrence, Kan., 1975]; *Papers*, 2:48–49, 92–93, 96, 102–3.)

8. Enclosure missing. Although ECS wrote this letter to SBA, she sent it first to Clara Colby, with this directive to send it along.

105 ❧ SBA TO HARRIET TAYLOR UPTON

Parker S.D.[1] June 10, 1890

My Dear Mrs Upton

Yours of the 5th inst—meets me here— It is just splendid of Judge Upton[2] not to take that $25— I will write & thank him as soon as possible— I should say—now—that you do not need to use the $25— for Judge Upton—you might use the whole $50— for the report—[3] I think Miss Ward[4] will direct packages of them—(of it) to the different points— Still—a better way perhaps will be to frank them—and then send all of them direct to Huron—and let the S.D. State secretary scatter them— But first—as soon as you can get a few—send a lot to me—at some of my points— I shall be in Huron from July 2^d to the 10th

The Farmers Alliance have done the idiotic thing of declaring themselves an Independent Party—& they are to meet in Huron to formulate their platform & nominate their candidates July 9th—[5] I feel awfully cut down about their action—as it loses to us <u>their</u> immense balance of power to compel the Republican Convention to put W.S. in their platform— But I cant talk about them—all I can do is to make as many converts as possible who, no matter how many parties there are—or whether they as parties endorse W.S. or not—will individually vote for WS.

Thanks for your "<u>scolding</u>." I shall try to hold my tongue & pen on the Blackwell kicks—save to a few of the tried & true—like unto you & Mrs Spofford— I surely shall not use any of the Dakota Fund for anything but its work—[6] I felt so ashamed of my neglect to send an order to Lucy Stone & thence to Mrs Spofford for the $25. for Judge Upton—that I did as I told you—but it gave you a text to make a splendid statement on the danger of carelessness— I think you had better invest the whole $50. in the report for Dakota Literature—it will be vastly better than any of the old leaflets— Lovingly yours

≈ Susan B. Anthony

≈ ALS, SBA Papers, NRU.

1. From the Farmers' Alliance convention in Huron on June 4, SBA traveled into the extreme southeastern corner of the state, attending meetings in Vermillion, Elk Point, and Centerville before arriving this day in Parker for the two-day Turner County Convention. For events at Centerville, see *Film*, 28:413.

2. William W. Upton (1817-1896) was Harriet Upton's father-in-law. He earned his title as a justice and later chief justice of the Oregon Supreme Court between 1864 and 1874. From 1877 to 1885, he was second comptroller of the Treasury in Washington, where he continued to practice law. The National-American owed him money for his work on securing its incorporation. (*NCAB*, 12:44-45.)

3. House of Representatives, Committee on the Judiciary, *Woman Suffrage*, 51st Cong., 2st sess., H. Rept. 2254, serial 2813. Issued on 29 May 1890, the report recommended passage of an amendment for woman suffrage, and SBA wanted it circulated in South Dakota.

4. Eliza Titus Ward (c. 1838-1907) was an activist in the District of Columbia Woman Suffrage Association by 1880 and prominent at the National association's conventions through the decade. Known for "notable administrative ability and financial sagacity," she was named auditor of the National-American Woman Suffrage Association at its founding. (Federal Census, 1880; *Washington Post*, 15 November 1907; unidentified clipping, 27 July 1890, in SBA scrapbook 16, Rare Books, DLC.)

5. SBA reached Huron ahead of the semi-annual meeting of the Farmers' Alliance and Knights of Labor and awaited an invitation to speak. It came on the meeting's first day, June 4. She opened by offering a resolution, that the Farmers' Alliance "pledge themselves as a body . . . to secure to the women of their households full civil rights," and proceeded to make what Alonzo Wardall described as a "ringing speech." In it she gave no hint that she anticipated the decision delegates made after she left town, to form a political party and run candidates against the Democrats and Republicans. By June 7, she knew what had happened and wrote to a friend, they were "wheedled by political schemers into forming a 3^d Party." She also knew by then that the meeting had resolved that "justice demands that no citizen be disfranchised on account of sex." The misstatement in this letter of June 10, that the Independent party

would write its platform in July, suggests she did not yet understand that the party's platform was written at Huron, without a suffrage plank. (SBA diary, 2-4 June 1890, and speech to Farmers' Alliance, and SBA to Jane S. Spofford, 7 June 1890, *Film*, 27:679ff, 28:391, 405-10; Diary of Alonzo Wardall, 4 June 1890, Alonzo and Elizabeth Wardall Collection, WaU.)

6. On SBA's swap of South Dakota funds to pay bills in Washington, see SBA to Jane S. Spofford, 7 June 1890.

106 ⇝ Priscilla Bright McLaren[1] to ECS

Newington House, Edinburgh, [*Scotland*] June 12, 1890.

My dearest Mrs. Cady Stanton:

Lord Hartington[2] has spoken at the Women's Liberal Union meeting, [ac]knowledging women's usefulness yet shrinking from giving them their just [ri]ghts. This has called forth an excellent article for us in the "Scotsman" [wh]ich until very recently was our great enemy.

I can't bear not to go the whole length with you in anything [fo]r I feel you have a far greater intellect than I have. You seem to have [no?] prejudices or adhesiveness to bind you to the past. It is not so with [me?]. I cannot go so far on the divorce question as you do. But I acknowledge [th]is with no feeling of superiority of judgement. I find my judgement wrong [ev]ery now and then.[3]

I used to wonder how it was that old persons grew more lax in [th]eir sentiments and feelings than when younger. But I think it must be [be]cause they ofttimes find results differ from their expectations. A day [or?] two ago I had proof of this. I thought if it were known that the "Women's [Pe]nny Paper" was the authorized medium for reporting the Woman Suffrage [Pr]oceedings that this might injure its sale.[4] I find the very reverse to be [tr]ue. Again, I was expressing the other day to some friends here my regret [of?] that, to me, unwise article about refusing the suffrage to married [wo]men so long as the law of coverture existed. These ladies replied: "Well, [we?] agree with you; but somehow we never understood or could see so clearly, [be]fore we read those articles and letters, how unjust and odious that law [of?] coverture was." I mused over all this and thought, Well, we need all [ki]nds of routes to lead us to the desired haven.

I saw the freedom of the city presented to Stanley yesterday.[5] It [is?] wonderful how refined he looks after all he has gone through. We live in [a] marvelous age.

You will rejoice over the latest success at Cambridge.[6] Thanks for [you]r last characteristic note. Ever your deeply grateful loving friend,

~ *Priscilla B. M'Laren.*

~ Typed transcript, ECS Papers, NjR. Square brackets surround letters obscured by binding.

1. Priscilla Bright McLaren (1815-1906) was a sister of John and Jacob Bright, the mother of Walter McLaren, and an astute politician in her own right. She became a good friend and ally of ECS in 1882, and she ensured that the suffrage society in Edinburgh sent a delegate to the International Council of Women in 1888. Since the death of her husband, Duncan McLaren, in 1886, she continued to live in their house in Edinburgh. (*Oxford DNB*; Holton, "From Anti-Slavery to Suffrage Militancy: The Bright Circle," 213-33. See also *Papers* 4.)

2. Spencer Compton Cavendish, marquess of Hartington (1833-1908), leader of the Liberal Unionist group in Parliament, addressed the Women's Liberal Unionist Association in London on 11 June 1890. Though opposed to woman suffrage, he praised women's great influence in politics through such associations. On June 12, an editorial in the *Scotsman* argued that women's indirect influence was precisely the reason they should have the vote. Politics would be better served by woman suffrage than by leaving women to exercise an ungoverned, indirect influence. (*Oxford DNB*; Edinburgh *Scotsman*, 12 June 1890.)

3. McLaren may respond to ECS's article "Divorce vs. Domestic Warfare," *Arena* 1 (April 1890): 560-69, *Film*, 28:324-33.

4. Billed as "The only Paper Conducted, Written, and Published by Women," the *Women's Penny Paper* began weekly publication in London in October 1888, edited by Henrietta Müller.

5. Henry Morton Stanley (1841-1904), the journalist and explorer, was feted throughout Britain in the spring and summer of 1890 after his return from Africa. The ceremonies in Edinburgh took place on June 11 before an audience of thousands. (*Oxford DNB*; Edinburgh *Scotsman*, 12 June 1890.)

6. McLaren refers to Philippa Fawcett's success in examinations at Cambridge University in the previous week, winning the highest honors in mathematics. As an indication of women's abilities, her triumph over the male candidates for degrees was widely celebrated, but the university persisted in its refusal to grant degrees to women. Philippa was the daughter of Millicent Garrett Fawcett and the late Henry Fawcett. (Rita McWilliams-Tulberg, *Women at Cambridge: A Men's University—Though of a Mixed Type* [London, 1975], 102; David Rubinstein, *A Different World for Women: The Life of Millicent Garrett Fawcett* [Columbus, Ohio, 1991], 107-8.)

107 ~ SBA TO ALICE ALT PICKLER

Canton S.D.¹ June 14/90

My Dear Mrs Pickler

I long to talk over the situation with you—

1st The Democrats have planted <u>their</u> <u>party</u> <u>squarely</u> against Woman Suffrage—so know just where to find that Party—²

2d The Farmers' Alliance <u>Party</u>—3d Party—has <u>ignored</u> in its platform both Prohibition & woman suffrage, & for the avowed object of <u>winning</u> the <u>votes</u> of the <u>Anti</u>-<u>Prohibition</u> & <u>Anti</u>-<u>Woman</u> <u>Suffrage</u> <u>Foreigners</u> among them—<u>to</u> <u>their</u> nominees— Though they passed a resolution—it isn't a committal of the <u>new party</u>—to stand for W.S. as a party measure—hence every one of their nominees will <u>play shy</u> of the question for fear he'll lose the votes of the Russians, Germans et al!! hence their influence while <u>seemingly</u> <u>friendly</u>—will be <u>virtually</u> against us!³

3d It remains to be seen, now, whether the Republicans at Mitchell will put a <u>square toed</u> <u>woman suffrage</u> <u>amendment</u> plank in their <u>party</u> platform—& thereby make it a <u>party</u> <u>measure</u>—to be advocated & urged upon every republican voter—⁴ If they will only do that—& also put in an <u>enforcement</u> <u>plank</u>—they'll carry the election with a whoop!! Do you not see—that by the Alliance playing shy—totally ignoring both reform measures in their platform—they to start with—alienate from their party all <u>true</u> <u>friends</u> of both—& leave them just ready to vote the Repub. ticket if that ↑party↓ does pledge itself to both reforms—

So to bring all our <u>guns</u> to bear on the Repub. Con. we must hold a state W.S. Con. at Mitchell August 25, 26—just prior to the Repub. Con—& you & the Maj. & every good & loyal Republican must be there to help pull down the scale on our side—& I will have some of our best National speakers there to help make our Con. splendid as to speaking, resolutions &c—⁵

Then I am just in receipt of a telegram from our State Pres. Mr Ramsey—saying—"Have Barker's recognition to day—have called Mass Convention July 8 at Huron"—so the skies are likely to be cleared of the Barker shadow—and I do hope no other <u>darker</u> <u>one</u> <u>will</u> come over the S.D. State association—⁶ Now you mustn't fail to be on hand—& dear Mrs Johnson⁷—& all of you help to make the Con. a success—and to make a Campaign Committee that will set the ball rolling in a most splendid manner—

Our meetings are going on very well—considering there is no <u>magnetic</u> <u>head</u> or <u>heart</u> or <u>hand</u> stretched out to the people from the head centre at Huron! What it needs to make things buzz is a true, earnest, <u>magnet</u> <u>soul</u> at the helm whose every pen scratch will enthuse everybody who reads it— Who shall that soul be? is the question! But do you think it all over & see if you can't resurrect from the thousands splendid people just the right one or ones to run this campaign— Lovingly your Friend

↙ *Susan B. Anthony*

↙ ALS, Major John A. Pickler Family Papers, 1865-1976, SdHi.

1. The Lincoln County Convention was in its second day in this town along the state's border with Iowa.

2. Suffragists appealed to the Democratic state convention, and members of the party's platform committee issued a minority report in favor of the constitutional amendment. Delegates, however, adopted a plank that read, "We are opposed to the proposed amendment to our state constitution striking out the word 'male' from the article on suffrage." (*Aberdeen Daily News*, 12, 13 June 1890.)

3. Equal suffrage was first in the list of a half-dozen resolutions adopted by the Farmers' Alliance; next in line was support for prohibition. Reacting to the same events, Republican Sarah Richards, treasurer of the equal suffrage association, described the alliance as having "deliberately expunged this principle from its political creed, relegating it to the rank of an appended resolution which no candidate will be expected to refer to, much less attempt to discuss and vindicate." ("What Will the Republicans Do About It?" unidentified and undated clipping, SBA scrapbook 16, Rare Books, DLC.)

4. The Republican party convention was scheduled to meet at Mitchell on August 28.

5. On June 15, SBA wrote a dozen letters asking leading suffragists to come into the state two days before the Republican convention and stay to lecture through the fall. (SBA diary, 1890, *Film*, 27:679ff.)

6. According to her diary, SBA received the telegram from Samuel Ramsey on June 10.

7. Philena Everett Johnson (c. 1843-?), who began married life in Cherokee, Iowa, settled in Highmore in 1883. She and her husband, Eli Johnson,

bought the local newspaper when they arrived, renamed it the *Highmore Herald*, and published it until 1892. Philena Johnson wrote for and edited the paper, and during the campaign, the *Herald* carried campaign news. Like other suffragists in the Dakotas, Johnson worked first in the state temperance union, organizing Highmore's local union in 1884. When the equal suffrage association chose new officers in July 1890, she was elected to succeed Samuel Ramsey as president. Johnson continued to lead in the state, as vice president of a newly organized state association in 1901 and delegate to the National-American association's meeting in 1909. Her son Royal Johnson helped the cause as attorney general of the state from 1910 to 1914 and a Repubican member of Congress from 1915 to 1933. (Federal Census, Cherokee County, Iowa, 1880, Hyde County, S.D., 1900, 1910; Kingsbury, *History of Dakota Territory*, 4:87-88; *History*, 5:254, 462, 523-24, 6:585, 588-89.)

108   SBA TO ALICE ALT PICKLER

[*South Dakota, before 2 July 1890*]¹

Dear Mrs Pickler

You will surely <u>not fail</u> to be at the Huron Con. July 8th— We must save the E.S.A. from the charges that are hurled at us—that we are <u>coquetting</u> with the Independent Party—² <u>I</u> know you are <u>not</u> doing so—and you know it is the last thing that I would countenance

But the Con. is called—& will be held—and you & I & Mr Pickler must save it & ourselves to the <u>true</u> position—so that we can go before the Repub. Con. at Mitchell & ask a plank—& get it—too— I could Guilotine the whole lot of the <u>Alliance schemers</u> to draw them off from being a balance of power to help us to win Woman Suffrage— But they've done it—& now we must not allow ourselves to <u>even seem</u> to be playing into their hands—

I wish I could go to you— What a muddle they are in—& <u>it</u> all through the <u>rule or ruin</u> policy!! but may it be held at bay—

Do you—too—be at the Ex. Com. meeting—at the Kent Hotel—Huron—on Wednesday evening—July 2^d—& Thursday A.M. July 3^d—which Mr Ramsey now promises to call—to appoint a <u>new</u> Secretary—a campaign Committee &c—&c— You & I & all of us must save the friends in the state from presenting a divided front— When I at last consented to the calling of the Con. at <u>Huron</u> the 8th was after Mr

Ramsey had telegraphed me at Canton—that the Ex. Com. <u>had called</u>— I <u>opposed</u> calling one then in so close conjunction with the Independents—for <u>fear</u> of being accused of just what they are—affiliation with that bolting faction—but I do not feel it best <u>now</u> to make a protest— only <u>you</u> & Mrs Johnson—Mrs DeVoe—& all of us—<u>Mr</u> <u>Pickler</u>—too— must see that our <u>cause</u> is not swamped!! Lovingly yours

↝ *Susan B. Anthony*

↝ ALS, Major John A. Pickler Family Papers, 1865-1976, SdHi.

1. Dated with reference to the executive committee meeting on July 2. Other references place the letter after June 10.

2. Pressure to reorganize the campaign and elect new officers of the equal suffrage association grew during June, leading to a call for a mass convention in Huron at the time of the Independent party's nominating convention in early July. The organizers and activists from across the state who issued the call agreed "that the campaign can be more successfully prosecuted by more united and determined action." Officers of the equal suffrage association reluctantly and belatedly signed on. When Republicans, frightened by the advent of the Independent party, read the call as an indication that suffragists had lined up in support of that party, timing of the mass meeting became at least as contentious as the plan to replace the officers. Editors attacked. The mass meeting was intended "evidently to bolster up the independents," the *Aberdeen Daily News* announced on June 24. It was an "insane scheme," the editor went on, one that "will alienate hundreds of republican voters." SBA, in pressing the Picklers to attend the meeting, encouraged a Republican presence. Evidence about her own earlier views of the call is contradictory, though local historians repeatedly assert that it was her doing: Prohibitionist Helen Gougar, who thought the convention necessary to improve the leadership, was sure that SBA agreed; Republican Sarah Richards, treasurer of the suffrage association, who thought the convention ill-timed, was equally sure that SBA opposed it. The selection of new officers on July 8 increased Republican numbers in the leadership and addressed one element of more united action by placing SBA on the executive committee. (Call for mass suffrage convention, *Woman's Tribune*, 5 July 1890; S. A. Richards to Alice Pickler, 23 June 1890, and Helen Gougar to Alice Pickler, Major John A. Pickler Family Papers, 1865-1976, SdHi; Helen Gougar to Editor, *Union Signal*, 19 June and 24 July 1890; Irene G. Adams to Editor, *Aberdeen Daily News*, 12 July 1890; Wardall, "Woman Suffrage in South Dakota," p. 5, *Film*, 28:871ff; Ross-Nazzal, "Emma Smith DeVoe and the South Dakota Suffrage Campaigns," 248-49; Cecelia M. Wittmayer, "The 1889-1890 Woman Suffrage Campaign: A Need to Organize," *South Dakota History* 11 [Summer 1981]: 213-14, 219-20.)

109 ECS TO SBA

Basingstoke Hants [*England*] August 7th [*1890*]

Dear Susan,

Do you remember the name of the man who gave the oration the 4th of July at Salt Lake City?[1] Do you remember how many people the big Tabernacle holds, if you do send these facts <u>to Mrs Colby</u>. I have just sent my letter to The Tribune on Salt Lake City our visit there in 71. I find no record of that anywhere   We had lost The Revolution so I am again thrown back on my true inwardness.[2] I made two stars at the point where these facts might come in as notes at the bottom. If I only had you at my right hand I could make my Rems far better, as I am now at the stage where we have no record whatever & I am entirely afloat on dates & names.

I see you are having a disagreeable time in Dakotah with Gougher & Bones.[3] <u>Matilda</u> sends me the papers.[4] She wants to keep me posted as to what your enemies say of your short comings, as if anything new could be said of either of us, between Harry & Bones we shall be kept humble. It is strange they have not the philosophy to see, that in impeaching the honor of their coadjutors, they hinder the cause they would promote. But what we have endured half a century cannot crush us now. If all the papers in the two Dakota's, should herald the news that you had been arrested & imprisoned for theft & slander, it would not make the slightest impression on me   I should not believe one word of it   Maggie is pursuing her studies at Chatauqua.[5] Theodore is rusticating for a month down in the South of France. Hattie & I have been speaking quite frequently in London   You see Lydia Becker is dead.[6] She was evidently the power here that held the forces together. Since she let go the helm the suffrage movement has been hopelessly demoralized the younger generation are all jealous of each other just as ours would be, if you should retire. Now all the dissatisfaction rests on you & me, if we were [*in margins of first page*] decapitated, it would rest by turn on all of them. adieu

E. C. S.

[*in margins of first and second pages*] Where is Mary. Hattie & I often laugh over that evening in Dan's room when we tried to get her off to bed before we uncorked the champagne⁷   When you write them give our kind regards

~ ALS, Clara B. Colby Papers, Archives Division, WHi.

   1. For "Reminiscences: A Week in Salt Lake City," *Film*, 28:580-88, ECS sought details about the visit she made with SBA en route to California in 1871.
   2. The last issue of the *Revolution* edited by ECS was dated 28 May 1870.
   3. During June 1890, Helen Gougar gave twenty lectures in seventeen counties in South Dakota and promised to raise one thousand dollars for the equal suffrage association thereafter. The much smaller sum that she raised was controlled, after the change in state leadership, by the state temperance union. During her month in the state, Gougar complained privately about Moses Barker's poor management of the speakers' schedules and SBA's ineffectiveness, and in the *Union Signal*, she condemned SBA's insistence on independence from the prohibitionists and reprised her attack on the National-American's decision to control the funds it raised (though she described it as a personal decision by SBA). SBA "is badly out of touch with these home workers," she wrote, referring to Helen Barker's temperance workers, "and being strange to the people she can not get her speakers before sufficient audiences, and much desultory work is the result. . . . The committee refuse to make her appointments, and she is a free lance, doing what she can." Gougar rescinded her criticism late in June and praised SBA's "wisdom." (Wardall, "Woman Suffrage in South Dakota," p. 8, *Film*, 28:871ff; Helen M. Gougar to Alice A. Pickler, 23 June 1890, Major John A. Pickler Family Papers, 1865-1976, SdHi; *Union Signal*, 19 June, 24 July 1890; Jennings, "Lake County Woman Suffrage Campaign," 401-2.)
   Marietta M. Wilkins Bones (1842-1901) of Webster was a disaffected South Dakota suffragist who haunted the amendment campaign with a stream of invective against SBA and contributed little else. Bones had been prominent in the territorial Woman's Christian Temperance Union and was named the National association's vice president for the territory in September 1882. Working with Matilda Gage in 1883, she appealed for woman suffrage to the constitutional convention and wrote up the experience for the *History of Woman Suffrage*. Late in 1889, however, she turned against both national organizations. At the temperance union's annual meeting, she walked out with other Republican women protesting Frances Willard's alliance with the Prohibition party and joined J. Ellen Foster in founding the Non-Partisan Woman's Christian Temperance Union. Back home in Webster, her local union turned her out. At about the same time, Gage recruited her as an ally against uniting the suffrage associations, and Bones left the National to join Gage in the Woman's National Liberal Union. She turned against SBA rather quickly: in

late November 1889, they spoke together to the Farmers' Alliance, and Bones praised SBA's speech; in February 1890, she was slandering SBA as a thief who stole forty thousand dollars. The press relished and nurtured the fight as one more way to mock the cause. In 1895, Bones announced that she opposed woman suffrage after all. She died in Washington, D.C. (*American Women*; *History*, 3:662-69; Kingsbury, *History of Dakota Territory*, 3:766-68, 770; Melanie Susan Gustafson, *Women and the Republican Party, 1854-1924* [Urbana, Ill., 2001], 66-71; Nancy Tystad Koupal, "The Wonderful Wizard of the West: L. Frank Baum in South Dakota, 1888-91," *Great Plains Quarterly* 9 [Fall 1989]: 210; *Aberdeen Daily News*, 20 November, 1 December 1889, 26 February, 3 May 1890; M. J. Gage to Harriet H. Robinson and Harriette R. Shattuck, 19 January 1890, Robinson-Shattuck Papers, MCR-S; *Chicago Daily Tribune*, 20 February 1890; *Washington Post*, 21, 22 February 1890, 12 July 1901; M. J. Gage to Thomas Clarkson Gage, 22 February 1890, Gage Collection, MCR-S.)

4. Matilda Gage probably sent the clippings from her home in Fayetteville, New York. Her recent arrival in South Dakota was noted in the *Aberdeen Daily News*, 18 October 1890.

5. Margaret Stanton's husband, Frank Lawrence, died from Bright's disease on 16 April 1890. When his health had deteriorated in the winter of 1890, he returned to California for treatment, and Margaret brought his body back to Council Bluffs for the funeral. She stayed with her in-laws for several months while she settled the estate. The Chautauqua Institution in Western New York, begun as a Protestant camp meeting and a place to train Sunday school teachers, obtained a university charter in 1883 and opened an extension school, modeled on the university extension movement in England, in the summer of 1889. (Council Bluffs *Daily Nonpareil*, 19, 25 April 1890, with assistance of Pottawattamie County Genealogical Society; William F. Channing to ECS, 7 May 1890, and ECS to Clara B. Colby, 16 June 1890, *Film*, 28:357-61, 422-29; Joseph E. Gould, *The Chautauqua Movement: An Episode in the Continuing American Revolution* [Albany, N.Y., 1961], 35-37; Theodore Morrison, *Chautauqua: A Center for Education, Religion, and the Arts in America* [Chicago, 1974], 49-50.)

6. Lydia Ernestine Becker (1827-1890), a hard-working founder of Britain's suffrage movement, former correspondent of the *Revolution*, and editor of the *Women's Suffrage Journal* since 1870, died on July 18. In recent years, ECS rarely spoke so well of Becker because they differed on the question of suffrage for married women, with Becker willing to compromise the cause of married women to gain parliamentary support for widows' and spinsters' suffrage. (*DNB*; Blackburn, *Women's Suffrage in the British Isles*, passim; Holton, *Suffrage Days*, 39-41. See also *Papers* 2-4.)

7. This is apparently a reference to an incident during SBA's birthday celebration.

110 ~ ECS TO CLARA BEWICK COLBY

[*Basingstoke, England, 15 August 1890*]

I find that the present Tribune just received has chapter XXX, so you will have to change the three I have sent to 31, 32, 33.[1] Have you received <u>four</u> packages from me, one speech & three Rems? Now you must stop scolding seeing that I am faithfully at work once more. I am awfully sick of these Rems. do you insist on my giving an account of myself for the twenty remaining years & running on until next April? Or do you say: hold enough. There is so much in the living present to write about. With what I have written in the Tribune thus far what is to be found in the history Ballot Box & Citizen,[2] I think my descendants can write me up fuller than the public will ever care to read. I am glad to [*sideways in margins*] see you are in Dakota but they are too poor to give you many subscribers[3]

~ AN on postal card, Clara B. Colby Papers, Archives Division, WHi. Postmarked at Basingstoke; addressed Beatrice, Nebraska.

1. The untitled chapter thirty, about lecturing in the Midwest, was published in *Woman's Tribune*, 2 August 1890, *Film*, 28:489–92. ECS had sent misnumbered chapters entitled "A Week in Salt Lake City," "California," and "California's Wonders"; Colby published them with the corrections in *Woman's Tribune*, 13, 27 September, 11 October 1890, *Film*, 28:580–88, 610–18, 646–59. Though ECS mentions a speech she sent to Colby, none appeared this fall in the *Tribune*.

2. These were two papers for which ECS served as a contributing editor, the *Ballot Box*, edited by Sarah Williams in Toledo, Ohio, from 1876 to 1878, and its successor, the *National Citizen and Ballot Box*, edited by Matilda Gage in Syracuse, New York, from 1878 to 1881.

3. Clara Colby delivered eighteen lectures in "the Black Hills Counties" in the western part of the state. (Wardall, "Woman Suffrage in South Dakota," p. 9, *Film*, 28:871ff.)

111 ~ ARTICLE BY ECS

[September 1890]

WYOMING ADMITTED AS A STATE INTO THE UNION.

A great event in the history of the race has just occurred in the United States, in the complete enfranchisement of women in a vast area covering 97,575 square miles. The admission of the Territory of Wyoming into the Union with an article in her Constitution securing to all the women within her borders full political rights, marks on the horologe of time a new epoch in which we are to witness the perfect equality of the sexes in government.[1]

After prolonged debate, the Bill passed the House of Representatives, March 26; and after months of painful suspense on the part of friends of the measure, it passed the Senate June 27, 1890, by a strict party vote, 29 Republicans to 19 Democrats.[2] The President was requested not to sign the Bill until the 4th of July, the natal day of the Republic, when the Colonies declared their independence and threw off the British yoke. It is peculiarly appropriate that the same day should be celebrated for woman's independence in the greater Republic; her complete enfranchisement from masculine domination in government. Having admitted the principle of the equal status of women in one State, it must sooner or later be conceded in all. By the passage of this Bill the women of Wyoming may now fill any United States office. They may be Congressmen, Senators, or even President of the United States. The magnitude and far reaching consequences of this step in legislation in a country of nearly 70,000,000 of people, cannot be overestimated.

The most encouraging feature of the admission of Wyoming into the Union, is that as a Territory she had already tried the experiment of Woman Suffrage for nearly twenty years, and so thoroughly satisfied were her people with the results, that only one adverse vote was cast in their constitutional convention.

Mr. Carey,[3] representative from Wyoming, in summing up his speech before Congress, said:

"Mr. Speaker,[4] after twenty years' experience with woman suffrage the people of that territory have deliberately formed a Constitution to be the supreme organic law of the new State, and have placed in Constitution a solemn inhibition of the denial or abridgment of that right on account of sex.

"The Territorial Legislature has asked by resolution for the admission of their State under the Constitution. The political organisations of the State, without regard to party, make the same prayer. No protest against it has been heard, no remonstrance, no petition against it has been presented to your committee nor to this body.

"No one dares to claim that it has not been beneficial to Wyoming and to her people. I quote the following words from a distinguished citizen of the territory:—'It has been stated that the best women do not avail themselves of the privilege of the elective franchise. This statement is maliciously false. The women of Wyoming vote with as much universality as men, and no State or Territory can boast of nobler and purer women. The foolish claim has also been made that the influence of the ballot upon women is bad. This is not true. It is impossible that a woman's character can be contaminated in associating with men for a few moments in going to the polls any more than it would be in going to the church or to places of amusement. On the other hand, women are benefited and improved by the ballot. Most women in Wyoming accumulate more or less property, and under our laws manage their property, though married, as if single. The management of business necessarily gives them new ideas, and brings a knowledge of affairs that none of us get but by experience. This makes them more intelligent, gives them enlarged ideas of life and its duties, instils higher aims and makes them better wives and mothers. The fact is, Wyoming has the noblest and best women in the world, because they have more privileges and know better how to use them.'"

There have been several attempts made to deprive women of their political rights during this long period, but overwhelming majorities in its favour have made all such attempts futile. Hence we may rest assured that there will be no retrogressive steps in that rich young State, where so many noble women have proved their capacity in political affairs. They have discharged their duties as jurors with marvellous wisdom and discretion.

The problem of Woman Suffrage is solved in Wyoming, and firmly established there beyond a peradventure. Scientists may now prate about the size of women's heads and the lack of grey matter in their brains; philosophers may tell us that the masculine element always has and always will dominate the universe; theologians, fresh from communion with their Creator, may prescribe woman's sphere according to "the Bible and the designs of Providence," and physicians may enlarge on the disabilities of the sex; but, in spite of all this, women are now full-fledged citizens in the United States, with their feet firmly planted on a territory, comprising a larger area than all Great Britain; a well-secured and certain inheritance to our daughters to the third and fourth generation.

It is over twenty years since Wyoming as a territory passed a Bill through her Legislature extending the right of suffrage to women. It was said at the time that the members, the majority being Democrats, did it partly as a joke, and partly to advertise the territory, hoping thereby to induce a large immigration of women; but whatever their object the Bill readily passed as the Republicans voted for it, and the Republican Governor signed the Bill.[5] The women being in favour of law and order, the large majority voted the Republican ticket, and thus changed at once the political power of the Territory, leaving the Democrats in the minority. They made several attempts afterwards to disfranchise the women but to no purpose. The best men in the Territory at once recognised the civilising power of women at the polls, in the courts, and in general society, and for all these years have remained steadfast to the principle.

Within the last year several Territories have become States, and all alike advised Wyoming not to put woman suffrage in her new Constitution, as it would prove a stumbling-block to her admission into the Union.[6] But her wisest politicians gave no heed to such advice; they said, we will take the noble women who have endured with us the hardships of pioneer life, into the Union, or we will remain with them in a Territory, until there are enough real men in Congress to admit us together. Fortunately there was a sufficient number there already to pass the Bill, after much opposition and prolonged debates, in which the old arguments that have been answered a hundred times, were made to do duty once more. Our chief opponents in Congress are Southern Democrats; their anxiety seemed to be, that if suffrage were extended to women, they would see in the near future, black women in the House or Senate, or even in the Presidential chair.[7] The frivolous objections made on both sides the great waters, in England and America alike, are unworthy of those who claim to be endowed with reason, men who have had the advantage of college drill in logic, mathematics, history, philosophy and science. But it is fair to suppose that they present the best arguments they can find, hence we must attribute their failure not to any lack of native strength, but to the paucity of the material at hand, on that side of the question.

I visited the Territory in 1870,[8] and saw the women who had voted, filled the offices of Justice of the Peace and Jurors, talked with them at the fireside, watched them in their domestic avocations, ate bread made by the same hands that had cast a ballot on election day, and found "marriage was not annulled, cradles abolished, nor stockings mended by the State." I was struck with the earnestness and the intelligence of the women, talking more about laws and constitutions, principles of government, and practical politics, than fashions, personalities, or their neighbour's private affairs. I was told that the women had discharged their duties with marvellous wisdom and discretion. Esther Morris presided for two years as Justice of the Peace, maintaining the most orderly court in the Territory, and not one of her decisions was ever reversed. The women were much amused with the financial view of the arduous jury duties of which they had heard so much. They said "we never earned three dollars a day more easily, sitting in comfortable chairs listening to arguments." The judge told me of a murder case that had just been tried, in which he was very curious as well as anxious to see whether they would render the verdict based on the evidence in the case, or be guided by their feelings. They felt the responsibility in deciding on the life of a human being, and passed the night in talking over the evidence with seriousness and care, and rendered their verdict "guilty." He said the change in the appearance of the Court-room, and the habits of the people were remarkable. As soon as the women appeared, everything was clean and in order, men came better dressed and smoking was abolished. In former times said the Judge, "the room was often so thick with smoke that I could hardly see how to give a decision." Before women went to the polls disorder and rowdyism prevailed, fisticuff fights were usual, and even the use of firearms was frequent, fraud and violence marked all the elections. And yet the first time the carriages rolled up loaded with women to vote, that rough pioneer crowd fell back in line, and with hats in hand, stood in perfect silence while the women performed as citizens. Woman's influence was at once felt in the choice of candidates, for it was known they would invariably oppose men of immoral character and bad habits.

At the last census Wyoming was returned as having a smaller percentage of illiteracy than any State or Territory in the Union.[9] Although her educational and charitable institutions are numerous and well sustained, yet she has no public debt. At all times women have manifested great public spirit and a conscientious interest in every department of government, especially in that of education. Wyoming is by no means an insignificant portion of the earth's surface, but one of the largest, and when its resources are developed, it will be one of the richest States in the Union. On July 25, 1868, Wyoming made its first appearance on the map of the American continent. By an Act of Congress it was cut out of the enormous Territory of Dakota; but it was many years before European maps ceased to name both Dakota and Wyoming "the great American desert." That vast territory is now populated and comprises three States admitted into the Union within the last year. The resources of Wyoming are varied and boundless. It is rich in agricultural productions, is well watered, as three of the largest rivers in North America have their sources there, and four others cross her boundaries on every side. It has from eight to ten millions of acres of spruce and pine forests, which with the melting snows on the mountains keep the atmosphere humid, and the smaller streams full most of the year. The oil and mineral resources are said to be boundless. Such are the natural advantages of the great State where woman has made a successful experiment of self-government, manifesting the necessary self-control and public spirit for a good citizen, and an officer of the State, and proving her capacity to the satisfaction of her co-adjutors, to fill any sphere where duty calls her. The history of Wyoming should close the debate on this question, as we now have abundant facts to contradict all the absurd suppositions and harrowing prophecies of the opposition.

The progress of the debate in Congress was watched with intense interest throughout the country; the galleries in the Capitol were crowded with ladies day after day. The passage of the Bill was hailed with the wildest enthusiasm, especially in Wyoming, and celebrated in all her chief cities with music and processions, flags and banners, with bonfires, guns, and cannon firing salutes throughout the day and far into the night. Preparations are being made for a greater celebration when her delegates return from Washington. Among other things, a company of thirty-one young girls of Cheyenne have been enrolled as the Wyoming State Guards, and have been uniformed and drilled to take part in the Statehood celebration.[10]

This is the first genuine Republic the world has ever seen; a government of the people, by the people, for the people. In Wyoming it can now be truly said, under our flag there is no caste nor class, no bond nor free, no male nor female, no Jew nor Gentile,[11] but all are one, by the provisions of our State Constitution. In one of his speeches, given at Harvard College, the late Wendell Phillips, one of our great prophets and reformers, said: "The first glimpse we get of Saxon blood in history is that line of Tacticus, in his 'Germany,' which reads, 'in all grave matters we consult our women.' Years hence, when robust Saxon sense has flung away Jewish superstition and Eastern prejudice, and put under its foot fastidious scholarship and squeamish fashion, some second Tacticus from the valley of the Mississippi will answer to him of the Seven Hills, 'In all grave questions we consult our women.'"[12] This prophecy, made only nine years ago, is already fulfilled. The statesmen of Wyoming have indeed echoed back to him of the Seven Hills, not only that "in all grave questions we consult our women," but that once more women enjoy the right of self-government, that the matriarchate, or mother-age, has come again. As England and America have thus far kept pace, step by step, on the question of women's emancipation, I venture to prophesy that the sunlight now shining on the wild mountain-tops of Wyoming will soon gild the venerable dome of St. Paul.[13]

~ *Elizabeth Cady Stanton.*

~ *Westminster Review* 134 (September 1890): 280-84.

1. ECS wrote about the admission of Wyoming on many occasions in 1890, each time with slight variations. See *Film*, 28:302, 354, 382, 457-60, 466, 867-70. The last of these, *Wyoming. The First Free State for Woman. July 4, 1890*, may be the text printed in Mitchell, South Dakota, at the request of SBA. (SBA diary, 23 June 1890, *Film*, 27:679ff.)

2. The House voted on March 27, not 26. After the Senate's vote on June 27, the bill returned to the House for approval on July 8 and was signed by the president on July 10.

3. Joseph Maull Carey (1845–1924) served as Wyoming's territorial delegate to Congress from 1885 to 1890, when he was elected to the Senate for one term in 1890. Although he spoke at length during debate on the admission of Wyoming, ECS misidentifies this quotation. The three paragraphs appear in the speech of Henry L. Morey, congressman from Ohio. (*BDAC*; *Congressional Record*, 51st Cong., 1st sess., 26 March 1890, p. 2693.)

4. That is, Thomas B. Reed.

5. On the bill's passage, see T. A. Larson, "Woman Suffrage in Wyoming," *Pacific Northwest Quarterly* 56 (April 1965): 57–66. John Allen Campbell (1835–1880) was appointed first governor of Wyoming Territory by President Ulysses Grant in April 1869. (*BDTerrGov*.)

6. In February 1889, Congress approved statehood for North and South Dakota, Montana, and Washington.

7. Concern about Wyoming's women overtaking the seats of power in Washington was a recurrent theme in the speeches of opponents to statehood. In one example, William Oates of Alabama and William Breckinridge of Kentucky debated whether Congress could refuse a seat to a woman elected from Wyoming. Joseph Washington of Tennessee opined: "it is not impossible or improbable that in the future some woman will sit in the chair now occupied by the Delegate; she will come with frills and flounces, with bonnet and bustle. (Laughter.) And when she arises and addresses the Chair, how will the Speaker recognize her? Sir, will it be the gentleman from Wyoming or the lady from Wyoming? (Renewed laughter.)" (*Congressional Record*, 51st Cong., 1st sess., 26 March 1890, pp. 2685, 2690.)

8. ECS went to Wyoming in 1871.

9. Details about Wyoming's resources, institutions, and future prospects were at hand in the report of the House Committee on the Territories and Joseph Carey's speech to the House. See House, Committee on the Territories, *Admission of Wyoming into the Union, Report*, 15 February 1890, 51st Cong., 1st sess., H. Rept. 39, Pt. 1, Serial 2807; and *Congressional Record*, 51st Cong., 1st sess., 26 March 1890, pp. 2672–83.

10. At the official celebration in Cheyenne on 23 July 1890, Therese A. Jenkins made the opening address; Esther Morris then presented the governor with a flag, a gift from the state's women; another local woman read her poem called "The True Republic"; and finally Amelia Post came forward to accept a copy of the state constitution, presented by the president of the constitutional convention. (I. S. Bartlett, ed., *History of Wyoming* [Chicago, 1918], 1:192–96.)

11. Gal. 3:28.

12. Wendell Phillips, *The Scholar in a Republic: Address at the Centennial Anniversary of the Phi Beta Kappa of Harvard College, June 30, 1881*. The

quotation from Phillips is apparently a loose translation of the Roman historian Cornelius Tacitus (c. 56–c. 120), *De origine et situ Germanorum*, chap. 8, sec. 2: "inesse quin etiam sanctum aliquid et providum putant, nec aut consilia earum aspernantur aut responsa neglegunt."

13. St. Paul's Cathedral in London.

112 ❧ SBA TO HARRIET TAYLOR UPTON

Huron, South Dakota, Sept. 1, 1890

Dear Mrs Upton

Yesterday & to day <u>are</u> <u>furiously</u> <u>hot</u> again— I did hope old sol's fury had spent itself— Your letters here—on my return from the Mitchell Con—where we had a splendid audiences of our own for the two days[1]—and splendid hearings before the Repub. Con—at the first— Rev O. Brown Rev. Anna Shaw, S. B. A.—Mrs Pickler & Mrs DeVoe spoke—at the second   only <u>our</u> Anna was <u>called</u> <u>out</u>—in a <u>lull</u> of the Con—and fully a thousand men jammed the hall—the vote of the delegates wa <u>543</u>[2]—which did <u>not</u> include the <u>four</u> <u>Yankton</u> <u>Reservation</u> <u>Indians</u>—who were by special resolution admitted—<u>invited</u> to seats in the Con. <u>without</u> <u>votes</u>!!!! <u>Good</u> <u>Heavens</u>— The Indian Bucks ahead of Civilized Women!! Then we had a splendid hearing before the Platform Committee—<u>but</u> <u>alas</u> we <u>got</u> <u>no</u> <u>mention</u> in their report—and none in the Con—save the courtesy of "<u>gabbling</u>"!!![3]

The Farmers Alliance men who hauled themselves off from the Repub. Party—<u>were</u> the <u>heavy</u> <u>weight</u> <u>in</u> the woman suffrage scale of the Repub. party—and by just so much was the party weakened on our side—& by so much strengthened on the enemy's side— So our <u>W.S.</u> <u>Amendment</u> is now left—just as it was left in the seven states that have voted on it before—without the <u>weight</u> of a good plank from in any party's platform—[4] The Independents have the advantage of having passed a resolution—in its favor— We are awfully cut down—but still bound to trudge on alone—and make the vote as large as possible—

Right about referring people to Mrs Colby for Judiciary & also for Senate Reports—[5] Lovingly but Hastily

❧ *Susan B. Anthony*

↢ ALS, on South Dakota Equal Suffrage Association letterhead, SBA Papers, NRU.

1. The rally on August 25 and 26 preceding the Republican convention was an enormous success, with large audiences that included many Republican delegates who heard speeches by Laura Johns, Henry Blackwell, Anna Shaw, Carrie Catt, Matilda Hindman, and SBA. Reports on state organizing by Alice Pickler, Philena Johnson, Emma DeVoe, and Elizabeth Wardall preceded discussion of a plan of work for the last two months of the campaign. (*Film*, 28:529-34.)

2. Henry Blackwell described the events to Lucy Stone. "We have made the best fight we could before the Platform Committee and have failed. The platform will contain *nothing* on Equal Suffrage. . . . But the ladies have been twice heard and Annie Shaw has covered herself with glory. She addressed the convention by invitation during a wait in the proceedings last evening & brought down the house in an admirable twenty minutes speech. If a vote of the Convention could have been had then & there, Miss Shaw could have carried almost everything. But the manipulation of the managers has been too shrewd to be overcome. There is a bitter & determined opposition to WS. by the worst element of the party & the representatives of the foreign voters. . . . The settled sentiment of the Convention (even of a majority of the Suffragists in it) is against naming it in the platform." He also noted that Boston's antisuffragists flooded the Republican convention with their remonstrance. (H. B. Blackwell to L. Stone, 27 August 1890, in Wheeler, *Loving Warriors*, 335-36.)

3. Three Yankton Sioux men were given seats but not votes at the Republican convention. At reservations east of the Missouri River, allotments of land were being made to tribal members in accordance with the Dawes Act of 1887; the Indians at Sisseton faced a deadline of 1892 and at Yankton a deadline of 1895, when land not granted to Indians would be open to white settlers. With an allotment came citizenship, and at this moment, the state constitution neither barred nor guaranteed voting rights to Indians no longer in tribal relations. The question would appear on the November ballot. The welcome extended to the Indians at the Republican convention became a staple of suffragists' storytelling, particularly in the speeches of Carrie Catt and Anna Shaw. The men grew dirtier and more numerous as the years passed, while indignation went beyond the details of their treatment by Republicans to emphasize their evident racial inferiority. (Schell, *History of South Dakota*, 333-34; Kingsbury, *History of Dakota Territory*, 3:658. See also Anna Shaw in *Anthony*, 2:687-88, and Carrie Catt in *Film*, 30:532-33.)

4. Kansas (1867), Michigan (1874), Colorado (1877), Nebraska (1882), Oregon (1884), Rhode Island (1887), and Washington Territory (1889).

5. Henry Blair's Senate report favoring passage of an amendment for woman suffrage was issued on 12 August 1890. Senate, Committee on Woman Suffrage, *Report*, 51st Cong., 1st sess., S. Rept. 1576, Serial 2711.

113 ➣ SBA TO OLYMPIA BROWN

Huron, South Dakota,[1] Sept. 3, 1890.

Dear Olympia

Not a lisp from you yet—[2] I feel really troubled lest you are not finding things in good shape—but the State Fair dates will soon come— then I shall see you at Aberdeen—and I do hope we can get settled somewhere near each other there—so I can see & know of you more— all was scurry, hurry at Mitchell—[3]

I have heard that a Post Card had come from you asking ↑that↓ letters be promply forwarded to you—which I trust Mr Bailey[4] attends to every day— The office now has daily—Mr Bailey, Mrs Johnson— Mrs Wardall & her lovely daughter Anna[5]—beside two or three women to put up packages each afternoon— It is a "<u>big job</u>" for them to keep eight speakers going—& supplied with literature— Dont fail to ask for packages of papers & tracts— Mrs Colby will undoubtedly send a roll of Tribunes to each speaker at each place—& perchance Alice Blackwell will send her Woman's Colum—too—so look out for mail at each place[6]

Mr Blackwell writes back that each & all of us female missionaries must be very careful to speak of the foreigners only in the most respectful manner— It took him an hour to re-convert a <u>Norwegian</u> who had been <u>repelled</u> from voting by one of our women at Highmore having "<u>abused</u>" the foreigners—the man said—but he got him back into the fold again—[7]

It is the most difficult sort of a campaign— The strongest argument to win the Prohibition men to vote for W.S.—is the very strongest one to drive from us the high license men— So the strongest testimony showing how ↑all↓ women's voting will lessen the ratio of the foreign vote & of the Catholic vote—is just the worst thing—in fact wholly estops all hope of winning the foreign born mens vote—& the Catholic vote— We are between two <u>distracting</u> dilemma's at every step—so I try to keep my talk on general principles—the bettering of women's chances for work & wages tyrany of taxation &c &c— But it is hardy possible to say anything—that will not hurt somebody—so each of us must be governed by our own true inwardness—as to what—& how to present our claims—[8]

I hope your head & bronchials & every bit of your body is ↑are↓ all well & strong & that you are having good audiences & making better speeches more to your own satisfaction than ever before— Come what may my dear—I shall always believe in Olympia Brown—and I trust come what may she will always believe in her Sincere friend

~ Susan B. Anthony

~ ALS, on South Dakota Equal Suffrage Association letterhead, Olympia Brown Papers, MCR-S.

1. According to her diary, SBA arrived in Huron by August 30 and stayed until September 9. (*Film,* 27:679ff.)

2. Olympia Brown reached South Dakota on 23 August 1890, in time to preach in two churches in Mitchell on the day Republican delegates arrived in town. Thereafter, she delivered fifty lectures in nineteen counties for the campaign, traveling some of the time with SBA. Brown wrote to SBA on this same day to report on her misadventures. (SBA to O. Brown, 2 August 1890, SBA diary, 23 August, 19-24 September 1890, *Film,* 27:679ff, 28:480-88; O. Brown to SBA, 3 September 1890, Major John A. Pickler Family Papers, 1865-1976, SdHi, not in *Film*; Wardall, "Woman Suffrage in South Dakota," p. 8, *Film,* 28:871ff.)

3. Aberdeen was the site of the South Dakota State Fair, whose managers allowed Emma DeVoe to organize a Woman's Day on September 17. Most of the chief speakers in the campaign were in attendance and borne in carriages in a parade of women that ended at a stage where they spoke about woman suffrage. (*Film,* 28:589-90.)

4. Will F. Bailey took the place of Moses Barker as the equal suffrage association's secretary in July. Helen Gougar, for one, had earlier recommended him for the thankless position. His performance as secretary earned nearly as much criticism as Barker's, without the added complaints about a high salary. Schedules and mail went awry. Directives late in the campaign that he also prepare financial reports suggest his duties were broad. Bailey was a young man, whose mother, Catharine, collaborated with Alice Pickler in organizing campaign events in Faulkton. He acquired a homestead in Faulk County at the end of 1890, and he may have moved to Meade County in the twentieth century. (H. Gougar to Alice Pickler, 23 June 1890, Major John A. Pickler Family Papers, 1865-1976, SdHi; SBA diary, 22 August, 4 October 1890, *Film,* 27:679ff; Ross-Nazzal, "Emma Smith DeVoe and the South Dakota Suffrage Campaigns," 252-53; U.S. Bureau of Land Management Records, on-line.)

5. Elizabeth A. Murray Wardall (1848-1917) was active in the Farmers' Alliance with her husband, Alonzo Wardall. Her column in the Alliance's

paper, the *Dakota Ruralist*, served as the principal outlet for news and schedules of the amendment campaign, and at the time of reorganization, she was elected to the suffrage association's executive committee. Only an occasional lecturer in 1890, she developed platform skills that later served the People's party. The Wardalls met in college in Iowa, married in 1868, moved to Dakota Territory in 1879 with four children, and left for Kansas in 1893. SBA would encounter them again at Populists' conventions in Omaha in 1892 and Topeka in 1894. After a decade or more in Kansas, the Wardalls settled in Washington State. There, Anna Wardall (c. 1869–?), the eldest child and married by then to William H. Scott, again worked alongside her mother (and Emma DeVoe) in the suffrage cause. Elizabeth Wardall became a Theosophist during her years in Kansas, and two of her sons held positions in the American Theosophical Society. (Federal census, Grant County, Dakota Terr., 1880, Kansas City, Mo., 1900, and Seattle, Wash., 1910; Guide, Alonzo and Elizabeth Wardall Collection, WaU; W. Scott Morgan, *History of the Wheel and Alliance and the Impending Revolution* [1891; reprint, New York, 1968], 301–2; Washington Equal Suffrage Association, *Washington Women's Cook Book* [Seattle, Wash., 1909]; obituary, *Messenger* 4 [9 February 1917]: 277, with thanks to Naomi Blumensaadt, Campbell Theosophical Library, Sydney, Australia.)

6. Beginning in 1888, Alice Blackwell published the *Woman's Column* weekly as a supplement to the *Woman's Journal* with the intention of providing copy about suffrage to the editors of local newspapers.

7. Henry Blackwell spent six weeks in South Dakota, visiting twenty counties and delivering thirty-five lectures. He arrived in time for private meetings with Republican leaders before the party convention. "I am trying to get a moderate plank *patting the women on the back*," he reported to his wife from Sioux Falls, "& paving the way for Republican help in the future when the exigency is less alarming than now." Lucy Stone received a letter on the theme of his (now missing) letter to SBA: "Miss Anthony is doing her very best. But our woman workers all make the mistake of seeming to censure men and of using sarcasm instead of a little harmless, good-natured taffy. Especially they speak sharply of *foreigners* & every time they do, the opponents use the fact to solidify the foreign voters. If only our women would not follow Mrs Stanton's foolish counsel & would use *womanly conciliation* we should be much more successful." Blackwell was himself circulating his pamphlet *The Elective Franchise* about woman suffrage as a counterweight to the immigrant vote. (H. B. Blackwell to L. Stone, 18, 23, 24 August, 2 September 1890, in Wheeler, *Loving Warriors*, 332–34, 338; Wardall, "Woman Suffrage in South Dakota," p. 8.)

8. Olympia Brown reached a similar conclusion about the constraints on each speaker. Writing to SBA on this same day, she repeated the refrain, "I spoke as well as I could avoiding of course politics religion indians foreigners negroes paupers tramps, prohibition temperance social evil &c &c &c &c." (O. Brown to SBA, 3 September 1890.)

114   SBA to Harriet Taylor Upton

Huron, South Dakota, Sept. 5 1890

Dear Harriet

Yours of Sept. 1st is just here this A.M—and my letter to Senator Palmer is already written—and in it I said ↑all↓ you suggested and more—[1] I said that ↑our movement for↓ woman's right to equality of rights & chances in the world—deserved & ↑ought to have↓ a corner & a recognition in the Worlds Fair—and I trusted he'd see to it that our great movement was respectfully treated & well represented there—&c &c—

It is too bad you didn't start earlier for the place on Ohio's part of the Board—but something will surely come to you & to our good cause—[2] I sent you Mrs Elwell's[3] last—and I ought to have sent you Mr Peter's[4] letter—it said if ↑for↓ no other reason—than the Ohio Presidents lack of purpose & interest to raise the requisite $400—women didn't deserve to vote—or did I send it to you—I cannot stop to look now— I shall count Mrs Southworths $100. to Mrs Colby direct—as of the Ohio sum—& with it—Mrs Elwell would have but a very few dollars to raise—to entitle us to Mr Peters $100—

Miss Smith's[5] success in Ohio—is about the same as on the Tribune—she cannot cooperate—she must boss!!— Yes I do read your Congressional Notes in the W.T. and they are excellent—[6] I am going to make you our next National President— You are not a public speaker—& so are just the one for all the speakers of all the states to concentrate upon— You can write—issue state papers & see & plan & do just what a Pres. should— now don't flutter over this—but study parliamentary rules of Speaker Reed & tell him I don't forgive his "press of work" so great that he couldn't say to me as much—as that he hoped the Republicans of S.D. would endorse the W.S. amendment that is to be voted upon—[7] Your father's letter had weight—and if we could have ↑had↓ a score of letters like his—from Reed, Hoar, et al— the weak knees—& weaker vertebrae of the trembling Republicans at Mitchell might have been strengthend to have put the W.S. plank in their platform— as it was the Resolution Com. lacked but <u>one vote</u> of doing it—and still—<u>that</u> it <u>wasn't</u> done—and thus it <u>isn't in the</u> <u>Republican platform</u>—strengthens the <u>enemy mightily</u>—<u>everywhere</u>—<u>among</u> <s>among</s> the people— The Independents are <u>mad</u> <u>at us</u>—because we won't come out <u>for them</u>—because of their friendly <u>resolution</u>—not plank—and <u>denounce</u> the <u>Republicans</u>— But we will do no such silly thing—all we can say is that the Democrats ↑have↓ made the <u>lowest bow</u>—to the <u>ignorance</u> & superstition of the enemy—the Republicans the <u>lower bow</u>—and the Indepedents the <u>low bow</u>!! All <u>alike</u> in <u>principle</u> have <u>discarded us from their platform</u>—though different in degree—not one of them gives us any <u>party help</u>—and nothing short of <u>actual endorsement</u>—is <u>other</u> than <u>against</u> us— I have been in the depths of despair—ever since the failure at Mitchell—for I did hope against hope—that we would get recognition there— And now my only hope of <u>relief</u> from my depression is to go out into the thick of the fight—& work so hard trying to convert individual men—as to in a degree forget that we are left alone—almost <u>denied</u>—as <u>was</u> Christ by his very apostles!!

How are we ever to cross ↑the↓ Jordan— No party will take us over until it feels it will die if it don't—and we cant make any party feel that it will die if it don't, <s>take us over,</s> until <u>we</u> are actually a part & parcel of its own number—& will sink its ship if it throws us overboard!!

But if we can convert just <u>one</u> more than ↑one↓ half the men left in this state—I shall be jubilant I know—but a I shant feel <s>that</s> under everlasting obligations for any <u>party</u> help—that is sure—

It wouldn't have <u>hurt</u> <u>any</u> Republican M.C. or Senator to have helped—& it wouldn't have hurt the Repub. Party of S.D. to have helped—but alike they didn't—so we struggle on single handed & alone—without hope—save of the slimmest sort— But don't worry about my feeling badly— I shall work & <u>seem</u> to <u>hope</u> to the end—but oh—<u>how</u> light hearted—we all should have felt—had we had the <u>Repub. party's</u> ↑help↓ that we had a moral right to— So here goes my wail—burn it—& go on hoping & making ↑the↓ men vote right— Lovingly yours

                                               Susan B. Anthony

ALS, on South Dakota Equal Suffrage Association letterhead, SBA Papers, NRU.

1. Thomas Palmer, who was elected president of the Columbian Commission on 27 June 1890, was preparing for the commission's meeting on September 17 at which the role of women would be decided.

2. The legislation authorizing the Columbian Exposition in Chicago, signed by the president in April, conceded a role for women in management, though not as men's equals. It required that a Board of Lady Managers be appointed by the Columbian Commission. When commissioners met in September, they agreed that each of them would nominate two women to the Board. Harriet Upton probably had expressed regret that she had not lobbied Ohio's commissioners for an appointment. (*Chicago Daily Tribune*, 17, 18 September 1890.)

3. Martha Hedger Elwell (1828–1909), of Willoughby, Ohio, presided over the Ohio Woman Suffrage Association from 1888 to 1891. She also spent many years active in the Woman's Christian Temperance Union. The complaint about her arose from new assignments given to presidents of state suffrage societies to raise money for the campaign in South Dakota. Campaign accounts for July 1890 showed New York, California, Pennsylvania, Ohio, and the District of Columbia as the top contributors, while the least amounts came from Massachusetts and Washington State. (Rosa L. Segur, "History of Woman Suffrage in the Maumee Valley," typescript, Toledo-Lucas County Public Library; *Willoughby Independent*, 27 August, 3 September 1909, with assistance of Sally Malone, Morley Library, Painesville, Ohio; *Woman's Tribune*, 16 August 1890.)

4. Oscar Glaze Peters (1842–1894), a wealthy businessman and philanthropist who founded the Columbus Buggy Company, pledged money to the South Dakota campaign payable if the Ohio state association raised four hundred dollars from other sources. In the final report of funds raised for South Dakota, he and Alice Peters are credited with giving one hundred dollars apiece. Alice and Oscar Peters had helped to revive Ohio's suffrage association in 1884 and continued to be active. (William Alexander Taylor, *Centennial History of Columbus and Franklin County, Ohio* [Chicago, 1909], 2:324–26; *Woman's Journal*, 29 December 1894; Accounts for South Dakota Campaign Fund, *Film*, 28:886ff.)

5. That is, Sara W. Smith.

6. Beginning in the *Woman's Tribune*, 16 August 1890, the customary column "Congressional Notes" was signed "H", presumably marking the start of Harriet Upton's authorship.

7. Thomas Reed declined SBA's request that he write a letter to South Dakota Republicans recommending woman suffrage. For three of the letters SBA did receive, see ECS to Republicans of South Dakota, undated; Clara Barton to SBA, 10 August 1890; and Ezra Taylor to SBA, 11 August 1890; all in *Film*, 28:508–11, 535.

115   Speech by ECS to the Bristol Women's Liberal Association

EDITORIAL NOTE: ECS and Harriot Blatch addressed the Bristol Women's Liberal Association at Redland Park Hall before "a large audience," according to the *Bristol Evening News*. Mother and daughter were on a week-long visit to Anna Maria Priestman, Mary Priestman, and Margaret Priestman Tanner, and the sisters arranged their engagement. When the speakers were done, the association adopted a message congratulating Congress on Wyoming statehood that "gratefully recognise[d] the strength and encouragement which this triumph of justice in America will be to constitutional freedom in England." (ECS to Miss Priestman, 24 August and 29 August 1890; to Anna Priestman, 8 September 1890; to Anna and Mary Priestman and Margaret Tanner, 13 October 1890; all in Millfield Papers, Archive, C. & J. Clark Ltd., Street, England, but not in *Film*; *Women's Penny Paper* 2 [18 October 1890]: 617, *Film*, 28:637.)

[9 October 1890]

Mrs Cady Stanton, who was warmly received, said she had been asked to tell them something about Wyoming, the first free State for woman. Some people perhaps, who had seen the bills announcing the meeting, believed that Wyoming was only a new way of spelling woman. (Laughter.) She wished there was a new way, not only of spelling woman, but of treating her also. (Hear, hear.) The day was dawning when the mother of the race would at last be recognised as a human soul, as a person endowed with inalienable rights; as a citizen of the State with an equal voice in the government; an equal factor in the social scale of being; a member of the Church Universal, to be guided in matters of faith by her own individual conscience and judgment; for political equality meant all this—civil, social, and religious freedom. The admission of Wyoming as a State into the Union, with a provision in her constitution for woman suffrage, was the second Declaration of Independence, as much more important in national life than that of 1776 as the moral status of woman in nature exceeded that of man, and as the fulfilment of a principle exceeded its proclamation.

Progress of Wyoming.

Twenty-one years ago the territory of Wyoming recognised woman as an equal factor in civilisation. Wyoming made its appearance on the map in 1868. An Act of Congress carved it out of the great American desert. It was one of the largest, and, when its resources were developed, would be one of the richest, States in the Union. There were already 110,000 inhabitants in the district. Women in Wyoming had the suffrage, sat upon juries, had been justices of the peace, and held other rights hitherto debarred to them. (Applause.) It was clear from the results of women's suffrage in Wyoming that men and women in council legislated better than men alone. In the Congress at Washington they had a committee which sat to inquire into all matters that concerned women. That was a step in advance of the English Parliament. (Hear, hear.) What was the question of women's suffrage that anyone should be afraid of it? It was merely a desire on the part of women to be on an equal footing with men. (Applause.)

~ *Bristol Evening News*, 10 October 1890.

116 ~ ECS to Margaret Stanton Lawrence

Basingstoke [*England*]   October 27th [*1890*]

Dear Madge,[1]

I have made a great improvement in my dress. You know how often you pulled my laces up in front saying "Mrs Southworth["]   Well right over my mantle peice hangs Hattie Brown[2]   I have been making a study of her tie & how nicely it stays up under her chin. I have laid aside all reading, philosophizing, speculations about the eternal past & future & devoted myself to the discovery of what kept this tie in place. At last my thoughts took this logical turn. "It must be fastened to something," it cannot be her skin, it cannot be sufficiently tight, to make the throat protrude & hold it underneath, it cannot be fastened with mucilage, as that would soil the lace & perchance irritate the skin, it cannot stay there of its own free will, for I have tied mine there so tight I could hardly swallow, & in a few minutes it worked down to the

Southworth mark. Yes, yes, after all this rodomontade of difficulties I returned to the original assertion. "It must be fastened to something" What can that be. Perhaps a ribbon tied round her throat. I pinned one as tight as I could bear it, fastened the ~~lace~~ ↑collar↓ with two bewitching bows of soft lace to the right & left, & ends hanging down, then I looked at Hattie's, "perfect," said I, & sat down full of satisfaction to read the morning paper. In the course of an hour I looked at myself in the mirror & lo! ribbon & all had stretched & settled down to the old place! With melancholy misgivings I returned to the tie train of thought, & suddenly my guardian angel, seeing the severe mental struggles through which I was passing said in dulcet tones "put a stiff collar on your dress"   I immediately sat down & sewed a stiff satin ribbon double on my dress. Filled with joy & hope I put it on, once more tied & pinned the lace, looked at myself then looked at Hattie. I made the bows just as large as hers, the ends just as long, & to my unspeakable delight, it remained ↑close up↓ under my chinn all day. The next morning I dressed my hair like Hatties high behind with only three puffs & with an abyding faith & confidence I adjusted my lace, thus concealing the throat which is not beautiful in age. With intense satisfaction I contemplated myself in the mirror several times during the day. I thought I detected a resemblace to Hattie!! Now I perceive another feature that must be concealed, <u>my ears</u>; they are very large, quite unnecessarily so. They cannot be cut off. I am so exhausted mentally & physically with the prolonged train of thought on the tie & throat question that really I am not able with my own unassisted common sense to cope with ↑the↓ ear problem. Hence I ask as a special favor that you & the aunts will set aside some evening, sacred to my interests & inform me what I can do to throw some gentle shadows over two of the most pronounced auricular organs, that ever dimmed the beauty of the side view, of one of Eves fair daughters. The ladies of Chicago are getting up subscriptions for busts of Susan & me for the great fair.[3] Must I appear there with these hereditary appendages on either side of my skull? As Dr Howard[4] is versed in the mysteries of Alchemy perhaps he knows of some chemical substances that might produce a marked shrinkage   I pause for some suggestions. It seems to me that half an inch might be taken from the lobe without detriment & if the entire edge could be rolled over once more that would take off another half inch. But where is the artist to be found equal to this work? Now take these grave questions into serious consideration & let me know what the Aunts [*sideways in margins*] say.⁵ They need not write me any homilies on vanity for an improvement is imperative, & quickly, too   Pass this on to cousin Liz,⁶ as she knows several magnetic cranks who might be able to do something outside the walks of the fixal sciences   With Love

≈ Mother

[*on separate sheet*] Tell the dear Aunts to profit now by my exhaustive experiments & hide their throats, & cousin Lizzie must do the same. The less that is seen of a woman on the shady side of sixty the better, as I told our old friend Mrs Bigelow who persisted in wearing decollète dresses until I took an "opportunity" with her in Paris. Cousin Liz would look fifty per cent better with soft lace close up under her chin. If the Aunts all appear at dinner with covered throats let me know, & now for ears!!

≈ ALS, in the collection of Coline Jenkins, Greenwich, Conn.

1. This use of Madge rather than Maggie for her daughter Margaret is rare but not unique in ECS's letters. Margaret had moved to New York City to live with ECS's sisters.

2. Harriet Cady Eaton Brown (1835–1893) was the daughter of Harriet Eliza Cady Eaton and a niece of ECS. In 1857, she married George Stewart Brown, head of the international banking house Alexander Brown & Sons, and lived in Baltimore. (Allen, *Descendants of Nicholas Cady*, 174–75.)

3. From several quarters, the idea arose of celebrating women's achievements at the Columbian Exposition by commissioning busts of notables. ECS refers to the work of Adelaide Johnson, commissioned by woman suffragists, in part to offset the attention paid to SBA by other sculptors. As SBA phrased it early in 1893, "I have been pretty well 'busted' the last year." Adelaide Johnson's sculptures of ECS and SBA occupied a crowded field, though hers is the best known of all the projects because some of the work survived and because its fund-raising left a well-marked trail. In other projects, Frances Willard announced plans for a bust of SBA, and through the pages of the *Union Signal*, raised money for a work that eventually fell to Lorado Taft. (Alice Blackwell also credited Willard with a commission to the sculptor Anne Whitney for a bust of Lucy Stone.) Some suffragists objected to Willard's omission of ECS. "Mrs. Stanton is the founder and mother of the organized work for the enfranchisement of women," Clara Colby explained in the *Woman's Tribune*. "She is also older than Miss Anthony, and stands to-day at the head of the united American suffrage hosts. There is also a very fine bust of Miss Anthony in existence recently made by a New York artist." Colby spoke for a

group of women in Washington who had already matched the sum of money raised by Willard's project in order to commission a bust of ECS. By the reference to a New York artist, Colby pointed to the sculptor Jonathan Scott Hartley, who received his commission from the Women's Memorial Association in New York City. Under the leadership of Elizabeth Thompson, a philanthropist who earlier underwrote printing costs of the *History of Woman Suffrage*, the association intended to place a statute of Mary Morris Hamilton and a bust of SBA at the exposition. Hartley had completed the bust in plaster, and in March 1891, the association set out to raise money enough for him to execute it in marble. Colby's survey of the field omitted Adelaide Johnson's first bust of SBA; it found little favor when it went on display during the National association's convention in 1887, and it later shattered while in transit across the Atlantic. Yet another bust of SBA was completed by the young sculptor Luella Varney in 1892 and exhibited in Rochester; whether Varney intended hers for the exposition is not known. (*Union Signal*, 15 May, 18 September 1890; *Woman's Tribune*, 17 May 1890; *New York Times*, 31 March 1891; *Woman's Journal*, 23 May 1891; "Ennobled in Marble," unidentified and undated clipping, winter 1892, SBA scrapbook 18, Rare Books, DLC; Blackwell, *Lucy Stone*, 273-74; SBA to Rachel G. Foster, 20 January 1887, and to F. E. Willard, 27 October 1890, and to Adelaide Johnson, 24 February 1892, and *Report of the Twenty-fifth Washington Convention, 1893*, p. 75, all in *Film*, 25:173-79, 28:691-94, 30:4-7, 31:200ff.)

4. Dr. Howard is unidentified.

5. Margaret lived at 8 West Fortieth Street, in a house inhabited by widows; it belonged to Tryphena Cady Bayard (1804-1891), the eldest of ECS's sisters and the widow of Edward Bayard, a well-known homeopathic physician in New York City, who died in September 1889. (City directory, 1889; Allen, *Descendants of Nicholas Cady*, 173; *New York Times*, 1 October 1889; *Woman's Tribune*, 10 May 1891.) The Bayards had shared it with other members of the Cady family for years. Harriet Cady Eaton usually lived there. Catherine Henry Cady Wilkeson (1820-?), the youngest of the sisters, was likely there too; it was her husband's address at the time of his death in December 1889. (City directory, 1889; *TroyFS*; C. H. Cady file, Emma Willard School Archives; *New York Times*, 3 December 1889.)

6. Cousin Liz is Elizabeth Smith Miller.

117 ~ INSCRIPTION BY SBA IN THE DIARY OF ALONZO WARDALL[1]

[*9 November 1890*]

SUN. NOV. 9, 1890. [*in Alonzo Wardall's hand*] Snow— Huron— Home

[*in SBA's hand*] A splendid Love-Feast—at the home of Mr & Mrs Wardall this lovely Sunday after the election—that leaves women still <u>subjects</u> and <u>not</u> <u>sovereigns</u>[2]—& of the company is their Sincere Friend & coworker

~ Susan B. Anthony

[*in signator's hand*] Helen G. Putnam[3]

[*in signator's hand*] Compliments of Dr Nettie C. Hall[4] Wessington Springs So Dak Nov 9—1890

[*in Alonzo Wardall's hand*] Gave dinner to 8 friends

~ Diary for 1890, Alonzo and Elizabeth Wardall Collection, WaU.

1. Alonzo A. Wardall (1845–1918), husband of Elizabeth and father of Anna, lost his post as vice president of the equal suffrage association in the July shakeup, and the Independent party consumed much of his time in the summer and fall. He nonetheless stayed friendly with the suffrage campaigners and occasionally attended their meetings. On November 9, when he hosted a dinner party for eight "in honor of Susan B. Anthony who goes away Monday," he opened his own diary to serve as a guest book. At the top of the page he followed his custom of recording the weather, and at the bottom, he stated the obvious. John and Emma DeVoe were also in attendance. Wardall's fourteen years in South Dakota, from 1879 to 1893, were more notable for his achievements as a reformer than for economic success. From an organizer of the Farmers' Alliance in the Dakotas, he rose to serve on the alliance's national executive board. His Alliance Insurance Companies of the Dakotas, providing fire, life, and hail insurance to members of the alliance, served as a model for national action. On the day he left South Dakota for the last time to move to Kansas, he noted in his diary, "14 years older—& many thousands of dollars worse than nothing financially— Small wonder that I am a calamity howler." (Morgan, *History of the Wheel and Alliance*, 301–2; Alonzo Wardall diary, 8 November 1890, 19 October 1893, Alonzo and Elizabeth Wardall Collection, WaU; Charles Postel, *The Populist Vision* [New York, 2007], 127.)

2. The final vote in South Dakota was yeas 22,972 and nays 45,682. (McPherson, *Hand-Book of Politics for 1892*, 144.)

3. Helen Grace Putnam (1840-1895) studied for the ministry at Meadville Theological Seminary and was ordained a Unitarian minister in the fall of 1889, when she was preaching in the church at Huron. Moving then to North Dakota, Putnam spent her remaining years as an itinerant missionary. Back in South Dakota for the suffrage campaign, she delivered forty-eight lectures in five counties. (Catherine F. Hitchings, "Universalist and Unitarian Women Ministers," *Journal of the Universalist Historical Society* 10 [1975]: 123-25; Wardall, "Woman Suffrage in South Dakota," p. 10, *Film*, 28:871ff.)

4. Nettie Crabb Weems Hall (c. 1842-1908), a physician and pharmacist, acquired a homestead in Jerauld County in 1882 while a widow and mother, remarried in 1884, lost her second husband in 1886, and became a lecturer on hygiene for the territorial temperance union. During the amendment campaign, Hall delivered forty-five lectures in eight counties. She left South Dakota in 1896 to join the planned community of Union and Confederate veterans in Fitzgerald, Georgia. (Federal Census, Renville, Minn., 1880; U.S. Bureau of Land Management Records, on-line; Jack Marken, ed., *The Making of a Community: A History of Jerauld County to 1980* [Wessington Springs, S.D., 1982], 63, 113, 114, 130, 225-26, 289-91; Wardall, "Woman Suffrage in South Dakota," p. 9.)

118   ECS TO MARGARET STANTON LAWRENCE

[*Basingstoke, England, 1 December 1890*]

Your postal this morning with good reports of the invalids gave us great pleasure. I am so glad that dear Try is better   Her death would indeed be a sad breaking up for all of us. We have all had in her a mother & a home. When she is gone we shall have no abyding place, where we can feel free to come & go in the family   Our thanksgiving party went off finely, the children were enchanted   A little boy was dressed up as Rip with his dog. The dog sat still & looked around as if conscious that he was part of the performance   Nora in black tights was a gnome struggling up a hill with a little barrel of whiskey on her shoulders. None of the children knew her. When Rip was finished, a big clothes hamper was brought in. Now said Hatty this has just arrived from Berlin   what do you think is in it. No answer but great expectations. So Hattie said I will touch the spring, up popped Nora covered with white cotton, she [*sideways in margins*] threw large cotton balls at each one containing a present. Then they all wanted to get into the basket so Harry lifted each one in & out

~ AN on postal card, in the collection of Coline Jenkins, Greenwich, Conn. Postmarked at Basingstoke; addressed to 8 West 40th street, New York.

119 ~ SBA TO CLARA BEWICK COLBY

[*before 13 December 1890*][1]

Not one of the new State parties that I have heard of has put a woman suffrage plank in its platform. Each and all of them, like the old Republican and Democratic parties, have welcomed women to work for them and have nominated women to some school offices. The new parties may have nominated more women, but not one of them has made woman's right to vote a party measure, requiring its nominees and its official papers to speak of it as one of the planks in its platform of principles. And until some great party does this thing, I shall not shout the praises of any one of them for nominations of women. The thing we are asking is not for men to put us into office, but for them to let us have the power to vote into office whomsoever we please.

~ *Woman's Tribune*, 13 December 1890.

1. "Much has been said," Clara Colby wrote to introduce this text, "about Miss Anthony's attitude towards the political parties. This is what she says for herself in a recent letter."

120 ~ ECS TO CLARA BEWICK COLBY

Basingstoke Hants [*England*] Dec 21st [*1890*]

Dear Mrs Colby,

I really cannot understand how my Rems are so long reaching you that you have had none in three weeks. I sent two in November one Rems & one an article on Annie Besant.[1] Then I sent another early in

December. The first was on Nebraska, the next on Michigan have you received them or are they lost. I mail one to day on the Centennial, you should certainly receive this in Washington by Jan 1st at the fartherest. I wish you would copy my article on Parnell from The Penny Paper, or better still from the January Westminster on "Patriotism & Chastity."[2] I had a letter from the editor John Chapman[3] yesterday he said he & his wife were delighted with it. It is Stead[4] & a set of canting saints to which Miss Müller & her social purity society[5] all join that have been the leading hounds on Parnell's trail trying to drive the ablest leader Ireland ever had from public life   Men have not been educated to Chastity why look for it? We might as well require that women, who have never been trained to Patriotism should be public spirited. Women are educated to a narrow domestic selfishness, hence their ambition centers in personal & family aggrandizement. Let us condemn the system that makes men & women what they are & not crucify the victims of our false standard of morals   I should love to see all your dear faces & be with you at the coming festivities but I shall not return before May, or or June & not then if Susan decides to come here. Hattie joins in kind regards, ever yours

≈ E. C. S.

≈ ALS, Clara B. Colby Papers, Archives Division, WHi.

1. The reminiscences resumed in *Woman's Tribune*, 6 December 1890, with "Texas, Nebraska, and the Mothers in New Civilizations." That was followed by "Campaign in Michigan" on 20 December 1890; "Annie Besant. Theosophy. English Schools. American Cake," on 27 December 1890; and "The Centennial Year" on 10 January 1891. See *Film*, 28:781-92, 818-33, 847-54, 899-908. Annie Wood Besant (1847-1933), one of England's most prominent radicals, was narrowing her interests since her conversion to Theosophy in 1889, but in conversations reported by ECS about Besant's visit to Harriot Blatch's house, she provided insights into her recent work in the Fabian Society, Social Democratic Federation, and London School Board, as well as Theosophy. (*Oxford DNB*; Joyce M. Bellamy and John Saville, *Dictionary of Labour Biography* [London, 1977], 4:21-31.)

2. Both articles bear the same title. For the first and shorter one in the *Women's Penny Paper*, see *Film*, 28:780. The second is below at January 1891. The uneasy quiet about Charles Parnell's adultery broke in mid-November 1890, when a court granted a divorce to William O'Shea and the press published details of Parnell's lengthy affair with Kate O'Shea. Calls for Parnell's resignation spread fast through the English press, the Catholic church, the

political establishment, and groups of social reformers. Early in December, a majority of Irish nationalists in Parliament rejected his leadership, and by month's end, Irish voters rejected him. (Frank Callanan, *The Parnell Split, 1890-91* [Syracuse, N.Y., 1992]; Kee, *Laurel and the Ivy*, 546-94.)

3. John Chapman (1821-1894), physician and publisher of the *Westminster Review*, lived in Paris with his second wife, Hannah Hughes MacDonald Chapman (1833-1916). (*Oxford DNB*; Gordon S. Haight, *George Eliot and John Chapman, with Chapman's Diaries*, 2d ed. [Hamden, Conn., 1969], 116.)

4. William Thomas Stead (1849-1912) was the crusading and morally righteous editor of the *Pall Mall Gazette* for seven years until January 1890, when he left to found the *Review of Reviews*. He turned on Parnell and urged Liberals to distance themselves from the adulterer, but he was hardly alone in the exploiting the scandal. (*Oxford DNB*.)

5. ECS probably refers to the National Vigilance Association, although by some accounts Müller had resigned from it by this date. At the association's annual meeting in November 1890, W. T. Stead found support for his insistence that Parnell had disqualified himself for public life. Müller shared that opinion, and she disputed every point in ECS's article when she published it. Parnell had committed crimes against chastity, and for that, women should demand his resignation. (*Women's Penny Paper* 3 [29 November 1890]: 87-88, and [6 December 1890]: 104.)

121 ~> ARTICLE BY ECS

[January 1891]

PATRIOTISM AND CHASTITY.

The old Latin proverb, *falsus in uno, falsus in omnia,* has been made to duty once more, used as a weapon to drive Charles Stewart Parnell from public life. It is said that he has violated the seventh commandment, and has thus rendered himself unfit for a political leader. Thousands of reformers have been holding him up in their analytical tweezers, during the last month, for a microscopic examination of his inmost thoughts and private relations. The pulpit, the press, and the people have taken the position that patriotism and chastity are convertible virtues, uniformly found in the same man, and that the lack of one precludes the exercise of the other.

But the business of the world has never been conducted on this line.

In availing ourselves of the skill of our fellow-men, in any special department, we do not ask whether they possess all the cardinal virtues. If we have a difficult case in court, we inquire for the most successful lawyer; if we have a child at death's door, we seek the most skilful physician; we ask no questions as to social life in either case, but avail ourselves of knowledge and wisdom when we need it. The *Pall Mall Gazette* originated a phrase which the press generally echoed, that, "men are not built in water-tight compartments, so that they can be sound in one part and not in another."[1] Now, the facts of life show that that is precisely the way men are built. History tells us of many men of broad culture and sympathy in all human conditions—statesmen, soldiers, scientists, and philosophers—devoted to the public good, yet faithless at their domestic altar. Lord Nelson, Lord Melbourne, the Duke of Wellington,[2] Daniel Webster, Henry Clay, Benjamin Franklin,[3] all rendered invaluable services to their country though they violated the popular standard of morality. Sir Charles Dilke was an able member of the House of Commons, and the women of England owe him a debt of gratitude for the persistent manner in which he helped to carry the Married Women's Property Bill. He never failed to vote in favour of Bills dealing with the protection of the civil and political rights of women. A leader in the suffrage movement once said:—"It would be more to the interest of women to have a Parliament composed of such men as Sir Charles Dilke, than one wholly of chaste angels in opposition." The press generally admits that Mr. Parnell has been a wise and skilful leader of the Irish party for the last ten years; while at the same time, it says he has had an entangling alliance in private life. Grover Cleveland was faithful to a marked degree in all the public offices he filled as Mayor, Governor, President of the United States; and yet his social life was not above reproach.[4] With a full knowledge of the facts of his life, many distinguished moralists voted for him, and he was elected by an overwhelming majority. At one time it was thought the social scandal would jeopardise his election; but sound Yankee common sense triumphed, and the verdict was, "here is a man with a clean public record, he shall serve us!" And so well did he serve his country, that, without doubt, he will again be the Democratic nominee for the Presidency. Lord Connemara, Governor of Madras,[5] is another example of the same principle. Though lacking in the virtues which make a good husband, he was honourable and efficient in his public duties, and so endeared himself to the people of Madras that they have sent, it is said, a petition to the Government asking that his resignation be declined.

If the women of England take up the position that there can be no true patriotism without chastity, they will rob some of the most illustrious rulers of their own sex of any reputation for ability in public affairs. The private lives of Cleopatra of Egypt, Elizabeth of England, Catherine of Russia[6] were all below the popular standard of their own times; and yet the pages of history glow with their brilliant achievements as rulers of nations. Weighed in this new balance, the queens of literature would be robbed of their laurels. Emerson, one of the purest of men, dwells on the rare and beautiful sentiment that runs through George Sand's *Consuelo*,[7] and who can deny the evidence of keen political insight, lofty ideas, and pure morality in the writings of such women as Mary Wollstonecraft, Frances Wright, and George Eliot:[8]—and yet all these rejected the English code of morals.

Certainly such examples go to prove that great souls may lack some virtues, and yet in an abounding measure possess many others. We must recognise the fact that patriotism and chastity belong to different spheres of action. The former is pre-eminently a masculine virtue, to which a man is trained from his earliest years. He may, in time, be the ruler of a nation; hence he must study the laws and practise the virtues needed to protect the public interests. He must be brave and courageous, ever ready to live or die for his country. Chastity, on the other hand, has in all ages been considered a feminine virtue. Women have been sedulously trained to regard this as their crowning glory, which best fits them for family life. Hence the vast majority of women are deficient in patriotism; they care but little for public interests; they are generally absorbed in a narrow, personal, and family selfishness. They are not to blame for their contracted outlook; it is the result of their education. In this view, it is equally absurd to deny patriotism to men because they lack chastity, as it would be to deny chastity to women because they lack patriotism. We are all what law, custom, and public sentiment have made us, alike fragmentary, some truth and some error bound up in every human soul. Through our whole system of jurisprudence we find a separate code of laws and morals for men and women recognised and enforced by the best authorities. We find woman, though the more important factor in social life, always placed in a subordinate position, and though she is declared to be the more helpless, on her shoulders are laid the heaviest responsibilities.

> "Many jurists," says Kent, vol. ii. p. 88, "are of opinion that the adultery of the husband ought not to be noticed or made subject to the same animadversions as that of the wife, because it is not evidence of such entire depravity, nor equally injurious in its effects upon the morals, good order, and happiness of domestic life. Montesquieu, Pothier, and Dr. Taylor all insist that the cases of husband and wife ought to be distinguished, and that the violation of the marriage vow, on the part of the wife, is the most mischievous, and the prosecution ought to be confined to the offence on her part."—*Esprit des Loix*, tome 3, 186; *Traité du Contrat de Mariage*, No. 516; *Elements of Civil Law*, p. 254.[9]

So long as the civil and canon law—Blackstone and the Bible—proclaim such distinctions, let us be honest and consistent, and repudiate these authorities, rather than ostracise the individual who is but a result of such teaching.

Like cyclones and earthquakes these sudden and violent attacks on the reputation of great men seem to be governed by no law, but the caprice of the elements. There never has been any true standard of social morality and none exists to-day. The true relation of the sexes is still an unsolved problem, that has differed in all latitudes and in all periods from the savage to civilised man. We have thus far had five forms of family life:—[10]

1st. The Consanguine Family:—the intermarriage of brothers and sisters in a group.

2nd. The Punaluan Family:—the intermarriage of several brothers to each other's wives in a group, and of several sisters to each other's husbands in a group.

3rd. The Syndyasmian Family:—the pairing of one man and woman for a season, with separation at the option of either husband or wife.

4th. The Patriarchal Family:—the marriage of one man to several wives.

5th. The Monogamian Family with legalised prostitution, our present form.

Such are the five defined systems with variations under each.[11] As there seems to be endless complaining and contention still, even under the present system, it is fair to suppose that we may pass through four or five more experiments before finding a satisfactory solution.

In the meantime, what constitutes chastity is the vital question. Like fashion in dress, it changes with time and latitude; its definition would be as varied as is public opinion on other subjects. Some would say that all legal relations of the sexes are chaste, and all illegal relations unchaste. Some would say that only those relations sanctioned by enduring friendship and love are chaste, that all others are unchaste. It is much more easy to say, what according to our clearest thinkers is not chaste, than what is so according to the present standard. The first definition Worcester[12] gives is continence. How many reformers even will accept this? Entire continence and no marriage is chastity for the Catholic priesthood. Unlimited license in marriage is chastity for the Protestant priesthood. A family of twelve children and an invalid wife casts no shadow on those who fill the most holy offices in the church. But a healthy, happy mother and child outside the bonds of legal wedlock, though, loving and beloved, are ostracised by the community as unchaste.

It is not my purpose or desire to say aught to lower the standard of high morality, only to ascertain in what it consists, and the most likely means by which it can be secured. To my mind, it is not by hounding men, but by the education, elevation, and emancipation of women, by training them to self-respect and a virtuous independence. It is no compliment to the strength and sagacity of women, to be always regarded as innocent victims and helpless dupes in these social catastrophes,—especially when they have reached years of discretion, and are quite able to protect their own reputation and the sacredness of their home life.

The one supreme lesson to be learned from the great upheaval that has just rent our political life is the futility of coercive measures in reformation. The spectacle of a whole nation hounding one man, and determined to administer summary punishment, is pitiful at a time, when those who love their fellow-men are asking for all the best moral appliances and conditions for the reformation of the criminal classes, instead of the old methods of punishment. Our leading thinkers in education, in prison discipline, and in the treatment of the insane have long since in no measured terms repudiated coercion and arbitrary punishment. Kindness and attraction are the corner-stones of the new system in all our educational and reformatory institutions. The child is not to be tyrannically regarded as a lump of clay to be moulded into any shape; but it is to be treated as a being of capacities and proclivities peculiar to itself, to be unfolded and developed. Force, either in the form of bodily infliction or mental lashing, has been abandoned by the experienced as wholly evil in its effects, both on the child and on the criminal. Acting on this principle, what right has a nation to turn all its enginery of denunciation on one human being for the violation of an unsettled question of morals, which even Cardinals and Bishops, Kings and Emperors ignore? The educator and the prison disciplinarian, following the old method, failed; and so long as the reform of humanity, according to that method, is attempted by public opinion, it will also fail. Indeed, these unethical systems turn the child into a dullard, the prisoner into a confirmed criminal, and force the statesman who has committed one fault into many others, force him, perchance, into such an attitude of supreme defiance that he is false to all the best feelings of his nature. While merciless hounding crushes those of tender sensibilities, it calls out savage and reckless retaliation in the more courageous, self-reliant men.[13]

The great lesson taught by the founder of our faith is charity: without that we are but sounding brass and a tinkling cymbal.[14] Could the Divine man, now worshipped in all our holy temples, appear again on earth, at this crisis of unhappy Ireland's history, and voice the same rebuke to the Pharisees of our day as in the past, how quickly would the pens now dipped in gall fall powerless from every hand, and the countless envenomed tongues be hushed to silence, as the nation's ear caught the stern message of charity. "He that is without sin among you, let him cast the first stone."[15]

~ *Elizabeth Cady Stanton.*

~ *Westminster Review* 135 (January 1891): 1–5.

1. London's *Pall Mall Gazette*, when under the editorship of W. T. Stead, led crusades for moral purity that included a vendetta against Charles Dilke and harassment of Charles Parnell.

2. From Britain, she names Horatio, viscount Nelson (1758–1805), naval hero; William Lamb, viscount Melbourne (1779–1848), politician and prime minister; and Arthur Wellesley, Duke of Wellington (1769–1852), military

general. Lord Nelson's six-year affair with the married Emma Hamilton produced one daughter. Lord Melbourne's sexual scandals included two suits brought against him by angry husbands. The Duke of Wellington had numerous affairs with English and French women.

3. From the United States, she names Daniel Webster (1782–1852), lawyer and politician; Henry Clay (1777–1852), politician; and Benjamin Franklin (1706–1790), revolutionary and scientist. Webster was believed to have fathered a son by a mulatto slave he later freed. Clay was said to have left his wife in Kentucky in order to make love to women in Washington. Franklin's wife raised his illegitimate son William.

4. Grover Cleveland's sexual indiscretions and illegitimate child became subjects of intense debate during the presidential election of 1884.

5. Robert Bourke, Baron Connemara (1827–1902), a Conservative politician and governor of Madras, was charged by his wife with cruelty and adultery in her petition for divorce, heard by a London court in late November 1890. (*Oxford DNB*.)

6. Rulers who combined sexuality with statecraft, these were: Cleopatra VII, queen of Egypt (69–30 B.C.); Elizabeth I, queen of England and Ireland (1533–1603); and Catherine II, empress of Russia (1729–1796).

7. George Sand was the pen name of Armandine Aurore Lucille Dupin (1804–1876), French novelist and sexual radical. In *Consuelo* (1842), she explored the human cost of imposing on women a dichotomy between sexual desire and maternal love. Ralph Waldo Emerson admired Sand for using the novel to explore human possibilities and freedom rather than to document social arrangements.

8. Pioneers in articulating woman's rights and challenging marriage, these were Mary Wollstonecraft, author of *A Vindication of the Rights of Women* (1792); Frances Wright (1795–1852), freethinking reformer in England and America; and George Eliot, English novelist.

9. For the source of this quotation from James Kent, *Commentaries on American Law*, see note at 3 December 1888, above.

10. ECS adapts a list by Lewis Henry Morgan (1818–1881), an American ethnologist whose studies of kinship among the Iroquois uncovered a matrilineal system of clans. His *Ancient Society* (1877), a synthesis of his anthropological work and historical research, aimed to track social evolution through all the stages of human history. Morgan placed this list at the start of his first chapter along with definitions of each type. In the first four instances, ECS paraphrased his definitions, but Morgan did not include legalized prostitution as the companion of monogamy in his definition of the fifth type. (*ANB*.)

11. Note in the source: "Morgan's *Ancient Society*."

12. Joseph Emerson Worcester (1784–1865), a lexicographer, was a rival of Noah Webster in the production of American dictionaries of the English language.

13. Note in the source: "In this fact lies, probably, the most intelligible

explanation of Mr. Parnell's recent aberrations. How, otherwise, can we understand his 'manifesto' which has astounded and grieved every well-wisher of the Home Rule cause; his violent antagonism to his, hitherto, zealous co-workers from whom he has alienated himself; and his extraordinary method of dominating the newspaper, *United Ireland.*—(Editors of the *Westminster Review.*)" The editor comments on elements of Parnell's self-defense. His manifesto, published on 29 November 1890, aimed to rouse supporters in Ireland in defense of his leadership against his parliamentary allies who wanted his resignation. In it, he charged, among many other things, that his troubles stemmed from interference by the Liberal party's leaders in deciding who should lead the Irish nationalists in Parliament. Back in Ireland in December, Parnell smashed into the offices of his newspaper, *United Ireland*, to oust opponents who had seized control.

14. 1 Cor. 13:1.

15. John 8:7.

122 ECS TO CLARA BEWICK COLBY

Basingstoke [*England*]   Jan 12th [*1891*]

Dear Mrs Colby,

Your postal received. Rems all right   I have written only one chapter on Nebraska & that you published. You have now two on The Centennial.¹ I am scratching round to see what next. I want you & Susan to polish up my Boston letter²   Add what I sent in regard to The Franchise League.³ It is the only suffrage organization that is based on principle demanding suffrage for women on the same basis as extended to men. Did you note Miss Müllers editorial last summer on the folly of asking suffrage for married women.⁴ Instead of specifying "widows & spinsters" as they once did, they say now, "except for those under coverture," which amounts to the same thing. Hattie & I have endeavored in letters to Susan to post you on the movement here. We want you to understand the situation so that you can give your influence to bring these English women up to the higher ground, where John Stuart Mill kept it as long as he lived. Mrs Peter Taylor⁵ one of the very first to move on the question always repudiated the widow & spinster bills   so did Mr & Mrs Jacob Bright.⁶ Get a clear statement of this, short & concise, in my Boston letter. If you think best you can change the letter into the form of a speech. Though as it is Susan can read & comment as she goes along. As I am on the ↑ground↓ & know how the land lies I may as well take the odium of saying that The Woman's Franchise League is the only branch of the woman movement based on principle. The others say, just let us get Parliamentary suffrage for widows & spinsters & then we will work for married women. The proof that they would not is shown in their silence as to municipal suffrage for married women   They have had that for 20 years & have not yet asked it for married women. When they get Parliamentary suffrage   they will still say wait until we get into office   then we will enfranchise you in a twinkling   All history shows, that the last class to enjoy any liberty is always opposed to new rights for those below them. Hattie joins in kind regards   cordially ever

~ E. C. S.

~ ALS, ECS Papers, DLC.

1. "Texas, Nebraska, and the Mothers in New Civilizations," 6 December 1890; "The Centennial Year," 10 January 1891; and "Centennial," 17 January 1891, *Film*, 28:791–92, 907–8, 924–26. "Campaign in Michigan" 20 December 1890, *Film*, 28:832–33, also fell in this sequence.

2. See below at 15 January 1891. ECS suggests in this letter that she mentioned the Women's Franchise League in her Boston letter, but such a reference does not appear in the published text.

3. In the company of Harriot Blatch in London, ECS attended meetings of the Women's Franchise League founded in 1889. Members of the league pursued the objective ECS urged Britain's suffragists to adopt when she was in England in 1882 and 1883: the franchise granted to women regardless of whether they were single, married, or widowed. This aim put its members at odds with suffragists who accepted language extending the parliamentary franchise only to women not under coverture and with those who favored a return to the ambiguous language used first in 1870 that left married women in a legal limbo but avoided tying suffrage to coverture. (Sandra Stanley Holton, "Now You See It, Now You Don't: The Women's Franchise League and Its Place in Contending Narratives of the Women's Suffrage Movement," in *The Women's Suffrage Movement: New Feminist Perspectives*, eds. Maroula Joannou and June Purvis [Manchester, England, 1998], 15–36; Holton, *Suffrage Days*, 76–82.)

4. Henrietta Müller wrote two editorials on the topic in the spring and summer of 1890. Her opposition to married women's suffrage derived not from political expediency or parliamentary possibilities but from the view that coverture rendered women unfit to vote. First destroy coverture, then allow married women to vote, she advised. "You cannot give *political* freedom to

one who is dispossessed of *personal* freedom," she wrote in the issue of May 24. A week later, she insisted that it was not only illogical to enfranchise women who lacked "the right to come and go," it was also unconstitutional. (*Women's Penny Paper* 2 [24 May 1890]: 366, and [31 May 1890]: 378.)

5. Clementia Doughty Taylor (1810-1908) was one of Britain's earliest advocates of woman suffrage in 1866 and a member of the executive committee of the Married Women's Property Committee from 1876 to 1882. Her husband, Peter Alfred Taylor (1819-1891), was a radical member of Parliament from 1876 to 1882. (Sally Mitchell, ed., *Victorian Britain, An Encyclopedia* [New York, 1988], and *Oxford DNB*, s.v. "Taylor, Clementia Doughty"; *Times* [London], 14 April 1908; Baylen and Gossman, *Modern British Radicals*, 2:497-99; *Who's Who of British Members of Parliament*, vol. 1.)

6. Jacob Bright (1821-1899), a younger brother of the great reformer John Bright, served as the parliamentary leader of woman suffragists in the early 1870s, and, as a member of Parliament until 1895, he was a strong advocate of votes for married as well as single women. (*Who's Who of British Members of Parliament*, vol. 2; Banks, *Biographical Dictionary of British Feminists, 1800-1930*.) Ursula Mellor Bright (1835-1915) shared her husband's political interests. She joined the Manchester suffrage society, worked against the Contagious Diseases Acts, and led the Married Women's Property Committee. The Brights joined the Women's Franchise League in 1890. (*Oxford DNB*; Holton, "From Anti-Slavery to Suffrage Militancy: The Bright Circle." See also *Papers* 4.)

123 ECS TO MARGARET STANTON LAWRENCE

[*Basingstoke, England, 12? January 1891*]¹

Now my blessed Madge do not worry about your possible future. Life is a march & a battle with most of us.² I have been wonderfully blest with health & earthly comforts all my life, but I have had my sorrows, trials & hardships but I never talk much about the shadows of life. In fact my settled feeling is, that in view of the miseries of the mass of makind, I have had more than my share of the good things, and you have had a fair share thus far. You have travelled about more than most women & had more liberty to do what you pleased than most. You have had good advantages of education & a large circle always of warm friends. So let us look on the bright side & be cheerful & happy & make our own sunshine wherever we are lovingly

mother

Love & kisses to my dear sisters & a thousand thanks [*sideways in margin*] for their kindness to you.

~ ALS incomplete, in the collection of Coline Jenkins, Greenwich, Conn. Envelope addressed to Mrs Stanton Lawrence, 8 West 40th street, New York U.S.A.

    1. Date from postmark. Opening pages missing.
    2. See note above at 15 February 1890.

124 ~ ECS TO LUCY STONE AND THE MASSACHUSETTS WOMAN SUFFRAGE ASSOCIATION

Basingstoke, Hants, England, Jan. 15, 1891.

Dear Lucy Stone: When I received your invitation to be present in person or by letter to celebrate the 40th anniversary of the first Woman's Rights convention held in Massachusetts,[1] I turned to the History of Woman Suffrage, Vol. I, Chap. VIII, to refresh my mind as to what was said and done on that occasion.[2]

    At no other convention have we ever had such an array of distinguished men and women on our platform. The resolutions, the speeches, the dignity and order of the proceedings, the whole tone of the meetings show rare organizing talent at the head. It was generally conceded at the time the marked success of the two Worcester conventions was due to Paulina Wright Davis more than to any other one person. With rare courage, persistence and executive ability, in the face of much opposition and many discouragements, she took the initiative steps unaided and alone. During my last visit in her beautiful home I looked over the many letters she had received from friends in England and America, in answer to hers, urging them to lend their influence to the success of the convention.[3] This correspondence alone showed the immense preliminary work she had done. She presided on both occasions, made out the programmes for the different sessions and took the entire financial responsibility. In giving me the details of what occurred behind the scenes, she said:

    "But, in spite of all the adverse winds, the meetings were successful and good. Oliver Johnson crowned the work with his splendid reports in the New York *Tribune*[4] which called out an able paper from Mrs. John Stuart Mill in the Westminister *Review*, and roused all England to thought on the question."[5]

How impossible it would have been for the half dozen women who adjourned from an anti-slavery meeting into a dark, dingy committee room to consult as to the wisdom of calling a convention, to foresee or estimate the far-reaching influences of their decision that day.[6]

England sent greetings through John Stuart Mill, Harriet Martineau and Mary Somerville.[7] France, through Helene Marie Weber and Jeanne Deroine, and Pauline Roland, written from the prison of St. Lazare, where they were incarcerated for their liberal opinions.[8] At this convention William Henry Channing presented a very radical paper on the social relations, which disappeared in a mysterious way and of which no report was ever given. I spoke to him about it in London. He said he never knew what became of it, but he thought some friend, for his reputation's sake, had cautiously suppressed it, as society was not ready for such liberal ideas.[9]

Through Mr. Channing I learned that Jeanne Deroine was living in poverty in London. So I called to see her one day in the outskirts of the great metropolis and found her comfortably situated with a son and daughter. I presented her Vol. I of the Woman Suffrage History. She was much pleased to see her letter to the Worcester convention in print. She seemed happy 'mid her plain surroundings, rejoicing in the larger freedom already accorded to women. In looking over the long list of speakers who made those conventions so brilliant and memorable I was oppressed with the thought of the many eloquent voices now hushed forever. Garrison, Phillips, Channing, Samuel J. May, Alcott, Emerson, the Burleighs, Stephen Foster, Abbie Kelley, Lucretia Mott, Ernestine L. Rose, Frances D. Gage, Sojourner Truth, Clarina I. H. Nichols, Abby Price, the Grimke sisters and many others,[10] represented by letter as well as in person, have all gone to the unknown land, leaving but a few of us who inaugurated the movement to rejoice over victories achieved and labor for those yet to come.

While I number the steps of progress that have been taken during the last half century, I cannot say that my heart is overflowing with gratitude when I consider the prolonged struggle we have made, the petitions we have rolled up, the appeals written, the conventions held, the legislatures besieged, the ecclesiastical councils invaded, the hand to hand fight for a foothold in the world of work, in the trades and professions, it all seems to me like a painful dream, in which one strives to run from some impending danger and yet stands still.

To talk to us to-day, after forty years of persistent effort, of patience, philosophy, and gratitude for privileges conceded is downright mockery. For what should we be thankful? That we have been robbed of our inheritance, of our rights of sovereignty, of person, property, children—alike defrauded of social, civil, and political equality. Because, forsooth, advancing civilization has wrung from our rulers a few privileges. Shall we be thankful as their subjects, when by every principle of our government and religion; by education and development we are the equals of at least one-half our rulers and infinitely superior to the rest. When every ship from the old world comes freighted with ignorance, poverty, and vice, to be manufactured into rulers for the women of this republic, when our rights of individual sovereignty are trodden into the dust by the wooden-shoed peasantry of Russia, Germany, Norway, and Sweden. Shall we boast of a few concessions to our demands, made here and there, and exclaim in triumph, "the world moves." It was such as these that defeated us in South Dakota, as well as in all the other States where the Woman Suffrage amendments have been submitted to the vote of the people.

And to whom and for what should we be grateful? Never was there a class battling for their rights thrown so wholly on their own resources or counseled to such suicidal measures. While in fighting their own battles men use their sharpest weapons and most pungent language, and attack the enemy at every point, they tell us to be patient, persuasive, and unaggressive and work on the same lines for, perchance, forty years longer. The public are accustomed to arguments in political rights. That demand is made respectable; it shocks no one, so they bid us sit, like Poe's raven on the door post, and sing suffrage forever and forever.[11] We must say nothing of equality in the church or the marriage relation, that would broaden the discussion and rouse a new source of opposition. The church women would leave our ranks and withdraw their subscriptions from our papers.

The fact is, no one regards our demands as requiring some prompt action. Our best friends seem to regard our reform as a kind of sentimental question to be referred to the limbo of romance, of no greater practical importance than who wrote the letters of Junius,[12] or whether Bacon wrote Shakespeare.[13]

After the discussion of half a century, look at the solitary champions we have had in Congress and State legislatures to present our petitions and plead our cause. Consider the silence of the press and the pulpit over the monstrous injustice of disfranchisement in a republic. They occasionally give some eloquent burst of a few paragraphs on the glory of motherhood and the sacredness of the fireside when some special outrage in society occurs, but they never probe beneath the surface and show that it is the general disrespect for the rights of all women that permits the individual wrong that ever and anon shocks society, like an earthquake.

Every man in South Dakota that did not vote for woman suffrage in the late election is responsible for every act of violence or injustice inflicted on the women of that State, for every insult offered to his mother, sister, wife, or daughter. Yes, 45,682 men, by their votes, told the ignorant foreigners and Indians that there was nothing sacred in womanhood; that men owed no allegiance to their mothers; that women in solitary places and little girls on their way to school were all alike fair game for the wily hunter. Such are the lessons taught by that young State just admitted into the Union. Again there were 6,000 more votes given to extend suffrage to the Indians than to women, practically saying that they preferred Indians to women as co-rulers within their borders. This is one of the most humiliating features of that election.[14]

We have now been compelled by our legislators to appeal to the riff-raff of eight different States and always with the same mortifying result, and I do hope women will never humble themselves again to repeat the experiment. Whether there is any connection between the defeat of this measure and the present uprising of the Indians it is difficult to ascertain, but if figures can express the contempt a State might feel for a class, the Indians may have understood the insult conveyed by the returns of the late election.[15]

When I first heard the news from South Dakota I remarked to my daughter that I hoped in our present humiliation the same old cup of consolation would not be pressed to our lips that we have drained to the very dregs eight times in succession. "Though you have not been victorious," say the comforters, "yet a great educational work has been accomplished." It is barely possible that women even might grow tired teaching in a school where the dullards never learn the A B C of human rights; never reward their educators with the slightest manifestation of sense, or the smallest pittance of a salary. Where do we see the evidence of "this great educational work accomplished." Some of our most gifted orators traveled over every inch of the ground in South Dakota, speaking wherever they could find ears to listen, for six months in succession, repeating all the great maxims of republican government, which the fathers had stated so clearly, that he that runs might read, and yet 45,682 men went to the polls and denied every one of them.

If, according to republican principles, as recognized in our Declaration of Rights and in our National Constitution, 60,000,000 of people are the legal heirs to these United States, by what principle of mathematics, or common honesty, are 30,000,000 in possession of the whole estate? There is no record on file anywhere that one-half the heirs abdicated their rightful position as owners. They never consented to such a wholesale robbery of all the daughters of the earth! No, our mothers were cunningly defrauded without knowing exactly how, when, or where, the deed was done.

If we complain to our self-constituted rulers of the injustice we suffer, they coolly tell us that this general awakening to our wrongs, and the many favors already granted, show that "a great educational work has been accomplished." Their coolness reminds me of an incident in the childhood of three boys I knew. One was a natural economist and loved to accumulate. He saved all his pennies in a little tin bank, while the two older brothers spent all the money given them from time to time.

One day Barnum's circus came to town,[16] and as they had no other resources they decided to rob the younger brother's bank, and by way of compensation, invited him to go also. He was very happy with this unusual attention, as they generally ran off and left him in the lurch, and he enjoyed the occasion most heartily. The brothers spared no pains to make him happy. They treated him to lemonade, tarts, candy, and peanuts, at the same time generously helping themselves. Days after, when the enthusiasm of the occasion had passed away, the little fellow found he had been robbed. The brothers promptly confessed, but begged him to remember what a rich treat he had, the great spectacular performance, the delicious lemonade, tarts, candy, and peanuts; and then "the great educational work accomplished for his brother in seeing the animals and the wonderful skill of man in their training; the rare lessons they had learned in the anatomy of the human body as seen in the grand and lofty tumbling; how small your sacrifice, dear brother, with all this knowledge achieved." Thus they so muddled the little boy's mind that at last he began to think he had been most generously treated.

This is just the way women's minds are confused to-day. When we complain of the degradation of disfranchisement, and of all the evils that flow therefrom, they point us to the change in woman's position from the time of Herod the king. They tell us of all the favors we receive—the best seats in the operas and theaters; the tid-bits at the table; the places we already hold in the colleges, trades and professions. All very well, gentlemen; but we have fought our way to the vantage ground we hold to-day, in spite of your opposition! Remember, too, that by taxation without representation our little tin banks have all been robbed to build the colleges, churches, capitols and public institutions. True, a great educational work has been accomplished; but as we eat the tarts and sip the lemonade in the great human circus, we would rather appear as equal, independent factors in the drama of life than as helpless victims of man's superior craft and cunning.

I am happy to say that the boys, after a few years were sorely troubled in conscience, when they remembered their act of injustice, and paid back to their younger brother, his money with interest. God grant the day may not be far off when there will be such an awakening among the men of this nation, that they too may hasten to make some restitution.

Fresh from communion with the noble men and women who submitted our case forty years ago to the judgment of a candid world, we must not linger in the valley of humiliation, but from their vantage-ground behold how insignificant are the struggles and disappointments of the past, in view of the boundless horizon that opens before us. Alone at the midnight hour, pondering their eloquent messages of faith and hope, they seem to pass transfigured before me, serenely pointing to diviner heights than we have yet reached; to sublimer duties than we have yet comprehended.

No; they are not gone; they linger with us still; their words and deeds gild many a page in history. From the realm invisible they speak, as ever, to those who listen and thrill our hearts again, as with the living voice.

Let us, then, weave immortal wreaths of praise and gratitude in memory of those whose lives were radiant with the love of justice, liberty and equality for every human soul, and hang our garlands on the altars where are inscribed the names of those who loved their fellow men. Yours, sincerely,

~ *Elizabeth Cady Stanton.*

~ *Woman's Tribune*, 31 January 1891.

1. The Massachusetts Woman Suffrage Association used a part of its annual meeting on 27 and 28 January 1891 to celebrate the fortieth anniversary of the First National Woman's Rights Convention at Worcester in 1850. In the absence of SBA, William Lloyd Garrison, Jr., read ECS's letter to the audience. Lucy Stone and Henry Blackwell regarded the event as an antidote to histories of woman's rights centered on the convention at Seneca Falls in 1848. As Stone explained to a friend in advance of this meeting in 1891, the meeting in 1850 "was the one really to stir the public thought— There is a report of the Seneca Falls meeting but I think it was made long after the meeting." (The North Star press published the report in 1848.) Or as Henry Blackwell explained to his daughter about Seneca Falls, "Very little notice was taken of it at the time." In 1870, Stone did not join the the twentieth anniversary celebration organized by Paulina Davis and the National Woman Suffrage Association, but in 1880, after the death of Davis, Stone appropriated celebrations of the anniversary for the Massachusetts association. (L. Stone to Antoinette L. B. Blackwell, 18 April & 5 July 1880, 18 September 1890, in Lasser and Merrill, *Friends and Sisters*, 216, 217, 260; H. B. Blackwell to Alice S. Blackwell, 7 August 1887, in Wheeler, *Loving Warriors*, 307; Blackwell, *Lucy Stone*, 95-99; Paulina Wright Davis, comp., *A History of the National Woman's Rights Movement, for Twenty Years* [New York, 1871], 6, 12-13; *Papers*, 2:362-68, 382; *Woman's Journal*, 30 October 1880.)

2. The chapter "Massachusetts," *History*, 1:201-89. In the course of this letter, however, ECS lost the distinction between the events of 1850, pages 215-26, and the Second National Woman's Rights Convention in 1851, also at Worcester, pages 226-42.

3. ECS described this, her last visit to Davis in December 1875, in the *History of Woman Suffrage*, 1:283. She also looked over Davis's papers when in Providence for her funeral in 1876; see *Papers*, 3:255.

4. The European edition of the *New York Tribune*, 29 October 1850, reported on the convention.

5. Harriet Taylor Mill, "The Enfranchisement of Women," *Westminster Review* 55 (July 1851): 149-61.

6. On this preliminary meeting in May 1850, see Davis, *History of the*

National Woman's Rights Movement, 12-13, and Lucy Stone's speech at the meeting of 1891, *Woman's Journal*, 14 February 1891.

7. ECS misread the chapter she consulted. On John Stuart Mill, the chapter in the *History of Woman Suffrage*, quoting at length from Davis, *History of the National Woman's Rights Movement*, refers to a letter he wrote to Paulina Davis in advance of the two-decade anniversary in 1870. See *History*, 1:219-20. For Harriet Martineau's letter to the second, not first, convention, see *History*, 1:229-31. Mary Fairfax Somerville (1780-1872) was an English astronomer whose name was mentioned several times during the convention 1850 because of her achievements but not on account of a letter written to the meeting.

8. Hélène-Marie Weber (1825-?), daughter of a Prussian officer and an Englishwoman, wrote to the first convention from her farm in Belgium to explain why she dressed in male clothing. American activists knew of her not only as a dress reformer but also as the author of ten tracts on woman's rights, published in 1844 and 1845, and as a successful agriculturalist. (*History*, 1:224, 822-23; Sarah J. Hale, *Woman's Record; or Sketches of all Distinguished Women From the Creation to A.D. 1868* [New York, 1872], 809-11.) Pauline Roland (1805-1852) wrote on 15 June 1851 from prison with Jeanne-Françoise Deroin (1805-1894) to the second convention. See *History*, 1:234-37.

9. An abstract of Channing's paper at the second convention is found in *History*, 1:233-34.

10. The reformers already identified are William Lloyd Garrison, Wendell Phillips, William H. Channing, Bronson Alcott, Ralph Waldo Emerson, Charles C. Burleigh, and Abby Kelley Foster. To these names ECS added William Henry Burleigh (1812-1871), brother of Charles; Stephen Symonds Foster (1809-1881), husband of Abby Kelley; Sojourner Truth (c. 1797-1883), formerly a slave in New York State; Sarah Moore Grimké (1792-1873) and her sister Angelina Emily Grimké Weld (1805-1879), the daughters of South Carolina slaveholders. Finally, she includes Abby Hills Price (1814-1878), an early antislavery activist, resident of the Hopedale community in Massachusetts, writer for the *Practical Christian*, and good friend of Abby Kelley and Paulina Davis. In 1870, Price attended the celebration organized by Davis. Leaving Massachusetts in 1853, she moved her family to the Raritan Bay Union in New Jersey for several years before opening her own business in Brooklyn. She was also a close friend of Walt Whitman. (Sherry Ceniza, *Walt Whitman and 19th-Century Women Reformers* [Tuscaloosa, Ala., 1998], 45-95; Davis, *History of the National Woman's Rights Movement*, 12-13, 15, 41; *Woman's Journal*, 25 May 1878.)

11. Edgar Allan Poe, "The Raven."

12. To the present day, no one has offered definitive proof about the identity of an author signing himself "Junius" whose political letters were published in London from 1769 to 1772.

13. That is, Francis Bacon.

14. The equation is misleading, as it compares the yea votes for the two

amendments without noting that to favor the amendment on Indian suffrage was to approve the *dis*franchisement of Indians still in tribal relations. ECS was not alone, however, in her reading. At the November election, voters in South Dakota defeated a constitutional amendment that read: "No Indian who sustains tribal relations, receives support in whole or in part from the government of the United States, or holds untaxable land in severalty, shall be permitted to vote at any election held under this constitution." The South Dakota constitution of 1889 said nothing about the voting rights of Native Americans, and it is unclear why the amendment was thought necessary. In the wake of the Dawes Act of 1887, states like North and South Dakota wanted to clarify the voting rights of Indians who severed their tribal relations, took an allotment of land, and thereby became federal citizens. North Dakota's constitution of 1889 addressed this new circumstance directly; among those defined as eligible to vote were "civilized persons of Indian descent who shall have severed their tribal relations two years next preceding such election." South Dakota made no such positive declaration. The defeated amendment seemed only to bifurcate the civil status of one race of residents without committing the state to recognize the voting rights of those who were citizens. The amendment lost by a vote of 29,053 to 38,632. (No. Dakota Constitution of 1889, Art. 5, sec. 121; C. H. Ellis, *History of Faulk County, South Dakota, Together with Biographical Sketches of Pioneers and Prominent Citizens* [Faulkton, S.D, 1909], 240; Jill E. Martin, "'Neither Fish, Flesh, Fowl, nor Good Red Herring': The Citizenship Status of American Indians, 1830–1924," in *American Indians and U.S. Politics: A Companion Reader*, ed. John M. Meyer [Westport, Conn., 2002], 51–72; Daniel McCool, Susan M. Olson, and Jennifer L. Robinson, *Native Vote: American Indians, the Voting Rights Act, and the Right to Vote* [New York, 2007], 10, 138; McPherson, *Hand-Book of Politics for 1892*, 144; with additional assistance from Jill E. Martin, Quinnipiac University.)

15. A reference to the Ghost Dance and Sioux War. A curious silence pervades sources and histories of the South Dakota amendment campaign about tension building in the western part of the state between the Sioux and the federal government. In March 1890, emissaries to the West brought back word of a messianic movement that would restore land and traditions to Indians; while Republicans met in the eastern part of the state in August, Sioux in the western part began the Ghost Dance; by election day, an investigation of the likelihood of war with the Sioux was underway, at the direction of the Secretary of War. The Massacre at Wounded Knee followed at the end of December 1890. (Robert M. Utley, *The Last Days of the Sioux Nation* [New Haven, Conn., 1963], 1–112; Philip S. Hall, *To Have This Land: The Nature of Indian/White Relations, South Dakota, 1888–1891* [Vermillion, S.D., 1991].)

16. P. T. Barnum entered the circus business in 1870, using his own name for the show. By 1887, in recognition of a new business partnership, the show came to be known as the circus of both Barnum and Bailey.

125 ⇝ ECS to William T. Stead

Basingstoke [*England*]   Jan 18th 1891

Dear Mr Stead,

I have been a faithful reader of the Review of Reviews ever since the first number appeared & have always taken it for granted that you gave your readers a fair idea of the contents of the magazines & the real spirit of the writers. But your review of my article on "Patriotism & Chastity" in the Westminster Review somewhat shakes my faith.[1]

You not only fail to give the spirit of my article, but in the one solitary sentence you quote, you leave out the main point, the reason why we preferred a Parliament composed of men like Sir Charles Dilke to all the chaste angels in opposition, "because he always voted & spoke in of all the bills relating to the rights of women." As you state it the preference rests on his questionable social morality

As the ancient oracles were permitted to speak twice, why may not the most dis↑tinguished↓ editor in Great Britain also & do me the justice to say, that it is evidently not my purpose to defend immorality, but to show that by our laws customs & religion, men are educated to the virtue of patriotism but not to respect chastity as a manly virtue. If you will take the trouble to read my article you will see my purpose is to teach a higher standard of morality for all men & women. [*sideways in margin*] sincerely yours,

⇝ *Elizabeth Cady Stanton*

⇝ ALS, ECS Papers, DLC.

   1. *Review of Reviews* 3 (January 1891): 60. Stead described the point of her article to be "that there has never been any true standard of social morality, and that none exists to-day.... No one knows what is chastity or what is not." As ECS notes, he quoted only the ironic sentence about Charles Dilke, attributed by ECS to an unnamed leader in the suffrage movement.

126   William T. Stead to ECS

London, January 21st, 1891

My dear Mrs Stanton,

Pray forgive me if I have done you any injustice. I will certainly insert a paragraph in my next Number with your disclaimer.[1]

Believe me, it is always a grief to differ from you. There are so few people who think seriously of such matters. I am, Yours very truly,

  W T Stead

~ TLS, on letterhead of the *Review of Reviews*, ECS Papers, DLC.

1. Stead did not publish ECS's disclaimer.

127   Lucy Stone to SBA

Dorchester, Mass. Jan 30, 1891

Dear Susan Anthony

What a mercy it was that you fell into the shelter and care of the Garrisons when so serious an illness came upon you![1] A home is better than a hotel at any time, but in case of sickness a home is indispendable. Of course everybody was disappointed that you could not be at the meeting so that they might at least see you.

Now that you are convalescing, and we trust, on the high road to recovery, and the meetings are over, we want to arrange for an informal reception at our office, so that those, or some of those who were sorry not to see you at the meeting may have a chance to do so.

I was too tired to-day to go with my two, and maybe you would have been too tired to see us, if I had gone. It is not quite the same when we are 72 as it is when we are 27. Still I am glad of what is left, and wish we might both hold out till the victory we have sought for is won. But all the same the victory is coming. In the after time the world will be the better for it. Trusting you may soon be well again, I am your fellow-worker,

                                        Lucy Stone

~ Transcript in hand of I. P. Boyer, Blackwell Papers, DLC.

1. Due to illness, SBA and Mary Livermore both missed their advertised appearance on 28 January 1891 at the annual meeting of the Massachusetts Woman Suffrage Association. After making the trip to Boston, SBA spent a week confined to the house of William and Ellen Garrison under a doctor's care. It is doubtful that she accepted Stone's invitation: the Garrisons put her on a sleeping car to Washington on February 2, Jane Spofford met her train with a carriage and rushed her to the Riggs House, and SBA explained to Rachel Avery that until that trip, she had not left the Garrisons' house for an entire week. (*Boston Evening Transcript*, 29 January 1891; SBA to Francis J. Garrison, 3 February 1891, SBA to R. G. F. Avery, 4 February 1891, and SBA to Ellen W. Garrison, 9 February 1891, in *Film*, 28:958–66, 984–87.)

128 ~ ISABELLA BEECHER HOOKER TO SBA

                                     Hartford, Ct., February 11, 1891.

Dear Susan:

Yours concerning Mrs Stanton has been received. I agree with you perfectly. She was never doing better work than now, perhaps; her writings as vigorous as ever and more carefully prepared. We will keep her in office and I hope she will live this side the water and only visit the other. Sincerely,

                                   Isabella Beecher Hooker.

~ Typed transcript, ECS Papers, NjR.

129 ECS TO CLARA BEWICK COLBY AND SBA

[Basingstoke, England, before 21 February 1891][1]

Dear Mrs Colby,

I have sent two speeches to Susan, one from Hattie on "Voluntary Motherhood" which I think well written & one from me on "The Matriarchate" or Mother age.[2] I fear my beloved Susan will not appreciate either as the word "suffrage" does not come ↑in↓, but they are alike valuable documents. When you get them set up, I would like to have them both struck off in tract form & I will the extra cost.[3] They are for the council & might be printed before & then distributed. If Susan reads mine, she need not read all the printed pages, but I want all published, for I think the superior position women held so long is a great fact for us.[4] I have been reading the whole year to glean these facts "Morgan's Ancient system," "Wilkinsons ancient Egypt"[5] and Karl Pearson[6] & have still many notes to use in articles for Magazines Why would it not be a good idea to enlarge your paper for two weeks for the conventions & thus get your matter out before the Journal. I would like to have Hatties name, "Mrs Stanton Blatch" put in the programme. She suggests one new thought that man is <u>destitute</u> of the paternal instinct. I suppose many would carp at that. There are always exceptions to all general rules, hence there may be a man here & there who would sacrifice himself as a mother does for his children. I have never seen one, but I have heard of such beings. I hope you & Susan will get up some decent resolutions & not publish such trash as you did last year. With love

E. C. S.

[*on separate sheet for SBA*] Gens, Gentis, Gentes, all pertaining to a <u>clan</u>[7]

Phratry a subdivision of a tribe.

The state	The tribes
The counties	The Phratries
The township	The Gentes

I think these are all the words that may be new to you.

[*on verso of same sheet*] I will try & grind out some good resolutions but do not let it be known that they are mine

~ ALS, Clara B. Colby Papers, Archives Division, WHi.

1. Dated to precede the start of the National Council of Women in Washington on 21 February 1891, the occasion for the speeches sent by ECS.

2. For ECS's speech, see *Film*, 28:1041-42. For a discussion of Harriot Blatch's speech, see DuBois, *Harriot Stanton Blatch*, 66-67. The matriarchate, or mother-age, was an era of human history shaped by women's power in culture and religion, an era that received considerable attention from nineteenth-century historians of ancient societies. For students of the history of the sexes, the mother-age challenged modern claims about women's physical inferiority and natural subjection to men. In ECS's hands, it offered "a new sense of dignity and self respect" and enhanced the prospect that women would again wield power.

3. Colby obliged by publishing an unusually long, twelve-page issue of the *National Bulletin* 1 (February 1891), *Film*, 28:1048-53, to accommodate both speeches.

4. ECS's manuscript of "The Matriarchate" is lost. The text contains lengthy quotations from her sources, and she may mean by the directions to SBA that she had pasted those passages into her manuscript. SBA read only portions of the speech, since the audience could read it in its entirety when published. Harriot Blatch's speech was not read aloud at all.

5. Sir John Gardner Wilkinson (1797-1875), the leading Egyptologist in Britain, wrote a number of books none of which bears precisely the title ECS assigns. *The Manners and Customs of the Ancient Egyptians* (1837) and *A Popular Account of the Ancient Egyptians* (1853) were often reprinted and widely available.

6. Karl Pearson (1857-1936), mathematician, philosopher of science, and founder of London's Men and Women's Club, caught ECS's attention with essays on the history of sex, including the mother-age, in *The Ethic of Freethought: A Selection of Essays and Lectures* (1888). She announced her interest in "Karl Pearson on the Matriarchate," *Women's Penny Paper* 3 [8 November 1890]: 38, *Film*, 28:717. (Judith R. Walkowitz, *City of Dreadful Delight: Narratives of Sexual Danger in Late-Victorian London* [Chicago, 1992], 135-69.)

7. On the separate sheet directed to SBA, ECS listed some of Lewis Morgan's unfamiliar terms about kinship and social organization. Not all of them appear in the published text of her speech.

130   "The Degradation of Disfranchisement": Address by ECS to the National-American Woman Suffrage Association

EDITORIAL NOTE: SBA read ECS's presidential address at the opening session of the National-American's Washington convention in Albaugh's Opera House on 26 January 1891. She prefaced her reading, according to the *Evening Star*, "by saying that she joined with all the audience in wishing that they were looking on the features of that noble woman and upon the snowy fringe that surrounds her sweet face." The text published here is that printed in the *Woman's Tribune*, with minor corrections from ECS's manuscript. ECS republished this speech in 1901, in anticipation of compiling a book of her speeches. (*Film*, 29:3, 28–54; 41:1040–44.)

[26 February 1891]

The degradation of disfranchisement begins with the birth into the class or caste to which the individual belongs. In the case of sex there is ever a lower depth for the woman, to whatever class or nationality she may belong, as she is not only subject to the powers above her, but to the man at her side. The bias of sex is apparent at the very hour of birth. If "a fine boy," the fact is announced in a tone of triumph that takes a minor key if "a little girl," unless in a family where boys are already at a discount. This bias of sex runs all through childhood and girlhood, regulating dress, amusements, and education. Though equally endowed with two legs and arms, the same number of vital organs, and the same love of liberty in thought and action, the girl's training is one of constant repression, crippled with her dress, and endless homilies on modesty, and propriety, while to the boy is accorded unlimited freedom.

It is a pertinent question, "Why are boys always at a premium?" It is simply because in our present civilization they belong to the ruling class, destined to be the active leaders in political, religious, and social life: to fill and hold all the places of responsibility, honor, emolument, and power; because, through centuries of injustice, oppression, and violence, they chance to be the dominant sex just now, they are supposed to be naturally superior, forgetting the long periods when woman reigned supreme, the source and center of all the first steps in civilization.

Some tender-hearted gentlemen object to our calling ourselves a distinct class. Well, we object to the fact as much as they do to the name. Nevertheless, as we have a different civil and moral code for men and women, as men make and execute the laws, are absolute rulers in the state, claim to be the inspired writers of Scripture and the divinely anointed heads of the church, and assume the office of High Priest at every family altar, and women are mere subjects in all their relations, we surely must belong to different classes of humanity. To say we do not, that woman is as free as man, is as absurd as the plea of the lawyer when talking to his client through the iron-door of a prison. After hearing his case he said: "You can not be imprisoned, you have violated no law." "But," replied the client, "I am in prison." "You cannot be." "But I am; if I am not, then open the door." So, I say, if we belong to the same class, then open the door and give us the same freedom you enjoy.

What is disfranchisement in a republic? It is in effect passing a bill of attainder in direct violation of article 1, section 10, of the National Constitution against all American citizens included in its provisions.[1] It is establishing a privileged class, dividing the people into rulers and subjects; one division to make laws for the other, not such laws as they make for themselves; for the discrimination is always based on the assumption that the ostracized classes are of an inferior order; that they have not common feelings and interests with themselves; that they need the supervision and protection of the rulers, as children need the care of their parents. Though the strongest of all human affections bind parents to their children, yet we see the best interests of the latter constantly sacrificed to the caprice, the selfishness, the will of parents; just as the ostracized classes are invariably sacrificed to their rulers, because in both cases, those in power are guided by their own interests, and not the welfare of the governed. And this governing is always done under the good fatherly name of "protection"! Such as the common law of England gave to Saxon wives and mothers; such as the United States gave the African race; such as Great Britain gives Ireland; such as the Czar of Russia gives his subjects, on the frozen plains of Siberia, and such as the eagle gives the lamb he carries to his eyrie!

Disfranchisement is the last lingering shadow of the old spirit of caste that has always divided humanity into classes of greater or less inferiority, some below even certain animals that were considered special favorites with Heaven. One can not contemplate these revolting distinctions among mankind without amazement and disgust. This spirit of caste that has darkened the lives of millions through the centuries still lives, persecuting the Jews to-day in Russia and Germany; that forbade them not many years ago to walk on the sidewalks of Paris, compelled always to take the center of the street with the horses, and denied admission to certain hotels in the fashionable watering places of the American Republic.

The discriminations against color and sex, in the United States, are but other forms of this same hateful spirit of caste, still sustained by our religion as in the past. It is the outgrowth of the false ideas of favoritism, ascribed to Deity, in regard to races and individuals, but which have their origin in the mind of man. Banish the idea of divine authority for these machinations of the human mind, and the power of the throne and the church, of a royal family and an apostolic order of succession, of kings and queens, of popes and bishops, and man's headship in the state, the church, and the home will be heard of no more forever. When woman understands the origin of all these assumptions, neither the eloquence of the pulpit, nor the arguments of Senators in Washington, will reconcile her to the degradation of disfranchisement.

All men of intelligence appreciate the power of holding the ballot in their own hands; of having a voice in the laws under which they live; enjoying the liberty of self-government. Those who have known the satisfaction of wielding political influence would not willingly accept again the degradation of disfranchisement. Yet men can not understand why women should feel aggrieved in being deprived of this same protection, dignity, and power. This is the Gibraltar of our difficulties to-day. We can not make men see that women feel the humiliation of their petty distinctions of sex, precisely as the black man feels those of color. It is no palliation of our wrongs to say that we are not socially ostracized as he is, so long as we are politically ostracized as he is not. That all orders of foreigners rank politically above the most intelligent, highly-educated women—native-born Americans—is indeed the most bitter drop in the cup of our grief, that we are compelled to swallow.

All distinctions in society are depressing and aggravating to the classes ostracized. Take a man of superior endowments, once respected and influential, but who through a series of misfortunes has lost wealth and position. He now sees men inferior to himself in the places of trust and influence, making palace homes for themselves and children, driving fine equipages while his children walk in shabby attire, ostracized by the circle where, by family intelligence and refinement, they belong, making them to feel every day of their lives the impassable gulf between riches and poverty. This man feels for himself, and doubly for his children, the degradation of even such evanescent distinctions between man and man. That glorious Scotch poet, Robert Burns,[2] from the depths of his poverty and despair might say triumphantly in an inspired moment, "A man's a man for a' that," but the sad wail through so many of his lines shows that he had tasted the bitterness of want, and hated all distinctions based on wealth.

No one doubts that woman feels all this as well as man: the humiliations of poverty, the bitterness of neglect, the pangs of envy and jealousy of those who enjoy pleasures and luxuries she does not possess. And yet, with the ever-turning wheel of fortune, these distinctions are transient—yours to-day, mine to-morrow; the same sad experiences, sooner or later, may come to all.

But the hateful spirit of class makes insurmountable distinctions that no turning wheel of fortune can change. Take that noble man, Robert Purvis, with wealth, education, and spotless character such as few white men possess, with a family of cultivated sons and daughters, and because a few drops of colored blood were supposed to flow in his veins he was denied in the city of Philadelphia all social communion with the society in which by birth and education he belonged, for he was a Moor,[3] and never a slave. Still he was denied equal freedom as a citizen, though a property-owner and tax-payer; denied equal advantages for his wife and children in public amusements, churches, means of travel, and opportunities for education. Does anyone doubt that the wife and daughters felt as deeply as the husband and sons the degradation of distinctions on the ground of color and race?

While it is possible that woman may feel precisely as man does all the invidious distinctions in society, based on wealth, position, classes, races, how can any one doubt that she feels the deeper degradation of disfranchisement, based on sex? This is the most unreasonable ground of all others, because it is insurmountable, antagonizing one vital principle in nature with another, when both are equally necessary to the very existence of either. To exalt the masculine principle in humanity, at the expense of the feminine, two elements that to produce harmony in society must be exactly equal in power to attract and repel, is as futile as to attempt the subjugation of the negative to the positive electricity: the centrifugal to the centripetal forces in nature, which, if it were possible to do, we should be hurled into our original chaos. Can there be any misery more real than proscriptive distinctions between those who in nature are the peers of each other in race, genius, wealth, and position, antagonizing brothers and sisters, husbands and wives; making rivals of men and women, in art, science, and literature, the whole realm of thought: instead of being helpmeets and guides, a constant inspiration to each other? Here is the secret of the infinite sadness of women of genius; for just in proportion as they occupy an even platform with man, they are surprised and aggravated with his assumptions of superiority and the artificial framework in society that makes him so; an assumption woman in her inner nature never concedes; an authority she utterly repudiates.

Again, the degradation of woman in the world of work is another result of her disfranchisement. Some deny that, and say look at the laboring classes of men; they have the ballot, yet they are still helpless victims of capitalists. They have the power and hold the weapons of defense, but have not yet learned how to use them. The bayonet, the sword, the gun are of no value to the soldier until he knows how to use them. Yet without these weapons of defense what could individuals and nations do in time of war for their own protection? The first step in learning to use a gun or a ballot is to own one.

In all the struggles of the human race for liberty there has never been one more complicated than the present demand for equality by woman. It is the only reform in which the class to be elevated has fought the prolonged battle for themselves, the only reform in which no appeal to the narrow self-interest of the dominant powers can be made, because it is the selfish interest of all alike to hold woman in subordination. Whenever it has been the interest of the ruling classes to extend new rights to those below them the battles have been fought for them, and victory secured with no effort on their part. The Southern slaves were emancipated and enfranchised because it was the interest of a political party to do so. The extension of suffrage to English laborers was for the same reason.[4] A sense of justice may have moved some of the actors in these battles, but self-interest carried both measures. The liberal party alike in both countries needed the vote to manipulate at their pleasure, and political rights to the lower orders of men made no essential change in the social and religious conditions of the nation.

But political equality for woman compels an entire change in our whole system of government, religion, social customs and industrial life.

Our reform is not lifting up an inferior order, but recognizing the rights of equals. It is more like two contending royal families for the crown and scepter, the right by blood to rule and reign, compelling man at last to share his liberty and power with his equals in virtue and intelligence and the ability to govern themselves. But man has the prestige of centuries in his favor, the force to maintain it, and he has possession of the throne, which is nine-tenths of the law. He has statutes and Scriptures, and the universal usages of society all on his side. And what have we? The settled dissatisfaction of half the race, the unorganized protests of the few, and the open resistance of still fewer. But we have truth and justice on our side and the natural love of freedom, and, step by step, we shall undermine the present form of civilization and inaugurate the mightiest revolution the world has ever witnessed. But its far reaching consequences increase the obstacles in the way of success, for the selfish interests of all classes are against us. The rulers in the state are not willing to share their power with a class over whom as equals they could never obtain absolute control, whose votes they could not manipulate to maintain the present conditions of injustice and oppression in every department of life.

As in the family the mother desires to see her children equally provided with the good things of life, so as an equal factor in the state, her influence would be for an equal distribution among all, for a system of political economy that would prevent the extremes of poverty and wealth, and secure clothes, food, shelter, and education to the whole people. Such, I believe, would be the policy of educated, enlightened women. The socialistic and the woman's rights movements are but equal throbs of one great impulse—toward liberty for all.

Again, the rulers in the church are hostile to liberty for a sex supposed for wise purposes to have been subordinated to man by divine decree. The equality of woman as a factor in religious organizations would compel an entire change in church canons, discipline, and authority, and many doctrines of the Christian faith. As a matter of self-preservation, the church has no interest in the emancipation of woman, as its very existence depends on her blind faith. What would the tragedy in the Garden of Eden be to a generation of scientific women? Instead of patiently trying to fathom the supposed spiritual significance of the serpent as the representative of Satan, and all the tergiversations involved in his communications with Eve, hers with Adam, and his with the Lord, and the final catastrophe, turned into the great unexplored wilderness, naked and helpless, to meet the terrible emergencies of the situation; instead of pondering all this in sorrow for the downfall of the race, they would relegate the allegory to the same class of literature as Aesop's fables.[5]

Society at large, based on the principle that might makes right, has in a measure excluded women from the profitable industries of the world, and where she has gained a foothold her labor is at a discount. Man occupies the ground and holds the key to the situation. As employer, he plays off the cheap labor of a disfranchised class against the employee, and thus in a measure undermines his independence, making wife and sister in the world of work the rivals of husband and father.

The family, too, is based on the idea of woman's subordination, and man has no interest, as far as he sees, in emancipating her from that despotism, by which his narrow, selfish interests are maintained under the law and religion of the country.

Here, then, is a fourfold bondage, so many cords tightly twisted together, strong for one purpose. To attempt to undo one is to loosen all. Conservatives are invariably clear-sighted in maintaining existing conditions, and see farther as to the ultimate effect of one step than radicals themselves; at least if we can believe what the latter admit is all they do see. Conservatives on this question have always maintained that political freedom for woman was antagonistic to all existing institutions, and that to sever one strand in her fourfold bondage was to loosen all.

Hence, however stoutly the advocates of suffrage have maintained that political equality for woman would not affect religious faith nor family life, whenever the question comes up in the halls of legislative or ecclesiastical assemblies, the argument invariably drifts to the divinely-ordained head of the state, the church, and the home; and the Bible is brought into requisition to prove the intentions of the Creator as to the sovereignty of man. Thus, in spite of all the efforts of the most politic adherents to keep the question of suffrage distinct, the opposition would uniformly consider the question of woman's political equality from every standpoint.

To my mind, if we had bravely untwisted all the strands of the fourfold cord that bound us, and demanded equality in the whole round of the circle, we should, perhaps, have had a harder battle to fight, and it would have been more effective and far shorter. Let us henceforth meet conservatives on their own ground, and admit that suffrage for woman does mean political, religious, industrial, and social freedom—a new and a higher civilization. By making these demands for liberty in all directions we should quadruple the agitation, as well as the antagonism, and meet all our opponents at the same time and answer every argument. Our enemies could not then jump from one point to another, thinking we would not pursue them, for we should sweep the whole board, demanding equality everywhere, and the reconstruction of all institutions that do not in their present status admit of it.

Woman's happiness and development are of more importance even than all man's institutions. If constitutions and statute laws stand in the way of woman's emancipation, they must be amended to meet her wants and needs, of which she is a better judge than man can possibly be. If church canons and scriptures do not admit of woman's equal recognition in all the sacred offices, then they must be revised in harmony with that idea. If the present family life is necessarily based on man's headship, then we must build a new domestic altar, in which the mother shall have equal dignity, honor, and power; and we do not propose to wait another century to secure all this; the time has come. Women understand the situation, and are organizing as never before. They have memories of freedom in the past and dreams of its realization in the future. There is a deep, unsatisfied longing in the soul of woman for freedom, growing stronger day by day, that sooner or later will burst all bounds and carry every barrier before her. There are instincts alike in man and beast that imperatively demand complete satisfaction.

In the distant northern plains, a hundred miles from the sea, in the midst of a Laplanders' village, a young reindeer raises his broad muzzle to the north wind, sniffing for the first time the ocean breeze. He stands still and stares at the limitless distance while a man may count a hundred. He grows restless from that moment, but he is yet alone. The next day a dozen of the herd look up from the cropping of the moss, sniffing the breeze; then the whole herd of young deer stand and gaze northward, breathing hard through their wide nostrils, jostling each other and stamping on the soft ground. They grow unruly, it is hard to harness them in the light sledge, the camp grows daily more unquiet. Then the Laps nod to one another, they watch the deer more closely, well knowing, sooner or later, what will happen.[6]

At last, in the northern twilight, the herd begins to move. The impulse is simultaneous, irresistible. Their heads are all turned in one direction. They move slowly at first, biting still here and there at the bunches of rich moss. Presently the slow step becomes a trot, they crowd closely together, while the Laps hasten to gather up their cooking utensils, their wooden gods, all their last unpacked possessions. The great herd break together from a trot to a gallop, from a gallop to a breakneck race. The distant thunder of their united tread reaches the camp for a few minutes and they are gone to drink of the polar sea. Ever swifter and more terrible in their motion, the ruthless herd has raced onward, crowding the weaker to death, careless of the slain, careless of food, careless of any drink, but the sharp salt water ahead of them. And when at last the Laplanders reach the shore, their deer are once more quietly grazing, once more tame and docile, once more ready to draw the sledge whithersoever they are guided.

Once in his life the reindeer must taste of the sea, in one long, satisfying draught, and if he is hindered he perishes. Neither man nor beast dare stand between him and the ocean in the hundred miles of his arrow-like path.

What a picture of human life is this; how like the march and battle of the race in its struggles to satisfy the instincts for freedom; for something of this same longing comes to every human soul, to taste for once the sweet waters of liberty from its fathomless, inexhaustible sources.

~ *Woman's Tribune*, 7 March 1891, corrected from AMs, also in *Film*.

1. Enumerating limits on the actions of states, this section of the Constitution of the United States bars states from passing bills of attainder and ex post facto laws. Woman suffragists argued that their disfranchisement was equivalent to both, as they fell victim to punishment without a judicial proceeding and suffered penalties for acts once deemed lawful.

2. Robert Burns (1759-1796), Scottish poet. His song "A Man's a Man for a' that" was an anthem to brotherhood.

3. With reference to Robert Purvis, "Moor" was a precise term about the north African origin of his grandmother, kidnapped in her native Morocco and sold into slavery. She later married a German, and their daughter married an Englishman. Purvis described his grandmother as "a full-blooded Moor of magnificent features and great beauty." (*Friends' Intelligencer* 55 [23 April 1898]: 336.)

4. In Great Britain, where property traditionally defined political rights, the Reform Bill of 1867, or Second Reform Bill, extended suffrage to male householders, and the Reform Bill of 1884, or Third Reform Bill, extended it to male ratepayers.

5. *Aesop's Fables* were ancient Greek stories of unknown authorship but attributed to Aesop.

6. ECS found these paragraphs about reindeer in F. Marion Crawford, *A Cigarette-Maker's Romance* (1890), pages 138-40 in the edition of 1912. On 17 March 1891, she told Clara Colby that the passage should have been marked as quotation; she had copied them, she said, from one of Crawford's novels but could no longer remember which one. (*Film*, 29:86-91.)

131 ❧ ECS TO CLARA BEWICK COLBY

[Basingstoke, England, 28 February 1891]

How is it that not one word of the Conventions reach this side except a puff of Miss Belgarnie[1] & 16 lines of F. Williards opening speech condemning Parnell!![2] Were these items here in the hands of friends beforehand or did they cable them? There is some hocus pocus about it. Is it Miss W's policy to make them think this side that that great convention of women endorsed her silly view of that case? Is the Irish cause nearer her heart than Parnell's? You remember she presented a resolution at the International to make us all endorse her temperance policy which I defeated on the spot.[3] Susan did not see the drift of the [*sideways in margins*] resolution & let it pass. She needs watching   Miss W. is a politician

❧ AN on postal card, Clara B. Colby Papers, Archives Division, WHi. Postmarked at Basingstoke; addressed to 1406 G street N.W. Washington D.C.

1. Florence Balgarnie (1856-1928), an English suffragist and temperance leader, attended the National Council of Women as a delegate of the British

Women's Temperance Association and the National-American's convention bearing greetings from the Central National Society for Women's Suffrage, several branches of the Women's Franchise League, and the Women's Trade Union Association. The Central National Society, of which she was full-time secretary, tried to get even more groups to sponsor her trip and endorse a message of congratulations about woman suffrage in Wyoming. (*Oxford DNB*; Ms. Minutes, 12 November 1890, Central National Society for Women's Suffrage, Women's Library, London; *Woman's Herald* 3 [21 February 1891]: 281, *Film*, 29:26.)

2. At the opening session of the National Council of Women, Frances Willard heralded "Parnell's present discrowned estate" as a signal triumph for women. No longer could public men be evaluated as "two characters," public and private; "when Parnell, great hero that he is, ruins one woman and despoils one home, his features as a hero are so blurred and distorted in the eye of nations that he must step down and out." (*Transactions of the National Council of Women of the United States, Assembled in Washington, D.C., February 22 to 25, 1891*, ed. Rachel Foster Avery [Philadelphia, 1891], 37–38.)

3. See above at 27 March 1888.

132 ECS TO CLARA BEWICK COLBY

Basingstoke [*England*] March 6th [*1891*]¹

Dear Clara

Now that I have landed in England you can copy my Rems from vol III Hist Woman Suff.² I have just read that chapter through carefully & note the following blunders which please correct in your vol. & also for The Tribune.

Page 924 Corney <u>Grain</u>³

In the note at the bottom, <u>South</u> <u>Place</u> church⁴ & again Corney <u>Grain</u>

Page 927. <u>James</u>⁵ instead of Hawthorne

945 <u>Strathfieldsaye</u> the name of the Duke of Wellingtons place⁶

951. would separate us <u>perchance</u> forever, put perchance in the 13th line⁷

On 5th line Mrs S<u>a</u>ville in the note too. Add too that her husband is a Col. in the British army, stationed at Aldershot near London

You will see that I was the one who inaugurated the International

Council.⁸ I talked it up all the time I was in England. Miss Becker strenuously opposed it   I think this will ↑give↓ you enough material for three numbers. I suppose this will find you back in Nebraska, with your little Indian baby in arms.⁹ Write me when you have time of the true inwardness of the convention   the unwritten history always the most interesting. How did Mr Blackwell disport himself? I trust you have not made him President, in the mean time I will write the others. I suppose you will have enough convention matter to fill your paper for weeks to come. If we had thought in time it would have been as well to unite with the Americans in separate organizations in the Council, & kept our distinct associations   I am afraid we shall always have trouble with Blackwell, & Lucy. You see they make a point of contradicting what I say.¹⁰ Paulina Davis was the sole mover of that Worcester con. I saw Lucy's letter saying she could not be there & it was better not to hold a con & in curt words too. But when she saw it was to be a success she went. I was right about Train yet H. B. B. contradicted my statement. The first thing to get absolute controul is to kill me & then whoever else dares to differ. But we shall see in due time   I am afraid we made a mistake when we took them in as even partners. The autocratic way Blackwell began gave me misgivings at the start. Well you have survived another convention, be thankful for that. With love good night yours as ever

≈ *Elizabeth Cady Stanton*

≈ ALS, Clara B. Colby Collection, CSmH. In *Film*, in error, at 6 March 1890.

 1. Details within this letter support assignment of the year 1891.
 2. Landing in England refers to the narrative of her reminiscences. On 16 May 1891, the *Woman's Tribune* published her account of reaching England in 1882, in *Film*, 29:197–99. For this and the articles that appeared weekly through June 1891, ECS corrected the recollections she published in *History*, 3:922–53.
 3. Richard Corney Grain (1844–1895) was an English entertainer and songwriter. Colby's correction introduced a new error.
 4. ECS preached in London's South Place Church in 1882 as a substitute for her friend Moncure Conway; the church's name is correct in the *Tribune*.
 5. Henry James (1843–1916) was an American novelist living in England. Colby corrected the name in *Woman's Tribune*, 23 May 1891, *Film*, 29:205–6. ECS dropped the sentence in *Eighty Years*.

6. Colby retained the misspelling in *Woman's Tribune*, 20 June 1891, *Film*, 29:251–52, leaving ECS to fix it in *Eighty Years*, 370.

7. Colby may have mislaid these instructions by the time she prepared *Woman's Tribune*, 27 June 1891, *Film*, 29:257–58. Rather than adding "perchance," Colby dropped the word "forever," to make the sentence end "would separate us." ECS accepted this change in *Eighty Years*, 374. Sybilla Savile (whose name ECS was misspelling anew) caught ECS's attention for her refusal to wear a hat to church. She was the wife of a professor of tactics at the Royal Military College. Colby left her name uncorrected, and ECS fixed it in *Eighty Years*. (Census of Britain, 1881; research by Dr. A. R. Morton, Archivist, Sandhurst Collection.)

8. Her account of plans for an international organization is in *History*, 3:951–53. ECS's concern implies that someone else was laying claim to the idea, but her rival has not been identified. Someone rewrote the passage for *Woman's Tribune*, 27 June 1891, so that it no longer forecast planning an international meeting but read: "and while this project has not yet been carried out, yet in a line with this, and carrying out the idea of intellectual cooperation of women to secure equal rights and opportunities for their sex, was the International Council of Women, which was held under the auspices of the National Woman Suffrage Association in Washington, D.C., March 1888." The new ending also appears in *Eighty Years*, 375.

9. This was Zintkala Nuni, a Lakota infant found on the site of the Massacre at Wounded Knee. Leonard Colby, Clara's husband, bid for and won the baby, and in January 1891 applied to adopt her under Nebraska law. His trophy attracted considerable attention, but Clara Colby did not return to Beatrice to take up her duties as mother until May 1891. (Renée Sansom Flood, *Lost Bird of Wounded Knee: Spirit of the Lakota* [New York, 1995].)

10. When William Garrison concluded his reading of ECS's letter to the fortieth anniversary meeting, Lucy Stone took the floor to dispute ECS's account of events in 1850. "[I]t is a mistake to say that Paulina Wright Davis was almost single-handed and alone in undertaking the preparations for the convention. Mrs. Davis took a very active part in getting up the meeting. But the success of the convention was the result of the labor of a number of people, not of any one. The 268 names signed to the call show in themselves that there was much co-operation. Mrs. Stanton was not present at the convention, and she has made a mistake in this particular; but what a spirited letter it is that she has sent us!" At another point in the program, Stone remininisced at length about her part in preliminary discussions about calling the convention of 1850. (*Woman's Journal*, 31 January, 14 February 1891.)

This composite picture commemorated a speaking tour across the congressional districts of Kansas in 1887, organized by Laura Mitchell Johns (1849–1935), bottom left, president of the Kansas Equal Suffrage Association. Representing the National Woman Suffrage Association were Susan B. Anthony and, bottom right, Rachel G. Foster (1858–1919). At the behest of Lucy Stone, Anna Howard Shaw (1847–1919), top left, joined them. The picture is probably the work of the D. McLeod Studio in Atchison, where the group arrived on October 20; that McLeod took the picture of Anthony is certain.
(Department of Rare Books and Special Collections, University of Rochester Library.)

Family and friends posed at the side entrance to 17 Madison Street, Rochester, in August 1888, during one of Elizabeth Cady Stanton's rare visits to the home of Susan B. Anthony. Anthony's niece Louise Mosher James stands at the left; Adeline Thomson, an old friend from Philadelphia, stands on the porch; Stanton's daughter Margaret Stanton Lawrence stands on the right. The photographer is unidentified.
(Courtesy of Coline Jenkins/Elizabeth Cady Stanton Trust.)

Alice Mary Alt Pickler (1848–1932)
(Courtesy of the State Archives of the
South Dakota State Historical Society.)

Emma Smith DeVoe (1848–1927)
(Carrie Chapman Catt Albums,
Catt3.10.2e, Bryn Mawr College
Special Collections.)

Alonzo A. Wardall (1845–1918)
(From W. Scott Morgan, *History of
the Wheel and Alliance and the
Impending Revolution*, courtesy of
Wisconsin Historical Society,
WHi-59467.)

Local leaders in the South Dakota amendment campaign of 1890. Alonzo Wardall, vice president of the state's Farmers' Alliance, and Alice Pickler, wife of a Republican congressman, pleaded for national assistance in the work and helped design the political strategy. Emma DeVoe, a musician, impressed everyone with her skills as an organizer.

Carrie Clinton Lane Chapman Catt (1859–1947) acquired considerable power in the National-American Woman Suffrage Association between 1890 and 1895. When she won approval for an Organization Committee under her leadership in 1895, she controlled the association's plan of work and most of its budget. Photograph from the New York portrait studio of Theodore C. Marceau, 1896.
(Courtesy of Wisconsin Historical Society, WHi–37234.)

Laura Clay (1849–1941) of Kentucky was the voice of the South in the new National-American Woman Suffrage Association and a formidable opponent of taking up topics other than suffrage. Though never elected to high office in the association, she served on the business committee for many years.
(Carrie Chapman Catt Albums, Catt4.15.3e, Bryn Mawr College Special Collections.)

Harriet Taylor Upton (1853–1945) of Ohio and Washington was entrusted with congressional work as soon as she made up her mind to work for suffrage; she had learned the ways of Congress from her father, Congressman Ezra Taylor. She later served as treasurer of the National-American Woman Suffrage Association.
(Courtesy of the Department of Rare Books and Special Collections, University of Rochester Library.)

"Elizabeth C., Susan B. and the Rochester U." was drawn by an unknown cartoonist in 1891, after Rochester's Political Equality Club hosted a reception for Elizabeth Cady Stanton and invited trustees and faculty from the University of Rochester to hear her case for coeducation. The cartoonist placed trustee Edward M. Moore at the gate; President David Hill, embracing his twin daughter and son, in the center medallion; and Susan B. Anthony at the head of a procession of girls ready for college. The caption read,

SUSAN B.—"Me, Elizabeth and the rest of 'em want to come to school."
DOCTOR M.—"That is all right, Susan, but there is not money enough to accommodate both sexes and you know the 'bread winners' must have the preference."
BREAD WINNERS IN THE DISTANCE.—"Get the ball, Tom; get the ball if you have to break a leg."
(Utica *Saturday Globe*, 24 October 1891, Rochester edition, Susan B. Anthony scrapbook 17, Rare Books Division, Library of Congress.)

"Stay Out! Come In," drawn by Myron A. Waterman for the Populist Ottawa Journal and Triumph in June 1894, depicted the response of Kansas state political conventions to the request that a constitutional amendment for woman suffrage be endorsed by the parties. Republicans not only refused but also reversed the party's stand in 1892.
(Susan B. Anthony scrapbook 21, Rare Books Division, Library of Congress, courtesy of Lynn Sherr.)

Mary Seymour Howell (1844?–1913).
Photograph by Aaron Veeder, Albany, New York.
(Carrie Chapman Catt Albums, Catt5.3.2d,
Bryn Mawr College Special Collections.)

Jean Frances Brooks Greenleaf (1831–1918).
(Carrie Chapman Catt Albums, Catt2.7.2b,
Bryn Mawr College Special Collections.)

Upstate New York produced leaders for the suffrage movement for half a century. Mary Howell of Albany worked closely with state legislators on woman's rights bills. In addition to work for the state association, she toured as a lecturer for the National and National-American associations in Kansas and South Dakota. Jean Greenleaf of Rochester succeeded Lillie D. Blake as president of the state suffrage association and led the New York State amendment campaign of 1894. Harriet Mills of Syracuse emerged during the amendment campaign as a valuable new worker who served as recording secretary during the campaign.

Harriet May Mills (1857–1913).
(Carrie Chapman Catt Albums,
Catt2.5.1b, Bryn Mawr College
Special Collections.)

At the Metropolitan Opera House, with their backs to the auditorium and the boxes draped with banners of women's organizations, participants and guests at the Reunion of Pioneers and Friends of Woman's Progress, also known as Elizabeth Cady Stanton's eightieth birthday party, posed for an "instantaneous photograph" by John C. Hemment. Hemment had designed his own apparatus and lights to photograph difficult subjects, usually sporting events. He later applied his talent to documenting the war in Cuba. A few people can be identified. Over Stanton's right shoulder, in a dark gown, is Mary

Lowe Dickinson who presided over the celebration. To Dickinson's left is John Hutchinson, the last survivor of the Hutchinson Family Singers, and to his left is May Wright Sewall. Standing on the left side of the picture, in a black robe, is Anna Howard Shaw; next to her, in an evening cape, is the singer Madame Antoinette Stirling. Over Stirling's left shoulder is Theodore Stanton. Reporters noted that Lillie Blake sat to Stanton's left and Susan B. Anthony to her right.
(*Leslie's Illustrated Weekly*, 28 November 1895, from Elizabeth Cady Stanton Papers, Special Collections and University Archives, Rutgers University Libraries.)

Ida Bell Wells (1862–1931) spent a week in Rochester at the end of March 1895 to mobilize antilynching sentiment. She and Susan B. Anthony appeared together at meetings several times, and Wells spent some nights at the Anthony house. Wells remembered frank conversations about whether national organizations of white reformers could survive if they practiced and endorsed racial equality. The picture is said to date from 1893.
(Courtesy of Special Collections Research Center, University of Chicago Library.)

A STREET VIEW OF THE CHURCH.

An artist's view of the crowds gathered in the slushy streets outside Rochester's Central Presbyterian Church during the funeral of Frederick Douglass on 26 February 1895. When the Douglass family arrived by train from Washington with the body, they were greeted by city officials, a regimental band, the police drill corps, and thousands of citizens. A hearse brought the body to city hall, where it lay in state through the morning. Early in the afternoon, a procession regrouped to accompany the hearse to the church, and a final procession formed for the journey to Mt. Hope Cemetery.
(Rochester *Union and Advertiser*, 26 February 1895, Douglass Scrapbook, "Obituaries, accounts of his funeral and other material," Central Library of Rochester and Monroe County.)

133   SBA TO LUCRETIA LONGSHORE BLANKENBURG[1]

Riggs House, Washington, D.C., March 11, 1891

My Dear

Is it true that our old friend Anna Dickinson is an Insane Hospital?—[2] Is it true that her household goods are about to be struck off at auction—to pay her debts?— And if true—what do you see to be done?— I have always sort of looked to you to keep me posted about Anna— Frances Willard writes that she thinks the friends ought to raise a fund to help her—& that she has pledged $100— Now—if any such move is made—I think you or your mother should be the parties to whom the money should be sent— Some reliable friend—like you—should see to the <u>spending</u> of the money—as well as the collecting of it— So do tell me what you see that I ought or can do in the matter—of money—[3] I have little—so little—that this A.M. I am deep in sadness—over the many things I <u>would</u> do to help others—and can't!!— So tell me—what I can get others to help to do—& believe me   Lovingly yours

                      ⤳ Susan B. Anthony

⤳ ALS, on NAWSA letterhead, National Woman's Party Papers, DLC.

1. Lucretia Longshore Blankenburg (1845–1937), the daughter of Philadelphia's pioneer doctor Hannah E. Myers Longshore (1819–1901), was a prominent reformer who became president of the Pennsylvania suffrage association in 1892. Blankenburg had grown up with Anna Dickinson, while her mother and Lucretia Mott fostered Dickinson's early career, and Hannah Longshore still provided financial assistance to Dickinson. (*NAW*; *ANB*; SBA to Frances E. Willard, 7 April 1891, *Film*, 29:136–41.)

2. Anna Dickinson was committed to an insane asylum as a pauper in late February 1891, and within weeks of the sensational news, at least two groups began raising money for her care and general support. In Brooklyn, Laura Holloway Langford raised money to pay for Dickinson's transfer to private care and announced plans for a fund of twenty thousand dollars. Soon Frances Willard acted in her capacity as president of the National Council of Women to start another fund to be managed as a trust by a Philadelphia banking firm, with Lucretia Blankenburg as the trust's secretary. "As she was a speaker

opening the way into the realm of oratory for all women who had the power to follow," Willard asked, "would it not be fitting that every woman who speaks ... should make a contribution to this fund, and that so far as practicable those who receive payment for their work on the platform should give to this fund the proceeds of a single address?" (Giraud Chester, *Embattled Maiden: The Life of Anna Dickinson* [New York, 1951], 253-68; J. Matthew Gallman, *America's Joan of Arc: The Life of Anna Dickinson* [New York, 2006], 180-86; L. H. Langford to Editor, *New York Times*, 8 March 1891; *Brooklyn Daily Eagle*, 9 April 1891; *Union Signal*, 2 April 1891; SBA to F. E. Willard, 7 April 1891.)

3. On SBA's solicitations in Washington for money for Dickinson's care, see SBA to Harriet T. Upton, 4 April 1891; SBA to L. L. Blankenburg, 5 April 1891; and SBA to F. E. Willard, 7 April 1891; all in *Film*, 29:117-20, 132-41.)

134 ~ ARTICLE BY ECS

[28 March 1891]

THE LORD CHANCELLOR.

The recent decision of the Lord Chancellor in the Jackson case, affecting as it does half the people in the British dominions, is the most important legal decision of the century.[1]

Over a hundred years ago Lord Chief Justice Mansfield gave his famous decision in the Somerset case, "That no slave could breathe on British soil," and the slave walked out of court a free man.[2]

The petty statutes that had so long held his race in bondage, with that one breath of justice, were abolished for ever in Great Britain, and the war of freedom, inaugurated by that decision, against the theory that one man could hold property in another, had since been steadily carried on in every latitude and longitude of the globe. Thus like the sunlight does the influence of a great principle pervade the darkest corners of the earth.

Like the great Chief Justice of the last century, the present Lord Chancellor, with a clearer vision than those about him, rises into a purer atmosphere of thought, and vindicates the principles of eternal justice and the dignity of British law by declaring all these old statutes obsolete, that make wives the bond slaves of their husbands.

In regard to the law so frequently cited, giving husbands the right to seize, imprison, and chastise their wives, he says:—

"I am of opinion that no such rights exist in law. I am personally of opinion that no such rights ever did exist in law. I am prepared to say that no English subject has a right to imprison another English subject, whether his wife or not, provided she was *sui juris*, and of responsible age." With this decision the wife walked out of the court a free woman. Thus verifying the declaration of one of America's great senators, Charles Sumner; that "all interpretations of statutes and constitutions in favour of liberty must in the broadest sense be just and legal."[3]

The passage of the Married Woman's Property Bill in 1882 was the first blow at the old idea of coverture, securing to wives their rights of property, the full benefits of which they are yet to realise, when more liberal and clearer minded men administer the laws.

The decision of the Lord Chancellor, March 18th, 1891, declaring the personal rights of married women, is still a more important blow, by just so much as the rights of person are more sacred than the rights of property.

And now if Mr. Gladstone, as the leader of the Liberal party, could see the dignity and magnitude of woman's demand for political equality, and in one of his inspired moments declare "that no British subject can be governed by laws and rulers in which she has no voice," he would strike the third and final blow against all forms of human slavery, giving to the most unfortunate and helpless of British subjects an equal share in the blessings of liberty.[4]

To every man once the opportunity is given to make himself immortal, and if Mr. Gladstone refuses to advocate the most vital question of his day, some other more eloquent voice will be heard in Parliament in the near future, demanding justice, liberty, and equality for the mothers of Great Britain.

Woman's Herald 3 (28 March 1891): 358.

1. In this case, Edmund Jackson held his wife, Emily, captive in his house because she would not return to him as wife of her own free will. After a divisional court of the Queen's Bench refused a writ of habeas corpus sought by relatives of Emily Jackson, they appealed the decision. The writ was granted, Emily Jackson was freed, and the court rejected the claim that any husband could imprison his wife for the purpose of restoring his conjugal

rights. Hardinge Stanley Giffard, Baron Halsbury (1823-1921), later 1st earl of Halsbury, was Lord Chancellor. ECS quotes from the opinion below. (Regina v. Jackson [1891] 1 Queen's Bench 671 [19 March 1891], in Court of Appeal; Shanley, *Feminism, Marriage, and the Law*, 177-83.)

2. In 1772, chief justice of the Court of King's Bench, William Murray, earl of Mansfield (1705-1798), freed the slave James Somersett, who was brought to England from Virginia, ruling that in the absence of positive law creating slavery, slaves could not lawfully be kept in England.

3. Charles Sumner (1811-1874), former senator from Massachusetts, was an eloquent advocate of equal civil and political rights for African-American men. Despite his refusal to take up the cause of women, his constitutional arguments provided woman suffragists with apt quotations. ECS paraphrases remarks he made in the Senate on 2 December 1873, urging immediate action on the supplementary Civil Rights Bill. In the wake of Reconstruction, he asserted, "a new interpretation is fixed upon the National Constitution, so that hereafter all its sentences, all its phrases, all its words, shall be interpreted broadly and emphatically for Human Rights." (*ANB*; Sumner, *Works*, 15:289.)

4. When ECS submitted nearly the same article to the *Woman's Tribune*, she lengthened this paragraph to say: "Could he follow the lead of the Lord Chancellor, and in considerating universal principles of justice forget the petty questions and successes of party politics, he would add new glory to the sunset of his life and shed a radiance over his political career such as no other act can give for the emancipation of women is the greatest question of human rights now demanding the attention of English statesmen." (18 April 1891, *Film*, 29:179.)

135   SBA TO OLIVIA BIGELOW HALL

Rochester N.Y. May 7, 1891

My Dear Mrs Hall

Your good letter is here— I reached home last Saturday night—[1] Am glad to be here—& glad to hear that you are well & that the dear Mary[2] is well again— Oh the many ills that human beings are heir to! Well it is to those who persevere & overcome them one & all that the crown comes to— Yes—I received that letter you speak of—and thought I answered it at the time—but alas I fail to be even decent as to the common courtesies so much of the time—

I am going to the <u>Ohio</u> W.S.A. Annual Convention at Warren—next week[3]—am to be the guest of Mrs Harriet Taylor Upton—at her father's house—the Hon—Ezra B. Taylor—who represents the Garfield, Wade & Giddings District[4]—then I return home for a week & them go to the May Anniversaries in Boston—the 25, 26, 27th of May—and them home for the summer

My Sister is making sundry improvements to the old homestead and I am to be the <u>housekeeper</u>—run the house—this year—& see if I can't do it O.K.!! Of course everybody <u>laughs</u>—but I'll show them! And I want, the first thing, a real <u>New</u> <u>York</u> <u>State</u> <u>woman</u> for the head of the kitchen—one who will keep the house from top to bottom—just as a first class woman would ↑if it were↓ her own! Is there such a woman to be had? My Sister says—"<u>No</u>"! but I believe "yes"!! It will be the simplest kind of housekeeping—for we have but very little furniture of any sort—my sister having sold & given away all but the few things she needed to furnish the upper floor of the house— She has rented the first floor for 6 or 8 years—and taken her meals out— And now, S. B. A. has moved into the <u>lower</u> <u>floor</u>—& has her nice bay-window bedroom up stairs—but we are to take lots of comfort—in having our friends come over to see us & sit at <u>our</u> <u>own</u> table <u>once</u> more—

How I wish I could meet you at Warren! Why not slip down & attend your own old state of Ohio Con. once more—with love to the daughters & the sons—& the Grand children[5]—I am—as ever—affectionately yours—

≈ *Susan B. Anthony*

≈ ALS, on NAWSA letterhead with address struck out, Olivia Bigelow Hall Papers, DLC.

1. From a month in Washington.

2. Mary Bigelow Hall DuBois (1846–?), the oldest of Olivia Hall's children, married Crines Hardenburgh DuBois in 1873. In the early years of their marriage, the couple lived in Grand Haven, Michigan, where Crines DuBois owned the *Daily Herald*. By 1880, they had moved to Minneapolis, where DuBois published and edited the *Saturday Evening Spectator*. (Bigelow, *Bigelow Family Genealogy*, 2:353; Wallace K. Ewing, *A Directory of People in Northwest Ottawa County*, 8th ed., electronic [Grand Haven, Mich., 2005], on-line Louthit District Library, Grand Haven, p. 389; *Cornell Alumni News* 27 [22 January 1925]: 214.)

3. On this meeting of the Ohio Woman Suffrage Association at Warren from 12 to 14 May 1891, see *Woman's Journal*, 6 June 1891.

4. Joshua Reed Giddings (1795–1864) won election to Congress as an anti-slavery Whig from Ashtabula County, Ohio, in 1838 and served until 1859.

Benjamin Franklin Wade (1800–1878), from the same county, entered the Senate in 1851 and served until 1869. James Abram Garfield (1831–1881) served in Congress from 1863 to 1880, when he was elected twentieth president of the United States. He lived in Hiram County. (*BDAC*.)

5. Olivia Hall was the mother of six children, and at the time of her husband's death in 1889, there were eight grandchildren. (Obituary for Israel Hall, unidentified and undated clipping, SBA scrapbook 14, Rare Books, DLC.)

136 ❧ SBA TO MARY POST HALLOWELL AND SARAH KIRBY WILLIS

Meriden Ct—May 21, 1891[1]

My Dear Friends Mary & Sarah

I reached ↑here↓ all safe & sound—but have kept up a thinking about Sister Mary & the house— She is bound not to get a <u>new</u> carpet for her up-stairs front room—and I want her to have a nice, light, bright, new carpet on her floor—so that her room will look as nice as mine— I can't bear to have her put down that old faded, worn, dull carpet again—

Now—wont you advise her to get a new one— She will need her old one to put on the back hall & the back bedrooms— She thinks she can patch up some old rags for them—but she can't—and I don't want her to drudge over patching them even if she could do it—

I have written her that I shall get a new <u>cheap</u> but pretty rug for the dining room floor—& ditto for the parlor floors—then for bay-window bedroom up stairs—I have the beautiful brussls rug of Julia Fosters—that Rachel gave me— So do go over & see her & how she gets on—and if possible help her to feel that she must get a new carpet for her room—I don't care how cheap a carpet—so it is bright & cheerful in it's look—I am awfully sorry to have to be away these two weeks— I did so want to be there to help her settle things—but I have told her & have written the same to night—that I want the <u>grained</u> <u>floors</u> to be kept the whole two weeks without a <u>mar</u> from anything on them—[2] If the paint & varnish can be left to get perfectly solid before a <u>foot</u> or a chair print is made on them—they'll be very nice—that is if the graining is well done!!

And I begged her—too—to persevere & have the kitchen woodwork grained again—that light yellow paint will soil as easily as white—almost—everything else is very nice— But don't tell her I urged you to coax her— She is awfully tired out with the job—and I should be too—if I had been it two months—

Well it is good to think of you at home—even if I cant be there to see you!! Lovingly yours

~ *Susan B. Anthony*

~ ALS, on letterhead of Winthrop Hotel, Mss. Collection, NRU. Envelope addressed "Mary H Hallowell 97 Plymouth Ave Rochester."

1. The Meriden Suffrage Club invited SBA to lecture at its second anniversary meeting on 22 May 1891, where she was joined by Isabella Hooker. (*Woman's Tribune*, 6 June 1891.)

2. Graining is the technique of giving painted wood the look of wood grain by applying darker paint and combing it.

137 ~ ROSALIND STANLEY HOWARD, COUNTESS OF CARLISLE[1] TO ECS

Naworth Castle, Carlisle. [*England*] May 24, 1891.

Dear Mrs Cady Stanton:

You honoured me some time ago by sending me some papers and by inviting me to see you. I should very greatly value the privilege of making your acquaintance and of hearing you talk, but it was not possible for me until now to cherish any hope of accepting your kind invitation. I am, however, going to London by to-night's train, to my London home, 1, Palace Green, Kensington, and if you would allow me to come down on Saturday, May 30, to Basingstoke, for the inside of the day, I should greatly enjoy doing so. I cannot sleep at Basingstoke, though you welcome me so kindly, because I can only take a week away from here altogether. But much can be learnt and much inspiration received in a few hours; therefore I shall gladly undertake the journey to you, just for that length of time. If I find you have already returned to America, I shall be greatly disappointed. Yours most respectfully and sincerely,

~ *Rosalind Carlisle.*

~ Typed transcript, ECS Papers, NjR.

1. Rosalind Frances Stanley Howard, countess of Carlisle (1845–1921) served at this time on the executive committee of the Women's Liberal Federation. There, allied with Eva McLaren, Jane Cobden, and others, she criticized the federation's reluctance to endorse woman suffrage and pressed for change. A year later, in May 1892, she won her point; Catherine Gladstone stepped down as the group's president, and many local groups as well as national leaders left the federation to establish a new auxiliary to the Liberal party. Lady Carlisle became president of the federation in 1893. She wrote to ECS from Naworth Castle near Carlisle, one of the properties of her husband's family. ECS left no record to indicate whether the visit proposed in this letter occurred, but in July 1891, ECS spent a week as a guest at Castle Howard, another family property. (*Oxford DNB*; Charles H. Roberts, *The Radical Countess: The History of the Life of Rosalind, Countess of Carlisle* [Carlisle, U.K., 1962], 114–18; Walker, "Party Political Women," 186–89; R. S. Howard to ECS, 8 and 10 June 1891, *Film*, 29:234, 239; ECS diary, 29–31 July 1891, *Stanton*, 2:275–78; *Eighty Years*, 429–30.)

138 ❧ SPEECH BY SBA TO THE NEW ENGLAND WOMAN SUFFRAGE FESTIVAL

EDITORIAL NOTE: Nine hundred people sat down to dinner at the New England Woman Suffrage Association's festival in Boston's Music Hall. An orchestra of female musicians entertained the guests until John D. Long, Lucy Stone, and SBA launched the program of some dozen speeches.

[27 May 1891]

Gov. Long[1]—The next subject is one with which none of us, I am sure, are personally familiar. It is "Pecuniary Independence." It may have some bearing upon the case which Mrs. Stone has related.[2] I have great pleasure in introducing to you, to speak upon that subject, a lady who is known throughout the length and breadth of this land, whose voice never wearies. Speaking of John G. Whittier,[3] somebody said, "The name of John G. is very familiar, but I think I never heard of Whittier before." Looking at this name, the name of Susan B. is exceedingly familiar, but has anyone ever heard of Anthony? (Laughter and applause.) I take great pleasure in presenting to you Miss Susan B. Anthony—not much accustomed to public speaking. (Laughter.)

Address of Miss Anthony.

Miss Anthony, who was repeatedly applauded, said:

Mr. President and Friends: A good deal accustomed, however, to opening the way for other people to speak. I should be more at home sitting in Gov. Long's chair telling the rest when to speak, than standing up and obeying his orders. I like the other place best.

A certain class of people are always telling you what happened when they were young. A certain other class are always telling what happened before they were married. So I am going to tell you something that happened—you can guess when. On a certain occasion I was a school teacher in the State of New York, the Empire State, and at the close of a few years' teaching, I was present at the New York State Teachers' Convention.[4] The audience contained at least a thousand women and about two hundred men. It was composed of the teachers of the State of New York. At that time no woman among them had ever dreamed of speaking in their conventions. They had a committee on resolutions, and that committee brought in a series as long as committees usually do, and among the resolutions was one declaring that teachers were not respected as were ministers, lawyers, and doctors. And one man made an address and demonstrated that the teacher did more and better for the world than did the lawyer. Another man showed of how much more value the teacher was to society than was the doctor; and yet another declared that the teacher did more to mould the morals of the world than the minister. And yet, said these men, while the minister and the lawyer and the doctor are all respected, and go into the best society, and sometimes are nominated and elected to high office, the teacher is spoken of slightingly, and often called a "Miss Nancy," or an "old grandmother." For an hour or two they discussed this question, and finally, sitting in the rear of the hall, I rose and said: "Mr. Chairman." The president was Prof. Davies of West Point notoriety, the author of Davies' Algebra and Arithmetic. Some of the old gray heads here, men and women, can remember when they studied that wonderful author, and puzzled their brains over his books. He was of magnificent proportions, always wearing the Websterian blue coat,[5] brass buttons and buff vest. He inserted his thumbs in his vest and said: "What will the lady have?" The idea had never entered his brain, or probably any other man's brain among them, that a woman could rise in a convention and address the Chair for the purpose of speaking. I said: "Mr. President and gentlemen, I would like to say a word upon the resolution under discussion." Then the president said: "What is the pleasure of the convention?" And he looked at the little handful of men on the platform and the few who sat in the front seats of the hall. And for thirty minutes I stood on my feet, bound to keep the floor, while those men argued the question whether a woman, a stranger to most of them—some of them had heard that she was a teacher—might speak in a teachers' convention. At length, by a very small majority, it was decided that she might speak.

If any of you ever tried to speak under such circumstances, you may possibly imagine how high in my throat my heart had risen. Nevertheless, I managed to say: "Mr. President and gentlemen, I have been greatly interested in your discussion, but it seems to me none of you quite comprehend the cause of the disrespect of which you complain. Do you not see that while society says a woman has not brains enough to be either a minister, a lawyer or a doctor, but has ample brains to be a teacher, every man of you who condescends to teach school tacitly acknowledges before all Israel and the sun that he has no more brains than a woman?" (Laughter and applause.) And I sat down. The next morning's newspaper said that no matter how angry Miss Anthony made the school-masters, it was evident that she had hit the nail on the head.

When Pres. Davies called the meeting to order next morning, he said: "I have been asked why women are not invited to speak in these conventions, why women are not appointed on committees to prepare reports to present here." And he stretched himself back, and said: "Look at this beautiful hall; these noble columns; look at the beautiful entablature; the symmetry of the shaft; the strength of the pedestal! Could I be instrumental in dragging from its proud elevation the beautiful entablature and trailing it in the dust and dirt that surround the pedestal?" To Prof. Davies, for a woman to prepare an essay or a report upon her experience as a teacher or upon the best methods of teaching,—for a woman to express an opinion in a public audience,—was to drag her down into the filth and dirt. Exactly what some people feel today, if women should go to the ballot-box and vote. Only I do not believe there is a person left today who feels that as great a degradation, as great a mischief would come to women from voting and from sitting upon the floors of the legislative halls of this country, as Prof. Davies and many of those men, so many years ago (for it was in 1853), felt would come to women if they should speak in public. A great change has come over the dream of the world since that time.

I have not touched, Mr. President, the subject that I was to speak upon, but I never did speak upon any subject, and therefore I didn't want to disappoint anybody. I was present at the first press club dinner in New York City, in 1869, at which women were present, a dinner at Delmonico's.[6] Mr. Simonton, the president of the Associated Press at that time, was master of ceremonies, and without the slightest notice to me that I was to say anything, he said: "Miss Anthony will respond to the toast, 'Why don't the women propose?'" And I said, "Simply because they are paupers; and so long as they are paupers, if a woman should ask a man to marry her, it would be virtually asking him to please to be so kind as henceforth to support her. It was not a delicate thing to do. But," I said, "grant the demand of the woman suffrage movement, that women shall have equal chances in the world of work, in the professions, that they shall not only be able to earn a subsistence but to get a competence and wealth,—then they will buy their own four-story brown stone fronts, and if they see a man that they think would contribute to the happiness of that home, they will not have the slightest delicacy about inviting him to come in." (Laughter.)

So there were two speeches of mine in the history of the ages, and I don't know whether I shall ever tell any better stories or feel any differently on this question.

Now, friends, I want to say one word with regard to politics. The mischief among our woman suffrage women today is that the moment a little handful of men in some obscure part of the country, in some particular State or in the nation, assemble themselves together and call themselves a political party, and put a woman suffrage plank in their platform, our women run off and help that party, and call it a third party; a little handful of men that were never heard of anywhere else. I want to warn our women against all such movements. There has never been a political party that has cared anything for women except in so far as women would help that party. Go back to the old Liberty party.[7] Go back to the Republican party in its organization. Women can never demonstrate their capacity to help men politically more than the women did in the old Liberty party, more than the women did in the formation of the Republican party, from the early days down to the present. Now we are told that a new party is forming, and that if the women will only go in and work side by side with the men in the organization of that party, they will take steps to enfranchise the women. Now, women, do not believe a word of it. If a body of men assemble, calling themselves a political party, and wishing to become a political party, if they have not the manhood, the love of justice, to declare openly and above board at their very first meeting that their first and primal plank means the enfranchisement of women, they will never do it under the sun. They are not going to have any "isms," never. And justice to women is an "ism" which they will not carry through. So it was in Cincinnati.[8] So it was in South Dakota. So it is everywhere where men come together to form a political party. They always leave the women out. So I warn you, better have nothing to do with any political party. Instead, just look for the man who declares for suffrage, and tell everybody, no matter what party he belongs to, to vote for that man and send him to the front. (Applause.)

~ *Woman's Journal*, 6 June 1891.

1. John Davis Long (1838–1915) served as governor of Massachusetts from 1880 to 1883 and Republican member of Congress from 1883 to 1889. He had endorsed woman suffrage while governor, cooperated with the state's suffrage societies while in the House of Representatives, and ignored the movement's divisions by hosting delegates to the National Woman Suffrage Association's Boston meeting at the State House in 1881. (*ANB*; *BDAC*; *Film*, 21:1046–48.)

2. Lucy Stone recounted what she called a secret and a fact. She exposed the secret that antisuffragists were soliciting donations for a fund to expand their work; someone had taken offense at the solicitation and contacted Stone. This she followed with a story of injustice caused by a wife's inability to make a will without her husband's consent. Her pitch for the festival to raise money for woman's rights concluded her remarks.

3. John Greenleaf Whittier (1807–1892), the poet and abolitionist, who lived in Massachusetts.

4. SBA repeated an anecdote she told at the festival on 30 May 1888, above.

5. The blue coat with brass buttons associated with the great American lawyer Daniel Webster.

6. At Delmonico's on 20 March 1869, the New York Press Club invited

women of the press to a dinner at which, as the *New York Tribune* reported, "the ordinary distinctions of sex were ignored." Women paid their own way and joined in the after-dinner speeches. James William Simonton (1823-1882), a journalist and agent of the Associated Press from 1867 to 1881, presided over the event. The *Tribune* thought SBA responded to the toast, "Why Should Women Propose?" but SBA reported in the *Revolution* that it was, "Why Don't the Men Propose?" (*Film*, 1:511, 13:425-28; *Papers*, 2:231-34.)

7. The Liberty party, organized in 1839, was the first attempt of antislavery men to test their strength in electoral politics. It nominated candidates for president in 1840 and 1844.

8. The National Union Convention, meeting at Cincinnati on 19 and 20 May 1891, resolved to form the People's party and adopted principles around which delegates from the Farmers' Alliance and Knights of Labor could rally. They agreed "That the question of universal suffrage be recommended to the favorable consideration of the various states and territories." Although this encouraged some suffragists, the convention's refusal to endorse prohibition damaged the hopes of Frances Willard, Helen Gougar, and others that the new coalition would cooperate with the Prohibition party. (Larry G. Osnes, "The Birth of a Party: The Cincinnati Populist Convention of 1891," *Great Plains Journal* 10 [Fall 1970]: 11-24; Jack S. Blocker, Jr., "The Politics of Reform: Populists, Prohibition, and Woman Suffrage, 1891-1892," *The Historian* 34 [August 1972]: 614-32.)

139 ❧ ECS TO SBA

[*Basingstoke, England, June? 1891*]¹

I rejoice that you are going to housekeeping. The mistake of my life was selling Tenafly. My advice to you, Susan, is to keep some spot you can call your own; where you can live and die in peace and be cremated in your own oven if you desire.

❧ *Anthony*, 2:707.

1. SBA's biographer, Ida Harper, placed this fragment amid events of June 1891 but indicated no date.

140   SBA TO J. MERRITT ANTHONY[1]

Rochester N.Y. July 8/91

My Dear Brother Merritt

During my visit in Keene Valley Essex Co. N.Y.—Mrs Banker[2]—my hostess—took me over to the old Adirondack home of Capt. John Brown—[3] And there we—Mr & Mrs Banker, Anna Shaw & myself— dined in the same old room Capt & Mrs Brown & all their children & friends used to take meals in—it is a good old farm house—with piazza on front & one side— In front is a small yard fenced off—which contains the Graves of old John Brown & his son ~~Owen~~ ↑Watson↓[4]— the head stone is of Granite—& ~~he~~ is the same one put at the head of his Grandfather—in 1777—& on it are cut the names & dates of ~~of~~ Capt John—his father John Brown & his Grandfather John Brown—three generations of John Browns— Covering more than one half [of?] the lot stands a great boulder with steps leading to the top of it—where is cut in large letters—John Brown—Dec. 2, 1859— It is a lovely plateau of pretty level land of 200 acres—surounded on all sides by the Adirondack Mountains— It shows that old John Brown had good taste as to a beautiful location for his home— Of all the Negroes who settled up there on the Gerrit Smith Lands—to entitle them to vote under the old property qualification law of New York—only one survives—he is aged & white haired—they say—but we didn't meet him—I am sorry to say—[5] In the little sketch—mention is made of Osawatomie— I thought of you all the day & wished you were there to tell of the olden days—& to enjoy the beaties of the spot on that loveliest of June days— I send you the book & the dried rose in memory of the day so rich to me—

I have just received three Semi Annual dividends of my $500— Old National Bank of Fort Wayne Ind—$75— That makes me 10 per cent on the $500— but, it is worth $1.35 = $675. x 8 = 54. annual ↑interest↓— So—if I was to sell the stock at the 1.35— and put the amount ~~at~~ ↑in an↓ 8 per cent bond & mortgage—I should get only $4. per year more— So I think I will not sell it—as I had thought to do—[6]

Now—what amount have you of mine—all together?— I would love dearly <u>not</u> to draw the interest—but with my house keeping expenses I shall be obliged to do so—hence—whenever interest money comes in— you may send it to me from time to time— I didn't draw <u>all</u> of my interest last ↑year did I?↓ And I <u>hope</u> I shant have to this year—but <u>expect</u> I shall—though if the friends continue thinking of my house keeping undertaking with checks to match—as they have done so far I may not be compelled to do so—

Lucy E. and Miss Thomson are coming the 15th inst & Miss Shaw the 20th the latter will be here off & on—as she has days between her lectures all the month—following—and I hope Lucy will stay a month surely & as much longer as she can plan her work to be here— She is looking better & weighing more than ever before— Now cant you & Mary come down & visit us—visit <u>Sister</u> <s>sister</s> <u>Susan</u> in her <u>first</u> <u>at-</u><u>tempt</u> at <u>running</u> a house all by her very self alone!! I do hope you can all come— Brother Dan. writes that they will help ↑keep↓ the house along by visiting us—but Sister Annie says not until September— I do not expect Mrs Stanton until last of August—& may be later—

Well—I feel that I am going to take lots of comfort being in my own house and entertaining my friends at <u>my</u> <u>very</u> <u>own</u> table— Of course Sister Mary laughs and doesn't believe I shall succeed—but at least she seems happy to let me prove that I <u>cant do it</u>—and that is a good deal— I haven't my splendid woman yet—but am expecting shell appear— everyday now— Mean time—Sister ↑Mary↓ provides & cooks & serves the meals in the kitchen—they are very, very simple—but splendid— and I enjoy them hugely—and if it weren't for entertaining our friends— I might continue—thus—but to see my friends & have them in my own house & at my own table is a pleasure I covet—& cannot forego— So I shall have a good housekeeper & hope to see all—& be ready to make them comfortable

⇜ AL incomplete, SBA Papers, DLC. Square brackets surround word torn from a corner.

1. Jacob Merritt Anthony (1834–1900), the youngest of SBA's siblings and known always as Merritt, lived in Fort Scott, Kansas, where he moved in 1869. He and his wife, Mary Almina Luther Anthony (1839–?), were the parents of Lucy E. Anthony. Like his older brother, he joined the antislavery migration to Kansas in 1856. By settling first in Osawatomie, he placed himself at a center of guerrilla warfare between abolitionists and proslavery raiders. The town was sacked by Border Ruffians in June 1856. John Brown and his sons were in

southeast Kansas to encourage armed resistance, and Anthony encountered them on several occasions during the summer. According to Anthony, he and Brown were together on the night of 29 August 1856 but fought separately on August 30 in the battle of Osawatomie. Anthony contributed to the legends about this event in an article for the *Leavenworth Times*, 14 February 1884. (Anthony, *Anthony Genealogy*, 173, 189; Andreas, *History of Kansas*, 2:1076; *Woman's Journal*, 23 June 1900.)

2. Henrietta M. Hull Banker (c 1830–1899), a New Englander who lived in the Boston vicinity until at least 1870, had been active in the Brooklyn suffrage association, the only beachhead held by the American Woman Suffrage Association in New York State. After the National-American association required Brooklyn suffragists to affiliate through the state society, Banker was elected state treasurer in 1890. She and her husband, George W. Banker (c. 1824–1899), were members of John White Chadwick's Unitarian church in the city and were very active in social services for working families and the poor and in establishing kindergartens. They were both patrons of the National Council of Women. Although the Bankers retained connections to Brooklyn after 1890 and returned often, most years they lived year-round in the Adirondacks at Ausable Forks, New York. The Bankers died within a few weeks of each in 1899. (Federal Census, Brooklyn, 1880; Minutes of annual meeting, New York State Woman Suffrage Association, 16–17 December 1890, *Film*, 28:803–12; *Woman's Journal*, 2 & 16 December 1899; *Brooklyn Daily Eagle*, 15 March 1896, 9 December 1899.)

3. John Brown (1800–1859), hanged for treason in 1859, after his raid against the federal armory at Harper's Ferry intended to start a revolt among slaves, was buried in North Elba, New York, on his farm. In 1870, Kate Field organized a group to purchase and preserve the farm and open it to visitors. In 1895, the group deeded the land to the State of New York for a public park. SBA signed the visitor's register on 25 June 1891. (*Film*, 29:253.)

4. The body of Watson Brown (1835–1859) was reburied at North Elba in 1882. Oliver Brown's body was moved to the gravesite in 1899.

5. In 1846, Gerrit Smith set aside land in the Adirondacks for three thousand farms of forty acres each to be given to African Americans. Two years later only twenty to thirty families had moved to the site, but whether farmed or not, the land could help black men to meet New York's requirement that they own property worth two hundred and fifty dollars to qualify to vote. See Ralph Volney Harlow, *Gerrit Smith: Philanthropist and Reformer* (New York, 1939), 242–46; John Stauffer, *The Black Hearts of Men: Radical Abolitionists and the Transformation of Race* (Cambridge, Mass., 2002), 134–44.

6. SBA was relying on her brothers for recommendations about interest-bearing investments. Her record of daily income and expenses, kept in her diaries, occasionally shows earnings sent by them. An overview of her assets and investments cannot be constructed from extant documents.

141 ❧ HARRIETTE ROBINSON SHATTUCK TO SBA

Malden [*Mass.*] Sept 8, 1891.

Dear Miss Anthony,

Some things that you have written to me and some things that you said to us when we called on you last winter,[1] have set me to thinking seriously whether the work of our branch association may not be done. Do <u>you</u> think so? Do you think that it would be better for the cause if there were not two branch associations in this state and do you think that the national work no longer needs us as a separate organization?[2]

You know we were started to champion the national leaders & to introduce the national methods & to make it possible for you and other nationals to be properly received in our state. So naturally your opinion in this matter is of value to me, and I greatly desire to hear from you regarding what you believe should be the future relation of our society to the work. ~~Will you not write me?~~ I wish also you would tell me whether our delegates are of sufficient importance at Washington, (in promoting the election of leaders with "national" ideas and in advocating national methods) to justify our existence as a separate organization for the purpose of sending them to help you & others of the national wing of the N-A

Personally I say frankly that I am very sorry the policy of the N-A has become narrower & that the opportunity is removed for the formation of independent auxiliaries like our own. It makes us seem to be in on sufferance and such a policy leads me, for one, to dislike any further auxiliaryship. But I am only one, and we have very independent members in our society.

Hoping to hear from you soon and also hoping that the work is progressing in Kansas which I know is your favorite vantage ground, (as well as in other states whenever anyone has the heart to pursue it), I am as ever   Yours sincerely

❧ *Harriette R Shattuck*

❧ ALS draft or file copy, on NWSA of Massachusetts letterhead, Robinson-Shattuck Papers, MCR-S.

1. At the Garrisons in January, when SBA was bedridden.

2. The National Woman Suffrage Association of Massachusetts had voted to become an auxiliary of the new National-American and maintain its identity separate from the Massachusetts Woman Suffrage Association. Shattuck, the group's president until 1892, was elected one of its delegates to the National-American convention in January 1890. Her letter to SBA anticipated a special meeting of the group in October 1891 to consider disaffiliating with the National-American, an idea rejected by all but one member. (*History*, 4:750–54.)

142 ECS TO HARRIOT STANTON BLATCH

26 West 61st st [*New York*]   Sept 14th [*1891*]

Dear Hattie

I date this at the flat though I am not yet there but am to go to morrow.[1] Your letter & postal from Theodore just received. I can just imagine how you felt as the wind howled round you. It was doing the same at sea   No, you saw the ladies saloon   the gentlemens room was over the dining room. My stewardess was such a sterling common sense character that I do believe I was the most comfortable soul on board   Most of the people men & women were very sick & cross growling at everything. I was calm happy & comfortable   The stewardess used to tell me how other ladies behaved & said I was the only one she ever attended so long who never spoke a cross or impatient word, & who was so easily suited. I got up twice in the night   she would turn on the light   fix the pillows along to board so I could easily turn out & in. Then I would turn over my pillows put some of Alice's[2] cologne on my [pkt?][3] & go to sleep. Tell A. that bottle was invaluable. Then she would open the port hole each time & fill the room with pure air. There was one little dry spot on deck where you left me where I sat hours every day. Then I found an easy corner in the dining room where I could nap   read. I had my stewardess sit by & knit when I slept with directions to wake me every time I snored. I told her when there was no one in the dining to let me snore but to push me the moment any one entered. As she snored about as badly as I did she looked on the habit with a due measure of charity   Well altogether I do not look back upon my voyage with any dread though every body said it was dreadful. I had anticipated so much misery that I was pleasantly disappointed Of course I was glad to land. The old stewardess stuck to me until she saw me safely in a carriage with Kit.[4] She carried my steamer chair round so as to have me rest at various points. When they were looking up the trunks there I sat in the midst of the hubbub hearing every body fretting about something foreigners cursing the country because they could not lay their hands instantly on their own baggage, & daming other people for having trunks precisely like theirs. They did not seem to think that a great vessel landing a thousand people might well take six hours to get all things distributed. Kit I am happy to say walked about like a gentleman, he neither swore nor blustered. The old german tagged at his heels & looked after me alternately, as if I were in the slightest danger of moving when I had a seat That western man's description of a lazy girl would apply to me, "The smartest girl he ever knew to keep a chair down"

~ AL incomplete, ECS Papers, DLC.

1. ECS was about to move into an eight-room apartment in a building with an elevator at this address that she would share with her daughter Margaret and son Robert. She joined the search for an apartment after her arrival in New York Harbor on August 31 aboard the North German Lloyd Line's *S.S. Ems.* (*Eighty Years*, 432-33.)

2. Alice Blatch (c. 1853-?), Harry Blatch's next younger sister, lived in Basingstoke. Harriot Blatch and ECS made a project of widening her horizons: she joined SBA's party to Italy in 1883, and to help her find an occupation, they introduced her to Emily Lord, a leader in the kindergarten movement. She took up kindergarten teaching, won election to the Basingstoke school board, and, after moving to London in the 1890s, served as a poor law guardian in Islington. In 1901, she married George Edwards, a much younger civil servant at Scotland Yard. (Census of Britain, 1881; Blatch and Lutz, *Challenging Years*, 68-70; DuBois, *Harriot Stanton Blatch*, 56, 173, 292n; *Papers*, 4:221-22, 226, 228.)

3. This appears to be one of the countless abbreviations for pocket handkerchief but its constituent letters are obscure.

4. That is, her son Henry, known within the family as Kit.

143 ❧ SBA TO LILLIE DEVEREUX BLAKE

Rochester N.Y. Sept. 22/91

My Dear Mrs Blake

Yours of yesterday is before me— I do not know what to say to you about the Isabella association—I am sure—[1] But it does look to me as if any building they can get the money for must be a very small affair as compared with that of the Lady Managers—built with Government money— I tried to talk with Mrs Hooker about last winter in Washington—when said—["]now Susan—I have studied the whole matter thoroughly and <u>know</u> whereof I am speaking—and don't you who <u>know</u> <u>nothing</u> meddle with it"—and so I haven't— So far as the statue is concerned—I fully <u>approve</u> it—and am willing to help all I can—[2] So I shall have to leave you just where you are— My Cousin—Dr Frances Dickinson is all enthusiasm about the Isabella—but I <u>know</u> nothing of it— I believe in Harriet Hosmer—and I want the Isabella statue—but I cannot see the need of a <u>feeble</u> no. 2. Woman's Pavillion—which the Dr Frances association can but be— Then the fact that Dr Julia Holmes Smith has retired—& that a new president has taken her place—doesn't token well to me—[3] Dr H. Smith is a very bright woman & I cannot but feel that she came to the conclusion that a splendid success was impossible—& so retired—but that I do not know.

Another thing I don't understand—that is how a member of the <u>Lady</u> M̶e̶m̶b̶e̶r̶ ↑Board↓ can at the same time—work for its best interest—and also for the best interest of another Board & another Pavillion Mrs Hooker assured me she could do so—& that there was no antagonism between the two objects—[4]

I am expecting Mrs Stanton Thursday evening—how glad I shall be to welcome her to my own bed & board—they, before, have always been first my mothers—then my oldest sisters, and then my mother's & sister Mary's—now—they are my very own—[5] I rent the house of my sister & run it myself—hiring the girl & catering for the table & all— and I do enjoy it hugely— When you ↑are↓ going through you must come & see if I don't do it nicely— Am glad I am to see you at the Auburn Con—[6] Sincerely yours

↭ *Susan B. Anthony*

↭ ALS, Lillie D. Blake Papers, MoSHi.

1. The Queen Isabella Association, organized in Chicago in August 1889, planned to erect a statue of Queen Isabella at the Columbian Exposition and an Isabella Pavilion on the fairgrounds. It launched a quarterly *Queen Isabella Journal* in January 1890 to attract donations. Founders included two doctors, a lawyer, a scholar, and a prominent activist, with headquarters in the medical office of SBA's cousin Frances Dickinson. As the association expanded its roster and opened offices in New York, Washington, and St. Louis, the group proved particularly attractive to professional women. SBA's forecast in this letter, that the Isabellas, as they were known, would collide with the official group overseeing women's participation in the fair, the Board of Lady Managers, proved accurate. Later, denied a permit to erect their own building on the fairgrounds, the Isabellas built a club house and dormitory nearby. (*Woman's Tribune*, 11 January 1890; Weimann, *Fair Women*, 28-30, 39-40, 55-56, 58-72.)

2. The Queen Isabella Association commissioned the American sculptor Harriet Goodhue Hosmer (1830-1908) to make a statue of Isabella, but they failed to raise sufficient funds for Hosmer to cast the statue in bronze. Instead, she shipped a statue molded in plaster that found a home at the fair's California Building. (*NAW*; *ANB*; *Woman's Journal*, 29 August 1891; Dolly Sherwood, *Harriet Hosmer: American Scuptor, 1830-1908* [Columbia, Mo., 1991], 325-27.)

3. Julia Holmes Smith presided over the Isabellas only through July 1891, though she remained as head of the Board of Directors until later that year. Eliza Allen Starr (1824-1901), a Chicago artist, convert to Catholicism, and author of *Isabella of Castile* (1889), replaced Smith as president of the association. (*NAW*; *Women Building Chicago*; *Queen Isabella Journal*, with special thanks to Corey Borenstein.)

4. Both Isabella Hooker and Frances Dickinson were Isabellas who also served on the Board of Lady Managers.

5. ECS was to be the guest of SBA for three weeks while the sculptor Adelaide Johnson worked in clay on the bust of ECS for the Columbian Exposition.

6. For the annual meeting of the New York State Woman Suffrage Association on November 10 and 11. See *Film*, 29:497-506.

144   SBA to Salome Merritt[1]

Rochester NY. Sept 22 1891.

My dear Doctor,

Yours of the 16th is before me— Mrs Shattuck had written me on the same subject— Really it is hardly worth while for your society to call itself a <u>state</u> <u>society</u>—unless it does work outside of a political class in <u>Boston</u>!! So far as any special <u>need</u> of its continuance on <u>my</u> <u>part</u>—or the Old Nationals part I do not know that any exists— And beside from what I saw when in Boston it seemed to me that very <u>nearly all</u> of <u>your members</u> were also members of the <u>old Mass. Society</u>— Isn't that so?— and if it is—it would seem unnecessary for you to keep up two organizations for the same end—namely to gain the suffrage—

Mrs Shattuck and Mrs Robinson talked with me last winter when they called at Mr Garrisons, I did not <u>advise</u> in the matter then and I do not like to do so now—

But so far as the National work is concerned—I have seen no disposition to change it <u>since</u> <u>the</u> <u>Union</u>! and I have not heard that any one who has attended the Washington D.C. meetings since that—have seen any disposition to change things from the old nationals ways— Have you heard of any such effort having been or to be made?

If your disbanding means the National or State association losing or not enjoying the sympathy of and cooperation of the members of <u>your</u> society—why then you had better hold them together for work in yours—while if by your disbanding your members simply remain with— or go into the old Mass Society—I cannot see that anything will be lost—

The National-American would have no less money from Mass with the members of the two societies combined in <u>one</u> <u>society</u>—and if you have <u>100 members</u>—those added to the Old Mass. will give it <u>two</u> delegates more than before—and they would undoubtedly endeavor to select from your <u>numbers</u> say Miss Hatch[2] & Dr. Merritt as delegates— so that the National would still have Miss Hatch—and her vote would be just as free & impartial as it has ever been—when representing the National Mass—I am sure—

But what I had thought you might do was to resolve yourselves into a <u>Political</u> <u>Equality</u> <u>Club</u>—and vote yourselves auxilliary to the Old Mass. State Society— What that old society wants is plenty of <u>auxilliary societies</u>—and <u>then</u> they should insist on amending the State Constitution so that the Presidents of all auxilliaries should be Vice Presidents of the State Society—and <u>members</u> of the State Executive Committee— and in order to get the Constitution thus amended—you & other societies must vote themselves auxilliary—& so go into the work systematically[3]

The <u>constitutions</u> of all the <u>State Societies ought</u> to be <u>amended</u> so as to be in line with the National Society—you see— The <u>only</u> <u>officers</u> of the <u>national</u> <u>board</u> to be elected by national society are the President, Vice Pres at large—secretaries, treasurer & auditors—all of the rest of the Executive Committee is made up of the presidents of the <u>States</u> who are elected by the members of their respective societies.

Thus you see I end as I began—by wishing you to act on your own best judgments—

Please forward this to dear Mrs Shattuck & so save my writing it all over again— I never have believed in or <u>practiced</u> <u>secession</u>—instead— I have always believed in & tried to practice—<u>full and free discussion</u>— and a <u>fair</u> vote—on all matters—and then abiding by the result—and that is what I hope to be able to do to the end— I did not form a second National twenty years ago—nor did I refuse to work with any one—but on the other hand—Those who could not abide by the vote of the majority—went to Cleveland & formed a second (2^d) society—called the American— <u>They</u> <u>refused</u> <u>to</u> <u>work</u> <u>with</u> <u>us</u>—you see—not we with them— So that when they after a score of years proposed to return & work with us—we simply welcomed them!!—that is all—and I do not like the spirit—that refuses to work with any one—for our one end of political emancipation—

Massachusetts is now the only state in which there are two societies— So if you do vote yourselves an auxilliary society—that one will be no more   But I do hope you will resurrect the Old Constitution & amend it so as to bring it in line of the Democratic idea—of the members of the local and county societies electing the members of the State Executive Board of officers   Hoping to hear from you I am very sincerely yours

Susan B. Anthony.

↢ Typed copy, Robinson-Shattuck Papers, MCR-S. Headed "Copied verbatim," and corrected throughout in the hand of Harriette Shattuck.

1. Salome Merritt (1843–1900), a physician in practice in Boston, had a notable record of leadership in women's urban reforms in the city. She was a founding member of the National Woman Suffrage Association of Massachusetts and became its president in 1893. (Howe, *Sketches of Representative Women of New England*, 299–301; *Woman's Journal*, 10 November 1900.)

2. Lavina Allen Hatch (1836–1903), a former school teacher, was another founding member of the National's auxiliary in Massachusetts, its secretary for seventeen years, and often one of its delegates to the Washington convention. Hatch also wrote the group's history for the *History of Woman Suffrage*. (Howe, *Representative Women of New England*, 114–17; *Woman's Journal*, 4 April 1903; *History*, 4:750–54.)

3. Members of the National Woman Suffrage Association of Massachusetts proudly differentiated their democratic governing structure from that of Lucy Stone's Massachusetts Woman Suffrage Association, in which all decisions were made by an appointed executive committee. When, in January 1892, the state association named a special committee to revise its constitution, members of the National auxiliary began a public discussion about making the document reflect the constitution of the National-American and introducing more democratic measures. In April, a new constitution allowed local suffrage clubs in the state to elect members to the state executive committee. (Evalyn L. Mason to Editor, *Boston Evening Transcript*, 9 February 1892, SBA scrapbook 18, Rare Books, DLC; Merk, "Massachusetts and the Woman-Suffrage Movement," 248–51.)

145 ↝ ECS TO THE EDITOR, *VOICE*[1]

Basingstoke, England [*before 1 October 1891*]

Editor of "The Voice."—To answer the question, "What changes, if any, should be made in the exercise of the right of suffrage in the United States?" I would say, in the first place, it should be extended to all women of sound mind and legal age on the same basis that it is now possessed by men. Women have the same interest in the laws and rulers under which they live as men have, and they should share equally in the responsibilities. According to the principles of the Declaration of Independence and the National Constitution, women have the same political rights men have, and it is equally their duty to exercise them.

I have always advocated universal suffrage, but in view of the immense number of foreigners every day landing on the shores of the United States, I have come to think seriously of an educational qualification. It would be impolitic and impracticable to take the suffrage from those who already possess it, but Congress might pass an act, saying that after 1895 no person shall be allowed to vote who cannot read and write the English language. That would give all here now who prize the right of suffrage sufficient time to learn the rudiments of our language and prevent those just landing from enjoying the same privilege until they too had gone through similar preparation. This would add new dignity to citizenship and make our people homogeneous by compelling all to speak in time the same language. As a measure of protection, we now limit the time at which foreigners may vote, but it is very difficult to make sure that this is successful. But to learn to read and write a language must necessarily take two or three years for the ordinary, dull, ignorant classes that crowd America's shores. By this means, we can be sure that they have been here the prescribed time. Those who desire this privilege very much can show their appreciation of it by diligent efforts to qualify themselves for its exercise. To make the right to vote a prize for some degree of education would not only be a protection against any sudden increase of the foreign vote, but it would dignify the suffrage in the eyes of our own people, and be a strong stimulus to all children to avail themselves of the privileges of education.

In making the legal age for America's educated sons as late as 21, shows that the fathers thought it needed some intelligence and experience to take part in government. If a well-educated American boy, born and brought up under our free institutions, must breathe the atmosphere of freedom so many years before he can with safety to the State be enfranchised, surely an ignorant foreigner, born and bred under Kings, Emperors and Czars, is not fit for the rights of sovereignty a few months after he touches our shores. I am opposed to all qualifications of sex, color or nativity because they are insurmountable. Neither time, education, property nor all the cardinal virtues can change a woman into a man, black to white, foreign to native. But ignorance can be changed into intelligence, and reading and writing are the tests to this end. There is nothing proscriptive in an educational qualification as the requirement, though great in its results, can be easily obeyed.

Again, to compel all foreigners to learn the English language helps to make our people homogeneous in character, literature, religion and social customs, and makes all, in time, alike loyal to the same form of government. English should be the only language taught in our public schools, for a difference in language keeps up the idea of different nationalities and prevents that peace and harmony that grows out of a feeling of oneness, of equality, of a perfect union of all in one great nation, governed by the people themselves.

~ *Elizabeth Cady Stanton.*

~ New York *Voice*, 1 October 1891.

1. Edward Jewitt Wheeler (1859–1922) edited the *Voice*, the paper of the Prohibition party, from 1884 to 1895. ECS contributed to a symposium on changes in suffrage laws. (*SEAP*.)

146 ~ Reception for ECS in Rochester

EDITORIAL NOTE: On the last evening of ECS's three-week visit to Rochester, the Political Equality Club hosted a reception for her at the Anthonys' house on Madison Street. ECS was announced to speak at 8:00 P.M. about coeducation, and invitations were extended to the trustees, president, and faculty of the University of Rochester. The event opened a new phase of mobilization in the project of several women's clubs to gain admission to the university for young women. At a time when the school's leaders hoped to garner more financial support among civic boosters, women's clubs had also taken their cause to the public by circulating petitions for coeducation. The chance to meet ECS and hear her match wits with the faculty drew two hundred guests as well as reporters from at least four local newspapers. Though in most respects, the *Rochester Herald*'s report of the discussion was very thorough, two other papers paraphrased prefatory remarks in which ECS "referred to the struggle which the Irish nation is making for its liberty and said that the struggle which the women of America and the other nations of the earth are making for their personal and political liberty is of no less importance." (William H. Pease, "The Gannetts of Rochester: Highlights in a Liberal Career, 1889–1923," *Rochester History* 17 [October 1955]: 18–20; Arthur J. May, *A History of the University of Rochester, 1850–1962*, ed. Lawrence Eliot Klein [Rochester, N.Y., 1977], 116–18; *Film*, 29:444–48.)

[15 October 1891]

"In thinking of this question I often wonder at the indifference manifested by women themselves as to their position. They seem to have no interest or enthusiasm on the subject. It is easy enough to get up enthusiasm among them upon almost any other subject. They will get enthusiastic about a donation to the minister or upon the subject of patch work quilts. Yet notwithstanding their apparent indifference I am sure that all women feel the injustice of their position. I contend that there never was a woman born who did not at some period of her life feel the humiliation of her position.

"So I suppose there is not a woman in Rochester that does not feel the injustice of girls being shut out of the university. Men argue that it is more important to educate boys than girls because the boys are to take part in the government of the state. And yet they frequently say that the position of wife and mother is the most exalted that any human being can occupy. If men are really serious in saying this what can they mean by saying that the education of our girls is a matter of much less importance than that of the boys? If the authorities of your university persist in this refusal to open its doors to women I suggest that you women make an effort to secure the establishment of a college here which shall be nonsectarian and co-educational. Your university I understand is sectarian and that may be one reason why it will not admit women, for the religious world has always held women in very light esteem.[1] We should demand the same equality in church as in state."

At this point Mrs. Stanton was interrupted by Miss Susan B. Anthony with the remark: "We have some of the professors of the university here, Mrs. Stanton, so perhaps we had better be careful what we say."[2]

"Well, if they are here I think that is a good reason for saying just what we think," was Mrs. Stanton's rejoinder. Continuing, she said:

"The experiment of educating boys and girls together has been tried and found perfectly safe and successful. It has been found best to educate them side by side. It is done in the primary and preparatory schools and I do not see why we should stop at the collegiate course. Horace Mann[3] has said that if only one half of the people can be educated women should have the preference. Suppose all wives and mothers for a single generation could be educated, what an influence that would have. Women are natural teachers. Many wise men are like oysters; they shut their lips and you can get nothing out of them. But what women know they can easily tell. When women get charge of the schools I think you will hear of no more whipping for disobedience. I understand that only the other day a girl was whipped by one of the male principals in this city. We are shocked at the idea of criminals being whipped in Delaware, but what can be more demoralizing to a girl than to be whipped by a man, and in the presence of other pupils? If co-education is demoralizing to girls how much more so must it be to be whipped by a man?"

At this point Miss Anthony stated that she had a letter of regret that she would like to read to the company. The letter is as follows:

> Miss Anthony: I wish to acknowledge for Mrs. Hill and myself[4] the invitation to attend the reception to be given Mrs. Stanton at your house and to express our regrets that we shall not be able to be present.
>
> Permit me to take this occasion to say, apropos of Mrs. Stanton's subject, that I am personally a strong believer in the higher education of women and trust that the day is not far distant when our city, which affords advantages to young men such as few cities offer, may provide equal facilities for the education of young women. It seems to me, also, that this should be done by our university, which I hope may from this time forward enter upon a career of larger usefulness to the citizens of Rochester. Very respectfully,
>
> DAVID J. HILL

There was hearty applause at the conclusion of Miss Anthony's reading of President Hill's letter. Mrs. Greenleaf[5] jokingly suggested that perhaps the fact that the president had a boy and girl in his family who began to tread life's pathway at the same time might have converted him to the doctrine of co-education. "Yes," said Mrs. Stanton, "that is significant as showing that providence approves of boys and girls being together."

Dr. Moore,[6] who had kept very quiet up to this time and had listened very attentively to Mrs. Stanton's remarks and Dr. Hill's letter now turned to the former and said: "I want to correct one statement that you have made. Our university is not sectarian as that term is usually understood. There is no more liberal or broad minded set of men than are contained in this board of trustees and I want to also say that there is no real opposition to women. We have long recognized that one of the needs of the city was an instruction for the higher education of women. With Lewis H. Morgan and Mr. Durand[7] I worked all of one winter 19 years ago to raise money enough to establish such an institution, but we were unsuccessful. We don't object to co-education. But our college is poor. The people of Rochester give it no money. Give us $200,000 and we will give you co-education. It is easy enough to say 'Let the girls come in and sit down with the boys,' but you must remember that double the number of students means double the number of teachers, or nearly so. So far from feeling that girls ought not to be educated we feel that they ought to be."

Mrs. Greenleaf wanted to know why it would not be a good idea for the college to receive only the young men and women of Rochester. "No, that wouldn't do," replied the doctor; "we don't want to be a local institution."

"But it seems to me you are worse than a local institution if you are sectarian," said Mrs. Stanton, "and you certainly are sectarian if you admit only one sex." This witty retort raised a merry laugh in which the doctor joined as heartily as the rest. In answer to a question put by Miss Anthony the doctor said that colored men were admitted to the university and that he was pleased to know that they were received on terms of perfect equality by the young men.[8] Then the doctor was subjected to a running fire of questions from a half dozen different ladies. He insisted that the education of men was of more importance than that of women because the men were the breadwinners. Mrs. Stanton could not agree with him on that point, and a good natured argument followed. "You must give up thinking of women simply as wives and mothers," said she, "and consider them as individuals." And finally after both had exhausted pretty much all of the ready argument on the question, Mrs. Stanton again turned the laugh on the doctor by telling him there was a "hitch somewhere in his philosophy."

Dr. S. A. Lattimore[9] was called upon to speak by Miss Anthony. He said that the fact that his mother, his wife and his children were all women ought to be sufficient indication of where he stood on the question. He had no faith in any argument against co-education that was based on a differentiation in the sexes. He was in favor of the higher education of women and he believed that the education of the sexes could best be accomplished together. The presence and companionship of the young women would have a salutary effect on the young men.

≈ *Rochester Herald*, 16 October 1891, SBA Scrapbook 17, Rare Books, DLC.

1. This question was the subject of debate in 1891, when outspoken Baptists challenged David Hill's leadership of the university, detecting a threat to denominational control in his modern curriculum and his appeals for support from civic leaders. (Aubrey Parkman, "President Hill and the Sectarian Challenge at the U. of R.," *Rochester History* 33 [October 1971]: 1-24.)

2. Those professors not identified below were Herman Le Roy Fairchild (1850-1943), who joined the faculty of the University of Rochester as professor of geology and natural history in 1888 (*WWW4*), and George Mather Forbes (1853-1934), who graduated from the University of Rochester in 1878 and returned as a professor of Greek in 1881. By 1891, he taught philosophy and education. (*WWW1*.)

3. Horace Mann (1796-1859), the noted educational reformer, promoted the education of girls and women while secretary of the Massachusetts state board of education from 1837 to 1848 and while president of Antioch College, a coeducational school, from 1853 until his death. (*ANB*.)

4. David Jayne Hill (1850-1932) was president of the University of Rochester from 1889 to 1896. Juliet Lewis Packer Hill (c. 1863-1923), his second wife, had just given birth to twins, a boy and a girl. (*ANB*; *New York Times*, 17 January 1923.)

5. Jean Frances Brooks Greenleaf (1831-1918), the wife of businessman and congressman Halbert S. Greenleaf, presided over the Political Equality Club of Rochester in 1888 and over the New York State Woman Suffrage Association from 1890 to 1896. (*American Women*; John Devoy, *Rochester and the Post Express. A History of the City of Rochester from the Earliest Times: The Pioneers and Their Predecessors, Frontier Life in the Genesee Country, Biographical Sketches* [Rochester, 1895], 162; "Jean Brooks Greenleaf," Rochester Regional Library Council website, *Western New York Suffragists: Winning the Vote*.)

6. Edward Mott Moore (1814-1902) was a distinguished surgeon and heart specialist who also served as a trustee of the University of Rochester. (*NCAB*, 12:55; *WWW1*.)

7. Frederick Lewis Durand (1816-1903) graduated from Yale College in 1836 and moved to Rochester to practice law in 1845. On another occasion Moore recounted how the three men raised one hundred and fifty thousand dollars for coeducation. Lewis H. Morgan also left money for women's educa-

tion to the university in his will in 1881 but in the form of a delayed bequest. (*Yale Obituary Record 1904*; Jesse Leonard Rosenberger, *Rochester, The Making of a University* [Rochester, N.Y., 1927], 239-41.)

8. The University of Rochester graduated its first African-American student in 1891. (Blake McKelvey, "Lights and Shadows in Local Negro History," *Rochester History* 21 [October 1959]: 16.)

9. Samual Allan Lattimore (1828-1913) was professor of chemistry and chairman of the executive committee of the faculty at the University of Rochester. (Peck, *History of Rochester and Monroe County, N.Y.*, 2:753-54; *WWW1*.)

147 ❧ SBA TO HARRIET TAYLOR UPTON

Rochester N.Y.—Oct. 22, 1891

My Dear Mrs Upton

Your Post-card is here this A.M—and Anna's[1] new dress is duly addressed to your care—and will go this afternoon or tomorrow—which will make it in ample time for the 27th— Tell her I took a squint at it—and pronounce it too clean & nice to travel in—and hence that she must wear it to speak in for awhile at least— I think she look fine in such a lovely blue with lovely blue braid trimmings!!

Mrs Greenleaf & Mrs Sanford[2] were here all the morning talking up state work— I told Mrs G. that I heard Mrs Perkins was sowing seeds of discord in Ohio—about auxilliaryship to the National![3] Do you believe that she & Olympia Brown are trying to alienate the friends where they go from the National? I know both were opposed to allowing the Americans to come back with the National—that is opposed to Union!—but now—since they are the two people I know of who stand out against Union—I don't see how or why they try to make disunion— Mrs Greenleaf—doesn't understand Mrs Perkins aim either—though she has known her for many years— Well I am sorry, sorry—and only wish I knew what to do o[r] say that would enable them to see that our strength lies in all being united in one great society for <u>political action</u>—no matter what our personal likes & dislikes may be— So if you see anything that will help me to bring content all round do tell me— We are too few to be split up!! Lovingly yours

❧ *Susan B. Anthony*

P.S—Tell Miss Shaw to get round here for as long a rest as possible before we go to Auburn—

~ ALS, on NAWSA letterhead, SBA Papers, NRU. Square brackets surround letter run off the page.

1. That is, Anna Shaw.
2. Mary Thayer Sanford (1853-?) grew up in Rochester, where her father, John M. Thayer, was a manager at the firm of Sargent and Greenleaf. In 1878, she married, as his second wife, John E. Sanford, a dentist. Known locally for her classes in art appreciation and encouragement of local artists, Sanford was also active in the Political Equality Club and state suffrage association. (Federal Census, Franklin County, Mass., 1860, Rochester, 1870, 1880, 1900, 1910, 1920; city directories, 1890 to 1899; Blake McKelvey, "The First Century of Art in Rochester—to 1925," *Rochester History* 17 [April 1955]: 16.)
3. The rumblings in Ohio may have signaled early organizing in the Midwest for the new Federal Suffrage Association, launched in March 1892. The cast of characters is the same. Sarah Perkins chaired the executive committee of Olympia Brown's new organization and later urged the Ohio association to withdraw from the National-American. She and Brown shared the view that the dues paid by auxiliaries to the national would be better spent in each state. (*True Republic* 1 [April 1892]: 4; *Wisconsin Citizen*, April 1892, in SBA scrapbook 18, Rare Books, DLC.)

148 ~ ECS TO ELIZA WRIGHT OSBORNE

26 West 61st [*New York*]   November 6th [*1891*][1]

Dear Eliza,

In a recent letter to Mrs Miller, speaking of the occasion when we last met,[2] you say, "why was Mrs Stanton so solemn"? to which I reply, Ever since an old German Emperor[3] issued an edict, ordering all the women under that flag to knit, when walking on the highway, when selling apples in the market place, when sitting in the parks, because "to keep women out of mischief their hands must be busy," ever since I read that, I have felt humiliated, whenever I have seen any daughters of our grand republic knitting, tatting, embroidering, or occupied with any of the ten thousand digital absurdities, that fill so large a place in the lives of Eve's daughters.

Looking forward to the scintillations of wit, the philosophical researches, the historical traditions, the scientific discoveries, the astronomical explorations the mysteries of theosophy palmistry, mental science, the revelations of the unknown world where angels & devils do congregate, looking forward to the discussions of all these grand themes, in meeting the eldest daughter of David & Martha Wright,[4] the neice of Lucretia Mott, the sister in law of William Loyd Garrison, a queenly looking woman five feet eight in height & well proportioned, with glorious black eyes rivalling even de Stael's in power & pathos, one can readily imagine the disappointment I experienced, when such a woman pulled a cotton wash rag from her pocket, & forthwith began to knit. With bowed head, fixing her eyes, & concentrating her thoughts on a rag one foot square: it was impossible for conversation to rise above the wash rag level. It was enough to make the most aged optimist solemn, to see such a wreck of glorious womanhood.

And still worse, she not only knit steadily hour after hour, but she bestowed the sweetest words of encouragement, on a young girl from the Pacific coast, who was embroidering rose buds on a rag, the very girl I had endeavored to rescue from the malestroom of embroidery, by showing her the unspeakable folly of giving her optic nerve to such base uses, when it was designed by the Creator, to explore the planetary world, with chart & compass to guide mighty ships across the sea, to lead the sons of Adam with divinest love from earth to heaven Only think the great leading nerve, by which we express ↑our↓ adoration of all that is good & glorious in earth & heaven, being subsidized to a cotten wash rag!!

Who can wonder that I was "solemn" that day. I made my agonized protest on the spot, but it fell unheeded & with a satisfied sneer Eliza knit on, & the young Californian continued making the rose buds as usual. I gazed into space & when alone wept for my degenerate countrywomen. I not only was "solemn" that day but I am profoundly solemn whenever I think of that queenly woman & that cotten wash rag. And yet one can buy a whole dozen of these useful appliances with red borders & fringed for twenty five cents!! Oh Eliza I beseech you knit no more, affectionately yours

Elizabeth Cady Stanton

As my dear Cousin rests under the curse of the old father of Frederick the Great, I send this for her to read, that she may understand why I was so depressed at times, during my recent visit.

↢ ALS, Garrison Papers, MNS-S.

1. Circumstances described in this letter and Osborne's reply date it to 1891. Inexplicably ECS changed the day of the month to November 12, when she published the letter in *Eighty Years*, 435–36. At the top of her first page, ECS pasted an unidentified clipping about German women who knit at the opera in modern times.

2. In October, ECS and SBA went together from Rochester to Geneva to visit Elizabeth Miller, and Eliza Osborne spent a day with the guests. (SBA to Ellen W. Garrison, 2 November 1891, *Film*, 29:456–57; *Eighty Years*, 434–38.)

3. Frederick William I, king of Prussia (1688–1740) instituted numerous practices to maximize production by enlarging the number of laborers. At the end of this letter ECS mentions his son, Frederick II (1712–1786), known as Frederick the Great.

4. David Wright (1805–1897), a lawyer in Auburn, New York, married Martha Coffin Wright in 1829.

149 ↣ SBA to George F. Hoar

Rochester N.Y. Dec. 10 1891

My Dear friend Senator Hoar

My niece sends me your reply to her[1]—in which you say "you had better not advertise me on your program &c"—and I want to lay before you what seems to me the importance of your consenting to let us put it there— It is that our movement may have the <u>weight</u> of <u>your influence</u> in all our advertisements of the coming Convention—a help to our cause that I fear you do not fully appreciate—when you think of saying "<u>No</u>" to us—[2]

If when the time comes—you find it impossible to be at our meeting—we will so announce—and be ready with another speaker to fill the time—

We want your <u>name</u> on our program—to show our opponents who read—that you stand for us & with us!! <u>We</u> all <u>know</u> <u>this</u> and are happy & proud of it—but the careless outside world thinks, and constantly taunts us, that <u>no</u> <u>men</u> of <u>place</u> & position—no men among men of affairs—are with us— So I beg of to allow us to put your name down for a <u>short</u> speech on one of the evenings— We shall have two women and one man—each evening—provided we can get the <u>one</u> <u>man</u>—and you are the one we most want—so I pray you let us announce you with the hope that you'll be on hand if possible— That is as nearly as any of us can pledge ourselves— Sincerely yours

～ *Susan B. Anthony*

P.S—Thanks for your cordial reply to my hope for a good friend at the head of our Select Committee on suffrage—³

～ ALS, on NAWSA letterhead, George F. Hoar Papers, MHi.

  1. SBA probably refers to Lucy E. Anthony, who served on the program committee for the Washington convention of 1892.
  2. SBA enclosed a copy of the call to the convention.
  3. See SBA to G. F. Hoar, 1 December 1891, *Film*, 29:536-41.

150 ～ SBA TO HARRIET TAYLOR UPTON

Rochester N.Y. Dec 10, 1891

Yes My Dear—

I know I ought to be in Washington—but you young people will have to pull the oar sometime—and this is a good time to begin— You are doing splendidly— But—if Cary & Warren¹ feel no pride in ↑Woman↓ Suffrage as the underlying principle of Wyoming & the nation—then they wont be of any special use on our committee— I thought they would be more enthusiastic than any other men could be— Well—do the best you can—and when I come I'll help you to carry out whatever you get started—

I wish I knew where I was to be <u>settled</u>—I can't bear to <u>change</u>—am expecting to hear from Mrs Lockwood² & Mrs Marble³ every day—as to head-quarters— I wonder if Miss Snow⁴ has both her houses full? Oh that the Spoffords were still in their old quarters & full & rich & happy!!

I wrote Senator Sherman⁵ the moment I saw the power put in his hands—but so he doesn't give us an <u>Ex-Rebel</u> for a chairman—we'll be content— just to think of <u>decent</u> <u>men</u>—<u>republicans</u>!—Congress after Congress placing Ex-Confederate soldiers to decide upon the destiny of <u>Loyal</u> <u>Women</u>!! My blood boils at the indignities our <u>friends</u> <u>heap</u> upon our poor disfranchised heads!— Lovingly yours

                         ↩ *Susan B. Anthony*

↩ ALS, on NAWSA letterhead, SBA Papers, NRU.

1. SBA had hoped, at the start of the Fifty-second Congress, that one of Wyoming's Republican senators would be appointed chairman of the Senate Select Committee on Woman Suffrage. They were Joseph Carey, not Cary, previously territorial delegate in the House, and Francis Emroy Warren (1844–1929), elected for the short term from 1890 to 1893 and returned in 1895 to serve until his death. (*BDAC*; SBA to George F. Hoar, 1 December 1891, *Film*, 29:536–41.)

2. For the first time in many years, the Riggs House was not available to be SBA's home and the National-American's headquarters during the Washington convention. The Spofford family left the business and moved out in 1891. Mary Smith Lockwood (1831–1922), a writer, worked on local arrangements for the Washington convention as a member of the District of Columbia suffrage association. Recognized for her skill in organizational work, she was named a commissioner-at-large to the Board of Lady Managers for the Columbian Exposition, presided over the Women's National Press Association, and led in founding the Daughters of the American Revolution. (*NCAB*, 3:266; *WWW4*; "Sketch of Mary S. Lockwood," *Daughters of the American Revolution Magazine* 56 [December 1922]: 710–11.)

3. Ella Marie Smith Marble (1850–?) was president of the District of Columbia suffrage association. She lived in Maine until the early 1880s, working as a writer and raising two children. About 1883, she moved to the Midwest, trying out Kansas before settling in Minneapolis. In short order, she presided over the city and state suffrage associations and held numerous offices in the Woman's Christian Temperance Union too. An offer to write for a daily paper in Washington took her east in 1888 or 1889, but she changed careers soon after her arrival. By 1891, she was proprietor of the New York Avenue School of Physical Culture, the city's first gymnasium for women, and of the Jenness Miller Emporium of Fashion, an outlet for the dress patterns and reform clothing of Annie Jenness-Miller. From teaching good health she moved to medicine; in 1895, she graduated from National University's College of Medicine. Her medical practice in Washington was last noted in the city directory of 1897, though her grown children continued to live and work in the city. (*American Women*; Federal Census, Paris, Me., 1880; "Dr. Ella M. S. Marble," *Woman's Medical Journal* 5 [March 1896]: 69; Washington city directories, 1891 to 1897; *History*, 4:136, 176, 201, 772, 835; Moldow, *Women Doctors in Gilded-Age Washington*, 53, 67, 69; *International Council of Women, 1888*, pp. 318–19, *Film*, 26:154ff.)

4. Sophronia C. Snow (1833–1904), a sister of Jane Snow Spofford and an active member of the National Woman Suffrage Association, had lived at the Riggs House with the Spoffords and left with them. Her address in 1892 was 1410 G Steet, Northwest, Washington, where Caleb Spofford also resided. (Federal Census, 1880; research by Katherine W. Trickey, Bangor, Me.; online transcription of gravestones in Locust Grove Cemetery, Hampden, Me., by Mike Desmarais, in possession of editors; city directory, 1892. See also *Papers* 4.)

5. John Sherman (1823–1900), Ohio Republican, served in the Senate from 1861 to 1877 and 1881 to 1897. Committee assignments fell to him as chairman of the Senate Republican Caucus Committee, a post he assumed on December 7 at the start of the Fifty-second Congress. (*BDAC*.)

151 ⇝ THOMAS B. REED TO SBA

Washington, D.C., 11 Decr 1891

Dear Miss Anthony:

I have got to say no again and for the same reason. I am under a heavier load than ever—[1]

You remember the long talk you and I once had on this whole matter and the reasons why I thought it unwise to mix politicians up with this movement. When the eleventh hour comes we shall flock in clamorous for pennies. Yours truly

⇝ T. B. Reed

⇝ ALS, on letterhead of The Shoreham, HM 10624, Ida Harper Collection, CSmH.

1. Presumably SBA invited Reed to speak at the upcoming Washington convention.

152   SBA to Harriet Taylor Upton

Rochester N.Y. Jan. 1st 1892

My Dear Mrs Upton

   I enclose Dr Frances Dickinsons letter—her head is level on <u>the point</u> to be made with the Committees & with Congress—men generally— We don't them to act upon the <u>merits</u> of the question but simply to pass the resolution that will permit the several States Legislatures act upon it—[1]

   My idea is that we must give that Committee a <u>half</u>—if not a <u>full</u> <u>hour</u> before the Committees—and the question is how will we be likely to get the <u>most</u> <u>complete</u> <u>presentation</u> of the subject—[2] By the three <u>members</u>—Blake, Colby & Dickinson concentrating all each can furnish into one paper—and let the <u>chairman</u>—Dr Frances—present it?—or for each one to make her own 15 minutes speech! <u>What</u> <u>we</u> <u>want</u> is to get the <u>best</u> <u>material</u> before the Coms. in the most condensed form—because the Com's will get the matter printed at <u>Uncle</u> <u>Sam's</u> expense for us!

   I wonder if you had better confer with Mrs Colby & see what she thinks— It is doesn't matter a fig who, nor how many gets the facts & arguments together—no who reads the paper—all we want is the <u>best</u> <u>product</u>! how can we get it—is the question?

   Then as to time of the Hearings—one might be <u>Saturday</u> A.M. the <u>16th</u>—and the other any morning during the week of the Con. or I forget about the days of ↑the↓ <u>meetings</u> of the House Judiciary—but you will be safe to arrange ↑for↓ any of the days from Jan 16 to Jan 23—

   Oh—dear—what a shame that we can't ↑present↓ our claim for <u>one</u> <u>entire</u> <u>half</u> of the people of this nation before the entire Congress—Senate & House of Representatives!— We have asked for our Hearings to be had in one & the other House over & over—always with a "<u>no</u>" to our request— And now with a set of men who never <u>heard</u>, much less <u>thought</u> of the <u>demand</u>—where's the hope!!—but <u>we'll</u> <u>peg</u> <u>away</u> on this line if it takes all of the twentieth century—so go ahead—[3]

   Mrs Stanton bids me stop for her—about Thursday or Friday of next week—and she'll go on to W. with me— So my heart is glad on that point—her ↑speech↓ title is to be—"The Solitude of Self"— Wont she make a splendid thing of it?

Oh—there are lots of things I want hear you talk over— Mrs Greenleaf writes of seeing you & says her Democratic M.C.[4] will obey orders—& so he will—he is a splendid fellow for recognizing equal rights for women—

But my anxiety now is to select the right women to go before the Committees Mrs Stanton "<u>swears</u>" she will never so humiliate herself again—as to beg <u>mere</u> <u>boys</u> to <u>grant</u> <u>her</u> <u>freedom</u>! but may be she'll change he mind—but we <u>must</u> have <u>Lucy Stone</u> for one—& <u>the</u> two <u>Southern</u> women—Meriwether[5] & Saxon—do you not say so— You needn't stop to write reply—only be thinking it over— Lovingly yours

⇜ *Susan B. Anthony*

[*sideways in margin*] I am so glad Mrs Spofford is home— I can hardly wait to get there— I know you've been & had a chat ere this

⇜ ALS, on NAWSA letterhead, SBA Papers, NRU.

1. Enclosure missing. Frances Dickinson chaired the National-American's Petition Committee, formed in 1890. With money given by a Chicago businessman for the purpose, committee members sought endorsements of a sixteenth, suffrage amendment from the American Federation of Labor, Grand Army of the Republic, Farmers' Alliance, and other societies with large memberships of men. Petitions were circulated to regional and local units of the groups. When Dickinson addressed the Senate Select Committee on Woman Suffrage on 20 January 1892, she stated that the effort garnered the support of one and a half million men. (*Woman's Journal*, 14 March 1891, *Woman's Tribune*, 6 February 1892, *Film*, 29:22-23, 1028-34.)

2. The congressional hearings this winter bore little resemblance to SBA's plan. Before the House Committee on the Judiciary on 18 January 1892, ECS, Lucy Stone, Isabella Hooker, and SBA spoke. (See below at date.) When she came before the Senate committee on January 20, SBA explained that since "the veterans were heard" by the House, "we propose this morning, to present to you the younger women who are at work in the several states." Dickinson and Colby were two among seventeen speakers on that occasion. (*Film*, 29:1028-52.)

3. A Democratic landslide changed the composition of House and Senate for the first session of the Fifty-second Congress that opened in December 1891. Republicans retained a majority in the Senate.

4. Halbert Stevens Greenleaf (1827-1906), Democrat from Rochester, New

York, served in the House of Representatives from 1883 to 1885 and returned in 1891 for one term. He was married to Jean Greenleaf and supported her work for woman suffrage. On 5 January 1892, he introduced a joint resolution to amend the Constitution to extend the right to vote to women at all federal elections. (*BDAC*; 52 Cong., 1st sess., H. Res. 14.)

5. Lide Parker Smith Meriwether (1829–1913), a sister-in-law of Elizabeth Avery Meriwether, was president of the Tennessee Woman's Christian Temperance Union from 1884 to 1897, a strong advocate of woman suffrage within the union, and founder in 1889 of the Memphis Equal Rights Association. She and Elizabeth Saxon worked together as organizers. (*American Women*; Wedell, *Elite Women and the Reform Impulse in Memphis*, passim; Shelby County, Tenn., on-line archives of death certificates.)

153   Eliza Wright Osborne to ECS, with Enclosure

Boston Jan 15th 1892

For Satan finds some mischief still for idle hands to do—[1]
Dear Mrs. S.

Why isn't that a good old saying & why wasn't that old German Emperor ↑very↓ wise which one was he by the way? I never saw anybody Knitting at the opera in Dresden, but at concerts—yes, & ~~mak~~↑work↓ing all sorts of pretty ~~things~~ fancy work, like the commendable young woman from the Pacific coast—

The prosaic side of life has been so steadily before me this last month or so, I have not been able to answer your light & most amusing letter, but I have appreciated it all the same, & thank you for making it possible to laugh & enjoy the fun. Dont think for a moment that I was so absurd as not to be amused, & to feel flattered by your letter, but I certainly never said you were solemn. I may have said quiet & the singing was charming that day. I must admit both you & Susan seemed tired

Our family muse[2] has been interviewed & has responded most devotedly to my request for a suitable answer to your letter, & here is what <u>he</u> says—& as I shall so soon see you, I will say farewell—& am always admiringly & affectionately your friend

Eliza W Osborne

ALS, Garrison Papers, MNS-S. Not in *Film*.

Enclosure

Dear Mrs. Stanton,
    In your skit
Against your sisterhood who knit,
    Or useful make their fingers,
I wonder if,—deny it not,
The habits of Lucretia Mott,
    Within your memory lingers!

In retrospective vision bright,
Can you recall dear Martha Wright
    Without her work or knitting?
The needles flying in her hands
On washing rags or baby's bands,
    Or other work as fitting?

I cannot think they thought the less,
Or ceased the company to bless
    With conversation's riches,
Because they thus improved their time,
And never deemed it was a crime
    To fill the hours' niches.

They even used to preach & plan
To spread the fashion, so that man
    Might have this satisfaction,
Instead of idling as men do,
With nervous meddling fingers too,
    Why not mate talk with action?

Both as a daughter & a niece,
I pride myself on every piece
    Of handiwork created;
While reveling in social chat,
Or listening to gossip flat,
    My gain is unabated.

That German Emperor you scorn,
Seems to my mind a monarch born,
    Worthy to lead a column;
I'll warrant he could talk & work,
And, neither being used to shirk,
    Was rarely ever solemn.

I could say more upon this head,
But must, before I go to bed,
    Your idle precepts mocking,
Get out my needles and my yarn,
And, caring not a single darn,
    Just finish up this stocking.

~ Ms in hand of E. W. Osborne, Garrison Papers, MNS-S. Not in *Film*.

1. Isaac Watts, "Against Idleness and Mischief," from his *Divine Songs for Children*.
2. William Lloyd Garrison, Jr.

154 ~ Executive Committee of the National-American Woman Suffrage Association

[16 January 1892]

The preliminary executive committee meeting was held Saturday afternoon, Jan. 16, in the Wimodaughsis parlors,[1] the Vice-president at large, Miss Susan B. Anthony, in the chair. Including the general officers, there were present 22 persons, representing nine State societies.

It was voted to use simply the words, "morning, afternoon and evening meetings," in order to do away with the confusion created by the phrase, "executive session," which had led some persons to think that the morning and afternoon meetings of the Association were not open to the public.

The chair appointed as Committee on Credentials Mrs. Jane H. Spofford, Mrs. E. M. S. Marble and Miss Mattie Shaw.[2]

The Plan of Work was discussed at some length.

Miss Laura Clay,[3] of Kentucky, moved to recommend to the convention that a Committee on Southern Work be continued,⁴ and that the convention devote earnest thought to the best methods of aiding and pushing its objects. She thought the Committee were discouraged about the work in the South. She, as a Southern woman, was not. She realized the difficulties. There was a good deal of suffrage sentiment in the South, but it was almost wholly unorganized. Both the Prohibition Party and the People's Party (national) are hesitating about adopting a suffrage plank, for fear it will cost them the support of the South. It is important to remove this difficulty, for politicians will not grant us suffrage from high moral motives alone. Progress in the South is likely to be very rapid when once started. When this Association has as many Southern States organized auxiliary to it as it has Northern States, the movement will be truly national.

Mrs. Hooker, of Connecticut, wanted to thank Miss Clay for every word she had said. Every effort of this Association during the coming year should be spent on the South, because of the great impetus given by the work in connection with the Columbian Exposition. It has already converted Mrs. Potter Palmer,[5] who has invited Mrs. Stone, Mrs. Wallace, Miss Willard[6] and other advocates of equal rights to address the Board of Lady Managers. She (Mrs. Hooker) attended the Franchise Reception given during the N.W.C.T.U. convention, at the *Woman's Journal* office, to which Southern women were especially invited; and of all the bright, strong, spirited addresses on suffrage that she had ever heard, those made by the Southern women on that occasion had been among the best.[7] She would like nothing better than to give two months to going through the South in behalf of the World's Fair, talking woman suffrage at the same time.

Mrs. E. M. S. Marble, of Washington, D.C., said that delightful responses had come from the South to the appeals in behalf of Wimodaughsis, and Georgia was going to have delegates here this year for the first time.[8] She favored work in the South.

Mrs. Lockwood,[9] of Washington, and Mrs. Demmon,[10] of Illinois, spoke to the same effect.

Rev. Anna H. Shaw asked Miss Lucy E. Anthony, who was present as the representative of Mrs. Rachel Foster Avery, to report what had already been done by the Committee on Southern Work.

Miss Lucy Anthony said they had obtained the addresses of more than a hundred persons in the South who favored woman suffrage, and had written to each of them, offering to send a lecturer to any place where the friends would raise $10 toward the cost, this Association to bear all the rest of the expenses. In reply to 128 letters conveying this offer, only about a dozen acceptances were received. All the other replies were most disheartening. The Committee had only succeeded in arranging for a series of five meetings, to be held in Maryland. There had been applications, also, for meetings in Georgia and Alabama, but at points too far apart to make it possible to send a speaker, except at great expense.

Miss Clay said she was encouraged nevertheless. The seed-sowing had to come first. The committee's proposition of a meeting wherever $10 could be raised was very liberal, and she was almost ashamed to ask for anything more; but she wished a speaker could be sent into some of the Southern States—say two of them—free of any charge except for the local expenses. Kentucky had a strong State society and did not need this; so she could speak with the more freedom of the needs of other Southern States.

Mrs. Olive Pond Amies,[11] of Pennsylvania, said that Mrs. Sibley,[12] president of the Georgia W.C.T.U., told her she had been converted at the Franchise Reception in Boston, and that she was going home to work for suffrage in Georgia.

Miss Susan B. Anthony said there were only two ways to break new ground—by going there to speak, or by going there to hold a convention, and in either case by paying your own bills.

Rev. Anna Shaw asked the treasurer if any contributions had come in during the year for the Southern work?

Mrs. Spofford: Only Mrs. Rachel Foster Avery's $1,000, and $100 from Mrs. Johnson,[13] of Kentucky.

Miss Blackwell thought more contributions would have been made if a notice of the fund to be raised for Southern work had been kept standing in the papers. People forgot about it. A contribution of literature had been made, in addition to the cash contributions mentioned. At the meeting of the business committee after last year's convention, it had been voted, instead of appropriating $300 apiece to send the *Woman's Journal* and *Woman's Tribune* to the families of Congressmen, to appropriate the same sum for the papers to be used for the Southern work—the editors of the *Journal* to have the privilege of dividing their $300 as they thought best between the *Journal* and the *Column*. Miss Anthony said that if they could obtain the addresses of any influential persons in the South, she wished they would send them the papers and charge it to this $300. With the help of friends in the South, the names and addresses of a great number of Southern ministers, teachers, legislators, etc., had been obtained, and the *Woman's Column* sent to them. Miss Blackwell said she had become interested in this work, and had been sending about twice as many papers as the whole appropriation of $300 would pay for; so that this might properly be counted as a contribution to the Southern work.

It was voted that a Committee on Southern Work be continued.

Miss Susan B. Anthony thought Kansas should be the principal object of effort until 1894. A proposal for a constitutional convention is pending there. We should work to get it carried. The next Legislature will decide everything relating to the constitutional convention, and we should work to secure the election of a progressive Legislature, who will let women both vote for the members of the constitutional convention and vote upon the constitution when submitted. In the eight States where suffrage amendments have been submitted heretofore, we have had only a few months between the submission of the amendment and the time when it was to be voted upon. Here we shall have two years to work. The fact of municipal suffrage being already granted gives us an advantage to start with, and the most widely circulated newspaper in the State has just declared for full suffrage.

Mrs. Josephine Patten,[14] of Kansas, moved that Kansas be made a special field of work for 1892.

Miss Blackwell thought it would be impossible at present to carry suffrage on a popular vote in any State, even in progressive Kansas. Public opinion was not yet educated up to it. But if the amendment were to be submitted, of course we wanted to get as large a vote for it as possible.

Mrs. Davis,[15] of Kansas, indorsed Miss Anthony's views; but money would be needed.

Mrs. Hooker would be glad to have something done for Kansas, but did not want the money diverted from the South.

Miss Clay thought the work in the South the more important. She should vote for the motion in regard to Kansas, but should regret to have any money diverted from the South under the impression that it would be better spent in Kansas. While the South is regarded as *solid* against suffrage, the politicians will do nothing for us.

Miss Anthony: That is true of national politics; but in the State politics of Kansas there is just now a special exigency which is going to carry woman suffrage there even if we do not work for it; but we should concentrate our work upon Kansas, because we want to carry it overwhelmingly.

Rev. Anna Shaw said that, in consequence of the independent voting of Kansas women, there was so much danger of municipal suffrage being repealed that we ought to concentrate our efforts upon Kansas for the next few years, for fear of losing what we already have. A backward step in Kansas would be an incalculable injury to the cause everywhere. The movement in Kansas at present is all to take municipal suffrage away—not because the women have not done well, but because they have done too well.

Miss Clay thought the backward movement in Kansas in regard to municipal suffrage was because public opinion elsewhere did not sustain it. It was hard for an isolated State like Kansas, Utah or Washington to maintain equal rights while surrounded by a hostile public opinion. The whole country should be educated, and the South particularly. Our most brilliant chance was lost when the constitutional convention of Mississippi failed to grant suffrage to women.[16] It was not the fault of this Association that the measure was lost, but she did not want anything of that sort to happen again.[17]

Mrs. Demmon indorsed this view.

Miss Anthony said that the work in Kansas would not hinder work in the South. Wherever the constitutional door was opened by men, it was our duty to get as good a vote as possible. The question would be submitted in Kansas whether we chose or not.

It was voted to recommend to the convention that Kansas be made a special field of work in 1892, and that a special committee be appointed on Kansas work.

Miss Shaw asked how we should use the Columbian Exposition to push our work. She would have the Association make a specialty of this—raise money to have our booth there, with our literature, our enrolments, etc. The Exposition will educate the Southern women and all other women, and it will be much easier to effect an entrance into the

South the year after the World's Fair than the year before it. Between now and 1893, that should be *the* work.

Mrs. Hooker expressed approval.

Miss Anthony: Mrs. May Wright Sewall advises that every State Suffrage Association try to secure space in its own State building at the World's Fair, and that the National-American should have space in the Woman's Building. Mrs. Potter Palmer has promised Mrs. Avery space for this Association.

Miss Clay proposed that this Association hold its annual meeting a few months later than usual next year, and have it at Chicago during the Exposition.[18] This would ensure a large and representative meeting. After discussion it was voted, almost unanimously, to recommend to the convention so to amend the by-laws as to allow the next annual meeting to be held in Chicago.

↩ *Woman's Journal*, 30 January 1892. Not in *Film*.

    1. At 1328 I Street, Northwest. The Wimodaughsis Society—its name constructed from the words 'wife,' 'mother,' 'daughter,' and 'sister'—was incorporated in 1890 to offer classes for women and provide a building to house headquarters for associations headed by women. Financed by the sale of five dollar shares, the club bought the fifteen-room house on I Street in the summer of 1891, and the National-American association opened an office there in 1892. By then the club had survived a nasty conflict about race, when Anna Shaw, as president, and the majority of directors refused to exclude Fannie Smith, an African-American school principal, from the club's classes. Although the decision, that "this incorporated stock company comes under the provisions of the civil rights bill" and could not exclude on the basis of race, caused some key members to quit the club, Wimodaughsis survived into the twentieth century. (Anna J. Cooper, "Woman Versus Indian," in *A Voice from the South: Anna Julia Cooper*, ed. Mary Helen Washington [New York, 1988], 80–84; Edward Ingle, *The Negro in the District of Columbia* [Baltimore, 1893], 59–60; Croly, *History of the Woman's Club Movement*, 347, 348; *Washington Post*, 3, 9 March 1891; *Woman's Journal*, 14 June, 6 September 1890, 21 March, 8 August, 14 November 1891, 23 January, 28 May, 19 November 1892; *Woman's Tribune*, 14 March 1891.)

    2. Mattie A. N. Shaw (c. 1867–?) was a niece of Anna Shaw and a delegate to the convention from Pennsylvania. It is likely that she changed her name to become Nicolas M. Shaw, using the given name of her grandmother. Anna Shaw described Nicolas as one of John Shaw's daughters; John Shaw's daughters in 1880 were named Mattie and Lizzie. After Nicolas Shaw's marriage to Samuel Fraser in 1903, she lived in Geneseo, New York, and worked in the state suffrage association. (Anna Howard Shaw and Elizabeth Jordan, *The*

Story of a Pioneer, [New York, 1915], 267; Federal Census, Big Rapids, Mich., 1880, and Geneseo, N.Y., 1910; *WWW3*, s.v. "Fraser, Samuel"; *History*, 6:448.)

3. Laura Clay (1849–1941) was the youngest of Cassius Clay's daughters and the last to surface as a forceful figure in the suffrage movement. Her older sisters straddled the divided movement for more than a decade, holding office in both associations, but Laura Clay became active through the American association, when she organized the Kentucky Equal Rights Association as an auxiliary in 1888. By the evidence at this meeting in 1892, she brought to the National-American skills as an infighter and a political vision that assigned highest priority to the South. (*NAW*; *ANB*.)

4. The National-American association created its Committee on Southern Work in 1891 (not in 1892, as often reported), when southern delegates lobbied hard for a plan of work that gave priority to calling conventions in the region's state capitals during legislative sessions. Delegates from other regions of the country raised objections about this redirection of resources: many states needed or wanted national aid for conventions, and the Blackwells wanted to focus on the territories rather than states. In the end, the plan of work stated that "if in addition to the Southern work it was found possible other conventions should be held." To carry out the plan, Rachel Avery, Jane Spofford, and Alice Blackwell were named as the new committee's members. Laura Clay was absent from the meeting in 1891. (*Woman's Journal*, 7 March 1891, and *Woman's Tribune*, 7 March 1891, *Film*, 29:10–12, 19–21; Paul E. Fuller, *Laura Clay and the Woman's Rights Movement* [Lexington, Ky., 1975], 57; Marjorie Spruill Wheeler, *New Women of the New South: The Leaders of the Woman Suffrage Movement in the Southern States* [New York, 1993], 115–16.)

5. Bertha Honoré Palmer (1849–1918), wife of Chicago's wealthy real estate and hotel magnate Potter Palmer, was elected president of the Board of Lady Managers in November 1890. At the time of her elevation to national prominence, she was already a force in Chicago's women's clubs, art collections, philanthropy, and conspicuous consumption. (*NAW*; *ANB*; *Women Building Chicago*.)

6. That is, Lucy Stone, Zerelda Wallace, and Frances Willard.

7. During the convention of the World's Woman's Christian Temperance Union in Boston, the Massachusetts Woman Suffrage Association and the Boston Woman Suffrage League hosted a reception for delegates on 17 November 1891. Special invitations were extended to southerners from states still lacking a franchise department of the temperance union, and Lucy Stone asked her guests to speak about their views of suffrage. (*Woman's Journal*, 28 November 1891.)

8. Daisy Miriam Howard DuBose (1862–1945), known in adulthood as Miriam, and her younger sister, Helen Augusta Howard (1865–1934), known as Augusta, were delegates from the Georgia Woman Suffrage Association that

they organized in 1890. Their efforts to direct the National-American's attention southward culminated in the choice of Atlanta for the convention in 1895. Both sisters apparently pulled back from activism after that event. Miriam DuBose, noted as a musician, married early, gave birth to a son about 1882, and later divorced. In 1920, she was employed as a stenographer in Columbus. Augusta moved to New York City in the 1920s and died there. (*American Women*, s.v. "DuBose, Miriam Howard"; Federal Census, 1870, 1880, and 1920; Certificate of Death, 30 April 1945, Georgia State Office of Vital Records; Kenneth Coleman and Charles Stephen Gurr, eds., *Dictionary of Georgia Biography* [Athens, Ga., 1983], s.v. "Howard, Helen Augusta"; Etta Blanchard Worsley, *Columbus on the Chattahoochee* [Columbus, Ga., 1951], 249-52; SBA diary, 6-9 February 1895, *Film*, 33:80ff.)

9. That is, Mary S. Lockwood.

10. Eliza Ann Van Patten Demmon (1838-1917), of Mount Carroll, Illinois, was treasurer of the state equal suffrage association. Her husband, John Farnsworth Demmon, who died a few months after this meeting in 1892, was described as "a Republican of active and decided type," and he too belonged to the suffrage association. He raised livestock on about fourteen hundred acres of farm land he owned in Whiteside and Carroll counties. (*Portrait and Biographical Album of Whiteside County, Illinois* [Chicago, 1883], 469; *Woman's Journal*, 11 June 1892; Federal Census, 1900; on-line Illinois Statewide Death Index.)

11. Olive Pond Amies (c. 1844-?), wife of Joseph Hay Amies, a Universalist minister, settled in Philadelphia about 1890, after an itinerant life in Lewiston, Maine, New Haven and Waterbury, Connecticut, and Scranton, Pennsylvania. Later in 1892, Joseph Amies, who lacked a church in Philadelphia, patented a new substance for paving roads, and started the Amies Pavement Company. Olive Amies joined him in the firm. Trained to be a teacher, she became a specialist in Sunday school education, joined the Association for the Advancement of Women and the Woman's Christian Temperance Union, and served as an officer and lecturer in Pennsylvania for the state suffrage society and temperance union. (*American Women*; *Papers Read at the Fourth Congress of Women, Held at St. George's Hall, Philadelphia, October 4, 5, 6, 1876* [Washington, D.C., 1877], 1; Philadelphia city directories, 1892 to 1894; Federal Census, Philadelphia, 1900, Delaware County, Pa., 1910;)

12. Jane Elizabeth Thomas Sibley (1838-1930) of Augusta presided over the Georgia Woman's Christian Temperance Union from 1883 to 1900. At the meeting in Boston in November 1891, she first declared herself a suffragist and promised to do her best "to get the Georgia W.C.T.U. to adopt the franchise department." In addition to temperance work, she was known for her teaching of Sunday schools, especially those for the children of workers at her husband's Sibley Cotton Mills. (*American Women*; *SEAP*; *Woman's Journal*, 28 November 1891.)

13. This is probably the same Mary H. Johnson, a vice president of the

Louisville Equal Rights Association, who contributed to the South Dakota campaign one hundred and fifteen dollars that she earned by her knitting. (*Anthony*, 2:676n; *History*, 4:668n; Accounts of the South Dakota Campaign Fund, 1890, *Film*, 28:886ff.)

14. Josephine M. Patten (c. 1845–?), though living in Washington, was a delegate from Kansas, where she had been a leader of the Beloit and Mitchell County suffrage associations and a delegate to state meetings. Raised in Maine, she married Alphonso Patten after he served in the Civil War, and the family lived in Biddeford until their move to Kansas about 1871. Alphonso Patten was a dentist in Maine and Kansas, but he moved his family to Washington about 1891 to take a job in the Treasury Department as an auditor for the post office. The Kansas association took advantage of Josephine Patten's proximity to the National-American's convention to name her a delegate again in 1893. The Pattens still lived in Washington in 1910. (Federal Census, Maine, 1870, Kansas, 1880, and District of Columbia, 1910; Kansas Census, 1885; *Minutes of the Kansas Equal Suffrage Association, At the First, Second, Third and Fourth Annual Meetings in 1884-5-7* [N.p., 1887?], 34, 35; *Register of Federal Officers, 1891*, 60.)

15. Martha Ann Powell Davis (1828–1900) of Kansas moved to Washington when her husband, John Davis, entered Congress in March 1891, as a Populist. Born in England and raised in the Midwest with her brother, the explorer John Wesley Powell, she married Davis in 1851 in Illinois and moved with him to Junction City, Kansas, in 1872. At this meeting, she was named to the Special Committee for Kansas. (Annie L. Diggs, "The Women in the Alliance Movement," *Arena* 32 [July 1892]: 178; *Kansas City Times*, 4 February 1888, and *Junction City Tribune*, 30 November 1900, in Kansas Biographical Scrapbooks, KHi; *TwCBDNA*; *BDAC*; *Papers*, 4:125.)

16. Clay refers to the Mississippi Constitutional Convention of 1890, called primarily to rewrite qualifications for voters in order to restore white supremacy. Clay shared Henry Blackwell's faith that limited woman suffrage, preferably through a literacy qualification for women, would accomplish the goal by increasing the white electorate. In 1890, Blackwell lobbied from afar for delegates to adopt his plan. Members of Mississippi's well-organized Woman's Christian Temperance Union had a similar idea, though based on a property qualification, but convention delegates rebuffed their request for a hearing. Although woman suffrage with a property qualification met with short-lived approval in the convention's franchise committee, in the end, delegates preferred placing insurmountable obstacles in the path of black men. Looking back at the convention, the legislative director of the Mississippi temperance union drew the same lesson that Clay did; "If there had been a simultaneous movement of women to support those brave men who took our part in the convention," she told a meeting in Boston in 1891, "I believe we should have got our vote." (H. B. Blackwell to Lucy Stone, 18 and 24 August 1890, and L. Stone to H. B. Blackwell, 1 September 1890, in Wheeler, *Loving*

Warriors, 332, 334, 337; *Woman's Journal*, 26 April 1890, 28 November 1891; William Charles Sallis, "The Color Line in Mississippi Politics, 1865-1915" [Ph.D., University of Kentucky, 1967], 298-319; Bradley G. Bond, *Political Culture in the Nineteenth-Century South: Mississippi, 1830-1900* [Baton Rouge, La., 1995], 232-51; Stephen Cresswell, *Rednecks, Redeemers, and Race: Mississippi after Reconstruction, 1877-1917* [Jackson, Miss., 2006], 116-20; A. Elizabeth Taylor, "The Woman Suffrage Movement in Mississippi, 1890-1920," *Journal of Mississippi History* 30 [February 1968]: 1-6; Wheeler, *New Women of the New South*, 113-15, 204, 234.)

17. At a later session, the Southern Committee was reconstituted as a body comprised of the presidents of the seven southern state auxiliaries, with power to select their own officers. The committee also received unusual authority to collect donations for its work directly rather than through the National-American. (*Woman's Tribune*, 13 February 1892, *Film*, 29:1011-13.)

18. This idea was defeated on January 19, after considerable argument. Isabella Hooker pointed out that the Columbian Exposition would not open in time for the convention of 1893 to be held there, and ECS told the delegates, "When Congress moves we'll move, and not till then." But the idea of a migratory convention had wide appeal. Vocal supporters of the change were Laura Clay, Alice Blackwell, Ella Marble, Claudia Murphy of Ohio, and Carrie Catt of Washington State. The *Washington Post*, whose reporter had inside access to someone during the entire convention, interpreted the discussion as "a fight between the East and the West, with the latter supported by the radical branch from the East." After a majority voted against the change, delegates from western states lodged a protest about a system of voting weighted in favor of easterners. (*Evening Star*, 20 January 1892, and *Washington Post*, 20 January 1892, *Film*, 29:995, 999.)

155 ~ "THE SOLITUDE OF SELF": SPEECH BY ECS TO THE HOUSE JUDICIARY COMMITTEE

EDITORIAL NOTE: Ice on the streets of Washington delayed the arrival of the women scheduled to speak before the House Committee on the Judiciary at ten o'clock on 18 February 1892. While the Washington convention of the National-American carried on its business, committee members heard from ECS, Lucy Stone, Isabella Hooker, and SBA. This was a hearing about Halbert Greenleaf's Joint Resolution, House Resolution 14, proposing a constitutional amendment extending to women voting rights only in federal elections. The customary woman suffrage amendment was not before the House of Representatives at the time. Nonetheless, according to the

Washington Post, ECS opened with an explanation of her topic; "she thought in twenty-four years she had covered everything that could be said on the sixteenth amendment, and wasn't going to repeat, but would talk on 'Individuality.'" The text here is that printed to mimic a government document in a pamphlet with other testimony given at the hearing. ECS delivered the speech again at the National-American's convention, and the *Woman's Tribune* published what it described as the speech delivered in the evening of February 18. Differences between the two texts are slight and most of them matters set by style sheets. Any differences in words are indicated in notes. ECS published the speech again in 1901 in the free-thought weekly *Boston Investigator*. The differences between the late text and those published in 1892 are substantive. Again, the differences are indicated in notes. What cannot be known now is whether the passages new to the 1901 text were recent changes. ECS was virtually blind in 1901; she was not rereading her speeches, nor was she writing for herself. There is some circumstantial evidence that the speeches were read to her, so it is possible that she revised aloud. It is equally possible that the manuscript she sent to the *Investigator* simply differed from the source used by typesetters in 1892. (*Congressional Record*, 52d Cong., 1st sess., 5 January 1892, p. 133; Ms minutes, House Committee on the Judiciary, and *Washington Post*, 19 January 1892, *Film*, 29:1016, 1025.)

[18 January 1892]

Mr. Chairman[1] and gentlemen of the committee: We have been speaking before Committees of the Judiciary for the last twenty years, and we have gone over all the arguments in favor of a sixteenth amendment which are familiar to all you gentlemen; therefore, it will not be necessary that I should repeat them again.

The point I wish plainly to bring before you on this occasion is the individuality of each human soul; our Protestant idea, the right of individual conscience and judgment—our republican idea, individual citizenship. In discussing the rights of woman, we are to consider, first, what belongs to her as an individual, in a world of her own, the arbiter of her own destiny, an imaginary Robinson Crusoe with her woman Friday on a solitary island.[2] Her rights under such circumstances are to use all her faculties for her own safety and happiness.

Secondly, if we consider her as a citizen, as a member of a great nation, she must have the same rights as all other members, according to the fundamental principles of our Government.

Thirdly, viewed as a woman, an equal factor in civilization, her rights and duties are still the same—individual happiness and development.

Fourthly, it is only the incidental relations of life, such as mother, wife, sister, daughter, that may involve some special duties and training. In the usual discussion in regard to woman's sphere, such men as Herbert Spencer, Frederic Harrison,[3] and Grant Allen[4] uniformly subordinate her rights and duties as an individual, as a citizen, as a woman, to the necessities of these incidental relations, some of which a large class of women may never assume.[5] In discussing the sphere of man we do not decide his rights as an individual, as a citizen, as a man by his duties as a father, a husband, a brother, or a son, relations some of which he may never fill. Moreover he would be better fitted for these very relations and whatever special work he might choose to do to earn his bread by the complete development of all his faculties as an individual.

Just so with woman. The education that will fit her to discharge the duties in the largest sphere of human usefulness will best fit her for whatever special work she may be compelled to do.

The isolation of every human soul and the necessity of self-dependence must give each individual the right to choose his own surroundings.

The strongest reason for giving woman all the opportunities for higher education, for the full development of her faculties, forces of mind and body;[6] for giving her the most enlarged freedom of thought and action; a complete emancipation from all forms of bondage, of custom, dependence, superstition; from all the crippling influences of fear, is the solitude and personal responsibility of her own individual life. The strongest reason why we ask for woman a voice in the government under which she lives; in the religion she is asked to believe; equality in social life, where she is a chief factor;[7] a place in the trades and professions, where she may earn her bread, is because of her birthright to self-sovereignty; because, as an individual, she must rely on herself. No matter how much women prefer to lean, to be protected and supported, nor how much men desire to have them do so, they must make the voyage of life alone, and for safety in an emergency they must know something of the laws of navigation. To guide our own craft, we must be captain, pilot, engineer; with chart and compass to stand at the wheel; to watch the wind and waves and know when to take in the sail, and to read the signs in the firmament over all.[8] It matters not whether the solitary voyager is man or woman. Nature having endowed them equally, leaves them to their own skill and judgment in the hour of danger, and, if not equal to the occasion, alike they perish.

To appreciate the importance of fitting every human soul for independent action, think for a moment of the immeasurable solitude of self. We come into the world alone, unlike all who have gone before us; we leave it alone under circumstances peculiar to ourselves. No mortal ever has been, no mortal ever will be like the soul just launched on the sea of life. There can never again be just such a combination of prenatal influences; never again just such environments as make up the infancy, youth, and manhood of this one. Nature never repeats herself, and the possibilities of one human soul will never be found in another. No one has ever found two blades of ribbon grass alike, and no one will ever find two human beings alike. Seeing, then, what must be the infinite diversity in human character, we can in a measure appreciate the loss to a nation when any large class of the people is uneducated and unrepresented in the government. We ask for the complete development of every individual, first, for his own benefit and happiness. In fitting out an army we give each soldier his own knapsack, arms, powder, his blanket, cup, knife, fork and spoon. We provide alike for all their individual necessities, then each man bears his own burden.

Again we ask complete individual development for the general good; for the consensus of the competent on the whole round of human interests; on all questions of national life, and here each man must bear his share of the general burden. It is sad to see how soon friendless children are left to bear their own burdens[9] before they can analyze their feelings; before they can even tell their joys and sorrows, they are thrown on their own resources. The great lesson that nature seems to teach us at all ages is self-dependence, self-protection, self-support. What a touching instance of a child's solitude; of that hunger of the heart for love and recognition, in the case of the little girl who helped to dress a Christmas tree for the children of the family in which she served. On finding there was no present for herself she slipped away in the darkness and spent the night in an open field sitting on a stone, and when found in the morning was weeping as if her heart would break. No mortal will ever know the thoughts that passed through the mind of that friendless child in the long hours of that cold night, with only the silent stars to keep her company. The mention of her case in the daily papers moved many generous hearts to send her presents, but in the hours of her keenest suffering she was thrown wholly on herself for consolation.[10]

In youth our most bitter disappointments,[11] our brightest hopes and ambitions are known only to ourselves; even our friendship and love we never fully share with another; there is something of every passion in every situation we conceal. Even so in our triumphs and our defeats.[12] The successful candidate for the Presidency and his opponent each have a solitude peculiarly his own, and good form forbids either to speak of his pleasure or regret. The solitude of the king on his throne and the prisoner in his cell differs in character and degree, but it is solitude nevertheless.

We ask no sympathy from others in the anxiety and agony of a broken friendship or shattered love. When death sunders our nearest ties, alone we sit in the shadow of our affliction. Alike mid the greatest triumphs and darkest tragedies of life we walk alone. On the divine heights of human attainments, eulogized and worshiped as a hero or saint, we stand alone. In ignorance, poverty, and vice, as a pauper or criminal, alone we starve or steal; alone we suffer the sneers and rebuffs of our fellows; alone we are hunted and hounded through dark courts and alleys, in by-ways and highways; alone we stand in the judgment seat; alone in the prison cell we lament our crimes and misfortunes; alone we expiate them on the gallows. In hours like these we realize the awful solitude of individual life, its pains, its penalties, its responsibilities; hours in which the youngest and most helpless are thrown on their own resources for guidance and consolation. Seeing then that life must ever be a march and a battle, that each soldier must be equipped for his own protection, it is the height of cruelty to rob the individual of a single natural right.[13]

To throw obstacles in the way of a complete education is like putting out the eyes; to deny the rights of property, like cutting off the hands. To deny political equality is to rob the ostracised of all self-respect; of credit in the market place; of recompense in the world of work; of a voice in those who make and administer the law; a choice in the jury before whom they are tried, and in the judge who decides their punishment. Shakespeare's play of Titus and Andronicus contains a terrible satire on woman's position in the nineteenth century[14]—"Rude men" (the play tells us) "seized the king's daughter, cut out her tongue, cut off her hands, and then bade her go call for water and wash her hands." What a picture of woman's position. Robbed of her natural rights, handicapped by law and custom at every turn, yet compelled to fight her own battles, and in the emergencies of life to fall back on herself for protection.

The girl of sixteen, thrown on the world to support herself, to make her own place in society, to resist the temptations that surround her and maintain a spotless integrity, must do all this by native force or superior education. She does not acquire this power by being trained to trust others and distrust herself. If she wearies of the struggle, finding it hard work to swim upstream, and allows herself to drift with the current, she will find plenty of company, but not one to share her misery in the hour of her deepest humiliation. If she tries to retrieve her position, to conceal the past, her life is hedged about with fears lest willing hands should tear the veil from what she fain would hide. Young and friendless, *she* knows the bitter solitude of self.

How the little courtesies of life on the surface of society, deemed so important from man towards woman, fade into utter insignificance in view of the deeper tragedies in which she must play her part alone, where no human aid is possible.

The young wife and mother, at the head of some establishment with a kind husband to shield her from the adverse winds of life, with wealth, fortune and position, has a certain harbor of safety, secure against the ordinary ills of life. But to manage a household, have a desirable influence in society, keep her friends and the affections of her husband, train her children and servants well, she must have rare common sense, wisdom, diplomacy, and a knowledge of human nature. To do all this she needs the cardinal virtues and the strong points of character that the most successful statesman possesses.

An uneducated woman, trained to dependence, with no resources in herself must make a failure of any position in life. But society says women do not need a knowledge of the world; the liberal training that experience in public life must give, all the advantages of collegiate education; but when for the lack of all this, the woman's happiness is wrecked, alone she bears her humiliation; and the solitude of the weak and the ignorant is indeed pitiable. In the wild chase for the prizes of life they are ground to powder.[15]

In age, when the pleasures of youth are passed, children grown up, married and gone, the hurry and bustle of life in a measure over, when the hands are weary of active service, when the old armchair and the fireside are the chosen resorts, then men and women alike must fall back on their own resources. If they cannot find companionship in books, if they have no interest in the vital questions of the hour, no interest in watching the consummation of reforms, with which they might have been identified, they soon pass into their dotage. The more fully the faculties of the mind[16] are developed and kept in use, the longer the period of vigor and active interest in all around us continues. If from a lifelong participation in public affairs a woman feels responsible for the laws regulating our system of education, the discipline of our jails and prisons, the sanitary condition of our private homes, public buildings, and thoroughfares, an interest in commerce, finance, our foreign relations, in any or all these questions, her solitude will at least be respectable, and she will not be driven to gossip or scandal for entertainment.

The chief reason for opening to every soul the doors to the whole round of human duties and pleasures is the individual development thus attained, the resources thus provided under all circumstances to mitigate the solitude that at times must come to everyone. I once asked Prince Krapotkin,[17] a Russian nihilist, how he endured his long years in prison, deprived of books, pen, ink, and paper. "Ah," he said, "I thought out many questions in which I had a deep interest. In the pursuit of an idea I took no note of time. When tired of solving knotty problems I recited all the beautiful passages in prose or verse I had ever learned. I became acquainted with myself and my own resources. I had a world of my own, a vast empire, that no Russian jailor or Czar could invade." Such is the value of liberal thought and broad culture when shut off from all human companionship, bringing comfort and sunshine within even the four walls of a prison cell.

As women ofttimes share a similar fate, should they not have all the consolation that the most liberal education can give? Their suffering in the prisons of St. Petersburg; in the long, weary marches to Siberia, and in the mines, working side by side with men, surely call for all the self-support that the most exalted sentiments of heroism can give.[18] When suddenly roused at midnight, with the startling cry of "fire! fire!" to find the house over their heads in flames, do women wait for men to point the way to safety? And are the men, equally bewildered and half suffocated with smoke, in a position to do more than try to save themselves?

At such times the most timid women have shown a courage and heroism in saving their husbands and children that has surprised everybody. Inasmuch, then, as woman shares equally the joys and sorrows of time and eternity, is it not the height of presumption in man to propose to represent her at the ballot box and the throne of grace, to do her voting in the state, her praying in the church, and to assume the position of high priest at the family altar?

Nothing strengthens the judgment and quickens the conscience like individual responsibility. Nothing adds such dignity to character as the recognition of one's self-sovereignty; the right to an equal place, everywhere conceded; a place earned by personal merit, not an artificial attainment, by inheritance, wealth, family, and position. Seeing, then, that the responsibilities of life rest equally on man and woman, that their destiny is the same, they need the same preparation for time and eternity. The talk of sheltering woman[19] from the fierce storms of life is the sheerest mockery, for they beat on her from every point of the compass, just as they do on man, and with more fatal results, for he has been trained to protect himself, to resist, to conquer. Such are the facts in human experience, the responsibilities of individual sovereignty. Rich and poor, intelligent and ignorant, wise and foolish, virtuous and vicious, man and woman, it is ever the same, each soul must depend wholly on itself.

Whatever the theories may be of woman's dependence on man, in the supreme moments of her life he can not bear her burdens. Alone she goes to the gates of death to give life to every man that is born into the world. No one can share her fears, no one can mitigate her pangs; and if her sorrow is greater than she can bear, alone she passes beyond the gates into the vast unknown.

From the mountain tops of Judea, long ago, a heavenly voice bade His disciples "Bear ye one another's burdens,"[20] but humanity has not yet risen to that point of self-sacrifice, and if ever so willing, how few the burdens are that one soul can bear for another. In the highways of

18 JANUARY 1892 ~ 431

Palestine; in prayer and fasting on the solitary mountain top; in the Garden of Gethsemane; before the judgment seat of Pilate; betrayed by one of His trusted disciples at His last supper; in His agonies on the cross, even Jesus of Nazareth, in those last sad days on earth, felt the awful solitude of self. Deserted by man, in agony he cries, "My God! My God! why hast Thou forsaken me?"[21] And so it ever must be in the conflicting scenes of life, in the long, weary march, each one walks alone. We may have many friends, love, kindness, sympathy, and charity to smoothe our pathway in everyday life, but in the tragedies and triumphs of human experience each mortal stands alone.[22]

But when all artificial trammels are removed, and women are recognized as individuals, responsible for their own environments, thoroughly educated for all positions in life they may be called to fill; with all the resources in themselves that liberal thought and broad culture can give; guided by their own conscience and judgment; trained to self-protection by a healthy development of the muscular system and skill in the use of weapons of defense, and stimulated to self-support by a knowledge of the business world and the pleasure that pecuniary independence must ever give; when women are trained in this way they will, in a measure, be fitted for those hours of solitude that come alike to all, whether prepared or otherwise. As in our extremity we must depend on ourselves, the dictates of wisdom point to complete individual development.

In talking of education how shallow the argument, that each class must be educated for the special work it proposes to do, and all those faculties not needed in this special work must lie dormant[23] and utterly wither for want of use, when, perhaps, these will be the very faculties needed in life's greatest emergencies. Some say, Where is the use of drilling girls in the languages, the sciences, in law, medicine, theology? As wives, mothers, housekeepers, cooks, they need a different curriculum from boys who are to fill all positions. The chief cooks in our great hotels and ocean steamers are men. In our large cities men run the bakeries; they make our bread, cake and pies. They manage the laundries; they are now considered our best milliners and dressmakers. Because some men fill these departments of usefulness, shall we regulate the curriculum in Harvard and Yale to their present necessities? If not, why this talk in our best colleges of a curriculum for girls who are crowding into the trades and professions; teachers in all our public schools, rapidly filling many lucrative and honorable positions in life? They are showing, too, their calmness and courage in the most trying hours of human experience.

You have probably all read in the daily papers of the terrible storm in the Bay of Biscay when a tidal wave made such havoc on the shore, wrecking vessels, unroofing houses, and carrying destruction everywhere.[24] Among other buildings the woman's prison was demolished. Those who escaped saw men struggling to reach the shore.[25] They promptly by clasping hands made a chain of themselves and pushed out into the sea, again and again, at the risk of their lives, until they had brought six men to shore, carried them to a shelter, and did all in their power for their comfort and protection.

What special school training could have prepared these women for this sublime moment in their lives? In times like this humanity rises above all college curriculums and recognizes Nature as the greatest of all teachers in the hour of danger and death.[26] Women are already the equals of men in the whole realm of thought, in art, science, literature, and government. With telescopic vision they explore the starry firmament and bring back the history of the planetary world.[27] With chart and compass they pilot ships across the mighty deep, and with skillful finger send electric messages around the globe. In galleries of art the beauties of nature and the virtues of humanity are immortalized by them on canvas and by their inspired touch dull blocks of marble are transformed into angels of light.

In music they speak again the language of Mendelssohn, Beethoven, Chopin, Schumann,[28] and are worthy interpreters of their great thoughts. The poetry and novels of the century are theirs, and they have touched the keynote of reform in religion, politics, and social life. They fill the editor's and professor's chair, and plead at the bar of justice, walk the wards of the hospital, and speak from the pulpit and the platform; such is the type of womanhood that an enlightened public sentiment welcomes to-day, and such the triumph of the facts of life over the false theories of the past.

Is it, then, consistent to hold the developed woman of this day within the same narrow political limits as the dame with the spinning wheel and knitting needle occupied in the past? No! no! Machinery has taken the labors of woman as well as man on its tireless shoulders; the loom and the spinning wheel are but dreams of the past; the pen, the brush, the easel, the chisel, have taken their places, while the hopes and ambitions of women are essentially changed.

We see reason sufficient in the outer conditions of human beings for individual liberty and development, but when we consider the self dependence of every human soul we see the need of courage, judgment, and the exercise of every faculty of mind and body, strengthened and developed by use, in woman as well as man.[29]

Whatever may be said of man's protecting power in ordinary conditions, mid all the terrible disasters by land and sea, in the supreme moments of danger, alone woman must ever meet the horrors of the situation; the Angel of Death even makes no royal pathway for her. Man's love and sympathy enter only into the sunshine of our lives. In that solemn solitude of self, that links us with the immeasurable and the eternal, each soul lives alone forever. A recent writer says:[30]

> I remember once, in crossing the Atlantic, to have gone upon the deck of the ship at midnight, when a dense black cloud enveloped the sky, and the great deep was roaring madly under the lashes of demoniac winds. My feeling was not of danger or fear (which is a base surrender of the immortal soul), but of utter desolation and loneliness; a little speck of life shut in by a tremendous darkness. Again I remember to have climbed the slopes of the Swiss Alps, up beyond the point where vegetation ceases, and the stunted conifers no longer struggle against the unfeeling blasts. Around me lay a huge confusion of rocks, out of which the gigantic ice peaks shot into the measureless blue of the heavens, and again my only feeling was the awful solitude.
>
> And yet, there is a solitude, which each and every one of us has always carried with him more inaccessible than the ice-cold mountains, more profound than the midnight sea; the solitude of self. Our inner being, which we call ourself, no eye nor touch of man or angel has ever pierced. It is more hidden than the caves of the gnome; the sacred adytum of the oracle; the hidden chamber of eleusinian mystery, for to it only omniscience is permitted to enter.

Such is individual life. Who, I ask you, can take, dare take, on himself the rights, the duties, the responsibilities of another human soul?

❦ *Hearing of the Woman Suffrage Association Before the Committee on Judiciary, Monday, January 18, 1892,* (N.p., n.d.), 1–5, in ECS Papers, DLC.

1. David Browning Culberson (1830–1900), Democrat of Texas and former officer in the Confederate army, served in the House of Representatives from 1875 to 1897. He became chairman of the House Judiciary Committee at the opening of the first session of the Fifty-second Congress. Ten Democrats, six of them southerners, and five Republicans made up the committee. Ezra Taylor of Ohio and Case Broderick of Kansas were strong supporters of woman suffrage. (*BDAC*.)

2. A reference to the fictional narrator of Daniel Defoe's novel *Robinson Crusoe* (1719), the heart of which is Crusoe's account of a solitary existence on a South American island after a shipwreck. Friday, the name Crusoe gave to a prisoner he freed from the control of pirates, became his companion and servant.

3. Frederic Harrison (1831–1923), a follower of Auguste Comte and president of London's Positivist Society, had recently lectured on "Woman's True Function," which he defined as "personal and not general, domestic and not public: . . . working through the imagination rather than through reason, by the heart rather than by the head." Women achieved their highest purpose, in the family, within the family, while outside of it they risked becoming "abortive men." (*Oxford DNB*; *Times* [London], 7 September 1891.)

4. Grant Blairfindie Allen (1848–1899), a Canadian who settled in England, was a follower of Herbert Spencer, known first for his scientific writing and later for his novels. To an upsurge of antisuffragism in England in 1889, he contributed "Plain Words on the Woman Question," declaring "that in the best-ordered community almost every woman should marry at twenty or thereabouts" and bear four children in order for the species to reproduce itself. The movement for woman's rights had misguidedly "subordinated the claims of the wives and mothers to the claims of the unmarried women." (*Oxford DNB*; *Popular Science Monthly* 21 [December 1889]: 170–81.)

5. In the *Woman's Tribune*, this reads, "neither of which a large class of women may ever assume," and the following sentence ends, "relations he may never fill." In the *Boston Investigator*, the latter sentence ends, "some of which he might never fill."

6. *Investigator* reads, "her faculties and forces of mind and body".

7. Both variants read, "where she is the chief factor."

8. *Investigator* reads: "the signs of coming storms in the firmament over all."

9. *Investigator* reads: "their own burdens. Before they can analyze".

10. The paragraph continues in *Investigator*: "When a girl may marry legally at twelve years of age, and barter away all that is most precious to pure and

innocent girlhood at the age of ten, you may as well talk of her safety with wild beasts in the tangled forests of Africa as in the present civilizations of England and America, the leading nations on the globe. These child-women desecrated and degraded thus early, learn the bitter solitude of self."

11. *Investigator* reads, "one's most bitter disappointments".

12. *Investigator* reads, "in every situation we conceal, alike in our triumphs and our defeats."

13. *Investigator* reads, "a single natural right, and the greatest of these is an equal voice in the Government under which we live."

14. William Shakespeare, *Titus Andronicus*, act 2, sc. 4, lines 960–69. The source of ECS's synopsis is unknown.

15. The paragraph continues in *Investigator*: "Every day our journals report the wreck of some circle in high life, in which the trusted custodians of social morality and family honor have sacrificed all to personal vanity. Every individual has an ambition to excel in some direction, and so long as a large class of women are trained simply for fashionable life, to dress with taste and attract attention, the foundations of home life must be as unstable as the sands of the sea."

16. *Investigator* reads: "The more fully all the faculties of the mind".

17. Pyotr Alekseyevich Kropotkin (1842–1921), known as Prince Kropotkin, was a Russian revolutionary and anarchist philosopher, who lived in England from 1886 to 1917. In 1887 he published *In Russian and French Prisons*, recounting his own prison time. ECS called on Kropotkin in London in 1888. (*Eighty Years*, 409–10.)

18. In *Investigator*, the sentence ends, "the most exalted sentiments of patriotism can give." A paragraph is then inserted: "Two women from high life in England have just been sentenced to solitary confinement for a term of years. They have fathers, husbands, brothers, sons, but none of these can minister now to their needs nor share their solitude. Alone they shudder over the past, and look with dread into the dark and weary days to come. What are the fine-spun theories of man's protecting power to them now?"

19. *Investigator* reads, "they need the same preparation. To talk of sheltering woman".

20. Gal. 6:2.

21. ECS names events in the final days of the life of Jesus, ending with his words from the cross, from Matt. 27:46 and Mark 16:34.

22. *Investigator* reads, "but in the tragedies that belong to all human experiences, each mortal stands alone."

23. Both printings of the speech in 1892 read, "those faculties not needed in this special walk must lie dormant." A correction was made in the 1901 printing.

24. This story might be recent: the eastern shores of Ireland, England, France, Spain, and Portugal endured immense damage from unusual hurricane-force winds that swept across the Atlantic in early November 1891. The

Bay of Biscay was hit on November 11. (*Monthly Weather Review* 19 [November 1891]: 264–65; *New York Times*, 12, 13 November 1891.)

25. *Investigator* reads, "Those who escaped, standing on the beach, saw men struggling to reach the shore."

26. In *Investigator*, the next sentence reads, "Women are already the equals of men in courage and heroism." The text then omits three sentences and resumes at "In music".

27. In this and the following sentence, retained in the *Tribune*, the final nouns are switched; the first ends, "bring back the history of the planetary spheres"; the second ends, "send electric messages around the world."

28. The German composers Felix Mendelssohn (1809–1847), Ludwig van Beethoven (1770–1827), and Robert Alexander Schumann (1810–1856), and the Polish composer Frédéric-François Chopin (1810–1849).

29. *Investigator* reads, "but when we consider the self-dependence of every human soul in all the tragedies of life, we see the need of courage, judgment, independence, skill, in the exercise of every faculty of mind and body strengthened and developed by use in woman, as well as man."

30. ECS recycled this quotation from her address of 27 May 1881 to the Free Religious Association, in *Papers* 4:85. Although she indicated in both instances that she quoted someone, the words are widely attributed to her. Her source is as yet undiscovered.

156 ⇝ Business Meeting of the National-American Woman Suffrage Association

> EDITORIAL NOTE: On the morning of 21 January 1892, the National-American's committee on resolutions reported, recommending various actions to be undertaken by suffragists in the states and urging Congress to pass an act protecting women's right to vote for members of the House of Representatives. The report was adopted without much debate, but ECS had learned of a fight in the committee over her resolution in favor of keeping the Columbian Exposition open on Sundays. She decided to bring the dispute to the convention floor.

[21 January 1892]

Mrs. Stanton then said she desired to present a resolution which she had sent to the committee and which had received at first a majority vote, but which afterwards had been reconsidered and rejected because so vehemently opposed. Objection was made by Miss Clay to the resolution being read, but by vote Mrs. Stanton was allowed to proceed.[1] Her resolution was as follows:

> *Whereas,* The purpose of the World's Fair to be held in Chicago, in 1893 is not only to show the progress of all nations in art, science, education and reform, but to bring the people in close fraternal relations, to cultivate the moral principles and religious emotions of all classes, and,
>
> *Whereas,* Sunday is the only day that the great army of working men and women can visit the Fair, therefore,
>
> *Resolved,* That it is the duty of the managers to open the gates, that the industrial classes may share in all the benefits of the Exposition and feel that new self-respect and dignity that the contemplation of the wonderful works of men must ever give.

A spicy discussion then followed. Mrs. Stanton advocated the resolution in an earnest manner. As her remarks were not taken down in short hand and as they expressed the same thought which appears in the February number of the *North American* in a communication from Mrs. Stanton,[2] the *Tribune* will republish this later.

Mrs. Hooker said she was very much in favor of the resolution, but was not in favor of this body passing it. She did not want to divide the suffrage forces.

Mrs. Stanton said she did not think this Association had ever wanted to find out that we all thought alike before advocating any measure.

Mrs. Lockwood was in favor of opening the gates on Sunday, but she thought this resolution should be better defined.[3] When the Board of Lady managers voted on the question, women who thought alike voted directly opposite, because the resolution was not definite. She was in favor of opening the gates for the arts, for sermons and music, but not for traffic and the bustle of machinery.

Lucy Stone regretted the resolution and thought it a thousand pities to bring in something to disturb the peace of the convention when it was not necessary. Mrs. Diggs[4] urged that the primary object of the organization was to carry Woman Suffrage, and we should present an undivided front. If we read the Congressional Record we would see that every day the petitions were pouring in from the W.C.T.U. and the churches.[5] Dr. Fannie Dickinson supported the resolution and urged it in behalf of the children.[6] Mrs. Colby also spoke in favor, bringing up the point that the Sunday breathing spot for thousands of Chicago's working classes had been appropriated for the fair, and now it was cruel to shut them out of the grounds on the only day when they could enjoy them.

Mrs. Saxon spoke of the good effect of opening the Exposition at New Orleans on Sunday.[7] The liquor saloons of the city were open on Sunday, but their patronage was much decreased by the fact of the Exposition being opened, and the day was exceptionally quiet and orderly.

Several others spoke against the resolution on the ground that it was not germane to the objects of the convention. Miss Clay moved to table the resolution, which being defeated Mrs. Stanton withdrew it, saying she had obtained the discussion which was her object in presenting it.[8]

Rev. Annie H. Shaw introduced a resolution asking the managers of the World's Fair not to allow the sale of liquor on the grounds. This was opposed on the same line as the preceding one, and also withdrawn.

~ *Woman's Tribune*, 30 January 1892.

1. According to the *Washington Post*, Clay raised two objections, that the resolution was not germane to the association's purpose and that no resolution should come to the floor without committee approval. (22 January 1892, *Film*, 29:1000.)

2. See below at start of February 1892.

3. Mary Lockwood, like Isabella Hooker and Frances Dickinson, served on the Board of Lady Managers. At their first meeting in late November 1890, the board voted in favor of Sunday closing but quickly reversed the vote. People in charge of the exposition, with huge bonds to pay off, worried about the financial impact of closing the grounds on Sunday. (*New York Times*, 29 November 1890.)

4. Annie LePorte Diggs (1848-1916), a leader among Populists in Kansas and member of the state suffrage association, was also a religious liberal who succeeded Lucretia Mott as a vice president of the Free Religous Association. (*NAW*; *ANB*.)

5. The Woman's Christian Temperance Union made it a special project to petition Congress to close the exposition on Sunday, joining the National Reform Association, the Young Men's Christian Association, and other proponents of state enforcement of a religious Sabbath. (Foster, *Moral Reconstruction*, 101-7.)

6. The *Washington Post* reported heated exchanges at this point between

Dickinson and Clay. To Clay's view that the resolution would alienate supporters of woman suffrage, Dickinson replied that voters wanted the fair open, and their support was more important. Clay retorted, "'I would like to introduce to Dr. Dickinson's notice the word honesty. Is it honesty to bring people thousands of miles here to a suffrage convention and then introduce them to a Sabbath observance society?' Dr. Dickinson made a spicy reply."

7. The World's Industrial and Cotton Centennial Exposition in New Orleans in 1885.

8. According to the *Washington Post*, at this point Carrie Catt moved to expunge this entire discussion from the minutes.

157 ~ ARTICLE BY ECS

[February 1892]

SUNDAY AT THE WORLD'S FAIR.

Some of our people are already passing resolutions in their convocations and rolling up petitions to Congress asking that the World's Fair in Chicago may be closed on Sundays, and it is important that those holding opposite views should be heard.

To my mind the fair should be open for many reasons. It is the only day that the laboring masses can enjoy it, as they are practically excluded every other day by the necessities of their condition. When the vast army of men who will construct the magnificent buildings and beautify the grounds, who day by day will lift the heavy machinery and foreign exhibits in place, desire to bring their wives and children to the exposition, Sunday will be the only day they will have leisure to do so; the only day, too, when farm-hands from the country, men and women from the workshops and the factories, clerks from the busy marts of trade, servants from their domestic vocations, can claim a few hours for recreation. When we consider the multitudes that comprise these classes and their immense value in the world of work, we appreciate the importance of their rights and interests in all the arrangements of society, whether for profit or pleasure. So far from the fair being closed on Sunday, it should be the one day especially reserved for the masses, when all those who have other opportunities should not crowd the exposition.

Though the Centennial Exposition in 1876 was closed on Sunday, yet favored statesmen, millionaires, and foreign diplomats visited every department on that day and viewed the exhibits at their leisure.[1] Whether the fair is open or not, the city of Chicago will inevitably be crowded on Sunday. People will come from all parts of the State, to look at each other, at the exposition buildings, the parks, and to enjoy whatever attractions the surroundings afford. If the exposition is closed, they must necessarily crowd less desirable places of amusement; hence if it is the best interests of the people those in authority aim at, they will keep the fair open on Sunday.

It is said that "those who watch the exhibits and serve the public through the week should have one day of rest." As their labors are transient, lasting only a few months, and as their surroundings are varied, beautiful, and entertaining, the tax on their time and patience would be light compared with the dreary monotony of the lives of ordinary laborers who spend year after year in dingy workshops and dark offices, or with multitudes of young men, sitting with bent shoulders, writing by artificial lights,—a class as much to be pitied as those who dig in the mines, scarcely ever seeing the light of day.

Those who can dispose of their time as they see fit can hardly appreciate what a Sunday at the World's Fair would be for large classes of their fellow men. It is difficult to see from what standpoint those women viewed the happiness of their fellow beings, who, in convention assembled, passed resolutions in favor of closing the fair on Sunday.

That noble Quakeress, Lucretia Mott, seeing that the laboring masses were practically excluded from the Centennial Exposition, made her protest against the injustice by never passing within the gates herself. With fifteen added years of experience one would think all American women might have reached a similar standard of justice and common-sense.

What is the duty of the State in this matter? Clearly, to do whatever conserves the welfare of the majority of the people. The minority have the right to stay away from the exposition on Sunday, but they have no right to throw obstacles in the way of a majority by influencing popular sentiment or securing legislative enactments to prevent them from enjoying that day in whatever way they may see fit, provided they do not infringe on the rights of the minority.

Again, in a financial point of view, the State has no right to cripple a great popular enterprise, wholly beneficial in its results, by any interference. The managers of the exposition, before everything is completed, must expend fabulous sums of money in realizing their ideal of what an exposition should be, and to close the gates the very day the greatest numbers could be there would be hostile to the interests of the managers as well as the happiness of the people. If to close the fair would drive the laboring masses to the churches, there to drop their dimes into the collection-boxes, there might be some reason for ecclesiastical interference. But the majority will not go to the churches, but rather crowd the drinking and gambling saloons, the restaurants, and the dance-houses, and make the city a pandemonium by night. But, after a long, well-spent day mid such fairy scenes as the exposition will present, wandering round the beautiful park or sailing on the lake, the majority would take the evening trains to their respective homes, with pleasant memories of all they had seen—enough to gladden the remaining days of the week.

If we would lift the masses out of their gross pleasures, we must cultivate their tastes for more refined enjoyments. The object of Sunday observance is primarily to give the people a day of rest and recreation, a change from their ordinary employments, a little space of time, in the hard struggle of life, for amusement. Sunday by common consent is the day set aside to use the best influences society possesses, to cultivate the religious emotions, the moral sentiments, to teach the dignity of humanity and the brotherhood of the race. It needs but little reflection to see what a potent influence in all these directions the World's Fair will be. The location is in every way most desirable. A magnificent park, whose shores are washed by an inland sea, vast buildings, that in grandeur and beauty of architecture have never been equalled, filled with the most wonderful productions of all that is new in art and science, from every nation on the globe—what an impressive scene this will be! With multitudes of men and women in happy companionship, now wandering through this museum of wonders, and now down the winding walks of the boundless park, now seated in that beautiful pavilion on the shores of Lake Michigan, watching the rolling waves break at their feet, or in the grand concert-hall listening to interpretations by Theodore Thomas, Seidl, or Damrosch,[2] of the divine melodies of the old masters—where else could such a rare combination of pleasures, mid such surroundings, be so easily provided for the people?

Here, too, in shady nooks gifted orators might speak to the multitudes on popular reforms or religious questions, for there are no meetings more impressive than those held in the open air, and many assemblies might be held in that vast space without interfering with each other.

If, then, the influence of the exposition on the minds of the people, can be alike entertaining and instructive, we may well ask, Why should it be closed on Sunday?

~ *Elizabeth Cady Stanton.*

~ *North American Review* 154 (February 1892): 254-56.

1. This exposition in Philadelphia marked the centennial of the Declaration of Independence.
2. These leading conductors were Theodore Thomas (1835-1905), at this time of the Chicago Symphony Orchestra; Anton Seidl (1850-1898), of the New York Philharmonic; and one or both of the brothers, Frank Heino Damrosch (1859-1937), chorus master at the Metropolitan Opera House, and Walter Johannes Damrosch (1862-1950), conductor of operas and symphony orchestras in New York.

158 ~ SBA TO LILLIE DEVEREUX BLAKE

Rochester N.Y. Feb. 13, 1892—

Dear Mrs Blake

Now here is the dilemma—[1] At the last Annual Con. at Auburn—a <u>state</u> Legislative Committee was appointed—consisting of Mrs Elnora M. Babcock[2]—Dunkirk—Mrs Harriet M. Goff[3]—135 Lefferts Place—Brooklyn—Mrs Mary E. Welch[4]—593—2^d Avenue, Lansingburg—and surely neither Mrs Greenleaf—as Pres. of the N.Y. State society—nor Miss Anthony—as Pres. of the National—should appoint <u>another</u> <u>Committee</u> of the <u>over</u> the <u>head</u> of <u>the one already in existence</u>!! I think you should at once consult with the Chairman of the Committee—& see if she will consign the Legislative work to <u>you</u>—and I will write her also—Why in the world didn't you look to this point in that last Ex. Com. meeting ↑last November,↓—when the Committees were appointed? I tell you Napoleon was right when he said "he who <u>makes</u> <u>his</u> <u>circum-</u>

stances is the master of the Situation"—⁵ You knew more of this question's being likely to come up this winter than either I or Mrs Greenleaf or any other one—and hence—it seems to me—you should have presented the need of an experienced Com—with its most active member near to Albany— I for one—felt it was a sort of off year—and that nothing was likely to come up in the Legislature requiring great skill—and so said nothing— Mrs Howell is in Kansas—else she would be there on the spot⁶—& could work without expense to the society— and you can with less expense than any other one of the Com. probably—because of your having a R.R. Pass—& I believe personal friends in Albany with ↑whom↓ you always stop— Isn't that so?— I have no doubt but that Mrs Babcock will say to you—go ahead & do the best you can—instead of her trying to go down— I think our conclusion— at the last Ex. Com. meeting at Washington was—that the Board of General Officers should be the Committee ↑on↓ Con. Con's. and itself, ↑and stand↓ ready to help whichever state should move for one— You can see that the National cannot—go ahead—contrary or without the perfect cooperation of the state— A letter from Mrs Greenleaf shows that she feels that the Standing Committee on Legislative work must ↑not↓ to be ignored—

I want you to do all you can—because I feel that you have faith in your ability to score a point!— And that is what I do not feel in myself— for I have not the slightest faith that the Legislature will ↑pass a law↓ either that ↑there shall be↓ one woman from each Cong. District a member of the Con. Con—nor↑or↓ that women shall be allowed to vote on the proposed amendment to strike male from the suffrage ↑clause↓— And our only hope of carrying such an am't ↑at the polls↓ would lie in women's being allowed to vote upon it themselves—and our having time to arouse them, to educate them—to believe in woman suffrage ↑enough to vote for it!↓!! Still the agitation will be ↑a↓ good education—⁷ But Hillism does not promise much reform-wise—⁸

What would be the minimum for your expenses to do what you feel should be done?— Does Mr Husted⁹ feel there is a chance for the introduction & passage of a Con. Con. Bill?— I have an idea it would have been moved before this if there were really a determination to push it through this Legislature?— Be sure you are right—before going ahead— I don't like us to be played with—any more than can be helped— Did you find who had any idea of framing the bill?

Well—I don't want to hinder from doing what you know will help along the cause—neither do I wish to interfere with the State Com—by overriding it by another & a National appointment— Do you see— Sincerely yours

↝ Susan B. Anthony

P.S—Why to think of Legislature granting women the slightest <u>touch</u> of the ballot or the Con. Con.—that is capable of having under consideration—with a fair prospect of passing it—such an atrocious Liquor or Saloon License Bill—[10] No! no! This Legislature will slam the door in our faces more angrily than ever one was slammed before— This Democratic Legislature is bound to <u>pave</u> the way for <u>Whiskey</u> <u>to</u> <u>win</u> in the ↑coming↓ <u>Presidential election</u>—hence no woman will be admitted!! S. B. A

↝ ALS, on NAWSA letterhead, Lillie D. Blake Papers, MoSHi.

1. Blake wrote SBA a few weeks earlier about the likelihood that New York's legislature, under Democratic control, would finally resolve years of partisan bickering about calling a constitutional convention that should have occurred in 1887. She wanted authority and salary from the state and the National-American associations to lobby the legislature in the matter. In an earlier reply, SBA cautioned Blake that she must consult with state president Jean Greenleaf and that the legislative work must be in the hands of the state executive committee. However, she encouraged Blake to think about a special committee and asked for her plan of work. Greenleaf intervened when she learned about Blake's expectations and SBA's preliminary response. (Charles Z. Lincoln, *The Constitutional History of New York* [Rochester, N.Y., 1906], 3:3-24; SBA to L. D. Blake, 9 February 1892, *Film*, 29:1064-68.)

2. Elnora E. Monroe Babcock (1852-1934) lived in Dunkirk, Chautauqua County, where she organized the town's Political Equality Club in 1889 and soon served as president of the county club until late 1893. Through her efforts the Chautauqua Assembly scheduled its first program on woman suffrage in 1891. After her appointment to the state society's legislative committee in the same year, she served for two years. The society then put her in charge of work with the press, for which she organized a statewide committee with members in every county. Her husband, John W. Babcock, a graduate of Cornell and former schoolteacher, was superintendent of the Dunkirk schools from 1881 to 1899. (*American Women*; *The Centennial History of Chautauqua County: A Detailed and Entertaining Story of One Hundred Years of Development* [Jamestown, N.Y., 1904], 2:473-74; *New York Times*, 30 December 1934.)

3. Harriet Newell Kneeland Goff (1828-?) was a noted temperance worker

and writer, active since 1870 and credited with the Prohibition party's early interest in woman suffrage. From Brooklyn, where she lived from the mid-1870s, she gained experience as a legislative lobbyist while trying to introduce police matrons into the city's jails. In 1892, she moved to Washington, D.C. (Brooklyn city directory, 1890; *American Women*; *SEAP*; Logan, *Part Taken by Women in American History*, 676-77.)

4. Mary E. Welch (c. 1824–?) was the wife of a dentist, S. P. Welch, in Lansingburgh, New York. (Federal Census, 1880; city directories, 1866, 1872, 1890.)

5. A more common rendering of Napoleon's idea is "I care nothing about circumstances; I make circumstances!"

6. As part of the National-American's pledge to assist the Kansas Equal Suffrage Association, Mary Howell joined the effort to hold thirty suffrage conventions and organize local suffrage societies across the state in February and March 1892. (*Report of the Twenty-fifth Annual Convention, 1893*, pp. 69-70, *Film*, 31:200ff.)

7. On February 8, Blake's New York City Woman Suffrage League petitioned the legislature to provide for equal representation of all citizens at the constitutional convention by allowing women to vote for delegates. (*Woman's Journal*, 13 February 1892.)

8. "Hillism" was synonymous with "bossism" in New York, where the Tammany Democrat David B. Hill, former governor and current senator, continued to dictate how the Democratic legislative majority should act.

9. James William Husted (1833–1892) had a distinguished career as a Republican in New York State politics, entering the Assembly in 1869, serving twenty-two consecutive years, and holding the post of Speaker of the Assembly six times. He was also, in the words of Mary Howell, "the great champion for the advancement of women in this State." He died on September 25 of this year. (*NCAB*, 25:53; *New York Times*, 26 September 1892; *Woman's Journal*, 8 October 1892.)

10. This bill, under debate and the object of protest meetings in New York and Albany in February 1892, became An Act to revise and consolidate the laws regulating the sale of intoxicating liquors, or Excise Act, signed by the governor on 30 April 1892. Critics charged that its provisions simply legitimated practices already achieved by bribery. It allowed some Sunday sales of liquor, created a special license for all-night sales, restricted police surveillance to the business hours specified in each license, and made it harder to sue liquor dealers, among other improvements. (*Laws of New York, 1892*, chap. 401.)

159 ⚘ SBA to Elizabeth Smith Miller

Rochester N.Y. Feb. 15, 1892.

My Dear Mrs Miller

Your good letter—and good check of $20— for the above fund are just here—¹ You doubtless saw in the ↑last Saturday mornings↓ Rochester Dem. & Chronicle's report of the <u>Historical society</u>, ~~at its last meeting~~ ↑that they↓ appointed a Committee to solicit & receive the money for the Anthony ↑Bust↓ Fund²—and how Mr Fitch³—its former editor spoke very laudatory of the movement to ↑thus↓ honor one of our own citizens— It is very gratifying to see the matter taken hold of by people ↑who were↓ never identified with our cause or with me personally. ~~to thus~~

I am expecting Mrs Colby this evening or tomorrow A.M—she is in Auburn, or was to be— It is very hard to move the public to feel enough interest in our question to turn out to a lecture— Mrs Sister Mary has had the Rochester Course ↑of five lectures↓ in hand—each of the three lectures given—proved to be <u>very cold</u> & stormy nights— hence, few, save those <u>holding season tickets</u>—attended—but she & Mrs L. C. Smith—each sold about 80 of those—making 160 tickets = $160— hence they are sure of not [sinking?] far short—but it does seem such a ↑<u>moral</u>↓ <u>loss</u> not to have every <u>seat filled</u>—after such expense of <u>labor</u> to arrange for them—

I am delighted that Nannie⁴ is improving—& I do hope she'll hold on to the knowledge to ↑keep↓ herself well in body & mind—

Mrs Stanton seemed so bright & splendid at Washington!— And I think "<u>The Solitude of Self</u>" is <u>her crowning speech</u>—and so thought able minds— Judge Taylor⁵—of the <u>Ohio, Garfield Cong. District</u>— said it surpassed anything he ever heard! it made those <u>ignorant</u> & <u>indifferent Southern</u> men on the Com. wipe the <u>tears</u> that would moisten their eyes—as she sat & stood there—alternately—and portrayed the <u>soul's utter aloneness</u> in <u>all the deepest experiences of life</u>!— It is too cruel that such ↑<u>mental</u>↓ powers must be hampered with such a <u>clumsy body</u>— oh—if we could only give her elasticity of limbs—and locomotive powers—but we must be thankful that we still have her marvelous <u>pen</u> <u>powers</u> to push along our work for the redemption of the race from <u>sex</u> <u>slavery</u>!! Lovingly yours

↝ *Susan B. Anthony*

N.B— Oh yes—about the books of your noble & sainted Father— I am glad you are bringing a lot out—<u>minus</u> of Mr O. B. F. unjust strictures—and I shall be glad to do what I can—[6] I think Charles E. Fitch— will too—he gave a very fine <u>eulogy</u> on your father but a few years ago in our Corinthian Hall— And Mrs Colby—I am sure will be able to put some copies in good hands—by offering them as a premium for a certain number of new subscribers— She can, & I am sure—<u>will</u> try & do the best she can— I read it at the time it came out at Mrs Stanton's— but I have not a copy of it— I remember of feeling all the way through that Mr Frothingham was incapable of understanding your father's <u>best part</u>—he seemed all the time squaring him by <u>his</u> <u>Cambridge student's</u> <u>rule</u>!—which wasn't the one to measure your father or Mr Garrison or any great reformer by— Mr F. did very well in writing the life of Theodore Parker[7]—but as <u>sad</u> <u>a</u> <u>failure</u> in writing that of dear, glorious Wm Henry Channing[8]—as he did in that of your father— He ought to have know <u>he</u> <u>couldn't</u> into the spirits that moved two such over-soul-men!! Lovingly yours S. B. A

So tell me exactly what & how you wish me to help in the distribution of the books— I will gladly second your plans!! S B A

↝ ALS, on Bust Fund letterhead, place corrected, Smith Family Papers, Manuscript Division, NN. Square brackets surround uncertain reading.

1. The top of SBA's stationery read "Lucretia Mott, Elizabeth Cady Stanton and Susan B. Anthony Bust Fund, Mrs. Jane H. Spofford, Treasurer, 1412 G Street, Washington, D.C." This committee, loosely affiliated with the National-American Woman Suffrage Association, raised money to pay for busts to go on display at the Columbian Exposition, although none for Mott was completed for that occasion. Its funds were directed to the sculptures by Adelaide Johnson.

2. Rochester *Democrat and Chronicle*, 13 February 1892. At an open meeting of the Rochester Historical Society, Charles Fitch suggested that the people of Rochester might "pay at least a portion toward the bust of Miss Anthony . . . . He spoke in praise of the work of the distinguished lady and said that when an impartial history of the latter part of the nineteenth century is written, Miss Anthony's name will stand very high among the list of noble men and women."

3. Charles Elliott Fitch (1835-1918) turned to journalism after many years as a lawyer and edited the *Democrat and Chronicle* from 1873 to 1890. Long active in the Republican party, he served as secretary of the New York Constitutional Convention in 1894. (*NCAB*, 4:492; *WWW1*.)

4. Anne Fitzhugh Miller (1856-1912), known as Nannie, lived with her mother in Geneva, New York. It was in the 1890s that she joined the suffrage movement as an organizer of political equality clubs in Ontario County and a regular participant in the state association. (*Geneva Daily Times*, 2 March 1912, and *Geneva Advertiser-Gazette*, 7 March 1912, courtesy of the Geneva Historical Society and Museum.)

5. That is, Ezra Taylor.

6. The topic is Octavius Brooks Frothingham, *Gerrit Smith, A Biography*, published late in 1877 and withdrawn by the publisher in March 1878 at Elizabeth Miller's insistence. She and her cousin John Cochrane objected to Frothingham's conclusion that Smith's assistance to John Brown before the raid on Harper's Ferry amounted to conspiracy against the United States. Since Miller owned the plates from which the book was printed, the author and publisher yielded to the family's demands. Frothingham revised his conclusions for a second edition that met the family's objections. A so-called third edition of the biography was not published until 1909, raising the question whether Miller, in 1892, had republished the book, as SBA wrote in this letter, or simply distributed copies of the second edition, published in 1878 and 1879. SBA kept an account of her own distribution of the book in the back pages of her diary for 1892. (*New York Times*, 13 March 1878; J. Wade Caruthers, *Octavius Brooks Frothingham, Gentle Radical* [University, Ala., 1977], 151-53; Ralph Volney Harlow, *Gerrit Smith, Philanthropist and Reformer* [New York, 1939], 449-54.)

7. *Life of Theodore Parker* (1874).

8. *Memoir of William Henry Channing* (1886).

160   From the Diary of SBA

[*29 February 1892*]

MONDAY, FEBRUARY 29, 1892. At home—17 Mad. st—Rochester Mrs Colby forwards letter from a colored man—John R. Taliaferro[1]—Amherst Nebraska—who says he drove 16 miles to Kearney to see & hear Miss Anthony—in the autumn of 1882[2]—& there she said colored men were sure to vote against W.S.—& hurt his feelings—& I wrote him—that I didn't mean the like of him—who was educated by a Quaker Samuel G.

Slocum[3]—of Evans Mills—Jeff. Co.—N.Y—& lived with such Quakers as Jennie M. Slocum—Canandaigua & Robert Howland[4] Union Springs— Miss Mary E. Post[5] of Rochester—but for ex-slaves & newly enfranchised men— he worked all of that Nov. 1882 election day at the Polls & his Township—Grant—[gave?] a majority for woman Suffrage— It is too cruel that in stating a general rule one is sure to hurt the exceptions—but so it ever is! with both women & colored men!

1. John R. Taliaferro (1849–?) was born in Virginia and came north to New York State during or after the Civil War; SBA suggests he attended the Howland School in Union Springs, Cayuga County, a Quaker school that educated freedmen. By 1870, Taliaferro lived and worked on the farm of Samuel Slocum in Jefferson County. His move to Nebraska came before 1880, when he lived alone and farmed in Grant Township, Buffalo County. Buffalo was one of the eleven counties in which voters approved the woman suffrage amendment in 1882. In 1900, Taliaferro was a day laborer in Kearney, Nebraska. SBA bought him a subscription to the *Woman's Tribune* at the time she answered his letter. (Federal Census, Jefferson County, N.Y., 1870, Buffalo County, Neb., 1880, 1900; SBA diary, account pages for February 1892, *Film*, 29:655ff.)

2. On 17 October 1882. See *Film*, 22:682.

3. While in New York, Taliaferro was in the care of Quaker families. Samuel G. Slocum (c. 1804–1874) owned a woolen factory and farm in LeRoy, Jefferson County. He employed Taliaferro as a farm hand and housed him with his family in 1870. Slocum's daughter Jane M. Slocum (1842–?) taught at the Howland School until she became a founder and vice president of the Granger Place School, a girls' seminary that opened in Canandaigua in 1876. Jane Slocum later left teaching to become a lecturer on political economy and worked in the Albany headquarters of the New York amendment campaign in 1894. (*Friends' Review* 27 [15 August 1874]: 826; Federal Census, 1870; Augustus Hopkins Strong, *Miscellanies in Two Volumes* [Philadelphia, 1912], 1:239–50; *1894. Constitutional-Amendment Campaign Year*, 7, 163.)

4. Robert Bowne Howland (1826–1916) graduated from Haverford College in 1843 and became a farmer as well as an educator. He presided over the Howland School from 1863 to 1876. (*Biographical Catalog of the Matriculates of Haverford College, 1833–1922* [Philadelphia, 1922], 28; Hugh Barbour et al., eds., *Quaker Crosscurrents: Three Hundred Years of Friends in the New York Yearly Meeting* [Syracuse, N.Y., 1995], 156.)

5. Mary E. Post (c. 1841–) was a student or young teacher at a girls' school in Union Springs in 1860, working with teachers who later taught at the Howland and the Granger Place schools. She followed her colleagues to Granger Place for a time and subsequently taught school in Rochester until 1907 or 1908, when she moved to Idaho. (Federal Census, Cayuga County, N.Y., 1860, Rochester, 1900; Rochester city directories, 1900 to 1908.)

⇜ Excelsior Diary 1892, n.p., SBA Papers, DLC. Square brackets surround uncertain reading.

161 ⇝ SBA to Elizabeth Smith Miller

Rochester N.Y. March 30/92

My Dear Mrs Miller

Your nice basket with its lovely contents all safe came yesterday forenoon—in good time for us to test the bit of cheese along with a fresh apple pie—spiced with a sprinkling of caraway seed— And we all pronounced it elegant—our all is composed of my sister Mary niece Anna O. Anthony—our youngest brother Merritt's youngest daughter—of Fort Scott—Kansas—going to school & taking violin lessons here this year!! And the jar of cream—well it is just luscious—our girl "Julia"[1] said— Well—what we buy everyday <u>called</u> <u>cream</u>—is not much like this! it is lovely—& the two jars of fruit—well—they'll be saved for some special occasion—when they'll be duly opened & eaten in memory of your own dear self—

The box of books is not yet arrived—but will doubtless appear during the day ~~Well~~ I shall take great pleasure in placing one in each of our city libraries! And will get the papers to notice the book— Mr Fitch—I know—will love to write an article on it and your noble father—he is a great admirer of him

I am wondering if you are going to make an effort to place them in the principal libraries of the country—that is where the book ought to be!! I have thus placed fifteen hundred sets of the History of Woman Suffrage—and not a hundred of them all have paid a dime for the work— And now that I have only about one hundred & fifty sets left— I am wishing I had the money—it would take about $7,000— to get out a second edition of 2,000 sets—and religiously place a set in every University, College, High School & city & village Library of the country—

I have sent Theodore Stanton about <u>100 sets</u>—which he has placed in the principal libraries of the continent—and another 100 sets to England—which are placed in libraries of the three kingdoms— And now I am packing a box for Lady Henry Somerset[2] to take home with her— I now feel that the best work I could do—would be to put this History within reach of every student in every school of every state— Not a day passes that I do not get letters asking for points to help boys & girls in their debates—and your fathers Life ought to be found by all students everywhere too. Love to Nannie & many thanks for your good thought of me—affectionately

↙ Susan B. Anthony

↙ ALS, on NAWSA letterhead, Smith Family Papers, Manuscript Division, NN.

1. Julia Ames, a young woman from Churchville, New York, worked as housekeeper at 17 Madison Street for more than a year. SBA's financial accounts are missing for 1891, so the date of her starting is unknown. Through all of 1892 and to the end of January 1893, SBA's accounts record payments of her share of Julia's monthly wages and regular sums paid to her for household expenses. Julia Ames returned in 1895 after some secretarial training, but SBA let her go, noting ruefully in her diary that Julia "hasn't the education no the quick perception to ever make a success of type writing & stenography." She may be the same Julia Ames listed in the census of 1900 as a boarder in Rochester who worked as a "machine hand." If so, she was twenty years old in 1892. (SBA diary, 1892 and 1893, pages of accounts, and 6 April 1895, *Film*, 29:655ff, 31:3ff, 33:80ff; Federal Census, 1900.)

2. Lady Isabella Caroline Somers-Cocks Somerset (1851–1921), known as Lady Henry Somerset, was president of the British Women's Temperance Association and a close friend of Hannah Whitall Smith, when she traveled to the United States in the fall of 1891 and met Frances Willard at the World's Woman's Christian Temperance Union meeting in Boston. The two women quickly became very close friends, and during the last years of Willard's life, she spent considerable time at one or another of Lady Henry's extensive properties in Britain. As a strong believer in woman suffrage and a member of the Women's Liberal Federation, Lady Henry tried, without much success, to import Willard's model of pushing temperance women toward advocacy of political rights. In April 1892, at the end of her visit to the United States, admirers in Boston staged an elaborate farewell at Tremont Temple. (*Oxford DNB*; Sarah Knowles Bolton, *Famous Leaders among Women* [New York, 1895], 250–71; Bordin, *Frances Willard, A Biography*, 197–200.)

162 ⇒ SBA to William Sulzer[1]

Rochester N.Y. April 10/92

Hon. Wm Sulzer   My Dear Sir

Many thanks for your good substitute—and I do hope you will push it to a vote that we may yet get from this very Legislature the right to vote on the ratification of the amendments proposed by the Constitutional Convention![2]

What a mean thing the Senate did do! To raise the plea of unconstitutionality for the governor to appoint delegates to the Con. Con—and then <u>knock</u> out <u>only three</u> of the proposed eleven—and that the <u>three</u> that represents the <u>one</u> <u>entire</u> <u>half</u> of the <u>people</u> of the state—who are <u>helpless</u> & <u>powerless</u> to <u>hurt</u> <u>the</u> <u>politicians</u> <u>who</u> <u>thus</u> <u>dared</u> <u>to</u> <u>rob</u> <u>them</u> of <u>the</u> <u>poor</u> <u>little</u> <u>privilege</u> of having <u>three</u> of their class to represent them!![3]

Why didn't Mr McCarran[4] & all of them carry their consciencious scruples far enough to knock out the 3 delegates of the Prohibition Party—and the 5 delegates for the <u>Labor</u> Party— Simply because those people <u>have votes</u> and could & would <u>hurt</u> <u>the</u> <u>men</u> who voted against their having the right of representation in the Convention— They simply made true the the old maxim—"to him (her) that hath not shall be taken even that which he (she) hath!["][5]

Now—my dear friend—when that bill comes back for the concurrence of the Assembly—will you not make a fight to <u>restore</u> the three women delegates—and at least compel every man to have his "<u>aye</u>" or "<u>nay</u>" <u>recorded</u> upon the question— It is such an <u>invidious discrimination</u>—that I want to see every <u>man</u> compelled to look himself in the face & <u>see his own ugliness</u>!!

I feel very grateful to you for your good work for woman and hope that you may still score new points on the line of political equality for women— I wonder if—now that our opponents have done us the mean thing of shutting us out of the Con. Con—you couldn't rush in a bill giving <u>school</u> suffrage to the women of the <u>thirty</u>—more or less—<u>cities</u> of the state? Wouldn't they let it go through out of <u>shere</u> <u>shame</u> of themselves? Do try it—& see if in these last moments of the session such a good thing can not be done for us taxed but unrepresented city women!!⁶ Again thanking you I am very sincerely yours

          ✌ *Susan B. Anthony*

✌ ALS, on NAWSA letterhead, William Sulzer Papers #1147, Department of Manuscripts and University Archives, NIC.

   1. William Sulzer (1863–1941), a Democrat at the start of a long political career, represented a Manhattan district in the New York Assembly from 1890 to 1894. He became Speaker in 1893, minority leader in 1894, and a year later he entered Congress. (*DAB, Supplement 3*; *BDAC*.)

   2. SBA refers to An Act to prevent discrimination on account of sex at elections, a bill granting full suffrage to women, to go into effect before the election of delegates for the constitutional convention. Sulzer reported it from the assembly's judiciary committee. It "substituted" for a bill written by Hamilton Willcox and introduced in March 1892 by Democratic assemblyman Hubbard R. Yetman "to relieve self-supporting women from disfranchisement and oppression." The bill's history is obscured by the fierce rivalry between Willcox and Lillie Blake. Willcox and Yetman had both bills ready in March; the full suffrage bill matched one Willcox wrote in 1880. But by Blake's account, when Sulzer saw an opportunity for passing full suffrage, his committee killed the Yetman bill, asked Mary Howell to draft a new bill, and substituted it. (*Woman's Journal*, 16, 23 April, 7 May 1892; *New York Times*, 16 April 1892; Assembly bill no. 1372, 18 March 1892, and Assembly bill no. 1372, 1507, 18 March 1892, in SBA scrapbook 18, Rare Books, DLC; SBA to Lillie D. Blake, 19 April 1892, *Film*, 30:134–37.)

   3. An Act to provide for a convention to revise and amend the constitution won legislative approval on 7 April 1892. In the bill approved by the assembly, eleven delegates would be appointed by the governor, of whom five would come from labor unions, three would be prohibitionists, and three would be woman suffragists. After raising questions about the constitutionality of appointed delegates, the state senate dropped only those allotted to woman suffragists. (*Laws of New York, 1892*, chap. 398; *Woman's Journal*, 9 April 1892; *New York Times*, 8, 16 April 1892.)

   4. Patrick Henry McCarren (1847–1909), a Democrat from Brooklyn, who served in the state senate from 1890 to 1893 and 1896 to 1908, moved to eliminate woman suffragists from the list of appointed delegates. (*DAB*.)

   5. Matt. 25:29.

   6. School suffrage for women in New York State differed according to residence. Since 1880, women could vote at school meetings or town meetings called to transact school business, effectively limiting the right to women in rural areas and very small towns. On 5 April 1892, a new law took effect that permitted women to vote for school commissioners, an office of county

government, and to do so by ballot at the state's general election. Still excluded from voting on matters concerning schools were women residing in chartered cities, where the charter itself would require amendment to enfranchise women. The school commissioners law, under which some women cast ballots in 1892, was later declared unconstitutional by the Court of Appeals of New York as a result of Matilda Gage's suit to have her name restored to the registration lists. (*History*, 3:423–30; *Laws of New York, 1892*, chap. 214; In re Matilda Joslyn Gage 141 New York Reports 112 [1894]; Paula Baker, *The Moral Frameworks of Public Life: Gender, Politics, and the State in Rural New York, 1870–1930* [New York, 1991], 74–78.)

163 ❧ HENRY B. BLACKWELL TO SBA

Boston, Apl 10 1892

Dear Miss Anthony

Your letter asking me to suggest "points" relative to getting planks in national conventions of parties is a reminder of 1872, when I succeeded in getting a resolution into the Rep. platform of state & nation.[1] I wish I could have a talk with you on the subject. In my judgment the <u>moral effect</u> of a resolution <u>naming</u> women kindly is very great, even if the suffrage is not endorsed in terms. On the other hand the refusal or neglect of parties to recognize women, when asked to do so, is a <u>loss</u> & a <u>hindrance</u>. Now a resolution directly endorsing woman suffrage <u>cannot</u> <u>be</u> <u>had</u> because the men who form these conventions are mostly opposed, or represent constituents mostly opposed. In 1872 Rutherford B. Hayes,[2] an old personal friend and the Ohio member of the Com on Resolutions said to me: "Personally I am in favor of woman suffrage, but the men who sent me here are not. It would not be right for me as their representative to urge a plank committing them to what they do not approve. If you will let me pare down your resolution I will try to get it in" I said to him: "Half a loaf is better than no bread. Here is my resolution. Do the best you can for us.["] The result was this:

> ["]The National Republican party is mindful of its obligations to the loyal women of America for their noble devotion to the cause of Freedom; their admission to wider spheres of usefulness is viewed with satisfaction, and the

honest demands of any class of citizens for additional rights is entitled to respectful consideration."

On the strength of having got this, I succeeded a few weeks later in getting from our Republican State Convention the resolution which Mrs. H H Robinson[3] is accustomed to style "Old Hail the Day"—as follows:

"<u>Resolved</u>: That we heartily approve of the recognition of the rights of women contained in the National republican platform; that the Republican party of Massachusetts, as the representative of liberty & progress, is in favor of extending suffrage on equal terms to all American citizens irrespective of sex and will hail the day when the educated intellect and enlightened conscience of Woman will find direct expression at the ballot box."

Now I thought that in getting my resolution reported and incorporated in the State Republican platform I had done a great thing. ~~But~~ We went into the campaign[4] and held the three largest Republican meetings held in Massachusetts at Boston, Worcester & Springfield for "Grant, Wilson,[5] and Woman Suffrage." But when the Legislature elected on that platform met, one half of the Republican members (and all the Democrats) voted against our bill for municipal woman suffrage.[6] And the adoption of that plank <u>followed by that defeat in the Legislature</u> made it forever impossible to get another one like it from any subsequent Rep. Convention in Mass.

In 1882, I succeeded in getting from the ↑Massachusetts↓ Democratic Convention which nominated Butler a flatfooted suffrage resolution,[7] but with similar result: The Democratic members of Legislature elected on a woman suffrage platform a large majority of them voted against our bill, & many of the Republicans, who would otherwise have voted for us, voted the other way to show their spite against the Democratic platform.[8]

I state these facts to show you that it really does us no good to try to commit parties by planks in platforms, to anything tangible—

In 1876 I went to Cincinnati hoping & expecting to secure another <u>general</u> expression for women like that of 1872. But I found there Mrs Spencer[9] of Washington & Mrs Harbert of Ills both bent on getting a specific out & out woman suffrage plank. They got a hearing before the Resolutions committee & Senator Hoar got Mrs Spencer a five minutes hearing (she wasnt heard for want of voice) before the Convention. And that was all we got—simply because we asked for too much. I thought it a mistake then & I think so now.[10]

I enclose two planks which are as definite and go as far as we can hope to secure.[11] In my judgment these might be secured if they are judiciously pushed. But they ought to be proposed and urged by women of the party— You ought to go to the Republicans, because you are in sympathy with the Republicans. Some Democratic woman (a Southern woman if possible) should go to the Democrats. In my judgment if you go to both, you will not succeed with either & as you are known to be Republican you will fail to enlist the Democrats & stand in the attitude of offering the Suffragists for sale for a plank, which after all commits nobody & secures nothing. I know how foolish and unjust a charge this is. But it will be made even by some of our own friends and be believed by our opponents, and do the cause harm.[12]

This leads me to ask you to consider seriously with me the relation suffragists should take towards the parties. I think we have made our great mistake in taking the "Mugwump" or "independent" position.[13] The logical result is to put us where the WC.T.U stands today viz. an ally of the Prohibition party & a rejected suitor of the People's party— To say "We will support the party that endorses our principle" sounds well, but results in side-tracking the Suffrage movement politically.

Now in England the suffragists have acted with greater political wisdom. There the women have gone on what I call the "helpmeet" theory instead of the impracticable mugwump "come-outer" theory. They have not nagged the parties for suffrage resolutions. They have gone into politics not as suffragists, but as Conservatives for the conservatives and for the Liberals as Liberals. The result has been that women have become a power in both parties. The Primrose League composed of Tory women who cared nothing for suffrage for themselves has made itself indispensable to the Conservatives, has converted a large proportion of conservative men and still better has converted themselves. The Liberal Women's Federation has kept itself in touch with the Liberals and in spite of Gladstone's ingrained aversion to woman suffrage and the more positive aversion of his wife &

daughter,¹⁴ the Liberal women have more than held their own with the men of the same stripe— The result is that both parties are steadily tending towards parliamentary suffrage for women.

Yesterday I asked Lady Somerset whether she thought that this siding of women with their respective parties in England had <u>promoted</u> woman suffrage? She said there was <u>no doubt</u> <u>of that</u>. She attributes the changed attitude of both parties largely to the respect they both feel for their own women allies.

Now in America so far ↑almost↓ the whole of this political work has been done ↑by our suffrage women↓ for the impracticable, fanatical, one-idead, powerless factions of extremists— ↑This has cost us Utah and Washington and the whole North West.↓¹⁵ Is it not time for us to urge the women who are <u>not</u> extremists, who are in sympathy with the parties to which their male friends belong—to organize <u>as Republicans</u> and <u>as Democrats</u>, leaving their own rights to be promoted by their political men. Women can only become interested in politics by becoming interested in parties & men can only be interested in woman suffrage by a consciousness that women are able & willing to do effective [*sideways in margin*] political work. If you do not feel able thus to subordinate our question—would you not find the right woman who will—you being the power behind the throne?

~ AL, on *Woman's Journal* letterhead, Blackwell Papers, DLC.

1. Blackwell and SBA both attended the Republican National Convention in Philadelphia that year. Blackwell offered the Republicans a plank adopted by the Massachusetts Republican party in 1871 that included a tribute to "loyal women" and an opinion that "the subject of suffrage for women is a question that deserves the most careful and respectful consideration." The Republican National Convention blunted the point by removing the reference to suffrage. (*History*, 3:277–78; *Appleton's Annual Cyclopaedia, 1871*, 493; *New York Times*, 29 August 1872; *Papers*, 2:497–502.)

2. At the time of the Republican National Convention, Rutherford Birchard Hayes (1822–1893), nineteenth president of the United States, had recently completed a term as governor of Ohio. Blackwell reported this conversation at the time to his wife. (H. B. Blackwell to Lucy Stone, 5 June 1872, in Wheeler, *Loving Warriors*, 244–45.)

3. Harriet Jane Hanson Robinson (1825–1911), journalist, historian, and widow of the respected Republican newspaper columnist, Warrington, was no friend of Henry Blackwell. Exasperated with Blackwell and Lucy Stone in

the late 1870s, she joined the National association, serving as her state's vice president, and in 1881 managed the National's annual meeting in Boston. With her daughter, Harriette Shattuck, she founded the National Woman Suffrage Association of Massachusetts in 1882. She reacted with abhorrence to the idea of uniting the suffrage societies; differences over national citizenship were too great, and "there can be no real Union with such dishonest people as the Blackwells." Late in 1892, she withdrew from suffrage activity. (*NAW*; *ANB*; Bushman, *"A Good Poor Man's Wife"*; Harriet Hanson Robinson Diaries, vol. 1, p. 87, Robinson-Shattuck Collection, MCR-S. See also *Papers* 3 & 4.)

4. During the presidential campaign of 1872, the Massachusetts Woman Suffrage Association agreed to pay their usual salaries to any of its agents who accepted work for the Republican party. (*History*, 3:279.)

5. Ulysses S. Grant (1822–1885), eighteenth president of the United States, ran for his second term in 1872 with Henry Wilson (1812–1875) as his vice presidential candidate. At the time, Wilson was a senator from Massachusetts. (*BDAC*.)

6. On the subsequent loss in the legislature, see *History*, 3:279. The same source indicates that state Republicans did adopt the suffrage plank for a few more years.

7. When the Massachusetts Democrats met in convention in Boston on 19 September 1882 to adopt their platform and nominate Benjamin Franklin Butler for governor, Blackwell was far away in Nebraska, working in that state's amendment campaign. The Democratic platform took an indirect route to woman suffrage, declaring as a principle, "Equal rights, equal powers, equal burdens, equal privileges, and equal protection by law under the government for every citizen of the republic, without limitation of race, or sex, or property qualification, whether it be by a tax on property or a poll-tax on persons." The party's plank on "freedom of the ballot" said nothing about sex. Neither Blackwell nor the *Woman's Journal* endorsed Butler's candidacy, though Butler's victory pushed Blackwell to credit suffragists with making their cause central to his election. Butler (1818–1893), a consistent supporter of woman suffrage, was the gubernatorial candidate of both the Democratic and Greenback parties. He served in Congress from 1867 to 1875 and 1877 to 1879. (*BDAC*; *Woman's Journal*, 4, 17 November 1882; *New York Times*, 19 September 1882; *Appleton's Annual Cyclopaedia, 1882*, 518.)

8. On the defeat of a bill for municipal suffrage in 1883, see *Woman's Journal*, 17, 24 February, and 3 March 1883. Democrats delivered thirty-one ayes and forty-eight nays; forty-eight Republicans voted aye and ninety-six said nay. At the time Blackwell thought that the "Democratic endorsement was a most excellent thing, and will bear good fruit in the future" (3 March).

9. Sara Jane Andrews Spencer (1837–1909), who ran the Spencerian Business College in Washington, emerged as a leading activist in the city's suffrage movement by 1871 and the chief of the National Woman Suffrage Association's

work in the capital by 1876. At the Republican National Convention of 1876, she and Elizabeth Harbert delivered the National's appeal for a plank in the platform supporting a citizen's right to vote. They appeared before the committee on resolutions, and after George Hoar presented their memorial to the full convention, Spencer spoke briefly to the delegates. At the time, Henry Blackwell said she "was not heard but looked well & did no harm." Rival accounts of events at the convention were published in the *Ballot Box* and the *Woman's Journal*. Spencer left the National association in 1880 in a dispute about supporting candidates in that year's presidential campaign. (*WWW1*; *Biographical Cyclopedia of Representative Men of Maryland and the District of Columbia* [Baltimore, 1879], 426–27; *Film*, 18:814–21; *Ballot Box*, July 1876; H. B. Blackwell to L. Stone, 16 June 1876, in Wheeler, *Loving Warriors*, 254; *Woman's Journal*, 24 June 1876. See also *Papers* 2 & 3.)

10. Blackwell forgets that the Republican platform of 1876 did include his resolution, "except the last clause for which 'respectful consideration' was substituted," as he reported from Cincinnati to his wife. In the *Woman's Journal* at the time, he took considerable pride in his success, writing that in his plank women's "equality of rights is approved, . . . In this respect the platform is far in advance of that of 1872." The plank read: "The Republican party recognizes with approval the substantial advances recently made toward the establishment of equal rights for women, by the many important amendments effected by Republican legislatures in the laws which concern the personal and property relations of wives, mothers, and widows, and by the appointment and election of women to the superintendence of education, charities, and other public trusts. The honest demands of this class of citizens for additional rights, privileges, and immunities should be treated with respectful consideration." (H. B. Blackwell to L. Stone, 16 June 1876, in Wheeler, *Loving Warriors*, 254; *Woman's Journal*, 24 June 1876; *National Party Platforms*, 54.)

11. Enclosures missing.

12. Blackwell gave the same advice in 1880, including the innuendo about selling oneself in exchange for a platform plank. "[It] will never do to seem to play fast and loose with political parties," he wrote in the *Woman's Journal*, 26 June 1880. "A woman who goes from the Convention of one party to that of another, and still another, no matter how pure her motives may be, will be likely to find herself rejected by all." For an antisuffragist's use of the charge, see *Kate Field's Washington* 6 (17 August 1892): 97.

13. Mugwumps were Republicans who bolted their party in 1884 and voted Democratic to protest the nomination of James G. Blaine for president. They fancied themselves independent. Further along in this letter Blackwell equates mugwumps and "come-outers," using a term more often applied to matters of faith, as when radicals objected to a church's stand on slavery and "came out" of fellowship. Both terms referred to leaving a group to which one once

belonged, a point about women's political affiliations on which SBA and Blackwell disagreed.

14. Mary Gladstone Drew (1847-1928), who acted as her father's assistant in his second term as prime minister, was discrete about her conversion to woman suffrage. (Sheila Gooddie, *Mary Gladstone, A Gentle Rebel* [Chichester, England, 2003]; Pat Jalland, *Women, Marriage and Politics, 1860-1914* [Oxford, 1986], 215.)

15. Although Utah seems an odd item in this list, Blackwell returns to his belief that prohibitionists were responsible for losses in the Pacific Northwest and elsewhere.

164   SBA to Harriet Taylor Upton

Rochester April 16/92

My Dear Mrs Upton

Yours of the 14th came yesterday— Glad you had a good time in Boston— I wrote Mr Stormont¹ to let the words—"of Massachusetts" stand— You it isn't naming the bill—but only the petition—and I was both surprised & delighted to learn that the only petition presented early in the session was sent by the National branch of Massachusetts— that means by Mrs Shattucks society—not Lucy Stone's!!² And I left it standing because that particular society ought to have the credit of doing what none of the rest of the state societies did, but what all ought to have done!! And I meant to have had this explanation waiting your return!!

Mr Blackwell's as a Schemer is prolific—but I have never yet know one of them to prove successful— If the Republican & Democratic women want to form attachments to the parties, all very well—but we as National Suffrage ↑Society↓ women do not—unless we wish to break our Association into flinders— He sent me forms of resolutions—that our ↑Pres. or↓ Vice-Pres at Large should try & get into the Repub. & Dem. platforms—perfectly shilly-shally things— I sent them to Mrs Stanton—just to set her soul on fire at him all political maneuverers on our platform— they have now gone to Anna Shaw for the same purpose—that they'll stir up her ire—I'm sure!!

By the way she now thinks she can run in here from Bradford Penn—

the 23^{d} inst—and stay four days— Don't you envy me the pleasure of a face to face chat with one ↑direct↓ from the field work!³

I just hope you'll start no sort of a League to help the Republican Party—until women are enfranchised— By the way the full suffrage Bill that passed our Assembly yesterday—will undoubtedly be knifed by the Senate or Governor! Still some time all three powers must blunder into giving their consent together! But it is too much to hope for! just yet— So I dont enthuse over it worth a cent!!⁴

The Olympia Brown & Perkins move—in its proposed object—is like the carrying of coals to New Castle!!—it is <u>Mrs Colby's</u> Committee work—pure & simple—that & nothing else!!⁵ And what good can come from <u>Olympia's airing</u> her disgruntlement I cannot see! <u>Under the ink & between the lines</u>—the <u>one & only reason</u> the Wisconsin Society—at the time I was at Milwaukee—of which they talk—did <u>not</u> vote itself <u>auxilliary</u> was because Olympia & Perkins worked against the auxilliaship—⁶ they had <u>personally persuaded</u> every one against it— and then couldn't prevent its being done then & there—except by the specious plan of getting the vote of all the local societies upon it!! It ↑is↓ just disheartening to see Olympia allow herself to be so small & petty— And dear Mrs Southworth—I am awfully sorry she's off the track too—⁷ She hasn't answered my last two or three letters—but I shall keep right on—without <u>knowing</u> that she hasn't—

I am delighted the way you are getting your Wimo. offices so nicely filled!!—⁸ Well—tell me all you see— Lovingly yours

↝ *Susan B. Anthony*

↝ ALS, SBA Papers, NRU. Inscribed in corner of first page "This is for the shelves," followed by illegible initials. The handwriting could be SBA's.

1. William Thomas Stormont (c. 1852–1926) was a printer in Washington, D.C. SBA wrote him about the opening paragraphs of the report of the hearing on 20 January 1892 before the Senate Select Committee on Woman Suffrage, published as a pamphlet entitled *Woman Suffrage*. Confusion arose because a petition from the National Woman Suffrage Association of Massachusetts occasioned the hearing, a fact stated twice at the report's opening, but speakers at the hearing represented the National-American association. (City directories, 1887 to 1892; *Washington Post*, 7 December 1926; *Film*, 29:1035–50.)

2. *Congressional Record*, 52d Cong., 1st sess., 16 December 1891, p. 67.

3. Plans changed, and on April 22 SBA took the train to Bradford, just

across the border with New York, southwest of Rochester, and stayed until April 25. She helped to found the Bradford Political Equality Club. (*Woman's Journal*, 7 May 1892; *Report of the Twenty-fifth Annual Convention, 1893*, pp. 14–15, 145, *Film*, 31:200ff.)

4. By a vote of seventy to thirty-four, the New York Assembly passed An Act to prevent discrimination on account of sex at elections, as amended to go into effect in July 1893, after the election of delegates to the constitutional convention. Section one of the bill read: "Every citizen, irrespective of sex, shall hereafter be entitled to vote for all and every officer hereafter to be elected in this State, and on any question submitted to a vote of the people, and it shall be unlawful to make any discrimination between citizens on account of sex at such elections." In the final days of the session, senators backing the bill were blocked by the leadership from bringing it to a vote. (*New York Times*, 16 April 1892; *Woman's Journal*, 23, 30 April, 7 May 1892.)

5. After their preliminary meeting in March 1892, officers of the new Federal Suffrage Association issued a call to join them at a public meeting in Chicago on May 10. Suffrage for women was not mentioned in the call. The group wanted "to obtain such legislation as will secure every citizen of the United States in the exercise of the right of suffrage, and also to advocate uniformity in the election of national officers." Taking their cues from Francis Minor, the association argued that states exercised unconstitutional power over federal voting rights. On the one hand, states refused to enfranchise females with undisputed federal citizenship. On the other hand, they allowed non-citizen males to vote in federal elections. Clara Colby chaired a new federal committee of the National-American association that also pursued Minor's ideas. In keeping with the association's resolutions of 1892, Colby circulated a petition for a "bill enabling women citizens of the United States to vote for members of the House of Representatives" and found a sponsor in Congress. While praising Colby's efforts, Olympia Brown asked why the National-American backed both Colby's proposal, based on the conviction that Congress could enfranchise women in federal elections through simple legislation, and the bill of Halbert Greenleaf, who believed federal suffrage for women required a constitutional amendment. This, Brown wrote, proved that the irreconcilable differences between the National and American associations lived on in a divided body. (*The Federal Suffrage Association: Its Origin and Constitution* [N.p., 1892]; Olympia Brown, ed., *Democratic Ideals: A Memorial Sketch of Clara B. Colby* [N.p., 1917], 47–48, 58–68; *Wisconsin Citizen*, May 1892, in SBA scrapbook 18, Rare Books, DLC; *Report of the Twenty-fifth Annual Convention, 1893*, pp. 101–6.)

6. In the *Wisconsin Citizen*, April 1892, Brown explained why the Wisconsin Woman Suffrage Association refused to be an auxiliary of the National-American association. Her account of the vote on affiliation, on 15 October 1889, was so far from the truth that another state leader immediately disputed

Brown's account. Chief among the reasons for independence were the falseness of uniting the American and National associations without anyone retracting the accusations made to justify division for twenty years; the National-American's impracticable and under-financed plan of work; its failure to provide services to states in exchange for auxiliary dues; Wisconsin's distance from annual meetings in Washington; and the pretense of national work led only by suffragists from the Northeast. (SBA scrapbook 18, Rare Books, DLC; Wisconsin meeting, *Film*, 27:484-91. See also note above at 12 October 1889.)

7. Louisa Southworth wrote a letter of support to the Federal Suffrage Association's meeting in March and, at the meeting in May, was named vice president of the eastern Mississippi division.

8. The National-American's new office in the house owned by Wimodaughsis.

165 ~ ISABELLA BEECHER HOOKER TO ECS

Hartford [*Conn.*] April 26, 1892

Dear Mrs Stanton

I send you a letter from Olympia Brown that is well worth your <u>careful reading</u>.¹ I wrote her in reply that I would go to Chicago at my own expense to help on the movement. <u>Congressional Districts</u> are the units of both State & National work—& I was sick of <u>delegate</u> State ~~Conventions~~ ↑Assctns↓ as basis of National Assctns. All we did at Washtn. was to nurse the Constitution—put our old Prest. on the shelf & decide that ↑as↓ we couldnt afford to hold two Conventions in a year—~~so~~ the one at Washington must be omitted & the different States have the honor.²

She has just written me another admirable letter—& I have replied in a letter which you will please read & <u>forward to her immediately</u>.³

I had expected to attend your lunch party ↑on the 7th↓ & then see you & talk the matter over—⁴ But I think now that I ought to go to Chicago directly from here & be there a few days beforehand to share the responsibility with Olympia. She has been in the right of it all the time & I wish I had staid by her. But perhaps it was well to capitulate— & now we can join this new Society with a clear conscience. We can work with both & still the field will not be half occupied.

I think now that I will go to Chicago from here on Friday May 6th— & I wish you would write me a letter containing your views which I may read to the Convention. With much love always yrs.

~ *Isabella B. Hooker*

~ ALS, Olympia Brown Papers, MCR-S.

1. Enclosure missing. At the top of her letter to ECS, Hooker wrote, "Please return Olympia's letter." The letter described Brown's plans for the Federal Suffrage Association.

2. At the Washington convention, delegates agreed to three of sixteen changes proposed to the National-American's constitution. Hooker overstates the success of those who wanted migratory meetings. She refers also to ECS's retirement from the presidency of the National-American and SBA's election. Despite her refusal to be a candidate, ECS received thirty-six votes to SBA's one hundred and twenty-one votes. The *Washington Post*'s unnamed informer alluded to a more complicated contest for leadership, predicting "the most exciting contest that has occurred over an election in the history of the association." The young women "aren't content to go along on the same old track," the reporter continued; they were ready to overthrow "sentiment" for old leaders. "Four slates with each a different head are made up, and each party is so firmly set on its candidate that the result of this first revolt is likely to be the election of another of the old-timers, or of a dark horse whose identity is not suspected." A day later, the *Post* had word that "one or two states will be cracked and forces concentrated. The president is liable to be a very active woman of the conservatives, and one highly venerated, while one of the younger candidates for president will turn into the accompanying vice president." (*Washington Post*, 19, 20 January 1892, *Film*, 29:999, 1025.)

3. Enclosure omitted. In this letter to Olympia Brown, 26 April 1892, Hooker agreed to attend the founding of the new association and expressed considerable frustration with the National-American. She recommended that an executive committee be empowered to make all decisions in the association and that meetings be held in Washington in years when the National-American "is trundling its huge bulk of speakers round among the States." Her idea that ECS be made president prompted ECS to write on the bottom of Hooker's letter, "Under no circumstances would I accept any office in any association. I want rest, to be free from all anxiety & friction. E. C. S."

4. See below at 7 May 1892.

166 ECS TO OLYMPIA BROWN

[*New York, after 26 April 1892*]

I was not laid on the shelf.[1] I resigned because I really did not wish to be President any longer. I had been chosen two years in succession by a large majority & should have been again had I chosen to accept the nomination   I am writing Mrs Hooker what I think of the situation & shall request her to forward the epistle to you. With kind regards

E. C. S.

ALS, Olympia Brown Papers, MCR-S. On verso of Isabella B. Hooker to ECS, 26 April 1892, and in *Film* at that date.

1. Olympia Brown made much of this point in the months leading up to the Federal Suffrage Association's founding. Answering Brown's queries about the election in February, Clara Colby assured her that ECS "could easily have been elected if she would have run, but she told everybody she would not run." In an editorial titled "Shelved," published in March, Brown described ECS as "set aside" from the presidency and predicted that the young members of the National-American would next year shelve SBA. (C. B. Colby to O. Brown, 6 February 1892 [on 1891 letterhead], Olympia Brown Papers, MCR-S; *Wisconsin Citizen*, March 1892, in SBA scrapbook 18, Rare Books, DLC.)

167 SPEECH BY ECS TO THE NEW YORK CITY WOMAN SUFFRAGE LEAGUE LUNCHEON

EDITORIAL NOTE: In the dining room of the Plaza Hotel at Fifth Avenue and Fifty-ninth Street, the New York City Woman Suffrage League hosted a Saturday luncheon for two hundred women to honor ECS. It was one in a series of events organized by Lillie Blake to give the suffrage movement a presence on the city's social calendar. Many writers and journalists were present; the president of Sorosis, the city's oldest woman's club, sat with the guest of honor; and members of the Daughters of the American Revolution filled a table. ECS "was received with a burst of enthusiasm which lasted some moments," according to Blake's report, and she proceeded to respond to the toast, "Fifty Years of Progress." After the event, typesetters at the *Woman's Tribune* made little sense of ECS's manuscript; here the editors have silently overridden many of their decisions about punctuation and paragraphs and corrected as best they could their obvious and numerous typographical errors. (*Woman's Journal*, 14 May 1892, *Film*, 30:173; Blake and Wallace, *Champion of Women*, 178-79.)

[7 May 1892]

In describing a man who was incapable of idealizing the facts of life, Wordsworth says, of his Peter Bell

> A primrose on the river's brim
> A yellow primrose was to him,
> And it was nothing more.[1]

As Peter trotted along the bank of the river, on his long eared mule, he said to himself no doubt, spring has come, there's the primrose. He had no thought of the mystery and poetry of its life, of the little seed sown gradually opening and stretching upward to the light: of the blossom, the bud, the full-grown flower and of the sweet traits in human character it represented.

Now, I would not, like Peter Bell, regard this most interesting gathering of most distinguished women, now engaged in many of the needed reforms of this time, as an ordinary feast given in my honor and nothing more, but as a beautiful tableaux of emancipated womanhood re-arising in the dawn of the new civilization, when the matriarchate shall be restored, and woman exalted to her proper plane, when the mother soul shall breath its love and mercy, its peace and harmony into every department of human life. The inspired sons of earth have long foreshadowed this coming day of exaltation. Go into the galleries of art and there you will find literature, philosophy, the sciences, the arts, the virtues, the graces, the seasons, day with its glorious dawn and night with its holy mysteries, all represented by woman. The glowing canvas and Parian marble alike revealing with much eloquence her birthright and her destiny.

Speaking of this fact one day to Mrs. Peter Bell, to me so poetical and full of promise, she said there was nothing mysterious or remarkable to her about it. The old painters, sitting alone in their studios, would very naturally be thinking of Eve's daughters and represent all their most beautiful conceptions in feminine forms. It would have been very stupid for them to be always painting and chiseling Hercules and Jupiter, grand specimens of their own sex. Perhaps, said she, as woman is now taking her place as novelist, poet and painter, we shall have the galleries filled, in due time, with her grand ideals of glorified manhood.

Fifty years on the horologe of time marks for us more changes than one could number even in the hours that we shall be here together. A scene like this fifty years ago would have been impossible; to have prophesied it, even, would have been considered one of the wildest vagaries of the human mind. Why Abigail Adams and Mercy B. Otis[2] with all their audacity in expressing their dissatisfaction with the Constitution the fathers framed, would never have dreamt of giving a grand feast to two hundred of their own sex in the best hotel in Boston. Even when Sorosis was formed, only a quarter century ago, it was thought a most dangerous innovation.[3] Everybody prophesied that the women who joined it, would lose all the feminine virtues. They said women had no organizing talent, that they had no *esprit de corps*, they were too envious and jealous to work together, and that a speedy dissolution of Sorosis was certain. But none of these predictions have proved true. Sorosis still lives. It is well organized. It has not suffered with envy, hatred and malice; those who have shared its friendships, its pleasures and advantages, have retained all the cardinal virtues they had when they first joined the association, and now we have clubs all over the country and their brilliant entertainments afford a feature peculiar to American life. I have passed the greater part of eight years in England and never saw so brilliant an assemblage of women devoted to the earnest, practical interests of life. English women have their clubs, some composed of women, alone, and some composed of men and women together, but they do not give delightful *recherche* entertainments that the Woman's League and Sorosis so frequently enjoy. I have never witnessed in the Old World a scene like this, significant of such probabilities for future organization and graver responsibilities than this gathering invites. The most our grandmothers thought of doing in their most audacious times was to slip into a little gallery, when their husbands had their festivities, to see them enjoy their viands and listen to their wit and wisdom.

Now let us do a little sum in subtraction to realize how far we have come. Take fifty from ninety-two and we have forty-two, the year, I believe, that General Harrison, the grandfather of our present President, ran for that office.[4] Well, that was the first time that women attended political meetings and took some interest in the old Whig party.

Whilst we have achieved many steps of progress in other directions, which I will leave for others to enumerate, woman's political status has not essentially changed. We are now on the eve of another presidential campaign. Our statesmen and politicians are full of enthusiasm as to the men and measures to be brought forward in the coming canvass. I note their speeches thus far in public, and their conversation in private, and though all the parties are alike searching for some vital issue on which to rouse the enthusiasm of the people, to carry the election for their candidates, neither of them are ready to trust the greatest question there is, the emancipation of women. The Republicans have not had a live question since slavery was settled, and if they would put a good, sound woman suffrage plank in their platform, they would sweep the country in November like a whirlwind. Perhaps, they will do it! If not, the Democrats may have the policy to do it. By voting down the property and educational qualifications in some states and extending the suffrage to all white men, the Democrats retained their political power with but few interruptions for half a century. If true to the principles of their great leaders, they would now devote themselves to the enfranchisement of women, they would gain a new lease of power, no doubt, for another half century. A handful of good men who are dissatisfied with the leading parties, now in solemn conclave formed a third, and styled themselves "The People's" party, with half the people left out, for, strange to say, they too are afraid to touch the woman question.[5] Talking with one of their leaders he said, the women ought to sustain the People's party as they were equally interested with men in their platform, which advances three vital measures, "cheap land, cheap money and cheap transportation." Ah! said I, as the men hold the land, handle the money and do the chief part of the travelling, we have not much interest in that platform. Suppose, said I, we had a little land, a few silver dollars in our pockets and took a trip on some railroad, for two cents a mile, you will not insure a woman against accident. The policies for women read "for death, only." What possible use would the money be to us on the other side of Jordan where, perhaps, gold, silver and greenbacks are all at a discount. I asked a president of one of these insurance companies why they made this invidious distinction between the sexes. He said, because women could make more staying in bed than at their usual occupations, they might stay there indefinitely, but men could make more at their usual business, hence, they would be up as soon as possible. But to return to the political parties, there are the Prohibitionists who have a woman suffrage plank in their platform.[6] Now, why do not the women all go for that party, wave their handkerchiefs, pin their bouquets in the buttonholes of the leaders, and talk it up as they have opportunity? For two reasons,

1st. They do not like the plank. While asking Congressional action on the manufacture and sale of intoxicating drinks, they remand us for all our personal and property rights to the several states. We claim, by the Fourteenth Amendment, to be citizens, first of the United States and second of the state wherein we reside. We demand national protection from the invasion of all our rights; the protection of the army and navy, the decisions of the Supreme Courts, the action of the picked men in Congress and State Legislatures. We do not hold our rights by so slender a tenure as the popular vote in the states. We have tried this plan with uniform humiliation and failure.

In the second place, we can gain nothing from a struggling party, that has no power to carry even the leading measure, by which it lives, moves and has its being. The Republican party has the power; it has made us, through many of its representatives fair promises in the past, which it did not redeem; it has coquetted with us, played with us, as a cat does with a mouse, but it has conferred some substantial benefits. It admitted Wyoming with woman suffrage into the Union; it gave us municipal suffrage in Kansas, and school suffrage in half the states of the Union; given women innumerable offices under government, and so, perhaps, as long as it is in power, it would be wise to stand by it until something better offers.

There is just one point I would suggest in closing, that good manners and sound philosophy alike, teach us to be thankful for all our blessings, for every step of progress achieved; we must remind those who withhold from us our inalienable rights to self government, that every new privilege conceded but makes our bondage more galling. Just in proportion, as through higher education, broader culture, a more comprehensive survey of the history and philosophy of human progress, woman attains an even platform with man, her position as subject while he is sovereign becomes day by day more intensely humiliating. This is grievous enough when our rulers are equals, but when by universal manhood suffrage you exalt above our heads all shades and types of manhood, foreign and native, and thus practically place the women of this republic under a foreign yoke, we have touched the lowest depths of political degradation.

But, aside from all pessimistic and humorous considerations, it is a grand spectacle, every four years, to see this great nation change its rulers, with such fair, orderly and well fought elections. And when the struggle is ended and the matter decided it is surprising to see with what good nature the one party accepts its defeat, and with what great dignity the other proclaims its victory; alike bowing to the will of the majority as the nations of the Old World do to the edict of a King.

As woman must suffer with man the evils of bad government, we are equally interested in all the questions of political life and though we have as yet no direct voice in public affairs, we have some influence and to that extent we have our duties and responsibilities, in the general welfare, to promote law and order, and secure the blessings of liberty, for all citizens in our great Republic.

~ *Woman's Tribune*, 14 May 1892.

1. William Wordsworth (1770–1850), *Peter Bell, A Tale in Verse* (1819), part 1, stanza 13.

2. By inclination and family connections at the center of revolutionary politics in Massachusetts, Abigail Smith Adams (1744–1818) wrote protests to her husband, John Adams, and Mercy Otis Warren (1728–1814), usually misnamed by ECS, wrote satires and histories as well as correspondence with political leaders.

3. Sorosis was founded in 1868, when New York's all-male press club laughed off Jane Cunningham Croly's attempt to attend a dinner for Charles Dickens. The club's members vied with the New England Woman's Club for position as the country's first club for women. (Karen J. Blair, *The Clubwoman as Feminist: True Womanhood Redefined, 1868–1914* [New York, 1980], 20–21.)

4. William Henry Harrison (1773–1841), ninth president of the United States

and grandfather of the twenty-third president, won election in 1840, not 1842, and died shortly after his inauguration.

5. The critical battle over woman suffrage in the platform of the People's party occurred earlier in the year, at the St. Louis Industrial Conference in February. Through intense negotiations to fuse a political party out of the diverse interests of farmers, laborers, southerners, northerners, and, for a time, prohibitionists, woman suffrage survived but as a supplementary resolution, not as a plank in the party's platform. (Blocker, "Politics of Reform," 624–29; Jack S. Blocker, Jr., *Retreat from Reform: The Prohibition Movement in the United States, 1890–1913* [Westport, Conn., 1976], 49–58.)

6. As the Prohibition party did not hold its national convention until late June 1892, ECS referred to earlier platforms based on states' rights. In 1892, the party abandoned that language and proclaimed the simple principle that "[n]o citizen should be denied the right to vote on account of sex, and equal labor should receive equal wages, without regard to sex." (*National Party Platforms*, 78, 92; Blocker, *Retreat from Reform*, 58–61.)

168 ❧ STATEMENT BY SBA

EDITORIAL NOTE: Chicago hosted the second biennial meeting of the General Federation of Women's Clubs from 11 to 13 May 1892, and other organizations took advantage of the gathering to schedule meetings of their own. The National Council of Women's executive committee met May 9 to 10, the Federal Suffrage Association held its first public meeting May 10, and officers of the National-American Woman Suffrage Association met informally on May 14. SBA was conspicuous in all the meetings but that of the Federal Suffrage Association. This interview, one of several conducted during her stay in the city, followed the National Council's meetings. (*Film*, 30:174–80, 184–92, 197–200; *True Republic* 1 [June 1892]: 4.)

[*c. 10 May 1892*]

It is not generally known that the idea of an organization of this sort had its origin with the redoubtable old-time leader of the suffrage movement, Susan B. Anthony. It was, however, she who conceived the idea of a National Council of Women. She is a member of the executive committee and is in Chicago expressly to attend its meetings. The same clear-headed accuracy as to data that has always distinguished her distinguishes her still. In fact, time deals very kindly with this truly remarkable woman. She does not in any way seem a day older than she did five years ago. With her strong face, her handsome black silk, jet trimmed gown with fine old filmy lace at neck and wrist and her breast knot of bright red carnations she is a picture which at once distinguishes itself from its surroundings. She is full of the same strong energy which has characterized her from the beginning of her career, with only this difference, there is a definite note of sadness in her voice when she speaks of the resignation of Elizabeth Cady Stanton as president of the suffrage organization, of which Miss Anthony, who was formerly vice president, is now the president. In speaking of this Miss Anthony hastens to say that Mrs. Stanton is just as enthusiastic for the cause as ever she was, and that she has resigned because she is so much of her time abroad, and not from any waning interest in the suffrage cause. "But even though she herself is unchanged, I feel the separation from her in the work very much indeed, for we were the complement of each other. She was a great word artist and I was a gatherer of facts. Now the truth is," said this great extempore speaker, leaning forward and lowering her voice to a confidential tone, "I can talk to the crack of the sky but I can't write any more than a school girl. Whatever has appeared with my name attached has been written by Mrs. Stanton. I have always brought my skeleton of facts to her and she has clothed it. Many a time have I tended the baby or made the pudding sauce while she wrote the article I wanted written. You see," continued Miss Anthony, "there are indeed few women who are gifted with the ability to speak well off hand and also to write well. In fact the only woman I know who is so gifted is Frances E. Willard. Mrs. Stanton and I were in every way suited to be yoke-fellows. For forty years we worked together without a shadow of ill feeling or jealously, many assertions to the contrary notwithstanding."

↞ *Chicago Evening Post*, 11 May 1892, scrapbook 39, IEWT, from *Temperance and Prohibition Papers*.

169 ECS TO SBA

[*New York, c. 17 May 1892*]¹

Dear Susan,

The New York Sun had an article about you and me having dissolved partnership.²

Have you been getting a <u>divorce</u> out in Chicago without notifying me? I should like to know my present <u>status</u>. I shall not allow any such proceedings. I consider our relation for <u>life</u>, so make the best of it. Yours

                          E. C. S.

❧ Typed transcript, ECS Papers, NjR. Transcription dated "Spring of 1870."

1. Dated with reference to the article mentioned by ECS.

2. New York *Evening Sun*, 16 May 1892. In the column "Women and Their Ways," it was reported that the "long partnership between Mrs. Stanton and Susan B. Anthony is about to be dissolved." The writer combined quotations similar to those reported in the Chicago press, above, with her own observations about SBA's fine character.

170 REMARKS BY SBA TO THE OHIO WOMAN SUFFRAGE ASSOCIATION

EDITORIAL NOTE: SBA spent two days at the eighth annual meeting of the Ohio Woman Suffrage Association in Salem, site of Ohio's first woman's rights convention. In the afternoon of May 26, she spoke during a contentious discussion about the Federal Suffrage Association, though the immediate context of these remarks is difficult to establish. When Sarah Perkins lobbied for the Ohio association to affiliate with the new group, she met with failure and a reprimand. The resolutions committee refused to affiliate and recommended a protest "against the action of any suffragists who organize any societies not auxilliary to the existing state and national associations, to perform work already taken up by them." All the delegates except Perkins voted to adopt the resolution. (Toledo *Woman's Recorder*, 2 June 1892, *Film*, 30:207-8.)

[26 May 1892]

Miss Anthony followed Mrs. Peters.[1] She gave a few historical reminiscences of suffrage work in America. She then referred to and scouted the idea that a bitterness existed between herself and Mrs. Cady Stanton, and stamped as false the statements of those persons who say that each one is persistently seeking to do the other injury. She said she believed that no two men could be found whose friendship exceeded that existing between Mrs. Cady Stanton and herself. She then read a letter from Mrs. Stanton,[2] addressed to the Michigan convention, which had failed to reach its destination before the adjournment of the convention, and she read the part that was applicable to the Salem convention; as Mrs. Stanton has as yet written no communication to this Ohio state convention. After the reading of the letter she spoke a few words to impress upon her hearers the necessity of local organization, by which better results in the movement must be attainable.

❦ Unidentified clipping, 27 May 1892, in SBA scrapbook 18, Rare Books, DLC.

1. Alice E. Heckler Peters (1845-1921) of Columbus spoke about what men said to her while she lobbied the legislature for a school suffrage law. The wife of Oscar G. Peters, Alice Peters took part in the Woman's Crusade in 1873 and joined the Woman's Christian Temperance Union at its founding. While remaining very active in the temperance union, she and her husband joined the effort to revive the Ohio Woman Suffrage Association in 1884. At this meeting the association elected her its representative on the executive committee of the National-American. (*American Women*; Taylor, *Centennial History of Columbus, Ohio*, 2:324-26; *History*, 4:877, 1101, 1104.)

2. ECS's letter has not been found. SBA attended the Michigan Equal Suffrage Association meeting on 4 May 1892. See *Film*, 30:163-65.

171   ➜   Remarks by SBA at Meeting during the Republican National Convention

EDITORIAL NOTE: With the Republican National Convention in session in Minneapolis, visiting woman suffragists addressed a large audience in the Hennepin Avenue Methodist Episcopal Church, at the corner of Tenth Street, on the evening of 8 June 1892. In addition to SBA, the speakers were Republican delegates from Wyoming, Ellen Foster of the Woman's National Republican Association, and Frederick Douglass. Missing from the platform were representatives of the new Federal Suffrage Association, also in town.

[8 June 1892]

If woman's enfranchisement does not appear as a plank in the next Republican platform it will not be Miss Anthony's fault. All day yesterday she was following about, as she expressed it, "on the ragged edge of the resolutions committee," and was only able to see the committeemen for a few moments' conference at 9 o'clock last night.[1] She looked somewhat worn and tired, therefore, when she mounted the platform to speak. In spite of this, however, she made a telling speech and gave in substance to the audience what she had told the committee on resolutions a short time before. She spoke of her 40 years of service in her cause and told the story of some of the obstacles and persecutions she had met with. She considered that the Republican party was already virtually pledged to woman's suffrage.

In the first place she said the municipal suffrage of 1887 in Kansas was carried by the Republican party. Again on the floor of congress in 1886, nine votes in the senate favored suffrage, all of them Republicans. In the House in 1884, 84 votes were given for that cause, all but four of them being Republican. The Democrats were opposed 104 strong. In 1887, when there was a discussion and vote on the amendment, 26 Republican votes were for it and the Democrats solid against it. Again in the Fifty-first congress a Republican committee brought in the first favorable report. In the admission of Wyoming as a state, with its suffrage constitution, the Republicans indorsed woman's enfranchisement. Wyoming, too, had elected women delegates to the national convention and no one thought of disputing their right.[2]

All that Miss Anthony asked in view of this was that the party openly and above board commit itself to woman's suffrage. The usual plank for a free ballot and fair count would be adopted this year and Miss Anthony urged the addition of the clause, "Without regard to sex."[3]

With the party pledged to this move, there would be no danger of the women flocking to third parties who were willing to incorporate a suffrage plank and Miss Anthony thought it would be easy to bring up 100 women to stump for the Republican party. In case Miss Anthony's resolutions are defeated in the committee her strong hope, she says, is that they will be adopted from the floor.

~ *Minneapolis Tribune*, 9 June 1892.

1. In addition to meeting with the platform committee on this day, SBA delivered to the chairman of the convention, William McKinley, the National-American's memorial for a suffrage plank in the party's platform on June 9, and she met again with the platform committee on June 10. On a separate occasion, Olympia Brown and Sarah Perkins met with the committee to present the Federal Suffrage Association's memorial seeking endorsement of women's right to vote for members of the House of Representatives. (*Minneapolis Times*, 9 June 1892, *Film*, 30:224; New York *Voice*, 16 June 1892, in SBA scrapbook 18, Rare Books, DLC; Brown, *Democratic Ideals*, 67-68; *Minneapolis Tribune*, 8 June 1892.)

2. Therese Alberta Parkinson Jenkins (1853-1936) and Cora Georgiana Snow Carleton (1844-1915) were alternate delegates to the Republican National Convention. Jenkins moved from Wisconsin to Wyoming about 1877 to marry a commissary clerk who later became a prosperous merchant in Cheyenne. Inspired by Frances Willard, she organized the local Woman's Christian Temperance Union in 1883, and advocacy of prohibition in the territory was her route to prominence. In 1891 the temperance union named her National Superintendent of the Franchise. For her work to protect woman suffrage in the new state constitution, she was singled out during celebrations of statehood to speak the congratulatory word for Wyoming's women. Jenkins joined the amendment campaigns in Colorado and Kansas in 1893 and 1894 as a speaker who could attest to the effects of woman suffrage. (*American Women*; Agnes Jenkins Metcalf, "Therese A. Parkinson Jenkins: A Prominent Wyoming Feminist," *Annals of Wyoming* 12 [October 1940]: 295-300.) Cora Carleton, from a large and distinguished Mormon family, was admitted to the Utah bar in 1872, at a time when her father was the territory's attorney general. She became territorial librarian two years later. Wyoming became her home in 1887, when she married George Wiley Carleton, a senator in that territory. The fact that she was named an alternate delegate to the Republican convention suggests activism as yet undiscovered in her new home. The Carletons moved to San Diego in 1906, where Cora Carleton continued her interest in

libraries and won election to the Board of Education just before her death. (Steven L. Staker and Colleen Y. Staker, "Utah's First Women Lawyers: Phoebe Wilson Couzins and Cora Georgiana Snow," *Utah Bar Journal* 6 [December 1993]: 10-12; Carol Cornwall Madsen, "'Sisters at the Bar': Utah Women in Law," *Utah Historical Quarterly* 61 [Summer 1993]: 217-19.)

3. The Republican platform of 1892 followed the party's usual form with regard to the franchise, with references to "every citizen" and a right to vote "guaranteed by the Constitution" but none to women as members of that citizenry. (*National Party Platforms*, 93.)

172 ❧ FROM THE DIARY OF SBA

[*8, 21 June 1892*]

WEDNESDAY, JUNE 8, 1892. In Minneapolis—at T. B. Walkers—[1] Did not get my hearing before the Republican resolution Committee until 9 P.M—then Ex. Gov—Foraker[2]—the chairman did not come out to Preside but Senator Jones of Nevada[3] officiated— I went from Hearing to M.E. Church Hennepin st—& spoke— Mrs Foster[4]—the Wyoming Delegates &c spoke—then I went to the Public Library to speak at an overflow meeting[5] [*9-20 June omitted.*]

1. Thomas Barlow Walker (1840-1928), wealthy lumberman and art collector, and his wife Harriet Granger Hulet Walker (1841-1917), noted philanthropist, hosted SBA during the Republican National Convention. The Walkers were Republicans, and their guests included J. Ellen Foster, with whom Harriet Walker worked in the Non-Partisan Woman's Christian Temperance Union. (*DAB*; *American Women*; *Minneapolis Journal*, 13 January 1917; "Harriet Granger Walker," typescript, T. B. Walker and Family Papers, MnHi.)

2. Joseph Benson Foraker (1846-1917) was former Republican governor of Ohio and an aspiring senator, who ran unsuccessfully for the Senate against John Sherman in 1892 but won election in 1896. (*ANB*.)

3. John Percival Jones (1829-1912), Republican, served in the Senate from 1873 to 1903. (*BDAC*.)

4. Judith Ellen Horton Avery Foster (1840-1910) had opposed Frances Willard's alliance with the Prohibition party and in 1888 formed the Non-Partisan Woman's Christian Temperance Union. In the same year she founded the Woman's National Republican Association, and at this national convention, the party recognized her group as its auxiliary. (*NAW*; *ANB*; Gustafson, *Women and the Republican Party*, 73-77.)

5. The library was on another corner of Tenth Street and Hennepin Avenue.

TUESDAY, JUNE 21, 1892. The National Presidential Nominating Convention in Chicago—[1]

I sat for Mr Tafft[2] this forenoon— Just as the Democracy were going to their Wigwam the rain just poured— Mrs Hooker arrived this evening—

Had a hearing before the Democratic Resolution Committee this evening—[3] Mr Watterson of Louisville Ky[4]—chairman— Gov Flower of N.Y.[5] very polite

1. SBA reached Chicago on June 19, carrying two thousand copies of a memorial from the National-American association to the Democratic National Convention. Her first business was to meet with Elizabeth Loomis, secretary of the Federal Suffrage Association. (SBA diary, 1892, and printed circular, *Film*, 29:655ff, 30:289–90.) For an account of this convention, the new Wigwam on Michigan Avenue erected for the purpose, and the rain, see R. Craig Sautter and Edward M. Burke, *Inside the Wigwam: Chicago Presidential Conventions, 1860–1996* (Chicago, 1996), 79–85.

2. Lorado Zadoc Taft (1860–1936) was a noted sculptor working in Chicago after he trained in Paris. Frances Willard arranged for him to make a bust of SBA for the Columbian Exposition, much to the chagrin of women artists. Taft began the work with photographs, until SBA could visit his studio. The only documented sittings for Taft occurred on these two days in June 1892. (*ANB*; *Union Signal*, 15 May, 18 September 1890, 11 August 1892; SBA to F. E. Willard, 27 October 1890, and SBA to Adelaide Johnson, 24 February, 28 November 1892, and SBA to L. Z. Taft, 30 April, 11 August 1892, all in *Film*, 28:691–94, 30:4–7, 150–51, 367–68, 576.)

3. According to the *Chicago Tribune*, SBA went before the committee with Olympia Brown and Jane McKinney of the Federal Suffrage Association. "They presented a joint memorial asking that a plank be inserted providing that suffrage belongs equally to every citizen of good character and legal age." That language came from the National-American's memorial. (*Chicago Daily Tribune*, 22 June 1892, *Film*, 30:288.)

4. Henry Watterson (1840–1921), editor of the *Louisville Courier-Journal*, chaired the party's platform committee when suffragists appeared before it in 1880, but in 1892, he was not a member of the committee. (*ANB*; *Papers*, 3:545–50.)

5. Roswell Pettibone Flower (1835–1899), a member of the resolutions committee, became governor of New York in 1892 as a Tammany Democrat, after serving in the House of Representatives from 1881 to 1883 and 1889 to 1891. (*ANB*; *BDAC*.)

≈ Excelsior Diary 1892, n.p., SBA Papers, DLC.

173 ❧ ECS TO ELLEN D. EATON[1]

26 West 61st [*New York*] June 22 [*1892*][2]

Dear Nellie,

I have had you often in my thoughts since my return from England & desired to know what was teeming in that busy brain. Having just received a letter from Daniel[3] with your direction I write to ask, if your arrangements for the summer are not already made, if you would like to spend three months with me up on the hills in Madison Co. We can have fine rooms, good board & pure air for $10.00 a week   I send you today some of my recent productions, which I want you to read   tell me what you think of my productions   Now do write me a few lines & give me some account of yourself. Sister Harriet & Hattie Brown spent a few days recently at the Fifth avenue Hotel. Hattie is very poorly both in mind & body. She feels the loss of her husband deeply.[4] Cady[5] is on his way home from Europe where he has been for the last three months   My sister is remarkably well but is very anxious about Hattie   I am living now in a flat with my youngest son & Maggie but we are all going into the country for the summer. With best love yours as ever

❧ *Elizabeth Cady Stanton*

❧ ALS, Ellen Dwight Eaton Papers, MCR-S.

1. Ellen Dwight Eaton (1832–?), known as Nellie, was a niece of Harriet Cady Eaton and a child of ECS's cousin Amos Beebe Eaton. Nellie and ECS met in 1860 and became fast friends. ECS once described her as an invalid. (Allen, *Descendants of Nicholas Cady*, 175; Sophie Selden Rogers, Elizabeth Selden Lane, and Edwin van Deusen Selden, *Selden Ancestry. A Family History, Giving the Ancestors and Descendants of George Shattuck Selden and His Wife Elizabeth Wright Clark* [Oil City, Pa., 1931], 167; ECS to Ann G. Phillips, before 9 January 1866, *Film*, 11:265–70. See also *Papers* 1 & 4.)

2. Year is supplied on the basis of the summer plan described.

3. This Daniel Cady Eaton (1834–1895), one of several of that name in the family, was Nellie Eaton's brother, a professor of botany. (*ANB*.)

4. George Stewart Brown (1834–1890), head of the international banking house Alexander Brown & Sons in Baltimore, died 19 May 1890. Hattie Brown's unspecified ailments brought an end to her life on 30 January 1893.

(*NCAB*, 1:474–45; *Representative Men of Maryland and District of Columbia*, 74–75; Frank R. Kent, *The Story of Alex. Brown & Sons* [Baltimore, 1950], 171–80.)

5. That is, Daniel Cady Eaton (1837–1912), Hattie Brown's brother and an art historian, already identified.

174 ~ From the Diary of SBA

[*22 June 1892*]

WEDNESDAY, JUNE 22, 1892. Dem. Con— Sat again this A.M. for Mr Taft— Mrs Hooker remained in Dem. Con—until 2 Oclock hoping to get a chance to speak before it!!

~ Excelsior Diary 1892, n.p., SBA Papers, DLC.

175 ~ Remarks by SBA to the Kansas Republican Convention

EDITORIAL NOTE: SBA accepted an invitation from the Kansas Equal Suffrage Association to address a two-day convention in Ottawa on 27 and 28 June 1892 and then accompanied Laura Johns and other officers to the Kansas Republican Convention in Topeka on 30 June. It was an unusual convention in that new leaders who favored reform as the best platform from which to compete with the Populists held a narrow majority among the delegates. As soon as the convention elected its chairman and committees, a delegate from Salina moved that the women of the equal suffrage association be offered seats on the convention floor, to which another delegate added that they should be offered not the floor but chairs. A short time later, the calls began for SBA to address the convention. According to Laura Johns, this was the first time that Republicans in Kansas had extended such an honor to a woman. (O. Gene Clanton, *Kansas Populism: Ideas and Men* [Lawrence, Kan., 1969], 122–23; *Topeka Daily Capital*, 1 July 1892, and *Report of the Twenty-fifth Annual Convention, 1893*, pp. 71–72, *Film*, 30:295–99, 31:200ff.)

[30 June 1892]

There were loud calls for Miss Susan B. Anthony, who with other members of the equal suffrage committee[1] sat to the right of the chairman's stand.[2] As she advanced to the platform she was greeted with the most cordial applause. Addressing the delegates as "Gentlemen of the Convention," she remarked, "I wish I could say 'Gentlemen and ladies of the convention' as they do in Wyoming." Then she continued: "Kansas is next to the best state in the union. Kansas is next to the best republican state in the union, but Wyoming stands at the head, because Wyoming has established a republican form of government in which every citizen, irrespective of color, nationality or sex has a voice. Kansas has established municipal suffrage, so Kansas is half as good a state as Wyoming."

Miss Anthony said she had addressed the committee on resolutions at the Minneapolis convention in the interest of equal suffrage. She had met with the democrats at Chicago and now she was on her way to the people's party convention at Omaha. Addressing herself to the Kansas convention, she said: "It is not the hour for you to be silent on any great principle of justice and right on which you have hitherto spoken. If you want to win back the honest, confiding men who have been cajoled and flattered into leaving your party, nothing will do more to bring that about than the adoption of an equal suffrage plank. If you will declare for the broad principle of equal justice to all, the best men will come back and register their vote with the republican party. It is not the time for you to cater to the lowest elements of society in Kansas. In the forty years of its existence, what has made the republican party so successful? The fact that it stood for great moral principles that fired the hearts of the best people of the nation, especially the women of the nation. The republican party practically stands for equal suffrage to the women. Every step for the enfranchisement of women has been taken by the republican party; every vote in congress in the interest of equal suffrage has been cast by the republicans."

Miss Anthony without mentioning his name, scored Senator Ingalls for having misrepresented the best feeling of Kansas, in that he ridiculed the efforts of the people of Kansas in the direction of equal rights for all women. Concluding she said: "I want you to send it out to the world that Kansas believes in a free ballot and a fair count to every citizen that lives on her soil, women included."

↝ *Topeka Daily Capital*, 1 July 1892.

1. Laura Johns listed the women in the group as herself, Elizabeth Hopkins, and May Belleville-Brown. Added to their party because they were present at the convention were Amanda Way and Mother Bickerdyke. A reporter included in his list Lucia O. Case, Nellie T. Butterfield, Olive P. Bray, Zu Adams, and Mrs. Noble Prentis. (*Report of the Twenty-fifth Annual Convention, 1893*, p. 71, *Film*, 31:200ff; *Topeka Daily Capital*, 1 July 1892.)

2. Frank L. Martin (1860–1929), delegate from Reno County, was the winning candidate for chairman of the Republican convention in the first test of strength for the reform-minded Republicans against the party bosses and conservatives. He practiced law in Hutchinson and, from 1891 to 1897, served as district court judge in Reno County. (Mullin Baldwin and Robert Morton Baldwin, eds., *Illustriana Kansas: Biographical Sketches of Kansas Men and Women of Achievement Who Have Been Awarded Life Membership in Kansas Illustriana Society* [Hebron, Neb., 1933] 738–39.)

176 ↣ FROM THE DIARY OF SBA

[*30 June 1892*]

THURSDAY, JUNE 30, 1892. At Topeka   Kansas State Republican Convention— A Hearing was given me before the Convention proper— & also before the Resolution Committee— Mrs Johns & Mrs Brown[1] of Salina spoke before the Com. also— We stayed at the Con. till 12 Oclock at night— there was a discussion on the Suffrage plank—but it was voted to stay in the platform—by—455 to 267[2]

1. May Belleville Brown Brown (1867–1936), a young mother and writer, became active in Salina's suffrage society in 1888, held office in the Kansas Equal Suffrage Association, and, during the amendment campaign of 1894, served as campaign secretary. In later years, she presided over the Kansas Federation of Women's Clubs and worked to promote public libraries. (*WWW1*; Baldwin and Baldwin, *Illustriana Kansas*, 159–61; "May Belleville Brown," *Chronicle Monthly Magazine* 3 [September 1894]: 16–18; *Kansas Library Bulletin* 5 [June 1936]: 5–6.)

2. The plank read: "We favor the submission to a vote of the people of an amendment to the constitution eliminating the disqualification of sex in the

enjoyment of the elective franchise." It was the only plank that stirred up significant debate and required a roll-call vote. When SBA left the convention at midnight, delegates were voting on candidates for governor. The balloting resumed the next morning.

~ Excelsior diary 1892, n.p., SBA Papers, DLC.

177 ~ REMARKS BY SBA AT MEETING DURING THE PEOPLE'S PARTY NATIONAL CONVENTION

EDITORIAL NOTE: At Unity Church in Omaha, an audience of four hundred people waited until ten o'clock in the evening to hear SBA, whose train from Kansas was delayed. They heard Clara Colby deliver her lecture on Wyoming, some remarks from Elizabeth Wardall, and a lengthy, sarcastic speech from Anna Shaw before a visibly tired SBA reached the church.

[2 July 1892]

A few minutes before 10 o'clock Miss Anthony came in and was introduced by Mrs. Colby. Those who have listened to Miss Anthony from year to year during the past quarter of a century were impressed probably more than ever before with the idea that Miss Anthony is a most extraordinary woman. There are very few men living who have traveled as far or made as many public addresses as this extraordinary woman, and yet she seems to be in good health and good for another decade at least of active work upon the platform. Owing to the lateness of the hour, Miss Anthony refrained from entering into an exhaustive discussion of the suffrage question, but simply presented a few points and nailed them down with her well known logic. It was not a very cheerful picture that she held up to the view.

HISTORY OF THE MOVEMENT.

She told about the first national convention visited by the advocates of woman's suffrage and the dismal failure of the attempt to get a woman's suffrage plank introduced. It was the democratic convention of 1868 held at New York.[1] She followed the history of the woman's cause all the way along and rejoiced in the fact that the republican state convention of Kansas had at last put a suffrage plank in the platform of the party. This was an entering wedge, she said, and the friends of the woman's cause would look for great things from the state of Kansas in the near future.

Miss Anthony related her experience before the platform committee at the republican convention in Minneapolis last month and also before the democratic convention in Chicago. She said that she [could] not help but notice that the delegates from Wyoming, where the women have the privilege of voting, were a great deal more obliging to the women who wanted to present the subject of suffrage to the committees than delegates who represented states where women had no vote. Let women get to the ballot once, the speaker said, and the leading politicians would be glad to show her the same consideration as they did the men. The republicans and democrats had made a great ado over the outrages practiced upon the Russian Jews, but refused to say a word about the injustice practiced upon female citizens of their own country.[2] The reason was plain. The Russian Jew might come over to the United States and have a vote, but the women, although a part of the bone and sinew of the country, have no vote and will have none so long as the men can hoodwink them with sentimental nonsense. Miss Anthony declared that nothing but a straight suffrage plank in the people's party platform would satisfy the advocates and workers for woman's rights at the ballot box.

≈ Unidentified clipping, 3 July 1892, SBA scrapbook 18, Rare Books, DLC. Square brackets surround word supplied by editors.

1. See *Papers*, 2:150–53, and *History*, 2:340–44.
2. Addressing the expulsion of Jews from Russia, the Republican platform "protest[ed] against the persecution of the Jews in Russia," while the Democrats called for the government "to use its prompt and best efforts to bring about a cessation of these cruel persecutions in the dominions of the Czar and to secure to the oppressed equal rights." (*National Party Platforms*, 88, 94.) A second, unidentified newspaper reported this paragraph somewhat differently; after SBA mentioned only the Democratic platform about Russia, she continued, "It says nothing of the half of its citizens who are taxed without representation, and has shut its eyes to the murder of one negro in every twenty-four hours for the last ten years." (*Film*, 30:305.)

178 ~ FROM THE DIARY OF SBA

[*2-4 July 1892*]

SATURDAY, JULY 2, 1892. At noon—took train for Omaha— When I arrived—with Miss Sofield[1]—at 8 P.M—Mrs Colby had advertised a meeting in Rev. Mr Mann's church—Unitarian—[2] Miss Shaw had arrived at the Paxton[3] a little before me—so she rushed to the church— & I reached there about 9.30

1. A daughter of her hosts in Washington, Kansas, this was probably Laura A. Sofield (1869-1952), later Swan. The Sofields moved to Kansas from Warren County, Illinois, sometime after 1880. Still residing in Washington in 1905, Laura was a widowed mother living with her widowed father. (SBA diary, 1 July 1892, *Film*, 29:655ff; Federal Census, Monmouth, Ill., 1880; Kansas Census, 1905, for Washington; Washington City Cemetery, on-line directory, copy in editor's files.)

2. Newton Maurice Mann (1836-1926) became minister of Omaha's First Unitarian Church in 1889, after serving eighteen years at Rochester's church, where SBA knew him well. (*DAB*.)

3. Built in 1882, the Paxton Hotel was at the intersection of Fourteenth and Farnam streets.

SUNDAY, JULY 3, 1892. In Omaha— Miss Shaw & I went to Exposition Building in the P.M—to a <u>working women's</u> meeting—[1] saw & Heard Master Workman Terence V. Powderly for the first time— I was asked to speak & did so—

Miss Shaw preached for Mr Mann in the A.M.   all—Mr Mann included—were very much pleased with her

1. Exposition Hall, on Capitol Avenue between Fourteenth and Fifteenth streets, was the site of a meeting called by the Working Women's Union, Assembly 718, Knights of Labor, to promote a home for working women in the city. When the scheduled speaker, Terence Vincent Powderly (1849-1924), was late to arrive, SBA was asked to fill the time with a speech. Powderly, a former machinist and onetime mayor of Scranton, Pennsylvania, became a member of the Knights of Labor in 1876 and the order's Grand Master Workman in 1879. Under his leadership the Knights led in organizing working women and cooperated with the Woman's Christian Temperance Union. Powderly came to Omaha because the Knights forged an alliance with the

People's party. He resigned from the order in 1893. (*Omaha Bee*, 4 July 1892; *ANB*.)

MONDAY, JULY 4, 1892. The Peoples Party (4th Party) National Con. Omaha Neb—which met in a most uncouth building called the Colliseum—not the first law of acoustics observed—[1] It was an ↑a↓ motley crowd of <u>disgruntled</u> men—from or of all the old parties—but quite as oblivious to the underlying principle of justice to women—as their first need as either of the old parties men & conventions even more so— The did even give Miss Shaw & me a hearing before their resolution Committee—[2]

1. A cavernous building erected in 1888 to house exhibitions and athletic events, the Coliseum underwent some renovations in 1890 to accommodate the city's large audience for opera. (Harlan Jennings, "Grand Opera in Nebraska in the 1890s," *Opera Quarterly* 11 [1995]: 97–118.)

2. At a meeting on Sunday afternoon, four women from the People's party, including Elizabeth Wardall, were delegated to call on members of the resolutions committee to seek a hearing for representatives of the National-American. But partisan loyalty worked against SBA at this convention. Populist suffragists felt bound by the decision made in St. Louis in February during negotiations over the terms on which their party was founded, to omit woman suffrage from the platform. As Annie Diggs told a reporter in Omaha, we argued all night in St. Louis to make suffrage part of the platform, "but when the vote was taken we were squarely beaten and then we resolved to let the larger and more momentous question take precedence. . . . I am more deeply impressed with the greater reforms necessary to be carried to successful conclusion before woman suffrage and prohibition shall obtain." (*Omaha Bee*, 2 & 4 July 1892, latter in *Film*, 30:306; Blocker, "Politics of Reform," 614–32.)

 Excelsior Diary 1892, n.p., SBA Papers, DLC.

179 ❧ SBA TO THOMAS B. REED

Rochester, N.Y., July 28th 1892

My Dear Friend

I am rejoiced to see that you are re-nominated by acclamation— I was proud of you & your brief speech at the Minneapolis Convention—[1] all I could have asked more, was that in your closing sentence—

telling of what the future glory of the Repub. Party would be—you should have added just the words "women as well as men"—after you said—"<u>every</u> United States citizen"— I exclaimed—"and with 'Tom.' Reed—<u>that</u> <u>means</u> <u>every</u> citizen—but to the outside world it means only men"— Why couldnt you, why couldnt Depew[2]—M'Kinley[3] et al— each and every one just have added the one word—& why couldn't the plank in the platform? When, oh when will it be <u>deemed</u> <u>expedient</u> to speak for the <u>full</u> application of <u>Rights</u> to all citizens—women included? Full of hope for all that is in store for us—I am very sincerely yours

↩ *Susan B. Anthony*

↩ ALS, on NAWSA letterhead, in the collection of Katharine B. Jenney, Alpine, Calif., and Jenney Microfiche, Thomas Brackett Reed Papers, MeB.

1. Reed had just been renominated as the Republican candidate for his congressional district in Maine. In a brief speech on the first day of the Republican National Convention, he hailed the party's glorious past and promised "a nobler future" of liberty for every citizen. (*Proceedings of the Tenth Republican National Convention, Held in the City of Minneapolis, Minnesota, June 7, 8, 9 and 10, 1892* [Minneapolis, 1892], 15.)

2. Chauncey Mitchell Depew (1834–1928), president of the New York Central Railroad and candidate for the Republican presidential nomination in 1888, was a delegate to the Republican National Convention. He nominated Benjamin Harrison for president. (*ANB*; *Republican National Convention, 1892*, 98–101.)

3. William McKinley (1843–1901), Republican of Ohio, served in the House of Representatives from 1877 to 1883 and 1885 to 1891, when he was elected governor of Ohio. He was chairman of the Republican National Convention. In 1897, he became the twenty-fifth president of the United States. (*ANB*.)

180 ↩ FROM THE DIARY OF SBA

[*7–9 August 1892*]

SUNDAY, AUGUST 7, 1892. At home— Mrs Hooker & dear Rachel Foster Avery with us— at evening dear Anna Shaw popped in upon us— She found she couldn't get to Buffalo from Olcott—so came back to Rochester—[1] Had a full & earnest discussion over Rev Olympia

Brown, and her forming her Federal Suffrage Society of the United States— Mrs H. unable to see that its effect could but be damaging— just as was that of the old division of Lucy Stone's & the American Society

 1. Olcott, New York, is on the shore of Lake Ontario and closer to Buffalo than to Rochester.

MONDAY, AUGUST 8, 1892. Rev Anna H. Shaw Chautauqua Assembly—by invitation from Bishop J. H. Vincent—[1] We were all called at 4.30 A.M—had breakfast & were in the carriage at 5.30—except Mrs Hooker— she waited until the 9.55 train & went to Lily Dale[2]—while Shaw—Foster-Avery & self went to Chautauqua— Met Louis Lapham at Buffalo & his mother—cousin Semantha & Nettie Vail at the Boat Landing—[3] Stopped at Hotel Athaneum—[4] at 2.30—the Great Auditorium was packed— George H. V. invited me—as a pioneer to sit on stage—& he introduced Anna—& she made the cleanest cut argument possible while the audience cheered & buoyed her up—so that she fairly floated—[5] Dr Buckle[6] sat just in front of her

 1. John Heyl Vincent (1832–1920), a bishop of the Methodist Episcopal church, established the Chautauqua Institution. By 1892, his son, George Edgar Vincent (1864–1941), had charge of setting up its summer programs, including lectures. That the father invited Anna Shaw signaled the importance assigned to this event when Shaw would make the case for woman suffrage and be answered the next day by one of Methodism's most powerful men and archenemy of woman suffrage, James Monroe Buckley. (*ANB*.)

 2. Isabella Hooker was scheduled to speak at the Cassadaga Lake Free Association, later known as Lily Dale, a spiritualist center that offered lectures during the summer season. Due to the prominence of western New York suffragist Marion Skidmore in founding and leading the association, the program from 1887 onward included regular appearances by prominent suffragists, whether or not they were spiritualists. SBA spoke there first in 1891 and returned in late August 1892. (Lecture by SBA, 15 August 1891, and SBA diary, 24–25 August 1892, *Film*, 29:340–41, 655ff, 45:388–90; W. H. Bach, *History of Cassadaga Camp, Compiled by W. H. Bach, and Presented as a Premium to the Patrons of the Sunflower* [N.p., 1899], 33–35.)

 3. They traveled through Buffalo and reached the assembly grounds by boat across Lake Chautauqua. Lewis Henry Lapham (1858–1934) was a son of SBA's second cousin and childhood friend Semantha Lapham Vail Lapham (1826–1905), both of New York City. Since the death of Semantha's husband in 1888, Lewis Lapham and his brother headed Henry G. Lapham & Co., their father's successful tannery and leather merchandising firm. By Nettie

Vail, SBA might mean Semantha Lapham's niece Annette Vail, a daughter of George Otis Vail who grew up in Buffalo. Possibly, she confused surnames and referred to Lewis Lapham's wife, Antoinette Dearborn Lapham (1861-?). (*Quaker Genealogy*, 3:198, 332; Aldridge, *Laphams in America*, 182-83, 256-57; *Friends' Intelligencer* 62 [1905]: 124; *NCAB*, 52:390; *New York Times*, 11 June 1934; William Penn Vail, *Moses Vail of Hungtington, L.I. Showing His Descent from Joseph (2) Vail* [N.p., 1947], 224.)

4. An ornate resort with sweeping porches overlooking Lake Chautauqua, the Hotel Athenaeum, built in 1881, sat at the center of the assembly grounds.

5. For Shaw's lecture, see *Chautauqua Assembly Herald*, 9 August 1892.

6. James Monroe Buckley (1836-1920), a Methodist minister, became editor of the church's *Christian Advocate* in 1880, wielding enormous influence through this weekly until his retirement in 1912. Within the General Conference of the Methodist church year after year, he led the forces opposed to the admission of women as delegates, a position he described as defensive, to stop the slide toward the ordination of women. Frances Willard and her Methodist allies were, he insisted, working against scripture. (*ANB*; "It Means Women as Traveling Preachers," *Christian Advocate*, 12 March 1891; *Chautauqua Herald Assembly*, 10 August 1892.)

TUESDAY, AUGUST 9, 1892. Rev. J. C. Bulkley—Chautauqua (Lake) Assembly— Spoke at 2.30—to about the same audience as Anna did the day before— But from his first sentence to his last—he never had his audience well in hand—and he felt the chill from it—evidently— not till he said "<u>Wyoming</u>"—was there a <u>cheer</u>—& that was just where he didn't want it— We could but feel he <u>gained us</u> converts—rather than lost us any— It was a weak attempt to make our claim a ridiculous one—his illustrations were so gross as to fail to provoke the laughter he expected— it was a sad spectacle for so able a man—[1]

1. For Buckley's lecture, see *Chautauqua Assembly Herald*, 10 August 1892. Woman suffrage, he reasoned first, violated the "feminine soul" and would "unfit woman for her position in the family." But a host of other prejudices emerged when he raised the spectre of woman suffrage empowering "all the Roman Catholic women," "the colored women of the South," "the foreigners," and "your domestics and servant girls." "You can imagine," he said to his Chautauqua audience, "the result this would bring about."

❧ Excelsior Diary 1892, n.p., SBA Papers, DLC.

181   REMARKS BY SBA TO THE MISSISSIPPI VALLEY CONFERENCE

EDITORIAL NOTE: The Iowa Woman Suffrage Association called the three-day Mississippi Valley Conference to coincide with its annual meeting on 20 September 1892 in Des Moines. In its structured agenda, focused on fundamentals of organizing, the conference bore the marks of Carrie Catt's planning. Catt had returned to Iowa for the summer of 1892 as an organizer. After SBA published a letter recommending that local, county, and state societies meet in regional councils, Catt won the approval of the Iowa association to announce the conference, and state leaders invited national leaders to attend. SBA was scheduled to be the lead speaker in a session on how to raise more money for suffrage work. She made the remarks here in the session on how to utilize the Columbian Exposition to advance the suffrage cause. Catt later reinvented the conference's history as an occasion of her innocent flaunting of protocol in the National-American, pioneering without permission, and shocking SBA. (*Woman's Journal*, 4 June 1892, *Film*, 30:222; Minutes, 21 June 1892, Records of Executive Committee of Iowa Woman Suffrage Society, 1892–1902, Women's Suffrage Records, Ia-HA; Mary Gray Peck, *Carrie Chapman Catt: A Biography* [1944; reprint, New York, 1975], 69.)

[20 September 1892]

A discussion followed, on "How can the World's Fair be utilized to the utmost to advance the interests of our cause?" Among those who took part were Rev. Olympia Brown, Miss Laura Clay, Senator Castle,[1] of Illinois, H. B. Blackwell and Miss Anthony. Miss Anthony explained what the National-American W.S.A. had done in regard to the Exposition. It was voted at the last Washington convention that the society's Committee on the Columbian Exposition, chosen the year before, should hold over, and that there should be added to it one member from each auxiliary State, to be chosen by the State. Mrs. Rachel Foster Avery is chairman of this committee, and the General Officers of the National-American also belong to it. Those members of this committee who were in Chicago last May at the gathering of the Federation of Women's Clubs, held a meeting with other friends to consult informally as to what it would be best to do for suffrage at the Fair.² It was voted to advise against having separate suffrage headquarters for the States at the Fair, as it would be hard to find women to stay for months at 44 different headquarters. We shall try to have one good suffrage headquarters, and welcome there all States and nations interested in suffrage. It was voted, on motion of Mrs. Colby, to try to have a good suffrage speech delivered at the noon hour every day, in the auditorium of the Woman's Building.³ Yesterday on my way through Chicago I visited Mrs. Potter Palmer, Mrs. Myra Bradwell⁴ and Mr. Bonney,⁵ and they all strongly approved of the plan. Mrs. Palmer thought it would be best not to limit the noon-day addresses to suffrage, but to have them on different subjects relating to the status of women. They will be advertised in the regular program of each day's proceedings. I wish every one, who knows of a woman competent to present any reformatory subject effectively, would send word to me at Rochester, N.Y., as we shall need to furnish a noon address every day for six months. But they must all be women with voices capable of filling an auditorium that seats 2500. An International Council of Women, to be held during the Exposition has been called by the Women's National Council of the United States, and the president of the latter society, Mrs. May Wright Sewall, has spent the summer abroad, holding parlor and public meetings in regard to the matter, and seeing influential women, including the Empress Frederick.⁶ I waited outside quarantine for five days to see Mrs. Sewall on her return, and finally saw her and talked with her for three hours. Mr. Bonney wishes to make the proposed International Council of Women an International Congress of Women instead, so that representative women who are doing important work in any country may participate, even if they are not delegates from any organization. The Exposition authorities have given the officers of the Women's National Council full charge of this World's Congress of Women.⁷ It is to be the opening Congress of the Exposition. The second will be the Press Congress, the third the Temperance Congress, in which woman suffrage is sure to be prominent. The Governmental Congress, to be held later, has one division on law reform, of which Mr. Palmer, of Michigan, is chairman; and he and Mr. Bonney and all the others want us to find the ablest women we can to speak with the men on each of the subjects to be treated at the Governmental Congress. This will give us the advantage of an audience of men. Woman suffrage will also be discussed at the Labor Congress. Now, under these circumstances, is it worth while for us to try to hold a separate International Suffrage Convention during the Fair? That is one of the things to be considered. As they said at one time that Congress was turned into an anti-slavery meeting, so the whole World's Fair seems to be turning into a woman suffrage meeting. The Committee on Government and Law Reform have appointed three of the oldest suffragists as an advisory council—Mrs. Stanton, Mrs. Stone and myself. I am anxious now, not as to what the Fair Committee will let women do, but how to find women who can do the things the Committee want done.

~ *Woman's Journal*, 1 October 1892.

1. Miles Beach Castle (1826–1900), of Sandwich, Illinois, was a businessman, banker, and publisher, who during his eight years as a state senator helped to pass legislation opening professions to women. For two decades, he held office in the Illinois Woman Suffrage Association. In March 1892, he was named president of the new Federal Suffrage Association. (Federal Census, 1880; *Chicago Legal News*, 11 August 1900; *History*, 4:599, 607n, 612.)

2. See *Film*, 30:197–200.

3. Many speeches in the noontime series were published in Mary Kavanaugh Oldham Eagle, ed., *The Congress of Women Held in the Woman's Building: World's Columbian Exposition, Chicago, U.S.A., 1893* (Chicago, 1894).

4. Myra Colby Bradwell (1831–1894), editor of the *Chicago Legal News* since 1868 and aggrieved party in *Bradwell v. Illinois* (1873), the Supreme Court opinion sustaining the state's right to bar her from the practice of law, played key roles in locating the Columbian Exposition in Chicago and placing women in its management. She and SBA lobbied together in Washington early in 1890. With both goals achieved, Bradwell was appointed to the Board of Lady Managers as one of the extra members from Chicago. (*NAW*; *ANB*; Weimann, *Fair Women*, 26–28, 38–39; SBA diary, entries for January 1890, *Film*, 27:679ff.)

5. Charles Carroll Bonney (1831–1903), a distinguished lawyer in Chicago, proposed and then directed the World's Congress Auxiliary, the series of international meetings concurrent with the Columbian Exposition. (*DAB*.)

6. Victoria Adelaide Mary Louise (1840–1901), daughter of Queen Victoria and widow of Emperor Frederick III of Germany.

7. On difficulties arising later in 1892 between May Sewall and the exposition's management over control of the congress of women, see Weimann, *Fair Women*, 524–30.

182 ~ ECS TO OLYMPIA BROWN

26 West 61st   New York Oct 15 [*1892*]

Dear Olympia

I see you are about to hold a state convention a good opportunity to distribute leaflets. I have sent a package to each of your officers as I found the list in your little paper for which receive my thanks[1]   I write specially to tell you that thousands of leaflets are piled up in Washington that should be going about all over our land doing missionary work. Thousands franked to go free all over the country   Now do write to Mrs Colby to send you a big package to distribute at your coming con. Let me know if you get the package I have sent you. If you & your secretary could sit down one day & send these leaflets to friends all over the state it might rouse many to action   I see you are actively & effectively at work & you have my best wishes for your success. I see no objection in that vast country to several organizations The Blackwells do most of their work in the New England association & I see no reason why the great west should not have a society officered by western women. We have no one woman broad enough to lead the whole nation. With kind regards yours sincerely

~ *Elizabeth Cady Stanton.*

I send you my leaflet on The World's Fair.[2] Do you agree with me

~ ALS, Olympia Brown Papers, MCR-S.

1. The Wisconsin Woman Suffrage Association met in Richland Center, 25 to 28 October 1892. The association's newspaper, the *Wisconsin Citizen*, was published from 1887 to 1917.

2. Probably this was "Shall the World's Fair be Open on Sunday," *Woman's Tribune*, 5 March 1892, *Film*, 30:22–23, and reprinted in the *National Bulletin* 1 (March 1892): 1–4, not in *Film*. ECS updated the essay, published as "Shall the World's Fair be Closed on Sunday?" *Woman's Tribune*, 25 February 1893, and *National Bulletin* 2 (February 1893): 1–4, *Film*, 31:362–67.

183   SBA TO HARRIET TAYLOR UPTON

Fort Scott Kansas[1] Oct. 21, 1892

My Dear

I fully intended to scribble a line to meet you & Anna Shaw & the dear Mrs Claypole[2] at the Akron meeting—though Sister Mary failed to forward your letter until this week—but alas—time was not at hand—[3] I spoke every night last week & made horrible Journies every day—& so far have spoken every night this week—but skip to night— I am at my youngest brothers—niece Lucy E's fathers—but leave at 9.20 tomorrow—& reach Howard at 7.08 evening—& go at once to the platform—& thence on & on through next week—then I go to Chicago Nov. 1st for a week—& hope to reach home by the 10th of Nov—and go to our N.Y. State Con. Nov. 14, 15, 16—

I cannot understand the fearful morbidity that has come over Olympia Brown—she had talked to the friends in Iowa of Miss Anthony's knowing <u>no</u> speaker but Miss Shaw—& she tried her hand at making friends feel as she does—but faild altogether— It is such a pity— Lovingly yours

                                       Susan B. Anthony

ALS, on NAWSA letterhead, place corrected, SBA Papers, NRU.

1. After the Kansas Republican Convention in June, Laura Johns approached the party's central committee with a suggestion that women be included in the roster of speakers for the fall campaign. The party accepted the services of SBA, Johns, and Mrs. T. J. Smith. SBA's assignment began on October 10 and required six lectures per week, each in a different town. (*Report of the Twenty-fifth Annual Convention, 1893*, p. 72, and SBA diary, 1892, *Film*, 29:655ff, 31:200ff.)

2. Katharine Benedicta Trotter Claypole (1847?–1901) was secretary of the Ohio Woman Suffrage Association and worked closely with Harriet Upton. She married the naturalist and geologist Edward W. Claypole as his second wife in 1879, raised his twin daughters who became scientists in their turn, and was acknowledged as her husband's collaborator. Edward Claypole taught at Buchtel College in Akron from 1883 to 1898, and Katharine joined the movement sometime after faculty members there helped to organize a local suffrage

society in 1889. In addition to her work for suffrage, she organized clubs and a local council of women's societies in Akron. The Claypoles moved to Pasadena in 1898. (*NCAB*, 13:259; Theodore B. Comstock, "Edward Waller Claypole," *American Geologist* 29 [January 1902]: 8-9; Katharine B. Claypole, "My Garden on an Onion," *Popular Science Monthly* 39 [May 1891]: 72-76; *Woman's Journal*, 8 June 1889.)

3. The annual meeting of the Nineteenth Congressional District of Ohio suffrage society gathered in Akron on 18 October 1892. ECS sent a letter to the meeting. See *Film*, 30:491-93.

184   ECS to Clara Bewick Colby

26 West 61st N.Y. Oct 25th [*1892*]

Dear Mrs Colby,

Mrs Miller sends me the enclosed.¹ Make a note of it in The Trib if you feel inclined.

Why not have a standing advertisements of leaflets at the end your books.² "Voluntary Motherhood" is a title that would attract many women. Would it not be well at at the coming convention in Syracuse to distribute a goodly number of leaflets.³ I have had more applications for my speech on The Solitude of Self than any I ever wrote. Are all those franked by Mr Upton⁴ distributed. We ought to make an effort to get Congress to reconsider their vote to close the The World's Fair on Sunday.⁵ My tract on that point should be broadcast now   Can you give me Miss Johnson's⁶ direction? There was a notice of her in Sunday's Sun   How are you getting on, do things look encouraging or do you feel like giving up   Susan & Mrs Johns determined to revolutionize Kansas   Just had a call from Mrs Blake she says the South is ready to listen to woman suff. With much love yours ever

        Elizabeth Cady Stanton

~ ALS, Clara B. Colby Papers, Archives Division, WHi.

1. Enclosure missing.

2. Each issue of the *Woman's Tribune* contained a long list of books recommended to its readers that could be purchased from the paper or earned as premiums for selling subscriptions.

3. Of the New York State Woman Suffrage Association.

4. ECS could refer to Harriet Upton's father-in-law, William Upton, or her husband, George Whitman Upton (1857–?).

5. In an appropriation bill for the Columbian Exposition, passed on 5 August 1892, Congress required that the fairgrounds be closed on Sunday. In Chicago, the fair's directors later decided to ignore the requirement and were sustained in their action by the Circuit Court of Appeals. (U.S. v. World's Columbian Exposition, 56 Federal Reporter 630 [C.C.N.D. Ill. 1893]; World's Columbian Exposition v. U.S., 56 Federal Reporter 654 [7th Cir. 1893].)

6. Adelaide Johnson (1859–1955), a resident of Washington, D.C., and Rome, was recruited in 1886 by Washington members of the National Woman Suffrage Association to sculpt a bust of SBA, and later, she agreed to make a bust of ECS. The New York *Sun*, 23 October 1892, described her at work in Rome on busts of ECS and Lucretia Mott. (*NAW Modern Period*.)

185 ❧ FROM THE DIARY OF SBA

[*25–27 October 1892*]

TUESDAY, OCTOBER 25, 1892. Kingman [*Kan.*][1] Was met at station by Mrs Parsons[2]—the wife of the Banker at 3.10 P.M— her parlor was full of ladies waiting to pay their respects— I barely passed around & shook hands with them & then went to bed—to try for a sleep— had taken the train at 6 sharp—& waited four hours at Conway Springs—

Had a big crowd in Opera House—& Mrs Parsons introduced me beautifully & a quartette of young women sang—& a young girl played the violin[3]

1. The city of Kingman is west of Wichita in Kingman County, south central Kansas. Traveling from El Dorado, east of Wichita, SBA took the long route, traveling southwest to a junction at Conway Springs and then northwest to Kingman.

2. Mary Sophronia Larned Parsons (1858?–1938) grew up in Champaign, Illinois, where her mother was a school superintendent. She graduated from the state university in 1878 and married Fernando Alston Parsons (1849–1927), an older graduate who stayed to work at the university. Before their marriage in 1881, Parsons joined Larned's father in business in Kansas. Over the next decade, he pursued multiple, successful ventures as a rancher, salesman, builder, investor, and banker, moving often. At Kingman, Fernando Parsons was cashier of the Farmers' and Drovers' Bank from 1890 to 1894. (Federal Census, Champaign, Ill, 1880; Franklin W. Scott, ed., *The Semi-*

Centennial Alumni Record of the University of Illinois [Urbana, Ill., 1918], 8-9, 18; William E. Connelly, *A Standard History of Kansas and Kansans* [Chicago, 1918], 4:2296-8; Cemetery Records of Champaign County, Illinois, vol. 9, Mount Hope Cemetery, Champaign—West Half, typescript, 1961, courtesy of the Urbana Free Library.)

3. Two buildings in Kingman were called opera houses. The one assigned to SBA proved wholly inadequate to the audience hoping to hear her; the standing room was filled long before the meeting started. A Miss Rodman played a violin solo. In her ninety-minute speech, SBA limited her endorsement of the Republican party: it was not "entirely right," but it was "most nearly right on the great moral questions." The local Republican newspaper continued, "She showed more clearly than has any other speaker that has been in Kingman the fallacy of hoping for reform through a new party, that the place to secure it was by making your influence felt in the primaries and conventions of parties which stand a show of success." (Kingman *Leader-Courier*, 27 October 1892.)

WEDNESDAY, OCTOBER 26, 1892. Stafford [*Kan.*][1] Left K. at 3.10—and reached Stafford at 5.30 Mrs Parsons had a nice dinner party—with Mr & Mrs Conkling[2]—Mrs Gillette[3]—& several others—the Repub. editors wife—but he—the Ed. was ill—so not there[4]

Stopped at the Grand Central Hotel!! had packed ~~Op~~ School House—made a good speech—[5] if were to stick to the business—think I could learn to make splendid points against 3^d Party swarms from the Repub. Party

1. The trip to Stafford in Stafford County took SBA a short distance northwest of Kingman. For reactions to her speech, see *Stafford Republican*, 27 October 1892, and Stafford *People's Paper*, 3 November 1892, neither in *Film*.

2. The midday meal in Kingman included the local Republican leadership. Ivan G. Conkling (1863-1933), secretary of the Kingman County Republican Central Committee and a lawyer in practice with his father, was accompanied by his wife, Antoinette Hinton Conkling (c. 1867-1940), known as Nettie, the daughter of a physician in Kingman. The Conklings left Kingman for Enid, Oklahoma, at the opening of the Cherokee Strip in 1893. (Federal Census, Schuyler County, N.Y., and Kingman, Kan., 1880; Branches and Twigs Genealogical Society of Kingman County, Kansas, *Kingman County Marriage Records, 1875-1913, 1917-1920* [Kingman, Kan., 1972], 48; Luther B. Hill, *A History of the State of Oklahoma* [Chicago, 1908], 2:443-45; Garfield County Genealogists, Inc., Enid Cemetery Records, on-line.)

3. Etta A. Goodson Gillett (1860-1930) was married to the chairman of the county Republican committee, Preston B. Gillett. (*A Biographical History of Central Kansas* [New York, 1902], 1:136-38; Walnut Hill Cemetery, Kingman, Kan., on-line records.)

4. Morton Albaugh (1862–1918), owner and editor of the Republican *Leader-Courier* and a member of the state Republican central committee, sent his wife, Eula Lee Houghton Albaugh (c. 1864–1947) to take his place. The Albaughs moved to Topeka when Republicans won the election of 1894. (Clippings on Morton Albaugh, Vertical files, KHi; *Topeka Daily Capital*, 30 April 1947.)

5. Built in 1886 and burned in 1902, this two-story hotel was on the northeast corner of Main and Broadway. Of the new brick schoolhouse, the *Stafford Republican* explained after SBA's appearance there, "by raising the connecting doors, and throwing the two upper rooms together, it makes the largest room in town for a public gathering; but this was far too small." (*Illustrated Souvenir of the Stafford County Republican* [Stafford, Kan., 1900], 5; Frank A. Steele, *A History of Stafford County* [N.p., 1982?], 94; *Stafford Republican*, 27 October 1892.)

THURSDAY, OCTOBER 27, 1892. Sterling [*Kan.*]—& county rally[1] Left Staford at 6.30— A.M. for Hutchinson—arriving in time take train west to Sterling—where I found ladies—Mrs Judge Ansel Clark[2]—Mrs English[3] & others waiting me— was guest of Mrs Clark— Instead of going in the parade—I went to bed—& a Quaker lady combed down her—put on my bonnet & shawl & rode in the carriage with my hostess & the Repub. women's club officers—in the procession—& no one suspected she wasn't Miss Anthony— It was the biggest rally of the season Judge Ady[4] of Newton spoke two hours in P.M. & I 20 minutes—& in the evening Judge Wood[5] & others spoke in the big tent—& I in the Opera House to a packed audience—[6]

1. Sterling's Republican rally in Rice County began with a morning parade consisting of more than two hundred vehicles, a marching band, veterans on the march, and children on bicycles. In the evening, four hundred men and boys made a torchlight procession. To reach her destination, SBA traveled east to Hutchinson to catch a westbound train. After this stop, two more lectures completed her commitment to the Republican party. (Sterling *Bulletin and Gazette*, 28 October 1892.)

2. Minnie Williston Clark (c. 1845–?) was the wife of Ansel Russell Clark (1842–1920). Before their marriage in 1881, she kept the boardinghouse where Clark lived in Sterling. Ansel Clark, a lawyer, served for thirteen years as an elected judge in Rice County. He and Minnie Clark had no children of their own but "cared for and reared, or assisted in rearing, twenty-five orphans to manhood and womanhood," according to his obituary. (Federal Census, 1880; "Report of the Memorial Committee," Bar Association of the State of Kansas, *Proceedings* [November 1920]: 17–18.)

3. Effie Caroline Bull English (1856–1898) and her husband John McCollister

English moved to Kansas in 1871, and after drought and fire ruined them in their first location, they settled in Rice County in 1874. At Sterling, John English became a wealthy loan agent and landowner. Effie English was active in the local Republican women's organization. (Federal Census, 1880; Connelly, *Standard History of Kansas and Kansans*, 5:2665.)

4. Joseph Wesley Ady (1851-1901) of Newton, Kansas, was the state's U.S. Attorney and a noted Republican orator. Early in 1893, he lost his bid to become United States senator. For reasons of health, he moved to Colorado Springs in 1895, where he reestablished his legal practice and his political influence. At this meeting in 1892, according to the local Republican paper, SBA spoke forty-five minutes, offering "an able discourse on 'Third Parties,' a subject upon which no one is better qualified to speak than she." (Hill P. Wilson, comp., *A Biographical History of Eminent Men of Kansas* [Topeka, Kan., 1901], 551; *Biographical History of Central Kansas*, 2:1082-84; *New York Times*, 30, 31 January 1893; Sterling *Bulletin and Gazette*, 28 October 1892.)

5. Joshua Gibson Wood (1841-1928), usually referred to as J. G., was a lawyer and Republican activist who lived in Topeka. After graduation from Oberlin College, he was admitted to the bar in Pennsylvania in 1868 and soon moved to Kansas. (Vertical files and Kansas Biographical Scrapbooks, KHi.)

6. Goodson's Opera House was erected in Sterling in 1880. In lieu of a report on her evening speech, the Republican editor opined that "[i]t is a tribute of praise in any political party when a woman of such comprehension and ability takes the platform in its interest." (*Bulletin and Gazette*, 28 October 1892.)

↭ Excelsior Diary 1892, n.p., SBA Papers, DLC.

186 ↬ SBA TO ECS

Rochester, N.Y., Nov. 27, 1892

My Dear Mrs Stanton

On my return from Buffalo—a visit to Miss Mulligan[1]—yesterday P.M—I found your note to Sister Mary— I am not gone daft—but I am overwhelmed with ten times more to do than I can possibly accomplish—

Mrs Sedgwick[2]—brought your Con. Con. letter to me at close of the second days meeting—but it was utterly impossible for me to crowd it into a single one of the sessions left— I descanted upon your letter—&

dear Mrs Colbys—in my last evening's brief speech—³ I haven't given ↑it↓ out to be printed—because I want to be with you & go over it carefully—first— I am clutching it—like a nugget of gold—for our Con. Con. campaign document—but since we failed to start the boom of it at the Syracuse Con—I think we'll wait doing it—until after the holidays—⁴

I ~~have~~ had several letters ↑from you↓ forwarded me while in Kansas— What a whirl-a-gig things have taken—⁵ I hope you have congratulated Mrs Lease⁶—on running for the U.S. Senate— She is smarter than any man of their party—and I just wish they would send her!! She has done more to win votes for that party than any man in it—and has richly earned the honor—

I was guest of Mrs Mary Bigelow Phillips⁷—at Syracuse—a part of the time—spent only one night at dear Mrs Sedgwicks— Mrs Israel Hall—of Ann Arbor was at her sisters—Mrs Phillips—and they are both to arrive here on Tuesday A.M—Mrs Hall on her way home—& Mrs Phillips—to accompany her this far— Mrs Hall is just as bright & earnest as ever— Dear a me—it is almost time to start for church— I cannot miss a sermon—when at home—and we all—Sister Mary— Niece Anna⁸ & self—go to Sarah Willis to dinner—of course Mary Hallowell—will be there too— I wish you were to be with ↑us↓ also— It is too cruel that you must be settled—fastened—so far away—so that I cant get to you without spending so much time & money— We ought to have our heads together for lots of the work before us now— Love to Maggie & Bob—& Congratulations to Kitt—⁹ It must be fun to see him petting a lovely little girl!! Well—a fellow is pretty sure to get hit—at last—even if he does escape for so many years— Lovingly yours

> Susan B Anthony

> ALS, on NAWSA letterhead, Katharine S. Day Collection, CtHSD.

1. Charlotte Mulligan (1844–1900) was a music teacher and critic; a philanthropist, known especially for her innovative work with boys; and the founder of Buffalo's Twentieth Century Club. ECS also knew her and incorporated descriptions of Mulligan's work into her speeches in the 1870s. Mulligan invited SBA to speak to the Graduates' Association, made up of alumnae of the Buffalo Female Academy, and also to consult about divisions among the city's suffragists. (*Charlotte Mulligan: Report of a Memorial Meeting Held at the Twentieth Century Club, November 9, 1914, with an Introduction* [Buffalo, N.Y., 1914?]; *Papers*, 3:341; SBA diary, 25 November 1892, and SBA

to Isabel Howland and Harriet M. Mills, 23 November 1892, *Film*, 29:655ff, 30:558-63.)

2. Deborah W. Gannett Sedgwick (1825-1901) of Syracuse hosted SBA for one night during the New York State Woman Suffrage Association meeting and gave a luncheon in her honor. She was the widow of Charles Baldwin Sedgwick, a leading lawyer in Central New York and antislavery congressman from 1859 to 1863, and the matriarch of a large family in the city. She shared a house with her son-in-law, John L. King. (*BDAC*; Charles H. Weygant, *The Sacketts of America, Their Ancestors and Descendants, 1630-1907* [Newburgh, N.Y., 1907], 209, 298; Mrs. Charles P. Gruman, "Oakwood Cemetery Records, Syracuse, New York," typescript, Daughters of the American Revolution of New York State, 1964, 1:380; SBA to Lydia A. A. Coonley, 22 November 1892, *Film*, 30:550-53.)

3. For SBA's final speech at the state meeting, see *Film*, 30:532-49. Reporters made no mention of letters from ECS or Clara Colby.

4. Plans changed for the suffrage association because the constitutional convention was to be postponed. Although not official until the legislature convened in January and amended chapter 398, it was already understood that the election of delegates would be delayed until the general election of 1893 and the convention would meet in May 1894. Lillie Blake saw the delay as advantageous because suffragists gained time to influence the election of delegates. The amended act of 1893, chapter 8, eliminated appointed delegates of all kinds but threw a crumb to women by stating that "any male or female citizen of this state" could be elected a delegate. (*Laws of New York, 1893*, chap. 8; *Woman's Journal*, 3, 10 December 1892.)

5. Populists won the governorship, a majority in the state senate and five seats in Congress, but did not control the assembly.

6. Mary Elizabeth Clyens Lease (1853-1933), lawyer, farmer, leader in the Farmers' Alliance and Knights of Labor, and former president of the Wichita Equal Suffrage Association, provided remarkable oratorical talent to the Kansas Populist party in the election of 1890 and to the national party in the presidential campaign of 1892. In the fall of 1892, she announced her willingness to be elected to the United States Senate, a move that pitted her against Populists who intended to select a Democrat as a favor returned for that party's support in the state election. Women in Kansas and elsewhere rallied around Lease's banner, while the Populist *Farmer's Wife* published their letters endorsing her candidacy. SBA's letter of support appeared in the *Chicago Tribune*. (*NAW*; *ANB*; *Papers*, 4:522-23; Richard Stiller, *Queen of Populists: The Story of Mary Elizabeth Lease* [New York, 1970], 179-83; Walter T. K. Nugent, *The Tolerant Populists: Kansas Populism and Nativism* [Chicago, 1963], 144-46; Peter H. Argersinger, *Populism and Politics: William Alfred Peffer and the People's Party* [Lexington, Ky., 1974], 152-57; *Farmer's Wife*, November, December 1892, in SBA scrapbook 18, Rare Books, DLC; SBA to M. C. Lease, *Film*, 30:724.)

7. Mary Bigelow Phillips (1827–1902), sister of Olivia Hall, grew up in Baldwinsville, New York, and moved to Syracuse after her marriage in 1852 to Lewis S. Phillips. Her husband died in 1883. (Patricia Bigelow, *Bigelow Family Genealogy*, 77.)

8. This niece was Anna Osborne Anthony (1874–1959), later Bacon, a daughter of Merritt Anthony. Like her sister and cousins, she spent time living with her aunts to pursue her education in Rochester. (Anthony, *Anthony Genealogy*, 189, 191; Virkus, *Compendium of American Genealogy*, 1:44; *Louisville Times*, 14 November 1959.)

9. Henry B. Stanton, Jr., known as Kit, was forty-eight years old when he married Mary O'Shea (c. 1873–?) on 5 November 1892. The wedding service was performed by the Catholic archbishop of New York at the Manhattan home of Mary's father, Patrick O'Shea, a prominent publisher of Catholic books. (*New York Times*, 8 November 1892, 14 March 1906; Federal Census, 1900; Charles G. Herbermann et al., eds. *The Catholic Encyclopedia* [New York, 1913], 11:28.)

187 ECS TO SBA

26 West 61st N.Y. Dec 24, [*1892*]

Dear Susan,

I enclose the letter you wished returned.[1] The Foremothers dinner went off successfully, your letter was read & applauded Annie Shaw gave a good speech full of humor, I never heard Mrs Blake do better, Isabella did well also.[2] I have suggested to Mrs Colby to make a leaflet of the occasion, as it is as great an event in our history as the first convention in Seneca Falls. Yours in haste

E. C. S.

As my speech was written out I have sent it to Mrs Colby

ALS, AF 66, Anthony Family Collection, CSmH.

1. Enclosure missing.

2. On 23 December 1892, the New York City Woman Suffrage League held the first of its Pilgrim Mothers' Dinners, a reception and luncheon for women to rival the New England Society's annual dinners for the male descendants of those who arrived on the Mayflower. One hundred and sixty-eight paying guests kicked off a tradition that lasted until 1906. Although the city league hosted the event and suffragists made the speeches, the event attracted women

from groups like the Colonial Dames, Daughters of the American Revolution, and Daughters of 1812. Speeches by Anna Shaw, Isabella Hooker, and Carrie Catt as well as SBA's letter of regret were mentioned but not quoted in Lillie Blake's account for the *Woman's Journal*. The *Woman's Tribune* later published ECS's speech with the title "Foremothers." (*Film*, 30:651-91; Blake and Wallace, *Champion of Women*, 180-81.)

188 ~ REMARKS BY SBA TO THE NATIONAL-AMERICAN WOMAN SUFFRAGE ASSOCIATION

EDITORIAL NOTE: At the first business meeting of the Washington convention, delegates took up a series of amendments to the National-American's constitution and bylaws. The most contentious of these were amendments to the first bylaw about annual meetings in Washington. Claudia Murphy of Ohio proposed that the executive committee be given the authority to decide where the annual meeting would take place. Rachel Avery of Pennsylvania proposed that the meeting be held in Washington during the first session of each Congress and that the executive committee decide where to convene in the alternate years. To manage a lively debate, delegates agreed to limit each speaker to one statement of no more than three minutes, but when SBA finally yielded the gavel to Anna Shaw and took the floor, they allowed her as much time as she needed. A slightly different version of her remarks was published in the official record of the meeting. Clara Colby described the *Tribune*'s version as "the gist of her remarks." Debate continued after SBA spoke, Murphy withdrew her motion, and delegates approved Avery's motion by a rising vote of thirty-seven to twenty-eight. (*Report of the Twenty-fifth Annual Convention, 1893*, pp. 41-53, *Film*, 31:200ff.)

[16 January 1893]

What is the end of our having a national organization? Women in the States have their specific aim, and that is the creation of public sentiment to influence their State Legislatures to give suffrage to women. Now, that is clear. My idea is that the people of each State should do their own work in their own State. The object of the National Association is not to educate the people in the school districts of the States. The sole object, it seems to me, is to bring the united influences of all the States combined upon Congress to get national legislation, and the very moment that you turn this great body and the end and aim of it into school district work you have changed it altogether. It is the State's business to do school district work, and, to make sentiment, it is our business to bring the power of all the national organization to bear upon Congress. You may talk as if we had not done anything in the last twenty-five years. I just wish you had been here then. You young women do not know anything about it. Here is Harriet Taylor Upton, who has been working for the past two years, and thinks she has been killed. (Vigorous protest from Harriet Upton.) There has been herculean work done here every year, and what is that work? When Jean Brooks Greenleaf stands on this floor she is not Mrs. Greenleaf, she is 1,436 woman suffragists of the State of New York, that is what she is. Now, then, we want to produce the effect in the school districts. When we have had those Congressional hearings from the year 1869 down to the present and every single Congress has given hearings before the committee to our best speakers. This National Association has paid the expense of a delegate from Oregon and one from California to appear before this committee and bring the influence of California and Oregon here. We do not as a national body go to California to influence that state body. Now there is Olivia B. Hall. She could pay a dozen lecturers to go over the State of Michigan and she might get Anna H. Shaw, the best lecturer you had in the United States, to go and speak in the school districts, without doing one-millionth part that Senator Tom Palmer did when he made that speech on the floor of the Senate.[1] That speech made by the Senator from Michigan was not only sent over the telegraphic wires all over the country, and synopses of that grand argument of his published in every paper from one ocean to the other, but it was published in full in every paper in the State of Michigan but one. How could you have gotten any of the suffrage speeches made published in even one hundred papers throughout the country? The W.C.T.U. is not parallel to our case at all. Our organization is for the purpose of working upon Congress to enfranchise half of the people and it is something we cannot secure in any other way but through Congress, and I believe in continuity. Nature abhors a vacuum and if this National Association deserts Washington some other body will come in and possess Washington and do the work. Last year we had representatives from twenty-three states and these twenty-three women, one from each state, went before the senate committee and brought the influence of those thousands of women they represented to bear on that committee. I shall feel that the death knell of this Association, of its power, of its influence, of its importance, is sounded if you unsettle the question; but I shall not bolt; I never did bolt; I shall submit to your decision. I detest all bolting parties. I am yours and I belong to you to the end.

~ *Woman's Tribune*, 18 January 1893.

1. Later published as *Universal Suffrage. Speech of Hon. Thomas W. Palmer, of Michigan, in the Senate of the United States, Friday, February 6, 1885* (Washington, D.C., 1885).

189 ~ SBA TO LAURA CLAY

Washington D.C. Jan. 30, 1893

Dear Miss Clay—

I enclose this paper of Mrs McDiarmid¹—which surely isn't strait— Did she send you $40— or $45? But whatever she sent you—this is not the full financial report of the Southern Com—is it?— Will you please make a full statement of the Com's receipts & disbursements—in good shape to be appended to our Treasurers financial report for 1892—and so help Mrs Upton to round out the report—

Then—in answer to the note you left for me—about furnishing a lecturer—Miss Shaw for the Southern States ↑Arkansas and Mississippi—↓ We would gladly do so—provided we were sure of having good arrangements made in the several places—but as you know getting up meetings—or rather getting audiences out to hear lectures is a fine art—and but but very very few can be found capable of the work—

Only five years ago—I was thoroughly advertised in Little Rock— Helena—Hot Springs—Fort Smith—and with lovely weather in the last of February—1889—² I spoke to Empty benches—very nearly—in each place—hence my faith for Anna Shaw's luck there is not very great— If at any place↑s↓ there is a ↑are↓ suffrage—or a Temperance associations—

that will work up on audiences—in 8 or 10 cities—right along—so that the speaker can go from place to without loss of time— You see—Miss Shaw is earning by her lectures from 5 to 6 hundred dollars a month— and our society cannot ask her to go South—unless we can make her whole financially—

The only way that I can see is for the Southern Committee to map out a series of meetings—↑& find a society or a person who will↓ engage the churches or halls—advertise the meetings—provide places for entertainment of the speaker &c. &c.— And I do not see how this can be done—in places where there is no person who understands the <u>how</u> to do it!!—

It has been my hope that some of our good speakers might make a winters pleasure trip—& speak in hotel parlors &c as they should go from city to city— So I do not see how our <u>business</u> <u>Committee</u> can <u>inaugurate</u> <u>lectures</u> in the South—in any other way than they are inaugurated at the North—that is by the few citizens there in each town talking & working up public sentiment until there is a nucleus of friends that will invite a speaker to come to their place— <u>I</u> have longed to go South for <u>thirty</u> <u>years</u>—and never could go—because I knew of no one to welcome me—and had not the money to go at my own expense— stop at hotels—hire halls—advertise lectures—& run my luck—all round— But if you can devise any plan—that will give promise of good audiences for Miss Shaw—our Com—will be glad to aid you in every way it can—but remember—with all the little mites—from the friends & the societies of the different states—our treasury is not equal to paying Miss Shaw for even <u>one months work</u> any where!!— So Lovingly & Hopefully—I am—

Susan B. Anthony

ALS, on NAWSA letterhead, Laura Clay Papers, Special Collections and Archives, KyU.

1. Enclosure missing. Clara A. Cox McDiarmid (1847–1899) of Little Rock, Arkansas, was the treasurer of the Southern Committee and president of the Arkansas Equal Suffrage Association. Raised in Kansas, she married a Union army veteran, an officer with the Fifty-fourth United States Colored Infantry, who stayed in Arkansas and held political office during Reconstruction. Clara McDiarmid was active in the temperance union, women's clubs, and the Grand Army of the Republic. By some accounts, she had also studied law.

(Andreas, *History of Kansas*, 903; Tom W. Dillard, "Pulaski People: Clara A. McDiarmid," *Pulaski County Historical Review* 26 [June 1978]: 27–28; A. Elizabeth Taylor, "The Woman Suffrage Movement in Arkansas," *Arkansas Historical Quarterly* 15 [Spring 1965]: 17–52; *Woman's Journal*, 12 August, 28 October 1899.) Contributions for southern work were sent directly to Laura Clay in Lexington. In Harriet Upton's financial report for 1892, accounts for southern work appeared under a heading for the Southern Committee and one for Rachel Avery's accounts of work in the South and Kansas. Both entries included Avery's transfer of fifty dollars to the Southern Committee at the time of its reorganization. The committee supplied no item list of its donations or expenditures, listing simply that forty dollars was spent "Through the treasurer by order of committee," and describing its other expenditure of forty-five dollars as "Cash on hand for committee." (*Woman's Journal*, 30 April 1892; *Report of the Twenty-fifth Annual Convention, 1893*, p. 155, *Film*, 31:200ff.)

2. After her niece's funeral in February 1889, SBA returned to the lecture circuit for a swing through Arkansas, speaking at Helena, Fort Smith, Little Rock, and Hot Springs between February 18 and 24. (*Woman's Tribune*, 9 March 1889.)

190 ❧ ECS TO ALICE S. BLACKWELL

26 West 61st Street, New York, Feb. 1 [*1893*].

To the Junior Editor of the Journal:

In the *Journal* of Jan. 28, in your review of the late Washington convention, you express a regret at the introduction of a resolution for opening the World's Fair on Sunday, as wholly foreign to the woman suffrage platform.[1]

In that connection, you quote the example of Wendell Phillips, in his objection to the discussion of marriage and divorce on the woman suffrage platform in a convention held in 1860.[2] Unfortunately for your purpose, Mr. Phillips' position on that occasion was wholly untenable. If the junior editor and her readers will turn to the Woman Suffrage History, Vol. I., Chap. XIV., they will see the whole debate, and that Mr. Phillips was not sustained by the facts in the case, or a single speaker on the platform; even Mr. Garrison protested, and Miss Anthony made one of the best impromptu speeches she ever made in her life. Mr. Phillips' rather audacious proposition, in a woman's convention, to sweep the whole subject from the platform, and not allow it to appear on the records, was lost by an overwhelming vote by the convention.

Mr. Phillips based his action on the assertion that "the laws of marriage and divorce bore equally on man and woman," therefore, they were not legitimate subjects for discussion in a suffrage convention. As all the speakers on the platform knew that the laws differed essentially for husbands and wives, we were amazed at his assertion. The day after the convention, I published a long summary of the laws in the *New York Tribune*, showing their injustice towards women (found in Chapter XIV).[3]

As I was responsible for this discussion, upwards of thirty years ago, and have received innumerable letters from fugitive wives, thanking me for the brave, true thoughts called out on that occasion, I feel that time has vindicated the action of the convention.

I will not ask space in your columns to vindicate the wisdom of the resolution I have tried to pass two years in succession in the suffrage convention, in favor of opening the World's Fair on Sunday. Thirty years more of experience may teach women that there is an intimate connection between their subject condition and the popular theology, and that they have a far deeper reason than man has for striving to preserve the secular nature of our government.

Can it be that the only political organization of women that we have had, of fifty years' standing, may not protest on the suffrage platform against an act of Congress that strikes at one of the most vital principles of our government?[4]

Elizabeth Cady Stanton.

Woman's Journal, 11 February 1893.

1. Alice Blackwell's report on the Washington convention chastised ECS for resubmitting her resolution about Sunday closing at the Columbian Exposition. "[Q]uestions of general public policy," she wrote, "where it is not proposed to make any difference in the treatment of the sexes, do not come within the scope of the Association." In the wake of the legislation that tried to enforce Sunday closing at the exposition, ECS's resolution gained new support in 1893. Although the resolutions committee rejected her resolution, her allies rewrote it as an affirmation of the separation of church and state and brought it to the floor. Laura Clay repeatedly insisted that any discussion of

the Sabbath violated the National-American's constitution, but her attempt to table the resolution failed by a vote of fifty to twenty-three. Other opponents, like Henry Blackwell, thought it impolitic to take a stand against the thousands of women who petitioned for Sunday closing. After heated debates spread over three sessions, the delegates finally voted that they "decline[d] to take action upon this resolution presented by the committee." (*Woman's Journal*, 28 January 1893; *Report of the Twenty-fifth Washington Convention, 1893*, pp. 85-88, 95-97, 115-16, and *Woman's Tribune*, 19 January 1893, *Film*, 31:200ff, 293-95.)

2. At the Tenth National Woman's Rights Convention. See above at 19 April 1890, and *Papers*, 1:418-31, 438-39, and *Film*, 9:612-75.

3. See *History*, 1:738-40, and *New York Tribune*, 30 May 1860, *Film*, 9:685.

4. Ellen Dietrick came to the defense of debate on the Sunday resolutions, and over the course of another month Alice Blackwell hammered home her disagreement. See *Woman's Journal*, 18 February, 4 & 18 March 1893.

191 ❧ "ORGANIZATION AMONG WOMEN AS AN INSTRUMENT IN PROMOTING THE INTERESTS OF POLITICAL LIBERTY": SPEECH BY SBA TO THE WORLD'S CONGRESS OF REPRESENTATIVE WOMEN

EDITORIAL NOTE: The program of the World's Congress Auxiliary at the World's Columbian Exposition opened on 15 May 1893 with a seven-day World's Congress of Representative Women. Drawing some of the largest audiences of any congress and crowding the new Art Memorial Building (now the Art Institute), the program provided hundreds of simultaneous sessions, many of them focused on a particular organization or profession of women. On the evening of May 20, SBA addressed one session of what was called a general congress on the topic of organization. She shared the stage with several other speakers, all addressing the subject from different vantage points. Three thousand people found space in Washington Hall to hear her.

[20 May 1893]

During the week of the presentation of the work of the various organizations that have been represented in this Congress, organizations from the Old World and the New, I have been curious to learn that "all roads lead to Rome." That is to say, it doesn't matter whether an organization is called the King's Daughters,[1] the partisan, or non-partisan Woman's Christian Temperance Union; whether it is called a Portia club, a sorosis, or a federation of clubs; a missionary society to reclaim the heathen of the Fiji Islands or an educational association; whether it is of the Jewish, of the Catholic, of the Protestant, of the Liberal, or the other sort of religion; somehow or other, everybody and every association that has spoken or reported has closed up with the statement that what they are waiting for is the ballot.

Another curious thing I have noted as I have listened to their reports is, that one association, the Federation of Clubs,[2] which is only three years old—not old enough to vote yet—can count forty thousand members;[3] that the Relief Associations of Utah, which is perhaps a quarter of a century old, reports thirty thousand members; that the Christian Temperance Union, which is yet but a little past its second decade, can report a half-million members; that the King's Daughters, only seven years old, can report two hundred thousand members; and so I might run through with all the organizations of the Old and the New worlds that have reported here, and I will venture to say that there is scarcely one of them that does not report a larger number than the Woman's Suffrage Association of the United States. Now why is it? I will tell you frankly and honestly that all we number is seven thousand. This is the number that reported this year to the national organization, which is an association composed of all the State societies and local societies that are united and that pay a little money. These other societies have a fee, or I suppose they do. But I want to say that all this great national suffrage movement that has made this immense revolution in this country, has done the work of agitation, and has kept up what Daniel Webster called it, "the rumpus of agitation,"[4] probably represents a smaller number of women, and especially represents a smaller amount of money to carry on its work than any other organization under the shadow of the American flag. We have known how to make the noise, you see, and how to bring the whole world to our organization in spirit, if not in person. I would philosophize on the reason why. It is because women have been taught always to work for something else than their own personal freedom; and the hardest thing in the world is to organize women for the one purpose of securing their political liberty and political equality. It is easy to congregate thousands and hundreds of thousands of women to try to stay the tide of intemperance; to try to elevate the morals of a community; to try to educate the masses of people; to try to relieve the poverty of the miserable; but it is a very difficult thing to make the masses of women, any more than the masses of men, congregate in great numbers to study the cause of all the ills of which they complain, and to organize for the removal of that cause; to organize for the establishment of great principles that will be sure to bring about the results which they so much desire.

Now, friends, I can tell you a great deal about what the lack of organization means, and what a hindrance this lack has been in the great movement with which I have been associated. If we could have gone to our State legislatures saying that we had numbered in our association the vast masses of the women; five millions of women in these United States who sympathize with us in spirit, and who wish we might gain the end; if we could have demonstrated to the Congress of the United States, and to the legislatures of the respective States, that we had a thorough organization back of our demand, we should have had all our demands granted long ago, and each one of the organizations which have come up here to talk at this great congress of women would not have been compelled to climax its report with the statement that they are without the ballot, and with the assertion that they need only the ballot to help them carry their work on to greater success. I want every single woman of every single organization of the Old World and the New that has thus reported, and that does feel that enfranchisement, that political equality is the underlying need to carry forward all the great enterprises of the world—I want each one to register herself, so that I can report them all at Washington next winter, and we will carry every demand which you want.

I want you to remember that Mrs. Rachel Foster Avery is to make the closing speech, and that this meeting is not adjourned; and I want all of you to bear in mind that the two young women who have made this Congress possible are my children. They were educated in this very small company, this small organization of which I am a member; and I am proud to say that that organization has graduated a great many first-class students, and among them none so near to my heart as May Wright Sewall and Rachel Foster Avery.[5]

↞ May Wright Sewall, ed., *World's Congress of Representative Women* (Chicago and New York, 1894), 463–66.

1. The International Order of the King's Daughters organized in 1886, incorporated in 1888, and added "and Sons" to its name in 1891. Interdenominational from the start, the order encouraged Christians to lend a hand through social services of each group's selection, such as day nurseries, homes for the aged, women's exchanges, and hospitals. (Sara F. Gugle, *History of the International Order of the King's Daughters and Sons, Year 1886 to 1930* [Columbus, Ohio, 1931].)

2. The General Federation of Women's Clubs organized in March 1890 at the instigation of Sorosis, the New York City club, to bring clubs into communication and mutual assistance. (*History*, 4:1050; Blair, *Clubwoman as Feminist*, 93–115.)

3. The National Woman's Relief Society was and is part of the central structure of the Church of Jesus Christ of Latter-day Saints, or Mormons, providing women with positions of leadership, albeit subordinate to the priesthood, and entrusting to them care of the needy and preparation against want. In the 1880s and 1890s, leaders of the Relief Society also led the effort to defend and regain woman suffrage in Utah. (*History*, 4:1052; Cheryll Lynn May, "Charitable Sisters," in *Mormon Sisters: Women in Early Utah*, ed. Claudia L. Bushman, new ed. [Logan, Utah, 1997], 224–39; *Encyclopedia of Mormonism*, 3:1190–1202.)

4. The phrase, reported incorrectly here, originated in an exchange between Daniel Webster and Wendell Phillips in 1852: when Webster dismissed the rub-a-dub of the abolitionist press, Phillips embraced the phrase, referring to "a 'rub-a-dub of agitation,' as ours is contemptuously styled." (Wendell Phillips, *Speeches, Lectures, and Letters* [1863; reprint, Boston, 1891], 36.)

5. May Sewall chaired the congress's committee on organization, and Rachel Avery was secretary to the committee.

192   REMARKS BY SBA TO THE WOMAN'S AUXILIARY CONGRESS OF THE PUBLIC PRESS CONGRESS

EDITORIAL NOTE: The Congress on the Public Press opened on 22 May 1893, and with it the complicated structure for women's participation in congresses went on display. Rather than integrating women into its committees, the World's Congress Auxiliary appointed women's committees "for Congresses suitable for the participation of women," and let those committees either plan sessions by and about women or push for women's inclusion on panels under the charge of men. On May 23, SBA was honored with a seat on the stage at a panel by and about women in journalism. At the conclusion of the scheduled program, the presiding officer asked SBA if she would speak. (Rossiter Johnson, ed., *A History of the World's Columbian Exposition Held in Chicago in 1893* [New York, 1898], 4:5-6.)

[23 May 1893]

Mrs. President[1] and Sisters, I might almost say daughters—I cannot tell you how much joy has filled my heart as I have sat here listening to these papers and noting those characteristics that made each in its own way beautiful and masterful. I would in no wise lessen the importance of these expressions by your various representatives, but I want to say that the words that specially voiced what I may call the up-gush of my soul were to be found in the paper read by Mrs. Swalm[2] on "The Newspaper as a Factor of Civilization." I have never been a pen artist and I have never succeeded with rhetorical flourishes unless it were by accident. I never made a peroration in oratory in my life, I think. At any rate, if I did, it was accidental and never with malice premeditated. But I have always admired supremely that which I could realize the least. The woman who can coin words and ideas to suit me best would not be unlike Mrs. Swalm, and when I heard her I said: "That is worthy of Elizabeth Cady Stanton."

While I have been sitting here I have been thinking that we have made strides in journalism in the last forty years. I recall the first time I ever wrote for a paper. The periodical was called the *Lily*.[3] It was edited—and quite appropriately—by a Mrs. Bloomer. The next paper to which I contributed was the *Una*.[4] These two journals were the only avenues women had through which to put themselves in type to any extent worthy of note before the war. The press was as kind as it knew how to be. It meant well and did all for us it knew how to do. We couldn't ask it to do more than it knew how. (Laughter.) But that was little enough and I tried an experiment in editing a newspaper myself. I started a paper and ran it for two years at a vast cost to every one concerned in it. I served seven years at lecturing to pay off the debt and interest on that paper and I considered myself fortunate to get off as easily as that.

We have had admirable papers this morning on journalism among the women of Canada.[5] The trouble with Canada is the dependence of the government and the dependence of the women. Dependence among women on the other sex in journalism is the bane of women. I remember well the days in New York when we couldn't get any kind of a report in the papers except in the way of a caricature. Things have changed and we are not caricatured now; but it isn't because we look any better than we did thirty or forty years ago. We don't look half so well. They called us cackling hens and other complimentary names. I can see the headlines now as they used to stare us in the face.

Now, if we could have controlled a paper in those days above a party and politics and everything else, we could have had fair representation. We have advanced, but there is a still further reach to be gained. The time has come when women should organize a stock company and run a newspaper on their own basis.[6] When woman has a newspaper which fear and favor cannot touch, then it will be that she can freely write her own thoughts. I do not mean that any individual woman should strive to get a newspaper of her own, but that all should combine. I fancy that Chicago is the place to start such a newspaper in, since Chicago has shown such superiority as a World's Fair city. We must have a great daily paper here edited, printed, and controlled by women. Now it is quite generally known, I suppose, that I am somewhat of a woman suffragist myself. (Laughter.) But in this daily paper I would not ask for any special phase of woman's ideas. I would ask that the paper be edited from woman's standpoint and not in the interests of any "ism." Let it be from woman's point of view just as a Republican paper is edited and filled with news from a Republican standpoint, and as a

Presbyterian periodical is given its tone from a Presbyterian point of view.

We need a daily paper edited and composed according to woman's own thoughts, and not as woman thinks a man wants her to think and write. As it is now the men who control the finances control the paper. As long as we occupy our present position we are mentally and morally in the power of men who engineer the finances. Horace Greeley once said that women ought not to expect the same pay for work that men received. He advised women to go down into New Jersey, buy a parcel of ground, and go to raising strawberries. Then when they came up to New York with their strawberries the men wouldn't dare to offer them half price for their produce.[7] I say, my journalistic sisters, that it is high time we were raising our own strawberries on our own land.

~ *Chicago Daily Tribune*, 24 May 1893.

1. Mary Hannah Krout (1851?–1927) presided over this session of the congress. Krout was an accomplished journalist, who began work at the *Crawfordsville Journal* in Indiana in 1879, moved to the *Terre Haute Express* as editor, and in 1888 joined the Chicago *Inter-Ocean*, where her duties included editing the "Woman's Kingdom." In later years, she reported for various papers from Hawaii, Australia, China, and England. No two sources on her life agree on her date of birth. (*American Women*; *WWW1*; Donald E. Thompson, comp., *Indiana Authors and Their Books, 1917–1966* [Crawfordsville, Ind., 1974].)

2. Pauline Given Swalm (1850–1934), a writer, worked alongside her husband as an editor of the *Herald* in Oskaloosa, Iowa. (Gue, *History of Iowa*, 4:257; gravestone, Woodland Cemetery, Des Moines, Iowa.)

3. Amelia Jenks Bloomer (1818–1894) published the first issue of the *Lily*, a temperance paper, in January 1849 in Seneca Falls, New York; moved it to Mount Vernon, Ohio, in 1853; and sold it in 1855, when she moved to Council Bluffs, Iowa. (*NAW*; *ANB*.)

4. Paulina Wright Davis published the *Una*, subtitled "A Paper Devoted to the Elevation of Woman," in Providence, Rhode Island, from 1853 to 1854. She moved it to Boston in January 1855, when Caroline Dall became coeditor. The paper ceased publication in October 1855.

5. Ethelwyn Wetherald spoke on women in Canadian art and literature; Eva Brodlique followed with a paper on women in Canadian journalism. (*Chicago Daily Tribune*, 23 May 1893.)

6. This vision caught the fancy of reporters. See, for example, SBA's interview with the *Chicago Daily Tribune*, 28 May 1893, *Film*, 31:485–86.

7. Possibly she directs her sarcasm at the report of the industrial committee charged by the New York woman's rights convention of 1853 to investigate

women and work. Horace Greeley chaired that committee. To relieve pressure on jobs open to women "at the base of the social edifice," the committee recommended an occupational ladder open to women. "Let her be encouraged to open a store, to work a garden, plan and tend an orchard," the committee advised. By "abstracting more and more of the competent and energetic" from the constricted job market for women, gradual improvement in women's wages would result. (*History*, 1:589-91.)

193 "The Moral Leadership of the Religious Press": Speech by SBA to the Public and Religious Press Congress

EDITORIAL NOTE: The Religious Press Congress was a division of the Public Press Congress, and on 27 May 1893, SBA was a scheduled speaker with an assigned topic. Six speakers preceded her, and, as the *Chicago Tribune* observed, "several of the papers read previously had scored the World's Fair authorities for an alleged defiance of the laws of God and man in opening the gates" on Sunday. Loud applause for these views, the *Tribune* opined, "only served to fire Miss Anthony with a zeal for her convictions in favor of the opposite side." The paper's headlines read, "Favors Open Gates. Susan B. Anthony Scores the Religious Newspapers." A stenographer provided notes for this report of her speech. (*Chicago Daily Tribune*, 28 May 1893, *Film*, 31:479.)

[27 May 1893]

I am asked to speak upon "The Moral Leadership of the Religious Press." For one who has for fifty years been ridiculed by both press and pulpit, denounced as infidel by both, it is, to say the least, very funny. Nevertheless I am glad to stand here to-day as an object lesson of the survival of the fittest, from ridicule and contempt. I was born into this earth right into the midst of the ferment of the division of the Society of Friends,[1] as it was called, on the great question which has divided all the religious peoples of Christendom, and my grandfather and grandmother[2] and my father, all Quakers, took the radical side, the Unitarian, which has been denounced as infidel.

I passed through the experience of three great reforms, not only with the secular press but with the religious press. The first one was that of temperance, in which my father was the very earliest man in all

Western Massachusetts who put liquor out of his store before he was even yet a married man. From that day in 1816 up to the day of his death, though a manufacturer and merchant nearly all of his life, he never sold a drop of liquor and scarcely ever tasted a drop. Very naturally my first reform work was in the cause of temperance, and I had my first little experience with the religious press on that question. It was no light affair. I can assure you.

I went as a delegate of the New York State Woman's Temperance Association to Syracuse, at the time of the holding of the great annual convention of the New York State Temperance Society, the men's society, and my credentials with the credentials of other women were presented.[3] When the committee reported it was adversely, that it was very well for women to belong to the temperance society, but wholly out of the way for them to be accepted as delegates or to speak or to take any part in the meetings, and I want to say to you that the majority of the men of that convention were ministers. They were not of one denomination or another, but they were of all denominations. I want to say for the comfort of everybody that the most terrible Billingsgate, the most fearful denunciation, and the most opprobrious epithets that I ever had laid on my head were spoken that day by those ministers; and when there was time to report the proceedings the whole religious press of the country, the liberal, the Unitarian, as well as the orthodox, came down on my head for obtruding myself there, claiming that St. Paul had said: "Let your women keep silence in the churches,"[4] and no one but an infidel would attempt to speak there. I submit that was not leadership in the right direction.

Then next came the anti-slavery movement. And nobody can say for a moment that either the religious pulpit or the religious press was a leader in the great work of breaking the chains of the millions of slaves in this country; but, on the other hand, church after church was rent in twain; the press—take the old New York *Observer* or the old New York *Advocate*[5]—used to make my hair stand straight for fear I might go to the bottomless pit because I was an abolitionist.

Then the next great question has been this woman question. When we started out on that the whole religious world was turned upside down with fright. We women were disobeying St. Paul; we women were getting out of sphere and would be no good anywhere, here or hereafter; and the way that I was scarified! I don't know, somehow or other the press both secular and religious, always took special pride in scarifying Miss Anthony. I used to tell them it was because I hadn't a husband or a son who would shoot the men down who abused me. Well, now they take special pains to praise. (Applause.) It is a wonderful revolution of the press.

I want to say that the religious press is exactly like the pulpit, and the religious press and pulpit are exactly in the position of the politician and of the political newspaper. The religious press has to be exactly what the people of the country want it to be, if it is not there is no support for the newspaper. The religious press, instead of being a leader in the great moral reform, is usually a little behind (applause,) and to-day, and I am glad Mr. Gilbert[6] has given me this chance to say it, I am glad that the spirit of freedom is abroad to-day, and that the people inside of the churches are demanding that the press shall be a leader in some sense.

People expect too much of the press and too much of the ministers. It is the pews that make the pulpit and decide what the pulpit shall be, and it is the constituents and subscribers for the religious papers that decide what the religious paper shall be, and therefore when you tell me that a minister is thus and so in opposing any great moral reform, or that the religious press and newspaper is thus and so, what do you tell me? You tell me that the majority of the people in the pews indorse that minister, that the majority of the church members who read that paper won't allow that editor to speak anything on the question. That is all. I am glad that the day is changing, and that the people are feeling that the press is a little laggard and want to whip it up a little.

Take the specific question of suffrage. It is but recently that the religious press has begun to speak in tolerably friendly terms in relation to us. Take the great Methodist Episcopal church; think of its having an editor chosen by the general conference, Mr. Buckley,[7] denounce the suffrage movement as something born—not of heaven, and yet if the vast majority of the members of the Methodist church were in favor of the enfranchisement of women and felt that it was a religious duty of the church to take its position in that direction, and of the religious newspaper, the organ of the society, to take position, Mr. Buckley would either be born again or else he would be slipped out of that editorial chair. He would be born again. He would believe in suffrage before he would lose his position.

I am not irreverent. I look to the public press. I look to the president of an organization, to the exponents of any society, religious or otherwise, as to the hands of the clock. They tell the time of day. Representing the suffrage movement, I stand to express the idea how high the tide has risen with the majority of the suffrage men and women of the day, and that is what a leader can do and but little more. We do not get very much ahead. We call ourselves leaders, but generally there are some down in the ranks a good deal ahead of us if they only had power to speak. I wish we had a great woman's rights press that knew how to speak the deepest and holiest thought of the best women of this country on the question of religious liberty, of political liberty, and of all liberty. And next to having such a press of our own is of course having the press of all the different denominations, of all the different political parties, of all the different interests in the country, come as near as possible to expressing our idea; and therefore, when I take up the Western Methodist paper, I forget what its name is, when I take up the *Advance*,[8] when I take up any of the Western religious newspapers I am made to feel that their editors have been born again into this recognition of the principle of equality of rights in the church for the women as well as for the men. I suppose the New York *Observer* and the New York *Advocate* and so on will have to lag behind until they are moved over on the ferry boat. However much they hold back, they have to go with the boat. I suppose these old papers will hang back just as long as they possibly can.

I cannot tell you how rejoiced I have been in listening to the papers which have been read here to see the liberality of spirit, to see the growing feeling of recognition of everybody who has inside what the Quakers used to call "the light that lighteth every man that cometh into the world," and consequently, the old Quaker preacher used to say, "every woman." He always had to add that. I have heard that preached in a singsong tone thousands of times, and that was the difference between the Quakers and the other religious sects. The Quakers always believed "consequently woman." Whatever right or duty or privilege was spoken of as having been obtained for man was "consequently for woman."

I think I have said it all, and I want to thank every editor of every liberal religious newspaper in the land for speaking on the side of perfect equality of rights to woman, for I believe that the first step toward religious equality is political equality, and I believe that our Puritan ancestors, in coming here for religious liberty, and first establishing political liberty, laid the foundation for religious liberty, and I do not believe religious liberty can exist anywhere except where political liberty has been thoroughly and fully established; and when we do have political liberty and equality fully established for the women of this country as it is for men, then you will see that the newspapers and the speakers and the politicians of the world will not be saying: "Oh, you cannot do anything with women, they are so bigoted religiously that you cannot get an idea into their heads." When the women are politically free they will dare to study all these great moral questions, and they will dare not only to study them but they will dare to write them and speak for them out of their souls.

One paper spoke of the opening of the gates of the Fair on Sunday. I have stood with my friend, Mrs. Stanton, from the beginning of the agitation, in favor of the opening of the gates on Sunday. Not because I do not venerate God and all his works, but because I do venerate God and all his works. (Applause.) Think of man allying himself to God and becoming almost a god in the creation of those wonderful works down in the White City.[9] I talked with a gentleman, Theodore Stanton, the son of my friend Mrs. Stanton, this very noon at the Palmer House lunch table, and he said: "Of all the fairs that I have ever attended, there was nothing there to begin to compare with the wonders which are gathered at Jackson Park, in this city." Now, friends look at that thing calmly for a moment, not from the standpoint of the bigotry of the pulpit or the backwardness of the press, but from your own heart of hearts and just see this; there are centered in that park, in those State and National and governmental buildings, the woman's building with all the rest, the very highest product of the human brain, the best brain, the highest moral development of this world. There are object lessons placed there for us to look at, and to say that for us to go there and study those wonderful productions of the hand and the brain of man is violating what we term the American Sabbath—is violating any injunction of God—well. I cannot understand it. To me, if I want to feel to venerate God, and if I want to feel that man is rising and approaching divinity itself, I go there and look at those wonderful productions.

Woman's Tribune, 17 June 1893.

1. SBA refers to the Separation of 1827 within the Society of Friends and the division of the Hicksite Friends from the Orthodox. Hicksites placed a greater emphasis on the divine in each individual and sought to limit the authority of elders and ministers. Many Hicksites, including Lucretia Mott, helped to shape Unitarianism, as SBA indicates.

2. Humphrey Anthony (1770-1866) and Hannah Lapham Anthony (1773-1841).

3. On this meeting of the New York State Temperance Society in June 1852, at which SBA, Amelia Bloomer, and Gerrit Smith were delegates of the Women's New York State Temperance Society, see *Film*, 7:263-72, and *History*, 1:485-88.

4. 1 Cor. 14:34.

5. The Presbyterian *New York Observer* and the Methodist *Christian Advocate* were periodicals of a genre known as family and religious papers, and both resisted social change.

6. Simeon Gilbert (1834-1917), minister and editor of the *Chicago Advance*, invited SBA and the other speakers in his capacity as chair of the Religious Press Congress. (Allibone Supplement; Johnson, *History of the World's Columbian Exposition*, 4:297.)

7. That is, James Buckley, editor of the *Christian Advocate*.

8. By western Methodist paper, SBA means the *North-Western Christian Advocate*, published in Chicago for the regional conference of the Methodist Episcopal church. The Chicago *Advance* was published by and for the Congregationalist church.

9. The World's Columbian Exposition was located in Jackson Park, at the edge of Lake Michigan on the city's south side. Congresses were held north of the exposition grounds in the building now housing the Art Institute of Chicago. The main exposition buildings in Jackson Park were referred to as the White City due to their exteriors of plaster painted white to create the impression of marble construction.

194 ❧ ELLIS MEREDITH[1] TO SBA

Denver, Colorado. June 14th, 1893.

My Dear Miss Anthony;

Yours of the 9th Inst. was read Monday night at the meeting of the E.S.A.[2] and you will doubtless hear from our corresponding secretary[3] in the near future; I believe she has already Mrs. Chapman.[4]

Are we to understand from your letter—you say that the National is not blessed with cash but that its wealth consists "in the ability of Mrs. Chapman and Mrs. Emma Smith DeVoe"—that though silver and gold you have none, such as you have you will give? Can Mrs. DeVoe raise her expenses as she goes along by using Mrs. Chapman's pledge-book system? I do not think there would be any difficulty in getting a list of places where speakers would be warmly received, and we will, of course, do what we can in the way of transportation through the state.

Practically speaking we have—well next to no money; the Attorney general[5] told us we would have no trouble in raising money; said there were fifty men in Denver who would be glad to give us $100 apiece; we were very glad to hear it, but so far have not discovered them. Mrs. Tyler[6] who has done some work organizing, and has managed to secure enough in membership fees, etc. to cover her expenses as she went along; she was thoughtless enough to go and have a [baby a]bout a year ago, and she has to devote part of her [*half a line torn away*] experienced worker we have. I do be- [*half a line torn away*] so far our Finance com- [*remainder of page torn away*] far better that it should come from women. There was some opposition in the House, but we had two thirds of the Senate;[7] I confess this was a surprise to me; suppose Mr. Armstrong's[8] bill had passed instead of ours—it would have meant the same thing, and we would have been just as anxious that it should become a law, but I dont believe any campaigning would have been done in any event, unless we did it; it is distinctly "our funeral"—I only hope we shall not be buried next fall.

Now let me explain as well as I can what we mean by a "quiet campaign": Do you remember Mrs. Nicholls?[9] She was a wheelhorse in 76–77; so was Judge Bromwell[10] and some other people that we have consulted; they say work among your friends, get votes for it; many who would vote against it will never discover it on their ballots unless you tell them; so far as party goes the Populists are pledged to it; the Republicans individually are not opposed, the election will be a comparatively quiet and unimportant one; make votes where you can, educate your friends so they will vote solidly for it and rouse as little opposition as possible. Judge Bromfield[11] is particularly strong on keeping all side issues, more especially temperance out of it entirely. Of course we may fail, but there is a very strong chance that our enemies may let it go by default, if only our friends are wide awake to the situation. We have the Australian system, and you know how prone the intelligent voter is to put his cross under the device and never cross names at all;[12] every ballot of that kind counts one for us. Do you understand our tactics better now?

Now as to making it a campaign issue; the election will not be one when party will count for much; the highest officer elected is the Sheriff; again, practically speaking the silver issue has united all parties; if it was a national election they would all vote for silver; it is only a county election, and there is a strong probability that men will be voted for, rather than party.[13]

You ask what we want; first, speakers who can organize and raise money sufficient to pay their way, and next floods of literature.

It is true that our Southern counties have not changed their spots nor their skins, although a "Greaser"[14] Senator told our Press chairman[15] that all the women down there had sat up nights to discuss our bill, and threatened to run him out of the county for voting against it, but it is also true that the rest of the state has changed radically. There are more people, and they are more intelligent; the mining districts I am told we can rely on, thanks to the labor organizations, and the silver speeches of Mrs. Lease and Mrs. Emery.[16] At the recent convention of the Department of Wyoming and Colorado G.A.R. and W.R.C. at Pueblo there was wild enthusiasm when Mrs. Gen. Carr,[17] president of the W.R.C. spoke for equal suffrage, and said it was to be voted on in the Fall.

Let me give briefly the reasons for the hope that is in us.

1. Two years ago the Legislature was either indifferent or opposed; the press ditto.[18] This year there were four bills for suffrage, not counting ours, and the press commented favorably in most instances; in fact I saw nothing against.[19]

2. Last fall the state went 12,000 Populist majority; women speakers helped to make that majority; equal suffrage is a Populist tenet, and those women made lots of friends for woman's cause.

3. The leading Republican paper of Denver has promised to help us. This paper, democratic, is not for,[20] but it is the policy of Mr. Patterson (whose wife you remember) not to say anything about it; this muzzles me to some extent, but I shall get in some good work nevertheless over my own signature, but this is on the side.

4. Last Fall at the W.C.T.U. convention the then Governor ↑(Routt)↓ spoke for equal suffrage.[21]

5. This winter at his inauguration the present Governor ↑(Waite)↓ also endorsed woman's suffrage.²²

6. The school elections all over the state called out more women voters than ever before, and in most instances they elected their candidates.

These are some of the straws that make us believe the wind is coming our way. Personally, I am afraid to hope; it seems as if victory would be too good to be true, but there are others who feel sure that we shall win. It would mean a great deal for the cause should we succeed. If you have time I would be glad to hear from you. I was born a suffragist, but from the time I read the advance sheets of the first volume of the history of Woman's Suffrage (sent to the St. Louis Globe-Democrat for review) when I was just a little girl, I have felt that you and Elizabeth Cady Stanton and Lucy Stone were the great triumverate to whom younger American women owe all the opportunities we have now or may gain in the future.²³ Feeling so you can understand that a word of encouragement from you would go a long way, and also that I dislike to feel that you think we have been rash and premature. Yours Sincerely

~ *Ellis Meredith Stansbury.*

~ TL carbon, damaged, on *Rocky Mountain News* letterhead, Ellis Meredith Collection, CoHi. "Ellis" added to name in handwriting.

1. Ellis Meredith (1865–1955) was vice president of the Colorado Equal Suffrage Association and a journalist. Born in Montana and raised chiefly in Missouri, she followed her father, Frederick Meredith, to Denver in 1885 when he went to work for the *Rocky Mountain News* as a printer and later managing editor. She too found work at the paper. "Ellis" was a penname, possibly formed from her initials "L. S."; in the 1890s she still sometimes identified herself as Lyl. She also varied her surnames. While married to Howard S. Stansbury from 1889 until their divorce in 1901, she often added Stansbury to her name, and after a second marriage in 1913 to Henry H. Clement, she occasionally used his surname. Meredith left Colorado for Washington, D.C., in the 1930s. She continued to write and was active in the Woman's National Democratic Club. ("Reminiscences of Frederick A. Meredith and Emily R. Meredith by Their Daughter, Ellis Meredith," typescript, Small Collection 288, MtHi; Federal Census, Cass County, Mo., 1880; *Woman's Who's Who 1914*; *American Women: Standard Biographical Dictionary, 1939-40*; *Washington Post*, 1 December 1955.)

2. On 3 April 1893, Colorado's Governor Davis Waite signed a bill that referred the question of woman suffrage to the voters, using the method laid

out in article seven of the state constitution by which a simple majority would decide the question rather than the higher numbers required to amend the constitution. Within weeks, SBA announced the need for "at least $20,000" in order to finance campaigns in Kansas, New York, and now Colorado. She did not foresee the severe economic depression that would make all efforts to raise money in 1893 extremely difficult. At the Columbian Exposition in May, Meredith made a personal appeal for money from the National-American, but previous pledges to New York and Kansas took precedence. Although accounts of Meredith's meetings in Chicago differ in most details, they agree that national leaders expressed little enthusiasm. Both SBA and Lucy Stone had committed time and resources to Colorado in the failed campaign of 1877. This letter is the earliest to survive in Meredith's correspondence with SBA after their meeting in Chicago. (*Woman's Journal*, 22 April 1893; Carolyn Stefanco, "Networking on the Frontier: The Colorado Women's Suffrage Movement, 1876-1893," in *The Women's West*, eds. Susan Armitage and Elizabeth Jameson [Norman, Okla., 1987], 265-76; Lucy Stone to Henry B. Blackwell, 21 May 1893, in Wheeler, *Loving Warriors*, 351; *History*, 4:513-14; Ellis Meredith, "Women Citizens of Colorado," *The Great Divide* 11 [February 1894]: 52-53; Peck, *Carrie Chapman Catt*, 73-74. See also *Papers* 3.)

3. Helen M. Reynolds (1852-1909), corresponding secretary, joined the campaign after following her younger sister Minnie to Denver from the East Coast. She staffed the campaign headquarters and reported for the *Woman's Journal*. When the campaign ended, she suffered a nervous breakdown, one serious enough to make her decline an offer to work for the National-American association. She later recovered and joined Carrie Catt in campaigns in Idaho and Montana. Reynolds moved east to New Jersey, probably at the time her sister left Denver in 1901. (Norwood Riverside Cemetery Stone Census, April 1999, from St. Lawrence County Historical Association, Canton, N.Y; Federal Census, Denver, 1900; Dolores Plested, "Amazing Minnie: A Nineteenth-Century Woman of Today," *Colorado Heritage* no. 1 [1994]: 19; *Woman's Journal*, 18 November 1893; Joseph G. Brown, *The History of Equal Suffrage in Colorado, 1868-1898* [Denver, Colo., 1898], 20-21; *History*, 4:515; *Rocky Mountain News*, 17 December 1893; Suzanne M. Marilley, *Woman Suffrage and the Origins of Liberal Feminism in the United States, 1820-1920* [Cambridge, Mass., 1996], 141-55; Rebecca J. Mead, *How the Vote Was Won: Woman Suffrage in the Western United States, 1868-1914* [New York, 2004], 65-66, 68-69, 153.)

4. Carrie Clinton Lane Chapman Catt (1859-1947), though already married to George Catt, still used the surname of her first husband, Leo Chapman, at this date. She entered the suffrage movement in Iowa as an organizer and lecturer, attended her first national convention in 1890, and joined the South Dakota campaign later that year. In 1892, the Catts moved to New York City, though Carrie Catt returned to Iowa to work that summer. The decision to send her to Colorado in 1893 established her as one of the movement's best

organizers, and she quickly capitalized on the victory to increase her power in the National-American. Catt introduced her "pledge books," mentioned below, in Iowa and found that promises of sums to be collected later raised much more money for suffrage work than direct collections of cash. (*NAW*; *ANB*; *Woman's Journal*, 10 October 1892.)

5. Eugene Engley (1853-1910) was state attorney general in 1893 and 1894, during the Populist administration. He studied law after his move to the territory in 1873, and while working in journalism and mining in southern Colorado, held public office as city and county attorney in a number of locations. In later years, he became attorney for the Western Federation of Miners and a state senator. (C. L. Swords and W. C. Edwards, comps., *Sketches and Portraitures of the State Officers and Members of the Ninth General Assembly of Colorado* [Denver, 1893]; on-line records of Colorado Legislators Past and Present, Colorado Joint Legislative Library.)

6. Louise Marie Tyler (1851-?) moved to Denver from Boston with her husband and children in 1890, after working as an organizer for either the New England or the Massachusetts suffrage association. She carried with her a letter of introduction from Lucy Stone, which no doubt helped her win election as president of the Colorado association in the fall of that year. She stepped down in 1892, but took charge of legislative lobbying and chaired the association's executive committee during the campaign. Tyler stayed in Denver until at least 1914, when she was a widow with teen-aged children. By 1930, she lived with her daughter and son-in-law in Montclair, New Jersey. (*History*, 4:432n, 509, 909, 6:61n; Brown, *History of Equal Suffrage in Colorado*, 17, 18, 20; Marilley, *Woman Suffrage and the Origins of Liberal Feminism*, 132; James Alexander Semple, *Representative Women of Colorado: A Pictorial Collection of the Women of Colorado Who Have Attained Prominence* [Denver, Colo., 1914], 163; Federal Census, 1900, 1910, 1930.)

7. What Meredith refers to below as "our bill" was House Bill 118, drafted by the Colorado Equal Suffrage Association and introduced by Populist member J. T. Heath on 16 January 1893. The bill won house approval by a vote of thirty-four to twenty-seven on March 8, with nearly solid support from Populists and strong opposition from Republicans. The state senate passed the bill twenty to ten on April 1, with a majority of the Republicans joining the Populists in support. (*Rocky Mountain News*, 2 April 1893; *House Journal of the General Assembly of the State of Colorado*, 975-76; *Senate Journal of the General Assembly of the State of Colorado*, 1585-87; *History*, 4:511-13; Billie Barnes Jensen, "Let the Women Vote," *Colorado Magazine* 41 [Winter 1964]: 13-25.)

8. Hamilton Armstrong (1857-1921) introduced Senate Bill 277 on 1 February 1893. Because it was identical to House Bill 118, the senators tabled it to await the arrival of Heath's bill. Armstrong was a bookbinder by trade, foreman at a large Denver bindery, head of the Denver Trades and Labor Assembly, general organizer for the western district of the American Federation of

Labor, and state senator from Arapahoe County, a Democrat elected as a Populist. In June 1893, he also lost his job at the bindery in retaliation for the Trades and Labor Assembly enforcing the eight-hour day at a cotton mill. After his service in the senate, Armstrong went into law enforcement in the Denver police department and the Arapahoe County sheriff's department. (Swords and Edwards, *Sketches and Portraitures of Ninth General Assembly of Colorado*; *Boulder Daily Camera*, 23 June 1893; Wilbur Fiske Stone, ed., *History of Colorado* [Chicago, 1918], 3:352–53; on-line William P. Horan Burial Records Index, Denver Public Library.)

9. Mary Plumb Nichols (1836–?), the wife of a retired lumber merchant, was a Denver artist, whose work was displayed at the Columbian Exposition. She joined the small group that reconstituted the Colorado Equal Suffrage Association in 1890, became its treasurer, and managed the state's contribution to the campaign in South Dakota. (Federal Census, 1880, 1910; Peter Hastings Falk, ed., *Who Was Who in American Art* [Madison, Conn., 1985]; Brown, *History of Equal Suffrage in Colorado*, 16–17.)

10. Henry Pelham Holmes Bromwell (1823–1903) served in Congress from Illinois before his move to Colorado in 1870. As a delegate to the constitutional convention of 1875 that prepared for statehood, Bromwell signed the minority report in favor of woman suffrage. Though he declined to serve as a judge in Colorado, his service as a county judge in Illinois in the 1850s earned him use of the title for life. (*BDAC*; *History*, 3:717–18.)

11. Meredith may have meant to type the name of Lewis C. Rockwell (1840–1897); in her report to the National-American in 1894, she mentioned early consultation with him about the campaign. Rockwell was named United States Attorney for Colorado Territory by President Grant, served in the convention that drew up the state constitution, and conducted a lucrative legal practice as a specialist in mining law. (*Portrait and Biographical Record of the State of Colorado* [Chicago, 1899], 164–65; *Report of the Twenty-sixth Washington Convention, 1894*, p. 185, *Film*, 32:326ff.)

12. With the Australian ballot, as adopted in Colorado in 1891, voters received a ballot printed by the government that included all the candidates and propositions. In previous elections, candidates, parties, and newspapers provided ballots showing only their chosen candidates or, as happened in some counties in the Colorado referendum of 1877, omitting propositions altogether.

13. Colorado's economy depended on silver, a fact evident to all in the depression of 1893. By the end of June, silver mining and smelting in the state were shut down. Republicans, Democrats, and Populists shared the belief that the United States needed free coinage of silver. On the impact of silver in Colorado politics and in the campaign for woman suffrage, see James Edward Wright, *The Politics of Populism: Dissent in Colorado* (New Haven, Conn., 1974), and Carolyn J. Stefanco, "Harvest of Discontent: The Depression of 1893 and the Women's Vote," *Colorado Heritage*, no. 2 (1993): 16–21.

14. A contemptuous term for Mexicans, in use since the 1840s.

15. Minnie Josephine Reynolds (1865-1936), later Scalabrino, moved to Denver from New York to write for the *Rocky Mountain News*. In the revitalized suffrage association, she was named press secretary. She also lobbied in the state senate to ensure passage of the suffrage referendum bill. During the campaign, she succeeded in lining up three-quarters of the state's newspapers to support the cause. Reynolds stayed in Colorado only until 1901, but her work for suffrage continued as a writer and organizer; she joined the Washington State campaign of 1910, and she introduced new suffrage societies into New Jersey. (Plested, "Amazing Minnie," 18-27; *History*, 4:511, 515.)

16. Sarah Elizabeth Van De Vort Emery (1838-1895), a writer and lecturer from Michigan and leader in that state's suffrage association, had a large Populist following. She wrote one of the basic texts of Populist economic thought, *Seven Financial Conspiracies Which Have Enslaved the American People* (1887). (*NAW*; Pauline Adams and Emma S. Thornton, *A Populist Assault: Sarah E. Van De Vort Emery on American Democracy, 1862-1895* [Bowling Green, Ohio, 1982].)

17. Mary L. Pease Carr (1837-1933) presided over the Colorado and Wyoming Department of the Woman's Relief Corps in 1893 and became national president in 1901. Her husband, Byron L. Carr, who later became Colorado's attorney general, was active in the affiliated Grand Army of the Republic, an organization of Union army veterans. The Carrs worked for the Colorado amendment from their home in Longmont, Boulder County. (*Portrait and Biographical Record of Denver and Vicinity, Colorado* [Chicago, 1898], 185-86; Brown, *History of Equal Suffrage in Colorado*, 55; *Longmont Ledger*, 28 April 1899, 3 March 1933, with assistance from the Longmont Public Library.)

18. The equal suffrage association tried to have a bill introduced in the Eighth General Assembly in 1891, but the measure was not taken up in time for action. (Meredith, "Women Citizens of Colorado," 52.)

19. In addition to the bill introduced by Hamilton Armstrong, these were House Bills 24 and 350 and Senate Bill 105.

20. Meredith wrote on the stationery of her employer, the *Rocky Mountain News*, owned by Thomas MacDonald Patterson (1839-1916). Katherine Grafton Patterson (1839-1902) held office in the Colorado Woman Suffrage Association during the campaign of 1877, and with her sister, she wrote the state's chapter in the *History of Woman Suffrage*. Despite the advocacy of his wife and daughters in 1893, Patterson would not permit the *News* to endorse woman suffrage during the campaign. (Sybil Downing and Robert E. Smith, *Tom Patterson: Colorado Crusader for Change* [Niwot, Colo., 1995]; *History*, 3:712-25.)

21. John Long Routt (1826-1907), Colorado's governor from 1876 to 1879 and 1891 to 1893, welcomed the Woman's Christian Temperance Union to Denver for its annual convention 28 October to 2 November 1892 with a warning: "You will never be able to accomplish this grand work you have

undertaken until you are allowed the ballot, and if I had it in my power I would give every one of you the ballot before I left my present position." Ellis Meredith added his name by hand, as she did in the next item on her list. (*BDGov*; *Union Signal*, 17 November 1892.)

22. Davis Hanson Waite (1825-1901), the candidate of the People's party, won the election of 1892 and was sworn in as governor of Colorado on 11 January 1893. Speaking at his inauguration, Waite was less enthusiastic about woman suffrage than Meredith suggested. Noting that "the heavens have not fallen" since women received school suffrage, he recommended "a law extending to the women of Colorado the right of suffrage at all municipal elections." (*BDGov*; *Inaugural Address of Governor Davis H. Waite to the Ninth General Assembly of the State of Colorado* [Denver, 1893], 48.)

23. On sending page proofs of the *History of Woman Suffrage*, volume one, to newspapers for reviews, see *Papers*, 4:67-68, and *Film*, 21:963-64, 970-75, 980-81, 984-85.

195 ⇒ SBA TO LYDIA AVERY COONLEY[1]

Rochester N.Y. June 22/93

My Dear Mrs Coonley

Your splendid word from Mrs Gross—written on Monday—came yesterday—Wednesday—but as yet—Thursday P.M—not a letter from Mrs Gross[2]—appears— It will surely come in the tomorrow mornings delivery— It is indeed splendid of Mrs Gross—and still more splendid of her good husband—not only to second her proposal to help along our good—but to increase it twice over— I didn't meet him—but I feel just as grateful—even more grateful—than if I had begged him to thus help us women— I was delightful of you to cheer my heart with the good news thus promptly too—

The weather is very hot here— We had a short but good shower yesterday—and it is not promising one this P.M—

I have just read aloud to my California brother-in-law Mr M'Lean[3]— the clipping your precious mother sent—[4] Judge Tourgees[5] surely settles Mr Ingalls[6] & Murat Halsteds[7] weak-kneed-ness!! on the 14th & 15th amendments—and that the protection of the Negro—is a <u>principle</u>—while <u>Prohibition</u> is a method—a <u>plan</u> of <u>dealing</u> <u>with</u> the Liquor question—hence that there is <u>no parallel</u> between the two questions—

this I have always tried to state—but Tourgee does it so strongly & clearly—he says "Prohibition is a <u>restrictive method</u>; citizenship an <u>enabling right</u>."[8]

I hope "<u>A Bystander's Notes</u>"—will continue to note all derelictions among our so called "<u>statesmen</u>"—"<u>politicians</u>" I fear—most of them—

So thank your dear mother for her thought of me—and with my dearest love to each & all of your loving & lovely household of faith—believe me ever & always Sincerely & gratefully yours

~ *Susan B. Anthony*

~ ALS, on NAWSA letterhead, SBA Collection, NR.

1. Lydia Arms Avery Coonley (1845–1924), later Ward, moved to Chicago in 1873 with her late husband, John Clark Coonley, and became active in cultural and reform activities; a member (and later president) of the Chicago Woman's Club, she also worked with the local suffrage movement and helped Jane Addams gain support for her social settlement at Hull-House. She spent summers in Wyoming, New York, where she and SBA became acquainted. SBA lived at Coonley's Chicago house for several weeks in May and June 1893. (*ANB*; *Women Building Chicago*.)

2. Emily Maude Brown Gross (1851–?) and Samuel Eberly Gross (1843–1913), friends of Lydia Coonley, later hosted SBA for a month at their mansion on Lake Shore Drive while Coonley went to New York. Samuel Gross earned fortune and fame as a designer and builder of subdivisions in Chicago with moderate-priced houses for the families of workingmen, and he was the model for Theodore Dreiser's character, Samuel E. Ross, in *Jennie Gerhardt*. Emily Gross, also known as Maude, was born in England, moved to Chicago with her family, and married Gross in 1874. Their one child died young. During the summer of 1893, she became infatuated with SBA; at the end of her visit, SBA noted "her affection & attention are phenomenal." Samuel and Emily Gross became close friends, visiting SBA in Rochester, making gifts of money and clothing, helping her causes, and providing a home in Chicago. The Grosses divorced in 1900, and Emily Gross stayed on in their mansion. (Emily Clark and Patrick Ashley, "The Merchant Prince of Cornville," *Chicago History* [December 1992]: 4–19; Emily Clark, "Samuel E. [G]ross: Dreiser's Real Estate Magnate," in *Dreiser's Jennie Gerhardt: New Essays on the Restored Text*, ed. James L. W. West III [Philadelphia, 1995], 183–93; *Chicago Daily Tribune*, 25 October 1893; Lillian Faderman, *To Believe in Women: What Lesbians Have Done for America—A History* [Boston, 1999], 27–30; SBA diary, 2 November 1893, SBA to E. B. Gross, 13 March 1899, SBA to S. E. Gross, 28 March 1900, S. E. Gross to SBA, 17 April 1900, *Film*, 31:3ff, 39:591, 41:156, 228.)

3. Aaron M. McLean (1812–1896), the widower of SBA's sister Guelma

McLean, lived in California with his daughter and her family. When he and his grandson traveled east for a visit, SBA returned to Rochester. (Baker Genealogical Ms., SBA Papers, MCR-S; SBA to Harriet T. Upton, 20 June 1893, and SBA to L. A. A. Coonley, 3 July 1893, *Film*, 31:511–14, 541–42.)

4. Susan Howes Look Avery (1817–1915), of Wyoming, New York, and Louisville, Kentucky, was the widow of Benjamin Franklin Avery, one of the nation's largest manufacturers of plows, and the mother of Lydia Coonley. In New York, Avery helped found the Warsaw Political Equality Club in 1891 and presided over countywide meetings of other local clubs for many years. In Louisville, she founded the Woman's Club, worked with Laura Clay on reform of married women's property laws, and supplemented the budget of the National-American's Southern Committee with her donations. (*WWW1*; Jane Kirk, "Susan Look Avery: A Nineteenth-Century Reformer," *Historical Wyoming* 24 [January 1978]: 57–64; Fuller, *Laura Clay and the Woman's Rights Movement*, 46, 57; Waldo R. Browne, *Chronicles of an American Home, Hillside (Wyoming, New York) and Its Family: 1858–1928* [New York, 1930].)

5. Albion Winegar Tourgée (1838–1905) was a writer and lawyer, living in Chautauqua County, New York, known for his unflinching commitment to equal rights for African Americans. Avery sent copies of his weekly column, "A Bystander's Notes," in the Chicago *Inter-Ocean*, in which he defended the Fourteenth and Fifteenth Amendments against a mounting cry to repeal them. (*ANB*; Mark Elliott, *Color-Blind Justice: Albion Tourgée and the Quest for Racial Equality from the Civil War to Plessy v. Ferguson* [New York, 2006]; Chicago *Inter-Ocean*, 10, 17 June 1893.)

6. John Ingalls had recently opposed repeal of the amendments, but, in the belief that the black and white races could never cooperate, he proposed instead that African Americans be sent to Africa. (*Chicago Daily Tribune*, 28 May 1893.)

7. Murat Halstead (1829–1908) was the former editor of the Cincinnati *Commercial Gazette*, once a powerful voice for midwestern Republicans. When he left Cincinnati, he became editor of the *Brooklyn Standard-Union*. Halstead, whom Tourgée thought had always suffered from "negrophobia," had opposed the Force Bill as inexpedient and called for repeal of the Reconstruction amendments; without public opinion behind national protection of voting rights, the Fifteenth Amendment was unenforceable, he wrote. What he called the "sovereignty of the community" in the South "must be respected wherever encountered." (*ANB*; Murat Halstead, "Review of Current Events," *Cosmopolitan, a Monthly Illustrated Magazine* 12 [January 1892]: 372–73; Chicago *Inter-Ocean*, 10 June 1893.)

8. Tourgée made this point to stop any further analogies between the impact of prohibition and of racial equality on the fortunes of a political party. They were not comparable commitments. (Chicago *Inter-Ocean*, 17 June 1893.)

196   SBA to Albion W. Tourgée

[*Rochester*] June 22/93

Dear Judge Tourgee

Mr Wm Dudley Foulke—the Chairman of the Department of ↑the↓ Government Congress ↑Committee↓ deputizes me to secure some able men to discuss the question of popular suffrage[1]—in general—or in some or all of its restrictions—and since mailing my scribble to you[2]— it comes to me that you ↑are↓ just the very man to set forth the whole subject— You see so many of our public men—politicians & editors— are like the ↑Iowa↓ republican[3]—and Ingalls &c—not <u>half</u> believing in the ballot—as the underlying principle of our government—and of all just governments—that they are unfitted to write on the subject—while you—are fit—because you do retain the belief in suffrage as a principle—

Now will you prepare a paper of thirty minutes say! The Congress is to be held from the 7th to the 15th of August— If possible—I would like you to ↑be↓ present & read it—but if that cannot be—I would love to have you deputize me to read it for you— I am to read Mrs Stanton's— and I should be proud to read yours—that is if you cannot be there to read it yourself—

Mrs Stanton's paper is to be on "<u>The essential nature of suffrage</u>["]— mine is to be "The <u>Protective</u> Power of Suffrage"—Lucy Stones—"The History of the woman suffrage movement in the United States["]—Mrs Livermore's—The Present status of suffrage in the U.S. Mrs Howe's "The Ethics of suffrage["]—Frederick Douglas on <u>Race</u> suffrage— But what I hope you will feel like doing—well—just the strongest thing you can think of— So I hope you'll say yes—and at once give me the title— so that I can announce it—

I do not know of a single person—man or woman—who feels the need of every citizen's being a voter as you do—unless it is my friend Mrs Stanton— It wont matter at all if your paper should treat of the essential nature of the suffrage— There cant be too much said at this time to emphasize the fact— So you needn't fear trenching upon any other persons ground—only just write your deepest & strongest thought—that the Congress Report may testify, ~~that~~ ↑may↓ carry down to posterity your good word— What is said in these Congresses will stand for all time—as the highest & best thought of the time—

Hoping to hear very soon that you will prepare this paper[4]—I am very sincerely yours

↬ Susan B. Anthony

↬ ALS, on NAWSA letterhead, Albion W. Tourgée Papers, NWefHi.

1. William Foulke headed the committee planning the Suffrage Congress, one of seven divisions within the Congress on Government, a responsibility he took over from Thomas Palmer early in the year. In June, the National-American association was given responsibility to organize a series of meetings within the Suffrage Congress. Tourgée accepted this invitation, and was scheduled for the same session as ECS on 12 August 1893. He sent his speech, and Theodore Sewall read it for him. (W. D. Foulke to Henry B. Blackwell, 11 February 1893, NAWSA Papers, DLC; Program of Department Congress of the National-American Woman Suffrage Association, SBA scrapbook 19, Rare Books, DLC; Chicago *Inter-Ocean*, 13 August 1893; *Woman's Journal*, 19 August 1893, *Film*, 31:593-94.)

2. SBA had just sent him an inscribed set of the *History of Woman Suffrage*, acknowledged by Tourgée on 7 July 1893, *Film*, 31:545-47.

3. See previous document. In the second of the columns sent to SBA, Tourgée replied at length to an unnamed Iowa Republican who protested that the Republican party could not survive being saddled with a responsibility for racial equality. (Chicago *Inter-Ocean*, 17 June 1893.)

4. Although Tourgée's reply is missing, SBA's next letter to him suggests its content. SBA's letter is somewhere in private hands; it was offered for sale in 1995 by a manuscript dealer who transcribed it for his catalogue. Tourgée explained his opposition to a federal amendment for woman suffrage on the grounds that the Constitution already protected women's right to vote. To this, SBA replied, "since you agree with us suffrage women that citizenship and suffrage ought to be synonymous—it doesn't matter whether they are made so by a new amendment to the U.S. constitution or by a new interpretation of the old amendments. . . . As many—I think more—of our friends believe with you as to the intention of the existing U.S. constitution and its amendments, I do not quarrel with those who take the view opposite to mine—for I well know that when we get a strong enough public sentiment there will be no difficulty in getting either a new amendment or a new interpretation—and I don't care which—so women are protected in what is—or ought to be—their 'citizen's right to vote.'" (SBA to A. W. Tourgée, 27 June 1893, in Catalogue of the Kenneth W. Rendell Gallery, Inc., 1995.)

197 SBA TO FREDERICK DOUGLASS

Rochester N.Y. June 25/93

My Dear Friend—

Mr Foulke—Chairman of the Committee of arrangements of the Government, Law Reform & Political Science Congress—to be held in the Art Palace—Chicago—from Aug. 7 to 15—writes me has failed to get any reply from you—though I gave him your address—when in Chicago—[1]

Now—he—and I too—wishes you to speak on the <u>race question</u>—or race suffrage—but—really—what I want you to do is to write out your strongest statement on Free Government—the whole underlying principle—or the one branch—as you prefer— What I want is that—<u>your paper</u> shall come along side of <u>Mrs Stantons</u>—which is to be on the Philosophy—or essential nature of suffrage—& on Friday afternoon August 14th— That is if you choose the whole question of ↑popular↓ suffrage as the basis of Gov't— What I want you to do—is to write or speak right of your very soul—the best & most needed thought you have— I want you to go down—to posterity—in <u>the published reports</u> of this Congress as having seen & said the very wisest & truest things <u>for</u> <s>our</s> ↑the↑ perpetuity of our government— Next to my pride that <u>Mrs Stanton</u> shall do her "<u>tippest toppest</u>" best—is my pride that Frederick Douglas shall do his— So write me—instanter—please—saying you'll do your level best to put your name & your thought by the side of Mrs Stantons in the great record books of these great World's Congresses— With kind regards to Mrs Douglass—and ever so many hopes that you'll say yes at once   I am very sincerely

Susan B. Anthony

ALS, on NAWSA letterhead, Frederick Douglass Papers, DLC.

1. Foulke had Douglass in mind for this assignment since at least February. Douglass spoke at a session of the Suffrage Congress on 9 August 1893, responding to a southerner's defense of white rule. On the same day, he made brief remarks at a session organized by the Federal Suffrage Association. (W.

D. Foulke to Henry B. Blackwell, 11 February 1893, NAWSA Papers, DLC; *Chicago Daily Tribune*, 10 August 1893; Chicago *Inter-Ocean*, 10 August 1893.)

198   SBA to Ellis Meredith

Rochester N.Y. July 16/93

My Dear Friend—& each & all interested in the getting of "male" voted out of Colorado's Constitution

I had a long conference with Mrs Carrie Lane Chapman—yesterday—in New York—& arrived home this A.M. to breakfast—and the result of it was—[1]

1st—That Mrs Chapman & Mrs DeVoe—would go to Denver—arriving Sept. 2d—to hold a conference there with not only the officers & members of your club—but with the leading <u>suffrage men & women</u>—a <u>private</u>—<u>not</u> a <u>public meeting</u>—to talk over the situation & to agree upon the <u>line</u> of <u>action</u>—for it <u>must be one line</u> of action—if success comes—not <u>every person</u> running off in his or her own sweet will & way—"a <u>free lance</u>"—as it is called— But on the other hand everybody who wants & works for success—must, for the time being—<u>know nothing</u>—push <u>nothing</u>—but suffrage, pure & simple—unadulterated with any assertions or pledges of <u>its use</u>—after women get their right—whether that shall be for or against this or that— <u>Our one aim</u> must be to get the <u>right for</u> women to have their opinions, on every question—counted at the ballot box—no matter what those opinions are—the <u>bad ones</u> as well as the good ones—we demand shall be counted!! This does seem so clear to me!

2d—We want you ↑(the friends there)↓—even before that date—to send me—Susan B. Anthony—67 Maple st—Chicago—Ill—where I go tomorrow[2]—a program—a statement of dates & places—when & where you will have meetings or lectures held—

3d—The money that Mrs Chapman & Mrs DeVoe shall raise by collections, contributions & pledges—shall ↑go↓ to pay their travelling & local expenses first— That is to say—the expenses incurred in getting up their meetings—or perhaps it would be better to say—all the money they raise shall go into the Colorado <u>Campaign</u> Fund—and say—one half of it go toward pay↑ing↓ your state speakers expenses—& the other half go toward paying the National speakers expenses— Of course our National association guarantees the expenses of both Mrs DeVoe & Mrs Chapman—but still we want the meetings to contribute toward them all that is possible—

4th—While you are planning the program—dont let a single <u>county political gathering</u> pass without have men pledged to secure the adoption of a resolution in favor of the amendment—

5th—Dont let a religious Convention—nor a County teachers Institute—nor the State teachers Con. pass without its adopting such a resolution— <u>For all possible</u> assemblages of <u>men</u> to pass such resolutions will help create sentiment on our side vastly faster than anything we can do in our separate meetings— And your County <u>Agricultural Fairs</u>—arrange to have Mrs DeVoe—or Mrs Chapman speak at as many as possible— Just go strait on with your quiet educational work—just as if you felt sure of success—and just as if this whole country wasn't in this fearful <u>panic</u> financially!!³

Now—dear friends—begin at once—to make plans for the best possible campaign—your own men & women—must turn in and help do the speaking—

6th—both Mrs Chapman & I think you should <u>hold no big meeting</u> in Denver or any of the large cities—until <u>after</u> you have held <u>ward meetings</u>—made a house to house canvass to get the names of men & women in favor—& those against— Do all you can in the wards of the cities—and in the voting precincts of the counties—all through September—say—and then in October—take the cities with big & rousing meetings—

But you—<u>first</u>—want quietly to get the people awakened all through every street & high-way—and then when you call a <u>County</u> Con. at the County seat—or a City Con—everybody having been visited & stirred up with speeches—talks & leaflets & papers—you see everybody will be ready to turn out to the County Conventions— So it looks to us— As most of the voters are in & near the largest settlements—you can see our plan means working up the places of densest populations!!

7th—Is not this statement clear—as to when & where to begin? If not write me—at once—to Chicago—and I will try again—

But now that we have settled upon giving you two splendid workers—I do hope you'll feel full of hope & courage to push ahead— But be Democrats, nor Republicans, nor Populists—dont be Prohibitionists nor Saloonists— Dont be Religionist nor agnostic—just be nothing but <u>woman & her disfranchised</u>—and bound to rescue her from the degradation of disfranchisement—all else to the contrary— Sincerely & affectionately yours

≈ *Susan B. Anthony*

N.B.—Now mark—↑neither↓ The National association nor its President—wishes to <u>dictate</u> your plan of campaign—<u>only</u> to <u>aid</u> <u>you</u> in <u>executing</u> <u>your</u> <u>own</u> <u>plan</u>— I want—when election day comes—Nov. 7th—whatever the result shall be, that you shall feel that ↑the↓ work has been prosecuted in accordance with the best judgement of the friends of suffrage <u>in</u> <u>Colorado</u>—and I want to feel—then—whatever the result—that the National has done all its power to ↑aid↓ you in carrying ↑out↓ <u>your</u> plans— All that I have said in foregoing pages ~~is~~ ↑I wish you to count as↓ merely suggestions—based on the experience I have had in eight states—Colorado one of them—16 years ago— That is—there is no hope for us—unless we know the man or men—in every <u>election</u> district in the state—who will devote himself to helping men to rightly scratch their tickets—the indifferent—the ignorant—the careless—as well as the friends—all want to be watched & helped at the last moment— Even Judges—in South Dakota scratched their tickets wrong— & voted against the amendment—when they intended to vote for it— So we want—<u>you</u> want intelligent men at every polling booth to see every ticket!!— S. B. A.

≈ ALS, on National Council of Women letterhead, Ellis Meredith Collection, CoHi.

1. SBA met Carrie Catt at the Park Hotel in New York City while en route from a visit to ECS in Glen Cove, Long Island, back to Rochester to pack for another trip to Chicago. According to her diary, this occurred not on July 15 but on July 16. Likely the diary is incorrect. Catt also wrote to Ellis Meredith on this date. (16 July 1893, Ellis Meredith Collection, CoHi.)

2. May Sewall and her husband were living at this address for the duration of the Columbian Exposition, and SBA was their guest for several weeks.

3. Progress of the Panic of 1893 could be traced in the failure of the Philadelphia and Reading Railroad in February, an April crisis in the size of the nation's gold reserves that backed the dollar, failure of the National Cordage Company in May, crash of the stock market on June 27, and collapse of hundreds of banks.

199   SBA TO ELLIS MEREDITH

                 67—Maple street   Chicago—Ill. Aug. 11/93

My Dear—

Your letter is here[1]—and we—in conference—have settled that Mrs Chapman is <u>our</u> <u>representative</u>—to go to Colorado—to consult with the friends there—and decide upon & help carry out—with them—<u>their plans</u>—[2] We do not—she does not wish to direct—but to get into rapport with the best men & women there—of all parties & classes and cooperate with them in settling upon the best plan of action—and the best means of executing it— We feel it very important that all should confer together— Have you called into your meeting the leaders of the Knights of Labor?—[3] I think you had better not make any <u>public</u> announcements of plans—until after Mrs Chapman arrives—& has seen & talked with the representatives of all parties & all organizations—that endorse suffrage— <u>Unity</u> of purpose—& action—is very important indeed the <u>only hope</u> of success— Every one must be willing to join in one general plan—and the more quietly you can work—the better— Sincerely & hopefully

                                       Susan B. Anthony

ALS, on NAWSA letterhead, Ellis Meredith Collection, CoHi.

    1. Meredith answered her letters from SBA and Carrie Catt, dated 16 July 1893, with a single one to SBA on 7 August 1893. Their suggestions were welcome, she wrote, but the impact of the depression threatened the feasibility of a campaign. "The great trouble with us is the lack of funds," she explained. "You have no idea how desparate things are." (Ellis Meredith Collection, CoHi, not in *Film*.)

    2. A special meeting of the National-American convened in Chicago on August 10 "to arrange for future work in Colorado and Kansas," as Henry Blackwell described its business. Only at this meeting did Carrie Catt's deployment to Colorado become official. The decision to send Emma DeVoe into Kansas rather than Colorado may have occurred at this meeting too. Participants also raised forty dollars for the campaign. (*Woman's Journal*, 19 August 1893.)

    3. The Woman's Christian Temperance Union had long cooperated with

the Knights of Labor, but only a few suffrage societies forged connections with the largest organized body of workingclass women. In Colorado, the Knights lobbied alongside suffragists during the legislative session to secure passage of the suffrage bill, and the national office sent one of the order's best organizers, Leonora Barry Lake, into the state to help with the campaign. (Mead, *How the Vote Was Won*, 62–63, 66–68.)

200 ~> "SUFFRAGE A NATURAL RIGHT": SPEECH BY ECS FOR THE WORLD'S CONGRESS ON GOVERNMENT

EDITORIAL NOTE: Although she accepted invitations for five lectures at congresses held in Chicago in the summer of 1893, ECS never left New York. On this occasion, SBA read ECS's lecture at the final session of the Congress on Government before an audience of one thousand people. Only a few manuscript pages of the text survive, and the lecture did not appear in print until the *Open Court* published it as an article in 1894 and reprinted it as a pamphlet. Whether ECS used that interval to emend the text is not known.

[12 August 1893]

The significance of suffrage and the power of the ballot have been idealised by statesman, poet, and artist alike, each in his own way. In the heated discussions on the enfranchisement of the Southern Freedmen, Charles Sumner, on the floor of the Senate, said:

> The ballot is the Columbiad of our political life, and every citizen who holds it is a full-armed monitor.[1]

In the early days of the anti-slavery and temperance struggles, in urging reformers to use their political power at the polls to accomplish their objects, the Rev. John Pierpont[2] said of the ballot:

> A weapon that comes down as still
> As snow-flakes fall upon the sod;
> But executes a freeman's will
> As lightning does the Will of God.

At the birth of the third French Republic, in one of the open squares in Paris a monument was raised to commemorate the advent of universal suffrage. The artist had carved various designs and mottoes on three sides of the shaft, and on the fourth stood a magnificent lion, his paw on the ballot-box, with a sphinx-like questioning look as to the significance of this new departure in government. He seemed to say, the sacred rights of humanity represented here I shall faithfully guard against all encroachments while the Republic stands.[3]

In our Republic to-day the social, civil, political, and religious rights of sixty-five millions of people all centre in the ballot-box, not guarded by a royal lion, but by the grand declarations of American statesmen at the foundation of our Government. In their inspired moments they sent their first notes of universal freedom echoing round the globe in these words: "All men are created equal." "All just governments derive their powers from the consent of the governed." "Taxation without representation is tyranny."

These are not glittering generalities, high-sounding platitudes with no practical significance, but eternal truths, on the observance of which depend the freedom of the citizen and the stability of the State. The right of suffrage is simply the right to govern one's self, to protect one's person and property by law. While individual rights, individual conscience and judgment are the basic principles of our republican government and Protestant religion, singularly enough some leading politicians talk of restricting the suffrage, and even suggest that we turn back the wheels of progress by repealing the fourteenth and fifteenth amendments, that charter of new liberties, irrespective of race, color, and previous condition of servitude.[4] It is well for such as these to consider the origin of rights.

In the early history of the race, when every man exercised his natural right of self-protection with the free use of the sling and the bow and arrow, it would have been the height of tyranny to deprive him of the rude weapons so necessary for his defence. It is equally cruel in civilised government to deprive the citizen of the ballot, his only weapon of self-defence against unjust laws and self-constituted rulers.

In the inauguration of government, when men made compacts for mutual protection and surrendered the rude weapons used when each one was a free lance, they did not surrender the natural right to protect themselves and their property by laws of their own making, they simply substituted the ballot for the bow and arrow.

Would any of these gentlemen who think universal suffrage a blunder be willing to surrender his right, and henceforth be subject to the popular will, without even the privilege of protest?

Does any thoughtful man really believe that he has a natural right to deprive another of the means of self-protection, and that he has the wisdom to govern individuals and classes better than they can govern themselves? England's experiment with Ireland, Russia with Poland,[5] the Southern States with Africans, the Northern States with women, all prove the impossibility of one class legislating with fairness of another.

The bitter discontent and continued protests of all these subject classes, are so many emphatic denials of the right of one man to govern another without his consent. Forbidden by law to settle one's own quarrels with the rude weapons of savage life, and denied their substitute in civilisation, the position of the citizen is indeed helpless, with his rights of person and property wholly at the mercy of others.

Such is the real position of all citizens who are denied the right of suffrage. They may have favors granted them, they may enjoy many privileges, but they cannot be said to have any sacred rights.

But we are told that disfranchisement does not affect the position of women, because they are bound to the governing classes by all the ties of family, friendship, and love, by the affection, loyalty, and chivalry that every man owes his mother, sister, wife, and daughter. Her rights of person and property must be as safe in his hands as in her own. Does woman need protection from the men of her own family?

Let the calendars of our courts and the columns of our daily papers answer the question. The disfranchisement of woman is a terrible impeachment of the loyalty and chivalry of every man in this nation. How few have ever penned one glowing period, or cast one vote for woman's emancipation.

Speaking of class-legislation, George William Curtis said:

> There is no class of citizens, and no single citizen, who can safely be intrusted with the permanent and exclusive possession of political power. It is as true of men as a class, as it is of an hereditary nobility, or of a class of property-holders. Men are not wise enough, nor generous enough, nor pure enough to legislate fairly for women. The laws of the most civilised nations depress and degrade women. The legislation is in favor of the legislating class.[6]

Buckle,[7] in his "History of Civilisation," says:

> There is no instance on record of any class possessing power without abusing it.

And even if all men were wise, generous, and honorable, possessed all of the cardinal virtues, it would still be better for women to govern themselves, to exercise their own capacities and powers in assuming the responsibilities of citizenship.

Whenever and wherever the right of suffrage has not proved beneficial, it has not been because the citizen had too many rights, but because he did not know how to use them for his own advantage.

We are continually pointed to the laboring masses and the Southern Freedmen to show the futility of suffrage. If our campaign orators in all the elections would educate the masses in the principles of political economy, instead of confusing them with clap-trap party politics, they would better understand their true interests and vote accordingly. Instead of repealing the fourteenth and fifteenth amendments, multiply schools, teachers, lecturers, and preachers in the South and protect the freedman in the exercise of his rights. Our mistake in the South, when we had the power, was not in securing to the blacks their natural rights, but in not holding those States as Territories until the whites understood the principles of republican government and the blessings of individual freedom for others as well as themselves.

George William Curtis says:

> There is no audacity so insolent, no tyranny so wanton, as the spirit which says to any human being, or to any class of human beings, "you shall be developed just as far as we choose, and as fast as we choose, and your mental and moral life shall be subject to our pleasure"![8]

John Stuart Mill says:

> There ought to be no pariahs in a full-grown and civilised nation; no persons disqualified except through their own default. . . . Every one is degraded, whether aware of it or not, when other people, without consulting him, take upon themselves unlimited power to regulate his destiny. No arrangement of the suffrage, therefore, can be permanently

satisfactory in which any person or class is peremptorily excluded; in which the electoral privilege is not open to all persons of full age who desire it.[9]

The distinctions lexicographers make between the elective franchise and suffrage, mark the broad difference between privileges and rights. While suffrage recognises the natural rights of the individual, the elective franchise recognises privileged classes. It is these contradictory definitions, of phrases some construe to mean the same thing, that has given rise to the theory that the suffrage is a political privilege.

Gratz Brown[10] eloquently said, on the floor of the Senate in that memorable discussion on the District of Columbia Suffrage Bill:

> Let this idea of suffrage as a political privilege that the few may extend or withhold at pleasure, crystallise in the minds of our people, and we have rung the death knell of American liberties.

The philosophy of suffrage covers the whole field of individual and national government. For the former it means self-development, self-protection, self-sovereignty. For the latter it means a rule of majorities: "the consensus of the competent," the protection of the people in all their public and private interests. I have always taken the ground that suffrage is a natural right, the status of the citizen in a republic is the same as a king on his throne; the ballot is his sceptre of power, his crown of sovereignty.

Whenever and wherever the few were endowed with the right to make laws and choose their rulers, the many can claim the same origin for their rights also. We argue the rights of persons from their necessities. To breathe, sleep, walk, eat, and drink, are natural rights, necessary to physical development. So the right to think, express one's opinions, mould public sentiment, to choose one's conditions and environments, are necessities for psychical development.

By observation, we decide the wants of animals, what they can do, their degree of intelligence and treat them accordingly. So in the study of human beings, we see their wants and needs, their capacities and powers and from their manifestations, we argue their natural rights. Children early show a determination to have their own way, a natural desire to govern themselves. Whoever touches their playthings without their consent arouses angry resistance, showing the natural desire to own property. From these manifestations in the human family, at all ages and in all latitudes, we infer that self-government, the protection of person and property against all encroachments, are natural rights.

Individual freedom comprises freedom in all departments of nature, the acknowledgment for every man of the full, free use of all his faculties. But it is the failure on the part of one individual to accord to others what he demands for himself, that causes the conflicts and disputes on all subjects. Each person strongly individualised maintains that his theories and line of action must be right, and those who differ from him necessarily wrong. Here comes in the great enemy of individual freedom: "the love of domination"; the strong hereditary feature of our animal-descent, which prevents the harmonious development of the oppressor as well as the oppressed.

The true use of this love of domination is in governing ourselves. Every person given to introspection is conscious of contending elements in himself, some urging him to the highest moral rectitude, under all circumstances, others tempting to a narrow selfish egoism to exalt one's self at the expense of his fellows. Here is the legitimate use of domination to control the evil in ourselves. As the chief business of life is character-building, we must begin by self-discipline, as thus only can we secure individual freedom. It is more hopeless to be the slave of our own evil propensities, than to be subject to the will of another.

This love of domination is the most hateful feature of human nature, antagonistic alike to the freedom of the individual and the stability of the State. Just as the love of domination retards the development of the individual, so it prevents the realisation of republican principles in government. Could this power find its legitimate exercise on the vices and crimes of society, on the fraud and corruption in high places, it would no longer be a dangerous element, but most beneficent in its influences and far reaching consequences on civilisation.

Herbert Spencer speaking of the nature of a new social science, says:

> It is manifest that so far as human beings, considered as social units, have properties in common, the social aggregates they form will have properties in common; so that whether we look at the matter in the abstract or the concrete, we reach the same conclusion. And thus recognising

both *a priori* and *a posteriori*, these relations between the phenomena of individual nature, and the phenomena of incorporated human nature, we cannot fail to see that the phenomena of incorporated human nature form the subject-matter of a science.[11]

In other words, the manifestations of the individual and of organised society being the same the interests of the individual and society lie in the same direction. We often hear of the necessity of sacrificing the individual to society, but no such necessity exists, as the rights of the individual and the citizen have the same origin and their public and private interests demand the same protection.

Individual freedom and self-government, citizenship and suffrage are synonymous. In demanding their own enfranchisement, have women been pursuing a shadow the last half century? In seeking political power do they abdicate that social throne where their influence is said to be unbounded?

No, no, the right of suffrage is not a mere shadow, but a substantial entity, that the citizen can wield for his own protection and his country's welfare. An individual opinion, counted on all questions of public interest is better than indirect influence, be it ever so far-reaching. Though influence, like the pure white light, is all-pervading, yet it is ofttimes obscured with passing clouds and nights of darkness;—like the sun's rays it may be healthy, genial, inspiring, though sometimes too direct for comfort, too oblique for warmth, too scattered for any given purpose. But as a prism by dividing the rays of light reveals to us the brilliant coloring of the atmosphere, and as the burning-glass by concentrating them in a focus intensifies their heat, so does the right of suffrage reveal the beauty and power of individual sovereignty in the great drama of national life,—while on a vital measure of public interest it unites the many voices of the people in a grand chorus of protest or applause.

~ *Open Court* 8 (1 February 1894): 3959–61.

1. "Equal Rights of All," delivered 5 and 6 February 1866, during Senate debate on the Fourteenth Amendment, Sumner, *Works*, 10:224.

2. John Pierpont (1785–1866) was a Unitarian minister, abolitionist, and poet. The lines are from "A Word from a Petitioner," a protest against congressional refusal to receive antislavery petitions, published in *Airs from Palestine, and Other Poems* (1840).

3. This colossal statue, "La République Française," was erected in the Place de la République in 1883.

4. For one notable example, see Jonathan C. Wickliffe, "Negro Suffrage a Failure: Shall We Abolish It?" *Forum* 14 [February 1893]: 797–804. The ideas of this distinguished Louisiana lawyer called out the modest defense of the amendments mounted by J. J. Ingalls in his syndicated column, *Chicago Daily Tribune*, 28 May 1893, and the harsh criticism of Albion Tourgée, Chicago *Inter-Ocean*, 10 June 1893.

5. The Russian Empire incorporated much of Poland in the nineteenth century, and the domination created a steady conflict over language, religion, participation in the economy, and nationalism.

6. "Equal Rights for Women," delivered 19 July 1867, on the floor of the New York Constitutional Convention, and published as a pamphlet with the same title in numerous editions.

7. ECS moved this quotation from the paragraph above; Curtis placed it after his sentence ending "possession of political power." Henry Thomas Buckle (1821–1862), a pioneer in the writing of scientific history, published *History of Civilization in England* between 1857 and 1861.

8. "Fair Play for Women," delivered 12 May 1870, before the American Woman Suffrage Association, and published as a pamphlet with the same title.

9. "Considerations on Representative Government," (1861), Mill, *Collected Works*, 19:470. ECS copied this from Curtis, "Equal Rights for Women," replicating his inaccurate ellipses.

10. Benjamin Gratz Brown (1826–1885) of Missouri entered the Senate as a radical Republican and served from 1863 to 1867. An early proponent of the idea that universal suffrage encompass the rights of women as well as black men, he spoke forcefully for woman suffrage during debate on the District of Columbia Suffrage Bill on 12 December 1866. ECS paraphrases his shock that fellow senators characterized suffrage as a privilege rather than a right. (*BDAC*; *Congressional Globe*, 39th Cong., 2d sess., 76.)

11. *The Study of Sociology* (1873), 59–60, though the sentences are not together in a single paragraph.

201   SBA to Harriet Taylor Upton

Leavenworth, Kansas,[1] Oct. 5, 1893

My Dear Harriet

Enclosed is the signature & voucher for $23. to Colorado—[2] I hope Mrs Chapman is hoping & expecting success out there the 7th of Nov!!

Every body here is full of belief that Kansas will be carried by an overwhelming majority in 1894!—³ I travelled with Dr Jones⁴—the Mayor of Topeka this forenoon—an he says Topeka will give the am't 3,000 majority!! I wish I <u>knew</u> their expectations were well founded— then I'd rush home and never turn another hand—but I doubt very much—therefore only good work in every Election District of the state is my order from this to November 1894!!!

This is my second trip to Kansas this Fall—and it was a fools errand—so far as the <u>State Fair</u>—for our women had not had the fact of my speaking there well advertised—

I return to Chicago Saturday night—shall be the guest of Mrs S. E. Gross Cor. Lake Shore Drive & Division street Chicago Ill—so pelt me there—

Dear Niece Lucy E. has held the Fort there at Chicago strait through all the hot weather— I want to talk up work— Oh—how I wish we had a pen-artist to boom our work in the papers!!— Lovingly yours

      ↝ *Susan B. Anthony*

↝ ALS, on letterhead of D. R. Anthony, SBA Papers, NRU.

1. SBA spent this day with her brother between events at Topeka and Lawrence. She had traveled from Chicago to Kansas City on August 31 with Carrie Chapman and Emma DeVoe to attend the opening rally of the Kansas amendment campaign that drew an audience of sixteen hundred people, and she filled six engagements to speak elsewhere in the state until September 19, when she returned to Chicago. After delivering ECS's speech to the Parliament of Religions at the Columbian Exposition on September 25, she was back in Kansas on October 4 to speak on equal suffrage day at the State Fair in Topeka.

2. Enclosure missing.

3. The Kansas legislature, by large majorities in both houses, agreed in March 1893 to submit a constitutional amendment for woman suffrage to the state's voters at the fall election of 1894.

4. Daniel C. Jones (1838–?), a medical doctor, was elected mayor of Topeka as a Republican in 1893. After service in the Civil War, he settled in Junction City, Kansas, in 1868. In 1875, he moved his practice to Topeka, and in 1895, he moved to Leavenworth to be the surgeon at the National Soldiers' Home. (*Portrait and Biographical Record of Leavenworth, Douglas, and Franklin Counties* [Chicago, 1899], 202–3.)

202   SBA to Ellis Meredith

Philadelphia Pa[1]—Nov. 23/93

My Dear Mrs Stansbury

Yours of the 9th inst is just here—forwarded from Rochester— I spent night before last ↑Monday↓ with dear Mrs Chapman[2]—& there read Miss Reynolds letter in the Woman's Tribune[3]—& Mrs C. read to me Miss Reynolds last letter to her—saying the majority had reached 7,000—and Mrs C. told me all about the work & all of you splendid workers in Colorado— Well—I can't yet believe it true—it is too good to be true! but Oh—how glad I am that at last we have knocked down our first State by the popular vote!!— It fills us with hope that we may knock down No. 2 & No. 3—Kansas & New York at the elections of 1894! Your splendid letter inviting me to be the guest of your dear Mother[4]—came duly—but <u>after</u> I had abandoned going to Colorado— and while I was in the whirl of packing & starting for home—[5] And when I was waiting for my carriage—to start for the N.Y. State Convention in New York—9 Oclock Wednesday night the 8th—a boy came with your telegram saying W.S. carried by 5,000 majority—[6] My heart bounded for joy—and I had my driver stop at our Rochester Democrat & Chronicle Office—& gave them the telegram & dictated the word for them to say—& rushed to Depot— Once in New York I was away from telegraph Office—& closetted with our Glorious Mrs Stanton—grinding out Resolutions & Plan of Campaign for the Convention—which opened the following Monday—[7] So while my heart was full of proudest kind of rejoicing for you ↑of Colorado↓ especially & our cause generally—I was so overwhelmed with trying to get the right things said in the papers & the Convention that I didn't stop to even look back with a telegram to you— I am awfully sorry—& when my name wasn't among those Miss Reynolds mentioned as sending you telegrams—I was awfully ashamed as well as sorry— But I know you knew & felt all the time that in heart & soul I was with you rejoicing more than words could tell. I am very glad of your rejoicing there on the spot—& glad you had Mrs Jenkins of Wyoming to help you—& still gladder that you had that little sentence from me—[8]

Well now about your big Jubilee the 25th inst—I am the only speaker here for the 23^d—at the annual meeting of the Penn. W.S.A.— And I am waiting here to attend it—but the minute it is over—I must hasten home to Rochester—where our N.Y. State campaign Committee are waiting for me to help them map out & start our big job of canvassing our 5,000— voting precincts—with meetings & literature—& petition—to roll up our Million names to carry into our Constitutional Convention—the first of May next— It is a herculean job—but we propose to compass it— Nothing short of this ↑educational work↓ will give us a chance of success in Nov. 1894— Dear Mrs Chapman—her cold & cough were better—and she is going right into our N.Y. campaign work— she is simply magnificent—

We are preparing the Call & Program for ↑our↓ National Washington D.C. Convention—to be held Feb. 15—to 20—1894—and the first evening—the 15th—and it happens to be my 74th birth—we are going to celebrate & Jubilate over Colorado—the 2^d star in the field of Blue in our Flag— Mrs Chapman is to make the speech—& put upon our flag the new star—& we hope some one or more of you "<u>free and independent</u>" women of Colorado will come down & speak at this session— who will be here? If none of you women can come—will your Congressman or either of your Senators speak for you— We shall try to get Judge Cary[9]—or Wyomings other senator or delegate to give the address of welcome to Colorado into our Suffrage Union!!—that is if we cannot get a Wyoming woman to do it— I wish we had the money to pay delegates expenses down—but we haven't—so must content ourselves with those who are able to come— Cant you as a newspaper woman get passes & so come? Well—I am so glad you are going to keep up your Leagues or Club—for political & governmental studies— men ought to join them—for they need the study as much as the— Yes—& do keep up your auxilliaryship with the National— Wyoming ought to have such clubs—& be auxilliary—too—but good night with good wishes for each & all of you dear women who fought the good fight, so possess the land of liberty— Lovingly—

⚐ *Susan B Anthony*

⚐ ALS, on NAWSA letterhead, Ellis Meredith Collection, CoHi.

1. SBA was in Philadelphia for the annual meeting of the Pennsylvania Woman Suffrage Association, held on this date. She was invited to speak at a memorial for Lucy Stone, who died on 18 October 1893. See *Film*, 31:782–85.

2. Leaving New York City for Philadelphia, SBA found Carrie Catt at the World Building, just back from Colorado. She accepted an invitation to spend the night at Catt's house in Bensonhurst. (SBA diary, 20 November 1893, *Film*, 31:3ff.)

3. *Woman's Tribune*, 18 November 1893, a report written by Helen Reynolds.

4. Emily Robinson Sorin Meredith (1836–1913). At this date, she probably resided on a farm at Fort Lupton, north of Denver. (Ellis Meredith, "Reminiscences of Frederick A. Meredith and Emily R. Meredith by Their Daughter," typescript, Small Collection 288, MtHi.)

5. Plans about SBA joining the Colorado campaign during its final week shifted several times. A telegram from Carrie Catt may have been the decisive factor in her decision to cancel the trip, but SBA was also very pessimistic about victory, and her letters tried as hard to prepare Meredith and others for defeat as to encourage them in their campaign. See SBA to E. Meredith, 10, 16, 20, 25 October, 4 November 1893, *Film*, 31:675–78, 687–90, 700–709, 725–28.

6. The New York State Woman Suffrage Association met in Brooklyn, 13 to 16 November 1893. See *Film*, 31:740–71. The meeting perfected plans for the campaign leading up to the constitutional convention of 1894. In the final tally, the referendum on women's enfranchisement Colorado passed by a vote of 35,698 to 29,461. The Rochester *Democrat and Chronicle*, 9 November 1893, reported SBA's news: "Last evening Susan B. Anthony received a dispatch from Mrs. Lyl Meredith Stansbury, of Denver, stating that suffrage was carried by a 5,000 majority. It is needless to say that our distinguished townswoman was happy. Her thousands of friends in Rochester will rejoice with her."

7. See below at 25 November 1893.

8. Admitting that Colorado suffragists "have been anxiously awaiting some word of congratulations from their great leader," Meredith summarized this letter in the *Rocky Mountain News*, 27 November 1893, and published an enclosed message to "Triumphant Friends in the West," *Film*, 31:779.

9. That is, Joseph M. Carey (not Cary), senator from Wyoming. He and Colorado's Senator Henry Teller both spoke at the National-American's celebration on 15 February 1894. Ellis Meredith was one of the state's two delegates to the convention, though she was snowbound en route and arrived late. *Report of the Twenty-sixth Annual Convention, 1894*, pp. 30–32, 89, 184–86, *Film*, 32:326ff.

203   PLAN OF WORK FOR THE NEW YORK STATE WOMAN SUFFRAGE ASSOCIATION

EDITORIAL NOTE: Although this plan of work for the New York amendment campaign was circulated over the signatures of officers of the New York State Woman Suffrage Association, it was no secret that ECS and SBA wrote it. As Jean Greenleaf described it a year later, the plan was "formulated by" ECS and "afterward adopted by the Convention." In advance of the association's annual meeting of 1893, SBA spent two days at ECS's apartment crafting the text. After SBA read the plan to the executive committee on November 13, Lillie Blake moved that it be presented to the delegates as a report of the committee, and the delegates approved it on November 15. The text was not changed to reflect a new element that the convention added to the plan: the association would compile figures about the property ownership and tax burden of women in New York's counties and submit that information to the constitutional convention along with petitions for woman suffrage. This printing of the plan in the *Woman's Journal* seems to be the earliest printing; small changes in wording were made in later texts published by the *Woman's Tribune*. (SBA diary, 10, 11 November 1893, and Minutes, New York State Woman Suffrage Association annual meeting, and New York *Sun*, 16 November 1893, all in *Film*, 31:3ff, 753, 755-71; *1894. Constitutional-Amendment Campaign Year*, 155.)

[25 November 1893]

The holding of a constitutional convention is always one of the most important events in the history of a State, and the coming one is especially so to the women of New York, as they are interested in securing an amendment that shall lift them from the degradation of disfranchisement.

To this end a great educational work must be accomplished by a thorough canvass of the State, not only in the cities, but in all the rural districts.

The State Suffrage Association proposes to hold a convention in every county with our best speakers, to organize societies, scatter leaflets, and circulate petitions asking that the word "male" be expunged from Article 2, Section 1, of the constitution, thus extending the right of suffrage to all women of legal age with the requisite qualifications. The presidents of the county societies must then hold meetings and appoint campaign committees in every election precinct, to carry on the same work.

As there are sixty counties in the State, each requiring a president of marked ability, and 4,892 voting precincts, demanding as many agents, we can readily see what an army of earnest, executive women is required to inaugurate this campaign. And, as all these persons must be interested in this movement and able to explain the object of the petition, they must be paid for their services.

This thorough canvass cannot be accomplished by voluntary parties circulating the petition as they are able to spare time from their other avocations, which has been the practice in years gone, but we must have well paid, executive persons, who will be responsible for the work done in each county.

It is no more the duty of one woman to do this work than of all women; and its duties are as varied as are the capacities of women; some to write, some to speak, some to circulate petitions, and some to contribute money to enable the others to do their work.

To this end, we must raise at least $50,000. And for this we look to men interested in this reform, and to women of wealth who do not take an active part in the campaign.

Many women say to us, with sorrow, "I cannot speak or write. What can I do to help this cause?" If you have position, give us your name; if you have wealth, give us your money. The least those who enjoy the luxuries of life—who "have all the rights they want"—can do, in this important hour, is to give generously of the money providentially entrusted to their care. If one fourth of the money women spend in jewelry and lace, in pictures and statuary were devoted to the education, elevation and enfranchisement of their sex, their own sons and daughters would enjoy the protection of a purer civilization than we have ever yet known. If every man and woman interested in this reform would give but one dollar, we should have the necessary sum for this great undertaking.

The one great obstacle in our way, reiterates the press of the nation, is that "women themselves do not want to vote." To silence this objection forever, we must now roll up a mammoth petition of at least a million names. The population of New York, in round numbers, is 6,000,000, and the number of voters in the State about 1,200,000. The women of legal age to vote would swell the number of those who could sign our petition to 2,400,000. Hence the proposal to get one million of signatures does not seem extravagant. An immense work, but one that can be accomplished by a thorough canvass of the State. To illustrate: New York counts 887 election districts. It would be the duty of the Chairman of the Campaign Committee to appoint agents in all their voting precincts, to go from house to house and give every voter the opportunity to sign the petition, as well as all women over twenty-one.

The importance of this year in the history of our movement, and the momentous consequences involved in the action of the coming constitutional convention, cannot be overestimated. This may be the only opportunity this generation of women will have to see the State Constitution so amended as to secure to them the rights, privileges and immunities of citizens. As a constitutional convention is held but once in twenty years, if women are not enfranchised now, those who have labored half a century for political equality will never taste the blessings of liberty that by the spirit of our institutions and a liberal interpretation of our constitution are guaranteed to every citizen of a Republic.

       Jean Brooks Greenleaf, Pres.,
       Mary S. Anthony, Cor. Sec.,
           Rochester, N.Y.
       Henrietta M. Banker, Treas.,
        Elm Cliff, Ausable Forks, N.Y.

~ *Woman's Journal*, 25 November 1893. Not in *Film* from this source.

204 ~ SBA TO LILLIE DEVEREUX BLAKE

        Rochester, N.Y., Dec. 11th 1893

Dear Mrs Blake

Yours is here— Your criticism of the <u>N.Y.</u> after each name is good— & I made the same—on the old New York paper & then neglected to correct the proof of this—[1] the other may be equally good—but the paper is printed—and if any letters to the ↑members of the↓ Council should come to the Head Quarters—the clerks here will forward them at once— I am glad you have called a conference on <u>Friday</u> evening—² I have invited Mrs Burt³ to meet me on Thursday P.M— My interview with her when in New York was very satisfactory— Mrs Chapman does not feel able to start into County Convention work—until after the Washington Convention— Mrs Howell as you see has begun already— I told her she & Miss Keyser⁴ were the young elephants sent across the bridge to see if ↑it↓ was strong enough ↑for the old ones.↓

How soon & upon what terms are you ready to go into the work—⁵ If we could get two sets of speakers we could hold ten conventions a week—but now that we cannot have either Mrs Chapman or Miss Shaw until—virtually—March 1ˢᵗ do you see the Speakers & the managers needed for the double work— We want <u>one</u> <u>lively</u> <u>manager</u> to stay through ↑each↓ Con. get there before & stay after—as well as through it—and see to everything possible—just as you or I manage a Con. not doing all the speaking, and yet being able to <u>fill in</u> all the chinks—and in case of the expected speakers failing to arrive—fill that gap—or rush out & find a minister or somebody else to do so— Miss Keyser—I imagine could do this splendidly—but can we have her outside of N.Y. city is the question? Do you think of any woman—or two or three of them—who could do this part of the job—[barely?] to go in & speak of an evening is nothing—comparatively speaking—or it requires only the <u>one</u> speaking talent—while the manager must have several other faculties—beside— Can you name <u>four</u> <u>good</u> speakers—and three good managers? Can you speak <u>five</u> nights in succession—& for how much?— of course the places will be near ↑together↓ so that there'll be a chance to rest each day—as well as make the journey to the next place—

I have pondered all the words of your long ago letter—and not a word of it lessens my intensity to roll up the million petition—but this I do see—that ↑the city of↓ New York's <u>quota</u> cannot be collected by any one not fully in the faith & spirit of the "big job"!⁶ But I feel sure some woman will be resurrected in the city who will go into the work with the enthusiasm & practical sagacity that will give us <u>one third</u> of the people of voting age— In the rural districts—we ought to ↑get↓ <u>more than one half</u>— Sincerely yours

Susan B. Anthony

↩ ALS, on Campaign Committee letterhead, year corrected, Lillie D. Blake Papers, MoSHi. Square brackets surround uncertain reading.

1. The object under discussion was new stationery for the New York State Constitutional Amendment Campaign Committee, with headquarters at 17 Madison Street, Rochester. Each line in the list of officers and their addresses, in the upper left corner, ended with "N.Y." Later printings of the stationery removed the offending redundancy. In the upper right corner, no addresses were provided for members of the campaign's advisory council—ECS, SBA, Blake, Mary Howell, and Carrie Catt.

2. On Friday, December 22, at Blake's house after the Pilgrim Mothers' Dinner. "Most of the members of the Executive Committee were present," Blake wrote in the *Woman's Journal*, "and we had with us Miss Anthony, Mrs. Howell, Miss Shaw and Mrs. Avery. The best methods of conducting the campaign in this city were fully discussed." (30 December 1893.)

3. Mary Towne Burt (1842-1898) was president of the New York State Woman's Christian Temperance Union and a senior member of the national union, having attended every convention since the first one in 1874. SBA met with her in November to discuss how to cooperate in the amendment campaign. The temperance union had adopted its own equal franchise petition, and SBA feared that dual petitions would divert the well-organized temperance membership from the suffragists' drive for one million signatures and also send a divided message to the constitutional convention. (*American Women*; *SEAP*; Frances W. Graham and Georgeanna M. Gardenier, *Two Decades: A History of the First Twenty Years' Work of the Woman's Christian Temperance Union of the State of New York* [Oswego, N.Y., 1894], 49; *1894. Constitutional-Amendment Campaign Year*, 141, 169, 220-22; SBA diary, 20 November 1893, *Film*, 31:3ff.)

4. Harriette Amelia Keyser (1841-1936) worked with the Church Association for the Advancement of the Interests of Labor, founded by the Episcopal Diocese of New York, at the time she joined the amendment campaign. She had supported herself in many ways, including a long stint as a stenographer for executives of the Western Union Telegraph Company. At this early stage of the campaign, she joined Mary Howell in the Adirondack region; later, she worked strictly for the New York City Woman Suffrage League as its organizer. (*WWW4*; Erma Conkling Lee, comp., *The Biographical Cyclopaedia of American Women* [1925; reprint, Detroit, 1974], 2:211-16; *New York Times*, 11 October 1936; *1894. Constitutional-Amendment Campaign Year*, 197-98)

5. SBA wrongly assumed that Blake would assist the campaign in upstate New York, where she had been organizing for a decade.

6. In several exchanges with Blake, SBA seemed to forget that the plan of work included an argument for paying wages to the people who circulated petitions. See 29 December 1893, below, and 3 January 1894, *Film*, 32:164-66. New York City suffragists, however, objected to conforming to a statewide

model for petitions and came up with an alternative. "Miss Anthony consulted me on the possibility of starting a house-to-house canvass in New York," Mary Putnam-Jacobi reported after the campaign. "I told her that I thought such a canvass would be impossible, and also useless. Few persons would sign a petition so presented, and their names would have little influence. The thing required was . . . simply to arouse sufficient interest among the women who had houses and large circles of friends." Petitions were signed at private parties or parlor meetings. Later, suffragists placed petition books and received signatures "at Sherry's, the fashionable confectioner and caterer on Fifth Avenue." (*1894. Constitutional-Amendment Campaign Year*, 217-20.)

205 ❧ SBA TO LILLIE DEVEREUX BLAKE

Rochester, N.Y., Dec. 29, 1893.

Dear Friend:—

¶1   Yours of yesterday is here. I am glad you have decided to begin work in New York, but am very sorry that you have resolved not to attempt the education of every voter in every precinct of the city, for when election day comes, Nov. 6, 1894, undoubtedly our fate will be in the hands of the voters of the state and if 1/6 of the whole number, those below Kings Bridge, are not educated into a knowledge of the good that will come from Woman Suffrage the rank and file of them will vote no. It does seem to me that your league committee should try to secure the co-operation of intelligent, influential men and women outside of your numbers. I am sure that there are many earnest women among those associated in Prof. Adler's society, for instance.[1]

¶2   About the tour of the 60 county conventions this spring, you seem not to comprehend the reasons why it should be made. None of my work has for its main spring the urging of the convention to propose the striking out of the word male, that they will do without any of our help. What I want to mass this great expression of favorable sentiment for—is—

¶3   <u>First</u>. To secure the embodiment of that amendment with the others that the convention considers <u>every</u> body demands, so that it will not be submitted as a <u>separate</u> measure![2]

¶4   <u>Second</u>. It is to influence the leaders of the two political parties in their nominating conventions next September, to endorse Woman Suffrage in their platforms and,

¶5   Third. It is that the political conventions having endorsed suffrage, the State Committees will instruct all their campaign speakers that the amendment may be spoken of and advocated in their meetings, and more than that, I hope to have created by that time so strong an impression as to the peoples demands that the committees will place some of our best <u>women</u> speakers in their regular political campaign meetings, all over the state. So that when the <u>last two months</u> before the election come, our state <u>suffrage</u> committee will not be obliged to run a <u>separate</u> Womans Convention Campaign, but instead, as I have said that our best speakers will be talking in the regular political meetings of both parties.

¶6   But, suppose we, by our house to house canvass of every voting precinct of the state, (outside of New York City) with the petitions, leaflets & lectures; with our township, and County meetings; and our big spring sweep of 60 county Conventions; suppose by all of this, we shall have succeeded in massing together a million signatures, and yet after all this work, we shall have failed to gain a single one of the points I have named, and our question goes to the voters, then every single man of them, black and white, native and foreign, will have been visited and talked with and plead with to vote <u>yes</u> on the amendment! And do you not think, since you are so sure that the final arbitrament of this amendment will be at the ballot-box, that by all this house to house, and man to man canvass, with every possible educational instrumentality, will be likely to give us a larger vote than we should otherwise get?

¶7   Of course if you feel that the county convention sweep this spring is useless, it will be of no use for the committee to ask you to be one of the speakers. I had thought that you might get the New York work so well under way that by Feb. 26, you would be ready to take your place and speak every one of the six nights for each of the six weeks from that time.

¶8   If you have such quantities of good names and addresses, I hope you will send them to Mrs. Greenleaf at once, for she and my sister are compassing sea and land to try to find reliable people to whom to write to take charge of the canvass in the several counties, so I hope you will send them right away. They can soon find out who are dead and who are moved away.

¶9 It is very amazing that all the people, especially the men, who want to make money out of this canvassing with the petitions should appeal to you. I have not seen a single letter sent to this office asking for employment in that way. I think it would be well for you, since you do not wish to employ such help, to send all such letters directly to Mrs. Greenleaf.

¶10 Yes the dinner was a splendid success. My cousins were delighted with the whole affair.[3] I saw the various reports in the New York papers, but it cost me $30 straight out of pocket—rather an expensive luxury—though the dinner itself was complementary— Sincerely yours,

~ *Susan B. Anthony*

P.S. Just as soon as you get the names of those who were at the dinner put on that petition book please send it to me. I got a letter this morning from a lady asking that her name shall be put upon it. Mrs. Wilkins.[4]

[*in SBA's hand*] P.S—With pen—you see I am not much at dictating to a stenographer yet— I running over these pages—I feel more than ever the mistake New York is making by failing to work in line with the plan of work adopted unanimously—I think—at the recent State Con in Brooklyn!! S. B. A

~ TLS, with handwritten emendations, on Campaign Committee letterhead, Lillie D. Blake Papers, MoSHi.

1. The Ethical Culture Society, a humanist group known for its advocacy of social reforms, was founded by Felix Adler in 1876. ECS and SBA both spoke to the society's women's conference on 23 December 1893. (*Woman's Tribune*, 16 December 1893; *Stanton*, 2:301-2; SBA diary, 1893, *Film*, 31:3ff.)

2. Delegates to earlier constitutional conventions submitted controversial changes to a separate vote of the electorate in order to protect routine changes. In 1867, for example, equal suffrage for African-American men was submitted separately, but in that instance voters rejected equal suffrage *and* the amended constitution.

3. The second Pilgrim Mothers' Dinner, held on 22 December 1893, attracted two hundred and fifty women, including SBA. (*Film*, 31:826-35.)

4. Mrs. Wilkins is unidentified.

Textual Notes

¶2	*ll.* 5–6	expression of favorable sentiment ~~is,~~ ↑for—is—↓
¶5	*l.* 1 beg.	Third. ↑It is that↓ the political
	ll. 9–11	as I have said ↑that↓ our best speakers will be talking in the ↑regular↓ political meetings of both parties.
¶6	*ll.* 2–6	petitions, leaflets ↑&↓ lectures↑;↓ ~~and~~ with out township, and County ~~Conventions~~ ↑meetings;↓ and our big ↑spring↓ sweep of ~~the~~ 60 county Conventions↑;↓ suppose↓ by all of ~~which~~ ↑this,↓ we shall have succeeded in massing together a million signatures, ~~suppose by~~ ↑and yet after↓ all this work, we shall have failed to ~~have~~ gain~~ed~~
	ll. 8–9	native and foreign, ~~has~~ ↑will have↓ been visited
¶7	*ll.* 3–4	the New York ↑work↓ so well under way
	l. 5	of the six nights for ~~all~~ ↑each of the↓ six weeks
¶9	*l.* 2	make money out of this canvassing ~~of~~ ↑with↓ the petitions
	l. 5	employ such help, to send ↑all↓ such letters
¶10	*ll.* 3–4	straight out of pocket. ↑rather an expensive luxury—though the dinner itself was complementary—↓

206 ❦ Appeal by ECS

[December 1893][1]

An Appeal to the Women of New York.

As a Convention will be held in this State in May 1894, to amend the Constitution the advocates of Woman Suffrage propose to make their demands again for enfranchisement. The methods adopted by the State Woman Suffrage Association to educate public sentiment are well set forth in the Campaign Plan of Work.

To strike the one word "male" out of the Constitution will be an act of momentous and far reaching consequences; lifting one half the people of the State from the degradation of disfranchisement; giving mothers new dignity, and honor; daughters added opportunities and respect in the world of work; securing for the pariahs of society, the most mournful figure in our civilization, protection and redemption.

Woman's emancipation means all this, yea more, for in her development man will find a reserved moral power to help him build up the ideal republic, to realize the golden age of purity and peace. The mother being the greatest factor in race building, her status in a nation must be the primal consideration.

Women who are ignorant or indifferent as to the advantages of a voice in the laws under which they live, must be urged to read and think on the question; members of the Convention must be asked to give the subject their serious consideration, to read the arguments of John Stuart Mill, Theodore Parker, Wendell Phillips and that magnificent speech of George William Curtis in the Convention of 1867.[2]

A man with a nice sense of justice, who believes in republican principles, could not read the able arguments on this question before the public in the last half century, without feeling that every educated citizen, who pays taxes and obeys the laws, should enjoy political equality. Franklin said long ago, "they who have no voice in the laws under which they live are slaves";[3] "what civil right is worth a rush, if my property can be taken from me without my consent?"

If the women of this State understood the significance of this right of suffrage, they would with united voice make the demand now. It simply means the right to govern one's self, to protect one's person and property by law. To the teacher it means a vote on her salary; to the property holder a reduction on her taxes; to the mother of school children a voice in the sanitary condition of the building and neighborhood and the choice of the teacher whose example her sons and daughters are to follow; to the philanthropist a voice in the charities and criminal legislation. Intelligent women cannot read of the abuses in our jails, prisons, asylums and hospitals without wishing they had the power to mitigate all this misery. The first step, to direct influence in these matters, is to secure the right of suffrage.

Large classes of women in this State are college graduates, teachers in our public schools, professors, lawyers, physicians, the pillars of the church, the guardians of our social life, filling honorable places in literature, in the press and the pulpit; surely all these must be fitted to exercise the right of self government and be sufficiently awake to their duties as citizens, to make the demand. To these then we appeal, for active, earnest work, in whatever direction they are able to exert the most influence.

From the devotees of fashion and the victims of want; from the ignorant and indifferent who take no note of the serious problems of life, whether found among those enervated by luxury or benumbed by ill-paid toil and ceaseless suffering; we can hope for no response. But intelligent thinking women will certainly spare no effort to relieve themselves from the disgrace of being classed in the political category with idiots, lunatics and criminals.

Women made their appeals in person in the last Convention of 1867.[4] Twenty-eight thousand sent in their petitions to have the word "male" struck from Article 2, Section 1, but the amendment they desired was not even submitted, such splendid friends even of woman's work and education as Horace Greeley deeming it too revolutionary and sweeping. Now behold the almost magical progress in sentiment all over the civilized world, which has brought to the advocacy of woman's political equality the wisest and most far-seeing statesmen as well as in large numbers the press and the pulpit who have heard the demand of the artisan and the agriculturist and who are now with ear against the nation's heart declaring that the hour is ripe for the removal of these ancient sex-limitations and restrictions. It only remains for the women of New York to come into touch with each other and speak with united voice at this time to gain the ear of the delegates to the Constitutional Convention and thus forever enshrine in the organic law of this State the equal political rights and privileges which are now the blessed possession of the women of Wyoming and Colorado. If this opportunity is lost, those who have long made the demand and earnestly labored for its accomplishment, will never enjoy the rights, privileges and immunities of republican government.

Injustice to 4,000,000 slaves corrupted the moral sense of the entire nation; we felt the palsying influence everywhere, in the State, the church and social life, in our literature, our commerce and the world of work. Can injustice to half the people of the entire nation be less dangerous to republican institutions? To make sex a badge of degradation, woman a dishonored class; the girl an inferior caste, at every fireside and in every cradle, is separating those who should be essentially one, who should be equals before the law.

Every principle of republican government is violated in the present position of woman, the corrupting influence of an exclusive masculine oligarchy, composed of every type and shade of mankind is felt in every department of life. The bribery and corruption in our elections and in the halls of legislation; in our courts where justice is openly bought and sold; defalcations in our banks; millions stolen in our railroads; trusted men, pillars in our churches, sitting in felon's garb in prisons today, for robbing widows and orphans of their inheritance; dishonesty and trickery in all the marts of trade, wholesale vices in the hidden haunts of sin, these are all common topics of discussion in the pulpit and the press and with the people; and yet the watchmen who cry the hours, say "all is well."

Think you that those who have plunged us into this moral chaos, can unaided retrieve the situation? Until they put away their deepest injustice, that of robbing one-half the people of their sacred right to a voice in the government, they cannot be honest in other relations. No man or woman can be thoroughly honest under present conditions and individual cases of dishonesty grow out of the dishonesty of man as a class towards woman as a class.

Philosophers tell us that the brain of man is already overweighted with the tangled problems of our complicated civilization and that to meet exigencies of the future, the race must be lifted a few degrees, some new force must be developed; some reserved power summoned to action. And where can this be found, but in the wisdom and virtue of the educated wives and mothers of the nation? Remember women of New York, you have equal interests with man in good government and in the near future you will have equal rights and duties and must assume equal responsibilities, if we are to realize on this continent a genuine Republic.

~ *Elizabeth Cady Stanton.*

~ *National Bulletin* 2 (December 1893): 1–2, in ECS Papers, DLC.

1. The issue of the *National Bulletin* with this appeal as its lead article bears the date December 1893, but it probably appeared after Colby published the identical text in the *Woman's Tribune*, 6 January 1894. Subsequently, Clara Colby devoted the entire January 1894 issue of the *Bulletin* to the New York campaign and reprinted this appeal on an inner page. At ECS's request, the reprint moved her name to just below the headline. (*Film*, 32:175–77.) For SBA's and ECS's temperamental correspondence with Colby about this essay, see *Film*, 31:820–21, 849–54, 856.

2. These classic speeches were reprinted many times by associations for woman's rights and suffrage; all four, for example, were in the list of tracts published by the American Equal Rights Association in 1867. They were John

Stuart Mill, *Suffrage for Women*; Theodore Parker, *Public Function of Woman*; Wendell Phillips, *Freedom for Women*; and George William Curtis, *Equal Rights for Women*.

3. To this point, she quotes Benjamin Franklin, "Some Good Whig Principles," as quoted by Charles Sumner in "Equal Rights of All," in Sumner, *Works*, 10:177. Sumner also supplied the remainder of her quotation, from James Otis, *The Rights of the British Colonies Asserted and Proved*, in Sumner, *Works*, 10:164. ECS could have also found both in SBA, "Is It a Crime for a U.S. Citizen to Vote?" *Papers*, 2:554-83.

4. On the campaign for woman suffrage at the New York Constitutional Convention of 1867, see *Papers*, 2:1-85, and *History*, 2:269-312.

207 ❦ From the Diary of SBA

[*1–7 January 1894*]

MON. JAN. 1, 1894. Sister Mary & self dined with Mr & Mrs Greenleaf— Dr & Mrs Sanford[1] there—Mrs Sargent[2] called— we had a pleasant day—

Yesterday—Dec 31, 1893 brother in law Aaron M. McLean rounded out his 81st year & started into his 82^d!!

1. John Edward Sanford (1846-?), born in Canada, was a dentist in Rochester and the husband of Mary T. Sanford. The Sanfords lived at 20 James Street. (Federal Census, 1880, 1900, 1910; city directories, 1890 to 1899.)

2. Angelina Morse Foster Sargent (1830-1907) was the wife of James Sargent, Halbert Greenleaf's partner in the Sargent and Greenleaf Lock Company. She and her husband contributed money to the amendment campaign. (*DAB*, s.v. "Sargent, James"; Charles Elliott Fitch, *Memorial Encyclopedia of the State of New York* [New York, 1916], 2:388-90; Mt. Hope and Riverside Cemetery Interment Records.)

TUES. JAN. 2, 1894. At home—& Mrs Greenleaf over—again— In the P.M. Mrs Martha R. Almy[1]—the Vice Pres at Large of the State W.S.A. from Jamestown—arrived— At once—she showed ability to take hold & understand the great work of mapping out the conventions of the sixty counties of the State—which gave me great heart & hope—

1. Martha Robinson Almy (1850-?), who had been active in the Chautauqua County Political Equality Club since its founding in 1888, arrived to plan the

conventions across New York State and attend to the correspondence and printing needed for each one. She later moved to the campaign's headquarters in Albany. Raised in Grand Rapids, Michigan, Almy graduated from New York's Genesee College in 1870, and after teaching school in her hometown, she came back to New York in 1871 to marry J. Eben Almy, a graduate of Syracuse University. Eben Almy pursued two careers, as a minister of the Methodist Episcopal church and a dentist, and the couple lived in various towns of Chautauqua County before settling in Jamestown. In 1893, Martha Almy ran unsuccessfully for county school commissioner as the Political Equality Club's candidate with the endorsement of the Prohibition party. After the amendment campaign, the state suffrage association put her in charge of its legislative work. In 1897, she was appointed a deputy factory inspector by the state. The Almys moved to Long Beach, California, after 1910, and Martha Almy, widowed by 1920, was still alive in 1927. (Downs, *History of Chautauqua County, N.Y.*, 1:352-53; *Alumni Record and General Catalogue of Syracuse University, 1872-'99, Including Genesee College, 1852-'71 and Geneva Medical College, 1835-'72* [Syracuse, N.Y., 1899], 274; Federal Census, 1880, 1910, 1920; *Cornell Alumni News* 30 [10 November 1927]: 84; *New York Times*, 5 August 1893; *1894. Constitutional-Amendment Campaign Year*, 148, 149, 156, 163; *History*, 4:857-60.)

WED. JAN. 3, 1894. 39th Annual Meeting—County School Commissioners & Superintendents—New Osborn House Hall—10 Oclock—[1]

Mrs Almy went over to this meeting and learned that tomorrow would be the time for Mrs Greenleaf to call on the County School Commissers to record themselves on the woman suffrage amendment—

1. The New York State Association of School Commissioners and Superintendents held a two-day meeting in Rochester.

THUR. JAN. 4, 1894. Mrs Greenleaf visited the School Commissioners meeting and they <u>tabled her resolution</u> by a large majority on the plea that theirs was not a <u>Woman's Rights Convention</u>!!

FRI. JAN. 5, 1894. Sister Mary self & Mrs Almy—also Mrs Sanford—dined with Mrs Greenleaf—to meet the Cattaraugus County ↑School↓ Commissioner—Miss [*blank*] Van Rensalaer[1] of Randolph—Catt. Co—She is a very bright woman—

1. Martha Van Rensselaer (1864-1932), a teacher, ran for school commissioner in 1893 as the candidate of the Cattaraugus County Political Equality Club, the county temperance union, and the Republican party. In the one year when women could vote for, as well as serve in, that office, she won handily;

reelection kept her in office until 1899. She later helped to develop extension services for rural women, headed Cornell's Department of Home Economics, and gained a national reputation in her field. (Baker, *Moral Frameworks of Public Life*, 74-76; *New York Times*, 25 October 1894; Cornell University Library, on-line biographies of Home Economics faculty.)

SAT. JAN. 6, 1894. All these day Mrs Almy & self have been working out the plan of Conventions—the arranging of   Miss Mary G. Hay[1] of Indianapolis arrived this day—& yesterday—to help in the campaign— all are delighted with her brightness— she is very like Anna Shaw in her quickness of perception—

1. Mary Garrett Hay (1857-1928) arrived to manage the campaign's county conventions. Within the year she became Carrie Catt's valued lieutenant as an organizer, but how Hay happened to join the New York campaign is not evident. She had worked principally in her state's temperance union, where she came to the attention of Zerelda Wallace and was guided into the suffrage movement. (*NAW*; *ANB*.)

SUN. JAN. 7, 1894. I went to Church— Sister Mary remained at home to work— She is overwhelmed with the many, many kinds of things to do and ways to turn[1]

Miss Hay went to 1st Presbyterian—Rev Millard[2]—& Mrs Almy went to with Marcenas Briggs—& family—[3]

1. Mary Anthony had charge of statewide work on the petition, the duties of corresponding secretary of the state association, and, as president of the Political Equality Club, responsibility for directing local circulation of the petition. She became, as Jean Greenleaf said, "the embodiment of perpetual activity." (*1894. Constitutional-Amendment Campaign Year*, 156-57.)

2. Nelson Millard (1835-1910) was pastor of Rochester's First Presbyterian Church. From 1872 to 1885, he led the church in Syracuse. (*New York Times*, 6 January 1910; Mt. Hope and Riverside Cemetery Interment Records.)

3. Marsenus H. Briggs (1850-1941) was a Rochester lawyer who served with SBA as a manager of the State Industrial School. He, his wife Elizabeth, and their three children lived at 657 East Main Street. (Federal Census, Rochester, 1880 and 1900, New York City, 1900; city directory, 1894.)

⚜ Excelsior Diary 1894, n.p., SBA Papers, DLC.

208 ~ SPEECH BY SBA TO THE GRAND RALLY IN ROCHESTER

EDITORIAL NOTE: A large rally in Rochester's City Hall on 8 January 1894 launched the New York State Constitutional Amendment Campaign in Monroe County. Here organizers succeeded in drawing voters into the campaign and attracting prominent Republicans as well as Democrats. Dozens of men from the legal profession, the university, the city's churches, and its businesses signed the call to the meeting. George F. Danforth, a retired state judge, presided. Men outnumbered women on the committee that drew up resolutions, and they made up nearly half of the large audience. After Danforth delivered a speech about the legal history of women, the Reverend Asa Saxe endorsed the cause in a few remarks and praised SBA. She "has been a troublesome woman for the last forty years, and may she continue to be troublesome till she gets justice," he said. (Rochester *Democrat and Chronicle*, 30 December 1893, SBA scrapbook 1876–1903, Manuscript Division, DLC; *Rochester Union and Advertiser*, 9 January 1894, *Film*, 32:181–82.)

[8 January 1894]

At the conclusion of Dr. Saxe's[1] remarks, Henry C. Maine,[2] as chairman of the committee on resolutions, presented the following amid great applause:

Whereas, We, citizens of Rochester, here assembled, believe that "In the course of human events, the time has come" when it is not only just but expedient to abolish the sex qualifications for voters; therefore,

Resolved, That it is the sense of this meeting that the word "male" should be stricken from the description of the qualifications of voters, as prescribed by the constitution of the state of New York.

Resolved, That we, citizens, the primary sources of authority in a republican government, urge, and, so far as we have authority, direct the representatives of this Senate district in the constitutional convention to use their votes and influence to give to citizens the rights of suffrage, without distinction of sex.

Resolved, That the citizens here assembled do hereby petition the constitutional convention to grant suffrage without distinction of sex.

When the handclapping died away, Judge Danforth[3] invited Miss Susan B. Anthony to speak to the resolutions. Enthusiastic cheering and applause greeted her as she came forward.

"I asked Dr. Moore,"[4] said Miss Anthony, "to second these resolutions, and what do you think he said? It was just this: 'I don't like them; they are not strong enough.' It is impossible to frame a resolution that will reach the ends of justice—for which we seek—but I can remember when nobody could write a resolution mild enough." Miss Anthony then pointed to the new banner over head and went on:

"We have now but the two stars to shine down upon us. They represent the states of Wyoming and Colorado. I have heard of the two little stars—New York and Kansas[5]—that are trying to shine, and I hope they may soon become stars of the first magnitude."

"Will the men of New York strike the word 'male' out of the constitution? That is the question. Thank God and the men of Colorado that a class of men holding absolute power over another class of human beings shared that right."

Miss Anthony told how in 1821 in this State the property qualification was stricken out of the ballot law only by permitting the 40,000 unfranchised to vote, and compared that halting reform with the spirit of Colorado.[6] "This meeting," she said, "gives us great hope. Little by little we have got all other rights and now we are going to get the suffrage. Mrs. Greenleaf and my sister Mary are getting the names for a great petition and we are going to strike out that word 'male.' The object in rolling up this petition is to stop the objection which Charles A. Dana[7] the editor of the Sun brings forth so often that women don't want to vote. I was in New York the other day and I called upon Mr. Dana and asked him how large a petition would be required to satisfy the public that women desired the ballot. He said: 'Well, Miss Anthony, I think a petition signed by 100,000 women would command the attention of the convention.' I told him we would carry to the constitutional convention a petition signed by 1,000,000 persons and he said, 'Miss Anthony, if you do you will win.'

"Agents and friends will go round from house to house. Every county seat will have a two-day convention and there will be an organization in every township. Tammany never had an organization such as this will be."[8] Miss Anthony told of her first campaign from 1850 to 1860 when every winter petitions were circulated.[9] She secured 13,000 names for property rights and only 4,000 for suffrage. In 1860 the property right clause was obtained and the power of the vagabond husband over the poor washerwoman's 50 cents was wrested away.[10] She further stated that she believed the discrimination against women in the matter of wages would only be done away with when women secured the ballot. Then they would organize and secure redress.

"We are going to hold the greatest canvass ever held in this State or in any other State or in this country or in any country of the world," she said. "We are going to do the greatest thing in the world. This evening we are simply going to open the great canvass that is to follow and extend throughout the State." (Applause.)

~ *Rochester Union and Advertiser*, 9 January 1894, SBA scrapbook 21, Rare Books, DLC.

1. Asa Saxe (1827–1908) had preached at Rochester's Universalist church since 1860. (*New York Times*, 9 June 1908; Mt. Hope and Riverside Cemetery Interment Records.)

2. Henry Clay Maine (1844–1922), journalist, astronomer, and civic leader, edited the *Democrat and Chronicle*. He was a pioneer in the forecasting of weather as well as a promoter of city parks. (Peck, *History of Rochester and Monroe County, N.Y.*, 2:1087–88.)

3. George Franklin Danforth (1819–1899), a Rochester lawyer, was a retired associate judge of the Court of Appeals of the State of New York. (*ACAB*; Charles Elliott Fitch, *Encyclopedia of Biography of New York* [New York, 1916], 1:66–67.)

4. That is, Edward M. Moore.

5. The press reported this state as "Arkansas."

6. New York's Constitution of 1821, Art. II, sec. 1, as amended in 1823, removed property qualifications for white males to vote, but the same constitution imposed a property qualification on men of color, and the discrimatory action was reaffirmed in the amendment of 1823.

7. Charles Anderson Dana (1819–1897) bought the New York *Sun* in 1867 and edited it for thirty years. According to a later report in his paper, SBA visited Dana in 1893 to talk about how to win his paper's support for woman suffrage, and because of their conversation, Dana should be credited with defining the campaign's strategy. (*ANB*; *Sun*, 6 May 1894, *Film*, 32:799–802.)

8. The well-oiled, Democratic machine in New York City. Monroe County led the state in the number of people, including nearly twenty thousand men, who signed petitions to the constitutional convention. New York City fell short by about eleven thousand names. On campaign work in Monroe County, see the report in *1894. Constitutional-Amendment Campaign Year*, 195–97.

9. See *History*, 1:577–619; *Film*, 7:840–1033; and *Papers*, 1:229–63.

10. *Laws of New York, 1860*, chapter 90, sometimes referred to as the Earnings Act.

209 ⇒ FROM THE DIARY OF SBA

[*8–26 January 1894*]

MON. JAN. 8, 1894. Rochester & Monroe County Grand Rally—on the Con. Con. Woman Suffrage amendment—City Hall—this evening—8 Oclock— A splendid audience— Judge Danforth Presided— Eugene T. Curtis[1] one of the Resolution Com—read Judge Raines[2] letter— Mr Maine—Ed. Dem & Chron Chair Com. on Resolutions— Prof. Lattimore—the 78th year—Dr E. M. Moore—on the platform— the speaking all good—& the meeting every way a success— Our Suffrage Flag—hung over the stage with its Colorado Star—added to its hitherto lone Star Wyoming—

 1. Eugene Thomas Curtis (1844–1910) left Williams College after two years to enlist in the Union army, returned to Rochester to work in a newspaper office, and entered various businesses. He owned the *Rochester Union and Advertiser*. (Fitch, *Memorial Encyclopedia of the State of New York*, 2:292.)
 2. Thomas Raines (1842–1924), an attorney in Rochester, was a former state treasurer and former county judge. (James Clark Fifield, ed., *The American Bar: Contemporary Lawyers of the United States and Canada* [Minneapolis, Minn., 1918], 470; *New York Times*, 12 August 1924.)

TUES. JAN. 9, 1894. Eugene Mosher[1]—the husband of our dear Sister Hannah died this evening at Friend's Hospital—at Frankford—near Philadelphia—after being there some three years—in a demented state—hardly knowing his own daughter Louise who often visited him— It is good that the spirit has taken its flight wholly—from that wreck of a body—

Took 9 AM train for Syracuse— met Sophie King[2]—& Mrs Eliz. Smith Miller at Station—& went to home of Mrs Charles B. Sedgwick De Witt st— Spoke for the P.E. Club at 4 and attended a splendid reception given by Mrs E. S. Janney[3]—everything very nice—the best people came

 1. Eugene Mosher (1819–1894) was the widower of SBA's sister Hannah and the father of Louise Mosher James. After a visit with him on 9 January 1893, SBA noted, "he barely knew me—did not know his own daughter."

(Chamberlain and Clarenbach, *Descendants of Hugh Mosher*, 128-29, 311-12; SBA diary, 1893, *Film*, 31:3ff. See also *Papers* 1-3.)

2. On the meeting in Syracuse, see *Film*, 32:186. SBA probably means M. Ophelia King (1855-1919), a sister of John Lord King, a Syracuse lawyer, Harvard graduate, and the widower of one of Dora Sedgwick's daughters. When John King's wife died in 1882, leaving two very young children, and his father-in-law died a year later, his house became home to his two children, his mother-in-law, and his younger sister, who moved to Syracuse from Springfield, Massachusetts. SBA stayed there on this visit. (Gruman, "Oakwood Cemetery Records, Syracuse, N.Y.," 1:253, 2:235; Federal Census, 1880 and 1900.)

3. Marie Regula Saul Jenney (1842-1922) was president of the Syracuse Political Equality Club. She was the daughter of German immigrants who moved to Syracuse soon after her birth in Boston. In their new home, her father had a short, contentious term as a Lutheran minister and started the city's first German newspaper. She married Edwin Sherman Jenney during the Civil War and raised four children. Edwin Jenney, who attended Kalamazoo College for a year, was a lawyer, a Democrat, and former city attorney. (Gruman, "Oakwood Cemetery Records, Syracuse, N.Y.," 1:239, 2:221; *Woman's Who's Who 1914*; *Historical Catalogue of the Students of Kalamazoo College and of Kalamazoo Theological Seminary, 1851-1902* [Kalamazoo, Mich., 1903], 60.)

WED. JAN. 10, 1894. Left Syracuse at at 12.20—stopped at home an hour—found a telegram from Niece Louise Mosher saying "father died last night["]—

Miss Mary G. Hay of Indianapolis went to Batavia to see about Hall &c to day—& got the price of Hall cut down from $40. to $10—

The Buffalo & Erie County Grand Rally this evening— Mrs Greenleaf stopped with Mr & <u>Miss</u> Tiffany[1]—& I with Dr Morris—[2] A good audience— meeting in its all—marred only by the <u>persistence</u> of Mrs Agusta Armstrong[3] thrusting herself into the niche of Chairman— which she was wholly incompetent to fill—

1. On the Buffalo rally, see *Film*, 32:187-88. Nelson Otis Tiffany (1842-1917), a widower and Republican businessman, was secretary and general manager of the Masonic Life Association, a national insurance company based in Buffalo. He chaired the committee of arrangements for this meeting. Martha Eliza (1870-1916), the second of his three children, was the meeting's secretary. (Henry Wayland Hill, ed., *Municipality of Buffalo, New York: A History, 1720-1923* [New York, 1923], 3:28-30; *Distinguished Successful Americans of Our Day, Containing Biographies of Prominent Americans Now Living* [Chicago, 1912], 58-59.)

2. Sarah Howe Morris (1832-1916), a physician, was the new president of the Buffalo Political Equality Club. Born in Maine, she went to work at the

Lowell mills as a teenager and graduated from medical school in Boston in 1869. She and her husband moved to Lockport, New York, in 1873 and to Buffalo in 1881. She was active in the state temperance union, heading its department on heredity in 1888 and later its project to install police matrons. Morris moved to California after 1900 and died in Santa Monica. (Federal Census, Lockport, 1880, Buffalo, 1900; Truman C. White, ed., *Our County and Its People: A Descriptive Work on Erie County, New York* [Boston, 1898], 2:51; *Los Angeles Times*, 22 July 1914; *New York Times*, 25 May 1916; *1894. Constitutional-Amendment Campaign Year*, 61–63, 189; Graham and Gardenier, *Two Decades: Woman's Christian Temperance Union*, 47, 56.)

3. S. Augusta Armstrong (1847–?), former president of the Buffalo Political Equality Club, was president of the Erie County club until the day after this meeting. Her skills as a presiding officer were put to the test when a man rose from the audience to insist that women did not want to vote. Armstrong was a spiritualist medium and wife of the doctor J. Stone Armstrong. Both New Yorkers, they married during the Civil War and spent some time in Philadelphia while he studied at the Jefferson Medical School. After his graduation in 1879, they settled in Buffalo. Augusta Armstrong informed the census taker in 1880 that she was an "electrician," a bold announcement of her spiritualist beliefs. In the final years of the century, her name recurs in spiritualist activities like summer camp at Lily Dale and preservation of the house where the Fox sisters launched American spiritualism. When her husband died in 1901, Augusta Armstrong moved to Florida, where she was still alive in 1930. (Federal Census, 1880, 1900, 1910, 1920, 1930; city directory, 1890; *Buffalo Medical Journal* 40 [April 1901]: 699; *1894. Constitutional-Amendment Campaign Year*, 149, 189.)

THUR. JAN. 11, 1894. Miss Wooden[1] of Indianapolis arrived to day— She will go through the County seat towns & arrange for meetings

Mrs G. & self devoted the forenoon to helping the women to organize an Erie County Campaign Committee— they elected Mrs Hawthorne[2] of Eden—Chairman—

When we reached home at 5.30—it was a blinding snow storm— [Tom?] & Mr G. awaited us— I took a cab home—found all going on well— Miss Vinnie R. Davis[3]—the Supt Franchise—arrived to talk the W.C.T.U. petition interference

1. Iva G. Fenton Wooden (c. 1859–1927) worked as "advance agent for conventions" in early stages of the New York campaign. Indianapolis may have become her home after marriage; she, her sisters, and widowed father all lived in Decatur County, Indiana, in 1880. By 1900, she had divorced, moved to Chicago, and found work as a stenographer. She maintained an interest in suffrage work, collaborated with Catharine Waugh McCulloch in state organizing, and in 1919, presided over a group called the Protestant Woman's

League of Illinois. (*1894. Constitutional-Amendment Campaign Year*, 164; Lewis A. Harding, ed., *History of Decatur County, Indiana: Its People, Industries and Institutions* [Indianapolis, 1915], 1:570-72; Federal Census, 1880, and Chicago, 1900; Catharine Waugh McCulloch Papers, Series VI of Mary Earhart Dillon Collection, MCR-S; on-line Illinois Statewide Death Index.)

2. Caroline Moore Hawthorne, variously described as of Eden or Alden, New York, won an election against Augusta Armstrong for Erie County president. She was returned to the post at the end of 1894. (*Buffalo Commercial*, 11 January 1894; *1894. Constitutional-Amendment Campaign Year*, 134, 148, 189.)

3. Vinnie R. Davis (c. 1863-?), who grew up in Orwell, New York, the daughter of a farmer, became superintendent of the franchise department of the New York temperance union in 1891. Of the rival petitions to the constitutional convention, Davis would later say it was regrettable "that co-operation during the campaign was not placed on an official basis by earlier intercommunication and conference." Although thirty-six thousand people signed the temperance union's petition, many union members chose to work through the campaign committee in their counties and to circulate the suffragists' petition. It was simply more efficient, Vinnie Davis explained; the temperance union's franchise department had inadequate resources to work alone. Davis became a proponent of state federations of suffrage, temperance, and other organizations that would coordinate amendment campaigns. (Federal Census, 1880; Graham and Gardenier, *Two Decades: Woman's Christian Temperance Union*, 49; *1894. Constitutional-Amendment Campaign Year*, 141, 169, 220-22.)

FRI. JAN. 12, 1894. Worked all the day trying to round out everything in line of letters— Wrote darling Niece Louise—H. Mosher James—of Phila. who has had the sad ordeal of looking after the last service to her father who died Tuesday night the 9th at Orthodox Friends Hospital at Frankford—near Phila— It was cruel that neither Sister Mary nor self could possibly go to her—without stopping the wheels of many other's work & the—

Mrs Davis, Mrs Almy, Mrs G. & self—talked & talked—& all agreed the W.C.T.U. petition a great hindrance—if not an utter defeat of our Million Petition— She left at 2.30—& I took the 10.25 train—which was 2 hours late—& because of it—my trunk [reached?] station & [*illegible*]

SAT. JAN. 13, 1894. Lecture this evening for the ↑Michigan↓ State University Lecture Association of Ann Arbor—W^m. W. Wedemeyer—Pres^1—first woman since war times—when Anna E. Dickinson—was thus honored— Gave my Power of the ballot to bring equal chances in the world of work & wages

Arrived two hours late   Guest of dear Mrs Israel Hall—   Mrs Stanton's thirty-years housekeeper—Amelia Willard[2]—now 71— & more came over from Ypsilanti to see me—& I must go to bed & sleep & be rested for the evening's work—so the poor woman had to go back without my answering her many questions about the children & Mrs Stanton—

A fine audience in the 3,000 capacity University Hall probably 1,500— a lovely evening—& Mrs Hall & daughters Louise & Charlotte[3] said I made good speech

1. For a snippet of SBA's speech, see *Film*, 32:210–11. For an example of her speech variously titled "The Power of the Ballot" and "Woman Wants Bread, Not the Ballot," see *Papers*, 3:215–19. William Walter Wedemeyer (1873–1913) was a law student at the University of Michigan. He later served one term in Congress. (*BDAC*.)

2. Amelia Willard (c. 1825–c. 1920) went to work for the Stantons at a young age in Seneca Falls and became the family's housekeeper, moving with them to New York and Tenafly. She died in Ypsilanti, Michigan, at age ninety-six. (*History*, 3:477n; *Eighty Years*, 203–5; G. Smith Stanton, "How Aged Housekeeper Gave Her All to Cause of Woman Suffrage," unidentified and undated clipping, Seneca Falls Historical Society; Federal Census, Tenafly, 1880. See also *Papers* 1–4.)

3. Two of Hall's six children, these were Charlotte Hall Eastman (1857–?), who lived in Chicago, and Marie Louise Hall Walker (1855–?), who lived in Ann Arbor. (Bigelow, *Bigelow Family Genealogy*, 2:353; obituaries of Israel Hall, SBA scrapbook 14, Rare Books, DLC.)

SUN. JAN. 14, 1894. At Ann Arbor   Guest of my dear dear friend Mrs Olivia Bigelow Hall—

Gave a lecture before the University Christian Association at 9 Oclock this A.M on the "Moral influence versus Political power"—to a fine audience in Newberry Hall—their own building—[1]

Staid in house all the P.M. & evening & as a result didn't sleep so well— I must have out of door exercise & air to sleep well—

1. Newberry Hall was built to house the University Christian Association in 1891. Rooms in the hall were also used for the congressional district meeting of the Michigan Equal Suffrage Association that opened on January 15. SBA attended the meetings for three days. See *Film*, 32:212–17.

MON. JAN. 15, 1894. Ann Arbor— Weather warm foggy & raining— [*No entries for 16–17 January*]

THUR. JAN. 18, 1894. Left Ann Arbor—at 11—arrived Toledo abot 1

P.M.—Cannie Mott—Mrs Hall—& self— we went to Miss Motts & had a quiet afternoon I taking a good sleep— Mrs Sarah Williams[1] & daughter called in the evening—

1. Sarah R. Langdon Williams (1822-1902) was one of the original members of the Toledo Woman Suffrage Association, a member of the National association's executive committee through the 1870s, and editor of the *Ballot Box* from 1876 to 1878. Two of her three daughters were alive; only Charlotte Langdon Williams Kumler lived in Toledo. (*In Search of Our Past: Women of Northwest Ohio* [Toledo, Ohio, 1987], 1:51-53; Waggoner, *History of Toledo and Lucas County, Ohio*, 641, 654; *History*, 3:503-4. See also *Papers* 2 & 3.)

FRI. JAN. 19, 1894. At Toledo—with Miss Anna C. Mott—the only child of Richard Mott—to celebrate the 25th anniversary of the W.S.A. of the city—formed by Mrs Stanton & self the 9th of March 1869!! at Mrs Halls house—

Splendid & large reception at Church of our Father Parlors in the P.M. 3 to 5—and packed church in the evening—[1] The 25 years report of work done was <u>splendid</u>   Mrs Segur[2] President, Mrs Bissell,[3] Mrs Fray[4] et al there—

1. On the events of 1869, see *History*, 3:503. For the anniversary in 1894, see *Film*, 32:224-27. The Church of Our Father was a Unitarian church.
2. Rosa L. Klinge Segur (1833-1906) immigrated from Germany with her parents as a child and spent most of her life in Toledo. A key figure in the city's suffrage society, she also held office in the state association and the National Woman Suffrage Association. (*American Women*; *Woman's Journal*, 5 January 1907.)
3. Sarah A. Secor Bissell (c. 1838-1921), wife of Edward Bissell, an attorney, was a charter member of the Toledo society, former member of the National association's executive committee, and officer of the state association. (Florence E. Allen and Mary Welles, *The Ohio Woman Suffrage Movement* [N.p., 1952], 31; Federal Census, 1880; *Yale Obituary Record 1895*; Ohio Death Certificate Index on-line, Ohio Historical Society.)
4. Ellen Sully Fray (1832-1903), at age sixteen, had accompanied her parents to the Rochester woman's rights convention of 1848. Married to Frank M. Fray in 1853, she moved to Fort Wayne, Indiana, and then in 1870 to Toledo. There she was active in the suffrage association and helped to found a women's literary club. At the time of her death she was a member of the Lucas County Board of Visitors to Charitable and Correctional Institutions and president of the Lucas County Woman Suffrage Association. (*American Women*; Waggoner, *History of Toledo and Lucas County, Ohio*, 731-32; *Ballot Box*, July 1876; *Woman's Journal*, 16 May 1903.)

SAT. JAN. 20, 1894. Took train—at 7.40 A.M. at Waggon Works—on Mich. Central—dozed all day—without fairly noticing the places we rolled by until the Porter sang out—Niagara Falls on the right side— the majest[ic?] waters pour over as ever—[1] at 8.20 we rolled into the Rochester Station— found Sister Mary—as overwhelmed with the Campaign mountain as ever—no not quite so much—

1. Wagon Works was the station at which to catch the Michigan Central's train from Toledo to Detroit. She then took the Canada Southern Railway across Ontario and back into the United States at Niagara Falls. Her trips between the Midwest and Rochester usually followed routes south of the Great Lakes.

SUN. JAN. 21, 1894. At Home— Sister Mary & self—& Mrs Almy heard Jenkins Lloyd Jones of Chicago preach for Mr Gannett[1]—on—"They have taken Our Lord away—& we know not where they have laid him"— It was a splendid Sermon— Mr Gannett asked me home to dinner with them— Mrs Blackall[2] & Mrs Kittridge[3] there also—

Called at the Greenleafs after Miss Mills[4] there—learned that Auntie Cook[5] died yesterday A.M. was found dead in her bed—so called at the house of Mrs Eliza J. Clapp who willed me $1000—which is not yet paid me— Mr Geo. Sawens is executor—

1. Jenkin Lloyd Jones (1843-1918), pastor of the Unitarian All Souls' Church in Chicago, was a promoter of the World's Parliament of Religions at the Columbian Exposition. Later in 1894, he organized the American Congress of Liberal Religious Societies, with SBA as one of its officers. He took as his text this day the words of Mary Magdalene, John 20:2. (*ANB*; *Film*, 32:875-77, 919-23, 930.) Jones spoke at the Unitarian Church led by William Channing Gannett (1840-1923). As a young man, Gannett attended the 1869 meeting in Milwaukee that organized the Wisconsin Woman Suffrage Association. He had worked closely with Jones in the Western Unitarian Conference, and the two men co-authored *The Faith that Makes Faithful* (1886). Gannett moved to Rochester in 1889, and SBA regularly attended his church, becoming good friends with him and his wife. (William H. Pease, "The Gannetts of Rochester: Highlights in a Liberal Career, 1889-1923," *Rochester History* 17 [October 1955]: 1-24.)

2. Sarah Colman Blackall (1836-1917) was a friend of long-standing who had joined the Women Taxpayers' Association of Monroe County in 1873, worked with the Political Equality Club, and was active in the Unitarian church. She and her husband, Burton F. Blackall, a former telegrapher who became an expert in fire alarm systems, were close friends of Frederick Douglass. (Hewitt, *Women's Activism and Social Change*, 208, 214; Victoria Sandwick

Schmitt, "Rochester's Frederick Douglass, Part Two," *Rochester History* 67 [Fall 2005]: 1-32; Mt. Hope and Riverside Cemetery Interment Records.)

3. Amelia Filley Kittredge (c. 1853-?) was the daughter of Mary Ann Powers Filley, an early suffragist and a moving spirit of women's mobilization against licensed prostitution in St. Louis. Amelia Filley married Darwin E. Kittredge in 1878, and the couple settled in Rochester about 1888. (*American Women*, s.v. "Filley, Mary A. Powers"; Henry Harrison Metcalf, *New Hampshire Women. A Collection of Portraits and Biographical Sketches* [Concord, N.H., 1895], 127; Federal Census, St. Louis, 1880, Haverhill, N.H., 1900, and Rochester, 1910, 1920; Rochester city directories 1889, 1894.)

4. Harriet May Mills (1857-1935) was recording secretary of the New York State Woman Suffrage Association, though she described herself as a recent convert to the cause. At the end of 1894, the association appointed her state lecturer and organizer. Mills was the daughter of Charles de Berard Mills of Syracuse, a noted abolitionist, lecturer, and student of Buddhism. After her graduation from Cornell in 1879, she taught school, became an authority on Robert Browning, and began her own career as a lecturer. Politics held her interest for the rest of her life: she presided over the state suffrage association from 1910 to 1913; after 1920 she worked in the Democratic party, where she became a friend of Eleanor Roosevelt; and she was the first woman to run for statewide office in New York. (*NCAB*, 15:374-75; *WWW4*; *New York Times*, 17 May 1935.)

5. Lucretia Cook (1814-1894) was a milliner, who for many years boarded with her widowed friend Eliza Jane Sawens Clapp (1822-1892) on Meigs Street. When Clapp died in 1892, her will provided an annuity for Cook and permission to live in Clapp's house for three years. Clapp, who died in July 1892, also left a bequest of one thousand dollars to SBA "to be used by her, in her discretion in promoting the cause of Woman's Rights so-called." Though the will stated that SBA should be paid within a year of Clapp's death, probate moved very slowly. One factor delaying the case was the executor's inability to sell Clapp's house to raise cash for bequests. SBA filed a petition for payment of a legacy with the surrogate court on 7 December 1893, and at a hearing on December 16, the executor was required to show cause to the court why she was not paid. (Estate of Eliza J. Clapp, case file 1892-122, Surrogate Court of Monroe County, New York; Federal Census, 1880; city directories, 1890 to 1893; Mt. Hope and Riverside Cemetery Interment Records.)

6. SBA confused two brothers who were nephews of Eliza Clapp. Possibly she knew George M. Sawens (1859-1927) because he lived in Rochester and found work as a groundskeeper at the State Industrial School while she served as a trustee. The executor of the estate was his older brother Russell W. Sawens (1855-1931), a housepainter who lived in Albion, New York. (Federal Census, Orleans County, N.Y., 1880 and 1900; Rochester city directory, 1890, 1893; Mt. Albion Cemetery, Albion, N.Y., on-line transcription of gravestones and cemetery records.)

MON. JAN. 22, 1894. Left Rochester at 10.30 for <u>Albion</u>—to attend the first—<u>Orleans</u> County—of our sweep of <u>60</u> County mass meetings[1] Mrs Spencer[2] met us—& took me to the School Sup't—Prof [blank] Green[3]—whose wife is a grand-daughter of Austin Cross—& daughter of Farrington Price—

Had a packed Court House—in evening—& a good audience in P.M. Miss Hay's managed nicely— good men & women came from every township—

1. On the convention in Orleans County, see *Film*, 32:235.
2. Eleanor M. Proper Spencer (1839–1899), the wife of a lawyer and sometime postmaster in Albion, was the Orleans County president for the New York State Woman Suffrage Association during the campaign. Orleans was considered an unorganized county, so she may have served at the behest of the state organization. (Federal Census, 1880; New York State Census, 1892; records of Mt. Albion Cemetery, Town of Albion, transcribed by Sharon A. Kerridge, 1997, copy in editor's files; *1894. Constitutional-Amendment Campaign Year*, 134, 148.)
3. Freeman A. Greene (1844–1900), a graduate of the University of Rochester, arrived in Albion in 1876 to become superintendent of its Union Free Schools. After the death of his first wife in 1884, he married Susan Ida Price (c. 1852-?) of Rochester. (Isaac S. Signor, ed., *Landmarks of Orleans County, New York* [Syracuse, N.Y., 1894], pt. 3, p. 42; New York State Census, 1892; records of Mt. Albion Cemetery, Town of Albion, transcribed by Sharon A. Kerridge, 1997, copy in editor's files.) SBA notes Susan Price's Quaker lineage. Austin Cross (c. 1793–1867) and his children moved to Rochester in the 1840s and joined the Rochester Monthly Meeting of the Society of Friends. His daughter Charlotte married Farrington Price of Poughkeepsie; widowed as a young mother, Charlotte Price moved back to Rochester to raise Susan Ida. (Federal Census, Poughkeepsie, 1850, Rochester 1860; Mt. Hope and Riverside Cemetery Interment Records.)

TUES. JAN. 23, 1894. Genessee County—Batavia— Free Will Baptist Church—in afternoon—& The Opera House—evening— Guest of Mrs Dr. [blank] Tozier—[1]

Left Albion 8.40—reach Rochester 9.45— Lunched at home—took train at 2.25—for Batavia—went to church found 200—best men & women there—& Harriet May Mills managing things finely—

Evening brought a packed house—& many left because of not finding even standing room— Made my Bread & Ballot speech here— Brain got fairly alive—so sleep never came till almost morning—

1. Emily A. Putnam Tozier (1840-1924) was married to Lemuel L. Tozier, one of Batavia's leading physicians. (F. W. Beers, ed., *Gazetteer and Biographical Records of Genesee County, N.Y., 1788-1890* [Syracuse, N.Y., 1890], pt. 1, pp. 312-33; Orrin Peer Allen, *The Allen Memorial. First Series. Descendants of Edward Allen of Nantucket, Mass., 1690-1905* [Palmer, Mass., 1905], 51; transcription of Old Batavia Cemetery records, in editor's files.)

WED. JAN. 24, 1894. Wyoming Co.—Warsaw—Methodist Church— Mrs Crossetts[1]—& Mrs Maude Humphrey's[2] guest—

Left Batavia at 8.33—reached Warsaw—10—dined with Mrs Crossett— rain & snow came—found a fair audience at 2.30— Miss Hay managed well made short talk—then in a driving snow storm—went to Mrs Humphreys—& to bed—was so sleepy— got up rested—& found M.E. Church well filled—spite of the storm— Mr Hayden Humphrey presided—made splendid speech in introducing me—& he said—after we got home—You made just the right speech for *this* audience— Miss Hay stopped at Mrs Hs also—& *little* Maude H. was jubilant in her welcome to Aunt Susan

1. On the convention in Wyoming County, see *Film*, 32:245-46. Ella Hawley Crossett (1853-1925) was president of the Warsaw Political Equality Club and Wyoming County Political Equality Club. Although raised in New York, she and her husband, John B. Crossett, lived in Chicago until sometime after the birth of their second daughter in 1882. In 1890, already well-established in Warsaw, she was named a state delegate to the National-American's convention in Washington. The skills she demonstrated in the campaign of 1894 propelled her into state leadership; she presided over the state association from 1902 to 1910. (*Woman's Who's Who 1914*; "Ella Hawley Crossett," Rochester Regional Library Council website, *Western New York Suffragists: Winning the Vote*.)

2. Lester Hayden Humphrey (1850-1902) was president of the Wyoming County National Bank and a salt manufacturer, with plants in upstate New York and Hutchinson, Kansas. He won election to the state senate as a Republican in 1895 and served until his death. At that time, Mariana Chapman described him as "[o]ur knight of the new chivalry," "our best friend in the Senate, always anxious to do his best for woman suffrage." Maude Milton Skinner Humphrey (1856-1897) grew up in Illinois and married there in 1875. Wyoming County sent her as a delegate to the state suffrage association in November 1893, and at the time of her death, she was a state officer. Maude Skinner Humphrey (c. 1879-?) was their youngest child and only daughter. (Federal Census, 1880; on-line Illinois statewide marriage index; *Woman's Journal*, 20 March 1897, 22 March 1902; Harry S. Douglass, ed. and comp., *Famous Sons and Daughters of Wyoming County, New York* [Warsaw, N.Y.,

1935], 64; Edgar L. Murlin, *The New York Red Book, An Illustrated Legislative Manual* [Albany, N.Y., 1897], 152-53; Rochester *Democrat and Chronicle*, 2 March 1897, *Film*, 36:918.)

THUR. JAN. 25, 1894. Yates Co. Pen Yan— Sheppard's Opera House Miss H. M. Mills—managed   Left Warsaw—7.25—reach R. 9—stopped till 11.50—reached Pen Yan—1.50—found Mrs Julia Sheppard— (John)[1] at Station—who took both Miss Mills & self to their palatial house— Small meeting—100—in P.M. Pretty chilly house—but spoke & then rushed back to Mrs Sheppards & went to bed—but sleep hardly came— had 200—or more at evening meeting— Judge Strauss[2] Presided & made good speech— Rev. Copeland[3]—M.E. Pastor Prayed— The Pastors—& 20 so called business men, sent Protest to headquarters—against our coming to Pen-Yan now because they were holding a revival meeting—all the churches together & they were giving their meeting this [evening?]— also the Yates Co. Teachers institute was in session—

1. John Shoemaker Sheppard (1840-1918) and Julia Morton Dodson Sheppard (1841-1918) were prominent residents of Penn Yan. John Sheppard's family were founders of the county; he graduated from Hamilton College in 1860, built a large lumber business, and acquired lands in the Midwest. A staunch Republican, he served in the state senate from 1896 to 1899. Julia Sheppard, who grew up in Illinois, was the state suffrage association's president for Yates County. (Lewis Cass Aldrich, ed., *History of Yates County, N.Y., With Illustrations and Biographical Sketches of Some of the Prominent Men and Pioneers* [Syracuse, N.Y., 1892], 284, 342, 525; Thompson P. Ege, *Dodson Genealogy, 1600-1907* [Philadelphia, 1908], 47-48; *The Sixth Decennial Catalogue of the Chi Psi Fraternity, 1902* [Auburn, N.Y., 1902], 220; *New York Times*, 7 July 1918; *1894. Constitutional-Amendment Campaign Year*, 134-35, 148.)

2. Local newspapers did not indicate who presided at this meeting, and SBA may have misnamed him. Possibly the man was Hanford Struble (1842-?), Yates County judge and surrogate.

3. Arthur Copeland (1860-1926) led the Methodist Episcopal church in Penn Yan from 1891 to 1894. He later became the chaplain at the state prison in Auburn. (*Alumni Record and General Catalogue of Syracuse University, 1872-'99*, 384; *New York Times*, 2 October 1926.)

FRI. JAN. 26, 1894. Decided to remain over & go through with this Yates Co. meeting—& see & hear Mrs Howell—& hold the Fort to the end of our meeting—to the best of our ability— the Ministers have made a special women's revival meeting this afternoon— it looks very like old times—to keep the women away from our meeting—[1]

1. SBA attended nine more county meetings in the next two weeks before heading south to address the Maryland Woman Suffrage Association in Baltimore on February 13 and reach Washington in time for the National-American's convention.

~ Excelsior Diary 1894, n.p., SBA Papers, DLC.

210 ~ REMARKS BY SBA TO THE NATIONAL-AMERICAN WOMAN SUFFRAGE ASSOCIATION

EDITORIAL NOTE: Competition for aid from the National-American Woman Suffrage Association set the tone of the annual Washington convention that opened on 15 February 1894. Over the protests of Laura Clay, who wanted all resources directed to the South, the executive committee recommended that the amendment campaigns in New York and Kansas both receive national assistance. Clay won the concession that she could make the southern case to the convention, and her repeated interjections, her collections from the floor of the convention, and her insistence that no northern state would grant suffrage to women until the South had risen to demand the right marked several sessions of the convention. At the first meeting of delegates, Lillie Blake and Laura Johns explained their needs. New York did not need money; it wanted speakers from neighboring states to aid the campaign. Kansas needed money, and New Yorkers objected strenuously to anyone from their state making a contribution to Kansas. During the debate, Clara Colby asked if woman suffrage would be submitted to New York's voters as part of the constitution or as a separate item. From her position as presiding officer, SBA answered the question. (*Report of the Twenty-sixth Annual Convention, 1894*, pp. 12-13, 17-26, 47-52, 140-49, *Film*, 32:326ff.)

[15 February 1894]

There is really a little bit of a division. The men are now planning at Albany to have the work of the constitutional convention submitted to a vote of the people, item by item in a great blanket sheet, and anybody can scratch it one way or another, just as they please. The point I want to make is this, that our great ultimatum depends on the rolling up of a petition of a million signatures; our only hope lies in the circulating of a gigantic petition, which we will bring first to the constitutional convention—we have no doubt about the convention, but we want to secure an expression of public sentiment that shall forever silence the cry that women don't want to vote. And in the second place we want to get the names of the men as a great political power, and when the two political parties meet, whichever is the first—the Democratic party at Saratoga, as last year, and then afterwards the Republican party, when they meet to make their political platforms and to nominate their candidates for the year, I expect to go, and if Mrs. Stanton is alive she will go too, and we are all going to be alive, and I want every single girl of every single state in the Union to stop writing to me and thinking I am going to die before this thing is through; we are all going to live in New York and Kansas until this work is done. If Mrs. Stanton and I are on terra firma, we are going to Albany or Saratoga. We will say, when we have got the names of half a million of the voters, is not that a strong enough expression to insure your putting a plank in your platform in favor of that amendment? And I tell you we shall get it. We shall pass over then to the next convention and we shall get the planks in both platforms; that is the ultimatum which I am fighting for. It is for an amendment. The Supreme Court, the Court of Appeals in the State of New York, has put its foot on the power of the Legislature to touch the subject.[1] The Supreme Court of the state of Michigan has put its foot on the power of the Legislature to extend another inch of suffrage.[2] The Supreme Courts have put their heads together, and the politicians have put their heads together all over the nation. We have got to go back to the people, the male people. We are going in for an amendment pure and simple, or we do not get it all, and we are getting up our petition in New York in order to do that. For myself, I have not the shadow of a doubt but that we will carry New York state next fall.

~ *Proceedings of the Twenty-sixth Annual Convention of the National-American Woman Suffrage Association, Held in Washington, D.C., February 15, 16, 17, 18, 19 and 20, 1894*, ed. Harriet Taylor Upton (Warren, Ohio, n.d.), 20–21.

1. A reference to the court's decision on school suffrage. See note above at 10 April 1892, SBA to William Sulzer.

2. In a pair of cases decided in October 1893, the Supreme Court of Michigan held the state's new municipal suffrage law to be invalid because the legislature lacked the authority to change the electorate without constitutional amendment. Its decision did not affect women's existing school suffrage. (Mary Stuart Coffin and Mary E. Burnett v. Board of Election Commissioners

of the City of Detroit, and Edward H. Kennedy and Henry S. Potter v. Hazen S. Pingree, Mayor et al., 97 Michigan Reports 188 [1893]; *History*, 4:764–65; Virginia Ann Paganelli Caruso, "A History of Woman Suffrage in Michigan," [Ph.D. diss., Michigan State University, 1986], 114–19.)

211 ECS TO CLARA BEWICK COLBY

26 West 61, [*New York, 28 February 1894*]¹

Dear Mrs Colby,

Susan read a speech of mine yesterday, which I do not want you to publish until I add   revise & improve as I wish to have it put into a leaflet for the campaign²   Several points need to be rounded out sharpened up to touch the ordinary mind. Did my leaflet "Suffrage a Natural Right" reach Washington in time for the convention.³ I have not seen Susan nor heard from her whether she received the package directed to her at the Riggs House   A friend of mine grafically describes her "like a devil in a whirlwind." He might have said angel or saint only I suppose he thought with supreme faith in Providence saints & angels would never be in a hurry. How did the Con. go off in Washington   A friend who attended all the sessions here that the only speech worth hearing was Anna Shaw's⁴   Owing to the storm the audiences were small until the last evening & then Mrs Catt was a failure   She was unbecomingly dressed they said & made no points & Judge Noah Davis⁵ wandered about in '46 aimlessly for three quarters of an hour. As it was up two flights of stairs I did not go. This report is not for The Tribune but for you, alone. Have you any of my leaflets on The Degradation of Disfranchisement?⁶ Yours sincerely

 Elizabeth Cady Stanton

ALS, Clara B. Colby Papers, Archives Division, WHi.

1. Dated with reference to the meeting of 27 February 1894, to which ECS refers.

2. Under the leadership of Lillie Blake, the New York County convention for the amendment campaign took place at Chickering Hall on February 26 and 27. Blizzard conditions existed on the first day. The speech SBA read for ECS became the essay "Women Do Not Wish to Vote," published in the *Woman's Tribune*, 17 March 1894, and in the *National Bulletin*, for distribution as a pamphlet, in April 1894. Both are in *Film*, 32:592–95, 598–600.

3. For text, see above at 12 August 1893. The Open Court Publishing Company in Chicago reprinted the speech as a pamphlet in 1894, *Film*, 32:277–85.

4. Switching her attention from Washington to New York City, ECS gossips about the county meeting at which Carrie Catt and Anna Shaw both spoke. Reporters praised but did not reproduce their speeches.

5. Noah Davis (1818–1902) was a retired judge with a long and distinguished career on the New York bench. According to reports in the press, his remarks at the campaign meeting on 27 Feburary 1894 covered the injustice of taxation without representation and the need for legislation against vice. ECS suggests that he reminisced about the New York constitutional convention of 1846. (*DAB*; *New York Tribune*, 28 February 1894, *Film*, 32:517.)

6. For text, see above at 26 February 1891. The speech was reprinted as *National Bulletin* 1 (March 1891).

212 ✍ SBA TO CLARA BEWICK COLBY

[*Binghamton, N.Y.? 23? March 1894*]¹

Dear Mrs Colby—

I have written Mrs Upton—to put <u>your</u> <u>name</u>—as Chairman of the Com. on Federal Suffrage—and drop—or not publish the other members—that you had last year—² You see you put on your Com— Olympia Brown—& Miss Hindman—who—each in her own state—refuses to let her society come into union with the National— Miss Hindman—wont allow her Allegany society to become auxilliary to the Penn. State society—& Mrs Gougar—is doing all she can to weaken the National society   And I—as President—of the National—cannot feel that <u>you</u>—as <u>chairman</u> of <u>one</u> of <u>its</u> <u>Committees</u>—and as one claiming to be a specially good friend of mine—should thus place ↑in the front the↓ women who are doing all in their power to <u>disintegrate</u>—instead of harmonizing & unifying the suffrage women of their state & national societies— ~~Most~~ ↑Many↓ of the women you have in your Committee—are not even members of any local or state society—to say nothing of being members of the National—and I want you to see with me—that we—our National officers—should place persons who care so little for our association on its committees—   It seems an <u>affront to me</u> to say the least for you to do such a thing—

So I have sent my note to Mrs Upton—to let the whole matter stand as the Committee voted it— Sara Smith has already resigned—so that leaves Colby & Bennett— And I have written her—& am writing Foster Avery, Dietrick[3]—Blackwell et al the same—to let the Com. stand thus—adding the name of H. Augusta Howard—to take the place of Sara—and then if Mrs Colby—persists in resigning—accept it—and place Mrs Root[4] of Michigan as Chairman— I see no other way than this—at this time— So all must make the best of it— I do hope you will let the matter rest—& not resign—but if you do resign—I have provided that Mrs Root shall be Chairman—[5]

2[d]—Have you sent a set of the Daily Tribunes to each of the persons contributing $1.— this year? If not yet done—as I ordered—to be done—out of the 5,000— copies I paid for—wont it be the better way for you to send a package of a 1,000— more or less wrappers to Mrs Upton—& let her direct them & return to you to put up the papers & mail— I want my promise to be kept with the contributors to our treasury—you see—

About Mrs Knox—I cannot engage a clerk now[6]—not until I cease to be on the wing— I have one of my old <u>Revolution</u> <u>Clerks</u>—in view—and if—when I visit her—next week—she seems to be in good heart—& equal to her old self—of 25 years ago—I shall try her—first—[7]

When I saw your item about sending the <u>Clerk money</u> to you—I intended to write you—because I saw you <u>hadn't noted</u> the vote of the society—that henceforth all the monies for the use of the different Committees should be sent to the Treasurer—with the word of direction as to where—they wanted it to go—and that is the way the Clerk hire money should go—and I have directed my Sister to forward it—the $5. to Mrs Upton— I have one contribution—but I send it to Mrs Upton—for I want we should begin to let our <u>Treasurer's books</u> show the actual facts as to the money contributed for association purposes— You see—we had no report from the Colorado—nor the Kansas—nor the Southern Committees—to go into the <u>general report</u> of the treasurer—[8]

↦ AL incomplete, on NAWSA letterhead, Clara B. Colby Collection, CSmH.

1. This date was written on the manuscript by archivists, and if it is correct, SBA was in Binghamton, New York. SBA to Clara Colby, 29 March 1894, *Film*, 32:642–49, continued their disagreement about the Federal Suffrage Committee and referred to this letter.

2. Harriet Upton was preparing the report of the convention of 1893. With authority given by the National-American to name members of the Federal Suffrage Committee in 1892, Clara Colby tapped women from thirty-nine states and one territory to serve. Many were active in the Federal Suffrage Association. Their names were published in the report of the convention of 1893. According to SBA, the Business Committee chose to change that authority in 1894, and the new report indicated some of the changes SBA described in this letter: a small committee, consisting of Clara Colby, Sallie Bennett, and Martha Root. (SBA to C. B. Colby, 29 March 1894, and *Report of the Twenty-fifth Annual Convention, 1893*, pp. 164-65, and *Report of the Twenty-sixth Annual Convention, 1894*, p. 235, *Film*, 31:200ff, 32:326ff.)

3. Ellen Virginia Battelle Dietrick (1847-1895) was the daughter of a Methodist minister from Ohio who helped separate West Virginia from the Confederacy at the start of the Civil War and died in a Union army camp in 1862. After her marriage in West Virginia in 1868, she lived for two decades in Covington, Kentucky, before moving to Boston. She was an accomplished writer with an "unsparing pen," according to William Garrison; at the time of her death it was said she contributed to every newspaper in Boston, "to all the prominent papers in New England and many in New York." The Massachusetts Woman Suffrage Association sent her as a delegate to the Washington convention first in 1891, but she disagreed with the Blackwells on most issues under discussion. She took ECS's side in the discussion of Sunday closing, and she argued for federal suffrage against Henry Blackwell's belief in state control. The National-American elected her one of its auditors in 1893, and in an unexplained swap the next year, she was elected auditor but traded jobs with Rachel Avery to become corresponding secretary. She also headed the committee on the press. Dietrick later joined the revising committee for the *Woman's Bible*, and when she died suddenly after an operation, ECS wrote of their collaboration "I feel as if I had been robbed of my right hand." (Descendants of Ebenezer Battelle, on-line genealogy by Marlene Morris and Susy Wetz, Newport Heritage Committee, Newport, Ohio; *Boston Herald*, 26 November 1895; *Boston Evening Transcript*, 26 November 1895; *Woman's Journal*, 30 November & 7 December 1895, the latter in *Film*, 34:585.)

4. Martha Elizabeth Snyder Root (1839-1904), of Bay City, Michigan, was among those in the National-American who favored the quest for federal suffrage. A Spiritualist, writer, hygenic reformer, promoter of cremation, and proponent of reforestation, Root was active in a host of organizations in the state promoting women's participation in public life. Her husband, Melvin A. Root, with whom she worked in all of her reform activities, published a compilation of laws *The Legal Condition of Girls and Women in Michigan* in 1894. ("Memorial Report," *Historical Collections: Collections and Researches Made by the Michigan Pioneer and Historical Society* 35 [1907]: 705-6; *Woman's Journal*, 16 April 1904; *History*, 4:6.)

5. Colby chose not to resign, though she reported to the meeting in 1895

that the committee did little during the year. A new chair was then named to the committee. (*Report of the Twenty-seventh Annual Convention, 1895*, p. 29, 115, *Film*, 33:552ff.)

6. The National-American's executive committee appropriated money for SBA to hire a clerk. See *Report of the Twenty-sixth Annual Convention, 1894*, p. 179. Mrs. Knox is unidentified.

7. Elizabeth C. Browne Chatfield (1843-1917) returned to live in her parents' house in Owego, New York, after the death of her elderly husband, Levi S. Chatfield, in 1884, and SBA stayed with her there when the state campaign reached Tioga County on March 28. As a young woman, she and her sister Julia came to work as clerks in the office of the *Revolution*, and SBA hired Lib, as she was known, as her secretary. She also organized the Decade Celebration of woman's rights in 1870 and tried her hand as SBA's lecture agent across New York later that year. (SBA diary, 28 March 1894, *Film*, 31:879ff; Federal Census, 1850; New York State Census, 1855, 1865; *New York Times*, 5 August 1884; *Owego Gazette*, 3 May 1917; with the assistance of the Tioga County Historical Society, Owego, N.Y. See also *Papers* 2.)

8. *Report of the Twenty-sixth Annual Convention, 1894*, pp. 221-26.

213 ⇝ SBA TO FRANKLIN G. ADAMS, WITH ENCLOSURE

Rochester, N.Y., April. 1st. 1894.

My Dear Mr. Adams:—

¶1 I cannot put my reasons exactly as I did in my scribble to you— but I have addressed a letter to our suffrage amendment campaign committee[1] in answer to the proposal not to get political endorsement, and enclose a copy thereof to you—[2]

¶2 I see Ex Congressman Morrill says <u>don't</u> put suffrage in the Republican platform—all that we have to do is to create such an agitation upon the question as to make the politicians see and feel and believe they will lose votes if they don't and gain if they do.[3]

¶3 Mr. Morrill knows very well that his reason is <u>not</u> to secure the best and <u>highest interests</u> for himself or his party, but simply <u>present success</u>!! The same is true of every other intelligent man, whether he realizes it or not, who says "<u>let the question</u> go to the ballot-box on its merits"!—that means every time to "let it go by default, we do not care enough for it to even say we believe in it!!"

¶4   What I see and hear of the wavering of our women troubles me more than anything else—We must exact justice, and if politicians do not give it, the curse be on their heads not on ours.

¶5   If I believed it would be impossible to get an amendment plank into the Republican platform, (for after all that is the party, the responsible party) I should never leave my work here, for it is as true here in New York as in Kansas, that our one and only hope of getting woman suffrage lies in getting it endorsed by our two leading parties, the Republican and Democratic. Our state conventions will not be held until the very last of August—and it will be an outrage for the Republicans of New York State, as it will be a thousand times greater one for the Republicans of Kansas, to throw the question overboard, for in Kansas the women have demonstrated that they are a help to the party.

¶6   Do you not see that what some newspaper scribbler has said, or written, the if Republicans or Populists do not espouse the suffrage amendment, St John[4] is lying in wait to spring his Prohibition Party into the arena with the fullest kind of a suffrage plank and pledge!! and thus make another attempt at demoralizing things in Kansas.

¶7   Why, if the Republicans had two grains of political sense, (foresight), they would see and know that for them to espouse the amendment and gain the glory, as they surely would, of lifting the women of the state into full suffrage, would be to give them new life, new prestige and power, greater and grander than they ever possessed, they surely would not be halting and belittling themselves with such idiotic stuff and nonsense as letting the amendment go to the electors of the state "on its own merits!!"

¶8   But, however, politicians may waver about it, our own suffrage women and men must not have a doubt but shout for full recognition in both platforms.

¶9   I hope I havent wearied you. I have sent a copy of the enclosed to Mrs. Otis[5] and one to Mrs. Thurston,[6] two members of the committee to whom I have not written on the subject. I have given[7] all of this and more too to Mrs. Johns and Mrs. Diggs.

¶10   I think the strongest of reasons on our side should be published in the papers, for while our committee is silent, the rank and file of the voters are having their minds filled with the stuff and nonsense of the mere office seekers of both of the parties.

¶11 I have heard that Judges Johnson[8] and Horton[9] <u>advised</u> not putting a plank in the Republican platform. If you think it would help them to see that such non-action would mean defeating the amendment at the polls, you may show them the enclosed. Sincerely yours,

~ Susan B. Anthony

~ TLS, with handwritten emendations, on Campaign Committee letterhead, Records of the Kansas State Historical Society, Correspondence Received, Department of Archives, KHi. Marked "Personal" in SBA's hand.

ENCLOSURE

Rochester, N.Y., April 1st. 1894.

To the Kansas W.S. Amendment Campaign Committee, Laura M. Johns, Bina M. Otis, Sarah A. Thurston, Anna L. Diggs, and others. My Dear Friends:—

¶12 I am in receipt of sundry letters and newspaper clippings telling of the demand on the part of many leaders of both the Republican and Peoples parties that you should relieve them from the embarrassment of your demand upon them to put a Woman Suffrage plank in their platform. And I hasten to tell you that such has been the appeal of politicians in every state in which an amendment has ever been submitted, and that it means simply, that either wittingly, or unwittingly, they are perfectly willing to see the amendment lost, exactly as it was lost in Kansas in 1867, when the Republican Party declared itself "Neutral," and then allowed their official campaign speakers to oppose it in every one of their meetings!!;—exactly as it was lost in Michigan in '74—Colorado, in '77—Nebraska, in '82—Oregon in '84—Rhode Island, in '86,—Washington in '89 and South Dakota in '90.

¶13 Let me illustrate by South Dakota in 1890, where the officers of the Farmers Alliance pledged me that if I would use my influence to get the friends to contribute money to send speakers to help, they would hold their alliance solid as a balance of power inside the Republican Party and thus ensure a plank in its platform, which, of course, would ensure the success of the amendment. Accordingly our National Association raised over $5,000, and sent its best speakers to canvass the state, when early in June, at a State Convention at

Huron, the Farmers Alliance resolved itself into the "Independent Party" with <u>only financial questions</u> to be <u>mentioned</u> in the <u>platform</u>. This not only permitted the speakers of the Independent Party to fail to advocate the suffrage amendment, but, the withdrawal of the Alliance men from the Republican Party left it so weakened in its weight of intelligence, that it, too, was silent on the amendment in its platform, and this meant that the Independent and Republican Party stump speakers were silent on the question in all of their Autumn Campaign meetings, while the Democratic Party stump speakers, true to their platform, spoke against woman suffrage throughout the campaign and worked vigorously against it at the polls on election day.

¶14 The election returns showed 70,000 voters. 40,000 of American born men and 30,000 of foreign born men, 24,000 of the Natives voted "yes" and 16,000 voted "No" and this minority of Native born "No's" put with the 30,000 foreign "No's" made an overwhelming majority against the amendment.[10]

¶15 Now look at Kansas. The Democratic Party has already most emphatically declared <u>against</u> the amendment, hence it will be in loyalty to their platform if every one of their editors and campaign speakers shall write and speak and vote against it. And if the two fractions of the old Republican Party, that used to make its magnificent majorities of sixty and eighty thousand, are now both silent on the question, it will be in good form for every Republican and Peoples Party editor and campaign speaker to be silent, or to oppose as he may choose.

¶16 Whereas, on the other hand, if each of the fractions of the Grand Old Party puts a solid suffrage plank in its platform, <u>that</u> will be the signal to every editor and stump speaker of each party, that it is not only in good order, but a requirement for approving words to be written and spoken; and, more than mere words of approval, party endorsement will mean the appliance of all the party machinery, of all the mechanical helps, that are used for carrying all other "party measures."

¶17 In fact, then, Republican and Peoples Party endorsement of the amendment will ensure to it the educational, mathematical and mechanical help of all the machinery of both parties, as against the opposition in the platform and all the party machinery of the Old

Democratic party of the state; while for them to fail to put an endorsement plank in their platforms will place both the Republican and Peoples parties virtually in <u>opposition</u> <u>with</u> the Democratic party for, as the old axiom has it "He that is not <u>for</u> me, is <u>against</u> me."[11] And surely when one party is bluntly outspoken against woman suffrage the others that are silent are not against the one!!

¶18 I cannot believe that any man who was ever a member of the Grand Old Republican Party of Kansas, will now betray the fundamental idea of his early education, that of "Equal rights to all." No, No, let every such man, by whatever name called, now give the weight of his influence, not only personally, but through his political party, for the completion of the grand work so nobly begun by the old Free State men of Kansas, in the extension to women of School Suffrage from the first, and of Municipal Suffrage since 1887. For their descendants not to do this is to prove themselves unworthy of the trust bequeathed them by their fathers, yes and their mothers, too!!

¶19 The only state in which woman suffrage has ever been carried by the popular vote was Colorado at the election of 1893; and in that state nearly every Republican and Peoples Party County Convention heartily endorsed it, they held no state conventions last year, and it was to this political party endorsement, more than to any one, or all other causes, that the women of Colorado are to-day rejoicing in their possession of the inestimable boon of political equality.

¶20 And I am sure that neither Rev. Anna Shaw, nor Mrs. Chapman Catt, and I <u>know</u> that I would never go a step to Kansas to work through the months of May and June, speaking from county to county, but for and with the expectation of helping to create so strong a demand upon the part of the voters as to cause them, in their county conventions, to instruct their delegates to their respective political state conventions to speak and work and vote for a full endorsement plank in their platforms!! And, if the rank and file of the voters of the state do not make this demand, and the State Conventions do not declare heartily and fully for woman suffrage, pledging themselves to do all in their power to aid it, the <u>amendment is defeated</u> just as surely as it was in Kansas twenty-seven years ago, just as surely as it was in the seven other states of which I have spoken; for, failure to endorse, says to the unthinking voters that woman's right to vote is not counted of sufficient moment to be made a party issue, hence that it is the wish or willingness of the leaders that they vote against it, and they will vote against it.

¶21 If the Party that holds the State Convention first puts the W.S. plank in its platform, the other will be sure not to be outdone and put even a stronger one in its platform, and then the Republican and Peoples party stump speakers will run the amendment campaign next fall, and the women whose political proclivities are with one or the other party will be left free to give their whole time and talents to help their own party to triumph, everywhere advocating the amendment along with the other party measures, and both parties would thus make women their strong allies. While if one party should not endorse and the other should, it is clear to be seen that women, at all human, must feel more kindly and work more energetically for their friends than for their open or silent opponents, for, as I have stated, silence will be opposition and the Republican or Peoples party can no more live and draw to itself the majority of the intelligent men of Kansas without taking to itself this truth than has the old democratic party been able to do so opposing the freedom & franchise of the whole people during the last score and ten years.

¶22 The trend of civilization is toward the completion of the experiment of a government of the <u>whole</u> people. Wyoming and Colorado have entered upon it, Kansas stands half way! the question now is, will she go forward—her two great parties, side by side, and place her women, who now enjoy the right of school and municipal suffrage on the proud platform of full political equality, or will she in attempting to stand still, slide back, and the women of her 288 cities be remanded to disenfranchisement? Not to go forward will be to go backward!! and I hope the men of Kansas will say "forward"!! Sincerely yours,

↬ *Susan B. Anthony*

↬ TLS, with handwritten emendations, on Campaign Committee letterhead, Records of the Kansas State Historical Society, Correspondence Received, Department of Archives, KHi.

1. Laura Johns chaired the National-American's Kansas Constitution Campaign Committee with the power to choose her co-workers. She chose ten Kansans, representing all political parties, and Carrie Catt, Alice Blackwell,

and Rachel Avery as national members. (*Proceedings of the Twenty-sixth Annual Convention, 1894*, pp. 144, 236, *Film*, 32:326ff.)

2. As Republicans and Populists lined up to do battle again for control of the state government in Kansas, leaders in both parties calculated that the referendum on woman suffrage would encumber them and should not be endorsed in their platforms. Suffragists had already encountered resistance from county Republican Clubs that met in late March to select delegates to the statewide Republican League convention on April 4.

3. Edmund Morrill was the presumptive gubernatorial candidate for the Republican party.

4. John P. St. John, leader of the state's Prohibition party.

5. Bina A. Numan Otis (c. 1847–1926) was president of the Woman's Progressive Political League and a member of the Kansas campaign committee. Described as "an excellent parliamentarian and impartial presiding officer," she was noted for consistent efforts to reduce tensions among suffragists with opposing partisan views. Otis grew up on a farm in New York State, and after her marriage to John Grant Otis in 1865, she joined him on a farm outside Topeka. The Grange and the Farmers' Alliance were her training grounds. During her husband's one term in the House of Representatives, she worked in his congressional office. (Andreas, *History of Kansas*, 573; Diggs, "Women in the Alliance Movement," 178; "Bina A. Otis," *Chronicle Monthly Magazine* 2 [September 1894]: 51–54.)

6. Sarah Abby Bray Thurston (1848–1918), who held office in the state temperance union and the equal suffrage association, would soon manage the campaign headquarters at Topeka. She also appeared on Republican platforms during the campaign to speak for the suffrage amendment. After graduation from the Salem Normal School and schoolteaching in Massachusetts, she married in 1871 and moved to Topeka. There she found work for many years at the Bank of Topeka, where her husband also worked, and hired herself out as an accountant to other businesses. In 1901, she formed her own title abstract company. Thurston and her husband provided a home for her older sister Olive P. Bray, another activist in the temperance and suffrage movements. The family left Topeka for Gloucester, Massachusetts, in 1917 or 1918. ("S. A. Thurston," *Chronicle Monthly Magazine* 3 [September 1894]: 25–27; Howard D. Berrett, ed., *Who's Who in Topeka* [Topeka, Kan., 1905], 122, 138, 139; *History*, 4:417, 639, 648, 1102; Topeka *State Journal*, 21 December 1918, and *Topeka Capital*, 22 December 1918, in Kansas Biographical File, KHi.)

7. From "committee" through "given," the words were handwritten by the typist to supply words that fell below the bottom of the sheet of paper.

8. William Agnew Johnson (1848–1937) won election to the supreme court in Kansas as an associate justice in 1884 and served until 1935. His wife, Lucy Brown Johnson, later headed the Kansas Federation of Women's Clubs and the Kansas Equal Suffrage Association. (*WWW1*; *NCAB*, 5:519.)

9. Albert Howell Horton (1837–1902), a Republican politician who often testified to the benefits of municipal suffrage, was the elected chief justice of the supreme court in Kansas. (*WWW1*; *NCAB*, 6:129–30; *Woman's Journal*, 13 September 1902.)

10. SBA's source for this breakdown of the South Dakota vote by nativity, one she repeats below at 4 May 1894, is not known.

11. A modification of Mark 9:40.

Textual Notes

¶1	*ll.* 3–4	political endorsement.↑, and enclose a copy thereof to you—↓
¶5	*l.* 6	parties, the Republican and Democratic, but our ↑. Our↓
¶6	*ll.* 1–2	scribble↑r↓ has said, if ↑or↓ written, the ↑if↓ Republicans or Populists ↑do not↓ espouse
	ll. 4–5	pledge!! and thus ↑make↓ another
¶7	*ll.* 1–2	(foresight), they ↑would↓ see and know
	ll. 4–5	give them full ↑new↓ life, new prestige
¶16	*l.* 7	that are used for such and ↑carrying↓ all other
¶18	*l.* 9	For the↑ir↓ descendants not
¶19	*ll.* 4–5	heartily endorsed it, ↑they held no state conventions last year↓ and it was to this political party
¶20	*l.* 16	hence it is the wish and ↑or↓ willingness of the
¶21	*ll.* 14–17	men of Kansas ↑without taking to itself this truth↓ than has the old democratic party been able to do so ↑opposing the freedom & franchise of the whole people↓ during the last score
¶22	*l.* 3	Kansas stands half ↑way!↓ the question now
	ll. 6–7	equality, or whether ↑will she↓ in attempting to stand still, she shall slide back, and the women

214 ~ SBA to Lillie Devereux Blake

Boonville, N.Y.[1] April 22/94

Dear Mrs Blake

I received yours a week ago or more—and have seen the New York papers from day to day— all goes well—so far as the <u>women go</u>!! but how are we to get at <u>the men</u>? Only in their regular political meetings next autumn—hence we must get planks in the platforms of both parties so that every speaker will be free to advocate the am't in their regular campaign speeches— With no woman's campaign can we get at the <u>voters</u>— I feel this more & more keenly every single day— We get one man to 5 and ten women—and yet we get a larger ratio of men than ever before— We must get our speeches & our literature before men!!

About the Con. Con—I have a letter from the veriest crank—who says she is wending her way to Albany so as to be there to besiege the Con. Con—Sarah F. Norton[2]—is her name— now she & Wilcox[3] will both on hand—and I see no way to have the matter fixed but to have all of the members understand that persons going before them must be duly authorized by the State Campaign Committee—signed by its chairman—Mrs Greenleaf— There must be a <u>head</u> to our forces—& surely there is none other than Mrs Greenleaf—and neither you, nor I, any more than Norton or Wilcox—should go with our views & plans unless authorized duly to do so by their State Com—

Surely if each man & woman goes on his or her own hobby—the members will be confused & disgusted beyond measure

I shall get home Sunday night—10 Oclock—stay two days & push on west—and I want to go with the feeling that in our approaches to the Con. Con—there is to be system & good order—each going as authorized to represent the Committee—not the individual—[4] So do write me there—so I can get it settled with Mrs Greenleaf— Hurriedly

～ S. B A—

～ ALS, on NAWSA letterhead, Lillie D. Blake Papers, MoSHi.

1. SBA's schedule in late April carried her into New York's northernmost counties. On April 21, she substituted for Mary Howell at a meeting in this village in Oneida County that drew an audience of more than three hundred people. She stayed through Sunday to catch up on sleep and correspondence before speaking to a union meeting of the Baptist and Presbyterian churches. On Monday, she headed to Watertown for the Jefferson County meeting. (SBA diary, 1894, *Film*, 31:879ff., 32:1ff.)

2. Sarah Frances Norton (c. 1840–1910) had once worked closely with SBA. She joined the Working Women's Association in 1868, wrote regularly for the *Revolution*, and toured New York State for woman suffrage in 1869. She later wrote for *Woodhull and Claflin's Weekly*. Her husband, Norris R. Norton, worked as a journalist and then as compiler of reports for the New York City Department of Health, until his death at the end of 1870 from complications of his war injuries. By 1894, Sarah Norton lived in Troy, New York, collecting a widow's pension; according to her obituary, she lost most of her money in 1893. (*New York Times*, 19 December 1870, 9 January 1910; *New York Tri-*

bune, 8 January 1910; city directories, Brooklyn, 1889, Troy, 1890; *Papers*, 2:143; Ellen Carol DuBois, *Feminism and Suffrage: The Emergence of an Independent Women's Movement in America, 1848-1869* [Ithaca, N.Y., 1978], 150, 160, 193.)

3. That is, Hamilton Willcox.

4. En route to Kansas, she stopped to attend a meeting of the Ohio Woman Suffrage Association.

215 ❦ Remarks by ECS to Parlor Meeting in New York City

EDITORIAL NOTE: A small and select group of guests gathered at 4 East Sixty-second Street, New York City, for a parlor meeting on 24 April 1894 to discuss the constitutional amendment campaign. Parlor meetings provided the city's suffragists with access to women of society who would never attend a public meeting; a hostess with sufficient space invited her friends, while suffragists sent a speaker. On this afternoon, several parlor meetings occurred simultaneously in the city. Though ECS was the announced speaker, she left most of the work to Harriot Blatch, who reached New York on April 14 and joined the campaign. ECS made a few remarks of her own on the chief news of the day, the emergence of organized antisuffragists, determined to defeat the constitutional amendment. (SBA diary, 14 April 1894, and ECS to Clara B. Colby, 19 April 1894, *Film*, 31:879ff, 32:746-47.)

[24 April 1894]

These women are enjoying the rights for which we have been working for half a century. It seems the highest of ingratitude that after our labors, and now that we are getting the key to the whole situation, so that we can keep what we have and get what we want, they should try to keep us out of it.[1]

Now, if you were all enfranchised women, you would not have to vote. And if you did want to vote, there would be no need of your being hustled away from the polls. If you made the laws, you could have just the kind of a place you wanted to vote in. We could open our churches for the purpose. The main security of the rights of the American citizen is the right to vote. If women are so much afraid of being mixed up with men—although I believe you will find men in most households—the ballot boxes can be carried around to the houses. They could be put in through a window, and one need never even see a man. You can be as exclusive as the women of the Turkish harem.

They say that women demoralize politics, and politics demoralize women. A gentleman said at a meeting the other evening that the women of Colorado had been demoralized by the franchise. As the privilege has been granted them only four months, and they have not had an opportunity to make use of it, I think the assertion was very strange. The Senators and Governors of Wyoming tell a different story.

~ *New York Times*, 24 April 1894.

1. The anti-woman suffrage campaign in New York State had just begun. On April 21, wives of powerful men in Brooklyn signed a protest against "this burdensome duty" of voting and distributed it to prominent women in other cities of the state. Jane Marsh Parker in Rochester had her copy by April 29, and Albany's elite remonstrants gathered in early May. Suffragists in Albany and Brooklyn reported feeling the impact of this new opposition, and antisuffragists in the constitutional convention made good use of their memorials against extending the vote to women. This contest among women attracted daily coverage in newspapers across the state, many examples of which are in SBA's scrapbooks. (*Brooklyn Daily Eagle*, 22 April 1894; Rochester *Post-Express*, 30 April 1894, in SBA scrapbook 20, Rare Books, DLC; *1894. Constitutional-Amendment Campaign Year*, 179–80, 191–93; *Revised Record of the Constitutional Convention of the State of New York, May 8, 1894 to September 29, 1894* [Albany, N.Y., 1900], 1:41–42, 59, 237, 348, 389, 392, 469, 652.)

216 ~ ECS TO THE EDITOR, NEW YORK *WORLD*

New York, 26 April 1894[1]

To the Editor of The World:

One of the most interesting features of the present agitation for woman suffrage is the organization of the women who are opposed to the demand. The apathy and indifference of women to their subject position in the past has been the greatest block to their growth and development. It has been the policy of their rulers to keep them separated and individualized as far as possible, lest by consultation and combination they should cement a rebellion. But now, happily in the crisis of this movement, the most indifferent class have been aroused to action. They have actually held meetings to discuss the greatest political question ever before the people of this State and organized themselves for public action. They propose to hold a succession of meetings, to circulate petitions and to do all in their power to prevent the enfranchisement of their sex.

To this end they will be obliged to do precisely what the advocates of suffrage are now doing—go from house to house with petitions, hold mass-meetings in Carnegie Hall and prepare able arguments to present in person to the Constitutional Convention soon to assemble in Albany. To neutralize the efforts the advocates of suffrage are now making they must follow in their footsteps and give them no quarter anywhere. They must send out their best speakers to hold meetings in every one of the sixty counties of the State and flood every school district with leaflets giving their strongest reasons for keeping the word "male" in article 2, sec. 1, of the Constitution. This will be a great educational work for the class hitherto so apathetic. We heartily welcome them to the field of battle. The leaders have already welcomed the reporters to the privacy of their homes and given them their political opinions, to be published in the leading journals.

The distinguished ladies in this movement are the wives of Judges. One said she voted over her teacup, with her feet on the fender, through stalwart sons. Being thoroughly informed on the political issues of the day, she told them how to vote, what men and measures to advocate. Another said, being very busy housecleaning and moving, she had no time to entertain the question. She could not even study up and tell her stalwart sons what to do, but she could teach her daughters that home was woman's sphere. Another thought that as politics had corrupted so many able men, women would be swept off their feet in no time.

But the wisest of the four was studying the State Constitution and she found it such dry reading that she doubted whether the women in the suffrage movement had ever made a study of that immortal document. She advises us all to read it, and throw our novels to the wind. That is good advice, and that is just what we did do forty years ago. It was through a knowledge of our system of jurisprudence and our Constitutions, State and national, that we learned the helpless condition of women in this republic. Now that the four Judges' wives intend to read the laws and Constitution of this State, to talk with reporters over their teacups on political questions, and lecture to their sons on the fundamental principles of government, and have the great declarations of the fathers impressed on their young minds, we shall hope to see in all our future homes beautifully embossed mottoes hung round the walls, suggestive of the political rights of citizens, such as:

"No just government can be formed without the consent of the governed";

"Taxation without representation is tyranny";

"Universal suffrage is the first truth and only basis of a genuine republic."

These will take the place—even in the nursery—of Mother Goose's melodies, and infant lips will sing the praises of Jefferson, Hancock and Adams.

Elizabeth Cady Stanton

~ New York *World*, 28 April 1894.

1. The New York *World* was the first of at least four city newspapers to print ECS's letter to the editor, but it removed the date she wrote it. The *New York Tribune*, 5 May 1894, published the date with the text. See *Film*, 32: 765-69.

217 ~ SPEECH BY SBA TO KANSAS CAMPAIGN RALLY, KANSAS CITY

EDITORIAL NOTE: A grand rally at Kansas City's Fifth Street Opera House was the first of one hundred county meetings planned for the Kansas amendment campaign. According to Laura Johns's account of the sequence of events (which differed from reports in local newspapers), SBA's speech followed a sharp discussion about the importance of winning suffrage planks in party platforms, led by Bina Otis. When SBA concluded her speech, the audience unanimously adopted her resolution in favor of pressing parties to endorse the amendment. After the Kansas City meeting ended on May 5, Johns, Carrie Catt, Anna Shaw, SBA, and other speakers traveled to Leavenworth for the second county rally. SBA did not repeat her speech, but Shaw introduced her resolution, and again the audience approved it. More than a week after the Kansas City rally and after his sister had left Leavenworth, D. R. Anthony published SBA's speech from an unknown source. The *Woman's Journal* picked it up from the *Leavenworth Times*, but mistakenly described it as delivered in Leavenworth, and newspapers reprinting from the *Woman's Journal* perpetuated the mistake. The *Journal*'s editors, however, pronounced it a fine speech, "full of good sense, on the paramount importance" of party support. ECS called it a "great speech" that should be scattered all over New York State. (*Kansas City Journal*, 5 May 1894, and ECS to Clara B. Colby, after 19 May 1894, *Film*, 32:790, 844–45; *Woman's Journal*, 19 & 26 May 1894.)

[4 May 1894]

Mrs. President[1] and Good Friends of Kansas: I come to you to-night not as a stranger, not as an outsider, but in spirit and in every sense, as one of you. My youngest brother came to this state in 1856, when a boy, scarce 21—I think he had never cast his first vote—and settled at Osawatomie. Old Captain John Brown slept in his bed the night before Price's raid down upon that settlement, and that boy followed and suffered in all the fortunes of those border ruffian days.[2] I shall never forget, when the word came back to our home at Rochester that out of the fifty settlers, on the 30th of August 1856, thirty had been shot dead and that for weeks after we believed that boy, my mother's youngest, was among the dead. Then in 1857, my elder brother, D. R. came to Leavenworth. He had come in 1854 with the first free state company and pitched his tent at Lawrence, but in 1857 he returned and settled in Leavenworth; and nobody will say that this brother has not fought a true and splendid battle for freedom from the day he set foot on Kansas soil until this day.

To preface, I want to say that when that great revolution, that great rebellion broke out in this country we of the woman's suffrage movement postponed our meetings, demanding the enfranchisement of women and organized ourselves into a great National Women's Loyal League with headquarters in the City of New York. We sent out thousands of petitions praying congress to abolish slavery as a war measure, and to those petitions we obtained 365,000 signatures. They were presented by Charles Sumner, that noblest Republican of them all, and it took two stalwart negroes to carry the petition into the senate chamber.[3] We did our work faithfully all those years. Other women scraped lint, made jellies, ministered to sick and suffering soldiers and in every way worked for the help of the government in putting down that rebellion. No man in the nation, no Republican leader worked more faithfully or loyally than did the women of this nation in every city and county of the north to aid the government in putting down that rebellion. (Applause.)

In 1865, I made my first visit in Kansas, and on the 4th of July by stage coach from Leavenworth to Topeka. Oh, how I remember those first acres and miles of cornfields I had ever seen in my life. How I remember that ride to Topeka and from there in an open mail wagon to Ottumwa where I was one of the speakers at that 4th of July celebration.[4] There was a professor of the university, I can't remember his name, who read the Declaration of Independence.[5] There were several men who made speeches. There was your national representative in congress, Sidney Clark,[6] who made a great speech, and I made my speech also. Those were the days, as you remember, just after the murder of Lincoln and the accession to the presidential chair of Andrew Johnson,[7] who had issued his proclamation for the reconstruction of Florida. So the question of the negro's enfranchisement was uppermost in the minds of many of the Republicans, though no one save Charles Sumner had dared to speak it out loud.

In that speech, I clearly stated that the government would never be reconstructed, that peace would never reign and justice would never be uppermost in this government until not only the blackmen were enfranchised but all the women of the entire nation as well. (Applause.)

The Republican men congratulated me upon my speech—the first part of it, every word I said about Negro suffrage, but declared that I should not have said a word about woman suffrage at such a critical hour. I sat down and spent two days there trying to reproduce what I had said and succeeded pretty well and it was published in the old Topeka *Commonwealth*, Father Baker's paper,[8] and if any one of you can procure the old files, you will find that old speech I wrote out—and it was a good one too. (Laughter.)

During that summer, I forget the precise date, I was sitting in my brother's office, (The *Bulletin*,) when the Associated Press dispatch came that Schenck, Jenks and Broomall[9] had made and seconded motions on the floor of the house of representatives at Washington to insert the word "male" in the second clause of the 14th amendment.

You remember the first clause: "All persons born or naturalized in the United States and subject to the jurisdiction thereof are citizens of the United States and of the state wherein they reside, and no person shall make or enforce any law that shall abridge the privileges and immunities of citizens." That was magnificent. Every woman of us saw that it covered the women of the nation as well as black men. The second section, as old Thad Stevens[10] drew it, said: "If any state shall disfranchise any of its citizens on account of color, all that class shall be counted out of the basis of representation"; but at once the enemy said, "Do you mean to say that if any state disfranchises its negro men, you are going to count all women out of the basis of representation?" And weak-kneed Republicans after having fought such a glorious battle surrendered. They could not stand the taunt, and Charles Sumner said he wrote over nineteen pages of foolscap in order to frame that second section so as not to virtually give countenance to the disfranchisement of the women of the nation, but he could not do it and so he with the rest subscribed to the amendment. "If any state shall disfranchise any of its *male* citizens all of that class shall be counted out of the basis of representation."

There was the first great surrender, and in all those years of transition, Elizabeth Cady Stanton, the great leader of our woman suffrage movement prior to the war, as she has been ever since, declared that because the Republicans proved unequal to that emergency, because they were willing to sacrifice the enfranchisement of the women of the nation, they would lose all, even the power of the black men in his right to vote. (Applause.)

But the leaders of the Republican party shouted back to Mrs. Stanton and Miss Anthony, "Keep silence, this is the Negro's hour." Even our glorious and magnificent Wendell Phillips who said "To talk to a black man of freedom without the ballot is mockery," joined in the cry. "This is the negroes hour" and we shouted back, "To talk to women of freedom without the ballot is mockery also."[11]

But timidity and cowardice, and lack of principle prevailed and they went on with the reconstruction of the government and the women were left out.

Then came in 1867 the submission by your state legislature of three amendments to your constitution. One providing that all men who had served in the rebel army should be disfranchised; that all black men should be enfranchised and that women should also be enfranchised. If there are any men who remember back to that legislature that submitted those three propositions for amendment, you will remember there was a great deal of discussion upon them; but nevertheless the three were submitted.[12]

By and by the Democrats held their state convention and they resolved they would have nothing to do with that modern fanaticism of women's rights. By and by the Germans held a meeting in Lawrence, and they did not like this new fangled idea that women must vote. And by and by the Republicans held their state convention and they resolved to be *"neutral."* And they were neutral precisely as England was neutral in the rebellion. (Laughter.) While England declared neutrality, she allowed the Shenandoah, the Alabama and other pirate ships to be fitted up in her ports to maraud the seas and take American vessels wherever they could find them.[13] The neutrality of the Republican party in 1867 was like unto this. Every one of the regular state committee's speakers, I won't call their names, some of them are dead and some of them are alive and have repented, and I do not want to tell bad things of the dead and I don't want to tell bad things of the living who have repented—therefore, if you will pardon me, I will not name them—I could call a whole string here—they each went up and down the state and the fact is, not a single accredited stump speaker appointed by the Republican committee advocated the woman suffrage amendment, and not only did not advocate it, but spoke against it.

So then, we had to run a separate woman's suffrage amendment campaign through the months of September and October. We did our best. Everywhere we went we had magnificent audiences and I think we had a larger ratio of men in our audiences in those olden times than we get now.

Election day came, that 5th day of November, 1867, and 9070 men voted yes, and over 18,000 noted no. And for the Negro Suffrage amendment, 10,500 voted yes, and the balance of them voted no. Both amendments were lost. Now, for the negro suffrage all the political power of the National Republican party and of the State Republican party was brought to bear to induce every Republican to vote *for*, whereas on the other hand, all the enginery and power of the Democratic party was against woman suffrage, all the enginery and power of the Republican party was against us, and many were so short sighted and so blinded that they absolutely declared that to vote for woman suffrage somehow was to vote against the negro. Just exactly like declaring here to-night if every woman in this house should expand her lungs and get into them all the oxygen possible was going to rob all of you fellows of enough to fill your lungs. That is just about the difference in giving everybody equal rights. Nobody is robbed, by letting everybody have equal rights and full rights.

Since 1867 eight other states have submitted the question. Let me run them over: In Michigan in 1874 the question was left to "go to the ballot box on its merits."[14] We raised our money and the best speakers of the east went into Michigan just as they came into Kansas—I myself was in the campaign for the last six weeks and addressed the largest audiences. No politician, not even Zac Chandler[15] himself, drew as large audiences as mine and every audience I spoke to voted a solid aye in favor of women's suffrage; and yet when the vote was taken only 40,000 men voted yes, while 80,000 voted no.

Then next came Colorado in 1877.[16] Again we buckled on our armor. Lucy Stone, Mr. Blackwell, myself and others went to that state and traveled over her magnificent mountains and through her equally magnificent valleys, paying ten cents for every mile we traveled on her railroads. In the southern counties where the Mexicans lived who could neither speak, read nor write the English language, I spoke to an audience as large as this in a lager beer saloon and those "Mexican Greasers," as we called them, stood all around the hall with their slouched hats down over their eyes and couldn't understand a word I said, yet by some hocus pocus or other, the Republicans of the state thought I could convert those ignoramuses to vote for woman suffrage. That is the work they left for us women to do. Then I went over into what is now Leadville. They were just moving the saloons from Ouray City which had been the big place there. I stood on (what you play balls on a table with a green cover.) (A voice.) ("A billiard table.") On a billiard table. (I haven't been in those places enough to know what they are.) But nevertheless I stood on a billiard table for my platform and I addressed that audience. "It was composed of men right out of their mines with their blouse shirts and old pipes, and while I was speaking, they were smoking, and every little while a man would go up to the bar and I heard the click, click of the glasses. Everything was going along smoothly until the room got so thick with smoke, and I couldn't speak any longer, I then told them when I got the right to vote my throat might get so hardened, so I could speak in an atmosphere thick enough to cut it with a knife, but I couldn't now. And they all put away their pipes, but not their whisky.

Governor Routt was in that meeting, and he said "Miss Anthony, the amendment is going to be carried. You see how all of these men have voted aye here. I have been all through the mountain camps, and all is going along splendidly. In Denver we have 400 negroes and we shall have a solid negro vote."[17] Then I said, "Governor, I don't know anything about your Denver negroes, but I do know the school in which they were educated, and slavery never taught either master or slave the love of equality for anybody but self. I don't believe it. I don't believe one out of a dozen of your Denver negroes will vote for the amendment." Now, what was the fact? When the election came not half a dozen of the whole 400 voted for the amendment. Do you suppose that men just coming into freedom themselves, just getting out of the clutches of tyranny, are going to vote away their power the next second? No. Intelligent men do not like to vote power out of their hands and ignorant men are less willing.

In the constitutional convention and in the legislature that submitted that amendment there were intelligent Mexicans, who made speeches and who voted in favor of our enfranchisement. The chairman of the suffrage committee of the constitutional convention, an educated Mexican, presented a most admirable report.[18] An intelligent Mexican may vote of his own accord for a woman suffrage amendment because of his own conviction; so may an intelligent Irishman or German vote his own convictions, and an intelligent negro, like Frederick Douglass and John M. Langston,[19] may vote for woman suffrage because of their individual intelligence. An intelligent saloon keeper or gambler may vote for woman suffrage because he believes every intelligent human being ought to have a voice in the government. All intelligent men will vote their own opinions at the ballot box, no matter whether there is a plank in the platform or not. But it is a fact that most of the rank and file of the electors will never vote for anything that is not in the platform.

The 6,666 men who voted for, were the white, intelligent, educated, native born men, the moral men. While on the other hand the 12,000 men who voted against, were the most ignorant foreign and native born men of every possible class, together with the few men who were left at that time in Colorado—I don't suppose there are any in Kansas today—the few bigoted men who really believed St. Paul's feelings would be hurt if they voted freedom to women. So that many of the most rigid churchmen voted together with the low-down, drinking, gambling, libertine men, foreign and native born, black and white, and made up the 12,000 noes.

And what was true of Colorado then has been true with every one of the other states. Let me run through them more hastily. Nebraska in 1882, for which our great national association raised $5,000, and sent twelve of our best speakers out to Nebraska for months before the election.[20] The Democrats resolved against us and the Republicans were again neutral. Oh, this neutrality. Beware of it, it is death! For the last two months of that campaign, I averaged six or seven nights a week in as many different places. In not a single Republican meeting was the amendment advocated. Not a single nominee for any office advocated that amendment. The very last night before the election I spoke in Fremont, and was the guest of the Hon. Theron Nye,[21] one of the best woman suffrage men in the state. When I entered the house I said: "Mr. Nye, I am sure at last I have got into the house of a nominee of the Republican party who has had his tickets printed *for* the amendment." "No," said Mr. Nye, "I am ashamed to say it, Miss Anthony, I have not, for there are just enough foreigners in my senatorial district who would have defeated me if I had dared thus to ask them to vote for woman's suffrage." And there you are.

Then came the movement in Oregon in 1884,[22] Rhode Island in 1886,[23] Washington in 1889,[24] and South Dakota in 1890. All these states left the question "*to go to the ballot box on its merits.*" The politicians expressed themselves all afraid they would *damage* the amendment if they put the plank in their platforms. All of them were sure that the best interests of the suffrage cause demanded silence on the part of the political nominees in their meetings, and so they were all silent, and each and all of the amendments were defeated by 3 and 4 to 1. I had vowed "By the Great Jehovah and the Continental Congress," that I would never again put on my bonnet and go to any state to work for a woman suffrage amendment until one party or the other or both of the two dominant parties of the state should put a plank in its platform. But in the fall of 1889 in Minneapolis, while attending the annual meeting of the Minnesota State Suffrage society, two gentlemen, the president and secretary of the South Dakota Farmers' Alliance, came to me there and begged me to help them in South Dakota, they had had poor crops, they had no money, and no speakers, nothing with which they could carry on a woman's suffrage campaign. Then I said to them what I have said to you, that I never would until a party had pledged itself to support the measure. Then those two men, the president and secretary of the South Dakota Farmers' Alliance pledged me that they would hold their Alliance men as the balance of power inside of the Republican party and thus compel it to put an endorsement plank in its platform; and you can see that in South Dakota, where there was not a city big enough to cover your two hands, scarcely at that time, the best majority of the men of South Dakota were Farmers' Alliance men and when the farmers of the state pledged me as these officers did, I said, "very well, on that pledge I will try once more," and I went back to our Washington convention and the secretary came there too, and reiterated the pledge that if we would raise the money and bring our speakers and help them to carry on this campaign they would carry the question to victory. And they knew as I knew that only political party help could carry it to victory.[25] So, in our national convention at Washington, that winter of 1890, once more the women put in their blood money, economized a whole year and more just to put in $25 to help carry on the South Dakota campaign as they had done over and over in these other campaigns. They believed that these men were going to hold to their promise and that at last we were going to carry one state. Five thousand dollars and over was raised. I was made manager of that money and we took over twelve speakers, more or less, and we held grand meetings and made a spring campaign as you are now making here. They had grand meetings, and on the 9th day of June there was held a state Farmers' Alliance convention in Huron and at the close of the very last session, they passed a resolution to form themselves into an Independent Party—to break off from the Republican party. And then they next resolved they would not have any "isms" in their platform. No "isms." Nothing but financial planks, and sub-treasury planks, and so forth were going into their platform, and they went home. And next the Republican state convention was held. These Farmers' Alliance men by forming a third party had drawn off a large majority of the best and most earnest woman's suffrage men of the Republican party, thereby weakening that party so that it couldn't endorse the amendment. Politics is the weighing, measuring and balancing of things, and when these thousands of Farmers' Alliance men took themselves out of the woman suffrage scale of the Republican party, the other scale pulled down and made woman suffrage kick the beam in that party. Whereas, if those Farmers' Alliance men had remained in the Republican party, and made themselves the balance of power as they had done for another measure, the year before, they would have compelled the Republican party to put the plank in their platform and then at every Republican campaign meeting the stump speakers would have advocated the measure. I knew that day that the Independent party was formed and the "no isms" resolution was passed, I knew that the amendment was killed. I knew it could not be carried just as well as I knew on the 3rd day of November of that year, because I knew then that not a single Independent party man would advocate woman suffrage in their meetings; and when no Republican plank came there was silence in their meetings also. So we had to run a little fall campaign ourselves. But whom did we get to attend our meetings. The women, and a little handful of superior men. It was a magnificent campaign. Miss Shaw was in it. Carrie Lane Chapman was in it and they learned a lesson. Your President, Mrs. Johns, was in that campaign and she had a lesson. Oh yes! while the Republican and Independent party platforms were silent not so with the Democratic party. It resolved to stand against the heresy of woman suffrage and talked against us everywhere.

Let us sum up South Dakota. The total vote was 70,000, 30,000 were foreigners—Scandinavians, Swedes, Norwegians, Russians, all classes—a very large ratio of Russians. Now, I am not going to talk against foreigners, I want you to understand that. I would not take the ballot from a single foreigner, the only thing I would deprive him of doing is voting that native born women may not have the right to vote as well as he. I am glad they may vote, I am glad there is one day in the year when every man can feel he is as good as every other man. One day in the year when every nabob has got to say, "Mister" and not "Sambo" or "Hans" or "Jim" or "Pat." I would be glad to reach the point where they would have to call women decent names one day in the year at least. (Laughter.) Of the American born men 24,000 voted yes and 16,000 voted no. So, that you perceive by a vote of 3 to 2 of those native born men we carried South Dakota but when the 30,000 foreigners' votes were counted with the 16,000 native voters we had a tremendous majority against us.

Now, my friends, the ratio of foreigners in South Dakota may be larger than here but South Dakota had other elements that were much more advantageous to our chances for success than you will find in Kansas. The South Dakota women had not had municipal suffrage. They had not made of themselves a balance of power in 285 cities of that state to search out every bootleg, every garret and cellar and thereby make themselves disagreeable to their "Best citizens," and there isn't a man in this state who wants these sinks of iniquity licensed and carried on that wants women to vote.

But at last, in Colorado we have won by the popular vote—but not without party endorsement—the enfranchisement of women. During the summer of 1893 nearly every Republican and People's and not a few Democratic county conventions put hearty planks in their platforms. When the fall campaign opened every political stump speaker was authorized to speak favorably upon the subject, and no man could oppose it unless he ran counter to the principles laid down in his party platform. That made it a truly educational campaign on the question to all the voters of the state.

A word to the wise is sufficient. Let every Kansas man who wants the suffrage amendment carried demand full and hearty endorsement of the measure by his political party—be it Democratic, Republican, People's or Prohibition—so that Kansas shall win as did her neighbor state, Colorado.

Your legislature of 1867 that submitted the proposition for women to vote passed a law making it obligatory upon the liquor seller, the saloon keeper you call him now, to get the signatures of one-half of the inhabitants to his petition for license, irrespective of color or sex.

* * *

The Republican party had made a party measure of the prohibition amendment. They had planks in their platform for its enforcement from year to year, until they were tired of fighting the liquor dealers in the state and the Democrats in the state and on the borders. They got tired of being taunted with the fact that they had not the power to enforce the law. Then, as a sheer political party necessity, just as much as it was a political party necessity of the Republican party in their reconstruction days at the close of the war to enfranchise the negroes, so it was a political party necessity in the state of Kansas, in 1887, to enfranchise the women of the cities of this state, because they needed a new balance of power to help them to elect officers that would enforce the law. Where could they go to get that new balance of power? Every single man in the state, native born and foreign, drunk or sober, outside of the state penitentiary, the idiot and the lunatic asylums, already had the right to vote. You could not enfranchise another man. You hadn't Indians enough, even if you brought them in, to help you to a new balance of power. You hadn't anybody but the women. As a dernier resort, as the only way of escape, the only way of getting help to carry out a party measure, the Republicans by a straight party vote—I can't remember it exactly, I think there were five Democrats between the senate and the house that voted in favor of the measure for the extension of municipal suffrage to the women of the cities of this state—but it was through a strict party vote that that privilege was extended to the women.

Now, this boon, this municipal vote, this political power was put in the hands of the women of this state by the old Republican party with its magnificent majorities—up to 82,000, you remember, the last time you bragged! It was before you had the division or quarrel in the family. It was by the grand old party, solid as it was in those olden days, that you gave suffrage to the women in your municipal elections.

Then, last year, and two years ago, after the division, after the People's party was organized, when the People's party state convention was held, and when the Republican party convention was held, each party put a plank in its platform declaring that the time had come for the submission of a proposition for full suffrage and the inference was, it could be none other, that both of those parties when they submitted it knew what they were about, and that it was an endorsement. I believe it. If I had not believed it, I never would have come to the state again and given my voice in the 25 or 30 different political meetings in telling the Republicans what a grand and glorious record they had made in the enfranchisement of black men not only, but in giving all the votes on the floor of congress that were ever given for women's enfranchisement, and being the party in this state that gave municipal suffrage to women. If I had not believed that when this party put a plank in their platform demanding the submission of the question, that they intended to stand by that question like men, I never would have raised my voice in meeting for any party or any set of men in the world. I will never speak, I have vowed it from the time I began to see suffrage through politics, I would never wave my handkerchief for either of the two great dominant parties that did not have a woman suffrage plank in their platform.

I consider, by every precedent of the past, by every pledge of the past, by the submission of the proposition, by the passage of the resolution through the legislature when the leaders and representatives of the two parties, the People's and Republican, vied with each other to see which would give the largest majority, they made the promise that they would make this measure a party measure, and I speak tonight to the two parties as the old Republican party. You are not the same men altogether, but you are the descendants, you are the allies of what was the grand old party. You are the children of that party; and I stand here tonight, and have come here, all the way from my home and from my state work, where this question is pending and where both of our great old parties, the Democratic and Republican, are going to put a woman's suffrage plank in their platform, I come out here that the Republicans and Populists of Kansas shall not be behind the Democrats and Republicans of New York.

I saw somewhere the Republicans were going to have their state convention the 6th of June. Though not the old Republican party it claims to be the lineal descendant of that party, having the name. When they meet on the 6th day of June I shall be ashamed if the telegraphic wires flash the word over the country, as was flashed from the Republican league the other day.[26] If there is a woman left in the state of Kansas after that convention is held who has any affiliation with the Republican party, any sympathy with it, who will float its banner, if it does not redeem its pledge, I will disown her; she is not one of my sort! (Applause.)

The People's party convention is held on the 12th of June. If that party shirks its responsibility and does not give a strong, hearty woman's suffrage plank in its platform, pledging itself to use all its party machinery, all its educational powers, all the mechanical manipulations of printing its ballots and of managing things at the polls, if that party does not make good that pledge, claiming to be the People's party, then I haven't any respect for any woman that will train in that company.

The Democrats have declared their purpose, you see. They are going to fight us. We expect it and I was going to say I was glad of it, only I do not know but I would be willing to have the fellow reputed to have the cloven foot be on our side rather than against us. What does the good book say, "He that is not for me is against me."[27] We know where the Democratic party is, it is against us. When the Republican and People's party say nothing for us they say everything against us. They do everything against us. No plank will be saying to every woman suffrage Republican campaign speaker and every woman suffrage People's party speaker "you must not advocate woman suffrage on the platform, for to do so will lose us the whisky vote, it will lose us the foreign vote." Hence, no plank for us means no word for us, and no word for us means everything against us.

Now, it comes your time, men of the Republican party, to choose whom you will have for your constituents, to make up the bone and sinew of your party, whether you will have the most ignorant foreigner, just landed on our shores, that has not learned a single principle of Republican government, whether you will lose two or three of those votes and gain the votes of all of us women, at future elections, or whether you will lose to-day a few votes of the high license or the low license Republicans, foreign or native, black or white, as the case may be, and gain to yourselves the women of your own households. That is the question. It has been stated in a newspaper article that Mrs. Johns could not have the suffrage plank put in the Republican platform in Saline county because it would lose the votes of the Scandinavians in that county.[28] Now, will those 1,000 Scandinavian men in Saline county be of more help to the Republican men or the People's party men of that county than are their own wives, mothers, daughters and sisters?

The crucial moment is upon you now, and I say unto you men of both parties, Republican and People's, you have driven the last nail in the coffin of this movement and banished all hope of carrying the question at the ballot box if you do not incorporate this question in your platforms. I know what you will say, I have talked with ever so many and heard from ever so many of the men of Kansas. I know what they all say. I read Governor Morrill's statement the other night, that they should let this question "go to the ballot-box on its merits" and don't let anybody speak of it in the political meetings and don't make a party measure of it. Why must we have the plank? Because no man wants to have the ballot—no man wants equality for women unless he is a well-educated man. The masses are rooted and grounded in the old prejudices of the inferiority of women, the subordination of women, and believe that woman was born merely to help man, to carry out his plans, and not to have any plans of her own whatsoever.

Now, friends, because that is true, because no man believes in political equality for women, except he is educated out of every bigotry, every custom, and every usage that he was born into, that no woman has a right to equality with man in the family, in the church and in the state, therefore it is that there can be no hope of the rank and file of men who toil from sunrise to sunset voting for this amendment, thus giving to women what is just and right. They must labor to gain bread to keep body and soul together. There is, there can be no possibility that those men can be reached, can be educated out of the prejudices into which they were born through any other instrumentality than that of the campaign meetings—the campaign papers of the political parties of which they are members.

Therefore, when you say this question is not to be a political party question, not to be in your platform, not to be discussed in your meetings, not to be advocated in your party papers, you simply say that these men are not to be educated upon this question.

Who are the men who come to our women's meetings? We have just finished fifty-nine out of the sixty counties in the state of New York. We had magnificent audiences, composed of people from the furthest townships in the county and in many of them every single township, with the largest opera houses packed, hundreds going away, who could not get in. Our audiences have been composed of five out of six or nine out of ten women and the one man out of six, the one man out of ten who was he? An educated, cultivated man who had lived through the experiences of life, who had come to realize that there was but one salvation for the race, one salvation for the country and that was through the equality of women, making woman the peer of man in every department of life.

How are we going to reach these other five men out of six, the other nine men out of ten who never come to our meetings. There is no way you see, if you have no discussion, no plank in your party platforms. If you do not put endorsement planks in your platforms then I say the fate of this measure is sealed. No use talking about it. You think your Kansas men are all going to vote independently. You imagine it. You are no more sanguine to-day than were all the men and women and myself included in 1867, with those free state men who had come out here, who had given up every comfort which human beings prize for the sake of liberty, who fought not only that first border ruffian warfare, but who had fought through the rebellion. And Kansas sent the biggest quota, I believe of any state to suppress the rebellion. Where would you ever expect to find a majority of men who would be more ready to grant to the women their equal rights if not among those old free state men? You haven't as glorious a batch of men in Kansas to-day by a long way as you had in Kansas in 1867. If you had told me then that a single one of those men would have gone to the ballot box and voted no, I should have felt like knocking you down. And yet some of them did. They went and voted no. They thought St. Paul and God and everyone else said no.

Do you mean to repeat the experiment of this state and South Dakota and the other nine states? If you do, do not have your party put a plank in the platform. Just have a "still hunt." A still hunt, when it is a work of education! My dear friends, I have worked enough in this state to save it if it is worth saving. All through that campaign of 1867, and since, three or four times, I have been out here, "free gratis and for nothing, without a cent to pay," as the Irishman said, and made the circuit of your state with Mrs. Johns, because I felt Kansas must be the first state in the Union to give. I never can be resigned to the fact that Wyoming comes in first and that Colorado gets in before Kansas does. Now, women, all is lost if you sit down here and supinely listen to any politician, any nominee. I don't care if he is the best friend of suffrage in the state, if he is a nominee, he won't want to put a plank in the platform—for if a man is a nominee he is a coward, he must reckon what he will lose or what he will gain. Daniel Webster said, "Ask the whole loaf and take what you can get." I appeal to you men and women who believe in suffrage, don't go "meaching" around about this matter but make the demand imperative! Say, "The plank must go in the platform!" Now I am going to give a resolution:

Whereas: From the standpoint of justice, political expediency and grateful appreciation of their wise and practical use of school suffrage from the organization of the state, and of municipal suffrage in our 285 cities for the past eight years, we, the citizens of Wyandotte county, descendants of the grand old party, with its magnificent majorities—now of the Republican and People's parties—which extended this partial suffrage to the women of Kansas in mass meeting assembled do hereby

Resolve: That we urgently request our delegates in their approaching state conventions to indorse the woman suffrage amendment in their respective platforms.

This resolution I consider adopted here, I want to say to you, my good friends of the Republican and People's party, I would never have made a journey here to convert a single man in Kansas. (Every man who can be has been already committed to this amendment.) I came for those who can be carried only and simply by party influence, who can be carried only by the plank and by the party mechanics that politicians know how to use and we woman do not. (Applause.)

~ *Leavenworth Times*, 13 May 1894. Ellipses in original.

1. Laura Johns chaired the meeting.
2. Sterling Price (1809–1867) was governor of Missouri from 1853 to 1857, when the proslavery raids occurred in Kansas, but the term Price's Raid is usually reserved for events in 1864, when he was a Confederate general and clashed with Union forces in Kansas and Missouri.
3. On 9 February 1864, when the first one hundred thousand names on a petition of emancipation were presented in the Senate. See *Papers*, 1:510–11n, and *Anthony*, 1:235.
4. See *Papers*, 1:550, and *Film*, 11:190–98.
5. John M. Rankin (c. 1829–?), president of the Western Christian University in Ottumwa, read the Declaration of Independence.
6. Sidney Clark (1831–1909) was a Republican congressman from Kansas from 1865 to 1871. While dining with SBA and her brother on 4 August 1865, he delivered advice about steering clear of woman's rights in her speeches. (*BDAC*; *Papers*, 1:552.)
7. Andrew Johnson (1808–1875) became president of the United States after the assassination of Abraham Lincoln. It was not his proclamation about Florida that SBA attacked in her speech but his proclamation about Mississippi, in which he based a new government on the state's antebellum constitution.
8. Floyd Perry Baker (1820–1909) was, in 1865, part owner of the *Kansas State Record*, published at Topeka. That paper merged with the *Commonwealth* a few years later. (Andreas, *History of Kansas*, 555.)
9. Republican members of the House of Representatives, these were Robert Cumming Schenck (1809–1890) of Ohio, Thomas Allen Jenckes (1818–1875) of Rhode Island, and John Martin Broomall (1816–1894) of Pennsylvania. They acted in December, not summer. (*BDAC*.)
10. Thaddeus Stevens (1792–1868) of Pennsylvania chaired the Joint Committee on Reconstruction where the language of the Fourteenth Amendment was drawn up. (*BDAC*.)
11. Wendell Phillips used the phrase "the Negro's hour" at the American

Anti-Slavery Society meeting in May 1865. See *Liberator*, 19 May 1865, and *Papers*, 1:549n, 564-65. On the quotation attributed to Phillips, see note above at 30 May 1888.

12. On the Kansas campaign, see *Papers*, 2:18n, 57, 58n, 92-93, 93-94n, 643-44, and *History*, 2:229-68, 928-34.

13. The *Alabama*, built in England, and the *Shenandoah*, built in Scotland, were warships of the Confederate Navy used worldwide to capture and destroy merchant ships loyal to the Union. Rather than treat their actions as piracy, Great Britain recognized the Confederate States of America as a belligerent nation whose ships were engaged in war.

14. On the Michigan campaign, see *Papers*, 3:80-87, 110-13, 120-28, and *History*, 3:516-22. The final tally against woman suffrage was 40,077 to 135,957.

15. Zachariah Chandler (1813-1879) was the Republican party boss of Michigan and United States senator. SBA made this comparison between his audiences and hers in her diary, 27 October 1874. (*BDAC*; *Papers*, 3:124-26.)

16. On the Colorado campaign, see *Papers*, 3:318-31, and *History*, 3:716-25. The final tally against woman suffrage was 6,612 to 14,053.

17. On her conversation with Routt, see *Papers*, 3:328, 330n, 4:428n.

18. Agapito Vigil (c. 1840-?), a farmer, was the delegate to the Colorado constitutional convention from Huerfano and Las Animas counties in southern Colorado. He supported woman suffrage in that convention and served on the executive committee of the Colorado suffrage association in 1877. (Federal Census, 1880; *History*, 3:717-18, 720n.)

19. John Mercer Langston (1829-1897), lawyer, former member of the House of Representatives from Virginia, founder of Howard University's law department, had long been an important spokesperson for the Republican party. (*ANB*.)

20. On the Nebraska campaign, see *Papers*, 4:61n, 139n, 176-77, 180, 183-91, 201-2, and *History*, 3:682-92.

21. Theron Nye (1828-1901), settled early in Fremont, Nebraska, before the Union Pacific Railroad came through town, and made a fortune from the sale of grain and farm implements. When the town was incorporated as a city, he won the first election for mayor in 1871. Later that decade, he served on the Dodge County Board of Commissioners. SBA was in Nebraska for nearly two months in 1882. (Daniel M. Carr, ed., *Progressive Men of Nebraska; A Book of Portraits. Dodge County Edition* [Fremont, Neb., 1902], 23, 35, 37, 55; William H. Buss and Thomas T. Osterman, eds., *History of Dodge and Washington Counties, Nebraska, and Their People* [Chicago, 1921], 1:62.)

22. See *Papers*, 4:308-9n, 422, 428n, and *History*, 3:777-79. Oregon's voters defeated the amendment 11,223 to 28,176.

23. See *Papers*, 4:552n, and *History*, 4:909-11. In April 1887, Rhode Island's voters defeated the measure 6,889 to 21,957.

24. An amendment for woman suffrage was submitted to Washington Territory's voters along with a new state constitution in November 1889. It

was rejected by a vote of 16,521 to 35,913. See *History*, 4:969-70, 1096—98.

25. The text reads "And they knew as I knew that no political party help could carry it to victory."

26. The Republican League met in Topeka on April 4 and 5. With the avowed purpose of educating voters and a promise "not to formulate party platforms or to nominate tickets," the league could and did dodge the question of woman suffrage. Delegates were warned "there must be absolute harmony in the ranks." In public view, only two items suggested a private contest: a meeting of the Woman's Republican Association scheduled for April 5 was called off, and the league offered a pat on the back to women, recognizing "the usefulness of the Kansas Woman's Republican association" and commending "the splendid work it has done and is doing for our party." (*Topeka Daily Capital*, 5 & 6 April 1894.)

27. Matt. 12:30.

28. At county Republican Club conventions in March, suffragists introduced resolutions in support of the amendment.

218 ~ From the Diary of SBA

[*4–5 May 1894*]

FRI. MAY 4, 1894. <u>Kansas Campaign</u>—Kansas City 5th Avenue Opera House—rough enough— Miss Shaw & self arrived at 9 A.M. & after being sent hither & yon to see people who didn't invite us we were landed at our good friends Mr & Mrs [*blank*] Simpsons[1]—who with their one son & daughter made us most welcome

Mrs Johns didn't arrive till P.M. no session till 8— I then made my speech on vital necessity of Planks in Platforms—of Repub. & Populist Platforms— It was given under a fearful pressure of opposition— Mrs Johns presiding never smiled, Miss Kimber[2] Mrs St Johns[3] double— whispered & scolded—with Miss Anthony's losing us a 1,000 votes by that— I never spoke under such a pressure—all had been wheedled into not demanding planks—

1. Samuel Newell Simpson (1826–1915) settled in Lawrence, Kansas, in 1854, and Kate Lyon Burnett Simpson (1833–1900) joined him there after their marriage in 1864. In 1877, the family moved to what became Kansas City, where Simpson was a major developer. Their sons Charles Lyon (1866–?) and Burnett Newell (1869–?) as well as an adopted daughter Nellie or Ellen Josephine (c. 1874–?) all still lived at the house of their parents. (Connelley,

Standard History of Kansas and Kansans [1918], 4:1999–2002; Kansas Census, 1895.)

2. Helen L. Kimber (c. 1864–?) was recognized as "the most successful organizer" in the amendment campaign. Born in Illinois, she grew up in Liberty, Kansas, and became a schoolteacher in Pittsburg and Parsons. As a Republican activist in the party as well as the suffrage organization, Kimber was at odds with SBA during the campaign and still angry with her ten years later. By then she was president of the equal suffrage association, a post she held for three terms to little effect. Giving up teaching sometime after 1895, she redirected her organizing skills into business, becoming a sales agent for the Union Pacific Land Company and establishing her own business in St. Joseph, Missouri, to buy and sell land in western Kansas and Mexico. ("Helen Kimber," *Chronicle Monthly Magazine* 3 [September 1894]: 27–28; *History*, 4:648, 655, 774, 5:13n, 19n, 6:193–94; Federal Census, 1870, and Kansas Census, Liberty Township, 1875; Kansas Census, Parsons, 1885 and 1895; Goldberg, *Army of Women*, 256; H. L. Kimber, "Kansas Women in Politics," *Civic Pride* 1 [April 1904]: 21–23; clippings, Biographical Scrapbooks, KHi.)

3. Susan Jane Parker St. John (?–1925), known as Jennie, was the wife of former governor John St. John and at one time the National association's vice president for Kansas.

SAT. MAY 5, 1894. Kansas City—Kansas Opening Spring Campaign for W.S. Constitutional Amendment— Miss Shaw, Mrs Chapman latter arrived this A.M—all present at day meetings— Mrs Johns, Miss Kimber & seemingly every one vexed with my last nights speech—

Miss Shaw went to Leavenworth at 6 P.M—she was ill all last night & to day—& Mrs J. classes her with me—in <u>killing</u> <u>the</u> <u>cause</u>—by flatly demanding Political party endorsement of the amendment—

Mrs Chapman spoke this evening—had a full house—Mrs Childs[1] of Iowa—Mrs Jenkins of Wyoming were speakers also—[2]

1. Rachel Lockwood Trumbull Child (1843–1933) was an activist from Iowa brought into the Kansas campaign. Carrie Catt may have recommended her for the work after meeting her through the Iowa suffrage association. When forty women in Dunlap organized a political equality club in 1892, Child was elected their president. Later that year she spoke to the annual meeting of the Iowa suffrage association and Mississippi Valley Conference and was elected to the state executive committee. But her involvement in the movement predated Catt's: she sent a letter to the anniversary of the Seneca Falls convention in 1878 in which she described suffrage as "the foundation of every radical reform." (*History of Harrison County, Iowa* [Chicago, 1891], 458–59; Elias Child, *Genealogy of the Child Childs and Childe Families, Of the Past and Present in the United States and the Canadas, from 1630 to 1881* [Utica, N.Y., 1881], 386; *National Citizen and Ballot Box*, August 1878, *Film*,

20:313–21; *Woman's Journal*, 30 April 1892; *History*, 4:647n; Works Progress Administration Gravestone Inscriptions Project, Pleasant Hill Cemetery, Harrison County, Iowa.)

2. Therese Jenkins also joined the Kansas campaign as a speaker.

⚜ Excelsior Diary 1894, n.p., SBA Papers, DLC.

219 ⚜ ECS TO MARY RICE LIVERMORE

26 West 61st N.Y. May 7 [*1894*]

Dear Mrs Livermore

Many thanks for your kind invitation. I am very sorry that Mrs Blatch cannot accept as I am very proud of her & should like to have all our Boston friends see & hear her. But she sails on on Wednesday.[1] As to myself the word "go" has lost all charm for me. I have arrived at that time of life when a good novel a rocking chair, my own bed & other personal comforts in an apartment house with no stairs to climb are all so necessary to my happiness that I cannot be tempted to new fields of labor, except those my pen can reach. You see the great uprising in this state. Mrs Blatch has spoken twice a day ever since she landed. The very day she landed she went straight from the ship to a parlor meeting to fill one of my engagements   You should be here to help us   Could you give July August September & October or any part of those months & make one grand campaign through all the counties of this state? I hope your festival will a grand success as it always is. With kind regards for Mr Livermore[2] & yourself yours as ever

⚜ *Elizabeth Cady Stanton*

⚜ ALS, Papers of ECS, NPV.

1. Livermore invited Harriot Blatch to speak at the Woman Suffrage Festival in Boston on 28 May 1894. Harriot returned to England on 9 May 1894.

2. Daniel Parker Livermore (1819–1899), married to Mary Livermore since 1845, was a retired Universalist minister. (Charles A. Howe, "Daniel and Mary Livermore: The Biography of a Marriage," *Proceedings of the Unitarian Universalist Historical Society* 19, pt. 2 [1982–1983]: 14–35.)

220   REMARKS BY ECS TO THE MASS MEETING IN NEW YORK CITY

EDITORIAL NOTE: New York City suffragists organized a mass meeting at Cooper Union in the evening of 7 May 1894. Two thousand people "filled every seat, packed every doorway, and made a human dado around the walls," according to a reporter. ECS's surprise entrance was the ceremonial highlight of the evening. With the stage lights down, "in the archway at the rear of the stage, appeared the silver-crowned figure, leaning on a cane and supported by her daughter. . . . [S]he came very slowly down the stage. As she advanced one set of lights after another was turned on, each added flash seeming to intensify the whiteness of her hair, until, as she reached her chair, the audience, too, turned white with waving handkerchiefs." In the sequence of short speeches, Samuel Gompers, president of the American Federation of Labor, preceded ECS, while Harriot Blatch, Father Ducey, and Henry George followed her. (New York *Sun*, 8 May 1894, *Film*, 32:816.)

[7 May 1894]

Mrs. Stanton had stood up and advanced to the front of the platform with the aid of her cane. She rested one hand on it and the other on the reading desk, bowing to the right and the left. Her fine head was thrown back, and the more they looked upon her the more enthusiastic the audience became. After a while she raised her hand and almost instantly they were still. There was none of that resumption of applause so common in mass-meetings. Mrs. Stanton did not expect to be present. She had even written a letter to be read, but at the last moment she decided she was strong enough to attend.[1]

In her deep, round musical voice she began to talk. There was no part of the room in which she could not be heard, and yet she did not speak loudly.

"They say that women cannot fight," she said. "They have met persecution, ridicule and jeers for fifty years, and it seems to me that is the best kind of fighting."

Again the fluttering handkerchiefs, the chorus of cries. Mrs. Stanton talked smoothly and epigrammatically, as one who knows all that can be learned of a subject, and with an earnestness and conviction of its absolute truth.

"Let no one tell us that suffrage is a privilege," she declared. "It is the foundation of the republic. The State has the right to regulate suffrage, but it has no right to deny it to any American citizen."

There was a mannish humor in much she said.

"We hear people talk of the effect of suffrage upon women. Well, women have school suffrage and sidewalk suffrage. I have met the women who have voted upon these questions and I cannot see that it changed them any. The women in England have suffrage in part. I have visited in their homes and I cannot see that it has destroyed the family. I was a guest at the house of Lady Carlisle and I found her and her ten children and her husband living in perfect peace and happiness."[2]

Scorns the Opposition.

"You hear people say, too, that all the good things will come about in time without this agitation. This reminds me of the clown in the classic fable who saw an archer bring down a bird. The clown said the archer might have saved his arrow: the fall would have killed the bird anyway."[3]

Father Ducey[4] placed his hands over his stomach and laughed with much heartiness. Dr. Mary Putnam Jacobi,[5] that modest little woman who has worked so hard and who has had the satisfaction of flooring every man who has met her in argument, was delighted.

Mrs. Stanton said she had read that the members of the Constitutional Convention were favorably disposed towards woman suffrage, but that the matter would be complicated by the women who would oppose it. She couldn't understand how any one could be influenced by the arguments of persons who didn't know what they were talking about, because these women admitted that they were so much occupied with home duties that they wouldn't have time to vote, and they did not have the time to look into the question. She had had time to keep house, bring up seven children and study these questions besides. Mrs. Stanton closed with an eloquent picture of what suffrage would accomplish, and when she sat down there was almost as much applause as when she was formally introduced.

~ New York *World*, 8 May 1894.

1. ECS to Eleanor B. Sanders, before 7 May 1894, *Film*, 32:803–6.
2. George James Howard, ninth earl of Carlisle (1843–1911), his wife Lady

Rosalind Carlisle, and some of their ten children hosted ECS at Castle Howard in July 1891.

3. In 1861, ECS confessed to Wendell Phillips that she appropriated this story for her lecture "Free Speech" from his lecture "The Pulpit." (*Papers*, 1:459-60; Phillips, *Speeches, Lectures, and Letters*, 272; ECS, *Free Speech*, in *Film*, 9:1092-95.)

4. Thomas James Ducey (1843-1909), a Roman Catholic priest in New York City, was a leading voice against municipal corruption and a social activist. (*NCAB*, 9:321-22; *WWW1*.)

5. Mary Corinna Putnam Jacobi (1842-1906), an eminent physician in New York City, led the city's "Volunteer Committee" in the campaign. Working parallel to the suffrage league, Jacobi's group invented the parlor meetings that encouraged elite women to sign petitions. (*ANB*; *1894. Constitutional-Amendment Campaign Year*, 217-20.)

221 ❧ Remarks by SBA to Committee on Suffrage, New York Constitutional Convention

EDITORIAL NOTE: New York's constitutional convention of 1894 met and adjourned on 8 May 1894, reconvened on May 22, and created its committees. The Committee on Suffrage held a short organizational meeting on May 23, at which members agreed to hold a special hearing in the Assembly Chamber on May 24 in order to accommodate SBA's need to return to Kansas. Despite the short notice, a large audience gathered to hear Jean Greenleaf and SBA. "Never did the great suffrage leader speak more grandly," according to the history of the campaign. "Never did she make the cause more clear." SBA opened with one of her standard lectures on suffrage and then tried to engage committee members in the kind of question period she often used on her lecture tours. (*Revised Record of the Constitutional Convention*, 1:20, 44, 46, 75; *1894. Constitutional-Amendment Campaign Year*, 8-9.)

[24 May 1894]

MISS ANTHONY'S CHALLENGE.

After Miss Anthony had spoken three-quarters of an hour she paused. She had given the familiar reasons for granting woman the ballot. She said that in the matter of voting the sex line had been broken, and that woman suffrage was a reform already begun. She said that in England women with a property qualification had voted for twenty-five years in municipal elections; that in Canada, Australia and all England's colonies women had a limited right to vote; that only last year in New Zealand the right had been made general, and that the New Zealand act had been made a law by the signature of a woman, Queen Victoria. She showed that in twenty-three States women could vote on school questions, in one on municipal affairs, and in one, the State of Wyoming, on all questions.

Then came her challenge to debate. She said she would like to answer any question which might be put to her.

Women here and there in seats smiled a smile of anticipated triumph. Chairman Goodelle[1] and the other members of the Committee on Suffrage moved uneasily in their places.

A brief, yet seemingly long, period of stillness followed. Not a man said a word. They were as if tongue-tied with fear of a woman, and that woman gray and bent with the burdens of seventy-four years.

At last Miss Anthony broke the silence. She seemed almost to taunt the men into saying something.

"You needn't be afraid, gentlemen," she said; "I am used to it. I have been stumping for forty years."

A burst of laughter came, to the great relief of the men.

Pursuing Her Advantage.

"It used to be said," went on Miss Anthony, "that a white man couldn't or wouldn't argue with a negro, only in those days they spelled negro with two g's. It is still said you can't argue with a woman, but if, as you enfranchised negroes, you will enfranchise women, you will find that you can argue with a woman. At any rate, here I am, and I want to be argued with."

Again came that disagreeable silence. Observing it, Miss Anthony stepped out more into the aisle, and, directing her eyes at ex-Speaker Alvord,[2] she lifted her hand and exclaimed: "There is Brother Alvord! He was our enemy in the Constitutional Convention of 1867, and may be against us now. What has he to say? Come, Mr. Alvord; what is your argument? What is your strongest argument?"

Miss Anthony laid great stress on the adjective strongest, and both that and the fact that she had singled out a champion of the other side to enter the lists with her, caused peals of laughter.

Ex-Speaker Alvord rose slowly and answered promptly, but deliberately: "We are sitting here as judges. We shall hear arguments and at the proper time we shall deliver our judgment."

He said more, but it was all to the same point. He was too shrewd to get into argument, too gallant to be anything but parliamentary and courteous.

Miss Anthony and the other women and, in fact, the assemblage generally regretted it, but Miss Anthony rallied and said she would tell how in the convention of 1867, when she had asked for objection to giving woman the right to vote, Horace Greeley, then a delegate, had risen and said: "The ballot and the bullet go together. You women want to vote; are you ready, too, to fight?"[3]

"I answered him," said Miss Anthony: "'Yes, Mr. Greeley, we are ready to fight,' and then, with a pause, 'Fight at the point of a goose quill, as you did.'

"But to-day we have no fighting. Peace is here, and we shall have no fighting, so that the question is not timely to-day."

One Man in Her Net.

After a few more remarks Miss Anthony again extended an invitation to the committee to ask questions. Her persistence was apparently worrying the men, so Chairman Goodelle said that the committee was there to listen but not to speak. Notwithstanding this, Delegate John Bigelow,[4] of New York, said he would like to have her account for the want of unanimity in her sex, many good women opposing the movement. Miss Anthony was applauded for the very first sentence of her reply:

"Just the way I used to explain the want of unanimity among the slaves before the war over the question whether they wanted to be free."

Then she said that no dependent class can be honest; that women were dependent; that because of this, because some have every comfort, they wish and care little for others, and because they do not wish to assume responsibility they oppose suffrage.

"We, however," asserted Miss Anthony, "are dependent upon ourselves, and for ourselves and the others like us we desire to vote. We desire and are willing to share all responsibilities with men."

She closed by comparing herself and her associates to Frederick

Douglass, and the women who do not want to vote to the sleek, well-fed, well-dressed, well-housed slaves of Henry Clay.

Mirabeau L. Towns[5] asked some questions apparently calculated to cause mirth. The effort failed dismally, and there were not a few hisses. Then Edward Lauterbach,[6] who apparently sees a compromise ahead, asked how it would satisfy the women if the suffrage were given them dependent upon an educational qualification. Miss Anthony replied that, while she believed in general suffrage, she had to remember that the women were at the mercy of the men and must take what would be given. If suffrage dependent upon an educational qualification were all that the men felt they could give them, the women would be pleased with that.

The committee then adjourned, but woman suffrage talk did not stop. Groups of delegates and women lingered, argued and debated for more than half an hour.

↩ New York *World*, 25 May 1894.

1. William Prevost Goodelle (1840?-1918), a Republican lawyer from Syracuse and a delegate-at-large to the convention, was named chairman of the suffrage committee. He did not favor woman suffrage, nor did he believe there existed a right to vote; voting was a duty imposed by the state in the best interests of the state. Speaking to convention delegates on August 15, he observed that nowhere had advocates of woman suffrage "shown that any certain, well-defined or tangible benefits would result, either to the State or to the women themselves, by the adoption of female suffrage." (Fitch, *Encyclopedia of Biography of New York*, 2:73-77; *New York Times*, 14 June 1918; *Revised Record of the Constitutional Convention*, 2:525-27.)

2. Thomas Gold Alvord (1819-1897) of Syracuse was a delegate to the constitutional conventions of both 1867 and 1894. A former lieutenant governor and frequent leader in the state assembly, he retired from politics in 1882. Explaining his vote against woman suffrage on 15 August 1893, Alvord predicted that "the Supreme Ruler of the universe will punish this attempted violation of that higher law laid down in holy writ and on nature's page, which points out clearly and plainly the duties and province of the two sexes." (*NCAB*, 2:413; *New York Times*, 27 October 1897; *Revised Record of the Constitutional Convention*, 2:541.)

3. Horace Greeley chaired the suffrage committee of the constitutional convention of 1867. For variations on the exchange he had with ECS and SBA, see *Papers*, 2:75-76; *Film*, 12:259-63; and *History*, 2:284.

4. John Bigelow, a Democrat, was elected a delegate from the eighth senatorial district in New York City. In debate on the convention floor in August, Bigelow made a point of challenging the arguments put forward by antisuffragists.

5. Mirabeau Lamar Towns (1850-1932), a Brooklyn Democrat who favored woman suffrage, was raised in Alabama and educated in Germany before he studied law in New York and began to practice. He was known as "the poet lawyer" for his habit of pleading cases in rhyme. Rhymes also softened the sarcasm of his address on suffrage at the constitutional convention on 14 August 1894, concluding with this verse: "Turn loose the jammers of dry rot, /Declaim against the female ballot, /Fill every heart with dreadful fears, / Regard not justice, mercy, pity, /Kill the measure in committee, /And woman's slaved for twenty years." (*New York Times*, 26 November 1932; *Revised Record of the Constitutional Convention*, 2:417-25.)

6. Edward Lauterbach (1844-1923), a Republican lawyer from New York City, was elected a delegate-at-large to the convention. He was one of the strongest advocates of woman suffrage in the convention. (Fitch, *Encyclopedia of Biography of New York*, 2:295-97; *New York Times*, 5 March 1923.)

222 ❧ FROM THE DIARY OF SBA

[*5-11 June 1894*]

TUES. JUNE 5, 1894. [*Topeka, Kan.*] The Republican <u>Women's</u> Association met this A.M.—Mrs Johns Pres—& a slimmer more nearly <u>nothing</u> lot of partisans I hope never to see—but for Miss Shaws & my rousing words—it looked as if they would not ask a plank—[1] J. Ellen Foster—present—to declare she was a Repub. 1st & a W.S. after— She spoke in Hamilton Hall in evening!!

[*written above the date*] At noon—this day—I went to Dr & Mrs Teffts— a nice home—[2]

[*added later at bottom of page*] Miss Shaw was with me in Repub Women's meeting

1. This was Laura Johns's last meeting as president of the Kansas Republican Women's Association. Minnie Morgan's resolution, believed by some to have come straight from party leaders, asked individual Republicans to give the amendment "its just and earnest consideration" and disclaimed "any desire to make it a test of party fealty." Even Ellen Foster thought it too weak for Kansas, and Johns announced that she would not work in the state if it were adopted. In its place, the group resolved to "ask the Republicans in Kansas state convention assembled to testify and advocate an equal ballot and a fair count to all citizens." Morgan was then elected to succeed Johns as president. (Topeka *Daily State Journal*, 6 June 1894, *Film*, 32:879-80.)

2. Herbert Kenyon Tefft (1848-1901) was a prominent doctor in Topeka. He moved to the state as a child and studied medicine after the Civil War at Bellevue Hospital Medical College in New York and Rush Medical College in Chicago. He then joined his father in practice. Emma A. Alkire Tefft (1855-1924) moved to Topeka before her marriage in 1874. (Andreas, *History of Kansas*, 580; Kansas Census, 1895; *Journal of the American Medical Association* 36 [6 April 1901]: 979; *Topeka State Journal*, 10 January 1924.)

WED. JUNE 6, 1894. Republican Party State Nominating Convention—met at 12 noon— Miss Shaw myself & others had seats on the platform because—there could be no other place fixed for women— Judge Peters[1] of Newton made Chairman—adjourned to appoint Committees till 3 P.M— during the recess brother D. R. & Nephew D. R., Jr.[2] called at Dr Teffts—but did not stay to or enter the Convention— brother D. R. in his paper The L. Times has opposed Mr Morrill for Governor all along— just as we reached the Hall—he said brother Merritt had an encounter with a "bull" the day before—which resulted in the killing of the beast—& the injury of brother Merritt—this was all—& we were parted—so I worried until Friday A.M. when Dr Tefft telephoned to L. to learn—& Maude's reply was that all were well at the farm & home

—at 5 P.M. Mrs Johns—Mrs Foster—Mrs Prentiss,[3] myself & Miss Shaw spoke [*continued on page for 5 June*] before the Resolution Committee of which Eskridge[4] was Chairman—he who was ↑27 years ago↓ & is to day one of the lowest & meanest opponents of woman's enfranchisement— the Com. let us talk—but too closed ears—heads & hearts—determined to ignore our appeals—

[*added above date but struck out*] Miss Shaw came this A.M no last evening—I think it was

1. Samuel Ritter Peters (1842-1910) was a member of the House of Representatives from 1883 to 1891, when he declined renomination in order to practice law in Newton, Kansas. A graduate of the University of Michigan Law School, he served as judge of the state's ninth judicial district from 1875 to 1883. (*BDAC*.)

2. Daniel Read Anthony, Jr., (1870-1931) graduated from the Michigan Military Academy in 1887 and the University of Michigan Law School in 1891. He later succeeded his father as editor of the *Leavenworth Times* and served in Congress from 1907 to 1929. (*BDAC*; *WWW1*; *New York Times*, 5 August 1831.)

3. Caroline E. Anderson Prentis (c. 1847-1932), better known as Mrs. Noble L. Prentis, was the second wife of a distinguished journalist and author, at this time associate editor of the *Kansas City Star*. Well known herself

among activist women and Republicans, Prentis filled a term as president of the Kansas and Western Missouri Social Science Club and was head of women's programs at the Ottawa Chautauqua Assembly. (Kansas Biographical Scrapbooks, KHi; *Topeka State Journal*, 11 & 12 February 1932.)

4. Charles Vernon Eskridge (1833-1900), publisher of the *Emporia Republican*, promoter of railroads, and Republican politician, ardently opposed woman suffrage in the campaign of 1867 and showed no signs of change when he chaired the resolutions committee for the state Republican party in 1894. (Joseph G. Gambone, ed., "The Forgotten Feminist of Kansas: The Papers of Clarina I. H. Nichols, 1854-1885, Part IV," *Kansas Historical Quarterly* 39 [Winter 1973]: 522-24; Andreas, *History of Kansas*, 853-54; Christopher Childers, "Emporia's Incongruent Reformer: Charles Vernon Eskridge, the *Emporia Republican*, and the Kansas Republican Party, 1860-1900," *Kansas History* 28 [Spring 2005]: 2-15.)

THUR. JUNE 7, 1894. Again we women went to the Repub. Con— to hear the Resolutions Com. report—and it was unanimous & <u>silent</u> not even a thank you—nor a hope for the aid of the women of the state—& not one of the 900 members of the Convention entered a protest against this utter ignoring of the W.S. Amendment— So, as a party—the Repub's say not even a word of hope for the success of our am't—nor for its respectful consideration & discussion in their campaign meetings—which mean's the friends mouths are shut—& the enemies mouths opened—<u>no</u> word for us—but every body [*illegible*] speak against—

[*written above date*] at Dr Teffts—

FRI. JUNE 8, 1894. In Topeka at Dr Teffts—212—West 8th street— Miss Shaw & self called at E.S.A. Head Quarters—Columbian Building—West 6th street—to get Mrs Johns to tell us the attitude she thought <u>the one</u> for us to take now that the Repub's had ignored our W.S. Amendment in their platform—but she gave us nothing—she seems utterly at sea—with no power to be or to do—but to <u>drift</u> <u>with</u> the <u>Repub. Party</u>— Miss Shaw took train for Eureka at 11.25—& after dinner—Mrs Tefft put me & my bag on board a College Avenue Car—& I went to Mrs T. L. Lyons[1]—1633—College ave. where Miss Shaw is to come Saturday noon & I hope Mrs Chapman Catt—Sunday A.M. [*probably added later*] and we three were all together there—

1. Nannie J. Wright Lyon (1847?-1929), whose given name may have been Hannah, was long active in the Topeka Equal Suffrage Association and worked also with the temperance union. She, her husband, Thomas Stewart Lyon (1833-1914), and their two children moved to Topeka from Indiana in 1880.

Thomas Lyon, a Republican, was a real estate and loan agent. Their son, William Maclay Lyon (1874–1933), known as Maclay, was a student at the University of Kansas. (Federal Census, 1880; Andreas, *History of Kansas*, 569–70; *Topeka State Journal*, 14 January 1914, 27 February 1929; *Minutes of the Kansas Equal Suffrage Association, At the First, Second, Third and Fourth Annual Meetings in 1884–5–7* [N.p., 1887?]; Louis H. Cornish, comp., *A National Register of the Society: Sons of the American Revolution* [New York, 1902], 378; Missouri, on-line archive of death certificates, s.v., "Lyon, Maclay.")

SAT. JUNE 9, 1894. In Topeka—Kansas—at Mr & Mrs Thos L. Lyons—1633—College avenue—to speak in Hamilton Hall—this evening with our Rev Anna H. Shaw she on woman first & Repub or Pop. afterwards—I on <u>Reasons</u> why neither of the Dominant parties can put a W.S. plank in platform—[1]

[*written later*] Had a fine crowd—Though the rain fell in torrents the thunder roared & the lightning flashed—

1. Annie Diggs presided at this Indignation Meeting that attracted seven hundred men and women. "Miss Anthony was milder in her remarks than the majority of the audience had been led to expect," the press reported. Anna Shaw, however, "proceeded to everlastingly rip the republican party up the back." (*Topeka Daily Capital*, 10 June 1894, *Film*, 32:892.)

SUN. JUNE 10, 1894. In Topeka—at Mrs Lyons— Miss Shaw to preach at the M.E. Church—Dr Embry's—who is opposed[1]

Mr & Mrs Lyon & son went with Miss Shaw— Mrs Chapman & self remained at home & talked over the fearfully embarrassing situation—

[*paragraph struck out on this page, describing events below at 13 June*] In the evening Mrs Johns & husband[2] & Mr [*blank*] drove out—but we couldn't get Mrs J. to make any statement as to what & how she would herself—or have us present the situation in view of the Repub. & no plank and the Pop & a plank

1. Alaric S. Embree (1843–1921) was the sometimes controversial pastor of Topeka's First Methodist Church from 1892 to 1895. After serving in the Civil War, Embree graduated from DePauw University and spent most of his career in Kansas. (Kansas Biographical Scrapbooks, KHi; *Topeka State Journal*, 18 October 1921.)

2. James Bennett Johns (c. 1844–?), married to Laura Johns since 1872 or 1873, pursued different business ventures in Salina. (Amy A. Mitchell, "Reminiscences of Laura Lucretia Johns," typescript, Alma Lutz Collection, NPV; Federal Census, Salina, Kan., 1910, and Los Angeles, 1920.)

MON. JUNE 11, 1894. In Topeka— The Progressive League women held a stirring meeting at 2 P.M— & resolved to demand plank of their party—[1]

In evening they held a meeting in Hamilton Hall—packed—Mrs Otis Presiding—Mrs Chapman making the principal speech—

1. Founded by Populists in 1893, the Women's Political Progressive League took a more independent stand toward its party's leaders than did the Republican Women's Association. Members stood for woman suffrage and the amendment. Bina Otis, league president, chaired both meetings. SBA spoke briefly at the afternoon session in Representative Hall, after which Annie Diggs introduced the resolution calling on the People's party "to place itself on record in favor of this measure of justice," the suffrage amendment. Twelve hundred people, three-quarters of them men, gathered in Hamilton Hall in the evening, when Carrie Catt gave the principal address. (Goldberg, *Army of Women*, 222-26; *Topeka Daily Capital*, 12 June 1894.)

⚬ Excelsior Diary 1894, n.p., SBA Papers, DLC.

223 ⚬ REMARKS BY SBA TO THE KANSAS PEOPLE'S PARTY CONVENTION

EDITORIAL NOTE: Delegates to the Kansas People's party convention were sharply divided about woman suffrage when they gathered in Topeka's Hamilton Hall on 12 June 1894. On the one side were fusionists who would steer clear of the topic in order to unite with Democrats, and on the other side were anti-fusionists for whom equal rights were too important to jettison for political advantage. Contests between the two camps filled most of the time on opening day. A pro-suffrage majority elected their candidate as temporary chairman, adopted rules that ensured debate on the subject, and stopped an attempt to adjourn before women spoke to the convention. While the resolutions committee argued over the party platform elsewhere, Carrie Catt addressed the delegates. Then came cries for SBA to be heard. (*Film*, 32:898-904; Argersinger, *Populism and Politics*, 172-76.)

[12 June 1894]

"Mr. Chairman[1] and fellow citizens, for I am a citizen and the women of Kansas are citizens. The only difficulty with us is that the other half, not of the same sex, have denied us our citizens' right to voice our sentiments in shaping the government. I am here in this state as I was here last week, to try to get a chance to influence the men who hold the destinies of the state in their hands to declare that in their opinion the time is come for the women of Kansas to have their political rights recognized and respected, and we have asked and shall ask of every political party that assembles in the state that this question of the enfranchisement of the women be indorsed. I am told that 80 per cent of the men who belong to your party are in favor of woman suffrage. I want you to understand that I belong to a party composed of the states prison birds, and the idiots and the lunatics that are confined. Now I don't like my company. Do you blame me for it? (Cries, no. no.) There is not a single party in Kansas but that ought to bow its head in shame at the thought of leaving the women of the state in company with such creatures. Are we to be left in the same category as idiots, lunatics and states prison birds?"

At the conclusion of Miss Anthony's address, W. G. Carpenter,[2] a delegate, arose and desired to address a few questions to her. Consent was granted. He asked:

"Miss Anthony, in the event that the people's party which is here in convention assembled, endorses woman suffrage, will you give us aid and help us to beat the republican party?"

Miss Anthony replied: "I have stood before the American people for forty years and in all that time have said that if either of the two leading parties of the state or the nation would put woman suffrage in their platform, for that party I would wave my pocket handkerchief. I don't know anything about the planks in any of the platforms. I will attend your meetings. I will give you the advantage of my name, and if you will give me an hour, I will talk for the women. I could not talk republicanism if I went into the republican party. I know nothing but woman suffrage."

This did not satisfy Mr. Carpenter and he propounded his second question:

"I ask you that in the event that the people's party here in this convention assembled endorses woman suffrage, will you go on the stump throughout this state and say that the people's party has stood by you and you want the men who are in favor of woman suffrage to help the people's party, who have had the courage of their convictions to stand up for women's suffrage?"

Miss Anthony—"I certainly shall."

❧ *Topeka Daily Capital,* 13 June 1894.

1. Ben S. Henderson (1843–?) was elected temporary chairman of the People's party convention and took the blame for failing to stop suffragists from endorsing the amendment in the party platform. A lawyer who arrived in Kansas in 1878, Henderson moved several times, lived in Winfield at the time of the convention, and moved to Kansas City soon after. Among Populists he was known as a woman suffragist, and in the fall of 1894, at the same time that he dropped out of the party's campaign, he also took on the legal defense of sexual radical Lois Waisbrooker against federal charges of obscenity. He explained his break with the party as a protest against Populist corruption, but historians oddly hostile to the suffragists' campaign have read his actions at the June convention and later as evidence that he was in the employ of the Republican party. (Andreas, *History of Kansas,* 1218; L. Wallace Duncan, comp., *History of Montgomery County, Kansas. By Its Own People* [Iola, Kan., 1903], 215–16; James C. Malin, *A Concern about Humanity: Notes on Reform, 1872–1912, At the National and Kansas Levels of Thought* [Lawrence, Kan., 1964], 131; Kansas Biographical Scrapbooks, KHi; Walter T. K. Nugent, "How the Populists Lost in 1894," *Kansas Historical Quarterly* 31 [Autumn 1965]: 245–55.)

2. Another newspaper identified this person as William H. Carpenter (1863–?), a former county attorney in Marion, Kansas, who became a Democratic leader in the state.

224 ❧ From the Diary of SBA

[*12–13 June 1894*]

TUES. JUNE 12, 1894. The Populist Party State Convention—& we were all there in force—in Hamilton Hall— We were all invited to Luncheon at Mrs John Mulvanes—[1] The Populist women—Mrs Diggs their leader— were in good earnest— They followed up the delegations & the Resolution Committee—never leaving them till they got a goodly minority pledged to report in favor of a plank—

1. Harriet N. Freeman Mulvane (1836–1901) moved to Topeka in 1868, after her marriage to John R. Mulvane. Her husband was president of the Bank

of Topeka. (Connelley, *Standard History of Kansas and Kansans* [1918], 3:1369–70; *Topeka Daily Capital*, 5 June 1901.)

WED. JUNE 13, 1894. Populist Convention Hamilton Hall The Resolution Com—13 majority—reported ignoring W.S. as did the Republican but the 8 minority report—after four hours discussion was adopted—& now begins the fray—the Repub's mad because Miss Shaw & Miss Anthony declared they'd "<u>whoop</u>" for the party that whooped for Woman Suffrage—[1]

Mrs Johns came out to Mrs Lyons this evening—but didn't give us the slightest cue as to how she would have the status of our case now put before the people

1. The resolutions committee divided on woman suffrage, thirteen to eight against support for the amendment. When the minority, including the sole female delegate, Eliza Hudson, brought a report to the floor of the convention, a long and furious debate ensued. Annie Diggs, though not a delegate, was invited to make the closing argument. By an overwhelming vote, the delegates rejected a bland substitute plank that endorsed the idea of a referendum on woman suffrage. By a vote of three hundred and thirty-seven to two hundred and sixty-nine, the delegates adopted the minority plank. It read: "The People's party came into existence and won its glorious victories on fundamental principles of equal rights to all and special privileges to none; therefore, we favor the pending constitutional amendment, but we do not regard it a test of party fealty." (Topeka *State Journal*, 13 June 1894, SBA scrapbook 22, Rare Books, DLC.)

~ Excelsior Diary 1894, n.p., SBA Papers, DLC.

225 ~ INTERVIEWS WITH SBA IN ROCHESTER, NEW YORK

EDITORIAL NOTE: SBA reached Rochester at dawn on 22 June 1894 to face a parade of reporters. Their interviews with her appeared in four local newspapers the next day, under headlines announcing "She Isn't a Populist." "One would think," she wrote in her diary, "I had committed the <u>Sin against</u> the Holy Ghost—in thanking the Populists for their good promise—& saying I preferred them no matter what their <u>financial</u> <u>vagaries</u>—with justice to women—to the Republicans no matter what their financial wisdom—<u>without</u> justice to women." The *Democrat and Chronicle*'s interview took place in the afternoon of June 22, followed by the *Rochester Union and Advertiser*'s interview on the morning of June 23. (SBA diary, 22-23 June 1894, *Film*, 31:879ff.)

[22 June 1894]

"I didn't go over to the Populists by doing what I did in Kansas," said Miss Anthony. "I have been like a drowning man for a long time, and have been waiting for someone to throw a plank to me. The Republicans of Kansas refused to throw a plank in my direction, but the Populists did not refuse. On the contrary, they threw an excellent plank in my direction, and I stepped on it. I didn't step on the whole platform, but just on the woman suffrage plank.

"I went forward at the close of the convention out there and told the men how glad I was to see one of the dominant parties take up woman suffrage. I said that I had been working and hoping for just such action for years, that we first thought of asking for the assistance of the big political parties twenty years ago, and ever since then had been at them. Here I said, is a party in power that is likely to remain in power, and if it will give its indorsement to our movement, we want that indorsement.

"I do not claim to know anything of the merits of the issues that brought the Populist party into existence. All I know about the party is that it is composed of the rank and file of the Republican party of the state, and that its existence is due to the fact that the men, who compose it, think that certain methods for the correction of existing evils in the national government that neither of the other big parties will try are methods likely to prove efficacious methods. I do not pretend to know whether the Populists are right. They are protestants against the existing order of things, and certainly no one will deny that there is ground for protest. I do not indorse their platform, but I would be one of the last to condemn an honest protest, such as they are making, until I knew that they were in the wrong.

"I am first and last for woman suffrage, and this much I will say: I would rather that those men who favor woman suffrage would have the conduct of the government than those who will do nothing for us should have it."

"But Miss Anthony," said the reporter, "it has always been generally understood that you are a strong Republican."

"Why has it been understood that I am a Republican?" asked Miss Anthony. "Simply because a majority of those men who have been inclined to give us what we want have been Republicans. I am speaking of the national legislators now. While a majority of the Republicans may not have been in favor of giving us suffrage, a majority of those who have been willing to give us our rights have been Republicans.

"Suppose the Republican party of this state, at its coming convention, refuses to entertain a proposition from us that it shall indorse woman suffrage. Suppose then that we go to the Democrats at their convention with the same request that we have made to the Republicans and the Democrats do as we ask them to do. Then my action with the Democrats would be just what it was with the Republicans of Kansas."

"Well, suppose that this situation that you have outlined should come about and you should get everything that you want from the constitutional convention and the people. Would you vote for the Democratic candidates at the first election at which you could legally cast a ballot?"

Miss Anthony pondered this question a moment and then said that she could not say what party she will vote with when she possesses the right to cast her ballot with men.

"Would you be an independent?" asked the reporter.

"No, I think not; I would join one of the dominant political parties. But I don't care to say anything about that now. I am for woman suffrage now and will work with any party of power that will help us. Remember I said 'with' not 'for.' The trouble for us all along has been the knowledge on the part of the politicians that we would vote intelligently. If the men who run the machines had thought that women could be handled by party leaders, we would have had our rights long ago."

Finally, Miss Anthony was asked to give her opinion of the prospects of the suffrage amendment to the constitution. She cared to say only that she considers it a favorable sign that the suffrage committee of the convention, in accepting adverse reports on a number of the amendments, reserved the woman suffrage proposition from its vote.[1]

Rochester *Democrat and Chronicle*, 23 June 1894.

[23 June 1894]

"I am a member of none of the political parties," said Miss Anthony. "We are striving to get our movement before the attention of every voter, so that he may intelligently understand what we want. Now, if we can get the great political parties to adopt a plank favoring our movement, why you see we obtain the aid to our cause of all their working machinery. It becomes a feature of the campaign, the party newspapers will discuss it, and we can have our workers and speakers go right into their mass meetings and address their audiences. In this way we can reach every voter.

"So in Kansas. There are two parties in that State, the Republicans and the People's party. We appealed to the Republicans, but they took no action either for or against. The Populists listened to us and have favored our movement. That allows us to present our facts at all their meetings throughout the State.

"As regards this State my position is the same. If the constitutional convention decides to submit our proposition to the people, we shall appeal to the first political convention held this fall. Suppose it is the Republican. Should they spurn us, we would appeal to the Democratic convention. Did they incorporate into their platform our proposition then our forces would work for that party. We want that party to be in power that favors woman suffrage."

~ *Rochester Union and Advertiser*, 23 June 1894.

1. In addition to woman suffrage, the suffrage committee of the convention in New York had before it more than two dozen proposals regarding qualifications for male voters, compulsory voting, and how new citizens would qualify to vote.

226 ~ ECS TO LILLIE DEVEREUX BLAKE

Thomaston Long Island[1]   June 26 [*1894*]

Dear Mrs Blake

An article of mine in The Sun & Recorder on Sunday looks like an abstract of your speech before the Con. con.[2] A singular coincidence I read your speech in The Journal yesterday very good   I took my facts from my old speech of '67.³ I think you made one mistake in using "men" as an adjective you should have said the "male" people especially as "male" is the word used in the Con. I send you Susans lamentations over Kansas quite equal to Isaiah & Jeremiah.⁴ But it is enough to make a saint swear to see women so wheedled by mere politicians. I think Susan & Annie Shaw took the right position Blackwell is a republican first & woman suffrage afterward.⁵ Kate Field calls it an "unholy alliance"⁶ I'll send you her paper. It is wonderful how tenderly new converts feel lest we should injure the cause. Kate has been converted within the last year & now sits in judgement on Susan. What is silver coinage, tariff, or income tax to us compared with our inalienable rights to life liberty & happiness? Yours as ever

～ E. C. S.

[*in margins of first page*] You need not return Susan's letter put it with your posthumous papers

～ ALS, Lillie D. Blake Papers, MoSHi.

1. ECS was again with Gat and Augusta Stanton in Nassau County, New York. Less than a month later she indicated that she wrote from Great Neck (below at July 20). It is not known if they moved or if ECS learned a different way to direct her mail. Thomaston, not yet a village and often referred to as Great Neck, did have its own post office.

2. *New York Recorder*, 24 June 1894, not in *Film*. This was the same open letter to constitutional convention delegates published by the *Woman's Tribune*, 30 June 1894, *Film*, 32:915. The *Woman's Journal*, 23 June 1894, published Lillie Blake's speech to the constitutional convention's suffrage committee on May 31. ECS's article and Blake's speech both reviewed the progress toward universal suffrage made by previous constitutional conventions and both urged that if "male" remained as a qualification for suffrage, then the preamble should be rewritten to begin, "We, the men people of the State of New-York."

3. ECS spoke in the Assembly Chamber to the judiciary committees of both houses of the New York legislature on 23 January 1867. See *Film*, 11:892–1046.

4. Enclosure missing. The Old Testament books of Isaiah and Jeremiah recount the dire prophecies of these two men. Isaiah's conviction about the triumph of righteousness, however, stands in contrast to Jeremiah's despair, memorialized in the word jeremiad.

5. In "The Situation in Kansas," *Woman's Journal*, 16 June 1894, Henry Blackwell opined, "If woman suffrage were the sole question at issue, the natural and proper thing would be to go with the Populists and fight it out on party lines.... But, such is not the case.... While the Populists deserve and

should receive the commendation due to courage and consistency, and have the enthusiastic support of all women who believe in the Populist programme, the State Woman Suffrage Association should remain non-partisan, and each individual woman should feel free to ally herself with whatever party she approves."

6. Kate Field (1838–1896), journalist and editor, published her weekly, *Kate Field's Washington*, from 1890 to 1895. Acquainted with ECS and SBA for several decades, she had kept her distance from the suffrage movement. In 1893 and 1894, she offered qualified support for the cause, first at the Columbian Exposition and later in a surprise appearance at the National-American's Washington convention. Her editorial about SBA and the Kansas Populists, "An Unholy Alliance," oozed scorn for the People's party and criticized SBA's alliance as old-fashioned politics by "barter and sale" and as an unseemly courtship and marriage. Suffragists should "keep away from all political conventions and turn their batteries on their own sex," she advised. (*Film*, 32:929; *NAW*; *ANB*; Gary Scharnhorst, *Kate Field: The Many Lives of a Nineteeth-Century American Journalist* [Syracuse, N.Y., 2008], 217–18; *History*, 4:235.)

227 ❧ ECS TO ANNA H. SHAW

Thomaston, P.O. Long Island [*N.Y.*] July 9th [*1894*]

Dear Anna Shaw,

Yes you & Susan did "stir them up" & to my mind you did the right thing.

Susan's plank the drowning is a good illustration. What is finance, tariff, tax on incomes to us compared with the ↑emancipation↓ of half the people of the country especially as all these questions cannot be wisely adjusted until viewed from the feminine as well as the masculine standpoint. "Must have <u>force</u> behind the ballot." Well look at the present complicated condition of our country, there is plenty of <u>force</u> on both sides, but they wait to settle their difficulties by <u>arbitration</u>!! Kind regards to all the faithful under your roof. yours as ever

❧ *Elizabeth Cady Stanton.*

❧ ALS, A-68 Mary Earhart Dillon Collection, Series XI, Box 20, MCR-S.

228 ~≈~ SBA TO ECS

Rochester, N.Y., July 19, 1894.

My Dear Mrs Stanton

Here are the <u>Kansas</u> Populist, Republican & Democratic platforms—[1] For the life of me I can't see any great difference—that should make such a howl against the Populists— The Prohibition Party's financial planks were nothing different[2]—the main points of difference is—that

<u>Dem's</u>	a flat-fotted against—the amendment[3]	
Repub's—	Silent	
Pops.—	———	for ——— ———
Prohibs[4]—	———	for ———

But the Republicans are cooling <u>down</u>—out there—and saying that every suffrage republican will vote <u>for</u>—no matter what his ↑party↓ platform says or doesnt say—that the suffrage Populists—will also—even the suffrage Democrats will also—

So that the good ↑that↓ will come—will be the discussion—& that is what we are after—

I tell you—I grow more & more restiff under the hateful subjection—every day— The utter complacency with which decent men bid us be patient—it is coming in due time—& then do nothing to help its coming— Lovingly yours

~≈~ *Susan B. Anthony*

[*on verso of second page*] N.B.—Please return these when you are done with them—I may need to refer to them—[5] S. B. A

~≈~ ALS, on Campaign Committee letterhead, Smith Family Papers, Manuscript Division, NN.

1. Enclosures missing. The Republican State Central Committee published the platforms of the state's four parties in a pamphlet, headed *The State Platforms*, available at the Kansas State Historical Society.

2. Populists and Republicans alike favored bimetallism, the use of both gold and silver to set the standard of money, and parity between government-

issued paper money and the two metals. With only slight difference in emphasis, the Prohibition party platform sought an expansion of the supply of money and unlimited coinage of silver.

3. The final plank of the Democratic platform read, "We oppose woman suffrage as tending to destroy the home and family, the true basis of political safety, and express the hope that the helpmeet and guardian of the family sanctuary may not be dragged from the modest purity of self-imposed seclusion to be thrown unwillingly into the unfeminine places of political strife."

4. Wording of the People's party plank is above at 13 June 1894. The Prohibition party plank read: "Recognizing the right of suffrage as inherent in citizenship, the Prohibition party stands unequivocally pledged to use its utmost efforts to secure the adoption of the pending constitutional amendment for the enfranchisement of the women of Kansas."

5. In a note to Elizabeth Miller, ECS wrote on this letter, "Read enclosed scraps & send to Susan".

229 ❧ ECS TO JOHN BIGELOW

Great Neck Long Island [*N.Y.*] July 20th [*1894*]

Hon John Bigelow Dear sir

Perhaps an amendment based on an educational & property qualification for woman suffrage, might meet with more favor.[1] Please propose it & much oblige yours sincerely

❧ *Elizabeth Cady Stanton.*

❧ ALS, John Bigelow Papers, NSchU.

1. Newspapers reported on this and the previous day that the constitutional convention's suffrage committee voted to report adversely all proposals for woman suffrage. This announcement came after difficult negotiations inside the committee. Earlier in July, members formed a sub-committee chaired by Edward Lauterbach to "investigate" what the committee could do. On July 17, Lauterbach's committee, by a narrow three to two vote, reported favorably on a proposal that the question of woman suffrage be sent to the voters as a separate question. Although the suffrage committee rejected that recommendation, the full constitutional convention eventually debated the proposal on separate submission. (Rochester *Democrat and Chronicle*, 14 & 20 July 1894, the former in *Film*, 32:962; *New York Times*, 18 July 1894.)

230 ❧ SBA to Elizabeth Smith Miller

Rochester, N.Y., July 25—1894.

My Dear Friend

Yours of Sunday is before me—its enclosures all right— Dear Mrs Greenleaf returned to Albany yesterday full of hope that the Con. Con. will reject the Majority report of the Committee—the friends in the Con. held a private meeting—& among them—they found there were 70 members ready to vote <u>for</u> submitting our amendment—the number needed is 88— No—I am not disappointed nor disheartened for myself—but I do feel very sorry for the thousands of new and young women who have had such strong hope of gaining our demand— I am used to having defeat every time—and know how to pick up & push on for another attack upon the enemy—

New York Republicans are nothing like as cruel as are the Kansas Republicans—for they have never pledged anything—whereas those of Kansas have— they by a strict party vote gave Municipal suffrage to the women—they almost solidly submitted the amendment—the women in return had almost without exception either carried the last elections in the 286 cities of the state over to the Republicans—or had greatly increased their old majorities— I think but with one exception—they owe their supremacy over the Democrats & Populists to the women of the cities— And no one dreamed of their <u>not</u> <u>endorsing</u> the am't when their State Con. should be held—but alas—their wire-pullers—to make sure of whipping the Populists—had made "<u>an</u> <u>unholy Alliance</u>"—ala Kate Field—with the German Democrats—that if they would vote the Republican ticket—their platform would be <u>silent</u> not ↑only↓ on Prohibition but on woman suffrage also— So the women of Kansas were traded off for the Whiskey Democracy—every one of whom can go into the Republican meetings this Fall and traduce women & their rights to their hearts content—while not a friend of ours will be permitted to advocate the measure— Even Mrs Johns—<u>begins</u> to <u>see</u> <u>this</u>—already— and then the Repub's expect me to shout halleluyahs to them—and not say a thank you to the poor but honest <u>old</u> <u>farmers</u> of the Populist party—for putting a plank in their platform— Well—I haven't fallen so

low as that yet—but it is awfully hard to hear all the cuts that come—
from all Republican quarters— But it always costs a good deal to seem
even to stand by the poor & despised— I enclosed an interview—not
very near but still about as good as can be—from a boy who knows very
little of politics & much less of our reform—[1] Lovingly yours

~ Susan B. Anthony

~ ALS, on Campaign Committee letterhead, Smith Family Papers, Manuscript Division, NN.

1. Enclosure missing.

231 ~ SBA TO ECS

Rochester, N.Y., Aug. 19, 1894.

My Dear Mrs Stanton

Your Post-Card of yesterday is here this noon— I couldn't possibly go to you on Friday—because I must be here Sept. 6th to receive my $1,000— Legacy—from Mrs Clapp—of this City—which is promised then[1]—and beside—I had just failed to meet Miss Shaw—in our flittings to and fro—and so decided to meet her at the Cassadaga Camp meeting—Lily Dale—Aug. 22d— And lo on getting home an invitation— pledging me $20— & expenses—was waiting which made it additionally pleasant & easy to go!! Then brother Dan's— D. R. Jr. is to be here ↑in↓ the last of this week—& perhaps Dan himself—then beside—it did seem to me I must have a little of my home— It is so delightful with just Sister Mary & myself—& our good girl Sarah!! Then after the 6th of Sept—will come the Republican Convention the 18th and the Democratic Convention the 25th at Saratoga—and of course I must be in Saratoga for that full week—[2] Then the Populist State Committee of Kansas is calling on me to fill my pledge in the October Campaign in that state—[3] And Mrs Greenleaf and all in this state are protesting & declaring I shall not give another ↑hour↓ to Kansas—that I owe all of myself to New York—and should, at once enter into the new campaign—the new attack upon the Legislature of 1895—for all our friends in the Con. Con. say that with our splendid petition to—and vote in the Con. Con. our demand has received such a momentum—as that—with the added work upon the State Conventions, and the 2 or 3 hundred thousand additional signatures to a petition direct to the Legislature, that body cannot, will not refuse to submit the proposition!![4] And should it do so—the next Legislature that can act upon it—ratify it—will be that of 1897—& passing that it will come to a vote at the election of that year—1897—thus we should virtually have <u>three years</u> of or for good solid educational work—added to the one we have just had—making us four solid years of educational work toward the immediate practical end of carrying our question to the electors of the state— The plan is to, at once, send into every county organizing & petition agents—to

1st Crystalize the Campaign Committees, county & local—into permanent Political Equality Clubs—and

2d to set them all at the work of securing as many <u>additional</u> signatures to the petition as possible—not <u>duplicate names</u> of those on the Con. Con. petitions—but names of all who did not sign that—this we are to do in the hope of yet reaching the <u>Million</u> for which we started!

Then I have a letter—giving me until <u>November 20</u>th to complete the Cyclopedia article—so that to get any time at all to be with you—I shall have to make two bites of a cherry—[5] Then there is another home attraction—and that is that the last of September Miss Willard & Miss Gordon are to bring Lady Henry Somerset—<u>Lady "Isabel"</u>—I like better—to visit me—and I must not miss this chance— I will see, tomorrow, if I cannot arrange so as not to be here the 6th of Sept—fix it so that my Lawyer can receive the money for me— If he can—then I will plan to go to you right after the 24th inst—& stay until Sept. 18th and then go again to you at once after the election for the two weeks—but my dear—do you make "<u>Jimmy Grind</u>" out that article so that I shall need only to say "<u>amen</u>" to it— The world is so full of work & in so many places at the same time—that I do not which thing to do first— Lovingly yours to start in anew—

                                           Susan B. Anthony

ALS, on NAWSA letterhead, AF 24(1), Anthony Family Collection, CSmH.

1. The attorneys were not ready for their day in court in September; "Oh the delays of the law—& the utter heedlessness of the lawyers as to a woman's time," SBA lamented in her diary. The pattern was repeated on October 3 and October 5. SBA signed the receipt for her legacy in Bourbon County, Kansas, on October 24. After inheritance taxes were subtracted from the bequest, she

received $943.25. (Estate of Eliza J. Clapp, case file 1892-122, Surrogate Court of Monroe County, New York; SBA diary, 5 September, 3, 5 October 1894, *Film*, 32:1ff.)

2. All chances for favorable action on woman suffrage from the constitutional convention ended on 15 August 1894. On August 2, the suffrage committee reported adversely on all amendments and gained the convention's approval for debate on Gideon Tucker's minority report on a proposal that voters should decide the question about removing "male" from the constitution. Made a special order of business for evening sessions of the convention, this debate began August 8. It continued into the evening of Thursday, August 9, resumed on Tuesday, August 14, and concluded on August 15. At the end of that Wednesday evening, the suffrage committee's report against taking any action on woman suffrage was sustained by a vote of ninety-eight to fifty-eight. The campaign then turned its attention to the state political conventions for endorsements. (*Revised Record of the Constitutional Convention*, 2:43-47, 192-223, 268-305, 404-46, 490-562; Document No. 43, "Minority Report from Mr. Tucker, of the Committee on Suffrage," 5:555-59.)

3. SBA joined the Populist party campaign in Kansas from October 24 to November 5, speaking in Kansas City, Fort Scott, Columbus, Girard, Lawrence, Enterprise, Holton, Burlington, Emporia, Clay Center, and Topeka. For reports of some of these events, see *Film*, 32:1095, 1102-5, 1112.

4. New York's constitution provided for amendments to be proposed to the legislature, approved by a majority of both houses, approved again by majorities in the subsequent legislature, and then submitted to the voters. It was this path that woman suffragists planned to follow in the wake of their defeat at the constitutional convention. (N.Y. Const. of 1846, Art. 13, sec. 1.)

5. This was their jointly authored entry "Women's Rights" in Charles Kendall Adams, ed., *Johnson's Universal Cyclopaedia, A New Edition*, 8:819-21, published in 1895 and in *Film*, 34:867-69. They had found a day to work on the entry in April 1894, and they resumed work at the end of November. (SBA to C. K. Adams, 16 September 1892; SBA diary, 15 April, 27 November-17 December 1894; and ECS to Clara B. Colby, 19 April 1894; all in *Film*, 30:417-19, 31:879ff, 32:1ff, 746-47.)

232 ECS TO THE EDITOR, NEW YORK *SUN*

Great Neck, L.I., [*N.Y.,*] Aug. 21, 1894.

To the Editor of The Sun—Sir:[1] I am asked how I feel about the action of the Constitutional Convention on the suffrage question.

Suppose I had had a fine estate left me, with executors who, as prodigals, were in extravagance, dissipation, fraud, and corruption, rapidly depriving my children and myself of the means of future livelihood. Then suppose I had applied to the courts to vindicate my rights, to appoint new executors, or to allow me to administer the estate. Then suppose my appeal was made to a small body composed mainly of very ordinary men, who said they could do nothing, that the case was not of sufficient consequence for the consideration of so august a body, or even to submit it for adjudication to a more ordinary body, the people.

In the nature of things how must a woman feel under such circumstances? Depressed, indignant, humiliated, anxious and apprehensive for the future. That is as I feel now.

The condition of our country, the disgraceful proceedings in Washington, the strikes, the terrible revelations of the wholesale corruption in our metropolis and in every department of Government, as well as in the business world, brought to light by investigating committees;[2] the rapid concentration of wealth in the hands of the few, all this fills me with apprehension as to the safety and stability of a government composed of men alone. Women and children have equal rights and interests in this heritage left us by the fathers, and I am not willing to trust our future welfare in such hands as administer our Government to-day.

If we stand parleying with such classes in power another half century the mass of the people will have no rights, privileges, or immunities for which to contend. We must prepare at once for political action, and inaugurate a people's party. Rejected by Republicans and Democrats, our political aristocracy, we must cast our lot with the laboring masses, of whom many thousand joined us in our petition for the right of suffrage.

If we are to save anything from the wreck of our national fortunes, we must try some new methods of action at once. When ninety-seven men can play football with the rights of half the people in the State, and that half meekly accept the abject condition of mere subjects, in a so-called republic, in direct violation of every principle of our Government, the women of the Empire State might as well be under the Czar of Russia as the American flag. We have plead our cause in Congress and courts and the halls of State legislation, but failed, thus far, at every point. What next? The excuse of the ninety-seven men who voted "No" was frivolous to the last degree. They said "the majority of the women of the State did not make the demand."

Have the majority of lawyers of the State asked for the proposed changes in the judiciary article?

Have the majority of the people in New York city asked for the proposed changes in the method of governing our metropolis?³

⇝ Elizabeth Cady Stanton.

⇜ New York *Sun*, 24 August 1894.

1. Charles A. Dana.
2. The Lexow Committee, created by the Republican-led state senate, began investigating corruption in New York City in the spring of 1894 and reported back to the legislature in January 1895. While committee members took a summer break, prosecutors pressed charges against city police officers, beginning in mid-July, and exposed the extent of Tammany Hall's use of the police force for graft.
3. Two of the largest changes under discussion in the constitutional convention, the first would reorganize the state's courts, while the second promised to reduce the legislature's direct governance of chartered cities. Neither measure was adopted by the convention until September. (Lincoln, *Constitutional History of New York*, 3:337-75, 626-52.)

233 ⇝ SPEECH BY SBA AT CASSADAGA LAKE FREE ASSOCIATION

> EDITORIAL NOTE: It was Woman's Day at Lily Dale on 22 August 1894; cottages were decorated with yellow bunting, banners hung from the camp's gates, and most of the twenty-four hundred people in the audience wore yellow ribbons. When Henry Blackwell, the morning's scheduled speaker, failed to show up, SBA accepted the request of the Chautauqua County Political Equality Club that she fill the time. Anna Shaw spoke for two hours in the afternoon. The county club reported that one hundred and seventy dollars was raised to help with the next stage of the New York State campaign. (*Woman's Journal*, 8 September 1894, *Film*, 32:1023.)

[22 August 1894]

"This is a Liberal Camp," said Miss Anthony, "in spirit and in truth. It is an interesting fact that the Spiritists of America are also woman suffragists and that every meeting which they hold in the name of Spiritism is also held in the name of woman's rights. If, instead of Spiritists, this great body of people called themselves Baptists, Presbyterians, Methodists or Catholics, their praises for the firm stand they have taken for the enfranchisement of the larger half of the people of this country would have been everywhere sung in song and told in story. But the suffragists of America have been also afraid to give voice to the 'thank you' which has always been in their hearts, for Spiritism in days gone by has been fully as unpopular as woman suffrage; and they were afraid if they displayed too great a gratitude for the indorsement of the Spiritists that the public would at once pronounce them Spirtists and they would thus be doubly damned. But there are a few of our members who are brave enough to rejoice in the damnation of orthodox religions and orthodox politics.[1]

"I am not so disappointed in the result with the Constitution Convention as I might be. It is an ill-wind that blows nobody good. This is not a Waterloo, but a Bunker Hill defeat.[2] It only means that we will take a breath, renew and double our forces and renew our attack. Had the Constitution Convention consented to submit the question of woman suffrage to the voters this fall, I doubt if we could have carried our point. The people at large are not educated up to it, and we should have had insufficient time to have enlightened them.

"Now what do we propose to do? Just this. We are going to present a 1,000,000 named petition to the New-York Legislature next winter to pass a resolution submitting the question of striking the word 'male' from the Constitution. This resolution will have to be passed upon by a second legislature in '97 before it comes to popular vote. So we will have two full years in which to do effective work in woman suffrage education. It is a mistake to suppose that the ballot for women is lost for at least 20 years to come. It will come in two years. I am certain of it. We have every reason to feel encouraged. In 1867 the Constitution Convention voted down the suffrage amendment by a vote of 140 to 19. In '94 the Convention stood 94 against and 58 in favor of woman suffrage. Note the ratio of increase in our favor. I tell you that in 1897 we shall win the long-fought fight. Dr. Vincent over at Chautauqua thinks he is teaching the young women to be only proficient in arts, sciences and religion. He will find that his chickens will turn out to be ducks. When he has given the young women the inch of education, they will take the ballot ell.[3] I want to say right here that the educational power in favor of universal freedom of thought which is continually flowing out from Lily Dale is not to be surpassed by any other lecture platform in the world."

Miss Anthony closed her remarks with a strong plea for money to carry on a systemized campaign. She said that their leaders were born economists and that they could do double the amount of agitation with half the money that men could. The first dollar ever contributed to the Constitution-convention work was contributed at Lily Dale last summer in a nest-egg of $59, which proved to be a magnet which attracted a multiplied sum, and she was going to give the camp a chance to do the same thing this year.[4]

~ *Buffalo Express*, 23 August 1894.

1. When this sentence appeared in the *Buffalo Express* and upset her religious friends, SBA disputed its accuracy. The misquotation led people to think she praised "Spiritualists at the expense of orthodox people." She had said, she wrote to a friend, "There are still a few of us brave enough to rejoice in every good word and work said and done by whomsoever, for women, and publicly express our thanks therefor, notwithstanding the 'denunciation' (not damnation) of orthodox religionists and orthodox politicians." (SBA to Friend, 29 August 1894, *Film*, 32:1038-39.)

2. At Waterloo in 1815, Napoleon's decisive defeat marked the end of his rule, whereas the Continental army's defeat at the Battle of Bunker Hill in 1775 did not determine the outcome of the American Revolution.

3. An English unit of measure.

4. At Lily Dale on 25 August 1892 (not 1893), before the New York Constitutional Convention was postponed, SBA raised money for the amendment campaign. (*Woman's Tribune*, 10 September 1892.)

234 ~ ECS TO THE EDITORS, *WOMAN'S JOURNAL*

[*before 1 September 1894*]

Editors Woman's Journal:

There is a growing feeling among thoughtful people that the thousands of uneducated foreigners landing every day on our shores should not so soon be admitted to the governing power of this country.[1] The law says they must be naturalized first, and be here a certain length of time; but who keeps the record of their arrival and the prescribed time from the steerage to the polls?

In a heated election, politicians care more for party success than for the welfare of the State, and then the "interested vote" buys up the "ignorant vote." I think we should have at least a qualification of reading and writing and ability to understand the English language. This would help to make our people homogeneous, and, as it would take most foreigners at least two years to accomplish this, we should be sure that they had been in the country long enough to know something of the spirit of its institutions. There are many good reasons why we should have an educational qualification.

1. It would limit the foreign vote.

2. It would decrease the ignorant native vote by stimulating the rising generation to learning. Children in the street would say to each other: "You better go to school if you hope to vote when you are twenty-one."

3. It would dignify the right of suffrage in the eyes of our people to know that some preparation was necessary for the exercise of so important a duty.

An attainable qualification in no way conflicts with our popular theory of "universal suffrage," of "suffrage a natural right." On the same principle that we say a man must be twenty-one for a legal voter, so we may say he must read and write the English language with ease and understanding.

We cannot take the right from those who already exercise it; but we can say that, after 1898, no one shall be permitted to vote unless he can read and write the English language.

One of the most patent objections to woman suffrage is the added ignorant and depraved vote that would still further corrupt and embarrass the administration of our Government.[2] Thus we are deprived of the influence of educated, virtuous, law-abiding women in our public affairs for fear of the ignorance of the masses. Several of the women who enrolled themselves as remonstrants in our late campaign in New York said they would favor educated woman suffrage, but they thought our ignorant vote was already far too large for the safety and stability of our Government.

The intelligent, organized laboring men were hampered in the recent strikes by the violent, unreasoning, ignorant voters, whose folly they could not control.[3]

It is the interest of the educated working-men, as it is of the women, that this ignorant, worthless class of voters should be speedily diminished. With free schools and compulsory education, there is no excuse in this country for ignorance of the elements of learning.

On this point the senior editor of the *Woman's Journal*, in a recent editorial, said:

> The recent serious disturbances throughout the West by large bodies of ignorant voters have intensified the very general feeling that suffrage should have certain reasonable limitations of personal character and intelligence. To reform politics we must reform the constituency. To recall a vested right is impossible, but to double the vote by admitting all women seems to many another step in a wrong direction. Why not extend suffrage to responsible, intelligent women only, on reasonable qualifications of personal fitness, and thus elevate the body politic? The admission of a new class offers a golden opportunity.

In a speech at South Framingham, Rev. Charles G. Ames recently said:

> Call a halt on unconditional cheap suffrage! Let me suggest a plan: From and after Jan. 1, 1901, let all new applicants for registration as voters pass an examination. Let those who can discriminate between the executive, legislative and judicial branches of government, men or women, be admitted, and let all others be excluded. We can no longer afford to include all masculine ignorance and exclude all feminine intelligence. Have a moderate qualification, easily ascertained, for all qualified citizens to enter, and no others. Take suffrage from no one who now has it, but enter the new century with a new set of books. "Strike for that which ought to be; God will bless the blows!"[4]

~ *Elizabeth Cady Stanton*

~ *Woman's Journal*, 1 September 1894.

1. The *Woman's Journal*, 4 August 1894, published two endorsements of educated suffrage, quoted by ECS below. The editors published the speech of Charles Ames, who moved from Philadelphia to Boston in 1889, at Woman's Day at a Chautauqua event in Massachusetts, in which he made the argument that "None should vote but those who know how." In an editorial, Henry Blackwell seconded Ames. The legal targets of ECS's ire in this response are

imprecise. New York and Massachusetts did require that immigrants become citizens before they were enfranchised, and citizenship required the kind of residence she recommended. However, eighteen states enfranchised immigrants as soon as they filed a declaration of intent to become citizens. Naturalized citizens seeking to vote in Massachusetts were already required to read and understand the federal and state constitutions before enfranchisement. In the northern states, Maine, Connecticut, and Wyoming had similar constitutional provisions, and in the South, North Carolina and Mississippi led the way. New York placed no such obstacle in the immigrant's path but it, along with California and Pennsylvania, imposed a waiting period between naturalization and enfranchisement, aimed at preventing a surge of new voters on the eve of an election. New York's proposed constitution of 1894 included a lengthening of that waiting period, but delegates rejected efforts to impose an educational qualification. (Alexander Keyssar, *The Right to Vote: The Contested History of Democracy in the United States* [New York, 2000], 117–59, Tables A.12, A.13; Lincoln, *Constitutional History of New York*, 3:78–80.)

2. This claim surfaced repeatedly at New York's constitutional convention, in the antisuffrage testimony offered to the suffrage committee on June 14 and in the delegates' debate in August. "We are now suffering in every State in this Union from the evil effects of a pauper and ignorant vote," one delegate declared in debate. "Now, if we allow the women to vote . . . I say we double that evil, and we endanger the stability and safety of the State." Under universal suffrage, he continued, "this ignorant vote, if you please, this pauper voter, if you please, would be doubled and the State would be at the mercy, not of its best, but probably of its worst citizens." (*Revised Record of the Constitutional Convention*, 2:287–88.)

3. Most notable was the Pullman Strike of the American Railway Union in June and July 1894.

4. The final lines of "For the Election," by George W. Clark, published in *The Liberty Minstrel* (1844).

235   SBA TO THOMAS E. BOWMAN[1]

Rochester, N.Y., Sept. 7th 1894.

My Dear friend Mr Bowman

Your very kind letter of Aug. 20th came duly—and every night— as my head was on my pillow—& I taking a review of the many things left undone—my resolve has been to answer your letter the very first thing the next morning—but alas, alas—my resolves—have failed! as you! What with my eye on the needs & wants of all the states—Kansas &

New York ↑most pressing, ~~and↓—the largest~~ of course—I am simply overwhelmed!!

I enclose you the new resolve of New-Yorkers to ~~reform~~ ↑reorganize↓ their forces—and march on to the Legislature!![2] The undertaking is herculean—but the momentum gained by the past years ↑unprecedented↓ work ↑and unparallelled gains↓ must not be lost!! And I <u>must</u> give myself to the officers here—to get all under way!!

Then the storm from somebody in Topeka—[3] I surely cannot imagine—who can have raised this ~~anew~~ ↑new outburst↓ <u>in agust,</u>—~~on~~ ↑based↓—so far as I can see, ↑on↓ <u>the incidents of last</u> ↑<u>May and</u>↓ <u>June</u>! certainly the "<u>true inwardness</u>" of it seems to ~~aim~~ ↑be that↓ of hitting and hurting all round! and because of this sort of shot-gun fire—it looks to me as if the article ↑of Aug 14↓ you enclosed,—& a similar one in the Chicago <u>Record</u>—of Aug 22^d—<u>from</u> Topeka,—~~and~~ bearing the same ear-marks[4]—had no other possible purpose but to get somebody—of our folks—to acknowledge there was a quarrel— They were <u>feelers</u> put out—to draw out somebody to answer the various charges—and I was very sorry to see <u>any</u> <u>sort</u> of notice taken of the scurrilous stuff! Still— I, like Mrs Johns,—rushed into the mesh—[5] I did it for the one purpose of exonerating ~~her~~ ↑Mrs Johns↓ from the ↑money↓ charges against her—and yet she writes me—I made the made the matter <u>vastly</u> <u>worse</u> for her!! Whereas in her rebuttal[6]—she gave herself away—by saying there was an interference of the National with the State—which—if there was—What was it?— The only measures—or attitude discussed ↑—or demanded by Miss Shaw & me↓—were that of <u>planks</u> in the Repub. ↑an↓ Pop. platforms—and that <u>no</u> <u>political</u> <u>party's</u> <u>interests,</u> should be allowed to sway us? Does Mrs Johns wish it understood that <u>she opposed us on either of those points</u>?—

The <u>in</u>harmony it seems to me—comes from Mrs Johns inability to accept—or offer opportunity—for a full & free interchange of opinions & views—at Kansas City May 4th, <u>before</u> opening the Spring Campaign!— She called no meeting of conference of her State Com—& the three national speakers ~~there~~ ↑there to help on the work— Mrs↓ Chapman Catt, Shaw & Anthony—~~and~~ ↑together with↓ other speakers from outside & inside the State—Mrs Jenkins, Mrs Child ↑Mrs Thurston, Miss Kimber↓ &c— I think full & free interchange of views & feelings at the beginning of the campaign would have resulted in all agreeing upon <u>one</u> <u>line</u> of action—instead of each going ↑out↓ alone & talking her own individual ideas—as to measures— But that cant be helped now—and all that grew out of it—ought to be dropped all round— I am sorry I put my word in that item to the Journal—and I am sure that Miss Shaw has had no hand in raising this late commotion—since she has had no correspondence with anybody in Topeka— The Journals article—was from <u>nobody's friend</u>—that I can see—but simply ↑from somebody who wished↓ to start up a <u>sensational</u> lot of stuff for the benefit of the trade!!

You say Mrs Johns has said nothing hard of any ↑one↓ that she expected ~~to~~ ↑would↓ report—or repeat it— No doubt—that is equally true of Miss Shaw & all other persons— I <u>know</u>—that Miss Shaw & Mrs Chapman Catt & myself—felt exactly the same as to the points of discussion—that is ↑that↓ the <u>one hope</u> of carrying the amendment <u>overwhelmingly</u>—which we were working for—lay in getting <u>planks</u> in both platforms—and thereby <u>opening</u> the doors of <u>both</u> parties ↑through their↓ <u>papers</u> & meetings for a <u>full</u> & <u>favorable</u> discussion of the question, ↑<u>not</u>↓ <u>as a party measure</u> ~~of both~~ ↑but as a great principle of justice to the women of their own households.↓ Had Maj. Morrill chosen—had the <u>decent</u> men taken the reigns of the <u>Republican</u> Party— & given the approving word—there would to day be no <u>party</u> hate on the subject—both parties orators & editors would be vieing with each other to see which could influence most men to vote for ~~it~~ ↑the amendment↓!!— While now—the republicans are like the ↑fabled↓ "dog in the manger"—~~addage~~—they wont allow their speakers to advocate the am't—and are mad because the populists do—and are making <u>friends</u> for themselves by it!!

Nobody can be so fearfully sorry as I—that <u>I</u> ↑and all our national speakers↓ <u>cannot stand</u> on the <u>Kansas republican platform</u>—and <u>urge the amendment</u>— I did my level best to get them to take the one step— that would ~~permit the discussion~~ ↑enable them to permit us to stand there—↓ they rejected it—and now spurn us!! I am awfully sorry! but because <u>they wont</u>—I dont propose to say <u>I wont</u> speak on the <u>only</u> ↑parties↓ <u>platform</u> opened to the discussion!!— And I feel sure that the returning good sense of all—will help them to see that my possition— my attitude—is the true one—that of knowing <u>no party</u>—save for <u>its allegiance</u> to <u>freedom</u> ↑and franchise↓ <u>to women</u>!! that ~~is~~ ↑to women, is now↓ the <u>over</u>-topping—underlying principle of all parties ~~now~~!!

I am in receipt of sundry papers setting forth the pitiable sacrifice of all principles of honor by Lewelling[7] & his officials—to all of which—

my inward response is—that is exactly the same in <u>kind</u>, if not in <u>degree</u>—as with Gov. Humphreys[8] and all administrations in the past that had to, or <u>did</u> bargain with the <u>anti</u> suffrage & <u>anti</u> prohibition men, to go <u>easy</u> with the enforcement laws!— I do not doubt the catering and pandering to hold on to and catch the <u>lowest</u> voters of the slums of the cities of the state— But Maj. Morrill, himself, can do no differently, if elected,—with Cy Leland,[9] Murdock,[10] & Eskridge, at ↑et al—at↓ the head of his management—and the bargain he knows they made with the <u>antis</u>—he like Lewelling must hold to the party ↑managers↓ contract,—and shut his eyes to violations of laws. of There is no escape for the <u>individual</u> officer—so long as each set of party managers—wire pullers—manipulate and contract with the lowest down violators of the laws of the state for the suppression of Dives, Joints, brothels &c. &c— Not until there is a balance of power to be courted & won—on the other side—can the <u>viscious</u> system be abolished. And no one knew this better than Morrill—and yet he accepted his nomination and consented to take ↑undertake↓ the execution of the "<u>unholy alliance</u>"—the henchmen of the party had made!!

Hence, my dear friend,—I have taken my position—that since <u>no party</u> & <u>no official of it</u>—<u>can</u> be other than what has ↑they have↓ been— both in <u>state</u> & <u>national</u> affairs—in Kansas and everywhere—until women are made a balance of power—to be consulted, catered to and <u>bargained with</u>, if you please,—my <u>one</u> deciding article <u>of</u> <u>party</u> <u>creed</u>— shall be that of <u>woman suffrage</u>— All other articles of <u>party</u> creeds—are not even a feathers weight ↑shall be with me as a drop in the bucket↓ as compared with this one <u>vital</u> <u>one</u>—hence I make it <u>my whole</u> <u>party creed</u>!!

I am as deeply and keenly interested in the many reforms in city, state & national government as any one can possibly be—but I know↑ing↓ that no right solution can come ↑of any↓ great question can be reached until the whole people have a voice in it—I give all of myself to the making it ↑getting the↓ whole people inside the body politic, so as to be able to begin making even the first equation of ↑any of↓ the problems.

Thanking you most heartily for your letter—and hoping you will always feel free to suggest or criticise—and assuring you that my effort has been & will be for justice & the harmony that grows out of it—↑and with love to dear Mrs Bowman—I am↓ Very sincerely yours—

Susan B. Anthony

↩ ALS, on NAWSA letterhead for 1894, AF 23, Anthony Family Collection, CSmH. Marked in SBA hand "Reply to Mr Bowman"; probably draft for typist.

1. The probable recipient of this letter was Thomas Elliott Bowman (1834–1896), a businessman in Topeka with whom SBA and Laura Johns stayed in 1892 on the eve of the state Republican convention. He was highly regarded by the equal suffrage association for his support. Bowman and his second wife, Eliza Wilson Bowman (1840–1931), moved to Kansas from Boston in 1879. After many years in silk manufacture, Bowman formed a profitable mortgage company in his new home. Eliza Bowman founded the city's first kindergarten and presided over the Topeka Kindergarten Association. With financial help from her husband and other prominent residents of the city, the association conducted nine schools and trained teachers. (James L. King, ed., *History of Shawnee County, Kansas, and Representative Citizens* [Chicago, 1905], 488–89; Topeka *State Journal*, 25 May 1896, 8 June 1931; SBA diary, 29 June 1892, *Film*, 29:655ff.)

2. Enclosure missing. Jean Greenleaf issued a broadside dated 1 September 1894 calling upon New York's suffragists to carry on with rallies and petition work in order to appeal for legislative action in 1895. (*1894. Constitutional-Amendment Campaign Year*, 161–62.)

3. "Called a Traitor. Mrs. Laura M. Johns Must Be Deposed, Say the Eastern Women Managers," Topeka *State Journal*, 14 August 1894. The article crafted a story out of disagreements in May 1894 about whether to seek endorsement of the suffrage amendment from state Republicans and enhanced the old news with a pronouncement alleged to come from Anna Shaw: "I have a trinity of traitors. They are Judas Iscariot, Benedict Arnold, and Laura M. Johns." The reporter also insisted that the National-American had raised thirty thousand dollars for the Kansas campaign but would not turn it over to state workers until Laura Johns was removed from office.

4. In a special report from Topeka, "Woman Suffrage Row," *Chicago Record*, 23 August 1894, told essentially the same story. After Emma DeVoe sent the *Record*'s article to her, SBA asked her help in understanding who benefited from the stories, "for it hurts ↑or hits↓ all round about equally—Mrs Johns—Miss Shaw & me . . . I wish you would enlighten me—for I cannot imagine?—It cannot be any Populist can it?" Still puzzling over the problem, she added, "I cannot believe it all came out of Miss Shaw's & my intense earnestness to get a plank in Republican platform—& yet I know of no other sin on our part." (SBA to E. S. DeVoe, 31 August 1894, *Film*, 32:1042–43.)

5. SBA's contribution to the uproar has not been located.

6. In the Topeka *State Journal*, 18 August 1894, Laura Johns declared the earlier article's falseness in nearly every particular. She pointed out that only two thousand and three hundred dollars had been pledged to the campaign, one thousand of which had been turned over to state workers. She was confident that the remainder would arrive when the pledges were paid. Johns

conceded that a difference of opinion about the authority of state and national suffrage organizations did exist, but she believed "that Miss Shaw had nothing whatever to do with the publication of statements which call out this letter. She is making no fight on any officer of the Kansas Suffrage organization, and will be chagrined and justly indignant when she finds herself made to appear as the sort of bushwhacker this article advertises her." The *Journal* insisted on the accuracy of its report.

7. Lorenzo Dow Lewelling (1846–1900), the Populist governor of Kansas, was a candidate for reelection. During the campaign, his performance was subjected to harsh and wide-ranging criticism, but SBA focuses on the intersection of anti-prohibition and anti-suffrage politics in Kansas. To win Democratic votes, Republicans and Populists avoided enforcement of prohibition and consequently backed away from woman suffrage. (*ANB*.)

8. Lyman Underwood Humphrey (1844–1915) was the Republican governor of Kansas from 1889 to 1893. (*BDGov*.)

9. Cyrus Leland, Jr., (1841–1917) was the Republican boss of Kansas. Rarely holding elective office himself, he wielded power through the party, in which he was a national committeemen for several decades as well as a state leader. (*Kansas City Star*, 30 August 1917, Vertical files, KHi.) For more on SBA's charges about Leland's deals with liquor dealers in the election of 1894, see her interviews in Topeka on 9 July 1895, *Film*, 34:228–31.

10. Thomas Benton Murdock (1841–1909), publisher of the Republican paper in El Dorado, Kansas, served intermittently in the state senate until the Populists' victories in 1892 and was a manager of the party's gubernatorial candidate in 1894. (Volney P. Mooney, *History of Butler County, Kansas* [Lawrence, Kan., 1916], 480–84.)

236 ~ ARTICLE BY ECS

26 West 61st Street, New York [3 November 1894]

EDUCATED SUFFRAGE JUSTIFIED.

"Universal suffrage is the first truth and only basis of a genuine republic."[1] There may be certain restrictions, however, for the exercise of this right, without denying the general principle.

We have had, at different times, in the several States, eleven different classes disqualified for the suffrage, namely, idiots, lunatics, criminals, paupers, minors, men who bet on elections, clergymen (by custom not constitution) those not possessing $250, those who could neither read nor write, all black men, and all women black and white. Nine of these are surmountable qualifications, supposed to exist for the best interests of the State, but from which the citizen, with time and effort, may easily escape.

By modern scientific appliances, the idiot may develop sufficient intelligence to provide for his own wants and protect his rights. The lunatic may become sane. The criminal may be pardoned and reform. The pauper may become capable of self-support. The minor may come of age. The men who bet on elections may awake to the dishonor of violating the State Constitution, which every good citizen is bound to support. The penniless by thrift may acquire $250. The ignorant may learn to read and write. The clergy can change their profession, or convince the people (as they have done) that an interest in the State in no way conflicts with their holy mission to save the souls of their people.

But for the remaining two classes the disqualifications are insurmountable. Neither time nor effort can change sex or color; hence such disqualifications are indeed opposed to every principle of a true republic. Regulating the suffrage is one thing; denying it absolutely is another.

It seems to me the proposition for "educated suffrage" made and reiterated in the *Woman's Journal*, is preëminently wise and timely.[2] A law providing that after 1898 those who vote must be able to read and write the English language would be an immense advantage to the individual and the State. With the ignorant and impecunious from the Old World landing on our shores by hundreds every day, we must have some restrictions of the suffrage for our own safety and for their education before they take part in the administration of the government. Every man of them should be compelled to read and write the English language before they are allowed to register themselves as voters. This would be a double blessing—to them and to the State.

A knowledge merely of the elements of learning would give a man greater aptitude for his duties in all relations of life. What is learned in the primary department in school is the foundation for all that is achieved in the higher classes. If a foreigner can read and write the English language intelligently, he has taken the first step towards understanding the spirit of our institutions and the duties of citizenship.

In reply to Mr. Garrison I would say:[3] Instead of repealing the educational law of Massachusetts, which he deems a mere travesty, I would draw the line a little higher, at intelligent reading and writing. To acquire this would take the ignorant foreigner at least two years, so we should be sure that he did not go straight from the steerage to the polls.

The proposition, as stated in the *Woman's Journal*, involves no injustice to women, but provides that all educated men and women shall vote on the same basis. True, we cannot take the suffrage from the ignorant men who already exercise it, not because they prize it so highly, but because no political party dare make the experiment. If Mr. Garrison belonged to a disfranchised class he might more keenly feel the humiliation of a foreign yoke, such as educated women endure to-day: tried in the courts by foreign jurors and witnesses, who scarcely understand the language in which the advocate pleads the case and the judge gives the charge.

As to Miss Anna Gardner's[4] point on "class legislation," a law that would affect alike men and women, black and white, rich and poor, foreign and native, can hardly be called "class legislation." A law that would compel all American citizens to acquire a knowledge of their own language before exercising the suffrage, would surely be a stimulus in the right direction. A law compelling all our foreign citizens to read and write the English language would make our whole people more homogeneous and united.

The greatest block in the way of woman's enfranchisement, is the fear of the "ignorant vote" being doubled. Wise men see what a strain it is on our institutions to-day, and object to any further experiment in that direction. I do not see that the ignorant classes need the suffrage more than the enlightened, but just the reverse. When a vessel is in danger on a stormy sea, we need skill and intelligence on the bridge and at the wheel, to protect those who are ignorant of the science of navigation. Just so in the State we need the highest intelligence and morality to govern a nation with justice and wisdom.

"The first desire of every enlightened mind," says Matthew Arnold, "is to take part in the great work of government."[5]

↦ *Elizabeth Cady Stanton.*

↤ *Woman's Journal*, 3 November 1894.

1. From Charles Sumner, "Equal Rights of All," in Sumner, *Works*, 10:201; Sumner himself quoted Alphonse de Lamartine.

2. Contributors and editors of the *Woman's Journal* carried on the discussion of universal and educated suffrage. Henry Blackwell's editorial on 20 October 1894 reminded readers that woman suffragists in Massachusetts had always supported the state's educational qualification for voting and sought the vote only for women who met that qualification. On October 27, he countered supporters of universal suffrage with examples from cities where immigrants made up a substantial part of the population and political corruption flourished; to provide universal suffrage in those circumstances produced "slavery of the masses to political bosses, and a bastard aristocracy of thieves, liquor-sellers and gamblers, and of bribed and brutal policemen."

3. William Lloyd Garrison, Jr., became the designated defender of universal suffrage as the debate continued, and the editors allowed him to respond to other contributors before their essays and letters were published. In the issue of October 20, he seconded views expressed by Anna Gardner and briefly challenged some points made by Henry Blackwell and ECS.

4. Anna Gardner (1816-1901), an antislavery activist in Massachusetts and former teacher of the freedmen in North and South Carolina and Virginia, returned to her native Nantucket at the end of Reconstruction to write and lecture. She published books of poetry and essays in 1881 and 1892. Gardner took issue with Henry Blackwell's editorial of August 4, accusing him of introducing "class legislation" and surrendering "the basic principle of the woman suffrage movement." Gardner distinguished between ECS and Blackwell. Unlike Blackwell, she noted, ECS had reiterated in her first letter on the subject the importance of universal suffrage to "a genuine Republic." (*American Women*; with the assistance of Barbara White.)

5. The English educator Thomas Arnold (1795-1842), not his son Matthew (1822-1888), expressed this view, recorded in Arthur Penrhyn Stanley, *The Life and Correspondence of Thomas Arnold, D.D.* In the eighth American edition, 1870, the quotation is on page 179.

237   Remarks by SBA to the Gospel Suffrage Meeting, Cleveland

EDITORIAL NOTE: Anna Shaw was in charge of this Sunday afternoon Gospel Suffrage Meeting, held during the annual convention of the Woman's Christian Temperance Union. SBA, in Cleveland for an executive committee meeting of the National-American association, was just one of the speakers but the only one to be introduced by Frances Willard. "Once we would not have allowed the yellow ribbon here," Willard told the crowd, "but now it is intertwined with our white all over this hall. . . . I am honored to present Susan B. Anthony."

[18 November 1894]

As Miss Anthony stepped briskly to the front of the platform a storm of applause burst from the audience and almost all in the hall rose to their feet. She said:

"There was a time when Miss Willard introduced me to an audience like this and jeopardized her official head. That was only twelve years ago. I am glad you know that there is but one way to reach the denied goal and that is by the ballot.[1] (Applause.)

"I am expected to talk on gospel suffrage. What is that? It must be a political system whereby truth and justice may come uppermost in the government. I should think that might be called gospel suffrage.

"What is a democratic-republican form of government? It is a system of mathematics. Every election is the solution of a mathematical problem. In order to make the government what it should be, those who desire the right thing should be enfranchised. All the business interests of this country by which money can be made is put into one political scale. All those businesses, or nine out of ten, are conducted by men. When you go to a political body you will find at every one lobbyists watching out for the interest of their particular business; on the other hand, of all the moral and religious and educational instrumentalities, nine out of ten are women, who are disfranchised. The material must therefore pull down the scale. Tammany will settle back into the same old conditions again. Women are working in every way for legislation to enable them to pursue their work effectively and [I] stand here to say that as a rule they get nothing."

Then Miss Anthony gave the history of the murder at Troy of the young man who was fighting for pure politics and explained why Gov. Flower obeyed the wave of Senator Murphy's hand rather than the wishes of the memorial of women of the country.[2]

"You can accomplish very little," continued Miss Anthony. "You must if you secure legislation have people behind you with ballots in their hands, a balance of power. Women, we might as well be beautiful Newfoundland dogs out baying at the moon as petitioning legislatures while we have no vote. (Applause.)

"When we go up to a legislature we want those whom we come to petition to know that we can by our votes make or break individual politicians. Now women, if you have not pity for yourselves or self-respect for yourselves to want to vote you ought to have sympathy enough for the few men who are associated with us and are helpless until we gain the ballot to want to vote.

"We stand on a par with lunatics, convicts and pardoned criminals in the eyes of ignorant men and small boys. You can't change that opinion until our laws are amended and respect us."

~ *Cleveland Plain Dealer*, 19 November 1894. Square brackets surround word supplied by editors.

1. In Washington, 26 October 1881. See *Papers*, 4:116–17; SBA to Harriet H. Robinson, 17 November 1881, *Film*, 22:143–44; and Bordin, *Woman and Temperance*, 118–19.

2. On election day, 6 March 1894, Bartholomew Shea killed Robert Ross in a political brawl at a polling place in Troy, New York. Shea worked for the notorious political machine of New York's Democratic senator from 1893 to 1899 and former mayor of Troy, Edward Murphy, Jr. (1836–1911). Ross, from a rival group, had pledged to stop illegal voting at the polls. On 10 July 1894, Shea was sentenced to death, but appeals delayed the execution for more than a year. In December 1894, Governor Roswell Flower refused to commute Shea's sentence to life imprisonment, his successor refused in February, and Shea died in the electric chair on 11 February 1896. (*BDAC*; *Century Illustrated Magazine* 48 [July 1894]: 470–71.)

238 ~ From the Diary of SBA

[*18–23 November 1894*]

SUN. NOV. 18, 1894. In Cleveland—at Mrs Louise Southworths—844—Prospect street—

Spoke at 5 P.M. in Music Hall—at a "Gospel Suffrage meeting"—!!

MON. NOV. 19, 1894. In Cleveland—in Mr Will Southworth's lovely bay window—down stairs bedroom—large with bath room & closet room—[1]

Held all day Business meeting of the National[2]—with—Shaw, Dietrick, Stone Blackwell, Upton & self—Mrs Avery & J. K. Henry—absent—[3]

The Lucy Stone Mite Box Fund—the sad bone of contention—but all of the Com. were for its being a National Fund—for our disposal for Kansas work—except A. S. B. who protested—& declared it was not for the treasury—but should go direct to the Kansas Campaign Com[4]

In evening—The active Suffrage women from twelve states met me—in Mrs Southworths parlors—discussing the relation of the National to the States—

1. William J. Southworth (c. 1857–?), the oldest of the Southworth children, took over the W. P. Southworth Company after the death of his father and resided in his parents' home. (Federal Census, 1880; city directory, 1894.)

2. A very brief notice of this meeting, technically a meeting of the business committee, is in *Film*, 33:4. The chief topic known to the local reporter was auditing accounts of the Kansas campaign. SBA described it in advance as a meeting to talk about plans for all the states. (SBA to Laura Clay, 6 September 1894, *Film*, 32:1058–59.)

3. Josephine Kirby Williamson Henry (1846–1928) was elected one of the National-American association's auditors at the convention in 1894. A native of Kentucky who lived in Versailles, she worked closely with Laura Clay in the Kentucky Equal Rights Association. Henry joined the committee for the *Woman's Bible*, and Clay's antipathy to that project brought their collaboration to an end in 1899. Henry was also active in the Prohibition party, running for office on the party ticket in 1890 and 1894 and, in advance of the election of 1900, making news as a possible presidential candidate for the party. In 1900, she founded the National Legislative League with Lillie Blake. (*American Women*; *New York Times*, 15 November 1897, 11 January 1928; Fuller, *Laura Clay and the Woman's Rights Movement*, 38–41, 184n.)

4. At the suggestion of Ellen Dietrick, the National-American leadership announced a Lucy Stone Birthday Memorial Fund to raise money for the Kansas campaign by distributing mite boxes decorated with Stone's picture. Women were asked to place their mites in the box during the year and send the accumulated funds to the association's treasurer on Stone's birthday, August 13. Neither the Kansas campaign committee nor treasurer Harriet Upton reported money from this source in year-end reports. The cost of manufacturing and distributing the boxes themselves was noted under disbursements. (*Woman's Journal*, 24 March, 14 April 1894, and *Report of the Twenty-seventh Convention, 1895*, pp. 30–38, 99–104; all in *Film*, 32:632, 737, 33:552ff. See also *Woman's Journal*, 10 March 1894.)

TUES. NOV. 20, 1894. In Cleveland visited the Ohio State Ex. Com. meeting in the Parlors of Unity Church—Mrs Everhard[1] presiding—Mrs Casement,[2] Mrs Claypole & others there— Mrs Southworth & Mrs Upton with me—then went

1. Caroline McCullough Everhard (1843–1902), president of the state suffrage association from 1890 to 1900, grew up and lived in Massillon, Ohio, where she inherited considerable property from her father and assumed his seat as a director of the city's bank. Her husband owned a quarry and conducted a

large business in stone and brick. According to Everhard's obituary, it was her property and the taxes she paid on it that caused her to join the suffrage movement after her father's death. She formed a local society about 1888, attended a state meeting soon after, and was immediately recognized as a leader for state work. (*American Women*; *Woman's Journal*, 3 May 1902.)

2. Frances Marion Jennings Casement (1840–1928) presided over the Ohio Woman Suffrage Association from 1885 to 1888. She is also credited with making an early appeal for union of the national suffrage societies. She and her husband, John S. Casement, a general in the Civil War and a major builder of the nation's railroads, hosted SBA on numerous occasions at their house in Painesville. (Tamburro, "Frances Jennings Casement," 162–76; Ruth Neely, ed., *Women of Ohio: A Record of Their Achievements in the History of the State* [Cincinnati, Ohio, 1939], 1:384; *WWW3*, s.v. "Casement, Dan Dillon.")

WED. NOV. 21, 1894. In Cleveland

THUR. NOV. 22, 1894. Left Cleveland—on the Boston Car—guest of Alice Stone Blackwell

Had long talk with her on her feelings toward the National &c—and hope she'll hereafter not suspect each & all of some under motive of not honoring her mother—for such distrust seems to have caused all of her lack of cordial feeling toward us all—especially Miss Shaw—

FRI. NOV. 23, 1894. At home—

❧ Excelsior Diary 1894, n.p., SBA Papers, DLC.

239 ❧ FRANCES E. WILLARD TO SBA

186 Commonwealth Avenue, Boston,   November 24th, 1894.

Beloved Susan,

As you know I kept faith with you about the resolution of co-operation, and I called it up in the Executive Committee when the Resolutions Committee failed to bring it in.[1] It was adopted not in the form in which I wrote it, but I think in the form in which some of your co-workers handed it in, and it was referred to the Executive Committee of the states to carry into effect "whenever practicable." There was quite a discussion, with this result: it is evident, Dearie, that the White Ribbon women do not intend in the smallest degree to conceal their temperance sentiments, but to go into the suffrage battle as "Home Protectionists," believing that in this way they can best enlist the home people and that we shall never get the ballot until the home people desire it.[2] Of course the suffrage societies will go into the work on the plane of justice pure and simple; so you see there is a difficulty about reconciling the two lines of argument. You know the National has not the slightest control over its state presidents and auxiliaries so long as they "pay their dues and don't drink." I am devotedly loyal and loving toward you, and I feel sure we shall always keep hand in hand and heart to heart; but I owe it to you to state the position as it now stands, and I saw plainly that the White Ribbon women meant to "stand by their guns," i.e., they cannot after twenty one years of a certain line of procedure, turn to any other, but will advocate suffrage as a means to an end—that end, the downfall of the liquor system, the gambling system, the system of legalized prostitution.

Beloved Susan, it was a great happiness to have you with us, and I hope you will come "every time." I hereby tender the warmest welcome to Baltimore where we go next year, and if your national Suffrage Convention were not so far away Lady Henry and I should certainly be there; but we shall probably remain pretty quiet until the Women's Council in Washington, where we shall hope to meet you again.[3] Believe me, Ever yours with tenderest sisterly affection,

~ *Frances E Willard*

[*handwritten*] Love to Sister Mary.

~ TLS, HM 10635, Ida Harper Collection, CSmH.

1. Frances Willard recommended to the temperance union's annual convention that cooperation with the woman suffrage movement be improved. After warning that separate petitions to legislators from temperance women sent a message about divisions among women, she urged the creation of "a state council made up of all the women's societies and on the executive committee of which the leaders of women in that state are represented." Short of that goal, there should be cooperation in "all that pertains to the building up of the suffrage propaganda among the people." Willard went on to say that California, Idaho, Utah, and North Dakota showed promise for work because Republicans and Populists in those states had made woman suffrage a part of their platforms. The resolution adopted by the convention's delegates said significantly less, though it endorsed the goals of "equality of citizenship" and "of combined and persistent efforts for securing the enfranchisement of woman." (*Union Signal*, 6 December 1894.)

2. For members of the Woman's Christian Temperance Union, the expression "home protection" connected their public and political work to traditional values like domesticity or woman's sphere. Willard used the phrase repeatedly in early years of her advocacy of woman suffrage. Twenty years later, as Willard indicates here, the expression was less about proper womanhood and more about preserving a distinctive purpose for the temperance union. On the history of the phrase, see Bordin, *Frances Willard: A Biography*, 100.

3. A triennial meeting of the National Council of Women of the United States was scheduled to open in Washington on 17 February 1895.

240 ECS TO THE EDITORS, *WOMAN'S JOURNAL*

26 West 61st Street, New York [*before 22 December 1894*].

Editors Woman's Journal:

The extracts from the speeches of Frederick Douglass and Wendell Phillips, quoted in the *Woman's Journal* by William Lloyd Garrison, have no significance from the disfranchised woman's standpoint.[1] An educational qualification for the colored race in the South, where there were no free schools, and they had been forbidden to read and write, and it was a penal offence to teach them, would have been the height of injustice. But in the North, where we have had free schools for centuries, and even in some States laws making education compulsory, there is no excuse for ignorance, and every stimulus to education should be applied to those who are to take part in government.

Mr. Phillips belonged to the governing class. He was in full possession of the rights and privileges of his class. Hence he had a direct power in protecting his own interests, as well as those of the State. Universal male suffrage did not place him below the ignorant native and foreign masses as women are. If he had been compelled to fight half a century for the smallest civil rights, if he had suffered the humiliation of seeing the cultured class to which he belonged, denied a voice in the government, while the ignorant masses, hostile to his class, had a direct influence in legislation, I think his opinion would have been essentially changed.

A rapidly increasing class of educated women demand the right of suffrage for their own protection, as well as for the best interests of the

State, and they have a right to call a halt on any farther enfranchisement of the ignorant masses, until the better element in society is fully recognized in the government. Our rulers have no excuse for their fears of the ignorant and vicious classes of women. They have it in their power to extend the suffrage to the best class, on an educational qualification. Begin with them until, in combination with the best class of men, the ignorance, poverty and vice of the remainder are reduced to a minimum. With compulsory education, and the same code of morals for man and woman in social life, there would be a gradual elevation of both sexes.

~ *Elizabeth Cady Stanton.*

~ *Woman's Journal*, 22 December 1894.

1. In the *Woman's Journal*, 3 November 1894, in a letter published just above ECS's letter, William Lloyd Garrison quoted at length from Frederick Douglass's speech "Lessons of the Hour," delivered in Washington on 9 January 1894. In the *Journal*, 8 December 1894, in a letter published just above another letter from ECS (see *Film*, 33:17), Garrison quoted a passage from the Phi Beta Kappa lecture of Wendell Phillips, delivered in 1881. Both men argued against restricted suffrage.

241 ~ Article by ECS

New York, Jan. 2, 1895.

Educated Suffrage Again.

It is not the principle of universal suffrage that I oppose, but ignorant, impecunious, immoral, "mankind suffrage," while sex is made a disqualification for all women.[1] I am opposed to the domination of one sex over the other. It cultivates arrogance in the one, and destroys the self-respect in the other. I am opposed to the admission of another man, either foreign or native, to the polling-booth, until woman, the greatest factor in civilization, is first enfranchised. An aristocracy of men, composed of all types, shades and degrees of intelligence and ignorance, is not the most desirable substratum for government. To subject intelligent, highly educated, virtuous, honorable women to the behests of such an aristocracy is the height of cruelty and injustice. Our government, religion, and social life are all on a masculine basis. Forces in man which, if complemented by the opposites in women, in moderation, are virtues, in excess are dangerous vices. His courage, his love of exploration and command, his violence, recklessness, love of money, display and strong drink, all unchecked—are responsible, in a measure, for our terrible accidents by land and sea, for our conflagrations and defalcations, for all the dishonor unearthed by investigating committees in every department of Government. The remedy for all this is education of the higher, more tender sentiments in humanity, the mother-thought omnipresent in every department of life. Her ideal must be represented in the State, the Church, and the home. This must be done before we can take another step in civilization. The key to all this is the right of suffrage, the ballot in the hands of woman.

To this end we must cry "halt" on "male suffrage" for the present, especially on the immense, increasing foreign element, chiefly male, and all a dead weight against women. In the Western States, where amendments to constitutions in favor of woman suffrage have been submitted, the foreign vote has been uniformly in the opposition, and the measure defeated. Hence, we must put up some barrier to hold this mighty multitude at bay. Time, naturalization papers, are a mere travesty. Who keeps watch of the 300,000 every year landing on our shores?[2] Are all these men so honest that they will not offer their votes until the legal time has expired?

But when we say, "You must read and write the English language intelligently," we lengthen the road from the steerage to the polls many miles, and in the meantime women can press their claims without encountering their worst enemies.

Other opponents say: "We are already struggling with the mass of ignorant voters; why ask us to enfranchise the vicious, ignorant women?" To deprive them of that excuse, we say again, Apply the educational qualification. That will hold another class at bay, until the best women are enfranchised, and their efforts, united with the best men, have time to make new conditions. The imperative need of the time is woman's influence in public life. It is the height of wisdom, as well as the best policy, to protest against further male accessions.

Our opponents of educated suffrage, from Mr. Garrison to Mrs. Stanton Blatch, all underestimate the value of the elements of education. The honest laboring man who can read and write intelligently has an immense advantage over one who cannot. The lessons we get from life's experiences are gilded by those we get from the spelling-book and school readers. Reading and writing are the tools with which the citizen can protect himself and dignify the State. That some people who are educated are vicious, and some who are uneducated are virtuous, is no argument against general education.[3] We must take a broader view, and in national life see if the country where people are educated does not occupy a higher position than the one where the masses are ignorant.

To get my standpoint clearly before Mrs. Stanton Blatch, I will take a supposititious case: Suppose that from the foundation of the German Government the women had reigned supreme; that the men were not allowed in the schools and colleges, the trades and professions; that they had no rights of property, wages or children, and no credit in the world of work; that they could not make contracts, nor sue or be sued; that, by constant petitioning for centuries, they had wrung a few civil rights from their oppressors, but that to all their prayers for political equality the women turned a deaf ear. Through all these years an untold number of ignorant foreign women had been landing on their shores to become a part of the governing power, while the men, of whom a majority were a highly educated, moral class, were mere pariahs, under this ignorant foreign mass. These wise, patriotic men not only suffered the humiliation of being under a foreign yoke, but they saw dangers to their country by the misgovernment of this ignorant aristocracy of sex, having absolute control in making laws and constitutions, and in administering every department of government.

Now what should we think of the common sense of these men, if, in the valley of disfranchisement, they sat singing paeans to "universal" womanhood suffrage, instead of blocking the way by an educational qualification that would be a real benefit to the voters, as well as to the State, and increase the chances of the men to secure political equality? "As self-preservation is the first law of nature," they would say, "we must stop this inflowing tide of foreign women, a dead weight against us. Some of our native-born women are in favor of our emancipation, but the foreigners always vote against us."

As Mrs. Stanton Blatch kindly takes me to Germany, and endows me with remarkable powers,[4] I will imagine myself a member of the Reichstag, eloquently urging the recognition of the best class of men, whose influence is needed in government, the suppression of the foreign vote for a season, and an educational qualification for all, that of sex being the most odious and unjust. Mrs. Stanton Blatch, also a member, whose fetich is universal womanhood suffrage, rises in opposition. "No, no," says she, "I object to all qualifications. Let the swelling tide of immigration flow in, and crown every woman as quickly as possible with the dignity of self-sovereignty." "But," I reply, "they are a dead weight against the admission of the best class of men, a new and much-needed element in government. We must have the united thought of man and woman for order and harmony."

William Lloyd Garrison, not allowed to be in the Reichstag on account of sex, sits in the valley with his confrères, advising them to stand by the principle of universal womanhood suffrage.

"Let us abide our time," says he, "if it takes to the crack of doom to enfranchise our sex." To strengthen his position, he quotes a few eloquent passages from the speeches of Frederick Douglass and Wendell Phillips. Some of the men inquired if these gentlemen were in a similar position with themselves? He replied, "No. They belonged to the governing class." "What do the women in the United States say, who, like us, are disfranchised?" "Some of them ask to have the suffrage restricted by property and educational qualifications, until their political rights are secured."

The large majority at once declared themselves of the same opinion, and sent a petition to the Reichstag next day to restrict woman suffrage, by several qualifications—property, education, birth and morality. The petition was laid on the table, and the men advised to remain in their sphere, and to attend to their business affairs, and make money to support their families, while the women administered the government. Men, being physically superior, were better fitted for the rough work of life, while women, in a warm house and comfortable chairs, made laws for their protection!

~ *Elizabeth Cady Stanton.*

~ *Woman's Journal*, 5 January 1895.

1. The editors described this as an open letter from ECS to Harriot Stanton Blatch. After reading her mother's letter above at 3 November 1894, Blatch joined the debate over educated suffrage with an open letter to ECS in the *Woman's Journal*, 22 December 1894, *Film*, 33:11. Blatch scoffed at ECS's assumptions that reading and writing alone taught enlightenment and that non-English speakers were ignorant. Voting rights, she suggested, might better be assigned by need or morals.

2. As ECS explained in her letter published in the *Woman's Journal*, 8 December 1894, *Film*, 33:17, the annual report of the United States Superintendent of Immigration, released in November, showed that 288,020 immigrants arrived in the United States between 1 July 1893 and 30 June 1894. Of those over sixteen years of age, 41,000 could not read or write. (*New York Times*, 26 November 1894.)

3. Blatch offered the example of southern slaveholders to underscore her point that educated people were fully capable of viciousness, and she extolled the intelligent proletarian who spoke only German as a useful citizen who would be punished by her mother's standard.

4. In one of many references to Germany in her letter, Blatch pointed to ECS's ignorance of the German language and imagined what her status would be in Germany if language were used as the measure.

242 ✎ SBA TO MARY S. ANTHONY

Louisville Ky¹—Jan. 13, 1895.

My Dear Sister Mary

I had an <u>old fashion</u> pious, cold & generally comfortless time at Wilmore—a <u>Methodist College</u>—they call—a fifth rate M.E. minister keeps— his wife has three little boys as near together as the law allows— they had some 30 or 40 boarders—² the water in my tumbler & basin froze hard during Friday night—though I had a fire on the grate until 10 Oclock—the pitcher of water—I had set on the mantle shelf— the halls below & above were icy cold & each of the twenty five girls had to get of her bed & make her own fire—³ it was a primitive place— the man & the wife & head teacher⁴ each labored to get my soul into rapport with Jesus— the two latter—came to my room after the lecture & asked to pray with me—& all this came from their learning that I belonged to the Hicksite—& <u>not</u> the orthodox Quakers— I was called at 5.30—took the train at 6.40—and reached here at 10—A.M— here we are at dear Susan Look Avery's son—Georges⁵— and so in clover— her youngest daughter came in from Anchorage yesterday noon—and has remained over—Mrs Helen Robinson⁶—the loveliest kind of a woman— Mrs C. C. & I have had a quiet Sunday— and we are take the train for Owensboro at 7.45 tomorrow Monday A.M—and next day to Paducah⁷

I hope you are making all things for Atlanta— If I didn't leave a wrapper—addressed to President & Mrs Hughes—Wilmore—Kentucky—which I think I didn't—will you, at once, send a set of the History with copy of International Council—& few copies of each of the tracts to them—& then will you address another copy and send to Miss Laura Clay—78 ↑North↓ Broadway—Lexington—Ky—that is send a set of History to each of them—

I shall hope to find a package at ~~Padu~~ Owensboro tomorrow & thence at each place we visit— no letter from you but you didn't know we were to be here— Tell Isabel[8]—I hope she & Mrs Sanford have solved all the difficulties & gotten a good copy of financial statement on the way to me at some point—this week— I can't get it out of my mind until I feast my eyes a perfected copy—and tell her not to fail to have a clear statement of both the petition & the tax matters—for Atlanta— I do hope Mrs Greenleafs State report will contain a concise statement or summary of each of the points— Lovingly

Susan B—

~ ALS, on NAWSA letterhead, place and year corrected, and letterhead of Burnet House, Cincinnati, Isabel Howland Papers, MNS-S.

1. SBA left home on 8 January 1895 for a long anticipated tour through the South arranged by Laura Clay. Unwilling to have sole responsibility for speaking at each stop, she asked Carrie Catt to join her. They reached Lexington, Kentucky, on January 9, and after their stop at Wilmore, they reached Louisville on January 12. (SBA to L. Clay, 13 March, 4, 6 September 1894, and 2 January 1895; SBA diary, 8-13 January 1895; *Report of the Twenty-seventh Annual Convention, 1895*, pp. 18-19, *Film*, 32:573-78, 1050-51, 1058-59, 33:80ff, 499-500, 552ff.)

2. On January 11, SBA spoke in the chapel of Asbury College (founded as Kentucky Holiness College) in Wilmore, Kentucky, where Laura Clay organized the Wilmore Equal Rights Association in 1894. Presiding over the college was John Wesley Hughes (1852-1932), its founder and owner. His wife, Mary Wallingford Hughes, headed the school's "Home Department." (Joseph A. Thacker, Jr., *Asbury College: Vision and Miracle* [Nappanee, Ind., 1990], 3-8, 29-30; *Catalogue of Asbury College, for 1894-'95 and Sixth Annual Announcement for 1895-'96* [Lexington, Ky., n.d.); obituary, Lexington *Leader*, n.d; all provided by Celia Eby, Archives and Special Collections, Kinlaw Library, Asbury College.)

3. Cold weather and houses ill-equipped for it were a theme throughout SBA's southern trip. Freezing temperatures gripped the South in January and February 1895.

4. Several women served on the faculty, and none was designated head teacher.

5. George Capwell Avery (1852–1911), a son of Susan L. Avery, worked in the family firm, B. F. Avery & Sons. (*WWW1*.)

6. Helen Blasdell Avery Robinson (1855–?), who married Charles Bonnycastle Robinson in 1877, came to town from her house in Anchorage, a small city outside Louisville. Her husband was president of the Beargrass Woolen Mills. (Browne, *Chronicles of an American Home*, 13–14, 37; city directory, 1890; Federal Census, 1900.)

7. At Owensboro on January 14, where SBA and Catt spoke in the room of the United States Circuit Court, SBA commented about the audience, "But, oh dear—the women are so W.C.T.U and so <u>little woman</u> suffrage." At Paducah on January 15, they spoke in the Cumberland Presyterian Church.

8. Isabel Howland (1859–1942), a niece of Emily Howland and 1881 graduate of Cornell University, was the corresponding secretary of the New York State Woman Suffrage Association. She was preparing *1894. Constitutional-Amendment Campaign Year. Report of the New York State Woman Suffrage Association. Twenty-sixth Annual Convention, Ithaca, N.Y., November 12–15* (1895). The financial statement for the amendment campaign (pp. 225–31), on which SBA spent time before her trip, proved to be especially difficult because the state treasurer's records were not well kept, and because the state treasurer handled only a fraction of all the money raised across the state. New York City and Brooklyn kept separate accounts. (*New York Times*, 6 December 1942; SBA diary, 26, 27 December 1894, and 3, 7, 8 January 1895; and SBA to Lillie D. Blake, 7 January 1895; all in *Film*, 32:1ff, 33:80ff, 513–14.)

243 ~> FROM THE DIARY OF SBA

[*19–20 January, 3–4, 10–11 February 1895*]

SAT. JAN. 19, 1895. Memphis—Tenn at Mrs Meriwethers—14 Talbot st—[1] at 9 A.M. went to Zions Hall with Mrs [*blank*] Cooper[2] & Mrs [*blank*] to a reception given by the colored womens Club—

at 10.30 to the Y. Men's Hebrew Associations Parlors—to a reception given by the Memphis Council—composed of 45 local women's associations—[3] only the 19th century club has not joined—& it was Julia Ward Howe's influence that kept it out—

This afternoon—we threw up Miss Clara Conway's reception[4]— given by her alumnie—at her school—that we might sleep & rest for the evening meeting at the Young Mens Hebrew Hall[5]

1. That is, Lide Meriwether, with whom SBA stayed from her arrival in Memphis on January 17 until her departure on January 20.

2. Florence P. Cooper (1856-1939), a schoolteacher, escorted SBA to Zion Hall on Beale Street to meet with the Coterie Migratory Assembly, a literary and social club of which she was president. Cooper was born in Mississippi, and in Memphis, she and her husband Edward became friends of Ida B. Wells. Cooper later led the Coterie into the National Federation of Afro-American Women in 1896, designating Mary Church Terrell as the club's delegate to the founding meeting in Washington. She helped to organize the National Association of Colored Women's subsequent meeting in Nashville in 1897. (Federal Census, 1880; city directory, 1890; Shelby County, Tenn., on-line archives of death certificates; Beverly G. Bond, "Every Duty Incumbent upon Them: African American Women in Nineteenth-Century Memphis," in *Trial and Triumph: Essays in Tennessee's African American History*, ed. Carroll Van West [Knoxville, Tenn., 2002], 218-20; *A History of the Club Movement among the Colored Women of the United States of America* [1902; reprint, Washington, D.C., 1978], 59, 121; *Minutes of the National Association of Colored Women at Nashville, Tenn., September 15th, 16th, 17th, and 18th, 1897* [Washington, D.C., 1901], 3-5; Paula J. Giddings, *Ida: A Sword among Lions: Ida B. Wells and the Campaign against Lynching* [New York, 2008], 145, 175.)

3. The Woman's Council Parlors were destroyed by fire on the day SBA and Carrie Catt arrived in Memphis, and events scheduled there were moved to the Young Men's Hebrew Association on Union Street. The council, organized in 1893, brought most of the city's many women's groups together for common programs. The Nineteenth Century Club, the city's literary club for elite women, was founded in 1890. Club members knew Julia Howe through the Association for the Advancement of Women, which held its congress in Memphis in 1892. (Wedell, *Elite Women and the Reform Impulse in Memphis*, 77-107.)

4. Clara Conway (1840-1904) was a nationally known teacher with her own school in Memphis to prepare girls for college. Locally, she was a founding member of the Nineteenth Century Club and once a candidate for city superintendent of schools. (*American Women*; Wedell, *Elite Women and the Reform Impulse in Memphis*, 15-19; *Woman's Journal*, 26 January 1895; Shelby County, Tenn., on-line archives of death certificates.)

5. On this second occasion for lectures in Memphis, SBA used familiar historical examples from her speech "Women Want Bread, Not the Ballot" to illustrate how political power could improve the wages of women. Catt did not repeat her earlier lecture about protecting Anglo-Saxon supremacy through woman suffrage, and instead, speaking after SBA, assured the audience that "the equal suffrage movement was no war upon men, but an attempt at cooperation with them." (*Memphis Commerical Appeal*, 18 January 1895, and *Memphis Avalanche*, 20 January 1895, *Film*, 33:533-34.)

SUN. JAN. 20, 1895. Spoke in Colored Church The Tabernacle at 11— Mrs C. C. also—[1] a wonderful assemblage—of all shades from jet black to absolute blonde white— Most pathetic— Mrs C. C.'s talk to them was lovely— "keep the soul on top"—she

Dined at Mrs Meriwethers—also Mrs Selden[2]—& several Unitarians— We left at 5.30— I here presented a set of History to Mrs M—& one to the Library of the Young Men's Hebrew Association[3] [*21 January-2 February 1895 omitted.*]

 1. Tabernacle Missionary Baptist Church on Turley Street.

 2. Elise Massey Selden (1851-1931), who hosted Carrie Catt on this visit to Memphis, organized the city's Nineteenth Century Club and was an early member of the local suffrage society. (Wedell, *Elite Women and the Reform Impulse in Memphis*, 78, 79, 83, 91, 97, 160n, 162n; Shelby County, Tenn., on-line archives of death certificates.)

 3. They took the train to New Orleans, where they spent the next three days. Carrie Catt then traveled into Mississippi, while SBA proceeded to Shreveport, Louisiana, and Birmingham, New Decatur, and Huntsville, Alabama. They reached Atlanta on January 30.

SUN. FEB. 3, 1895. 27th ought to be Wash. Con De Give's Opera House—Atlanta Georgia—[1]

Rev Anna H. Shaw preached— ["]The Heavenly Vision" at 3 P.M. in the Opera House—packed to suffocation—the stage & all standing room—& hundreds turned away by the Police—

Dr Hathorne[2] had preached <u>against</u> us in the morning—Baptist— which stirred Anna to greater power—

In the evening ↑our↓ women spoke in various white & colored churches—but I sat in Parlors & held Council with all who came in—[3]

 1. The National-American's annual convention opened on 31 January 1895, at DeGive's Opera House, at the corner of Peachtree and Pryor streets. Built in 1893, the house had a capacity in excess of two thousand people. See *Film*, 33:552-651.

 2. James Boardman Hawthorne (1837-1910), of Atlanta's First Baptist Church, preached against woman suffragists before they gathered in the city. Taking a published sermon of Anna Shaw's as his text, he denounced these women, who "defy, not only the Bible and the law of God, written on their own beings, but that unconquerable and eternal social sentiment which despises every woman who confesses to such unwomanly aspirations." Shaw handled him roughly at the National's session on the morning of February 2, and on this occasion, she repeated the sermon Hawthorne had criticized a week earlier.

The same morning Hawthorne opened his service by denouncing the notion held by "manly women" that God was both mother and father as "something worse than medieval superstition." "This is a specimen of the new gospel which we shall hear when these feminine haters of Pauline theology get possession of our pulpits and invert God's order." Hawthorne, ordained in 1859, took over the church in Atlanta in 1884, after a long career across the South. He played a prominent part in the state's temperance movement. (George Braxton Taylor, *Virginia Baptist Ministers. Fifth Series, 1902-1914, with Supplement* [Lynchburg, Va., 1915], 253-67; *Atlanta Constitution*, 28 January, 4 February 1895; Shaw and Jordan, *Story of a Pioneer*, 307-8.)

3. A parlor for delegates was located in the Aragon Hotel, at the corner of Peachtree and Ellis streets.

MON. FEB. 4, 1895. 27th Annual National Con—Atlanta—Georgia

Went to the Atlanta University at 9— A.M. and talked to the colored students—[1] at 10— went into Executive Com. meeting in Hotel Aragon— until 2 P.M.—and 3.30 went to High School Assembly Ro ↑in afternoon↓ again until dark—[2]

Then dressed in Velvet & was whirled to colored Bethel Church— met Bishop Turner[3] there—& Mrs Merrick[4] & I talked to a 1000 or more—some <u>whiter</u> than me— Still doomed to go with the blackest— Then returned to the Aragon Reception—shook hands with the hundreds that surged through[5] [*4-9 February 1895 omitted.*]

1. Sponsored by the American Missionary Association, Atlanta University was one of the leading colleges opened for African Americans at the end of the Civil War. Martha Schofield accompanied SBA and made the introductions to the students, and Isabel Howland spoke at the conclusion of SBA's remarks. To an audience largely of girls, SBA recommended that "before you take to yourselves the luxury of a husband, earn your *own* money, buy your *own* home and live in it, then your husband can't put you out of it—and if *he* does n't do right *you* can put *him* out." (*Bulletin of Atlanta University*, no. 63 [March 1895]: 3-4, *Film*, 33:662-63.)

2. See *Report of the Twenty-seventh Annual Convention, 1895*, pp. 50-51, *Film*, 33:552ff. SBA struck out an event that took place the next day, when she and Mary Anthony met with one hundred high school alumnae in Atlanta.

3. The Bethel African Methodist Episcopal Church was the city's oldest African-American church and one of the largest meeting spaces available to African Americans in Atlanta. More than one thousand people heard SBA and Caroline Merrick. Henry McNeal Turner (1834-1915), a bishop in the African Methodist Episcopal church, was an important political as well as religious leader, whose ideas of reform for the African American community carried him into territory associated with white women's reforms. Besides issuing this invitation to hear from woman suffragists, he cooperated with the Woman's

Christian Temperance Union on local prohibition laws and, against church policy, ordained a woman to the ministry. (*ANB*.)

4. Caroline Elizabeth Thomas Merrick (1825-1908) was the woman's rights pioneer of Louisiana and had hosted SBA in 1885. (Glenn R. Conrad, ed., *A Dictionary of Louisiana Biography*, [New Orleans, 1988]; *NAW*; *Papers*, 3:417-20.)

5. The Georgia Woman Suffrage Association and the Atlanta Equal Suffrage Association hosted this reception for delegates.

SUN. FEB. 10, 1895. Arrived at Aiken S.C. at 7.15—found all in bed— But Miss Schofield[1] soon had her fires going— she had taken home with her from Atlanta—Emily Howland, Mrs Hubbard[2]—Mr & Mrs Tilney[3] of Phila—Dr Jane Myers[4] & Mrs Blankenburg—Phebe Wright,[5] the Canada Friend, & Miss McCoun[6] of Brooklyn—& my arrival made nine—

The weather cold but bright & lovely— we visited the Old Peoples Home—some 10 or 12—all 70 or over— Old <u>Pompey</u> told of his Slavery life—no Patrick Henry could have writhed under bondage more [bitterly?] than did Pompey— George Washington—another character— Talk about the loveliness of the patriarchal family! every slave with a spark of the love of liberty in his soul rebelled against it—

1. Martha Schofield (1839-1916), raised near Philadelphia, went south to teach former slaves on the Sea Islands of South Carolina at the end of the Civil War and moved inland in 1868 to establish the Schofield Normal and Industrial School at Aiken. While battling for the rights of African Americans during Reconstruction, she maintained close ties to northern suffragists. In 1878, she attended the Third Decade Celebration in Rochester, and more recently she attended the meeting in Atlanta as a delegate of the South Carolina Equal Rights Association. (*NAW*; *ANB*; Katherine Smedley, "Martha Schofield and the Rights of Women," *South Carolina Historical Magazine* 85 [January 1984]: 195-210.)

2. Mary N. Rice Hubbard (1824-1909), a delegate from New York to the Atlanta convention, took over her husband's extensive business interests in White Creek, Washington County, after his death in 1884 and proved to be a capable businesswoman. A leader in the local Political Equality Club, Hubbard attended the state suffrage convention in 1893 and the Washington convention in 1894. (William L. Stone, ed., *Washington County, New York: Its History to the Close of the Nineteenth Century* [New York, 1901], 247-49; on-line transcription of records, Woodlands Cemetery, Cambridge, N.Y., copy in editors' files.)

3. Robert Tilney (1839-1918) and Anna Robinson Longstreth Tilney (1841-1925), Philadelphia Quakers and writers, were delegates to the convention from Pennsylvania. Robert Tilney, an Englishman who served in the Union

army, was editor of the *American Newspaper Annual* from 1879 to 1908. Anna Tilney, whose mother was a friend of Lucretia Mott, was a member of Philadelphia's New Century Club as well as the suffrage association. (John W. Jordan, ed., *Colonial Families of Philadelphia* [New York, 1911], 2: 1538-40; *Friends' Intelligencer* 82 [1925]: 477.)

4. Jane Viola Myers (1831-1918), a physician in Philadelphia who earned her degree at the Penn Medical University in 1855, was the youngest sister of two other doctors, Mary Frame Myers Thomas of Indiana and Hannah E. Myers Longshore also of Philadelphia. (Frederick C. Waite, "The Three Myers Sisters—Pioneer Women Physicians," *Medical Review of Reviews* 39 [March 1933]: 114-20.)

5. Phebe C. Whitson Wright (1824-1916), of a Quaker family on Long Island and the widow of James B. Wright, lived in Sea Girt, New Jersey, and was a delegate of the state's suffrage association to the convention in Atlanta. Martha Schofield referred to her as an aunt and noted her role raising money in New York for her school in Aiken. (Delight W. Dodyk, "Education and Agitation: The Woman Suffrage Movement in New Jersey" [Ph.D. diss., Rutgers University, 1997], 725; *Quaker Genealogy*, 3:504; *Friends Intelligencer* 36 [1879]: 234, and 73 [1916]: 237, 315; M. Schofield to Eliza Schofield, 6? April? 1895, Schofield Papers, Record Group 5, PSC-Hi.)

6. Pamelia Townsend Underhill McCoun (1828-?) was a cousin of Phebe Wright and a delegate from the New York state association to the Atlanta convention. Raised on Long Island, she married out of meeting, lived in Buffalo for many years, and returned to Long Island in the 1880s. (*Quaker Genealogy*, 3:426, 459, 460, 502.)

MON. FEB. 11, 1895. Aiken S.C. Court House—Martha Schofield—who has kept a Boarding & Industrial School for Colored youth here for 30 years— This mornings light found the ground white & the trees weighted down with snow—and the cold & snow together—kept her ↑100↓ day scholars at home—save 8 or 10—so I could see & talk only to the boarding scholars— she took me to the shops Carpenter, Harness, blacksmith &c— Had small but best representative audience—the Baptist minister presented me[1]—all of went in an Omnibus— The Court House was icy cold [tho?] it had two stoves & one grate fire going at red heat—[2]

1. Edward Earle Bomar (1861-1947) was pastor of Aiken's First Baptist Church from 1893 to 1899. Schofield quoted him as saying, "'we should all be students after the truth, you know I am a conservative but no matter how much we differ from these ladies, we welcome them to our town, and I am a Student.'" (Wendell H. Rone, *A History of the Daviess-McLean Baptist Association in Kentucky, 1844-1943* [Owensboro, Ky., 1943], 369-70; Landrum

Cemetery, Landrum, S.C., gravestone transcription by W. D. Floyd, copy in editor's files; Martha Schofield to Eliza Schofield, 6? April? 1895, Schofield Papers, Record Group 5, PSC-Hi.)

2. Helen Morris Lewis of North Carolina preceded SBA with a fifteen minute review of southern organizing. SBA urged political parties to realize the long-term potential of being known as the party that enfranchised women— what Schofield called "one of her <u>real</u> political speeches," aimed more at the men than the women. (*Charleston Evening Post*, 13 February 1895, *Film*, 33:672; Martha Schofield to Eliza Schofield, 6? April? 1895.)

🌿 Excelsior Diary 1895, n.p., SBA Papers, DLC. Square brackets surround uncertain readings.

244 🌿 ECS TO CLARA BEWICK COLBY

26 West 61st   N.Y. Feb 16th [*1895*]

Dear Mrs Colby,

Do you intend to keep The Tribune going for two or three years to come? <u>I have been told half a dozen times that it was on its last legs</u>!! If you hope to go on would you like to begin, "The Woman's Bible" a chapter each week.¹ I have the whole of the Penteteuch ready, & can commence at once. We formed a revision committee of a dozen women in England & America eight years ago but four only did any work & the project seemed so herculean that it was suspended. But I have always felt that it would be a big thing to do. Frances Lord ran through the Bible with a concordance & found that only about one tenth part made any mention of women. So it would only need a volumn of about 300 pages to do the whole thing. Now my plan would be this. 1st Form a new committee,² say of one dozen, assign to each a portion of the scripture. Mrs Blatch & I have already gone over the Penteteuch Whilst we are perfecting that & running it through your paper, they can be writing theirs. As you publish each week, you send a copy to each one of the committee for approval or dissent, to add to or take from, as short & concise as possible. Leaving the final decision with five of the committee whom we may choose, for example you, me, Mrs Dietrick, Olympia Brown, Mrs Livermore. If we make any money on it divide it between those who <u>actually</u> do the work. I was talking to a publisher about it. He said he thought it would have a great sale   The Woman's Bible!! by a revising committee of women!!

Men have never made the most of the varied spheres filled by women in the scriptures. In this work we shall touch no creeds nor faiths none of the thirty nine articles of the Confession of Faith, simply what is said of women.³ Now what do you think of the project? will you join   will you publish. When set up you could strike it off in leaflets if we thought best. I will send you a chapter that you may see my idea of how the work should be done, & you talk with some of the most liberal women in The Council now in Washington   Yours as ever

~ E. C. S.

We bought some cheap Bibles to cut. My plan is as you will see, to quote in small print, & make the commentaries larger. If you decide to carry on The Tribune, & print the Bible, let me know at once & I will make up the committee & send their names with the plan of work. If you decide to begin next week ~~illegible see~~ you might say something of what we propose. Ask Mrs Dietrict if she will be one of the revising com. The commentaries must be short & crisp, not too voluminous

~ ALS, Clara B. Colby Papers, Archives Divison, WHi. "Rec'd. & Ans'd. Feby. 16th, 1895" typed in corner of first page.

1. "When I read of the ferocious attack of the Baptist clergymen on woman during the recent convention in Atlanta," ECS explained to a reporter from the New York *World* in March, "it seemed to me the time had come" to resume work on the *Woman's Bible*. (*Film*, 33:803–4; Kern, *Mrs. Stanton's Bible*, 135-36.)

2. On occasion in the winter of 1895, ECS mentioned several members of her original committee of 1886 whom she thought would continue the work. In February, she named Olympia Brown, Sara Underwood, and Mary Livermore. In mid-March, she included Phebe Hanaford's name and added that manuscripts by Ellen Burr and Helen Gardener were still in her possession. On March 25, she sent Colby a list of women who had agreed to serve on the *new* revising committee: they were Lillie Blake, Harriot Blatch, Olympia Brown, Ellen Burr, Carrie Catt, Clara Colby, Ellen Dietrick, Matilda Gage, Helen Gardener, Phebe Hanaford, Isabella Hooker, Mary Livermore, Frances Lord, Lady Isabella Somerset, Louise Thomas, Sara Underwood, and Frances Willard. A month later, Alice Scatcherd, Eva Ingersoll, Josephine Henry, and Catherine Stebbins were added. A list published early in May added Lucinda Chandler and Elizabeth Grannis. (ECS to C. B. Colby, 27 February, 25 March, and before 27 April 1895, and Interviews, 17 March and 11 May 1895, *Film*, 33:760–63, 803–4, 845–46, 950, 1012–14.)

3. ECS blended the names for two different documents, the Westminster Confession of Faith of the Presbyterian church, written during the English Civil War, and the Thirty-nine Articles of the Anglican and Episcopal churches, dating from the reign of Elizabeth I, that together defined the major Protestant faiths.

245 ~ FUNERAL OF FREDERICK DOUGLASS

EDITORIAL NOTE: Frederick Douglass died at home on 20 February 1895, soon after his return from a meeting of the National Council of Women. Over the next four days, plans for his memorial service were drawn up, announced in the press, and then revised; a male-only program was adjusted late on February 24 to make room for a delegation from the National Council. During that interval, SBA "sent no end of telegrams and letters" to ECS in New York, urging her to write a tribute to Douglass, and she called on Helen Douglass. On the twenty-fifth, with the District of Columbia schools closed and many businesses shut, thousands of mourners filed in the east door of the Metropolitan African Methodist Episcopal Church, past the coffin, and out the west door; thousands more jammed the street in front of the church hoping to find space at the afternoon service. SBA, May Sewall, and Anna Shaw, the National Council's delegation, were placed last on the program. In its report of the event, the *Woman's Tribune* included remarks made by SBA. *In Memoriam: Frederick Douglass*, prepared by Helen Douglass, provides a more careful rendering of ECS's tribute. (SBA diary, 20, 24 February 1895, and ECS to Harriot S. Blatch, after 25 February 1895, *Film*, 33:80ff, 759.)

[25 February 1895]

I endorse all that has been said here. My last word with Frederick Douglass was this; 'You must be at the celebration of Mrs. Stanton's 80th birthday anniversary in November and say your good word on the occasion.' He replied, I shall be there and ready with my word. Never did he seem in more vigor and graciousness than he was that afternoon. And now I will read a tribute sent by Mrs. Stanton whom Frederick Douglass loved more than all the others in the ranks of the woman suffragists.

~ *Woman's Tribune*, 2 March 1895.

February 21, 1895.

Taking up the morning *Tribune*, the first words that caught my eye thrilled my very soul. "Frederick Douglass is dead!" What vivid memories thick and fast flashed through my mind and held me spellbound in contemplation of the long years since first we met.

Trained in the severe school of slavery, I saw him first before a Boston audience, fresh from the land of bondage. He stood there like an African prince, conscious of his dignity and power, grand in his physical proportions, majestic in his wrath, as with keen wit, satire and indignation he portrayed the bitterness of slavery, the humiliation of subjection to those who in all human virtues and capacities were inferior to himself. His denunciation of our national crime, of the wild and guilty fantasy that men could hold property in man, poured like a torrent that fairly made his hearers tremble.

Thus I first saw him, and wondered as I listened that any mortal man should have ever tried to subjugate a being with such marvelous powers, such self-respect, such intense love of liberty.

Around him sat the great anti-slavery orators of the day, watching his effect on that immense audience, completely magnetized with his eloquence, laughing and crying by turns with his rapid flights from pathos to humor. All other speakers seemed tame after Douglass. Sitting near, I heard Phillips say to Lydia Maria Child: "Verily, this boy, who has only just graduated from the 'southern institution' (as slavery was called), throws us all in the shade." "Ah," she replied, "the iron has entered his soul and he knows the wrongs of slavery subjectively; the rest of you speak only from an objective point of view."

He used to preach a sermon in imitation of the Methodist clergy, from the text, "Servants, Obey your Masters," which the people were never tired of hearing. Often after he had spoken an hour shouts would go up from all parts of the house, "Now, Douglass, give us the sermon." Some of our literary critics pronounced that the best piece of satire in the English language.

The last time I visited his home in Anacostia, I asked him if he ever had the sermon printed. He said "No." "Could you reproduce it?" said I. He said, "No; I could not bring back the old feeling if I tried, and I would not if I could. The blessings of liberty I have so long enjoyed, and the many tender friendships I have with the Saxon race on both sides of the ocean, have taught me such sweet lessons of forgiveness that the painful memories of my early days are almost obliterated, and I would not recall them."

As an orator, writer and editor, Douglass holds an honored place among the gifted men of his day. As a man of business and a public officer he has been pre-eminently successful; honest and upright in all his dealings, he bears an enviable reputation.

As a husband, father, neighbor and friend, in all social relations he has been faithful and steadfast to the end. He was the only man I ever knew who understood the degradation of disfranchisement for woman. Through all the long years of our struggle he has been a familiar figure on our platform, with always an inspiring word to say. In the very first convention he helped me to carry the resolution I had penned demanding woman suffrage.

Frederick Douglass is not dead! His grand character will long be an object lesson in our national history; his lofty sentiments of liberty, justice and equality, echoed on every platform over our broad land, must influence and inspire many coming generations!

~ *Elizabeth Cady Stanton.*

~ Helen Pitts Douglass, *In Memoriam: Frederick Douglass* (Philadelphia, 1897), 44–45. Not in *Film* in this version.

246 ~ ECS TO CLARA BEWICK COLBY

20 West 61st   N.Y. March 4th [*1895*]

Dear Clara

Miss Willard & Lady Henry Somerset called on me yeseterday & I told them about The Woman's Bible & they said they would give their names on the Revising Committee[1]   But do not announce it as we should be flooded with names which we do not want yet. When we get it running the way way we think best it will be time enough.[2] I have enough ready to run until June 1st   Have you Lady Henry's direction? Yours sincerely

~ *Elizabeth Cady Stanton.*

~ ALS, Clara B. Colby Papers, Archives Division, WHi.

1. ECS wanted evangelical women to collaborate with her on the *Woman's Bible*. Indeed, she envisaged a complex conversation, in which each woman would speak "from her standpoint. . . . Our book would then be comments from the surface the plain English, the spiritual, the symbolical, the evangelical the liberal, the Protestant the Catholic, the Jew the Gentile's various standpoints; it would be a lesson to all men, of toleration & wisdom such as never before been possible." Frances Willard had already published commentaries on key passages in the New Testament on which men based their exclusion of women from preaching, and she had long contested men's translations and literal interpretations. She predicted that little about church polity would change "until women share equally in translating the sacred text. That they should do so is most desirable, and young women of linguistic talent ought to make a speciality of Hebrew and New Testament Greek in the interest of their sex." When she and Lady Somerset called on ECS on March 3, the subject turned to collaboration on the *Woman's Bible*. As the editor of the *Union Signal*, 25 April 1895, explained the agreement they reached that day, Willard and Somerset "agree[d] to be members of a committee to prepare an exegesis of those passages in the Bible that relate to woman's position in the church and state, with the understanding that Miss Elizabeth W. Greenwood and a number of women evangelists should be associated with themselves and other leading women in the undertaking." Willard and Somerset sailed for England soon after this conversation, but Greenwood, who lived in Brooklyn, was in conversation with ECS for several months. ECS herself revealed the agreement in the interview with the New York *World* two weeks later. (*Eighty Years*, 452; Frances Willard, *Woman in the Pulpit* [Boston, 1888], 31; Statement on Woman's Bible, 16 April 1895, National Office Correspondence, 1895, Woman's Christian Temperance Union, IEWT, from *Temperance and Prohibition Papers*; ECS to C. B. Colby, 21 February, 14 May 1895, and Interview, 17 March 1895, *Film*, 33:745-48, 803-4, 34:16-21.)

2. ECS's first five commentaries on the Book of Genesis were published in the New York *World*, 17 March 1895. The series began in the *Woman's Tribune*, 23 March 1895, and appeared weekly through the issue of 8 June 1895, with contributions by ECS, Lillie Blake, and Clara Colby. Although the series continued through the summer, the sequence no longer followed the order of books in the Bible but rather what was ready to publish. New to the project in June, July, and August were Louisa Southworth and Ellen Dietrick. In the fall, the authors resumed a more orderly progression through the Old Testament, with significant contributions from Phebe Hanaford, Susan Wixon, Clara Neymann, and again, Louisa Southworth.

247 ~ LILLIE DEVEREUX BLAKE TO SBA, WITH REPLY

[29 March 1895]

COPY OF LETTER FROM MRS. L. D. BLAKE, MAR. 29, 1895.[1]

Do you know I cannot reconcile myself to the idea of the Nat. Council taking charge of the Stanton Birthday.[2] In the first place, how can this change be made? At Atlanta it was voted by the N.A.W.S.A. that they would take charge; how can this action be set aside? I think great dissatisfaction will be created if it is. Then Mrs. Stanton stands for Suffrage above all else, and should be honored by our Societies, while to have <u>the</u> celebrations under the charge of the Pres. Kings Daughters,[3] an orthodox affair, seems very much out of taste. Still again, I do not think any one will make the celebration such a success as you will, and then we ought to have <u>you</u> preside—you, the long time companion and co-worker with our dear leader, are the person who should be at the head and, with your admirable manner as a presiding officer, you will give a tone to it that no else will. It will be lifeless under the proposed arrangements and vital with you. Mrs. Catt and others with whom I have talked, feel just as I do, and anyway how can it be done? As I said at first, after the vote at Atlanta, how can the celebration be taken away from the N.A.W.S.A.?

~ L. D. B.

COPY OF MISS ANTHONY'S REPLY.

You are the only person I have heard of, who fails to see the higher honor coming to Mrs. Stanton, in having her 80th birthday Celebration mothered by a great national body, composed of twenty different National Societies, instead of by our <u>one</u> out of the twenty. To me, it will be second only in power and far-reaching, to that of the National Council's adopting the splendid resolutions and sending a delegation of its members, bearing a wreath of ivy and laurel, to the funeral of the Frederick Douglass!![4] Surely, for all classes of women—liberals, orthodox, Jewish, mormon, suffrage and anti-suffrage, native and foreign, black and white,—to unite in paying a tribute of respect to the life and work of the greatest woman reformer, philosopher and statesman of the century, seems to me to be the realization of Mrs. Stanton's most optimistic dream. I am continually surprised and delighted at the action of Council in both instances. It shows a breadth and comprehensiveness on the part of the leaders of its twenty in one organization of which I am very proud. To be sure Mrs. Stanton stands for Suffrage first, last and all the time, and the conservative women who join in this celebration, do so knowing and rejoicing that she stands thus for a fully free and enfranchised womanhood.

Yes, both the N.Y. State and National Societies voted to celebrate the day; but we did not, in either capacity, vote not to let anybody but our own members have a hand in it. Why don't you see that for Anthony to head the fray, preside at the celebration, be general master of ceremonies, would reduce it to a mere mutual admiration affair!! The celebration is not, my dear, taken away from us. We, the Suffragists, will have our modicum of time to set forth what Mrs. Stanton has done for our specific cause—temperance women will have their chance to confess to her—educational, industrial and all classes. Oh no, my dear, it is not possible that the greater can be less than one of the parts that compose it!! At any rate, the fate of the celebration is in the hands of the greater which includes the less, and our political demand is but one of the less, that make up the greater.

I am hoping Mrs. Dickinson will soon get out her first statement of the fact and general plan of the Council's undertaking. Well I trust you will soon be able to see, and seeing enjoy, the tribute <u>of</u> and <u>by</u> <u>all</u> women—more than if it were by but a part of them.

≈ S. B. A.

≈ TCL, on NAWSA letterhead for 1894, Anthony-Avery Papers, NRU. Was enclosed in SBA to Rachel F. Avery, 2 April 1895, and in *Film* at that date.

1. SBA's typist made a copy of Blake's letter to SBA and SBA's reply. SBA enclosed the copy in a letter to Rachel Avery on 2 April 1895 and also sent a copy to Mary Dickinson with assurances that she should "<u>hold</u> the celebration <u>reins</u> in her own hands." "I wanted her to see ↑in it↓," SBA told Avery, "the wisdom of your suggestion to her on Mrs Blake's ambition &c."

2. At its recent meeting in Washington, the National Council of Women voted to organize a grand birthday celebration for ECS on November 12. Blake believed that the National-American association had already decided to host such an event, but records of the meeting in Atlanta did not support her view.

Delegates directed local suffrage clubs to use the occasion for "a public or social meeting." As president of the suffrage league in ECS's hometown, Blake may have assumed that her local celebration would be the premier event. She also could have picked this fight at the behest of ECS. In her autobiography, in a passage written soon after her birthday, ECS made no secret of her belief that a party given by woman suffragists would have been more appropriate. (*History and Minutes of the National Council of Women*, pp. 246-48, and *Proceedings of the Twenty-seventh Annual Convention, 1895, Film*, 33:552ff, 710ff; *Eighty Years*, 458.)

3. Mary Lowe Dickinson (1839-1914) succeeded May Sewall as president of the National Council of Women in 1895. A poet, novelist, teacher, professor of literature, and editor, Dickinson also distinguished herself as a leader in women's organizations, notably as the longtime leader of the King's Daughters. At the National-American's convention in 1894, she took the stage to declare her conversion to woman suffrage. (*WWW1*; *Woman's Who's Who 1914*; Mary Simmerson Logan, *The Part Taken by Women in American History* [Wilmington, Del., 1912], 713-15; *New York Times*, 9 June 1914; Washington *Evening Star*, 17 February 1894, *Film*, 32:449.)

4. The National Council of Women had also adopted a memorial resolution to honor Frederick Douglass, drafted by delegates from the National-American Woman Suffrage Association, Woman's Christian Temperance Union, Woman's Republican Association of the United States, and Woman's Relief Corps. It noted that Douglass paid "his last tribute to woman's progress" on the final day of his life, claimed him as "a friend and champion" of the woman's movement, and praised his aid in their search "for education, for industrial independence, and for political equality." (*Washington Post*, 24 February 1895, and *History and Minutes of the National Council of Women*, pp. 243-44, *Film*, 33:688-89, 710ff; *In Memoriam: Frederick Douglass*, 80-81.)

248 ❧ SBA TO ELIZA GRAY WHITING[1]

Rochester, N.Y., April 2, [*1895*].

Mrs. Eliza R. Whiting, Springfield, Mass.
My dear friend:—

Your note with Mr. Bonney's letter, came duly.[2] What a "Tempest in a teapot" the South has gotten up over the Council's resolutions of respect to the greatest colored man, orator, statesman, philosopher, the world ever saw. They seem to think nothing, but an endorsement of Miscegenation, in these respectful notices. They are charmingly oblivious of the fact that his bleached out complection with that of the black faces of the negros, whom we meet in the streets in the North and South, give evidence that something more than respectful attention was paid by the Anglo-Saxon men of the nation to the colored women.[3]

I have been home a little over two weeks and have but three more before I start for California.[4] Why does not the Republican send you over to San Francisco to write home letters of the wonderful gathering of Pacific Slope women? As you know, Miss Shaw is going with me and henceforth I propose always, wherever I go, to take along with me an orator. I should like also to be able to take along a good newspaper correspondent, such as you are, for instance. Lovingly yours,

~ Susan B. Anthony

~ TLS, on NAWSA letterhead for 1894, year uncorrected, Papers of SBA, NPV.

1. Eliza Rose Gray Whiting (c. 1846–?) worked for the *Springfield Republican* along with her husband, Charles G. Whiting, the paper's literary editor. She also served as secretary of Springfield's Union Relief Association from 1893 to 1910 and was active in the Northeast in the movement for coordinated charitable services. She was a member of the National-American association and attended the convention of 1892 as a delegate from Massachusetts. (*NCAB*, 9:365; *Springfield Republican*, 3 May 1910; Washington *Evening Star*, 19 January 1892, and *Report of the Twenty-sixth Annual Convention, 1894*, p. 101, both in *Film*, 29:994, 32:326ff.)

2. Whiting published Charles Bonney's tribute to Frederick Douglass in the *Springfield Republican*, 3 March 1895, and returned it to SBA. Written at SBA's request, the letter had not been read aloud at the funeral for lack of time. SBA sent the original to Helen Douglass on March 19. (SBA to H. P. Douglass, 19 March 1895, *Film*, 33:813–16; *In Memoriam: Frederick Douglass*, 45.)

3. News of white women paying tribute to Frederick Douglass set off a firestorm in the South. One Georgia editor wrote that a society "that applauds a white woman eulogist of a negro whose life was spent in advocating social equality is no better than the negro who is eulogized." Atlanta's Rev. J. B. Hawthorne, already infamous for his attacks on everyone associated with the National-American, reinvigorated his offensive in a public letter. He found "unmistakable significance" in the fact that the National Council of Women "devoted a day to the glorification of a dead negro who had been the chief apostle of the infamous doctrine of miscegenation. Does not this notable event forewarn the women of this country of the terrible vortex to which these feminine eulogists would lead them?" Anna Shaw later conflated this uproar with Hawthorne's behavior during the annual convention, leading historians

astray. (*Atlanta Constitution*, 1 March 1895; Shaw and Jordan, *Story of a Pioneer*, 307; Wheeler, *New Women of the New South*, 22.)

4. SBA's trip to California in the company of Anna Shaw was timed to coincide with the six-day Pacific Coast Woman's Congress in San Francisco and to spark preparations for a state amendment campaign in 1896. She arrived about May 20 and left on July 5, splitting her time between the Bay Area and Southern California. The public aspects of her visit included at least eight large meetings, twenty engagements to lecture, and numerous receptions. Behind the scenes she mediated a dispute between rival state suffrage leaders that had come before the National-American's executive committee in Atlanta, pushed local leaders to form a campaign committee through which various women's groups could collaborate, and saw her old friend Elizabeth Clark Sargent elected to head the committee.

249 ~ MEETING OF THE POLITICAL EQUALITY CLUB OF ROCHESTER

[4 April 1895]

Miss Ida B. Wells,[1] the colored advocate of freedman's rights, was present yesterday afternoon at the regular meeting of the Political Equality Club, held at the Watson house on North Clinton street.[2] The usual number of members attended the meeting and the session was productive of many interesting features.

Miss Susan B. Anthony gave an interesting talk concerning the treatment accorded colored people at the recent Atlanta convention, and commented upon the humiliations which the educated freedmen were subjected by the Southern delegates who attended the convention. Many of the former, she stated, refused to come to the sessions of the convention, owing to their self respect which prevented their forcing themselves into company so manifestly uncongenial.[3]

Miss Wells followed Miss Anthony. Among other illustrations given by her, to show the advancement which has been made by the freedmen in the South, she told of a young colored woman, a student at the Memphis medical college, who recently graduated and carried off the honors to the exclusion of thirty male students in the same class.[4] Her success did not meet with the appreciation it deserved, from the hands of her class mates, who refused to make her valedictorian. Miss Wells stated that, during the last ten years, 1,000 colored people had been lynched in the South. In 1893 160 met death at the hands of mobs and, last year, the number summed up 180.[5]

At the conclusion of Miss Wells's remarks the following resolutions were offered and adopted:

"Whereas, Reliable information has reached us through the personal knowledge of our friend of human rights, Miss I. B. Wells, that the barbarous practice of lynching, not only men, but women, without judge or jurors—on suspected, not proven crime, and sometimes without even a charge of crime, is still in practice in the South and West, and has been repeated within the last month, in the lynching of two women, one a white in Nebraska, charged with having been a witness against cattle thieves, the other a colored woman in Fayetteville, Tenn., only suspected of having burned a house some six months before,[6] therefore, be it

"Resolved, That the Woman's Political Equality Club of Rochester deplore and denounce such degraded and neglected conditions of any portion of our people as admits of such atrocities without arousing speedy retribution and reform by our governmental officials, through a thorough investigation, and the application of stringent measures for the protection of the disfranchised portion of our people, who are thus rendered helpless and without redress, and also for the safety of our whole community."[7]

↝ Rochester *Democrat and Chronicle*, 5 April 1895.

1. Ida Bell Wells (1862–1931), later Wells-Barnett, arrived in Rochester on 28 March 1895 for a weeklong visit, filled with lectures and meetings to protest the lynching of African Americans. A schoolteacher in Memphis for nearly a decade and a newspaperwoman in the same city, Wells became the unmatched and most vocal opponent of lynchings after 1892. Rochester's African Methodist Episcopal Zion Church and activists in its congregation hosted her visit, and a number of churches and clubs invited her to speak. Before their encounter at this meeting, SBA had called on Wells at the home of Adam and Anna Morse and introduced her to an audience at Plymouth Church on March 31. (*NAW*; *ANB*; Rochester *Democrat and Chronicle*, 28, 29, 30 March, 1, 2 April 1895.)

2. The Watson House at 61 North Clinton Street housed the headquarters of the Women's Educational and Industrial Union.

3. According to the *Rochester Union and Advertiser*, 5 April 1895, *Film*, 33:886, SBA specified that "the colored people were allowed only in the top gallery."

4. Wells probably refers to Francis W. Puryear, an African-American woman who graduated in 1895 from Meharry Medical College in Nashville (not Memphis), Tennessee. ("Our Lady Asclepiads," *Journal of the National Medical Association* 60 [March 1968]: 136, 154.)

5. Wells used statistics both to shock her audiences into recognizing the scale of the problem and to undermine the belief that violence and murder committed by whites were responses to rapes committed by blacks. She could show that charges of rape (not to be confused with the actual crime) accounted for a small percentage of known lynchings and thus underscore her point that lynching was better understood as a reign of terror. The numbers she provided in this speech were also available in her pamphlet *The Red Record: Tabulated Statistics and Alleged Causes of Lynching in the United States*, published in 1895.

6. In March 1895, Mrs. W. E. Holton was lynched in Keya Paha County, Nebraska, by cattle thieves. The Fayetteville lynching has not been identified. (*New York Times*, 19 March 1895.)

7. The newspaper's text of the resolution is corrected here to match the manuscript of its author, Lewia C. Smith, within the club's minutes. (*Film*, 33:887-93.)

250 ≫ FROM THE DIARY OF SBA

[*4–9 April 1895*]

THUR. APRIL 4, 1895. At Home   In evening Sister Mary & self went over & called on Miss Wells & Mrs Gannetts—[1]

1. Mary Thorn Lewis Gannett (1854–1952), wife of William Gannett, was one of Rochester's leading reformers and organizers, joining the Political Equality Club and the Women's Educational and Industrial Union and also founding new groups, like the Unitarian church's Woman's Alliance. Though Wells misremembered William Gannett's name, she later spoke fondly of her visit with the Gannetts. (Pease, "The Gannetts of Rochester,"; *New York Times*, 27 October 1952; Ida B. Wells, *Crusade for Justice: The Autobiography of Ida B. Wells*, ed. Alfreda M. Duster [Chicago, 1970], 231.)

FRI. APRIL 5, 1895. At home—   Got off 20 letters or more—& in P.M. went to Dr Farleys[1]—to listen reading of Sally Holly's letters—extracts by Carrie Putnam—which carried us back to the olden times—   Took Miss Wells to Young Peoples Party—but found no supper—so came home to cold water & bread & butter—[2]

1. Porter Farley (1840-1919), a physician, was the grandson of Samuel D. Porter, a leading abolitionist in Western New York and supporter of Frederick Douglass. (Columbia University, *Alumni Register, 1754-1931* [New York, 1932], 267; genealogical records, Porter Family Papers, NRU.) Caroline Putnam later prevailed upon John White Chadwick to edit *A Life for Liberty: Anti-Slavery and Other Letters of Sallie Holley* (1899).

2. Possibly this refers to an activity at the Unitarian Church, although its social group for youth was called the Young Folks' Club. The paltry meal started Wells's stay at 17 Madison Street with the Anthonys.

SAT. APRIL 6, 1895. At home—with Type writer— paid off Julia Ames— She hasn't the education no the quick perception to ever make a success of type writing & stenography

SUN. APRIL 7, 1895. Sunday A.M. Sister Mary went to hear Mr Gannett— Miss Wells to colored church[1]—& at 1 we all went to Dr & Mrs Sanfords to dinner—then to 2^d Baptist Church— Dr Anderson[2] introduced Miss Wells to a good audience—& she began "My country tis of thee"—which they had sung—& clearly proved it wasn't her country— At close it rained— Sister Mary went with her to Rev Stuarts[3] to tea— & then to 1st Baptist Church—& there was a still larger audience— at close of her speech a <u>Texas</u> Theological student brutally asked questions—which answered beautifully—& at last I threw in my word—that proscription of color was rampant here in Rochester &c[4]

1. The African Methodist Episcopal Zion Church on Favor Street.
2. Frederick Lincoln Anderson (1862-1938) was the pastor of Rochester's Second Baptist Church from 1888 to 1900, when he left to teach at the Newton Theological Seminary. Wells was announced to speak at the Second Baptist church in the afternoon and the First Baptist church in the evening. (*WWW4*; Rochester *Democrat and Chronicle*, 6 & 8 April 1895.)
3. Joseph William Alexander Stewart (1852-1947) was the pastor of Rochester's First Baptist Church from 1887 to 1903. He then became dean of the Rochester Theological Seminary. (*WWW2*.)
4. The questions came from a Texan enrolled at the Rochester Theological Seminary. Headlines in the next day's newspapers highlighted SBA's remarks. She had "jumped to her feet," the press reported, "and in a voice full of emotion said she would tell the gentleman from the South why it was that the negroes did not come North. 'It is because . . . they get no better treatment in the North than they do in the South.' The animated manner in which Miss Anthony denounced the treatment of the negroes in the city of Rochester carried her audience into the highest pitch of excitement and enthusiasm. It is doubtful if a more eloquent plea for the wiping out of race distinctions has

been heard in many a day." The Texan was silenced by the "outburst of approval on the part of the audience" that followed SBA's remarks. (*Rochester Herald*, 8 April 1895, and *Rochester Union and Advertiser*, 8 April 1895, *Film*, 33:905-6; Wells, *Crusade for Justice*, 227-28.)

MON. APRIL 8, 1895. Ida B. Wells of Memphis—guest— Went to see Mrs Fullam[1] about dresses for California trip— Told typewriter Anna Dorsey[2]—to ask Miss Wells if she would like to dictate her letters & have them written on the type writer— When I returned—I found Miss Wells scribbling away—& said couldn't you dictate & let Anny type write for you— "oh yes—if I had had a chance"— then I went to my room & said—"You didn't understand me did you to ask Mrs W."— ["]Yes—she said—but I didn't choose to write for a colored woman"— I engaged to work for you! Well—when I ask an employee to do a favor to a guest I expect her to comply— so the little fatherless & homeless girl of 20—left— The Presbytery's ↑members↓ this A.M. passed a resolution against Lynching—[3]

1. Sarah J. Mylacraine Fullam had made and repaired some of SBA's dresses for at least a decade, beginning before she married Frank Fullam in the late 1880s. By this date, she no longer advertised herself as a dressmaker and may have worked only for private clients. (City directories, 1885, 1888, 1894, 1895; SBA diary, 1888, cash account page for August, *Film*, 25:869ff.)

2. Anna Dorsey worked for SBA for one week and four days before this dismissal, according to the cash account for April in SBA diary, 1895, *Film*, 33:80ff.

3. The local Presbyterian Ministers' Association denounced lynchings "as cruel, inhuman and as a lasting reproach to our liberty and laws. We pledge our united influence against this evil and toward the formation of a public sentiment founded upon a higher respect for law and life." (*Rochester Union and Advertiser*, 8 April 1895, *Film*, 33:906.)

TUES. APRIL 9, 1895. At home— Miss Wells here to supper— Democrat Reporter called[1]—gave him the story of Miss Wells & the Clerk at Burke's store[2]—that of my type writer &c—but the Dem. Chron never published it—nor did it allude to the outrage editorially— At 9 Oclock Miss Wells left & went to her colored friend's Mrs Morse—[3]

1. The reporter came to Madison Street to interview SBA about false charges leveled against her by Anna Dickinson about outstanding debts from the *Revolution* that SBA paid in full on 16 April 1874. See *Film*, 33:914, and *Papers*, 3:71.

2. On Monday, April 8, Ida Wells and Mary Anthony went shopping at

Burke, Fitz Simons, Hone & Company, a large department store, and were approached by a manager who disputed SBA's charges about segregation in the North. (City directory, 1895; Wells, *Crusade for Justice*, 228.)

3. Anna A. Morse (c. 1858–1941), a member of the Zion Church, helped to welcome Wells at the railroad station on March 28 and took Wells to her house at 60 Favor Street, where Wells stayed until her move to Madison Street. SBA called on Morse and Wells and met young Anna, a fourteen year-old whose story of being barred from a public school social was the poignant tale at the center of SBA's protest against local segregation when she spoke on April 7. The senior Anna Morse was born in Alabama and moved to Rochester after her marriage to Adam Morse and the birth of several children in the South. Adam Morse's occupations varied: he was a waiter in 1895; at other times he worked as a coachman, porter, and university janitor. He too was active in the community, taking a part in Rochester's funeral of Frederick Douglass. (Rochester *Democrat and Chronicle*, 28, 30 March, 9 April 1895; *Rochester Herald*, 9, 10 April 1895, in SBA scrapbook 34, Rare Books, DLC; city directories, 1895 to 1900; Mt. Hope and Riverside Cemetery Interment Records; Wells, *Crusade for Justice*, 227–29.)

⇒ Excelsior Diary 1895, n.p., SBA Papers, DLC.

251 ⇒ ECS TO CLARA BEWICK COLBY

26 West 61   N.Y. April 26 [*1895*]

Dear Mrs Colby

I send you a long letter from Mrs Gage on Copyright of Woman's Bible.[1] Will you see Mr Spofford & do what must be done. Is it better to have it in my name alone or with Mrs Gage? I will remit what it costs to do the thing & your time   Send her copy of The Tribune   I shall leave the copy right business to you if you will see to it

⇒ *E C S*

⇒ ALS, Clara B. Colby Papers, Archives Division, WHi.

1. According to Matilda Gage, ECS suggested copyright in both their names in a letter of early April that asked Gage to file the appropriate forms. When Gage did nothing about it, ECS wrote again on April 26 to say that she had forwarded Gage's directions about how to proceed to Clara Colby who would take care of the matter. (M. J. Gage to C. B. Colby, 17 & 30 May 1895, Clara B. Colby Papers, Archives Division, WHi.)

252 ❧ ECS TO CLARA BEWICK COLBY

[*New York, after 26 April 1895*]

Dear Mrs Colby

I thought in sending Mrs Gages letter I had asked you some questions about copyright   I wanted to know before adding Mrs Gages name if that gave her any right over the contents of the book or the proceeds from it[1]   As I expect to do the publishing, find the money do all the correspondence   I do not wish to complicate my work by any other rights   Find out the rights involved & if it would be complimentery only to Mrs Gage without giving her any rights then do it

❧   E. C. S.

❧ ALS, Clara B. Colby Papers, Archives Division, WHi.

1. Gage knew nothing of ECS's reservations and learned that Colby obtained copyright in the name only of ECS by pushing Colby and ECS for answers late into May. While Gage subsequently lashed out at both women for their betrayal of her interests, she did not indicate how the conversation with ECS about copyright began, nor offer evidence about why she deserved copyright. The incident bears the familiar marks of ECS assenting to someone's request and later reconsidering or taking other advice. Despite her initial excitement about working on the *Woman's Bible*, Gage had dropped out of the project. Moreover, in a fit of pique in 1893, she swore never again to work on anything with ECS. When ECS named the members of her original committee to a reporter from the New York *World* in mid-March 1895, Gage was not in the list. Correspondence on the subject between Gage and ECS must have begun at about that time, though the letters are missing. By March 25, ECS knew that Gage wanted to join her new committee. By early May, before the copyright dispute played itself out, Gage had reserved the books of Matthew and Revelations for herself. In a missing letter in which ECS confessed her decision about the copyright, received by Gage on May 30, she also offered, according to Gage, to pay her for some work on the Pentateuch. Gage's first commentaries were published in the spring of 1897. (Interviews, 17 March & 11 May 1895, ECS to C. B. Colby, 25 March, 14 & 30 May 1895, and M. J. Gage to ECS, 28 May 1895, *Film*, 33:803-4, 845-46, 1012-14, 34:16-21, 114-15, 121-24; M. J. Gage to C. B. Colby, 17 & 30 May 1895, Clara B. Colby Papers, Archives Division, WHi; M. J. Gage to T. C. Gage, 2 December 1886, 11 July

1893, Gage Collection, MCR-S; Kern, *Mrs. Stanton's Bible*, 169-70; Sally Roesch Wagner, *Matilda Joslyn Gage: She Who Holds the Sky* [Aberdeen, S.D., 1998], 63-65.)

253 ❧ LADY ISABELLA SOMERSET TO ECS

Reigate Priory, England. June 5th, 1895.

My dear Mrs. Cady Stanton,

Thank you for your most kind letter written at the end of March.¹ My great difficulty with regard to your scheme has been in the fact that part of your revised edition of the Bible was issued before the rest of the committee had seen it, and we were much blamed because we had associated ourselves with a scheme in which people of different views were not represented, as almost everyone held the same view, and that was not one that found acceptance with the women for whom we work.² I think Miss Willard gave a list of names to your daughter, and I am quite sure you will understand we are placed in a somewhat difficult situation owing to the fact that we have to stand as representatives of large organizations and are not free to act as individuals. If women of Conservative opinions could be associated with you it would make the scheme much easier for us. I know that you have asked me for the names of two distinguished English women, but I find it most difficult to get anyone to join now that some part of the manuscript has been published, as people do not understand how they can come into a revision a portion of which is already accomplished. I have not yet been able to see Mrs. Blatch, but hope to meet her very soon. It was a great pleasure to see you, and I shall not forget your kind and cordial welcome. Believe me, Yours most warmly,

❧ *Isabel Somerset*

❧ TLS, on British Women's Temperance Associaton letterhead, ECS Papers, DLC.

1. This letter of March has not been found. Frances Willard wrote to ECS on April 27 to say that her sojourn in England made it inconvenient to serve on the committee. She went on to advise ECS about working with evangelicals: "They feel that the Bible as the word of God must be handled by those who regard it as such in order to evolve such a result as they are willing to look

upon with any degree of confidence," she wrote. They are more attuned to exegesis by men than women, she continued, "because the clergy have so long been regarded by them as the special channel of communication so far as the sacred oracles are concerned." Willard placed herself among a small group of evangelicals who "believe[d] in the right of private judgment, no matter whether the one who does the judging is a man or a woman." On May 21, ECS asked Willard and Somerset to reconsider their withdrawal from the committee and "give the 'Woman's Bible' the influence of your names and of the highest truth your mature thought on the Scriptures has revealed." After restating her vision of diverse points of view, ECS asked, "Would it not be a greater blessing to women at large, a stronger proof of your faith in your own religious opinions, for you to comment on what I have written and show wherein I am in error, and thus illumine the Woman's Bible with your truth, than to withdraw?" ECS subsequently reframed her letter to Willard as an article for the *Woman's Tribune*. (*Film*, 34:89.)

2. Attention to the articles appearing in the *Woman's Tribune* and in other papers across the country, especially in May 1895, stirred members of the Woman's Christian Temperance Union to wonder how they were implicated in the *Woman's Bible*. The *Union Signal*'s editor tried to clear up confusion over the book's name by pointing out that the object was to write commentaries, not a new Bible, and she reiterated that the union had no role at all. She did, however, explain on May 30, that "Miss Willard was requested . . . to write upon certain passages in the Scriptures relating to women, and consented provided there would be a sufficient number of evangelical Christian women on the commentary committee to make the work an orthodox one." Noting the recent agitation in the press, the editor assured her readers that Willard had contributed nothing to the project so far and was likely to retire from it soon.

254 ~ ECS TO AUGUSTA J. CHAPIN[1]

26 West 61st N.Y. June 6th [*1895*]

Dear Miss Chapin

You ask about our final work. That is the difficult point for decision, how to get the whole book in print & in the hands of the Revising Committee for ↑before↓ our General assembly meets is the question. We cannot get many papers to publish anything regularly & more not at all   I have thought of one plan & would like to know how it strikes you. Divide the whole into six parts & publish in cheap form, paper cover, as fast as we can get each one ready, then place all in the hands of each member of the Revising Committee say two or three weeks or months before we meet for the final revision. Then we would be in a measure be prepared for intelligent discussion being familiar with what each one had contributed.

What do you think of this plan? Can you propose anything better? Suppose we try the experiment with The Penteteuch. I have been through all those books once, published all of Genesis, the last chapter will be in the next Woman's Tribune   Some comments have been made on these. Suppose you make some comments on the different books, criticisms on mine or general remarks on the whole & we publish Part I   I think it would stir up the whole committee to work now in their summer vacation, & simplify the work before us. Yes you understand the plan aright each one writes over her own name with the right to comment on each other, & each one a voice & vote as to what shall be finally bound up in The Woman's Bible.

To be handsomely bound, good print   good paper & illustrations if we can raise the money. I would like an illustration of Huldah in the College surrounded by the wise men, Deborah with Barak leading the army, Vashti in all her womanly pride & dignity defying the orders of King Ahasuerus, Esther in the councils of state, &c &c I would like to have a grand & beautiful book. The women learned in Hebrew & Greek & biblical criticism should do their best to gild its pages, & from every stand point we should have their opinions   I want Jew & Gentile Catholic & Protestant leading women in all nations & denominations to give us their opinions on woman's position in the Bible & of the authority & inspiration of its teachings

But alas! when a woman like Frances Willard was frightened from such a grand enterprize by my garden scene the little tableax of the women the snake & the apple in whom shall we put our trust[2]   Her flight made me think of

> "Little Miss Lynch sat on a bench
>   Eating some curds & whey
> When along came a spider
>   And sat down beside her
> And frightened Miss Lynch away"[3]

With kind regards yours sincerely

Elizabeth Cady Stanton.

Send this to Miss Willard it might amuse her. E. C. S.

~ ALS, GLC 5508.233, Gilder Lehrman Collection, Gilder Lehrman Institute of American History. Not in *Film*.

1. Augusta Jane Chapin (1836-1905), member of the Revising Committee for the *Woman's Bible*, was a Universalist minister, the second woman to be ordained in that church after Olympia Brown. She spent most of her career in the Midwest, and was probably living at this time in Chicago, although she was nominally the minister of a church in Omaha. Returning to school in the 1880s, she earned a master of arts degree from the University of Michigan, and in 1893, while she helped organize the Parliament of Religions at the Columbia Exposition, Lombard University awarded her an honorary doctorate of divinity. In addition to preaching, she taught literature at several universities, including the University of Chicago. Chapin's connections to the suffrage movement were casual but long-lasting ones; while based in Milwaukee in 1869, she presided at the suffrage convention held during the winter tour of ECS and SBA, and a year later, she held office in Iowa's state suffrage association. (*NAW*; Hanson, *Our Woman Workers*, 432-37; *American Women*; *Papers*, 2:227.)

2. ECS's commentary on Genesis, 3:1-24, the verses recounting the Fall, was published in the New York *World*, 17 March 1895, and *Woman's Tribune*, 6 April 1895, *Film*, 33:803-4, 902. She began by asking with Adam Clarke whether to read the scene as an allegory or a literal account, noting that Clarke stumbled on the talking snake but urged a literal reading nonetheless. After adding that botanists now knew apples did not grow in the Middle East, she mused, "If the serpent and the apple are to be withdrawn thus recklessly from the tableaux, it is feared that with advancing civilization the whole drama may fall into discredit." In a familiar gloss on the temptation, she praised Eve's "intense thirst for knowledge, that the simple pleasures of picking flowers and talking with Adam did not satisfy."

3. On variants of the traditional nursery rhyme "Little Miss Muffet," see Iona and Peter Opie, eds., *The Oxford Dictionary of Nursery Rhymes* (Oxford, England, 1951), 323-24, though "Miss Lynch" on "a bench" is not among those listed.

255 ❧   SBA TO NANNIE WRIGHT LYON

[c. 22 July 1895]

I must just say how I have laughed over the men's howling over the idea that the women might possibly take our advice and sit down with folded hands refusing to do another thing to help them until the right of self government was accorded.[1] Their agony over the bare suggestion of such a dilemma only proves it to be the true thing to do. Remember that Napoleon said: "Watch your enemy. Learn what he wants you not to do and do it."[2]

Wouldn't it be fun if the women of every household, of which the men voted against their rights would just say, "Run your house alone then"; and the church women say to Dr. Buckley and Bishop Vincent, "Then run your church alone."

But alas, women have too much of the spaniel nature I fear to do other than lick the hand that smites them.

I did not expect to be connected with the resolution but it proves just the word to stir up the lions.

What did the Republican party do to carry the amendment? Absolutely nothing. But by their silence in their platform virtually said to every man, "better not."

Well, after this wind blows over you must all begin to work again. It is no use letting the amendment go to the voters until at least two of the larger parties have endorsed it and endorsed it so that they can't go back on their word when the crucial convention comes just before election. Lovingly yours,

❧   *Susan B. Anthony.*

❧ Unidentified and undated clipping, SBA scrapbook 23, Rare Books, DLC.

1. Nannie and Thomas Lyon hosted a luncheon for SBA on her stop in Topeka between trains on 9 July 1895. According to a reporter among the guests, when SBA was asked what the state's suffragists should be doing, she replied, "They ought to withdraw from all their charitable work and let the men run things for awhile. . . . I say that the women of Kansas should sit by and fold their hands. If they would stop their helping the men for six months, we would have equal suffrage granted us." SBA resumed her travel, and two days

later, at Topeka's annual suffrage picnic, the suggestion surfaced as a resolution for discussion. Under the headline "Miss Anthony's Spite," the *Daily Capital*, published the resolution. It began, "Whereas, 117,000 Kansas men declared themselves against female suffrage at the late election and 31,000 showed their opposition by remaining silent," and it recommended the boycott apply to "any religious, charitable, moral reform or political association." After a lively debate, the picnickers postponed a vote on the measure until August. The news spread quickly from Topeka as scores of humorless editors across the country denounced the idea and SBA as "spiteful," "babyish," and "foolish." Interviewed while passing through Chicago on July 15, SBA joked about men's fears that "all women should cease even to cook dinner," but she also refused to call the idea ridiculous. Had men been denied the vote, she suggested, "they would not merely sit down and fold their hands." When the Rochester *Democrat and Chronicle* interviewed her on July 21, she "defended her position with vigor." It made sense to her that men should be left to run charitable institutions alone, she told Clara Colby the next day, "as they have voted to run the government alone— I see nothing but Patrick Henryism in it." (SBA diary, 9 July 1895; Topeka *Daily State Journal*, 10 July 1895; *Topeka Daily Capital*, 12 July 1895; Chicago *Inter-Ocean*, 16 July 1895; Rochester *Democrat and Chronicle*, 22 July 1895; SBA to C. B. Colby, 22 July 1895; all in *Film*, 33:80ff, 34:231, 233, 236, 254-55, 256-60.)

2. Among his military maxims, Napoleon advised "never to do what the enemy wishes you to do, for this reason alone, that he desires it." (*The Military Maxims of Napoleon*, trans. George C. D'Aguilar, ed. David G. Chandler [London, 2002], 61.)

256 ~ SBA TO ECS

Rochester, N.Y., July 24, 1895.

Well! Well! My Dear

It is really good to see your pen-tracks once more— No—I don't want my name on that Bible Committee— You fight that battle—and leave me to fight the secular—the political fellows— I haven't seen a half dozen of The Tribunes or Journals since I went to California—so haven't read yours or any one's Comments— I know your doing good because you are making Rome Howl— So go ahead—but do at least have the members of your Committee of those who have even read the Bible once through—consecutively—in their lives— I simply don't want the enemy to be diverted from my practical ballot fight—to that of scoring me for belief one way or the other about the bible— The religious <u>part</u>—has <u>never</u> <u>been</u> <u>mine</u>—you know—and I wont take it up—so long as the men who hold me in durance vile—wont care a dime what the Bible says—all they care for is what the <u>saloon</u> says— So go ahead—in your own way—and let me stick to my own—

Did you give your name to Marguerita Arlina Hamm[1]—for her <u>new</u> women's Press Club?— She must <u>not</u> use <u>mine</u>— I hear she has done so—tell her she must drop it off her list—no one has a right to use my name before asking me—not even that dear little woman must do it—

Are you preparing your Bible for a book? If so who is going to publish it?

I see Mrs Colby announces she is going to omit her paper this summer—or some weeks of it— That will just finish it— The friends everywhere seem to have lost heart over The Tribune—her Coxeyism—her Indian Religionists puffings—& now her Dress Page—there doesn't seem to be any consecutiveness about her paper—[2] If she hadn't such piles of encumbrances—her house, boy, indian &c, &c, if she were <u>free</u> footed—she would be just the person to come strait & help me dig through the mountain piles in our back garret— Alas I know of no one to look to.

Rachel—Mrs Chapman Catt & Mrs Upton are to be Saturday night—to enlightmen of things in general—Program for your Celebration for one thing— Rachel & the Council President Mrs Dickinson have had the matter in hand— If you think of any points you'd like to have made—please write them to me instanter— I do we can make your 80th birth day tell tremendously—the world over—so do put your thought to it & write me at once— It is dark—so must stop—take the 10.37 train to night for Lakeside Assembly Ohio—to speak—shall be back Saturday night—[3]

Oh how I do wish you were where I could run in to chat over—but we are always so far apart— Lovingly yours

≈ *Susan B. Anthony*

[*on verso, ECS to Clara Bewick Colby*] I get my share of criticism too. You need not return. Read & burn.

≈ ALS, on NAWSA letterhead, AF 24(2), Anthony Family Collection, CSmH.

1. Margherita Arlina Hamm (1867–1907), a journalist, organized the Woman's Suffrage Press Association in the summer of 1895 and announced that ECS,

SBA, and Mary Livermore were lifetime members of its advisory council. Hamm was the group's president, and her list of officers included Harriette Keyser, Lillie Blake, Carrie Catt, Ellen Dietrick, Rachel Avery, Anna Shaw, Laura Johns, and Harriet Upton. Members pledged to provide reliable suffrage news for papers across the country, essentially the job assigned to the press committee of the National-American. By quoting an interview with ECS in its publicity, the association linked itself to the cause, but in one undated article, the group made grander claims about its origins. It was "a natural outgrowth" of Carrie Catt's plan of work for the National-American; it was "affiliated with the New York City Woman Suffrage League and the State League, thereby coming under the direct auspices of the National Council of Women and with the National American Woman Suffrage Association." Neither the national nor the New York suffrage societies mentioned the press association in reporting work done in 1895. (*NAW*; "Woman's Organizations," *Arthur's Home Magazine* 65 [August 1895]: 687–89; undated and unidentified clipping, at July? 1895, *Film*, 34:288.)

2. In what would become a familiar litany of complaints about the way Clara Colby used her newspaper to explore her many passions, SBA referred first to Coxey's Army of workers who marched on Washington in the early spring of 1894 in support of public works to ease the staggering unemployment following the Panic of 1893. The paper also reflected an interest in eastern religions that Colby shared with many Americans in the last decade of the century. Finally, Colby had taken up dress reform, giving the subject a full page of her four-page paper.

3. SBA agreed to substitute for an ailing Anna Shaw at the Lakeside Chautauqua Assembly on the shore on Lake Erie.

257 ❧ ECS TO CLARA BEWICK COLBY

26 West 61st   N.Y. July 29th [1895]

Dear Mrs Colby,

Your pathetic letter touches my very heart. I only wish I were worth enough to help you in your struggles but my income only just meets my necessities.¹ I do not understand with your financial responsibilities, why you adopt old men & children, & try to publish a paper.

As we are all limited in our powers & capacities why shoulder burdens we cannot carry. You have cut yourself off from the sympathies of many friends, by assuming ↑burdens↓ you were not compelled to do in justice to yourself nor humanity. If you are interested in the topics you treat & gain subscribers thereby that is the line to follow, that is common sense which every editor would understand. Susan has one idea & she has no patience with any one who has two. I cannot sit on the door post like Poe's raven & sing suffrage evermore[2] I am deeply interested in all the live questions of the day. I asked Mrs Chandler to take my place in The Tribune until she had published Timothy as I am busy with The Penteteuch now in the hands of the Publisher as soon as I get that out I will go on with the next books for Part. II. She writes me that you declined taking hers, why? I wanted her to put what she had written in ship shape like mine ready for the printer.[3] She published them in a Chicago paper all in a heap that I should be obliged to arrange all over before it could go into The Woman's Bible[4] It is amazing after all the directions published in The Tribune no one knows how to do the work. I have heaps of manuscript sent me in pencil & pale ink that I cannot read, running all over the Bible on every possible subject except "the status of woman" that I cannot use. The stupidity of the human family surpasses all understanding. You would suppose the paper we published telling in detail what & how to do the work would be all sufficient, but no after I send that they come back with questions already answered therein. I think you better write Mrs Chandler to fix hers up in chapters of two columns with her texts in fine print & send me Hers would probably run a month, by that time I should be ready for Part II. With kind regards & deep sympathy yours ever

≈ *Elizabeth Cady Stanton*

≈ ALS, Clara B. Colby Papers, Archives Division, WHi.

   1. The thoughtless act of sending Colby the letter with SBA's criticism of her now required ECS to make amends.

   2. See note above at 18 February 1890.

   3. In May 1895, ECS informed Colby, "I have told others they cannot have room in your paper except to comment on what you & I say that they must find publishers elsewhere." Lucinda Chandler had done so. An entire page of the Sunday *Chicago Times-Herald*, 30 June 1895, was devoted to her commentaries on the New Testament's first and second books of Timothy. (ECS to C. B. Colby, c. 14 May 1895, *Film*, 34:16–21.)

   4. In the *Woman's Tribune*, 27 April 1895, *Film*, 33:950, contributors were directed to buy a copy of the English Revised Version of the Bible, cut out the half dozen or more verses desired for comment, paste the text at the head of a paper, write the comments below "with *black* ink," and style a heading from

examples already published. In her choice of translation, Chandler followed ECS's directions better than ECS did herself: ECS was publishing verses from the King James Version while Chandler used the English Revised Version. Chandler prefaced her response to biblical passages with a lengthy essay on the teachings of Paul, and along with commentaries, she included sections that she headed "The Gospel of the New Dispensation According to Woman." These alternative gospels described a new Christianity of exalted womanhood and direct communion with God and scripture, unmediated by clergy. Either Chandler or ECS laid a heavy editorial hand on the work before it appeared in the *Woman's Bible*, part two; sections were omitted, parts of the alternative gospels became commentaries, and scriptural verses were quoted from the King James Version.

258 ≫ FRANCES E. WILLARD TO ECS

Reigate, Surrey, England. August 1st. 1895

My dear Mrs. Stanton,

We have taken your advice and "dropped the subject." You have shown us your large heartedness in appreciating the difficulty of our position, and we have never mentioned you except in terms of reverence and affection, but as we certainly do differ on the question of the Bible it is better that we do not try to work together on that one subject.[1] Miss Greenwood[2] wrote me that she thought everything was now satisfactory between us, and we are rejoiced to think so. Believe me, dear Friend, it has been Lady Henry's purpose and mine from the first to manifest to all concerned the affection and regard we feel for you as a mighty pioneer in the work of uplift for one half the human race. Believe me Yours with warm affection,

≫ *Frances E Willard*

≫ TLS, on World's Woman's Christian Temperance Union letterhead, Scrapbook 2, Papers of ECS, NPV.

1. Questions within the Woman's Christian Temperance Union mounted as the press stayed on the subject of Frances Willard's connection to the *Woman's Bible*. An editorial in the *Union Signal*, 11 July 1895, backed off somewhat from an earlier history of talks between ECS and Willard to say that ECS was premature in announcing Willard's participation without awaiting "the responses of the various evangelical names" mentioned in their interview. If the evangelical women "should decline to be associated with the

committee," the editor continued, "Lady Henry Somerset and Miss Willard feel that their names must not remain on the list, as it would not then fairly represent the women of the churches who have always been the co-workers of these two white ribbon leaders." On 8 August 1895, the editor streamlined the news: "While we are about it, we may as well reiterate that Miss Willard and Lady Henry Somerset have nothing whatever to do with the 'Woman's Bible.'"

2. Elizabeth Ward Greenwood (1850–1922), Superintendent of Evangelical Work for the Woman's Christian Temperance Union and president of the union's local in Brooklyn, was put in touch with ECS by Frances Willard to collaborate on the *Woman's Bible* as one of several evangelical women added to the committee. Though not ordained, Greenwood ministered to a Congregational church each summer and served as pastor of a large mission in Brooklyn. (*American Women*; *Alumni Record of Wesleyan University, Middletown, Conn.*, 3d ed. [Hartford, Conn., 1883], 184; *Chicago Times-Herald*, 13 May 1895, *Film*, 33:1012–14; *New York Times*, 29 November 1922.)

259 ECS TO ROBERT L. STANTON

Peterboro, [*N.Y.*] 10 A.M. Saturday, August [*10*], 1895.[1]

My dear Bob:—

I look out on a clean beautiful lawn and some magnificent trees older than I am. The air is bracing and delicious, and I feel like a bird set free from a cage. The entire household is just setting out in three carriages for a picnic. The house is full. Everything in and about, clean, sweet and lovely. I have little table to myself for meals and sit in the library in a big cosy chair by an open window. I hate being crowded at a table, with elbows in my ribs on each side, and to listen to incoherent gabble, half a dozen persons talking at the same time.

But to begin at the hour we parted. I had comfortable seats in the train, plenty of air, took off my bonnet, put a veil over my head and soon fell asleep. No stops until we reached Albany in two hours and three quarters. The scenery all the way up the Hudson was lovely, the air cool, and cinders abundant. From Albany on, through the valley of the Mohawk, it was not so pleasant and seemed much warmer. We reached Utica at one and waited almost twenty minutes. The mail train was not crowded. I got the conductor to open the door, so that we had a current of air almost strong enough to blow us out of our seats.

At Canistota, Mr. Lewis and his coach were in waiting order. Mr.

Lewis himself and one of his confrères were at the door to conduct me tenderly down the steps and across the rails to the coach, where stood almost a dozen men waiting to see me ascend. I saw at a glance that this was impossible without some extra appliances. The men whom I have steadily abused for half a century ran in all directions for boxes, which being judiciously arranged, made a convenient ladder. So with a man on each side to boost and support and a very tall strong one in the carriage to whose horny hands I clung with feminine tenacity, I reached my destination. The big man leaped out on the right side, the smaller men removed the various boxes, big and little, the coachman cracked his whip, and, after paying Mr. Lewis four dollars for his carriage and one for the baggage piled on another vehicle, away we went.

I made a very pretty speech to the dear men, thanking them for all their efforts individually and collectively, with this peroration:

"When you are eighty, gentlemen, I hope a bevy of strong women will aid you under similar difficulties."

I threw them each a warm farewell kiss, they raised their hats, and the curtain fell.

The drive up to Peterboro was delightful. The clouds obscured the sun, the air was cool, and the carriage, with the top down, was easy and large. We ate some delicious pears that Maggy had provided. We drove up in front of the old castle a little before five. My dismounting was as eventful as the ascent. The step of the carriage was rickety and considered unsafe for my weight. The guests filled the piazza. One ran and got a stool, another a big dictionary, a third Clark's "Commentaries,"[2] the first book as a support to the stool and the second to lay on the stool to shorten the distance. Then with one male guest on one side and a second on the other, I backed down and out amid the congratulations of the assembled multitude.

After resting a short time, we went to our respective chambers, disrobed, brushed and washed off the cinders and then dressed for high tea. We sat on the piazza and chatted all the evening and retired early. I had a delightful bed and slept sweetly. It never did seem so delightful here. But now I shall take a nap. So adieu,

~ *Mother.*

~ Typed transcript, ECS Papers, NjR.

1. The Stanton children omitted a day of the month from their transcript of the letter. Writing from New York City on August 8, ECS directed that her

mail thereafter be sent to Peterboro, New York, in Madison County. There she spent a month with her cousins in the house of Gerrit Smith, a place frequented in her youth and the site of her introduction to Henry Stanton. (*Eighty Years*, 453-55.)

2. Adam Clarke (1762-1832) published *The Holy Bible, with a Commentary and Critical Notes* between 1810 and 1826 in eight volumes. ECS consulted it often while at work on the *Woman's Bible*.

260 ❦ SBA TO CLARA BEWICK COLBY

Rochester N.Y. Aug 26/95

My dear niece Clara B. C.

Yours of Saturday the 24th to sister Mary is here to day—and "Richard is so nearly himself again"—that he—<u>she</u> will report progress—¹ My ↑oldest and↓ dearest Rochester friend—Mary H Hallowell—came yesterday P.M. and took me a half hours drive into the outskirts of the city—and this P.M. she has given me a drive of an hour or more—thus you see I ↑am↓ making daily progress—but too slow for my swift winged longings to be about my masters business as of yore

It is awfully hard to have to be too lazy for anything—but don't magnify the lapse—it is just a month to day—since I simply collapsed—the whole of me coming to a sudden stand still like a clap of thunder in a clear sky—without note or warning— I have had nothing ↑that might be called↓ pain—simply inaction— I tell my nurse² I expect to pass on to the beyond without knowing what excrutiating pain is—but my temperature ran for days up to 103 & 4—but no more—it seems a long long time—since that 26th July noon-day at Riverside— Just say—Miss Anthony after her enforced rest—absolute do nothingness of a whole month—will soon be left to herself—both Doctor & nurse having decided her capable to go along without their farther ministrations.— But of the blessings of a trained nurse—to boss one—as the mother does her baby!!

Yes—you may have the Herald—Miss Müller speaks of³—she says write to Mr. W. O. Judge⁴—144 Madison Avenue—New York—will you in turn give me Miss Müllers exact P.O. address—she has only Maidenhead—

No Pagan or Barbarous nation can suffer greater cruelties & outrages than does this of ours— The Negro lynchings are something blood-curdling—& the myriads of <u>wife</u> murders—pass almost unnoticed—though they blister over our newspapers—

Your Postal—the other day—alluding to death of some aged person under your roof—was all greek to me—but so you did what seemed your duty—all is well—each one of us must decide her own work & worship— Lovingly yours

Susan B. Anthony

ALS, on NAWSA letterhead, Clara B. Colby Collection, CSmH.

1. For quotation, see note above at 31 December 1888. SBA suffered momentary heart failure and fainted while speaking at Lakeside, Ohio, on July 26. The first reports that she had died were soon followed by premature reports of her recovery. Harriet Upton escorted her to Rochester on July 27, and officers of the National-American held a meeting at 17 Madison Street on July 28. Of that occasion SBA wrote in her diary, "I feeling awfully stupid," and for three weeks she wrote nothing further. Not until Mary Anthony substituted for her sister in Warsaw, New York, on August 3 did the press return to the story and realize that SBA was seriously ill, confined to her bed, and cared for by a resident nurse. (*Film*, 33:80ff.)

2. According to SBA's diary on August 29, when the nurse completed her work, this was Magdalene Kelly McCutcheon, a Canadian woman. Who served as her physician is not known.

3. Henrietta Müller's *Women's Penny Paper* became the *Woman's Herald* on 3 January 1891, without change of volume or issue numbers.

4. William Quan Judge (1851–1896), an immigrant to New York from Ireland and a lawyer, was a leading Theosophist and president of the independent American Theosophical Society. (*ANB*.)

261   Parker Pillsbury to SBA

Henniker, N.H. 21 Sept. 1895.

Not much of a letter my dear and now venerable Friend, not much of a letter but at least a billet, that you may know you are not forgotten.

Not forgotten certainly in your calamity, nor in your decline of years.

We have heard of your late illness, and of your more recent relapse in the hands of the artist—the latter denoting great weakness of the system, and warning to constant prudence and care for your health as you come down to "Life's latest stage."[1]

But hold on, my dear, <u>our</u> dear Susan, hold on to the latest hour possible. So we all pray and hope.

You have seen great and glorious changes, almost Revolutions in your long and busy life.

But yet, how much remains to be encountered and accomplished!

We shall hope you may live to see one grand achievement: <u>The equal civil and political Rights of all Men and all Women, before the Law.</u>

Then you may well say "Lord, now lettest thou thy servant depart in Peace; for mine eyes have seen thy Salvation."[2]

It is well that the Birth Day of Mrs. Stanton be celebrated. Would that I could be there to witness the august scenes and beholdings of the occasion!

But since my illness of last year, I have not been so far from home. Nor is it probable that I shall ever see New York again. I have not been in Boston for more than a year and a half!

Last week, I ventured to Portland for a few days, and so far, no harm seems to have come of it. But you know how almost certain Paralysis is to repeat itself, and some time soon—and so I am almost always bidden to beware!

Mind and body are both victims to the disease; but it seems to me so far, that the spirit remains intact. Is that super added argument for the eternity of the soul? It may be; but I do not need it. That is already secured—the intrepid Col. Ingersoll to the contrary, notwithstanding.[3]

But this must close so soon as you are told that wife and daughter,[4] here with me, send their love and wishes that you were near them that they could minister to your needs, [*in margin of first page*] and my own assurances that I am ever, forever your sincere friend and brother,

~ *Parker Pillsbury.*

~ ALS, ECS Papers, DLC. Marked for excerpts by Ida Harper.

1. SBA slowly regained strength. After three weeks and four days under the care of a nurse, she was able to bathe and dress herself on August 30. On September 16, in an incident reported across the country, she arrived at a photographer's studio in Rochester and fainted again.

2. Luke 2:29–30.

3. Robert Ingersoll described immortality as a hope born of love and affection, having nothing to do with Christian or any other theology and lacking a known basis in the natural world. "In my judgment," he wrote in a letter of 1887, "no human being knows whether there is another life or not,—and whether there is or not should make no particular difference with us. If there

is no other life, we should make the best of this—if there is another life, we should still make the best of this." (R. G. Ingersoll to Lucien I. Chapman, 3 June 1887, in *The Letters of Robert G. Ingersoll*, ed. Eva Ingersoll Wakefield [New York, 1951], 288–89.)

4. Helen Buffum Pillsbury Cogswell (1843–?), the only child of Parker and Sarah Pillsbury, lived with her parents, even after her marriage in 1888 to a close family friend P. Brainard Cogswell. Her husband died at the end of October 1895. (Robertson, *Parker Pillsbury*, passim.)

262 ~ SBA TO ECS

Rochester, N.Y., September 30, 1895.

My dear Mrs. Stanton:—

Yours of yesterday is just here this morning.

The next "Bulletin" is to be gotten out very soon, and Mrs. Chapman Catt is its editor and has absolute control over it,[1] but I haven't any doubt that she would be very happy to put in the notice of your publication of reminiscences.[2]

I cannot comprehend how it is that Mrs. Blake does not know where the celebration is to be held. Metropolitan Opera House has been the one named and printed all through. Mrs. Dickinson has her plan of celebration pretty well started and I think it an excellent one, and she will now be at her home, 230 West 59th street, very soon, and then she is to call all her committees together for conference and map out the work for each. I have recommended to her Mrs. Blake's name on two very important committees—those of decoration and entertainment, and I hope Mrs. Blake and all the representative women of the different women's clubs—literary, political, scientific, etc., in the city will co-operate with Mrs. Dickinson in making the celebration a grand success. I am writing Mrs. Blake to inform her that the last issue of the "Woman's Journal" gives the Council's entire plan and invitation to everybody. I do not understand why the "Tribune" does not publish it, except that that old Bible business blisters over all its pages.

I am feeling splendidly and you need not worry a speck about me. I intend to be on hand at my cousin, Mrs. Lapham's, some days before the celebration so as to get coached as what to say when my turn comes to speak.

No, the Bulletin has not been sent to the friends abroad because Mrs. Catt only printed only 1000 copies for the especial purpose of sending to the Presidents of the local clubs throughout this country, to stir them up to celebrate your birthday; so there were not enough to send abroad; but she is going to get another out immediately on her return, which will be Thursday of this week, and you can send to her any little short notice that you like. She had quite a lot of short items for the last one, but her article on the celebration was so long that it crowded out everything else.

I had a very sweet letter of sympathy from Matilda yesterday,[3] and I have written her to-day telling her that I hope she will be able to attend your celebration.

Thanks for Mrs. Osborne's letter; I will write her and answer her questions.

I see that dear Mr. John Hooker has met with an accident and broken his hip. I shall write them. I am awfully sorry for the wild imaginations of dear Mrs. Hooker as to herself and dear Olympia. I surely have never had anything for either of them but the best love, so when you write her or any one, I think with your knowledge of me and of my feelings towards each and all of the workers in our movement, you might do me the justice to say that you <u>know</u> all such charges against me to be false. I think I should do that much for you assuredly, if any one came to me with grievances against you. Very lovingly yours,

~ TL, on NAWSA letterhead, AF 24(3), Anthony Family Collection, CSmH. Signed for SBA by Emma B. Sweet.

1. This was the *National Suffrage Bulletin*, issued by Carrie Catt's Organization Committee of the National-American from September 1895 to 1901. Sent free to the presidents of local suffrage clubs, it suggested, wrote Catt, "what to do and how to do it. It is not designed to keep the reader informed upon the ethics of woman suffrage, but to inspire her to do practical work to bring the reality." Clara Colby's more idiosyncratic *National Bulletin* did not long survive the competition. ("Report Organization Committee of National-American Woman Suffrage Association, Annual Convention, 1895," *Supplement to National Suffrage Bulletin*, February 1896, in SBA scrapbook 25, Rare Books, DLC.)

2. ECS did advertise a book of reminiscences at the end of 1895, but plans changed. After making substantial changes to the articles already published in the *Woman's Tribune*, she published the book as *Eighty Years and More* in 1898.

3. That is, Matilda Gage.

263 ❧ SBA to Ascha Harter Reynolds[1]

Rochester, N.Y., November 1, 1895.

My Dear Friend:—

Yours of October 26th is before me.

If I were demanding the enfranchisement of women as a measure of expediency, to gain some particular end, I should think it necessary to go into a long explanation and make a tremendous effort to answer all your questions; but since I demand it simply on the ground of <u>justice</u> and because I believe every intelligent person who is governed should have the right to give or withhold his or her consent from that government—no matter on which side of any question he or she may be, I would simply answer: No harm can come to a country which shall make this principle its <u>foundation stone</u>. If I knew that a vast majority of the women of the country would vote Presbyterianism into vogue and shut all liberal mouths, I still would maintain that all women should be enfranchised. Again, if I knew that the vast majority would vote the way the Catholic priests should tell them, I still would be for woman's enfranchisement. And, again, if I knew that the vast majority of the women of the country would vote with the saloon power, I still would insist upon it that women should have the right to vote.

You see, the difficulty with people is, that they are all the time quaking and worrying themselves to death about what measure will be voted up or down after women are enfranchised. If all of the evils which you have foreshadowed in your letter should be the result of the first election in which women vote, there would be but one thing for us, who feel ourselves more intelligent than the majority, to do, and that is, to set about educating the rank and file of the women who carried the election in the direction which we considered wrong. So, I never try to prove to anybody exactly which way every woman will vote, for every individual woman of us will go to the ballot-box and come just as near as we possibly can to voting in favor of our own hobby, whatever that may be.

Wyoming, Colorado and New Zealand[2] have proved the groundlessness of every fear which has ever been expressed. Thus, you see, I have no trouble in answering your question: "Will the enfranchisement of women benefit the country under all the existing circumstances cited?" My answer is, <u>Yes</u>, no matter though the heavens should fall, but I always know the heavens <u>won't</u> fall when justice is done.

When women as a class hold the ballot in their hands, all of us who are liberals will be able to have some influence with men's organizations, whether they be Presbyterian, Catholic, or any other sort of organization.

My secretary[3] will make a copy of your letter, and I will see what sort of a discussion and conclusion can be secured in our Political Equality Club here.

I am glad you wrote me and hope you keep up your interest and do all you can to educate every man and woman you meet to work for the enfranchisement of women. Very sincerely yours,

～ *Susan B. Anthony*

～ TLS, on NAWSA letterhead, Osborne Family Collection, NSyU. Inscribed in margin to Thomas Mott Osborne, "N.B. Please return this, as I wish to preserve it. A. H. R."

1. Ascha Hudson Harter Reynolds (1833–1916), of Auburn, New York, identified herself to SBA as an admirer of Matilda Gage and someone "wholly with you in the work of enfranchising woman." She had, however, come to "<u>doubt</u> the <u>utility</u> of woman's <u>vote</u> at the present time," she explained, because women "generally act under the control of opinions, prepared by those on whom they lean." This was especially true of women in Protestant and Catholic churches, who want to "cast their ballots in furtherance of those church interests; instead of the <u>broad</u> <u>principles</u> on which our Republic is based." Reynolds was the widow of Jacob Henry Harter, a Universalist minister who left the church for spiritualism, and the wife of George L. Reynolds, an inventor. In 1906, she sent a copy of her letter to SBA and the original of SBA's reply to Thomas Mott Osborne to help him make the best possible case against woman suffrage. By then the scales had tipped: "<u>disastrous</u> results" would come of the enfranchisement of women devoted to "(self-styled) 'Orthodox Christianity,'" she told him. (A. H. H. Reynolds to SBA, 26 October 1895 [not in *Film*], and A. H. H. Reynolds to T. M. Osborne, 1 November 1906, Osborne Family Collection, NSyU; Federal Census 1880, 1900, 1910; Fort Hill Cemetery, Auburn, N.Y., on-line interment roster; John B. Buescher, *The Other Side of Salvation: Spiritualism and the Nineteenth-Century Religious Experience* [Boston, 2004], 111–14.)

2. By the Electoral Act of 1893, signed in September of that year, parliamentary suffrage was given to white settler women and Maori women in New Zealand. The new voters mobilized quickly to participate in the general election held two months later. On the law and its context, see Patricia Grimshaw, *Women's Suffrage in New Zealand* (Aukland, N.Z., 1972), 86–95; Grimshaw, "Settler Anxieties, Indigenous Peoples and Women's Suffrage in the Colonies of Australia, New Zealand and Hawai'i, 1888 to 1902," in *Women's Suffrage in Asia: Gender, Nationalism and Democracy*, eds. Louise Edwards and Mina Roces (London, 2004), 220–39; and Neill Atkinson, *Adventures in Democracy: A History of the Vote in New Zealand* (Dunedin, N.Z., 2003), 81–100. For indications of contact between SBA and New Zealand's leaders, see SBA to Katherine W. M. Sheppard, 7 November 1893, *Film*, 31:734; and Grimshaw, *Women's Suffrage in New Zealand*, 95.

3. Emma Biddlecome Sweet (1862–1951) became SBA's stenographer and typist in October 1895. She grew up in Macedon, New York, and moved to Rochester as a young woman to study stenography and typing and find work more congenial than teaching. After her marriage to Fred Gilbert Sweet in 1883, she continued to work. Sweet belonged to the Unitarian Church and the Political Equality Club. SBA employed her over many years, and Sweet became her frequent travel companion. (E. B. Sweet to SBA, 7 September 1895, and SBA diary, 30 December and account pages for October, 1895, *Film*, 30:80ff, 34:333; "Emma B. Sweet," Rochester Regional Library Council website, *Western New York Suffragists: Winning the Vote*; Emma C. Donk, Life of Emma B. Sweet, typescript, supplied by author.)

264 ≫ SBA TO ANNA E. DICKINSON

Rochester, N.Y. Nov. 5, 1895—

My Darling Anna

It is lovely to see your pen-tracks once more—as I opened the envelope—I said—"Why this looks like Anna Dickinson's writing["]—& turning to the last page sure enough—there it was Anna E. Dickinson—the same dear old name—[1] It don't matter if its contents do seem a wee bit scolding—I'm awfully glad to ↑know↓ you still live—and that I have a chance to tell you that my <u>motherly love</u>—my elderly sister's love—has never abated for my <u>first Anna</u>— I have had several lovely ↑<u>Anna</u>↓ girls—"<u>nieces</u>"—they call themselves now a-day—since my <u>first Anna</u>—but none of them—ever has or ever can fill the niche in my heart that you did—my dear— Now—I must see you when I get to New York— I take the 9.05—train tomorrow—Wednesday A.M—and shall stop at my Quaker cousins—Mrs H. G. Lapham—no 10—east 68th street—and shall be there tomorrow evening— Oh how I do wish you would come up there & let us have a dear old face to face look & talk—

I am so glad you wrote me—because it gives me a chance to send you the invitation to Mrs Stanton's 80th birth day reception—and I want you to sit on the stage as the pioneer ↑woman↓ speaker to save the nation in its times of perils— You will come wont you?— Our Hotel Head Quarters are to be the Vendome—on Broadway two blocks below the Opera House[2]—& I am going to be there with the dear old friends who come from a distance— Mrs Hallowell—at whose house our glorious Phillips used always stop—& her aunt Mrs Willis & my sister Mary will be there—and dear Dr Longshore—aunt Jane & Mrs Blankenburg[3]—and I do not know who else—but I do want to take you on my arm & introduce you to the young women who have come among us these later years— You will come to me, or let me come to you—at the earliest moment—after my arrival in New York— My! wouldn't I like to go to Del Monicos as of old![4] Well my dear—we'll talk when we meet—till then   Lovingly your old & best friend—

~ Susan B. Anthony

~ ALS, on NAWSA letterhead, Anna Dickinson Papers, DLC.

1. Although Dickinson's letter does not survive, it was one of many she wrote in November and December 1895, accusing the people who raised money for her in 1891 of criminal libel. Some of the other victims of this new twist in Dickinson's mind were Robert Purvis, Hannah Longshore, and Frances Willard. (Gallman, *America's Joan of Arc*, 200-1.)

2. The Vendome Hotel, at Broadway and Forty-first Street, was a short walk from the Metropolitan Opera House, at Broadway and Thirty-ninth Street.

3. That is, Hannah Longshore, her sister Jane Myers, and her daughter Lucretia Blankenburg.

4. Delmonico's, New York's most famous restaurant, allowed women to eat in public without male escorts. At the peak of Anna Dickinson's career in the late 1860s, she and SBA dined there. At that time the restaurant was located at Fifth Avenue and Fourteenth Street.

265 ❧ FROM THE DIARY OF SBA

[*6–9 November 1895*]

WED. NOV. 6, 1895. Took 9.05 train for New York— Mrs Eastwood & her 77 years old mother[1] on same train— we each had lunch—so dined together—with a cup of tea from the Porter

Found cousin S. V— Lapham—waiting or expecting me—took seat at table at once— Cousin Carrie Vail Ladd spending the winter—also Mrs Rockwell studying music—Piano— Son John called & son Louis & wife spent evening— Cousin Lizzie not able to come out—[2]

1. Ellen Clara Bigelow Eastwood (1840–1911) traveled with her widowed mother, Clara Kathan Bigelow (1816–1897), known as Clarissa. Ellen Eastwood, the wife of a Rochester merchant, was one of the city's busier activists, involved with the Ethical Club, Women's Educational and Industrial Union, committees to bring coeducation to the University of Rochester, and Daughters of the American Revolution, to name a few of her affiliations. In later years, she held office in the state federation of women's clubs. (Gilman Bigelow Howe, *Genealogy of the Bigelow Family of America* [Worcester, Mass., 1890], 318; Peck, *History of Rochester and Monroe County, N.Y.*, 1:464; Rochester *Democrat and Chronicle*, 4 & 6 July 1911; Mt. Hope and Riverside Cemetery Interment Records.)

2. At Semantha Lapham's were her oldest son John Jesse Lapham (c. 1852–1911), her niece Caroline Ruth Elizabeth Vail Ladd (1836–1913), and Lewis and Antoinette Lapham. John Lapham worked with his brother in their father's firm, Henry G. Lapham & Co. SBA thought his wife's name was Elizabeth W. Lapham, although genealogies give her name as Mary E. Walker Lapham. Carrie Vail Ladd, as SBA knew her, was the daughter of SBA's childhood friend and cousin Aaron Rogers Vail. Before the death of her husband in 1882, Ladd lived in East Orange, New Jersey, but she spent her time back in her native Vermont thereafter. Mrs. Rockwell is unidentified. (Albridge, *Laphams in America*, 182–83, 256; *New York Times*, 12 February 1911; SBA to Emilie Van Biel, 19 December 1894, *Film*, 33:44–45; Vail, *Moses Vail*, 222; Federal Census, 1880.)

THUR. NOV. 7, 1895. In New York Cousin Semantha sent me to call on Mrs Dickinson & then on Mrs Stanton—in Cab— found Mrs Stanton well—& working on her speech—which she read to me—but which I criticised—saying she should treat the moral—the intellectual work done in ↑the↓ church—as in t̶h̶e̶ ↑she↓ treated it done in the State—&c—

FRI. NOV. 8, 1895. N.Y. State W.S.A. Convention at Newburg, Orange Co—[1]

was at Mrs Stanton's when telegram from Pres. Greenleaf—to go to Newburg & speak this evening & be let off for Monday evening the 11th—which I gladly did—reaching N. at 5.30—& going first to Palatine Hotel—& meeting ever so many—Eliz. Smith Miller, daughter Nannie & Sister in Law—Bessie[2]—also Miss Emily Howland—& Mrs Eliza Osborn—&c— thence to the lovely home of Mrs C. E. Jenkins[3]—a mile out of city— Mrs Blake guest there also— A rainy muddy night—with a small but good audience— Martha R. Almy spoke on "New Occasions"—& said new attitude needed—sweetness of manner & elegance of dress—must take place of scolding men & wearing Bloomers— this stirred me—so that I just ran over the early list—Mary Wollstonecraft Frances Wright —Ernestine L. Rose—[*continued on page for 7 November*] Nichols—Paulina Davis—Lucy Stone, Frances D. Gage—Lucretia Mott & E C. Stanton—each without her peer among any of our College graduate young women of today—

    1. See *Film*, 34:458-65. The Palatine Hotel hosted many delegates and provided headquarters; meetings were held in the Academy of Music.

    2. Elizabeth Fitzhugh Smith (c. 1840-1918), known as Bessie, was the widow of Elizabeth Miller's brother, Green Smith. (Genealogical file, Geneva Historical Society, N.Y.)

    3. Charles S. Jenkins (1822-1905) and Caroline E. Macy Jenkins (1835-1911) lived outside the city of Newburgh in Balmville. Husband and wife were members of Quaker families originally from Nantucket, and Charles Jenkins worked for many years in the business of ships and sailing. He was president of the Newburgh Savings Bank. Caroline, or Carrie, Jenkins served as an officer of the city's Young Women's Christian Association, and in 1899, helped to organize the New York State Household Economic Association. (John J. Nutt, comp., *Newburgh, Her Institutions, Industries and Leading Citizens* [Newburgh, N.Y., 1891], 153, 175; *New York Times*, 26 July 1899, 29 September 1905, 20 June 1911.)

SAT. NOV. 9, 1895. N.Y. State W.S.A. annual Con—Newburg—N.Y—to be the guest of Mrs C. S. Jenkins—Maple Hill—

Mrs Jenkins took me to the Opera House this A.M— I spent A.M. & till 4 P.M. in the meeting   lunching at Hotel— Mrs Greenleaf re-elected— Mrs Almy—not—self-seeking hasn't paid in one case— Took train at 5 P.M. & reached Cousin Semanthas after 7—& dear Miss Vorse[1] soon had nice supper for me—

Miss Shaw arrived in Newburg at 8 & went direct to Opera House—she & Lucy E. were gues of dear Miss Taft—[2]

1. Susan Vorse was, in SBA's words, "companion, nurse & housekeeper" to Semantha Lapham. (SBA diary, 26 November 1894, *Film*, 32:1ff.)

2. Clara Taft (1839–?) lived at 291 Liberty Street. She hosted SBA during the amendment campaign. (City directories, 1889, 1892, 1894, 1896, 1898, 1900; Federal Census, 1900; SBA diary, 14 March 1894, *Film*, 31:879ff.)

❧ Excelsior Diary 1895, n.p. SBA Papers, DLC.

266 ❧ Statements by SBA and ECS: "If Women Came to Congress, What Would be the Result?"

EDITORIAL NOTE: The syndicated columnist Frank Carpenter, known as "Carp," posed the question about the effect of women in Congress to a number of men and women, supplied postal cards for their replies, and constructed a column from the "necessarily short" answers he received. The column opened with the responses of SBA and ECS, whose handwritten cards are in *Film*, 34:472–74. Carpenter instructed newspapers not to use the column before 10 November 1895. Editors selected which entries to publish, and in some newspapers, ECS's reply was omitted.

[10 November 1895]

When women come to Congress, both the men and the women will be put on their best behavior—morally, intellectually, socially—because the sexes together always inspire each other to be and to do their best. The huge cuspidors at every seat will be banished, the heating registers will no longer emit the fumes of burned tobacco juice; the two houses and the corridors will cease to be filled with tobacco smoke thick enough to cut with a knife. The desks will not be used as foot benches; decency and good order will be observed in the discussions, and the proprieties of civilized society will obtain. Then justice, not bargain and sale, will decide legislation. May the good time come speedily!

❧ *Susan B. Anthony.*

The result would be:

1st. Justice, liberty and equality for women.

2d. It would lighten the burdens of men.

3d. It would improve the manners of statesmen at the Capitol, and society at large in the city.

4th. It would give us united thought of man and woman on all the vital questions of the hour, introducing a moral element into the discussion of questions now viewed only from a material standpoint, and thus promote the welfare of the nation and the stability of the republic.

~ *Elizabeth Cady Stanton.*

~ Proofsheet, Frank G. Carpenter Papers, DLC. Not in *Film* in this version.

267 ~ FROM THE DIARY OF SBA

[*10–11 November 1895*]

SUN. NOV. 10, 1895. In New York— Spent day at Mrs Stantons— Cousin sending me in Carriage   all these days are dark & rainy—

MON. NOV. 11, 1895. In New York— Went to The Vendome & found dear Mrs Southworth—& one of her ministers—Miss Murdock[1]—with her— Spent all day trying to find Rachel—but she was at office hard at work—

1. Marion Murdoch (1848–1943), sometimes Murdock, shared the ministry at Cleveland's Unity Church from 1893 to 1899 with her friend Florence Buck. (*American Women*; Cynthia Grant Tucker, *Prophetic Sisterhood: Liberal Women Ministers of the Frontier, 1880–1930* [Boston, 1990], 35–40; Samuel A. Eliot, ed., *Heralds of a Liberal Faith*, vol. 4, *The Pilots* [Boston, 1952], 56; on-line index to California Death Records.)

~ Excelsior Diary 1895, n.p. SBA Papers, DLC.

268 ❧ Speech by ECS to the Reunion of the Pioneers and Friends of Woman's Progress

EDITORIAL NOTE: At the Metropolitan Opera House, on her eightieth birthday, ECS occupied center stage on a throne-like chair a little higher than the ones on either side for SBA and Mary Dickinson. Around her were close friends, pioneers in professions and reforms, delegates from the constituent societies of the National Council of Women, and family members. One reporter counted five Stanton children, two daughters-in-law, and a number of nieces and nephews. Children and grandchildren of old friends like Martha Wright, Lucretia Mott, and William Lloyd Garrison were in attendance. "The boxes," one member of the audience wrote to a friend, "were all taken by the different Women's Societies, whether Woman's rights or not & each club decorated their box with flowers, banners, flags & lights. Indeed it was a very fine sight." Musicians performed between speeches, and the evening concluded with stereopticon views projected onto the darkened stage, illustrating women's lives then and now across fifty years. "[F]or instance," wrote the member of the audience to her friend, "courting—a couple sitting together, the man holding the yarn while the young woman wound— Then was presented a boy & girl riding alongside each other on a bicycle!" ECS's address fell in the middle of the lengthy program. She rose to accept the audience's salute and reassure the men in the audience, lest they think from all they heard "that the new woman is going to crowd them entirely off the planet. I want to assure you all that, as long as you have mothers, wives, and sweethearts, they will look out for your welfare." She also said, "[a]s I am not able to stand very long, nor to talk loud enough, I have invited Miss Helen Potter to read what I have to say to you." For many years Helen Potter had impersonated ECS on lecture platforms across the country. (Elizabeth E. Pike to Caroline Putnam, 21 November 1895, ECS Papers, DLC.)

[12 November 1895]

In thanking the friends present, and through the press the many clubs of women throughout the country who are celebrating my birthday to-night, and in response to the many letters and telegrams I have received from the Old World and the New, I would say to one and all that in demanding justice and equality for all women I have secured larger liberties for myself.[1]

I am well aware that all these public demonstrations are not so much tributes to me as an individual as to the great idea I represent—the enfranchisement of women.

It is a long time, near half a century, since a few persons met in 1848, in a little Methodist church in Seneca Falls, to discuss the status of women under the laws of New York.

That was the first woman's rights convention ever held in the world, and here the first demand was made for woman suffrage.[2] A declaration was read and signed by most of those present, and a series of radical resolutions adopted. But the majority of women ridiculed the idea of political rights for themselves, the press caricatured the convention, the pulpit denounced it, and some who took part withdrew their names, and appeared no more on our platform. But above this wave of clamor[3] that rolled from Maine to Louisiana, arose the clarion voice of Phillips; "This is the inauguration of the most momentous reform yet launched upon the world, the first organized protest against the injustice that has brooded for ages over the character and destiny of one-half the human race."[4]

Within two years conventions were held in half a dozen different States, letters of sympathy came from women in this country, from Italy, France and Germany, all taking an active part in the revolutions of 1848. Just at that time, too, the earthquakes began in California, showing that old mother earth sympathized in the general upheaval, in the rebellion of her daughters against the creeds and codes and customs of effete civilizations. And the invisibles began at that time to knock and move tables, gradually awakening a deep interest in psychological manifestations.[5] But I will not use any of my allotted time in dwelling on the past and noting the steps of progress, except to say that James Mott,[6] a dignified Quaker, presided over the first convention, and his noble wife Lucretia, and her sister, Martha Wright, and Frederick Douglass were the leading speakers. Paulina Wright Davis called the first convention in old Massachusetts,[7] and Lucy Stone kept the watch fires of liberty burning there until the day of her death.[8] She was the first woman in the nation to protest against the marriage laws at the altar, and to manifest sufficient self respect to keep her own name, to represent her individual existence through life. Frances D. Gage responded to the call for Ohio, Mary F. Thomas for Indiana, Lucinda Stone[9] for Michigan, Mary Grew for Pennsylvania, Elizabeth B. Chace[10] for Rhode Island, Ernestine L. Rose, a beautiful Polish lady, and Antoinette Brown[11] made their appeals in most of the States and before several legislative assemblies. Matilda Joslyn Gage and Susan B. Anthony made their debut on our platform in 1852.[12] Later came Mary A. Livermore, Isabella Beecher Hooker and Julia Ward Howe, Rev. Phebe Hanaford,[13] Rev. Olympia Brown and others, who all did good service. Those who follow will pay fitting tributes to all these noble women.[14] I have just two thoughts I wish to emphasize.

1. Woman's sphere. That ground has been travelled over so often that there is not a single tree nor flower nor blade of grass to be found anywhere. Yet excursions of men are continually going to survey that old worn-out land. Ever since Eve left Paradise, the trend of thought has been in the direction of woman's sphere. Those who could write in prose or verse have written about it. Those who could orate have talked about it. Statesmen have declared its limits in laws and constitutions; bishops in Scriptures and sermons; editors in journals, and scientists in osseous formations, muscles, nerves, and the size and quality of the feminine brain. They have sung in chorus the same old song, and will continue, like Poe's raven to sing it "evermore," unless some one shall arise to solve this tangled problem.[15] Fortunately, to remove this subject from human thought and give place to more profitable discussions, I arose on the 12th of November, in the year of our Lord 1815, and have spent a greater part of my life in elucidating this question. I propose now to give you the result of my explorations. Those who are capable of drawing logical conclusions from facts will leave this house to-night with their minds forever at rest as to the limits of woman's sphere. While Franklin, Kane, Greeley and Peary[16] have been sailing mid the Polar ices to find the North Pole, I have been travelling in the realm of the possibilities to find woman's sphere and the voting poll. Spyglass in hand, I have crossed the imaginary lines of diameter and circumference bounding its limits; I took reckonings at every degree of latitude and longitude; in the temperate, frigid and torrid, Arctic and Antarctic zones. In halting one day I found an old document, said to have been written at the dawn of creation, when the Gods were in consultation about the creation of man. They said:

> Let us make man in our own image, male and female, and give them dominion over the whole earth and every living thing therein.[17]

They did so. Here we have the first title-deed to this green earth, given alike to man and woman, and the first hint of "God's intentions." Those who will make some logical concessions must admit that wherever woman has been and maintained a foothold, and whatever she has done and done well, it must have been the "Creator's intentions" that she should occupy that position and do that special work. Unless you admit this, you impeach the wisdom of the Creator and exalt the woman as able to set at defiance the laws of her being. While everything in the universe moves according to immutable law, the sun, the moon, the stars and every planet revolving in its own elliptic, the fish of the sea, the birds of the air, all in their appointed places, moving together in harmony, how can woman get out of her sphere? The moment you declare she is, you make her all-powerful, greater than her Maker. To do this she must defy the laws of attraction, cohesion and gravitation, the centripetal and centrifugal forces, the positive and negative electricity, to be scattered into space, herself, and be seen no more forever.

Instead of this fatal escapade, lo! she is here; tied to the planet just as man is, and compelled to follow in his footsteps. He is happy and contented, and always stays in his sphere, and nobody writes or talks about it. He has gone everywhere and done everything his genius made possible; diving to ocean depths, he gives us pictures of coral caves and the monsters of the sea; sailing with his balloon in the blue ether, he tells us of the wonders above the clouds. With his railroads he has linked together the Rocky and Alleghany mountains, the Atlantic and Pacific, and with his ocean cable he has anchored continents side by side and welded the nations of the earth in one. The seven wonders of the world are so many tributes to his genius; the magnificent cathedrals, the museums, the libraries, the art galleries—all proclaim his divine origin, his creative powers.

He has labored by turns in every department of science and industry, and has gathered knowledge and riches from every quarter of the globe. He has filled all stations, high and low, governed nations, led armies, and by his marvellous inventions has shifted the heavy burdens of labor from human shoulders to tireless machines. Every day he has some new surprise in store for us, and new promises of the future, when we are to make the journey of life by electricity, when all our present modes of locomotion, even the bicycle, will be thrown into the shade. He will thus make life like a sweet dream, the realization of a fairy land.

Thus we see that women need no longer knit or weave, make butter or cheese. Cunning arms and fingers of steel now do it all. Women need no longer cook or wash or iron or bake or brew, for men do it all in restaurants, laundries, bakeries and breweries. Women need no longer sew, for with cunning machines men now make underclothes for women and children, and even the man-milliner bonnets and the tailor-made dresses are superior to what women themselves can produce. And man is not only making our earthly dwelling all that we could desire, but he is giving us new and delightful anticipations of the life to come. Learned revising committees have cast serious doubts on the Inferno and the Prince of Darkness. They have even, in the last version of the New Testament, eliminated the words "hell" and "everlasting punishment," a most praiseworthy concession to the emotional nature of women and children. They have even added some new touches of gladness and hospitality to our heavenly home. Instead of a frowning judge, driving three-fourths of the human race like goats into outer darkness and despair, we have pictures of a loving father who welcomes us to his presence; instead of a bigoted Peter at the gate questioning our entrance there, smiling angels open wide the portals, and all shades and colors of humanity walk in together—Jew and Gentile, bond and free, white and black, rich and poor, male and female, without regard to color, sex, or previous condition of servitude.[18]

This is the beautiful vision liberal Doctors of Divinity and Spiritualists give us of the future. Milton and Dante,[19] they say, threw their doleful poems into the Jordan as they passed over; and Swedenborg,[20] on the shore, got out an expurgated edition of his melancholy prose writings. Now, I suppose, carping women all over the house are saying to their neighbors, "Where do we come in? If man is such a wonderful being, and fills all space, where is our sphere?" Why it is plain to every rational mind that if man is everywhere and women must of necessity remain on the planet, then their sphere is the same. They are and ever must be indissolubly bound together, as mother, father, husband, wife, brother, sister, in childhood, in marriage, in all life's struggles, ever sharing each other's joys and sorrows. With tears of affection and immortal wreaths they perform the last sad offices of love and friendship for each other, and in the bosom of mother earth, side by side, they rest at last together.

Yes, the spheres of man and woman are the same, with different duties according to the capacity of the individual. Woman, like all created things, lives, moves, and has her being obedient to law, exploring with man the mysteries of the universe and speculating on the glories of the hereafter. In the words of Tennyson[21] they must be together

> Everywhere,
> Two heads in council, two beside the hearth,
> Two in the tangled business of the world,
> Two in the liberal offices of life,
> Two plummets dropped for one to sound the abyss
> Of science and the secrets of the mind.

The question is no longer the sphere of a whole sex but of each individual. Women are now in the trades and professions, everywhere in the world of work. They have shown their capacity as students in the sciences, their skill as mariners before the mast, their courage as rescuers in lifeboats. They are close on the heels of man in the arts, sciences and literature; in their knowledge and understanding of the vital questions of the hour, and in the every day practical duties of life. Like man, woman's sphere is in the whole universe of matter and mind, to do whatever she can, and thus prove "the intentions of the Creator."

2. The other thought I would emphasize is the next step in progress we should take in our march to complete emancipation. We who have made our demands on the State have nearly finished this battle. The principle is practically conceded.

We now have full suffrage in Colorado, Wyoming and Utah;[22] municipal suffrage in the great State of Kansas, and school suffrage in half the States of the Union. They have had municipal suffrage in Great Britain and her colonies for over twenty years, and some form of suffrage, on a property qualification, either in person or by proxy, in several European countries. Most of those who fought this battle have passed to another sphere of action, and our younger coadjutors will ere long, like Miriam of old, with timbrels and dances and songs of victory,[23] lead the hosts of women into the promised land of freedom. As learned bishops and editors of religious newspapers are warning us against further demands for new liberties, and clergymen are still preaching sermons on the "rib origin," and refuse to receive women as delegates to their synods, it is evident that our demands for equal recognition should now be made of the Church for the same rights we have asked of the State for the last fifty years, for the same rights, privileges and immunities that men enjoy. We must demand that the canon laws, the Mosaic code, the Scriptures, prayer books and liturgies be purged of all invidious distinctions of sex, of all false teaching as to woman's origin, character and destiny. To make her the author of sin, cursed in her maternity, subordinate in marriage, an afterthought in the creation, and all by the command of God, was so to overweight her in the scale of being that centuries of civilization have not as yet been able to lift the burden. Charles Kingsley said long ago, "This will never be a good world for women until the last remnant of the canon law is swept from the face of the earth,"[24] and Lord Brougham[25] echoed back the same sentiment as to the civil law for women. "It is," said he, "a disgrace to the Christianity and civilization of the nineteenth century." Here is the opinion of two distinguished men as to women's degraded position under the canon and civil law in Church and State. Can it be that what such men see and denounce women themselves do not feel and repudiate?

3. We must demand an equal place in the offices of the Church, as pastors, elders, deacons; an equal voice in the creeds, discipline, and all business matters, in synods, conferences and general assemblies.

Women of wealth are all the time giving large sums of money to build and maintain churches; they fill the pews each returning Sunday; they swell the numbers of the devotees; they supply the enthusiasm for revival seasons, and worship the priesthood. They are ever loyal to the sons of Aaron, the house of Levi, the very powers that through the centuries have done more to block their way to freedom than all other influences put together. It is the perversion of the religious element in woman that has held her for ages the patient victim under the car of Juggernaut, on the funeral pyre, in iron shoes, in the Turkish harem, in the Catholic nunnery, and in the Protestant world beggars ever for fairs, donation parties, church decorations, embroideries of altar clothes, surplices and slippers. In return for this devotion they are entertained with sermons from the texts: "I suffer not a woman to speak in the churches"; "As Christ is the head of the Church, so is man the head of the woman."[26]

4. Women must demand that all unworthy reflections on the dignity and sacred office of the mother of the race be expunged from religious literature, such as the allegory as to the creation of woman and St. Paul's assumption as to her social status. These ideas conflict with the Golden Rule and the fifth commandment: "Honor thy mother," and should no longer be rehearsed in the pulpit.[27] Such sentiments cannot inspire the rising generation with respect for their mothers.

5. We must demand that the pulpit be no longer desecrated by men who read passages of Scripture or preach from texts that teach subordination of one-half the human race to the other.

What sight could be more inexpressibly sad and comic than a young man fresh from Princeton, preaching his first sermon to a congregation of educated middle-aged women from the text: "Wives, obey your husbands"; "If you would know anything, ask your husbands at home."[28] In view of the character and higher education of the women of the present day, the time has fully come for the Church to take an advance step on this question. Jewish women should demand an expurgated edition of their liturgy. It must be very humiliating to them to have every man stand up in the Synagogue each returning Sabbath day, and say: "I thank thee, O Lord, that I was not born a woman."[29] Nothing that has ever emanated from the brain of man is too sacred to be revised and corrected. Our National Constitution has been amended fifteen times, our English system of jurisprudence has been essentially modified in the interest of women, to keep pace with advancing civilization. And now the time has come to amend and modify the canon laws, prayer books, liturgies and Bibles. Gladstone said the American Constitution, considering the circumstances under which it was written, is the most wonderful document that ever emanated from the brain of man.[30] Yet from time to time, with the growth of the people, amendments were demanded. So with our statute laws. Why should we hold the Mosaic code and church decretals more sacred than the Saxon civil code and the legal opinions of Blackstone, Story and Kent?[31] The trouble in both cases is that the laws and customs in Church and State alike are behind the public sentiment of our day and generation.

Woman's imperative duty at this hour is to demand a thorough revision of creeds and codes, Scriptures and constitutions. Petitions for a sixteenth amendment to the National Constitution for the enfranchisement of women have been annually presented to Congress for the last quarter of a century. Similar petitions for equal recognition in the Church should now every year press into the synods, conferences and general assemblies.

Twenty-five years ago a church in Illinois was rent in twain because some women persisted in praying in the weekly meetings. Ten years ago the Presbyterian General Assembly discussed this question for three days, and finally passed a resolution leaving the matter to the discretion of the pastor. Now women not only pray in church meetings, but on many public occasions, in missionary and charitable conventions. Fifteen years ago the General Conference of the Methodist Episcopal Church, by a large majority, voted down a resolution to ordain women as missionaries, and four years ago they voted down a resolution to ordain women as lay delegates; while thus far this autumn every State conference held has given a majority vote in favor of women as lay delegates. Last May (1895), the Episcopal Church of California passed a resolution that women might vote in vestry meetings, and also be eligible as church officers.[32] When the Church obeys the command, "Honor thy mother," and the State heeds the declaration, "Equal rights to all"; when the two powers join hands to exalt the mother of the race, who has gone to the very gates of death to give every man life and immortality, then we shall see the dawn of a new day in woman's emancipation. When she awakes to the beauty of science, philosophy, true religion and pure government, then will the first note of harmony be touched; then will the great organ of humanity be played on all its keys, with every stop rightly adjusted, and with louder, loftier strains, the march of civilization will be immeasurably quickened.

❧ *Woman's Tribune*, 28 December 1895.

1. Lists of letters, telegrams, and gifts sent to the celebration are in *Woman's Tribune*, 28 December 1895, *Film*, 34:488–90.

2. The editors of the *Woman's Journal* did not let ECS's history appear in print without redaction and comment. They cut short this sentence at "in the world," deleted ECS's claim that "the first demand" for suffrage arose at Seneca Falls, and substituted ellipses without explanation. (23 November 1895.)

3. The *Woman's Journal* text of the speech reads "above this wave of petty clamor".

4. A slight variation on the second paragraph of *The Speech of Wendell Phillips, to the Convention in Worcester, Oct. 1851*, published in several series of *Woman's Rights Tracts* in the 1850s and kept in print after the war.

5. The Fox sisters of Hydesville, New York, first heard the rappings of spirits in 1848, setting in motion a spiritualist movement that overlapped with secular reforms.

6. James Mott (1788–1868) of Philadelphia, businessman and reformer.

7. Returning to the Blackwell family's objections to crediting Paulina Davis with organizing the convention of 1850, the editors added a footnote here. "The first Woman's Rights Convention held in Massachusetts, which was also the first National Woman's Rights Convention held anywhere, met at Worcester in 1850. It was called by Harriot K. Hunt, Eliza J. Kenney, Lucy Stone, Abby Kelley Foster, Paulina Wright Davis, Dora Taft, and Eliza J. Taft.—Eds. *Woman's Journal*."

8. ECS's brushstrokes were too small for the editors, who added a footnote to this sentence. "Lucy Stone," they wrote, "gave her first lecture for woman suffrage in 1847, and during the next ten years travelled through a large part of the United States and Canada, lighting up 'the watchfires of liberty' all along her way.—Eds. *Woman's Journal*."

9. Lucinda Hinsdale Stone (1814–1900) was noted for her work in women's education and the club movement as well as woman suffrage. (*NAW*; *ANB*.)

10. Elizabeth Buffum Chace (1803–1899) was an early supporter of William Lloyd Garrison and a leader in her state's suffrage association. (*NAW*; *ANB*.)

11. Later Brown Blackwell.

12. At the Third National Woman's Rights Convention, held in Syracuse, New York, in 1852.

13. Phebe Ann Coffin Hanaford (1829–1921) was the second woman to be ordained by the Universalist church. (*NAW*.)

14. The program included addresses by notable women on religion, education, philanthropy, moral progress, suffrage, literature, art, medicine, foreign missions, the progress of colored women, industries, woman's progress, and human progress. Julia Ward Howe, Fannie Barrier Williams, Harriette Keyser, J. Ellen Foster, Harriet Hosmer, and Mary Burt were some of the speakers.

15. See note above at 18 February 1890.

16. The work of these Arctic explorers spanned the years of ECS's public life: John Franklin (1786–1847), an Englishman, was lost on his final voyage; Elisha Kent Kane (1820–1857), an American, made two trips in the 1850s, one of them in search of Franklin; Adolphus Washington Greely (1844–1935) commanded an American expedition in 1881; and Robert Edwin Peary (1856–1920) returned from his third Arctic expedition in 1894.

17. A revision of Gen. 1:26–27, passages in which God created man and woman simultaneously.

18. ECS borrows language from the Fifteenth Amendment to the Constitution of the United States that bars states from denying the right to vote "on account of race, color, or previous condition of servitude."

19. The English poet John Milton and the Italian poet Dante (1265-1321).
20. Emanuel Swedenborg (1688-1772), a Swedish mystic and writer whose followers organized the Church of the New Jerusalem.
21. Alfred, Lord Tennyson, "The Princess," pt. 2, lines 155-60. Tennyson (1809-1892) was the leading poet of the Victorian age.
22. Though the proclamation admitting Utah to statehood was not signed until 4 January 1896, voters approved a new state constitution that restored woman suffrage on 5 November 1895.
23. Exod. 15:20-21.
24. Charles Kingsley (1819-1875) wrote this sentence in a letter to John Stuart Mill in 1870, explaining why he had withdrawn from the woman suffrage movement. Canon law, in his mind, rendered women unfit to lead their own emancipation. (*Charles Kingsley: His Letters and Memories of His Life*, ed. Frances Grenfell Kingsley [New York, 1877], 416-19.)
25. Henry Peter Brougham, baron Brougham and Vaux (1778-1868), a champion of law reform in the House of Lords, introduced the married women's property bill of 1857 (rejected by Parliament) and argued in debate on the divorce act of 1857 (passed by Parliament) for granting women more causes to obtain a divorce. The source of this quotation has not been found. (*DNB*; Holcombe, *Wives and Property*, 62-63, 88-89; Shanley, *Feminism, Marriage, and the Law*, 35-48.)
26. Dicta of the apostle Paul as reported in 1 Cor. 14:34 and Ephe. 5:23.
27. Matt. 7:12 and Exod. 20:12.
28. Ephe. 5:22 and 1 Cor. 14:35.
29. From the morning prayer service in Isaac Leeser, ed. *The Book of Daily Prayers for Every Day in the Year* (Philadelphia, 1848), 7.
30. See note at 25 March 1888 above.
31. Legal commentators William Blackstone, Joseph Story, and James Kent.
32. In the last three decades of the nineteenth century, leaders in most Protestant denominations faced challenges to men's monopoly of the governance and teaching in institutions with large and active female memberships. The debates, votes, and dissension over ordination, licensing, public prayer, and roles in governance were widely reported in the newspapers. Students of the phenomenon usually write sectarian accounts without the ecumenical (and historical) perspective ECS employed in this speech. The Methodist Episcopal church drew particular attention among organized women, in part because the chief defenders of its patriarchal leadership, like J. M. Buckley, were colorful celebrities; in part because its putative democratic structure with elected lay delegates exposed it to political argument; and in part because it was the dominant church in the Woman's Christian Temperance Union. Frances Willard mobilized her sizeable forces on the issue of equality in her own church. ECS's list of notable moments in this history is idiosyncratic and difficult to date. (Kern, *Mrs. Stanton's Bible*, 248 n.14; Lois A. Boyd and R. Douglas Brackenridge, *Presbyterian Women in America: Two Centuries of a Quest for Status* [Westport, Conn., 1983]; Hilah F. Thomas and Rosemary

Skinner Keller, eds., *Women in New Worlds: Historical Perspectives on the Wesleyan Tradition* [Nashville, Tenn., 1981]; Richard L. Greaves, ed., *Triumph over Silence: Women in Protestant History* [Westport, Conn., 1985]; *Los Angeles Times*, 17 May 1895.)

269 ❧ FROM THE DIARY OF SBA

[*12–13 November 1895*]

TUES. NOV. 12, 1895. Mrs Elizabeth Cady Stanton's 80th Birth day—to be celebrated by the National Council—& by all women—in the Metropolitan Opera House New York city—with Mrs S. on the stage—& I trust, too, in many, many other cities & villages throughout the country

Niece Louise & cousin Ellen Squier—Sister Mary—Dr Myers & Dr Longshore & ever so many came to the Vendome—

The Opera House was well filled—the papers said 3,000 & everything went of well—fully a 100 telegrams came with greetings to Mrs S.—

I spent night at Vendome—↑room↓ 69—corner of Broadway & 41st streets—& the roar & thunder of Cars & Waggons kept me awake every hour the whole night— it was fearful—

WED. NOV. 13, 1895. In New York Took an 8 Oclock breakfast with May Wright Sewall—she returning to her Theodore[1] at Poughkeepsie— then came others & I staid & talked till nearly lunch time— then went to Mrs Stanton's & had cast taken of my single hand & then with it clasped with Mrs Stantons—& the Italians pronounced it good cast—[2] Then I rushed back to cousin Semanthas

Reception at <u>Savoy</u> Parlors at 3—[3] Cousin Ellen & Louise went— Nephew Wendell Mosher came— after supper I simply went to bed— & he & Louise came—

1. Theodore Lovett Sewall (?–1895), suffering from tuberculosis, died on December 23. A graduate of Harvard College in 1874, he conducted a boys' classical school in Indianapolis until 1889, and after his marriage in 1880, he and May Wright Sewall founded the city's Girls' Classical School. (*Historical Register of Harvard University, 1636–1936* [Cambridge, Mass., 1937], 231; *Woman's Journal*, 4 January 1896.)

2. This was the project of Mary E. B. Culbertson (1864–1929), known as Meb, a sculptor from Richmond, Indiana. The clasped hands of ECS and SBA were said to be the most interesting of all the famous hands she modeled in what became a New York fad. She told another guest at the birthday celebration that copies were "to be sold thro the various clubs & leagues." (*Oswego Times*, 17 December 1897; Elizabeth E. Pike to Caroline Putnam, 21 November 1895, ECS Papers, DLC; Beverly Yount, comp., *Tombstone Inscriptions in Wayne County, Indiana* [Fort Wayne, Ind., 1968], 1:52; *Who's Who among Earlhamites* [Richmond, Ind., 1916], 44.)

3. Henry and Fanny Garrison Villard hosted this reception at the Hotel Savoy. See *Film*, 34:520–21.

❦ Excelsior Diary 1895, n.p. SBA Papers, DLC.

Appendix A

ALICE BLACKWELL'S MEMORANDUM ON DISCUSSIONS ABOUT UNION

3 Park Street, Boston, December 25, 1887.

Dear Miss Foster: The arrangement between Miss Anthony and my mother was this, as expressed in the letter I read to Miss Anthony Friday morning, to which she took no exception: The committees appointed respectively by herself and Mrs. Stone shall each agree upon a common name, a common constitution, and a common list of officers for the first year; and the subsequent acceptance of these by each association will thereafter constitute the two societies one society.

At the conference between Miss Anthony and my mother on Wednesday afternoon, Miss Anthony said she preferred not to make any propositions herself at that time, but to listen first to what our side had to suggest.

My mother then read a series of points that she had jotted down, as what she would like and should consider feasible. These suggestions are all purely informal, and may be added to or subtracted from by the committee into whose hands the whole matter will be put. They were substantially as follows, though a few have been a little more fully elaborated since, and one or two were not mentioned on Wednesday, but were talked over between Miss Anthony and my father on Friday morning. I thought you would probably prefer to have them all together, as your reason for wanting them written out was to give your committee a general idea of what our committee was likely to propose, and to let them be thinking it over in advance. And we should be glad if Miss Anthony would send us a similar informal list of the things she would like and would consider feasible.

1. Name, either of the following: The United Woman Suffrage Societies, National American Woman Suffrage Association, American

Equal Suffrage Association. (Mrs. Stone liked the first-mentioned best, and Miss Anthony the second. I think there would be no objection to the second.)

2. Object, to secure suffrage to the women of the United States.

3. A delegate basis, such as may be mutually agreed upon.

4. Duly accredited State delegates alone to be entitled to vote at business meetings.

5. Presidents of State societies to be *ex-officio* Vice-Presidents of the National American, and chairmen of State executive committees to be *ex-officio* members of the National American Executive Committee.

6. Men and women to be eligible to office and membership on equal terms.

7. After a mutually satisfactory constitution has been agreed upon, it shall not be altered except after full notice to all members (through the woman suffrage papers or otherwise) of the exact change proposed.

8. A provision like that of the National Woman's Christian Temperance Union, by which no department of the National work is binding on the States or on individuals.

9. Each State to have supreme control of its own State work, and the National American to have supreme control of the National work.

10. Headquarters at Boston, and also at Washington while Congress is in session.

11. All woman suffrage papers to be treated upon an equal footing, and no discrimination made for or against any one of them.

12. Where there are two State societies in the same State, that they be requested to unite; and if they fail to do so, that the original State society be the one recognized by the National American.

13. Since many members of the National society regard Mrs. Stone as the cause of the division, and many members of the American regard Mrs Stanton and Miss Anthony as the cause of it, Mrs. Stone suggested that it would greatly promote a harmonious union for those three ladies— Mrs. Stanton, Miss Anthony, and herself—to agree in advance that they would none of them take the presidency of the united association.

Negotiations between the American and National Woman Suffrage Associations in Regard to Union, ed. Rachel G. Foster, (N.p., 1888), 3–4, in *Film*, at 20 April 1888.

Appendix B

OF CONSTITUTIONS, BYLAWS, AND UNION

1886
Constitution of the National Woman Suffrage Association

EDITORIAL NOTE: The National association made few changes to its bare-bones constitution after 1869, and no procedures for amendment were included in the text. From minutes of executive sessions, it can be detected that changes to the bylaws occurred with some frequency, but no one has yet located a copy of the association's bylaws. The constitution as it stood in 1886 was published in the program for the Eighteenth Annual Washington Convention, in the Robinson-Shattuck Papers, scrapbook 57, MCR-S.

Article 1. This organization shall be called the National Woman Suffrage Association.

Article 2. The object of this Association shall be to secure National Protection for women in the exercise of their citizens' right to vote.

Article 3. All citizens of the United States, subscribing to this Constitution, and contributing not less than one dollar annually, shall be considered members of the Association, with the right to participate in its deliberations.

Article 4. The officers of this Association shall be a President, a Vice-President from each of the States and Territories, Corresponding and Recording Secretaries, a Treasurer, and an Executive Committee of not less than five.

Article 5. A quorum of the Executive Committee shall consist of nine, and all the officers of this Association shall be *ex-officio* members of such Committee, with power to vote.

Article 6. All Woman Suffrage Societies throughout the country shall be welcomed as auxiliaries, and their accredited officers or duly appointed representatives shall be recognized as members of the National Association.

1888–1889
Basis of Representation, National Woman Suffrage Association

EDITORIAL NOTE: For the final eight years of its existence, the National association struggled to balance its original structure as a society of individual members with practical objections to allowing members on the East Coast, especially in Washington, to dominate annual meetings. Nearly every year from 1882, a committee on a basis of representation, chaired by Harriette Shattuck, introduced into the bylaws schemes for voting by delegates assigned on the basis of individual and auxiliary memberships in the states; nearly as often, the annual meeting adopted the plan one year but tinkered with it the next to quiet complaints from people in attendance. In the *Woman's Tribune*, 20 October 1888, Harriette Shattuck announced the basis of representation in effect for the Washington convention of 1889.

Each vice-president of the National W.S.A. shall, at least once a year, call together the members for the current year of the N.W.S.A. resident in her state or territory, and from this assembly elect delegates to the annual Washington convention. Or if this is not practicable, she shall (*after consultation with and with the approval of the executive committee for her state or territory*) appoint such delegates from the members by correspondence therewith. Each state or territory is entitled to one delegate and one more for every twenty-five members of the N.W.S.A. for the current year. The delegates actually present shall be entitled to cast as many votes as the membership of their state or territory commands. Or, delegations not full, may complete their quota with members present at the convention who are residents of their state or territory.

Any state suffrage association, whether an auxiliary of the National W.S.A. or not may send two delegates, each of whom shall have one vote.

Any suffrage association, state or local, which pays annually into the national treasury twenty-five per cent. of its membership fees, shall be styled a paying auxiliary and shall be entitled to three delegates, and one additional delegate to every twenty-five members above a membership of fifty; and the delegates actually present may cast the whole number of votes to which the association they represent is entitled.

The members of paying auxiliaries shall also be considered members of the National W.S.A.

When a national vice-president is also the president of a state "paying auxiliary," she need not call together the members of the National W.S.A. but may convert them in the basis of representation for the state association of which she is president, and summon them to all meetings when delegates are chosen for the National W.S.A. conventions.

All credentials, from whatever organizations, must be signed by the vice-president of the National W.S.A. for the state or territory from which the delegate is sent.

All officers of the National W.S.A. shall be *ex-officio* delegates at large with the power to vote. Members who are neither officers nor duly accredited delegates, may be present at business meetings, but (with the exception of members from isolated states or territories where there is no suffrage society) such members shall speak and vote only by the unanimous consent of the delegation.

1888
UNION CONSTITUTION PROPOSED BY THE
AMERICAN WOMAN SUFFRAGE ASSOCIATION

EDITORIAL NOTE: Henry Blackwell, in his capacity as secretary to the American association's conference committee, submitted this constitution on 29 March 1888 to the National's conference committee as a basis for uniting the two societies. Along with it, he sent a full slate of officers for the new society. This constitution was based, Blackwell wrote, "chiefly upon that of the National W.C.T.U., a society which, in point of efficient organization, was thought to be an excellent model." This text was published by Blackwell in the *Woman's Journal*, 5 May 1888.

1. The name of this Society shall be the (Union Woman Suffrage Association, or the) National American Woman Suffrage Association.

2. The object of this Association shall be to secure suffrage to the women of the United States, by appropriate National and State legislation.

3. The general officers of this Association shall be a President, ten Vice-Presidents at large, Chairman of Executive Committee, a Corresponding Secretary, a Foreign Corresponding Secretary, a Recording Secretary, and a Treasurer. The President of each auxiliary State or Territorial Woman Suffrage Association shall be *ex-officio* Vice-President of the general Woman Suffrage Association. The general officers, with

the Vice-Presidents from the States, heads of departments, and National Organizers and Lecturers, shall constitute the Executive Committee, of whom fifteen members actually assembled shall constitute a quorum; but three-fifths may act by correspondence in response to a circular addressed to every member of the Executive Committee no less than fifteen days beforehand by the President, Chairman of Executive Committee, and Corresponding Secretary.

Superintendents of departments and National Organizers and Lecturers shall be proposed by the Executive Committee, and elected at the annual meeting.

4. The annual meeting shall consist of the Executive Committee, auxiliary State and Territorial Corresponding Secretaries and Treasurers, National Superintendents of departments, National Organizers and Lecturers, one delegate at large from each auxiliary State or Territorial Society, and one additional delegate for every five hundred paying members. The District of Columbia shall be represented on the same basis as a Territory.

5. Any State or Territorial Woman Suffrage Association may become auxiliary to the general Woman Suffrage Association, by subscribing to this Constitution.

6. The annual meeting, at which the officers shall be elected, shall be held at such time and place as may be determined by the Executive Committee of the general Woman Suffrage Association.

7. Each auxiliary State Association shall pay annually to the general treasury ten cents per member of the State Association.

8. This Constitution may be altered or amended by a two-thirds vote of all the delegates present at any annual meeting and entitled to vote, provided the proposed amendment has been submitted in writing at the previous annual meeting; and it shall be the duty of the Recording Secretary to enter such proposed amendment in full on the minutes, for publication.

9. Any person may become a member of the general Association by subscribing to the Constitution and paying the sum of one dollar, from which the general Association shall refund to his or her State and local Treasurer (if any) the amount of their respective dues. If there is no State or local Society where the person comes from, then the general Society shall keep all the money.

10. All woman suffrage papers shall be treated by the general Association upon an equal footing, and no discrimination made for or against any one of them.

11. This Society shall have a headquarters for Congressional work at Washington during the session of Congress, a headquarters at Chicago for a lecture bureau, and a headquarters at Boston for suffrage literature.

12. No distinction on account of sex shall ever be made in membership or eligibility to office in this Society.

13. No officer or representative of the general organization shall go into any State to work in behalf of the National American Woman Suffrage Association, except with the written approval of the President and Corresponding Secretary of the State Society or Societies.

By-Laws.

Duties of Officers.

1. The President may, through the Corresponding Secretary, call special meetings of the Executive Committee, when he or she may deem it necessary, or at the written request of ten members of the Executive Committee, the topics to be considered at such meeting to be stated in the call; at least fifteen day's notice to be mailed to each member of the Executive Committee; and shall perform all other duties usual to such office.

2. The Corresponding Secretary shall perform all the duties usual to such office, and shall also send to each State Corresponding Secretary, at least two months before the general annual meeting, a blank for his or her report for the current year, from which the Secretary of the National American Woman Suffrage Association shall collate his or her own report to the annual meeting.

3. The Recording Secretary shall attend all meetings of the Association, and of the Executive Committee, and keep a correct record of the same; shall send to each member of the Executive Committee a notice of such meetings; shall apprise members of committees of their appointment, and officers of the Society of their election; at the first session of each annual meeting shall read in their order the minutes of all meetings of the Executive Committee since the last annual meeting, and shall perform all other usual duties.

4. The Foreign Corresponding Secretary shall conduct the foreign correspondence.

5. The Treasurer shall keep accurate account of all receipts and disbursements, and present a detailed report thereof at each annual meeting; and shall pay no bill except on an order signed by the President and Recording Secretary. The fiscal year shall end two weeks before the annual meeting, and the books shall then be closed. At the annual meeting the Treasurer shall give the Corresponding Secretary the number of delegates to which each State is entitled, according to the amount of dues paid; and shall perform all other usual duties.

6. The Superintendents shall originate, advise, and direct plans of work relating to their several departments; correspond and co-operate with State Superintendents, and report to annual meeting work accomplished and proposed. They shall furnish an itemized account of their receipts and expenditures.

7. The officers, with the exception of Vice-Presidents of States, shall be elected by ballot, on the morning of the last day but one of the annual meeting.

8. Each delegation may fill its quota by visiting members from its own State. If any State President is absent, said State may be represented on the Executive Committee by a member of its delegation, chosen by said delegation.

9. Tellers shall be appointed by the annual meeting, and the members of same shall proceed to vote by ballot.

10. The Executive Committee may fill any vacancies occurring in the interim of annual meetings.

11. The following committees shall be chosen on the first day of the annual meeting: Credentials, Finance, Business, Resolutions. The last shall consist of one delegate from each State chosen by its delegation.

12. The Executive Committee, superintendents, and organizers and lecturers shall meet in joint session, previous to the annual meeting, to prepare a plan of work to be submitted to said meeting.

13. An Auditing Committee and a Committee on Railroad Rates shall be appointed by the general officers in the interim of the annual meetings.

14. The Committee on Credentials shall approve such as are signed by President and Secretary of State or Territorial Societies represented; and shall report to the convention setting forth the whole number of delegates present.

15. The Finance Committee shall consist of three or more.

16. The Business Committee shall consist of three, chosen by the Executive Committee from their own number. They shall, in conference

APPENDIX B 741

with the local committee of the city where the annual meeting is held, provide speakers for all public services outside of the business meetings.

17. All documents and announcements from the general officers shall be sent to the State Societies through their respective Presidents or Corresponding Secretaries.

18. No new department of work shall be created, except on recommendation of the Executive Committee and vote of the annual meeting. Co-operation with any department shall be discretionary in each State.

19. These By-laws may be amended by a two-thirds vote of the members present at any annual meeting and entitled to vote therein.

1889–1890
Constitution of the National Woman Suffrage Association and the National-American Woman Suffrage Association

> EDITORIAL NOTE: During the same business meeting in 1888 at which delegates of the National association sent the message to Henry Blackwell that a joint convention of the two societies should be called to draft a constitution and elect officers, delegates also voted to create a subcommittee on constitutional revision, charged to report back in 1889. As chair of the executive committee, Matilda Gage oversaw the election of subcommittee members and chose May Sewall to lead it. What prompted the action is nowhere stated in the record, but by revising the constitution at this juncture, the National could set its own standard if union went forward. Late in 1888, the American association responded to the National's terms, stating that if agreement could be reached on a new constitution in advance of union, their members would consent to an election of officers in joint convention. That agreement was reached by representatives of the American and the National in January 1889. Rather than voting just to approve the constitution as a plan for union, delegates to the National's convention proceeded to adopt it as their own, creating confusion over when it would go into effect. The American association regarded the constitution of 1889 as that of a new National-American society, and its leaders circulated a text slightly different from that the National adopted. Differences are indicated in the text below. The National's new constitution was published in the *Woman's Tribune*, 16 February 1889; the *Woman's Journal*, 2 March 1889, published the National-American's constitution.

Article I. The name of this Association shall be "The National Woman Suffrage Association."

Article II. The object of this Association shall be to secure protection in their right to vote to the women citizens of the United States by appropriate National and State legislation.

Article III. *Section 1.* All citizens of the United States, subscribing to this Constitution and paying not less than one dollar annually into the treasury of this Association, shall become members thereof and shall be entitled to attend all its meetings, to participate in all discussions that may arise and to receive Reports and other documents published by it. [*added in National-American text:* but such membership shall not carry with it the right to vote.]

Section 2. The payment of fifty dollars ($50.00) into the treasury of this Association shall constitute any citizen of the United States a life member of the Association, with all the privileges belonging to regular annual members.

Article IV. *Section 1.* The officers of this Association shall be a President, a Vice-President at Large, a Recording secretary, a Corresponding secretary, a Treasurer, a Chairman of the executive committee and two Auditors. The officers named in this section shall be nominated by an informal ballot at a business session of the Annual Convention of the Association. The three persons receiving the highest number of votes for any office, shall be considered the nominees of the Convention for that office, and the will of the Association shall be taken by a formal ballot.

Section 2. Wherever state and territorial Associations auxiliary to the National Woman Suffrage Association exist, the Presidents of such Associations shall be considered Vice-Presidents of the National association, representing therein their respective states and territories.

Section 3. Each State or Territorial auxiliary Association shall elect from its membership one person to serve on the Executive Committee of the National Association.

Section 4. The President of the National Woman Suffrage association shall appoint a Vice-President to represent on its Executive Board, any State or Territory where no state or territorial association exists auxiliary to the National association.

Section 5. The officers enumerated in the preceding sections of this article shall constitute the Executive Committee of this association; of these officers fifteen shall constitute a quorum for the transaction of business.

Section 6. The Executive Committee shall elect annually from the veterans of our cause, ten or more Honorary Vice-Presidents.

Article V. This Constitution may be amended by a majority vote, at any annual meeting, notice of the amendment having been given at any preceding annual meeting.

By-Laws.

By-Law I. For the accomplishment of the object specified in Article II of its Constitution this Association shall seek to concentrate the efforts of all the advocates of woman suffrage in the United States by the following methods. (1) It shall hold annually in Washington one meeting of delegates (according to the basis of representation stated in By-law II) for the transaction of business, the election of officers and the advocacy of its principles; and it may hold one or more other conventions annually for the advocacy of its principles. (2) It shall form State or Territorial associations auxiliary to itself in every state and territory where none such now exists, and, recognizing the authority of its auxiliaries, in their respective states and territories, it shall promote their local work by every means in its power. (3) It shall publish tracts, speeches and other documents and shall furnish the same to state and local suffrage associations and to individuals at actual cost. (5) It shall prepare and circulate petitions to Congress and to state and territorial Legislatures on behalf of the political and civil equality of woman. (6) It may employ one or more organizers and lecturers and take such other measures for the promotion of woman suffrage as the Executive Committee shall determine upon, subject always to the will of the association.

By-Law II. Basis of Representation. *Section 1.* Any state or territorial woman suffrage association, and (in a state or territory where there is no state or territorial suffrage organization auxiliary to the National woman suffrage association) any local woman suffrage association may become auxiliary to the National woman suffrage association by paying into the treasury of the National association, annually twenty-five cents (.25) per member of its entire membership.

Section 2. It shall be the duty of the Treasurer of each auxiliary association to send to the Treasurer of the National woman suffrage association, before January 1st in each year, a list certified to by its President or recording secretary, of the members of said organization for the current year.

Section 3. Every such auxiliary association shall be entitled to send three delegates to the annual Convention of the National woman suffrage association, and one delegate in addition for every twenty-five members above a membership of fifty. The delegates actually present may cast the whole number of votes to which the auxiliary association is entitled.

Section 4. Any state or territorial woman suffrage association which is not auxiliary to the National woman suffrage association may send one delegate to the annual meeting of the National association.

Section 5. All officers of the National woman suffrage association shall be *ex-officio* delegates at large and every such officer shall be entitled to one vote in all the business meetings of the association.

[*added in National-American text: Section 6.* Where there are two State societies in one State, both of them auxiliary to the National-American, the president of each shall be a vice-president of the National-American; and each shall elect its own representative on the National-American executive board, and be entitled to one delegate for each twenty-five members.]

By-Law III. Credentials.

All delegates (except the delegates at large specified in section 5 of by-law II) must present credentials properly signed by the President and the recording secretary of the organization represented. Membership cards, properly signed by the treasurer of the National woman suffrage association shall serve as credentials for the members of that body who are not delegates from other bodies.

By-Law IV. The Executive Committee of the National woman suffrage association shall hold one session preceding the opening of each annual Convention in Washington and another session after the conclusion of such Convention; and the Committee having in charge the arrangements for the Annual Convention shall always take cognizance of such meetings of the Executive Committee and make provision for them.

By-Law V. The decisions reached by the Executive Committee shall be presented in the form of recommendations at the business sessions of the Convention.

By-Law VI. Every delegate shall be entitled to one vote on all questions, but only on election of officers shall the delegates be entitled to cast the full vote to which the organizations represented by them are entitled.

By-Law VII. The committee on Resolutions shall consist of one person from each state and territory, elected by the delegation from the organization represented.

By-Law VIII. At the concluding business session of each annual Convention, the President of this association shall appoint the following committees, each committee to consist of three persons, viz: a Committee on Credentials to have in charge the credentials of delegates to the next annual Convention; a Committee on program to arrange the program for the next annual meeting; and a Congressional Committee to have in charge the direct Congressional work during the year which shall intervene between the time of its appointment and the next annual Convention in Washington.

By-Law IX. The report of the Treasurer up to the 1st of the January preceding the annual Washington Convention shall be read at the first business session of that body.

INDEX

Academy of Music (Newburgh), 716
Adam Bede (Eliot), 154
Adams, Abigail Smith, 467, *470n*
Adams, Franklin George, *1n*; letter from SBA, 586–91; letter to SBA, 1
Adams, John, 151, *158n*, 254, 598
Adams, Nehemiah, 288, *292n*
Adler, Felix, 11, *12n*
adultery: and character, 336–41
Ady, Joseph Wesley, 498, *499n*
Aesop's Fables, 366
African Americans: in Calif., 186; and Colo. campaign, 604; in Leavenworth, 189–91, 194–95. *See also* suffrage, African-American
African Methodist Episcopal Zion Church (Rochester), 690
aging: ECS on, 200, 328–30, 429, 618; L. Stone on, 356–57; P. B. McLaren on, 302
Aiken, S.C.: SBA in, 675–76; SBA speaks in, 676
Albaugh, Eula Lee Houghton, 497, *498n*
Albaugh, Morton, 497, *498n*
Albaugh's Opera House (Washington), 93, 360
Albert (prince consort), 152, *158n*
Albion, N.Y.: SBA speaks in, 577
Alcott, Amos Bronson, 250, *263n*, 347
Allegheny City, Pa.: conservatory for, 191–92
Allen, Grant Blairfindie, 425, *434n*
Allen's Opera House (Jamestown, N.Y.), 134
Almy, Martha Robinson, *563–64n*, 575; and N.Y. association, 716; and N.Y. campaign, 563, 564, 565, 572
Alvord, Thomas Gold, 622–23, *624n*
American Equal Rights Association, 53, 252, 298, 299–300n
American Woman Suffrage Association: annual meetings of, 3, 52–56, 160, 162n; constitution of, 65n, 67n; proposes union, xxv, 52–53, 54–56, 68; responds to National association, 160, 162n
American Woman Suffrage Association conference committees, 69n, 109, 112–13, 162n, 168; constitution proposed by, 736–40
Ames, Charles Gordon, 3, *5n*; and educated suffrage, 649
Ames, Fanny Baker, 3, *5n*
Ames, Julia, 450, *451n*, 690
Amies, Olive Pond, *421n*; at suffrage meeting, 416

Ancient Society (Morgan), 339, 358
Anderson, Frederick Lincoln, 690, *690n*
Andersonville Prison, 146
Ann Arbor, Mich.: SBA in, 572–73; SBA speaks in, 221, 226. *See also* Michigan, University of
Anthony, Anna E. Osborne, 177, *180n*, 387; in Washington, 237, 271
Anthony, Anna Osborne, 500, *502n*; in Rochester, 450
Anthony, Annette, *134n*; death of, 134
Anthony, Daniel, 178, *180n*, 516
Anthony, Daniel Read, *42n*; introduces SBA, 41, 42; and Kan. history, 599; mayoral campaign of, 194–95; mentioned, 387; in Rochester, 641; in Topeka, 626; in Washington, 237, 271, 309
Anthony, Daniel Read, Jr., 626, *626n*, 641
Anthony, Hannah Lapham, 516, *521n*
Anthony, Humphrey, 516, *521n*
Anthony, Jacob Merritt, *387–88n*; accident of, 626; and Kan. history, 386, *387–88n*, 599; letter from SBA, 386–87; SBA visits, 494
Anthony, Lucy Elmina, *7n*; and Columbian Exposition, 547; education of, 15; health of, 16–17n; mentioned, 4, 163, 406, 494, 717; in Rochester, 134, 387; at suffrage meeting, 415–16
Anthony, Lucy Read, 243, *245n*, 392
Anthony, Mary Almina Luther, 387, *387–88n*
Anthony, Mary Stafford, *16n*; as home-owner, 377, 378–79, 387, 392–93; and I. B. Wells, 689, 690, 691, *691–92n*; leads Rochester lecture series, 446; letter from SBA, 669–70; mentioned, 15, 134, 494, 499, 563, 641, 663, 706, 714; in New York, 730; and N.Y. campaign, 553, 564, 565, 567, 572, 575; in Washington, 237, 271, 309
Anthony, Maude, *7n*; in Leavenworth, 626; in Rochester, 204; in Washington, 4, 237, 271
Anthony, Susan B.: birthday of, 237–38, 240–43, 245, 271, 283; descriptions of, 210, 471–72; ECS criticizes, 137–38, 142, 201, 701–2; gifts for, 164–65; health of, 163, *163–64n*, 356–57, 706–7, 707–8, *707n*, 709; as housekeeper, 377, 378–79, 387, 392–93; letters from ECS, 9–11, 297–98, 308–9, 358–59, 385, 473, 502, 638; letters to ECS, 499–500, 641–42, 699–700, 709–10; religious views of, 177–78; and

747

(Anthony, Susan B., *continued*)
  Republican party, 58–59, 74, 126, 137–38, 139, 456, 634; views of union, 53n, 56, 69, 74–75, 75n, 165, 178–80, 234–35, 270, 395; and *Woman's Bible*, 699–700
Anthony, Susie B., *180n*; death of, 177–78
antisuffragists: ECS mocks, 595–98, 620; in Mass., 151; in N.Y., 596n, 623, 648
appeals: "To the Women of New York" (ECS), 559–62
Aragon Hotel (Atlanta), 673–74
Arkansas: SBA's trip to, 505
Armstrong, Hamilton, 522, *526–27n*
Armstrong, S. Augusta, 570, *570–71n*
Arnold, Matthew, 101, *106n*, 150, 657
Arnold, Thomas, *658n*; quoted, 657
articles: "Educated Suffrage Again" (ECS), 665–68; "Educated Suffrage Justified" (ECS), 655–57; "The Great Trial" (ECS), 198–99; "Let the Blue Laws Rest" (ECS), 191–94; "The Lord Chancellor" (ECS), 374–75; "Parties or Platforms" (ECS), 135–38; "Patriotism and Chastity" (ECS), 336–41; "Sunday at the World's Fair" (ECS), 439–42; "What Should be Our Attitude Towards Political Parties" (ECS), 285–90; "Wyoming Admitted as a State into the Union" (ECS), 312–17
Asbury College: SBA speaks at, 669
Association for the Advancement of Women, 10
Atlanta, Georgia: SBA in, 673–74
Atlanta University: SBA speaks at, 674
Australian ballot, 522–23
Avery, George Capwell, *671n*; hosts SBA, 669
Avery, Rachel G. Foster: and Columbian Exposition, 490, 511; gifts to SBA, 378; letters from SBA, 220–21, 225; mentioned, 163, 415, 416, 419, 660; and National-American, 584, 700; and National association, 162, 168, 170, 219; and National conference committee, 166; in Rochester, 487; and SBA's birthday, 245. *See also* Foster, Rachel G.
Avery, Susan Howes Look, 529–30, *531n*, 669

Babcock, Elnora E. Monroe, 442, 443, *444n*
Bacon, Francis, 47, *51n*, 349
Bailey, Will F., 321, *322n*
Bain, George Washington, 221, *222n*
Baker, Floyd Perry, 600, *614n*
Baldwin, Charles A., 198–99, *199n*
Balgarnie, Florence, 369, *369–70n*
Ballot Box (Toledo), 311
Banker, George W., *388n*; hosts SBA, 386
Banker, Henrietta M. Hull, *388n*; hosts SBA, 386; and N.Y. campaign, 553

Barber, Lucy Sweet, 121n
Barker, Helen Morton, *277n*; and So. Dak. campaign, 274–76, 281–82
Barker, Moses, *282–83n*; and So. Dak. campaign, 281, 304–5
Barnum's circus, 350
Barrau de Muratel, Caroline Françoise Coulomb de, 33, *35n*
Bartlett, Paul Wayland, 32, *34n*
Bartol, Emma Jemima Welchman, 271, *273–74n*
Barton, Clara, 123
Basingstoke, England: ECS in, 7–8, 9–11, 20–22, 70–72, 77, 90–91, 293, 297–98, 308, 311, 328–30, 333–34, 334–35, 343–44, 345, 346–52, 355, 358–59, 369, 370–71, 385
Batavia, N.Y.: meeting in, 577
Baum, Maud Gage, 202, *203n*
Bayard, Tryphena Cady, 330, *331n*, 333, 346
Becker, Lydia Ernestine, 308, *310n*, 371
Beethoven, Ludwig van, 432, *436n*
Bellamy, Edward, *203n*; *Looking Backward*, 202, 208
Bennett, Sarah Lewis Clay, *279n*; and National-American, 584; at suffrage meeting, 278
bequests: by E. A. McConnell, 220, 221–22n; by E. J. S. Clapp, 575, 641, 642–43n
Besant, Annie Wood, 334, *335n*
Bethel African Methodist Episcopal Church (Atlanta), 674
Bible: commentaries on, 20–21; in public schools, 72. *See also* men of the Bible; *Woman's Bible;* women of the Bible
biblical quotations and references: charity in, 341; death in, 242, 708; to devils, 141; to Fifth Commandment, 726, 727; friendships of women in, 241; to Garden of Eden, 366, 696, 697n; to Genesis, 696; to Golden Rule, 148, 726; lamentations in, 636; love in, 71, 136; loyalty in, 611; men's dominion in, 50; to parable of ten virgins, 97; to Paul's views of women, 196, 517, 726; to Pentateuch, 20, 677, 696, 702; to Pharisees, 341; resistance to change in, 250; resurrection in, 575; self-reliance in, 97; self-sacrifice in, 430; simultaneous creation in, 722; to sins of fathers, 156; social distinctions in, 317; teachings of Jesus in, 72, 430–31; to Timothy, 702; transformation in, 179–80; wandering in, 78, 100, 284
bicycle: and dress reform, 207
Bigelow, Clara Kathan, 715, *715n*
Bigelow, Jane Tunis Poultney, 32, *34n*, 330
Bigelow, John, *34n*; letter from ECS, 639; and N.Y. campaign, 623, 639; in Paris, 32
Biggs, Caroline Ashurst, 86, *87n*
Binghamton, N.Y.: SBA in, 583–84

Bissell, Sarah A. Secor, 574, *574n*
Blackall, Sarah Colman, 575, *575–76n*
Blackstone, William, 47, *51n*, 339; and double standard, 153; mentioned, 726; quoted, 176
Blackwell, Alice Stone, *57n*; and American conference committee, 168; criticizes ECS, 507-8, 508-9n; and her father, 270, 297; letter from ECS, 507-8; letter to R. G. Foster, 732-33; at meeting on union, 57, 59-64; and National-American, 584, 660, 662; and plans for union, 55, 68, 69-70n, 74, 215, 231-32, 732-33; at suffrage meetings, 270, 416-17; and *Woman's Column*, 321
Blackwell, Antoinette Louisa Brown, 84, *85n*, 97, 250, 721
Blackwell, Henry Browne, *53n*; and 1872 election, 454-55; and American association, 52-53, 219; and American conference committee, 109, 117-19; and Colo. campaign, 603; and educated suffrage, 649; his own historian, 213n; 297-98, 298-99n, 308, 371; and Kan. campaign, 636-37n; letter from National association, 118-19; letter to SBA, 454-57; and plans for union, xxvi, 216, 732, 736-40; on political parties, 460; as Republican, 636; and So. Dak. campaign, 321, 323n; and suffrage factions, 54-55, 270; at suffrage meetings, 269, 286, 289, 291n, 490
Blair, Henry William, *6n*, 240; and amendment, 4, 75; letter from SBA, 75-76
Blake, Lillie Devereux, *17n*; and constitutional centennial, 37-38; and ECS birthday, 683, 709; and International Council, 86-87, 108-9; letters from ECS, 593-94, 635-36; letters from SBA, 37-38, 74-75, 86-87, 215-16, 392-93, 442-44, 553-54, 556-58, 683-84; letter to SBA, 683; mentioned, 110, 251; and National-American, 410; and National association, 170; and National conference committee, 117, 119, 166-67; and N.Y. association, 442-44, 716; and N.Y. campaign, 553-54, 556-58, 635-36; at Pilgrim Mothers' Dinner, 502; and *The Question*, 15-16; on South, 495; views of union, 111-12, 117
Blankenburg, Lucretia Longshore, *373n*, 675, 714; letter from SBA, 373
Blatch, Alice, 390, *391n*
Blatch, Harriot Eaton Stanton, xxvi-xxvii, 333; debates educated suffrage, 666-68, 668-69n; letter from ECS, 390-91; in London, 308; mentioned, 10, 11, 77, 90, 221, 225, 230, 232, 278, 293, 296, 335, 694; as mother, 32-33; and N.Y. campaign, 618; at suffrage meeting, 268;

and "Voluntary Motherhood," 358; and *Woman's Bible*, 677
Blatch, Nora Stanton, *24n*, 333; education of, 32-33; letter from ECS, 23-24
Blatch, William Henry, Jr., 32-33, *35n*, 334
Bloomer, Amelia Jenks, 143, 514, *515n*
Bomar, Edward Earle, 676, *676–77n*
Bones, Marietta M. Wilkins, *309–10n*; and So. Dak. campaign, 308
Bonney, Charles Carroll, 491, *492n*, 685
Boonville, N.Y.: SBA in, 593-94
Boston: SBA in, 59-64; SBA speaks in, 123-25, 380-84
Boston Music Hall, 123-24, 380
Bourke, Robert (Baron Connemara), 337, *342n*
Bowen, Thomas Mead, *76–77n*; and Senate committee, 75-76
Bowman, Eliza Wilson, 653, *654n*
Bowman, Thomas Elliott, *654n*; letter from SBA, 650-53
Boyd's Opera House (Omaha), 141, 143
Boyles, Hannah Dickinson, 238, *239n*, 271
Bradwell, Myra Colby, 491, *492n*
Bremer, Fredrika, 95, *104n*
Briggs, Marsenus H., 565, *565n*
Bright, Jacob, 343, *345n*
Bright, John, 8, *9n*, 259, 260
Bright, Ursula Mellor, 343, *345n*
Brighton Beach Hotel (Brooklyn), 205, 209
Bristol, England: ECS speaks in, 327-28
Bromwell, Henry Pelham Holmes, 522, *527n*
Brontë, Charlotte, 241, *244n*
Brooklyn, N.Y.: ECS speaks in, 205-7; SBA speaks in, 209-10
Broomall, John Martin, 600, *614n*
Brougham, Henry Peter (Baron Brougham and Vaux), *729n*; quoted, 725
Brown, Benjamin Gratz, *546n*; quoted, 543
Brown, George Stewart, 479, *479–80n*
Brown, Harriet Eaton, 328-29, *330n*, 479
Brown, John, *388n*; farm of, 386; in Kan., 599
Brown, May Belleville Brown, 482, *482n*
Brown, Olympia, *12n*; and federal suffrage, 461, 463, 487-88; letters from ECS, 200-201, 211-13, 465, 493; letters from SBA, 177-80, 321-22; mentioned, 11, 250, 710, 721; and National-American, 403, 494, 583; and National association, 168; and National conference committee, 64, 119, 166; and So. Dak. campaign, 319; at suffrage meetings, 269, 490; and *Woman's Bible*, 677
Brown, Watson, 386, *388n*
Browning, Elizabeth Barrett, 95, *104n*
Buckle, Henry Thomas, *546n*; quoted, 542
Buckley, James Monroe, *489n*, 698; and woman suffrage, 488, 489, 518

Buffalo, N.Y.: ECS and SBA in, 134; meeting in, 570–71
Bullard, Laura J. Curtis, 32, *35n*
Burleigh, Charles Calistus, 99, *105n*, 347
Burleigh, William Henry, 347, *353n*
Burns, Robert, 363, *369n*
Burr, Frances Ellen, 4, *6n*; and Hartford Equal Rights Club, 176n
Burt, Mary Towne, *555n*; and N.Y. campaign, 554
busts: of ECS, 329, 330–31n; of SBA, 446, 447n, 478, 480
Butler, Benjamin Franklin, 455, *458n*
Byron, N.Y.: ECS and SBA speak in, 132
"A Bystander's Notes" (Tourgée), 529–30

Caesar, Julius, 241, *244n*
California: rights of African Americans in, 186; SBA's trip to, 686, 691, 699
Callanan, Martha Coonley, 219, *219–20n*
Cambridge University, 303
Campbell, Margaret West, 219, *220n*
Canada: women's journalism in, 514. *See also* Toronto, Canada
canon law: and women, 725
Canton, So. Dak.: SBA in, 304–5
Carey, Joseph Maull, 313, *318n*, 407, 549
Carleton, Cora Georgiana Snow, 475, *476–77n*, 477
Carlisle, Lady. *See* Howard, Rosalind Frances Stanley (countess of Carlisle)
Carnegie, Andrew, 149, *157n*
Carpenter, Frank G., 717
Carpenter, Julia Louise Gage, 202, *203n*
Carpenter, William H., 630–31, *631n*
Carr, Mary L. Pease, 523, *528n*
Casement, Frances Marion Jennings, 661, *662n*; proposes union, 55
Cassadaga Lake Free Association: SBA speaks to, 645–47
Castle, Miles Beach, 490, *492n*
Catherine II (empress of Russia), 338, *342n*
Catt, Carrie Clinton Lane Chapman, 525–*26n*; and Colo. campaign, 521–22, 535–38, 546, 548, 549; and ECS birthday, 683, 709–10; and Kan. campaign, 590, 617, 627, 628, 629, 651–52; and National-American, 700, 709, 710; and N.Y. campaign, 554, 582; and So. Dak. campaign, 607; on southern tour, 669; at suffrage meeting, 439n
Cavendish, Spencer Compton (marquess of Hartington), 302, *303n*
Cecil, Robert Arthur Talbot Gascoyne- (marquess of Salisbury), *106n*; quoted, 101, 150
Centennial Exposition (1876), 440
Chace, Elizabeth Buffum, 721, *728n*

Chace, Jonathan, *76–77n*; and Senate committee, 75–76
Chambers, Eliza Anne, *121n*; views of union, 116
Chandler, Lucinda Banister, *73n*; and secular state, 70–72, 128; and *Woman's Bible*, 702
Chandler, Zachariah, 603, *615n*
Channing, William Henry, 99, *105n*, 250, 251, 347
Chant, Laura Ormiston Dibbin, *87n*; and International Council, 86, 90
Chapin, Augusta Jane, *697n*; letter from ECS, 695–97; and *Woman's Bible*, 695–97
Chapman, Carrie Clinton Lane. *See* Catt, Carrie Clinton Lane Chapman
Chapman, Hannah Hughes MacDonald, 335, *336n*
Chapman, John, 335, *336n*
chastity: lacks definition, 340; women trained for, 338–39
Chatfield, Elizabeth C. Browne, 584, *586n*
Chautauqua, N.Y.: SBA in, 488–89
Chester County, Pa., 3
Chicago: SBA in, 478, 480, 538; SBA interviewed in, 471–72; SBA speaks in, 509–11, 513–15, 516–20. *See also* World's Columbian Exposition
Chicago Advance, 519
Chicago Record, 651
Child, Lydia Maria Francis, 99, *105n*, 680
Child, Rachel Lockwood Trumbull, *617–18n*; and Kan. campaign, 617, 651
Choate, Rufus, *50n*; quoted, 42–43
Chopin, Frédéric-François, 432, *436n*
Christian Advocate, 517, 519
Christian Science, 36
Christian Union (New York), 175, 176
Christmas: customs, 163
church and state, separation of: ECS explains, 70–71; interest of women in, 508; need to protect, 191–92, 257, 440; as strength of government, 102–3
churches: equality for women in, 256–57, 725–27; and slavery, 517; and temperance, 517; and woman suffrage, 517–18
Church of Our Father (Washington), 9, 217
church property, taxation of, 72
Cibber, Colley: quoted, 163, 706
A Cigarette-Maker's Romance (Crawford), 367–68
citizenship: national protection of, 131–32, 469; and solitude, 424; and voting rights, 532, 533n, 545
Civil War: women's contributions to, 599–600
Claflin, Tennessee Celeste, 86–87, *89n*
Clapp, Eliza Jane Sawens, *576n*; bequest to SBA, 575, 641, 642–43n

Clark, Ansel Russell, 498, *498n*
Clark, George Waldo: quoted, 649
Clark, Helen Priestman Bright, 259-60, *265-66n*
Clark, Minnie Williston, 498, *498n*
Clark, Sidney, 600, *614n*
Clarke, Adam, 705, *706n*
Clay, Henry, 337, *342n*, 624
Clay, Laura, *420n*; letter from SBA, 505-6; mentioned, 669; at suffrage meetings, 414-15, 416, 417-18, 419, 436-37, 438, 438-39n, 490
Clay, Mary Barr, *120n*; and International Council, 108; and National conference committee, 117, 119; at suffrage meeting, 166; views of union, 112, 116
Claypole, Katharine Benedicta Trotter, 494, *494-95n*, 661
Cleopatra VII (queen of Egypt), 338, *342n*
Cleveland, Grover, 102, *107n*, 337
Cleveland, Ohio: SBA in, 658-62; SBA speaks in, 658-60
Cobbe, Frances Power, 241, *244n*
Cockrell, Francis Marion, *77n*; and Senate committee, 75
coeducation: advocated, 399-402
Cogswell, Helen Buffum Pillsbury, 708, *709n*
Colby, Clara Dorothy Bewick, *6n*, 37; and federal suffrage, 461, 583-84; and H. B. Blackwell, 297, 298; Lakota baby of, 371; lectures in Rochester, 446; letters from ECS, 7-8, 70-72, 140-42, 159, 208, 210, 223-24, 278, 297-98, 311, 334-35, 343-44, 358-59, 369, 370-71, 495, 582, 677-78, 681, 692, 693, 700, 701-2; letters from SBA, 334, 583-84, 706-7; mentioned, 143-44, 202, 249, 275, 319, 324, 448, 491, 500; and National-American, 410, 493; and National association, 4; and National conference committee, 64, 119, 166; and national enrollment, 167; in Omaha, 483, 485; and So. Dak. campaign, 311, 311n; at suffrage meeting, 438; views of union, 168-70; and *Woman's Bible*, 677-78; and *Woman's Tribune*, 16, 29, 70, 72, 308, 321, 447, 502, 700
Coleridge, John Duke (Baron Coleridge), 206, *207-8n*
Coliseum (Omaha), 486
Colorado: school suffrage in, 524; woman suffrage in, 590, 591, 608, 613, 712, 724
Colorado amendment campaign (1877), 588, 603-5
Colorado amendment campaign (1893), 521-24, 526n; C. Catt's plan for, 535-36; national assistance for, 535-38, 538n; votes cast, 548, 550n
Colorado Equal Suffrage Association, 521

Colorado People's party, 523
Columbus, Christopher, 218, *219n*, 228
Commentaries on American Law (Kent), 153, 339
Commentaries on the Laws of England (Blackstone), 176
common law: and right of suffrage, 144, 254
"Concerning Men" (Craik), 39
Conkling, Antoinette Hinton, 497, *497n*
Conkling, Ivan G., 497, *497n*
Connecticut Woman Suffrage Association, 234
Connemara, Lord. *See* Bourke, Robert (Baron Connemara)
consent of the governed, 711; and Civil War, 44-45
Conservative party (Great Britain), 7; and women, 456. *See also* Primrose League
"Considerations on Representative Government" (J. S. Mill), 542-43
constitutional amendment for woman suffrage: action urged on, 75-76; advocated, 424; in House, 58, 59n, 76; object of National-American, 504; opposed by J. J. Ingalls, 48-50; petitions for, 410, 411n; rejected by Senate, xxiv; in Senate, 75
Consuelo (Sand), 338
Conway, Clara, 671, *672n*
Conway, Moncure Daniel, 11, *12n*
Conway Springs, Kan., 496
Cook, Lucretia, *576n*; death of, 575
Cook, Tennessee Celeste Claflin. *See* Claflin, Tennessee Celeste
Coonley, Lydia Arms Avery, *530n*; letter from SBA, 529-30
Cooper, Florence P., 671, *672n*
Cooper Union (New York), 619
Copeland, Arthur, 579, *579n*
copyright: international, 102
Corday, Charlotte, 199, *200n*
Costelloe, Mary Smith, 293, *293n*
Coterie Migratory Assembly (Memphis), 671
Couzins, Phoebe Wilson, 46, *51n*, 140
Cowin, John Clay, 199, *199-200n*
Coxe, Arthur Cleveland, 206-7, *208n*
Craik, Dinah Mulock, 39, *40n*
Crawford, Francis Marion: quoted, 367-68
Cross, Austin, 577, *577n*
Crossett, Ella Hawley, 578, *578n*
Culberson, David Browning, 424, *434n*
Cumback, William, 254, *264n*
Curtis, Eugene Thomas, 569, *569n*
Curtis, George William, *247n*, 251, 560; quoted, 247, 541, 542
Cushing, Harriet Smith, 181, 186, *187n*

Dall, Caroline Wells Healey, *79n*, 250; and

(Dall, Caroline Wells Healey, *continued*)
International Council, 78–79, 81; letters from SBA, 78–79, 80–81
Damrosch, Frank Heino, 441, *442n*
Damrosch, Walter Johannes, 441, *442n*
Dana, Charles Anderson, 567, *568n*
Danforth, George Franklin, 567, *568n*, 569
Dansville, N.Y.: ECS seeks health in, 223, 225; ECS speaks in, 230
Dante, 723, *729n*
Davies, Charles, 124, *125n*, 381–83
Davis, Edward Morris, 99, *105n*
Davis, Maria Mott, 236, *237n*
Davis, Martha Ann Powell, *422n*; at suffrage meeting, 417
Davis, Noah, 582, *583n*
Davis, Paulina Kellogg Wright, 99, *105n*; mentioned, 250, 716; and woman's rights conventions, 346–47, 371, 720, 728n
Davis, Vinnie R., 571–72, *572n*
Dawes, Anna Laurens, 283, *284n*
Dawes, Electa Allen Sanderson, 283, *284n*
Dawes, Henry Laurens, *284n*; letter from SBA, xxv, 283–84
death: of Annette Anthony, 134; of E. Mosher, 569, 570, 572; of F. Douglass, 679; of F. E. Lawrence, 310n; of F. Miller, 82; of L. Cook, 576; of L. E. Becker, 308; SBA on, 177–78; of Susie B. Anthony, 177
Debate on Woman Suffrage in the Senate of the United States, 4
deceased wife's sister bill, 212
Declaration of Independence, 42–43
DeGive's Opera House (Atlanta), 673
The Degradation of Disfranchisement (ECS), 582
"The Degradation of Disfranchisement" (ECS), 360–68
Deland, Margaret Wade Campbell, 143, *143n*
Delmonico's (New York), 714
Demmon, Eliza Ann Van Patten, *421n*; at suffrage meeting, 415, 418
Democratic party: convention of 1868, 483; convention of 1892, 478, 480, 484; and woman suffrage, 469; and Wyoming statehood, 315. *See also* Kansas Democratic party; Massachusetts; South Dakota
Depew, Chauncey Mitchell, 487, *487n*
Deroin, Jeanne-Françoise, 347, *353n*
The Destiny of Man Viewed in the Light of His Origin (Fiske), 148
Detroit, Mich.: SBA speaks in, 221, 226
DeVoe, Emma Smith, *273n*; and Colo. campaign, 522, 535–36, 538n; letter from SBA, 654n; and So. Dak. campaign, 270, 307, 319
Dickinson, Anna Elizabeth, *205n*; financial aid for, 373, 373–74n; letter from SBA, 713–14; mentioned, 572; SBA praises, 204
Dickinson, Charles, 238, *239n*, 271
Dickinson, Frances, *239n*; and Columbian Exposition, 392; and National-American, 410; at suffrage meeting, 437–38, 438–39n; in Washington, 238, 271
Dickinson, Mary Lowe, *685n*; and ECS birthday, 683, 684, 700, 709, 715–16, 719
Dickinson, Melissa, 238, *239n*, 271
Dietrick, Ellen Virginia Battelle, *585n*; and National-American, 584, 660, 661n; and *Woman's Bible*, 677, 678
Diggs, Annie LePorte, *438n*, 486n; and Kan. campaign, 587, 588, 631; at suffrage meeting, 437
Dilke, Charles Wentworth, 90, *91n*, 92, 337, 355
Dilke, Margaret Maye Smith, 88n, 90, *91n*, 92
disfranchisement: degradation of, 124–25; impact of, 360–68; and inequality, 209
divorce: divides suffragists, 286–88, 507–8; federal investigation of, 258; in France, 287; in Ill., 196; uniform laws of, 135–36, 203
"Divorce and the Proposed National Law" (Gardener), 258
Dominion Women's Enfranchisement Association: SBA speaks to, 226
Dorsey, Anna (typist), 691
Douglas, Stephen Arnold, 288, *292n*
Douglass, Frederick, *84n*; attacks on, 685–86; and Columbian Exposition, 532, 534; ECS recalls, 680–81; funeral of, 679–81; and International Council, 83–84; letters from SBA, 83–84, 534; quoted, 124; at Seneca Falls convention, 83, 720; tributes to, 683–84, 685–86, 685n; and unrestricted suffrage, 664, 665n, 668; and woman's rights, 251, 297, 604, 623–24
Douglass, Helen Pitts, 83, *84n*, 534
dress: bicycle's impact on, 207; fashionable, 207; reform in, 11
Drew, Mary Gladstone, 456–57, *460n*
DuBois, Mary Bigelow Hall, 376, *377n*
DuBose, Daisy Miriam Howard, 415, *420–21n*
Ducey, Thomas James, 620, *621n*
Duniway, Abigail Jane Scott, *170n*; and National association, 169; and National conference committee, 166
Dunnell, Mark Hill, 284, *284n*
Durand, Frederick Lewis, 401, *402–3n*

Eastman, Charlotte Hall, 573, *573n*
Eastman, Mary F., *121n*; and National conference committee, 117, 119; and National Council, 139

Eastwood, Ellen Clara Bigelow, 715, *715n*
Eaton, Daniel Cady (1834-1890), 479, *479n*
Eaton, Daniel Cady (1837-1912), 32, *34n*, 479
Eaton, Ellen Dwight, *479n*; letter from ECS, 479
Eaton, Harriet Eliza Cady, *33n*, 330, 346, 479; in Johnstown, N.Y., 33n
economic inequality: in Britain, 22; ECS describes, 138, 644; overcome, 208
Edinburgh *Scotsman*, 302
Edmunds-Tucker Act, 247
"Educated Suffrage Again" (ECS), 665-68
"Educated Suffrage Justified" (ECS), 655-57
education: of women, 48, 303, 425-26, 427-29, 431-33
election of 1800, 254
election of 1848, 137
election of 1888: and National association, 126-27, 129-30n; Prohibition party in, 135-38; and women, 152, 161
election of 1892: suffragists prepare for, 454-57, 460
Eliot, George, 47, *51n*, 95, 154, 241, 338
Elizabeth I (queen of England), 338, *342n*
Elwell, Martha Hedger, 324, *326n*
Emancipation Proclamation, 43, 261
Embree, Alaric S., 628, *628n*
Emerson, Ralph Waldo, *244n*; mentioned, 250, 338, 347; quoted, 241
Emery, Sarah Elizabeth Van De Vort, 523, *528n*
"The Enfranchisement of Women" (H. T. Mill), 347
England, Julia. *See* Johnson, Julia England
Engley, Eugene, 522, *526n*
English, Effie Caroline Bull, 498, *498-99n*
Ensign, James Edwin, 199, *200n*
Episcopal church: in California, 727
equality, intellectual, 47
equality, physical, 77
"Equal Rights for Women" (Curtis), 541
"Equal Rights of All" (Sumner), 539, 560, 655
Equal Rights party, 128, 130-31n
Erie County, N.Y.: amendment campaign in, 570-71
Eskridge, Charles Vernon, 626, *627n*, 653
etiquette: of social calls, 79, 80-81, 83
Evans, Mary Ann. *See* Eliot, George
Everhard, Caroline McCullough, 661, *661-62n*
Ex parte Yarbrough (1884), 262, 267n
Exposition Hall (Omaha), 485
Fairchild, Herman Le Roy, 399, *402n*
"Fair Play for Women" (Curtis), 541
Farley, Porter, 689, *690n*
Farmers' Alliance, xxv; in So. Dak., 216-17n, 226, 227n, 269, 274, 300, 301-2n, 304, 306, 319, 588, 606-7. *See also* South Dakota Independent party

Fawcett, Philippa, 303n
federal elections bills, 261, 266-67n
federal suffrage, 462n
Federal Suffrage Association, 403, 404n; ECS's views of, 493; founding of, 461, 462n, 463; SBA's reaction to, 488
federal surplus, 102
feminine element, 364
Fenton, Elizabeth Scudder, *133n*; hosts ECS and SBA, 133-34
Field, Kate, 636, *637n*, 640
Fifteenth Amendment: resistance to, 529, 540, 542
Fifth Avenue Hotel (New York), 479
Fifth Street Opera House (Kansas City), 598, 616
First Baptist Church (Leavenworth), 41, 42
First Baptist Church (Rochester), 690
Fiske, John, *157n*; quoted, 148
Fitch, Charles Elliott, 446, 447, *448n*, 450
Flower, Roswell Pettibone, 478, *478n*, 659
Foraker, Joseph Benson, 477, *477n*
Forbes, George Mather, 399, *402n*
"For the Election" (Clark), 649
Fort Scott, Kan.: SBA in, 494
Forum (New York), 39
Foster, Abigail Kelley, 99, *105n*, 250, 347
Foster, Judith Ellen Horton Avery, *477n*; and Kan. campaign, 625, 626; at Republican convention, 477
Foster, Julia Manual, 4, *7n*
Foster, Julia T., 4, *7n*, 77, 378
Foster, Rachel G., *4n*; and constitutional centennial, 38; and International Council, 26, 28, 82, 85, 92, 122; letter from A. S. Blackwell, 732-33; letters from SBA, 2-4, 15-19, 26-27, 69, 75n; marriage of, 162n; at meeting on union, 57, 59-64; and National association, 2-4; and National conference committee, 64, 119; and plans for union, 68, 74, 732-33. *See also* Avery, Rachel G. Foster
Foster, Stephen Symonds, 347, *353n*
Foulke, William Dudley, *120n*; and American association, 54, 112, 219; and Columbian Exposition, 532, 533n, 534; at suffrage meetings, 268, 278, 286-87, 291n
Foundry (Washington), 9
Fourteenth Amendment: and black suffrage, 261-63; quoted, 48-49, 600-601; resistance to, 529, 540, 542; and woman suffrage, 261-63, 469
France: divorce in, 287; and universal suffrage, 539-40
Franklin, Benjamin, 337, *342n*; quoted, 560
Franklin, John, 721, *728n*

Fray, Ellen Sully, 574, *574n*
Frederick II (king of Prussia), 405, *406n*
Frederick William I (king of Prussia), 404, *406n*
Fremont, Neb., 605
Friends, Society of (Quakers): Hicksite, 516, 669; and SBA's family, 516; and women, 519
"Friendships of Women" (ECS), 240–42
Frothingham, Octavius Brooks, 297, *299n*; as biographer, 447
Froude, James Anthony, 101, *106n*, 150
Fullam, Sarah J. Mylacraine, 691, *691n*

Gage, Frances Dana Barker, 99, *105n*, 250, 347, 716, 721
Gage, Helen Leslie Gage, 202, *203n*
Gage, Matilda Joslyn, *12n*, 251, 710; absence of from meeting, 166, 170n; criticizes *Looking Backward*, 202; criticizes SBA, 126–29, 225–26n; and International Council, 19, 28, 84; letter from ECS, 214; letters to ECS, 126–29, 201–3; letter to meeting, 169; and liberal union, xxvi, 214, 215n, 223–24, 234–35, 236–37, 278; mentioned, 721; and National association, 37–38, 126–27, 129–30n, 162; and National conference committee, 117, 119; quoted, xxiii; SBA criticizes, 178, 248; undermines SBA, 308; views of union, 215n, 248; and *Woman's Bible*, 22, 692, 693; as a writer, 10
Gage, Thomas Clarkson, 202, *203n*; hosts SBA, 226
Galton, Francis, *159n*; quoted, 156
Gannett, Mary Thorn Lewis, *689n*; and I. B. Wells, 689
Gannett, William Channing, 575, *575n*, 690
Gardener, Helen Hamilton, 11, *12n*, 214; debates W. A. Hammond, 77; on divorce, 258; and International Council, 77; and *Woman's Bible*, 22
Gardner, Anna, 657, *658n*
Garfield, James Abram, 377, *377–78n*
Garrison, Ellen Wright, 122, *123n*; in Washington, 236, 238, 271
Garrison, Francis Jackson, *122n*, 296; letter from SBA, 122
Garrison, Helen Eliza Benson, 210, *210–11n*
Garrison, William Lloyd, *105n*; as abolitionist, 296, 297, 447; quoted, 23, 95; and woman's rights, 99, 250, 287–88, 347, 507
Garrison, William Lloyd, Jr., 122, *123n*, 405; debates educated suffrage, 656–57, 658n, 664, 665n, 666, 668; verse of, 413–14; in Washington, 236
General Federation of Women's Clubs, 510
Genessee County, N.Y.: amendment campaign in, 577

Geneva, N.Y.: ECS in, 223–24
George, Henry, 127, *130n*
Gerrit Smith, A Biography (Frothingham), 447, 450, 451
Geyer, Elizabeth, 186, *188n*
Giddings, Joshua Reed, 377, *377–78n*
Giffard, Hardinge Stanley (Baron Halsbury), 374–75, *375–76n*
Gifford, Josephine Fenton, 133, *133n*
Gilbert, Jeannette Fenton Hegeman, 133, *133n*
Gilbert, Simeon, 518, *521n*
Gillett, Etta A. Goodson, 497, *497n*
Girls' Latin School (Boston), 48
Gladstone, Catherine Glynne, 8, *9n*, 456–57
Gladstone, William Ewart, 47, *51n*; on divorce, 258, 287; quoted, 101, 150; on U.S. Constitution, 101, 150, 726; and woman suffrage, 375, 456
Goff, Harriet Newell Kneeland, 442, *444–45n*
Goodelle, Henry Prevost, 622–23, *624n*
Goodson's Opera House (Sterling, Kan.), 498
Gordon, Anna Adams, 163, *164n*, 642
Gougar, Helen Mar Jackson, *67n*; criticizes SBA, 309n; ECS commends, 141–42; ECS criticizes, 212–13; and National-American, 583; and National conference committee, 64, 119, 166; and Prohibition party, 221, 222–23n; and So. Dak. campaign, 308, 309n; views of union, 231, 233n
Grain, Richard Corney, 370, *371n*
Grand Army of the Republic, 523
Grand Central Hotel (Stafford, Kan.), 497
Grant, Ulysses S., 455, *458n*
Great Britain: fishing dispute with, 102; women and partisanship in, 7–8, 456–57. *See also* Ireland
"The Great Trial" (ECS), 198–99
Greeley, Horace, *70n*, 297, 561, 623; quoted, 69, 74; on woman's work, 515
Greely, Adolphus Washington, 721, *728n*
Greene, Freeman A., 577, *577n*
Greene, Susan Ida Price, 577, *577n*
Greenleaf, Halbert Stevens, 411, *411–12n*, 571; and federal suffrage, 423; hosted SBA, 563
Greenleaf, Jean Frances Brooks, *402n*, 575; hosts SBA, 563; and N.Y. association, 403, 442, 443, 444n, 716; and N.Y. campaign, 553, 557–58, 563, 564, 567, 570, 571, 572, 594, 640–41, 670; and Political Equality Club, 400, 401; at suffrage meeting, 504; in Washington, 411
Greenwood, Elizabeth Ward, 703, *704n*
Grew, Mary, 2, 4, *5n*, 721
Griffing, Josephine Sophia White, 99, *105n*
Grimké, Sarah Moore, 347, *353n*

Gripenberg, Alexandra, 86, *87–88n*
Groff, Lewis A., 199, *200n*
Gross, Emily Maude Brown, 529, *530n*, 547
Gross, Samuel Eberly, 529, *530n*
Grover, Alonzo Jackson, 32, *33–34n*
Grover, Alonzo Jackson, Jr., 32, *33–34n*
Grover, Nettie Corrine Smith, 32, *33–34n*
Grubb, Sophronia Farrington Naylor, 270, *272n*

Hall, Israel, 165, *165–66n*
Hall, Nettie Crabb Weems, 332, *333n*
Hall, Olivia Bigelow, *165–66n*, 221; hosts SBA, 573; letters from SBA, 164–65, 376–77; at suffrage meeting, 504; in Syracuse, 500; in Toledo, 574
Hallowell, Anna Coffin Davis, 236, *237n*
Hallowell, Mary H. Post, *238n*; letter from SBA, 378–79; mentioned, 500, 714; and SBA's convalescence, 706; in Washington, 237, 271
Halstead, Murat, 529, *531n*
Hamilton, Alexander, *159n*; quoted, 155
Hamilton Hall (Topeka), 625, 628, 629
Hamilton House (Washington), 80
Hamlet (Shakespeare): quoted, 210
Hamm, Margherita Arlina, 700, *700–701n*
Hammond, William Alexander, 77, *78n*
Hanaford, Phebe Ann Coffin, 721, *728n*
Hancock, John, 151, *158n*, 598
Harbert, Elizabeth Morrison Boynton, *16n*, 455–56; and National conference committee, 117, 119; and *New Era*, 15–16
Harberton, Florence Wallace Legge Pomeroy (viscountess), 11, *13n*
Harper, Ida A. Husted, 169, *174n*
Harrison, Benjamin, 468
Harrison, Caroline Lavinia Scott, 269, *269n*
Harrison, Carter Henry, 127, *130n*
Harrison, Frederic, 425, *434n*
Harrison, William Henry, 468, *470–71n*
Hartford Equal Rights Club: letter from ECS, 175–76
Hartington, Lord. *See* Cavendish, Spencer Compton (marquess of Hartington)
Hatch, Lavina Allen, 394, *396n*
Hawthorne, Caroline Moore, 571, *572n*
Hawthorne, James Boardman, *673–74n*; attacks suffragists, 673; and F. Douglass, 685, *686–87n*
Hawthorne, Nathaniel, 154, *159n*
Hay, Mary Garrett, *565n*; and N.Y. campaign, 565, 570, 577, 578
Hayes, Rutherford Birchard, 454, *457n*
Hempstead, N.Y.: ECS in, 200–201, 208, 210, 211–13, 214, 230
Henderson, Ben S., 629, *631n*
Henderson, Martha Y. Tiffany, 133, *133n*
Hennell, Sara Sophia, 241, *244n*

Henry, Josephine Kirby Williamson, 660, *661n*
Hereditary Genius (Galton), 156
Hiawatha, Kan.: SBA in, 41
Higginson, Thomas Wentworth, 251, *263n*, 297
Hill, David Jayne, *402n*; letter to SBA, 400
Hill, Juliet Lewis Packer, 400, *402n*
Hinckley, Frederic Allen, *291n*; at suffrage meeting, 286, 288, 291n
Hindman, Matilda, 55, *173n*, 281, *283n*; and National-American, 583; at suffrage meeting, 169
history: and suffrage factions, 211–12, *213n*, 246–47; of suffrage movement, 252–53, 261–62; of woman's rights, 94, 96–98, 249–51
History of Civilization in England (Buckle), 542
History of European Morals (Lecky), 153–54
History of the Rise and Influence of the Spirit of Rationalism (Lecky), 251
History of Woman Suffrage, 100, 251, 297, 298, 346, 347, 370, 507–8; distribution of, 14, 450–51; second edition of, 3, 164–65, 450
Hoar, George Frisbie, 85, *85n*, 456; letter from SBA, 406–7
Holley, Sallie, 241, *244n*, 689
Holloway, Laura Carter, *205n*; letter from SBA, 204. *See also* Langford, Laura Carter Holloway
The Holy Bible, in the Authorized Version (Wordsworth), 20
The Holy Bible, with a Commentary and Critical Notes (Clarke), 705
Hooker, Isabella Beecher, *119n*; in Chicago, 478, 480; and Columbian Exposition, 392; and federal suffrage, 463–64, 487–88; and H. B. Blackwell, 297; letter from SBA, 234–35; letter to ECS, 463–64; letter to SBA, 357; at Lily Dale, 488; mentioned, 111, 179, 250, 465, 710, 721; and National association, 168; and National conference committee, 117, 119, 166–67; at Pilgrim Mothers' Dinner, 502; in Rochester, 487–88; and spiritualism, 178; at suffrage meetings, 415, 417, 419, 437; views of union, 114–15, 463
Hooker, John, 234, *235n*, 710
Horton, Albert Howell, 588, *593n*
Hosmer, Harriet Goodhue, 392, *393n*
Hôtel Meurice (Paris), 32
Hotel Savoy (New York), 730
housekeeping: and ECS, 385; SBA tries, 377, 378–79, 387, 392–93
Howard, Dr. (of New York), 329
Howard, George James (earl of Carlisle), 620, *620–21n*
Howard, Helen Augusta, *420–21n*; and National-American, 415, 584

Howard, Kan., 494
Howard, Rosalind Frances Stanley (countess of Carlisle), *380n*, 620; letter to ECS, 379
Howe, John Homer, 185, *188n*
Howe, Julia Ward, 63, *67n*, 671, 721; and American association, 219; and Columbian Exposition, 532; at suffrage meeting, 269, 270
Howell, Mary Catherine Seymour, *174n*; and Kan. campaign, 443; and National association, 169; and N.Y. campaign, 554, 579
Howland, Emily, 675, 716
Howland, Isabel, *671n*; and N.Y. campaign, 670
Howland, Robert Bowne, 449, *449n*
Hubbard, Mary N. Rice, 675, *675n*
Hughes, John Wesley, 669, *670n*
Hughes, Mary Wallingford, 669, *670n*
Humphrey, Lester Hayden, 578, *578-79n*
Humphrey, Lyman Underwood, 653, *655n*
Humphrey, Maude Milton Skinner, 578, *578-79n*
Humphrey, Maude Skinner, 578, *578-79n*
Hunt, Mary Hannah Hanchett, 107
Huron, So. Dak.: SBA in, 319, 321-22, 324-25, 332
husbands' rights: in England, 374-75
Husted, James William, 443, *445n*
Hutchinson, John Wallace, 243, *245n*, 249
Hutchinson, Kan., 498
Huxley, Thomas Henry, 72, *73n*

Illinois: temperance women in, 186
immigrants: and English language, 656-57; ignorance of, 348, 647-48; impact of, 397-98; numbers of, 666, *669n*; oppose woman suffrage, 666; in So. Dak., 269-70, 321-22, 607-8
Indiana: SBA visits, 19
Indianapolis: SBA visits, 18-19
Indiana Woman Suffrage Association, 231, 233n
individualism, 152
Ingalls, John James, *4on*; forsakes black suffrage, 529, 532; opposes woman suffrage, 39, 40n, 42-50, 52n, 184, 187-88n; SBA criticizes, 42-50, 481; "The Sixteenth Amendment," 39, 40n, 41, 42-50
Ingersoll, Robert Green, 11, *12n*, 224, 708
international arbitration, 101-2
International Council of Women, 36, 162, 209; call to, 24-26, 27-28; ECS's address of welcome to, 93-103; foreign delegates to, 86-87, 88-89n, 90-92; plans for, 3-4, 9-11, 15, 17, 18-19, 94-95; program for, 10-11, 18, 77, 78-79, 81, 83-84; and religion, 11, 19; reporting of meetings,
122; temperance session of, 107-9, 369; and woman suffrage, 24, 27n
International Order of the King's Daughters, 510, 683
interviews: SBA in Chicago, 471-72; SBA on Populist endorsement, 632-35
Iowa Woman Suffrage Association. *See* Mississippi Valley Conference
Ireland: Britain's policies toward, 11, 541; and Home Rule, 253, 289
Isabella (queen of Castile), *229n*; reputation of, 228-29, 229-30n; statue of, 392. *See also* Queen Isabella Association

Jackson, James Caleb, *157n*; quoted, 148-49
Jacobi, Mary Corinna Putnam, 620, *621n*
jails: matrons for, 46
James, Alvan T., 238, *239n*, 271
James, Elizabeth Knight, 238, *239n*, 271
James, Helen Louise Mosher: and father's death, 569, 570, 572; in New York, 730; in Washington, 238, 271. *See also* Mosher, Helen Louise
James, Henry, 370, *371n*
Jamestown, N.Y.: ECS and SBA speak in, 134
Jefferson, Thomas, *51n*, 151, 254, 598; and Declaration of Independence, 43; quoted, 255
Jenckes, Thomas Allen, 600, *614n*
Jenkins, Caroline E. Macy: hosts SBA, 716, *716n*
Jenkins, Charles S.: hosts SBA, 716, *716n*
Jenkins, Helen Mar Philleo, 221, *223n*
Jenkins, Therese Alberta Parkinson, *476-77n*; and Colo. campaign, 549; and Kan. campaign, 617, 651; at Republican convention, 475, 477
Jenney, Marie Regula Saul, 569, *570n*
Jews: discrimination against, 362; women's place among, 726
Joan of Arc, 199, *200n*, 255
Johns, James Bennett, 628, *628n*
Johns, Laura Lucretia Mitchell, *2n*; and Kan. campaign, 587, 588, 599, 611, 613, 616-17, 625-28, 632, 651-52; mentioned, 1, 495; and National conference committee, 64, 117, 119, 166, 169; as Republican, 482, 625, 627, 640; and So. Dak. campaign, 607; views of union, 54, 114
Johnson, Adelaide, 495, *496n*
Johnson, Andrew, 600, *614n*
Johnson, Helen Hunt, 14, *14-15n*
Johnson, Jane Maria Abbott, 14, *14-15n*
Johnson, Julia England, 133, *133n*
Johnson, Mary H., 416, *421-22n*
Johnson, Oliver, *14-15n*, 347; letter to SBA, 14
Johnson, Philena Everett, 305, *305-6n*, 307, 321
Johnson, William Agnew, 588, *592n*

Johnson's Universal Cyclopaedia, A New Edition (Adams), 642
John Ward, Preacher (Deland), 143
Jones, Daniel C., 547, *547n*
Jones, Jenkin Lloyd, 575, *575n*
Jones, John Percival, 477, *477n*
Judge, William Quan, 706, *707n*
Junius, 349
juries: male only, 198–99; women on, 46–47, 185, 315

Kane, Elisha Kent, 721, *728n*
Kansas: congressional district meetings in, 39, 40n; history of, 43, 599; municipal suffrage in, 1, 2n, 39, 181–87, 417–18, 590, 724; prohibition in, 46, 51n, 182–83, 195; school suffrage in, 590
Kansas amendment campaign (1867), 588, 590, 601–3, 612–13; history of, 297–98, 298–99n
Kansas amendment campaign (1894): ECS's views of, 636, 637; funds for, 660–61; hopes for, 547, 548; meeting of, 616–17; and National-American, 417–18; People's party in, 629–35; Republican party in, 625–28; tensions in, 651–53
Kansas City, Kan.: SBA speaks in, 598–614, 616–17
Kansas Democratic party: opposes woman suffrage, 589–90, 610–11; platform, 638, 639n
Kansas Equal Suffrage Association: considers protest, 698, 698–99n; meeting of, 1, 2n; proposes union, 54; at Republican convention, 481, 482
Kansas People's party: and 1894 election, 588; convention of, 631–32; endorses woman suffrage, 640–41; platform, 638; and prohibition, 652–53; SBA addresses convention of, 629–31; SBA campaigns for, xxvi, 638, 641, 643n, 652; and woman suffrage, 609–10, 632, 632n, 633, 635
Kansas Prohibition party: platform, 638, 639n
Kansas Republican League, 610, 616n
Kansas Republican party: and 1867 amendment campaign, 602–3; and 1894 election, 586–88, 613–14; convention of, 626–27; endorses woman suffrage, 482, 483–84, 609–10; ignores woman suffrage, 626–27, 633, 635, 640, 652; loses election, 500, 501n; and municipal suffrage, 161, 609; platform, 638; and prohibition, 608–9, 653; SBA addresses convention of, 480–82; SBA campaigns for, 494, 496–99
Kansas Republican Women's Association: meeting of, 625
Kansas State Historical Society: donations to, 1, 2n

Kennett Square, Pa., 2–3
Kent, James, *158n*, 726; quoted, 153, 339
Keyes, Mrs. (of Leavenworth), 189
Keyser, Harriette Amelia, 554, *555n*
Kimber, Helen L., 616–17, *617n*, 651
"Kin beyond Sea" (Gladstone), 101, 150, 726
King, Elizabeth Biechler, 153, 158n; murder trial of, 198–99
King, M. Ophelia, 569, *570n*
Kingman, Kan.: SBA speaks in, 496, *497n*
Kingsley, Charles, *729n*; quoted, 725
Kittredge, Amelia Filley, 575, *576n*
Klumpke, Anna Elizabeth, 32, *34n*
Knights of Labor, 538
knitting: defended, 412–14; ECS objects to, 404–5
Knox, Mrs., 584
Knox-Little, William John, 175, *176–77n*
Kollock, Florence Ellen, 11, *12–13n*
Kropotkin, Pyotr Alekseyevich, 429, *435n*
Krout, Mary Hannah, 513, *515n*

Ladd, Caroline Ruth Elizabeth Vail, 715, *715n*
Lakeside, Ohio: SBA speaks in, 700, 706
Lamb, William (viscount Melbourne), 337, *341–42n*
Langford, Laura Carter Holloway, 373–74n. *See also* Holloway, Laura Carter
Langston, John Mercer, 604, *615n*
Lapham, Antoinette Dearborn, 488, *488–89n*, 715
Lapham, Elizabeth Walker, 715
Lapham, John Jesse, 715, *715n*
Lapham, Lewis Henry, 488, *488–89n*, 715
Lapham, Semantha Lapham Vail, 488, *488–89n*; hosts SBA, 709, 714, 715, 717, 718, 730
Lathrap, Mary Torrans, 221, *222n*
Lattimore, Samuel Allan, 401–2, *403n*, 569
Lauterbach, Edward, 624, *625n*
Lawrence, Frank Eugene, *160n*; death of, 310n; illness of, 159
Lawrence, Margaret Livingston Stanton, xxvii; education of, 308; and husband's illness, 159; letters from ECS, 328–30, 333–34, 345–46; mentioned, 133, 230, 479, 500, 694, 705; at suffrage meeting, 268
Lease, Mary Elizabeth Clyens, *501n*; in Colo., 523; favored for U.S. Senate, 500
Leavenworth, Kan., 41; municipal election 1887, 186, 188n; municipal election 1889, 181–87, 189–91, 194–95; race relations in, 189–91, 194–95; SBA in, 177–87, 189–90, 194–95, 546–47; SBA speaks in, 42–50, 181–87, 189–90, 194–95
Lecky, William Edward Hartpole, *158n*; quoted, 153–54, 251
Leland, Cyrus, Jr., 653, *655n*

"Let the Blue Laws Rest" (ECS), 191–94
Lewelling, Lorenzo Dow, 652–53, *655n*
Lewis, Mr. (at Canistota), 704–5
Liberal party (Great Britain), 7–8; and women, 456–57. *See also* Women's Liberal Federation
Liberty party, 137, 383
Life of Theodore Parker (Frothingham), 447
Lily (Seneca Falls), 513–14
Lily Dale. *See* Cassadaga Lake Free Association
Lincoln, Abraham, 44, *51n*, 261, 600
Lincoln Music Hall (Washington), 249, 268
Livermore, Daniel Parker, 618, *618n*
Livermore, Mary Ashton Rice, 63–64, *67n*, 123, 721; and Columbian Exposition, 532; letter from ECS, 618; and *Woman's Bible*, 677
Lloyd, Mary Charlotte, 241, *244n*
Lockwood, Belva Ann Bennett McNall, 128, *130–31n*
Lockwood, Mary Smith, 407, *408n*; at suffrage meetings, 415, 437
London *Daily News*, 7
Long, John Davis, 380–81, *384n*
Longshore, Hannah E. Myers, 373, *373n*, 714, 730
Looking Backward (Bellamy), 202, 208
Lord, Henrietta Frances, 20, *21n*, 22; and *Woman's Bible*, 677
Lord, Martha Mott, 236, *237n*
"The Lord Chancellor" (ECS), 374–75
Loucks, Henry Langford, 216–17n, 606
Louisville, Ky.: SBA in, 669–70
Love, Alfred Henry, 128, *131n*
Lucas, Margaret Bright, 260, *266n*
Lucy Stone Mite Box Fund, 660–61, 661n
Luther, Martin, 152, *158n*
lynching: condemned in Rochester, 687–88, 690, 691; SBA condemns, 706–7
Lyon, Nannie J. Wright, *627–28n*; hosts SBA, 627, 628, 632; letter from SBA, 698
Lyon, Thomas Stewart, *627–28n*; hosts SBA, 627, 628, 632
Lyon, William Maclay, *627–28n*, 628

McCarren, Patrick Henry, 452, *453n*
McCarthy, Justin, *292n*; quoted, 289
McConnell, Elizabeth Amanda, 220, *221–22n*
McCoun, Pamelia Townsend Underhill, 675, *676n*
McCutcheon, Magdalene Kelly, 706, 707n
McDiarmid, Clara A. Cox, 505, *506–7n*
Mackenzie, Robert, 101, *106n*
McKinley, William, 487, *487n*
McLaren, Priscilla Bright, *303n*; on aging, 302; letter to ECS, 302–3
McLaren, Walter Stowe Bright, 7–8, *9n*
McLean, Aaron M., *530–31n*; birthday of, 563; in Rochester, 529

McLean, Guelma Penn Anthony, 243, *245n*
Maine, Henry Clay, 566, *568n*, 569
Maine, Henry James Sumner, 101, *106n*, 150, 212
Mallon, Patrick, 220, *221–22n*
Manderson, Charles Frederick, 141, *142n*
Mann, Charles, *5–6n*; as editor, 10; printing business of, 3
Mann, Horace, 399, *402n*
Mann, Newton Maurice, 485, *485n*
Mansfield, Lord. *See* Murray, William (earl of Mansfield)
Marble, Ella Maria Smith, 407, *408n*; at suffrage meeting, 414, 415
marriage: and dependency, 210, 383, 428, 430; equality in, 175–76; open discussion of, 286–87; uniform laws of, 135–36, 203
married women: and suffrage, 302, 343–44, 344–45n
Married Women's Property Act (1848), 94
married women's property rights: in England, 144, 156–57n, 375
Martin, Frank L., 481, *482n*
Martin, Victoria Claflin Woodhull. *See* Woodhull, Victoria Claflin
Martineau, Harriet, 241, *244n*, 347
Mary Stuart (queen of Scots), 199, *200n*
masculine element, 364
Massachusetts: antisuffragists in, 151; Democratic party in, 455; educated suffrage law of, 649–50n, 655–57, 658n; municipal suffrage in, 455; Republican party in, 455; school suffrage in, 41, 42n
Massachusetts Woman Suffrage Association, 389, 394–95, 396n, 460; letter from ECS, 346–52
Massey, Gerald, 11, *12n*
matriarchate, 317, 358
Matthews, William D., 194–95
May, Samuel Joseph, 251, *263n*, 347
Mazzini, Guiseppe, 241, *244n*, 296
Meharry Medical College, 687
Melbourne, Lord. *See* Lamb, William (viscount Melbourne)
Memoir of William Henry Channing (Frothingham), 447
Memphis, Tenn.: SBA in, 671–73
Memphis Woman's Council, 671, 672n
Mendelssohn, Felix, 432, *436n*
men of the Bible: Aaron, 196; Barak, 696; David, 196; King Ahasuerus, 696; Moses, 196; Paul, 196; Solomon, 196
Merchant of Venice (Shakespeare): characters in, 199
Meredith, Ellis, *524n*; letters from SBA, 535–37, 538, 548–49; letter to SBA, 521–24
Meredith, Emily Robinson Sorin, 548, *550n*
Meriden, Conn.: SBA in, 378–79

Meriwether, Lide Parker Smith, *412n*; hosts SBA, 671, 673; and National-American, 411
Merrick, Caroline Elizabeth Thomas, 674, *675n*
Merritt, Salome, *396n*; letter from SBA, 394–95
Methodist Episcopal church: General Conference, 727
Metropolitan Opera House (New York), 709, 714, 719
Mexican-Americans: and Colo. campaigns, 523, 603
Michigan: municipal suffrage in, 581, 581–82n
Michigan, University of: SBA lectures at, 572–73
Michigan amendment campaign, 588, 603
Mill, Harriet Hardy Taylor, 92, *93n*; "Enfranchisement of Women," 347
Mill, John Stuart, 90, *91n*, 92, 146, 347; and married women's suffrage, 343; mentioned, 560; quoted, 542–43
Millard, Nelson, 565, *565n*
Miller, Anne Fitzhugh, 446, *448n*, 451; and N.Y. association, 716
Miller, Caroline Hallowell, 82, *82n*; and National conference committee, 166
Miller, Elizabeth Smith, *37n*; letter from ECS, 142–43; letters from SBA, 36, 446–47, 450–51, 640–41; mentioned, 330, 404, 405, 495; and N.Y. association, 716; in Syracuse, 569
Miller, Francis, *82n*; death of, 82
Miller, Samuel Freeman, 46, *51n*
Mills, Harriet May, *576n*; and N.Y. campaign, 575, 577, 579
Milton, John, 287, *291n*, 723
Milton, Pa.: SBA speaks in, 80
Mind Cure, 16, 17n, 36, 77
Minneapolis, Minn.: SBA in, 215–16, 475–77, 605–6
Minnesota Woman Suffrage Association: annual meeting of, 606; and So. Dak. campaign, 269–70
Minor, Francis: quoted, 254
Minor, Virginia Louisa Minor, *120n*; and National conference committee, 166; and views of union, 113
Minor v. Happersett (1875), 120n, 262, 267n
Mississippi Constitutional Convention (1890): and woman suffrage, 418, 422–23n
Mississippi Valley Conference: SBA speaks to, 490–92
Molly Maguires, 253
Monroe County, N.Y.: amendment campaign in, 566–68, 568n, 569
Montesquieu, Charles-Louis de Secondat (Baron de la Brède et de Montesquieu), 153, *158n*, 339
Moore, Edward Mott, 400–401, *402n*, 567, 569

"The Moral Leadership of the Religious Press" (SBA), 516–20
moral standards: inequality of, 153–55, 339
Morgan, Lewis Henry, *342n*, 358, 401; quoted, 339
Morrill, Edmund Needham, *59n*; and 1894 election, 586, 611, 626, 652, 653; hosts SBA, 58
Morris, Esther Hobart McQuigg Slack, *51n*, 315; as justice of the peace, 46
Morris, Sarah Howe, 570, *570–71n*
Morse, Anna A., 691, *692n*
Mosher, Arthur Anthony, 238, *239–40n*, 271
Mosher, Carolyn Louise Mixer, 271, *273n*
Mosher, Eugene, 569, 569–70n, 570, 572
Mosher, Hannah Lapham Anthony, 243, *245n*, 569
Mosher, Helen Louise, 134, *134n*. See also James, Helen Louise Mosher
Mosher, Martha Beatrice Brown, 271, *273n*
Mosher, Wendell Phillips, 271, *273n*, 730
mothers: duties of, 175–76
Mott, Anna Caroline, *273n*; hosts SBA, 574; in Washington, 271
Mott, James, 720, *728n*
Mott, Lucretia Coffin, *105n*, 405; at Seneca Falls convention, 720; and Sunday closing, 440; and woman's rights, 99, 250, 347, 716
Mott, Richard, 271, *273n*, 574
Müller, Frances Henrietta, 11, *12n*, 36; and C. S. Parnell, 335; and married women's suffrage, 343, 344–45n; and *Woman's Herald*, 706
Mulligan, Charlotte, 499, *500–501n*
Mulock, Dinah Maria. See Craik, Dinah Maria Mulock
Mulvane, Harriet N. Freeman, 631, *631–32n*
municipal suffrage, 61–62, 98; in England, 144, 156–57n; in Kan., 1, 2n, 39, 161, 181–87, 189–91, 469; in Mich., 581, 581–82n; as obstacle to full suffrage, 608
Murdoch, Marion, 718, *718n*
Murdock, Thomas Benton, 653, *655n*
Murphy, Edward, Jr., 659, *660n*
Murray, William (earl of Mansfield), 374, *376n*
Myers, Jane Viola, 675, *676n*, 714, 730

Napoléon I (emperor of France), 47, *51n*; quoted, 442–44, 698
Naquet, Alfred-Joseph, 287, *291–92n*
National-American Woman Suffrage Association: and 1892 election, 454–57, 460, 475–76, 477, 478, 480, 483–84, 486; auxiliaries of, 212, 215–16, 218–19, 231, 233n, 234, 389, 394–95, 403, 404n, 461, 462–63n; business committee of, 660–62; and Colo. campaign, 521–22, 535–38,

(National-American, *continued*)
538n, 546, 549; and Columbian Exposition, 324, 418–19, 436–38, 490–92, 532–33, 533n, 534; committees of, 410, 411n; constitutions of, 215–16, 231–32, 463, 464n, 740–44; and ECS's birthday, 683–84, 684–85n, 709–10; executive committee of, 414–19; and federal suffrage, 461, 462n, 463, 583–84, 585–86n; and Kan. campaign, 417–18, 445n, 581, 586, 591–92n, 651–53, 660–61; leadership of, 245, 246–47; and national citizenship, 389, 394, 503–5; and N.Y. campaign, 580–81; organization committee of, 709–10; pays SBA's clerk, 584; rejected constitution of, 736–40; size of, 510; and So. Dak. campaign, 269–71, 271–72n, 274–76, 281–82, 294, 295n, 324, 326n, 606; and southern work, 414–19, 420n, 423n, 505–6, 506–7n, 580; and state associations, 661; treasurers' reports of, 505, 506–7n, 584

National-American Woman Suffrage Association's annual conventions: debate resolutions on Sabbath, 436–38, 507–8; ECS addresses, 249–63, 360–68; ECS criticizes, 278, 285–90; ECS's resolutions for, 263–64n, 265n, 266n; I. B. Hooker criticizes, 463, 464n; location of, 419, 423n, 463, 503–5; plans for 1890, 217–19, 225; plans for 1892, 406–7, 409, 410–11; plans for 1894, 549; resolutions for, 359; SBA addresses, 503–5, 580–81; SBA describes, 268–69, 673–74, 687, 688n

National Citizen and Ballot Box (Syracuse), 311

National College for the Deaf: admits women, 80–81

National Council of Women, 663; and Columbian Exposition, 491; and ECS's birthday, 683–84, 684–85n, 719; ECS speech for, 358–59; and F. Douglass, 683, 685–86, 685n, 686–87n; meetings of, 369, 471–72, 678; plans for, 139. *See also* Reunion of the Pioneers and Friends of Woman's Progress

National Reform Association, 128, 131n, 191
National Suffrage Bulletin, 709–10, 710n
National Union Convention, 384
National Vigilance Association, 335
National Woman's Relief Society, 510
National Woman's Rights Convention, First (1850): commemorated, 346–52
National Woman's Rights Convention, Second (1851), 346
National Woman's Rights Covention, Tenth (1860), 287–88, 507–8
National Woman Suffrage Association: and 1888 election, 126–29; appeals to Democratic party, 126–27; appeals to Greenback-Labor party, 127; appeals to Republican party, 126, 129–30n; basis of representation in, 61, 65n, 735–36; bequests to, 220, 221–22n; committees of, 168–69; and congressional district meetings, 39, 40n; and constitutional centennial, 37–38; constitutions of, 168, 215–16, 734, 740–44; debates plan for union, 109–19; executive committee of, 169–70; executive sessions of, 109–19, 166–69, 246–47, 248; and individual memberships, 62, 65n; and International Council, 95; and membership of men, 61, 65n; and national enrollment, 29–30, 31n, 167; in Pa., 2–4, 5n, 15–16; reporting meetings of, 4; responds to American association, 117–19; statements of purpose, 61–62, 66n

National Woman Suffrage Association conference committees: letter to H. B. Blackwell, 118–19; members of, 64, 67n, 166; reports to National association, 109–19

National Woman Suffrage Association of Indiana: meeting of, 18

National Woman Suffrage Association of Massachusetts, 389, 390n, 394–95, 396n; petitions Congress, 460

National Woman Suffrage Association's Washington conventions: of 1889, 166–70; ECS skips, 166–70; plans for 1889, 159, 160–62, 163, 165; plans for 1890, 179–80, 210, 215–16, 217–19, 231–33, 234–35, 236–37

Native Americans: and citizenship, 319, 320n
naturalization: and voting rights, 647–48
Nebraska amendment campaign, 448–49, 588, 605
Nebraska Woman Suffrage Association: annual meeting of, 140–42, 143–56
Nelson, Horatio (viscount), 337, *341–42n*
Nelson, Julia Bullard, *271n*; and So. Dak. campaign, 269–70
Newburgh, N.Y.: SBA in, 716–17
new departure, 262
New England Woman Suffrage Association, 493
New England Woman Suffrage Festival: plans for, 122; SBA speaks to, 123–25, 380–84
New Era (Chicago), 15–16
New Jersey: and woman suffrage, 144, 254
newspapers: Sunday, 191–94; women's need for, 514–15, 519
Newton, Richard Heber, 11, *12n*
Newton, Sylvina M. Dewey, *132n*; hosts ECS and SBA, 132–33

New York (city): amendment campaign in, 554, 557, 582; ECS speaks in, 595–96, 619–20; SBA in, 715–17, 730
New York (state): antisuffragists in, 596n, 623, 648; liquor laws in, 444; married women's property in, 94; political bosses in, 443; Prohibition party in, 128, 131n; school suffrage in, 452–53, 453–54n, 581; woman suffrage in, 452, 453n, 461, 462n
New York amendment campaign, 618; appeals to legislature, 641–42, 643n, 646, 651, 654n; appeals to women, 559–62; hopes for, 548; meetings of, 566–68, 569–71, 577–79, 595–96, 619–20; meetings of described, 593–94, 612; petitions of, 552–53, 554, 555–56n, 567–68, 571–72; plan of work for, 551–53, 553–54, 556–58; plans for, 548, 549, 554, 556–57, 563, 565, 572, 593–94; political parties in, 635; and temperance union, 554, 555n, 571–72
New York City Woman Suffrage League: luncheon for ECS, 463, 465–70. *See also* Pilgrim Mothers' Dinners
New York constitution: of 1821, 567
New York Constitutional Convention (1867), 560, 561, 622, 623, 646
New York Constitutional Convention (1894): defeats woman suffrage, 643–45, 646; preparations for, 442–44, 444n, 445n, 452, 453n, 499–500, 501n; SBA speaks to, 621–24; suffrage committee of, 639n, 640
New York Democratic party, 641
New York *Evening Sun*, 473
New York Observer, 517, 519
New York Press Club, 383
New York Recorder, 636
New York Republican party, 641
New York State Association of School Commissioners and Superintendents, 564
New York State Teachers' Association, 124, 381–83
New York State Temperance Society: bars women, 517
New York State Woman Suffrage Association: annual meetings of, 494, 499–500, 548, 550n, 551, 716–17; plan of work, 551–53
New York *Sun*, 636; letter from ECS, 643–45
New York *Voice:* letter from ECS, 396–98
New York *World*, 228; letter from ECS, 596–98
New Zealand: woman suffrage in, 622, 712, 713n
Neymann, Clara Low, 11, *12n*, 72; and National conference committee, 117, 119; views of union, 114
Nichols, Clarina Irene Howard, 99, *105n*, 250, 347, 716

Nichols, Mary Plumb, 522, *527n*
Nightingale, Florence, 255, *265n*
Nineteenth Century Club (Memphis), 671
Non-Partisan Woman's Christian Temperance Union, 510
North American Review: ECS writes for, 437, 439–42
North Elba, N.Y.: SBA in, 386
North Pole: search for, 242, 721
North-Western Christian Advocate, 519
Norton, Sarah Frances, 594, *594–95n*
Nussey, Ellen, 241, *244n*
Nye, Theron, 605, *615n*

Oberlin College, 48, 250
occupations: equal access to, 46, 724; women's need of, 425, 427–28, 431–32
Ohio Woman Suffrage Association: annual meeting of, 376–77; executive committee, 661; and National-American, 403; SBA speaks to, 473–74
Omaha, Neb.: ECS in, 140–42, 159, 175–76, 196; ECS speaks in, 143–56; murder in, 153, 158n, 198–99; SBA in, 483–86
Omaha Bee: ECS writes for, 191–94; quoted, 145
Omaha Republican: ECS writes for, 198–99
Open Court (Chicago), 20; ECS writes for, 22
Oregon: suffrage campaign in, 588, 605
"Organization among Women" (SBA), 509–11
Orleans County, N.Y.: amendment campaign in, 577
Osawatomie, Kan., 386, 599
Osborne, Eliza Wright, *237n*, 710; letter from ECS, 404–5; letter from SBA, 236–37; letter to ECS, 412–14; and N.Y. association, 716; at suffrage meeting, 236; in Washington, 238, 271
Otis, Bina A. Numan, *592n*; and Kan. campaign, 587, 588, 629
Ottumwa, Kan.: SBA speaks in, 600
Ouray, Colo., 603
The Outlook for Women, A Sermon (Jackson), 148–49
Owensboro, Ky., 669, 671n

Pacific Coast Woman's Congress, 686
Paducah, Ky., 669, 671n
Palatine Hotel (Newburgh), 716
Pall Mall Gazette (London), 337
Palmer, Bertha Honoré, *420n*; and Columbian Exposition, 415, 419, 491
Palmer, Thomas Witherell, *77n*; and amendment, 504; and Columbian Exposition, 324, 491; mentioned, 85, 275; and Senate committee, 75–76
panic of 1893, 536
Paris, France: ECS describes, 32–33; ECS in, 23–24, 31–33

Parker, Jane Marsh, 237, *238n*
Parker, So. Dak.: SBA in, 300–301
Parker, Theodore, 250, *263n*, 560
parliamentary procedure, 170
Parnell, Charles Stewart, 253, *264n*, 335; ECS defends, 335, 336–41
Parnell, Delia Tudor Stewart, 11, *13n*
Parsons, Mary Sophronia Larned, 496, *496–97n*, 497
Patience, or Bunthorne's Bride (Gilbert and Sullivan): quoted, 210
patriotism: men trained for, 338
"Patriotism and Chastity" (ECS), 335, 336–41, 355
Patten, Josephine M., *422n*; at suffrage meeting, 417
Patterson, Katherine Grafton, 523, *528n*
Patterson, Thomas MacDonald, 523, *528n*
Patton, William Weston, 196, *197n*
Paxton Hotel (Omaha), 485
Peabody, Andrew Preston, 85, *85n*
Pearson, Karl, 358, *359n*
Peary, Robert Edwin, 721, *728n*
Peckam, J. (of Byron, N.Y.), 132
Pennock, Deborah Ann Yerkes, 2–3, *5n*
Pennsylvania: organizing in, 2–4, 5n, 15–16
Pennsylvania Woman Suffrage Association: annual meeting of, 549
Penn Yan, N.Y.: meeting in, 579
People's party: convention of 1892, 483–86; and woman suffrage, 384, 468–69. *See also* Colorado People's party; Kansas People's party; National Union Convention
Perkins, Sarah Maria Clinton, *120n*; and federal suffrage, 461; and National conference committee, 117, 119, 166; views of union, 112, 403
Personal Rights Association (London): invitation to ECS, 295–96
Peter Bell, A Tale of Verse (Wordsworth), 466
Peterboro, N.Y.: ECS in, 704–5
Peters, Alice E. Heckler, 474, *474n*
Peters, Oscar Glaze, 324, *326n*
Peters, Samuel Ritter, 626, *626n*
Philadelphia: SBA in, 57–59, 75–77, 548–49
Phillips, Mary Bigelow, 500, *502n*
Phillips, Wendell, 99, *105n*, 297; and F. Douglass, 680; mentioned, 250, 261, 287, 347, 560, 714; opposes discussion of marriage, 507–8; quoted, 124, 601, 720; "Scholar in a Republic," 317; and unrestricted suffrage, 664, 665n, 668
Phipps, Henry, Jr., 191, *194n*
Pickler, Alice Mary Alt, *294–95n*; letters from SBA, 294, 304–5, 306–7; and So. Dak. campaign, 319
Pickler, John Alfred, *277n*; and So. Dak. campaign, 275, 304, 306, 307

Pierpont, John, *545n*; quoted, 539
Pierre, So. Dak.: SBA in, 220–21
Pilgrim Mothers' Dinners: ECS describes, 502; SBA attends, 558
Pillsbury, Parker, 83, *84–85n*; letter to SBA, 707–8
Pillsbury, Sarah H. Sargent, 83, *84–85n*, 708
Place de la République (Paris), 539–40
Plaza Hotel (New York), 465
Poe, Edgar Allan, *265n*; "The Raven," 256, 348, 702, 721
political education: women's need of, 145–46, 206–7, 257–59
Political Equality Club: of Rochester, 216, 687–88; of Syracuse, 569
political parties: roles of in state campaigns, 319, 324–25, 334, 557, 581, 586–91, 593–94, 598–614, 632–35, 653; suffragists' affiliations with, 161, 285–90, 456–57, 644; women's roles in, 137, 152, 161, 384, 457, 468–70
Poppleton, Andrew Jackson, 141, *142n*
Portsmouth, Iowa: ECS in, 142–43
Post, Amy Kirby, *84n*; and International Council, 83
Post, Mary E., 449, *449n*
Pothier, Robert-Joseph, 153, *158n*, 339
Potter, Helen L.: reads ECS's speech, 719
Powderly, Terence Vincent, 485, *485–86n*
Prentis, Caroline E. Anderson, 626, *626–27n*
Prentis, Mrs. Noble L. *See* Prentis, Caroline E. Anderson
Presbyterian General Assembly: and women, 727
Presbyterian Ministers' Association (Rochester): denounces lynching, 691
presidential suffrage, 61–62, 66n
Price, Abby Hills, 347, *353n*
Price, Farrington, 577, *577n*
Price, Sterling, 599, *614n*
Primrose League, 7–8, 72
"The Princess" (Tennyson), 724
prohibition: conflicts with woman suffrage, 29, 220–21, 269–70, 275–76, 286, 288, 290, 321–22, 640, 653; in Kan., 46, 51n, 182–83, 195; in So. Dak., 220–21, 222n
Prohibition party: and 1888 election, 131–32; ECS endorses, 135–38; and F. E. Willard, xxiv–xxv, 139; M. J. Gage criticizes, 126–29; mentioned, 76; platforms of, 127, 135–36, 161, 469; and temperance union, 58. *See also* New York (state)
prostitution: in London, 154–55; in Sioux City, 46–47, 184–85
Purcell, William, 228, *229n*
Purinton, Charles S., 122, *123n*
Purinton, Harriett S. Furguson, 57, *57n*, 122
Purinton, James, Jr., 122, *123n*

Purvis, Robert, *84n*, 240, 251; discrimination against, 363; and International Council, 83
Purvis, Tacy Townsend, 83, *84n*
Putnam, Caroline F., 241, *244n*, 689
Putnam, Helen Grace, 332, *333n*

Queen Isabella Association, 392, 393n
The Question (New York), 16
"The Question of Divorce" (Gladstone), 258

Raines, Thomas, 569, *569n*
Ramsey, Samuel Albert, *282n*, 304, 306–7; letter from SBA, 281–82
Rankin, John M., 600, *614n*
"The Raven" (Poe), 256, 348, 702, 721
Reconstruction, 600
Reed, Thomas Brackett, *59n*, 324; and amendment, 58, 59n, 76; letters from SBA, 58–59, 486–87; letter to SBA, 409; mentioned, 313; and National-American, 409
Regina v. Jackson (1891), 374–75
Reid, Elizabeth Jesser, 241, *244n*
religion: and public schools, 206; and woman's bondage, 141, 212, 224
Religio-Philosophical Journal (Chicago), 196
"Reminiscences" (ECS): plans for, 370–71; reactions to, 202, 297–98, 298–99n; work on, 210, 278, 308, 311, 334–35, 343–44
Republican Clubs: national convention of, 74
republican government: achieved in Wyoming, 317; and individual rights, 424–25, 540, 543, 544; power of ballots in, 659; superiority of, 98–99, 101–2
Republican party: in 1892 election, 468, 469, 475–77, 484; and black suffrage, 600–601; convention of 1888, 126, 129–30; ECS criticizes, 136–38; platform of 1872, 454–55; platform of 1876, 455–56, 459; and SBA, 74, 137–38; in So. Dak., 304, 306, 319, 320n, 324–25; and suffrage amendment, 76; and woman suffrage, 469, 475–76, 486–87; and women, 58–59; and Wyoming statehood, 283–84, 469, 475. *See also* Kansas Republican party; South Dakota Republican party
Reunion of the Pioneers and Friends of Woman's Progress, 709–10, 714, 719–27, 730
Review of Reviews, 355
Revolution (New York), 100, 308, 514
revolutions of 1848, 720
Reynolds, Ascha Hudson Harter, *712n*; letter from SBA, 711–12
Reynolds, Helen M., 521, *525n*, 548
Reynolds, Minnie Josephine, 523, *528n*
Rhode Island: suffrage campaign in, 288, 588, 605

Richmond Hotel (Buffalo), 16
Riggs House (Washington): residence of SBA, 2, 78–79, 80–81, 82, 83–84, 86–87, 122, 226–27, 231–33, 234–35, 274–76
Robert Elsmere (Ward), 142–43
Robinson, Charles, 298, *300n*
Robinson, Harriet Jane Hanson, 394, 455, *457–58n*
Robinson, Helen Blasdell Avery, 669, *671n*
Robinson Crusoe (Defoe): characters in, 424
Rochester, N.Y.: ECS in, 398–402; SBA speaks in, 221, 226, 566–68, 569
Rochester, University of: campaign for coeducation in, 398–402
Rochester convention of 1848: commemorated, 94
Rochester *Democrat and Chronicle*, 446, 548, 691
Rochester Historical Society: and SBA bust, 446, 447n
Rochester Theological Seminary, 690
Rockwell, Lewis C., 522, *527n*
Rockwell, Mrs. (in New York), 715
Rocky Mountain News (Denver), 523
Rogers, Caroline Gilkey, 202, *203n*
Rogers, Elias F., 202, *203n*
Rogers, May, 70, 72, *73n*
Rogers, Nathaniel Peabody, 99, *105n*
Roland, Jeanne-Marie Philipon, 95, *104n*
Roland, Pauline, 347, *353n*
Root, Martha Elizabeth Snyder, *585n*; and National-American, 584
Rose, Ernestine Louise Siismondi Potowski, *247–48n*, 250, 347, 716, 721; atheism of, 247
Ross, Robert: murder of, 659, 660n
Rousseau, Jean-Jacques, 43, *51n*
Routt, John Long, 523, *528–29n*, 604
Russell, Elizabeth B., 80, *81n*
Russia: and expulsion of Jews, 484; extradition treaty with, 102; and Poland, 541

St. John, John Pierce, 221, *222n*; and 1894 election, 587
St. John, Sarah Jane Parker, 616–17, *617n*
Salem, Ohio: SBA in, 473–74
Salisbury, Lord. *See* Cecil, Robert Arthur Talbot Gascoyne- (marquess of Salisbury)
Salt Lake City, Utah, 308
Sand, George, 95, *104n*, 338, *342n*
Sanford, John Edward, 563, *563n*; and I. B. Wells, 690
Sanford, Mary Thayer, 403, *404n*, 563; and I. B. Wells, 690; and N.Y. campaign, 564, 670
Sargent, Angelina Morse Foster, 563, *563n*
Savile, Sybilla, 370, *372n*
Sawens, George M., 575, *576n*

Sawens, Russell W., 575, *576n*
Saxe, Asa, 566, *568n*
Saxon, Elizabeth Lyle, *174n*; and National-American, 411; and National association, 169; at suffrage meeting, 438
The Scarlet Letter (Hawthorne), 154
Scatcherd, Alice Cliff, *88n*; and International Council, 86, 90
Schenck, Robert Cumming, 600, *614n*
Schofield, Martha, *675n*; hosts SBA, 675–76
Schofield Normal and Industrial School, 675–76
"The Scholar in a Republic" (Phillips): quoted, 317
school suffrage, 98, 469, 724; in Colo., 524; in Mass., 41, 42n; in N.Y., 452–53, 453–54n, 581; in Wis., 30, 31n
Schumann, Robert Alexander, 432, *436n*
Scofield, Anna Bishop, *134n*; hosts ECS and SBA, 134
Second Baptist Church (Rochester), 690
Sedgwick, Deborah W. Gannett, 499–500, *501n*, 569
Segur, Rosa L. Klinge, 574, *574n*
Seidl, Anton, 441, *442n*
Seidl Society, 204, 205n; ECS speaks to, 205–7; SBA speaks to, 209–10
Selden, Elise Massey, 673, *673n*
Seneca Falls convention of 1848, 720, 727n; commemorated, 25, 27, 83, 94
Severance, Caroline Maria Seymour, 250, *263n*
Sewall, Harriet Winslow List, *84n*; and International Council, 83
Sewall, May Eliza Wright Thompson, *16n*, 28, 37–38; and Columbian Exposition, 419, 491, 511; ECS criticizes, 278; and International Council, 15, 17, 18–19, 26–27; letter from SBA, 231–33; mentioned, 85; and National association, 168–69, 219; and National conference committee, 64, 109–13, 117, 119, 166; and National Council, 139; in New York, 730; and plans for union, 215; and SBA's birthday, 245; at suffrage meeting, 287
Sewall, Samuel Edmund, *84n*; and International Council, 83; mentioned, 251
Sewall, Theodore Lovett, 730, *730n*
Seward, Elizabeth Irene Helton, 231, *233n*
Shakespeare, William, 47, *51n*, 349; *Hamlet*, 210; *Merchant of Venice*, 199; *Titus Andronicus*, 427–28
"Shall the World's Fair be Open on Sunday" (ECS), 493, 495
Shattuck, Harriette Lucy Robinson, *65–66n*, 394, 395; mentioned, 111, 460; and National association, 61; and National conference committee, 64, 117, 119; at suffrage meeting, 166–67, 169; views of union, 113–14, 170–71n, 173–74n

Shaw, Anna Howard, *41n*; and American conference committee, 112–13, 168; at Chautauqua, 488–89; and International Council, 107; and Kan. campaign, 590, 616–17, 625, 626, 627, 628, 632, 636, 651–52, 654n; in Kan., 41; letter from ECS, 637; letter from SBA, 41; at Lily Dale, 641; mentioned, 386, 387, 403, 404, 504, 565, 686; and National-American, 505–6, 660, 662; and N.Y. association, 717; and N.Y. campaign, 554, 582; in Omaha, 485, 486; in Pa., 460–61; at Pilgrim Mothers' Dinner, 502; rivals of, 494; in Rochester, 487–88; and So. Dak. campaign, 319, 607; at suffrage meetings, 269, 415, 416, 418–19, 438, 673; and temperance union, 658
Shaw, Mattie A. N., 414, *419–20n*
Shaw, Mme. (of Sioux City), 47, 184–85
Sheldon, Ellen Harriet, 28, *29n*
Sheppard, John Shoemaker, 579, *579n*
Sheppard, Julia Morton Dodson, 579, *579n*
Sheppard's Opera House (Penn Yan), 579
Sherman, John, 407, *409n*
Short, Mme. (of Sioux City). *See* Shaw, Mme.
Sibley, Jane Elizabeth Thomas, 416, *421n*
Simonton, James William, 383, *384–85n*
Simpson, Burnett Newell, 616, *616–17n*
Simpson, Charles Lyon, 616, *616–17n*
Simpson, Ellen Josephine, 616, *616–17n*
Simpson, Kate Lyon Burnett, 616, *616–17n*
Simpson, Samuel Newell, 616, *616–17n*
Sioux City, Iowa: prostitution in, 46–47, 184–85
Sioux War, 349
"The Sixteenth Amendment" (Ingalls), 39, 40n, 41, 42–50
Slocum, Jane M., 449, *449n*
Slocum, Samuel G., 448–49, *449n*
Slosson, Achsah Louise Lilly, 186, *189n*
Smith, Elizabeth Fitzhugh, 716, *716n*
Smith, Elizabeth Oakes Prince, 250, *263n*
Smith, Gerrit, 250, *263n*, 297, 386, 450
Smith, Hannah Whitall, *13n*, 26; letter from ECS, 293
Smith, Julia Holmes Abbot, *163–64n*; cares for SBA, 163; and Columbian Exposition, 392
Smith, Lewia C. Hannibal, *238n*; leads Rochester lecture series, 446; in Washington, 237, 271
Smith, Lucy Boardman, 237, *238n*
Smith, Sara Wisner Winthrop, *171n*; mentioned, 278; and National-American, 584; and National association, 219; in Ohio, 324; at suffrage meeting, 167, 168
Snow, Sophronia C., 407, *409n*
Snowden, Mrs. (of Washington), 80

Socialist Labor party, 128
Sofield, Laura A., 485, *485n*
"The Solitude of Self" (ECS), 423–34; mentioned, 411; praised, 446
"Some Good Whig Principles" (Franklin), 560
Somerset, Lady Isabella Caroline Somers-Cocks, *451n*, 457; and *History of Woman Suffrage*, 450–51; letter from ECS, 694–95n; letter to ECS, 694; mentioned, 642, 663; and *Woman's Bible*, 681, 694, 703
Somerville, Mary Fairfax, 347, *353n*
Sorosis (New York), 467
South Dakota: Democratic party in, 304, 305n, 589; immigrant population of, 269–70, 272n, 321–22; and Native Americans, 319, 320n, 349; prohibition in, 275–76, 277n
South Dakota amendment campaign: money for, 220, 225, 227, 269–70, 271–72n, 275–76, 281–82, 300–301, 324; plans for, 216, 216–17n, 220–21, 226, 227, 269–70, 274–76, 281–82, 294; political realignment in, 300, 301–2n, 304, 319, 588–89; votes cast, 332, 333n, 348, 349–50, 589, 607–8
South Dakota Equal Suffrage Association, 216–17n, 226, 227–28n, 270, 271–72n, 274; and National-American, 281–82, 294; new leadership for, 304–5, 307n; resolutions about SBA, 294, 295n
South Dakota Independent party, 306, 319, 325, 589; founded, 300, 301–2n; platform of, 304, 305n; and woman suffrage, 384
South Dakota Republican party, 269, 606–7
Southworth, Louisa Stark, *171–72n*; donations of, 324; and federal suffrage, 461; hosts SBA, 660–62; mentioned, 328–29; and national enrollment, 167; in New York, 718
Southworth, William J., 660, *661n*
speeches and remarks: ECS, "The Degradation of Disfranchisement," 360–68; ECS, "Friendships of Women," 240–42; ECS, "The Solitude of Self," 423–34; ECS, "Suffrage a Natural Right," 539–45; ECS, "Woman's Duty to Vote," 143–56; ECS in N.Y. amendment campaign, 595–96, 619–20; ECS to Bristol Women's Liberal Association, 327–28; ECS to reception in Rochester, 399–402; ECS to reunion of pioneers, 719–27; ECS to suffrage league luncheon, 465–70; SBA, "The Moral Leadership of the Religious Press," 516–20; SBA, "Organization among Women," 509–11; SBA in N.Y. amendment campaign, 566–68; SBA to Cassadaga Lake Free Association, 641, 645–47; SBA to gospel suffrage meeting, 658–60; SBA to Kan. People's party, 629–31; SBA to Kan.

Republicans, 480–82; SBA to meeting in Minneapolis, 475–76; SBA to meeting in Omaha, 483–84; SBA to meetings in Leavenworth, 42–50, 181–87, 189–90, 194–95; SBA to Mississippi Valley Conference, 490–92; SBA to National-American conventions, 503–5, 580–81; SBA to National association, 246–47; SBA to N.Y. constitutional convention, 621–24; SBA to Ohio association, 473–74; SBA to Public Press Congress, 513–15; SBA to suffrage festival, 123–25, 380–84
Spencer, Eleanor M. Proper, 577, *577n*
Spencer, Herbert, 72, *73n*, 425; quoted, 544–45
Spencer, Sara Jane Andrews, 455–56, *458–59n*
Sperry, Hannah Bassett, *172n*; and National association, 168, 219
spiritualism, 36, 720; SBA's praise for, 645–46
Spofford, Ainsworth Rand, 202, *203n*, 692
Spofford, Caleb Wheeler, 232, *234n*, 236; leaves Riggs House, 407
Spofford, Jane H. Snow, *20n*, 28, 300–301; and H. B. Blackwell, 297; hosts SBA, 79, 80–81; leaves Riggs House, 407; mentioned, 19, 85, 122, 220, 268, 411; and National association, 219; and National conference committee, 166; at suffrage meeting, 414, 416
Springer, William McKendree, 203, *203–4n*, 280
"Springer Amendment to the Federal Constitution" (Waite), 203
Squier, Ellen Hoxie, 238, *239n*, 271, 730
Squier, Lucien Bertrand, 238, *239n*, 271
Staël, Germaine de, 95, *104n*
Stafford, Kan.: SBA speaks in, 497
Stanley, Henry Morton, 303, *303n*
Stansbury, Ellis Meredith. *See* Meredith, Ellis
Stansbury, Lyl Meredith. *See* Meredith, Ellis
Stanton, Augusta E. Hazleton, 230, *230n*
Stanton, Daniel Cady, xxvii
Stanton, Elizabeth Cady: on aging, 200, 328–30, 429, 618; birthday of, xxii–xxiii, xxv–xxvi, 679, 683–84, 700, 708, 709–10, 719–27, 730; health of, 223, 232–33, 446–47; letters from SBA, 499–500, 638, 641–42, 699–700, 709–10; letters to SBA, 9–11, 297–98, 308–9, 358–59, 385, 473, 502; religious initiative of, 11, 212–13, 224, 256–57; SBA commends, 15, 47, 204, 472, 474, 532, 601; SBA describes, 19; SBA scolds, 710; sits for artists, 32; at suffrage meetings, 110–17, 249–63, 424, 436–38; as traveler, 390–91, 704–5; views of illness, 159; views of union, 201, 211–12, 223–24, 252–53, 297, 371; weight of, 210

Stanton, Elizabeth Cady, Jr., 23–24, *24n*, 33
Stanton, Gerrit Smith, *xxvii*, 230
Stanton, Henry Brewster, 243, *245n*
Stanton, Henry Brewster, Jr., *xxvii*; helps his mother, 391; marriage of, 500
Stanton, Marguerite Marie Berry, 32, *35n*
Stanton, Mary O'Shea, 500, *502n*
Stanton, Robert Livingston (1859–1920), *xxvii*, 479, 500; letter from ECS, 704–5
Stanton, Robert Livingston (1885–1974), 23, *24n*
Stanton, Theodore Weld, *xxvii*; in Chicago, 520; ECS visits, 23–24; and *History of Woman Suffrage*, 450; mentioned, 22, 36, 390; news of, 308
states' rights: and citizenship, 469; and suffrage, 131–32, *132n*
Stead, William Thomas, *336n*; and C. S. Parnell, 335; letter from ECS, 355; letter to ECS, 356
Stearns, Ozora Pierson, 271, *274n*
Stearns, Sarah Burger, *217n*; hosts SBA, 216; letter from SBA, 269–71
Stearns, Stella Burger, 271, *274n*
Stearns, Susan M., 271, *274n*
Stearns, Victor Alonzo, 271, *274n*
Stepniak, Sergei, 102, *106–7n*
Sterling, Kan.: SBA speaks in, 498, *499n*
Stevens, Thaddeus, 600, *614n*
Stewart, Joseph William Alexander, 690, *690n*
Stone, Lucinda Hinsdale, 721, *728n*
Stone, Lucy, *53n*; and 1888 election, 139, *140n*; on aging, 356–57; and American association, 219; and Colo. campaign, 603; and Columbian Exposition, 415, 492, 532; criticizes ECS, 371, *372n*; ECS criticizes, 201; ECS praises, 250; family's history of, *728n*; and International Council, 79, 83–84, 88–*89n*; and Kan. campaign, 297, 298; and leadership of united societies, 63, 64, *67n*, 112–15, 165, 179, 201, 733; letter from ECS, 346–52; letter from SBA, 57; letters to SBA, 52–53, 68, 356–57; marriage of, 720–21; at meeting on union, 59–64; mentioned, 97, 122, 460, 716; and National-American, 411; and plans for union, xxvi, 732–33; proposes union, 52–53, 68; remembered, 660, *661n*, 662; and suffrage factions, 488; at suffrage festival, 380; at suffrage meeting, 437; views of union, 54–56, 74, 178–80
Stormont, William Thomas, 460, *461n*
Story, Joseph, 153, *158n*, 726
Stowe, Emily Howard Jennings, 226, *228n*
Struble, Hanford, 579, *579n*
Stuart, James, 8, *9n*
The Study of Sociology (Spencer), 544–45

suffrage: history of, 45; a natural right, 620; a privilege, 44–45; and self defense, 540–41, 543
suffrage, African-American, 600–601; under siege, 261–63, 529–30
suffrage, educated: C. G. Ames advocates, 649; as compromise, 624, 639; ECS advocates, 397–98, 647–49, 655–57, 664–68; H. B. Blackwell advocates, 649, *658n*
suffrage, manhood: ECS objects to, 470, 664–66
suffrage, universal: ECS supports, 397, 648, 655, 665
suffrage, woman: acceptance of, 96–97; impact of, 315–16, 328; justice of, 711–12; need for, 209–10; and other reforms, 366–67; won in Wyoming, 312–17
Suffrage a Natural Right (ECS), 582
"Suffrage a Natural Right" (ECS), 539–45
Sullivan, Margaret Frances Buchanan, 11, *13n*
Sulzer, William, *453n*; letter from SBA, 452–53
Sumner, Charles, *376n*; and black suffrage, 600, 601; and loyal league, 599; quoted, 375, 539, 560, 655
"Sunday at the World's Fair" (ECS), 439–42
Sunday closing, 72, 191–92; and Columbian Exposition, 436–38, 439–42, 493, 495, 507–8, 520
Swain, Adeline Morrison, *121n*; views of union, 116
Swalm, Pauline Given, 513, *515n*
Swedenborg, Emanuel, 723, *729n*
Sweet, Emma Biddlecome, 712, *713n*
Syracuse, N.Y.: SBA speaks in, 569

Tabernacle Missionary Baptist Church (Memphis), 673
Tacitus, Cornelius, *318–19n*; quoted, 317
Taft, Clara, 717, *717n*
Taft, Lorado Zadoc, 478, *478n*, 480
Taliaferro, John R., 448–49, *449n*
Tammany, 567
Taylor, Clementia Doughty, 343, *345n*
Taylor, Ezra Booth, *40n*; and amendment, 39; and house hearing, 446; mentioned, 377
Taylor, Helen, *13n*; and International Council, 11, 86, 88–89n, 90–92; letter from ECS, 90–91; letter to SBA, 91–92
Taylor, John, 153, *158n*, 339
Taylor, Peter Alfred, 343, *345n*
teachers: wages of, 381–83
Tefft, Emma A. Alkire, *626n*; hosts SBA, 625, 626, 627
Tefft, Herbert Kenyon, *626n*; hosts SBA, 625, 626, 627
Tennyson, Alfred, Lord, *729n*; quoted, 724

Thomas, Maria Louise Palmer, *140n*; and National Council, 139
Thomas, Mary Frame Myers, 19, *19–20n*, 721
Thomas, Theodore, 441, *442n*
Thomaston, N.Y.: ECS in, 635–36
Thomson, Mary Adeline, *37n*; in Rochester, 134, 387; travels with SBA, 36; in Washington, 238, 271
Thurston, Sarah Abby Bray, 587, 588, *592n*, 651
Tiffany, Martha Eliza, 570, *570n*
Tiffany, Nelson Otis, 570, *570n*
Tilney, Anna Robinson Longstreth, 675, *675–76n*
Tilney, Robert, 675, *675–76n*
Tilton, Theodore, 32, *35n*, 297; quoted, xxiii
Titus Andronicus (Shakespeare), 427–28
Tod, Isabella Maria Susan, 11, *13n*
Toledo, Ohio: SBA in, 573–75
Toledo Woman Suffrage Association: anniversary of, 574
Topeka, Kan.: SBA in, 480–82, 625–32; SBA speaks in, 628
Topeka *State Journal*, 651, 652, 654n
Toronto, Canada: SBA speaks in, 226
"To the Women of New York" (ECS), 559–62
Tourgée, Albion Winegar, *531n*; and Columbian Exposition, 533n; letters from SBA, 532–33, *533n*; and national citizenship, 529–30
Towns, Mirabeau Lamar, 624, *625n*
Tozier, Emily A. Putnam, 577, *578n*
Tragical History of King Richard the Third (Cibber), 706; quoted, 163
Train, George Francis, *12n*; in Kan. campaign, 297–98, 371; quoted, 10
Triumphant Democracy (Carnegie), 149
Troy, N.Y.: murder in, 659
Truth, Sojourner, 347, *353n*
Trygg, Maria Alexandra, *88n*; and International Council, 86
Tucker, Gideon John, *229n*; letter to SBA, 228–29
Turner, Henry McNeal, 674, *674–75n*
Tyler, Louise Marie, 522, *526n*
Tyndall, John, 72, *73n*

Una (Providence), 514
Underwood, Benjamin Franklin, *21n*, 22, 196; letter from ECS, 20–21
Underwood, Sara A. Francis, *21n*; letters from ECS, 20–22, 196; and *Woman's Bible*, 22
Union Labor party, 127–28
Union Signal (Chicago): ECS writes for, 135–38
United Labor party, 127

U.S. Congress: when women enter, 717–18
U.S. Constitution: article 1, sec. 10, 361; article 6, 71, 102; attempts to put God in, 71, 102, 128–29, 136, 191; centennial of, 37–38, 218
U.S. House of Representatives: hearings of, 423–34; Judiciary Committee, 410–11, 411n; Judiciary Committee, reports of, 300, 301n, 319; Wyoming statehood in, 280, 280–81n
U.S. Senate: amendment in, 75, 76n; Suffrage Committee, 75–76, 407–8, 410–11, 411n; Suffrage Committee, reports of, 319, 320n; vote on amendment, xxiv
U.S. Supreme Court: and *Ex parte Yarbrough*, 262, 267n; and *Minor v. Happersett*, 120n, 262, 267n
United States v. Susan B. Anthony (1873), 137
Unity Church (Omaha), 483, 485
Universal Suffrage. Speech of Hon. Thomas W. Palmer, 275, 504
Upton, George Whitman, 495, *496n*
Upton, Harriet Taylor, *40n*; hosts SBA, 376–77; letters from SBA, 39, 300–301, 319, 324–25, 403–4, 407–8, 410–11, 460–61, 494, 546–47; and National-American, 505, 583, 584, 660, 700; and Ohio association, 661; at suffrage meeting, 504
Upton, William W., 300, 301, *301n*, 495
Utah Territory: state constitution approved in, 724, 729n
Utah Territory Woman Suffrage Association: and National association, 247, 248n

Vail, Annette, 488, *488–89n*
Van Rensselaer, Martha, 564, *564–65n*
Vendome Hotel (New York), 714, 718, 730
Venturi, Emilie Ashurst Hawkes, *296n*; letter to ECS, 295–96
Victoria (queen of England), 150, 151–52, *158n*, 622
Victoria Adelaide Mary Louise (empress of Germany), 491, *492n*
Vigil, Agapito, 604, *615n*
Vincent, George Edgar, 488, *488n*, 646
Vincent, John Heyl, 488, *488n*, 698
"Voluntary Motherhood" (Blatch), 495
Vorse, Susan, 717, *717n*

Wade, Benjamin Franklin, 377, *377–78n*
wages of women: inequality of, 135–36, 381–83
Waite, Charles Burlingame, *156n*; and common law rights, 144; on divorce law, 203
Waite, Davis Hanson, 524, *529n*
Walker, Harriet Granger Hulet, *477n*; hosts SBA, 477

Walker, Mary Edwards, 87, *89n*
Walker, Mary Louise Hall, 573, *573n*
Walker, Thomas Barlow, *477n*; hosts SBA, 477
Wallace, Zerelda Gray Sanders, 128, *129n*; and Columbian Exposition, 415; quoted, 126; at suffrage meeting, 269
Ward, Eliza Titus, 300, *301n*
Ward, Mary Augusta Arnold, 142-43, *143n*
Ward, Mrs. Humphrey. *See* Ward, Mary Augusta Arnold
Wardall, Alonzo A., 216-17n, *332n*, 606; hosts SBA, 332
Wardall, Anna, 321, *322-23n*
Wardall, Elizabeth A. Murray, 321, *322-23n*, 486n; hosts SBA, 332
Warren, Francis Emroy, 407, *408n*
Warren, Mercy Otis, 467, *470n*
Warsaw, N.Y.: meeting in, 578
Washington, George, 254, *264n*
Washington Territory: suffrage campaign in, 588, 605; suffrage overturned in, 29, 30n
Watson House (Rochester), 687
Watterson, Henry, 478, *478n*
Watts, Isaac: quoted, 412
Weber, Hélène-Marie, 347, *353n*
Webster, Daniel, 47, *51n*, 337, 342n; quoted, 510, 613
Wedemeyer, William Walter, 572, *573n*
Welch, Mary E., 442, *445n*
Weld, Angelina Emily Grimké, 347, *353n*
Wellesley, Arthur (duke of Wellington), 337, *341-42n*, 370
Wellington, Duke of. *See* Wellesley, Arthur (duke of Wellington)
Wells, Ida Bell, *688n*; in Rochester, 687-92
Westminster Review: ECS writes for, 312-17, 335, 336-41
"What Should be Our Attitude Towards Political Parties" (ECS), 285-90
Wheeler, Edward Jewitt, 396, *398n*
Whiting, Eliza Rose Gray, *686n*; letter from SBA, 685-86
Whittier, John Greenleaf, 380, *384n*
"Who Were Voters in the Early History of This Country?" (Waite), 144
Wilbour, Charles Edwin, 32, *34-35n*
Wilbour, Charlotte Beebe, 32, *34-35n*
Wilkeson, Catharine Henry Cady, 330, *331n*, 346
Wilkins, Mrs. (of N.Y.), 558
Wilkinson, Sir John Gardner, 358, *359n*
Willard, Amelia, 573, *573n*
Willard, Frances Elizabeth Caroline, *13n*; and 1888 election, 139; and A. E. Dickinson, 373, 373-74n; and C. S. Parnell, 369, 370n; and Columbian Exposition, 415; ECS criticizes, 212-13; and International Council, 19, 107-9, 209, 369; introduces SBA, 658, 659; as leader, 288; letter from ECS, 694-95n; letters from SBA, 29-30, 131n, 163, 274-76; letters to ECS, 694-95n, 703; letters to SBA, 139, 662-63; mentioned, 26, 58, 128-29, 642; and National association, 163; and National Council, 139; and Prohibition party, xxiv-xxv, 139; SBA praises, 472; and *Woman's Bible*, 681, 682n, 694, 694-95n, 696-97, 703
Willard, Frederick W., 41, *41-42n*
Willard, Julia H. Dustin, 41, *41-42n*
Willard, Mary Hill Thompson, 163, *164n*
Willcox, John Keappock Hamilton, *120-21n*, 594; at suffrage meeting, 115-16
Williams, Sarah R. Langdon, 574, *574n*
Willis, John Henry, 201, *201n*
Willis, Sarah L. Kirby Hallowell, *238n*; letter from SBA, 378-79; mentioned, 500, 714; in Washington, 237, 271
Wilmore, Ky.: SBA speaks in, 669
Wilson, Henry, 455, *458n*
Wimodaughsis Society (Washington), 414, 415, 419n, 461
Wisconsin: school suffrage in, 30, 31n
Wisconsin Citizen (Racine), 493
Wisconsin Woman Suffrage Association: annual meetings of, 211, 213n, 493; and National-American, 461, 462-63n
Wollstonecraft, Mary, 95, *104n*, 338, 342n, 716
Woman's Bible: contributions to, 702; copyright of, 692, 693; design of, 695-96; plans for, 677-78, 681; reactions to, 699-700; SBA comments on, xxvi, 699-700
Woman's Bible committee, 22, 678n, 681, 693-94n, 694, 695-96, 699, 703
Woman's Christian Temperance Union, xxiv-xxv; in 1888 election, 128; annual meetings of, 523, 658-60, 662-63; annual report of, 30; and International Council, 107-9; as model for united societies, 61, 64, 211, 733, 736; and People's party, 456; and Prohibition party, 58, 139, 456; size of, 232, 510; and So. Dak. campaign, 270, 272n, 274-76; and southern states, 415; state focus of, 504; and suffrage campaigns, 554, 555n, 571-72, 662-63, 663n; and Sunday closing, 437, 438n; and *Woman's Bible*, 694, 695n, 703, 703-4n
Woman's Column (Boston), 321
"Woman's Duty to Vote" (ECS), 143-56
Woman's Herald (London): ECS writes for, 374-75
Woman's Journal (Boston), 100, 635, 709; and Blackwell family, 297; ECS writes for, 655-57, 665-68; letters from ECS, 647-49, 664-65; and plans for union, 64, 165
"Woman's Legal Right to the Ballot" (Minor), 254

INDEX ~ 769

Woman's Relief Corps, 523
Woman's Suffrage Press Association, 700
Woman's Tribune (Beatrice, Neb.), 100, 321, 548, 584, 709; ECS comments on, 70, 72; and ECS's "Reminiscences," 278; H. T. Upton writes for, 324; and International Council, 122; letter from SBA, 226–27; mailed to So. Dak., 275; and plans for union, 64, 165; SBA comments on, 700; and *Woman's Bible*, 677–78, 692, 696, 700, 702, 702n
Woman Suffrage. Speech of Hon. Henry W. Blair, 4
women: universal experience of, 95–96
women of the Bible: Deborah, 196, 260, 696; Elizabeth, 241; Esther, 260, 696; Huldah, 196, 207, 260; Mary, 241; Miriam, 724–25; Naomi, 196, 241; Phoebe, 241; Priscilla, 241; Ruth, 196, 241; Tryphena, 241; Tryphosa, 241; Vashti, 260, 696
Women's Franchise League, 343–44, 344n
Women's Liberal Federation, 7–8, 456
Women's Loyal National League, 261, 599–600
Women's National Liberal Union: and ECS, 214, 223–24, 234–35; meeting of, 278, 279n; plans for, 214, 215n; and SBA, 234, 236–37
Women's New York State Temperance Society, 517
Women's Penny Paper (London), 302; ECS writes for, 335
Women's Political Progressive League: meeting of, 629
Wood, Joshua Gibson, 498, *499n*
Wooden, Iva G. Fenton, 571, *571–72n*
Woodhull, Victoria Claflin, 86–87, *89n*
Worcester, Joseph Emerson, 340, *342n*

"A Word from a Petitioner" (Pierpont), 539
Wordsworth, Christopher, *21n*; and Pentateuch, 20
Wordsworth, William, *470n*; quoted, 466
World's Columbian Exposition: busts for, 329, 330–31n, 478, 480; ECS address for, 539–45; Government Congress of, 532–33, 534, 539–45; Lady Managers of, 392; and National-American association, 324, 490–92; Public Press Congress of, 513–15; Religious Press Congress of, 516–20; SBA addresses congresses of, 509–11, 513–15, 516–20; and southern states, 415; and Sunday closing, 436–38, 439–42, 495, 496n, 507–8, 520; Woman's Congress of, 491, 509–11; women's part in, 235, 236n
World's Industrial and Cotton Centennial Exposition, 438
Wright, David, 405, *406n*
Wright, Flora McMartin, *33n*; letter from ECS, 31–33
Wright, Frances, 338, *342n*, 716
Wright, Martha Coffin Pelham, 236, *237n*, 405; mentioned, 250; at Seneca Falls convention, 720
Wright, Phebe C. Whitson, 675, *676n*
Wyoming: rights of women in, 328; statehood, 280, 283–84, 293, 312–17, 327–28; woman suffrage in, 481, 591, 613, 622, 712, 724
"Wyoming Admitted as a State into the Union" (ECS), 312–17
Wyoming County, N.Y.: amendment campaign in, 578
Wyoming Territory: woman suffrage in, 185

Yates County, N.Y.: amendment campaign in, 579
Young Men's Hebrew Association (Memphis), 671–72, 672n